# Organization Theory and Design

## THIRD CANADIAN EDITION

**Richard L. Daft**

VANDERBILT UNIVERSITY

**Ann Armstrong**

ROTMAN SCHOOL OF MANAGEMENT,
UNIVERSITY OF TORONTO

**NELSON EDUCATION**

CELEBRATE LIFELONG LEARNING

1914–2014: Nelson Education celebrates 100 years of Canadian publishing

# NELSON / EDUCATION

**Organization Theory and Design, Third Canadian Edition**
by Richard L. Daft and Ann Armstrong

**Vice President,
Editorial Higher Education:**
Anne Williams

**Executive Editor:**
Jackie Wood

**Marketing Manager:**
Dave Stratton

**Developmental Editor:**
Rachel Eagen

**Photo Researcher:**
Christine Elliott

**Permissions Coordinator:**
Christine Elliott

**Content Production
Manager:**
Christine Gilbert

**Production Service:**
MPS Limited

**Copy Editor:**
Karen Rolfe

**Proofreader:**
MPS Limited

**Indexer:**
Shan Young

**Design Director:**
Ken Phipps

**Managing Designer:**
Franca Amore

**Interior Design:**
Sharon Lucas

**Cover Design:**
Sharon Lucas

**Cover Image:**
Melissa McKinnon

**Compositor:**
MPS Limited

**Library and Archives Canada
Cataloguing in Publication**

Daft, Richard L., author

Organization theory and design/
Richard L. Daft, Vanderbilt
University, Ann Armstrong,
Rotman School of Management,
University of Toronto.—Third
Canadian edition.

Includes bibliographical references
and indexes.
ISBN 978-0-17-653220-8 (bound)

1. Organization.  2. Organizational
sociology—Case studies.
3. Organizational sociology—
Textbooks. I. Armstrong, Ann,
1951–, author II. Title.

HD58.8.D33 2014   658.4
C2014-902150-X

ISBN-13: 978-0-17-653220-8
ISBN-10: 0-17-653220-X

In loving memory of my mother (1918–2000),
over whom death has no dominion.

AA

# About the Authors

**Richard L. Daft, Ph.D.,** is the Brownlee O. Currey, Jr., Professor of Management in the Owen Graduate School of Management at Vanderbilt University. Professor Daft specializes in the study of organizational theory and leadership. Professor Daft is a Fellow of the Academy of Management and has served on the editorial boards of *Academy of Management Journal, Administrative Science Quarterly,* and *Journal of Management Education.* He was the Associate Editor-in-Chief of *Organization Science* and served for three years as Associate Editor of *Administrative Science Quarterly.*

Professor Daft has authored or co-authored 12 books, including *Management* (Cengage/South-Western, 2010), *The Leadership Experience* (Cengage/South-Western, 2008), and *What to Study: Generating and Developing Research Questions* (Sage, 1982). He also published *Fusion Leadership: Unlocking the Subtle Forces That Change People and Organizations* (Berrett-Koehler, 2000, with Robert Lengel). He has authored dozens of scholarly articles, papers, and chapters. His work has been published in *Administrative Science Quarterly, Academy of Management Journal, Academy of Management Review, Organizational Dynamics, Strategic Management Journal, Journal of Management, Accounting Organizations and Society, Management Science, MIS Quarterly, California Management Review,* and *Organizational Behavior Teaching Review.* Professor Daft has been awarded several government research grants to pursue studies of organization design, organizational innovation and change, strategy implementation, and organizational information processing.

Professor Daft is also an active teacher and consultant. He has taught management, leadership, organizational change, organizational theory, and organizational behaviour. He has been involved in management development and consulting for many companies and government organizations, including Allstate Insurance, American Banking Association, Bell Canada, Bridgestone, National Transportation Research Board, NL Baroid, Nortel, TVA, Pratt & Whitney, State Farm Insurance, Tenneco, Tennessee Emergency Pediatric Services, the United States Air Force, the United States Army, J. C. Bradford & Co., Central Parking System, USAA, United Methodist Church, Entergy Sales and Service, Bristol-Myers Squibb, First American National Bank, and the Vanderbilt University Medical Center.

**Ann Armstrong, Ph.D.,** has been an instructor at the Rotman School of Management for the past 17 years. She was the Director of the Social Enterprise Initiative, where she was responsible for increasing the School's involvement in the nonprofit/social enterprise sectors through curriculum design, research, and community engagement. Now Ann teaches environmental and social innovation in the Rotman Commerce program as well as organizational behaviour in the B.A.Sc. Engineering program. Ann also teaches change management in the Executive Development Program as well as in the MBiotech and Innovation Programs at the University of Toronto at

Mississauga. Ann is currently working on a SSHRC–supported research project that looks at the social economy of Ontario and, in particular, social businesses.

She has written articles on a broad range of subjects, from diversity in the nonprofit sector to case studies on green social enterprises. Ann has co-authored a textbook on Canada's social economy with Drs. Jack Quarter and Laurie Mook. With Joan Condie, Ann adapted Nelson and Quick's *ORGB* for the Canadian market; the textbook is now in its second Canadian edition.

Ann earned her Ph.D. in organizational behaviour from the University of Toronto. She has received several teaching awards, including the Gilmour Award and the Annual Rotman Teaching Award in both the MBA and BCom programs. In addition, she sits on several not-for-profit boards and consults on organization design and change for clients in the nonprofit and social enterprise sectors.

# Brief Contents

# Contents

# Preface

When I was approached to prepare a Canadian version of the ninth edition of Dr. Daft's *Organization Theory and Design,* I was excited to build on his wonderful book. In the process, I learned so much about Canada and, particularly, the variety of organizations that spans from sea to sea to sea. As I worked on the third Canadian edition, I was reminded of the richness of the Canadian experience. I hope that I have been able to capture that richness for both the students and the faculty who will use this book. Our organizations are remarkably diverse, as we are! I hope that this edition excites you about the variety—and the impact—of our organizations.

## Distinguishing Features of the Third Canadian Edition

The Canadianization of Dr. Daft's book has been extensive. However, a number of U.S. and international examples were retained or updated to accurately represent Canada's role in the world.

Each chapter has a *Dilbert* strip to highlight the chapter's concepts in a light-hearted or cynical but insightful way. Scott Adams, the creator of *Dilbert*, reminds us that when we listen to our egos, rather than to analysis, we may make poor decisions.[1] I hope this book's contents will help you subordinate your ego and instead use good theory, supported by solid research, so that you can be an effective organizational actor.

**Leading by Design** The Leading by Design features describe organizations that have undergone a major shift in organizational design, strategic direction, values, or culture as they strive to be more competitive in today's turbulent global environment. Many of these organizations are applying new design ideas, such as network organizing, e-business, or temporary systems for flexibility and innovation. Examples of Leading by Design organizations include Four Seasons, Médecins sans Frontières (MSF), Manitoba Telecom Services, Dell, and WestJet Airlines.

**Book Marks** Book Marks, a special feature of this text, are book reviews that reflect current issues of concern for managers working in real-life organizations. These reviews describe the varied ways organizations are meeting the challenges of today's changing environment. Book Marks in the third Canadian edition include a review of Andrea Mandel-Campbell's *Why Mexicans Don't Drink Molson,* Joel Bakan's *The Corporation: The Pathological Pursuit of Profit and Power,* and Andrew Heinztman's *The New Entrepreneurs: Building a Green Economy for the Future.*

**Case Examples** This edition contains new examples to illustrate theoretical concepts. Many examples are Canadian, and all are based on real organizations. They include Teleflex Canada, Metropolitan College, The Daily Grind Inc., The Big Carrot, and Vancity. Some are international, such as Apple Inc.'s Foxconn Test.

**In Practice** There are many cases used within chapters to illustrate specific concepts. They include Bombardier Inc., Harvard Business School, Garrison Guitars, Aravind Eye Hospital, Joe Fresh Style, Apotex, McCain Foods, Doepker Industries, lululemon athletica, zappos.com, and Experiencepoint, to name a few.

**A Look Inside** This feature introduces each chapter with a relevant and interesting organizational example. Many examples are Canadian, and all are based on real organizations. Examples include Air Canada, Alcan, Tim Hortons, Manitobah Mukluks, and Anishinabek Nation.

**ACT!** ACT, which stands for Apply-Compare-Think, helps students personalize their understanding of the chapter's concepts.

**You and Design** This feature is designed to help students achieve a personal and practical understanding of the material by answering short questionnaires about a key concept in each chapter.

**Text Exhibits** Frequent exhibits are used to help students visualize organizational relationships, and some of the artwork has been redone to communicate concepts more clearly.

**Summary and Interpretation** The Summary and Interpretation section tells students how the chapter points are important in the broader context of organizational theory.

**Cases for Analysis** These cases are tailored to chapter concepts and provide a vehicle for student analysis and discussion.

**Integrative Cases** The integrative cases at the end of the text are designed to encourage in-depth discussion and involvement. Many are new to this edition. The cases include IKEA: Scandinavian Style, The Hospital for Sick Children (SickKids®), Costco: Join the Club, "Ramrod" Stockwell, Make Green Delicious: Sustainability at Jamie Kennedy Kitchens, The Donor Services Department, The War of the Woods: A Forestry Giant Seeks Peace, Chiquita in Colombia, Genocide in Rwanda: Leadership, Ethics and Organizational "Failure" In a Post-Colonial Context, and The International Career Opportunity: From Dream to Nightmare in Eight Weeks.

# New Concepts

Some concepts have been added or expanded in this edition. Updated material has been provided on culture, learning, and performance; virtual network organization structures; applying ethics to create socially responsible organizations; lean manufacturing; e-commerce; political tactics for increasing and using managerial power; and the use of global coordination mechanisms for transferring knowledge and innovation. Many ideas are aimed at helping students learn to design organizations for an environment characterized by uncertainty; a renewed emphasis on ethics and social responsibility; and the need for a speedy response to change, crises, or shifting customer expectations. In addition, coping with the complexity of today's global environment is explored thoroughly. To help students see the relationships among the concepts, I have designed a course/concept map, which is presented in Chapter 1.

In the third edition, students are challenged directly to look at the various theories critically. For example, students are alerted to importance of looking beyond the "accepted wisdom" on topics such as lean manufacturing and globalization and more generally to the implicitly capitalist framework of organizational theory.

## Chapter Organization

Each chapter is highly focused and is organized into a logical framework. Many organization theory textbooks treat material in sequential fashion, such as "Here's View A, Here's View B, Here's View C," and so on. *Organization Theory and Design* shows how these views apply in organizations. Moreover, each chapter sticks to the essential point. Students are not introduced to extraneous material or confusing methodological squabbles that occur among organizational researchers. The body of research in most areas points to a major trend, which is discussed here. Several chapters develop a framework that organizes major ideas into an overall scheme.

As I was working on the book, I often solicited ideas from my undergraduate and graduate students; I am sure that they will see their impact! The combination of organization theory concepts, book reviews, examples of organizations recommended by the students, case illustrations, experiential exercises, self-reflection tools, and other teaching devices is designed to effectively meet students' learning needs.

## Chapter Changes in the Third Canadian Edition

At the suggestion of the thoughtful reviewers, more small and medium-sized organizational examples were added throughout the text. The book now has 12 chapters. Key material from a previous chapter has been incorporated in other chapters; for example, the balanced scorecard was added to Chapter 2 as one reviewer suggested.

- Chapter 1: Organizations and Organizational Theory

  - The Air Canada story has been updated.

  - The history of the discipline receives more prominent attention.

  - International and nonprofit examples have been added.

  - Evergreen and the Brick Works has been added as an In Practice box.

- Chapter 2: Strategy, Organizational Design, and Effectiveness

  - Both updated and new organizational examples, such as Volvo Car Corporation, are included. More nonprofit examples are also included.

    – There is a new Book Mark, *Good Strategy Bad Strategy: The Difference and Why It Matters.*

    – The new Case for Analysis, "I want there to be!": Apple Inc.'s Foxconn Test, describes the challenges faced by Apple in its dealings with Foxconn.

- Chapter 3: Fundamentals of Organizational Structure

    – There is a new In Practice box about Mountain Equipment Co-op's governance and structure.

    – The Microsoft In Practice box was updated.

- Chapter 4: The External Environment

    – The introduction looks at how organizations come and go to the extent they can adjust to the demands of their environments.

    – A new In Practice box looks at Kraft's challenges in meeting changing customers' tastes.

    – The Joe Fresh In Practice box was updated to include the tragic fire at its supplier's factory in Bangladesh.

- Chapter 5: Interorganizational Relationships

    – A new In Practice box on Google was added.

    – Shazam's current competitive landscape was added.

- Chapter 6: Designing Organizations for the International Environment

    – Cole + Parker's innovative business model was described.

    – A discussion on the concerns about globalization was added.

    – The BRANDAID Project In Practice box was updated to highlight its international reach.

    – A new In Practice box, Impact Hub, describes a values-driven and organic international organization.

- Chapter 7: Manufacturing and Service Technologies

    – The new A Look Inside box describes the design and manufacturing process of Manitobah Mukluks, an Aboriginal organization that produces stylish mukluks.

    – A new In Practice box describes Eyecandy, a small company in Halifax that combines old and new technologies.

    – A new In Practice box looks at how Sealy uses lean manufacturing principles.

    – A critique of lean manufacturing is included.

- Chapter 8: Organization Size, Life Cycle, and Decline

    – A new In Practice box was added that looks at the fallout from the tsunami in Japan at the Shizugawa Elementary School Evacuation Centre, and discusses the limitations of top-down bureaucracy at Toyota Motors.

- The current threats to Sears Canada's future were added to the In Practice about Eaton's demise.

- The In Practice box on the Grackle Coffee Company was updated.

- Chapter 9: Organizational Culture and Ethical Values

  - A discussion on organizational identity was added.

  - A new In Practice box on zappos.com discusses the importance and impact of culture.

  - Several In Practice boxes were updated.

- Chapter 10: Innovation and Change

  - New material about Kurt Lewin's influence on change was added.

  - The differences between the concepts of innovation and change were highlighted.

- Chapter 11: Decision-Making Processes

  - A new In Practice box describes the series of decisions that contributed to BlackBerry's considerable difficulties.

  - Some statistics were updated.

- Chapter 12: Conflict, Power, and Politics

  - Etsy was added as an example of conflict in an artisanal organization.

  - Both the Bennett Jones and Conrad Black examples were updated.

  - A discussion on the importance of empowerment was added.

  - An updated account of Semco's empowerment strategy was included.

## References

1. S. Adams, "The Loser Decision" (2007) at http://dilbertblog.typepad.com/the_dilbert_blog/2007/07/the-loser-decis.html (accessed March 30, 2014).

## About the Nelson Education Teaching Advantage (NETA)

The **Nelson Education Teaching Advantage (NETA)** program delivers research-based instructor resources that promote student engagement and higher-order thinking to enable the success of Canadian students and educators. To ensure the high quality of these materials, all Nelson ancillaries have been professionally copy-edited.

Be sure to visit Nelson Education's **Inspired Instruction** website at http://www.nelson.com/inspired to find out more about NETA. Don't miss the testimonials of instructors who have used NETA supplements and seen student engagement increase!

**Planning Your Course:** *NETA Engagement* presents materials that help instructors deliver engaging content and activities to their classes. **NETA Instructor's Manuals** not only identify the topics that cause students the most difficulty, but also describe techniques and resources to help students master these concepts. Dr. Roger Fisher's *Instructor's Guide to Classroom Engagement* accompanies every Instructor's Manual.

**Assessing Your Students:** *NETA Assessment* relates to testing materials. *NETA Test Bank* authors create multiple-choice questions that reflect research-based best practices for constructing effective questions and testing not just recall but also higher-order thinking. Our guidelines were developed by David DiBattista, psychology professor at Brock University and 3M National Teaching Fellow, whose research has focused on multiple-choice testing. All Test Bank authors receive training at workshops conducted by Prof. DiBattista, as do the copy editors assigned to each Test Bank. A copy of *Multiple Choice Tests: Getting Beyond Remembering*, Prof. DiBattista's guide to writing effective tests, is included with every Nelson Test Bank.

**Teaching Your Students:** *NETA Presentation* has been developed to help instructors make the best use of Microsoft® PowerPoint® in their classrooms. With a clean and uncluttered design developed by Maureen Stone of StoneSoup Consulting, **NETA PowerPoints** features slides with improved readability, more multi-media and graphic materials, activities to use in class, and tips for instructors on the Notes page. A copy of *NETA Guidelines for Classroom Presentations* by Maureen Stone is included with each set of PowerPoint slides.

**Technology in Teaching:** *NETA Digital* is a framework based on Arthur Chickering and Zelda Gamson's seminal work "Seven Principles of Good Practice In Undergraduate Education" *(AAHE Bulletin*, 1987) and the follow-up work by Chickering and Stephen C. Ehrmann, "Implementing the Seven Principles: Technology as Lever" *(AAHE Bulletin*, 1996). This aspect of the NETA program guides the writing and development of our **digital products** to ensure that they appropriately reflect the core goals of contact, collaboration, multimodal learning, time on task, prompt feedback, active learning, and high expectations. The resulting focus on pedagogical utility, rather than technological wizardry, ensures that all of our technology supports better outcomes for students.

## Instructor Resources

All instructor ancillaries for *Organization Theory and Design* are available at **http://www.nelson.com/orgtheory3e** and also through the Instructor Resource Center at **http://www.nelson.com/login** or **http://login.cengage.com**. These rich supplements give instructors the ultimate tool for customizing lectures and presentations.

**NETA Test Bank:** This resource includes over 400 multiple-choice questions written according to NETA guidelines for effective construction and development of higher-order questions. Also included are approximately 265 true/false and 50 essay questions.

The NETA Test Bank is available in a new, cloud-based platform. **Testing Powered by Cognero®** is a secure online testing system that allows you to author, edit,

and manage test bank content from any place you have Internet access. No special installations or downloads are needed, and the desktop-inspired interface, with its drop-down menus and familiar, intuitive tools, allows you to create and manage tests with ease. You can create multiple test versions in an instant, and import or export content into other systems. Tests can be delivered from your learning management system, your classroom, or wherever you want.

**NETA PowerPoint:** Microsoft® PowerPoint ® lecture slides for every chapter feature key figures, tables, and photographs from *Organization Theory & Design*. NETA principles of clear design and engaging content have been incorporated throughout, making it simple for instructors to customize the deck for their courses.

**Image Library:** This resource consists of digital copies of figures, short tables, and photographs used in the book. Instructors may use these jpegs to customize the NETA PowerPoint or create their own PowerPoint presentations.

**NETA Instructor's Manual:** This resource is organized according to the textbook chapters and addresses key educational concerns, such as typical stumbling blocks students face and how to address them. Other features include learning objectives and suggested activities to increase student engagement, as well as answers to exercises and cases.

**Day One:** Day One—Prof InClass is a PowerPoint presentation that instructors can customize to orient students to the class and their text at the beginning of the course.

## Student Ancillaries

**CourseMate** The more you study, the better the results. Make the most of your study time by accessing everything you need to succeed in one place. The **Course-Mate** site for *Organization Theory & Design* includes:

- An interactive eBook with highlighting, note taking, and an interactive glossary
- Interactive learning tools, including:
  - quizzes
  - flashcards
  - games
  - review questions
  - . . . and more!

Visit **NELSONbrain.com** to start using CourseMate. Enter the Online Access Code from the card included with your text. If a code card is **not** provided, you can purchase instant access at **NELSONbrain.com**.

## Acknowledgements for the Third Canadian Edition

First, I would like to thank Dick Daft. He not only wrote a wonderful book, but also sent me useful material. Among my Rotman School of Management colleagues, I would like to thank (former) Dean Roger Martin and Associate Dean Joel Baum, who have supported my textbook writing. I thank my colleagues Alan Saks and Uli Menzefricke, both seasoned textbook writers, for orienting me to the realities of writing a textbook! I thank Alison Kemper for her work on Chapter 2 for the first Canadian edition.

The reviewers made an especially important contribution. They praised many features, were critical of things that didn't work well, and offered valuable suggestions. I was impressed by the constructive nature of their feedback. Thanks to

Kelly Dye
*Acadia University*

Kai Lamertz
*Concordia University*

John Hardisty
*Sheridan College*

Stefan Litz
*St. Francis Xavier University*

Cammie Jaquays
*Trent University*

Dayna Patterson
*York University*

Ruthanne Krant
*Georgian College*

The team at Nelson Education is amazing! Alwynn Pinard, Acquisitions Editor, was a good advocate for this book and others that I completed with her. Jackie Wood took over in the latter stages of this edition and I was glad to work with her again! Karen Rolfe, freelance copy editor, found my errors and made valuable suggestions. I have now worked with Karen four times and have been so fortunate! Christine Elliott, permissions and photo researcher, worked so diligently to ensure that the permissions were received in a timely way and was patient with my last-minute submissions. Christine Gilbert, Production Project Manager; Dave Stratton, Marketing Manager; and Susan Calvert, Director of Content and Media Production, worked hard to ensure that the book would be well received by students and faculty alike. I would like to thank Naman Mahisauria for his patience as we worked on the last stages of book production. I would like to thank A. Nayyer Samsi for finding elusive typos and helping to maintain consistency in the language. The third Canadian edition would not have been completed if not for Rachel Eagen, Developmental Editor, who kept me on track. She was patient in the extreme! I was also delighted to reconnect with Lesley Mann, Managing Developmental Editor, who was my developmental editor for the first edition of this book. Finally, I want to thank my friends and especially my family, who heard more about the book than they wanted to hear, and listened!

*Ann Armstrong*

# 1

# Organizations and Organization Theory

Jelle-vd-Wolf / Shutterstock.com

# A Look Inside

## Air Canada

Air Canada filed for bankruptcy protection on April 1, 2003. Robert Milton, CEO and chair, was ridiculed for managing a monopoly into bankruptcy! However, under his leadership, Air Canada emerged from bankruptcy on September 30, 2004. Air Canada cut thousands of jobs, renegotiated contracts with its 30,000 unionized employees, slashed fares, and eliminated free drinks and meals on many of its flights. In November 2005, Robert Milton was named CEO of the year by *Report on Business* magazine, which lauded Milton for managing the massive restructuring of Air Canada and for repositioning the airline to offer smaller, more cost-efficient planes for regional routes. "While Air Canada spilled almost five billion dollars in red ink between 2000 and 2004 and wiped out billions more in shareholder value ..., [it] is poised to post a healthy profit [in 2005 and 2006]."[1]

## Background

Air Canada has had a bumpy history since it was founded as Trans-Canada Airlines in 1937. As Canada's national airline, it started with three planes and $5 million. Forty years later, it had revenues of more than $500 million and 90 planes. In 1977, Air Canada was reorganized under the *Air Canada Act*. In 1988, Air Canada was privatized and 43 percent of its shares sold to the public. The privatization was designed to level the competitive environment between Air Canada and its chief competitor, Canadian Airlines International (CAI). In 1989, the privatization was complete. By 1991, CAI was suffering financially and the two airlines began merger talks.

The 1992 recession in North America hit both airlines hard. Both were losing a million dollars a day as passenger volumes dropped dramatically. Air Canada suspended its freight operations and laid off more than 2,000 employees. Air Canada then suggested a merger with CAI, which the latter accepted. However, Air Canada had second thoughts about managing the $7.7 billion debt and the deal did not proceed.

The federal government deregulated flights between Canada and the United States and, in 1999, suspended the *Competition Act* to let the two airlines discuss restructuring. At that time, the Onex Corporation attempted, unsuccessfully, to buy Air Canada. By year's end, Air Canada won its bid for CAI after it received more than 50 percent of CAI's shares and struck a deal with American Airlines for its 25 percent stake in CAI.

Soon after September 11, 2001, as Air Canada's losses continued to mount, it asked the federal government for $4 billion in aid, cut 5,000 jobs, and grounded 84 planes. In early 2002, Air Canada announced its biggest loss—$1.25 billion! In late 2002, it announced that it would no longer issue paper tickets for domestic flights. Job cuts continued and, in 2003, Air Canada filed for bankruptcy protection. After difficult and often acrimonious negotiations, both with potential investors and the unions representing Air Canada's staff, Air Canada took flight again.

Air Canada was restructured; Robert Milton became CEO and chair of a new parent company, ACE Aviation Holdings. The company also welcomed an American investor, Cerberus Capital Management, which invested $250 million. ACE Aviation Holdings debuted on the Toronto Stock Exchange on October 1, 2004. Its shares traded at $20 and have traded in the range of $16 to $32 since. In the summer of 2005, Air Canada had a profit of $168 million in the preceding quarter and had an average plane capacity of 80 percent.

### Competition Heats Up

As Air Canada was recovering from its near-death experience, two new airlines entered the Canadian industry—WestJet Airlines (WestJet) and Jetsgo. They offered cheap, no-frills flights and were able to take one-third of Air Canada's domestic business. Although Jetsgo went out of business, WestJet continues to thrive.

WestJet was founded in 1996 by four Calgary entrepreneurs. They modelled their low-fare airline on Southwest Airlines in the United States. WestJet took off with 220 employees and three planes that flew between five cities. Since then, WestJet has grown dramatically and flies throughout Canada and into the United States. In 2000, the four founders received the Ernst & Young Entrepreneur of the Year Award and, in 2003, WestJet was named Canada's second most respected corporation in an Ipsos Reid survey of 255 of Canada's leading CEOs.[2]

Soon after, WestJet found itself in an industrial espionage scandal. Air Canada accused WestJet executives of spying by tapping into its website and of stealing confidential information. Air Canada filed a $220 million lawsuit against WestJet. WestJet did not deny the accusations; the vice president of strategic planning for WestJet resigned. Clive Beddoe, president of WestJet, apologized and WestJet paid $15.5 million to settle the suit. "WestJet, which typically casts itself as the David to Air Canada's Goliath, admitted in a joint statement … that its campaign of online snooping 'was both unethical and unacceptable' and offered a rare apology to Air Canada and Robert Milton …."[3]

### The Survivor

Robert Milton survived the turbulence at Air Canada. When asked what he had learned about himself as he was vilified throughout the restructuring process, he commented,

> When you know your game—and I believe I do know the airline industry—and you know where you've got to take them, sometimes you just have to put your head down and just drive through the walls and just stop listening to all the people who tell you that it can't be done. Because a lot of those people that said it couldn't be done are now awfully quiet. And so it really was about knowing the business and knowing how we had to change and now I think even those that weren't too happy recognize they're a lot better off.[4]*

### The Successor

While Milton survived and did well—he earned about $83 million between 2005 and 2009 in his position as chair and CEO of ACE Aviation Holdings—trouble loomed for Air Canada. In 2009, it rehired Calvin Rovinescu who had been the chief restructuring officer in 2004 to become the next president and CEO of Air Canada. His challenge was "to rescue a company that was being strangled by debts, a massive pension deficit, shrinking traffic and more nimble competitors."[5] Air Canada has been successful in controlling costs. As a result, Air Canada's profit margins increased from −1.5 percent in 2008 to 3.6 percent in 2012.[6]

Rovinescu was known for his aggressive style when he was the chief restructuring officer. However, more recently, he has become focused on employee empowerment as he believes that leadership comes from the middle, which requires engaged employees. While Rovinescu was named 2013 CEO of the Year, it was a bumpy start for Air Canada in 2014. One flight skidded off an icy runway, a military veteran suffering from post-traumatic stress syndrome was prevented from flying with her support dog, and Air Canada lost snowboards of two Australian Sochi Olympics hopefuls. Air Canada remains one of the country's most disliked organizations.[7]

---

*"Robert Milton, Chairman & CEO, ACE Aviation" from CNN.com; 10/9/2006. Used with permission.

### Competing On Price

Recently, Air Canada joined the discount airline market and now competes with Porter Airlines and WestJet. Air Canada's Rouge service and WestJet's Encore service are both designed to compete on price and in some cases are offering 50 percent reductions on certain routes. As well, Encore is expected to compete head-on with Air Canada on its smaller regional hubs. Air Canada needs to be concerned as "[by] expanding to more locations, Encore also sets up its parent carrier for international expansion, eventually allowing, say, someone from Brandon to go on an Italian holiday in Rome entirely on WestJet planes."[8] Similarly, Air Canada faces competition from Porter Airlines as it adds locations and increases the numbers of jets in its fleet.

## Organization Theory in Action

Welcome to the exciting, complex, and often surprising world of organization theory. The shifting fortunes of Air Canada illustrate organization theory in action. Everyone at the company was deeply involved in organization theory every day at work. However, managers did not fully understand how the organization related to the environment or how it should function internally. Familiarity with organization theory helped Robert Milton and his management team analyze and diagnose what was happening and the changes needed to keep the company competitive. Organization theory gives us the tools to explain Air Canada's birth, decline, and rebirth and to understand Air Canada's turnaround. It helps us explain what happened in the past, as well as what may happen in the future, so that we can manage organizations more effectively.

Before exploring the field of organization theory and design any further, please complete the You & Design feature to assess your overall approach to organization design.

## YOU & DESIGN

### Evolution of Style

This questionnaire asks you to describe yourself. For each item, give the number "4" to the phrase that best describes you, "3" to the item that is next best, and on down to "1" for the item that is least like you.

1. My strongest skills are
   ___**a.** Analytical skills
   ___**b.** Interpersonal skills
   ___**c.** Political skills
   ___**d.** Flair for drama

2. The best way to describe me is
   ___**a.** Technical expert
   ___**b.** Good listener
   ___**c.** Skilled negotiator
   ___**d.** Inspirational leader

3. What has helped me the most to be successful is my ability to
   ___**a.** Make good decisions
   ___**b.** Coach and develop people
   ___**c.** Build strong alliances and a power base
   ___**d.** Inspire and excite others

4. What people are most likely to notice about me is my
   ___**a.** Attention to detail
   ___**b.** Concern for people
   ___**c.** Ability to succeed in the face of conflict and opposition
   ___**d.** Charisma

*(Continued)*

**5.** My most important leadership trait is
___**a.** Clear, logical thinking
___**b.** Caring and support for others
___**c.** Toughness and aggressiveness
___**d.** Imagination and creativity

**6.** I am best described as
___**a.** An analyst
___**b.** A humanist
___**c.** A politician
___**d.** A visionary

**Scoring:** Compute your scores according to the following rater. The higher score represents your way of viewing the organization and will influence your management style.

Structure = 1a + 2a + 3a + 4a + 5a + 6a = _____
Human Resource = 1b + 2b + 3b + 4b + 5b + 6b = _____
Political = 1c + 2c + 3c + 4c + 5c + 6c = _____
Symbolic = 1d + 2d + 3d + 4d + 5d + 6d = _____

**Interpretation:** Organization managers typically view their world through one or more mental frames of reference. (1) The *structural frame* of reference sees the organization as a machine that can be economically efficient with vertical hierarchy and routine tasks that give a manager the formal authority to achieve goals. This manager way of thinking became strong during the era of scientific management when efficiency was everything. (2) The *human resource frame* sees the organization as its people, with manager emphasis given to support, empowerment, and belonging. This manager way of thinking gained importance after the **Hawthorne studies**. (3) The *political frame* sees the organization as a competition for scarce resources to achieve goals, with manager emphasis on building agreement among diverse groups. This frame of reference reflects the need for organizations to share information, have a collaborative strategy, and have all parts working together. (4) The *symbolic frame* sees the organization as theatre, with manager emphasis on symbols, vision, culture, and inspiration. This manager frame of reference is important for managing an adaptive culture in a learning organization.

Which frame reflects your way of viewing the world? The first two frames of reference—structural and human resource—are important for newer managers at the lower and middle levels of an organization. These two frames usually are mastered first. As managers gain experience and move up the organization, they should acquire political and collaborative skills (Chapter 12) and also learn to use symbols to shape cultural values (Chapter 9). It is important for managers not to be stuck in one way of viewing the organization because their progress may be limited.

Source: Roy G. Williams and Terrence E. Deal, *When Opposites Dance: Balancing the Manager and Leader Within* (Palo Alto, CA: Davies-Black, 2003), pp. 24–28. Reprinted with permission.

## ■ Topics

The Air Canada case illustrates many of the topics in the book. We see the importance of choosing the right **change strategy** and then designing the right structure. We see the importance of the changing environment and its impact on Air Canada's effectiveness. We see the adoption and impact of electronic technology. We learn that organizations go through life cycles and face crises along the way. We also see that organizations face ethical challenges, and tough decisions must be made and conflict addressed.

Of course, the concepts of organization theory are not limited to Air Canada. The Ganong family has an acute understanding of the impact of changing environmental conditions on their New Brunswick chocolate business, which was founded in 1837. Ganong employs about 400 and sells its chocolates in North America and the United Kingdom. David Ganong notes that "[you've] got four moving parts underneath this business ... exchange rates, corn syrup, sugar and cocoa."[9] In 2008, Ganong looked outside the family for a CEO whose challenge was to manage the four moving parts more effectively, as Canada's chocolate industry

**Apply**

What can you apply from the Air Canada saga to help you be an effective organizational actor?

had lost half its manufacturing capacity.[10] Global organizations such as IBM, Hewlett-Packard, and Ford Motor Company have all undergone major structural transformations using concepts based in organization theory. Organization theory also applies to nonprofit organizations such as Free the Children, the Heart and Stroke Foundation, local arts organizations, colleges and universities, and the Starlight Children's Foundation of Canada. Rock groups such as the Rolling Stones benefit from an appreciation of organization theory (see this chapter's Leading by Design box).

Organization theory draws lessons from organizations such as the Rolling Stones, IBM, and Air Canada and makes those lessons available to students and managers. The story of Air Canada's rebirth is important because it demonstrates that even large, successful organizations are vulnerable, lessons are not learned automatically, and organizations are only as strong as their decision makers. Organizations are not static; they continuously adapt to shifts in the external environment. Today, many companies are facing the need to transform themselves into dramatically different organizations because of new challenges in the environment.

# The Evolution of Organization Theory and Design

Organization theory is not a collection of facts; it is a way of thinking about organizations. Organization theory is a way to see and analyze organizations more accurately and deeply than we otherwise could. The way to see and think about organization theory is based on patterns and regularities in organizational design and behaviour. Organization scholars search for these regularities, define them, measure them, and make them available to the rest of us. The facts from the research are not as important as the general patterns and insights into organizational functioning.

## Historical Perspectives

Organizational design and management practices have varied over time in response to changes in the larger society. The modern era of management theory began with the classical management perspective in the late 19th and early 20th centuries. The emergence of the factory system during the Industrial Revolution posed problems that earlier organizations had not encountered. As work was performed on a much larger scale by a larger number of workers, people began thinking about how to design and manage work in order to increase productivity and help organizations attain maximum efficiency. The classical perspective, which sought to make organizations run like efficient, well-oiled machines, is associated with the development of hierarchy and bureaucratic organizations and remains the basis of much of modern management theory and practice. In this section, we will examine the classical perspective, with its emphasis on efficiency and organization, as well as other perspectives that emerged to address new concerns, such as employee needs and the role of the environment. Elements of each perspective are still used in organizational design, although they have been adapted and revised to meet changing needs.

**Efficiency Is Everything.** Pioneered by Frederick Winslow Taylor, **scientific management** postulates that decisions about organizations and job design should be based on precise, scientific study of individual situations.[11] To use this approach, managers develop precise, standard procedures for doing each job; select workers with appropriate abilities; train workers in the standard procedures; carefully plan work; and provide wage incentives to increase output. Taylor's approach is illustrated by the unloading of iron from railcars and reloading finished steel for the Bethlehem Steel plant in 1898. Taylor calculated that with correct movements, tools, and sequencing, each man was capable of loading 43 tons per day instead of the typical 11.3 tons. He also worked out an incentive system that paid each man $1.85 per day for meeting the new standard, an increase from the previous rate of $1.15. Productivity at Bethlehem Steel shot up overnight. These insights helped to establish organizational assumptions that the role of management is to maintain stability and efficiency, with top managers doing the thinking and workers doing what they are told.

**How to Get Organized.** Another subfield of the classical perspective took a broader look at the organization. Although scientific management focused primarily on the technical core—on work performed on the shop floor—**administrative principles** looked at the design and functioning of the organization as a whole. For example, Henri Fayol proposed 14 principles of management, such as "each subordinate receives orders from only one superior" (unity of command) and "similar activities in an organization should be grouped together under one manager" (unity of direction). These principles formed the foundation for modern management practice and organizational design.

The scientific management and administrative principles approaches were powerful and gave organizations fundamental new ideas for establishing high productivity and increasing prosperity. Administrative principles in particular contributed to the development of **bureaucratic organizations**, which emphasized designing and managing organizations on an impersonal, rational basis through elements such as clearly defined authority and responsibility, formal record keeping, and uniform application of standard rules. Although the term *bureaucracy* has taken on negative connotations in today's organizations, bureaucratic characteristics worked extremely well for the needs of the Industrial Age. One problem with the classical perspective, however, is that it failed to consider the social context and human needs.

**What About People?** Early work on industrial psychology and human relations received little attention because of the prominence of scientific management. However, a major breakthrough occurred with a series of experiments at a Chicago electric company, which came to be known as the **Hawthorne Studies**. Interpretations of these studies concluded that positive treatment of employees improved their motivation and productivity. The publication of these findings led to a revolution in worker treatment and laid the groundwork for subsequent work examining treatment of workers, leadership, motivation, and human resource management. These human relations and behavioural approaches added new and important contributions to the study of management and organizations.

However, the hierarchical system and bureaucratic approaches that developed during the Industrial Revolution remained the primary approach to organizational design and functioning well into the 1970s and 80s. In general, this approach worked well for most organizations until the past few decades. However, during the 1980s, it began to lead to problems. Increased competition, especially on a global scale, changed the playing field.[12] North American companies had to find a better way.

The 1980s produced new organizational cultures that valued lean staff, flexibility, rapid response to the customer, motivated employees, caring for customers, and quality products. Over the past two decades, the world of organizations has undergone even more profound and far-reaching changes. The Internet and other advances in information technology, globalization, rapid social and economic changes, and other challenges from the environment call for new management perspectives and more flexible approaches to organizational design.

## ■ Current Challenges

Research into hundreds of organizations provides the knowledge base to make Air Canada and other organizations more effective. For example, challenges facing organizations today are quite different from those of the past, and thus the concept of organizations and organization theory is evolving. The world is changing more rapidly than ever before. Surveys of top executives indicate that coping with rapid change is the most common problem facing managers and organizations.[13] Some specific challenges are dealing with globalization, ensuring high standards of ethics and social responsibility, responding rapidly to environmental changes and customer needs, managing the digital workplace, and supporting diversity.

**Globalization.** The cliché that the world is getting smaller is dramatically true for today's organizations. With rapid advances in technology and communications, the time it takes to exert influence around the world from even the most remote locations has been reduced from years to only seconds. Markets, technologies, and organizations are increasingly interconnected.[14] Today's organizations have to feel "at home" anywhere in the world. Companies can locate different parts of the organization wherever it makes the most business sense: top leadership in one country, technical brainpower and production in other locales. A related trend is to contract out some functions to organizations in other countries or to partner with foreign organizations to gain global advantage. India's Wipro used to sell cooking oils; today, its 15,000 employees develop sophisticated software applications, design semiconductors, and manage back-office solutions for giant companies from all over the world, including Origin Energy, Home Depot, and Sony. Korea's Samsung Electronics, which has manufacturing plants in 14 countries, has long supplied components for U.S. computer firms, and it designed a new laptop that it will manufacture for Texas-based Dell Computer. Samsung's global presence includes 111 subsidiaries in the form of production subsidiaries, sales subsidiaries, distribution subsidiaries, research laboratories, and eight overseas business divisions representing North America, Europe, China, Southeast Asia, Southwest Asia, Central and South America, CIS, the Middle East, and Africa.[15] Exhibit 1.1 presents a simplified design of an organization with regional headquarters and functional divisions and centres.

Many of Intel's new chip circuits, for example, are designed by companies in India and China. These organizations can do the job for 50 to 60 percent less than organizations based in the United States or Canada, creating new advantages

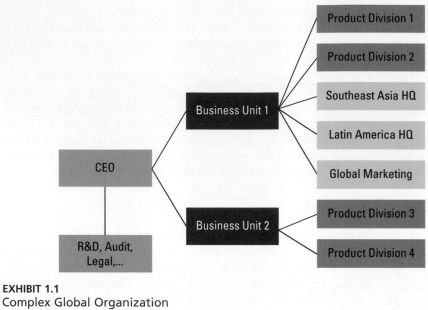

**EXHIBIT 1.1**
Complex Global Organization
Source: Ann Armstrong.

as well as greater competition for North American organizations.[16] This growing interdependence means that the environment for companies is becoming extremely complex and competitive. Organizations have to learn to cross lines of time, culture, and geography in order to survive. Companies, large and small, are searching for the right structures and processes that can help them reap the advantages of global interdependence and minimize the disadvantages.

**Ethics and Social Responsibility.** Ethics and social responsibility have become two of the hottest topics in organizations today. The list of executives and major corporations involved in financial and ethical scandals continues to grow. The sordid story of high-flying Enron Corporation, where managers admitted they inflated earnings and hid debt through a series of complex partnerships, was just the beginning. Executives profited handsomely from the fraud at Enron, but when the company collapsed, employees and average investors lost billions. Arthur Andersen LLP, the company's auditor, was found guilty of obstruction of justice for improperly shredding documents related to the Enron investigation. Martha Stewart, who built a multimillion-dollar style empire, has served time in jail, convicted of lying about why she unloaded shares of ImClone Systems stock just before the price plunged. And Yale University's School of Management forced out the head of its corporate governance institute over alleged expense-account abuse.[17] The CEO of Hotel-Dieu Grace Hospital in Windsor was fired in 2011 after the hospital's reputation had been tarnished by scandal as a result of significant surgical and diagnostic errors.[18] On almost any day, the news will contain an account of some organization embroiled in an ethical scandal. In 2013, Canada was rocked by the Senate expenses scandal and the Rob Ford scandal in Toronto, to name only two; both received international attention.

# Leading *by Design*

## The Rolling Stones

They may be really old, but they keep on rocking and rolling after more than 50 years in the music business! The Rolling Stones have enjoyed phenomenal commercial success in recent decades, generating billions of dollars in revenue from record sales, song rights, concert tickets, sponsorships, and merchandising.

The Rolling Stones group was recently cited as one of the world's ten most enduring organizations, according to a study commissioned by consulting firm Booz Allen Hamilton. One reason for the Stones' success is that the band operates like an effective global business organization. The Stones have set up a solid organizational structure, with different divisions to run different aspects of the business, such as touring or merchandising. At the top of the organization is a core top management team made up of the four band members: Mick Jagger, who acts as a sort of CEO; Keith Richards; Charlie Watts; and Ronnie Wood. This core team manages a group of somewhat autonomous yet interlocking companies that include Promotour, Promopub, Promotone, and Musidor, each dedicated to a particular part of the overall business. At times, depending on what's happening in the organization, each company might employ only a few dozen people. When the band is touring, on the other hand, head count soars and the organization resembles a flourishing start-up company. Jagger himself keeps a close eye on the market-price range for concert tickets so that the band can

keep its prices competitive. That sometimes means cutting costs and increasing efficiency to make sure the organization turns a profit. The Stones also recognize the importance of interorganizational partnerships, cutting sponsorship deals with big companies such as Sprint, Anheuser-Busch, and Microsoft, which reportedly paid $4 million for the rights to "Start Me Up" for the launch of Windows 95. And the group hires lawyers, accountants, managers, and consultants to keep in touch with changes in the environment and manage relationships with customers (fans), partners, employees, record companies, promoters, and tour sites. Jagger learned from the early days that creativity and talent aren't enough to ensure success—in the mid-1960s, the band was selling millions of records but still living hand to mouth. Today, effective control systems and widespread information sharing make sure that doesn't happen.

"You don't start to play your guitar thinking you're going to be running an organization that will maybe generate millions," Jagger says. Yet by understanding and applying organization theory, the Rolling Stones have become one of the most successful organizations ever in the music industry—and the wealthiest rock 'n' roll band on the planet.[19] The Rolling Stones have enjoyed such success as they do not reinvent themselves: they "flout the rules … and invest their remaining energy in staying just the same"[20] while adapting to new audiences and new technologies.

Although some executives and officials continue to insist that it is a few bad apples involved in all the wrongdoing, the public is quickly forming the opinion that all corporate executives are crooks.[21] It is disgusted with the whole mess, and leaders face tremendous pressure from the government and the public to hold their organizations and employees to high ethical and professional standards. Gwyn Morgan, founding (and retired) CEO of EnCana Corporation, for example, urges business leaders to pursue business as a "calling" to address some of the public's concerns by "both teaching and role modelling ethical behaviours for the young Canadians who will determine the kind of Canada we will become."[22]

**Speed of Responsiveness.** A third significant challenge for organizations is to respond quickly and decisively to environmental changes, organizational crises, or shifting customer expectations. For much of the 20th century, organizations operated in a relatively stable environment, so managers could focus on designing structures and systems that kept the organization running smoothly and efficiently. There was little need to search for new ways to cope with increased competition, volatile environmental shifts, or changing customer demands. Today, globalization and advancing technology have accelerated the pace at which organizations in all industries must roll out new products and services to stay competitive.

Today's customers also want products and services tailored to their exact needs. Companies that relied on mass production and distribution techniques must be prepared with new computer-aided systems that can produce one-of-a-kind variations and streamlined distribution systems that deliver products directly from the manufacturer to the consumer. Another shift brought about by technology is that the financial basis of today's economy is increasingly *information*, not machines and factories. Of concern to organizational leaders is that the primary factor of production becomes knowledge, to which managers must respond by increasing the power of employees. Employees, not production machinery, have the power and knowledge needed to keep the company competitive.

Considering the turmoil and flux inherent in today's world, the mindset needed by organizational leaders is to expect the unexpected and be ready for rapid change and potential crises through nimble organizational designs. Crisis management has moved to the forefront in light of terrorist attacks; a tough economy, rocky stock markets, and weakening consumer confidence; widespread ethical scandals; and, in general, an environment that may shift dramatically at a moment's notice.

**The Digital Workplace.** Some traditional managers feel particularly awkward in today's technology-driven workplace. Organizations have been engulfed by information technology that affects how organizations are designed and managed. In today's workplace, many employees perform much of their work on computers and may work in virtual teams, connected electronically to colleagues around the world. In addition, organizations are becoming enmeshed in electronic networks. The world of e-business is booming as more and more business takes place by digital processes over a computer network rather than in physical space. Some companies have taken e-business to very high levels to achieve amazing performance. Dell Computer pioneered the use of end-to-end digital supply-chain networks to keep in touch with customers, take orders, buy components from suppliers, coordinate with manufacturing partners, and ship customized products directly to consumers. This trend toward *disintermediation*—eliminating the middleperson—is affecting every industry, prompting a group of consultants at a Harvard University conference to conclude that businesses today must either "Dell or Be Delled."[23] These advances mean that organizational leaders not only need to be technologically savvy but also are responsible for managing a web of relationships that reaches far beyond the boundaries of the physical organization, building flexible e-links between a company and its employees, suppliers, contract partners, and customers.[24]

**Diversity.** Diversity is a fact of life that no organization can afford to ignore. As organizations increasingly operate on a global playing field, the workforce—as well as the customer base—is changing dramatically. Many of today's leading organizations have an international face. Look at the makeup of the international consulting firm McKinsey & Co. In the 1970s, most consultants were American, but by the turn of the century, McKinsey's chief partner was from India; only 40 percent of consultants were American; and the firm's international consultants came from 40 different countries.[25] Now, McKinsey consultants represent more than 100 nationalities and speak over 120 languages.[26]

The demographics of the Canadian population and workforce are also shifting. In 2005, Statistics Canada developed a demographic projection of the Canadian population in 2017. The study projects that (1) Canada will have a population of

33 to 36 million, of whom 6.4 to 8.5 million will be members of visible minorities, and (2) half the members of visible minorities will be South Asian or Chinese, followed by Blacks at one to 1.2 million.[27] Population growth will be from immigration. Today's average worker is older, and many more women, visible minorities, and immigrants are seeking job and advancement opportunities. A report by RBC Financial Group argues that "immigrants, women, and baby boomers approaching retirement will need to play more significant roles in the country's workforce, as Canada needs to capitalize on the broader economic benefits that a more diverse population has to offer."[28] This growing diversity brings a variety of challenges, such as maintaining a strong organizational culture while supporting diversity, balancing work and family concerns, and coping with the conflict brought about by varying cultural styles.

Managing diversity may be one of the most rewarding challenges for organizations competing on a global basis. For example, research has indicated that women's style of doing business may hold important lessons for success in the emerging global world of the 21st century. Yet the glass (or plastic) ceiling persists, keeping women from reaching positions of top leadership.[29]

## Purpose of This Chapter

This chapter explores the nature of organizations and organization theory today. Organization theory has developed from the systematic study of organizations by scholars. Concepts are obtained from living, ongoing organizations. Organization theory can be practical, as illustrated in the Air Canada case. It helps us understand, diagnose, and respond to emerging organizational needs and problems.

The next section begins with a formal definition of organization and then explores introductory concepts for describing and analyzing organizations. Next, the scope and nature of organization theory are discussed more fully. Succeeding sections examine the development of new organizational forms in response to changes in the environment, and how organization theory can help people manage complex organizations in a rapidly changing world. The chapter closes with a brief overview of the themes to be covered in this book.

## What Is an Organization?

Organizations are ubiquitous but are hard to see. We see outcroppings, such as a tall building, a computer workstation, or a friendly employee, but the whole organization is vague and abstract and may be scattered among several locations, even around the world. We know organizations are there because they touch us every day. Indeed, they are so common that we take them for granted. We hardly notice that we are raised in a family, have our health cards registered in a provincial government agency, are educated in schools and universities, are raised on food produced by local organic farmers or agribusinesses, are treated by doctors engaged in a joint practice, buy a house built by a construction company and sold by a real estate agency, borrow money from a bank, turn to police and fire departments when trouble erupts, use moving companies to change residences, receive an array of benefits from government, spend 40 (or more) hours a week working in an organization, and are even laid to rest by a funeral home.[30]

# ■ Definition

Organizations as diverse as a family, a prison, a hospital, and Air Canada have characteristics in common. The definition used in this book to describe organizations is as follows: **organizations** are (1) social entities that are (2) goal directed, (3) designed as deliberately structured and coordinated activity systems, and (4) linked to the external environment.

The key element of an organization is not, of course, a building or a set of policies and procedures; organizations comprise people and their relationships with one another. An organization exists when people interact with one another to perform essential functions that help attain goals. Recent trends in management recognize the importance of human resources, with most new approaches designed to empower employees with greater opportunities to learn and contribute as they work together toward common goals.

Managers deliberately structure and coordinate organizational resources to achieve the organization's purpose. However, even though work may be structured into separate departments or sets of activities, most organizations today are striving for greater horizontal coordination of work activities, often using teams of employees from different functional areas to work together on projects. Boundaries between departments, as well as those between organizations, are becoming more flexible and diffuse as companies face the need to respond to changes in the external environment more rapidly. An organization cannot exist without interacting with customers, suppliers, competitors, and other elements of the external environment. Today, some companies are even cooperating with their competitors, sharing information and technology to their mutual advantage.

# ■ Types of Organizations

Some organizations are large, multinational corporations. Others are small, family-owned shops. Some manufacture products such as automobiles or computers, whereas others provide services such as legal representation, banking, or medical services. Later in this text, Chapter 7 will look at the distinctions between manufacturing and service technologies. Chapter 8 discusses size and life cycle and describes some differences between small and large organizations.

Another important distinction is between for-profit businesses and nonprofit organizations. All of the topics in this text apply to nonprofit organizations such as the Salvation Army, the World Wildlife Fund, the Communist Party of Canada, the London Police Service, and Toronto's Hospital for Sick Children, just as they do to such businesses as Timothy's World Coffee, eBay, or Holiday Inn. However, there are some important differences to keep in mind. The primary difference is that managers in businesses direct their activities toward earning money for the company, whereas managers in nonprofits direct their efforts toward generating some kind of social impact. The unique characteristics and needs of nonprofit and public-sector organizations created by this distinction present difficult challenges for organizational leaders.[31] As you can see from Exhibit 1.2, the London Police Service has an overarching purpose of community service.

Financial resources for nonprofits come from government grants and individual and corporate donations, rather than from the sale of products or services to customers. In businesses, managers focus on improving the organization's products and services to increase sales revenues. In nonprofits, however, services are typically provided to

**EXHIBIT 1.2**
London Police Service
(London, Ontario)
Mission Statement

## MISSION

The London Police Service is committed to providing a safe and secure community through community partnerships and by striving to attain the highest level of professionalism and accountability.

## VISION

Recognizing that our strength stems from our partnerships with all sectors of the community, we envision an organization structured to meet the changing needs of citizens and our profession. Our success in accomplishing this goal depends on our ability to:

- Provide optimum public safety and security to enhance the quality of life in the community;
- Foster trusting, caring partnerships with the community in all its diversity;
- Develop effective communications within our organization and with those we serve;
- Promote a safe and equitable workplace, allowing for the professional development of employees to their fullest potential;
- Promote training and life long learning; and
- Acquire and use resources efficiently and responsibly.

## STATEMENT OF VALUES

The London Police Service, in pursuit of its mission, believes in providing quality service with the highest possible degree of excellence, based upon the principles of fairness, integrity, honesty, and respect for human dignity.

Employees are reminded to familiarize themselves with the Mission Statement, Statement of Values, and Vision of Success, and to embrace these goals as we collectively strive to provide the most effective police service for our citizens.

Source: London Police Service, Mission Statement, at
http://www.police.london.ca/AboutLPS/MissionStatement.htm (accessed June 2, 2008).

nonpaying clients, and a major problem for many organizations is securing a steady stream of funds to continue operating. Nonprofit managers, committed to serving clients with limited funds, must focus on keeping organizational costs as low as possible and demonstrating a highly efficient use of resources.[32] Another problem is that, since nonprofit organizations do not have a conventional "bottom line," managers often struggle with the question of what constitutes organizational effectiveness. It is easy to measure dollars and cents, but nonprofits have to measure intangible goals such as "improve public health" or "make a difference in the lives of the disenfranchised."

Managers in nonprofit organizations also deal with many diverse stakeholders and must market their services to attract not only clients (customers) but also volunteers and donors. Some nonprofits have responded to such challenges by developing new organizations. In 2001, Big Brothers and Sisters of Canada and Big Sisters Association of Ontario merged so that each partner organization could better serve more clients. The merger was also designed to reduce confusion in the eyes of the funders and the public that having two organizations with similar names and mandates had created. Moreover, it was an opportunity to pool the resources and expertise of the two organizations.[33] However, not all members of the Big Sisters Association of Ontario supported the merger as they believed that girls' interests would not be as well served by the new organization. They formed new, small, community-based organizations that continue the original social mandate.

Some nonprofits have created social enterprises that are designed to use business practices to achieve social missions. They have two bottom lines and often three—economic, social, and environmental. Social enterprises are emerging as an important organizational form in Canada and elsewhere. While there is ongoing debate about what precisely constitutes a social enterprise, it can be defined as "a form of community economic development in which an organization exchanges services and goods in the market as a means to realizing its social objectives or mission."[34] In addition to using the market to realize their missions, many social enterprises get support from government, individuals, and foundations. Social enterprises work towards self-sufficiency while focussing on their social objectives. Some social enterprises focus on training, others on providing employment. There are virtual social enterprises as well. Key is the equal and joint focus on the social and the economic. Eva's Phoenix Print Shop, described in Chapter 3, is one of Canada's best-known social enterprises.

The organizational design concepts discussed throughout this book, such as setting goals and measuring effectiveness, coping with environmental uncertainty, implementing effective control mechanisms, satisfying multiple stakeholders, and addressing issues of power and conflict, apply to nonprofit organizations such as Big Brothers and Big Sisters just as they do to Microsoft, Purolator Courier, or Air Canada, as described in the chapter–opening example. These concepts and theories are adapted and revised as needed to fit unique needs and problems.

## ■ Importance of Organizations

It may seem hard to believe today, but organizations as we know them are relatively recent in the history of humankind. Even in the late 19th century there were few organizations of any size or importance—no labour unions, no trade associations, and few large businesses, nonprofit organizations, or governmental departments. What a change has occurred since then! The development of large organizations transformed all of society, and, indeed, the modern corporation may be the most significant innovation of the past 120 years.[35] This chapter's Book Mark examines the rise of the corporation and its significance in our society. Organizations are central to people's lives and exert a tremendous influence.

Organizations are all around us and shape our lives in many ways. But what contributions do organizations make? Why are they important? Exhibit 1.3 highlights seven reasons organizations are important to you and to society. First, organizations bring together resources to accomplish specific goals. Consider Bombardier, which designs and builds planes for the business, regional, and amphibious markets, as well as trains. Putting together an airplane is an incredibly complex and labour-intensive job, involving many different kinds of components built to the highest standards of quality.

Organizations also produce goods and services that customers want at competitive prices. Bill Gates, who built Microsoft into a global powerhouse, asserts that the modern organization "is one of the most effective means to allocate resources we've ever seen. It transforms great ideas into customer benefits on an unimaginably large scale."[36]

Companies look for innovative ways to produce and distribute desirable goods and services more efficiently. Two ways are through e-business and through the use of computer-based manufacturing technologies. Redesigning organizational structures and management practices can also contribute to increased efficiency.

## Book Mark 1.0   HAVE YOU READ THIS BOOK?

### The Company: A Short History of a Revolutionary Idea
By John Micklethwait and Adrian Wooldridge

"The limited liability corporation is the greatest single discovery of modern times," is one conclusion of the concise and readable book, *The Company: A Short History of a Revolutionary Idea* by John Micklethwait and Adrian Wooldridge. Companies are so ubiquitous today that we take them for granted, so it may come as a surprise that the company as we know it is a relatively recent innovation. Although people have joined together in groups for commercial purposes since ancient Greek and Roman times, the modern company has its roots in the late 19th century. The idea of a *limited liability company* that was legally an "artificial person" began with the *Joint Stock Companies Act,* enacted by the London Board of Trade in 1856. Today the company is seen as "the most important organization in the world." Here are a few reasons:

- The corporation was the first autonomous legal and social institution that was within society, yet independent of the central government.
- The concept of a limited liability company unleashed entrepreneurs to raise money because investors could lose only what they invested. Increasing the pool of entrepreneurial capital spurred innovation and generally enriched the societies in which companies operated.
- The company is the most efficient creator of goods and services that the world has ever known. Without a company to harness resources and organize activities, the cost to consumers for almost any product we know today would be impossible to afford.
- Historically, the corporation has been a force for civilized behaviour and provided people with worthwhile activities, identity, and community, as well as a paycheque.
- The Virginia Company, a forerunner of the limited liability corporation, helped introduce the revolutionary concept of democracy to the American colonies.
- The modern multinational corporation began in Britain in the third quarter of the 1800s with the railroads, which built rail networks throughout Europe by shipping into each country the managers, materials, equipment, and labour needed.

During the past few years, it seems that large corporations have been increasingly in conflict with societies' interests. Yet large companies have been reviled throughout modern history—consider the robber barons at the beginning of the 20th century—and the authors suggest that recent abuses are relatively mild compared to some historical incidents. Everyone knows that corporations can be scoundrels, but overall, Micklethwait and Wooldridge argue, their force has been overwhelmingly for the cumulative social and economic good.

*The Company: A Short History of a Revolutionary Idea*, by John Micklethwait and Adrian Wooldridge, is published by The Modern Library.

Organizations create a drive for innovation rather than a reliance on standard products and outmoded ways of doing things.

Organizations adapt to and influence a rapidly changing environment. Consider Google, provider of the Internet's most popular search engine, which continues to adapt and evolve along with the evolving Internet. Rather than being a rigid service, Google is continually adding technological features that create a better service by accretion. At any time, Google's site features several technologies in development so that engineers can get ideas and feedback from users.[37] Google buys companies to add to its portfolio of services and now owns YouTube and DoubleClick, to name just two. However, when it bought Motorola in 2012 for $12 billion, Google's decision was questioned and many wondered what Google was thinking! The answer emerged in 2013 with the development of the Moto X, a customizable leading-edge smartphone being built in the United States.[38] Some large businesses have entire departments charged with monitoring the external environment and finding ways to adapt to or influence that environment. One of the most significant changes in the external environment today is globalization. Organizations such as Coca-Cola,

**EXHIBIT 1.3**
Importance of
Organizations

Alcan, Labatt Breweries of Canada, and IBM are involved in strategic alliances and partnerships with companies around the world in an effort to influence the environment and compete on a global scale.

Through all of these activities, organizations create value for their owners, customers, and employees. Managers analyze which parts of the operation create value and which parts do not; a company can be profitable only when the value it creates is greater than the cost of resources. Air Canada Jazz, a subsidiary of ACE Aviation Holdings, offers flights to 68 destinations, offering competitive pricing choices. Similarly, Porter Airlines offers flights to 14 destinations as well as seasonal flights to Mt. Tremblant and Myrtle Beach, S.C., while providing both competitive prices and superior service.

Finally, organizations have to cope with and accommodate today's challenges of workforce diversity and growing concerns over ethics and social responsibility, as well as find effective ways to motivate employees to work together to accomplish organizational goals.

Organizations shape our lives, and well-informed managers can shape organizations. An understanding of organization theory enables managers to design organizations to function more effectively.

## Perspectives on Organizations

There are various ways to look at and think about organizations and how they function. Two important perspectives are the open-systems approach and the organizational—configuration framework.

# Open Systems

One significant development in the study of organizations was the distinction between closed and open systems.[39] A **closed system** would not depend on its environment; it would be autonomous, enclosed, and sealed off from the outside world. Although a true closed system cannot exist, early organizational studies focused on internal systems. Early management concepts, including scientific management, leadership style, and industrial engineering, were closed-system approaches because they took the environment for granted and assumed the organization could be made more effective through internal design. The management of a closed system would be quite easy. The environment would be stable and predictable and would not intervene to cause problems. The primary management issue would be to run things efficiently.

An **open system** must interact with the environment to survive; it both consumes resources and exports resources to the environment. It cannot seal itself off. It must continuously adapt to the environment. Open systems can be enormously complex. Internal efficiency is just one issue—and sometimes a minor one. The organization has to find and obtain needed resources, interpret and act on environmental changes, dispose of outputs, and control and coordinate internal activities in the face of environmental disturbances and uncertainty. Every system that must interact with the environment to survive is an open system. The human being is an open system. So are the planet Earth; Iqaluit, the capital of Nunavut; and Air Canada. Indeed, one problem at Air Canada was that top managers seemed to forget they were part of an open system. They isolated themselves within the bureaucratic culture and failed to pay close attention to what was happening with their customers, suppliers, and competitors. The rapid changes over the past few decades, including globalization and increased competition, the explosion of the Internet and e-business, and the growing diversity of the population and workforce, have forced many managers to reorient toward an open-systems mindset and recognize their business as part of a complex, interconnected whole.

To understand the whole organization, we must view it as a system. **A system** is a set of interacting elements that acquires inputs from the environment, transforms them, and discharges outputs to the external environment. The need for inputs and outputs reflects dependency on the environment. Interacting elements mean that people and departments depend on one another and must work together.

Exhibit 1.4 illustrates an open system. Inputs to an organizational system include raw materials and other physical resources, employees, information, and financial resources. The transformation process changes these inputs into something of value that can be exported back to the environment. Outputs include specific products and services for customers and clients. Outputs may also include employee satisfaction, pollution, and other byproducts of the transformation process.

A system comprises several **subsystems**, as illustrated at the bottom of Exhibit 1.4. These subsystems perform the specific functions required for organizational survival, such as boundary spanning, production, maintenance, adaptation, and management. The production subsystem produces the product and service outputs of the organization. Boundary subsystems are responsible for exchanges with the external environment. They include activities such as purchasing supplies or marketing products. The maintenance subsystem maintains the smooth operation and upkeep of the organization's physical and human elements. The adaptive subsystems are responsible for organizational change and adaptation. Management is a

**Compare**

Compare various organizations that you experience every day. What do they have in common and what makes them different?

**EXHIBIT 1.4**
An Open System and
Its Subsystems

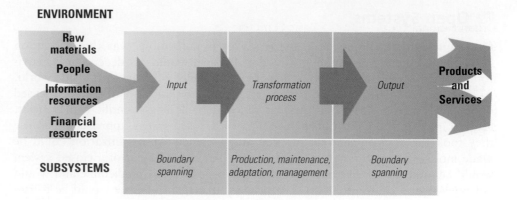

distinct subsystem, responsible for coordinating and directing the other subsystems of the organization.

## ◼ Organizational Configuration

Various parts of the organization are designed to perform the key subsystem functions illustrated in Exhibit 1.5. One framework proposed by the esteemed Canadian scholar, Henry Mintzberg, suggests that every organization has five parts.[40] These parts, illustrated in Exhibit 1.5A, and elaborated in Exhibit 1.5B, include the technical core, top management, middle management, technical support, and administrative support. The five parts of the organization may vary in size and importance depending on the organization's environment, technology, and other factors.

**Technical Core.** The technical core includes people who do the basic work of the organization. It performs the production subsystem function and actually produces the product and service outputs of the organization. This is where the primary transformation from inputs to outputs takes place. The technical core is the production department in a manufacturing firm, the teachers and classes in a university, and the medical activities in a hospital. At Air Canada, the technical core includes pilots, flight attendants, and baggage handlers.

**Management.** Management is a distinct subsystem, responsible for directing and coordinating other parts of the organization. Top management provides direction,

**EXHIBIT 1.5A**
Five Basic Parts of an
Organization
Source: Based on Henry
Mintzberg, *The Structuring
of Organizations* (Englewood
Cliffs, N.J.: Prentice-Hall, 1979),
215–297; and Henry Mintz-
berg, "Organization Design:
Fashion or Fit?" *Harvard
Business Review* 59 (January–
February 1981): 103–116.

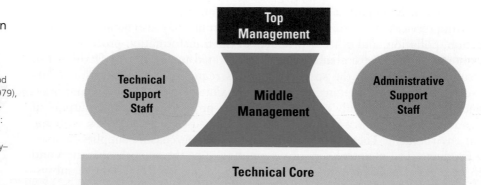

**EXHIBIT 1.5B**
## Organizational Types and Their Basic Components

| | SIMPLE STRUCTURE | MACHINE BUREAUCRACY | PROFESSIONAL BUREAUCRACY | DIVISIONALIZED FORM | ADHOCRACY |
|---|---|---|---|---|---|
| **Key Means of Coordination** | Direct supervision | Standardization of work | Standardization of skills | Standardization of outputs | Mutual adjustment |
| **Key Part of Organization** | Strategic apex | Technostructure | Operating core | Middle line | Support staff (with operating core in operating adhocracy) |
| **STRUCTURAL ELEMENTS** | | | | | |
| **Specialization of Jobs** | Little specialization | *Much horizontal and vertical specialization* | *Much horizontal specialization* | Some horizontal and vertical specialization (between divisions and headquarters) | *Much horizontal specialization* |
| **Training and Indoctrination** | Little training and indoctrination | Little training and indoctrination | *Much training and indoctrination* | Some training and indoctrination (of division managers) | Much training |
| **Formalization of Behaviour—Bureaucratic/Organic** | *Little formalization—organic* | *Much formalization—bureaucratic* | *Little formalization—bureaucratic* | Much formalization (within divisions)—bureaucratic | *Little formalization—organic* |
| **Grouping** | Usually functional | *Usually functional* | Functional and market | *Market* | Functional and market |
| **Unit Size** | Wide | Wide at bottom, narrow elsewhere | Wide at bottom, narrow elsewhere | Wide at top | Narrow throughout |
| **Planning and Control Systems** | Little planning and control | Action planning | Little planning and control | Much performance control | Limited action planning (esp. in administrative adhocracy) |
| **Liaison Devices** | Few liaison devices | Few liaison devices | Liaison devices in administration | Few liaison devices | Many liaison devices throughout |
| **Decentralization** | Centralization | Limited horizontal decentralization | Horizontal and vertical decentralization | Limited vertical decentralization | Selective decentralization |
| **SITUATIONAL ELEMENTS** | | | | | |
| **Age and Size** | Typically young and small | Typically old and large | Varies | Typically old and very large | Typically young (operating adhocracy) |
| **Technical System** | Simple, not regulating | Regulating but not automated, not very complex | Not regulating or complex | Divisible, otherwise like machine bureaucracy | Very complex, often automated (in administrative adhocracy), not regulating or complex (in operating adhocracy) |
| **Environment** | Simple and dynamic; sometimes hostile | Simple and stable | Complex and stable | Relatively simple and stable; diversified markets (esp. products and services) | Complex and dynamic; sometimes disparate (in administrative adhocracy) |
| **Power** | Chief executive control; often owner-managed; not fashionable | Technocratic and external control; not fashionable | Professional operator control; fashionable | Middle-line control; fashionable (esp. in industry) | Expert control; very fashionable |

Note: *Italic* type in columns 2–6 indicates key design parameters.

Source: Reprinted by permission of *Harvard Business Review*. From "Organization Design: Fashion or Fit?" by Henry Mintzberg, 59 (January–February 1981): 6–7. Copyright © 1981 by the Harvard Business School Publishing Corporation; all rights reserved.

strategy, goals, and policies for the entire organization or major divisions. Middle management is responsible for implementation and coordination at the departmental level. In traditional organizations, middle managers are responsible for mediating between top management and the technical core, such as implementing rules and passing information up and down the hierarchy.

**Technical Support.** The technical support function helps the organization adapt to the environment. Technical support employees such as engineers and researchers scan the environment for problems, opportunities, and technological developments. Technical support is responsible for creating innovations in the technical core, helping the organization change and adapt. Technical support at Air Canada is provided by Air Canada Technical Services.

**Administrative Support.** The administrative support function is responsible for the smooth operation and upkeep of the organization, including its physical and human elements. This includes human resource activities such as recruiting and hiring, establishing compensation and benefits, and employee training and development, as well as maintenance activities such as cleaning buildings and servicing and repairing machines. Administrative support functions in a corporation such as Air Canada might include the human resource department, organizational development, the employee cafeteria, and the maintenance staff.

In practice, the five parts are interrelated and often serve more than one subsystem function. For example, managers coordinate and direct other parts of the system, but they may also be involved in administrative and technical support. In addition, several of the parts serve the *boundary spanning* function mentioned in the previous section. For example, in the administrative support realm, human resource departments are responsible for working with the external environment to find quality employees. Purchasing departments acquire needed materials and supplies. In the technical support area, research and development (R&D) departments work directly with the external environment to learn about new technological developments. Managers perform boundary spanning as well. The important boundary-spanning subsystem is embraced by several areas, rather than being confined to one part of the organization.

# Dimensions of Organizational Design

The systems view pertains to dynamic, ongoing activities within organizations. The next step for understanding organizations is to look at dimensions that describe specific organizational design traits. These dimensions describe organizations in much the same way that personality and physical traits describe people.

Organizational dimensions fall into two types: structural and contextual, illustrated in Exhibit 1.6. **Structural dimensions** provide labels to describe the internal characteristics of an organization. They create a basis for measuring and comparing organizations. **Contextual dimensions** characterize the whole organization, including its size, technology, culture, environment, and goals and strategy. They describe the organizational setting that influences and shapes the structural dimensions. Contextual dimensions can be confusing because they represent both the

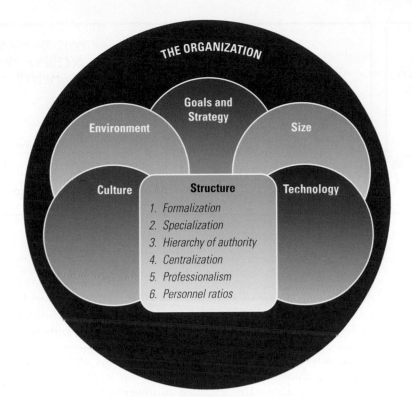

organization and the environment. Contextual dimensions can be envisioned as a set of overlapping elements that underlie an organization's structure and work processes. To understand and evaluate organizations, we must examine both structural and contextual dimensions.[41] These dimensions of organizational design interact with one another and can be adjusted to accomplish the purposes listed earlier in Exhibit 1.3.

1. *Formalization* refers to the amount of written documentation in the organization. Documentation includes procedures, job descriptions, regulations, and policy manuals. These written documents describe behaviour and activities. Formalization is often measured by simply counting the number of pages of documentation within the organization. Large universities, for example, tend to be high on formalization because they have several volumes of written rules for things such as registration, dropping and adding classes, student associations, residence governance, and financial assistance. A small, family-owned business, in contrast, may have almost no written rules and would be considered informal.

2. *Specialization* is the degree to which organizational tasks are subdivided into separate jobs. If specialization is extensive, each employee performs only a narrow range of tasks. If specialization is low, employees perform a wide range of tasks in their jobs. Specialization is sometimes referred to as the division of labour.

3. *Hierarchy of authority* describes who reports to whom and the span of control for each manager. The hierarchy is depicted by the vertical lines on an organizational chart. See Exhibit 1.7 for an unorthodox way of using an organization

**EXHIBIT 1.7**
Using an Organizational Chart!

chart. The hierarchy is related to span of control (the number of employees reporting to a supervisor). When *spans of control* are narrow, the hierarchy tends to be tall. When spans of control are wide, the hierarchy of authority will be shorter.

4. *Centralization* refers to the hierarchical level that has authority to make a decision. When decision making is kept at the top level, the organization is centralized. When decisions are delegated to lower organizational levels, it is decentralized. Organizational decisions that might be centralized or decentralized include purchasing equipment, establishing goals, choosing suppliers, setting prices, hiring employees, and deciding marketing territories.

5. *Professionalism* is the level of formal education and training of employees. Professionalism is considered high when employees require long periods of training to hold jobs in the organization. Professionalism is generally measured as the average number of years of education of employees, which could be as high as 20 in a medical practice and less than 10 in a catering company.

6. *Personnel ratios* refer to the deployment of people to various functions and departments. Personnel ratios include the administrative ratio, the clerical ratio, the professional staff ratio, and the ratio of indirect to direct labour employees. A personnel ratio is measured by dividing the number of employees in a classification by the total number of organizational employees.

## ■ Contextual Dimensions

1. The organization's *goals and strategy* define the purpose and competitive techniques that set it apart from other organizations. Goals are often written down as an enduring statement of company intent. A strategy is the plan of action that describes resource allocation and activities for dealing with the environment and for reaching the organization's goals. Goals and strategies define the scope of operations and the relationship with employees, customers, and competitors.

2. The *environment* includes all elements outside the boundary of the organization. Key elements include the industry, government, customers, suppliers, and financial community. The environmental elements that affect an organization the most are often other organizations.

**Think**

Think of the organization as an entity distinct from the individuals who work in it. Use the language of design to describe the organization according to its size, formalization, decentralization, specialization, professionalism, and personnel ratios.

3. *Size* is the organization's magnitude as reflected in the number of people in the organization. It can be measured for the organization as a whole or for specific components, such as a plant or division. Because organizations are social systems, size is typically measured by the number of employees. Other measures, such as total sales or total assets also reflect magnitude, but they do no indicate the size of the human part of the system.

4. An organization's *culture* is the underlying set of key values, beliefs, understandings, and norms shared by employees. These underlying values may pertain to ethical behaviour, commitment to employees, efficiency, or customer service, and they provide the glue to hold organization members together. An organization's culture is unwritten but can be observed in its stories, slogans, ceremonies, dress, and office layout.

5. *Technology* refers to the tools, techniques, and actions used to transform inputs into outputs. It concerns how the organization actually produces the products and services it provides for customers and includes things such as flexible manufacturing, advanced information systems, and the Internet. An automobile assembly line, a college classroom, and an overnight package delivery system are technologies, although they differ from one another.

The 11 contextual and structural dimensions discussed here are interdependent. For example, large organizational size, a routine technology, and a stable environment all tend to create an organization that has greater formalization, specialization, and centralization. More detailed relationships among the dimensions are explored in later chapters of this book.

These dimensions provide a basis for the measurement and analysis of characteristics that cannot be seen by the casual observer, and they reveal significant information about an organization. Consider, for example, the dimensions of EllisDon Construction and the Museum of Contemporary Canadian Art (MOCCA) compared with those of Tim Hortons.

## In Practice
### EllisDon, MOCCA, Tim Hortons

### EllisDon

EllisDon, founded in 1951 by two brothers in London, Ontario, has become a leading international construction company. It has undertaken projects in Europe, the Middle East, the Caribbean, and the United States. The projects range in size from several thousand to several hundred million dollars. It sees itself as a "construction services" company, offering services such as construction and project management, design and build services, and health and safety consulting. EllisDon has 1,200 employees and offices across Canada and in the United States, Greece, Dubai, the United Arab Emirates, and St. Lucia. One of its best-known projects is the building of the world's first sports stadium with a retractable roof, the Toronto SkyDome, now known as the Rogers Centre.

Donald Smith, EllisDon's founder, recruited individuals with a sense of adventure and entrepreneurial drive. "The company's defining characteristic emerged very early on: EllisDon was prepared to assume risk. We were seen as innovative and dynamic in our approach to a construction challenge. Above all, we were seen as builders."[42]

EllisDon is often ranked in the top three of Canada's best employers. In 2013, it was ranked Canada's second best employer.[43] EllisDon's president and CEO, Geoff Smith, believes that the "key to industry leadership is creating a culture of independent thought, of individual confidence, openness, initiative and enjoyment. We believe that success doesn't necessarily lie in the larger innovations, but in the smaller daily breakthroughs that occur on the sites, in the hard work, and in finding ways to say yes when a client asks. That is the way great companies, and great places to work, are built."[44]

### MOCCA

MOCCA, founded in 1999, has a mandate to exhibit, research, collect, and promote innovative art by Canadian artists "whose works engage and reflect the relevant stories of our times." MOCCA is a nonprofit, arms-length agency of the City of Toronto's Culture Division. Its permanent collection numbers 400 works of art by 150 artists. MOCCA has presented more than 40 exhibitions of contemporary Canadian and international works in eight countries. "It is MOCCA's belief that this local-to-global investment in Canadian arts and culture will strengthen our ability to serve the artistic, cultural and general public communities of Toronto, Canada and beyond." MOCCA has a staff of seven and is supported, in part, by memberships.[45]

### Tim Hortons

Tim Hortons achieves its competitive edge through human resource efficiency and internal cost efficiency. A standard formula is used to build each store, with similar displays and uniform food and beverage products and branded items. In 2006, Tim Hortons opened its 3,000th store and continues to expand. To gain efficiencies from scale, Tim Hortons has automated a number of tasks such as franchise agreement invoicing, electronic funds transfer, accounts receivable and payable, sales order management and purchasing, taxation control, inventory, and warehousing.[46]

---

EllisDon is a medium-sized construction services organization that ranks quite low on formalization, specialization, and centralization. Employees work on different projects. Tim Hortons is much more formalized, specialized, and centralized. There, efficiency by managing costs is more important than innovation, so most activities are guided by standard regulations. The percentage of nonworkflow personnel is kept to a minimum. In contrast, MOCCA is small and ranks low on formalization, specialization, and centralization. MOCCA needs to be flexible in design so that it can achieve its creative goals.

Structural and contextual dimensions can thus tell us a lot about an organization and about differences among organizations. Organizational design dimensions are examined in more detail in later chapters to determine the appropriate level of each dimension needed to perform effectively in each organizational setting.

## ■ Performance and Effectiveness Outcomes

The whole point of understanding varying perspectives and the structural and contextual dimensions of organizations is to design the organization in such a way as to achieve high performance and effectiveness. Managers need to adjust structural and contextual dimensions and organizational subsystems to most efficiently and effectively transform inputs into outputs and provide value. **Efficiency** refers to the amount of resources used to achieve the organization's goals. It is based on the quantity of raw materials, money, and employees necessary to produce a given level of output. **Effectiveness** is a broader term, meaning the degree to which an organization achieves its goals. Simply put, efficiency is "doing things right" while effectiveness is "doing the right thing."

To be effective, organizations need clear, focused goals and appropriate strategies for achieving them. Strategy, goals, and approaches to measuring effectiveness will be discussed in detail in Chapter 2. Many organizations are using new technology to improve efficiency and effectiveness. For example, Air Canada became the first airline to introduce self-service express check-in kiosks in Canada. Purolator Courier uses technologically sophisticated package-handling equipment and computerized logistics systems to reduce delivery time for cross-border shipping. Google

**Apply**

Visit www.vault.com and www.glassdoor.ca to learn about the different organizational cultures. How can you apply an understanding of organizational culture in planning your career?

has introduced a pay-by-phone system that will enable consumers to pay for their purchases using Android smartphones.[47]

However, achieving effectiveness is not a simple matter because different people want different things from the organization. For customers, the primary concern is high-quality products and services at a reasonable price, whereas employees are mostly concerned with adequate pay, good working conditions, and job satisfaction. Managers carefully balance the needs and interests of various stakeholders in setting goals and striving for effectiveness. This is referred to as the **stakeholder approach**, which integrates diverse organizational activities by looking at various organizational stakeholders and what they want from the organization. A **stakeholder** is any group within or outside the organization that has a stake in the organization's performance. The satisfaction level of each group can be assessed as an indication of the organization's performance and effectiveness.[48]

Exhibit 1.8 illustrates various stakeholders and what each group wants from the organization. Organizations often find it difficult to simultaneously satisfy the demands of all groups. A business might have high customer satisfaction, but the organization might have difficulties with creditors or supplier relationships might be poor. Consider Walmart. Customers love its efficiency and low prices, but the low-cost emphasis the company uses with suppliers has caused friction and anger. Some activist groups argue that Walmart's tactics are unethical because they force suppliers to lay off workers, close factories, and outsource to manufacturers from low-wage countries. One supplier said clothing is being sold at Walmart so cheaply that many North American companies couldn't compete even if they paid their workers nothing. The challenges of managing such a huge organization have also led to strains in relationships with employees and other stakeholder groups, as evidenced by recent gender discrimination suits and complaints about low wages.[49]

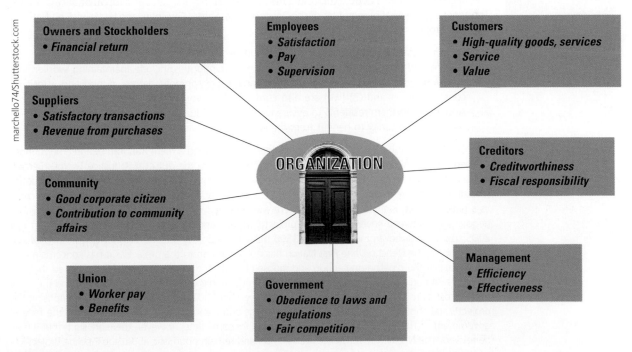

**EXHIBIT 1.8**
Major Stakeholder Groups and What They Expect

Stakeholder interests sometimes conflict, such as when unions demand wage increases that might hurt shareholders' financial returns or require a switch to lower-cost suppliers. In nonprofit organizations, the needs and interests of clients sometimes conflict with restrictions on use of government funds or contributions from donors. In reality, it is unreasonable to assume that all stakeholders can be equally satisfied. However, if an organization fails to meet the needs of several stakeholder groups, it is probably not meeting its effectiveness goals. Recall from the opening case Air Canada's problems with satisfying employees, customers, creditors, unions, stockholders, and government regulators.

Research has shown that the assessment of multiple stakeholder groups is an accurate reflection of organizational effectiveness, especially with respect to organizational adaptability.[50] Moreover, both profit and nonprofit organizations care deeply about their reputations and attempt to shape stakeholders' perceptions of their performance.[51]

Managers strive to at least minimally satisfy the interests of all stakeholders. When any one group becomes seriously dissatisfied, it may withdraw its support and hurt future organizational performance. Satisfying multiple stakeholders can be challenging, particularly as goals and priorities change, as illustrated by the example in the In Practice box.

## In Practice

### Mackenzie Valley Natural Gas Pipeline Project (The Pipeline Project)

The proposed Mackenzie Pipeline Project is enormous; it proposes to develop natural gas fields in the Mackenzie Delta of the Northwest Territories and deliver the gas to market through a 1,300 kilometre pipeline built along the Mackenzie Valley. It is a multibillion dollar project that is expected to create 2,600 jobs. There are five business partners in the proposed venture: Imperial Oil, Shell Canada, Exxon Mobil Canada, Conoco Phillips Canada, and the Aboriginal Peoples' Group (APG). The APG was formed in 2000 to represent the interests of the First Nations peoples of the Northwest Territories and consists of members of the Dehcho Dene, Sahtu, Gwich'in, and Inuvialuit First Nations.

The project makes two commitments:

(1) [The] Mackenzie Gas Project respects the peoples of Canada's North and the land, wildlife and environment that sustains them. Our priorities include maintaining worker and public safety at all times and caring for the environment before, during and after construction … and (2) [we] are also committed to working with Aboriginal and non-Aboriginal northern residents to ensure northern individuals, communities and businesses have an opportunity to benefit from the Project.[52]

Even though the 30 First Nations stakeholder groups signed a memorandum of agreement under the aegis of the APG, the project has been controversial from the outset. Mr. Justice Thomas Berger, in his 1977 report to assess the impact of a pipeline, wrote "[We] are at our last frontier. It is a frontier that all of us have read about, but few of us have seen. Profound issues, touching our deepest concerns as a nation, await us there."[53] In 2004, there was renewed momentum for building the pipeline but negotiations between governments, the project partners, and the First Nations groups stalled. In July 2005, the federal government pledged $500 million to address the socioeconomic concerns of the First Nations. The Dehcho Dene First Nation has not signed on to the project as it has concerns about the impact of the pipeline on caribou and moose habitats and traplines. The APG has stated that the Dehcho's 34 percent share will be held for them. Production is estimated to start in 2014 and the costs of the project are estimated to be $16 billion. In November 2007, the joint review panel, comprising the project's stakeholders, concluded its public hearings and planned to report its findings to the federal government.[54] The Pipeline Project has been stalled for some time; however, there are signs that it may be revived. The Northwest Territories are keen on and remain optimistic about the Pipeline Project.[55]

This example provides a glimpse of how difficult it can be for managers to satisfy multiple stakeholders. In all organizations, managers have to evaluate stakeholder concerns and establish goals that can achieve at least minimal satisfaction for major stakeholder groups.

**The Environment.** Many problems occur when all organizations are treated as similar, which was the case with scientific management and administrative principles approaches that attempted to design all organizations alike. The structures and systems that work in the retail division of a conglomerate will not be appropriate for the manufacturing division. The organizational charts and financial procedures that are best for an entrepreneurial Internet firm such as eBay or Google will not work for a large food-processing plant.

**Contingency** means that one thing depends on other things, and for organizations to be effective, there must be a "goodness of fit" between their structure and the conditions in their external environment.[56] What works in one setting may not work in another setting; there is not one best way. Contingency theory means "it depends." For example, some organizations experience a certain environment, use a routine technology, and desire efficiency. In this situation, a management approach that uses bureaucratic control procedures, a hierarchical structure, and formal communication would be appropriate. However, free-flowing management processes work best in an uncertain environment with a nonroutine technology. The correct management approach is *contingent* on—depends on—the organization's situation.

Today, almost all organizations operate in highly uncertain environments. Thus, we are involved in a significant period of transition, in which concepts of organization theory and design are changing as dramatically as they did with the dawning of the Industrial Revolution.

## ■ Contemporary Organizational Design

To a great extent, managers and organizations are still imprinted with the hierarchical, bureaucratic approach that arose more than a century ago. Yet the challenges presented by today's environment—globalization, diversity, ethical concerns, rapid advances in technology, the rise of e-business, a shift to knowledge and information as organizations' most important form of capital, and the growing expectations of workers for meaningful work and opportunities for personal and professional growth—call for dramatically different responses from people and organizations. The perspectives of the past do not provide a road map for steering today's organizations. Managers can design and orchestrate new responses for a dramatically new world.

Today's organizations and managers may be seen as shifting from a mind-set based on mechanical systems to one based on natural and biological systems. These changing beliefs and perceptions affect how we think about organizations and the patterns of behaviour within organizations.

For most of the 20th century, 18th-century Newtonian science, which suggests that the world functions as a well-behaved machine, continued to guide managers' thinking about organizations.[57] The environment was perceived as orderly and predictable, and the role of managers was to maintain stability. This mind-set worked quite well for the Industrial Age.[58] Growth was a primary criterion for organizational success.

Over the 20th century, organizations became large and complex, and boundaries between functional departments and between organizations were distinct. Internal structures grew more complex, vertical, and bureaucratic. Leadership was based on solid management principles and tended to be autocratic; communication was primarily through formal memos, letters, and reports. Managers did all the planning and "thought work," while employees did the manual labour in exchange for wages and other compensation.

The environment for today's organizations, however, is anything but stable. With the turbulence of recent years, managers can no longer maintain an illusion of order and predictability. The science of **chaos theory** suggests that relationships in complex, adaptive systems—including organizations—are nonlinear and made up of numerous interconnections and divergent choices that create unintended effects and render the universe unpredictable.[59] The world is full of uncertainty, characterized by surprise, rapid change, and confusion. Managers can't measure, predict, or control in traditional ways the unfolding drama inside or outside the organization. However, chaos theory also recognizes that this randomness and disorder occurs within certain larger patterns of order. The ideas of chaos theory suggest that organizations should be viewed more as natural systems than as well-oiled, predictable machines.

Many organizations are shifting from strict vertical hierarchies to flexible, decentralized structures that emphasize horizontal collaboration, widespread information sharing, and adaptability. According to Christopher White, a minister in the United Church of Canada, "adaptability, tenacity, courage, endurance, humour, tolerance for ambiguity, and the capacity to live in paradox are all needed as we move together into the ever-shifting present. We have to find a way to sprint the marathon, while at the same time rooting ourselves in the values that have withstood the tests of centuries."[60] As the ministry of the United Church changes, the organization needs to design more adaptable structures. The United Church of Canada, the largest Protestant denomination in Canada, continues to increase its social justice work while ministering to its membership of three million in 3,500 congregations. One of its social justice activities is a partnership in KAIROS, a "coalition of Canadian churches, church based agencies and religious organizations dedicated to promoting human rights, justice and peace, viable human development and universal solidarity among the peoples of the Earth."[61] The Church's organizational chart shows the changing nature of its work; for example, there are executive ministers for "ethnic ministries, faith formation and education, justice, global and ecumenical relations, ministries in French, support to local ministries, financial services and stewardship, information technology services, ministry employment policies and services, and resource production and distribution."[62]

Businesses and other nonprofit organizations today also need greater flexibility and adaptability. Many managers are redesigning their companies toward something called the learning organization. The **learning organization** promotes communication and collaboration so that everyone is engaged in identifying and solving problems, enabling the organization to continuously experiment, improve, and increase its capability. The learning organization is based on equality, open information, little hierarchy, and a culture that encourages adaptability and participation, enabling ideas to bubble up from anywhere to help the organization seize opportunities and handle crises. In a learning organization, the essential value is problem solving, as opposed to the traditional organization designed for efficient performance.

# ■ Efficient Performance versus the Learning Organization

As managers struggle toward the learning organization, they are finding that specific dimensions of the organization—the interconnected elements of structure, tasks, systems, culture, and strategy—have to change.

**From Vertical to Horizontal Structure.** Traditionally, the most common organizational structure has been one in which activities are grouped together by common work from the bottom to the top of the organization. Generally, little collaboration occurs across functional departments, and the whole organization is coordinated and controlled through the vertical hierarchy, with decision-making authority residing with upper-level managers. This structure can be quite effective. It promotes efficient production and in-depth skill development, and the hierarchy of authority provides a sensible mechanism for supervision and control in large organizations. However, in a rapidly changing environment, the hierarchy becomes overloaded. Top executives are not able to respond rapidly enough to problems or opportunities.

In the learning organization, the vertical structure that creates distance between managers at the top of the organization and workers in the technical core is disbanded. Structure is created around horizontal workflows or processes rather than departmental functions. The vertical hierarchy is dramatically flattened, with perhaps only a few senior executives in traditional support functions such as finance or human resources. Self-directed teams are the fundamental work unit in the learning organization. Boundaries between functions are practically eliminated because teams include members from several functional areas. In some cases, organizations do away with departments altogether. For example, at Oticon Holding A/S, a Danish company that introduced the world's first digital hearing aid, there are no organizational charts, no departments, no functions, and no titles. Employees are continuously forming and re-forming into self-directed teams that work on specific projects.[63]

**From Routine Tasks to Empowered Roles.** Another shift in thinking relates to the degree of formal structure and control placed on employees in the performance of their work. Recall that scientific management advocated precisely defining each job and how it should be performed. A **task** is a narrowly defined piece of work assigned to a person. In traditional organizations, tasks are broken down into specialized, separate parts, as in a machine. Knowledge and control of tasks are centralized at the top of the organization, and employees are expected to do as they are told. A **role**, in contrast, is a part in a dynamic social system. A role has discretion and responsibility, allowing the person to use his or her discretion and ability to achieve an outcome or meet a goal. In learning organizations, employees play a role in the team or department, and roles may be continually redefined or adjusted. There are few rules or procedures, and knowledge and control of tasks are located with workers rather than with supervisors or top executives. Employees are encouraged to take care of problems by working with one another and with customers. Delta Hotels, founded in British Columbia, emphasizes the importance of creating a healthy and engaged workplace through two programs—"Response-Ability and Power to Please." The programs are designed to give employees both the responsibility and authority to deal with workplace issues. Employees are also part of planning groups for improving processes; the housekeeping staff, for example, is involved in recommending cleaning supplies, designing effective cleaning processes,

**Compare**

Identify an organization that competes in a turbulent environment with one that competes in a placid one. What design differences would you predict based on the theory in this chapter?

and creating amenity packages. According to Bill Pallett, senior vice president, People, Resources and Quality, "[If] you have an engaged workforce, you have a loyal customer and if you have a loyal customer base, you're going to increase share value."[64]

**From Formal Control Systems to Shared Information.** In young, small organizations, communication is generally informal and face-to-face. There are few formal control and information systems because the top leaders of the company usually work directly with employees in the day-to-day operation of the business. However, when organizations grow large and complex, the distance between top leaders and workers in the technical core increases. Formal systems are often implemented to manage the growing amount of complex information and to detect deviations from established standards and goals.[65]

In learning organizations, information serves a very different purpose. The widespread sharing of information keeps the organization functioning at an optimal level. The learning organization strives to return to the condition of a small, entrepreneurial firm in which all employees have complete information about the company so they can act quickly. Ideas and information are shared throughout the organization. Rather than using information to control employees, a significant part of a manager's job is to find ways to open channels of communication so that ideas flow in all directions. In addition, learning organizations maintain open lines of communication with customers, suppliers, and even competitors to enhance learning capability. Magna International, the giant auto parts manufacturer, for example, has set up MIND (Managing Innovative New Developments). It is a web-based program designed to encourage employees to submit new product and process ideas across the organization. Employees are rewarded appropriately for successful ideas.[66] Information technology also plays a key role in keeping people across the organization connected.

**From Competitive to Collaborative Strategy.** In traditional organizations designed for efficient performance, strategy is formulated by top managers and imposed on the organization. Top executives think about how the organization can best respond to competition, efficiently use resources, and cope with environmental changes. In the learning organization, in contrast, the accumulated actions of an informed and empowered workforce contribute to strategy development. Since all employees are in touch with customers, suppliers, and new technology, they help identify needs and solutions and participate in strategy making. In addition, strategy emerges from partnerships with suppliers, customers, and even competitors. Organizations become collaborators as well as competitors, experimenting to find the best way to learn and adapt. Boundaries between organizations are becoming diffuse, with companies often forming partnerships to compete globally, sometimes joining in nodes or virtual network organizations that are connected electronically.

**From Rigid to Adaptive Culture.** For an organization to remain healthy, its culture should encourage adaptation to the external environment. A danger for many organizations is that the culture becomes ossified, as if set in concrete. Organizations that were highly successful in stable environments often become victims of their own success when the environment begins to change dramatically. One of the reasons for the demise of Eaton's, whose mail-order catalogue achieved near biblical status, was that "Eaton's management failed at numerous stages to understand the strategic contours involved in the terrain of successfully turning around a company ...."[67] The cultural values, ideas, and practices that helped attain success were detrimental to effective performance in a rapidly changing environment.

In a learning organization, the culture encourages openness, equality, continuous improvement, and change. People in the organization are aware of the whole system, how everything fits together, and how the various parts of the organization interact with one another and with the environment. This whole-system mind-set minimizes boundaries within the organization and with other organizations. In addition, activities and symbols that create status differences, such as executive dining rooms or reserved parking spaces, are discarded. Each person is a valued contributor and the organization becomes a place for creating a web of relationships that allow people to develop and apply their full potential. Consider the Boston Pizza franchise's emphasis on the importance of training its employees, which it articulates in its mission statement. Its mission is "to be a world class franchisor through selecting and training people to profitably manage an outstanding foodservice business."[68] The emphasis on treating everyone with care and respect creates a climate in which people feel safe to experiment, take risks, and make mistakes, all of which encourage learning.

No company represents a perfect example of a learning organization, although many of today's most competitive organizations have shifted towards ideas and forms based on the concept of a living, dynamic system. Some of these organizations are spotlighted throughout this book in the Leading by Design boxes.

Managers today are involved in a struggle as they attempt to change their companies into learning organizations. The critical challenge for managers is to maintain some level of stability as they actively promote change toward the new way of thinking, to navigate between order and chaos. One organization that is transforming into a learning organization is Evergreen and its Brick Works.[69]

---

## In Practice
### Evergreen and the Brick Works

Evergreen, a charity, was founded with the express purpose of bringing communities and nature together for the benefit of both. Its vision states that "Evergreen envisions a sustainable society where individuals live in harmony with and contribute meaningfully to their local environment. Evergreen will be at the forefront of the movement to create this society, by empowering communities, by creating innovative resources and by transforming educational values."

Evergreen has partnered with various corporations to achieve its mission of bringing communities and nature together. To illustrate, Evergreen works with Fido, a wireless company, which is encouraging its customers to adopt paperless billing and then using the proceeds from the program to support tree planting across Canada. Evergreen also has a long-time partnership with Toyota Canada and its dealerships to support the Evergreen Learning Grounds program, which has distributed more than $2 million in grants to over 1,700 schools and day cares across the country. Since 2005, Evergreen has worked with Home Depot Canada to provide more than 100 communities across Canada with the funding, tools, materials, and volunteers needed to complete urban stewardship projects through the Rebuilding Nature Grant Program.

The Brick Works is Evergreen's most ambitious project. It is a $55 million project in downtown Toronto to redevelop an abandoned brick works to create an innovative and educational organization. Its development was and continues to be informed by two central purposes: (1) to provoke new ideas about the relationship between nature, people and cities, and (2) to capitalize on the Brick Works unique natural and industrial heritage setting. By Evergreen's work of engaging and educating the community about diverse nature-based experiences, people will be able to witness the benefits of nature firsthand, giving them a renewed sense of place and inspiring them to become active participants in shaping a more sustainable future.[70]

The scope of the Brick Works is social as well as sustainable. It is a social enterprise. It generates revenues through such sources as native plant sales, office and event rental fees, the café, and summer camps. It uses its earned income to increase its educational reach in the form of new programs and services that improve environmental quality and promote health and wellness. It is a triplebottom-line organization that measures its success on environmental, social, and financial indicators that are captured on a tool that blends social accounting with the balanced scorecard, discussed later in the book.

The Brick Works is very much a work-in-progress and by choice. It is committed to learning as the thinking about and knowledge of sustainability grow. It follows the principle of design incompletion, which recognizes that design is an iterative process. Design does not stop—rather, design must be reconceived and change as change occurs.[71] The Brick Works has an Outward Bound Canada site, and a chimney court where children learn about edible gardens. In 2013, Evergreen hosted the Meeting of the Minds Conference, an invitation-only event that brings together 350 innovative thinkers from all around the globe to discuss how to create and enhance sustainable cities.

**Think**

Think about how you can become a competent, influential manager by using the frameworks that organization theory provides to interpret and understand your organization.

# Framework for the Book

What topic areas are relevant to organization theory and design? How does a course in management or organizational behaviour differ from a course in organization theory? The answer is related to the concept called level of analysis.

## Levels of Analysis

Four **levels of analysis** normally characterize organizations, as illustrated in Exhibit 1.9. The individual human being is the basic building block of organizations. The human being is to the organization what a cell is to a biological system. The next higher system level is the group or department. These are collections of individuals who work together to perform group tasks. The next level of analysis

**EXHIBIT 1.9**
Levels of Analysis in Organizations
Source: Based on Andrew H. Van De Ven and Diane L. Ferry, *Measuring and Assessing Performance* (New York: Wiley, 1980), 8; and Richard L. Daft and Richard M. Steers, *Organizations: A Micro/Macro Approach* (Glenview, Ill: Scott, Foresman, 1986), 8.

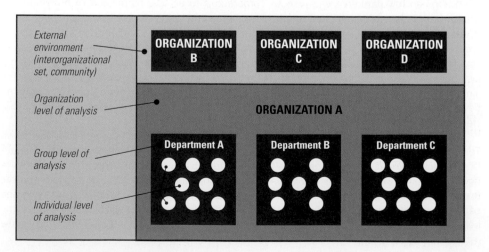

is the organization itself. An organization is a collection of groups or departments that combine into the total organization.

Organizations themselves can be grouped together into the next higher level of analysis, which is the interorganizational set and community. The interorganizational set is the group of organizations with which a single organization interacts. Other organizations in the community also make up an important part of an organization's environment.

Organization theory focuses on the organizational level of analysis but with concern for groups and the environment. To explain the organization, we should look at not only its characteristics but also the characteristics of the environment and of the departments and groups that make up the organization. The focus of this book is to help you understand organizations by examining their specific characteristics, the nature of and relationships among groups and departments that make up the organization, and the collection of organizations that make up the environment.

Are individuals included in organization theory? Organization theory does consider the behaviour of individuals, but in the aggregate. People are important, but they are not the primary focus of analysis. Organization theory is distinct from organizational behaviour.

**Organizational behaviour** is the micro approach to organizations because it focuses on the individuals within organizations as the relevant units of analysis. Organizational behaviour examines concepts such as motivation, leadership style, and personality, and is concerned with cognitive and emotional differences among people within organizations.

**Organization theory** is a macro examination of organizations because it analyzes the whole organization as a unit. Organization theory is concerned with people aggregated into departments and organizations, and with the differences in structure and behaviour at the organization level of analysis. Organization theory is the sociology of organizations, while organizational behaviour is the psychology of organizations.

A new approach to organization studies is called *meso theory*. Most organizational research and many management courses specialize in either organizational behaviour or organization theory. **Meso theory** (meso means "in between") concerns the integration of both micro and macro levels of analysis. Individuals and groups affect the organization, and the organization in return influences individuals and groups. To thrive in organizations, managers and employees need to understand multiple levels simultaneously. For example, research may show that employee diversity enhances innovation. To facilitate innovation, managers need to understand how structure and context (organization theory) are related to interactions among diverse employees (organizational behaviour) to foster innovation because both macro and micro variables account for innovation.[72]

Organization theory is directly relevant to top- and middle-management concerns and partly relevant to lower management. Top managers are responsible for the entire organization and must set goals, develop strategy, interpret the external environment, and decide organizational structure and design. Middle management is concerned with major departments, such as marketing or research, and must decide how the department relates to the rest of the organization. Middle managers must design their departments to fit work-unit technology and deal with issues of power and politics, intergroup conflict, and information and control systems, each of which is part of organization theory. Organization theory is only partly concerned with lower management because this level of supervision is concerned with employees who operate machines, input data, teach classes, and sell goods. Organization theory is concerned with the big picture of the organization and its major departments.

## Plan of the Book

The topics within the field of organization theory are interrelated. Chapters are presented so that major ideas unfold in logical sequence. Part 1 introduces the basic idea of organizations as social systems and the nature of organization theory. This discussion provides the groundwork for Part 2, which is about strategic management, organizational design, effectiveness, and the fundamentals of organizational structure. Organizations are open systems that exist for a purpose. This part examines how managers help the organization achieve its purpose, including the design of an appropriate structure, such as a functional, divisional, matrix, or horizontal structure. Part 3 looks at the various open-system elements that influence organizational structure and design, including the external environment, interorganizational relationships, and the international environment.

Parts 4 and 5 look at processes inside the organization. Part 4 describes how organizational design is related to such factors as manufacturing and service technologies; control; and organizational size, life cycle, and decline. Part 5 shifts to dynamic processes that exist within and between major organizational departments and includes topics such as culture and ethical values; innovation and change; decision-making processes; and conflict, power, and politics. Exhibit 1.10 illustrates the core concepts in the book and can serve as a *course map*.[73]

## Plan of Each Chapter

Each chapter begins with an organizational case to illustrate the topic to be covered. Theoretical concepts are introduced and explained in the body of the chapter.

**EXHIBIT 1.10**
Core Concepts and
Course Map
Source: Copyright © 2008 by
Ann Armstrong.

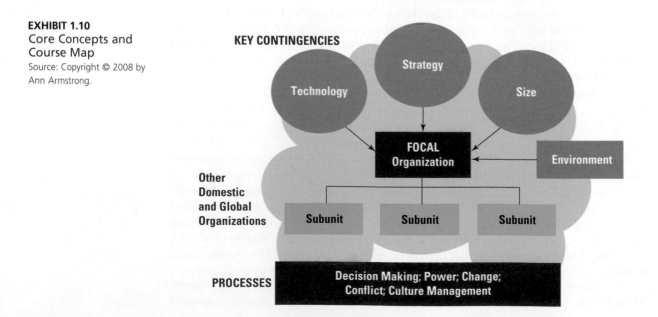

Several *In Practice* segments are included in each chapter to illustrate the concepts and show how they apply to real organizations. *Book Marks* are included in most chapters to present organizational issues that managers face right now. These book reviews discuss current concepts and applications to deepen and enrich your understanding of organizations. The *Leading by Design* examples illustrate the dramatic changes taking place in management thinking and practice. *act!*, apply-compare-think, is designed to link the theoretical concepts with your own experiences. In addition each chapter includes a *You and Design* to personalize the content further. Each chapter closes with a "Summary and Interpretation" section that reviews and explains important theoretical concepts.

## Summary and Interpretation

One important idea in this chapter is that organizations are systems. In particular, they are open systems that must adapt to the environment to survive. Various parts of the organization are designed to perform the key subsystem functions of production, adaptation, maintenance, management, and boundary spanning. Five parts of the organization are the technical core, top management, middle management, technical support, and administrative support.

The focus of analysis for organization theory is not individual people but the organization itself. Relevant concepts include the dimensions of organizational structure and context. The dimensions of formalization, specialization, hierarchy of authority, centralization, professionalism, personnel ratios, size, organizational technology, environment, goals and strategy, and culture provide labels for measuring and analyzing organizations. These dimensions vary widely from organization to organization. Subsequent chapters provide frameworks for analyzing organizations with these concepts.

Many types of organizations exist. One important distinction is between for-profit businesses, in which managers direct their activities toward earning money for the company, and nonprofit organizations, in which managers direct their efforts to generating some kind of social impact. Managers strive to design organizations to achieve high performance and effectiveness. Effectiveness is complex because different stakeholders have different interests and needs that they want satisfied by the organization.

Increasingly, turbulence and complexity have replaced stability and predictability as defining traits for today's organizations. Some of the specific challenges managers and organizations face include coping with globalization; maintaining high standards of ethics and social responsibility; achieving rapid response to environmental changes, organizational crises, or new customer expectations; shifting to a technology-based workplace; and supporting diversity.

These challenges are leading to changes in organizational design and management practices. The trend is away from highly structured systems based on a mechanical model toward looser, more flexible systems based on a natural, biological model. Many managers are redesigning companies toward the learning organization, which is characterized by a horizontal structure, empowered employees, shared information, a collaborative strategy, and an adaptive culture.

Many concepts in organization theory pertain to the top- and middle-management levels of the organization. This book is concerned more with the topics of those levels than with the operational-level topics of supervision and motivation of employees, which are discussed in courses on organizational behaviour.

Finally, it is important that you read the material in the textbook with a critical lens by examining assumptions and accepted wisdom. Some argue that management textbooks have an implicit undeclared bias in favour of capitalism, even though its failings have become glaringly evident in the recent years of economic turbulence and uncertainty. Others note that textbooks may perpetuate a particular ideology. For example, some argue "[if] propaganda is the systematic propagation of an ideology, then inasmuch as the texts push a managerial ideology, often uncritically, the answer to this question is a resounding "yes."[74] Whatever views you have on this issue, it is vital for you to question and to evolve your own views, based on rigorous thought and introspection. Then you will become a more thoughtful organizational actor.

## ■ Key Concepts

administrative principles, p. 8
bureaucratic organizations, p. 8
change strategy, p. 6
chaos theory, p. 30
closed system, p. 19
contextual dimensions, p. 22
contingency, p. 29
effectiveness, p. 26
efficiency, p. 26
Hawthorne Studies, p. 8
learning organization, p. 30
level of analysis, p. 34
meso theory, p. 35

open system, p. 19
organization, p. 14
organizational behaviour, p. 35
organization theory, p. 35
role, p. 31
scientific management, p. 8
stakeholder approach, p. 27
stakeholder, p. 27
structural dimensions, p. 22
subsystems, p. 19
system, p. 19
task, p. 31

## ■ Discussion Questions

1. What is the definition of *organization*? Briefly explain each part of the definition.
2. What is the difference between an open system and a closed system? Can you give an example of a closed system? How is the stakeholder approach related to this concept?
3. Explain how Mintzberg's five basic parts of the organization illustrated in Exhibit 1.5 work. If an organization had to give up one of these five parts, which one could it survive the longest without? Discuss.
4. A handful of companies on the Fortune 500 list are more than 100 years old, which is rare. What organizational characteristics do you think might explain 100-year longevity?
5. What is the difference between formalization and specialization? Do you think an organization high on one dimension would also be high on the other? Discuss.
6. What does *contingency* mean? What are the implications of contingency theories for managers?
7. What are the primary differences between an organization designed for efficiency and one designed for flexibility? Discuss the pros and cons of each approach for today's organizations.

# ■ Chapter 1 Workbook: Measuring Dimensions of Organizations*

Analyze two organizations along the dimensions shown below. Indicate where you think each organization would fall on each of the scales. Use an X to indicate the first organization and an asterisk (*) to show the second.

You may choose any two organizations you are familiar with, such as your place of work; the university; a student organization; your faith-based organization; or your family.

| Formalization | | | | | | | | | | | |
|---|---|---|---|---|---|---|---|---|---|---|---|
| Many written rules | 1 | 2 | 3 | 4 | 5 | 6 | 7 | 8 | 9 | 10 | Few rules |
| **Specialization** | | | | | | | | | | | |
| Separate tasks and roles | 1 | 2 | 3 | 4 | 5 | 6 | 7 | 8 | 9 | 10 | Overlapping tasks |
| **Hierarchy** | | | | | | | | | | | |
| Tall hierarchy of authority | 1 | 2 | 3 | 4 | 5 | 6 | 7 | 8 | 9 | 10 | Flat hierarchy of authority |
| **Technology** | | | | | | | | | | | |
| Product | 1 | 2 | 3 | 4 | 5 | 6 | 7 | 8 | 9 | 10 | Service |
| **External Environment** | | | | | | | | | | | |
| Stable | 1 | 2 | 3 | 4 | 5 | 6 | 7 | 8 | 9 | 10 | Unstable |
| **Culture** | | | | | | | | | | | |
| Clear norms and values | 1 | 2 | 3 | 4 | 5 | 6 | 7 | 8 | 9 | 10 | Ambiguous norms and values |
| **Professionalism** | | | | | | | | | | | |
| High professional training | 1 | 2 | 3 | 4 | 5 | 6 | 7 | 8 | 9 | 10 | Low professional training |
| **Goals** | | | | | | | | | | | |
| Well-defined goals | 1 | 2 | 3 | 4 | 5 | 6 | 7 | 8 | 9 | 10 | Goals not defined |
| **Size** | | | | | | | | | | | |
| Small | 1 | 2 | 3 | 4 | 5 | 6 | 7 | 8 | 9 | 10 | Large |
| **Organizational Mindset** | | | | | | | | | | | |
| Mechanistic system | 1 | 2 | 3 | 4 | 5 | 6 | 7 | 8 | 9 | 10 | Biological system |

## Questions

1. What are the main differences between the two organizations you evaluated?
2. Would you recommend that one or both of the organizations have different ratings on any of the scales? Why?

*From DAFT. *Organization Theory and Design*, 10E. © 2010 South-Western, a part of Cengage Learning, Inc. Reproduced by permission. www.cengage.com/permissions

## Case for Analysis: Teleflex Canada: A Culture of Innovation*

Teleflex Canada, a division of Teleflex Inc., manufactured a range of products, including marine hydraulic steering systems, trim components for marine propulsion, heating equipment for both the truck and bus industries, a range of proprietary fluid controls, and field cookstoves for the U.S. Army. Over the past 30 years, Teleflex Canada grew from sales of a few million dollars to more than $160 million in 2004. The company has a reputation as a world leader in the design and manufacture of hydraulic and thermal technology products. Within Teleflex Canada there was a consensus that continual innovation in product design, manufacturing, and marketing was critical to the success of the organization.

In 2005, Teleflex Canada executives were faced with various questions: Would size inhibit the ability to innovate? Would increased corporate centralization at Teleflex Inc. impact Teleflex Canada's ability to respond quickly to new market opportunities? At the Teleflex Inc. corporate level, different questions were being asked: Could the culture of innovation in Teleflex Canada be transferred to other parts of the company? What was the appropriate level of corporate support and control necessary to foster innovation and high performance at Teleflex Canada and at other Teleflex business units?

### Teleflex Inc.

Teleflex Inc., a diversified manufacturing company, was headquartered in Limerick, Pennsylvania, just outside Philadelphia. The company had three principal business segments: Commercial, Medical, and Aerospace.

### Commercial

The Commercial segment manufactured various products for automotive, marine, and industrial markets, including manual and automatic gearshift systems; transmission guide controls; mechanical and hydraulic steering systems; vehicle pedal systems; heavy-duty cables; hoisting and rigging equipment for oil drilling and other industrial markets; mobile auxiliary power units used for heating and climate control in heavy-duty trucks, industrial vehicles, and locomotives; and fluid management products for automobiles and pleasure boats.

### Medical

The Medical segment manufactured health care supply and surgical devices including anesthesiology devices, sutures, ligation solutions, chest drainage systems, and high-quality surgical and orthopedic instruments.

### Aerospace

The Aerospace segment manufactured products for the commercial and military aerospace, power generation, and industrial turbine machinery markets. Aerospace businesses provided repair products and services for flight and ground-based turbine engines; manufactured precision-machined components and cargo-handling systems; and provided advanced engine surface treatments. Products in the Commercial segment were generally produced in higher unit volumes than that of the company's other two segments.

In the fiscal year ended December 31, 2004, Teleflex's consolidated sales were $2.49 billion, with 48 percent coming from the Commercial segment, while Medical and Aerospace represented 30 percent and 22 percent, respectively. With approximately 21,000 employees and major operations in more than 70 locations worldwide, Teleflex Inc. operations were highly decentralized, with dozens of small profit centers and a corporate office consisting of a few senior executives and support staff. A few years ago, a major effort was begun to redefine Teleflex as a unified operating company that shared people, products, and processes across divisions and business units. The objective of the reorganization was to establish some common operational standards to improve productivity. Not surprisingly, in a company where autonomy had always been the hallmark of business unit activity, increased efforts at standardization, consolidation, and sharing of resources were met with some managerial resistance at the business unit level.

### Teleflex Canada

Teleflex Canada, based in Richmond, British Columbia, in the metropolitan Vancouver area, had been one of the best performing business units within Teleflex for several decades. Through internal development, licensing, and acquisition, its growth rate averaged 20 percent per year for 25 years. Total sales in 2004 were about $160 million. Teleflex Canada designed and produced a variety of products utilizing hydraulic and thermal technologies.

### Marine and Industrial Hydraulic Systems

Teleflex Canada was created in 1974 when Teleflex Inc. purchased part of Capilano Engineering, a small machine shop in Vancouver that was developing hydraulic steering systems for boats. At that time, another Teleflex unit was producing marine steering systems with mechanical cable steering. Teleflex management knew that as marine engines got larger and more powerful, mechanical steering would become obsolete because it could no longer provide the necessary comfort and safety.

Teleflex Canada's hydraulic steering systems—SeaStar, SeaStar Pro, and BayStar—were designed to enable more comfortable control of pleasure boats. These products fundamentally changed the marine steering industry. In 2004 Teleflex Canada sold more than 100,000 SeaStar systems, an increase of more than 30 percent over the previous year (retail prices for the higher-end products ranged from about $1,200–$1,500 per system, while lower-end systems were about $250). The company had an estimated 95 percent market share in North America and 50 percent share in markets outside the continent. Teleflex Canada's steering products were usually among the highest-priced products available in the marketplace.

The marine steering industry had two main market segments. One segment included stern drive engine companies like Volvo Penta that would purchase a private label steering system and integrate it with their engine to provide a complete steering and controls package to boat builders. A second segment was the marine distribution and dealer network that sold Teleflex-branded products to boat companies and individual boat owners. Sales of marine products were split almost equally between original equipment manufacturers like Volvo Penta and aftermarket dealers.

In addition to steering systems, Teleflex Canada also produced components for marine engine companies like Bombardier and Volvo Penta. These products were referred to as industrial actuation systems.

### Energy

Teleflex Canada was successful in applying its boat-based technology to the needs of other markets. In 1985 Teleflex Canada began licensing an engine governor technology for large diesel trucks. In 1990 an auxiliary heater business for large trucks and buses was purchased from Cummins, which led to the development of the ProHeat vehicle heater product line. The heater technology was adapted in 1997 to create cookstoves, called modern burner units (MBUs), for use in army field kitchens. A major contract was signed with the U.S. military for the production of MBUs. By 1999 Teleflex was producing 10,000 MBUs per year for military purposes.

## Innovation, Technology, and Product Development

Teleflex Canada innovation focused on product and market development that solved customer problems or created new markets. Much of Teleflex Canada's success has come about because a demand was identified for new products in niche markets that were ready for a change in technology. As explained by a Teleflex Canada executive:

*Our fundamental belief is that we don't use any technology that is not proven. We call ourselves product developers. We will not develop any technology that cannot be robust and highly reliable with a low repair requirement. We take existing technology and tweak it to make it better. ... We usually don't invent anything radically new (although sometimes new technology had to be invented to solve a customer's problem). We are a company that has been innovative in applications engineering. We focus on products we know we can sell because we are close to the market and know the customers. ... Innovation at Teleflex Canada involves three questions:*

1. *How do we exploit existing technology?*
2. *How do we develop reliable and robust products from that technology?*
3. *How do we penetrate and dominate some market niche with that product?*

*For example, we are looking for new areas where we can use electro-hydraulic applications. There are other markets where this technology could work, such as dental chairs and hospital beds or suspensions systems for lawn and garden equipment. These are markets that will pay a premium for a customer-built system using hydraulics.*

The next sections discuss some product development activities at Teleflex Canada.

### Seastar Development

When Teleflex Inc. acquired Capilano Engineering, the intent was to expand into new markets. At that time, the company was producing a heavy-duty commercial hydraulic steering system. In 1978 Teleflex Canada introduced Syten, the world's first low-cost hydraulic system for the mass pleasure boat market. Cost was a big factor because Syten competed against low-priced mechanical steering systems. Unfortunately, Syten's plastic parts deteriorated when used beyond their mechanical capability, leading to unsatisfied customers and a risk that Teleflex Canada would lose its position in hydraulic steering. At that time, Teleflex Canada had about 10% of the hydraulic steering market (the largest competitor had a share of about 80%).

Teleflex Canada developed a new hydraulic steering system called SeaStar, which was introduced in 1984. SeaStar became the leading product on the market. In 1989 the new SeaStar was introduced. The mandate for the development team was smaller size to expand the potential market, lower cost, and better performance. Using some patented technology (a floating spigot), the new Seastar was 30% cheaper to produce, 18% more efficient, and sold at the same price as the older model. In 1993 Seastar Pro was introduced and was very successful in the Bass boat market where performance was the primary purchase criterion. BayStar, introduced in 2002 for the lower-end market, was very successful (although it cannibalized sales of a mechanical steering system produced by another Teleflex division).

Again, a Teleflex Canada executive explains:

*To regain our reputation in the marketplace, we had to come out with an overkill approach with the product. We developed a much more sophisticated and rugged all-metal system, which became SeaStar. This decision involved heated internal debates because the development costs were substantial. This required a lot of trust from Bim Black (Teleflex Inc. Chairman and former CEO). He was willing to take some risk in the investment. There were a lot of skeptics. But, the hydraulics technology was well-proven and being used in automotive systems. We were applying existing technology to a customized marketplace. From a technology perspective, the risk was not high. From a market point of view, we knew that our current line of cables (from another Teleflex Inc. business unit) was not going to satisfy customers as boat engines got bigger and more difficult to steer.*

*We have 35 patents but the technology was not earth-shattering. The marketplace wanted higher horsepower and more comfort, and we were able convince people to change to hydraulics. ... Harold (Copping, Teleflex Canada President at the time) kept a nice fence between corporate and Teleflex Canada. And we were small enough to fall under the radar screen at corporate. For example, we were able to order some tooling without approval.*

*When the development of SeaStar was done, the marine industry was going through a downturn. Our competitors were laying off engineers and trying to survive. We kept our engineers developing products. When we came out of the downturn, we had new products that allowed us to grow.*

*There are two keys to the success of SeaStar over the years. One, we always kept innovating. Our competitors would copy our designs and in about six months we would have a better product on the market. Since our products were 30 percent–40 percent better than the competition, we could keep our margins up. As time went on, the performance gap narrowed. But, because we built scale economies through our size and innovated in manufacturing, we have the lowest cost. So, we have the lowest cost and the best performing product. Two, a lot of our success is through innovation on the shop floor to ensure that we had a cost-effective product. The corporation pushed us to use more advanced machine tools and to be more analytical. SeaStar involved innovation in technology, product development, marketing, and manufacturing processes that were developed at the shop floor level. The product designs were enhanced because of the manufacturing processes, some of which must be kept in-house because they are proprietary.*

*Also, having a good product is only part of the story. You also need to sell the product. To me, selling is like being a farmer. You go out and spread some seeds, water them daily, and eventually they come to fruition. I always fought corporate—they kept telling me to close the deal. I was very patient. I was very generous with our product. I would give away our product and let them try it. I am out there constantly talking with customers, looking at the competition.*

*Our competitors are getting better, but our market share makes it difficult for other companies to compete on cost. We continue to focus on being the best and never giving any customers an excuse to go looking elsewhere. ... One day, all boats will steer as comfortably as cars. That has been my passion. To make that happen. I have never deviated from it.*

### Energy Product Development

ProHeat, an auxiliary power and climate control system for trucks and buses, was introduced in 1992.

*To get into heaters we bought a product line from Cummins Engine. Cummins was not successful with the product so we bought the remaining inventory. This got our foot in the door, and it is much easier to start a business when you have something to sell. When we did the deal with Cummins, we had already concluded that the product [the truck heater] was not any good. We did the deal anyway because it got us into a new market that we thought we could serve better with new products.*

*We never actually produced any of the Cummins products, but we learned a lot about the market. There was a clear demand for a product that could be used to heat trucks and was more fuel-efficient than leaving the engine idling. We were able to figure out the type of product innovation that was necessary and spent about two years bringing the product to market. The first truck heater was ProHeat in 1992. Once we had some success in the Canadian market, we looked to the U.S. market. We needed a different product because of air conditioning. Teleflex usually doesn't like to start from scratch so we looked around for a possible acquisition. We bought a small company in Ontario that had a product. That allowed us to get into the market.*

*We then took the truck heater to the transit bus market. We started talking to different city bus companies and were able to adapt our technology for the bus market. These were not huge leaps, and to us they seemed very obvious. We never say build it and they will come. We try to get the order first and then build the product. We start by selling concepts along with our credibility in the market.*

The development of the truck heater, along with several other products, including a heater for tents used by the military, provided Teleflex Canada with a solid base of experience in combustion technology. This led to the development of the military cookstove called the MBU. The MBU used the same combustion technology as the truck heater and could be used as a block heater, passenger heat source, barbeque, or oven.

The MBU project started with an inventor who had built a prototype stove. The inventor was able to convince the U.S. Army to put the project out for bid based on the specifications he had developed in his prototype. Harold Copping described how the military cookstove project got started:

*We understood the military market. When we did our licensing deal for the tent heater, we had an understanding that we would not develop a cookstove. Eventually, we agreed to license the technology for the cookstove. I visited the military and made sure the funding was in place. I knew the U.S. Army liked the design, and I saw a huge opportunity for Teleflex. I saw this as a chance to back a winner and take a gamble. We put together a team of some of our best people to develop a working prototype. It was not a big risk because I knew that we had very good burner technology and I knew the Army liked the people and the design. We were in their good books because we had had great success with previous projects for them. We spent $500,000 and it worked out well. Our people improved the inventor's design and made it manufacturable and safer.*

Another Teleflex executive added the following comments about product development:

*To make these programs work, it started at the very top of Teleflex Inc. There were skunk works going on, but they were tolerated. When we were trying to diversify the business, Harold protected us from the operations mentality. For each of the key projects, we put a dedicated team together whose priority was not operations. For several programs we moved engineers out of the building to off-site locations. We wanted these engineers to worry about the development project, not the stuff that was in production. We wanted their full attention on the product development. There has to be a wall between development and existing operations. The next challenge is how to reintegrate the new business into operations and try to avoid the us-and-them attitude. Operations people like stability, and design engineers like change.*

You need a focused team that says "our mission is to capture this market." In other groups in Teleflex, there is not the same acceptance about product development teams that may take years to bring a product to market. They ask: how can you justify that over the next quarter?

## Teleflex Canada Culture

Harold Copping describes some of the characteristics of the Teleflex Canada culture:

*I joined the company two years after the acquisition [by Teleflex Inc.]. My strength was an ability to recognize the strengths of other people. I cared a lot about people enjoying their work and doing interesting jobs. We had one person who was a mechanical genius but very difficult to work with. He was a great source of innovation in improved manufacturing methods and quality. He had a very temperamental personality, and in the early days there were fisticuffs on the shop floor and all kinds of things that should not happen. I protected him because I recognized how much he could do. We had another engineer who was brilliant and could think out of the box. He was off the wall and I had to protect him on two occasions against his bosses. I believed something good was going to come out of this guy [he is still at Teleflex Canada].*

*Right from the beginning, there was a nucleus of very good people in Teleflex Canada in terms of inventive creativity and willingness to solve problems and make things happen. There was some adversity that forced us to work together, such as vast quantities of products being returned by customers [the first innovative hydraulic steering system]. This helped me understand who contributed to solutions and who didn't. It also allowed me to play on the theme that if we did not do this right, the corporation will take it away from us. This was our chance to show them that we could manufacture in Vancouver.*

*We had discipline but we also had freedoms. We allowed a pretty free rein on innovation, and at the same time were adding systems and standardization. I tried to build the organization around a spirit of independence and risk-taking with a passionate group of people. I wanted the organization to work around the innovative people even if they were eccentric and hard to work with. Enthusiasm and passion are variables that are not measurable. I maintain that one degree of passion is worth 10 degrees of efficiency. All of our customers could sense the enthusiasm. People really cared at Teleflex Canada.*

*We had a culture of admiration for people with innovative engineering talent. We were also strongly motivated to never to [be] second-class. There were drivers in the marketplace that pushed us to excel, and there was a constant focus on continuous improvement.*

*You have to create an identity and differentiation that is different from the rest of the corporation. If you lose the identity, you become an employee. You don't have the nice feeling of being part of a cause and a culture that you understand. Therefore, there has to be some symbolism around the identity and also some competition with other divisions of Teleflex. We tried to identify threats so that people would be scared and there would never be complacency. We used threats to draw people together. Some of our greatest successes came about when there was a lot of adversity because of customer problems or breakdowns.*

Other managers echoed Harold Copping's views:

*Harold was able to maintain a chemistry between the group of individuals that had to make it happen. That is easier when you are a small company. Harold surrounded himself with people who were passionate about what they believed in. If there was a common denominator, it was passion to be the best and the most successful. If you did not believe in this, you were gone. We were almost competing with each other but still working together as a team. The chemistry was as good as it could have been.*

*Everybody can question anyone about technical details. We have always had a culture that allows people to question everything. Everyone realizes that they are in a position where they could be questioned. We all have egos, but people have to check them at the door at Teleflex Canada. Harold knew that if you put people on too high a pedestal, it can cost you money. ... Harold was the president, but he did not have his own parking space. People related to that. He did not try to be better than anyone.*

*We had some people who were unorthodox but were real technical geniuses. We also had some managers who were eternal optimists. If you have a negative attitude, it will kill entrepreneurial thinking.*

Managerial commitment to Teleflex Canada was another key element in the company culture, as indicated by the following statement:

*After the reorganization in May 2004, we realized there were a few businesses that were in serious trouble. The first company I was asked to visit was in Ontario. Within the first few hours of discussion, I discovered that the fundamental issue was the uncontrolled financial expense relative to a declining market. I was asked to run the company as general manager for the next 3–4 months. This was not the best time from a personal perspective: I was in the middle of building a new house (acting as general contractor) and had a number of personal issues involving the sale of my current house and dealing with the planned move of my family.*

*I spoke to my wife and family the next day, and we both agreed that the need for me to work in Ontario was greater than the need for me to continue as general contractor for the house. She rearranged her work schedule, and my parents stepped in to help get the kids to their various*

*activities. On May 30, 2004, I took the red-eye from Vancouver and went straight into work on arrival in Toronto. For the next 8 months I flew out every Sunday night, spent long hours at work from Monday to Thursday, and flew back for the weekend. Even the weekend we moved into our new house, I flew back on Friday, moved into the house, and flew out on Sunday. I appreciated the opportunity Teleflex Canada had provided me over the past few years, and this was my way of showing them how dedicated I was to the company's success.*

## Teleflex Inc. and Teleflex Canada

Harold Copping described the relationship between Teleflex Canada and Teleflex Inc.:

*I was running a remote subsidiary in a decentralized company. That was a huge advantage. From the very outset, I had a feeling of positive support from corporate and a feeling that I was controlling my own destiny. I tried to help the staff understand that it was really up to us, and I tried to create a culture where we controlled our own destiny.*

*The relationship was not "control by corporate." It was "help being available from corporate." We had people available from corporate to help teach us about quality and engineering. I always felt that I could choose to use the corporate resources that were available to me. If I could use local resources cost effectively, I did so. I pushed back when someone tried to force corporate resources on me ... Access to the corporation definitely played a role in our progress. [Chairman] Bim [Black] fostered a climate of cross-pollination between divisional and general managers by holding interesting meetings, although as the company got bigger there were fewer meetings. These meetings were very good in helping us know where to go and who to call. I used to find an excuse to visit other Teleflex facilities.*

*There was enough interaction and influence from corporate to allow people to create successful business relationships [with other parts of Teleflex Inc.]. Since they were not forced by corporate, only the viable relationships occurred. If we could help each other, we did. The attitude was based on open markets. ... There were many benefits to being part of a large corporation. It was a nice environment to be in. As we got bigger, we were increasingly under the microscope.*

*We did not know the word* core competence *at the time. By the early 1980s we began to think that we were not really limited to the marine market. We were small enough and far enough away from corporate that nobody really cared what we did. We could explore new opportunities without being unduly restrained. As long as we were making money and growing, we had a lot of latitude. Nobody restricted me—freedom was a big factor.*

## Pull-Through Strategy

Rather than designing products and then looking for channels through which to sell them, Teleflex Canada focused on end users. Executives described this strategy as a pull-through strategy:

*Our strategy in the truck business is pull-through. The reason why ... the truck companies [OEM manufacturers] put our ProHeat product on the truck is because the customer [the truck fleet operators] wanted it. The same thing happens with SeaStar. The boat builders buy it from us but the customer [the boat buyer] demands it.*

*A pull-through strategy is pragmatic. I can call on OEMs all day long but if no end users are asking for the product, we won't sell anything. We still have to negotiate with OEMs, but they don't get to make the call. It is the fleet customer who says we want ProHeat. We are trying to keep our products from becoming commodities, where the OEMs only care about price. They never ask for better— they only ask for cheaper. A lot of companies are confused about who their customers really are. The OEM is not the customer; the OEM is the channel. The customer is the person who will actually use the product.*

*The SeaStar technology was developed for a market that was prepared to pay a premium for higher comfort. People have asked, "why don't you leverage this technology into high volume sectors like automotive?" The problem with those markets is that the pricing pressures are intense and the volumes are much higher. We build about a half-million steering systems per year. Plus, we see automotive as more of a commodity market. Marine customers are using surplus funds to buy their products. Nobody has to own a boat. Boats are not a commodity, and we can demand a higher premium in the marine market. We have never entered another steering market.*

*We want to move boats closer to car steering comfort levels. Our next level of product innovation is to take comfort to a new level through power steering. We thought we would sell 2,000 power steering systems this year and it looks like we will sell 20,000. The boat builders initially resisted the shift to power steering. We gave the boat builders the new systems to try. Our philosophy is not to sell to the boat builders; we want them to buy it from us.*

*It does not matter what the technology is. The market will decide. Everybody is willing to pay a fair price for fair value. ... We always try to be a few steps ahead of our customers. For example, we have an expensive power steering system for 60–100–foot luxury yachts. It is a very technical product and there are varying levels of expertise within the boat building companies. We believe that if we want to capture a bigger share of the market, we will have to simplify the technology and make it "bubba-proof."*

*That is what we strive for: how do we make our product better and easier for our customers to use. Since our competitors are followers, they cannot think like this.*

## The Future

As Teleflex Canada executives looked towards the future, they were faced with various issues, such as the degree of vertical integration, the relationship with Teleflex Inc., managing the size of the organization, and the future for new product development.

### Vertical Integration

Teleflex Canada had always been vertically integrated. There was a consensus that, in the future, there would be less vertical integration.

*All our customers want us to be as cost-effective as possible. In the past we were incredibly vertically integrated. For example, when we started with ProHeat, we needed various parts, like a flame sensor, a compressor, a blower, and a water pump. Nobody built any of these parts to our specs, so we developed them ourselves from scratch. What are we doing developing a flame sensor? There are companies out there who should be able to do these things better than us. We spent a lot of money doing a lot of things, and we would have been better served if we had had the option to look outside. We developed some stuff that we had no business developing. As a general rule, we will buy technology rather than develop technology. We will develop new products. That is not the way we got here, but it is the way we need to go.*

*We have developed a strategic plan that involves core and non-core capabilities. We went through all our manufacturing processes and asked what is really core from process and intellectual property points of view. We have to protect intellectual property. We identified about 80% of our manufacturing processes as noncore.*

*We are going to try to shift from [being] a manufacturer to an integrator and a tester. We will only fabricate what is considered absolutely core for protecting our manufacturing and quality processes and our intellectual property. Everything else is up for grabs. If we cannot be competitive here, the work will go elsewhere. We will be going through a rapid change. We want to focus on marketing, sales, product development and engineering, prototyping, final assembly, and testing. Fabrication and subassembly may go elsewhere. We want to be an OEM or a tier 1 player.*

Not everyone was in complete agreement that the shift from manufacturer to integrator and tester was the basis for a unique strategy. According to one manager:

*Every company in the world is trying to be an early adopter with low-cost manufacturing and outsourcing of* non-core activities. That is not a strategy—that is good business practice. If you lose the ability to innovate on the production floor, you lose some of the ability to lower costs. That is my fear with off-shore production. Also, how are we going to protect key product designs and innovation when we spread work out to partners?

## Relationships With Teleflex Inc.

Within all of Teleflex Inc. there was an ongoing debate about the merits of centralization and unified operating processes. Within Teleflex Canada, this debate was particularly relevant given the history of the subsidiary (i.e., 3,000 miles from headquarters) and its successful innovations:

The bigger area of conflict from a corporate unified perspective involves market and product development, who owns it, and how do we keep the innovation happening. With more centralization going on, how do you make sure you don't kill the entrepreneurialism? Everybody knows that if you go completely centralized, you totally lose the innovation. What we have agreed on is that product development has to stay close to the market. There has to be some consolidation at a group level but not at a corporate level. We are creating centers of excellence such as hydraulics and power generation.

I understand the need for centralization. I also understand that the centralization pendulum usually swings too far. As far as the centralization of patent attorneys, this will take away from our ability to get prompt intellectual property. We will get it, but it will be slower. It is critical to understand your intellectual property before you spend too much time in development. Centralization of HR may also affect us. For example, corporate edicts about raises may make it hard to keep engineers, since Vancouver is such a hot tech area.

If you take away all of the divisional autonomy, you cripple the divisions. Before, purchases for $25,000 or less could be approved at the division. Now everything has to go to corporate. Unless you are yelling or screaming, it can be a two- or three-month process to get approval. Because of Sarbanes-Oxley, things have to be done in a specific way. Too many rules will take away someone's incentive to stick their neck out and try something different. The old environment is gone, but we will make it happen somehow.

## Managing Size

Teleflex Canada had grown rapidly over the past three decades. Size has brought a variety of challenges, as the following comments demonstrate:

We went from $4.5 million when I started to $160 million today. Every time we made a big jump in revenue,

there were benefits and downsides. Getting big can be a problem, which is one reason Harold split the company into three divisions—he saw that we were getting too big.

The problem with growth is that as you get bigger, it gets more difficult to manage and control. Then you get to a point where the corporation becomes huge and the latest flavor of the month comes in, like "go to China for your raw materials." Now the buzz word is "cut costs, cut costs." If all we focus on is cutting costs, we will stifle the entrepreneurialism, and that is the beginning of the end. Once you stifle entrepreneurialism, passion, and creativity, you become like any other corporation. Margins will drop because you cannot be fast and innovative. You slowly start losing. We are on the edge.

As we get bigger we have to follow more processes, sign more forms; and by the time you get done, it is too late. It is not how big you are that makes you successful—it is how fast you are to market. In efforts to consolidate, we are risking our fast response time. When we were smaller, I could get things done in 24 hours. Now it takes forever.

We have always been known as a company that solved customer problems. We were very good at getting to the root cause of the problem. When a customer calls us, we take care of them. This got us a lot of respect and market share, and this was not the way our competitors did it. As we get bigger we may not be able to react quickly enough.

To keep our edge, we need to keep up with the technology, move fast, and make sure quality does not suffer as we experiment with offshore sourcing. Basically, we need to continue to deliver what we promise. Do not take cost-cutting to the point where it affects what you have promised your customers.

One way we are trying to deal with size is with the Virtual Development Center. We are leaving too many opportunities on the table. This Center will be a small group that acts as an interface between the customers and the divisions. The Center will have two main objectives: one, to make sure the customers get proper focus from the people best qualified to deal with their problems; and two, to make sure the development project goes to the appropriate division. ... Our goal is to provide a customer with a conceptual design in 7 days and a prototype within 30 days. In a way, we are trying to break free of the shackles of size by responding quickly to customers. Once we have a customer, we will put the product into the appropriate division to develop it, make it manufacturable, optimize it, etc.

There is a limit to how big the firm can get and still be innovative and entrepreneurial. It is easier with smaller groups. Once an organization gets over 150 people, it should be subdivided. You need to strike the right balance between operational efficiency, serving the customer well, and maintaining a spirit of identity. ... Balancing operational efficiency with subdividing the organization is more of a challenge because there are tradeoffs. When people work together in subunits and depend on each other for overall success, politics is minimized. The challenges are to work with people and stay connected with people at every single level. If people believe that they succeed together and make things happen together, they will have some job security and will reap some rewards. It is much easier to excite people about a portion of the business rather than the whole business.

### Forward Thinking: New Product Development and New Technologies

New product development was central to the success of Teleflex Canada and central to continued growth. Executives were generally confident that the organization would continue to develop and exploit existing technologies. Some comments about the marine area are as follows:

I don't see an issue with product development. The bigger challenge is dealing with new technologies. The risk is that our existing products get replaced by new technologies in which we have no expertise. Take steering systems. We know that hydraulics will go away eventually, and the market will demand more comfort at lower prices. The boat builders may integrate steering into their outboards. Most stern drive engine steering uses a cable with a power steering system.

We will have to reduce costs and develop more robust designs for larger outboard engines. There will be new technologies that replace hydraulic steering. Electro over hydraulic with programmable tension and torque levels is the next generation and will come out soon. The next shift will be to electro-mechanical actuation or steer-by-wire, which is disruptive technology. We believe we can bring this to market, and we had the foresight to realize that we were going to become an electronics company. Five years ago we engaged a local university professor—an expert in fault tolerant systems—to work with us privately on steer-by-wire. Corporate and other engineers did not know we were doing this. We scavenged the money where we could and eventually bought an equity stake in an offshoot company owned by the university and the professor. When corporate found out what we were doing, they saw that it made sense and gave us steer-by-wire responsibility for the corporation. We are going

to be ready with a steer-by-wire product when the world is ready for the technology.

We are also trying to develop new products for boats. We know that we will lose market share when hydraulic steering goes away. We also know that the engine companies want to integrate steering with their engines. We need to be forward-looking and help our customers sell their products. We need to make sure we are the company that the engine manufacturer wants as the integrator. Our plan is to develop new business with Yamaha, Bombardier, and other engine companies.

### Conclusion

Teleflex Canada had provided a high margin contribution to the Teleflex corporation for many years. Would success breed complacency and stagnation? Or, would Teleflex Canada continue to grow, innovate, and develop new products? According to one executive:

We can't get fat and lazy, because that will be the beginning of the end. We have to continue to solve our customers' problems and make their lives easier. As long as we do what we promise and don't get arrogant, we will be fine. If we start acting like an 800-pound gorilla, customers will find a way to deal with us. We need to work with our customers and make their lives easier. It is a fine line and you need to know where the line is. Most of our boat builders are entrepreneurs; there are no barriers to entry in the boat business. This helps keep the automotive mentality out of this industry.

### Assignment Questions

1. What does innovation mean at Teleflex Canada? Why is innovation necessary at Teleflex Canada?
2. Why has Teleflex Canada been so successful in introducing new products?
3. What role do organizational factors play in supporting innovation?
4. Are there threats to continued innovation at Teleflex Canada?
5. Can the Teleflex Canada approach to innovation be implemented in other organizations?

PART 2

# Organizational Purpose and Structural Design

# 2

# Strategy, Organizational Design, and Effectiveness

CANADIAN PRESS/Colin Perkel

## Tim Hortons

Which company has taken hold in the everyday lives of Canadians? Many would argue that it is Tim Hortons, which has created its own slang ("double double"),[1] made its stores part of every busy Canadian street corner, spawned a phenomenon in which people arrive at work or at school with a "Tims," and consistently promoted Canadian culture and sports in its advertising and sponsorships. In a hugely popular move, it operated a store for Canadian troops stationed in Kandahar, Afghanistan.[2]

NHL hockey star Tim Horton opened a coffee and doughnut shop in Hamilton, Ontario, in 1964 in order to earn income in the off-season. Soon afterward, he met Ron Joyce, a local police officer, who joined the business. By 1967, Joyce was a partner, and in 1974, he bought out the Horton family after Tim's death to become its sole owner. The chain has grown rapidly between 1964 and 2012—in 1964, there was only one store in Hamilton, Ontario, but by 2012, there were 3,295 locations in Canada, 714 across 10 U.S. states in the northeast and midwest, and five locations in the United Arab Emirates.[3]

In Canada, Tim Hortons is synonymous less with doughnuts than with coffee. It has been able to break out of the narrowly defined market typical of Krispy Kreme to anchor its brand in coffee. "While doughnuts play an important role in our product mix, they aren't the key to our growth or our success," said Patti Jameson, a spokesperson for Tim Hortons, noting that the company's restaurants also sell bagels, sandwiches, soups and coffee, with coffee providing close to 50 percent of sales. The company sees room for more stores in Canada.[4] Tim Hortons sells about two billion cups of hot and iced coffee annually, second only to Starbucks.[5]

By centring its brand on coffee, Tim Hortons has gained enormous success. It has a 62 percent market share in the Canadian coffee segment. The second largest share is that of Starbucks, at 7 percent.[6] The anchoring effect of coffee allows the company to explore other products and revise its mix as necessary. At the end of the day, however, the products are all branded as Tim Hortons. The company topped *Canadian Business*'s annual survey of best-managed brands in 2004, 2005, and 2006.[7] In 2010, it was ranked as Canada's most trusted brand but slipped to second place in 2011 to the Jean Coutu Group. The difference in the scores of the two brands is slight, however.[8] In 2013, Tim Hortons was ranked the sixth most influential brand in Canada, after Google, Facebook, Microsoft, Apple and Visa.

Tim Hortons has had an interesting history of ownership and governance. At first, Tim Horton both owned and managed it. Then Ron Joyce became a partner in the ownership and management. Upon Horton's death, Joyce became the sole owner. When Ron Joyce needed funds to expand, he didn't issue stock to the public but instead borrowed money, retaining his sole ownership. (Canadian companies with publicly listed shares of stock are subject to extensive regulation. Their executives must report annually to the shareholders and regularly to a board of directors.) In 1995, as Joyce approached retirement age, he sold Tim Hortons to the American fast-food chain Wendy's. In spite of its place in Canadian society, its head office was Dublin, Ohio, and the company was no longer under Canadian ownership. The latest shift in the company's structure happened in 2006, when investors demanded that the company be spun off from Wendy's. Today, the company's head office is in Oakville, Ontario, and the stock is listed on the New York and Toronto exchanges.

Tim Hortons has achieved success only through attention to its brand. Unlike Starbucks, which sells its enticing aroma, sophisticated music, comfortable seats, attentive staff, and welcoming atmosphere, Tim Hortons has been able to sell itself not only as a destination, but also as part of typically Canadian experiences outside its doors. Tim Hortons has driven the high level of Canadian out-of-the-home coffee drinking. Due in part to the high number of drive-through outlets, "Timmies" are seen in workplaces, at meetings, in rinks, and anywhere Canadians gather. The company sponsors activities that enhance its image as a deeply Canadian company: Timbits Minor Sports Program, free swimming at community pools and holiday skating at local arenas, and summer camp for underprivileged children.

However, the company's ability to sell coffee to people on their way to work has not compromised its ability to attract Canadians to its stores. In recognizing Tim Hortons as one of the top ten brands in Canada in 2010,[9] Interbrand focuses on this capacity: "Canada's beloved Tim Hortons sells coffee but truly produces loyalty and ranks number six. With market penetration in Canada that makes even global giant Starbucks roast with envy, Tim Hortons is the country's fourth place after home, work, and the hockey rink."[10] Company research indicates that approximately 46 percent of customers visit four or more times per week, a marker of the company's success at making a visit to Tim's part of daily routines in Canada.[11]

Top managers such as Ron Joyce and his successor, Paul House, are responsible for positioning their organizations for success by establishing goals and strategies that can help the company be competitive. An organizational goal is a desired state of affairs that the organization attempts to reach.[12] A goal represents a result or end point toward which organizational efforts are directed. It specifies where energy and resources are to be used. In 2012, House set a goal of continued growth in the Canadian market; he believed that there was room for another 700 locations in Canada.[13] The goal fits with the company's overall strategy of gradual expansion into adjacent areas, retaining Canadian identity, and maintaining consistency. Even so, Tim Hortons faces significant competitive pressure from McDonalds: "A market share battle is brewing in the fast-food sector, with Tim Hortons confronting an unprecedented challenge to its decades-long reign as Canada's coffee-and-doughnut icon."[14] However, according to Marc Caira, President and CEO,

> We are setting out to be bold, different and daring. We envision a Tim Hortons that is one of the industry's most consumer-centric brands, leveraging technology to build our understanding of emerging consumer insights and to connect with them in new and innovative ways. We are focusing on flawless execution and creating the ultimate guest experience. We are asserting our coffee and food leadership, simplifying our operations and pursuing differentiated innovation. Our team is aligned, focused and committed to strong execution and market leadership.[15]*

The choice of goals and strategy affects organizational design, as we will discuss in this chapter.

## ■ Purpose of This Chapter

Typically top managers give direction to organizations. They set goals and develop the plans for their organization to attain those goals. The purpose of this chapter is to help you understand the types of goals that organizations pursue and some of the competitive strategies managers use to reach those goals. We will examine two significant frameworks for determining strategic action and look at how strategies affect organizational design. The chapter also describes the most popular approaches to measuring the effectiveness of organizational efforts. To manage organizations well, managers need a clear sense of how to measure effectiveness. Before reading any further, complete the You & Design feature to assess your strengths in strategic thinking and doing.

# YOU & DESIGN

## Your Strategy/Performance Strength

As a potential manager, what are your strengths concerning strategy formulation and implementation? To find out, think about how you handle challenges and issues in your school work or job. Then circle "a" or "b" for each of the following items depending on which is more descriptive of your behaviour in work situations. There are no right or wrong answers.

1. When keeping records, I tend to be
   a. Very careful about documentation.
   b. More haphazard about documentation.

2. If I run a group or a project, I
   a. Have the general idea and let others figure out how to do the tasks.
   b. Try to figure out specific goals, timelines, and expected outcomes.

3. My thinking style could be more accurately described as
   a. Linear thinker, going from A to B to C.
   b. Thinking like a grasshopper, hopping from one idea to another.

4. In my office or home things are
   a. Here and there in various piles.
   b. Laid out neatly or at least in reasonable order.

5. I take pride in developing
   a. Ways to overcome a barrier to a solution.
   b. New hypotheses about the underlying cause of a problem.

6. I can best help strategy by making sure there is
   a. Openness to a wide range of assumptions and ideas.
   b. Thoroughness when implementing new ideas.

7. One of my strengths is
   a. Commitment to making things work.
   b. Commitment to a dream for the future.

8. I am most effective when I emphasize
   a. Inventing original solutions.
   b. Making practical improvements.

**Scoring:** For *strategic formulator* strength, score one point for each "a" answer circled for questions 2, 4, 6, and 8, and for each "b" answer circled for questions 1, 3, 5, and 7. For *strategic implementer* strength, score one point for each "b" answer circled for questions 2, 4, 6, and 8, and for each "a" answer circled for questions 1, 3, 5, and 7. Which of your two scores is higher and by how much? The higher score indicates your *strategy strength*.

**Interpretation:** Formulator and implementer strengths are important ways managers bring value to strategic management and effectiveness. Managers with implementer strengths tend to work on operative goals and performance to make things more efficient and reliable. Managers with formulator strength push toward imaginative strategies and like to think about mission, vision, and dramatic breakthroughs. Both styles are essential to strategic management and organizational effectiveness. Strategic formulators often use their skills to create whole new strategies and approaches, and strategic implementers often work with strategic improvements, implementation, and measurement. If the difference between your two scores is two or less, you have a balanced formulator/implementer style and work well in both arenas. If the difference is 4–5, you have a moderately strong style and probably work best in the area of your strength. And if the difference is 7–8, you have a distinctive strength and almost certainly would want to contribute in the area of your strength rather than in the opposite domain.

Source: Adapted from Dorothy Marcic and Joe Seltzer, *Organizational Behavior: Experiences and Cases* (South-Western, 1998), 284–287, and William Miller, *Innovation Styles* (Global Creativity Corporation, 1997).

# The Role of Strategic Direction in Organizational Design

An organization is created to achieve some purpose, which is often decided by the chief executive officer (CEO) and the top management team. Top executives decide on the end purpose the organization will strive for and determine the direction it will take to accomplish it. It is this purpose and direction that shapes how the organization is designed and managed. Indeed, *the primary responsibility of top management is to determine an organization's goals, strategy, and design, therein adapting the organization to a changing environment.*[16] Middle managers do much the same for major departments within the guidelines provided by top management. On the other hand, many nonprofits see these issues as the board's responsibility.[17] The relationships through which top managers provide direction and then design are illustrated in Exhibit 2.1.

The direction-setting process typically begins with an assessment of the opportunities and threats in the external environment, including the degree of change, uncertainty, and resource availability, which we discuss in more detail in Chapter 4.

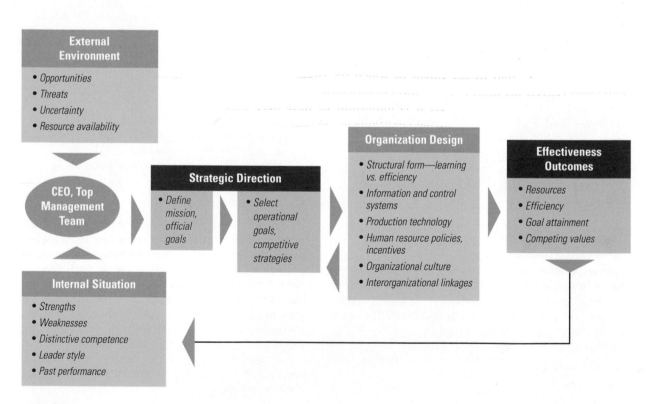

**EXHIBIT 2.1**

Top Management Role in Organization Direction, Design, and Effectiveness

Source: Adapted from Arie Y. Lewin and Carroll U. Stephens, "Individual Properties of the CEO as Determinants of Organization Design," unpublished manuscript, Duke University, 1990; and Arie Y. Lewin and Carroll U. Stephens, "CEO Attributes as Determinants of Organization Design: An Integrated Model," *Organization Studies* 15, no. 2 (1994), 183–212.

Managers also assess internal strengths and weaknesses to define the company's distinctive competence compared with other firms in the industry.[18] The assessment of internal environment often includes an evaluation of each department and is shaped by past performance and the leadership style of the CEO and top management team. The next step is to define the overall mission and official goals based on the correct fit between external opportunities and internal strengths. Specific operational goals or strategies can then be formulated to define how the organization is to accomplish its overall mission.

In Exhibit 2.1, you can see that organizational design reflects the way goals and strategies are implemented. Organizational design is the administration and execution of the strategic plan. Organization direction is implemented through decisions about structural form, including whether the organization will be designed for a learning or an efficiency orientation, as discussed in Chapter 1, as well as choices about information and control systems, the type of production technology, human resource policies, culture, and linkages to other organizations. Changes in structure, technology, human resource policies, culture, and interorganizational linkages will be discussed in subsequent chapters. Also, note the arrow in Exhibit 2.1 running from organizational design back to strategic direction. This means that strategies are often made within the current structure of the organization, so that current design constrains or puts limits on goals and strategy. More often than not, however, the new goals and strategy are selected based on environmental needs, and then top management attempts to redesign the organization to achieve those ends.

Finally, Exhibit 2.1 illustrates how managers evaluate the effectiveness of organizational efforts—that is, the extent to which the organization realizes its goals. This chart reflects the most popular ways of measuring performance, each of which is discussed later in this chapter. It is important to note here that effectiveness outcomes feed back into the internal environment, so that past performance of the organization is assessed by top management in setting new goals and strategic direction for the future.

The role of top management is important because managers can interpret the environment differently and develop different goals. For example, when William Weldon became CEO, in 2002, of Johnson & Johnson, he recognized an underlying need for greater collaboration and information sharing among Johnson & Johnson's disparate divisions. Johnson & Johnson is an extremely complex organization, made up of more than 200 different companies organized into three divisions: drugs, medical devices, and diagnostics. The company has thrived by giving its various businesses almost complete autonomy. However, Weldon believed the system had to change to thrive in today's shifting environment. Weldon set goals that required managers to build alliances across the three major divisions.[19] "If you are going to have a successful corporate program, it has to be directed from the top," says Weldon. He could be talking about cost-cutting initiatives or a new talent-management protocol.[20] Johnson & Johnson, one of the world's most admired companies, has been recognized for its successful strategies; for example, it was honoured by the United Nations in 2011 with the Humanitarian of the Year Award for its leading role in the Healthy Mother, Healthy Child initiative.[21]

The choices top managers make about goals, strategies, and organizational design have a tremendous impact on organizational effectiveness. Remember that goals and strategy are not fixed or taken for granted. Top managers and middle managers must select goals for their own units, and the ability to make such

**Apply**

How can you apply performance measurement as you progress in your career?

choices largely determines organizational success. Organizational design is used to implement goals and strategy and also determines organization success. We will now discuss further the concept of organizational goals and strategy, and in the latter part of this chapter we will discuss various ways to evaluate organizational effectiveness.

# Organizational Purpose

Organizations are created and continued in order to accomplish something. All organizations, including Johnson & Johnson, Dalhousie University, Cineplex Odeon, the Royal Bank of Canada, the United Church of Canada, the Assembly of First Nations, the local dry cleaner and the neighbourhood milk store, exist for a purpose. This purpose may be referred to as the overall goal, or mission. Different parts of the organization establish their own goals and objectives to help meet the overall goal, mission, or purpose of the organization.

Many types of goals exist in an organization, and each performs a different function. One major distinction is between the officially stated goals, or **mission**, of the organization and the operative goals the organization actually pursues.

## Mission

The overall goal for an organization is often called the mission—the organization's reason for existence. The mission describes the organization's vision, its shared values and beliefs, and its reason for being. It can have a powerful impact on an organization.[22] The mission is sometimes called the **official goals**, which refers to the formally stated definition of business scope and outcomes the organization is trying to achieve. Official goal statements typically define business operations and may focus on values, markets, and customers that distinguish the organization. Whether called a mission statement or official goals, the organization's general statement of its purpose and philosophy is often written in a policy manual or the annual report. The vision, mission, strategy, and values statement for Endeavour, Volunteer Consulting for Non-Profits is shown in Exhibit 2.2. Note also that an organization's *vision* and mission are different. While the mission focuses on goals, the vision captures the core ideology and the envisioned future for an organization. The core ideology describes the values of the organization while the envisioned future articulates what the organization aspires to become.[23]

One of the primary purposes of a mission statement is to serve as a communication tool.[24] The *mission statement* communicates to current and prospective employees, customers, investors, suppliers, and competitors what the organization stands for and what it is trying to achieve. A mission statement communicates legitimacy to internal and external stakeholders, who may join and be committed to the organization because they identify with its stated purpose. Most top leaders want employees, customers, competitors, suppliers, investors, and the local community to look on them in a favourable light, and the concept of legitimacy plays a critical role.[25] The corporate concern for legitimacy is real and pertinent. Consider the accounting firm Arthur Andersen, which was accused of obstructing justice

**EXHIBIT 2.2**
Endeavour: Volunteer
Consulting for
Non-Profits

### VISION

We envision a world where access to professional consulting services is not a barrier to non-profits in achieving their goals, regardless of their financial capacity.

### MISSION

Endeavour is dedicated to enabling non-profit organizations to improve and sustain their community impact.

### VALUES

- Committed: We are committed to delivering sustainable value to organizations that exist for a social benefit. As a volunteer organization, we appreciate the talent and time given to us by our members and strive to reflect this commitment fully to impact performance of our non-profit clients.
- Collaborative: We function in an inspiring environment of transparency and teamwork. As a volunteer consulting organization, we not only understand that collaboration is critical to our performance, but also that it is crucial to develop long-term meaningful relationships with our volunteers, clients and community.
- Inclusive: We promote inclusiveness both internally and externally. We value diversity in our members, advisors and volunteers as well as in our clients and projects. We welcome diversity in opinion and ideas.
- Impactful: We engage on strategic management issues to help non-profit organizations improve their impact. Working for clients and projects limited for resources, we challenge ourselves to provide pragmatic and impactful solutions.
- Growth-oriented: We strive toward organizational, community, professional and personal growth.

Source: Endeavour Volunteer Consulting for Non-Profits http://www.endeavourvolunteer.ca/about-us/ Used with Permission.

by shredding accounting documents related to the Enron investigation. Once the previously respected global firm lost legitimacy with clients, investors, and the public, it was all but dead. In the post-Enron environment of weakened trust and increasing regulation, many organizations face the need to redefine their purpose and mission to emphasize the firm's purpose in more than financial terms.[26] Companies where managers are sincerely guided by mission statements that focus on their social purpose, such as LifeLabs' "At every step in the testing process, from collection to reporting, our goal is to deliver caring, compassionate, quality service that contributes to enhanced patient care" or ArcelorMittal Dofasco's "Our product is steel. Our strength is people" typically attract better employees, have better relationships with external parties, and perform better in the marketplace over the long term.[27]

## ■ Operative Goals

**Operative goals** designate the ends sought through the actual operating procedures of the organization and explain what the organization is actually trying to do.[28] Operative goals describe specific measurable outcomes and are often

**Compare**

Compare the mission and the operative goals of two dissimilar organizations that you know well. What differences did you note?

concerned with the short run. Operative goals typically pertain to the primary tasks an organization must perform, similar to the subsystem activities identified in Chapter 1.[29] These goals concern overall performance, boundary spanning, maintenance, adaptation, and production activities. Specific goals for each primary task provide direction for the day-to-day decisions and activities within departments.

**Overall Performance.** Profitability reflects the overall performance of for-profit organizations. Profitability may be expressed in terms of net income, earnings per share, or return on investment. Other overall performance goals are growth and output volume. Growth pertains to increases in sales or profits over time. Volume pertains to total sales or the amount of products or services delivered. For example, Volkswagen's Audi division was targeted to sell 1.2 million cars in 2011. It has experienced such rapid growth that it plans to create 10,000 new jobs by 2020 to meet demand from China and North America.[30]

Government and nonprofit organizations such as social service agencies or labour unions do not have goals of profitability, but they do have goals that attempt to specify the delivery of services to clients or members within specified expense levels. In 2006, the Government of Québec set numeric targets for the participation of women on its public boards together with a timetable to achieve them; by mid-December 2011, all 23 public boards had to have an equal number of men and women.[31] Growth and volume goals also may be indicators of overall performance in nonprofit organizations. Treasury Board of Canada Secretariat encourages the government to manage its contracts with nonprofits and charities through service-level agreements.[32]

**Resources.** Resource goals pertain to the acquisition of needed material and financial resources from the environment. They may involve obtaining financing for the construction of new plants, finding less-expensive sources for raw materials, or hiring top-quality technology graduates. Resource goals for McGill University include attracting top-notch professors and students. Honda Motor Company has resource goals of obtaining high-quality auto parts at low cost. United Way of Greater Toronto sets annual fundraising targets, which it frequently exceeds, in order to help maintain social programs in the Toronto area. In 2012, it set a goal of $116 million and raised $116.1 million even as the world was still recovering from some difficult times.[33]

**Market.** Market goals relate to the market share or market standing desired by the organization. Market goals are the responsibility of marketing, sales, and advertising departments. An example of a market goal is Honda's desire to overtake Toyota Motor Company as the number-one seller of cars in Japan. Honda has surpassed Nissan to become number two in Japan, and the recently introduced Fit subcompact has eclipsed the Toyota Corolla as the best-selling car in that market and became the top-selling car in November 2013 ahead of the Prius.[34] In the toy industry, Canada's Mega Bloks, now owned by Mattel, achieved its goal of doubling its share of the toy building block market to 30 percent. The giant of the industry, Denmark's Lego, is re-evaluating strategies to try to regain the market share it has lost.[35]

**Employee Development.** Employee development refers to the training, promotion, safety, and growth of employees. It includes both managers and workers. Strong employee development goals are one of the characteristics common to organizations that regularly show up on *Report on Business*'s list of "50 Best Employers in Canada." For example, Wellington West Capital, an employee-owned financial services firm in Winnipeg, received the award for five years in a row between 2006 and 2010.[36] Two of its seven principles centre on people: the company identifies and recruits the best, and is confident in the quality of its staff. *The Globe and Mail* notes that "[companies] fare better when managers coach workers up the corporate rungs."[37]

**Innovation and Change.** Innovation goals pertain to internal flexibility and readiness to adapt to unexpected changes in the environment. Innovation goals are often defined in terms of the development of specific new services, products, or production processes. The 3M Company has a goal that 30 percent of sales come from products that are less than four years old.[38] In the 2014 *Fast Company* rankings of the world's most innovative companies, Apple fell to 14th place while Twitter is ranked thirteenth. Google tops the list. The organization ranked 49th is Alta Bicycle Share, which launches bike sharing programs around the world.[39] The four examples highlight that there are many different forms of innovation.

**Productivity.** Productivity goals concern the amount of output achieved from available resources. They typically describe the amount of resource inputs required to reach desired outputs and are thus stated in terms of "cost for a unit of production," "units produced per employee," or "resource cost per employee." Managers at Akamai Technologies, which sells Web content delivery services, keep a close eye on sales per employee to see if the company is meeting productivity goals. Akamai's chief financial officer, Timothy Weller, sees this statistic as "the single easiest measure of employee productivity." Boeing Company installed a new moving assembly line for the 737 aircraft to increase productivity. Once the wings and landing gear are attached, each plane is dragged toward the door at two inches a minute, with workers moving along with it on a float-like apparatus.[40]

# Leading *by Design*

## Four Seasons

Hotels are often terrible workplaces. The nonmanagement jobs are often physically tough. Housekeepers have to wrestle large mattresses and heavy linens. Cleaners work with hazardous chemicals. The jobs are often low paying, and the workers seldom achieve any recognition or status. A 2002 study of San Francisco workers found that

> In addition to physical job demands, 83 percent of the room cleaners reported constant time pressure. Other job stressors often reported include lack of respect from supervisors (40 percent), poor job security (52 percent), and poor job promotion prospects

(61 percent). On average, 30 percent of the room cleaners experienced an imbalance between their work efforts and the material and nonmaterial rewards they receive. This imbalance is an indicator for job stress. In addition, 38 percent of the room cleaners experienced high levels of job strain, measured as the combination of high job demands and little job control. Both these findings suggest that more than a third of the room cleaners experience high levels of job stress.[41]

Since the mid-1990s, Unite Here has been fighting difficult but successful organizing campaigns among hotel workers,

*(Continued)*

fuelled by dissatisfaction over wages and working conditions.[42] "Turnover rates throughout the industry, according
to the American Hotel & Motel Association, are 158 percent
for front-line employees and 129 percent for managers."[43]

Four Seasons, the Canadian-based luxury hotelier,
believes in doing things differently from the rest of the
industry. Its employee turnover rates are 25 percent for all
Four Seasons employees, and 19 percent for managers.[44]
The company has never missed being listed as one of the
"100 Best Companies to Work for in America." Until Four
Seasons restructured the company in 2007, its stock traded
at 40 to 50 times earnings, far higher than most others in
the industry. Why is this hotel considered much more valuable than its competitors? Does part of the answer lie in the
relationships it builds with its staff?

Izzy Sharpe thinks so. The celebrated founder of the company believes that the experience of luxury must be based in
exemplary service. He believes that the employees providing
that service cannot do it well if they are not supported,
encouraged, and led by managers committed to them.

Take the time Mercedes Simon applied for a job cleaning
the public bathrooms in the Westlake Village hotel. "People
were very polite, but I didn't really get it at first," she says
of the four successive rounds of interviews she was asked
to undergo.

But then, as she sat down for a break in the cafeteria
on her first day, the hotel's manager walked up to her.
"May I bring you something, Mercedes?" he asked with
a smile.

Stunned by his graciousness, let alone by the fact that
he remembered her name, "I said, 'Oh, no, thanks,'" she
recalls sheepishly. "But that's when I realized this place
really is different. It made me want to work here."[45]

This attention to service, which results in enormous
brand equity, is no accident: Sharpe has been building it
into every management decision for decades. The Four Seasons' human resource policies are not about emulating best
practices; they are designed to be an integral part of the
company's strategy to make profits.

Successful organizations use a carefully balanced set of operative goals. Although
profitability goals are important, some of today's best companies recognize that a
single-minded focus on bottom-line profits may not be the best way to achieve high performance. Increasing numbers of companies are using triple-bottom-line accounting,
a system in which companies assess their environmental and social performance as
well as their profits.[46] Innovation and change goals are increasingly important, even
though they may initially cause a decrease in profits. Employee development goals are
critical for helping to maintain a motivated, committed workforce.

## ■ The Importance of Goals

Both official goals and operative goals are important for the organization, but they
serve very different purposes. Official goals and mission statements describe a value
system for the organization; operative goals represent the primary tasks of the organization. Official goals legitimize the organization; operative goals are more explicit
and well defined.

Operative goals can provide employees with a sense of direction, so that they
know what they are working toward. This can help motivate employees toward
goal accomplishment, especially if employees are involved in setting the targets.
The events at Walkerton, Ontario's water plant provide a negative illustration of
the motivating power of goals: "In May 2000, Walkerton's drinking water system
became contaminated with deadly bacteria, primarily *Escherichia coli* O157:H7.1.
Seven people died, and more than 2,300 became ill. The community was devastated.
The losses were enormous. There were widespread feelings of frustration, anger,
and insecurity." Justice Dennis O'Connor's report concludes that cuts to the inspections budget of the Ministry of the Environment were part of the chain of events
that led to the disaster. "In February 1996, the Cabinet approved the budget reductions in the face of the warnings of increased risk to the environment and human

health." The Conservative provincial government of the mid-1990s did not intend to reduce the quality of drinking water, but its goal of reducing expenditures was paramount. With many fewer provincial inspections, public utilities commissioners and staff were neither accountable for nor motivated to do their work.[47] Managers need to understand the power of goals and use care when setting and implementing them. Another important purpose of goals is to act as guidelines for employee behaviour and decision making. Appropriate goals can act as a set of constraints on individual behaviour and actions so that employees behave within boundaries that are acceptable to the organization and larger society.[48] They help define the appropriate decisions concerning organizational structure, innovation, employee welfare, or growth. Finally, goals provide a standard for assessment. The level of organizational performance, whether in terms of profits, units produced, degree of employee satisfaction, level of innovation, or number of customer complaints, needs a basis for evaluation. Operative goals provide this standard for measurement.

# A Framework for Selecting Strategy and Design

To support and accomplish the direction determined by organizational mission and operative goals, managers have to select specific strategy and design options that will help the organization achieve its purpose and goals within its competitive environment. In this section, we examine a couple of practical approaches to selecting strategy and design.

A **strategy** is a plan for interacting with the competitive environment to achieve organizational goals. Some managers think of goals and strategies as interchangeable, but for our purposes, *goals* define where the organization wants to go and strategies define how it will get there. For example, a goal might be to achieve 15 percent annual sales growth; strategies to reach that goal might include aggressive advertising to attract new customers, motivating salespeople to increase the average size of customer purchases, and acquiring other businesses that produce similar products. Strategies can include any number of techniques to achieve the goal. The essence of formulating strategies is choosing whether the organization will perform different activities than its competitors or will execute similar activities more efficiently than its competitors do.[49] Magna International Inc., for example, has decided to change its acquisitions strategy. In the past, it bought small or distressed companies that were being sold off. As the company is cash rich, in 2011 and beyond, it plans to buy "big targets." Don Walker, CEO, comments that "[we] believe we will continue to be a consolidator in the industry."[50]

As noted in Chapter 1, it is important to examine accepted wisdom. For example, some thinkers argue that strategies are essentially narratives or fiction. The narratives are not false but rather accounts that are created to persuade others to act.[51] Still others argue that strategies need to be understood as organizational myths. "Common themes run through organizational tales such as[:] the creation story, the journey for 'the grail', dragon slaying. Because these are common themes, they are used by managers as one way of making sense of the their experiences in the world. Myths then become the foundation for our 'knowing.'"[52] From this perspective, strategies—or myths—can be seen as another sense-making act. In Chapter 9, we will revisit the importance of myths and stories when we examine the impact of culture in shaping organizations.

Two models for formulating strategies are the Porter model of competitive strategies and Miles and Snow's strategy typology. Each provides a framework for competitive action. After describing the two models, we will discuss how the choice of strategies affects organizational design.

## ■ Porter's Competitive Strategies

Michael E. Porter studied a number of businesses and introduced a framework describing three competitive strategies: low-cost leadership, differentiation, and focus.[53] The **focus strategy**, in which the organization concentrates on a specific market or buyer group, is further divided into *focused low-cost leadership* and *focused differentiation*. This yields four basic strategies, as illustrated in Exhibit 2.3. To use this model, managers evaluate two factors, competitive advantage and competitive scope. With respect to advantage, managers determine whether to compete through lower cost or through the ability to offer unique or distinctive products and services that can command a premium price. Managers then determine whether the organization will compete on a broad scope (competing in many customer segments) or a narrow scope (competing in a selected customer segment or group of segments).

**Differentiation.** In a **differentiation strategy**, organizations attempt to distinguish their products or services from others in the industry. An organization may use advertising, distinctive product features, exceptional service, or new technology to achieve a product perceived as unique. This strategy usually targets customers who are not particularly concerned with price, so it can be quite profitable. Toronto-based Cervélo bicycles,[54] Roots clothing, and Jaguar automobiles are examples of products from companies using a differentiation strategy. Service firms such as Four Seasons Hotels and utilities such as Bullfrog Power use a differentiation strategy as well.

**EXHIBIT 2.3**
Porter's Competitive Strategies
Source: Adapted from *Competitive Advantage: Creating and Sustaining Superior Performance* by Michael E. Porter, Copyright © 1985, 1988 by Michael E. Porter; and from Stonehouse, G. and B. Snowden (2007) Competitive Advantage Revisited, Michael Porter on Strategy and Competitiveness, *Journal of Management Inquiry*, 16, 3, 256–273.

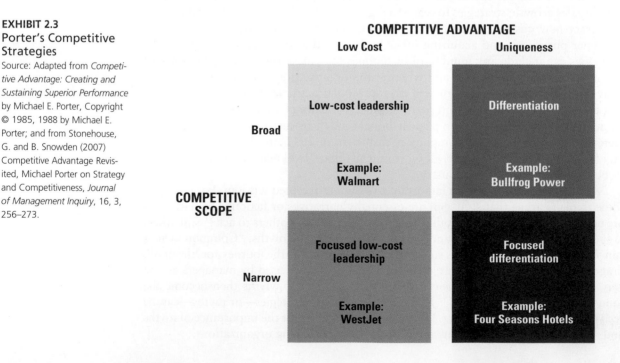

A differentiation strategy can reduce rivalry with competitors and fight off the threat of substitute products because customers are loyal to the company's brand. However, companies must remember that successful differentiation strategies require a number of costly activities, such as product research and design and extensive advertising. Companies that pursue a differentiation strategy need strong marketing abilities and creative employees who are given the time and resources to seek innovations.

**Low-Cost Leadership.** The **low-cost leadership strategy** tries to increase market share by emphasizing low cost compared to competitors. With a low-cost leadership strategy, the organization aggressively seeks efficient facilities, pursues cost reductions, and uses tight controls to produce products or services more efficiently than its competitors. One good example of a focused low-cost leadership strategy is WestJet.

The low-cost leadership strategy is concerned primarily with stability rather than taking risks or seeking new opportunities for innovation and growth. A low-cost position means a company can undercut competitors' prices and still offer comparable quality and earn a reasonable profit.

**Think**

Think about how you can use a differentiation strategy to market yourself in job interviews.

## In Practice

**WestJet Airlines Limited (WestJet)**

For decades, new airlines have fought to end Air Canada's domination of the Canadian market. Canadian, WardAir, Caledonia, and others have started with a base in the West and worked to compete with Air Canada's long-established routes and reputation. In 1996, Clive Beddoe, Mark Hill, Tim Morgan, and Donald Bell founded WestJet to serve the country from Winnipeg to Vancouver. It grew quickly and generated profits like Southwest, the low-cost airline it wished to emulate.

WestJet has succeeded through constant, planned, incremental growth. In contrast to more established carriers, it quickly identifies and abandons strategies, markets, and technologies that are unprofitable. (It no longer flies to Gander, San Francisco, San Diego, or LaGuardia; moved its eastern hub from Hamilton to Toronto; and abandoned plans to buy Boeing 737-600s.) Like Ryanair and Southwest, its counterparts in Europe and the United States, WestJet uses new, high-efficiency aircraft. WestJet staff are compensated in part through profit sharing, in an attempt to reduce pressure to unionize and minimize labour costs. WestJet watches its costs closely, allowing every point in market share to be realized as profits.[55] WestJet's 2013 implementation of its premium service for the business market strategy has not gone smoothly. It introduced three fare bundles with no promotion so some passengers unknowingly sat in premium seating. WestJet's CEO, Gregg Saretsky, admitted that the rollout "wasn't pretty."[56]

A low-cost strategy can help a company defend against current competitors because customers cannot find lower prices elsewhere. In addition, if substitute products or potential new competitors enter the picture, the low-cost producer is in a better position to prevent loss of market share.

**Focus.** With Porter's third strategy, the focus strategy, the organization concentrates on a specific regional market or buyer group. The company will try to achieve either a low-cost advantage or a differentiation advantage within a narrowly defined market. In a curious strategic move, Héroux-Devtek, based in Longueuil,

Québec, sold off its profitable businesses to focus on the landing-gear segment of the aerospace industry. The immediate impact of the change in strategy was a lower fourth-quarter profit.[57] One good example of a focused strategy is Edward Jones, a St. Louis–based brokerage house. The firm has succeeded by building its business in rural and small-town North America and providing investors with conservative, long-term investments. An example of a focused differentiation strategy is Puma, the German athletic-wear manufacturer. Ten years ago, Puma was on the brink of bankruptcy. CEO Jochen Zeitz, then only 30 years old, revived the brand by targeting selected customer groups, especially armchair athletes, and creating stylish shoes and clothes that are setting design trends. Puma is "going out of its way to be different," says analyst Roland Könen, and sales and profits reflect the change. Puma has been profitable every year since 1994, and enjoyed record sales growth in 2010.[58]

When managers fail to adopt a competitive strategy, the organization is left with no strategic advantage and performance suffers. Porter found that companies that did not consciously adopt a low-cost, differentiation, or focus strategy, for example, achieved below-average profits compared to those that used one of the three strategies. Many Internet companies have failed because they did not develop competitive strategies that would distinguish them in the marketplace.[59] On the other hand, eBay and Google have been highly successful with coherent differentiation strategies. The ability of managers to devise good strategy through careful diagnosis, guided by policy and supported by action steps is key, as further discussed in this chapter's Book Mark.

Porter's competitive strategy model has been criticized for being too generic and therefore of minimal use to managers. As well, the model does not account for organizations that are successful even though they are not pursuing one particular strategy.[60]

## ■ Miles and Snow's Strategy Typology

Another business strategy typology was developed from the study of business strategies by Raymond Miles and Charles Snow.[61] The Miles and Snow typology is based on the idea that managers seek to formulate strategies that will be congruent with the external environment. Organizations strive for a fit among internal organization characteristics, strategy, and the external environment. The four strategies that can be developed are the prospector, the defender, the analyzer, and the reactor.

**Prospector.** The **prospector** strategy is to innovate, take risks, seek out new opportunities, and grow. This strategy is suited to a dynamic, growing environment, where creativity is more important than efficiency. Nike, which innovates in both products and internal processes, exemplifies the prospector strategy. For example, it has introduced a line of shoes based on designs that can be produced using recycled materials and limited amounts of toxic chemical-based glues.[62] Even the Volvo Car Corporation, known better for following a defender strategy, is following a prospector strategy thanks to its owner, Li Shufu, CEO of Zhejiang Geely Holding Group. The next In Practice describes Li's strategy.

**Defender.** The **defender** strategy is almost the opposite of the prospector. Rather than taking risks and seeking out new opportunities, the defender strategy is concerned with stability or even retrenchment. This strategy seeks to hold onto current customers, but it neither innovates nor seeks to grow. The defender is concerned primarily with internal efficiency and control to produce reliable, high-quality

In Practice

**Volvo Car Corporation (Volvo)**

For several years Volvo has focused on stability, seeking to hang on to customers who appreciate the brand's reputation for safe, reliable family vehicles. But Li Shufu, the company's hard-charging Chinese owner, is setting a new course for the company, aiming to expand aggressively into the luxury car market and compete head-on with the likes of BMW and Mercedes. Li's company, Zhejiang Geely Holding Group, acquired Volvo from Ford in a landmark deal in 2010.

Li has clashed with Volvo's European CEO, Stefan Jacoby, who wants to move more slowly away from the company's tradition of modest style, but the two eventually agreed on an ambitious turnaround plan that involves $10 billion in investment over a five-year period and a goal of doubling worldwide sales to 800,000 vehicles by 2020. The plan to build three new manufacturing plants in China has been scaled back to one, but Li still wants to build more as soon as possible.

In April 2011, Volvo introduced the Concept Universe, an upscale vehicle that reflects the goal of moving into snazzier luxury models. The car's underpinning, called SPA for "scalable platform architecture," was designed to be able to accommodate a larger car in the future. China's emerging class of rich consumers "behave outrageously," Li says, and he wants Volvo to offer innovative, electrifying designs that turn heads and win new customers. Sales in China are a growing part of the auto business, and Li says Volvo has no future unless it caters to the flashier tastes of emerging rich consumers in that country.[63]

---

products for steady customers. This strategy can be successful when the organization exists in a declining industry or a stable environment. As the market for department stores has declined over the last 30 years, Canadians saw the Hudson's Bay Company and Eaton's adopt different approaches to the defender strategy. Eaton's tried every possible innovation in its last years, but none was successful enough to save the company. HBC, on the other hand, has carefully monitored its margins and spending, maintained its discount brand (Zellers) in order to successfully compete with Walmart, and survived as one of Canada's only two national department stores. As well, HBC hired Bonnie Brooks in 2008 to revamp its brand. She dropped many underperforming product lines and brought in trendy product lines such as Coach and Top Shop. Like many Canadian companies, Zellers' recent purchase by U.S.–based Target signals its success rather than failure. However, it is still too early to tell if Target's entering the Canadian market through its purchase of Zellers signals success. Target plans to open 100 to 150 stores across Canada in 2013 and 2014. Its strategy in Canada appears to be essentially the same as it uses in the United States: "[We] know that 70% of Canadians know the Target brand and that 10% are already shopping our stores, so we know that there's a strong affinity there and we want to deliver on that."[64]

**Analyzer.** The **analyzer** tries to maintain a stable business while innovating on the periphery. It seems to lie midway between the prospector and the defender. Some products will be targeted toward stable environments in which an efficiency strategy designed to keep current customers is used. Others will be targeted toward new, more dynamic environments, where growth is possible. The analyzer attempts to balance efficient production for current product lines with the creative development of new product lines.[65] We can see this strategy in use at Rogers Communications. Rogers works within mature markets such as cable TV, where it has a significant but stable revenue base and few opportunities for new customers. However, the company explores growth strategies in areas such as wireless data transfer.

**Reactor.** The **reactor strategy** is not really a strategy at all. Rather, reactors respond to environmental threats and opportunities in an ad hoc fashion. In a reactor strategy, top management has not defined a long-range plan or given the organization an explicit mission or goal, so the organization takes whatever actions seem

## Book Mark 2.0        HAVE YOU READ THIS BOOK?

### Good Strategy Bad Strategy: The Difference and Why It Matters
By Richard Rumelt

Richard Rumelt, the Harry and Elsa Kunin Chair in Business and Society at UCLA's Anderson School of Management, points out that "winging it is not a strategy." Corporate leaders are always talking about strategy, but Rumelt says many of them are just winging it. "Too many organizational leaders say they have a strategy when they do not," writes Rumelt in *Good Strategy Bad Strategy: The Difference and Why It Matters.* Instead, he explains, they have fallen prey to "the creeping spread of bad strategy."

#### HOW TO TELL A BAD STRATEGY FROM A GOOD ONE

Some carefully devised strategies founder or fail due to managers' miscalculations or flawed decisions, but what Rumelt calls bad strategy is something else entirely and can be identified by several characteristics. First, many executives mistake goals for strategy. Have you ever heard a CEO proclaim that his company's strategy is "to grow by 20 percent a year" or "to increase profits by 15 percent?" These desired outcomes, emphasizes Rumelt, are not strategy. Goals define where you want the organization to go, whereas "strategy is how you are going to get there." The following are three other ways to tell a bad strategy from a good one.

- *It Fails to Define the Problem.* "A good strategy does more than urge us forward toward a goal or vision; it honestly acknowledges the challenges we face and provides an approach to overcoming them," Rumelt writes. Managers can't craft a good strategy unless they clearly define the challenge or problem. If managers have failed to identify and analyze the obstacles they're aiming to overcome, then they have a bad strategy.
- *It Is Based on Weak or Fuzzy Objectives.* A good strategy is focused. Managers have to carefully choose a few clearly defined goals to pursue, which means other goals have to be set aside. Bad strategy results when managers pursue what Rumelt calls "a dog's dinner of goals"—a long list of desires, objectives, and things to do. Another problem many managers fall prey to is the "blue sky goal." This kind of lofty

objective inspires a wish-driven strategy that "skips over the annoying fact that no one has a clue how to get there."
- *It Is Mostly Fluff.* Fluff refers to a "superficial restatement of the obvious combined with a generous sprinkling of buzzwords." Good strategy is clearly stated, based on a careful analysis of problems, opportunities, and sources of strength and weakness, and focuses on actionable objectives. It builds a bridge between the current state of affairs and the desired outcome with specific strategic actions. A "flurry of fluff designed to mask the absence of thought" is a clear sign of a bad strategy.

#### THREE ELEMENTS OF GOOD STRATEGY

What follows is a summary of the elements of good strategy:
- *Diagnosis.* A careful analysis of the challenges and problems facing the organization comes first. To conduct this analysis, managers define specific critical issues in the environment in order to simplify the complexity of the situation.
- *A Guiding Policy.* This is an overall approach that managers choose for how the organization will cope with or overcome the challenges. The guiding policy is designed to give the organization a distinctive advantage over competitors.
- *Coherent Action Steps.* Good strategy always specifies how the organization will achieve the strategic goals. Execution is often the hardest part and includes action steps that are coordinated to facilitate the accomplishment of the guiding policy.

*Good Strategy Bad Strategy* is not only thought-provoking but also an enjoyable read. Using examples ranging from Hannibal's defeat of a larger Roman army at Cannae in 216 BC to Steve Jobs' rescue of Apple in the late 20th and early 21st centuries, Rumelt shows us what a good strategy is—and how it can make the difference between success and failure.

*Good Strategy Bad Strategy: The Difference and Why It Matters*, by Richard Rumelt (2011), is published by Crown Business.

to meet immediate needs. Although the reactor strategy can sometimes be successful, it can also lead to failed companies. The last few years of the now defunct Eaton's, as mentioned above, can be seen as an example of a reactive company. Some large, once highly successful companies, such as Xerox and Kodak, are struggling because managers failed to adopt a strategy consistent with consumer trends. In recent years, managers at McDonald's, long one of the most successful fast-food franchises in the world, have been attempting to find the appropriate strategy. McDonald's had a string of disappointing quarterly profits as competitors continued to steal market share. Franchisees grew aggravated and discouraged by the uncertainty and lack of clear strategic direction for the future. Recent innovations such as healthier food options have revived sales and profits, but managers still are struggling to implement a coherent strategy.[66] More recently, McDonald's has been transforming its stores' look and feel through the largest makeover in its history. "McDonald's has to change with the times," says Jim Carras, senior vice president of domestic restaurant development for the giant chain. "And we have to do so faster than we ever have before."[67] The Miles and Snow typology has been widely used, and researchers have tested its validity in a variety of organizations, including hospitals, colleges, banking institutions, industrial products companies, and life insurance firms. In general, researchers have found some support for the effectiveness of this typology for organization managers in real-world situations.[68]

## How Strategies Affect Organizational Design

Choice of strategy affects internal organization characteristics. Organizational design characteristics need to support the firm's competitive approach. For example, a company wanting to grow and invent new products looks and "feels" different from a company that is focused on maintaining market share for long-established products in a stable industry. Exhibit 2.4 summarizes organizational design characteristics associated with the Porter and Miles and Snow strategies.

With a low-cost leadership strategy, managers take an efficiency approach to organizational design, whereas a differentiation strategy calls for a learning approach. Recall from Chapter 1 that organizations designed for efficiency have different characteristics from those designed for learning. A low-cost leadership strategy (efficiency) is associated with strong, centralized authority; tight control; standard operating procedures; and emphasis on efficient procurement and distribution systems. Employees generally perform routine tasks under close supervision and control and are not empowered to make decisions or take action on their own. A differentiation strategy, on the other hand, requires that employees be constantly experimenting and learning. **Structure** is fluid and flexible, with strong horizontal coordination. Empowered employees work directly with customers and are rewarded for creativity and risk taking. The organization values research, creativity, and innovativeness over efficiency and standard procedures.

The prospector strategy requires characteristics similar to a differentiation strategy, and the defender strategy takes an efficiency approach similar to low-cost leadership. Because the analyzer strategy attempts to balance efficiency for stable product lines with flexibility and learning for new products, it is associated with a mix of characteristics, as listed in Exhibit 2.4. With a reactor strategy, managers have left the organization with no direction and no clear approach to design.

*act!*

**Apply**

Apply the Miles and Snow typology by assessing what strategy your university/college appears to be using. What evidence did you use in your assessment?

**EXHIBIT 2.4**
Organizational
Design Outcomes of
Strategy

| PORTER'S COMPETITIVE STRATEGIES | MILES AND SNOW'S STRATEGY TYPOLOGY |
|---|---|
| **Strategy:** Differentiation | **Strategy:** Prospector |
| **Organizational Design:** | **Organizational Design:** |
| • Learning orientation; acts in a flexible, loosely knit way, with strong horizontal coordination | • Learning orientation; flexible, fluid, decentralized structure |
| • Strong capability in research | • Strong capability in research |
| • Values and builds in mechanisms for customer intimacy | **Strategy:** Defender |
| • Rewards employee creativity, risk taking, and innovation | **Organizational Design:** |
| **Strategy:** Low-Cost Leadership | • Efficiency orientation; centralized authority and tight cost control |
| **Organizational Design:** | • Emphasis on production efficiency; low overhead |
| • Efficiency orientation; strong central authority; tight cost control, with frequent, detailed control reports | • Close supervision; little employee empowerment |
| • Standard operating procedures | **Strategy:** Analyzer |
| • Highly efficient procurement and distribution systems | **Organizational Design:** |
| • Close supervision; routine tasks; limited employee empowerment | • Balances efficiency and learning; tight cost control with flexibility and adaptability |
|  | • Efficient production for stable product lines; emphasis on creativity, research, risk taking for innovation |
|  | **Strategy:** Reactor |
|  | **Organizational Design:** |
|  | • No clear organizational approach; design characteristics may shift abruptly, depending on current needs |

Source: Based on Michael E. Porter, *Competitive Strategy: Techniques for Analyzing Industries and Competitors* (New York: The Free Press, 1980); Michael Treacy and Fred Wiersema, "How Market Leaders Keep Their Edge," *Fortune* (February 6, 1995), 88–98; Michael Hitt, R. Duane Ireland, and Robert E. Hoskisson, *Strategic Management* (St. Paul, Minn.: West, 1995), 100–113; and Raymond E. Miles, Charles C. Snow, Alan D. Meyer, and Henry J. Coleman, Jr., "Organizational Strategy, Structure, and Process," *Academy of Management Review* 3 (1978), 546–562.

## ■ Other Factors Affecting Organizational Design

Strategy is one important factor that affects organizational design. Ultimately, however, organization design is a result of numerous contingencies, which will be discussed throughout this book. The emphasis placed on efficiency and control versus learning and flexibility is determined by the contingencies of strategy, environment, technology, size and life cycle, and organizational culture. The organization is designed to "fit" the contingency factors, as illustrated in Exhibit 2.5.

For example, in a stable environment, the organization can have a traditional structure that emphasizes vertical control, efficiency, specialization, standard procedures, and centralized decision making. However, a rapidly changing environment may call for a more flexible structure, with strong horizontal coordination and collaboration through teams or other mechanisms. Environment will be discussed in detail in Chapter 4. In terms of size and life cycle, young, small organizations are generally informal and have little division of labour, few rules and regulations,

**EXHIBIT 2.5**
Contingency Factors
Affecting Organiza-
tional Design

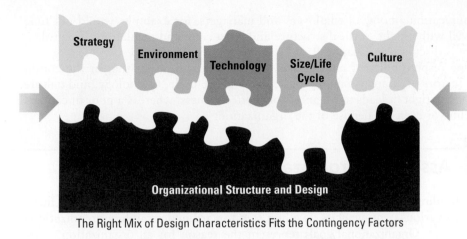

Strategy
Environment
Technology
Size/Life Cycle
Culture

**Organizational Structure and Design**

The Right Mix of Design Characteristics Fits the Contingency Factors

and ad hoc budgeting and performance systems. Large organizations such as Coca-Cola, Sony, or General Electric, on the other hand, have an extensive division of labour, numerous rules and regulations, and standard procedures and systems for budgeting, control, rewards, and innovation. Size and stages of the life cycle will be discussed in Chapter 8.

Design must also fit the workflow technology of the organization. For example, with mass production technology, such as a traditional automobile assembly line, the organization functions best by emphasizing efficiency, formalization, specialization, centralized decision making, and tight control. An e-business, on the other hand, might need to be informal and flexible. Technology's impact on design is discussed in detail in Chapters 7 and 10.

In Canada, companies also consider other questions unique to our culture, geography, and history. A basic question for organizations that operate nationwide is how to structure themselves in Québec and English Canada. Neither a functional scheme (production, marketing, research and development, etc.) nor product divisions reflect the differences in language, culture, and law between Québec and English Canada. Moreover, companies financed and governed as publicly held entities are subject to foreign takeover. Such iconic Canadian companies as Hudson's Bay Company (the oldest continuously operated incorporated company in the world), Alcan, and virtually all companies in Alberta's oil patch are owned by non-Canadians. Nortel and Thomson moved their head offices out of Canada; Canadian markets, know-how, and resources are valuable to the entire world. Business managers in Canada are obligated to ensure their companies become as valuable as possible: the strategy and structure of Canadian companies is devoted to gaining value, not retaining Canadian ownership or control. It is an issue that has attracted the interest of Canadians within and outside the business community. Will future business leaders be constrained in their search for value? Will they be able to use foreign ownership and financing as a means to survive and thrive, as did Tim Hortons, which later returned to Canada-based autonomy, larger and stronger? Or will we see the continuing "hollowing out" of Canadian head offices as foreign takeovers dominate the news? Will the structure of our companies help determine the future?

A final contingency that affects organization design is organizational culture. An organizational culture that values teamwork, collaboration, creativity, and open communication among all employees and managers, for example, would not function well with a tight, vertical structure and strict rules and regulations. The role of culture is discussed in Chapter 9.

One responsibility of managers is to design organizations that fit the contingency factors of strategy, environment, size and life cycle, technology, and culture. Finding the right fit leads to organizational effectiveness, whereas a poor fit can lead to decline or even the demise of the organization.

## Assessing Organizational Effectiveness

Understanding organizational goals and strategies, as well as the concept of fitting design to various contingencies, is a first step toward understanding organizational effectiveness. **Organizational goals** represent the reason for an organization's existence and the outcomes it seeks to achieve. The next few sections of the chapter explore the topic of effectiveness and how effectiveness is measured in organizations.

Recall from Chapter 1 that organizational effectiveness is the degree to which an organization realizes its goals.[69] *Effectiveness* is a broad concept. It implicitly takes into consideration a range of variables at both the organizational and departmental levels. Effectiveness evaluates the extent to which multiple goals—whether official or operative—are attained.

*Efficiency* is a more limited concept that pertains to the internal workings of the organization. Organizational efficiency is the amount of resources used to produce a unit of output.[70] It can be measured as the ratio of inputs to outputs. If one organization can achieve a given production level with fewer resources than another organization, it would be described as more efficient.[71]

Sometimes efficiency leads to effectiveness. In other organizations, efficiency and effectiveness are not related. An organization may be highly efficient but fail to achieve its goals because it makes a product for which there is no demand. Likewise, an organization may achieve its strategic goals but be inefficient.

Overall effectiveness is difficult to measure in organizations. Organizations are large, diverse, and fragmented. They perform many activities simultaneously, pursue multiple goals, and generate many outcomes, some intended and some unintended.[72] Managers determine what indicators to measure in order to gauge the effectiveness of their organizations. One study found that many managers have a difficult time with the concept of evaluating effectiveness based on characteristics that are not subject to hard, quantitative measurement.[73] However, top executives at some of today's leading companies are finding new ways to measure effectiveness, including the use of such "soft" indications as "customer delight" and employee satisfaction. A number of approaches to measuring effectiveness look at which measurements managers choose to track. These *contingency effectiveness approaches* are discussed in the next section.

**Compare**

Compare, in detail, the differences between efficiency and effectiveness by examining two organizations you know well.

## Contingency Effectiveness Approaches

Contingency approaches to measuring effectiveness focus on different parts of the organization. Organizations bring resources in from the environment, and those resources are transformed into outputs delivered back into the environment, as shown in Exhibit 2.6. The **goal approach** to organizational effectiveness

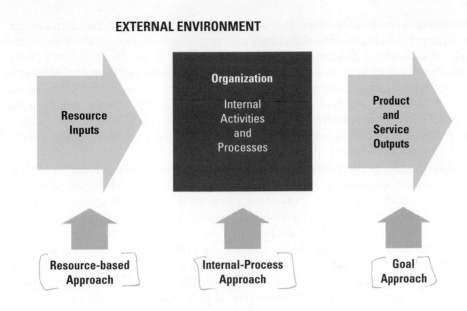

**EXHIBIT 2.6**
Contingency Approaches to the Measurement of Organizational Effectiveness

is concerned with the output side and whether the organization achieves its goals in terms of desired levels of output.[74] The **resource based approach** assesses effectiveness by observing the beginning of the process and evaluating whether the organization effectively obtains resources necessary for high performance. The **internal-process approach** looks at internal activities and assesses effectiveness by indicators of internal health and efficiency. Each has its strengths but each is limited in its scope.

## ■ Resource-based Approach

The resource-based approach looks at the input side of the transformation process shown in Exhibit 2.6. It assumes organizations must be successful in obtaining and managing valued resources in order to be effective. From a resource-based perspective, organizational effectiveness is defined as the ability of the organization, in either absolute or relative terms, to obtain scarce and valued resources and successfully integrate and manage them.[75]

**Indicators.** Obtaining and successfully managing resources is the criterion by which organizational effectiveness is assessed. In a broad sense, indicators of effectiveness according to the resource-based approach encompass the following dimensions:

- Bargaining position—the ability of the organization to obtain from its environment scarce and valued resources, including financial resources, raw materials, human resources, knowledge, and technology
- The abilities of the organization's decision makers to perceive and correctly interpret the real properties of the external environment
- The abilities of managers to use tangible (e.g., supplies, people) and intangible (e.g., knowledge, organizational culture) resources in day-to-day organizational activities to achieve superior performance
- The ability of the organization to respond to changes in the environment.

**Usefulness.** The resource-based approach is valuable when other indicators of performance are difficult to obtain. In many not-for-profit and social welfare organizations, for example, it is hard to measure output goals or internal efficiency. Some for-profit organizations also use a resource-based approach. For example, Mathsoft, which provides a broad range of technical-calculation and analytical software for business and academia, evaluates its effectiveness partly by looking at how many top-rate PhDs it can recruit. CEO Charles Digate believes Mathsoft has a higher ratio of PhDs to total employees than any other software company, which directly affects product quality and the company's image.[76]

Although the resource-based approach is valuable when other measures of effectiveness are not available, it does have shortcomings. For one thing, the approach only vaguely considers the organization's link to the needs of customers in the external environment. A superior ability to acquire and use resources is important only if resources and capabilities are used to achieve something that meets a need in the environment. Critics have challenged that the approach assumes stability in the marketplace and fails to adequately consider the changing value of various resources as the competitive environment and customer needs change.[77] The resource-based approach is most valuable when measures of goal attainment cannot be readily obtained. The Government of British Columbia, for example, can easily see if it has reached the number of child care spaces it set as a goal for a particular year and use its results to adapt its strategy to ensure success.

## ■ Internal-Process Approach

In the internal-process approach, effectiveness is measured as internal organizational health and efficiency. An effective organization has a smooth, well-oiled internal process; employees are happy and satisfied; and department activities mesh with one another to ensure high productivity. This approach does not consider the external environment. The important element in effectiveness is what the organization does with the resources it has, as reflected in internal health and efficiency.

**Indicators.** One indicator of internal-process effectiveness is the organization's economic efficiency. However, the best-known proponents of a process model are from the human relations approach to organizations. Writers such as Chris Argyris, Warren G. Bennis, Rensis Likert, and Richard Beckhard have all worked extensively with human resources in organizations and emphasize the connection between human resources and effectiveness.[78] Writers on organizational culture and organizational excellence have stressed the importance of internal processes. Results from a study of nearly 200 secondary schools showed that both human resources and employee-oriented processes were important in explaining and promoting effectiveness in those organizations.[79]

There are seven indicators of an effective organization as seen from an internal-process approach:

1. Strong organizational culture and positive work climate
2. Team spirit, group loyalty, and teamwork
3. Confidence, trust, and communication between workers and management
4. Decision making near sources of information, regardless of where those sources are on the organizational chart
5. Undistorted horizontal and vertical communication; sharing of relevant facts and feelings

6. Rewards to managers for performance, growth, and development of subordinates and for creating an effective work group
7. Interaction between the organization and its parts, with conflict that occurs over projects resolved in the interest of the organization.[80]

**Usefulness.** The internal-process approach is important because the efficient use of resources and harmonious internal functioning are ways to assess organizational effectiveness. Today, most managers believe that happy, committed, actively involved employees and a positive organizational culture are important measures of effectiveness. Innovative and highly successful clothing company American Apparel is having problems because CEO and founder Dov Charney feels free to engage in consensual sexual relationships with his staff. "I've had relationships, loving relationships, that I'm proud of," he says. "I think it's a [U.S.] First Amendment right to pursue one's affection for another human being."[81] This departure from contemporary corporate norms may be reducing the impact of the company's achievements in creating an anti-sweatshop, locally made, constantly evolving line of casual clothing for young, urban North Americans. Although its business model is extremely promising, its human relations and organizational culture are under fire. In May 2007, three former employees sued Charney for sexual harassment at work. As well, American Apparel has had declining sales, financing problems and production problems.[82] (A group of Canadian investors saved American Apparel from bankruptcy by investing $15 million in 2011. One of the investors comments that "[we] are contrarian investors and look for opportunities where the market has discounted companies for reasons that are temporary . . . American Apparel is a perfect example of that.")[83] In contrast, Four Seasons Hotels, a luxury chain of hotels with headquarters in Toronto, reflects smooth internal processes. Treating employees well is considered key to the organization's success. Workers at each hotel select a peer to receive the Employee of the Year award, which includes an expenses-paid vacation and a $1,000 shopping spree.[84]

The internal-process approach also has shortcomings. Total output and the organization's relationship with the external environment are not evaluated. Another problem is that evaluations of internal health and functioning are often subjective, because many aspects of inputs and internal processes are not quantifiable.

## ■ Goal Approach

The goal approach to effectiveness consists of identifying an organization's output goals and assessing how well the organization has attained those goals.[85] This is a logical approach because organizations do try to attain certain levels of output, profit, or client satisfaction. The goal approach measures progress toward attainment of those goals. For example, the Toronto Transit Commission (TTC) centres its business plan around the number of riders per year. Its authoritative planning document is the Ridership Growth Strategy.[86] The TTC has become a victim of its own success: because of the city's capital budget constraints,[87] it is unable to keep up with the demand for service.[88]

**Indicators.** The important goals to consider are operative goals. Efforts to measure effectiveness have been more productive using operative goals than using official goals.[89] Although official goals tend to be abstract and difficult to measure, operative goals reflect activities the organization is actually performing. Organizations often have multiple (and conflicting) operative goals.

**Usefulness.** The goal approach is used in business organizations because output goals can be readily measured. Business firms typically evaluate performance in terms of profitability, growth, market share, and return on investment. However, identifying operative goals and measuring performance of an organization are not always easy. Two problems that must be resolved are the issues of multiple goals and subjective indicators of goal attainment.

Since organizations have multiple and conflicting goals, effectiveness often cannot be assessed by a single indicator. High achievement on one goal might mean low achievement on another. Moreover, there are department goals as well as overall performance goals. The full assessment of effectiveness considers several goals simultaneously. Most organizations use a balanced approach to measuring goals. For instance, the vision of Diavik Diamond Mines does not mention creation of profits for the shareholders of Rio Tinto, but states, "Our vision is to be Canada's premier diamond producer, creating a legacy of responsible safety, environmental, and employee development practice and enduring community benefit."[90] Senior managers cannot ignore the mandate to create profits for the parent company, but the organization's stated goal is to be Canada's premier diamond producer. Can it reach this goal, fulfill its obligations to the parent, and still build an exemplary legacy in the other three areas? How will the company know the areas are balanced? How will it know that its work is optimal? Operational goals are difficult to measure and achieve because of their diversity.

# In Practice
## Loblaw

Loblaw, which is owned by George Weston Limited, was the dominant grocer of Canada throughout the 1980s and 90s. President Dave Nichol pioneered the use of private-label groceries as high-margin items uniquely available at Weston's own stores. On the strength of the President's Choice products, Loblaw could brand itself as the highest-quality grocer and charge correspondingly high prices. Such items as "Decadent" chocolate chip cookies and "Memories of Szechuan" peanut sauce attracted customers who were unable to find these products elsewhere. Selling private-label products with premium prices drove the company's margins up from the 2 to 4 percent margins normal in the industry to a staggeringly high 6 percent.

However, in 2005, the company's margins had fallen to 4.7 percent. Management discovered that customers were not happy to purchase a bag of milk in a 3,000 m² superstore in which the dairy section could be more than 100 m from the car. Loblaw bought Maple Leaf Gardens, intending to convert it to a superstore, but was unable to finance the conversion and fulfill its promise of a new kind of "icing" in this location.

When Galen G. Weston, the new, 34-year-old head of the company, took over in late 2006, he was faced with unhappy customers, heavily financed real estate, and investors who wanted returns commensurate with other Canadian grocers. The company had lost $6 billion in value over the last two years. What could Weston, the heir to his parents' vast holdings, do to ensure that the company would return to its prior position as Canada's leader?

In February 2007, he announced the new plan. Profits would go up 10 percent a year. Loblaw would cut prices, increase marketing, improve staffing, and become more innovative. "In other words, the plan involves taking a hit to revenue while increasing expenses, yet profit margins are supposed to go up."[91]

Is this a recipe for success? Can the company achieve these goals simultaneously? What are the indicators Loblaw management should measure to ensure their strategy is on track? Can they measure the improvement in their staffing? How? What about innovation? Which indicators should be most likely to point to or "lead" profits? "We continue to make progress on our overall renewal plan," said Galen G. Weston, executive chairman, Loblaw Companies Limited. "However, we are now [in 2010] in the critical period of heightened risk for the infrastructure and information technology components of the plan. As previously stated, we expect investments associated with this to continue to negatively impact our operating income during this period."[92] The plan has not gone particularly well. One CIBC World Markets' analyst wrote in 2012, "after seven years of optimistic rhetoric from various management teams, investors can be forgiven for rolling their eyes at the latest pronouncements,..."[93] George Weston Limited bought Shoppers Drug Mart in 2013 for $12.4 billion; this move signals a new strategic direction. According to the former President of George Weston Limited, Pavi Binning, the health and wellness market is an attractive investment space and he expects future acquisitions to be in that space.[94]

The other issue to resolve with the goal approach is how to identify operative goals for an organization and how to measure goal attainment. Business organizations often have objective indicators for certain goals, such as profit or growth. However, subjective assessment is needed for other goals, such as employee welfare or social responsibility. Someone has to go into the organization and learn what the actual goals are by talking with the top management team. Once goals are identified, subjective perceptions of goal attainment have to be used when quantitative indicators are not available. Managers rely on information from customers, competitors, suppliers, and employees, as well as their own intuition, when considering these goals.

See Exhibit 2.7 for an illustration of a PowerPoint "strategy" that organizations will want to avoid!

## ■ An Integrated Effectiveness Model

The three approaches—goal, resource-based, and internal-process—to organizational effectiveness described earlier all have something to offer, but each one tells only part of the story. The **competing-values model** tries to balance a concern with various parts of the organization rather than focusing on one part. This approach to effectiveness acknowledges that organizations do many things and have many outcomes.[95] It combines several indicators of effectiveness into a single framework.

**EXHIBIT 2.7**
Strategy by PowerPoint!
DILBERT ©2009 Scott Adams. Used By permission of UNIVERSAL UCLICK. All rights reserved.

The model is based on the assumption that there are disagreements and competing viewpoints about what constitutes effectiveness. Managers sometimes disagree over which are the most important goals to pursue and measure. In addition, stakeholders have competing claims on what they want from the organization, as described in Chapter 1. One tragic example of conflicting viewpoints and competing interests comes from NASA. After seven astronauts died in the explosion of the space shuttle *Columbia* in February 2003, an investigative committee found deep organizational flaws at NASA, including ineffective mechanisms for incorporating dissenting opinions between scheduling managers and safety managers. External pressures to launch on time overrode safety concerns with the *Columbia* launch. As Wayne Hale, the NASA executive charged with giving the go-ahead for the next shuttle launch, puts it, "We dropped the torch through our own complacency, our arrogance, self-assurance, sheer stupidity, and through continuing attempt[s] to please everyone."[96] NASA is an extremely complex organization that operates not only with different viewpoints internally but also from the U.S. Congress, the U.S. president, and the expectations of the American public.

The competing-values model takes into account these complexities. The model was originally developed by Robert Quinn and John Rohrbaugh to combine the diverse indicators of performance used by managers and researchers.[97] Using a comprehensive list of performance indicators, a panel of experts in organizational effectiveness rated the indicators for similarity. The analysis produced underlying dimensions of effectiveness criteria that represented competing management values in organizations.

**Indicators.** The first value dimension pertains to organizational focus, which is whether dominant values concern issues that are *internal* or *external* to the firm. Internal focus reflects a management concern for the well-being and efficiency of employees, and external focus represents an emphasis on the well-being of the organization itself with respect to the environment. The second value dimension pertains to organizational structure, and whether *stability* versus *flexibility* is the dominant structural consideration. Stability reflects a management value for efficiency and top-down control, whereas flexibility represents a value for learning and change.

The value dimensions of structure and focus are illustrated in Exhibit 2.8. The combination of dimensions provides four approaches to organizational effectiveness, which, though seemingly different, are closely related. In real organizations, these competing values can and often do exist together. Each approach reflects a different management emphasis with respect to structure and focus.[98]

A combination of external focus and flexible structure leads to an **open-systems emphasis**. Management's primary goals are growth and resource acquisition. The organization accomplishes these goals through the subgoals of flexibility, readiness, and a positive external evaluation. The dominant value is establishing a good relationship with the environment to acquire resources and grow. This emphasis is similar in some ways to the resource-based approach described earlier.

The **rational-goal emphasis** represents management values of structural control and external focus. The primary goals are productivity, efficiency, and profit. The organization wants to achieve output goals in a controlled way. Subgoals that facilitate these outcomes are planning and goal setting, which are rational management tools. The rational-goal emphasis is similar to the goal approach described earlier.

The **internal-process emphasis** is in the lower-left section of Exhibit 2.8; it reflects the values of internal focus and structural control. The primary outcome is a stable organizational setting that maintains itself in an orderly way. Organizations that are well established in the environment and simply want to maintain their current

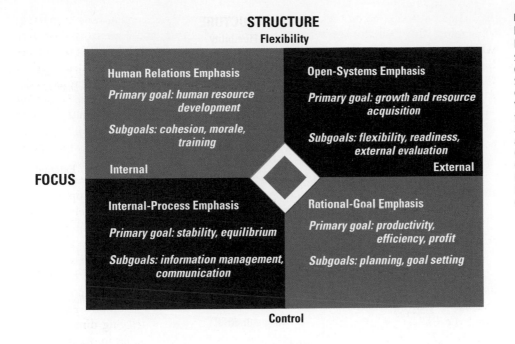

**STRUCTURE**
**Flexibility**

**Human Relations Emphasis**

*Primary goal: human resource development*

*Subgoals: cohesion, morale, training*

Internal

**Open-Systems Emphasis**

*Primary goal: growth and resource acquisition*

*Subgoals: flexibility, readiness, external evaluation*

External

**FOCUS**

**Internal-Process Emphasis**

*Primary goal: stability, equilibrium*

*Subgoals: information management, communication*

**Rational-Goal Emphasis**

*Primary goal: productivity, efficiency, profit*

*Subgoals: planning, goal setting*

**Control**

**EXHIBIT 2.8**
**Four Approaches to Effectiveness Values**
Source: Adapted from Robert E. Quinn and John Rohrbaugh, "A Spatial Model of Effectiveness Criteria: Toward a Competing Values Approach to Organizational Analysis," *Management Science* 29 (1983), 363–377; and Robert E. Quinn and Kim Cameron, "Organizational Life Cycles and Shifting Criteria of Effectiveness: Some Preliminary Evidence," *Management Science* 29 (1983), 33–51.

position reflect this emphasis. Subgoals include mechanisms for efficient information management and communication. Although this part of the competing-values model is similar in some ways to the internal-process approach described earlier, it is less concerned with human resources than with other internal processes that lead to efficiency.

The **human relations emphasis** incorporates the values of an internal focus and a flexible structure. Here, management concern is for the development of human resources. Employees are given opportunities for autonomy and development. Management works toward the subgoals of cohesion, morale, and training opportunities. Organizations adopting this emphasis are more concerned with employees than with the environment.

The four cells in Exhibit 2.8 represent opposing organizational values. Managers decide which goal values will take priority in the organization. The way two organizations are mapped onto the four approaches is shown in Exhibit 2.9.

Organization A is a young organization concerned with finding a niche and becoming established in the external environment. Primary emphasis is given on flexibility, innovation, the acquisition of resources from the environment, and the satisfaction of external constituencies. This organization gives moderate emphasis to human relations and even less emphasis to current productivity and profits. Satisfying and adapting to the environment are more important. The attention given to open-systems values means that the internal-process emphasis is practically nonexistent. Stability and equilibrium are of little concern.

Organization B, in contrast, is an established business in which the dominant value is productivity and profits. This organization is characterized by planning and goal setting. Organization B is a large company that is well established in the environment and is primarily concerned with successful production and profits. Flexibility and human resources are not major concerns. This organization prefers stability and equilibrium to learning and innovation because it wants to take advantage of its established customers.[99]

**EXHIBIT 2.9**
Effectiveness Values
for Two Organizations

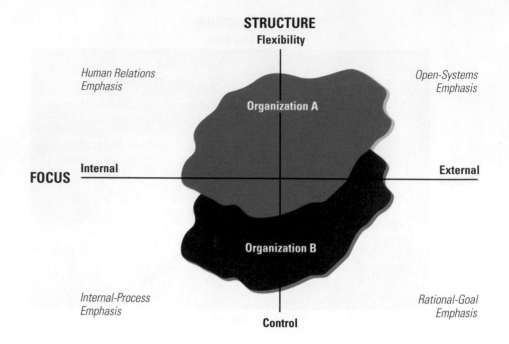

**STRUCTURE**
**Flexibility**

*Human Relations
Emphasis*

*Open-Systems
Emphasis*

**Organization A**

**FOCUS**     **Internal**                                **External**

**Organization B**

*Internal-Process
Emphasis*

*Rational-Goal
Emphasis*

**Control**

**Usefulness.** The competing-values model makes two contributions. First, it integrates diverse concepts of effectiveness into a single perspective. It incorporates the ideas of output goals, resource acquisition, and human resource development as goals the organization tries to accomplish. Second, the model calls attention to effectiveness criteria as management values and shows how opposing values exist at the same time. Managers must decide which values they wish to pursue and which values will receive less emphasis. The four competing values exist simultaneously, but not all will receive equal priority. For example, a new, small organization that concentrates on establishing itself within a competitive environment will give less emphasis to developing employees than to the external environment.

The dominant values in an organization often change over time as organizations experience new environmental demands or new top leadership.

**Think**

Think about how you determine your own effectiveness as an organizational actor. What metrics would you use?

## ▇The Balanced Scorecard

Many organizations use a combination of metrics for measuring organizational performance and effectively controlling the organization. A recent control system innovation is to integrate internal financial measurements and statistical reports with a concern for markets and customers, as well as employees. The **balanced scorecard** (BSC) is a comprehensive management control system that balances traditional financial measures with operational measures relating to an organization's critical success factors.[100] A balanced scorecard contains four major perspectives, as illustrated in Exhibit 2.10: financial performance, customer service, internal business processes, and the organization's capacity for learning and growth.[101]

Within these four areas, managers identify key performance indicators the organization will track. The *financial performance* reflects a concern that the organization's activities contribute to improving short- and long-term financial performance. It includes traditional measures such as net income and return on investment.

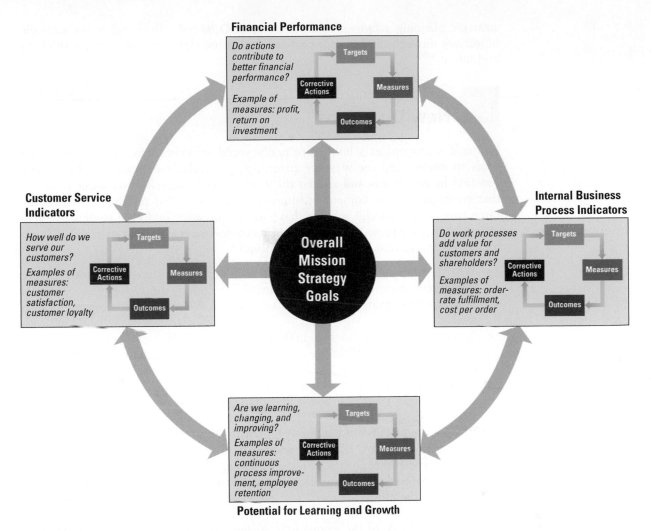

**EXHIBIT 2.10**

Major Perspectives of the Balanced Scorecard

Based on Robert S. Kaplan and David P. Norton, "Using the Balanced Scorecard as a Strategic Management System," *Harvard Business Review* (January–February 1996), 75–85; Chee W. Chow, Kamal M. Haddad, and James E. Williamson, "Applying the Balanced Scorecard to Small Companies," *Management Accounting* 79, no. 2 (August 1997), 21–27; and Cathy Lazere, "All Together Now," *CFO* (February 1998), 28–36.

*Customer service indicators* measures things such as how customers view the organization as well as customer retention and satisfaction. *Business process indicators* focus on production and operating statistics, such as order fulfillment or cost per order. The final component looks at the organization's *potential for learning and growth*, focusing on how well resources and human capital are being managed for the company's future. Measurements include things such as employee retention, business process improvements, and the introduction of new products. The components of the scorecard are designed in an integrative manner so that they reinforce one another and link short-term actions with long-term strategic goals. Managers can use the scorecard to set goals, allocate resources, plan budgets, and determine rewards. The BSC can be used by nonprofit organizations as well as for-profit organizations. For example, Kenya Red Cross used the BSC as part of its strategic planning activity. Arthur Omolo, CFO, noted, "[looking] at the strategic objectives through the four perspectives gave more clarity to the strategic thinking and intent."[102]

## New Directions

Strategic management scholars are really social scientists who employ statistical tools to understand the way organizations, particularly companies, change and function in our society and around the world. Most researchers use large data sets that encompass many companies, numerous variables, and multiple years. At the same time, a few careful scholars have used field work and case studies of small groups of organizations to develop deeper and narrower veins of material. What are the big questions that strategy tries to answer?

- Why do so many firms look alike and why are there differences? How do these differences shape different performance?
- How do firms gain, store, and use knowledge? What makes a company innovative?
- When do companies choose to make an alliance with another company rather than buy their products? What are the costs and gains? What are the conditions that make this a good choice?
- What kind of oversight do corporate boards provide? What kinds of relationships between investors, board and managers exist, and what influences their structures?
- What is the function of contracts? Of trust? Of monitoring? Under which conditions does a company use one or another to protect its interests?
- How do companies change with the increasing globalization of trade?
- Why do particular industries cluster in some cities and not in others?
- What are the effects of social and political institutions on the performance of firms?
- What is the role of the company in society? In what ways are companies constrained by ethical expectations?

Some strategy scholars are now asking whether they are working on the right problems and asking the right questions; for instance, few scholars have brought their skills to bear on highly controversial questions, like the future of the oil patch in Canada in the midst of global warming, or the increasing impact of income inequality in a globalized economy. The quickly shifting dynamics of a global economy and a disintegrating environment invite new perspectives and create new lines of research into corporate roles, characteristics, and behaviours.

Even the blogosphere has discovered strategy. Two blogs that cover the field are www.orgtheory.net and www.organizationsandmarkets.com, reflecting its sociological and economic roots. These blogs gather the reflections of many different scholars from various academic traditions. Posts include "The Network of Inuit Languages" and "Three Frontiers of Science that Sociologists Should Really Care About" on orgtheory.net, and "9-11, Strategic Management, and Public Policy" and "Economic Darwinism during Recessions" on organizationsandmarkets.com. Each lists its own blogroll with sites of interest to commerce, business, and management students.

## Summary and Interpretation

This chapter discussed organizational goals and the strategies that top managers use to help organizations achieve those goals. Goals specify the mission or purpose of an organization and its desired future state; strategies define how the organization will reach its goals. The chapter also discussed the impact of strategy on organization design and how designing the organization to fit strategy and other contingencies can lead to organizational effectiveness. The chapter then examined some of the most popular approaches to measuring effectiveness; that is, how well the organization realizes its purpose and attains its desired future state.

Organizations exist for a purpose; top managers define a specific mission or task to be accomplished. The mission statement, or official goals, makes explicit the purpose and direction of an organization. Official and operative goals are a key element in organizations because they meet these needs—establishing legitimacy with external groups and setting standards of performance for participants.

Managers must develop strategies that describe the actions required to achieve goals. Strategies may include any number of techniques to achieve the stated goals. Two models for formulating strategies are Porter's competitive strategies and the Miles and Snow strategy typology. Organization design needs to fit the firm's competitive approach to contribute to organizational effectiveness.

Assessing organizational effectiveness reflects the complexity of organizations as a topic of study. No one measure will guarantee an unequivocal assessment of performance. Organizations must perform diverse activities well—from obtaining resource inputs to delivering outputs—to be successful. Contingency approaches use output goals, resource acquisition, or internal health and efficiency as the criteria of effectiveness. The competing-values model is a balanced approach that considers multiple criteria simultaneously. No approach is suitable for every organization, but each offers some advantages that others may lack.

From the point of view of managers, the goal approach to effectiveness and measures of internal efficiency are useful when measures are available. The attainment of output and profit goals reflects the purpose of the organization, and efficiency reflects the cost of attaining those goals. Other factors such as top-management preferences, the extent to which goals are measurable, and the scarcity of environmental resources may influence the use of effectiveness criteria. In nonprofit organizations, where internal processes and output criteria are often not quantifiable, resource acquisition may be the best available indicator of effectiveness.

From the point of view of people outside the organization, such as academic investigators or government researchers, the competing-values model of organizational effectiveness may be preferable. This model acknowledges different areas of focus (internal, external) and structure (flexibility, stability), and allows managers to choose among approaches—human relations, open systems, rational goal, or internal-process—in order to emphasize the values they wish to pursue.

## ■ Key Concepts

analyzer, p. 65
competing-values model, p. 75
defender, p. 64
differentiation strategy, p. 62
focus strategy, p. 62
goal approach, p. 70
human relations emphasis, p. 77
internal-process approach, p. 71
internal-process emphasis, p. 76
low-cost leadership strategy, p. 63
mission, p. 56

official goals, p. 56
open-systems emphasis, p. 76
operative goals, p. 57
organizational goals, p. 70
prospector, p. 64
rational-goal emphasis, p. 76
reactor strategy, p. 66
resource-based approach, p. 71
strategy, p. 61
structure, p. 67

## ■ Discussion Questions

1. Discuss the role of top management in setting organizational direction.
2. How might a company's goals for employee development be related to its goals for innovation and change? to goals for productivity? Can you discuss ways these types of goals might conflict in an organization?
3. What is a goal for the class for which you are reading this text? Who established this goal? Discuss how the goal affects your direction and motivation.
4. What is the difference between a goal and a strategy as defined in the text? Identify both a goal and a strategy for a campus or community organization with which you are involved.
5. Discuss the similarities and differences in the strategies described in Porter's competitive strategies and Miles and Snow's typology.
6. Do you believe mission statements and official goal statements provide an organization with genuine legitimacy in the external environment? Discuss.
7. Suppose you have been asked to evaluate the effectiveness of the police department in a medium-sized community. Where would you begin, and how would you proceed? What effectiveness approach would you prefer?
8. What are the advantages and disadvantages of the resource-based approach versus the goal approach for measuring organizational effectiveness?
9. What are the similarities and differences between assessing effectiveness on the basis of competing values versus the stakeholder approach described in Chapter 1? Explain.
10. A noted organization theorist once said, "Organizational effectiveness can be whatever top management defines it to be." Discuss.

## ■ Chapter 2 Workbook: Identifying Company Goals and Strategies*

Choose three companies, either in the same industry or in three different industries. Search the Internet for information on the companies, including annual reports. For each company, look particularly at the goals expressed.

|  | Articulated Goals | Strategies from Porter Used |
|---|---|---|
| Organization 1 |  |  |
| Organization 2 |  |  |
| Organization 3 |  |  |

## Questions

1. Which goals seem most important?
2. Look for differences in the goals and strategies of the three companies and develop an explanation for those differences.
3. Which of the goals or strategies should be changed? Why?

4. Compare your table with those of other students and look for common themes. Which companies seem to articulate and communicate their goals and strategies best?

*From DAFT. *Organization Theory and Design*, 10E. © 2010 South-Western, a part of Cengage Learning, Inc. Reproduced by permission. www.cengage.com/permissions

## Case for Analysis: Jones Soda*

In an energetic, enormously candid interview, Jones Soda's founder shares some stories about the building blocks of his business.

### Juice Guise

I was thrown into the beverage industry without any aspirations to be in the beverage industry. I didn't wake up one morning and say I want to be in the beverage industry. What happened was, I was in the *ski industry*. I was fairly young at the time. My father was a psychiatrist and he was, like, "You've got to go to school." And I'm, like, "Dude, I get paid to go to ski right now. I've got a sweet car. You're on drugs if you think I'm giving this up. I've got my own credit card. I'm paid to ski. What are you thinking?" This was in Edmonton, Alberta.

I basically blew him off, and when I realized that I wasn't good enough [at skiing], and that school was probably the right option, I was so stubborn that I couldn't do it. I couldn't go to school because I told him I didn't need it. But I also realized I wasn't good enough to be a professional skier of any great magnitude. I was 22, 23 at the time. I had travelled Europe and done all the things you do after high school. To make a long story short, I started a fruit stand. The ski industry pays you for 12 months, but you only work nine, so you have these paid summer vacations.

The guy I was buying my fruit from said, "You've got to look at this orange juice from Florida." I did the due diligence on the OJ market in Canada. And it's 55% of a $365-millon industry. There's no premium fresh-squeezed frozen OJ, yadda, yadda, yadda. So I sold my car and brought this OJ up from Florida to Canada. And that's how I got into the beverage industry.

I got US $14,400 for my car. It was a Chiraco. It was a sweet Chiraco. But it wasn't too gooey. Just the right amount of goo on it. It was a beautiful car. I sold the car to buy the OJ. It was a product called Just Picked. The guy who sold it to me was from New York and the company was from Florida. And the first batch he sold to me was the extra-thick stuff. So I had 1,440 cases. And this stuff was so thick you could stick a spoon in. So I was going to restaurants to sell it with champagne. The solids would

separate. So you'd have a clump of crap. And I'm, like, "Oh my god, I've got all this OJ. What am I going to do?" So I'm walking up and down the street, telling people it'll lower their cholesterol, it's got fibre, you can eat it with a spoon. It was horrible. It tasted really good, but it was absolutely horrible in quality. It actually caught on. The next year the sales were $12,500 for the entire company. I was able to fight through that.

The Jones Soda story is really one of determination and fighting through challenges that most companies would never have to. No one's given us anything. Everything we've done, we've had to fight for, probably harder than we should have. The fighting is getting less and less now.

After the OJ started to take off, I started to import other beverages and built a distribution company, a beverage distribution company, in Vancouver. We sold Snapple, Arizona Ice Tea, Pepsi, Coke, we were selling tons of different beverages. We were the largest independent beverage distributor in Western Canada.

That was by 1994, 1995. We built the business to about $6.9 million in sales. One of the problems was, I didn't like dealing with the suppliers and I wanted to create my own brand. Because I had seen all these companies come to me and say, hey sell my crap in Canada.

If someone asked me at 18, is this what you dreamt to do? I would say no. The reality is that it's been a weird game to get to where I'm at now. But at the age of 41, I'm very qualified to do what I do. I understand the consumers better than a lot of people do.

### Not Necessarily Needed

Around this time, we started to import concentrated root beer. We were bottling a root beer. So I started to understand how to make soda. So we started Urban Juice and Soda and by 1994, we were flying. Sales were going through the roof. Snapple sold to Gatorade for $1.6 billion, 432 new ice teas are coming out.

*Reproduced with permission of FAST COMPANY INC., from "Jonesing for Soda" by Ryan Underwood. Used with permission of Fast Company Copyright © 2011. All rights reserved.

I'm saying, this is crazy. I'm seeing this stuff come flying at me. People are knocking on the door every day trying to get me to sell their stuff. Then I said, I don't want to sell other people's stuff anymore. That's horrible. It's not fun. It's not yours.

But the world doesn't need any more of this stuff. Because nobody cares when this stuff goes off the market. If Jones Soda fell off the face of the earth today—or if I got hit by a bus and the company got closed down, nobody would lose any sleep over it. And that's the attitude you have to take today. That's the attitude we took in 1995–96. It's more relevant today because of consolidation in the biz world. It's more relevant today because of the Internet and the number of channels. But it's still relevant and was relevant in 1995. The reality is that consumers don't need our stuff. I don't mean to say that. But when you start thinking that way—a lot of time, business people, marketers convince themselves that people need their stuff. They're passionate about how you need my new widget. You need it!

The fact is, you *don't* need it! And as soon as you get off the fact that you don't need it you become, in my opinion, you become a better marketer, you get a better understanding of your customer. You're not listening to your customer when you tell them, "You need me." You listen to [your] customers when you say, "You really don't need me." Coca-Cola sold 500 million cans of soda yesterday. I think a consumer can find a cold beverage somewhere if they really need to. Let's just get this stuff clear. Clearly, let's call an ace an ace. Nobody's going to lose any sleep, no one's going to get dehydrated. That's a fundamental difference, I believe, between marketers and brand builders. Brand builders realize that brands need to be accepted by the consumer and that it's a privilege and honour for someone to pay $1.70 for a bottle of Jones Soda. I'm very honoured by that.

## The Rules

I came to that insight pretty early on in the game because when you're selling so many widgets—here I had a distribution warehouse, where I have 600 different beverages and I realized that all I'm doing is moving one to the other and nobody really gives a rat's ass. But I wasn't inundated with the culture of a big company. I didn't have the three or four years of big-time corporation. And by not going to business school—and I wish I had gone to biz school in order to learn the game—but I'm so glad I didn't learn to believe in the rules. That's a key component of what I do: I'm not convinced that I don't have to play by anybody's rules. Well, that's not true. We have three. A. The world doesn't need another soda. B. We don't believe people need our soda. C. We can't play by anybody's rules. If we adhere to those three things, then we're going to create an emotional connection with our consumers, we're going to

be bigger than a lot of companies think we can get because we're doing the right thing, and we're going to have a lot of fun doing it.

## Passionate Brands

Great brands are built because people are passionate about them. The very first case of Jones Soda went to the founder of Nike, Phil Knight. He got the first case of Jones Soda. I don't know if he ever saw it. But he sent a letter—I don't know if he signed it or if his secretary signed it. I don't care; it's framed in the boardroom. I just really like what he was doing. One of the things about Jones Soda, I always viewed Jones as an accessory. So when we looked at companies to emulate, we never looked at beverage companies. It doesn't make any sense. If I'm trying to be a leader in a category, why look at the big guys because I'm just going to try and follow what they're doing. So the approach has always been to say I don't care what anybody does in the beverage industry. I really don't. They're going to do what they're going to do, so who gives a rat's ass. We've got to do what we've got to do. You have to know what they're doing, but you don't have to follow what they're doing.

If you don't like Jones Soda, if you're not into it, I don't give a rat's ass. I'm not going to change my formula to please you. That's a very profound statement because if you talk to companies today, they say the customer's always right. Well, no. Forget that. The customer's not always right. If you are always trying to cater to all of the customers you have, you have no soul. You have to define yourself.

You're always going to piss people off. We had people pissed off that we had a salt and pepper shaker on our label, because they said it was promoting "racial commingling." You are an idiot. It's a salt and pepper shaker. There was a cue ball, and that was promoting cocaine. There was a Zippo lighter and that was promoting "smoking and weed." The point is, fine, have a nice day. But I'm not going to pull those off. Now do I have a kid being beaten? No. I had a salt and pepper shaker.

A great brand is going to evoke passion. You're going to love it or hate it. And I'm good with that. I'm good with people loving us. And I'm good with people hating us.

## On Health and Humour

My daughter drinks one Jones a week. And I'm good with that. We don't sell two litres. It's a treat. And everybody wigs out on it, saying it causes obesity. It's the fact that you drink 44 fluid ounces of this stuff. Ten years ago the average size of a soda was 12 ounces. Now, the average size is 43 ounces. Well, you don't have to be a rocket scientist to do the math, you morons. So we sell in 12-ounce. That's it. Have a nice soda. If you're going to drink a gallon of soda, you better figure out that that's a lot of sugar. The reality is that Jones can be a powerful brand. We can be a powerful brand by—we're selling 12-packs in Target now. That's going to show me how we stack up against Coke and Pepsi. And so far, we're doing better than they thought we would do. And we're doing better than I thought we would do. And the reality is that we haven't advertised it. Nobody knows about it. But then, you're going to see our turkey and gravy holiday pack. That stuff is outrageous. No one's going to come up with mashed potato flavour, green bean, and fried onions. Fruitcake, which is disgusting, and cranberry sauce.

I can't drink a case of the stuff. No, it's more about having fun. What I really wanted to do with the turkey and gravy, I wanted to say we're not afraid to do it. And now what we're making fun of is the whole carb thing. Now you can have a carb-free turkey and gravy dinner. We're just going to hammer away and make it a big, big parody.

One year on April Fool's Day we sent a press release saying we were acquired by John Deere. That was hilarious. You sold out man! It was a joke, dude. We spelled Deere wrong. It was one of the funniest things we've ever done. We said they wanted their own weed-flavoured soda. We came up with that stuff and people went ballistic. We were getting phone calls: "I can't believe you sold out. You sold out to the big guy." Dude, it was a tractor company. It's really very harmless. I mean we live in a society today where there's a lot of stuff going on. We've got wars, we've got terrorism, we've got fuel prices, we've got elections, we've got a very divided country right now. And if Jones can throw some realistic humour, that's harmless.

## Patently Personalized

I don't want to be a soda company. I have no desire to say Jones is just a soda company. I have a desire to say Jones is a lifestyle company. Look at what we did with myjonesmusic.com.

In 1997, Ernest von Rosen [developer of Jones' website] and I were in Vancouver, he was saying, Dude we're getting a ton of baby photos. I'm like, yeah, we are. He's like how many baby photos do you really want to see on a bottle of Jones soda? But these people love their baby photos—of course they do, and we're fired up about it. So he said I've got this guy by the name of Vaclav—and Vaclav is from Eastern Europe. He doesn't speak any English. He speaks in white board. You know these guys, they just have a white board and they talk in white board? So this is 1997, we're now thinking about people emailing photos. In 2004, this is no big deal. Photos are flying across email. But in 1997, nobody's talking about this stuff. So we're talking about it. So Vaclav creates myjones and myjones, we get the patent for. So we own the patent for customizing branded merchandising over a computer network. Our value is not so much as a soda company. Our value is as a company that can create ideas like myjones, myjonesmusic, and create the stuff that's truly in tune with our consumers in a positive way.

## Getting Real

Look at somebody like Jon Stewart. Why is he so funny and so in synch with people? Because he's real. And Coke says it's real. But saying it and being it are two different things. So if you say it, you better be it. My daughter, she couldn't give a rat's ass about Coke. And her friends—she's 10, they're 10—they don't care because it's *everywhere*. It's nothing new, it's nothing special. That's what big companies have forgotten. The most important thing is not about money.

If somebody said to me, Peter I want to give you $100 million, and I want you to launch a successful brand tomorrow, I'd say take your money and walk away. You want to give me $10 million and five years to do it, I'll knock the ball out of the park. It's not about money, it's about time.

We have people who come up to our door—they've travelled from, say, Utah—to go to the Jones mecca.

And they cry when they're here. It's soda, dude. But I totally get it. People get fired up about Jones because it's theirs. It's not my soda. When you buy a bottle of Jones Soda there is a person's name on the bottle who took the photo. That is their soda. And when you go to a Target and buy a 12-pack of Jones, there are seven people's names on this. Seven people are saying, "This is my stuff." The most important thing is that whenever you do something with real people, it gets real. And that's the difference between saying you're real and being real.

Now I'm scamming. Companies are paying me to give talks. I think it's a pretty good gig. They'll pay me 10 grand to come talk to them. Maybe if I write a book, I get can that up there more. I do a good job and all the money goes to charity—so it's not a total scam. So far we've built two schools.

Our customers, they can spot BS. And that's totally kosher. If you don't live up to what you say you're going to do, like being real, they throw you under the bus. You just feed their existing perception of companies. Right or wrong, that's the way it is.

## And a Child Shall Lead Them

We're going to invoke an advisory board of kids. We're going to do it online. It's going to be like a reality TV show. One is actually going to be a board member. Somebody, 16–17 years old, is actually going to be a director of the company. Now that's absolutely insane. But it's not. It's totally sane. You know, I'm reading Barrons about having directors approve their advertising. These guys are 70 years old! How the heck can he approve anything about anything? How can they approve it? I'm just saying, I couldn't approve advertising for golfing or something. And I shouldn't approve it.

The way marketing has taught us to talk about demographics is BS. Let's look at the 35–40 year olds. That's where their income is. But if you're going to be their aspirational brand, then you really have to look lower than the 35 year old. There's not a 35-year-old woman looking to a 45-year-old woman to see how she dresses. They're looking at a 25 year old. And they're finding the balance between a 25 year old and a 35 year old. So the aspiration always goes down. Everybody knocks Jones, says you're a kid's soda. Sweet, if I'm a 12- to 24-year-old brand. It's not the actual demographic you're aiming for, it's the aspirational demographic.

I'd like for people to talk about Jones the same way they talk about brands such as Diesel Jeans. Puma, Diesel, Nike. I want to be in that category. I don't want to be Coke or Pepsi. I like Puma because they created a category in a category. Diesel because they're always relevant, always fresh, always on target.

### Listen and Learn

If you're able to give your customers the ability to give you info and you listen to them from their perspective, not everything they say will make sense. Not everything they do will be right. But you will know more about what you have to do based on the info you have. Because it's one component, but [a] very critical component.

Focus groups are toilet paper: They're only used to cover your ass. You can get a focus group to tell you anything you want. When we do focus groups, tastings really, we have two choices: Does it taste good, or does it taste like crap? Yummy or crappy? Good or bad? It's not rocket science. And you get really good information. You have to be careful to make a distinction between getting the answers you want and honest answers.

People get cash-itis—meaning they have cash and they think they have to spend it to drive revenues, etc. You've got cash, and you've got to do the right thing with it. Cor-

porations think they can buy these kids and the kids are saying, screw you, you're a loser. That's the simple math. You have to have time to allow kids to discover you.

### Built to Spill (Over)

Execution is where we need to improve. That's where we can get better. If you judge our company, for the last seven years we've been playing in the minors. And then last year, we got called up to the majors with Panera, Barnes and Noble. And we were sitting on the bench. This year we got to the plate once. With Target. In 2004 we got called up to the plate. From a baseball analogy, we've been in the minors for a long time. Now we've got something to prove. So obviously execution is something we have to improve. And if we're hitting in all aspects, this thing is going to go.

First thing is you change the rules. The Target deal is rule-breaker that is unbelievable [sic]. For the beverage industry, we took their game and shoved it up their ass. I watched Richard Branson try to do it by playing by the rules. He couldn't do it. It's so easy to scale this up by not playing by the rules. It's so hard to scale by playing by rules.

To steal a line from Sam Cook from Boston Beer, we don't sell as much as Coke or Pepsi spill in a day. There's so much room to grow—Coke and Pepsi are so big—we've got a long way to go before anyone notices. I'm more interested in growing geographically—both domestic and international—than by volume, to boost brand equity.

### Assignment Questions

1. What strategy is Jones Soda using?
2. Is the strategy sustainable? Why or why not?
3. Are there ethical concerns here that need to be addressed?

## Case for Analysis: "I want there to be!": Apple Inc.'s Foxconn Test*

### "Made in America"!?

"I want there to be! I want there to be!" Timothy Cook, Apple's former Chief Operations Officer (COO) and current Chief Executive Officer (CEO) answered emphatically, when asked by *All Things Digital* co-hosts Kara Swisher and Walt Mossberg, in May 2012, why Apple does not launch its very own manufacturing plant in mainland China, or why Apple does not initiate a move for its China-based assembly lines to the United States.[1] An operations

expert with a Fuqua MBA, Cook was determined to join Apple just five minutes after meeting his former boss, the charismatic Steve Jobs, then Apple's CEO.[2]

Ironically, Cook contrasts with the late Jobs who, when asked similar questions about the potential of a resurgence in American manufacturing in February 2011, stated to U.S. President Barack Obama, "Those jobs aren't coming back." Unsurprisingly, on his very first television interview with NBC's *Rock Center* (December 2012) since taking over from

Jobs, Cook announced that one of the existing Mac lines would be manufactured exclusively in the U.S. in 2013.[3]

Despite his enthusiasm and optimism, Cook still converges with Jobs that it is about skilled workers that Apple does not leave China entirely to manufacture everything in the US.[4] Long been credited with developing Apple's overseas supply chain, according to one former high-ranking Apple executive, Cook decided to move much of its manufacturing to Asia because it can "scale up and down faster" and "Asian supply chains have surpassed what's in the U.S."[5] Other Apple executives, in fact, acknowledge the key advantages of Chinese manufacturers, in addition to skilled workers, are "scale, flexibility, [and] diligence."[6] Defending Apple's *low-cost* strategy in making iPhones overseas, one executive once said, "We don't have an obligation to solve America's problems. Our only obligation is making the best product possible." Projecting an even more pragmatic yet critical view, another concurred, "We shouldn't be criticized for using Chinese workers… The U.S. has stopped producing people with the skills we need."[7]

Arguably, whether or not Apple shall or will be able to deliver this new "Made in America" strategy in the long run depends not only on its own will, but also on the key contingencies shaped by its major Chinese manufacturer, namely, the Foxconn Technology Group (Foxconn, for short). Insights into future strategic trajectories of both Apple and Foxconn would not be complete without a closer look at the increasingly complex "Made in the USA vs. China" perspectives, convergent and divergent, shaped by what Foxconn is, how Foxconn operates, and thus why Foxconn achieves its core manufacturing competencies.

## Foxconn 101

*Electronics Contract Manufacturer Giant.* Founded in 1974 by Terry Gou, Hon Hai Precision Industry Co., Ltd. (trading as Foxconn), is a Taiwanese multinational electronics contract manufacturer. With factories in Asia, Europe, Mexico and South America, Foxconn assembles about 40 percent of global consumer electronics products sold.[8] Currently the world's largest manufacturer of this kind, Foxconn has a market capitalization of US$33,423 million (as of October 28, 2013)[9] and 1.23 million employees (2012). This manufacturing giant has made the miracles of Apple, BlackBerry, Dell, Hewlett-Packard, Motorola, Nintendo, Nokia, Sony, Toshiba, and many others.

*Mega campus under military-style management.* As of 2012, Foxconn has established 15 Foxconn campuses in nine mainland Chinese cities. With the largest in Longhua Township, Shenzhen, this mega campus has been referred to as "Foxconn City." The biggest technological park in China, this 2.3-square-kilometre campus houses about 300,000 (one-third of Foxconn's workforce in the country), with a wide range of amenities such as dormitories, banks, hospitals, bookstores, soccer fields, basketball courts, track and field, swimming pools, supermarkets, cafeterias and restaurants, and many others.

Gou's *military-style* ideology governs Foxconn's managerial practices across all levels of factory floors in Foxconn. "Outside the laboratory," says Gou, "there is no high-technology, only execution of discipline." Gou also firmly and openly states his belief that group benefit is more important than that of individual workers. Gou's managerial ideal has been consistently applied to all Foxconn factories to deliver the core Foxconn competencies: "speed, quality, engineering services, flexibility and monetary cost saving.[10] Not surprisingly, when Jobs once demanded a change in the iPhone glass screen (to prevent it from getting scratched) just six weeks before its scheduled launch, recalled a former executive, one Apple executive immediately flew to Southern China's Shenzhen Special Economic Zone to address the overtly urgent issue pressed by Jobs.[11] As a result, 8,000 Foxconn employees were woken up in the middle of the night to outfit glass screens; within just a few days, more than 10,000 iPhones were produced daily.[12]

*Suicidal cluster.* Foxconn's high speed of product delivery and hence Apple's market triumph could have never been possible without substantial human capital costs. In fact, Foxconn has struggled in recent years with critical labour and worker safety problems. A spate of worker suicides at Shenzhen's mega Foxconn city has marked this crisis. A startling 13 young Chinese migrant workers (ranging in age from 17 to 20s; nine men and four women) attempted or committed suicide (e.g., jumping from buildings) at Shenzhen Foxconn production facilities between January and May 2010.[13] After the 12th jump, one worker blog said, "To die is the only way to testify that we ever lived. Perhaps for the Foxconn employees and employees like us—we who are called *nongmingong*, rural migrant workers, in China—the use of death is simply to testify that we were ever alive at all, and that while we lived, we had only despair."[14]

*The young labourers.* Recent scholarly work[15] suggests that the underlying cause of Foxconn's tragedies was primarily due to the oppressive management regime that drives workers to meet the extreme production demands; however, deeper labour issues associated with the changing socio-cultural demographics of the younger-generation workers invite scrutiny. Who are these workers? What do they desire for? How do they cope with their Foxconn experience? Representing the second-generation Chinese migrant workers, these workers, relative to their parents, have higher levels of education. With the radical social and cultural changes in mainland China, these younger workers may have a higher awareness for self-promotion and development. Given their stronger values towards personal growth, they may desire to see progression in their career beyond a life-long career with assembly lines like Foxconn's. Importantly, unlike the majority of their parents whose primary motives were to earn their living and eventually return to raise a family, the younger generation may have a relatively lower desire of returning home after working in factories. Consequently, a "no-way-back" mentality, coupled with a high level of self-awareness and the Chinese changing reality, directly and/or indirectly, contribute to their overall (dis)satisfaction with their Foxconn's experience (SACOM, 10, October 2010).

## Apple in Response

In response to Foxconn's tragedy, according to the Apple Supplier Responsibility Progress Reports (2012), Apple worked with Foxconn to launch an employee assistance program (EAP) at its Shenzhen facility later in 2010. The EAP offers free psychological counselling to workers, giving advice on their personal and professional concerns. During 2011, Apple customized to meet higher worker needs and began working with three more suppliers to establish EAPs at their largest facilities. In addition to counselling services, the EAPs help build support networks and arrange social activities for workers. "The programs are designed by mental health experts who specialize in issues that are common among workers in China" (Apple Supplier Responsibility Progress Reports, 2012, p. 8).

Not until 2012, did Apple become the first electronics company to be admitted to the Fair Labor Association (FLA), "a coalition of universities, non-governmental organizations (NGOs), and businesses committed to improving the well-being, safety, fair treatment, and respect of workers" (Apple Supplier Responsibility Progress Reports, 2013, p. 12). In February 2012, Apple asked the FLA to conduct special voluntary audits of their biggest final assembly suppliers, including Foxconn factories in Shenzhen and Chengdu, China. "With unrestricted access to our operations, the FLA completed one of the most comprehensive and detailed assessments in the history of manufacturing—in scale, in scope, and in transparency. This independent assessment covered an estimated 178,000 workers and included interviews with 35,000 workers."

In March 2012, two years after Foxconns's suicidal cluster phenomenon, the FLA published its findings with recommendations. Subsequently, accepting the FLA's findings and recommendations, Apple and Foxconn created a 15-month action plan with target dates for completion. Among the recommendations, for example, Foxconn has "engaged consultants to provide health and safety training for employees, improved its internship program, and increased access to unemployment insurance for its migrant workers, as well as for all workers in Shenzhen" (Apple Supplier Responsibility Progress Reports, 2013, p. 8).

## What's Next?

Over the past six or so years, Apple has expanded professional development opportunities for workers through the Supplier Employee Education and Development (SEED) program. The Apple-designed program offers workers classes in topics such as finance, computer skills, and the English language. In addition, SEED programs partner with Chinese universities to allow workers to earn associate degrees (Apple Supplier Responsibility Progress Reports, 2012). In fact, the program began as a pilot at Shenzhen's Foxconn facility as early as in 2008 and has expanded to all final assembly sites in 2011. According to Apple, more than 60,000 workers have participated in SEED training. As a result, Apple evaluated the SEED program as desirable and successful, stating that "SEED participants have higher morale and are promoted more often than other employees" (Apple Supplier Responsibility Progress Reports (2012, p. 27). Yet, it still appears unclear as to how such a program, combined with other worker assistance and development initiatives (e.g., the EAPs), can jointly (re)shape Chinese young workers' overall well-being.

Today, Apple has become the world's largest electronics company by market capitalization; Foxconn has most of the contracts of the world's major consumer electronic brands.[16] Cook recently said, "We never had an objective to sell a low-cost phone. Our primary objective is to sell a great phone and provide a great experience, and we figured out a way to do it at a lower cost."[17] Then what's next for both Apple and Foxconn, do you think?

## Assignment Questions

1. Apply the "Top management role in organization direction, design, and effectiveness" framework and analyze the 2010 Foxconn suicidal cluster phenomenon, assuming your role as either Steve Jobs or Terry Gou:
   a. What are the most pressing environmental issues (external and internal)?
   b. What are the primary organizational design issues?
   c. How would you (re)define organizational effectiveness to build a socially responsible company?
2. Should Apple be (entirely) responsible for the practices of its general suppliers and particularly, Foxconn?
3. What does Cook's new "Made in America" strategy mean for both Apple and Foxconn?
4. In light of both Cook's new strategy and Apple and Foxconn's chronologies in implementing the EAPs and SEED, evaluate the viability of such programs given the changing demographics of Chinese younger migrant workers in the transforming Chinese labor market.

*Prepared by Xiao Chen, Ph.D., Department of Leadership and Organization Management, School of Economics and Management, Tsinghua University, Beijing, China.

---

[1] Based on Kaplan and Norton, "The Balanced Scorecard"; Chow, Haddad, and Williamson, "Applying the Balanced Scorecard"; and C. A. Latshaw and Y. Choi, "The Balanced Scorecard and the Accountant as a Valued Strategic Partner," *Review of Business* 23, no. 1 (2002), 27–29.

[2] A. Omolo, "Our Experience with the Balanced Scorecard Strategy Development Process," Kenya Red Cross (2010) at http://balancedscorecard.org/Portals/0/PDF/KenyaRedCrossBSC.pdf (accessed March 11, 2014).

[3] Daniel Eran Dilger, "Tim Cook: 'I Want There to Be' American-made Apple products," Apple Insider (May 29, 2012) at http://appleinsider.com/articles/12/05/30/tim_cook_i_want_there_to_be_american_made_apple_products (accessed March 11, 2014).

[4] "Video of Apple CEO Tim Cook at D10 Now Available," Apple Insider (May 30, 2012) at http://appleinsider.com/articles/12/05/30/video_of_apple_ceo_tim_cook_at_d10_now_available (accessed March 11, 2014).

[5] "Apple CEO Tim Cook Announces Plans to Manufacture Mac Computers in USA," Apple Insider (December 6, 2012) at http://rockcenter.nbcnews.com/_news/2012/12/06/15708290-apple-ceo-tim-cook-announces-plans-to-manufacture-mac-computers-in-usa?lite (accessed March 11, 2014).

[6] Ibid.

[7] Josh Ong, "Apple's Overseas Manufacturing Operations Offer Flexibility, Not Just Savings – Report," Apple Insider (January 12, 2012) at http://appleinsider.com/articles/12/01/22/apples_overseas_manufacturing_operations_offer_much_needed_flexibility_not_just_savings.html (accessed March 11, 2014).

[8] Ibid.

[9] Ibid.

[10] Charles Duhigg and Keith Bradsher "How the U.S. Lost Out on iPhone Work," New York Times (January 21, 2012) at http://www.nytimes.com/2012/01/22/business/apple-america-and-a-squeezed-middle-class.html?_r=1& (accessed March 11, 2014).

[11] Hon Hai, "Quarterly Reports" at http://www.foxconn.com/Investors_En/Financial_Information.html?index=1&target=QuarterRevenueReport.html (accessed March 11, 2014).

[12] Hon Hai, "Business Philosophy" (2013) at http://www.foxconn.com/GroupProfile_En/BusinessPhilosophy.html (accessed March 11, 2014).

[13] "Apple's Overseas Manufacturing Operations Offer Flexibility, Not Just Savings – Report."

[14] Ibid.

[15] Jenny Chan and Ngai Pun "Suicide as Protest for the New Generation of Chinese Migrant Workers: Foxconn, Global Capital, and the State," *The Asia-Pacific Journal*: Japan Focus (2010) at http://www.japanfocus.org/-Ngai-Pun/3408 (accessed April 14, 2014).

[16] David Barbosa, "Former Foxconn Managers Detained in a Bribery Case," New York Times (January 22, 2014) at http://www.nytimes.com/2014/01/23/business/foxconn-ex-managers-detained-in-bribery-inquiry.html?_r=0 (accessed March 11, 2014).

[17] Rebecca Greenfield, "Tim Cook: Apple Will Never, Ever Make a Cheap iPhone," (September 12, 2013) The Wire.com at http://www.thewire.com/technology/2013/09/tim-cook-apple-will-never-ever-make-cheap-iphone/69601 (accessed March 11, 2014).

## ■ Chapter 2 Workshop: Competing Values*

Phase 1: Rank-order the items below according to your own beliefs.

Phase 2: Rank-order the items according to the priorities that you believe are assigned to the values in the business world.

Phase 3: Form groups of three to six to act as a top decision making team of a large corporation. Try to reach genuine consensus on the rankings using your own beliefs.

Phase 4: Share the rankings of three phases and discuss as a class.

### Values to Rank-Order†

- Career growth and development of individuals
- Concern for personnel as individuals
- Efficiency
- Ethics
- Managerial and organizational effectiveness
- Political responsibility
- Profits
- Providing gods and services for society
- Quality of goods and services
- Social responsibility

---

†Michael Morris "Modifying the Values in Business Exercise to Examine Holier-than-Thou Attitudes toward Profits," *Journal of Management Education* 5, 34–36, 1980.

# 3

# Fundamentals of Organizational Structure

Lee Brown / Alamy

## Desjardins Group (Desjardins)

Desjardins is one of the best-known credit unions in the world (see photo). It was founded more than 100 years ago by Alphonse Desjardins in Lévis, Québec. Desjardins' mission is

To contribute to the economic and social well-being of people and their communities within the compatible limits of our field of activity by:

- developing an integrated cooperative network of secure and profitable financial services on a permanent basis, owned by the members and administered by them, and a network of complementary financial companies with a competitive return, also controlled by the members; and
- educating the public, and in particular our members, officers and employees, about democracy, the economy, solidarity, and individual and collective responsibility.[1]*

The number one financial institution in Québec and the sixth largest cooperative financial group in the world, Desjardins upholds its presence through its caisses, business centres, subsidiary distribution networks, and virtual networks. Desjardins is present in Ontario, Manitoba, and New Brunswick through its components and its affiliated cooperative caisse networks, and through Desjardins Credit Union. Several subsidiary businesses are also active in all Canadian provinces.

When in the United States, members and clients can count on the services offered by Desjardins Bank and Caisse centrale Desjardins to support them in their business development or to help make their lives easier when they travel. On the global stage, Desjardins is actively involved in international cooperation, supporting four million people in some 20 developing and emerging countries.

Every caisse and credit union is a financial services cooperative that serves and protects the interests of its members. Desjardins Business Centres are owned by the caisses in the area and, together, they meet the needs of the members in their community. Together, subsidiaries, caisses, credit unions, and business centres offer their 5.8 million members and clients a full range of financial products and services. Under the leadership of Monique Leroux, Desjardins has been lauded for its performance, its organizational culture, and its social responsibility commitment, and has received various awards such as the British magazine *The Banker*'s 2010 Bank of the Year.[2]

In 2014, Desjardins bought the Canadian arm of State Farm, an American mutual insurer. As a result of the acquisition, Desjardin will become the country's second-largest property and casualty insurer. Desjardins has been pursuing a growth strategy with a focus on increasing its presence across Canada.[3] As Exhibit 3.1 illustrates, Desjardins is a complex organization designed according to the principle of democratic control by the members. In light of its recent acquisitions, we can predict that the organization will become more complex.

---

Organizations use various structural alternatives to help them achieve their purpose and goals. Nearly every firm needs to undergo structural reorganization at some point to help meet new challenges. Structural changes are needed to reflect new strategies or respond to changes in other contingency factors such as environment, technology, size and life cycle, and culture. For example, the Catholic Church is reorganizing to meet the challenges of a dwindling and aging

---

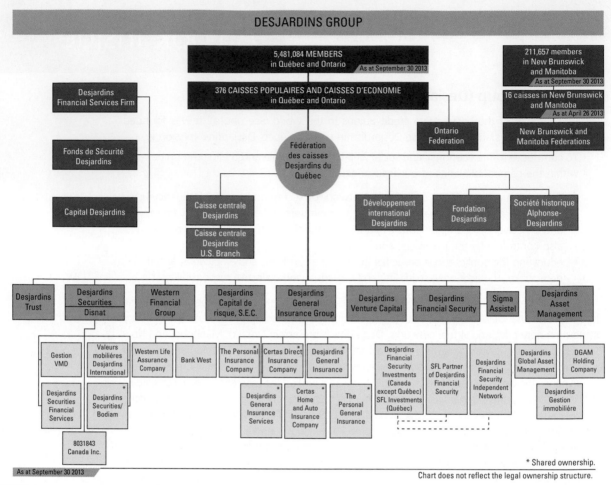

**EXHIBIT 3.1**
Desjardins' Organization Structure—September 30, 2013

Source: ©2014 Desjardins Group. http://www.desjardins.com/ca/about-us/desjardins/governance-democracy/structure/group-organization-chart (accessed January 23, 2014). Used with permission.

corps of priests, financial pressures and scandals, shifting demographics, and sexual, and ethical scandals. The traditional top-down, authoritarian management style is being re-evaluated in an effort to improve decision making and put resources in places where they're needed most.[4] The current pope, Francis, has been recognized for his "…efforts to unclog the Vatican's stultifying bureaucracy, to bring more transparency to its dealings and to revitalize the ranks of prelates…"[5]

## ■ Purpose of This Chapter

This chapter introduces basic concepts of organizational structure and shows how to design structure as it appears on the organization chart. First, we define structure and provide an overview of structural design. Then an information-processing perspective explains how to design vertical and horizontal linkages to provide needed information flow. The chapter next presents basic design options, followed by strategies for grouping organizational activities into functional, divisional, geographical, matrix, horizontal, virtual network, or hybrid structures. The final section examines how the

## YOU & DESIGN

### The Pleasure/Pain of Working on a Team

Your approach to your job or schoolwork may indicate whether you thrive on a team. Answer the following questions about your work preferences. Please answer whether each item is Mostly True or Mostly False for you.

|  | Mostly True | Mostly False |
|---|---|---|
| 1. I prefer to work on a team rather than do individual tasks. | _____ | _____ |
| 2. Given a choice, I try to work by myself rather than face hassles of group work. | _____ | _____ |
| 3. I enjoy the personal interaction when working with others. | _____ | _____ |
| 4. I prefer to do my own work and let others do theirs. | _____ | _____ |
| 5. I get more satisfaction from a group victory than an individual victory. | _____ | _____ |
| 6. Teamwork is not worthwhile when people do not do their share. | _____ | _____ |
| 7. I feel good when I work with others, even when we disagree. | _____ | _____ |
| 8. I prefer to rely on myself rather than others to do a job or assignment. | _____ | _____ |

**Scoring:** Give yourself one point for each odd-numbered item you marked as Mostly True and one point for each even-numbered item you marked Mostly False. Your score indicates your preference for teamwork versus individual work. If you scored 2 or fewer points, you definitely prefer individual work. A score of 7 or above suggests that you prefer working in teams. A score of 3–6 indicates comfort working alone and in a team.

**Interpretation:** Teamwork can be either frustrating or motivating depending on your preference. On a team you will lose some autonomy and have to rely on others who may be less committed than you. On a team you have to work through other people and you lose some control over work procedures and outcomes. On the other hand, teams can accomplish tasks far beyond what an individual can do, and working with others can be a major source of satisfaction. If you definitely prefer individual work, then you would likely fit better in a functional structure within a vertical hierarchy or in the role of individual contributor. If you prefer teamwork, then you are suited to work in the role of a horizontal linkage, such as on a task force or as an integrator, and would do well in a horizontal or matrix organization structure.

Source: Based on Duffy, Michelle K., Stark, Shaw, "Preference for Group Work, Winning Orientation, and Social Loafing Behavior in Groups," *GROUP & ORGANIZATION MANAGEMENT* vol. 32 no. 6 699–723. Copyright © 2007 by Sage Publications Inc. Journals. Reproduced with permission of SAGE Publications via Copyright Clearance Center.

application of basic structures depends on the organization's situation and outlines the symptoms of structural misalignment. Before delving into the chapter, complete the You and Design feature to assess your views on working in one type of structure, teams.

## Organizational Structure

There are three key components in the definition of **organizational structure:**

1. Organizational structure designates formal reporting relationships, including the number of levels in the hierarchy and the span of control of managers and supervisors.

2. Organizational structure identifies the grouping together of individuals into departments and of departments into the total organization.
3. Organizational structure includes the design of systems to ensure effective communication, coordination, and integration of efforts across departments.[6]

These three elements of structure pertain to both vertical and horizontal aspects of organizing. For example, the first two elements are the structural framework, which is the vertical hierarchy.[7] The third element pertains to the pattern of interactions among organizational employees. An ideal structure encourages employees to provide horizontal information and coordination where and when needed.

Organizational structure is reflected in the organization chart. It isn't possible to see the internal structure of an organization the way we might see its manufacturing tools, offices, or products. Although we might see employees going about their duties, performing different tasks, and working in different locations, the only way to actually see the structure underlying all this activity is through an organization chart. An organization chart is the visual representation of a whole set of underlying activities and processes in an organization at a particular point in time. The organization chart can be quite useful in understanding how an organization works. It shows the various parts of an organization, how they are interrelated, and how each position and department fits into the whole. The concept of an organization chart, showing what positions exist, how they are grouped, and who reports to whom, has been around for centuries.[8] The use of the organization chart for business stems largely from the Industrial Revolution. As we discussed in Chapter 1, as work grew more complex and was performed by greater and greater numbers of workers, there was a pressing need to develop ways of managing and controlling organizations. The type of organizational structure that grew out of these efforts in the late 19th and early 20th centuries was one in which the CEO was placed at the top and everyone else was arranged in layers below. The thinking and decision making are done by those at the top, and the physical work is performed by employees who are organized into distinct, functional departments. This structure was quite effective and became entrenched in business, nonprofit, and military organizations for much of the 20th century. However, this type of vertical structure is not always effective, particularly in rapidly changing environments. Over the years, organizations have developed other structural designs, many of them aimed at increasing horizontal coordination and communication and encouraging adaptation to external changes. This chapter's Book Mark argues that structural and management innovations have been sources of organizational competitive advantage. In this chapter, we will examine five basic structural designs and show how they are reflected in the organization chart.

**Apply**

Apply the practice of representing organizational structures through charts by preparing an organization chart for an organization with which you are familiar. What insights did the process and the chart reveal?

## Information-Processing Perspective on Structure

The organization should be designed to provide both vertical and horizontal information flow as necessary to accomplish the organization's overall goals. If the structure does not fit the information requirements of the organization, people either will have too little information or will spend time processing information that is not vital to their tasks, thus reducing effectiveness.[9] However, there is an inherent tension between vertical and horizontal mechanisms in an organization. While vertical

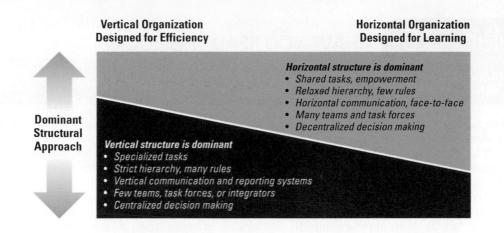

**Vertical Organization Designed for Efficiency**

**Horizontal Organization Designed for Learning**

**Dominant Structural Approach**

*Horizontal structure is dominant*
- Shared tasks, empowerment
- Relaxed hierarchy, few rules
- Horizontal communication, face-to-face
- Many teams and task forces
- Decentralized decision making

*Vertical structure is dominant*
- Specialized tasks
- Strict hierarchy, many rules
- Vertical communication and reporting systems
- Few teams, task forces, or integrators
- Centralized decision making

**EXHIBIT 3.2**
The Relationship of Organizational Design to Efficiency versus Learning Outcomes

linkages are designed primarily for control, horizontal linkages are designed for coordination and collaboration, which usually means reducing control.

Organizations can choose whether to orient toward a more traditional organization designed for efficiency, which emphasizes vertical communication and control, or toward a more contemporary learning organization, which emphasizes horizontal communication and coordination. Exhibit 3.2 compares organizations designed for efficiency with those designed for learning. An emphasis on efficiency and control is associated with specialized tasks, a strict hierarchy of authority and rules, vertical reporting systems, few teams or task forces, and **centralized** decision making, which means problems and decisions are funnelled to top levels of the hierarchy for resolution. Emphasis on learning is associated with shared tasks, a horizontal hierarchy, few rules, face-to-face communication, many teams and task forces, and informal, **decentralized** decision making. Decentralized decision making means decision-making authority is pushed down to lower organizational levels. Organizations may have to experiment to find the correct degree of centralization or decentralization to meet their needs. For example, one study found that three large school districts that shifted to a more flexible, decentralized structure performed better and more efficiently than large districts that were highly centralized.[10] On the other hand, decentralized companies such as Procter & Gamble have found a need in recent years to build in more centralized communication and control systems to keep these huge, global corporations functioning efficiently. Thus, managers are always searching for the best combination of vertical control and horizontal collaboration, centralization and decentralization, for their own situations.[11]

## ▪ Vertical Information Linkages

Organizational design should facilitate the communication among employees and departments that is necessary to accomplish the organization's overall task. Linkage is defined as the extent of communication and coordination among organizational elements. **Vertical linkages** are used to coordinate activities between the top and bottom of an organization, and are designed primarily for control of the organization. Employees at lower levels should carry out activities consistent with top-level goals, and top executives must be informed of activities and accomplishments at the lower levels. Organizations may use any of a variety of structural devices to

# Book Mark 3.0    HAVE YOU READ THIS BOOK?

## The Future of Management
By Gary Hamel with Bill Breen

Management breakthroughs such as the principles of scientific management, divisionalized organization structure, and using brand managers for horizontal coordination have created more sustained competitive advantage than any hot new product or service innovation, says Gary Hamel in *The Future of Management,* written with Bill Breen. Wait a minute—haven't those ideas been around since—well, forever? Exactly the point, says Hamel. In fact, he points out that many of today's managers are running 21st-century organizations using ideas, practices, and structural mechanisms invented a century or more ago. At that time, the principles of vertical hierarchy, specialization, bureaucratic control, and strong centralization were radical new approaches developed to solve the problem of inefficiency. They are too static, regimented, and binding today when the pace of change continues to accelerate. Today's organizations, Hamel argues, have to become "as strategically adaptable as they are operationally efficient."

### SOME STRUCTURAL INNOVATORS
Hamel suggests that the practice of management must undergo a transformation akin to that which occurred with the Industrial Revolution and the advent of scientific management. Here, from *The Future of Management,* are a few examples that offer glimpses of what is possible when managers build structure around principles of community, creativity, and information sharing rather than strict hierarchy:

* *Whole Foods Market.* Teams are the basic organizational unit at Whole Foods, and they have a degree of autonomy nearly unprecedented in the retail industry. Each store is made up of eight or so self-directed teams that oversee departments such as fresh produce, prepared foods, dairy, or checkout. Teams are responsible for all key operating decisions, including pricing, ordering, hiring, and in-store promotions.
* *W. L. Gore.* W. L. Gore's innovation was to organize work so that good things happen whether managers are "in control" or not. Gore, best known for Gore-Tex fabric, lets employees decide what they want to do. There are no management layers, few titles, and no organization charts. As at Whole Foods, the core operating units are small teams, but at Gore, people can choose which teams to work on and can say no to requests from anyone. Yet Gore also builds in strong accountability—people are reviewed by at least 20 of their peers every year.
* *Visa.* Everybody's heard of Visa, but few people know anything about the organization behind the brand. Visa is the world's first almost entirely virtual company. In the early 1970s, a group of banks formed a consortium that today has grown into a global network of 21,000 financial institutions and more than 1.3 billion cardholders. The organization is largely self-organizing, continually evolving as conditions change.

### HOW TO BE A MANAGEMENT INNOVATOR
Most companies have a system for product innovation, but Hamel notes that few have a well-honed process for management innovation. *The Future of Management* provides detailed steps managers can take to increase the chances of a breakthrough in management thinking. Hamel considers the rise of modern management and organization design the most important innovation of the 20th century. It is time now, though, for 21st-century ideas.

Source: *The Future of Management,* by Gary Hamel with Bill Breen, is published by Harvard Business School Press, 2007.

achieve vertical linkage, including hierarchical referral, rules and plans, and vertical information systems.[12]

**Hierarchical Referral.** The first vertical device is the hierarchy, or **chain of command,** which is illustrated by the vertical lines in Exhibit 3.1. If a problem arises that employees don't know how to solve, it can be referred up to the next level in the hierarchy. When the problem is solved, the answer is passed back down to lower levels. The lines of the organization chart act as communication channels.

**Rules and Plans.** The next linkage device is the use of rules and plans. To the extent that problems and decisions are repetitious, a rule or procedure can be established so employees know how to respond without communicating directly with their manager. Rules provide a standard information source enabling employees to be coordinated without actually communicating about every task. A plan also provides standing information for employees. The most widely used plan is the budget. With carefully designed budget plans, employees at lower levels can be left on their own to perform activities within their resource allotment.

**Vertical Information Systems.** A **vertical information system** is another strategy for increasing vertical information capacity. Vertical information systems include the periodic reports, written information, and computer-based communications distributed to managers. Information systems make communication up and down the hierarchy more efficient. Vertical information systems are an important component of vertical control at software maker Oracle.[13]

In today's world of corporate financial scandals and ethical concerns, many top managers, like Oracle's Larry Ellison, are considering strengthening their organization's linkages for vertical information and control. The other major issue in organizing is to provide adequate horizontal linkages for coordination and collaboration.

## ■ Horizontal Information Linkages

Horizontal communication overcomes barriers between departments and provides opportunities for coordination among employees to achieve unity of effort and organizational objectives. **Horizontal linkage** refers to the amount of communication and coordination horizontally across organizational departments. Its importance is articulated by comments made by Lee Iacocca when he took over Chrysler Corporation in the 1980s.

> What I found at Chrysler were thirty-five vice presidents, each with his own turf.... I couldn't believe, for example, that the guy running engineering departments wasn't in constant touch with his counterpart in manufacturing. But that's how it was. Everybody worked independently. I took one look at that system and I almost threw up. That's when I knew I was in really deep trouble.... Nobody at Chrysler seemed to understand that interaction among the different functions in a company is absolutely critical. People in engineering and manufacturing almost have to be sleeping together. These guys weren't even flirting![14]

During his tenure at Chrysler, Iacocca pushed horizontal coordination to a high level. Everyone working on a specific vehicle project—designers, engineers, and manufacturers, as well as representatives from marketing, finance, purchasing, and even outside suppliers—worked together on a single floor so they could constantly communicate.

Horizontal linkage mechanisms often are not drawn on the organization chart, but nevertheless are part of organizational structure. The following devices are structural alternatives that can improve horizontal coordination and information flow.[15] Each device enables people to exchange information.

**Information Systems.** A significant method of providing horizontal linkage in today's organizations is the use of cross-functional information systems.

**Compare**

Compare the structure of your college or university with the structure of the bank or credit union you use. What are the key differences and what accounts for them?

Computerized information systems can enable managers or front-line workers throughout the organization to routinely exchange information about problems, opportunities, activities, or decisions. For example, Siemens, a large international conglomerate headquartered in Germany, uses an organization-wide information system that enables 450,000 employees around the world to share knowledge and collaborate on projects to provide better solutions to customers. The information and communications division collaborated with the medical division to develop new products for the health care market.[16]

Some organizations also encourage employees to use the company's information systems to build relationships all across the organization, aiming to support and enhance ongoing horizontal coordination across projects and geographical boundaries. CARE International, one of the world's largest private international relief organizations, enhanced its personnel database to make it easy for people to find others with congruent interests, concerns, or needs. Each person in the database has listed past and current responsibilities, experience, language abilities, knowledge of foreign countries, emergency experiences, skills and competencies, and outside interests. The database makes it easy for employees working across borders to seek out each other, share ideas and information, and build enduring horizontal connections.[17]

**Direct Contact.** A higher level of horizontal linkage is direct contact between managers or employees affected by a problem. One way to promote direct contact is to create a special **liaison role.** A liaison person is located in one department but has the responsibility for communicating and achieving coordination with another department. Liaison roles often exist between engineering and manufacturing departments because engineering has to develop and test products to fit the limitations of manufacturing facilities. At Johnson & Johnson, former CEO William C. Weldon set up a committee comprising managers from R&D and sales and marketing. The direct contact between managers in these two departments enables the company to determine which new drugs to pursue and market. Weldon also created a new position to oversee R&D, with an express charge to increase coordination with sales and marketing executives.[18] Another approach is to locate people close together so they will have direct contact on a regular basis.

**Task Forces.** Liaison roles usually link only two departments. When linkage involves several departments, a more complex device such as a task force is required. A task force is a temporary committee composed of representatives from each organizational unit affected by a problem.[19] Each member represents the interest of a department or division and can carry information from the meeting back to that department.

**Task forces** are an effective horizontal linkage device for temporary issues. They solve problems by direct horizontal coordination and reduce the information load on the vertical hierarchy. Typically, they are disbanded after their tasks are accomplished.

Organizations have used task forces for everything from organizing the annual company picnic to solving expensive and complex manufacturing problems. One example was the executive automotive committee formed by DaimlerChrysler former CEO Jürgen Schrempp. This task force was set up specifically to identify ideas for increasing cooperation and component sharing among Chrysler, Mercedes, and Mitsubishi. The task force started with a product road map, showing all

Mercedes, Chrysler, Dodge, Jeep, and Mitsubishi vehicles to be launched over a ten-year period, along with an analysis of the components they would use, so task force members could identify overlap and find ways to share parts, and cut time and costs.[20] However, the much-hyped 1998 merger between equals was a failure for two reasons: (1) it was really a takeover of Chrysler by Daimler and (2) the savings and marketing clout the two expected from the merger did not materialize. In less than ten years, the companies were again separate entities.[21]

**Full-Time Integrator.** A stronger horizontal linkage device is to create a full-time position or department solely for the purpose of coordination. A full-time **integrator** frequently has a title such as product manager, project manager, program manager, or brand manager. Unlike the liaison person described earlier, the integrator does not report to one of the functional departments being coordinated. He or she is located outside the departments and has the responsibility for coordinating several departments. For example, General Motors has brand managers who are responsible for marketing and sales strategies for each of GM's new models.[22]

The integrator can also be responsible for an innovation or change project, such as coordinating the design, financing, and marketing of a new product. An organization chart that illustrates the location of project managers for new product development is shown in Exhibit 3.3. The project managers are drawn to the side to indicate their separation from other departments. The arrows indicate project

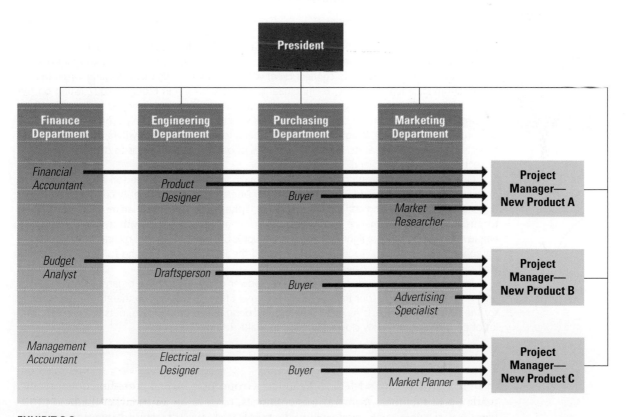

**EXHIBIT 3.3**
Project Manager Location in the Structure

**Think**

Think about how to be a project manager for one of your school or work teams. What activities would you use to be an effective integrator?

members assigned to the new product development. New Product A, for example, has a financial accountant assigned to keep track of costs and budgets. The engineering member provides design advice, and purchasing and marketing members represent their areas. The project manager is responsible for the entire project. He or she sees that the new product is completed on time, is introduced to the market, and achieves other project goals. The horizontal lines in Exhibit 3.3 indicate that project managers do not have formal authority over team members with respect to giving pay raises, hiring, or firing. Formal authority rests with the managers of the functional departments, who have formal authority over subordinates.

Integrators need excellent people skills. Integrators in most companies have a lot of responsibility but little authority. The integrator has to use expertise and persuasion to achieve coordination. He or she spans the boundary between departments and must be able to get people together, maintain their trust, confront problems, and resolve conflicts and disputes in the interest of the organization.[23]

**Teams.** Project teams tend to be the strongest horizontal linkage mechanism. **Teams** are permanent task forces and are often used in conjunction with a full-time integrator. When activities among departments require strong coordination over a long period of time, a cross-functional team is often the solution. Special project teams may be used when organizations have a large-scale project, a major innovation, or a new product line.

**In Practice**

**Imagination Limited (Imagination)**

Imagination has ten offices in Europe, the Americas, and Asia. Its mission is communication: "[No] matter the channel or the audience, we conceive, develop and deliver communication that has relevance, immediacy and clarity, to connect client with consumer."[24] Its clients include Virgin Mobile for which Imagination created a 16-city global road show for Virgin Mobile's 2007 listing on the New York Stock Exchange. Imagination has received many accolades for its work. Founded in 1978, Imagination is Britain's largest design firm, and its structure is based entirely on teamwork. At the beginning of each project, Imagination puts together a team of designers, writers, artists, marketing experts, information specialists, and representatives of other functional areas to carry out the entire project from beginning to end.

One of its most interesting projects was to make waiting in a 700-person lineup to get into Skyscape, an attraction inside Britain's Millennium Dome, a fun experience. According to Imagination's director of marketing and strategic planning, "[the] work was quite mad, really.... We wanted to push the queue experience to a new place."[25] Imagination started with a team of in-house employees—an architect, a lighting designer, a graphic designer, and a film director. Later, a choreographer joined the team. Together they designed the Journey Zone and the TalkZone so that the wait would be part of the experience.

Imagination understands the value and the power of teamwork. The organization is nonhierarchical by design—only four individuals have formal titles—and everyone therefore is responsible for the success of a project. As one of the graphic designers, Martin Brown, puts it, "[we've] got a lot of performers and a few clowns. Enough to make it funny."[26]

Hewlett-Packard's Medical Products Group uses **virtual cross-functional teams**, made up of members from various countries, to develop and market medical products and services such as electrocardiograph systems, ultrasound imaging technologies, and patient monitoring systems. A **virtual team** is one that is made up of organizationally or geographically dispersed members who are linked primarily through advanced information and communications technologies. Members frequently use the Internet and collaborative software to work together, rather than meeting face to face.[27]

Ford Motor Company provides another good illustration of the use of teams for horizontal coordination.

**In Practice**
**Ford Motor Company (Ford)**

The demand for hybrid vehicles is growing quickly, but many people want more than the small cars from Toyota and Honda that were first on the market. Ford Motor Company vowed to be the first auto manufacturer to come out with a hybrid SUV. CEO Bill Ford raved for years about plans for a new model that would handle like a muscular V6 but sip tiny amounts of gas and produce minuscule emissions. The Escape Hybrid SUV would be the most technologically advanced vehicle Ford had ever made, and perhaps its most important since the Model T.

The problem was, the Escape Hybrid was a dramatically different product for Ford and involved nine new major technologies, which Ford wanted to develop in-house rather than licensing patents from Toyota's hybrid system. Introducing even one major technological breakthrough was a challenge for Ford's traditional design and engineering process. Typically, researchers and product engineers haven't worked closely together at Ford—in fact, they were located in different buildings a half-mile apart. To meet the demanding schedule for getting the Escape Hybrid on the market, Ford created a sort of hybrid team, made up of scientists and product engineers from far-flung departments, now working side by side, creating and building software and hardware together, then working with production personnel to bring their creation to life. The team's leader, Prabhaker Patil, was himself a hybrid, a PhD scientist who had started out working in Ford's lab and then crossed over to hands-on product development. Patil was careful to select team members he knew would be open to collaboration. Although in the past problems were "tossed over the wall," they would now be ironed out collaboratively. The approach was revolutionary for Ford, and it led to amazing breakthroughs.

The Escape Hybrid team was given nearly complete autonomy, another rarity for Ford. Because the team was allowed to be entrepreneurial, their productivity zoomed. Decisions that once would have taken days were made on the spot. As a result, the team met the demanding schedule, and the Ford Escape Hybrid was introduced right on time—and to amazing success. It was named the best truck of the year at the 2005 North American International Auto Show, and Ford will use the technologies the team developed to introduce four more hybrid vehicles.[28] For example, in late 2007, Ford delivered the first 20 Escape plug-in hybrid vehicles for road testing.[29] Since its launch, the Escape Hybrid has sold well and received various awards for its engine design and its environmental friendliness. In 2010, Ford Motor Company of Canada sold more vehicles than any other company and much of its sales growth came from its utility and truck product lines.[30]

Just as Ford Motor Company first made the automobile accessible to the everyday consumer, it has taken a bold step by introducing a team-based structure to bring the hybrid to a mass market. A study by the Freedonia Group estimates that the hybrid car and light truck market will rise to 7.8 million units by 2020.[31] Most automakers outside Japan have been shortsighted by failing to invest in hybrid technology.[32] Therefore, Ford had an early lead, thanks largely to the communication and collaboration made possible by the team approach. Many of today's organizations are using teams as a way to increase horizontal collaboration, spur innovation, and speed new products and services to market.

Exhibit 3.4 summarizes the mechanisms for achieving horizontal linkages. These devices represent alternatives that managers can select to increase horizontal coordination in any organization. The higher-level devices provide more horizontal information capacity, although the cost to the organization in terms of time and human resources is greater. If horizontal communication is insufficient, departments

**EXHIBIT 3.4**
Ladder of Mechanisms
for Horizontal Linkage
and Coordination

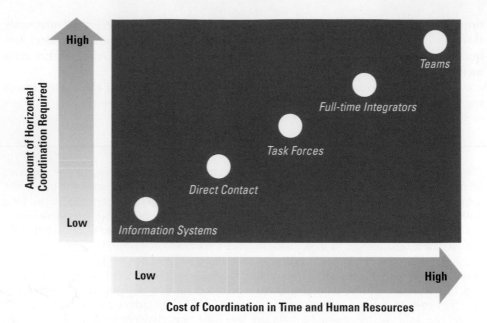

will find themselves out of synchronization and will not contribute to the overall goals of the organization. When the amount of horizontal coordination required is high, managers should select higher-level mechanisms.

# Organizational Design Alternatives

The overall design of organizational structure indicates three elements—required work activities, reporting relationships, and departmental grouping options.

## Required Work Activities

Departments are created to perform tasks considered strategically important to the company. For example, in a typical manufacturing company, work activities fall into a range of functions that help the organization accomplish its goals, such as a human resource department to recruit and train employees, a purchasing department to obtain supplies and raw materials, a production department to build products, a sales department to sell products, and so forth. As organizations grow larger and more complex, more and more functions need to be performed. Organizations typically define new departments or divisions as a way to accomplish tasks deemed valuable by the organization. Today, many companies are finding it important to establish departments such as information technology or e-business to take advantage of new technology and new business opportunities.

## Reporting Relationships

Once required work activities and departments are defined, the next question is how these activities and departments should fit together in the organizational hierarchy.

Reporting relationships, often called the chain of command, are represented by vertical lines on an organization chart. The chain of command should be an unbroken line of authority that links all persons in an organization and shows who reports to whom. In a large organization like Motorola or Ford Motor Company, 100 or more charts are required to identify reporting relationships among thousands of employees. The definition of departments and the drawing of reporting relationships define how employees are to be grouped into departments.

## ■ Departmental Grouping Options

Five possible options for departmental groupings are a functional grouping, divisional grouping, multifocused (or matrixed) grouping, horizontal grouping, and virtual network grouping. **Departmental grouping** affects employees because they share a common supervisor and common resources, are jointly responsible for performance, and tend to identify and collaborate with one another.[33] For example, if a credit manager were shifted from the finance department to the marketing department, he or she would work with salespeople to increase sales, thus becoming more liberal with credit than when he or she was located in the finance department.

**Functional grouping** places together employees who perform similar functions or work processes or who bring similar knowledge and skills to bear. For example, all marketing people work together under the same supervisor, as do manufacturing and engineering people. All people associated with the assembly process for generators are grouped together in one department. All chemists may be grouped in a department different from biologists because they represent different disciplines.

**Divisional grouping** means people are organized according to what the organization produces. All the people required to produce toothpaste—including personnel in marketing, manufacturing, and sales—are grouped together under one executive. In huge corporations such as EDS, some product or service lines may represent independent businesses, such as A. T. Kearney, a management consulting firm, and Wendover Financial Services.

**Multifocused grouping** means an organization embraces two structural grouping alternatives simultaneously. These structural forms are often called the matrix design. Domestic matrix structures will be discussed in more detail later in this chapter, and global matrix structures are addressed in Chapter 6. An organization may need to group by function and product division simultaneously or perhaps by product division and geography.

**Horizontal grouping** means employees are organized around core work processes, the end-to-end work, information, and material flows that provide value directly to customers. All the people who work on a core process are brought together in a group rather than being separated into functional departments.

**Virtual network grouping** is the most recent approach to departmental grouping. With this grouping, the organization is a loosely connected cluster of separate components. In essence, departments are separate organizations that are electronically connected for the sharing of information and completion of tasks. Departments can be spread all over the world rather than located together in one geographical location.

Each structural design alternative has significant strengths and weaknesses, to which we now turn.

# Functional, Divisional, and Geographical Designs

Functional grouping and divisional grouping are the two most common approaches to structural design.

## Functional Structure

In a **functional structure**, activities are grouped together by common function from the bottom to the top of the organization. All engineers are located in the engineering department, and the vice president of engineering is responsible for all engineering activities. The same is true in marketing, R&D, and manufacturing.

With a functional structure, all human knowledge and skills for specific activities are consolidated, providing a valuable depth of knowledge for the organization. This structure is most effective when in-depth expertise is critical to meeting organizational goals, when the organization needs to be controlled and coordinated through the vertical hierarchy, and when efficiency is important. The structure can be quite effective if there is little need for horizontal coordination. Exhibit 3.5 summarizes the strengths and weaknesses of the functional structure.

One strength of the functional structure is that it promotes economy of scale within functions. Economy of scale results when all employees are located in the same place and can share facilities. Producing all products in a single plant, for example, enables the plant to acquire the latest machinery. Constructing only one facility instead of separate facilities for each product line reduces duplication and waste. The functional structure also promotes in-depth skill development of employees. Employees are exposed to a range of functional activities within their own department.[34] The functional structure allows the organization to accomplish functional goals.

The main weakness of the functional structure is a slow response to environmental changes that require coordination across departments. Decisions may pile up, so the vertical hierarchy becomes overloaded. There may be poor horizontal coordination among departments. Other disadvantages of the functional structure are that innovation is slow because of poor coordination, and each employee has a restricted view of overall goals.

**EXHIBIT 3.5**
Strengths and Weaknesses of the Functional Organizational Structure

| STRENGTHS | WEAKNESSES |
|---|---|
| 1. Allows economies of scale within functional departments | 1. Slow response time to environmental changes |
| 2. Enables in-depth knowledge and skill development | 2. May cause decisions to pile up, hierarchy overload |
| 3. Enables organization to accomplish functional goals | 3. Leads to poor horizontal coordination among departments |
| 4. Is best with only one or a few products | 4. Results in less innovation |
| | 5. Involves restricted view of organizational goals |

Source: Adapted from *Organizational Dynamics*, (Winter 1979), Robert Duncan, "What Is the Right Organization Structure? Decision Tree Analysis Provides the Answer," p. 429, Copyright 1979, with permission from Elsevier.

Some organizations perform very effectively with a functional structure. However, as the organization expands, it may have problems coordinating across departments, requiring stronger horizontal linkage mechanisms.

## Functional Structure with Horizontal Linkages

Today, there is a shift toward flatter, more horizontal structures because of the challenges described in Chapter 1. Very few of today's successful companies can maintain a strictly functional structure. Organizations compensate for the vertical functional hierarchy by installing horizontal linkages, as described earlier in this chapter. Managers improve horizontal coordination by using information systems, direct contact between departments, full-time integrators or project managers, task forces, or teams. One interesting use of horizontal linkages occurred at Karolinska Hospital in Stockholm, Sweden, which had 47 functional departments. Even after top executives cut that to 11, coordination was still woefully inadequate. The team set about reorganizing workflow at the hospital around patient care. Instead of bouncing a patient from department to department, Karolinska now envisions the illness-to-recovery period as a process with "pit stops" in admissions, X-ray, surgery, and so forth. The most interesting aspect of the approach is the new position of nurse coordinator. Nurse coordinators serve as full-time integrators, troubleshooting transitions within or between departments. The improved horizontal coordination dramatically improved productivity and patient care at Karolinska.[35] Karolinska is effectively using horizontal linkages to overcome some of the disadvantages of the functional structure.

**In Practice**
**Mountain Equipment Co-op (MEC)**

MEC is one of Canada's most successful cooperatives and its excellence in governance and sustainability has been often recognized.[36] (An In Practice in Chapter 9 has more about MEC's values and awards.) MEC was founded in 1971 by a group of students at UBC. It sold sporting equipment not otherwise available in Canada such as avalanche beacons, climbing ropes, and ice crampons. The founders charged a one-time fee of five dollars to join. The fee remains five dollars; it can be considered a share. In 2012, its total sales were $302 million, an 11.8 percent increase from 2011.

Like Desjardins, described at the beginning of the chapter, MEC is part of Canada's social economy but is a co-op rather than a credit union. "A co-op is a democratically owned business structure in which members pool their resources to obtain a benefit."[37] Co-ops are characterized by seven design principles: (1) voluntary and open membership, (2) democratic member control, (3) member economic participation, (4) autonomy and independence, (5) education, training and information, (6) cooperation among cooperatives, and (7) concern for community.

MEC has a flat functional structure, integrated through its democratic decision-making mechanisms. Its hierarchy consists of the board of directors, the CEO, and various vice presidents in charge of Information, Production, Human Resources, Finance, Marketing, to name a few. At the VP level, there is a director of Sustainability and Community. The last level in the hierarchy consists of a material development manager, an ethical sourcing director, store sustainability coordinators, and a community programs manager.[38]

## Divisional Structure

The term **divisional structure** is used here as the generic term for what is sometimes called a product structure or strategic business units. With this structure, divisions

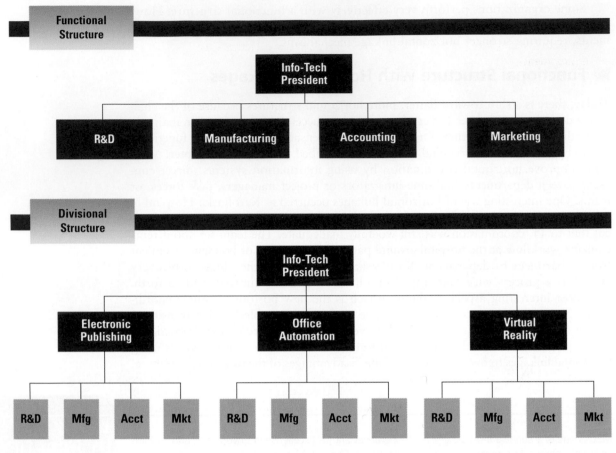

**EXHIBIT 3.6**
Reorganization from Functional Structure to Divisional Structure at Info-Tech

can be organized according to individual products, services, product groups, major projects or programs, divisions, businesses, or profit centres. The distinctive feature of a divisional structure is that grouping is based on organizational outputs.

The difference between a divisional structure and a functional structure is illustrated in Exhibit 3.6. The functional structure can be redesigned into separate product groups, and each group contains the functional departments of R&D, manufacturing, accounting, and marketing. Coordination across functional departments within each product group is maximized. The divisional structure promotes flexibility and change because each unit is smaller and can adapt to the needs of its environment.

Moreover, the divisional structure decentralizes decision making, because the lines of authority converge at a lower level in the hierarchy. The functional structure, by contrast, is centralized, because it forces decisions all the way to the top before a problem affecting several functions can be resolved.

Strengths and weaknesses of the divisional structure are summarized in Exhibit 3.7. The divisional organizational structure is excellent for achieving coordination across functional departments. It works well when organizations can no longer be adequately controlled through the traditional vertical hierarchy, and when goals are oriented toward adaptation and change. Giant, complex organizations

| STRENGTHS | WEAKNESSES |
|---|---|
| 1. Suited to fast change in unstable environment<br>2. Leads to customer satisfaction because product responsibility and contact points are clear<br>3. Involves high coordination across functions<br>4. Allows units to adapt to differences in products, regions, customers<br>5. Best in large organizations with several products<br>6. Decentralizes decision making | 1. Eliminates economies of scale in functional departments<br>2. Leads to poor coordination across product lines<br>3. Eliminates in-depth competence and technical specialization<br>4. Makes integration and standardization across product lines difficult |

**EXHIBIT 3.7**
Strengths and Weaknesses of the Divisional Organizational Structure

Source: Adapted from *Organizational Dynamics*, (Winter 1979), Robert Duncan, "What Is the Right Organization Structure? Decision Tree Analysis Provides the Answer," p. 431, Copyright 1979, with permission from Elsevier.

such as General Electric, Nestlé, and Johnson & Johnson are subdivided into a series of smaller, self-contained organizations for better control and coordination. In these large companies, the units are sometimes called divisions, businesses, or strategic business units. The structure at Johnson & Johnson includes 204 separate operating units, including McNeil Consumer Products, makers of Tylenol; Ortho Pharmaceuticals, which makes Retin-A and birth-control pills; and J&J Consumer Products, the company that brings us Johnson's Baby Shampoo and Band-Aids. Each unit is a separately chartered, autonomous company operating under the guidance of Johnson & Johnson's corporate headquarters.[39] Microsoft Corporation uses a divisional structure to develop and market different software products.

**In Practice**
**Microsoft Corporation (Microsoft)**

Bill Gates co-founded Microsoft in 1975 and built it into the most profitable technology company in the world. But as the company grew larger, the functional structure became ineffective. Employees began complaining about the growing bureaucracy and the snail's pace for decision making. A functional structure was just too slow and inflexible for a large organization operating in the fast-moving technology industry.

To speed decision making and better respond to environmental changes, top executives created seven business units based on Microsoft's major products: Windows Group; Server Software Group; Mobile Software Group; Office Software Group; Video Games and XBox Group; Business Software Group; and MSN-Internet Group. Each division is run by a general manager and contains most of the functions of a stand-alone company, including product development, sales, marketing, and finance.

What really made the structure revolutionary for Microsoft, at the time, was that the heads of the seven divisions were given the freedom and authority to run the businesses and spend their budgets as they saw fit to meet goals. The general managers and chief financial officers for each division set their own budgets and manage their own profit and loss statements. Previously, the two top executives, Bill Gates and Steven Ballmer, were involved in practically every decision, large and small. Managers of the divisions are charged up by the new authority and responsibility. One manager said he feels "like I am running my own little company."[40]

In the summer of 2013, Microsoft announced a major change in its design to improve decision making, to address customer complaints and to become more nimble. The strategy, named
Microsoft One, involves redesigning its engineering function into four divisions: devices, operating
systems, cloud service and applications. It previously had eight. Departments such as marketing are
no longer part of product divisions but are company-wide. Ballmer, retiring in 2014 after 13 years
as CEO, explains, "[we] are rallying around a single strategy as one company—not a collection of
divisional strategies"[41] This major change was seen by industry analysts as a sign that Microsoft
was in trouble. Microsoft has faced the impact of lagging personal computer sales, criticisms of
its operating system, poorly timed product launches, and global backlash about its apparent close
relationship with US intelligence agencies.[42]

---

The reduced, albeit hybrid, divisional structure has several strengths that are of
benefit to Microsoft.[43] This structure is suited to fast change in an unstable environment and provides high product or service visibility. Since each product line has its
own separate division, customers are able to contact the correct division and achieve
satisfaction. Coordination across functions is excellent. Each product can adapt to
requirements of individual customers or regions. The divisional structure typically
works best in organizations that have multiple products or services and enough personnel to staff separate functional units. At corporations such as Johnson & Johnson
and Microsoft, decision making is pushed down to the lowest levels. Each division
is small enough to be quick on its feet, responding rapidly to changes in the market.

One disadvantage of using divisional structures is that the organization loses
economies of scale. Instead of 50 research engineers sharing a common facility in a
functional structure, ten engineers may be assigned to each of five product divisions.
The critical mass required for in-depth research is lost, and physical facilities have to
be duplicated for each product line. Another problem is that product lines become
separate from each other, and coordination across product lines can be difficult. As
one Johnson & Johnson executive said, "We have to keep reminding ourselves that
we work for the same corporation."[44] There was some concern at Microsoft that
the independent divisions might start offering products and services that conflict
with one another.

Companies such as Xerox, Hewlett-Packard, and Sony have a large number
of divisions and have had real problems with horizontal coordination. Sony is far
behind in the business of digital media products partly because of poor coordination.
Apple's iPod quickly captured 60 percent of the American market versus 10 percent
for Sony. The digital music business depends on seamless coordination. Sony's
Walkman didn't even recognize some of the music sets that can be made with the
company's SonicStage software, and thus didn't mesh well with the division selling
music downloads. Sony has set up a new company, called Connect Co., specifically to
coordinate among the different units for the development of digital media businesses.[45]
Unless effective horizontal mechanisms are in place, a divisional structure can cause
real problems. One division may produce products or programs that are incompatible
or compete with products sold by another division. Customers are frustrated when a
sales representative from one division is unaware of developments in other divisions.
Task forces and other linkage devices are needed to coordinate across divisions. A
lack of technical specialization is also a problem in a divisional structure because
employees identify with the product line rather than with a functional specialty.
R&D personnel, for example, tend to do applied research to benefit the product line
rather than basic research to benefit the entire organization.

## ◼ Geographical Structure

Another basis for structural grouping is the organization's users or customers. The most common structure in this category is geography since each region of the country may have distinct tastes and needs. Each geographic unit includes all functions required to produce and market products or services in that region. Large nonprofit organizations such as Habitat for Humanity, Make-a-Wish Foundation, and United Way frequently use a type of geographical structure, with a central headquarters and semi-autonomous local units. The national organization provides brand recognition, coordinates fundraising services, and handles some shared administrative functions, while day-to-day control and decision making is decentralized to local or regional units.[46] The Leading by Design on page 110 describes the design for Médecins sans Frontières, the world's leading international medical relief organization, which has five centres in Europe and 14 national sections around the world.

For multinational corporations, self-contained units are created for different countries and parts of the world. Some years ago, Apple Computer reorganized from a functional to a geographical structure to facilitate manufacture and delivery of Apple computers to customers around the world. Apple used the structure to focus managers and employees on specific geographical customers and sales targets. See Exhibit 3.8 for an example of a geographical structure.

The strengths and weaknesses of a geographic divisional structure are similar to the divisional organization characteristics listed above in Exhibit 3.7. The organization can adapt to specific needs of its own region, and employees identify with regional goals rather than with national goals. Horizontal coordination within a region is emphasized rather than linkages across regions or to the national office.

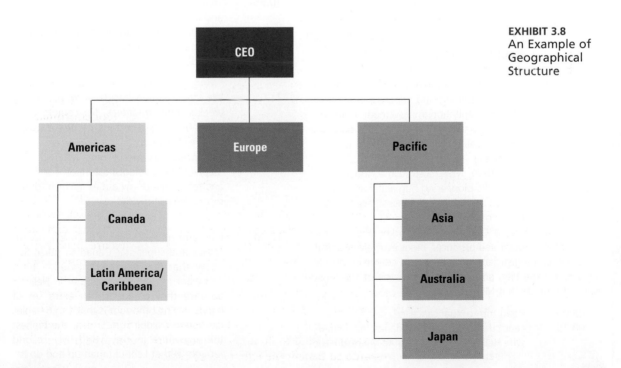

**EXHIBIT 3.8**
An Example of Geographical Structure

# Leading *by Design*

## Médecins sans Frontières (MSF)

MSF was started in 1971 by a small group of French doctors and journalists who had worked in Biafra, a short-lived independent state in Nigeria. The founders wanted to create an autonomous way to respond to public health crises, free of economic, religious, or political influence. MSF's Charter states that

- Médecins Sans Frontières offers assistance to populations in distress, to victims of natural or man-made disasters and to victims of armed conflict, without discrimination and irrespective of race, religion, creed or political affiliation.
- Médecins Sans Frontières observes neutrality and impartiality in the name of universal medical ethics and the right to humanitarian assistance and demands full and unhindered freedom in the exercise of its functions.
- Médecins Sans Frontières' volunteers promise to honour their professional code of ethics and to maintain complete independence from all political, economic and religious powers.
- As volunteers, members are aware of the risks and dangers of the missions they undertake and have no right to compensation for themselves or their beneficiaries other than that which Médecins Sans Frontières is able to afford them.[47]*

MSF starts a project when it identifies a humanitarian crisis: first, a medical team is sent to assess the situation and report its findings and recommendations to the operations department in one of its five operational offices. The operations department makes the decision to proceed and determines the medical priorities. The work can involve massive vaccination campaigns, training and supervision of local medical staff, water and sanitation improvement, data collection, feeding, physical and mental health care, maternal and pediatric care, medical and drug supplies distribution, rehabilitation of hospitals and clinics, and HIV/AIDS care and prevention.[48] In 1999, MSF received the Nobel Peace prize in recognition of its pioneering humanitarian work—MSF relief workers had brought medical assistance to more than 80 countries, 20 of which were in conflict.

Michael White, a Canadian aid worker and award-winning film director and producer, blogs evocatively about his work as a logistician administrator in charge of supply logistics for the Pieri project [in Sudan]—one of the most isolated projects that MSF runs.

| | |
|---|---|
| 08:00 | Road trip to Yuai cancelled. |
| 08:15 | Learn that our beloved Sudanese nurse/midwife Hellen needs to return to Khartoum for |

an undisclosed amount of time for personal reasons (a solid blow to the team—we just lost our African Mom).

. . .

| | |
|---|---|
| 09:20 | Hear screams of life-halting horror coming from our medical clinic more than 200 metres away. |
| 09:30 | Learn that a middle-aged man has passed away from unknown causes in our Inpatient Department (IPD). |
| 10:00 | The deceased is from a village over a day's walk away, and his wife, daughter and son have no way to remove or dispose of the corpse. |
| 10:01 | It's Sunday and we're short staff, which in this case is the same thing as a short straw. |
| 10:30 | Nothing in my life has prepared me for this. Flies and fecal fluids have filled the middle-aged man's tukul. He's naked and dead and I'm breathing and confused by the simplicity of it all. I can taste the smell of death in the back of my mouth. I keep thinking the middle-aged man is going to move and it scares me a lot. |
| 10:35 | Thankfully John Yany (pronounced Yang) and a guard crawl into the tukul ahead of me and roll the middle-aged man onto a stretcher. To be honest I don't think I could have done it. |

. . .

| | |
|---|---|
| 11:01 | We start digging beside a couple of the week's other tragedies. No cemetery, no markers ... just mounds of death in the middle of a field. |
| 11:10 | Maina and six men from Pieri including Stephen Mai, our logistical supervisor, come and relieve me of my duties. (Which for the record are not my duties.) |

. . .

| | |
|---|---|
| 12:50 | Our amazing 29-year-old Dutch doctor Ortillia and super-star Canadian nurse Sue know that I've never witnessed a birth and want to. Sue suggests that in Hellen's absence they could use an extra set of hands. My first thought is that 1 in 6 babies die during childbirth in Sudan, the highest toll anywhere in the world. My second thought is that I should man up and do it! |

*(Continued)*

1:35    Without the aid of any drugs this woman has withstood a barrage of contractions, and an episiotomy and has barely made a sound.

1:40    The mood suddenly shifts when Ortillia calmly mentions to Sue that the umbilical cord is wrapped around the baby's neck. With only basic medical tools at their disposal, the [women] continue their inspired work, while for the first time since arriving I'm grateful that the woman in labour doesn't speak English.

1:41    I can't stop watching Sue and Ortillia do their thing. They are so calm and never once let on that there may be a problem. But there is a problem, a huge one.

1:42    Ortillia performs some orchestrated moment of magic with her arms and like that the baby appears untangled in front of Sue and its Mom.

1:42    Silence surrounds us.

1:42    Everyone and everything is soundless. It feels like we somehow stepped into a vacuum. In my mind I start chanting . . . Cry . . . Cry . . . Cry . . . Time passes with a glacial sense of speed. Please cry!

1:43    For those of you who have heard the first cry of a newborn, you know that there is no sweeter sound on earth. It's a boy and I'm never having sex again!†

. . .

I don't know how to reconcile the divergent nature of that Sunday. I've learned that the Sudanese circle of life is the same as anywhere else; [its] circumference is just a lot smaller. I have always had a very difficult time with the concept of life and death. Ever since I was old enough to understand death it has frightened me more than I believe is either normal or healthy. Notorious B.I.G. summed it up best, when talking about Tupac's demise. "Death, there ain't no comin' back from that shit." While I don't pretend to know if that's true, I do understand that although death is inevitable, sickness and suffering doesn't always have to be. To that end MSF's work in Sudan and around the world is a tribute to human compassion, and inspired action.[49]

. . .

As you can see from Exhibit 3.9, MSF is structured geographically. The structure of MSF fits well with its purpose and its strategy.

*www.msf.ca/en/about/charter/charter.html. Used with permission from Médecins Sans Frontières Canada.
†www.msf.ca/blogs/MikeW.php. Used with permission from Médecins Sans Frontières Canada.

## Matrix Structure

Sometimes an organization's structure needs to be multifocused in that both product and function or product and geography are emphasized at the same time. One way to achieve this is through the **matrix structure**. The matrix can be used when both technical expertise and product innovation and change are important for meeting organizational goals. The matrix structure often is the answer when organizations find that the functional, divisional, and geographical structures combined with horizontal linkage mechanisms will not work.

The matrix is a strong form of horizontal linkage. The unique characteristic of the matrix organization is that both product division and functional structures (horizontal and vertical) are implemented simultaneously, as shown in Exhibit 3.10. The product managers and functional managers have equal authority within the organization, and employees report to both of them. The matrix structure is similar to the use of full-time integrators or product managers described earlier in this chapter (Exhibit 3.3), except that in the matrix structure the product managers (horizontal) are given formal authority equal to that of the functional managers (vertical).

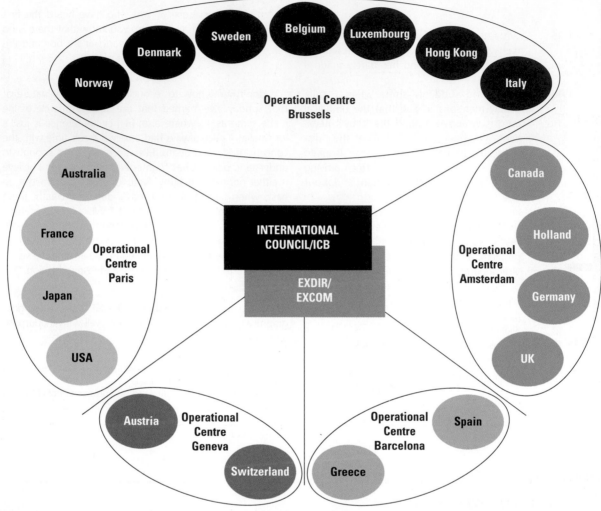

**EXHIBIT 3.9**
Unofficial MSF Organization Chart

Note: As of mid-2008, the organization chart of Médecins Sans Frontières (Doctors Without Borders), featuring 19 national sections, did not include 11 so-called "new entities" in places such as Brazil, India, Ireland, South Africa, and the United Arab Emirates. Affiliated organizations such as the Campaign for Access to Essential Medicines, Epicentre, and the Drugs for Neglected Diseases initiative were also not included in this chart. Please consult www.msf.org for current information about MSF and links to national websites.
Source: Ann Armstrong in consultation with MSF Canada, 2008. Used with permission from Médecins Sans Frontières Canada.

## Conditions for the Matrix

A dual hierarchy may seem an unusual way to design an organization, but the matrix is the correct structure when the following conditions are met:[50]

- *Condition 1.* Pressure exists to share scarce resources across product lines. The organization is typically medium sized and has a moderate number of product lines. It feels pressure for the shared and flexible use of people and equipment across those products. For example, the organization is not large enough to assign engineers full-time to each product line, so engineers are assigned part-time to several products or projects.

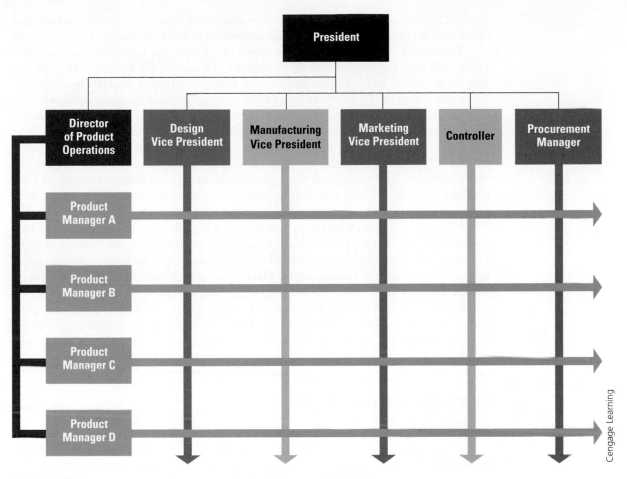

**EXHIBIT 3.10**
Dual-Authority Structure in a Matrix Organization

- *Condition 2.* Environmental pressure exists for two or more critical outputs, such as for in-depth technical knowledge (functional structure) and frequent new products (divisional structure). This dual pressure means a balance of power is needed between the functional and product sides of the organization, and a dual-authority structure is needed to maintain that balance.
- *Condition 3.* The environmental domain of the organization is both complex and unstable. Frequent external changes and high interdependence between departments require a large amount of coordination and information processing in both vertical and horizontal directions.

Under these three conditions, the vertical and horizontal lines of authority must be given equal recognition. A dual-authority structure is thereby created so the balance of power between them is equal.

Referring again to Exhibit 3.10, assume the matrix structure is for a clothing manufacturer. Product A is footwear, product B is outerwear, product C is sleepwear, and so on. Each product line serves a different market and customers. As a medium-sized organization, the company must effectively use people from manufacturing, design, and marketing to work on each product line. There are not enough designers to warrant a separate design department for each product line, so the designers are shared across product lines. Moreover, by keeping the manufacturing, design, and marketing functions intact, employees can develop the in-depth expertise to serve all product lines efficiently.

The matrix formalizes horizontal teams along with the traditional vertical hierarchy and tries to give equal balance to both. However, the matrix may shift one way or the other. Many organizations have found a balanced matrix hard to implement and maintain because one side of the authority structure often dominates. As a consequence, two variations of matrix structure have evolved—the functional matrix and the product matrix. In a **functional matrix**, the functional bosses have primary authority and the project or product managers simply coordinate product activities. In a **product matrix**, by contrast, the project or product managers have primary authority and functional managers simply assign technical personnel to projects and provide advisory expertise as needed. For many organizations, one of these approaches works better than the balanced matrix with dual lines of authority.[51]

All kinds of organizations have experimented with the matrix, including hospitals, consulting firms, banks, insurance companies, government agencies, and many types of industrial firms.[52] This structure has been used successfully by large global organizations such as Procter & Gamble and Unilever, and in local plants such as the Cummins Engine plant in Jamestown, New York, which fine-tuned the matrix to suit its own particular goals and culture. Project-based organizations often use the matrix structure. For example, Defence Research and Development Canada, whose purpose is to inform, enable, and respond to Canada's defence and security priorities, is structured as a matrix to connect the people and departments that direct, deliver, and exploit knowledge about national and international innovations in military operations.[53]

## ■ Strengths and Weaknesses

The matrix structure is best when environmental change is high and when goals reflect a dual requirement, such as for both product and functional goals. The dual-authority structure facilitates communication and coordination to cope with rapid environmental change and enables an equal balance between product and functional bosses. The matrix facilitates discussion and adaptation to unexpected problems. It tends to work best in organizations of moderate size with a few product lines. The matrix is not needed for only a single product line, and too many product lines make it difficult to coordinate both directions at once. Exhibit 3.11 summarizes the strengths and weaknesses of the matrix structure based on what we know of organizations that use it.[54]

**EXHIBIT 3.11**
Strengths and Weaknesses of the Matrix Organizational Structure

Source: Adapted from *Organizational Dynamics*, (Winter 1979), Robert Duncan, "What Is the Right Organization Structure? Decision Tree Analysis Provides the Answer," p. 431, Copyright 1979, with permission from Elsevier.

| STRENGTHS | WEAKNESSES |
|---|---|
| 1. Achieves coordination necessary to meet dual demands from customers | 1. Causes participants to experience dual authority, which can be frustrating and confusing |
| 2. Flexible sharing of human resources across products | 2. Means participants need good interpersonal skills and extensive training |
| 3. Suited to complex decisions and frequent changes in unstable environment | 3. Is time consuming; involves frequent meetings and conflict-resolution sessions |
| 4. Provides opportunity for both functional and product skill development | 4. Will not work unless participants understand it and adopt collegial rather than vertical-type relationships |
| 5. Best in medium-sized organizations with multiple products | 5. Requires great effort to maintain power balance |

The strength of the matrix is that it enables an organization to meet dual demands from customers in the environment. Resources (people, equipment) can be flexibly allocated across different products, and the organization can adapt to changing external requirements.[55] This structure also provides an opportunity for employees to acquire either functional or general management skills, depending on their interests.

One disadvantage of the matrix is that employees experience dual authority, reporting to two bosses and sometimes juggling conflicting demands. This can be frustrating and confusing, especially if roles and responsibilities are not clearly defined by top managers.[56] Employees working in a matrix need excellent interpersonal and conflict-resolution skills, which may require special training in human relations. The matrix also forces managers to spend a great deal of time in meetings.[57]

**Apply**

Apply your self-knowledge and determine if you have the skills necessary to work in a matrix structure.

## In Practice
### Englander Steel

As far back as anyone could remember, the steel industry in England was stable and certain. Then in the 1980s and 90s, excess European steel capacity, an economic downturn, the emergence of the mini mill electric arc furnace, and competition from steelmakers in Germany and Japan forever changed the English steel industry. By the turn of the 21st century, traditional steel mills in the United States, such as Bethlehem Steel and LTV, were facing bankruptcy. Mittal Steel in Asia and Europe's leading steelmaker, Arcelor, started acquiring steel companies to become world steel titans. The survival hope of small traditional steel manufacturers was to sell specialized products. A small company could market specialty products aggressively and quickly adapt to customer needs. Complex process settings and operating conditions had to be rapidly changed for each customer's order—a difficult feat for the titans.

Englander Steel employed 2,900 people, made 400,000 tonnes of steel a year (about one percent of Arcelor's output), and was 180 years old. For 160 of those years, a functional structure worked fine. As the environment became more turbulent and competitive, however, Englander Steel managers realized they were not keeping up. Fifty percent of its orders were behind schedule. Profits were eroded by labour, material, and energy cost increases. Market share declined.

In consultation with outside experts, the president of Englander Steel saw that the company had to walk a tightrope. It had to specialize in a few high-value-added products tailored for separate markets, while maintaining economies of scale and sophisticated technology within functional departments. The dual pressure led to an unusual solution for a steel company: a matrix structure.

Englander Steel had four product lines: open-die forgings, ring-mill products, wheels and axles, and sheet steel. A business manager was given responsibility for and authority over each line, which included preparing a business plan and developing targets for production costs, product inventory, shipping dates, and gross profit. The managers were given authority to meet those targets and to make their lines profitable. Functional vice presidents were responsible for technical decisions. Functional managers were expected to stay abreast of the latest techniques in their areas and to keep personnel trained in new technologies that could apply to product lines. With 20,000 recipes for specialty steels and several hundred new recipes ordered each month, functional personnel had to stay current. Two functional departments—field sales and industrial relations—were not included in the matrix because they worked independently. The final design was a hybrid matrix structure with both matrix and functional relationships, as illustrated in Exhibit 3.12.

Implementation of the matrix was slow. Middle managers were confused. Meetings to coordinate orders across functional departments seemed to be held every day. However, after about a year of training by external consultants, Englander Steel was on track. Ninety percent of the orders were delivered on time, and market share recovered. Both productivity and profitability increased steadily. The managers thrived on matrix involvement. Meetings to coordinate product and functional decisions provided a growth experience. Middle managers began including younger managers in the matrix discussions as training for future management responsibility.[58]

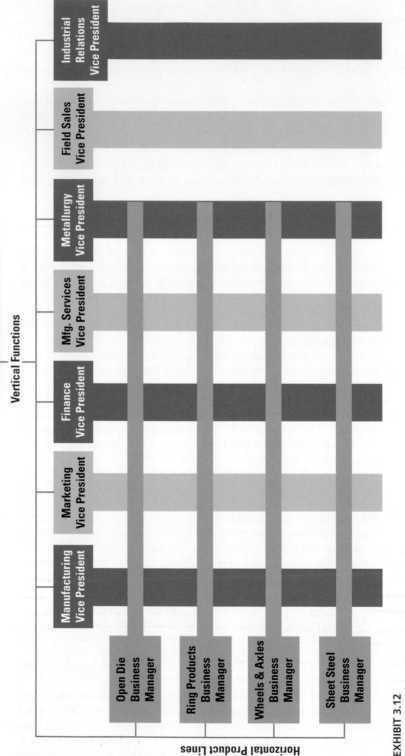

**EXHIBIT 3.12**

**Matrix Structure for Englander Steel**

Source: Based on Frank Ostroff, *The Horizontal Organization* (New York: Oxford University Press, 1999); John A. Byrne, "The Horizontal Corporation," *BusinessWeek* (December 20, 1993), 76–81; and Thomas A. Stewart, "The Search for the Organization of Tomorrow," *Fortune* (May 18, 1992), 92–98.

**EXHIBIT 3.13**
Matrix Structure—A Special Design!

This example illustrates the appropriate use of a matrix structure. The dual pressure to maintain economies of scale and to market four product lines gave equal emphasis to the functional and product hierarchies. Through continuous meetings for coordination, Englander Steel achieved both economies of scale and flexibility.

If managers do not adapt to the information and power sharing required by the matrix, the system will not work. Managers must collaborate with one another rather than rely on vertical authority in decision making. In addition, managers must work hard at maintaining the power balance between the members of the matrix. Exhibit 3.13 provides a comic and cynical view of matrix structure!

# Horizontal Structure

A recent approach to organizing is the **horizontal structure**, which organizes employees around core processes. Organizations typically shift toward a horizontal structure during a procedure called re-engineering. **Re-engineering**, or *business process re-engineering*, basically means the redesign of a vertical organization along its horizontal workflows and processes. A **process** refers to an organized group of related tasks and activities that work together to transform inputs into outputs that create value for customers.[59] Re-engineering changes the way managers think about how work is done; rather than focusing on narrow jobs structured into distinct functional departments, managers emphasize core processes that cut horizontally across the organization and involve teams of employees working together to serve customers. Examples of processes include order fulfillment, new product development, and customer service.

A good illustration of process is provided by claims handling at Progressive Casualty Insurance Company. In the past, a customer would report a vehicle accident to an agent, who would pass the information to a customer service representative, who, in turn, would pass it to a claims manager. The claims manager would batch the claim with others from the same territory and assign it to an adjuster, who would schedule a time to inspect the vehicle damage. Today, adjusters are organized into teams that handle the entire claims process from beginning to end. One member handles claimant calls to the office while others are stationed in the field. When an adjuster takes a call, he or she does whatever is possible over the phone. If an inspection is needed, the adjuster contacts a team member in the field and schedules an appointment immediately. Progressive now measures the time from call to inspection in hours rather than the seven to ten days it once took.[60]

When a company is re-engineered to a horizontal structure, all the people throughout the organization who work on a particular process (such as claims handling or order fulfillment) have easy access to one another so they can communicate and coordinate their efforts. The horizontal structure virtually eliminates both the vertical hierarchy and old departmental boundaries. This structural approach is largely a response to the profound changes that have occurred in the workplace and the business environment over the past 15 to 20 years. Technological progress emphasizes computer- and Internet-based integration and coordination. Customers expect faster and better service, and employees want opportunities to use their minds, learn new skills, and assume greater responsibility. Organizations mired in a vertical mindset have a hard time meeting these challenges. Thus, numerous organizations have experimented with horizontal mechanisms such as cross-functional teams to achieve coordination across departments or task forces to accomplish temporary projects. Increasingly, organizations are shifting away from hierarchical, function-based structures to structures based on horizontal processes.

## ■ Characteristics

An illustration of a company re-engineered into a horizontal structure appears in Exhibit 3.14. Such an organization has the following characteristics:[61]

- Structure is created around cross-functional core processes rather than tasks, functions, or geography. Thus, boundaries between departments are obliterated. Ford Motor Company's Customer Service Division, for example, has core process groups for business development, parts supply and logistics, vehicle service and programs, and technical support.
- Self-directed teams, not individuals, are the basis of organizational design and performance.
- Process owners have responsibility for each core process in its entirety. For Ford's procurement and logistics process, for example, a number of teams may work on jobs such as parts analysis, purchasing, material flow, and distribution, but a process owner is responsible for coordinating the entire process.
- People on the team are given the skills, tools, motivation, and authority to make decisions central to the team's performance. Team members are cross-trained to perform one another's jobs, and the combined skills are sufficient to complete a major organizational task.
- Teams have the freedom to think creatively and respond flexibly to new challenges that arise.
- Customers drive the horizontal corporation. Effectiveness is measured by end-of-process performance objectives (based on the goal of bringing value to the customer), as well as customer satisfaction, employee satisfaction, and financial contribution.

**EXHIBIT 3.14**
**A Horizontal Structure**
Source: Based on Frank Ostroff, *The Horizontal Organization* (New York: Oxford University Press, 1999); John A. Byrne, "The Horizontal Corporation," *BusinessWeek* (December 20, 1993), 76–81; and Thomas A. Stewart, "The Search for the Organization of Tomorrow," *Fortune* (May 18, 1992), 92–98.

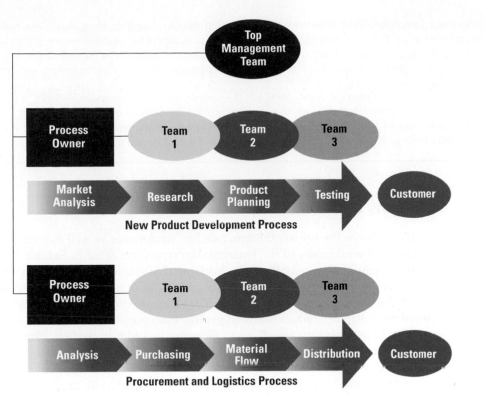

- The culture is one of openness, trust, and collaboration, focused on continuous improvement. The culture values employee empowerment, responsibility, and well-being.

The Chemainus Sawmill, described below, re-engineered a traditional sawmill into a team-based structure supported by multiskilling training and pay-for-skills compensation systems.

## In Practice
**Chemainus Sawmill (Chemainus)**

The Chemainus Sawmill, which re-opened in 1985, is the fifth in the 150-year history of sawmilling in the small town of Chemainus on Vancouver Island. The town is also known for its large murals on the exterior walls of many of its buildings. The outdoor art gallery received international recognition in 1985 when Chemainus won first prize in the global Downtown Revitalizations Awards competition.

When the sawmill reopened, its mission was "to be first choice with customers and with the community."[62] It was structured to meet seven goals: (1) to provide a high-value product in terms of size, grade, and presentation; (2) to provide dependable delivery; (3) to respond proactively to market demands through organizational flexibility; (4) to respond to feedback; (5) to provide rewarding work; (6) to provide a safe and healthy workplace; and (7) to develop and to maintain trust within the sawmill and the community.[63]

The sawmill has several teams. There are six production teams with varying numbers of work stations for log prep, log breakdown, trim, grading, merchandising, and yard. There is also a team of shippers. The operators and the shippers are expected to rotate through all the work stations in their teams to become multiskilled and to train others in the skills they have mastered. The operators report to a shift foreperson who, in turn, reports to a department foreperson. The shippers report to a yard foreperson. The maintenance team consists of several millwrights, filers, electricians, oilers, and mechanics. They report to charge hands who, in turn, report to the maintenance supervisor. Lastly, there is the management team, headed by the mill manager, which consists of the operations superintendent, the personnel supervisor, the accountant, the sales superintendent, and other managerial staff.

Central to nurturing the team concept at the sawmill is its communications network, a series of meetings of the production team, the crew, and others to obtain employee input. As well, each production team has an official team representative. The workers are represented by Local 1-80 of the International Woodworkers of America. The sawmill is now owned by Weyerhaeuser.

## ■ Strengths and Weaknesses

As with all structures, the horizontal structure has weaknesses as well as strengths. The strengths and weaknesses of the horizontal structure are listed in Exhibit 3.15.

The most significant strength of the horizontal structure is that it can dramatically increase the organization's flexibility and response to changes in customer needs because of the enhanced coordination. The structure directs everyone's attention toward the customer, which leads to greater customer satisfaction as well as improvements in productivity, speed, and efficiency. In addition, because there are no boundaries between functional departments, employees take a broader view of organizational goals rather than being focused on the goals of a single department. The horizontal structure promotes an emphasis on teamwork and cooperation, so that team members share a commitment to meeting common objectives. Finally, the horizontal structure can improve the quality of life for employees by giving them opportunities to share responsibility, make decisions, and contribute significantly to the organization.

A weakness of the horizontal structure is that it can harm rather than help organizational performance unless managers carefully determine which core processes are

**EXHIBIT 3.15**
Strengths and
Weaknesses of the
Horizontal Structure

| STRENGTHS | WEAKNESSES |
|---|---|
| 1. Promotes flexibility and rapid response to changes in customer needs | 1. Determining core processes is difficult and time consuming |
| 2. Directs the attention of everyone toward the production and delivery of value to the customer | 2. Requires changes in culture, job design, management philosophy, and information and reward systems |
| 3. Each employee has a broader view of organizational goals | 3. Traditional managers may balk when they have to give up power and authority |
| 4. Promotes a focus on teamwork and collaboration | 4. Requires significant training of employees to work effectively in a horizontal team environment |
| 5. Improves quality of life for employees by offering them the opportunity to share responsibility, make decisions, and be accountable for outcomes | 5. Can limit in-depth skill development |

Source: Based on Frank Ostroff, *The Horizontal Organization: What the Organization of the Future Looks Like and How It Delivers Value to Customers* (New York: Oxford University Press, 1999); and Richard L. Daft, *Organization Theory and Design*, 6th ed. (Cincinnati, Ohio: South-Western, 1998), 253.

critical for bringing value to customers. Simply defining the processes around which to organize can be difficult. In addition, shifting to a horizontal structure is complicated and time consuming because it requires significant changes in culture, job design, management philosophy, and information and reward systems. Traditional managers may balk when they have to give up power and authority to serve instead as coaches and facilitators of teams. Employees have to be trained to work effectively in a team environment. Finally, because of the cross-functional nature of work, a horizontal structure can limit in-depth knowledge and skill development unless measures are taken to give employees opportunities to maintain and build technical expertise.

# Virtual Network Structure

The virtual network structure extends the concept of horizontal coordination and collaboration beyond the boundaries of the traditional organization. Many of today's organizations farm out some of their activities to other companies that can do it more efficiently. **Outsourcing** means to contract out certain corporate functions, such as manufacturing, information technology, or credit processing, to other companies. This is a trend in all industries that is affecting organizational structure.[64] The advantages of outsourcing are of an operational and strategic nature. "Operational advantages usually provide for short-term trouble avoidance, while strategic advantages offer long term contribution in terms of maximizing opportunities."[65] Accenture, for example, handles all aspects of information technology for the British food retailer J. Sainsbury's. Companies in India, Malaysia, and Scotland manage call centre and technical support for North American computer and cell phone companies. Entire chunks of General Motors' and BMW's automobiles are engineered and built by outside contractors such as Magna International. Fiat Auto is involved in multiple complex outsourcing relationships, with other companies handling logistics, maintenance, and the manufacturing of some parts.[66]

These interorganizational relationships reflect a significant shift in organizational design. A few organizations carry outsourcing to the extreme and create a virtual network structure. With a **virtual network structure**, sometimes called a *modular structure*, illustrated in Exhibit 3.16, the firm subcontracts many or most of its major processes to separate companies and coordinates their activities from a small headquarters organization.[67]

## How the Structure Works

The virtual network organization, illustrated in Exhibit 3.16, may be viewed as a central hub surrounded by a network of outside specialists. Rather than being housed under one roof or located within one organization, services such as accounting,

*act!*

**Compare**

Compare the essential characteristics of the horizontal and the virtual network structures. What similarities do you see?

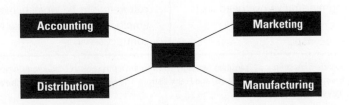

**EXHIBIT 3.16**
Virtual Network Structure
Source: Adapted from David Nadler and Michael Tushman, *Strategic Organization Design* (Glenview, Ill: Scott Foresman, 1988), 68.

design, manufacturing, marketing, and distribution are outsourced to separate companies that are connected electronically to a central office. Organizational partners located in different parts of the world may use networked computers or the Internet to exchange data and information so rapidly and smoothly that a loosely connected network of suppliers, manufacturers, and distributors can look and act like one seamless company. The virtual network form incorporates a free-market style to replace the traditional vertical hierarchy. Subcontractors may flow into and out of the system as needed to meet changing needs.

With a network structure, the hub maintains control over processes in which it has world-class or difficult-to-imitate capabilities and then transfers other activities— along with the decision making and control over them—to other organizations. These partner organizations organize and accomplish their work using their own ideas, assets, and tools.[68] The idea is that a firm can concentrate on what it does best and contract out everything else to companies with distinctive competence in those specific areas, enabling the organization to do more with less.[69] The network structure is often advantageous for start-up companies.

## ■ Strengths and Weaknesses

Exhibit 3.17 summarizes the strengths and weaknesses of the virtual network structure. One of the major strengths is that the organization, no matter how small, can be truly global, drawing on resources worldwide to achieve the best quality and price, and then selling products or services worldwide just as easily through subcontractors. The network structure also enables new or small organizations to develop products or services and get them to market rapidly without huge investments in factories, equipment, warehouses, or distribution facilities. The ability to arrange and rearrange resources to meet changing needs and best serve customers gives the network structure flexibility and rapid response. New technologies can be developed quickly by tapping into a worldwide network of experts. The organization can continually redefine itself to meet changing product or market opportunities.

**EXHIBIT 3.17**
Strengths and Weaknesses of the Virtual Network Structure

| STRENGTHS | WEAKNESSES |
|---|---|
| 1. Enables even small organizations to obtain talent and resources worldwide<br>2. Gives a company immediate scale and reach without huge investments in factories, equipment, or distribution facilities<br>3. Enables the organization to be highly flexible and responsive to changing needs<br>4. Reduces administrative overhead costs | 1. Managers do not have hands-on control over many activities and employees<br>2. Requires a great deal of time to manage relationships and potential conflicts with contract partners<br>3. There is a risk of organizational failure if a partner fails to deliver or goes out of business<br>4. Employee loyalty and organizational culture might be weak because employees feel they can be replaced by contract services |

Source: Based on Linda S. Ackerman, "Transition Management: An In-Depth Look at Managing Complex Change," *Organizational Dynamics* (Summer 1982), 46–66; and Frank Ostroff, *The Horizontal Organization* (New York: Oxford University Press, 1999), Fig 2.1, 34.

A final strength is reduced administrative overhead. Large teams of staff specialists and administrators are not needed. Managerial and technical talent can be focused on key activities that provide competitive advantage while other activities are out-sourced.[70]

The virtual network structure also has a number of weaknesses.[71] The primary weakness is a lack of control. The network structure takes decentralization to the extreme. Managers do not have all operations under their jurisdiction and must rely on contracts, coordination, and negotiation to hold things together. This also means increased time spent managing relationships with partners and resolving conflicts.

A problem of equal importance is the risk of failure if one organizational partner fails to deliver, has a plant burn down, or goes out of business. Managers in the headquarters organization have to act quickly to spot problems and find new arrangements. Finally, from a human resource perspective, employee loyalty can be weak in a network organization because of concerns over job security. Employees may feel that they can be replaced by contract services. In addition, it is more difficult to develop a cohesive organizational culture. Turnover may be higher because emotional commitment between the organization and employees is low. With changing products, markets, and partners, the organization may need to reshuffle employees at any time to get the correct mix of skills and capabilities.

## Hybrid Structures

It is important to note many structures in the real world do not exist in the pure forms we have outlined in this chapter. Organizations often use a **hybrid structure** that combines characteristics of various approaches tailored to specific strategic needs. Most companies combine characteristics of functional, divisional, geographical, horizontal, or network structures to take advantage of the strengths of various structures and to avoid some of the weaknesses. Hybrid structures tend to be used in rapidly changing environments because they offer the organization greater flexibility.

One type of hybrid that is often used combines characteristics of the functional and divisional structures. When a corporation grows large and has several products or markets, it typically is organized into self-contained divisions of some type. Functions that are important to each product or market are decentralized to the self-contained units. However, some functions that are relatively stable and require economies of scale and in-depth specialization are also centralized at headquarters. The departments provide services for the entire organization. For example, Rogers Communications, has three business units—wireless, cable and telecom, and media—as well as functional support across the organization.

Exhibit 3.18 illustrates another hybrid structure. Ford Motor Company's Customer Service Division, a global operation made up of 12,000 employees serving nearly 15,000 dealers, provides an example of this type of hybrid. Beginning in 1995, when Ford launched its "Ford 2000" initiative to become the world's leading automotive firm in the 21st century, top executives grew increasingly concerned about complaints regarding customer service. They decided that the horizontal model offered the best chance to gain a faster, more efficient, integrated approach to customer service. Several horizontally aligned groups, made up of multiskilled teams, focus on core processes such as parts supply and logistics (acquiring parts and getting them to dealers quickly and efficiently),

**EXHIBIT 3.18**
Hybrid Structure
at Ford Motor
Company's Customer
Service Division

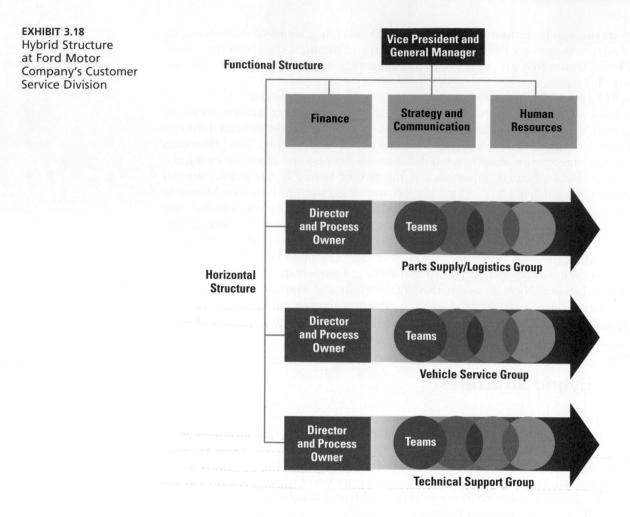

vehicle service and programs (collecting and disseminating information about repair problems), and technical support (ensuring that every service department receives updated technical information). Each group has a process owner who is responsible for seeing that the teams meet overall objectives. Ford's Customer Service Division retained a functional structure for finance, strategy and communication, and human resources departments. Each of these departments provides services for the entire division.[72]

## Applications of Structural Design

Each type of structure is applied in different situations and meets different needs. In short, design follows purpose. In describing the various structures, we touched briefly on conditions such as environmental stability or change and organizational size that are related to structure. Each form of structure—functional, divisional, matrix, horizontal, network, hybrid—represents a tool that can help managers make an organization more effective, depending on the demands of its situation.

## Structural Alignment

Ultimately, the most important decision that managers make about structural design is to find the right balance between vertical control and horizontal coordination, depending on the needs of the organization. Vertical control is associated with goals of efficiency and stability, while horizontal coordination is associated with learning, innovation, and flexibility. Exhibit 3.19 shows a simplified continuum that illustrates how structural approaches are associated with vertical control versus horizontal coordination. The functional structure is appropriate when the organization needs to be coordinated through the vertical hierarchy and when efficiency is important for meeting organizational goals. The functional structure uses task specialization and a strict chain of command to gain efficient use of scarce resources, but it does not enable the organization to be flexible or innovative. At the opposite end of the scale, the horizontal structure is appropriate when the organization has a high need for coordination among functions to achieve innovation and promote learning. The horizontal structure enables organizations to differentiate themselves and respond quickly to changes, but at the expense of efficient resource use. The virtual network structure offers even greater flexibility and potential for rapid response by allowing the organization to add or subtract pieces as needed to adapt and meet changing needs from the environment and marketplace. Exhibit 3.19 also shows how other types of structure defined in this chapter—functional with cross-functional linkages, divisional, and matrix—represent intermediate steps on the organization's path to efficiency or innovation and learning. The exhibit does not include all possible structures, but it illustrates how organizations attempt to balance the needs for efficiency and vertical control with innovation and horizontal coordination. In addition, as described in the chapter, many organizations use a hybrid structure to combine characteristics of these structural types. There are many structural choices and, as the Canadian Inquisition organization, described below, shows, one possibility is a web of inclusion.[73] The web of inclusion is more circular

**Think**

Think about how to design the correct balance between vertical control and horizontal coordination to meet the needs of the organization.

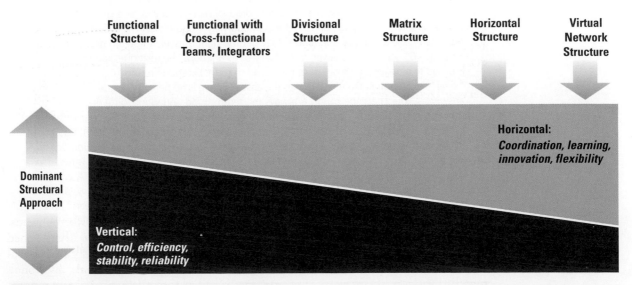

**EXHIBIT 3.19**
Relationship of Structure to Organization's Need for Efficiency versus Learning

than hierarchical and builds from the centre out, while creating new connections. Webs of inclusion allow

> …organizations to draw on the widest possible base of talent, a huge advantage in an economy based on knowledge. They allow resources to flow to where they're needed. They undermine the tendency to become hierarchical. They put organizations more directly in touch with those they serve, and make partnerships easier to achieve. Perhaps most importantly, they break down the old industrial-era division between the heads of organizations and the hands—those who come up with ideas and those who execute them.[74]*

## In Practice
### The Canadian Inquisition (The Inquisition)

The Inquisition is a trivia league formed in 1986 in Toronto. The participants call it a cooperative pub trivia league as there is no formal organizational structure. There are 15 to 16 teams with five players per team in a game. There are about 130 players in the league, including the quiz masters, who ask the questions. Games take place at various Toronto pubs on Monday nights; there are three seasons per year and a final competition for a total of 33 games per year. Players include teachers, programmers, reporters, editors, cab drivers, and real estate agents. Each team has a captain who is responsible to ensure that the players know where the game is being played and to line up substitute players, if necessary. The captain meets the team at the start of the season to discuss any rule changes and to review the finances. Players pay three dollars per game to cover costs such as photocopying and buying trophies. A volunteer treasurer for the Inquisition manages the league's bank account. Another volunteer compiles the statistics, and prizes are awarded every season for winning teams, individual scores, and team performance in the Canadiana and stinker rounds. The website is maintained, as well, by a volunteer.

The Inquisition is a loose, self-sustaining organization that has survived on trust, cooperation and commitment.[75]

### The Rules

One team sits out each season and takes care of writing the questions, organizing the schedule, and running the games. A game consists of 10 rounds with 10 questions in each round. Each question is first posed to an individual player: if he or she gives the correct answer, the team gets two points. If the individual player doesn't get the answer, the whole team can discuss the question, and if they get the right answer, the team gets one point. You have 60 seconds to answer, individually or as a group. The next question in the round is posed to a player on the opposite team, and so forth. Except on round 10, one team can't "steal" from another team that misses the answer; there is no penalty for guessing a wrong answer…. The challenge round is always the tenth round and works differently from the others. First of all, there are six categories of questions, with two questions per category. Each player gets to pick the category they want (unless that category is used up). You have 30 seconds to answer (for two points) but if you don't get the answer the question goes to the person opposite you on the other team. He or she then has 20 seconds to answer for one point…. The league final (championship) game has three teams, not two. A wildcard team, the team that scored the greatest number of "question" points gets to play, plus the teams with the best win-loss records in each division (ignoring the wildcard team). There are still ten rounds of questions, but normally each round is divided into triplets with a common theme under a more general theme such as "science" or "geography." There is usually a video round, and sometimes there are more imaginative question formats such as identifying objects or substances, or interpreting a hand gesture.[76]

---

*Books, The Web of Inclusion: A New Architecture for Building Great Organizations, http://www.sallyhelgesen.com/books.cfm?isbn=0385423640, accessed February 21, 2011.

## ■ Symptoms of Structural Deficiency

Top executives periodically evaluate organizational structure to determine whether it is appropriate to changing organizational needs. Many organizations try one organizational structure and then reorganize to another structure in an effort to find the right fit between internal reporting relationships and the needs of the external environment. As a general rule, when organizational structure is out of alignment with organizational needs, one or more of the following **symptoms of structural deficiency** appear.[77]

- *Decision making is delayed or lacking in quality.* Decision makers may be overloaded because the hierarchy funnels too many problems and decisions to them. Delegation to lower levels may be insufficient. Another cause of poor-quality decisions is that information may not reach the correct people. Information linkages in either the vertical or horizontal direction may be inadequate to ensure decision quality.
- *The organization does not respond innovatively to a changing environment.* One reason for lack of innovation is that departments are not coordinated horizontally. The identification of customer needs by the marketing department and the identification of technological developments in the research department must be coordinated. Organizational structure also has to specify departmental responsibilities that include environmental scanning and innovation.
- *Employee performance declines and goals are not being met.* Employee performance may decline because the structure doesn't provide clear goals, responsibilities, and mechanisms for coordination. The structure should reflect the complexity of the market environment and be straightforward enough for employees to effectively work within.
- *Too much conflict is evident.* Organizational structure should allow conflicting departmental goals to combine into a single set of goals for the entire organization. When departments act at cross-purposes or are under pressure to achieve departmental goals at the expense of organizational goals, the structure is often at fault. Horizontal linkage mechanisms are inadequate.

## New Directions

Gareth Morgan of York University is one of the most influential organizational theorists, here and around the world. He argues that "[all] theories of organization and management are based on implicit images or metaphors that lead us to see, understand, and manage organizations in distinctive yet partial ways."[78] Morgan provides eight images or metaphors through which we can understand organizations: organizations as (1) machines, (2) organisms, (3) brains, (4) cultures, (5) political systems, (6) psychic prisons, (7) flux and transformation, and (8) instruments of domination. Exhibit 3.20 provides some detail about each of the images. Morgan argues that managers need to look at organizations through the different images so that they can get a rich and accurate understanding of their organizations to make more informed decisions. He notes that "[the] concept of organization is a product of the mechanical age. Now that we are living in an electronic age, new organizing principles [or images] are necessary."[79]

**EXHIBIT 3.20**
**Morgan's Eight Metaphors**

- *Machines:* Efficiency, waste, maintenance, order, clockwork, cogs in a wheel, programs, inputs and outputs, standardization, production, measurement and control, design
- *Organisms:* Living systems, environmental conditions, adaptation, life cycles, recycling, needs, homeostasis, evolution, survival of the fittest, health, illness
- *Brains:* Learning, parallel information processing, distributed control, mindsets, intelligence, feedback, requisite variety, knowledge, networks
- *Cultures:* Society, values, beliefs, laws, ideology, rituals, diversity, traditions, history, service, shared vision and mission, understanding, qualities, families
- *Political systems:* Interests and rights, power, hidden agendas and back room deals, authority, alliances, party-line, censorship, gatekeepers, leaders, conflict management
- *Psychic prisons:* Conscious and unconscious processes, repression and regression, ego, denial, projection, coping and defence mechanisms, pain and pleasure principle, dysfunction
- *Flux and transformation:* Constant change, dynamic equilibrium, flow, self-organization, systemic wisdom, attractors, chaos, complexity, butterfly effect, emergent properties, dialectics, paradox
- *Instruments of Domination:* Alienation, repression, imposing values, compliance, charisma, maintenance of power, force, exploitation, divide and rule, discrimination, corporate interest

Sources: Yousefi, M.H. (2005) *Organizational Metaphors*, www.mhy-page.com/images/1.pdf, accessed February 21, 2011; and Morgan, G. (2006) *Images of Organization*, Thousand Oaks, CA: Sage Publications.

One new organizing principle is that of the boundaryless organization. The term was apparently coined by Jack Welch, in the late 1980s.[80] He believed that boundaries in organizations prevent organizations from achieving high levels of success as organizations become consumed by turf wars. There are four types of boundaries: the vertical or hierarchical, the horizontal or interunit, the geographic, and the external or interorganizational.[81] Boundaryless organizations learn to permeate their boundaries so that they can be more flexible and responsive to their stakeholders. They are also able to generate good ideas as they are nimble in structure.[82]

## Summary and Interpretation

Organizational structure must accomplish two things for the organization. It must provide a framework of responsibilities, reporting relationships, and groupings, and it must provide mechanisms for linking and coordinating organizational elements into a coherent whole. The structure is reflected on the organization chart. Linking the organization into a coherent whole requires the use of information systems and linkage devices in addition to the organization chart.

It is important to understand the information-processing perspective on structure. Organizational structure can be designed to provide vertical and horizontal information linkages based on the information processing required to meet the organization's overall goal. Managers can choose whether to orient toward a traditional organization designed for efficiency, which emphasizes vertical linkages such as hierarchy, rules and plans, and formal information systems, or toward a contemporary learning organization, which emphasizes horizontal communication and coordination. Vertical linkages are not sufficient for most organizations today. Organizations provide horizontal linkages through cross-functional information systems, direct contact between managers across department lines, temporary task forces, full-time integrators, and teams.

Alternatives for grouping employees and departments into overall structural design include functional grouping, divisional grouping, multifocused grouping, horizontal grouping, and network grouping. The choice among functional, divisional, and horizontal structures determines where coordination and integration will be greatest. With functional and divisional structures, managers also use horizontal linkage mechanisms to complement the vertical dimension and achieve integration of departments and levels into an organizational whole. With a horizontal structure, activities are organized horizontally around core work processes. A virtual network structure extends the concept of horizontal coordination and collaboration beyond the boundaries of the organization. Core activities are performed by a central hub while other functions and activities are outsourced to contract partners. The matrix structure attempts to achieve an equal balance between the vertical and horizontal dimensions of structure. Most organizations do not exist in these pure forms, using instead a hybrid structure that incorporates characteristics of two or more types of structure. Ultimately, managers attempt to find the correct balance between vertical control and horizontal coordination.

Finally, an organization chart is only so many lines and boxes on a piece of paper. The purpose of the organization chart is to encourage and direct employees into activities and communications that enable the organization to achieve its goals. The organization chart provides the structure, but employees provide the behaviour. The chart is a guideline to encourage people to work together, but management must implement the structure and carry it out.

## ■ Key Concepts

## ■ Discussion Questions

1. What is the definition of *organizational structure?* Does organizational structure appear on the organization chart? Explain.
2. How do rules and plans help an organization achieve vertical integration?
3. When is a functional structure preferable to a divisional structure?
4. Why do large corporations tend to use hybrid structures?
5. What are the primary differences between a traditional organization designed for efficiency and a more contemporary organization designed for learning?
6. What is the difference between a task force and a team? Between a liaison role and an integrating role? Which of the four provides the greatest amount of horizontal coordination?
7. What conditions usually have to be present before an organization should adopt a matrix structure?
8. The manager of a consumer products firm said, "We use the brand manager position to train future executives." Do you think the brand manager position is a good training ground? Discuss.
9. Why do companies using a horizontal structure have cultures that emphasize openness, employee empowerment, and responsibility? What do you think a manager's job would be like in a horizontally organized company?
10. How is structure related to the organization's need for efficiency versus its need for learning and innovation? How can managers tell if structure is out of alignment with the organization's needs?
11. Describe the virtual network structure. Why do you think this is becoming a good structural alternative for some of today's organizations?

## ■ Chapter 3 Workbook: You and Organizational Structure*

To better understand the importance of organizational structure in your life, do the following assignment.

Select one of the following organizations to design:

- A copy and printing shop
- A travel agency
- A sports rental (such as snowmobiles) in a resort area
- A bakery

### Background

Organization is a way of gaining some power against an unreliable environment. The environment provides the organization with inputs, which include raw materials, human resources, and financial resources. There is a service or product to produce that involves technology. The output goes to clients, a group that must be nurtured. The complexities of the environment and the technology determine the complexity of the organization.

### Planning Your Organization

1. Write down the mission or purpose of the organization in a few sentences.
2. What are the specific tasks to be completed to accomplish the mission?

3. Based on the specifics in number 2, develop an organization chart. Each position in the chart will perform a specific task or is responsible for a certain outcome.
4. You are into your third year of operation, and your business has been very successful. You want to add a second location a few miles away. What issues will you face running the business at two locations? Draw an organization chart that includes the two business locations.
5. After five years, the business has five locations in two cities. How do you keep in touch with it all? What issues of control and coordination have arisen? Draw an up-to-date organization chart and explain your rationale for it.
6. Twenty years later you have 75 business locations in 5 provinces. What are the issues and problems that must be dealt with through organizational structure? Draw an organization chart for this organization showing how information will flow within the organization.

---

*From DAFT. *Organization Theory and Design*, 10E. © 2010 South-Western, a part of Cengage Learning, Inc. Reproduced by permission. www.cengage.com/permissions

## Case for Analysis: Aquarius Advertising Agency*

The Aquarius Advertising Agency is a middle-sized firm that offered two basic services to its clients: (1) customized plans for the content of an advertising campaign (for example, slogans and layouts) and (2) complete plans for media (such as radio, TV, newspapers, billboards, and Internet). Additional services included aid in marketing and distribution of products and marketing research to test advertising effectiveness.

Its activities were organized in a traditional manner. The organization chart is shown in Exhibit 1. Each department included similar functions.

Each client account was coordinated by an account executive who acted as a liaison between the client and the various specialists on the professional staff of the operations and marketing divisions. The number of direct communications and contacts between clients and Aquarius specialists, clients and account executives, and Aquarius specialists and account executives is indicated in Exhibit 2. These sociometric data were gathered by a consultant who conducted a study of the patterns of formal and informal communication. Each intersecting cell of Aquarius personnel and the clients contains an index of the direct contacts between them.

Although an account executive was designated to be the liaison between the client and specialists within the agency, communications frequently occurred directly between clients and account managers and executives and bypassed the specialists. These direct contacts involved a wide range of interactions, such as meetings, telephone calls, e-mail messages, and so on. A large number of direct communications occurred between agency specialists and their counterparts in the client organization. For example, an art specialist working as one member of a team on a particular client account would be occasionally contacted directly by the client's in-house art specialist, and agency research personnel had direct communication with research people of the client firm. Also, some of the unstructured contacts often led to more formal meetings with clients in which agency personnel made presentations, interpreted and defended agency policy, and committed the agency to certain courses of action.

Both hierarchical and professional systems operated within the departments of the operations and marketing divisions. Each department was organized hierarchically with a director, an assistant director, and several levels of authority. Professional communications were widespread and mainly concerned with sharing knowledge and techniques, technical evaluation of work, and development of professional interests. Control in each department was exercised mainly through control of promotions and supervision of work done by subordinates. Many account executives, however, felt the need for more influence, and one commented:

*Creativity and art. That's all I hear around here. It is hard as hell to effectively manage six or seven hotshots who claim they have to do their own thing. Each of them tries to sell his or her idea to the client, and most of the time I don't know what has happened until a week later. If I were a despot, I would make all of them check with me first to get approval. Things would sure change around here.*

The need for reorganization was made more acute by changes in the environment. Within a short period of time, there was a rapid turnover in the major accounts handled by the agency. It was typical for advertising agencies to gain or lose clients quickly, often with no advance warning, as consumer behaviour and lifestyle changes emerged and product innovations occurred.

An agency reorganization was one solution proposed by top management to increase flexibility in this unpredictable environment. The reorganization would be aimed at reducing the agency's response time to environmental changes and at increasing cooperation and communication among specialists from different departments. The top managers are not sure what type of reorganization is appropriate. They would like your help analyzing their context and current structure and welcome your advice on proposing a new structure.

### Assignment Questions

1. Analyze Aquarius in terms of the five contextual variables. How would you describe the environment, goals, culture, size, and technology for Aquarius?
2. Design a new organization structure that takes into consideration the contextual variables in the case and the information flows.
3. Would a matrix structure be feasible for Aquarius? Why or why not?

---

*Adapted from John F. Veiga and John N. Yanouzas, Aquarius Advertising Agency, *The Dynamics of Organization Theory* (St. Paul, Minn.: West, 1984), 212–217, with permission.

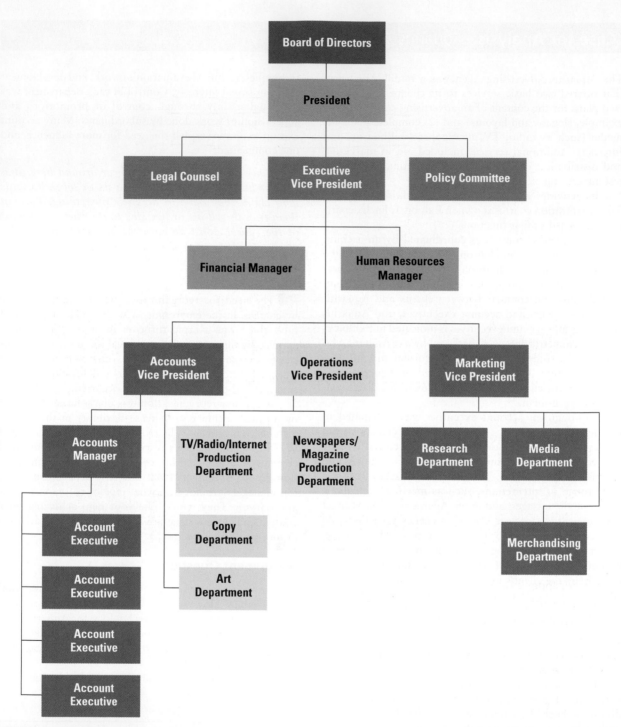

**EXHIBIT 1**
Aquarius Advertising Agency Organization Chart

Adapted from John F. Veiga and John N. Yanouzas, Aquarius Advertising Agency, *The Dynamics of Organization Theory* (St. Paul, Minn.: West, 1984), 212–217, with permission.

| | Clients | Account Manager | Account Executives | TV/Radio Specialists | Newspaper/Magazine Specialists | Copy Specialists | Art Specialists | Merchandising Specialists | Media Specialists | Research Specialists |
|---|---|---|---|---|---|---|---|---|---|---|
| **Clients** | X | F | F | N | N | O | O | O | O | O |
| **Account Manager** | | X | F | N | N | N | N | N | N | N |
| **Account Executives** | | | X | F | F | F | F | F | F | F |
| **TV/Radio Specialists** | | | | X | N | O | O | N | N | O |
| **Newspaper/Magazine Specialists** | | | | | X | O | O | N | O | O |
| **Copy Specialists** | | | | | | X | N | O | O | O |
| **Art Specialists** | | | | | | | X | O | O | O |
| **Merchandising Specialists** | | | | | | | | X | F | F |
| **Media Specialists** | | | | | | | | | X | F |
| **Research Specialists** | | | | | | | | | | X |

**EXHIBIT 2**
**Sociometric Index of Aquarius Personnel and Clients**

F = Frequent—daily

O = Occasional—once or twice per project

N = None

Adapted from John F. Veiga and John N. Yanouzas, Aquarius Advertising Agency, *The Dynamics of Organization Theory* (St. Paul, Minn.: West, 1984), 212–217, with permission.

## Case for Analysis: Eva's Phoenix Print Shop*

*I just wanted to keep you posted that I'm still with Astley-Gilbert and I'm no longer a receiver but now I'm working in the Offset Bindery Department as a helper. I'm learning how to use the folder machine and the stitcher as well. I get a lot of overtime plus my situation in life seems to be getting a little better. I want to thank you for all your help, I couldn't have done it without your support. (2006 graduate)*

### Introduction

Described in 2007 by *Print Action Magazine* as "Canada's leading social program with printing ties," Toronto's Eva's Phoenix Print Shop is a socially and environmentally responsible commercial printer that helps homeless and at-risk youth achieve self-sufficiency. The enterprise is an initiative of Eva's Initiatives, an award-winning charity for homeless youth.

Operating since 2002, it is the only print based social enterprise working with youth in Toronto, and virtually the only location where one can gain significant mechanical skills training in print. The Print Shop is guided by an Advisory Board comprised of senior corporate and graphic industry professionals as well as three youth graduates, each of whom works in graphics.

### Organization Design

Critical to the enterprise's success is "careful integration": both between social and commercial elements of the enterprise, and between the enterprise and the Eva's Phoenix housing and employment facility. The current extent to which the social and commercial elements are integrated within the enterprise itself delivers useful synergy. Examples include effective use of shared physical plant, as well as cross-fertilization of staff skills and knowledge. In terms of integration with the "host" Eva's Phoenix, there are positives, but a further degree of separation will be beneficial for both elements. The plan to shift the print shop to an adjacent site would preserve the benefit of, for example, immediate access for Eva's Phoenix youth, and create greater commercial workflow efficiency with larger and dedicated space. Expansion will require a review of what legal structure best suits the enterprise's long-term objectives in relation to those of its parent, Eva's Initiatives. See Exhibit 3.1 for the organization chart.

### Social Operations

The print training department of Eva's Phoenix Print Shop is called Foundations of Print. Every quarter up to eight youth receive hands-on print training. They are not paid, but receive supports such as a transit pass, access to housing at Eva's Phoenix, math tutoring, and honoraria for completed assignments and good attendance. Youth who complete training are supported to apply for full-time work in the graphics industry.

Foundations of Print currently costs approximately $190,000 per year, and is paid for by the United Way's Toronto Enterprise Fund as well as corporate, foundation, and individual contributions.

### Commercial Operations
### Print Services:

- Design, offset/digital print, finishing (cut, fold, stitch, collate, shrink-wrap, drill)
- MAC and PC: Quark, Photoshop, Illustrator, InDesign
- Customers include PricewaterhouseCoopers LLP, TD Bank, Toronto Hydro, Scotia Capital, United Way, Salvation Army, Bombardier.

Current operating costs are approximately $180,000. The 2007 objective is to sell approximately $300,000 of print for a gross profit of $120,000 and a net loss of $55,000. The goal is to break even in fiscal 2009, with a stretch goal of 2008. Longer term (three to five years) the Print Shop wants the commercial department to generate a profit to help pay for Foundations of Print. As the business grows, the Print Shop also envisions hiring some graduates to join the team on a permanent basis.

### Pivotal Point in Enterprise Development

The enterprise started in 2002. At that time funding came from several sources, including the Rotary Club, the United Way, a corporate donor, and the federal government. The federal government contract required that youth be paid for on-the-job training. At any given time, four to six youth with little or no graphics experience were working on live customer jobs and training at the same time. Despite frequent contract changes and disruptions, the enterprise achieved strong social results, but the business achieved little growth and suffered with ongoing quality control issues. The business challenges were exacerbated by not having the "right people on the bus."

A 2005 strategic review, led by an MBA research intern, led to pivotal change. First, the enterprise withdrew from participation in the federal government contract, electing to increase revenues from corporate, foundation, and individual sources. This decision allowed the leadership team to draw on four years of experience and implement changes that would benefit both the social and business bottom lines. The new structure required a clearer separation between training and production, without losing the synergy created by their interaction.

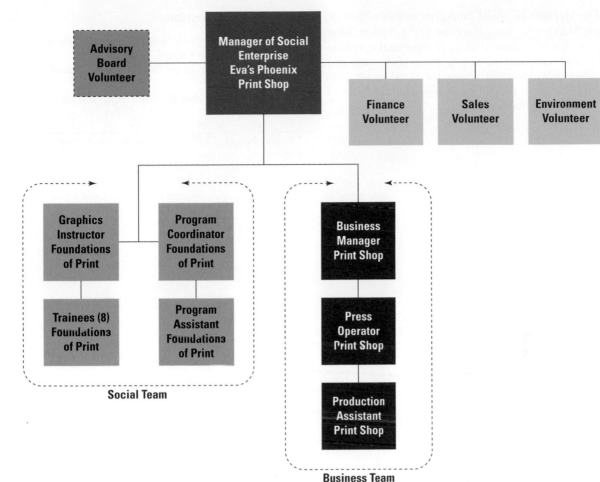

**EXHIBIT 1**
Eva's Phoenix Print Shop
A. Macdonald (2007) Eva's Phoenix Print Shop. Used with Permission.

The key move was a redefinition of roles, which, fortuitously, led to the right people joining the bus, and in the right seats!

Under the government regulated structure concurrent teaching and production created ongoing conflicting priorities. Learning at such a beginner level is better with a dedicated instructor because youth build a foundation of knowledge in a logical sequence. On the business side, having an experienced business manager and press operator led to immediate improvements in quality and productivity. Overall shop infrastructure was used more effectively—stretching use over a 12-hour, rather than an 8-hour, time frame. In one year the enterprise doubled the number of youth participants and increased sales by 250 percent.

The Print Shop is a 2007 Toronto Community Foundation Vital Ideas Award Winner, recognizing "leading edge programs that combine experience, expertise and ingenuity to create practical solutions that strengthen Toronto's vital signs." In addition, it was selected by Vancouver's Vancity Foundation as one of eight Canadian social enterprises to contribute to an 18-month initiative to develop common tools for Demonstrating Value.

Through its Vital Ideas Award, the Print Shop is working with Resiliency Canada to implement a "strength-based model." This model, instead of focusing on the negative risks and barriers associated with the homeless youth, directly involves youth in identifying both strengths and challenges, and tracking their progress over time with our support. Elements of this tracking model are comprised of youth intake assessment, service plan development, evaluation protocol, and database system. From an organizational point of view this model will ensure consistency in data evaluation and articulation of long-term outcomes.

The Manager of Social Enterprise at Eva's Phoenix, Andrew Macdonald, was chosen by *Print Action Magazine* as one of Canada's 50 most influential people in graphic communications, noting that: "Eva's Phoenix Print Shop provides opportunities for at-risk youth with much needed press and pre-press skills for the heart of Canada's printing community."

## Assignment Questions

1. How does the Print Shop integrate the social and the economic in its design?
2. What are some of the innovative features of the Print Shop?
3. Do you think that the Print Shop should expand? If so, how?

---

*A. Macdonald (2007) Eva's Phoenix Print Shop. Used with Permission.

# Open-System Design Elements

# The External Environment

Art Directors & TRIP / Alamy

## Nokia

Nokia (see photo) became the world's leading maker of cell phone handsets in 1998, and the giant Finnish company looked poised to run rivals out of the handset business for good. But by 2004, products that didn't match consumer needs and strained relationships with major customers had cost Nokia nearly a fifth of its 35 percent global market share. Revenue growth shifted into reverse and the stock took a nosedive.

What went wrong? For one thing, Nokia missed the hottest growth sector in cell phones, the market for mid-range models with cameras and high-resolution colour screens. Nokia's leaders chose instead to pump hundreds of millions of dollars into the development of "smart-phones" that allow consumers to get on the Internet, play video games, listen to music, and watch movies or television shows. The problem was, the new phones proved too bulky and expensive for many consumers, who began turning instead to cheaper, stylish models from Motorola, Samsung, and Siemens. The clamshell design, in particular, which allowed users to fold the phone in half when it wasn't in use, fuelled a new cell phone boom in Europe and North America. Nokia had stuck to the "candy bar" handset and was caught without a competitor in the battle. Nokia also neglected some of its biggest customers. Mobile operators such as Orange SA, France Telecom SA's wireless unit, pushed for customized phones with special features that their customers wanted, but Nokia was slow to respond.

These missteps allowed rivals to gobble up market share. To get Nokia back on track, leaders cranked up the introduction of new mid-range phones, slashed costs on low-end models for developing countries, and promised mobile operators to tailor phones to their specifications. Nokia also continues to invest heavily in gadgets that feature advanced software. The key question is: Will customers want the gadgets Nokia is developing?[1] In 2011, Nokia and Microsoft entered a strategic alliance to take on Apple and Google in the smartphone market. One analyst notes that "[this] is a very frank admission that Nokia's platform strategy has failed and underlines the seriousness of Nokia's position...."[2] Nokia sees 2011 and 2012 as transition years and has brought in a non-Finn Microsoft executive to execute the new strategy.

Nokia is experiencing its strongest sales in China due to a growing demand for less expensive phones in rural areas. It remains to be seen if the company's new, technologically advanced products will catch on in the marketplace. Nokia sales and profits were stagnant while those of rival Samsung Electronics of Korea are booming.[3] Nokia became profitable in 2012 after 18-months of large losses. Even so, one analyst noted that, "[the] fourth quarter 2012 was the bottom line for Nokia...Significant results need to be delivered this year starting right from the first quarter. From 2013 Nokia has only two options: either significantly grow sales or change its strategy, radically."[4] Nokia is selling its handset division to Microsoft even as the division's sales continue to drop. And, "[the] sale of the phone business is a big change for the Finnish company, which once dominated the global smartphone market."[5]

---

Many companies, like Nokia, face tremendous uncertainty in dealing with the external environment. The only way a high-tech company like Nokia can continue to grow is through innovation, yet unless the company makes products that people want to buy, the huge investments in research and development will not pay off.

Similarly, whatever happened to MySpace? Well, it is still around, but maybe not for long. At one time, MySpace ruled social networking. Then Facebook came along. After several attempts to revitalize the once-dominant company, including management layoffs and a shift in strategic direction, MySpace is no longer even considered a competitor. In January 2011, the company laid off about half of its 1,000 or so employees. Users had declined to fewer than 55 million, whereas Facebook was reporting more than 600 million. Yet Facebook has provided opportunities for other companies too. Zoosk, a fast-growing online dating service, owes its existence to Facebook. The company originally launched as an application on Facebook and experienced rapid user growth.

Changes in the environment, such as the appearance of a new business model such as Facebook, can create both threats and opportunities for organizations. "Facebook is both a great competitor and a benefactor here in Silicon Valley," said one venture capitalist. "Anyone who's trying to get the attention of the young Internet user now has to compete with [Facebook's] dominant position.... On the other hand, they have opened up a lot of opportunities." With its wide reach, powerful influence, and growing ambitions, Facebook is considered both a friend and a foe to most technology companies, including Yahoo, eBay, Google, and Microsoft. But the environment is always changing. As one executive put it when talking about MySpace's decline: "There's a lot of people who wonder if the same thing will happen to Facebook."[6] In 2013, Facebook lost one-third of its American teen users; however, the number of its Instagram users has increased.[7] Even so, some alarmists worry that Facebook may lose 80 percent of its users by 2017.[8]

All organizations—not just Internet companies such as Facebook, Zoosk, and Google, but traditional firms like Toyota, Goldman Sachs, General Electric, and Hudson Bay Company—face tremendous uncertainty in dealing with events in the external environment and often have to adapt quickly to new competition, economic turmoil, changes in consumer interests, or innovative technologies.

Take a few minutes now to see what sort of environment your mind-set best fits by completing the You and Design feature.

# YOU & DESIGN

## Mind and Environment

Does your mind best fit an organization in a certain or an uncertain environment? Think back to how you thought or behaved as a student, employee, or formal or informal leader. Please answer whether each item was Mostly True or Mostly False for you.

|  | Mostly True | Mostly False |
|---|---|---|
| 1. I always offered comments on my interpretation of data or issues. | _____ | _____ |
| 2. I welcomed unusual viewpoints of others even if we were working under pressure. | _____ | _____ |
| 3. I made it a point to attend industry trade shows and company/school events. | _____ | _____ |
| 4. I explicitly encouraged others to express opposing ideas and arguments. | _____ | _____ |
| 5. I asked "dumb" questions. | _____ | _____ |
| 6. I enjoyed hearing about new ideas even when working toward a deadline. | _____ | _____ |
| 7. I expressed a controversial opinion to bosses and peers. | _____ | _____ |
| 8. I suggested ways of improving my and others' ways of doing things. | _____ | _____ |

*(Continued)*

Some companies are surprised by shifts in the environment and are unable to quickly adapt to new competition, changing consumer interests, or innovative technologies. Music World and Sam the Record Man went out of business in the wake of Apple's iPod and other new channels that allow music lovers to download just what they want. Traditional music retailers are surviving only by diversifying into new areas or forming partnerships to create their own downloading services. Similarly, in the airline industry, major carriers that used the traditional hub-and-spoke system, invented by American Airlines, were pummelled by smaller, nimbler competitors such as Ryanair and Southwest Airlines, which can prosper in today's difficult environment by keeping operations costs ultra-low.[9]

The external environment, referred to throughout this chapter as "the environment," including international competition and events, is the source of turbulence, uncertainty, and major threats confronting today's organizations. The environment often imposes significant constraints on the choices that managers make for an organization.

## ■ Purpose of This Chapter

The purpose of this chapter is to develop a framework for assessing environments and how organizations respond to them. First, we will identify the environmental domain and the sectors that influence the organization. Then, we will explore two major environmental forces on the organization—the need for information and the need for resources. Organizations respond to these forces through structural design, planning systems, and attempts to change and control elements in the environment.

## The Environmental Domain

In a broad sense the environment is infinite and includes everything outside the organization. However, the analysis presented here considers only those aspects of the environment to which the organization is sensitive and must respond to survive. Thus, **organizational environment** is defined as all elements that exist outside the boundary of the organization that have the potential to affect all or part of the organization.

The concept of environment in the discipline of organizational theory and design looks at the **green environment** only indirectly. In a thought-provoking article, Paul Shrivastava argues that organization studies uses "denatured, narrow and parochial concepts of organizational environment" and goes on to argue that "[at] the present time, when environmental crises proliferate around the world, nature-centred organizational theories are particularly important."[10] This is particularly important as it is organizations, and their managers, that are responsible for much of the damage to the natural environment. In recognition of the environmental costs of its work, the National Hockey League Players Association (NHLPA) and the David Suzuki Foundation in late 2007 created a partnership that includes the NHLPA Carbon Neutral Challenge and a program promoting action on climate change and environmental responsibility. "…NHLPA members are doing their part to reduce global warming through the NHLPA Carbon Neutral Challenge. This initiative, researched and designed specifically for the players by the David Suzuki Foundation, involves individual NHL players purchasing carbon credits to offset the carbon footprint produced by their extensive travel schedule. Over 500 players have already taken the challenge, with hundreds more expected to jump aboard…."[11]

The environment of an organization can be understood by analyzing its domain within external sectors. An organization's **domain** is the chosen field of action. It is the territory an organization stakes out for itself for its products, services, and markets served. Domain defines the organization's niche and defines those external sectors with which the organization will interact to accomplish its goals.

The environment comprises several **sectors** or subdivisions of the external environment that contain similar elements. Ten sectors can be analyzed for each organization: industry, raw materials, human resources, financial resources, market, technology, economic conditions, government, sociocultural, and international. The sectors and a hypothetical organizational domain are illustrated in Exhibit 4.1; the sectors can be further subdivided into the task environment and general environment.

## ■ Task Environment

The **task environment** includes sectors with which the organization interacts directly and that have a direct impact on the organization's ability to achieve its goals. The task environment typically includes the industry, raw materials, and market sectors, and perhaps the human resources and international sectors.

The following examples illustrate how each of these sectors can affect organizations:

- In the *industry* sector, Netflix has been a disruptive force in the home entertainment industry since it began in 1997. First, it virtually wiped out the retail video rental business. The biggest player in video rentals, Blockbuster, went bankrupt in the fall of 2010. Now Netflix is becoming a major competitive threat to television and movie providers, offering unlimited movies and television shows streamed to viewers' computers or other devices for a low monthly fee. Cable television long controlled home entertainment, but subscriptions fell for the first time in the cable companies' history in late 2010.[12] Netflix has moved successfully into producing its own content such as *House of Cards* and *Orange Is the New Black*. Its success is based, in part, on using Big Data. NetFlix has access to "… 30 million 'plays' a day, including when you pause, rewind and

*act!*

**Apply**

How can you—should you—apply the movement to developing green organizations in your career planning?

**EXHIBIT 4.1**
An Organization's
Environment

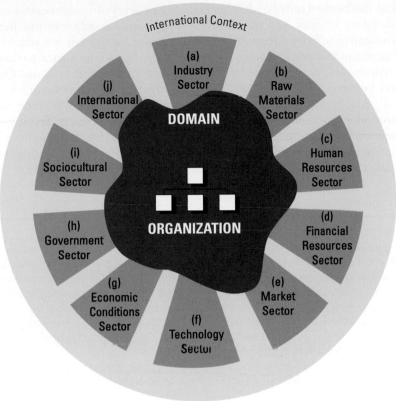

fast forward, four million ratings by Netflix subscribers, three million searches as well as the time of day when shows are watched and on what devices."[13]

- An interesting example in the *raw materials sector* concerns the beverage can industry. Steelmakers owned the beverage can market until the mid-1960s, when Reynolds Aluminum Company launched a huge recycling program to gain a cheaper source of raw materials and make aluminum cans price competitive with steel.[14]

- In the *market sector*, smart companies are paying close attention to the "Generation C" consumer. Generation C refers to people born after 1990, who will make up about 40 percent of the population in the United States, Europe, Brazil, Russia, India, and China by 2020, and about 10 percent of the rest of the world. For this generation, the world has always been defined by the Internet, mobile devices, social networking, and continuous connectivity. This huge cohort of consumers wants a different approach to products and services than do their parents and grandparents.[15] See the next In Practice for the impact of rapidly changing food tastes on Kraft Foods.

- The *human resources sector* is of significant concern to every organization. Research shows that while secondary and postsecondary systems of education are producing graduates with good literacy and numeracy skills, there remains a gap between the demand for workers with strong literacy and numeracy skills and the supply of Canadians who possess them. "Many of Canada's competitors have recognized the need to increase the level and equitable distribution of adult literacy and numeracy skills. The United Kingdom, Sweden, Ireland,

and the Netherlands have all increased their level of investment in adult skills, including literacy and numeracy."[16] However, Canada has not increased its investment in talent development and training for the last ten years.[17]

- For many companies today, the *international sector* is also a part of the task environment because of globalization and intense competition. Outsourcing has become a hot-button issue, with companies in industries from toy manufacturing to information technology sending work to lower-wage countries to become more competitive. Biotechnology and life sciences firms once seemed immune to the trend, but that too is changing. Large drug manufacturers are facing pressures as smaller firms gain cost advantages by outsourcing to companies such as WuXi Pharmatech in Shanghai or Biocon in India.[18]

**In Practice**

**Kraft Foods (Kraft)**

Keeping up with consumers' rapidly changing tastes is a real headache for big food companies such as Kraft and Nestlé SA. A few years ago, Kraft was at the top of the food chain, with a portfolio of brands including Philadelphia, Jell-O, Oreo, and Ritz. But growing consumer concerns over obesity and food-related health issues have taken a huge toll on Kraft's earnings. In response, the company looked for growth primarily by expanding its organic and gourmet product offerings rather than pushing macaroni and cheese or cookies and crackers. In addition, Kraft's CEO, Irene Rosenfeld, developed a three-year strategy in 2010 that focused on "[delighting] global snacks consumers. It's a growing category around the world. It's got very attractive margins."[19] In 2011, Rosenfeld announced that Kraft was splitting into two separate publicly traded companies. This restructuring occurred soon after Kraft's much criticized acquisition of Cadbury. While both revenue and net income increased,

> it became quickly evident that Kraft was having issues with its identity. It had abruptly become the world's largest snack company, but at its heart Kraft was still in the groceries business. It now had a pair of enormous, yet distinct, product portfolios. The company had wandered too far away from its core business and consumers.[20]

It is still too early to see whether the split will make Kraft more successful in meeting its customers' changing tastes.

## ■ General Environment

The **general environment** includes those sectors that might not have a direct impact on the daily operations of a firm but will indirectly influence it. The general environment often includes the government; sociocultural, technology, and financial resources sectors; and the economy. These sectors affect all organizations eventually. Consider the following examples:

- In the *government sector*, European Union (EU) environmental and consumer protection legislation could cause challenges for some North American firms. For example, one rule requires chemical makers that do business in EU countries to run safety and environmental impact tests on more than 30,000 chemicals, a process that could cost these companies more than $7 billion. Other regulations require companies to pick up the tab for recycling the products they sell in the EU.[21]
- Shifting demographics is a significant element in the *sociocultural sector*. A 2011 study by Statistics Canada found that foreign-born people make up almost 21 percent of Canada's population. As the birth rate declines, immigration

**EXHIBIT 4.2**
Technology Changes Quickly!

is expected to be the primary source of labour. Almost one in five is a visible minority and in nine municipalities in Canada, the visible minorities are the majority.[22] ProMation Engineering, located in Mississauga, Ontario, produces robotics for the automotive industry, and has 77 employees who speak a total of 27 languages![23]

- The *technology sector* is an area in which massive changes have occurred in recent years, from digital music and video recorders to advances in cloning technology and stem-cell research. Exhibit 4.2 highlights the speed of technological change today! One technology having a tremendous impact on organizations is online software that allows people to easily create and maintain blogs. One estimate is that, in early 2005, 23,000 new blogs were being created each day, with everyday people widely publishing information on everything from bad customer service to poor product performance.[24] By early 2006, there were 100 million blogs around the world, and they continue to proliferate.[25] In 2010, there were about 152 million blogs, and 25 billion tweets were sent and the numbers continue to increase.[26]

- All organizations have to be concerned with *financial resources*, but this sector is often foremost in the minds of entrepreneurs starting a new business. Ken Vaughan started a gas-mask business to take advantage of a boom in the asbestos-removal business. When the boom ended, it looked like Neoterik Health Technologies would end too. But after the terrorist attacks of September 11, 2001, Vaughan attracted the attention of venture capitalists, who were eager to invest financial resources in a company that could profit from concerns over U.S. security.[27]

- General *economic conditions* often affect the way a company does business. Germany's two most celebrated daily newspapers, the *Frankfurter Allgemeine Zeitung* and the *Süddeutsche Zeitung*, expanded pell-mell during the economic boom of the late 1990s. When the economy crashed, both papers found themselves in dire financial circumstances and have had to cut jobs, close regional offices, scrap special sections, and cut out customized inserts.[28] The economic meltdown of 2008–2009 had far-reaching impacts on economies, companies, and consumers around the world. Lehman Brothers went bankrupt, Bear Stearns and Merrill Lynch were taken over by commercial banks, Iceland went bankrupt, to name only a few casualties. The crisis had its origin in the "biggest housing and credit bubble in history."[29] While Canada was not affected as badly as the United States and other countries, its automotive sector, for example, suffered during the economic meltdown.[30]

## ■ International Context

The international sector can directly affect many organizations, and it has become extremely important in the last few years. In addition, all domestic sectors can be affected by international events. Despite the significance of international events for today's organizations, many of us fail to appreciate the importance of international events and still think domestically. Think again. Even if you stay in your hometown, your company may be purchased tomorrow by the English, Americans, Japanese, or Germans. The Japanese alone own thousands of North American companies, including steel mills, rubber and tire factories, automobile assembly plants, and auto parts suppliers.[31] For example, Sleeman Breweries, Canada's third-largest beer producer, was taken over by Japan's Sapporo Breweries in 2006.[32]

The distinctions between foreign and domestic operations have become increasingly irrelevant. For example, in the auto industry, Ford owns Sweden's Volvo, while Chrysler, still considered one of America's Big Three automakers, was owned by Germany's DaimlerChrysler and is now partners with Italy's Fiat. Toyota is a Japanese company but it has built more than ten million vehicles in North American factories. In addition, Canadian organizations are involved in thousands of partnerships and alliances with firms all around the world. For example, Sea Breeze Power Corporation, headquartered in Vancouver, is a member of the Methane to Markets Partnership, which is "an international initiative that advances cost-effective, near-term methane recovery and use as a clean energy source. The goal of the Partnership is to reduce global methane emissions in order to enhance economic growth, strengthen energy security, improve air quality, improve industrial safety, and reduce emissions of greenhouse gases."[33] These increasing global interconnections have both positive and negative implications for organizations. Because of the significance of the international sector and its tremendous impact on organizational design, this topic will be covered in detail in Chapter 6.

The growing importance of the international sector means that the environment for all organizations is becoming extremely complex and extremely competitive. However, every organization faces uncertainty domestically as well as globally. Consider how changing elements in the various environmental sectors have created uncertainty for advertising agencies such as Ogilvy & Mather.

*act!*

**Compare**

Conduct research to compare the characteristics of Sleeman Breweries before and after it was sold to Sapporo Breweries. Are there any significant differences?

## In Practice

**Ogilvy & Mather**

On November 9, 2007, Ogilvy & Mather received the Grand Prix at the Cassies Awards for its work on Dove's campaign for the Dove Self-Esteem Fund. According to Nancy Vonk, co-chief creative officer, "[It's] been the best year ever in many, many ways … [We] really turned a corner from the traditional ad agency perch … to approaching the task in a much more holistic way and in a media-neutral way."[34]

However, it was not too long ago that Ogilvy & Mather, one of the most respected advertising agencies on Madison Avenue and beyond, was reduced to competing for business in a live online auction. The agency won the account, but that eased the pain only slightly. The world has changed dramatically since Ogilvy & Mather's founders made deals with corporate CEOs over golf games and could reach 90 percent of the North American public with a prime-time commercial on network television. Today, agency executives frequently have to dicker with people from their clients' procurement department, who are used to beating down suppliers on the price of cardboard boxes or paper bags. Clients want to get the best deal, and they want to see a whole lot more than a couple of television spots.

The economic decline that followed the crash of the dot-coms and the September 11, 2001 attacks in the United States led to the worst advertising recession in more than half a century. (The 2008–2009 recession had the same effect.) Marketing budgets were often the first to be cut, and worldwide ad spending declined 7 percent in 2001. The agencies laid off 40,000 employees, nearly 20 percent of their workforce. The weak economic climate also led to a major change in how corporations pay for advertising. Up until that time, most clients paid their agencies a 15 percent commission on media purchases rather than paying them directly for their work. Today, though, many companies have cut out commissions altogether. Corporate procurement departments are demanding that the agencies clearly spell out their labour costs and how they are billing the client. The agencies are having a hard time making the shift.

And that's not even the biggest problem for ad agencies. Traditionally, agencies have relied on television and print media, but that's just not working anymore. The Internet, video on demand, smartphones, and video games are taking up a larger and larger percentage of people's time. Corporations are clamouring for more innovative low-key approaches, such as product placements in video games or products integrated into television shows and music events, as well as lower-cost options such as direct mail and Internet advertising. Yet the agencies have been slow to adapt, still clinging to the notion that making good half-million-dollar 30-second television commercials will pay off.

The combination of weak economic conditions, media fragmentation, new technologies, and changing habits has the advertising industry reeling. Although many of these developments had been predicted for some time, the big agencies were caught unaware when they actually came to pass. As Ogilvy & Mather's CEO, Shelly Lazarus, says of the past, "These have not been the best years."[35] In 2008, Lazarus stepped down as Chair-Global CEO and was replaced by Miles Young. However, she maintained her role as Chair of Ogilvy Group until 2012 and continues to be one of the most powerful women in business in North America.[36]

---

Advertising agencies aren't the only organizations having difficulty adapting to massive shifts in the environment. In the following sections, we will discuss in greater detail how organizations can cope with and respond to increasing environmental uncertainty and instability.

## Environmental Uncertainty

How does the environment influence an organization? The patterns and events occurring in the environment can be described along several dimensions, such as whether the environment is stable or unstable, homogeneous or heterogeneous, simple or complex; the *munificence*, or amount of resources available to support the organization's growth; whether those resources are concentrated or dispersed; and the degree of consensus in the environment regarding the organization's intended domain.[37] These dimensions boil down to two essential ways the environment influences organizations: (1) the need for information about the environment and (2) the need for resources from the environment. The environmental conditions of complexity and change create a greater need to gather information and to respond based on that information. The organization is also concerned with scarce material and financial resources, and with the need to ensure availability of resources.

Environmental **uncertainty** applies primarily to those sectors that an organization deals with on a regular, day-to-day basis. Recall the earlier discussion of the general environment and the task environment. Although sectors of the general environment—such as economic conditions, social trends, or technological changes—can create uncertainty for organizations, determining an organization's environmental uncertainty generally means focusing on sectors of the *task environment*, such as how many elements the organization deals with regularly, how rapidly these elements change, and so forth. To assess uncertainty, each sector of the organization's task environment can be analyzed along dimensions such as stability or instability and degree of complexity.[38] The total amount of uncertainty felt by an organization is the uncertainty accumulated across environmental sectors.

Organizations must cope with and manage uncertainty to be effective. Uncertainty means that decision makers do not have sufficient information about environmental factors, and they have a difficult time predicting external changes. Uncertainty increases the risk of failure for organizational responses and makes it difficult to compute costs and probabilities associated with decision alternatives.[39] The remainder of this section will focus on the information perspective, which is concerned with uncertainty created by the extent to which the environment is simple or complex and the extent to which events are stable or unstable. Later in the chapter, we discuss how organizations control the environment to acquire needed resources.

*act!*

**Think**

Think about what it means, in practical terms, to cope with uncertainty.

## Simple–Complex Dimension

The **simple–complex dimension** concerns environmental complexity, which refers to heterogeneity, or the number and dissimilarity of external elements relevant to an organization's operations. The more external factors that regularly influence the organization and the greater number of other organizations in an organization's domain, the greater the complexity. A complex environment is one in which the organization interacts with and is influenced by numerous diverse and different external elements. In a simple environment, the organization interacts with and is influenced by only a few similar external elements.

Aerospace firms such as Boeing Company and Europe's Airbus operate in a complex environment, as do universities. Universities span a large number of technologies and are continually buffeted by social, cultural, and value changes. Universities must also cope with ever-changing government regulations, competition for quality students and highly educated employees, and scarce financial resources for many programs. They deal with granting agencies, professional and scientific associations, alumni, parents, foundations, legislators, community residents, international agencies, donors, corporations, and athletic teams. This large number of external elements makes up the organization's domain, creating a complex environment. On the other hand, a family-owned hardware store operating in the suburbs competes in a simple environment. The store does not have to deal with complex technologies or extensive government regulations, and cultural and social changes have little impact. Human resources are not a problem because the store is run by family members and part-time help. The only external elements of real importance are a few competitors, suppliers, and customers.

## Stable–Unstable Dimension

The **stable–unstable dimension** refers to whether elements in the environment are dynamic. An environmental domain is stable if it remains the same over a period of months or years, or experiences readily predictable change. Under unstable conditions, environmental elements shift abruptly and unexpectedly. Environmental

## Book Mark 4.0 HAVE YOU READ THIS BOOK?

### Confronting Reality: Doing What Matters to Get Things Right*
By Lawrence A. Bossidy and Ram Charan

The business world has changed in recent years and will continue to change at an increasingly rapid pace. That's the reality that spurred Larry Bossidy, retired chairman and CEO of Honeywell International, and Ram Charan, a noted author, speaker, and business consultant, to write *Confronting Reality: Doing What Matters to Get Things Right*. Too many managers, they believe, are tempted to hide their heads in the sand of financial issues rather than face the confusion and complexity of the organization's environment.

#### LESSONS FOR FACING REALITY
For many companies, today's environment is characterized by global hyper-competition, declining prices, and the growing power of consumers. Bossidy and Charan offer some lessons to leaders for navigating a fast-changing world.

- *Understand the environment as it is now and is likely to be in the future, rather than as it was in the past.* Relying on the past and conventional wisdom can lead to disaster. Kmart, for example, stuck to its old formula as Walmart gobbled its customers and carved out a new business model.
- *Seek out and welcome diverse and unorthodox ideas.* Managers need to be proactive and open towards conversing with employees, suppliers, customers, colleagues, and anyone else they come in contact with. What are people thinking about? What changes and opportunities do they see? What worries them about the future?
- *Avoid the common causes of manager failure to confront reality: filtered information, selective hearing, wishful thinking, fear, emotional overinvestment in a failing course of action, and unrealistic expectations.* For example, when sales and profits fell off a cliff at

data-storage giant EMC Corporation in early 2001, managers displayed a bias toward hearing good news and believed the company was experiencing only a blip in the growth curve. When Joe Tucci was named CEO, however, he was determined to find out if the slump was temporary. By talking directly with top leaders at his customers' organizations, Tucci was able to face the reality that EMC's existing business model based on high-cost technology was dead. Tucci implemented a new business model to fit that reality.

- *Ruthlessly assess your organization.* Understanding the internal environment is just as important. Managers need to evaluate whether their company has the talent, commitment, and attitude needed to drive the important changes. At EMC, Tucci realized his sales force needed an attitude shift to sell software, services, and business solutions rather than just expensive hardware. The arrogant, hard-driving sales tactics of the past had to be replaced with a softer, more customer-oriented approach.

#### STAYING ALIVE
Staying alive in today's business environment requires that managers stay alert. Managers should always be looking at their competitors, broad industry trends, technological changes, shifting government policies, changing market forces, and economic developments. At the same time, they should work hard to stay in touch with what their customers really think and really want. By doing so, leaders can confront reality and be poised for change.

*Confronting Reality: Doing What Matters to Get Things Right*, by Lawrence A. Bossidy and Ram Charan (2004), Crown Business Publishing.

domains seem to be increasingly unstable for most organizations. This chapter's Book Mark examines the volatile nature of today's business world and gives some tips for managing in a fast-shifting environment.

Instability may occur when competitors react with aggressive moves and countermoves regarding advertising and new products, as happened with Nokia, described in the chapter opening. Sometimes specific, unpredictable events—such as Janet Jackson's so-called wardrobe malfunction at the 2004 Super Bowl half-time show, accounts of anthrax-laced letters being sent through the mail, the SARS crisis, or the discovery of heart problems related to pain drugs such as Vioxx and

Celebrex—create unstable conditions. Today, "hate sites" on the Internet, such as *Ihatemcdonalds.com and Walmartsucks.com*, are an important source of instability for scores of companies. In addition, freewheeling bloggers can destroy a company's reputation virtually overnight. Kryptonite's reputation in bicycle locks plummeted after a blog posted that the locks could be opened with a Bic pen. Within ten days, Kryptonite announced a free product exchange that would cost it about $10 million.[40]

Although environments are more unstable for most organizations today, an example of a traditionally stable environment is a public utility.[41] A gradual increase in demand may occur, which is easily predicted over time. Toy companies, by contrast, have an unstable environment. Hot new toys are difficult to predict, a problem compounded by the fact that children are losing interest in toys at a younger age, their interest captured by video games, cable TV, and the Internet. Adding to the instability for toy makers such as Mattel and Hasbro is the shrinking retail market, with big toy retailers going out of business trying to compete with discounters such as Walmart. Toy manufacturers often find their biggest products languishing on shelves as shoppers turn to less-expensive knock-offs produced for Walmart by low-cost manufacturers in China.[42] Besides, the major toy makers have had to make massive recalls because of concerns about the lead content of many of the toys made in China.[43]

## ◼ Framework

The simple–complex and stable–unstable dimensions are combined into a framework for assessing environmental uncertainty in Exhibit 4.3. In the *simple, stable* environment, uncertainty is low. There are only a few external elements to contend with, and they tend to remain stable. The *complex, stable* environment represents somewhat greater uncertainty. A large number of elements have to be scanned, analyzed, and acted upon for the organization to perform well. External elements do not change rapidly or unexpectedly in this environment.

Even greater uncertainty is felt in the *simple, unstable* environment.[44] Rapid change creates uncertainty for managers. Even though the organization has few external elements, those elements are hard to predict, and they react unexpectedly to organizational initiatives. The greatest uncertainty for an organization occurs in the *complex, unstable* environment. A large number of different elements impinge upon the organization, and they shift frequently or react strongly to organizational initiatives. When several sectors change simultaneously, the environment becomes turbulent.[45]

A beer distributor functions in a simple, stable environment. Demand for beer changes only gradually; for example, there had been little change in demand for domestic beer. Beer remains the drink of choice for Canadians but recently it is being challenged by wine sales. In 2011, stores sold $20.3 billion of beer, up 2 percent from the previous year.[46] The distributor has an established delivery route, and supplies of beer arrive on schedule. Appliance manufacturers and insurance companies are in somewhat stable, complex environments. A large number of external elements are present, but although they change, changes are gradual and predictable.

Toy manufacturers are in simple, unstable environments. Organizations that design, make, and sell toys, as well as those that are involved in the clothing or music industry, face shifting supply and demand. Most e-commerce companies focus on a specific competitive niche and, hence, operate in simple but unstable environments as well. Although there may be few elements to contend with, such as technology and competitors, they are difficult to predict and change abruptly and unexpectedly.

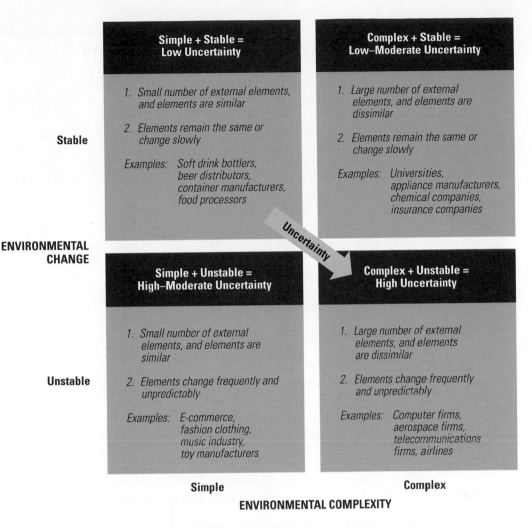

**ENVIRONMENTAL CHANGE**

**Stable**

**Simple + Stable =
Low Uncertainty**

1. Small number of external elements, and elements are similar

2. Elements remain the same or change slowly

Examples:  Soft drink bottlers, beer distributors, container manufacturers, food processors

**Complex + Stable =
Low–Moderate Uncertainty**

1. Large number of external elements, and elements are dissimilar

2. Elements remain the same or change slowly

Examples:  Universities, appliance manufacturers, chemical companies, insurance companies

*Uncertainty*

**Unstable**

**Simple + Unstable =
High–Moderate Uncertainty**

1. Small number of external elements, and elements are similar

2. Elements change frequently and unpredictably

Examples:  E-commerce, fashion clothing, music industry, toy manufacturers

**Complex + Unstable =
High Uncertainty**

1. Large number of external elements, and elements are dissimilar

2. Elements change frequently and unpredictably

Examples:  Computer firms, aerospace firms, telecommunications firms, airlines

**Simple**                **Complex**

**ENVIRONMENTAL COMPLEXITY**

**EXHIBIT 4.3**
**Framework for Assessing Environmental Uncertainty**
Source: Adapted and reprinted from "Characteristics of Perceived Environments and Perceived Environmental Uncertainty," by Robert B. Duncan, published in *Administrative Science Quarterly* 17 (1972), 313–327, by permission of *The Administrative Science Quarterly*. Copyright © 1972 by Cornell University.

The telecommunications industry and the airline industry face complex, unstable environments. Many external sectors are changing simultaneously. In the case of airlines, in just a few years they were confronted with an air-traffic controller shortage, price cuts from low-cost carriers such as WestJet Airlines, soaring fuel prices, the entry of new competitors, a series of major air-traffic disasters, and a drastic decline in customer demand following the September 11, 2001, terrorist attacks. WestJet Airlines faces possible competition from NewAir & Tours, a Calgary-based carrier that flies travellers in smaller cities to larger ones. NewAir & Tours was started by four former WestJet Airlines executives.[47] NewAir & Tours has since changed its name to Enerjet and offers workforce air transportation and charter services.[48]

# Adapting to Environmental Uncertainty

Once you see how environments differ with respect to change and complexity, the next question is, "How do organizations adapt to each level of environmental uncertainty?" Environmental uncertainty represents an important contingency for organizational structure and internal behaviours. Recall from Chapter 3 that organizations facing uncertainty generally have a more horizontal structure that encourages cross-functional communication and collaboration to help the organization adapt to changes in the environment. In this section we discuss in more detail how the environment affects organizations. An organization in a certain environment will be managed and controlled differently from an organization in an uncertain environment with respect to positions and departments; buffering and boundary spanning; differentiation and integration; organic versus mechanistic management processes; and planning, forecasting, and responsiveness. Organizations need to have the right fit between internal structure and the external environment.

## Positions and Departments

As the complexity and uncertainty in the external environment increases, so does the number of positions and departments within the organization, which in turn increases internal complexity. This relationship is part of being an open system. Each sector in the external environment requires an employee or department to deal with it. The human resource department deals with unemployed people who want to work for the company. The marketing department finds customers. Procurement employees obtain raw materials from hundreds of suppliers. The finance group deals with bankers. The legal department works with the courts and government agencies. Many companies have added e-business departments to handle electronic commerce and information technology departments to deal with the increasing complexity of computerized information and knowledge management systems.

## Buffering and Boundary Spanning

The traditional approach to coping with environmental uncertainty was to establish buffer departments. The purpose of **buffering roles** is to absorb uncertainty from the environment.[49] The technical core performs the primary production activity of an organization. Buffer departments surround the technical core and exchange materials, resources, and money between the environment and the organization. They help the technical core function efficiently. The purchasing department buffers the technical core by stockpiling supplies and raw materials. The human resource department buffers the technical core by handling the uncertainty associated with finding, hiring, and training production employees.

A newer approach some organizations are trying is to drop the buffers and expose the technical core to the uncertain environment. These organizations no longer create buffers because they believe being well connected to customers and suppliers is more important than internal efficiency. For example, John Deere has assembly-line workers visiting local farms to determine and respond to customer concerns. Whirlpool Corporation pays hundreds of customers to test computer-simulated products and features.[50] Opening up the organization to the environment makes it more fluid and adaptable.

**Boundary-spanning roles** link and coordinate an organization with key elements in the external environment. Boundary spanning is primarily concerned with the exchange of information to (1) detect and bring into the organization information about changes in the environment and (2) send information into the environment that presents the organization in a favourable light.[51]

Organizations have to keep in touch with what is going on in the environment so that managers can respond to market changes and other developments. A study of high-tech firms found that 97 percent of competitive failures resulted from lack of attention to market changes or the failure to act on vital information.[52] To detect and bring important information into the organization, boundary personnel scan the environment. For example, a market-research department scans and monitors trends in consumer tastes. Boundary spanners in engineering and R&D departments scan new technological developments, innovations, and raw materials. Boundary spanners prevent the organization from stagnating by keeping top managers informed about environmental changes. Often, the greater the uncertainty in the environment, the greater the importance of boundary spanners.[53]

One new approach to boundary spanning is business intelligence, which refers to the high-tech analysis of large amounts of internal and external data to spot patterns and relationships that might be significant. For example, the federal government provides business intelligence through its Innovation in Canada branch.[54] However, according to a 2005 Ipsos Reid poll, the use of business intelligence is neither extensive nor sophisticated, and focuses only on knowledge management, data mining, environmental scanning, and competitive intelligence.[55]

Business intelligence is related to another important area of boundary spanning, known as *competitive intelligence* (CI). Membership in the Society of Competitive Intelligence Professionals has more than doubled since 1997, and colleges are setting up master's degree programs in CI to respond to the growing demand for these professionals in organizations.[56] Competitive intelligence gives top executives a systematic way to collect and analyze public information about rivals and use it to make better decisions.[57] Using techniques that range from Internet surfing to digging through trash cans, intelligence professionals dig up information on competitors' new products, manufacturing costs, or training methods, and share it with top leaders.

In today's turbulent environment, many successful companies involve everyone in boundary-spanning activities. People at the grass-roots level are often able to see and interpret changes or problems sooner than managers, who are typically more removed from the day-to-day work.[58] At Ottawa-based and IBM-owned Cognos, which sells planning and budgeting programs to large corporations, any of the company's 3,000 employees can submit scoops about competitors through an internal website called Street Fighter. Each day, R&D and sales managers pore over the dozens of entries. Good tips are rewarded with prizes.[59]

The boundary task of sending information into the environment to represent the organization is used to influence other people's perception of the organization. In the marketing department, advertising and salespeople represent the organization to customers. Purchasers may call on suppliers and describe purchasing needs. The legal department informs lobbyists and elected officials about the organization's needs or views on political matters. Many companies set up their own web pages to present the organization in a favourable light. For example, to counteract hate sites that criticize its labour practices in developing countries, Nike created websites specifically to tell its side of the story.[60]

All organizations have to keep in touch with the environment. Here's how Joe Fresh Style, a growing fashion retailer that markets high-quality inexpensive apparel, spans the boundary in the shifting environment of the fashion industry.

## In Practice
### Joe Fresh Style

Joe Mimran has been creating fashion trends for many years. Mimran is a chartered accountant by training and practised his profession for a couple of years before joining his mother and his brother in their small clothing company. The family eventually hired designer Alfred Sung and soon the Alfred Sung brand was a success in Canada and in the United States. In 1983, Alfred Sung was described as the King of Fashion by *Maclean's*.

Then Mimran realized that he was missing out on the casual apparel business, so "[he] started to play around with a bunch of concepts and came up with the notion of being vertically integrated with one thumbprint from beginning to end, so nobody would tamper with the vision."[61] Mimran decided to start Club Monaco on Queen Street West in Toronto; the company grew rapidly. In 48 months, 50 new stores opened in Canada and around the world. According to Mimran, "[the] brand was very urban-driven...because of this, growth in Canada was limited."[62] He also ventured into home furnishings through his Caban stores. In 1999, he sold both Club Monaco and Caban to the Ralph Lauren Corporation and did well on the sale.

After the sale, Mimran started Joseph Mimran and Associates and worked with a few clients. He was approached by Loblaw Companies to develop an apparel line—the Joe Fresh Style line. Now available in many Loblaw stores, the line consists of classic but stylish casuals with an average price of $15. The line has been well received and is continuing to grow in its range of apparel. According to Mimran, he is able to keep the prices low by "[being] really smart with...fabric and color choices. It's that simple. You have to understand the production process,...Of a hundred [fabric] swatches, you have to pick the right one." He goes on to note that "Canadian customers are very much value-driven,...They prefer classics that run to the core. And they really love fashion."[63] Joe Fresh Style's "cheap chic" has been so successful that it launched more stand-alone boutiques in Canada and a pilot store in Manhattan, NYC, in 2011.[64]

Joe Fresh experienced a shock from its environment when a tragic fire engulfed a factory in Bangladesh in 2013, the worst disaster in the Bangladeshi garment industry. While some companies said they would no longer source from Bangladesh, Joe Mimran took a different position. He argued, "more can be done to make the apparel industry 'a force for good' in the world by working with local authorities to improve conditions."[65]

## ■ Differentiation and Integration

Another response to environmental uncertainty is the amount of differentiation and integration among departments. Organizational **differentiation** is "the differences in cognitive and emotional orientations among managers in different functional departments, and the difference in formal structure among these departments."[66] When the external environment is complex and rapidly changing, organizational departments become highly specialized to handle the uncertainty in their external sector. Success in each sector requires special expertise and behaviour. Employees in an R&D department thus have unique attitudes, values, goals, and education that distinguish them from employees in manufacturing or sales departments.

A seminal study by Paul Lawrence and Jay Lorsch examined three organizational departments—manufacturing, research, and sales—in ten corporations.[67] This study found that each department evolved toward a different orientation and

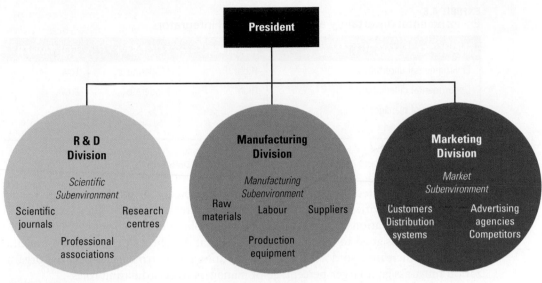

**EXHIBIT 4.4**
Organizational Departments Differentiate to Meet Needs of Subenvironments

structure to deal with specialized parts of the external environment. The scientific, manufacturing, and market subenvironments identified by Lawrence and Lorsch are illustrated in Exhibit 4.4. Each department interacted with different external groups. The differences that evolved among departments within the organizations are shown in Exhibit 4.5. To work effectively with the scientific subenvironment, R&D had a goal of quality work, a long time horizon (up to five years), an informal structure, and task-oriented employees. Marketing was at the opposite extreme. It had a goal of customer satisfaction, was oriented toward the short term (two weeks or so), had a very formal structure, and was socially oriented.

One outcome of high differentiation is that coordination among departments becomes difficult. More time and resources must be devoted to achieving coordination when attitudes, goals, and work orientation differ so widely. **Integration** is the quality of collaboration among departments.[68] Formal integrators are often required to coordinate departments. When the environment is highly uncertain, frequent changes require more information processing to achieve horizontal coordination, so integrators become a necessary addition to the organizational structure. Sometimes integrators are called liaison personnel, project managers, brand managers, or coordinators. As illustrated in Exhibit 4.6, organizations with highly uncertain environments and

**EXHIBIT 4.5**
Differences in Goals and Orientations among Organizational Departments

| CHARACTERISTIC | R&D DEPARTMENT | MANUFACTURING DEPARTMENT | MARKETING DEPARTMENT |
|---|---|---|---|
| Goals | New developments, quality | Efficient production | Customer satisfaction |
| Time horizon | Long | Short | Short |
| Interpersonal orientation | Mostly task | Task | Social |
| Formality of structure | Low | High | High |

Source: Based on Paul R. Lawrence and Jay W. Lorsch, *Organization & Environment* (Homewood, Ill.: Irwin, 1969) 23–29.

**EXHIBIT 4.6**
Environmental Uncertainty and Organizational Integrators

| INDUSTRY | PLASTICS | FOODS | CONTAINER |
|---|---|---|---|
| Environmental uncertainty | High | Moderate | Low |
| Departmental differentiation | High | Moderate | Low |
| Percentage of management in integrating roles | 22% | 17% | 0% |

Source: Based on Jay W. Lorsch and Paul R. Lawrence, Environmental Factors and Organizational Integration, *Organizational Planning: Cases and Concepts* (Homewood, Ill.: Irwin and Dorsey, 1972), 45.

**Apply**

Apply the idea of fit between the characteristics of the environment and organization structure by examining your university or college. What did you observe?

a highly differentiated structure assign about 22 percent of management personnel to integration activities, such as serving on committees, on task forces, or in liaison roles.[69] In organizations characterized by very simple, stable environments, almost no managers are assigned to integration roles. Exhibit 4.6 shows that, as environmental uncertainty increases, so does differentiation among departments; hence, the organization must assign a larger percentage of managers to coordinating roles.

Lawrence and Lorsch's research concluded that organizations perform better when the levels of differentiation and integration match the level of uncertainty in the environment. Organizations that performed well in uncertain environments had high levels of both differentiation and integration, while those performing well in less-uncertain environments had lower levels of differentiation and integration.

## ■ Organic versus Mechanistic Management Processes

Another response to environmental uncertainty is the amount of formal structure and control imposed on employees. Tom Burns and G. M. Stalker observed 20 industrial firms in England and discovered that external environment was related to internal management structure.[70] When the external environment was stable, the internal organization was characterized by rules, procedures, and a clear hierarchy of authority. Organizations were formalized. They were also centralized, with most decisions made at the top. Burns and Stalker called this a **mechanistic** organizational system.

In rapidly changing environments, the internal organization was much looser, free-flowing, and adaptive. Rules and regulations often were not written down or, if written down, were ignored. People had to find their own way through the system to figure out what to do. The hierarchy of authority was not clear. Decision-making authority was decentralized. Burns and Stalker used the term **organic** to characterize this type of management structure.

Exhibit 4.7 summarizes the differences between mechanistic and organic systems. As environmental uncertainty increases, organizations tend to become more organic, which means decentralizing authority and responsibility to lower levels, encouraging employees to take care of problems by working directly with one another, encouraging teamwork, and taking an informal approach to assigning tasks and responsibility. Thus, the organization is more fluid and is able to adapt continually to changes in the external environment.[71]

The learning organization, described in Chapter 1, and the horizontal and virtual network structures, described in Chapter 3, are organic organizational forms used by companies to compete in rapidly changing environments. Guiltless Gourmet, headquartered in New Jersey, sells low-fat tortilla chips and other high-quality snack foods. The company shifted to a flexible network structure to remain competitive

**EXHIBIT 4.7**
Mechanistic and Organic Forms

| MECHANISTIC | ORGANIC |
| --- | --- |
| 1. Tasks are broken down into specialized, separate parts.<br>2. Tasks are rigidly defined.<br>3. There is a strict hierarchy of authority and control, and there are many rules.<br>4. Knowledge and control of tasks are centralized at the top of the organization.<br>5. Communication is vertical. | 1. Employees contribute to the common tasks of the department.<br>2. Tasks are adjusted and redefined through employee teamwork.<br>3. There is less hierarchy of authority and control, and there are few rules.<br>4. Knowledge and control of tasks are located anywhere in the organization.<br>5. Communication is horizontal. |

Source: Adapted from Gerald Zaltman, Robert Duncan, and Jonny Holbek, *Innovations and Organizations* (New York: Wiley, 1973), 131. Copyright © 1973 by John Wiley & Sons, Inc. Reproduced with permission of John Wiley & Sons, Inc.

when large companies such as Frito-Lay entered the low-fat snack-food market. The company redesigned itself to become basically a full-time marketing organization, while production and other activities were outsourced. An 18,000-square-foot plant in Austin, Texas, was closed and the workforce cut from 125 to about 10 core people who handle marketing and sales promotions. The flexible structure allows Guiltless Gourmet to adapt quickly to changing market conditions.[72]

## ■ Planning, Forecasting, and Responsiveness

The whole point of increasing internal integration and shifting to more organic processes is to enhance the organization's ability to quickly respond to sudden changes in an uncertain environment. It might seem that in an environment where everything is changing all the time, planning is useless. However, in uncertain environments, planning and environmental forecasting actually become *more* important as a way to keep the organization geared for a coordinated, speedy response. Japanese electronic giants such as Toshiba and Fujitsu, for example, were caught off-guard by a combination of nimble new competitors, rapid technological change, deregulation, the declining stability of Japan's banking system, and the sudden end of the 1990s technology boom. Lulled into complacency by years of success, Japan's industrial electronics companies were unprepared to respond to these dramatic changes and lost billions.[73]

When the environment is stable, the organization can concentrate on current operational problems and day-to-day efficiency. Long-range planning and forecasting are not needed because environmental demands in the future will be the same as they are today.

With increasing environmental uncertainty, planning and forecasting become necessary.[74] Planning can soften the adverse impact of external shifts. Organizations that have unstable environments often establish a separate planning department. In an unpredictable environment, planners scan environmental elements and analyze potential moves and countermoves by other organizations. Planning can be extensive and may forecast various scenarios for environmental contingencies. With scenario building, managers mentally rehearse different scenarios based on anticipating various changes that could affect the organization. Scenarios are like stories that offer alternative, vivid pictures of what the future will look like and how managers will respond. Royal Dutch/Shell Oil has long used scenario building and has been a leader in speedy response to massive changes that other organizations failed to perceive until it was too late.[75]

**Compare**

Compare two organizations whose degree of environmental uncertainty is different. What structural differences do you observe?

# ding *by Design*

## ...toba Telecom Services (MTS)

Manitoba Telecom Services (MTS) is the leading telecommunications company in Manitoba. The company handles local telephone service throughout Manitoba, and also offers cellular communication, paging, and group communication networks and long-distance service throughout the province. The company's MTS Media subsidiary produces advertising and information directories, especially through the Internet. Another subsidiary, Qunara, provides consulting services on information security, web management, and information management. MTS also owns a 40 percent share in Bell West, a local and long-distance communications carrier. MTS was formerly known as the Manitoba Telephone System, a public utility owned and managed by the province of Manitoba. The utility became a public for-profit company in 1996. MTS also owns MTS Allstream whose national broadband fibre network spans more than 24,300 kilometres.[76] MTS has had a rocky history but, by 2003, it was being described as the belle of the telco ball by *Canadian Business*. It has most of the local and long-distance phone service and 60 percent of the Internet service in the province. Its principal competitors are Shaw Communications and Rogers Wireless Communication.[77]

In 1993, MTS and its union, the Communication, Energy & Paperworkers Union, engaged in a joint work redesign of its operator services. The redesign project was named M-POWER (i.e., Professional Operators with Enhanced Responsibilities). The catalyst for the redesign was a power surge in MTS's Winnipeg office after which operators began to experience shocks. A work stoppage was ordered; however, a technical analysis found no problems with the equipment. A joint committee of management and union representatives was created to understand and remedy the situation. It was at the urging of Gareth Morgan, whose work was described briefly in Chapter 3, that the joint committee was created. The committee identified and canvassed all the key stakeholders.

The redesign committee developed an action statement to guide its work: "To trial organizational and managerial systems and processes that will improve the working environment by reorganizing work, improving communication, [and] empowering employees and managers to be more directly involved in decisions while maintaining and improving the level of customer service."[78] The redesign committee made nine recommendations: (1) the creation of small teams of operators, (2) the immediate removal of remote monitoring of the operators, (3) the implementation of extensive cross-training, (4) personalizing customer service, (5) removing restrictions on operators' trades, (6) increasing scheduling and work flexibility, (7) increasing training for the operators, (8) increasing the product knowledge of the operators, and (9) dedicating training space. Most of the recommendations were followed and both management and union were pleased with the process and the outcome.[79]

Planning, however, cannot substitute for other actions, such as effective boundary spanning and adequate internal integration and coordination. The organizations that are most successful in uncertain environments are those that keep everyone in close touch with the environment so they can spot threats and opportunities, enabling the organization to respond immediately. The Leading by Design box provides an example of useful planning to respond to an unexpected event.

## Framework for Organizational Responses to Uncertainty

The ways environmental uncertainty influences organizational characteristics are summarized in Exhibit 4.8. The change and complexity dimensions are combined and illustrate four levels of uncertainty. The low-uncertainty environment is simple

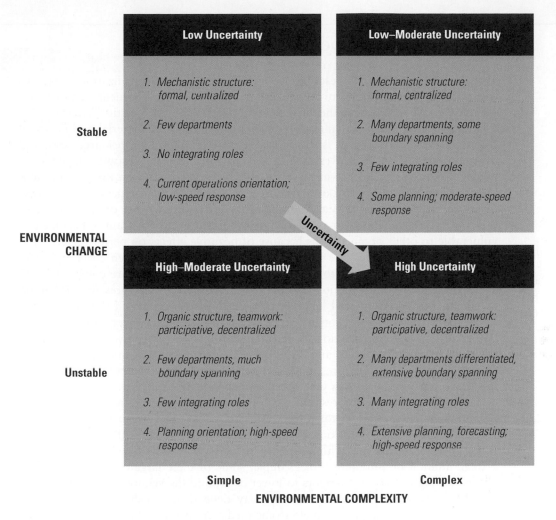

**EXHIBIT 4.8**
Contingency Framework for Environmental Uncertainty and Organizational Responses

and stable. Organizations in this environment have few departments and a mechanistic structure. In a low–moderate uncertainty environment, more departments are needed, along with more integrating roles to coordinate the departments. Some planning may occur. Environments that are high–moderate uncertainty are unstable but simple. Organizational structure is organic and decentralized. Planning is emphasized and managers are quick to make internal changes as needed. The high-uncertainty environment is both complex and unstable and is the most difficult environment from a management perspective. Organizations are not only large and have many departments, but they are also organic. A large number of management personnel are assigned to coordination and integration, and the organization uses boundary spanning, planning, and forecasting to enable a high-speed response to environmental changes.

## Resource Dependence

Thus far, this chapter has described several ways in which organizations adapt to the lack of information and to the uncertainty caused by environmental change and complexity. We turn now to the third characteristic of the organization–environment relationship that affects organizations, which is the need for material and financial resources. The environment is the source of scarce and valued resources essential to organizational survival. Research in this area is called the resource-dependence theory. **Resource dependence** means that organizations depend on the environment but strive to acquire control over resources to minimize their dependence.[80] Organizations are vulnerable if vital resources are controlled by other organizations, so they try to be as independent as possible. Organizations do not want to become too vulnerable to other organizations because of negative effects on performance.

Although companies like to minimize their dependence, when costs and risks are high they also team up to share scarce resources and be more competitive on a global basis. Formal relationships with other organizations present a dilemma to managers. Organizational linkages require coordination,[81] and they reduce the freedom of each organization to make decisions without concern for the needs and goals of other organizations. Interorganizational relationships thus represent a trade-off between resources and autonomy. To maintain autonomy, organizations that already have abundant resources will tend not to establish new linkages. Organizations that need resources will give up independence to acquire those resources.

Dependence on shared resources gives power to other organizations. Once an organization relies on others for valued resources, those other organizations can influence managerial decision making. When a large company such as IBM, Motorola, or BMW forges a partnership with a supplier for parts, both sides benefit, but each loses a small amount of autonomy. For example, some of these large companies are now putting strong pressure on vendors to lower costs, and the vendors have few alternatives but to go along.[82] In much the same way, dependence on shared resources gives advertisers power over print and electronic media companies. For example, as newspapers face increasingly tough financial times, they are less likely to run stories critical of advertisers. Though newspapers insist advertisers do not get special treatment, some editors admit there is growing talk of the need for advertiser-friendly newspapers.[83]

## Controlling Environmental Resources

**Think**

Think about what ways you can reduce your resource dependence or increase your resource munificence.

Organizations maintain this balance between linkages with other organizations and their own independence through attempts to modify, manipulate, or control other organizations.[84] To survive, the focal organization often tries to reach out and change or control elements in the environment. Two strategies can be adopted to manage resources in the external environment: (1) establish favourable linkages with key elements in the environment and (2) shape the environmental domain.[85] As a general rule, when organizations sense that valued resources are scarce, they will use such strategies rather than go it alone. Notice how dissimilar these strategies are from the responses to environmental change and complexity described in Exhibit 4.8. The dissimilarity reflects the difference between responding to the need for resources and responding to the need for information.

## ■ Establishing Interorganizational Linkages

**Ownership.** Companies use ownership to establish linkages when they buy a part of or a controlling interest in another company. This gives the company access to technology, products, or other resources it doesn't currently have.

A greater degree of ownership and control is obtained through acquisition or merger. An acquisition involves the purchase of one organization by another so that the buyer assumes control. A merger is the unification of two or more organizations into a single unit.[86] These forms of ownership reduce uncertainty in an area important to the acquiring company. Over the past few years, there has been a huge wave of acquisition and merger activity in the telecommunications industry, reflecting the tremendous uncertainty these organizations face. According to the law firm McMillan Binch Mendelsohn, Canadian M&A activity in 2006 was higher than any year since the technology boom of 2000, buoyed by a strong economy, low interest rates, high energy and commodity prices and continued cross-border activity. Continuing trends include: increased involvement by private equity funds (particularly U.S.–based funds), Chinese participation, large cross-border transactions, increased income trust activity (particularly after the October 31, 2006, announcement by the federal government that the favourable tax treatment accorded to income trusts will come to an end), increased willingness to launch hostile and competing bids, increased institutional shareholder activism and growing recognition of national security interests in the context of M&A transactions. In addition, cash continues to be king in competitive auctions (e.g., Falconbridge and Inco transactions).[87]

---

**In Practice**

**TSX Group and Montréal Exchange**

After some sparring between the Toronto and Montréal exchanges, "Canada's largest stock and derivatives exchanges have made it official, striking a $1.3 billion marriage pact."[88] The federal finance minister had urged the two organizations to put aside their differences and join forces for the national interest. Both the New York Mercantile Exchange and the Intercontinental Exchange had expressed interest in acquiring the Montréal Exchange. The new organization was named the TMX Group and is managed from Toronto. However, derivatives trading stayed in Montréal at the same location and with the same management. Montréal exchange shareholders received a half Toronto exchange share and $13.95 for each of the shares in the Montréal derivatives exchange. When the merger was approved, Montréal exchange shareholders owned 18 percent of the new exchange and Toronto exchange shareholders owned the remainder.

The merger created an organization that has the size to compete and to expand globally. The Montréal exchange has a stake in the Boston Options Exchange, and the organization plans to expand further in the United States. According to Richard Nesbitt, CEO of the Toronto Exchange, "[this] combination grows out of a common vision for the future of the Canadian capital markets.... Customers in Canada and internationally will benefit from increased liquidity levels, accelerated product development, a fully diversified product suite, and superior technology."[89] Cost savings from the merger are estimated to be $25 million per year. One analyst referred to the proposed merger as a "not-so-stunning [but positive] move"[90] in the long run. The merged organization, in 2011, pursued another merger, with another exchange, the London Stock Exchange. Had the merger succeeded, it would have created the world's largest exchange. The proposed merger was more contentious as it was international in scope and would leave the London Stock Exchange with 55 percent ownership of the new exchange. The proposed merger was terminated and any other possible mergers would face many federal and provincial hurdles.[91]

**Formal Strategic Alliances.** When there is a high level of complementarity between the business lines, geographical positions, or skills of two companies, the firms often go the route of a strategic alliance rather than ownership through merger or acquisition.[92] Such alliances are formed through contracts and joint ventures.

Contracts and joint ventures reduce uncertainty through a legal and binding relationship with another firm. Contracts come in the form of *licence agreements* that involve the purchase of the right to use an asset (such as a new technology) for a specific time and *supplier arrangements* that contract for the sale of one firm's output to another. Contracts can provide long-term security by tying customers and suppliers to specific amounts and prices. For example, Italian fashion house Versace has forged a deal to license its primary asset—its name—for a line of designer eyeglasses. McCain's contracts for an entire crop of russet potatoes to be certain of its supply of French-fries. It also gains influence over suppliers through these contracts and has changed the way farmers grow potatoes and the profit margins they earn, which is consistent with the resource-dependence theory.[93] Large retailers such as Walmart and Home Depot are gaining so much clout that they can almost dictate contracts, telling manufacturers what to make, how to make it, and how much to charge for it. Many music companies edit songs and visual covers of their albums to cut out "offensive material" in order to get their products on the shelves of Walmart, which sells many millions of CDs annually.[94]

*Joint ventures* result in the creation of a new organization that is formally independent of the parents, although the parents will have some control.[95] In a joint venture, organizations share the risk and cost associated with large projects or innovations. AOL created a joint venture with Venezuela's Cisneros Group to smooth its entry into the Latin American online market. In 2006, CUBANIQUEL Corporation and Sherritt International developed a joint venture to increase productive capacity of nickel and cobalt mining in Cuba and Canada with capital from both partners.[96]

**Cooptation, Interlocking Directorates. Cooptation** occurs when leaders from important sectors in the environment are made part of an organization. It takes place, for example, when influential customers or suppliers are appointed to the board of directors, such as when the senior executive of a bank sits on the board of a manufacturing company. As a board member, the banker may become psychologically coopted into the interests of the manufacturing firm. Community leaders can also be appointed to a company's board of directors or to other organizational committees or task forces. These influential people are thus introduced to the needs of the company and are more likely to include the company's interests in their decision making.

An **interlocking directorate** is a formal linkage that occurs when a member of the board of directors of one company sits on the board of directors of another company. The individual is a communications link between companies and can influence policies and decisions. When one individual is the link between two companies, this is typically referred to as a **direct interlock**. An **indirect interlock** occurs when a director of company A and a director of company B are both directors of company C. They have access to one another but do not have direct influence over their respective companies.[97] Recent research shows that, as a firm's financial fortunes decline, direct interlocks with financial institutions increase. Financial uncertainty facing an industry also has been associated with greater indirect interlocks between competing companies.[98]

**Executive Recruitment.** Transferring or exchanging executives also offers a method of establishing favourable linkages with external organizations. For example, each year the aerospace industry hires retired generals and executives from the U.S. Department of Defense. These generals have personal friends in the department, so the aerospace companies obtain better information about technical specifications, prices, and dates for new weapons systems. They can learn the needs of the defence department and are able to present their case for defence contracts in a more effective way. Companies without personal contacts find it nearly impossible to get a defence contract. Having channels of influence and communication between organizations serves to reduce financial uncertainty and dependence for an organization.

**Advertising and Public Relations.** A traditional way of establishing favourable relationships is through advertising. Organizations spend large amounts of money to influence the taste of consumers. Advertising is especially important in highly competitive consumer industries and in industries that experience variable demand. Advertising is a major part of Apple's strategy to increase its market share for its computer line; its advertisements focus on Apple's innovations with taglines such as "Think Different." which remains one of its most famous.

Public relations is similar to advertising, except that stories often are free and aimed at public opinion. Public relations people cast an organization in a favourable light in speeches, in press reports, and on television. Public relations attempts to shape the company's image in the minds of customers, suppliers, and government officials. For example, in an effort to survive in this antismoking era, tobacco companies have launched an aggressive public relations campaign touting smokers' freedom of choice.

## ■ Controlling the Environmental Domain

In addition to establishing favourable linkages to obtain resources, organizations often try to change the environment. There are four techniques for influencing or changing an organization's environmental domain.

**Change of Domain.** The ten sectors described earlier in this chapter are not fixed. The organization decides which business it is in; the market to enter; and the suppliers, banks, employees, and location to use—and this domain can be changed.[99] An organization can seek new environmental relationships and drop old ones. An organization may try to find a domain where there is little competition, no government regulation, abundant suppliers, affluent customers, and barriers to keep competitors out.

Acquisition and divestment are two techniques for altering the domain. Bombardier, maker of Ski-Doo snowmobiles, began a series of acquisitions to alter its domain when the snowmobile industry declined. CEO Laurent Beaudoin gradually moved the company into the aerospace industry by negotiating deals to purchase Canadair, Boeing's de Havilland unit, business-jet pioneer Learjet, and Short Brothers of Northern Ireland.[100]

**Political Activity, Regulation.** Political activity includes techniques to influence government legislation and regulation. Political strategy can be used to erect regulatory barriers against new competitors or to quash unfavourable legislation. Corporations also try to influence the appointment to agencies of people who are sympathetic to their needs. Canadian defence contractors, for example, have lobbied the American military to get work on the U.S. missile shield system. Ron Kane, vice president of the Aerospace Industries Association of Canada, notes that "it's an area where Canadian industry has been very successful in the past, supporting U.S. military programs..."[101] However, involvement in the program was rejected, in 2005, by Prime Minister Paul Martin. In 2007, Stephen Harper did speak in favour of supporting the program.[102]

## In Practice
### Walmart

In the late 1990s, Walmart discovered a problem that could hamper its ambitious international expansion plans—U.S. negotiators for China's entry into the World Trade Organization had agreed to a 30-store limit on foreign retailers doing business there. Worse still, executives for the giant retailer realized they didn't know the right people in Washington to talk to about the situation.

Until 1998, Walmart didn't even have a lobbyist on the payroll and spent virtually nothing on political activity. The issue of China's entry into the WTO was a wake-up call, and Walmart began transforming itself from a company that shunned politics to one that works hard to bend public policy to suit its business needs. Hiring in-house lobbyists and working with lobbying organizations favourable to its goals has enabled Walmart to gain significant wins on global trade issues.

In addition to concerns over global trade, Walmart has found other reasons it needs government support. In recent years, the company has been fighting off legal challenges from labour unions, employees' lawyers, and federal investigators. For example, the United Food and Commercial Workers International Union helped Walmart employees file a series of complaints about the company's overtime, health care, and other policies with the National Labor Relations Board, leading to dozens of class-action lawsuits. In turn, Walmart poured millions of dollars into a campaign that presses for limits on awards in class-action suits and began lobbying for legislation that bars unions from soliciting outside retail stores. Although that legislation failed, top executives are pleased with their lobbyists' progress. Yet they admit they still have a lot to learn about the best way to influence government legislation and regulation in Walmart's favour.[103]

In Canada, Walmart has fought attempts to unionize its stores. The United Food and Commercial Workers were successful in organizing the Jonquière, Québec, Walmart store; it was the first North American Walmart store to have a union. However, Walmart closed the Jonquière store soon after and fired the store's 200 workers. The workers tried to launch a class action suit against Walmart but the Québec Court of Appeal declined to hear the case. The Court's decision upheld a November 2005 decision by the Québec Superior Court that the firing of the unionized workers was best decided by the province's labour relations board.[104]

In addition to hiring lobbyists and working with other organizations, many CEOs believe they should do their own lobbying. CEOs have easier access than lobbyists and can be especially effective when they do the politicking. Political activity is so important that "informal lobbyist" is an unwritten part of almost any CEO's job description.[105]

**Trade Associations.** Much of the work to influence the external environment is accomplished jointly with other organizations that have similar interests. For example, most large pharmaceutical companies belong to Pharmaceutical Research and Manufacturers of America. Manufacturing companies are part of the Canadian Manufacturers and Exporters, and retailers are part of the Retail Council of Canada. Microsoft and other software companies join the Initiative for Software Choice (ISC). By pooling resources, these organizations can pay people to carry out activities such as lobbying legislators, influencing new regulations, developing public relations campaigns, and making campaign contributions. There are more specialized trade associations such as the Hellenic Canadian Board of Trade, the Confectionery Manufacturers Association of Canada, the Music Industries Association of Canada, and Trade Team PEI.

**Illegitimate Activities.** Illegitimate activities represent the final technique companies sometimes use to control their environmental domain. Certain conditions, such as low profits, pressure from senior managers, or scarce environmental resources, may lead managers to adopt behaviours not considered legitimate.[106] Many well-known companies have been found guilty of unlawful or unethical activities. Examples include payoffs to foreign governments, illegal political contributions, excessive promotional gifts, and wiretapping. At formerly high-flying companies such as Enron and WorldCom, pressure for financial performance encouraged managers to disguise financial problems through complex partnerships or questionable accounting practices. In the Canadian airlines industry, for example, intense competition between Air Canada and WestJet resulted in an industrial espionage case, as discussed in Chapter 1's A Look Inside. "In the spring of 2004, Air Canada sued WestJet for $220 million for logging on more than 240,000 times to an internal website that contained passenger-load data. WestJet, a discount carrier, then sued Air Canada for, among other things, hiring private investigators who dressed as garbage collectors to retrieve documents from the home of a former executive." WestJet apologized and took responsibility for the unethical act.[107]

One study found that companies in industries with low demand, shortages, and strikes were more likely to be convicted for illegal activities, implying that illegal acts are an attempt to cope with resource scarcity. Some nonprofit organizations have been found to use illegitimate or illegal actions to bolster their visibility and reputation as they compete with other organizations for scarce grants and donations.[108] A 2007 series of *Toronto Star* articles highlighted questionable practices of a few charities. One charity, International Charity Association Network (ICAN), has been suspended by the Charities Directorate. ICAN is not allowed to issue tax receipts and must warn potential donors that it is under suspension.[109]

# ■ Organization–Environment Integrative Framework

The relationships illustrated in Exhibit 4.9 summarize the two major themes about organization–environment relationships discussed in this chapter. One theme is that the amount of complexity and change in an organization's domain influences the need for information and hence the uncertainty felt within an organization. Greater information uncertainty is resolved through greater structural flexibility and the assignment of additional departments and boundary roles. When uncertainty is low, management structures can be more mechanistic, and the number of departments and boundary roles can be fewer. The second theme pertains to the scarcity of material and financial resources. The more dependent an organization is on other organizations for those resources, the more important it is to either establish favourable linkages with those organizations or control entry into the domain. If dependence on external resources is low, the organization can maintain autonomy and does not need to establish linkages or control the external domain.

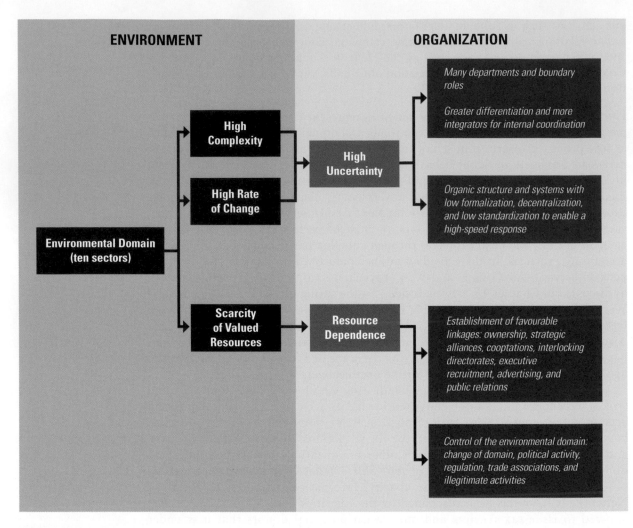

**EXHIBIT 4.9**
Relationship between Environmental Characteristics and Organizational Actions

## Summary and Interpretation

The external environment has an overwhelming impact on management uncertainty and organization functioning. Organizations are open social systems. Most are involved with hundreds of external elements. The change and complexity in environmental domains have major implications for organizational design and action. Most organizational decisions, activities, and outcomes can be traced to stimuli in the external environment.

Organizational environments differ in terms of uncertainty and resource dependence. Organizational uncertainty is the result of the stable–unstable and simple–complex dimensions of the environment. Resource dependence is the result of scarcity of the material and financial resources needed by the organization.

Organizational design takes on a logical perspective when the environment is considered. Organizations try to survive and achieve efficiencies in a world characterized by uncertainty and scarcity. Specific departments and functions are created to deal with uncertainties. The organization can be conceptualized as a technical core and departments that buffer environmental uncertainty. Boundary-spanning roles provide information about the environment.

The concepts in this chapter provide specific frameworks for understanding how the environment influences the structure and functioning of an organization. Environmental complexity and change, for example, have specific impact on internal complexity and adaptability. Under great uncertainty, more resources are allocated to departments that will plan, deal with specific environmental elements, and integrate diverse internal activities. Moreover, when risk is great or resources are scarce, the organization can establish linkages through the acquisition of ownership and through strategic alliances, interlocking directorates, executive recruitment, or advertising and public relations that will minimize risk and maintain a supply of scarce resources. Other techniques for controlling the environment include a change of the domain in which the organization operates, political activity, participation in trade associations, and illegitimate activities.

Two important themes in this chapter are that organizations can learn and adapt to the environment and that organizations can change and control the environment. These strategies are especially true for large organizations that command many resources. Such organizations can adapt when necessary but can also neutralize or change problematic areas in the environment.

## ■ Key Concepts

| | |
|---|---|
| boundary-spanning roles, p. 153 | interlocking directorate, p. 162 |
| buffering roles, p. 152 | mechanistic, p. 156 |
| cooptation, p. 162 | organic, p. 156 |
| differentiation, p. 154 | organizational environment, p. 141 |
| direct interlock, p. 162 | resource dependence, p. 160 |
| domain, p. 142 | sectors, p. 142 |
| general environment, p. 144 | simple–complex dimension, p. 148 |
| green environment, p. 142 | stable–unstable dimension, p. 148 |
| indirect interlock, p. 162 | task environment, p. 142 |
| integration, p. 155 | uncertainty, p. 147 |

## ■ Discussion Questions

1. Define *organizational environment*. Would the task environment of a new Internet-based company be the same as that of a government welfare agency? Discuss.
2. What are some forces that influence environmental uncertainty? Which typically has the greatest impact on uncertainty—environmental complexity or environmental change? Why?
3. Why does environmental complexity lead to organizational complexity? Explain.
4. Discuss the importance of the international, compared to domestic, sector, for today's organizations. What are some ways in which the international sector affects organizations in your city or community?

5. Describe *differentiation* and *integration*. In what type of environmental uncertainty will differentiation and integration be greatest? least?
6. Under what environmental conditions is organizational planning emphasized? Is planning an appropriate response to a turbulent environment?
7. What is an organic organization? What is a mechanistic organization? How does the environment influence organic and mechanistic structures?
8. Why do organizations become involved in interorganizational relationships? Do these relationships affect an organization's dependency? Performance?
9. Assume you have been asked to calculate the ratio of staff employees to production employees in two organizations—one in a simple, stable environment and one in a complex, shifting environment. How would you expect these ratios to differ? Why?
10. Is changing the organization's domain a feasible strategy for coping with a threatening environment? Explain.

## ■ Chapter 4 Workbook: Organizations You Rely On*

Below, list eight organizations you somehow rely on in your daily life. Examples might be a restaurant, a clothing store, a university, your family, the post office, the telephone company, an airline, a pizzeria that delivers, your place of work, and so on. In the first column, list those eight organizations. Then, in Column 2, choose another organization you could use if the ones in Column 1 were not available. In Column 3, evaluate your level of dependence on the organizations listed in column 1 as Strong, Medium, or Weak. Finally, in Column 4, rate the certainty of that organization being able to meet your needs as High (certainty), Medium, or Low.

| Organization | Backup Organization | Level of Dependence | Level of Certainty |
|---|---|---|---|
| 1. | | | |
| 2. | | | |
| 3. | | | |
| 4. | | | |
| 5. | | | |
| 6. | | | |
| 7. | | | |
| 8. | | | |

*From DAFT. Organization Theory and Design, 10E. © 2010 South-Western, a part of Cengage Learning, Inc. Reproduced by permission. www.cengage.com/permissions

## Questions

1. Do you have adequate backup organizations for those of high dependence? How might you create even more backups?
2. What would you do if an organization you rated high for dependence and high for certainty suddenly became high dependence and low certainty? How would your behaviour relate to the concept of resource dependence?

*From DAFT. *Organization Theory and Design*, 10E. © 2010 South-Western, a part of Cengage Learning, Inc. Reproduced by permission. www.cengage.com/permissions.

# Case for Analysis: The Paradoxical Twins: Acme and Omega Electronics*

## PART I

In 1986, Technological Products of Fort Erie was bought out by a Cleveland, Ohio, manufacturer. The Cleveland firm had no interest in the electronics division of Technological Products and subsequently sold two plants that manufactured computer chips and printed circuit boards to different investors. Integrated circuits, or chips, were the first step into microminiaturization in the electronics industry, and both plants had developed some expertise in the technology, along with their superior capabilities in manufacturing printed circuit boards. One of the plants, located in nearby Walden, was renamed Acme Electronics; the other plant, within the city limits of Fort Erie, was renamed Omega Electronics, Inc.

Acme retained its original management and upgraded its general manager to president. Omega hired a new president who had been a director of a large electronic research laboratory and upgraded several of the existing personnel within the plant. Acme and Omega often competed for the same contracts. As subcontractors, both firms benefited from the electronics boom and both looked forward to future growth and expansion. The world was going digital, and both companies began producing digital microprocessors along with the production of circuit boards. Acme had annual sales of $100 million and employed 550 people. Omega had annual sales of $80 million and employed 480 people. Acme regularly achieved greater net profits, much to the chagrin of Omega's management.

### Inside Acme

The president of Acme, John Tyler, was confident that, had the demand not been so great, Acme's competitor would not have survived. "In fact," he said, "we have been able to beat Omega regularly for the most profitable contracts, thereby increasing our profit." Tyler credited his firm's greater effectiveness to his managers' abilities to run a "tight ship." He explained that he had retained the basic structure developed by Technological Products because it was most efficient for high-volume manufacturing. Acme had detailed organization charts and job descriptions. Tyler believed everyone should have clear responsibilities and narrowly defined jobs, which would lead to efficient performance and high company profits. People were generally satisfied with their work at Acme; however, some of the managers voiced the desire to have a little more latitude in their jobs.

### Inside Omega

Omega's president, Jim Rawls, did not believe in organization charts. He felt his organization had departments similar to Acme's, but he thought Omega's plant was small enough that things such as organization charts just put artificial barriers between specialists who should be working together. Written memos were not allowed since, as Rawls expressed it, "the plant is small enough that if people want to communicate, they can just drop by and talk things over."

The head of the mechanical engineering department said, "Jim spends too much of his time and mine making sure everyone understands what we're doing and listening to suggestions." Rawls was concerned with employee satisfaction and wanted everyone to feel part of the organization. The top management team reflected Rawls's attitudes. They also believed that employees should be familiar with activities throughout the organization so that cooperation between departments would be increased. A newer member of the industrial engineering department said, "When I first got here, I wasn't sure what I was supposed to do. One day I worked with some mechanical engineers and the next day I helped the shipping department design some packing cartons. The first months on the job were hectic, but at least I got a real feel for what makes Omega tick."

### Assignment Questions—Part I

1. What are Acme and Omega's goals?
2. What impact do top managers have on the goals?
3. Are the goals to be achieved with different strategies?

### Part II

In the 1990s, mixed analog and digital devices began threatening the demand for the complex circuit boards manufactured by Acme and Omega. This "system-on-a-chip" technology combined analog functions, such as sound, graphics, and power management, together with digital circuitry, such as logic and memory, making it highly useful for new products such as cellular phones and wireless computers. Both Acme and Omega realized the threat to their futures and began aggressively to seek new customers.

In July 1992, a major photocopier manufacturer was looking for a subcontractor to assemble the digital memory units of its new experimental copier. The projected contract for the job was estimated to be $7 million to $9 million in annual sales.

Both Acme and Omega were geographically close to this manufacturer, and both submitted highly competitive bids for the production of 100 prototypes. Acme's bid was slightly lower than Omega's; however, both firms were asked to produce 100 units. The photocopier manufacturer told both firms that speed was critical because its

*Adapted from John F. Veiga, The Paradoxical Twins: Acme and Omega Electronics, in John F. Veiga and John N. Yanouzas, *The Dynamics of Organizational Theory* (St. Paul: West, 1984), 132–138, with permission.

president had boasted to other manufacturers that the firm would have a finished copier available by Christmas. This boast, much to the designer's dismay, required pressure on all subcontractors to begin prototype production before the final design of the copier was complete. This meant Acme and Omega would have at most two weeks to produce the prototypes or would delay the final copier production.

## Assignment Question—Part II

1. Which organization do you think will produce better results? Why?

## Part III

### Inside Acme

As soon as John Tyler was given the blueprints (Monday, July 13, 1992), he sent a memo to the purchasing department asking to move forward on the purchase of all necessary materials. At the same time, he sent the blueprints to the drafting department and asked that it prepare manufacturing prints. The industrial engineering department was told to begin methods design work for use by the production department supervisors. Tyler also sent a memo to all department heads and executives indicating the critical time constraints of this job and how he expected that all employees would perform as efficiently as they had in the past.

The departments had little contact with one another for several days, and each seemed to work at its own speed. Each department also encountered problems. Purchasing could not acquire all the parts on time. Industrial engineering had difficulty arranging an efficient assembly sequence. Mechanical engineering did not take the deadline seriously and parceled its work to vendors so the engineers could work on other jobs scheduled previously. Tyler made it a point to stay in touch with the photocopier manufacturer to let it know things were progressing and to learn of any new developments. He traditionally worked to keep important clients happy. Tyler telephoned someone at the photocopier company at least twice a week and got to know the head designer quite well.

On July 17, Tyler learned that mechanical engineering was far behind in its development work, and he "hit the roof." To make matters worse, purchasing had not obtained all the parts, so the industrial engineers decided to assemble the product without one part, which would be inserted at the last minute. On Thursday, July 23, the final units were being assembled, although the process was delayed several times. On Friday, July 24, the last units were finished while Tyler paced around the plant. Late that afternoon, Tyler received a phone call from the head designer of the photocopier manufacturer, who told Tyler that he had received a call on Wednesday from Jim Rawls of Omega. He explained that Rawls's workers had found an error in the design of the connector cable and taken corrective action on their pro-

totypes. He told Tyler that he had checked out the design error and that Omega was right. Tyler, a bit overwhelmed by this information, told the designer that he had all the memory units ready for shipment and that, as soon as they received the missing component on Monday or Tuesday, they would be able to deliver the final units. The designer explained that the design error would be rectified in a new blueprint he was sending over by messenger and that he would hold Acme to the Tuesday delivery date.

When the blueprint arrived, Tyler called in the production supervisor to assess the damage. The alterations in the design would call for total disassembly and the unsoldering of several connections. Tyler told the supervisor to put extra people on the alterations first thing Monday morning and to try to finish the job by Tuesday. Late Tuesday afternoon, the alterations were finished and the missing components were delivered. Wednesday morning, the production supervisor discovered that the units would have to be torn apart again to install the missing component. When John Tyler received the news, he again "hit the roof." He called industrial engineering and asked if it could help out. The production supervisor and the methods engineer couldn't agree on how to install the component. John Tyler settled the argument by ordering that all units be taken apart again and the missing component installed. He told shipping to prepare cartons for delivery on Friday afternoon.

On Friday, July 31, fifty prototypes were shipped from Acme without final inspection. John Tyler was concerned about his firm's reputation, so he waived the final inspection after he personally tested one unit and found it operational. On Tuesday, August 4, Acme shipped the last fifty units.

### Inside Omega

On Friday, July 10, Jim Rawls called a meeting that included department heads to tell them about the potential contract they were to receive. He told them that as soon as he received the blueprints, work could begin. On Monday, July 13, the prints arrived and again the department heads met to discuss the project. At the end of the meeting, drafting had agreed to prepare manufacturing prints, while industrial engineering and production would begin methods design.

Two problems arose within Omega that were similar to those at Acme. Certain ordered parts could not be delivered on time, and the assembly sequence was difficult to engineer. The departments proposed ideas to help one another, however, and department heads and key employees had daily meetings to discuss progress. The head of electrical engineering knew of a Japanese source for the components that could not be purchased from normal suppliers. Most problems were solved by Saturday, July 18.

On Monday, July 20, a methods engineer and the production supervisor formulated the assembly plans, and production was set to begin on Tuesday morning. On Monday afternoon, people from mechanical engineering, electrical engineering, production, and industrial engineering got together to produce a prototype just to ensure that there would be no snags in production. While they were building the unit, they discovered an error in the connector cable design. All the engineers agreed, after checking and rechecking the blueprints, that the cable was erroneously designed. People from mechanical engineering and electrical engineering spent Monday night redesigning the cable, and on Tuesday morning, the drafting department finalized the changes in the manufacturing prints. On Tuesday morning, Rawls was a bit apprehensive about the design changes and decided to get formal approval. Rawls received word on Wednesday from the head designer at the photocopier firm that they could proceed with the design changes as discussed on the phone. On Friday, July 24, the final units were inspected by quality control and were then shipped.

### Assignment Questions—Part III

1. Which organization was more effective at developing the prototype and meeting the deadlines? Was its level of effectiveness due to the goals chosen by top management?

2. Predict which organization will get the final contract. Why?

### Part IV

Ten of Acme's final memory units were defective, whereas all of Omega's units passed the photocopier firm's tests. The photocopier firm was disappointed with Acme's delivery delay and incurred further delays in repairing the defective Acme units. However, rather than give the entire contract to one firm, the final contract was split between Acme and Omega with two directives added: (1) maintain zero defects and (2) reduce final cost. In 1993, through extensive cost-cutting efforts, Acme reduced its unit cost by 20 per cent and was ultimately awarded the total contract.

### Assignment Questions—Part IV

1. How can Acme's success be explained? Did Acme's goals seem more appropriate? Did stakeholder satisfaction play a role?
2. Overall, who was more effective, Acme or Omega? Explain.

---

## Case for Analysis: Vancity: Doing Good, Doing Well

*"Amid change and uncertainty, we're remaining true to our roots. We are Main Street, not Wall Street—independent and local, member-owned and based on cooperative principles."*

—*Excerpt from message from the CEO and chair, Vancity, 2008*

It was a typical cloudy spring day in Vancouver in April 2009. As Vancity chief executive officer (CEO) Tamara Vrooman looked out of the 11th floor window from her Terminal Avenue head office, she wondered if the gloomy weather outside was a fitting backdrop for the difficult decision facing Vancity's board. Recognized for its community values and commitment to social justice, Vancity was being forced by the ongoing financial crisis to consider repricing its line of credit offerings. Such a move was sure to be unpopular with the organization's customers, who also happened to be its owners (members) due to Vancity's structure as a Cooperative. "How could such a decision be implemented," she wondered, "without breaking the trust that members had in the institution?" If the board decided not to reprice the loans, how would the estimated shortfall of $24 million be covered? In short, how should Vancity balance its own financial viability with its members' expectations?

The immediate problem relating to repricing loans also raised broader questions for Vancity's strategy going forward: How should Vancity differentiate itself from other financial institutions? To what extent should Vancity stick to its cooperative roots versus focusing on making money that it would then plough back into the community? What should the measures of success be for the institution going forward?

## Vancity Background: History and Culture

Vancity was founded by a handful of local and former prairie residents following the Second World War, starting off on the corner of a desk in the Dominion Bank building at Victory Square. In a relatively short time, the credit union changed the nature of banking in Greater Vancouver: it was the first to loan money to the post-war wave of immigrants to help them buy their first homes (primarily Italians on Vancouver's Eastside); it was the first to lend to women without their husbands' signatures; and, it was the first to employ new technology to provide daily interest. In more recent years, Vancity pioneered social responsibility and environmental sustainability, becoming the first carbon neutral organization in the province and the first financial institution in North America to do so.[1]

When Vrooman took over as CEO of Vancity in September 2007, she joined an institution with a long history in British Columbia (BC)—one that had become Canada's largest credit union. Formerly the deputy minister

of finance in BC, Vrooman had overseen the province's annual $100 billion borrowings and helped allocate its $36 billion budget. A history graduate from the University of Victoria, Vrooman had not previously run a financial institution; however, she was widely admired for her role in the public sector, and Vancity's board recognized that her skills and background easily compensated for her lack of direct experience.

Net earnings at Vancity had been in decline for four years from 2004 through 2007; however, there was a turnaround in 2008, with earnings increasing at 43 per cent (see Exhibit 1), and Vrooman was committed to building on this positive change.

In the face of the financial crisis gripping the world in 2008 and 2009, trust in traditional financial institutions such as the major banks was eroding. Despite this declining trust Vancity continued to attract new members, with membership increasing from 407,070 to 409,202 in the first quarter of 2009. Vancity was perceived to be different from other financial institutions, and comments from members reflected this perception:

- "Vancity is the type of organization that one can be proud to be associated with. It sets the bar very high

**EXHIBIT 1**
**Vancity Financial Highlights (for the year ended December 31)**

| STATEMENT OF EARNINGS (IN THOUSANDS OF DOLLARS) | 2008 | 2007 | 2006 | 2005 | 2004 |
|---|---|---|---|---|---|
| Total interest income | 813,996 | 729,649 | 632,258 | 517,774 | 466,492 |
| Total interest expense | 482,389 | 448,781 | 352,826 | 244,918 | 211,416 |
| Net interest income | 331,607 | 280,868 | 279,432 | 272,856 | 255,076 |
| Provision for credit losses | −27,108 | −16,323 | −11,208 | −7,525 | −9,968 |
| Other income | 92,747 | 84,583 | 89,211 | 75,823 | 68,039 |
| Net interest and other income | 397,246 | 349,128 | 357,435 | 341,154 | 313,147 |
| Salaries and employee benefits | 187,037 | 173,746 | 160,876 | 146,982 | 133,330 |
| Other operating expenses | 134,653 | 124,760 | 124,569 | 115,771 | 105,062 |
| Earnings from operations | 75,556 | 50,622 | 71,990 | 78,401 | 74,755 |
| Unusual item | 0 | 0 | 0 | 1,359 | 18,848 |
| Earnings after unusual item | 75,556 | 50,622 | 71,990 | 79,760 | 93,603 |
| Distribution to community and members | 16,977 | 10,822 | 15,805 | 16,626 | 19,578 |
| Provision for income taxes | 11,762 | 7,045 | 10,885 | 16,012 | 16,838 |
| **Net earnings** | **46,817** | **32,755** | **45,300** | **47,122** | **57,187** |
| **Statistics** | | | | | |
| Return on average assets | 0.33% | 0.25% | 0.38% | 0.46% | 0.63% |
| Return on equity | 7.2% | 5.7% | 8.4% | 9.6% | 13.0% |
| Membership | 407,121 | 387,762 | 354,663 | 337,107 | 302,032 |
| No. of employees | 2,564 | 2,408 | 2,385 | 2,340 | 2,050 |

Source: Vancity *Annual Report,* 2008.

in many areas: diversity, service and respect for its members, community involvement and support."—Member since 1975.

- "This is one financial institution that sees things the right way-from the member's point of view."—Member since 2008.
- "They give me all the financial services I need, and they support the community."—Member since 2004.

Over time, traditional financial institutions were also moving toward a greater community focus, but Vancity continued to lead in this area. The company had developed a statement of values out of a highly consultative process involving a broad cross-section of staff, directors, members and representatives of the communities in which it operated (see Exhibit 2). Every two years the organization reported how well it lived up to its values and commitments in an externally verified accountability report. In one of these reports it also listed four short-term goals[2]:

1. Build on our financial strength: While we continue to show solid growth, we need to respond to the new market dynamics by growing in a more balanced way. Because of the asset-backed commercial paper market failure, capital to fund loans is scarcer and the cost of those funds has increased. To maintain healthy capital we need to balance loan growth with deposit growth. Serving and deepening relationships with our existing members and clients will be a priority. We will also be monitoring our costs and closely watching the markets and our performance to stay on track.

**EXHIBIT 2**
## Vancity Statement of Values and Commitments

**MISSION:**

To be a democratic, ethical, and innovative provider of financial services to our members. Through strong financial performance, we serve as a catalyst for the self-reliance and economic well-being of our membership and community.

**PURPOSE:**

Working with people and communities to help them thrive and prosper.

**VALUES:**

**Integrity:** We act with courage, consistency and respect to do what is honest, fair and trustworthy.
**Innovation:** We anticipate and respond to challenges and changing needs with creativity, enthusiasm and determination.
**Responsibility:** We are accountable to our members, employees, colleagues and communities for the results of our decisions and actions.

**COMMITMENTS:**

We make the following commitments in order to live our purpose and values in how we do business. Our aim is to strengthen Vancity's long term business while contributing to the well-being of our members, staff, communities and the environment.

We will be responsible and effective financial managers so Vancity remains strong and prospers. This means we will:

- make sound business decisions to achieve solid financial results
- manage risks responsibly to safeguard Vancity's assets
- prudently exercise fiduciary responsibility with members' deposits

We will provide you with outstanding service and help you achieve your financial goals. This means we will:

- treat you with respect and dignity
- give you trustworthy advice about your financial options
- offer products and services that meet your unique needs and provide good value
- protect your right to privacy
- ensure that low income and marginalized members have access to necessary financial services

**EXHIBIT 2 CONTINUED...**

We will provide meaningful opportunities for you to have input in setting the direction of the credit union. This means we will:

- make it easy and straightforward to vote and provide you with information to make informed decisions
- offer multiple channels for you to provide us with input and feedback
- address your concerns in a timely manner

We will ensure, that Vancity is a great place to work. This means we will:

- create a workplace that is healthy, diverse, stimulating, and rewarding
- provide the leadership, tools, resources and opportunities for employees to do their best work and achieve their full potential
- respect and honour employees' responsibilities to their families, friends and communities

We will lead by example and use our resources and expertise to effect positive change in our communities. This means we will:

- leverage our unique skills and expertise as a financial institution to create solutions to social, environmental and economic issues
- model and advocate socially and environmentally responsible business practices
- seek business partners that practice progressive employee relations, contribute to the well-being of their communities and respect the environment
- invest our dollars responsibly in the communities in which we live and work

We will be accountable for living up to our commitments. This means we will:

- make continuous and measurable progress in meeting our commitments
- involve our members, staff and communities in measuring our performance and report the findings in a public, externally verified report.

Source: Vancity *Accountability Report*, 2006–07.

2. Increase our commitment to community leadership: We are much more than a financial institution with a diverse array of products, competitive rates and convenient access. We also use our resources and expertise to positively change our community and environment in three focus areas: acting on climate change, facing poverty, and growing the social economy. Driving positive change is part of our co-operative roots and we believe it is critical to our future success; it is who we are, and it is what brings many staff and members to the Vancity Group and differentiates us from other financial institutions. We plan to build on this core strength and celebrate our successes more with employees and members. By engaging staff and members, and by embedding community leadership throughout our organization, this differentiator will set us apart and inspire our members, partners and the community.

3. Build operational excellence: We plan to reduce bureaucracy and move, decision making closer to where decisions are made. We've formed a small task force of senior leaders to lead this work. Process improvements, a technology strategy and other changes to support this goal will begin immediately.

4. Revive our spirit of innovation and entrepreneurial thinking: We know employees have innovative ideas about all aspects of our business. We need to create the culture and tools to tap into that creativity, assess and implement their very best ideas, and truly leverage innovation.

Vancity believed that its approach to business was not only the right thing to do from an ethical perspective, but that it also made good business sense. To the extent that its customers (members) subscribed to its values, Vancity was able to attract new members and grow; in addition, to the extent that Vancity's efforts in the community encouraged social and economic development, they also created a stronger platform for Vancity to operate upon. The benefits of Vancity's approach were also seen in other ways; for example, its branch in the crime-ridden, downtown Eastside was seen as an integral part of the community and as a result—and in contrast to most of the other businesses in the area—had never been robbed.

## Cooperative Structure

As a cooperative, Vancity's governance structure was quite different from that of a traditional corporation. Vancity was owned and controlled by its customers (members) and functioned to serve the needs of these members. The members contributed capital to finance the organization and all members, regardless of the amount of capital they invested, had an equal vote in selecting the cooperative's board of directors.

As a financial cooperative, Vancity was committed to the Co-operative Principles of the International Co-operative Alliance. These seven principles were seen as the foundation of its identity as a credit union[3]:

1. Voluntary and open membership,
2. Democratic member control,
3. Member economic participation,
4. Autonomy and independence,
5. Education, training and information,
6. Co-operation among co-operative,
7. Concern for community.

Vancity was not the only financial cooperative in British Columbia, though it was the largest. As of the end of 2007, there were 49 credit unions in the province with 368 branch locations and approximately 500 automated teller machines (ATMs), serving more than 1.6 million members. Generally, one out of every three British Columbians belonged to a credit union. Together, BC credit unions held more than $42 billion in assets and employed approximately 7,000 British Columbians. BC credit unions returned an average of $35 million annually to members in dividends and patronage refunds.[4]

## Social Finance[5]

Vancity had a long history of social engagement and community support: the board was committed to furthering this agenda and was in the process of defining a new strategy for the group built around social finance and a new approach to wealth generation. This new approach was based on principles of social justice, environmental sustainability and community well-being. Partly in reaction to recent market conditions and growing concerns about the role of financial institutions in encouraging speculation and excessive indebtedness, Vancity's social finance mission had an orientation of enhancing asset building tied to productive uses. This mission would take established corporate social responsibility (CSR) initiatives and embed them into Vancity's core business model to generate wealth for Vancity by improving the well-being of its community. Vancity used the following working definition in its operations: "Social Finance is an entrepreneurial and risk-based discipline of investment in enterprises—business, not-for-profit and cooperative—which uses a stable of capital pools and Vancity's convening power to generate economic, social, and environmental benefits and creates wealth and community well-being."

The social finance strategy would see the development of new products and a focus on different market segments. In commercial real estate, for example, the focus would shift from financing traditional real estate developments to affordable housing and green buildings. New opportunities would be sought in banking the unserved, enhancing food security and fostering the development of clean technologies.

Decision-making to implement the new strategy would be guided by the following key principles:

1. We will operate in an atmosphere of trust, transparency and transformational leadership.
2. We will build on our existing legacy of expertise, member relationships and community networks.
3. Social Finance is a profitable business model with metrics on social, environmental and financial outcomes.
4. Social Finance plays a leadership role at Vancity in the journey to our Vision, creating synergies across the Vancity group, and supporting our ethical standards.
5. We will put capital at measured risk for community benefit.
6. We will work to build assets and enhance cash flows for our members to build their sustainability and that of our community through a broad range of financial offerings.
7. Our commitment to research and innovation will allow us to identify and serve underserved markets.

## Financial Crisis

The financial crisis that hit world markets in late 2008 marked the end of a speculative bubble, driven by ever-increasing real estate prices in major markets. Accompanied by poor lending practices, particularly in the United States, and new forms of financial engineering, the crisis had undermined the stability of the entire financial system. Believing that real estate prices were on a permanent upward slope, some lenders had abandoned their traditionally prudent practices and offered mortgage loans to consumers who could not afford to make the interest payments once initial discounts had been exhausted. So-called NINJA loans were made to people with no income, no jobs and no assets. Other financial institutions repurchased these loans and repackaged them as collateralized debt obligations and, in turn, sold them on to others. The result was an enormous volume of new financial instruments with unknown risk, but which were acutely sensitive to a downturn in the housing markets.

Beginning in the fall of 2008, the turmoil in global financial markets started to have effects on economies around the world, and governments hastened to take action. By April 2009, several of the largest financial institutions in the world had ceased to exist as independent entities and many others were surviving due to government bailouts. Canadian banks were in relatively good shape, but the Canadian economy was not immune to global economic pressures. Monetary policy was being used aggressively worldwide as an economic stimulus and the Bank of Canada dropped its key overnight lending rate six times in six months, down to a historic low of 0.25 per cent. In December 2007, the rate had stood at 4.5 per cent; in announcing another rate reduction on April 21, 2009, Bank of Canada Governor Mark Carney indicated his intention to keep interest rates at this level at least through June of 2010.

The Bank of Canada rate was the key lending rate in the economy, and all financial institutions adjusted their own lending rates based on changes in this rate. Prime interest rates in Canada, charged by financial institutions to their best corporate accounts, had accordingly dropped to 2.25 per cent by April 2009. Other lending rates were generally pegged to the prime rate, and Vancity charged interest rates of prime plus or minus certain percentage points on its credit lines. These lines of credit, offered to customers with a good credit rating, were generally, but not always, secured by physical property. To offer these facilities, financial institutions collected deposits from their customers and used the funds to lend out. With a low prime rate, the difference between the interest rates paid to depositors and those charged to borrowers (the spread) had narrowed dramatically.

## Repricing Loans

The problem facing Vancity was that as lending rates declined, so did the margins on outstanding loans. In March 2009, Vancity's credit line portfolio amounted to approximately $2.3 billion. Some $1.8 billion of this was in secured debt, but 83 per cent of this debt was at or below the prime rate. Almost all other financial institutions had already repriced their loans to customers, generally by raising interest rates by one per cent across the board. The annualized loss to Vancity if they did not follow this practice was estimated at $24 million, based on existing outstanding loans. Should customers draw down their credit lines to the maximum authorized, the annualized loss to Vancity could increase to $45 million. Such drawing down of credit lines would also force Vancity to fund these loans at the expense of other member needs.

The total number of customers affected was approximately 80,000, but 5,500 of these were considered high priority as they held 80 per cent of the outstanding loans.

A customer contact plan had been drafted involving telephone calls to key customers, branch communications and mailings, but would need to be finalized based on expected reactions.

Unlike most commercial banks, Vancity's credit lines could not be repriced without customer acceptance. Vancity could not simply send a letter to customers informing them of a rate increase, as other financial institutions had done, as their contracts did not allow for such action to be taken. Vancity had the right to cancel the loans, but could not change the credit terms unilaterally. Cancelling ("calling") loans, or even threatening to do so, would have to be a last resort for Vancity.

The decision of whether or not to reprice loans was a very contentious one for Vancity. Some board members argued strongly that it was a violation of trust and could irrevocably damage the relationship that Vancity had with its members. Furthermore, they argued, it was the wrong thing to do in terms of the institution's high standards of ethics and fairness. Others argued that Vancity had no choice, pointing to the unusual financial circumstances, the competitive context and its obligation to safeguard the capital provided by its members.

Vancity had considered maintaining a prime rate above that of other financial institutions. While this could remove the need for repricing of the credit line portfolio, it would cause problems for the remainder of Vancity's prime-related products, which would then be priced uncompetitively high and would be out of line with those of all other Canadian financial institutions. This would, in turn, send a message that Vancity was charging rates higher than others in the market.

Vancity had also considered setting a prime rate for its credit line products separate and distinct from its regular prime rate. This option was rejected, as Vancity had no history of offering differential prime rates and none of its customer agreements or promotional materials allowed for such a distinction.

The company recognized the risks inherent in going to its members and asking them to sign new agreements at higher rates. It was likely that some members would not agree to the new terms, and more punitive actions would then have to be taken. Complaints from members about a cash grab could also undermine Vancity's reputation and have broader consequences for member relations and customer loyalty.

## Decision

As she walked to the boardroom, Vrooman could not help going over in her mind the pros and cons of the pricing decision. Was this the right move to make? Would Vancity's members accept the need for the change? What did the decision mean for the relationship that Vancity had with its members? What did it mean for the Group's new social finance agenda?

## Assignment Questions

1. How have policy makers responded to the global financial crisis, and what effect is this having on Vancity?
2. How is Vancity different from a commercial bank?
3. What is Vancity's business strategy?
4. Should Vancity reprice its loans?

[1] "Co-operative Opportunities in BC—A Discussion Paper," prepared for Vancity for the Business Council of British Columbia Opportunity BC 2020 Program, www.bcbc.com/Documents/2020200909_Vancity.pdf, accessed November 4, 2009.

[2] Vancity Accountability Report, 2006–07.

[3] Vancity *Co-operative Principles*, ww.vancity.com/AboutUs/OurValues/CooperativePrinciples/, accessed November 24, 2009.

[4] Vancity Accountability Report, 2006–07.

[5] "Social Finance Strategy: A New Approach to Wealth Generation," Vancity internal document, 2009.

# 5

# Interorganizational Relationships

Gary Tramontina/Bloomberg/Getty Images

Purpose of This Chapter

**Organizational Ecosystems**
Is Competition Dead? • The Changing Role of Management
• Interorganizational Framework

**Resource Dependence**
Resource Strategies • Power Strategies

**Collaborative Networks**
Why Collaboration? • From Adversaries to Partners

**Population Ecology**
Organizational Form and Niche • Process of Ecological Change
• Strategies for Survival

**Institutionalism**
The Institutional View and Organizational Design • Institutional Similarity

**Summary and Interpretation**

## Toyota Motor Corporation (Toyota)

Toyota (see photo) is considered the standard setter in developing, managing, and sustaining relationships with its network of nearly 200 suppliers. The Toyota Group, as the network is called, creates a strong identity of co-existence and co-prosperity, reciprocity, and knowledge transfer. Toyota is governed by 14 management principles. They include a focus on the long term in decision making; a commitment to getting quality right from the outset; a culture of relentless reflection, continuous learning, and improvement; and developing deep relationships with its suppliers. Principle 11 states "Respect your extended network of partners and suppliers by challenging them and helping them to improve."[1]

Toyota's underlying strategy for its supplier relationships is *keiretsu*, a tight network of suppliers that learns and prospers alongside the parent organization. Toyota sources about 80 percent of its manufacturing costs from its outside suppliers and works to ensure that the relationships are mutually advantageous. To that end, Toyota conducts joint improvement activities, shares information intensively but selectively develops its suppliers' technical capabilities, supervises its suppliers, turns supplier rivalry into opportunity, and understands how suppliers work. For example, Toyota has a guest engineer program whereby its suppliers send their engineers to Toyota's facilities for two or three years to work with Toyota's engineers to learn about and to contribute to the Toyota Way.

According to Toyota's management, its tight relationships with its suppliers have resulted in faster production times so that it can design a new car in 12 to 18 months, compared to the industry norm of 24 to 36 months. Moreover, Toyota reduced its manufacturing costs on the Camry by 25 percent in the 1990s while scoring top spot on the J.D. Powers customer satisfaction surveys. When compared to the top three North American manufacturers, Toyota is the most productive; Toyota requires 27.9 hours per vehicle for assembly while Ford and Chrysler require 37 and 35.9 hours, respectively.[2]

---

Organizations of all sizes in all industries are rethinking how they do business in response to today's chaotic environment. One of the most widespread trends is to reduce boundaries and increase collaboration between companies, sometimes even between competitors. Today's aerospace companies, for example, depend on strategic partnerships with other organizations. Bombardier and Boeing, a U.S. aerospace company, are both involved in multiple relationships with suppliers, competitors, and other organizations. Global semiconductor makers have been collaborating while competing for years because of the high costs and risks associated with creating and marketing a new generation of semiconductors.

Global competition and rapid advances in technology, communications, and transportation have created amazing new opportunities for organizations, but they have also raised the cost of doing business and made it increasingly difficult for any company to take advantage of those opportunities on its own. In this new economy, webs of organizations are emerging. A large company like General Electric develops a special relationship with a supplier that eliminates intermediaries by sharing complete information and reducing the costs of salespeople and distributors. Several small companies may join together to produce and market noncompeting products. You can see the results of interorganizational collaboration when movies such as the *Harry Potter* series are launched. Before seeing the movie, you might read a cover story in entertainment magazines, see a preview clip or chat live with the stars at an online site, find action toys being promoted through a fast-food franchise, and notice retail stores loaded with movie-related merchandise. For some blockbuster movies, coordinated action among companies can yield millions in addition to box-office and DVD profits. In the new economy, organizations think of themselves as teams that create value *jointly* rather than as autonomous companies that are in competition with all others.

## ■ Purpose of This Chapter

This chapter explores the most recent trend in organizing, which is the increasingly dense web of relationships among organizations. Companies have always been dependent on other organizations for supplies, materials, and information. The question is how these relationships are managed. At one time it was a matter of a large, powerful company like General Electric or Johnson & Johnson tightening the screws on small suppliers. Today, a company can choose to develop positive, trusting relationships. Or a large company like General Motors might find it difficult to adapt to the environment and hence create a new organizational form, such as Saturn, to operate with a different structure and culture. The notion of horizontal relationships described in Chapter 3 and the understanding of environmental uncertainty in Chapter 4 lead to the next stage of organizational evolution, which is horizontal relationships across organizations. Organizations can choose to build relationships in many ways, such as appointing preferred suppliers, establishing agreements, business partnering, joint ventures, or even mergers and acquisitions.

Interorganizational research has yielded perspectives such as resource dependence, collaborative networks, population ecology, and institutionalism. The sum total of these ideas can be daunting, because it means managers no longer can rest in the safety of managing a single organization. They have to understand how to manage a whole set of interorganizational relationships, which is a great deal more challenging and complex. The cartoon in Exhibit 5.1 illustrates the benefits of such relationships!

The You and Design feature asks you to assess your own relationships as evidenced by the nature of your networking.

**EXHIBIT 5.1**
The Benefits of Interorganizational Relationships!

## YOU & DESIGN

### Personal Networking

Are you a natural at reaching out to others for personal networking? Having multiple sources of information is a building block for partnering with people in other organizations.

To learn something about your networking, answer the following questions. Please answer whether each item is Mostly True or Mostly False for you in school or at work.

| | Mostly True | Mostly False |
|---|---|---|
| 1. I learn early on about changes going on in the organization and how they might affect me or my job. | _____ | _____ |
| 2. I network as much to help other people solve problems as to help myself. | _____ | _____ |
| 3. I join professional groups and associations to expand my contacts and knowledge. | _____ | _____ |
| 4. I know and talk with peers in other organizations. | _____ | _____ |
| 5. I act as a bridge from my work group to other work groups. | _____ | _____ |
| 6. I frequently use lunches to meet and network with new people. | _____ | _____ |
| 7. I regularly participate in charitable causes. | _____ | _____ |
| 8. I maintain a list of friends and colleagues to whom I send cards. | _____ | _____ |
| 9. I maintain contact with people from previous organizations and school groups. | _____ | _____ |
| 10. I actively give information to subordinates, peers, and my boss. | _____ | _____ |

**Scoring:** Give yourself one point for each item marked as Mostly True. A score of 7 or higher suggests very active networking. If you scored three or less, reaching out to others may not be natural for you and will require extra effort.

**Interpretation:** In a world of adversarial relationships between organizations, networking across organizational boundaries was not important. However, in a world of interorganizational partnerships, many good things flow from active networking, which will build a web of organizational relationships to get things done. If you are going to manage relationships with other organizations, networking is an essential part of your job. Networking builds social, work, and career relationships that facilitate mutual benefit. People with large, active networks tend to enjoy and contribute to partnerships and have broader impact on interorganizational relationships.

## Organizational Ecosystems

**Interorganizational relationships** are the relatively enduring resource transactions, flows, and linkages that occur among two or more organizations.[3] Traditionally, these transactions and relationships have been seen as a necessary evil to obtain what an organization needs. The presumption has been that the world is composed of distinct businesses that thrive on autonomy and compete for supremacy. A company may be forced into interorganizational relationships depending on its needs and the instability and complexity of the environment.

One current view argues that organizations are now evolving into business ecosystems. An **organizational ecosystem** is a system formed by the interaction of a community of organizations and their environment. An ecosystem cuts across traditional industry lines. A company can create its own ecosystem. Microsoft travels in four major industries: consumer electronics, information, communications, and personal computers. Its ecosystem also extends to hundreds of suppliers, including Hewlett-Packard and Intel, and millions of customers across many markets. Cable companies such as Rogers Communications are offering home phone service as well as wireless, television, and Internet services, and telephone companies such as Bell Canada are now in the satellite television business.

Apple Computer is arguably having greater success as an entertainment company with its iPod and iTunes Music Store than it ever had as a computer manufacturer. In 2013, for example, Apple topped the list of the most admired companies for the sixth consecutive year.[4] Apple's success grows out of close partnerships with other organizations, including music companies, consumer electronics firms, smartphone makers, other computer companies, and even car manufacturers.[5] Samsung of South Korea is the major supplier of parts in Apple's iPhone—its components account for more than $80 in each iPhone. A key component also comes from a subsidiary of the automotive parts manufacturer, Magna International.[6] Apple and Microsoft, like other business ecosystems, develop relationships with hundreds of organizations cutting across traditional business boundaries. The first Case for Analysis details the ecosystem that Apple has spawned.

**Apply**

Apply what you learned about your networks and your networking skill from the You and Design feature to expand your own network.

## ■ Is Competition Dead?

No company can go it alone under a constant onslaught of international competitors, changing technology, and new regulations. Organizations around the world are embedded in complex networks of confusing relationships—collaborating in some markets, competing fiercely in others. Indeed, research indicates that a large percentage of new alliances in recent years have been between competitors. These alliances influence organizations' competitive behaviour in varied ways.[7]

Traditional competition, which assumes a distinct company competing for survival and supremacy with other stand-alone businesses, no longer exists because each organization both supports and depends on the others for success, and perhaps for survival. However, most managers recognize that the competitive stakes are higher than ever in a world where market share can crumble overnight and no industry is immune from almost instant obsolescence.[8] In today's world, a new form of competition is in fact intensifying.[9]

Organizations now need to coevolve with others in the ecosystem so that everyone gets stronger. Consider the wolf and the caribou. Wolves cull weaker caribou, which strengthens the herd. A strong herd means that wolves must become stronger themselves. With coevolution, the whole system becomes stronger. In the same way, companies coevolve through discussion with each other, shared visions, alliances, and managing complex relationships. Chapters.Indigo.ca and its retail partners are an example of this approach.

In an organizational ecosystem, conflict and cooperation frequently exist at the same time. Mutual dependencies and partnerships have become a fact of life in business ecosystems, so is competition dead? Companies today may use their strength to win conflicts and negotiations, but ultimately cooperation carries the day. For example, Intel reversed itself and became involved in supporting the One Laptop

Per Child Foundation even though the head of the Foundation and Intel's chair had feuded publicly. As William Swope, Intel's Director of Corporate Affairs put it, "By aligning here we are going to help more kids."[10]

At Google, there's a whole team dedicated to giving business to the competition. If people don't like Google products, such as Gmail or Google Maps, the Google team makes it easy for them to move their data free of charge to any competitor's website. Google has never tried to lock users into its products, believing that when people spend more time online—wherever they spend it—everyone benefits. Helping your competitors get more business might seem like a strange way to run a business, but Google managers don't think so. Take the Google Chrome browser. It's small potatoes compared to Microsoft's Internet Explorer, but Chrome has slowly eaten away at Microsoft's market share. Yet Google Chrome is free and open source, which means any other browser that wants to incorporate pieces of the software can freely do so. What if Microsoft copied entire chunks of Chrome's programming code and built a better Explorer? That's great, says Google. Similarly, Google makes its smartphone's operating platform Android free to any handset manufacturer that wants to use it. It created the first real competition to the iPhone, and the open-source approach means there are now many more people using Android-based phones than iPhones. Google believes giving away its technology leads to further Internet advances, which not only fits with Google's mission of improving the way people connect with information but also means Google gets more business—and gets stronger.

Collaboration, Google managers say, is essential to innovation. Consider the recently released Google Body Browser, an interactive 3-D simulation of the human body that allows users to peel back layers of the body and zoom in to study specific organs, bones, muscles, and more. At this time, Body Browser is still a work in progress, but it could be a hit with medical schools as well as other users (and advertisers). So far, few browsers outside of Google's most recent version of Chrome can support such a sophisticated tool. Others will catch up, of course, and that's fine with Google because that will spur even further advances.[11]

Google's emphasis on cooperation might be tested in coming years as it moves more steadily into markets now dominated by Apple. In addition to smartphones, Google is also moving into other businesses, such as digital music services, that put it in direct competition with a tough rival. "Open systems don't always win," warned Steve Jobs, Apple's co-founder and former CEO, who always kept tight control and close watch over his company's products.[12]

Similarly, as part of the Toronto Port Lands area redevelopment, two rivals have united to build the largest studio complex in Toronto. Although movie mogul Paul Bronfman had lost a bid to build a major film studio in the area to Sam Reisman, a developer, the two have partnered to build the Filmport studio complex. As Bronfman put it, "Sam won the deal fair and square, but we've always had a great relationship and I'm glad that I could get involved.... Toronto is losing out to other cities and this studio will help put Toronto back on the map [as Hollywood North]."[13] The first phase of the Filmport project will create the largest sound stage in North America and, once completed, Filmport is expected to be more than three million square feet. It expects to have competition from another studio, Pinewood Studios, which has access to the expertise of the largest European studio. But, according to Reisman, "I think it will help in attracting more production to the city. No different than having more stores in a plaza, it gives people options and at this point we can't be accused of overcapacity."[14] The facility opened in 2008 with no studio tenant.[15] Since then, it has become the Pinewood Toronto Studios and was named, in 2011, one of the reasons to love Toronto by *Toronto Life*.[16] Three studios were added in 2013. Pinewood Toronto Studios has helped Toronto to become the third largest production centre in North America and is home to films such as *Pacific Rim* and *Robocop*.[17]

## ■ The Changing Role of Management

Within business ecosystems, managers learn to move beyond traditional responsibilities of corporate strategy and designing hierarchical structures and control systems. If a top manager looks down to enforce order and uniformity, the company is missing opportunities for new and evolving external relationships.[18] In this new world, managers think about horizontal processes rather than vertical structures. Important initiatives are not just top down but also cut across the boundaries separating organizational units. Moreover, horizontal relationships, as described in Chapter 3, now include linkages with suppliers and customers, who become part of the team. Business leaders can learn to lead economic coevolution. Managers learn to see and appreciate the rich environment of opportunities that grows from cooperative relationships with other contributors to the ecosystem. Rather than trying to force suppliers into low prices or customers into high prices, managers strive to strengthen the larger system evolving around them, finding ways to understand this big picture and to contribute.

This is a broader leadership role than ever before. For example, the Global Business Coalition on HIV/AIDS, Tuberculosis, and Malaria (GBC) has spent seven years developing an alliance of over 200 international companies dedicated to combating the AIDS epidemic through the business sector's unique skills and expertise. Headquartered in New York, GBC maintains regional offices in Beijing, Geneva, Johannesburg, Nairobi, and Paris; "it harnesses the individual and collective power of the world's top corporations to fight AIDS at the local, national, and international levels."[19] GBC is also in the process of merging with the Transatlantic Partners Against AIDS. Its Canadian members include Alcan, Bank of Nova Scotia, Barrick Gold, BMO Financial Group, Indigo Books and Music, Power Corporation of Canada, Royal Bank of Canada, Sun Life Financial, and TD Financial Group.

## ■ Interorganizational Framework

Understanding this larger organizational ecosystem is one of the most exciting areas of organizational theory. The models and perspectives for understanding interorganizational relationships ultimately help managers change their role from top-down management to horizontal management across organizations. A framework for analyzing the different views of interorganizational relationships is in Exhibit 5.2. Relationships among organizations can be characterized by whether the organizations are dissimilar or similar and whether relationships are competitive or cooperative. By understanding these perspectives, managers can assess their environment and adopt strategies to suit their needs. The first perspective is called resource-dependence theory, which was briefly described in Chapter 4. It describes rational ways organizations deal with each other to reduce dependence on the environment. The second perspective is about collaborative networks, wherein organizations allow themselves to become dependent on other organizations to increase value and productivity for both. The third perspective

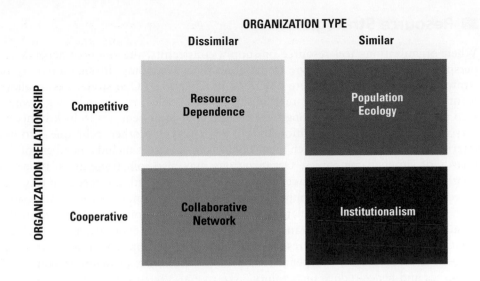

**ORGANIZATION TYPE**

EXHIBIT 5.2
A Framework of
Interorganizational
Relationships
*Thanks to Anand Narasimham
for suggesting this framework.

is population ecology, which examines how new organizations fill niches left open by established organizations, and how a rich variety of new organizational forms benefits society. The final approach is called institutionalism and explains why and how organizations legitimate themselves in the larger environment and design structures by borrowing ideas from each other. These four approaches to the study of interorganizational relationships are described in the remainder of this chapter.

**Compare**

Compare the ecosystems of the computer and automotive industries to see how they differ, and why.

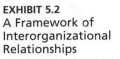

# Resource Dependence

Resource dependence represents the traditional view of relationships among organizations. As described in Chapter 4, resource-dependence theory argues that organizations try to minimize their dependence on other organizations for the supply of important resources and try to influence the environment to make resources available.[20] Organizations succeed by striving for independence and autonomy. When threatened by greater dependence, organizations will assert control over external resources to minimize that dependence. Resource-dependence theory argues that organizations do not want to become vulnerable to other organizations because of negative effects on performance.

The amount of dependence on a resource is based on two factors. First is the importance of the resource to the organization, and second is how much discretion or monopoly power those who control a resource have over its allocation and use.[21] Organizations aware of resource dependence tend to develop strategies to reduce their dependence on the environment and learn how to use their power differences. For example, one study of Canadian university athletic departments found that they perceived that the central administration of universities had considerable control over them.[22] Another study of Canadian sports organizations reports that linkages are increasing between nonprofit sports organizations, governments, and corporations. The linkages are designed to help the organizations to share resources and to coordinate their work.[23] In 2006, Swimming Canada and the Red Cross of Canada become partners: Swimming Canada is to promote the Red Cross's safety messages and the Red Cross is to identify potential competitive swimmers.[24]

## ■ Resource Strategies

When organizations feel resource or supply constraints, the resource-dependence perspective says they manoeuvre to maintain their autonomy through a variety of strategies, several of which were described in Chapter 4. One strategy is to adapt to or alter the interdependent relationships. This could mean purchasing owner-ship in suppliers, developing long-term contracts or joint ventures to lock in neces-sary resources, or building relationships in other ways. Another technique is to use interlocking directorships, which means boards of directors include members of the boards of supplier companies. Organizations may also join trade associations to coordinate their needs, sign trade agreements, or merge with another firm to guar-antee resources and material supplies. Some organizations may take political action, such as lobbying for new regulations or deregulation, favourable taxation, tariffs, or subsidies, or push for new standards that make resource acquisition easier. Orga-nizations operating under the resource-dependence philosophy will do whatever is needed to avoid excessive dependence on the environment to maintain control of resources and hence reduce uncertainty.

## ■ Power Strategies

In resource-dependence theory, large, independent companies have power over small suppliers.[25] For example, power in consumer products has shifted from ven-dors such as Rubbermaid and Procter & Gamble to the big discount retail chains, which can demand—and receive—special pricing deals. Walmart has grown so large and powerful that it can dictate terms with virtually any supplier. Consider Levi Strauss, which for much of its 150-year history was a powerful supplier, with a jeans brand that millions of people wanted and retailers were eager to stock. "When I first started in this business, retailers were a waystation to the consumer," says Levi's CEO Philip Marineau. "Manufacturers had a tendency to tell retailers how to do business." But the balance of power has shifted dramatically. In order to sell to Walmart, Levi Strauss had to overhaul its entire operation, from design and production to pricing and distribution. For example, Levi jeans used to go from factories to a company-owned distribution centre where they were labelled, packed, and sent on to retailers. Now, to meet Walmart's desire to get products quickly, jeans are shipped already tagged from contract factories direct to Walmart distribu-tion centres, where Walmart trucks pick them up and deliver them to individual stores.[26] When one company has power over another, it can ask suppliers to absorb more costs, ship more efficiently, and provide more services than ever before, often without a price increase. Often the suppliers feel that they have no choice but to go along, and those that fail to do so may go out of business.

Many organizations manage supply-chain relationships by using the Internet and other intellective technologies, creating linkages between the organization and their external partners to exchange data. Companies such as Apple, Samsung, and Tesco, to name a few, are connected electronically so that everyone along the supply chain has almost transparent information, in a timely way. In 2010, Apple was named the best-performing supply chain in the world for the third year in a row.[27]

Power is also shifting in various industries. For decades, technology vendors have been putting out incompatible products and expecting their corporate customers to assume the burden and expense of making everything work together. Those days are coming to an end. When the economy began declining, big corporations cut back their spending on technology, which led to stiffer competition among vendors and gave corporate customers greater power to make demands. Microsoft and Sun Microsystems, which have been waging war for 15 years, recently buried the hatchet and negotiated a collaboration agreement that will smooth the way for providing compatible software products.[28]

## Collaborative Networks

Traditionally, the relationship between organizations and their suppliers has been an adversarial one. Indeed, North American companies typically have worked alone, competing with each other and believing in the tradition of individualism and self-reliance. Today, however, thanks to an uncertain global environment, a realignment in corporate relationships is taking place. The **collaborative-network** perspective is an emerging alternative to resource-dependence theory. Companies join together to become more competitive and to share scarce resources. Technology companies join together to produce next-generation products. Large aerospace firms partner with one another and with smaller companies and suppliers to design next-generation jets. Large pharmaceutical companies join with small biotechnology firms to share resources and knowledge and spur innovation. Nonprofit organizations often build bridges or bond to deal with the impact to their survival that environmental changes in the social sector bring.[29] Consulting firms, investment companies, and accounting firms may join in an alliance to meet customer demands for expanded services.[30] As companies move into their own uncharted territory, they are also racing into alliances.

### Why Collaboration?

Why all this interest in interorganizational collaboration? Major reasons are sharing risks when entering new markets, mounting expensive new programs and reducing costs, and enhancing organizational profile in selected industries or technologies. Cooperation is a prerequisite for greater innovation, problem solving, and performance.[31] In addition, partnerships are a major avenue for entering global markets, with both large and small firms developing partnerships overseas and in North America.

North Americans have learned from their international experience just how effective interorganizational relationships can be. Both Japan and Korea have long traditions of corporate clans or industrial groups that collaborate and assist each other. North Americans typically have considered interdependence a bad thing, believing it would reduce competition. However, the experience of collaboration in other countries has shown that competition among companies can be fierce in some areas even as they collaborate in others. It is as if the brothers and sisters of a single family went into separate businesses and want to outdo one another, but they still love one another and will help each other when needed.

Interorganizational linkages provide a kind of safety net that encourages long-term investment and risk taking. Companies can achieve higher levels of innovation and performance as they learn to shift from an adversarial to a partnership mind-set.[32] In many cases companies are learning to work closely together. Consider the following examples:

- Angiotech, a pharmaceutical and medical device company headquartered in Vancouver, has partnered with Boston Scientific Corporation to market coronary stent systems in Japan.[33]
- International pharmaceuticals giant Pfizer collaborates with more than 400 companies on research and development projects and co-marketing campaigns. For example, Pfizer has earned billions from co-promotion of Warner-Lambert's Lipitor, a drug for treating elevated cholesterol.[34]
- Leave No Trace Canada is a nonprofit organization whose mission is to promote and to inspire responsible outdoor recreation through education, research, and partnerships. To fulfill its mission, it has partnerships with co-operatives, governments, and business associations.[35]
- Small companies are banding together to compete against much larger firms. The Ontario Craft Brewers was formed in 2005 to increase awareness about members' beers with the goal of increasing their market share from four percent in 2005 to 12 percent by 2014. The Government of Ontario provided money to support the brewers' marketing campaign.[36] Since then, (1) the number of craft breweries in Ontario has increased to 47 from 31 in 2005, (2) sales of Ontario craft beer reached approximately $190 million in 2010, representing a five percent share of the Ontario beer market, (3) in 2011, Ontario's craft beers led LCBO sales in all categories, including wine and spirits—with nearly 45 percent sales growth, and (4) Ontario's craft breweries won 19 awards at the 2012 Canadian Brewing Awards.[37]

**Think**

Think about how to form partnerships that might benefit you.

## ■ From Adversaries to Partners

Once-bitter rivalries among suppliers, customers, and competitors are now being replaced with partnerships between them. In North America, collaboration among organizations initially occurred in not-for-profit social service and mental health organizations where public interest was involved. Community organizations collaborated to achieve greater effectiveness and better use scarce resources.[38] With the push from international competitors and international examples, hard-nosed business managers began shifting to a new partnership paradigm on which to base their relationships.

A summary of this change in mind-set is in Exhibit 5.3. More companies are changing from a traditional adversarial mind-set to a partnership orientation. Evidence from studies of companies such as General Electric, Toyota, Whirlpool, Harley-Davidson, and Microsoft indicate that partnering allows reduced cost and increased value for both parties in a predatory world economy.[39] Rather than organizations maintaining independence, the new model is based on interdependence and trust. Performance measures for the partnership are loosely defined, and problems are resolved through discussion and dialogue. Managing strategic relationships with other firms has become a critical management skill, as discussed in this chapter's Book Mark. In the new orientation, people try to add value to both sides and believe in high commitment rather than suspicion and competition. Companies work toward equitable profits for both sides rather than just for their own benefit. The new model is characterized by lots of shared information, including electronic linkages for automatic ordering and face-to-face discussions to provide corrective feedback and solve problems. Sometimes people from other companies are on-site to

| TRADITIONAL ORIENTATION: ADVERSARIAL | NEW ORIENTATION: PARTNERSHIP |
|---|---|
| Low dependence | High dependence |
| Suspicion, competition, arm's length | Trust, addition of value to both sides, high commitment |
| Detailed performance measures, closely monitored | Loose performance measures, problems discussed |
| Price, efficacy, own profits | Equity, fair dealing, both profit |
| Limited information and feedback | Electronic linkages to share key information, problem feedback, and discussion |
| Legal resolution of conflict | Mechanisms for close coordination, people on-site |
| Minimal involvement and up-front investment, separate resources | Involvement in partner's product design and production, shared resources |
| Short-term contracts | Long-term contracts |
| Contract limiting the relationship | Business assistance beyond the contract |

**EXHIBIT 5.3**
Changing Characteristics of Interorganizational Relationships

Source: Based on Mick Marchington and Steven Vincent, "Analysing the Influence of Institutional, Organizational, and Interpersonal Forces in Shaping Inter-Organizational Relations," *Journal of Management Studies* 41, no. 6 (September 2004), 1029–1056; Jeffrey H. Dyer, "How Chrysler Created an American Keiretsu," *Harvard Business Review* (July/August 1996), 42–56; Myron Magnet, "The New Golden Rule of Business," *Fortune* (February 21, 1994), 60–64; and Peter Grittner, "Four Elements of Successful Sourcing Strategies," *Management Review* (October 1995), 41–45.

enable very close coordination, as we saw in the chapter-opening example. Partners are involved in each other's product design and production, and they invest for the long term, with an assumption of continuing relations. Partners develop equitable solutions to conflicts rather than relying on legal contractual relationships. Contracts may be loosely specified, and it is not unusual for business partners to help each other outside whatever is specified in the contract.[40]

This new partnership mind-set can be seen in a number of industries. Microsoft hired contract manufacturer Flextronics to not only build but also help design Xbox, its electronic game console.[41] Many supermarkets and other retailers rely on key suppliers to help them determine what goes on the store shelves. A large vendor such as Procter & Gamble, for example, analyzes national data and makes recommendations for what products the store should offer, including not only P&G's brands, but also products from its competitors.[42] A large company in England that supplies pigments to the automobile, plastics, and printing industries has a long-standing interdependent relationship with a key chemicals supplier, with the two organizations sharing information about their long-term business needs so that any changes in products or processes can benefit both sides.[43]

In this new view of partnerships, dependence on another organization is seen to reduce rather than increase risks. Greater value can be achieved by both parties. By being embedded in a system of interorganizational relationships, everyone does better by helping each other. This is a far cry from the belief that organizations do best by being autonomous and independent. Sales representatives may have a desk on the customer's factory floor, and they have access to information systems and the research lab.[44] Coordination is so intimate that it's sometimes hard to tell one organization from another. The next In Practice describes how Bombardier and its suppliers are linked together almost like one organization in building the Continental, a "super-midsize" business jet that can comfortably fly eight passengers nonstop from coast to coast.

## Book Mark 5.0   HAVE YOU READ THIS BOOK?

**Managing Strategic Relationships: The Key to Business Success***
By Leonard Greenhalgh

What determines organizational success in the 21st century? According to Leonard Greenhalgh, author of *Managing Strategic Relationships: The Key to Business Success*, it's how successfully managers support, foster, and protect collaborative relationships both inside and outside the firm. The book offers strategies for managing relationships between people and groups within the company and with other organizations. Effectively managing relationships generates a sense of commonwealth and consensus, which ultimately results in competitive advantage.

### MANAGING RELATIONSHIPS IN A NEW ERA

Greenhalgh says managers need a new way of thinking to fit the realities of the new era. Here are a few guidelines:

* *Recognize that detailed legal contracts can undermine trust and goodwill.* Greenhalgh stresses the need to build relationships that are based on honesty, trust, understanding, and common goals instead of on narrowly defined legal contracts that concentrate on what one business can give to the other.
* *Treat partners like members of your own organization.* Members of partner organizations need to be active participants in the learning experience by becoming involved in training, team meetings, and other activities. Giving a

partner organization's employees a chance to make genuine contributions promotes deeper bonds and a sense of unity.

* *Top managers must be champions for the alliance.* Managers from both organizations have to act in ways that signal to everyone inside and outside the organization a new emphasis on partnership and collaboration. Using ceremony and symbols can help instill a commitment to partnership in the company culture.

### CONCLUSION

To succeed in today's environment, old-paradigm management practices based on power, hierarchy, and adversarial relationships must be traded for new-era commonwealth practices that emphasize collaboration and communal forms of organization. The companies that will thrive, Greenhalgh believes, "are those that really have their act together—those that can successfully integrate strategy, processes, business arrangements, resources, systems, and empowered workforces." That can be accomplished, he argues, only by effectively creating, shaping, and sustaining strategic relationships.

*\*Managing Strategic Relationships: The Key to Business Success*, by Leonard Greenhalgh, is published by The Free Press, 2001.

## In Practice
### Bombardier

In an assembly plant on the edge of Mid-Continent Airport in Wichita, Kansas, a new plane is taking shape as great chunks of it are rolled in and joined together. Not counting rivets, it takes just a dozen big parts—all manufactured elsewhere—to put Bombardier's Continental together. Those big subassemblies come from all over the world—the engines from Phoenix, Arizona; the nose and cockpit from Montréal; the mid-fuselage from Belfast, Northern Ireland; the tail from Taichung, Taiwan; the wings from Nagoya, Japan; and other parts from Australia, France, Germany, and Austria. When production is up to full speed, it will take just four days to put a plane together and get it in the air.

In the past, most executive-jet companies have made major parts in-house. Bombardier, instead, relies heavily on suppliers for design support and the sharing of development costs and market risks. The company is intertwined with about 30 suppliers, a dozen or so of which have been involved since the design stage. At one point, about 250 team members from Bombardier and 250 from outsider suppliers worked together in Montréal to make sure the design would be good for everyone involved. Bombardier has so far invested about $250 million in the Continental, but suppliers have equalled that amount in development costs. In addition to sharing costs, the supplier companies also share the risks. "They haven't got a contract that says, 'You're going to sell us twenty-five wings a year for the next 10 years.' If the market's there, it's there, and if it's not, it's not," says John Holding, who is in charge of Bombardier's engineering and product development.[45]

Integrating partners so that everyone benefits from and depends on the others—and managing this multinational, multi-company endeavour—is no easy task, but with development costs for a new plane reaching more than $1 billion, the partnership approach just makes sense.[46]

---

By breaking down boundaries and becoming involved in partnerships with an attitude of fair dealing and adding value to both sides, today's companies are changing the concept of what makes an organization. The type of collaborative network illustrated by Bombardier is also being used by a growing number of automotive companies, including Volkswagen and General Motors. These companies are pushing the idea of partnership further than ever before, moving somewhat toward a network approach to organizational design.

## Population Ecology

This section introduces a different perspective on relationships among organizations. The **population-ecology perspective** differs from the other perspectives because it focuses on organizational diversity and adaptation within a population of organizations.[47] A **population** is a set of organizations engaged in similar activities with similar patterns of resource utilization and outcomes. Organizations within a population compete for similar resources or similar customers, such as financial institutions in the Edmonton area would do.

Within a population, the question asked by ecology researchers is about the large number and variation of organizations in society. Why are new organizational forms that create such diversity constantly appearing? The answer is that individual organizational adaptation is severely limited compared to the changes demanded by the environment. Innovation and change in a population of organizations take place through the birth of new forms and kinds of organizations more so than by the reform and change of existing organizations. Indeed, organizational forms are considered relatively stable, and the good of a whole society is served by the development of new forms of organization through entrepreneurial initiatives. New organizations meet the new needs of society more than established organizations that are slow to change.[48]

What does this theory mean in practical terms? It means that large, established organizations often become dinosaurs. As discussed in the previous chapter, large airlines that rely on a hub-and-spoke system have had tremendous difficulty adapting to a rapidly changing environment. Hence, new organizational forms are emerging that fit the current environment, fill a new niche, and, over time, take away business from established companies. Bullfrog Power, for example, provides 100 percent green electricity to Ontario and Alberta residents and businesses, and is changing the landscape of electricity generation.[49]

Why do established organizations have such a hard time adapting to a rapidly changing environment? Michael Hannan and John Freeman, originators of the population-ecology model of organization, argue that there are many limitations on the ability of organizations to change. The limitations come from heavy investment in plants, equipment, and specialized personnel; limited information; established viewpoints of decision makers; the organization's own successful history that justifies current procedures; and the difficulty of changing organizational culture. True transformation is a rare and unlikely event in the face of all these barriers.

For example, large equipment makers such as Cisco, Nortel Networks, and Sun Microsystems have felt the pinch as they lose million-dollar deals to used-equipment brokers. Another recent change is the development of corporate universities within large companies like Motorola and FedEx. There are more than 2,000 corporate universities, compared to just 200 a few years ago. One reason they've developed so quickly is that companies can't get desired services from established universities, which are too stuck in traditional ways of thinking and teaching.[50]

According to the population-ecology view, when looking at an organizational population as a whole, the changing environment determines which organizations survive or fail. The assumption is that individual organizations suffer from structural inertia and find it difficult to adapt to environmental changes. Thus, when rapid change occurs, old organizations are likely to decline or fail, and new organizations emerge that are better suited to the needs of the environment.

The population-ecology model is developed from theories of natural selection in biology, and the terms *evolution* and *selection* are used to refer to the underlying behavioural processes. Theories of biological evolution try to explain why certain life forms appear and survive, whereas others perish. Some theories suggest the forms that survive are typically best fitted to the immediate environment.

Some years ago, *Forbes* magazine reported a study of American businesses over 70 years, from 1917 to 1987. Of the 22 that remained in the top 100, only 11 did so under their original names. The environment of the 1940s and 1950s was suitable to Woolworth, but new organizational forms like Walmart became dominant in the 1980s. In 1917, most of the top 100 companies were huge steel and mining industrial organizations, which were replaced by high-technology companies such as IBM and Merck.[51] Two companies that seemed to prosper over a long period were Ford and General Motors, but they are now being threatened by world changes in the automobile industry. Meanwhile, technology continues to change the environment. The expansion of the Internet into many consumers' households has brought a proliferation of new organizations such as Facebook, Google, Skype, and eBay.

No company is immune to the processes of social change. More and more Canadian firms are being bought by international companies and there is concern that the Canadian economy is being hollowed out. In response to the concern, a federal panel was set up in 2007 to review foreign ownership and to examine the *Investment Canada Act*.[52] On the other hand, Canadian National Railway has been buying up American railways; in 2007, it bought the major portion of the Elgin, Joliet, and Eastern Railway (EJ&E) for US$300 million.[53]

## ■ Organizational Form and Niche

The population-ecology model is concerned with **organizational form**. Organizational form is an organization's specific technology, structure, products, goals, and personnel, which can be selected or rejected by the environment. Each new organization tries to find a **niche** (a domain of unique environmental resources and needs) sufficient to support it. The niche is usually small in the early stages of an organization but may increase in size over time if the organization is successful. If a niche is not available, the organization will decline and may perish.

From the viewpoint of a single firm, luck, chance, and randomness play important parts in survival. New products and ideas are continually being proposed by both entrepreneurs and large organizations. Whether these ideas and organizational forms survive or fail is often a matter of chance—whether external circumstances happen to support them. Success or failure of a single firm is predicted by the characteristics of the environment as much as by the skills or strategies used by the organization.

**Apply**

How can you apply an ecology model to your career success?

## Process of Ecological Change

The population-ecology model assumes that new organizations are always appearing in the population. Thus, organization populations are continually undergoing change. The process of change in the population is defined by three principles that occur in stages: variation, selection, and retention. These stages are summarized in Exhibit 5.4.

- **Variation** means the appearance of new, diverse forms in a population of organizations. These new organizational forms are initiated by entrepreneurs, established with venture capital by large corporations, or set up by a government seeking to provide new services. Some forms may be conceived to cope with a perceived need in the external environment. In recent years, a large number of new firms have been initiated to develop computer software, to provide consulting and other services to large corporations, and to develop products and technologies for Internet commerce. Other new organizations produce a traditional product such as steel, but do it using minimal technology and new management techniques that make the new companies, such as steel company Nucor, far more able to survive. Organizational variations are analogous to mutations in biology, and they add to the scope and complexity of organizational forms in the environment. This chapter's Leading by Design box describes a new organizational form conceived by a British entrepreneur to capitalize on advances in information technology and wireless text messaging.
- **Selection** refers to whether a new organizational form is suited to the environment and can survive. Only a few variations are "selected in" by the environment and survive over the long term. Some variations will suit the external environment better than others. Some prove beneficial and thus are able to find a niche and acquire the resources from the environment necessary to survive. Other variations fail to meet the needs of the environment and perish. When there is insufficient demand for a firm's product and when insufficient resources are available to the organization, that organization will be "selected out." For example, Shazam, described in the Leading by Design box, was launched in mid-2002. If demand for the new service

**EXHIBIT 5.4**
Elements in the Population-Ecology Model of Organizations

does not continue to grow, or if the company cannot obtain needed resources, the company will be selected out and cease to exist. (In 2008, Shazam had become established and, for example, was on Facebook and is now has its own App.)

- **Retention** is the preservation and institutionalization of selected organizational forms. Certain technologies, products, and services are highly valued by the environment, and the retained organizational form may become a dominant part of the environment. Many forms of organization have been institutionalized, such as government, schools, churches, and automobile manufacturers. McDonald's, which owns 43 percent of the fast-food market and provides the first job for many teenagers, has become institutionalized in North American life.[54]

Institutionalized organizations like McDonald's seem to be relatively permanent features in the population of organizations, but they are not permanent in the long run. The environment is always changing, and if the dominant organizational forms do not adapt to external change they will gradually diminish and be replaced by other organizations. McDonald's has had to address consumers' view that Burger King and Wendy's provide fresher, higher-quality food at better prices. In addition, chains such as Subway and Quiznos are offering today's health-conscious customer an alternative to fast-food burgers and fries. In response, McDonald's has launched the "latest evolution of the Canadian Balanced Lifestyles program, [promoted by] Canadian hockey legend Wayne Gretzky."[55] In the 2010 annual consumer satisfaction survey, McDonald's consumer satisfaction decreased even though its sales increased. Unless it adapts effectively, McDonald's may no longer be competitive in the fast-food market.[56]

# Leading *by Design*

## Shazam—It's Magic!

Many people have had the experience of hearing a song they like on the radio or in a dance club and waiting in vain for the DJ to identify it. Shazam, a mobile-phone music service launched in the United Kingdom in August 2002, came to the rescue. The next time a cell phone user hears that mystery tune, he or she simply dials a four-digit number on the cell phone, lets the music play into the handset, and moments later receives a text message with the artist and song title. The user can forward a 30-second clip of the track to friends, or download the song directly to his or her phone. The song can then be legally copied from the mobile phone to a computer and shared between multiple devices.

Shazam's magic happens through the use of a pattern-recognition software algorithm developed by the company's chief scientist. The algorithm picks out the salient characteristics of a tune and matches them against a massive music database. The company, founded by Californian entrepreneur Chris Barton, calls the process "tagging," and users in the United Kingdom alone have already tagged

more than 5.5 million music tracks. Users can go online and see a list of all the songs they've tagged.

Shazam's success depends on collaborative partnerships with mobile-phone companies, major record labels, software companies, and others. A recent partnership with Swiss-based SDC (Secure Digital Container) AG provides the technology that enables a complete "tag to download" in three simple steps, allowing users to purchase music on the move. A strategic alliance with MTV Japan helped Shazam expand to about 40 million mobile-phone subscribers in Japan. Deals with international mobile operators and media companies throughout the North America, Europe, and Asia make Shazam's service available to more than one billion mobile-phone users worldwide.

The mobile-phone companies offer tagging as a premium service to their customers and pay Shazam a cut of the profits. Since tagging promises to drive up call times, most mobile-phone companies are interested. And the record labels' interests are served by getting new music

*(Continued)*

in front of consumers. Word-of-mouth recommendations are a powerful means of driving music sales, so the idea of people all over the world forwarding 30-second clips of their new songs has music companies paying attention. The service has proven to be a good predictor of future hits in Britain, so the music industry closely watches Shazam's weekly chart of tagged prerelease tracks.

Shazam is the world's first in music recognition and one of the brightest new ideas in the world of technology. With multiple deals and a presence in 12 countries, it is clear that Shazam is suited to the environment and has found a solid niche. However, managing the complex network of global relationships will be a challenge for managers of the small company, and it remains to be seen if they can take a good idea and build a lasting organization.[57] And it now faces some competition from SoundHound Inc. and MusixMatch.[58] SoundHound alone had 170 million users in 2013.[59]

From the population-ecology perspective, the environment is the important determinant of organizational success or failure. The organization must meet an environmental need, or it will be selected out. The process of variation, selection, and retention leads to the establishment of new organizational forms in a population of organizations.

## ■ Strategies for Survival

Another principle that underlies the population-ecology model is the **struggle for existence**, or competition. Organizations and populations of organizations are engaged in a competitive struggle over resources, and each organizational form is fighting to survive. For example, since coming out from under the protection of the *Companies' Creditors Arrangement Act* in April 2006, Stelco has lost $240 million as it overestimated demand from the automotive sector and underestimated the role steel imports play in Canada. CEO Rodney Mott "[held] a garage sale of ... noncore assets that were somehow core enough to survive the restructure attempt under [the Act]"[60] so that Stelco might survive.

The struggle is most intense among new organizations, and both the birth and survival frequencies of new organizations are related to factors in the larger environment. Factors such as size of urban area, percentage of immigrants, political turbulence, industry growth rate, and environmental variability have influenced the launching and survival of newspapers, telecommunication firms, railroads, government agencies, labour unions, and voluntary organizations.[61]

In the population-ecology perspective, generalist and specialist strategies distinguish organizational forms in the struggle for survival. Organizations with a wide niche or domain, that is, those that offer a broad range of products or services or that serve a broad market, are **generalists**. Organizations that provide a narrower range of goods or services or that serve a narrower market are **specialists**. In the business world, Indigo.ca started with a specialist strategy, selling books over the Internet, but evolved to a generalist strategy with the addition of music, DVDs, greeting cards, toys, and other products, plus partnering with other organizations to sell a wide range of products online. An organization such as inuitart.ca, whose product line includes traditional Holman packing dolls of the Northwest Territories, would be considered a specialist, whereas Mattel is a generalist, marketing a broad range of toys for children of all ages.[62]

Specialists are generally more competitive than generalists in the narrow area in which their domains overlap. However, the breadth of the generalist's domain serves to protect it somewhat from environmental changes. Though demand may decrease for some of the generalist's products or services, it usually increases for others at the same time. In addition, because of the diversity of products, services, and customers, generalists are able to reallocate resources internally to adapt to a changing environment, whereas specialists are not. However, because specialists are often smaller companies, they can sometimes move faster and be more flexible in adapting to changes. [63]

Managerial impact on company success often comes from selecting a strategy that steers a company into an open niche. Consider how Apotex has thrived in the generic drug sector.

## In Practice
### Apotex

Using his mother's life savings as collateral, Barry Sherman founded Apotex in 1974. "Notoriously litigious (and persistent), [CEO] Sherman has filed hundreds of lawsuits against manufacturers that have blocked Apotex from making cheap clones of their products."[64] He has also sued researchers and, in 2007, sued his cousin for $8 million.[65] On the other hand, he gives away 20 percent of his income every year and drives a modest car.

Apotex has grown to become the nation's largest pharmaceutical company, with 5,000 employees in research, development, manufacturing, and distribution facilities around the world. It specializes in the production and distribution of generic drugs. Apotex produces more than 250 generic drugs in approximately 4,000 dosages and formats that fill 60 million prescriptions annually in Canada alone.

Apotex exports its drugs to 115 countries and has subsidiaries, joint ventures, or licensing agreements in the Czech Republic, Mexico, China, Poland, New Zealand, France, Italy, and other countries. Apotex also researches, develops, and manufactures fine chemicals, nonprescription and private-label medicines, and disposable plastics for medical use. It controls several health-related companies, including Winnipeg-based Cangene and U.S.-based Barr Laboratories, the pharmacist to Walmart. Apotex's annual worldwide sales in 2006 were $900 million. In 2005, Apotex spent $153 million in research and development.[66]

Apotex manufactures Apo-TriAvir, a drug used for the treatment of HIV infection, a drug that the Rwandan government wanted to buy. Rwanda is the first country in the world to use global trade rules to override pharmaceutical patents and import generic drugs. Rwanda is buying 260,000 packs of Apo-TriAvir, which combines three patented brand-name drugs: zidovudine, lamivudine, and nevirapine. The announcement by Rwanda is the first step for Apotex to get a licence that will allow it to produce and export the drug. In 2007, Apotex received the necessary permissions to distribute the drug in Rwanda.[67] Besides, Apotex has an agreement with Médecins Sans Frontières and has stockpiled Apo-TriAvir for distribution in Africa.[68]

## act!

### Compare

Compare the generalist and specialist strategies.

Apotex isn't immune from the volatility and uncertainty inherent in the industry, but it found a niche that put the company on a solid foundation for survival over the long term. CEO Sherman chose a specialist strategy, focusing on generic drugs.

## Institutionalism

The institutional perspective provides yet another view of interorganizational relationships.[69] Organizations are highly interconnected. Just as companies need efficient production to survive, the institutional view argues that organizations need legitimacy from their stakeholders. Companies perform well when they are perceived by the larger environment to have a legitimate right to exist. Thus, the **institutional perspective** describes how organizations survive and succeed through congruence between an organization and the expectations from its environment. The **institutional environment** is composed of norms and values from stakeholders (customers, investors, associations, boards, government, and collaborating organizations). The institutional view believes that organizations adopt structures and processes to please outsiders, and these activities come to take on rule-like status in organizations. The institutional environment reflects what the greater society views as correct ways of organizing and behaving.[70]

**Legitimacy** is defined as the general perspective that an organization's actions are desirable, proper, and appropriate within the environment's system of norms, values, and beliefs.[71] Institutional theory thus is concerned with the set of intangible norms and values that shape behaviour, as opposed to the tangible elements of technology and structure. Organizations must fit within the cognitive and emotional expectations of their audience. For example, people will not deposit money in a bank unless it sends signals of compliance with norms of wise financial management. Consider also your municipal government and whether it could raise property taxes for increased police services if community residents did not approve.

Most organizations are concerned with legitimacy. Corporations are paying attention to their social responsibility rankings. In 2010, Mountain Equipment was ranked first in *Corporate Knights'* annual listing of Best 50 Corporate Citizens. Alcan, Vancity Savings Credit Union, Dofasco, and Hydro-Québec round out the top five.[72] The top five organizations in the 2012 rankings are Desjardins Group, Vancity Savings Credit Union, Co-operators Group Limited, CNR Company, and Royal Bank of Canada.[73] Many corporations actively shape and manage their reputations to increase their competitive advantage, and managers are searching for new ways to bolster legitimacy in the wake of ethical and financial scandals at such well-known companies as Boeing, Enron, and WorldCom. One U.S. company that has built a reputation as a highly ethical and socially responsible company is Johnson & Johnson, where managers stress the company's commitment to customers, employees, and the broader community. In 2010, Johnson & Johnson ranked in first place on the CSR Index that is based on a survey of 7,790 online U.S. consumers conducted in January and February 2010. After the survey, Johnson & Johnson announced that that it had misled regulators and consumers by using company-paid contractors to buy defective Motrin painkiller products from store shelves rather than announce a recall. CEO William Weldon commented, "This was not one of our finer moments."[74]

Walmart has not been seriously damaged by criticisms, but managers know that how the company is perceived by customers and the public plays a big role in long-term success. Walmart is extremely powerful today, but its power could decline if the company's actions are not considered legitimate and appropriate. Walmart's recent green commitments may help the company to combat its image problems. In 2007, for example, Walmart Canada announced that it was buying green electricity from Bullfrog Power for the next three years and, as a result, it became the nation's largest commercial purchaser of green power.

The fact that there is a payoff for having a good reputation is verified by a study of organizations in the airline industry. Having a good reputation was significantly related to higher levels of performance measures such as return on assets and net profit margin.[75] Ireland's low-cost airline, Ryanair, may be an exception, however, as it known for its abysmal service and predatory pricing and yet continues to do well. It has spawned a web site, www.ihateryanair.org which details many of Ryanair's problems. Nevertheless, in 2010, its profit doubled from the previous year.[76]

Walmart has been pilloried in the film *Walmart, The High Cost of Low Price.* For the first time in its history, Walmart is facing a serious legitimacy problem. A combination of factors has led to a decline in the company's reputation and a growing criticism of its practices.

People naturally begin to distrust corporations that grow so large and dominant as Walmart. It is the world's largest corporation and has substantial bargaining power with its suppliers to cut costs. "Walmart is so big and so centralized that it can all at once hook Chinese and other suppliers into its digital system. So—wham—you have a large switch to overseas sourcing in a period quicker than in the old rules of retailing."[77] In addition, the company's size has brought a host of new management challenges. Publicity about cleaning contractors using illegal immigrants in U.S. Walmart stores tarnished the company's once pristine image. Walmart's early-1990s' claim to "Buy American" has quietly been shelved as the company has more than doubled its imports from China since then. And some critics charge that manufacturers of everything from bras to bicycles have had to close plants, lay off workers, and outsource to low-wage countries in order to survive in the face of Walmart's cost-cutting demands. Employee complaints about low pay, and a damaging gender-discrimination suit, have compounded the company's image problems.

Walmart's 1998 foray into the German market was unsuccessful, and the company shut down its German outlets in 2006. "Walmart's attempt to apply the company's proven U.S. success formula in an unmodified manner to the German market turned out to be nothing short of a fiasco."[78] Walmart's approach ran afoul of German labour laws and traditions. In addition, Walmart underestimated the extent of the differences between the U.S. and German markets; for example, it provided pillow cases that fit North American pillows but did not fit German pillows! Walmart's exit from Germany cost the company $1 billion.[79]

Consumers are still captivated by Walmart's low prices, but there is growing concern and criticism about the high social and economic costs of the company's low-cost approach. "Shoppers could start feeling guilty about shopping with us," says Walmart spokeswoman, Mona Williams. "Communities could make it harder to build our stores.[80] According to a McKinsey study, between two and eight percent of consumers do not shop at Walmart because of its practices. "Walmart operates on such razor thin margins, and [the market] demands such strong quarter-over-quarter sales, that the total impact of the public relations swirl could be devastating in the short and long term."[81]

---

In interacting with outsiders, Ryanair has made a name for itself in being remarkably raucous and aggressive. The company regularly uses events and news to make bold, irreverent, statements, either through explicit sexual references or harsh criticism of governments, other companies, or even consumers. Unusual as it may seem, Ryanair has found a remarkably efficient way of generating free publicity for itself through these statements.[82] Paradoxically, it uses its negative reputation to its advantage so it is seen as a cheap anti-airline that people want to try. However, it is doubtful that Ryanair can continue to act illegitimately and succeed.

The notion of legitimacy answers an important question for institutional theorists. Why is there so much homogeneity in the forms and practices of established organizations? For example, visit banks, high schools, hospitals, government departments, or business firms in a similar industry, in any part of the country, and they will look strikingly similar. When an organizational field is just getting started, such as e-commerce, diversity is the norm. New organizations fill emerging niches. However, once an industry becomes established, there is an invisible push toward similarity.

**Think**

Think about how you can enhance your legitimacy.

# The Institutional View and Organizational Design

The institutional view also sees organizations as having two essential dimensions—technical and institutional. The technical dimension is the day-to-day work, technology, and operating requirements. The institutional structure is that part of the organization most visible to the outside public. Moreover, the technical dimension is governed by norms of rationality and efficiency, but the institutional dimension is governed by expectations from the external environment. As a result, the formal structures of some organizations reflect the expectations and values of the environment rather than the demand of work activities. This means that an organization may incorporate positions or activities (equal employment officer, e-commerce division, chief ethics officer) perceived as important by the larger society to increase its legitimacy and survival prospects, even though these elements may decrease efficiency. For example, many small companies set up websites, even though the benefits gained from the site are sometimes outweighed by the costs of maintaining it; having a website is perceived as essential today. The formal structure and design of an organization may not be rational with respect to workflow and products or services, but it may ensure survival in the larger environment.

Organizations adapt to the environment by signalling their congruence with the demands and expectations stemming from cultural norms, standards set by professional bodies, funding agencies, and customers. Structure is something of a facade disconnected from technical work through which the organization obtains approval, legitimacy, and continuing support. The adoption of structures thus might not be linked to actual production needs, and might occur regardless of whether specific internal problems are solved.[83]

# Institutional Similarity

Organizations have a strong need to appear legitimate. In so doing, many aspects of structure and behaviour may be targeted toward environmental acceptance rather than toward internal technical efficiency. Interorganizational relationships thus are characterized by forces that cause organizations in a similar population to look like one another. **Institutional similarity**, called *institutional isomorphism* in the academic literature, is the emergence of a common structure and approach among organizations in the same field. Isomorphism is the process that causes one unit in a population to resemble other units that face the same set of environmental conditions.[84]

Exactly how does increasing similarity occur? How are these forces realized? These three core mechanisms are *mimetic forces*, which result from responses to uncertainty; *coercive forces*, which stem from political influence; and *normative forces*, which result from common training and professionalism.[85]

**Mimetic Forces.** Most organizations, especially business organizations, face great uncertainty. It is not clear to senior executives exactly what products, services, or technologies will achieve desired goals, and sometimes the goals themselves are not clear. In the face of this uncertainty, **mimetic forces**, the pressure to copy or model other organizations, occur.

When executives see an innovation that they consider useful, the innovative practice or process is quickly copied. An example is the proliferation of Wi-Fi hotspots in cafes, hotels, and airports. Starbucks was one of the first companies to adopt Wi-Fi, enabling customers to use laptops and mobile devices at Starbucks stores. The practice has rapidly been copied by both large and small companies, from Holiday Inns to the local deli. Many times, this modelling is done without any clear proof that performance will be improved. Mimetic processes explain why fads and fashions occur in the business world. Once a new idea starts, many organizations grab onto it, only to learn that the application is difficult and may cause more problems than it solves. This was the case with the recent merger wave that swept many industries. The past two decades have seen the largest merger and acquisition wave in history, but evidence shows that many of these mergers did not produce the expected financial gains and other benefits. The sheer momentum of the trend was so powerful that many companies chose to merge not because of potential increases in efficiency or profitability but simply because it seemed like the right thing to do.[86] Downsizing of the workforce is another trend that can be attributed partly to mimetic forces. Despite some evidence that massive downsizing actually hurts organizations, managers perceive it as a legitimate and effective means of improving performance.[87]

Techniques such as outsourcing, reengineering, Six Sigma quality programs, and the balanced scorecard have all been adopted without clear evidence that they will improve efficiency or effectiveness. The one certain benefit is that management's feelings of uncertainty will be reduced, and the company's image will be enhanced because the firm is seen as using the latest management techniques. One study of 100 organizations confirmed that those companies associated with using popular management techniques were more admired and rated higher in quality of management, even though these organizations often did not reflect higher economic performance.[88] Perhaps the clearest example of official copying is the technique of benchmarking that occurs as part of the total quality movement. *Benchmarking* means identifying who's best at something in an industry and then duplicating the technique for creating excellence, perhaps even improving it in the process.

The mimetic process works because organizations face continuous high uncertainty, they are aware of innovations occurring in the environment, and the innovations are culturally supported, thereby giving legitimacy to adopters. This is a strong mechanism by which a group of banks, high schools, or manufacturing firms begin to look and act like one another.

**Coercive Forces.** All organizations are subject to pressure, both formal and informal, from government, regulatory agencies, and other important organizations in the environment, especially those on which a company is dependent. Coercive forces are the external pressures exerted on an organization to adopt structures, techniques, or behaviours similar to other organizations. As with other changes, those brought about because of coercive forces may not make the organization more effective, but it will look more effective and will be accepted as legitimate in the environment. Some pressures may have the force of law, such as government mandates to adopt new pollution-control equipment. Health and safety regulations may demand that a safety officer be appointed. New regulations and government oversight boards have been set up for the accounting industry following widespread accounting scandals.[89]

Coercive pressures may also occur between organizations where there is a power difference, as described in the resource-dependence section earlier in this chapter. Large retailers and manufacturers often insist that certain policies, procedures, and techniques be used by their suppliers. When Honda picked Donnelly Corporation of the United States to make all the mirrors for its U.S.-manufactured cars, Honda insisted that Donnelly implement an employee-empowerment program. Honda managers believed the partnership could work only if Donnelly learned how to foster collaborative internal relationships.

Organizational changes that result from coercive forces occur when an organization is dependent on another; when there are political factors such as rules, laws, and sanctions involved; or when some other contractual or legal basis defines the relationship. Organizations operating under those constraints will adopt changes and relate to one another in a way that increases homogeneity and limits diversity.

**Normative Forces.** According to the institutional view, the third reason organizations change is normative forces. **Normative forces** are pressures to change to achieve standards of professionalism, and to adopt techniques that are considered by the professional community to be up-to-date and effective. Changes may be in any area, such as information technology, accounting requirements, marketing techniques, or collaborative relationships with other organizations.

Professionals share a body of formal education based on university degrees and professional networks through which ideas are exchanged by consultants and professional leaders. Universities, consulting firms, trade associations, and professional training institutions develop norms among professional managers. People are exposed to similar training and standards and adopt shared values, which are implemented in organizations with which they work. Business schools teach finance, marketing, and human resource students that certain techniques are better than others, so using those techniques becomes a standard in the field. In one study, for example, a radio station changed from a functional to a multidivisional structure because a consultant recommended it as a "higher standard" of doing business. There was no proof that this structure was better, but the radio station wanted legitimacy and to be perceived as fully professional and up-to-date in its management techniques.

Companies accept normative pressures to become like one another through a sense of obligation or duty to high standards of performance based on professional norms shared by managers and specialists in their respective organizations. These norms are conveyed through professional education and certification and have almost a moral or ethical requirement based on the highest standards accepted by the profession at that time. In some cases, though, normative forces that maintain legitimacy break down, as they recently did in the accounting industry, and coercive forces are needed to shift organizations back toward acceptable standards.

An organization may use any or all of the mechanisms of mimetic, coercive, or normative forces to change itself for greater legitimacy in the institutional environment. Firms tend to use these mechanisms when they are acting under conditions of dependence, uncertainty, ambiguous goals, and reliance on professional credentials. The outcome of these processes is that organizations become far more homogeneous than would be expected from the natural diversity among managers and environments.

## Summary and Interpretation

This chapter has been about the important evolution in interorganizational relationship. At one time, organizations considered themselves autonomous and separate, trying to outdo one another. Today, more organizations see themselves as part of an ecosystem. The organization may span several industries and will be anchored in

## Case for Analysis: Apple*

### July 9, 2007

Steve Jobs had plenty of problems to contend with as he sauntered onstage for his first speech after returning to the top of Apple in 1997. He faced a shrinking market for his Mac computers, bloated costs, and a severe shortage of cash. But on that day, Jobs chose to talk to the Mac faithful mostly about another problem: Apple's growing isolation. Despite the company's reputation for making the world's finest PCs, very little software or add-on gear worked with the Mac. "Apple lives in an ecosystem, and it needs help from other partners," said Jobs. "And it needs to help other partners."

Jobs then did the unthinkable, inviting arch-nemesis Bill Gates to join him on stage via videoconference to announce details of a deal to forget any patent claims in exchange for $150 million, and a promise by Microsoft Corp. (MSFT) to continue making a Mac-compatible version of its ubiquitous Office software.

Today, that Apple Inc. (AAPL) ecosystem has morphed from a sad little high-tech shtetl into a global empire. Once known for defining the digital future but never fully capitalizing on it, Apple has been transformed into tech's most influential hit-maker. More than 200,000 companies have signed on in the past year to create Apple-compatible products, a 26 percent increase from the year before. That includes software makers such as gamemaker Electronic Arts Inc. and corporate supplier VMware, drawn by Mac sales that are growing three times faster than the overall PC market. A cottage industry of iPod accessories continues to blossom into something far more substantial. Consider that this year, some 70 percent of new U.S.–model cars have iPod connectors built in, and about 100,000 airline seats will have the same. And Apple's online iTunes Music Store has become the world's third-largest music retailer after Wal-Mart Stores Inc. (WMT) and Best Buy Co. (BBY)

### Joining the Jobs Club

With the June 29 debut of the iPhone, Apple seems poised to extend its reach even further. A new flock of partners, from AT&T Corp. to Salesforce.com Inc. (CRM), is set to jump on the bandwagon for the slick phone/Web browser/music player/camera. Sure, the hype prior to iPhone's launch bordered on ridiculous; (Comedy Central [VIA] Stephen Colbert joked that the iPhone launch is the second most important event in human history, after the birth of Christ). But phonemakers such as Nokia (NOK) and Motorola (MOT), and carriers like Verizon (VZ), are waiting nervously to see if Apple can remake the U.S. cellular business by determining what services consumers get and leaving the carriers out of the loop.

As long as Apple stays on its game, leading providers of everything from silicon chips to Hollywood flicks will feel pressure to strike deals to Jobs' liking. Apple can confer brand hipness on its partners. And its ascendence in markets like cell phones and who knows what else in the future may impose a new focus on more consumer-friendly parts, software, and services. But to be part of the Jobs club, you give up a certain amount of independence on everything from design to identity to pricing.

Jobs is upending two decades of conventional wisdom about the nature of competition in digital markets. Since the rise of Microsoft and Intel's "Wintel" PC standard in the 1980s, the assumption has been that markets would be dominated by those that could set technical standards—say, Microsoft in operating systems or Intel in microprocessors—and then benefit as thousands of others competed to build products on top of these "platforms."

But Apple's strategy is far simpler: Focus on making the best product, and rewards will follow. In fact, Apple's new partners are signing up in spite of, rather than because of, Jobs' rules of engagement. Apple makes little pretense of building a level playing field, but routinely picks favorites—such as Google for building mapping and video applications for the iPhone. And rather than aim for the most partners, Apple focuses on attracting the best ones. As a result, the Mac and iPod feel more like a gated, elitist community, with Apple keeping close watch over who gets in. "The notion of a platform is a very PC-oriented way of looking at the world," says Silicon Valley financier Roger McNamee. "Consumers just want a great experience. They don't buy platforms."

Consider how Apple changed expectations about portable music devices. There were plenty of MP3 players around before the iPod arrived in 2001. Now, if the iPhone works as advertised, it could similarly redefine the mobile-phone experience. As any BlackBerry or Treo owner knows, all of the 25 million smartphones sold last year offer similar capabilities, such as Web browsing and e-mail. But none has captured the heart of the mainstream consumer. And on paper, at least, the iPhone erases myriad frustrations faced by hundreds of millions of phone users—from maddeningly complex menus, to the inability to find a contact while on a call.

Spin it out a few years, and it's not hard to see why many companies want to be on Apple's side. [U.S.] iPhone buyers now sign up for an AT&T cellular package via iTunes. In the future, maybe they'll also be able to sign up for all the broadband and data services needed to power their Macs, iPods, and future Apple products (can you say: "I want my Apple iHomeTheater"?) and make them work together. That would play to Apple's strength—making the complex simple. "What you end up with is a kind of Apple archipelago—this cluster of islands in this big digital sea that are great places to hang out," says Silicon Valley futurist and consultant Paul Saffo.

Of course, Apple's products have to continue to delight—a real question for the iPhone, which doesn't even have a physical keyboard. But if Apple succeeds, it could raise itself and its ecosystem above the cacophony of industry giants now battling to "own" the digital consumer. The telephone and cable companies try to take advantage of their control of customers' access to video, data, and voice content. Google Inc. (GOOG) and Yahoo! Inc. (YHOO) want to leverage their power as online concierge for millions of consumers. Apple comes at it from the device perspective: If it can control the gadget you use to connect with all those other platforms, it increases its control over what you do, and how much you pay (99 cents a song, for example).

There are lots of phone carriers and cable companies, each with fairly similar offerings. Google and Yahoo are powerful in their own right, but they can't totally control their destiny since Web users are a click away from using another search engine or portal. For now, though, Apple is head and shoulders above others in making the actual machines you use to pull up Web pages, music, TV shows, movies, and soon, perhaps, phone conversations. Says David Sanderson, head of Bain & Co.'s global media practice: "We're moving from a distributor-driven paradigm to a consumer-driven paradigm—and Apple gets consumers."

And not just any consumers, but those who will pay a premium. The Mac is gaining share despite an average price tag of $1,400, nearly twice that of the typical PC. iPod shoppers still paid an average price of $181 in May, 15 percent above other music players. The iPhone is even more audaciously priced. The [US]$499 base price compares with an average $66 for a regular phone, or $160 for a smartphone such as a BlackBerry or Treo, says NPD Group Inc. analyst Stephen Baker.

## The Compatibility Factor

None of this would have come about if Jobs hadn't had his epiphany about reaching out beyond the insular world of the Mac. The Office deal was a symbolic first step, but the real wake-up call came with the 2003 decision to do a Windows-compatible version of iTunes. Rather than hurt Mac sales, as some feared, this opened the floodgates on iPod sales by making the device usable by the 98 percent of computer users who ran Windows. Another milestone came when the company switched from PowerPC processors made by IBM (IBM) to Intel's far more popular chips. This made it possible for Macs to run Windows (an important insurance policy to many Mac newbies) and made it far easier for software developers to adapt their programs for Apple's products.

Consider the perspective of one big video-game producer, Electronic Arts. In the early 1980s, about half of the people working at EA's Redwood City (Calif.) campus were Apple alumni. Yet EA stopped making Mac-compatible games later in the decade, when Apple turned its attention to corporate markets. EA co-founder Bing Gordon recalls his shock when Apple's then-CEO John Sculley said in 1987 that "there is no home-computer market." Says Gordon: "They were working so hard to get respect, the last thing they wanted was for people who wore suits to think of the Mac as a toy." Predictably, game sales on the Mac plummeted, making it even less worthwhile for EA to make the big investments to adapt its PC games to run on the Mac's unique innards.

But because today's Intel-based Macs don't look much different from any Windows PC from EA's perspective, Gordon says it should be cheaper to churn out Mac games than, say, adapting them to game consoles like the Sony (SNE) PlayStation or Nintendo (NTDOY) Wii. With the Mac rapidly gaining share with younger shoppers, EA has announced plans to release its new *Harry Potter* game and three other titles on the Mac this summer.

Another rarely mentioned advantage is Apple's so-called developer program. Once iPod sales began skyrocketing in 2003, the company worked with makers of portable speakers, music-player cases, and other add-on gadgets. And Apple is working on the most mobile platform of all. Since BMW first added an optional iPod connector in the glove compartment of many of its 2004 models, carmakers including Chrysler (DCX), Ford (F), and Honda (HMC) have followed suit. General Motors Corp.'s (GM) 2008 Cadillac CTS will come with a center console that features the iPod's "rotate and click" interface, not only for pulling music off an iPod but also for playing the radio or listening to CDs or satellite radio. "It's about getting to your music, not having to learn a new set of tricks for each service," says James Grace, the 27-year-old GM manager who leads the project.

With the iPhone, Apple seems ready to open up opportunities for software developers who were mostly shut out from the iPod. On June 11, it announced that any Web 2.0 program designed to work with Apple's Safari browser would work on the iPhone. That means such popular sites as MySpace, Digg, or Amazon.com will be able to adapt their services to take advantage of the device—say, by adding a virtual button on their sites so that iPhone users could actually place a phone call with a fellow Netizen, rather than just trade e-mails or post messages.

To be sure, many developers gripe that this approach is a far cry from letting them create applications designed from the ground up to work directly with the iPhone. That's a privilege Apple has conferred on only a few partners, such as Google. But "it's a good first step," says Digg Chairman Jay Adelson, who expects Apple to become more inclusive as time goes by. "For now, it's a very strange kind of controlled system—because they have these insanely high bars [for reliability and user experience] that they want to hit."

Many partners won't wait for a formal invite. Despite doubts about the iPhone's usefulness to serious business-people, Salesforce.com is working on an iPhone version of its sales management software. "It's not just about market share, it's about showing what is possible and what is cool," says CEO Marc Benioff. And more than 150 developers have registered to attend an ad hoc "iPhone Developers Camp" in San Francisco on July 6, to trade ideas and create new applications.

But if the Apple orchard is growing, it is still no Eden. For those partners that make the cut, Apple enforces a brutal perfectionism. "The stereotype is that they're this loosey-goosey California company, but nothing could be further from the truth," says Gary Johnson, the former CEO of chipmaker PortalPlayer Inc., which roared to prosperity by providing the electronic brains of the first generations of iPods. Johnson says that whenever a project fell off track or a part fell short of Apple's needs, its engineers were demanding "root cause analysis" and explanations within 12 hours. "You could pacify other customers by putting 10 engineers on a plane to see them. Not Apple."

## "An Unreasonableness"

Working with Apple can be exhausting. Johnson says the company almost never issued documents outlining its technical requirements, preferring to keep things oral to avoid a paper trail that might be leaked. And no supplier was given a full picture of what exactly Apple was working on: Everything was on a "need to know" basis. "There's an unreasonableness," says Johnson. "It's as though your entire reason for being is to serve them." Yet he adds he has no hard feelings: "It wasn't a malicious thing. It's almost machine-like. You may have friendships or business relationships, but they don't really count." Johnson found that out on an April morning in 2006, when he learned Apple had decided not to use a chip that had been under development for more than a year and was expected to bring in half of PortalPlayer's sales. The company's stock crashed 50 percent when Johnson told Wall Street a few days later. Seven months later, it was purchased by Nvidia Corp. (NVDA) for $357 million—half of its peak market cap.

Suppliers of TV shows, movies, and other video content have their own reasons for being wary of joining the Apple ecosystem. They know what happened in the music industry. Jobs created a kind of reverse razor-and-blades model with the iPod, where Apple sells lucrative razors (music players) and the studios are stuck selling cheapo blades (music). Hollywood has resisted Jobs' vision for placing movies on the iPod and iPhone. Only movies from Walt Disney Co. (DIS) (where Jobs is the largest individual shareholder) and Paramount Pictures (VIA) have licensed

movies to iTunes. The 52 million TV shows and movies sold so far by Apple amounts to fewer than two videos per iPod.

This makes Apple's newest partnership with AT&T (T) for iPhone service all the more intriguing. Since the iPhone was announced in January, many observers have wondered if Jobs pulled another fast one, using his consumer cred to win unprecedented influence over the $140 billion cellular-phone business. Normally, carriers in the U.S. control how cell-phones are priced and marketed, right down to deciding whether they will turn on capabilities built into the phones, such as wireless music downloading. But that's not how Apple rolls. Apple defined the 16 services that are highlighted on the iPhone homepage, and users sign up for them via iTunes, not on AT&T's homepage or in its stores.

Has AT&T set itself up to be marginalized? The carrier stands to steal subscribers from its rivals; CEO Randall L. Stephenson said on June 19 that of the 1.1 million people who had inquired about the iPhone, 40 percent were not currently signed up with AT&T. But analysts say Apple will earn a luxurious 35 percent gross margin on each of the $500 devices. AT&T is offering a $59 base plan for phone and data services—roughly $20 less than the cost for corporate e-mail devices like Treo. Besides potentially taking a bite out of AT&T's margins, this could cause its other handset makers to demand sweeter deals, too.

But the real test will be whether Jobs can change the way consumers think about a phone. This is Apple's first entry into a preexisting mass market, and those other phone manufacturers can't afford to let Jobs rewire things to suit Apple's strengths. Some already have rolled out cheaper products that, if not exactly as capable as the iPhone, may be close enough. Will most consumers eventually choose to save money, even at the expense of a bit of elegance? History says they will, according to Harvard Business School professor Clayton M. Christensen: "The world always ends up thanking innovators for their cool products—but won't pay for them. There are forces of gravity at work."

Now there's a matchup worth watching: Steve Jobs vs. gravity.

## Assignment Questions

1. Why would Steve Jobs want to partner with Bill Gates?
2. What is Apple's strategy? Is it effective?
3. According to Christensen, in his book *The Innovator's Dilemma*, the world thanks innovators for new products but won't buy them. Does his statement hold for Apple in general and for its iPhone, in particular?

## Case for Analysis: Hugh Russel, Inc.*

The following story is a personal recollection by David Hurst of the experience of a group of managers in a mature organization undergoing profound change.... The precipitating event in this change was a serious business crisis....

When I joined Hugh Russel Inc. in 1979, it was a medium-sized Canadian distributor of steel and industrial products. With sales of $535 million and 3,000 employees, the business was controlled by the chairman, Archie Russel, who owned 16 percent of the common shares. The business consisted of four groups—the core steel distribution activities (called "Russelsteel"), industrial bearings and valves distribution, a chain of wholesalers of hardware and sporting goods, and a small manufacturing business....

The company was structured for performance.... The management was professional, with each of the divisional hierarchies headed by a group president reporting to Peter Foster in his capacity as president of the corporation. Jobs were described in job descriptions, and their mode of execution was specified in detailed standard operating procedures. Three volumes of the corporate manual spelled out policy on everything from accounting to vacation pay. Extensive accounting and data processing systems allowed managers to track the progress of individual operations against budgets and plans. Compensation was performance-based, with return on net assets (RONA) as the primary measure and large bonuses (up to 100 percent of base) for managers who made their targets.

At the senior management level, the culture was polite but formal. The board of directors consisted of Archie's friends and associates together with management insiders. Archie and Peter ran the organization as if they were majority owners. Their interaction with management outside of the head office was restricted to the occasional field trip...

### Crisis

Nine months after I joined the company as a financial planner, we were put "in play" by a raider and, after a fierce bidding war, were acquired in a hostile takeover. Our acquirer was a private company controlled by the eldest son of an entrepreneur of legendary wealth and ability, so we had no inkling at the time of the rollercoaster ride that lay ahead of us. We were unaware that not only did the son not have the support of his father in this venture but also he had neglected to consult his two brothers, who were joint owners of the acquiring company! As he had taken on $300 million of debt to do the deal, this left each of the brothers on the hook

for a personal guarantee of $100 million. They were not amused, and it showed!

Within days of the deal, we were inundated by waves of consultants, lawyers, and accountants: each shareholder seemed to have his or her own panel of advisers. After 6 weeks of intensive analysis, it was clear that far too much had been paid for us and that the transaction was vastly overleveraged. At the start of the deal, the acquirer had approached our bankers and asked them if they wanted a piece of the "action." Concerned at the possible loss of our banking business and eager to be associated with such a prominent family, our bankers had agreed to provide the initial financing on a handshake. Now, as they saw the detailed numbers for the first time and became aware of the dissent among the shareholders, they withdrew their support and demanded their money back. We needed to refinance $300 million of debt—fast....

### Change

The takeover and the subsequent merger of our new owner's moribund steel fabricating operations into Hugh Russel changed our agenda completely. We had new shareholders (who fought with each other constantly), new bankers, and new businesses in an environment of soaring interest rates and plummeting demand for our products and services. Almost overnight, the corporation went from a growth-oriented, acquisitive, earnings-driven operation to a broken, cash-starved company, desperate to survive. Closures, layoffs, downsizing, delayering, asset sales, and "rationalization" became our new priorities.... At the head office, the clarity of jobs vanished. For example, I had been hired to do financial forecasting and raise capital in the equity markets, but with the company a financial mess, this clearly could not be done. For all of us, the future looked dangerous and frightening as bankruptcy, both personal and corporate, loomed ahead.

And so it was in an atmosphere of crisis that Wayne Mang, the new president (Archie Russel and Peter Foster left the organization soon after the deal), gathered the first group of managers together to discuss the situation. Wayne Mang had been in the steel business for many years and was trusted and respected by the Hugh Russel people. An accountant by training, he used to call himself the "personnel manager" to underscore his belief in both the ability of people to make the difference in the organization and the responsibility of line management to make this happen. The hastily called first meeting consisted of people whom Wayne respected and trusted from all over the organization. They had been selected without regard for their position in the old hierarchy.

The content and style of that first meeting were a revelation to many! Few of them had ever been summoned to the head office for anything but a haranguing over their budgets. Now they were being told the complete gory details of the company's situation and, for the first time, being treated as if they had something to contribute. Wayne asked for their help.

During that first meeting, we counted nineteen major issues confronting the corporation. None of them fell under a single functional area. We arranged ourselves into task forces to deal with them. I say "arranged ourselves" because that was the way it seemed to happen. Individuals volunteered without coercion to work on issues in which they were interested or for which their skills were relevant. They also volunteered others who were not at the meeting but, it was thought, could help. There was some guidance—each task force had one person from the head office whose function it was to report what was happening back to the "center"—and some members found themselves on too many task forces, which required that substitutes be found. But that was the extent of the conscious management of the process.

The meeting broke up at 2:00 a.m., when we all went home to tell our incredulous spouses what had happened....

The cross-functional project team rapidly became our preferred method of organizing new initiatives, and at the head office, the old formal structure virtually disappeared. The teams could be formed at a moment's notice to handle a fast-breaking issue and dissolved just as quickly. We found, for example, that even when we weren't having formal meetings, we seemed to spend most of our time talking to each other informally. Two people would start a conversation in someone's office, and almost before you knew it, others had wandered in and a small group session was going. Later on, we called these events "bubbles;" they became our equivalent of campfire meetings....

Later, when I became executive vice president, Wayne and I deliberately shared an office so we could each hear what the other was doing in real time and create an environment in which "bubbles" might form spontaneously. As people wandered past our open door, we would wave them in to talk; others would wander in after them. The content of these sessions always had to do with our predicament, both corporate and personal. It was serious stuff, but the atmosphere was light and open. Our fate was potentially a bad one, but at least it would be shared. All of us who were involved then cannot remember ever having laughed so much. We laughed at ourselves and at the desperate situation. We laughed at the foolishness of the bankers in having financed such a mess, and we laughed at the antics of the feuding shareholders, whose outrageous manners and language we learned to mimic to perfection.

I think it was the atmosphere from these informal sessions that gradually permeated all our interactions—with employees, bankers, suppliers, everyone with whom we came into contact. Certainly, we often had tough meetings, filled with tension and threat, but we were always able to "bootstrap" ourselves back up emotionally at the informal debriefings afterward....

Perhaps the best example of both the change in structure and the blurring of the boundaries of the organization was our changing relationships with our bankers. In the beginning, at least for the brief time that the loan was in good standing, the association was polite and at arm's length. Communication was formal. As the bank realized the full horror of what it had financed (a process that took about 18 months), the relationship steadily grew more hostile. Senior executives of the bank became threatening, spelling out what actions they might take if we did not solve our problem. This hostility culminated in an investigation by the bank for possible fraud (a standard procedure in many banks when faced with a significant loss).

Throughout this period, we had seen a succession of different bankers, each of whom had been assigned to our account for a few months. As a result of our efforts to brief every new face that appeared, we had built a significant network of contacts within the bank with whom we had openly shared a good deal of information and opinion. When no fraud was found, the bank polled its own people on what to do. Our views, presented so coherently by our people (because everyone knew what was going on), and shared so widely with so many bankers, had an enormous influence on the outcome of this process. The result was the formation of a joint company-bank team to address a shared problem that together we could solve. The boundary between the corporation and the bank was now blurred: to an outside observer, it would have been unclear where the corporation ended and the bank began....

Our corporation had extensive formal reporting systems to allow the monitoring of operations on a regular basis. After the takeover, these systems required substantial modifications. For example...we had to report our results to the public every quarter at a time when we were losing nearly 2 million dollars a week! We knew that unless we got to our suppliers ahead of time, they could easily panic and refuse us credit. Hasty moves on their part could have had fatal consequences for the business.

In addition, our closure plans for plants all over Canada and the United States brought us into contact with unions and governments in an entirely different way. We realized that we had no option but to deal with these audiences in advance of events.

I have already described how our relationship with the bankers changed as a result of our open communication. We found exactly the same effect with these new audiences. Initially, our major suppliers could not understand why we had told them we were in trouble before we had to. We succeeded, however, in framing the situation in a way that enlisted their cooperation in our survival, and by the time the "war story" was news, we had their full support. Similarly, most government and union organizations were so pleased to be involved in the process before announcements were made that they bent over backward to be of assistance. Just as had been the case with the bank, we set up joint task forces with these "outside" agencies to resolve what had become shared problems. A significant contributor to our ability to pull this off was the high quality of our internal communication. Everyone on the teams knew the complete, up-to-date picture of what was happening. An outside agency could talk to anyone on a team and get the same story. In this way, we constructed a formidable network of contacts, many of whom had special skills and experience in areas that would turn out to be of great help to us in the future.

The addition of multiple networks to our information systems enhanced our ability both to gather and to disseminate information. The informality and openness of the networks, together with the high volume of face-to-face dialogues, gave us an early-warning system with which to detect hurt feelings and possible hostile moves on the part of shareholders, suppliers, nervous bankers, and even customers. This information helped us head off trouble before it happened. The networks also acted as a broadcast system through which we could test plans and actions before announcing them formally. In this way, not only did we get excellent suggestions for improvement, but everyone felt that he or she had been consulted before action was taken....

We had a similar experience with a group of people outside the company during the hectic last 6 months of 1983, when we were trying to finalize a deal for the shareholders and bankers to sell the steel distribution business to new owners. The group of people in question comprised the secretaries of the numerous lawyers and accountants involved in the deal....

We made these secretaries part of the network, briefing them in advance on the situation, explaining why things were needed, and keeping them updated on the progress of the deal. We were astounded at the cooperation we received: our calls were put through, our messages received prompt responses, and drafts and opinions were produced on time. In the final event, a complex deal that should have taken nine months to complete was done in three. All of this was accomplished by ordinary people going far beyond what might have been expected of them....

We had been thrust into crisis without warning, and our initial activities were almost entirely reactions to issues that imposed themselves upon us. But as we muddled along in the task forces, we began to find that we had unexpected sources of influence over what was happening.

The changing relationship with the bank illustrates this neatly. Although we had no formal power in that situation, we found that by framing a confusing predicament in a coherent way, we could, via our network, influence the outcomes of the bank's decisions. The same applied to suppliers: by briefing them ahead of time and presenting a reasonable scenario for the recovery of their advances, we could influence the decisions they would make.

Slowly we began to realize that, although we were powerless in a formal sense, our networks, together with our own internal coherence, gave us an ability to get things done invisibly. As we discussed the situation with all the parties involved, a strategy began to emerge. A complicated financial/tax structure would allow the bank to "manage" its loss and give it an incentive not to call on the shareholders' personal guarantees. The core steel distribution business could be refinanced in the process and sold to new owners. The wrangle between the shareholders could be resolved, and each could go his or her own way. All that had to be done was to bring all the parties together, including a buyer for the steel business, and have them agree that this was the best course to follow. Using our newfound skills, we managed to pull it off.

It was not without excitement: at the last minute, the shareholders raised further objections to the deal. Only the bank could make them sell, and they were reluctant to do so, fearful that they might attract a lawsuit. Discreet calls to the major suppliers, several of whose executives were on the board of the bank, did the trick. "This business needs to be sold and recapitalized," the suppliers were told. "If the deal does not go through, you should probably reduce your credit exposure." The deal went through. By the end of 1983, we had new owners, just in time to benefit from the general business recovery. The ordeal was over.

## Assignment Questions

1. Briefly describe whether events in this case support or refute each of the resource-dependence, collaborative network, population ecology, and institutional perspectives. Why or why not?
2. Do you think the changed relationships with other organizations could have occurred without internal company changes? Explain.
3. Hugh Russel seemed to increase its legitimacy and power by developing relationships with other companies. Does this make sense to you as general strategy for *powerless* organizations?

*Reprinted by permission of Harvard Business School Press. From *Crisis and Renewal: Meeting the Challenge of Organizational Change*, by David K. Hurst (Boston: Harvard Business School Press, 1995), pp. 53–73. Copyright © 1995 by the Harvard Business School Publishing Corporation; all rights reserved.

# ■ Chapter 5 Workshop: Ugli Orange Case*

1. Form groups of three members. One person will be Dr. Roland, one person will be Dr. Jones, and the third person will be an observer.
2. Roland and Jones will read only their own roles, but the observer will read both.
3. Role-play: Instructor announces, "I am Mr./Ms. Cardoza, the owner of the remaining Ugli oranges. My fruit export firm is based in South America. My country does not have diplomatic relations with your country, although we do have strong trade relations."

The groups will spend about 10 minutes meeting with the other firm's representative and will decide on a course of action. Be prepared to answer the following questions:
   a. What do you plan to do?
   b. If you want to buy the oranges, what price will you offer?
   c. To whom and how will the oranges be delivered?
4. The observers will report the solutions reached. The groups will describe the decision-making process used.
5. The instructor will lead a discussion on the exercise addressing the following questions:
   a. Which groups had the most trust? How did that influence behaviour?
   b. Which groups shared more information? Why?
   c. How are trust and disclosure important in negotiations?

## Role of "Dr. Jones"

You are Dr. John W. Jones, a biological research scientist employed by a pharmaceutical firm. You have recently developed a synthetic chemical useful for curing and preventing Rudosen. Rudosen is a disease contracted by pregnant women. If not caught in the first four weeks of pregnancy, the disease causes serious brain, eye, and ear damage to the unborn child. Recently, there has been an outbreak of Rudosen in your state, and several thousand women have contracted the disease. You have found, with volunteer patients, that your recently developed synthetic serum cures Rudosen in its early stages. Unfortunately, the serum is made from the juice of the Ugli orange, which is a very rare fruit. Only a small quantity (approximately 4,000) of these oranges were produced last season. No additional Ugli oranges will be available until next season, which will be too late to cure the present Rudosen victims.

You've demonstrated that your synthetic serum is in no way harmful to pregnant women. Consequently, there are no side effects. The production and distribution of the serum as a cure for Rudosen has received regulatory approval. Unfortunately, the current outbreak was unexpected, and your firm had not planned on having the compound serum available for six months. Your firm holds the patent on the synthetic serum, and it is expected to be a highly profitable product when it is generally available to the public.

You have recently been informed on good evidence that R. H. Cardoza, a South American fruit exporter, is in possession of 3,000 Ugli oranges in good condition. If you could obtain the juice of all 3,000 you would be able to both cure present victims and provide sufficient inoculation for the remaining pregnant women in the state. No other state currently has a Rudosen threat.

You have recently been informed that Dr. P. W. Roland is also urgently seeking Ugli oranges and is also aware of Cardoza's possession of the 3,000 available. Dr. Roland is employed by a competing pharmaceutical firm and has been working on biological warfare research for the past several years. There is a great deal of industrial espionage in the pharmaceutical industry. Over the past several years, Dr. Roland's firm and yours have sued each other for infringement of patent rights and espionage law violations several times.

You've been authorized by your firm to approach Cardoza to purchase the 3,000 Ugli oranges. You have been told he will sell them to the highest bidder. Your firm has authorized you to bid as high as $250,000 to obtain the juice of the 3,000 available oranges.

## Role of "Dr. Roland"

You are Dr. P. W. Roland. You work as a research biologist for a pharmaceutical firm. The firm is under contract with the U.S. government to do research on methods to combat enemy uses of biological warfare.

Recently several World War II experimental nerve gas bombs were moved from the United States to a small island just off the U.S. coast in the Pacific. In the process of transporting them, two of the bombs developed a leak. The leak is currently controlled by government scientists, who believe that the gas will permeate the bomb chambers within two weeks. They know of no method of preventing the gas from getting into the atmosphere and spreading to other islands and very likely to the West Coast as well. If this occurs, it is likely that several thousand people will incur serious brain damage or die.

You've developed a synthetic vapor that will neutralize the nerve gas if it is injected into the bomb chamber before the gas leaks out. The vapor is made with a chemical taken from the rind of the Ugli orange, a very rare fruit. Unfortunately, only 4,000 of these oranges were produced this season.

You've been informed on good evidence that R. H. Cardoza, a fruit exporter in South America, is in possession of 3,000 Ugli oranges. The chemicals from the rinds of all 3,000 oranges would be sufficient to neutralize the gas if the vapor is developed and injected efficiently. You have been informed that the rinds of these oranges are in good condition.

You have learned that Dr. J. W. Jones is also urgently seeking to purchase Ugli oranges and that he is aware of Cardoza's possession of the 3,000 available. Dr. Jones works for a firm with which your firm is highly competitive. There is a great deal of industrial espionage in the pharmaceutical industry. Over the years, your firm and Dr. Jones's have sued one another for violations of industrial espionage laws and infringement of patent rights several times. Litigation on two suits is still in process.

The U.S. government has asked your firm for assistance. You've been authorized by your firm to approach Cardoza to purchase 3,000 Ugli oranges. You have been told he will sell them to the highest bidder. Your firm has authorized you to bid as high as $250,000 to obtain the rinds of the oranges.

Before approaching Cardoza, you have decided to talk to Dr. Jones to influence him so that he will not prevent you from purchasing the oranges.

---

*By Robert House, Joseph Frank Bernstein Professor of Organizational Studies; Professor of Management, Wharton University of Pennsylvania. Used with permission.

# 6

# Designing Organizations for the International Environment

Theo Wargo/WireImage/Getty Images

## Alcan

Alcan planned to invest $1.5 billion to expand an aluminium smelter in Hafnarfjordur, Iceland. The ISAL smelter is the oldest in Iceland and has been operating since 1969. Hafnarfjordur is a small port suburb of Iceland's capital, Reykjavik. Hafnarfjordur has been a commercial port since the 1300s. Myth claims that the port is full of elves and mystical creatures, the Hidden Folk, who live on rocks near the town's centre.

Alcan had an agreement with the Icelandic government for access to cheap hydroelectricity to run the smelter and was planning to increase output from 180,000 to 460,000 tonnes annually. However, Alcan misjudged the reaction of the 25,000 citizens of Hafnarfjordur. In a referendum held in the spring of 2007, 50.3 percent voted against allowing the government to move a highway and rezone land as part of the proposed expansion of the ISAL smelter. Many citizens opposed the expansion because of environmental concerns. Alcan lost the referendum by 88 votes. Michel Jacques, President and CEO of Alcan's primary metal group, says that the company will review the results carefully—"[we] will consider our options—if we can improve our project to make it more in line with people's expectations, we will do that."[1]

Other aluminium producers have gone to Iceland as its natural terrain—rivers from its glaciers along with the geothermal energy beneath its volcanic rocks—creates the potential for the massive amounts of energy that smelters need to produce aluminium. The smelters are facing opposition from Iceland's environmental and citizens' groups as they are concerned about their impact on Iceland's wilderness.[2] Iceland's best-known singer Bjork, recently expressed her concern about the sale of the Icelandic power company HS Orka to Vancouver-based Magma Energy Corp. by holding a karaoke protest marathon as well as addressing the country's parliament. Magma Energy Corp. has acquired a 98.53 percent in HS Orka.[3] Since then, part of HS Orka has been sold to several Icelandic pension funds.[4]

B efore you learn more about doing business internationally, complete the You & Design feature to learn about your own approach.

## YOU & DESIGN

### Are You Ready to Fill an International Role?

Are you ready to negotiate a sales contract with someone from another country? Coordinate a new product for use overseas? Companies large and small deal on a global basis. To what extent do you display the behaviours below? Please answer each item as Mostly True or Mostly False for you.

| Are You Typically: | Mostly True | Mostly False |
|---|---|---|
| 1. Impatient? Do you have a short attention span? Do you want to keep moving to the next topic? | ___ | ___ |
| 2. A poor listener? Are you uncomfortable with silence? Does your mind think about what you want to say next? | ___ | ___ |

*(Continued)*

3. Argumentative? Do you enjoy arguing for its own sake?  _____  _____

4. Not familiar with cultural specifics in other countries? Do you have limited experience in other countries?  _____  _____

5. Placing more emphasis on the short-term than on the long-term in your thinking and planning?  _____  _____

6. Thinking that it is a waste of time getting to know someone personally before discussing business?  _____  _____

7. Legalistic to win your point? Holding others to an agreement regardless of changing circumstances?  _____  _____

8. Thinking "win/lose" when negotiating? Trying to win a negotiation at the other's expense?  _____  _____

**Scoring:** Give yourself one point for each Mostly True answer. A score of 3 or lower suggests that you may have international style and awareness. A score of 6 or higher suggests low presence or awareness with respect to other cultures.

**Interpretation:** A low score on this exercise is a good thing. [North] American managers often display cross-cultural ignorance during business negotiations compared to counterparts from other countries. [North] American habits can be disturbing, such as emphasizing areas of disagreement over agreement, spending little time understanding the views and interests of the other side, and adopting an adversarial attitude. [North] Americans often like to leave a negotiation thinking they won, which can be embarrassing to the other side. For this quiz, a low score shows better international presence. If you answered "Mostly True" to three or fewer questions, then consider yourself ready to assist with an international negotiation. If you scored six or higher "Mostly True" responses, it is time to learn more about how business people behave in other national cultures before participating in international business deals. Try to develop greater focus on other people's needs and an appreciation for different viewpoints. Be open to compromise and develop empathy for people who are different from you.

Source: Adapted from Cynthia Barnum and Natasha Wolniansky, "Why Americans Fail at Overseas Negotiations," *Management Review* (October 1989), 54–57.

When an organization decides to do business in another country, managers face a whole new set of challenges. Despite the challenges of doing business internationally, most companies today think the potential rewards outweigh the risks. Canadian companies have long been involved in international business, but interest in global trade is greater now than ever before. Companies have set up foreign operations to produce goods and services needed by consumers in other countries, as well as to obtain lower costs for producing products to sell at home. In return, companies from Japan, Germany, and the United Kingdom compete with Canadian companies on their own turf as well as abroad. Domestic markets for many companies are becoming saturated, and the only potential for growth lies overseas. In 2005, Magna International recognized the importance of becoming a global organization and hired Mark Hogan "to prepare the world's most diversified Tier 1 supplier of automotive systems for the new global order." "The best way to characterize Magna," he says, "is as a Canadian company that grew its North American business in the 1970s and 80s. In the 1990s, it then focused its attention on growth in Europe, which it did quite successfully. This decade is devoted to making sure we stay competitive in North America and Europe, but to also grow our base of business in Asia—both from a manufacturing standpoint and a customer standpoint."[5]

For e-commerce companies, expanding internationally is becoming a priority. Google, for example, entered the Chinese market but is considered "another imported also-ran"[6] as it competes with Baidu, which does 78 percent of Chinese Internet searches. When Google threatened to pull out of China over free speech, investors bought Baidu shares and its stock price rose about 170 percent in 2010.[7] Baidu is the second most popular website in the world, after Google.[8]

Succeeding on a global scale isn't easy. Organizations have to make decisions about strategic approach; how best to get involved in international markets, policies, and laws; and how to design the organization to reap the benefits of international expansion.

## ■ Purpose of This Chapter

This chapter will explore how managers design organizations for the international environment. We begin by looking at some of the primary motivations for organizations to expand internationally, the typical stages of international development, and the use of strategic alliances as a means for international expansion. Then the chapter examines global strategic approaches and the application of various structural designs for global advantage. Next, we discuss some of the specific challenges global organizations face, mechanisms for addressing them, and cultural differences that influence the organization's approach to designing and managing a global firm. Finally, the chapter takes a look at an emerging type of global organization, the *transnational model*, that achieves high levels of the varied capabilities needed to succeed in a complex and volatile international environment.

## Entering the Global Arena

As recently as 30 years ago, many companies could afford to ignore the international environment. However, the world is becoming a unified global field; today's companies must think globally or get left behind. Extraordinary advancements in communications, technology, and transportation have created a new, highly competitive landscape. Products can be made and sold anywhere in the world, communications are instant, and product-development and life cycles are growing shorter. No company is isolated from global influence. Some large so-called American companies such as Coca-Cola and Procter & Gamble rely on international sales for a substantial portion of their sales and profits. On the other hand, organizations in other countries search for customers in North America. Sony of Japan gets much of its game business sales from North America and European consumers. Sales of the PlayStation 4 were strong in North America in early 2014 ahead of the Japanese launch.[9] And even small companies can be actively involved in international business through exports and online business. Cole + Parker, founded in London, Ontario, makes socks that "start businesses"; it sells its socks online and through its retail network. Cole + Parker has partnered with Kiva, a microfinance organization. "Proceeds from each purchase of our socks [are] loaned to support entrepreneurs in poverty. So literally, purchasing a few pairs of socks can start multiple start ups around the world. And that is how our socks start businesses, thus the one for many business model."[10] Similarly, Boréalis, located in Magog, Québec, has established social responsibility standards for multinationals to ensure that

**Apply**

How can you apply "going global" in your role as a university or college student?

their international projects are sustainable. "For Boréalis, community involvement is global, encompassing providing financial aid to college and university groups involved in international aid trips, offering apprenticeships to foreign students, and giving back to the countries in which they work."[11]

## ■ Motivations for Global Expansion

Economic, technological, and competitive forces have combined to push many companies from a domestic to a global focus. In some industries, being successful now means succeeding on a global scale. The importance of the global environment for today's organizations is reflected in the shifting global economy. As one indication, *Fortune's* list of the Global 500, the world's 500 largest companies, indicates that economic clout is being diffused across a broad global scale. Although the United States accounts for the majority of the Global 500 revenues, a number of smaller and less-developed countries are growing stronger. According to the 2010 Global 500, the United States has the most global giants, followed by Japan and China. Canada's most highly ranked company, Manulife Financial, ranked in 208th place.[12] In general, three primary factors motivate companies to expand internationally: economies of scale, economies of scope, and low-cost production factors.[13]

**Economies of Scale.** Building a global presence expands an organization's scale of operations, enabling it to realize **economies of scale**. The trend toward large organizations was initially sparked by the Industrial Revolution, which created pressure in many industries for larger factories that could seize the benefits of economies of scale offered by new technologies and production methods. Through large-volume production, these industrial giants were able to achieve the lowest possible cost per unit of production. However, for many companies, domestic markets no longer provide the high level of sales needed to maintain enough volume to achieve scale economies. The Running Room, for example, entered the U.S. market in 2007 as the domestic market was saturated. It started its expansion in the Minneapolis, Minnesota area, but growth has been slow. Seven years later, it opened only its tenth store in the United States.[14] Entering American markets has not been easy for Canadian companies—retailers especially as "[they] have grossly underestimated the competitiveness of the American market.... Americans are take-no-prisoners type retailers."[15]

In an industry such as automobile manufacturing, for example, a company would need a tremendous share of the domestic market to achieve scale economies. Thus, an organization such as Chrysler was forced to become international in order to survive. Economies of scale also enable companies to obtain volume discounts from suppliers, lowering the organization's cost of production.

**Economies of Scope.** A second factor is the enhanced potential for exploiting **economies of scope.** *Scope* refers to the number and variety of products and services a company offers, as well as the number and variety of regions, countries, and markets it serves. Having a presence in multiple countries provides marketing power and synergy compared to the same size firm that has presence in fewer countries. For example, an advertising agency with a presence in several global markets gains a competitive edge serving large companies that span the globe. Cossette Communication Group, an advertising company best known for its Bell Canada campaign featuring beavers Frank and Gordon, bought Dare Digital Ltd. of London, the United Kingdom as an entry point into European markets. Its foray into the U.S. market had not been particularly successful but Cossette continues to build its American business. As Claude Lessard, CEO, chair and president noted, "[we'll] never be in the top five in the U.S. (Cossette ranks 15th in North America and 25th internationally)...[but] we want to be much more aggressive winning new clients and making acquisitions."[16] Economies of scope can also increase a company's market power as compared to competitors, because the company develops broad knowledge of the cultural, social, economic, and other factors that affect its customers in varied locations and can provide specialized products and services to meet those needs.

**Compare**

Compare the key differences between economy of scale and economy of scope.

**Low-Cost Production Factors.** The third major force motivating global expansion relates to **factors of production**. One of the earliest, and still one of the most powerful, motivations for North American companies to invest abroad is the opportunity to obtain raw materials and other resources at the lowest possible cost. Organizations have long turned overseas to secure raw materials that were scarce or unavailable in their home country. In the early 20th century, tire companies went abroad to develop rubber plantations to supply tires for North America's growing automobile industry. Today, American paper manufacturers such as Weyerhacuser and U.S. Paper, forced by environmental concerns to look overseas for new timberlands, are managing millions of acres of tree farms in New Zealand.[17]

Many companies also turn to other countries as a source of cheap labour. Textile manufacturing in the United States is now practically nonexistent as companies have shifted most production to Asia, Mexico, Latin America, and the Caribbean, where the costs of labour and supplies are much lower. Between 1997 and 2002, the percentage of clothing sold in the United States but manufactured elsewhere rose to around 75 percent, an increase of nearly 20 percent in five years. A check of the "Made in" tags at one Gap store found clothing made in 24 countries, in addition to the United States.[18] Gildan Activewear, which makes casual apparel such as T-shirts, sports shirts, and fleeces, has been shifting its production to low-cost factories in Central America and the Caribbean. It has done so to boost profits.[19] It shut down its two remaining Montréal factories and laid off 1,365 Mexican workers in early 2007. According to Laurence Sellyn, Gildan Activewear's chief financial and administrative officer, "[we] regret that these closures are necessary in order to be globally competitive...[but] the economic case for consolidating offshore is compelling."[20] Globalization has had a significant impact on Canada's garment industry. There are only few companies—such as Canada Goose and Second Denim Co.—that actually manufacture clothing in Canada, and they are aware of the uncertain future they face.[21]

Other organizations have gone international in search of lower costs of capital, sources of cheap energy, reduced government restrictions, or other factors that lower the company's total production costs. Companies can locate facilities wherever it makes the most economic sense in terms of needed employee education and skill levels, labour and raw materials costs, and other production factors. Automobile manufacturers such as Toyota, BMW, General Motors, and Ford have built plants in South Africa, Brazil, and Thailand, where they can pay workers less than one-tenth of what workers earn in higher-wage, developed countries. In addition, these countries typically offer dramatically lower costs for factors such as land, water, and electricity.[22] However, they have also lower environmental and health and safety standards. Foreign companies also come to North America to obtain favourable circumstances. Japan's Honda and Toyota and Switzerland's Novartis, for example, have built plants or research centres in North America to take advantage of incentives, to find skilled workers, and to be closer to major customers and suppliers.[23]

## ■ Globalization Issues

While economic factors seem to be the main drivers of globalization, it remains a controversial strategy. Globalization is not new in Canada. Canada was involved in global industrial systems with the British Empire. Even earlier, Québec, known as New France, played a key role in global agricultural systems. It appears the globalization existed in Greco-Roman times, Parthian societies, and ancient Chinese dynasties, to name a few.[24]

Protests against globalization began in earnest in 1999 in Seattle. The protesters were a varied group such as unions worried about job losses, environmentalists worried about pollution, and labour groups worried about working conditions. Many of the concerns raised by the Seattle protestors have been empirically verified. For example, economists have found that competition from China has lowered wages and increased unemployment in the United States.[25] Protests continue and often focus on the role of both the World Bank and the International Monetary Fund. Antiglobalization activists are concerned that both organizations are "imposing Western-style capitalism on developing countries without regard to the social effects."[26] One of the key thinkers and activists in the antiglobalization movement is our own Naomi Klein whose book *No Logo* has had global impact.

As mentioned in Chapter 1, it is important for you to look critically at organizational ideas and practices. Whether you are for or against globalization, it is important to understand that it is a complex and nuanced issue that has consequences beyond economic benefit.

## ■ Stages of International Development

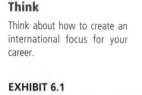

**Think**

Think about how to create an international focus for your career.

No company can become a global giant overnight. Managers have to consciously adopt a strategy for global development and growth. Organizations enter foreign markets in a variety of ways and follow diverse paths. However, the shift from domestic to global typically occurs through stages of development, as illustrated in Exhibit 6.1.[27] In stage one, the **domestic stage,** the company is domestically oriented, but managers are aware of the global environment and may want to consider initial foreign involvement to expand production volume and realize economies of scale.

**EXHIBIT 6.1**
**Four Stages of International Evolution**

|  | I. DOMESTIC | II. INTERNATIONAL | III. MULTINATIONAL | IV. GLOBAL |
|---|---|---|---|---|
| Strategic Orientation | Domestically oriented | Export-oriented multidomestic | Multinational | Global |
| Stage of Development | Initial foreign involvement | Competitive positioning | Explosion | Global |
| Structure | Domestic structure, plus export department | Domestic structure, plus international division | Worldwide geographic, product | Matrix, transnational |
| Market Potential | Moderate, mostly domestic | Large, multidomestic | Very large, multinational | Whole world |

Source: Based on Nancy J. Adler, *International Dimensions of Organizational Behavior*, 4th ed. (Cincinnati, Ohio: South-Western, 2002), 8–9; and Theodore T. Herbert, "Strategy and Multinational Organization Structure: An Interorganizational Relationships Perspective," *Academy of Management Review 9* (1984), 259–271.

Market potential is limited and is primarily in the home country. The structure of the company is domestic, typically functional or divisional, and initial foreign sales are handled through an export department. The details of freight forwarding, customs problems, and foreign exchange are handled by outsiders.

In stage two, the **international stage,** the company takes exports seriously and begins to think multidomestically. **Multidomestic** means competitive issues in each country are independent of other countries; the company deals with each country individually. The concern is with international competitive positioning compared with other firms in the industry. At this point, an international division has replaced the export department, and specialists are hired to handle sales, service, and warehousing abroad. Multiple countries are identified as a potential market. Artisan bread maker Ace Bakery, once a ten-seat Toronto bakery, has expanded internationally. It now sells its par-baked bread, which accounts for 60 percent of its sales, across Canada, and in New York, Michigan, and the Bahamas. The Bahamas operations began in 2005 when a chef at a five-star hotel couldn't find high-quality bread locally. Ace Bakery has grown considerably in its 15 years of operation—it has 300 employees and annual sales under $50 million. It commits 10 percent of pretax profit in the regions where it does business by investing in organic farming, culinary scholarships, and food and nutrition programs for the poor.[28]

In stage three, the **multinational stage,** the company has extensive experience in a number of international markets and has established marketing, manufacturing, or research and development facilities in several foreign countries. The organization obtains a large percentage of revenues from sales outside the home country. Explosion occurs as international operations take off, and the company has business units scattered around the world along with suppliers, manufacturers, and distributors. Examples of companies in the multinational stage include Sony of Japan, and Coca-Cola of the United States. Walmart, although it is the world's biggest company, is just moving into the multinational stage, with only 18.5 percent of sales and 15.8 percent of profits from international business in 2003.[29] By 2011, Walmart's fortunes shifted from the North American to its international markets. Global net sales increased 4.4 percent, led by an 11.5 percent surge in the company's international sales to almost $28 billion; however, net U.S. sales, which include new stores open less than a year, edged up 0.6 per cent to almost $63 billion. Walmart may be moving into the global stage.[30]

The fourth and ultimate stage is the **global stage,** which means the company transcends any single country. The business is not merely a collection of domestic industries; rather, subsidiaries are interlinked to the point where competitive position in one country significantly influences activities in other countries.[31] Truly **global companies** no longer think of themselves as having a single home country, and, indeed, have been called *stateless corporations.*[32] This represents a new and dramatic evolution from the multinational company of the 1960s and 1970s.

Global companies operate in truly global fashion, and the entire world is their marketplace. Organizational structure at this stage can be extremely complex and often evolves into an international matrix or transnational model, which will be discussed later in this chapter.

Global companies such as Nestlé, Royal Dutch/Shell, Unilever, and Matsushita Electric may operate in more than 100 countries. The structural problem of holding together this huge complex of subsidiaries scattered thousands of miles apart is immense.

# ■ Global Expansion Through International Strategic Alliances

One of the most popular ways companies get involved in international operations is through international strategic alliances. Companies in rapidly changing industries such as media and entertainment, pharmaceuticals, biotechnology, and software might have hundreds of these relationships.[33] QLT, for example, a Vancouver-based biopharmaceutical company specializing in the fields of ophthalmology and dermatology, has co-development agreements with Novartis Ophthalmics, and, through QLT USA, has agreements with Pfizer, Sanofi-Synthelabo, Astellas Pharma, Medi-Gene AG, and Mayne Pharma PTY Ltd.[34]

Typical alliances include licensing, joint ventures, and consortia.[35] For example, pharmaceutical companies such as Merck, Eli Lilly, Pfizer, and Warner-Lambert cross-license their newest drugs to one another to support industry-wide innovation and marketing and offset the high fixed costs of research and distribution.[36] A **joint venture** is a separate entity created with two or more active firms as sponsors. This is a popular approach to sharing development and production costs, and penetrating new markets. Joint ventures may be with either customers or competitors.[37] Competing Chinese firms Shanghai Automotive Industries and Nanjing Automobile Corporation have partnered to develop new models so that they can compete globally; in 2007, they signed a "comprehensive co-operation agreement on design, production and sales."[38] Swiss food company Nestlé and French cosmetics giant L'Oréal engaged in a joint venture to develop Inneov, a nutritional supplement intended to improve the health of skin.[39] MTV Networks has joint ventures with companies in Brazil, Australia, and other countries to expand its global media presence.[40]

Companies often seek joint ventures to take advantage of a partner's knowledge of local markets, achieve production cost savings through economies of scale, share complementary technological strengths, or distribute new products and services through another country's distribution channels. Nortel Networks, for example, developed joint ventures with China Putian and LG Electronics to get access to the Asian markets.[41] Robex Resources, a gold exploration and development company, and Geo Services International, an international company operating in Mali, have an agreement that enables the two to combine their technological power and increase the success of gold exploration and drilling projects in certain areas.[42] The steel unit of Tata Group is planning to spend $32 million to assess the viability of developing iron ore deposits located on the Québec–Labrador border. According to the CEO of the Canadian partner, the development of the iron ore "...will generate long-term jobs, taxes, and infrastructure for the First Nations and other surrounding communities."[43] ICICI Bank, one of India's largest financial services providers, entered into a joint venture with Lombard, one of Canada's oldest property and casualty insurance companies, to launch its general insurance business in India.[44]

Another increasingly popular approach is for companies to become involved in **consortia**, groups of independent companies—including suppliers, customers, and even competitors—that join together to share skills, resources, costs, and access to one another's markets. Airbus Industrie, for example, is a consortium comprising French, British, and German aerospace companies that has been successfully battering U.S. giant Boeing.[45] Consortia are often used in other parts of the world, such as the *keiretsu* family of corporations in Japan. In Korea, these interlocking company arrangements are called *chaebol*. See the next In Practice for an intriguing alliance that links artisans and companies to develop sustainable aid.

A type of consortium, the global virtual organization, is increasingly being used and offers a promising approach to meeting worldwide competition. The virtual organization refers to a continually evolving set of company relationships that exist temporarily to exploit unique opportunities or attain specific strategic advantages. A company may be involved in multiple alliances at any one time. Oracle, a software company, is involved in as many as 15,000 short-term organizational partnerships at any time.[46] Some executives believe shifting to a virtual approach is the best way for companies to be competitive in the global marketplace.[47]

---

The BRANDAID Project is a global marketing initiative to bring prosperity to artisans by closing the market divide between poorer and richer countries. Its co-founders include Tony Pigott, CEO of JWT Canada; David Belle, filmmaker; and Paul Haggis, Oscar-winning director. The five market principles it applies are (1) helping developing world artisans create prosperity; (2) bridging the market divide with world-class marketing partners and Hollywood patrons to grow online sales for artisan producers; (3) building an online community where developing-world artisans can showcase their work to a new era of consumers who engage global culture; (4) supporting better living and working conditions in artisan communities with capacity building, skills training, health and education; and (5) paying artisans their asking price in advance of sales and share in the profits.[48]

BRANDAID's partners include CARE, UNESCO, Ciné Institute, and the Saatchi Gallery. It uses the UNESCO Award of Excellence for handicrafts criteria, and looks for sources of high quality art, sculpture, home decor, textiles, ceramics and jewellery. Its suppliers are master-artisan-led, community-based microenterprises. Through the BRANDAID Foundation, it funds capacity building and skills training so that the communities become stronger. The artisans share in the profits and some of the profits go back to the Foundation to support its work.

The BRANDAID Haiti project, for example, is focused on rebuilding two communities devastated by the 2010 earthquake by revitalizing the metal artists of Croix de Bouquets and the papier mâché artisans of Jacmel. Another goal of BRANDAID Haiti is to provide a market for the work of the talented artisans. According to the project's development director, Thor Burnham, "[The] multiplier effect of the artisan community is huge."[49] As a result, the income of the artisans increases substantially.

The Macy's Group sells some of the work of the papier mâché artisans through its Heart of Haiti collection that is part of its Shop for a Better World program. Besides, The Bay has created a pop-up store and an online store to sell the work of the Haitian artisans. According to the President and Co-founder of BRANDAID, Cameron Brohman, "They're very unique products, designed by Canadian designers and made by Haitian master artisans so that collaboration has produced some very exciting, very new-looking designs."[50] BRANDAID now is considering its own move into other countries.

**In Practice**

**The BRANDAID Project (BRANDAID)**

*act!*

**Apply**

How could you apply the BRANDAID model in other organizational types?

---

## Designing Structure to Fit Global Strategy

As we discussed in Chapter 3, an organization's structure must fit its situation by providing sufficient information processing for coordination and control while focusing employees on specific functions, products, or geographic regions. Organizational design for international firms follows a similar logic, with special interest in global versus local strategic opportunities.

## ■ Model for Global Versus Local Opportunities

When organizations venture into the international domain, managers strive to formulate a coherent global strategy that will provide synergy among worldwide operations for the purpose of achieving common organizational goals. One dilemma they face is choosing whether to emphasize global **standardization** versus national responsiveness. Managers must decide whether they want each global affiliate to act autonomously or whether activities should be standardized across countries. These decisions are reflected in the choice between a globalization versus a multidomestic global strategy.

The **globalization strategy** means that product design, manufacturing, and marketing strategy are standardized throughout the world.[51] For example, the Japanese took away business from Canadian and American companies by developing similar high-quality, low-cost products for all countries. The Canadian and American companies incurred higher costs by tailoring products to specific countries. Black & Decker became much more competitive internationally when it standardized its line of power hand tools. Other products, such as Coca-Cola, are naturals for globalization, because only advertising and marketing need to be tailored for different regions. In general, services are less suitable for globalization because different customs and habits often require a different approach to providing service. Walmart has had trouble transplanting its successful North American formula without adjustment. In Indonesia, for example, Walmart closed its stores after only a year. Customers didn't like the brightly lit, highly organized stores, and, because no haggling was permitted, they thought the goods were overpriced.[52] On the other hand, Bombardier has enjoyed success in Germany and employs 7,000 people at its seven production facilities. Tim's Canadian Deli in Germany has enjoyed success too—it has 75 employees who run three restaurants and a wholesale bakery supplying cafés and supermarkets with Canadian baked goods such as blueberry and chocolate muffins.[53]

Other companies in recent years have also begun shifting away from a strict globalization strategy. Economic and social changes, including a backlash against huge global corporations, have prompted consumers to be less interested in global brands and more in favour of products that have a local feel.[54] However, a globalization strategy can help a manufacturing organization reap economy-of-scale efficiencies by standardizing product design and manufacturing, using common suppliers, introducing products around the world faster, coordinating prices, and eliminating overlapping facilities. By sharing technology, design, suppliers, and manufacturing standards worldwide in a coordinated global automotive operation, Ford saved $5 billion in three years.[55] In addition, Ford and Toyota had some discussions about some sort of relationship.[56] Details were vague but the relationship would focus on possible environmental technology tie-ups.

A **multidomestic strategy** means that competition in each country is handled independently of competition in other countries. Thus, a multidomestic strategy would encourage product design, assembly, and marketing tailored to the specific needs of each country. Some companies have found that their products do not thrive in a single global market. For example, people in different countries have very different expectations for personal-care products such as deodorant or toothpaste. The French do not drink orange juice for breakfast, and laundry detergent is used to wash dishes, not clothes, in parts of Mexico. As another example of a multidomestic strategy, Procter & Gamble tried to standardize diaper design, but discovered that

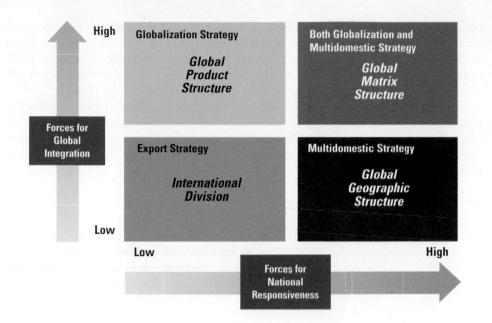

**EXHIBIT 6.2**
**Model to Fit Organization Structure to International Advantages**
Source: From Roderick E. White and Thomas A. Poynter, "Organizing for Worldwide Advantage," *Ivey Business Journal*. Adapted by permission of the Richard Ivey School of Business, the University of Western Ontario, London, Ontario, Canada. Copyright © 1999, Ivey Management Services. One time permission to reproduce granted by Richard Ivey School of Business Foundation on January 24, 2014.

cultural values in different parts of the world required style adjustments to make the product acceptable to many parents. In Italy, for example, designing diapers to cover the baby's navel was critical to successful sales.[57]

Different global organizational designs, as well, are better suited to the need for either global standardization or national responsiveness. Recent research on more than 100 international firms based in Spain has provided further support for the connection between international structure and strategic focus.[58] The model in Exhibit 6.2 illustrates how organizational design and international strategy fit the needs of the environment.[59]

Companies can be characterized by whether their product and service lines have potential for globalization, which means advantages through worldwide standardization. Companies that sell diverse products or services across many countries have a globalization strategy. On the other hand, some companies have products and services appropriate for a multidomestic strategy, which means local-country advantages through differentiation and customization to meet local needs.

As indicated in Exhibit 6.2, when forces for both global standardization and national responsiveness in many countries are low, simply using an international division with the domestic structure is an appropriate way to handle international business. For some industries, however, technological, social, or economic forces may create a situation in which selling standardized products worldwide provides a basis for competitive advantage. In these cases, a global product structure is appropriate. This structure provides product managers with authority to handle their product lines on a global basis and enables the company to take advantage of a unified global marketplace. In other cases, companies can gain competitive advantages through national responsiveness—by responding to unique needs in the various countries in which they do business. For these companies, a global geographic structure is appropriate so that each country or region will have subsidiaries modifying products and services to fit that locale. A good illustration is the advertising firm of Ogilvy & Mather, which divides its operations into four primary geographic regions because advertising approaches need to be modified to fit the tastes, preferences, cultural values, and government regulations in different parts of the world.[60] Children are frequently used to advertise products in Canada, but in France this approach is against the law. The competitive claims of rival products regularly seen on North American television would violate government regulations in Germany.[61]

In many instances, companies will need to respond to both global and local opportunities simultaneously, in which case the global matrix structure can be used. Part of the product line may need to be standardized globally, and other parts tailored to the needs of local countries. Let's discuss each of the structures in Exhibit 6.2 in more detail.

## ■ International Division

As companies begin to explore international opportunities, they typically start with an export department that grows into an **international division**. The international division has a status equal to the other major departments or divisions within the company and is illustrated in Exhibit 6.3. Although the domestic divisions are

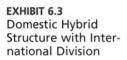

**EXHIBIT 6.3**
Domestic Hybrid Structure with International Division

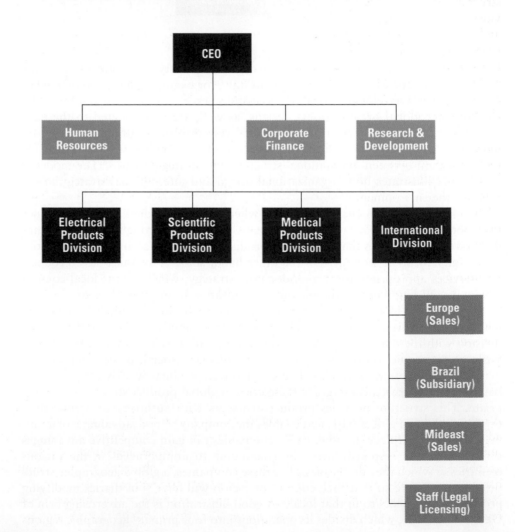

typically organized along functional or product lines, the international division is organized according to geographic interests, as illustrated in the exhibit. The international division has its own hierarchy to handle business (licensing, joint ventures) in various countries, selling the products and services created by the domestic divisions, opening subsidiary plants, and in general moving the organization into more sophisticated international operations.

Although functional structures are often used domestically, they are less frequently used to manage a worldwide business.[62] Lines of functional hierarchy running around the world would extend too long, so some form of product or geographic structure is used to subdivide the organization into smaller units. Firms typically start with an international department and, depending on their strategy, later use product or geographic division structures.

## ■ Global Product Structure

In a **global product structure**, the product divisions take responsibility for global operations in their specific product area. This is one of the most commonly used structures through which managers attempt to achieve global goals because it provides a fairly straightforward way to effectively manage a variety of businesses and products around the world. Managers in each product division can focus on organizing international operations as they see fit and directing employees' energy toward their own division's unique set of global problems or opportunities.[63] In addition, the structure provides top managers at headquarters with a broad perspective on competition, enabling the entire corporation to respond more rapidly to a changing global environment.[64]

With a global product structure, each division's manager is responsible for planning, organizing, and controlling all functions for the production and distribution of its products for any market around the world. The product-based structure works best when a division handles products that are technologically similar and can be standardized for marketing worldwide. The global product structure works best when the company has opportunities for worldwide production and sale of standard products for all markets, thus providing economies of scale and standardization of production, marketing, and advertising.

Alcan has used a form of worldwide product structure, as illustrated in Exhibit 6.4. In this structure, Bauxite & Alumina, Primary Metal, Engineered Products, and Packaging groupings are responsible for manufacture and/or sale of products worldwide. The product structure is great for standardizing production and sales around the globe, but it also has problems. Often the product divisions do not work well together, competing instead of cooperating in some countries, and some countries may be ignored by product managers.

## ■ Global Geographic Structure

A regionally based organization is well suited to companies that want to emphasize adaptation to regional or local market needs through a multidomestic strategy, as noted in Exhibit 6.2. The **global geographic structure** divides the world into geographic regions, with each geographic division reporting to the CEO. Each division has full control of functional activities within its geographic area. For example, Nestlé, with headquarters in Switzerland, puts great emphasis on the autonomy of regional managers who know the local culture. The largest branded food company

**EXHIBIT 6.4**
Alcan's Organization
Chart—as of April 2007
Source: Alcan Inc. (April 2007)
at http://www.alcan.com/
web/publishing.nsf/content/
About+Alcan++Company+
Structure/$file/Alcan_Inc_
April2007.pdf (accessed July 2,
2008). Used with permission.

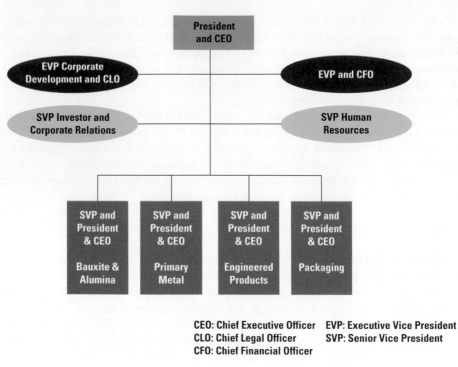

CEO: Chief Executive Officer    EVP: Executive Vice President
CLO: Chief Legal Officer    SVP: Senior Vice President
CFO: Chief Financial Officer

**act!**

**Compare**

Compare the different kinds
of global designs and evaluate
their strengths and weaknesses.

in the world, Nestlé rejects the idea of a single global market and uses a geographic structure to focus on the local needs and competition in each country. Local managers have the authority to tinker with a product's flavouring, packaging, portion size, or other elements as they see fit. Many of the company's 8,000 brands are registered in only one country.[65]

Companies that use this type of structure have typically been those with mature product lines and stable technologies. They can find low-cost manufacturing within countries, as well as meeting different needs across countries for marketing and sales. However, several business and organizational trends have led to a broadening of the kinds of companies that use the global geographic structure.[66] The growth of service organizations has outpaced manufacturing for several years, and many, but not all, services must occur on a local level. In addition, to meet new competitive threats, many manufacturing firms are emphasizing the ability to customize their products to meet specific needs, which requires a greater emphasis on local and regional responsiveness. All organizations are compelled by current environmental and competitive challenges to develop closer relationships with customers, which may lead companies to shift from product-based to geographic-based structures.

The problems encountered by senior management using a global geographic structure result from the autonomy of each regional division. For example, it is difficult to do planning on a global scale—such as new-product R&D—because each division acts to meet only the needs of its region. New domestic technologies and products can be difficult to transfer to international markets because each division thinks it will develop what it needs. Likewise, it is difficult to rapidly introduce products developed offshore into domestic markets, and there is often duplication of line and staff managers across regions.

Nestlé is currently struggling to adapt its global geographic structure in an effort to cut costs and boost efficiency. Because regional divisions act to meet specific needs in their own areas, tracking and maintaining control of costs has been a real problem. One analyst referred to Nestlé as "a holding company, with hundreds of companies reporting in."[67] Nestlé needs to find ways to increase efficiency and coordination without losing the benefits of the global geographic structure.

---

**In Practice**
**McCain Foods Limited (McCain)**

McCain Foods, a privately owned multinational family business, is the world's largest producer of frozen French fries (and other foods). It processes nearly one-third of the world's French fries. Its plants around the world have a total production capacity of more than one million pounds of potato products an hour! Its products are sold in 110 countries, and McCain has factories on five continents. In 2005, it opened an $18 million potato processing plant in Ahmedabad, India. In 40 years, McCain morphed from a small Florenceville, New Brunswick, company to one that has 55 production facilities that employ 20,000 people worldwide.[68]

McCain's statement of purpose and values notes that "we will 'drink the local wine': we are multicultural and care about our people, our families, and our local communities."[69] In addition to its many plants, McCain has licensing agreements in some countries, such as Switzerland, for the manufacture and distribution of its products. McCain did not enter the American market until 1997 when it bought Ore-Ida from Heinz for $500 million. In 2001, it acquired a frozen appetizer manufacturer, Anchor Food Products.[70] The company's expansion has been guided by the corporate cornerstone of drinking the local wine. According to Howard Mann, president and CEO until 2003, "[We] never march in and say [do] it this way"[71] as tastes can differ significantly. For example, North Americans prefer a thin, crispy French fry while the British prefer a thicker French fry.

While McCain has succeeded globally as it recognized the need to accommodate global differences, it has been marred by familial conflicts. In the mid-1990s, the two brothers who co-founded McCain, Harrison and Wallace, fought bitterly about who should succeed them. Wallace wanted his son, Michael, to take over while Harrison wanted outside management to run McCain. A New Brunswick court found in favour of Harrison McCain. Howard Mann, a non-family member, became CEO of McCain in 1995, and Wallace McCain was removed from the company he had co-founded. (Even so, the two brothers reconciled before Harrison McCain's death.) Wallace McCain and his two sons, Michael and Scott, then took over Maple Leaf Foods.[72]

---

## ■ Global Matrix Structure

**A global matrix structure** is similar to the matrix described in Chapter 3, except that for multinational corporations the geographic distances for communication are greater and coordination is even more complex. Exhibit 6.5 illustrates a global matrix structure. The matrix works best when pressure for decision making balances the interests of both product standardization and geographic localization, and when coordination to share resources is important. For many years, Asea Brown Boveri (ABB), an electrical equipment corporation headquartered in Zurich, used a global matrix structure that worked extremely well to coordinate a 200,000-employee company operating in more than 140 countries.

Many international firms apply a global hybrid or mixed structure, in which two or more different structures or elements of different structures are used. Hybrid structures are typical in highly volatile environments. Siemens AG of Germany, for example, combines elements of functional, geographic, and product divisions to respond to dynamic market conditions in the multiple countries where it operates.[73]

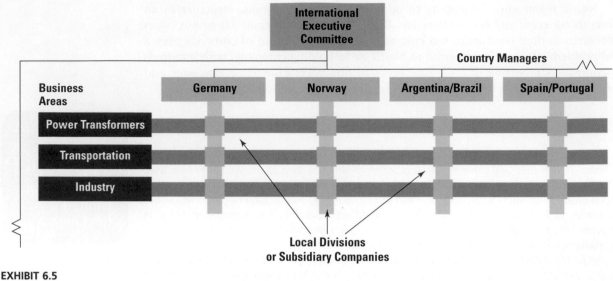

**EXHIBIT 6.5**
Global Matrix Structure

# Leading *by Design*

## Asea Brown Boveri Ltd. (ABB)

ABB has given new meaning to the notion of "being local worldwide." ABB owns 1,300 subsidiary companies, divided into 5,000 profit centres located in 140 countries. ABB's average plant has fewer than 200 workers and most of the company's 5,000 profit centres contain only 40 to 50 people, meaning almost everyone stays close to the customer.[74] For many years, ABB used a complex global matrix structure to achieve worldwide economies of scale combined with local flexibility and responsiveness.

At the top are the chief executive officer and an international committee of eight top managers, who hold frequent meetings around the world. Along one side of the matrix are 65 or so business areas located worldwide, into which ABB's products and services are grouped. Each business area leader is responsible for handling business on a global scale, allocating export markets, establishing cost and quality standards, and creating mixed-nationality teams to solve problems. For example, the leader for power transformers is responsible for 25 factories in 16 countries.

Along the other side of the matrix is a country structure; ABB has more than 100 country managers, most of them citizens of the country in which they work. They run national companies and are responsible for local balance sheets, income statements, and career ladders. The German president, for example, is responsible for 36,000 people

across several business areas that generate annual revenues in Germany of more than $4 billion.

The matrix structure converges at the level of the 1,300 local companies. The presidents of local companies report to two bosses—the business area leader, who is usually located outside the country, and the country president, who runs the company of which the local organization is a subsidiary.

ABB's philosophy is to decentralize to the lowest levels. Global managers must be open, patient, and multilingual. They must work with teams made up of different nationalities and be culturally sensitive. They craft strategy and evaluate performance for people and subsidiaries around the world. Country managers, by contrast, are regional line managers responsible for several country subsidiaries. They must cooperate with business area managers to achieve worldwide efficiencies and the introduction of new products. Finally, the presidents of local companies have both a global boss—the business area manager—and a country boss, and they learn to coordinate the needs of both.[75]

ABB is a large, successful company that achieved the benefits of both product and geographic organizations through this matrix structure. However, over the past several years, as ABB has faced increasingly complex competitive issues, leaders have transformed the company toward a complex structure called the transnational model, which will be discussed later in this chapter.

Organizations like McCain and Nestlé that operate on a global scale frequently have to make adjustments to their structures to overcome the challenges of doing business in a global environment. In the following sections, we will look at some of the specific challenges organizations face in the global arena and mechanisms for successfully confronting them.

# Building Global Capabilities

There are many instances of well-known companies that have trouble transferring successful ideas, products, and services from their home country to the international domain. We talked earlier about the struggles Walmart is facing internationally, but Walmart isn't alone. In the early 1990s, PepsiCo. set a five-year goal to triple its international soft-drink revenues and boldly expanded its presence in international markets. Yet by 1997, the company had withdrawn from some of those markets and had to take a nearly $1 billion loss from international beverage operations.[76] Hundreds of North American companies that saw Vietnam as a tremendous international opportunity in the mid-1990s are now calling it quits amid heavy losses. Political and cultural differences sidetracked most of the ventures. Only a few large companies, such as Citigroup's Citibank unit and Caterpillar's heavy-equipment business, have found success in that country.[77] However, smaller companies such as InoWeb Global, a merger of InoWeb Canada and ADKT located in Hanoi have enjoyed some success.[78] Managers taking their companies international face a tremendous challenge in how to capitalize on the incredible opportunities that global expansion presents.

## The Global Organizational Challenge

There are three primary segments of the global organizational challenge: greater complexity and differentiation, the need for integration, and the problem of transferring knowledge and innovation across a global firm. Organizations have to accept an extremely high level of environmental complexity in the international domain and address the many differences that occur among countries. Environmental complexity and country variations require greater organizational differentiation, as described in Chapter 4.

At the same time, organizations must find ways to effectively achieve coordination and collaboration among far-flung units and facilitate the development and transfer of organizational knowledge and innovation for global learning.[79] Although many small companies are involved in international business, most international companies grow very large, creating a huge coordination problem. For example, Toyota's value added (i.e., the sum of total wages, pretax profits, depreciation, and amortization) was $US30.4 billion while Vietnam's gross domestic product was nearly the same at $US31.3 billion![80]

**Increased Complexity and Differentiation.** When organizations enter the international arena, they encounter a greater level of internal and external complexity than anything experienced on the domestic front. Companies have to create a structure to operate in numerous countries that differ in economic development, language, political systems and government regulations, cultural norms and values, and infrastructure such as transportation and communication facilities. For example, although most international firms have their headquarters in wealthier, economically developed countries, smart managers are investing heavily in less-developed countries in Asia, Eastern Europe, and Latin America, which offer huge new markets for their goods and services. In the area of e-commerce, the number of Internet users and the amount of online sales are booming in Latin America, so companies such as Dell and America Online quickly set up online stores and services for customers in that region. Over the past few years, China has become a major centre for international business, including burgeoning local companies as well as big foreign corporations such as Nokia, IBM, Volkswagen, and BMW.[81]

Another factor increasing the complexity for organizations is that a growing number of global consumers are rejecting the notion of homogenized products and services, calling for greater response to local preferences. Even McDonald's, perhaps the ultimate example of standardization for a world market, has felt the need to be more responsive to local and national differences. In France, where consumers have been resentful of the fast-food chain's incursion, McDonald's boosted sales even as its North American restaurants stalled by remodelling stores to include features such as hardwood floors, wood-beam ceilings, and comfortable armchairs, and by adding menu items such as espresso, brioche, and more upscale sandwiches.[82]

All this complexity in the international environment is mirrored in a greater internal organizational complexity. Recall from Chapter 4 that, as environments become more complex and uncertain, organizations grow more highly differentiated, with many specialized positions and departments to cope with specific sectors in the environment. Top management might need to set up specialized departments to deal with the diverse government, legal, and accounting regulations in various countries, for example. More boundary-spanning departments are needed to sense and respond to the external environment. In addition, organizations might implement a variety of strategies, a broader array of activities, and a much larger number of products and services on an international level in order to meet the needs of a diverse market.

**Need for Integration.** As organizations become more differentiated, with multiple products, divisions, departments, and positions scattered across numerous countries, managers face a tremendous integration challenge. As described in Chapter 4, integration refers to the quality of collaboration across organizational units. The question is how to achieve the coordination and collaboration that is necessary for a global organization to reap the benefits of economies of scale, economies of scope, and labour and production cost efficiencies that international expansion offers. Even in a domestic firm, high differentiation among departments requires that more time and resources be devoted to achieving coordination because employees' attitudes, goals, and work orientations differ widely. Imagine what it must be like for an international organization, whose operating units are divided not only by goals and work attitudes but also by geographic distance, time differences, cultural values, and perhaps even language as well. Companies must find ways to share information, ideas, new products, and technologies across the organization. The next In Practice highlights how new structural elements and an emphasis on integration helped Impact Hub to create an equitable global network.

The Hub was founded in central London, UK, in 2005. Its genesis was the antiglobalization movement. As one of the co-founders, Jonathan Robinson, said, "There was a huge amount of criticism of the current economic models but almost no attention to different models of progress."[83] The purpose of the Hub was to catalyze ideas by being a hybrid between an incubator, learning lab, and a community. "Our goal is to jointly create platforms and experiences that inspire, connect and enable individuals and institutions around the world to sustainably impact society. Through our direct and collaborative efforts we support journeys of impact on many different levels."[84]

Soon there were 200 members in Hub London and hubs formed around the world. By 2008, there were nine hubs in cities such as Johannesburg and Amsterdam. There were, however, no formal agreements about how to grow and to structure the emerging hubs. The international hubs were essentially social franchises that were expected to pay a franchisee fee. While the hub network continued to grow, the organization faced a cash crunch when some hubs did not pay their fees. By 2010, the tensions were too acute to ignore and so Hub leaders met to design a new global organization. What emerged was a co-ownership model whereby the local hubs would own the global hub. While the local hubs would still pay a fee and contribute a portion of revenues, the amounts would be significantly smaller. Each hub then signed on and together they created a network that they named Impact Hub; it is governed by a hub association board. What the hubs have created is a global process and design that marries passionate activism, managerial talent, and entrepreneurism. "There are hundreds of Hub makers around the world who hold the network ethos very dearly and are ready to fight for it. It's this strong personal connection—our having built something together—that unites us."[85]

**In Practice**
**Impact Hub**

**Transfer of Knowledge and Innovation.** The third piece of the international challenge is for organizations to learn from their international experiences by sharing knowledge and innovations across the enterprise. The diversity of the international environment offers extraordinary opportunities for learning and the development of diverse capabilities.

Organizational units in each location acquire the skills and knowledge to meet environmental challenges that arise in that particular locale. Much of that knowledge, which may be related to product improvements, operational efficiencies, technological advancements, or myriad other competencies, is relevant across multiple countries, so organizations need systems that promote the transfer of knowledge and innovation across the global enterprise. One good example comes from Procter & Gamble. Liquid Tide was one of P&G's most successful American product launches in the 1980s, but the product came about from the sharing of innovations developed in diverse parts of the firm. Liquid Tide incorporated a technology for helping to suspend dirt in wash water from P&G headquarters in the United States, the formula for its cleaning agents from P&G technicians in Japan, and special ingredients for fighting mineral salts present in hard water from company scientists in Brussels.[86]

Most organizations tap only a fraction of the potential that is available from the cross-border transfer of knowledge and innovation.[87] There are several reasons for this:

- Knowledge often remains hidden in various units because language, cultural, and geographic distances prevent top managers from recognizing it exists.
- Divisions sometimes view knowledge and innovation as power and want to hold onto it as a way to gain an influential position within the global firm.

- The "not-invented-here" syndrome makes some managers reluctant to tap into the know-how and expertise of other units.
- Much of an organization's knowledge is in the minds of employees and cannot easily be written down and shared with other units.

Organizations have to find ways to encourage both the development and sharing of knowledge, implement systems for tapping into knowledge wherever it exists, and share innovations to meet global challenges.

## ■ Global Coordination Mechanisms

Managers meet the global challenge of coordination and transferring knowledge and innovation across highly differentiated units in a variety of ways. Some of the most common are the use of global teams, stronger headquarters planning and control, and specific coordination roles.

**Global Teams.** The popularity and success of teams on the domestic front allowed managers to see firsthand how this mechanism can achieve strong horizontal coordination, as described in Chapter 3, and thus recognize the promise teams held for coordination across a global firm as well. **Global teams**, also called *transnational teams*, are cross-border work groups made up of multiskilled, multinational members whose activities span multiple countries.[88] Typically, teams are of two types: intercultural teams, whose members come from different countries and meet face-to-face, and virtual global teams, whose members remain in separate locations around the world and conduct their work electronically.[89] Heineken formed the European Production Task Force, a 13-member team comprising multinational members, to meet regularly and come up with ideas for optimizing the company's production facilities across Europe.[90] The research unit of BT Labs has 660 researchers spread across the United Kingdom and several other countries who work in global virtual teams to investigate virtual reality, artificial intelligence, and other advanced information technologies.[91] The team approach enables technologies, ideas, and learning in one country to rapidly spread across the firm via the constant sharing of information among team members.

The most advanced and competitive use of global teams involves simultaneous contributions in three strategic areas.[92] First, global teams help companies address the differentiation challenge, enabling them to be more locally responsive by providing knowledge to meet the needs of different regional markets, consumer preferences, and political and legal systems. At the same time, teams provide integration benefits, helping organizations achieve global efficiencies by developing regional or worldwide cost advantages and standardizing designs and operations across countries. Finally, these teams contribute to continuous organizational learning, knowledge transfer, and adaptation on a global level.

**Stronger Headquarters Planning.** A second approach to achieving stronger global coordination is for headquarters to take an active role in planning, scheduling, and control to keep the widely distributed pieces of the global organization working together and moving in the same direction. In one survey, 70 percent of global companies reported that the most important function of corporate headquarters was to "provide enterprise leadership."[93] Without strong leadership, highly autonomous divisions can begin to act like independent companies rather than coordinated parts of a global whole. To counteract this, top management may delegate responsibility and decision-making authority in some areas, such as adapting products or services to meet local needs, while maintaining strong control through centralized management and information systems that enable headquarters to keep track of what's going on and coordinate activities across divisions and countries. Plans, schedules, and formal rules and procedures can help ensure greater communication among divisions and with headquarters, and foster cooperation and synergy among far-flung units to achieve the organization's goals in a cost-efficient way. Top managers can provide clear strategic direction, guide far-flung operations, and resolve competing demands from various units. For example, Sony's Sir Howard Stringer emphasized his resolve to promote collaboration and creativity to produce "new products, new ideas, new strategies, new alliances, and a shared vision."[94]

**Specific Coordination Roles.** Organizations may also implement structural solutions to achieve stronger coordination and collaboration.[95] Creating specific organizational roles or positions for coordination is a way to integrate all the pieces of the enterprise to achieve a strong competitive position. In successful international firms, the role of top functional managers, for example, is expanded to include responsibility for coordinating across countries, identifying and linking the organization's expertise and resources worldwide. In an international organization, the manufacturing manager has to be aware of and coordinate with manufacturing operations of the company in various other parts of the world so that the company achieves manufacturing efficiency and shares technology and ideas across units. A new manufacturing technology developed to improve efficiency in Ford's Brazilian operations may be valuable for European and North American plants as well. Manufacturing managers are responsible for being aware of new developments wherever they occur and for using their knowledge to improve the organization. Similarly, marketing managers, HR managers, and other functional managers at an international company are not only involved in activities for their particular location but also coordinating with their sister units in other countries.

Although functional managers coordinate across countries, country managers coordinate across functions. A country manager for an international firm has to coordinate all the various functional activities to meet the problems, opportunities, needs, and trends in the local market, enabling the organization to achieve multinational flexibility and rapid response. The country manager in Venezuela for a global consumer products firm such as McCain would coordinate everything that goes on in that country, from manufacturing to HR to marketing, to ensure that activities meet the language, cultural, government, and legal requirements. The country manager in India or France would do the same for those countries. Country managers also help with the transfer of ideas, trends, products, and technologies that arise in one country and might have significance on a broader scale.

Some organizations create formal network coordinator positions to coordinate information and activities related to key customer accounts. These coordinators would enable a manufacturing organization, for example, to provide knowledge and integrated solutions across multiple businesses, divisions, and countries for a large customer such as Walmart.[96] Top managers in successful global firms also encourage and support informal networks and relationships to keep information flowing in all directions. Much of an organization's information exchange occurs not through formal systems or structures but through informal channels and relationships. By supporting these informal networks, giving people across boundaries opportunities to get together and develop relationships and then ways to keep in close touch, executives enhance organizational coordination.

International companies today have a hard time staying competitive without strong interunit coordination and collaboration. Those firms that stimulate and support collaboration are typically better able to leverage dispersed resources and capabilities to reap operational and economic benefits.[97] Benefits that result from interunit collaboration include the following:

- *Cost savings.* Collaboration can produce real, measurable results in cost savings from the sharing of best practices across global divisions.
- *Better decision making.* By sharing information and advice across divisions, managers can make better business decisions that support their own unit as well as the organization as a whole.
- *Greater revenues.* By sharing expertise and products among various divisions, organizations can reap increased revenues. For example, more than 75 people from BP's various units around the world flew to China to assist the team developing an acetic acid plant there. As a result, BP finished the project and began realizing revenues sooner than project planners had expected.
- *Increased innovation.* The sharing of ideas and technological innovations across units stimulates creativity and the development of new products and services. Recall the example of Procter & Gamble mentioned earlier, in which P&G developed Liquid Tide based on ideas and innovations that arose in a number of different divisions around the world.

# Cultural Differences in Coordination and Control

Just as social and cultural values differ from country to country, management values and organizational norms of international companies tend to vary depending on the organization's home country. Organizational norms and values are influenced by the values in the larger national culture, and these in turn influence the organization's structural approach and the ways managers coordinate and control an international firm.

## National Value Systems

Studies have attempted to determine how national value systems influence management and organizations. One of the most influential was conducted by Geert Hofstede, who identified five dimensions of national value systems that vary widely across countries.[98] According to Hofstede, "[Culture] is more often a source of conflict than of synergy. Cultural differences are a nuisance at best and often a disaster."[99] For example, two of his five dimensions that seem to have a strong impact within organizations are power distance and uncertainty avoidance. High power distance means that people accept inequality in power among institutions, organizations, and people. Low **power distance** means that people expect equality in power. High uncertainty avoidance means that members of a society feel uncomfortable with uncertainty and ambiguity, and thus support beliefs that promise certainty and conformity. Low **uncertainty avoidance** means that people have a high tolerance for the unstructured, the unclear, and the unpredictable. (More recently, a sixth dimension, based on Minkov's World Values Survey data analysis for

93 countries, has been added, called Indulgence versus Restraint. Indulgence stands for a society that allows relatively free gratification of basic and natural human drives related to enjoying life and having fun. Restraint stands for a society that suppresses gratification of needs and regulates it by means of strict social norms.)[100]

The value dimensions of power distance and uncertainty avoidance are reflected within organizations in beliefs regarding the need for hierarchy, centralized decision making and control, formal rules and procedures, and specialized jobs.[101] In countries that value high power distance, for example, organizations tend to be more hierarchical and centralized, with greater control and coordination from the top levels of the organization. On the other hand, organizations in countries that value low power distance are more likely to be decentralized. A low tolerance for uncertainty tends to be reflected in a preference for coordination through rules and procedures. Organizations in countries where people have a high tolerance for uncertainty typically have fewer rules and formal systems, relying more on informal networks and personal communication for coordination. This chapter's Workbook lets you delve further into the five dimensions and their impact.

More recent research by Project GLOBE (Global Leadership and Organizational Behavior Effectiveness) has supported and extended Hofstede's assessment. Project GLOBE used data collected from 18,000 managers in 62 countries to identify nine dimensions that explain cultural differences, including those identified by Hofstede.[102] The GLOBE project's cultural dimensions are described in Exhibit 6.6.

**act!**

**Think**

Think about Canada's value systems. What are some critical and defining values that characterize Canada?

**EXHIBIT 6.6**
**The GLOBE Project's Nine Cultural Dimensions**

| GLOBE DIMENSIONS | CHARACTERISTICS |
| --- | --- |
| Power Distance | Extent to which a society expects power to be distributed equally |
| Gender Egalitarianism | Degree to which society discourages gender role differences and inequality |
| Uncertainty Avoidance | Extent to which society relies on rules, procedures, and policies to minimize ambiguity and unpredictability of the future |
| Collectivism 1 (institutional collectivism) | Degree to which a society encourages and rewards collective action and resource distribution |
| Collectivism 2 (in-group collectivism) | Extent to which members express pride and cohesiveness in their relations with others |
| Future Orientation | Extent to which members engage in such behaviours as planning for and investing in the future |
| Assertiveness | Extent to which members are confrontational toward each other |
| Performance Orientation | Extent to which a society rewards individuals for innovation |
| Humane Orientation | Extent to which a society encourages altruism and caring for others |

Source: Based on Tirmizi, S.A. (2008) The Impact of Culture in Multicultural Teams, in Halverson, C.B., and S.A. Tirmizi (eds.) Effective Multicultural Teams, New York: Springer, pp. 30–31. With kind permission from Springer Science + Business Media B.V.

The nine dimensions provide more detail and depth than Hofstede's dimensions in helping managers to understand cultural differences.

Although organizations do not always reflect the dominant cultural values, studies have found rather clear patterns of different management structures when comparing countries in Europe, North America, and Asia. For example, Gesteland outlines four major cultural value patterns, which he calls logical patterns, that characterize countries around the world.[103]

- *Deal-focused versus relationship-focused*. Deal-focused cultures, such as those in North America, Australia, and Northern Europe, are task oriented, while relationship-focused cultures, including those in the Middle East, Africa, Latin America, and Asia, are typically people oriented. Deal-focused individuals approach business in an objective and impersonal way. Relationship-focused individuals believe in building close personal relationships as the appropriate way to conduct business.

- *Informal versus formal*. Informal cultures place a low value on status and power differences, whereas formal cultures are typically hierarchical and status conscious. The unconstrained values of informal cultures, such as those in the United States and Australia, may insult people from formal, hierarchical societies, just as the class-consciousness of formal groups, such as cultures in most of Europe and Latin America, may offend the egalitarian ideals of people in informal cultures.

- *Rigid time versus fluid time*. One part of the world's societies is flexible about time and scheduling, while the other group is more rigid and dedicated to clock time. Conflicts may occur because rigid-time types often consider fluid-time people undisciplined and irresponsible, while fluid-time people regard rigid-time folks as arrogant, demanding, and enslaved by meaningless deadlines.

- *Expressive versus reserved*. Expressive cultures include those in Latin America and the Mediterranean. Reserved cultures are those in East and Southeast Asia as well as Germanic Europe. This distinction can create a major communication gap. People from expressive cultures tend to talk louder and use more hand gestures and facial expressions. Reserved cultures may interpret raised voices and gesturing as signals of anger or instability.

Exhibit 6.7 highlights how you should *not* behave when addressing international cultural differences.

**EXHIBIT 6.7**
Cultural Insensitivity
Source: DILBERT © 2010 Scott Adams. Used By permission of UNIVERSAL UCLICK. All rights reserved.

# ■ Three National Approaches to Coordination and Control

Let's look at three primary approaches to coordination and control as represented by Japanese, European, and North American companies.[104] It should be noted that companies in each country use tools and techniques from each of the three coordination methods. However, there are broad, general patterns that illustrate cultural differences.

**Centralized Coordination in Japanese Companies.** When expanding internationally, Japanese companies have typically developed coordination mechanisms that rely on centralization. Top managers at headquarters actively direct and control overseas operations, whose primary focus is to implement strategies handed down from headquarters. A recent study of R&D activities in high-tech firms in Japan and Germany supports the idea that Japanese organizations tend to be more centralized. While German firms leaned toward dispersing R&D groups out into different regions, Japanese companies tended to keep these activities centralized in the home country.[105] This centralized approach enables Japanese companies to leverage the knowledge and resources located at the corporate centre, attain global efficiencies,

## Book Mark 6.0   HAVE YOU READ THIS BOOK?

### Why Mexicans Don't Drink Molson: Rescuing Canadian Business from the Suds of Global Obscurity*
By Andrea Mandel-Campbell

In her incisive analysis, Mandel-Campbell argues that Canadian companies do not have the gumption to become global brand leaders. She argues that we need, as a country, to get over our inferiority complex if we are to project ourselves internationally,

Her account of Molson's inability to become a global brand is illuminating. In the 1970s, Molson was about the same size as the Netherlands' Heineken. In 30 years, Heineken has become the world's fourth-largest brewery with 115 breweries in more than 65 countries. In contrast, Molson does not have a single brand in the world's top 20! Rather than expanding into emerging markets such as Russia and China, Molson sold half its breweries to Australian and American brewers and diversified into hardware. Molson had an opportunity to enter the Chinese market in the 1980s when China's Tsingtao Brewery was insolvent and searching for a $20 million investment. Molson did not invest in China but did invest in Brazil. Molson did not provide its own brand to the large South American market but did bring Brazilian beer to the Canadian market! Molson had once been a powerful organization; founded in 1786, it once had steamships, a bank, and even its own currency, but it is not the global player it could have been.

Mandel-Campbell provides many other vivid examples of Canadian companies that ignored or failed to see the importance of investing globally. In her last chapter, aptly titled "A New Approach to Parenting," she offers some useful prescriptions. She argues that the Government of Canada has a critical role in fostering global competitiveness—it must have a clear strategy and goal. "The fundamental question that government policy makers should ask themselves is, how can Canadians graduate from being telemarketers, middle managers, and commodity producers to not only running, but leading, globally oriented enterprises? (p. 287) She goes on to recommend that industrial policy should be used to promote successful organizations and not to protect failing ones. Mandel-Campbell's other prescriptions are a strong call for Canada, its companies, and its people to become much more entrepreneurial and ambitious and, in short, "to grow up." (p. 311) As she notes in her penultimate sentence, "Canada has all the makings of a global leader. The question is whether it wants to be one." (p. 312).

*Why Mexicans Don't Drink Molson: Rescuing Canadian Business from the Suds of Global Obscurity, by Andrea Mandel-Campbell, is published by Douglas & McIntyre.

and coordinate across units to obtain synergies and avoid turf battles. Top managers use strong structural linkages to ensure that managers at headquarters remain up-to-date and fully involved in all strategic decisions. However, centralization has its limits. As the organization expands and divisions grow larger, headquarters can become overloaded and decision making slows. The quality of decisions may also suffer as greater diversity and complexity make it difficult for headquarters to understand and respond to local needs in each region.

China is a rapidly growing part of the international business environment, and limited research has been done into management structures of Chinese firms. Many China-based firms are still relatively small and run in a traditional family-like manner. However, similar to Japan, organizations typically reflect a distinct hierarchy of authority and relatively strong centralization. Obligation plays an important role in Chinese culture and management, so employees feel obligated to follow orders directed from above.[106] Interestingly, though, one study found that Chinese employees are loyal not just to the boss, but also to company policies.[107] As Chinese organizations grow much larger, more insight will be gained into how these firms handle the balance of coordination and control.

**European Firms' Decentralized Approach.** A different approach has typically been taken by European companies. Rather than relying on strong, centrally directed coordination and control as in the Japanese firms, international units tend to have a high level of independence and decision-making autonomy. Companies rely on a strong mission, shared values, and informal personal relationships for coordination. Thus, great emphasis is placed on careful selection, training, and development of key managers throughout the international organization. Formal management and control systems are used primarily for financial rather than technical or operational control. With this approach, each international unit focuses on its local markets, enabling the company to excel in meeting diverse needs. One disadvantage is the cost of ensuring, through training and development programs, that managers throughout a huge, global firm share goals, values, and priorities. Decision making can also be slow and complex, and disagreements and conflicts among divisions are more difficult to resolve.

**North America: Coordination and Control Through Formalization.** Many North American companies that have expanded into the international arena have taken a third direction. Typically, these organizations have delegated responsibility to international divisions, yet retained overall control of the enterprise through the use of sophisticated management control systems and the development of specialist headquarters staff. Formal systems, policies, standards of performance, and a regular flow of information from divisions to headquarters are the primary means of coordination and control. Decision making is based on objective data, policies, and procedures, which provides for many operating efficiencies and reduces conflict among divisions and between divisions and headquarters. However, the cost of setting up complex systems, policies, and rules for an international organization may be quite high. This approach also requires a larger headquarters staff for reviewing, interpreting, and sharing information, thus increasing overhead costs. Finally, standard routines and procedures don't always fit the needs of new problems and situations. Flexibility is limited if managers pay so much attention to systems that they fail to recognize opportunities and threats in the environment.

Clearly, each of these approaches has advantages. But as international organizations grow larger and more complex, the disadvantages of each tend to become more pronounced. Because traditional approaches have been inadequate to meet the demands of a rapidly changing, complex international environment, many large international companies are moving toward a new kind of organization form, the *transnational model*, which is highly differentiated to address environmental complexity, yet offers very high levels of coordination, learning, and transfer of organizational knowledge and innovations.

## The Transnational Model of Organization

The **transnational model** represents the most advanced kind of international organization. It reflects the ultimate in both organizational complexity, with many diverse units, and organizational coordination, with mechanisms for integrating the varied parts. The transnational model is useful for large, multinational companies with subsidiaries in many countries that try to exploit both global and local advantages as well as technological advancements, rapid innovation, and global learning and knowledge sharing. Rather than building capabilities primarily in one area, such as global efficiency, national responsiveness, or global learning, the transnational model seeks to achieve all three simultaneously. Dealing with multiple, interrelated, complex issues requires a complex form of organization and structure.

The transnational model represents the most current thinking about the kind of structure needed by complex global organizations such as Philips NV, illustrated in Exhibit 6.8. Headquartered in the Netherlands, Philips has hundreds of operating units all over the world and is typical of global companies such as Unilever, Matsushita, or Procter & Gamble.[108]

Achieving coordination, a sense of participation and involvement by subsidiaries, and a sharing of information, knowledge, new technology, and customers is a tremendous challenge. For example, a global corporation like Philips is so large that size alone is a huge problem in coordinating global operations. In addition, some subsidiaries become so large that they no longer fit a narrow strategic role defined by headquarters. While being part of a larger organization, individual units need some autonomy for themselves and the ability to have an impact on other parts of the organization.

The transnational model addresses these challenges by creating an integrated network of individual operations that are linked together to achieve the multidimensional goals of the overall organization.[109] The management philosophy is based on *interdependence* rather than either full divisional independence or total dependence of these units on headquarters for decision making and control. The transnational model is more than just an organizational chart. It is a managerial state of mind, a set of values, a shared desire to make a worldwide learning system work, and an idealized structure for effectively managing such a system. Several characteristics distinguish the transnational organization from other global organization forms such as the matrix, described earlier.

1. Assets and resources are dispersed worldwide into highly specialized operations that are linked together through interdependent relationships. Resources and capabilities are widely distributed to help the organization sense and respond to diverse stimuli such as market needs, technological developments, or consumer trends that emerge in different parts of the world. However, managers forge interdependent relationships among the various product, functional, or

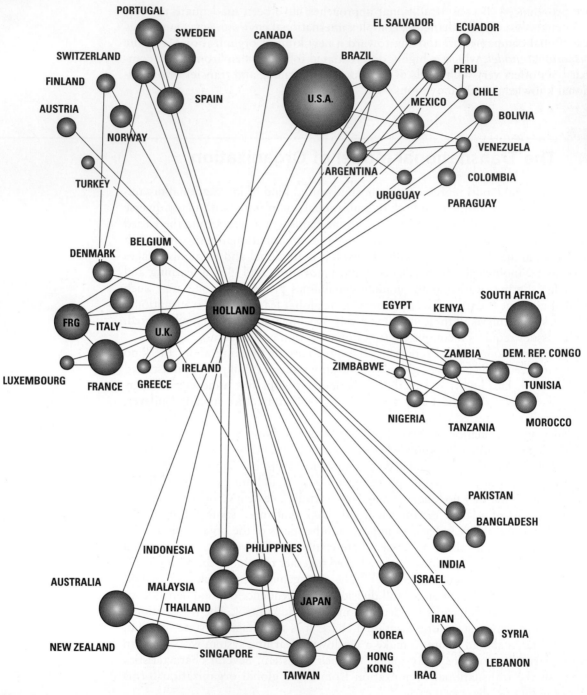

**EXHIBIT 6.8**
International Organizational Units and Interlinkages within Philips NV
Source: Sumantra Ghoshal and Christopher A. Bartlett, "The Multinational Corporation as an Interorganizational Network," *Academy of Management Review* 15 (1990), 605; permission conveyed through Copyright Clearance Center, Inc.

geographic units. Mechanisms such as cross-subsidiary teams, for example, compel units to work together for the good of their own unit as well as the overall organization. Rather than being completely self-sufficient, each group has to cooperate to achieve its own goals. Such interdependencies encourage the collaborative sharing of information and resources, cross-unit problem solving, and collective implementation demanded by today's competitive international environment. Materials, people, products, ideas, resources, and information are continually flowing among the dispersed parts of the integrated network. In addition, managers actively shape, manage, and reinforce informal information networks that cross functions, products, divisions, and countries.

2. Structures are flexible and ever-changing. The transnational operates on a principle of flexible centralization. It may centralize some functions in one country yet decentralize other functions among its many geographically dispersed operations. An R&D centre may be centralized in Holland and a purchasing centre may be located in Sweden, while financial accounting responsibilities are decentralized to operations in many countries. A unit in Hong Kong may be responsible for coordinating activities across Asia, while activities for all other countries are coordinated by a large division headquarters in London. The transnational model requires that managers be flexible in determining structural needs based on the benefits to be gained. Some functions, products, and geographic regions by their nature may need more central control and coordination than others. In addition, coordination and control mechanisms will change over time to meet new needs or competitive threats.

3. Subsidiary managers initiate strategy and innovations that become strategy for the corporation as a whole. In traditional structures, managers have a strategic role only for their division. In a transnational structure, various centres and subsidiaries can shape the company from the bottom up by developing creative responses and initiating programs in response to local needs and dispersing those innovations worldwide. Transnational companies recognize each of the worldwide units as a source of capabilities and knowledge that can be used to benefit the entire organization. In addition, environmental demands and opportunities vary from country to country, and exposing the whole organization to this broader range of environmental stimuli triggers greater learning and innovation.

4. Unification and coordination are achieved primarily through organizational culture, shared vision and values, and management style, rather than through formal structures and systems. The transnational structure is essentially a horizontal structure. It is diverse and extended, and it exists in a fluctuating environment so that hierarchy, standard rules, procedures, and close supervision are not appropriate. Achieving unity and coordination in an organization in which employees come from a variety of different national backgrounds, are separated by time and geographic distance, and have different cultural norms is more easily accomplished through shared understanding than through formal systems. Top leaders build a context of shared vision, values, and perspectives among managers who in turn cascade these elements through all parts of the organization. Selection and training of managers emphasize flexibility and open-mindedness. In addition, people are often rotated through different jobs, divisions, and countries to gain broad experience and become socialized into the organizational culture. Achieving coordination in a transnational organization

is a much more complex process than simple centralization or decentralization of decision making, and requires shaping and adapting beliefs, culture, and values so that everyone participates in information sharing and learning.

Taken together, these characteristics facilitate strong coordination, organizational learning, and knowledge sharing on a broad global scale. As you can see from Exhibit 6.8, the transnational model is truly a complex and messy way to conceptualize organizational structure, but it is becoming increasingly relevant for large, global firms that treat the whole world as their playing field and do not have a single country base. The autonomy of organizational parts gives strength to smaller units and allows the firm to be flexible in responding to rapid change and competitive opportunities on a local level, while the emphasis on interdependency enables global efficiencies and organizational learning. Each part of the transnational company is aware of and closely integrated with the organization as a whole so local actions complement and enhance other company parts.

## Summary and Interpretation

This chapter has examined how managers design organizations for a complex international environment. Almost every company today is affected by significant global forces, and many are developing overseas operations to take advantage of global markets. Three primary motivations for global expansion are to realize economies of scale, exploit economies of scope, and achieve scarce or low-cost factors of production such as labour, raw materials, or land. One popular way to become involved in international operations is through strategic alliances with international firms. Alliances include licensing, joint ventures, and consortia.

Organizations typically evolve through four stages, beginning with a domestic orientation, shifting to an international orientation, then changing to a multinational orientation, and finally moving to a global orientation that sees the whole world as a potential market. Organizations typically use an export department, then use an international department, and eventually develop into a worldwide geographic or product structure. Geographic structures are most effective for organizations that can benefit from a multidomestic strategy, meaning that products and services will do best if tailored to local needs and cultures. A product structure supports a globalization strategy, which means that products and services can be standardized and sold worldwide. Huge global firms might use a matrix structure to respond to both local and global forces simultaneously. Many firms use hybrid structures by combining elements of two or more different structures to meet the dynamic conditions of the global environment.

Succeeding on a global scale is not easy. Three aspects of the global organizational challenge are addressing environmental complexity through greater organizational complexity and differentiation, achieving integration and coordination among the highly differentiated units, and implementing mechanisms for the transfer of knowledge and innovations. Common ways to address the problem of integration and knowledge transfer are through global teams, stronger headquarters planning and control, and specific coordination roles. Managers also recognize that diverse national and cultural values influence the organization's approach to coordination and control. Three varied national approaches are the centralized coordination and control typically found in many Japanese-based firms, a decentralized approach common among European firms, and the formalization approach often used by North American–based international firms. Most companies, however, no matter their home country, use a combination of elements from each of these approaches.

Many companies are also finding a need to broaden their coordination methods and are moving toward the transnational model of organization. The transnational model is based on a philosophy of interdependence. It is highly differentiated yet offers very high levels of coordination, learning, and transfer of knowledge across far-flung divisions. The transnational model today represents the ultimate global design in terms of both organizational complexity and organizational integration. Each part of the transnational organization is aware of and closely integrated with the organization as a whole so that local actions complement and enhance other company parts.

## ■ Key Concepts

<table>
<tr><td>consortia, p. 220</td><td>globalization strategy, p. 222</td></tr>
<tr><td>domestic stage, p. 218</td><td>international division, p. 224</td></tr>
<tr><td>economies of scale, p. 216</td><td>international stage, p. 219</td></tr>
<tr><td>economies of scope, p. 216</td><td>joint venture, p. 220</td></tr>
<tr><td>factors of production, p. 217</td><td>multidomestic strategy, p. 222</td></tr>
<tr><td>global companies, p. 219</td><td>multidomestic, p. 219</td></tr>
<tr><td>global geographic structure, p. 225</td><td>multinational stage, p. 219</td></tr>
<tr><td>global matrix structure, p. 227</td><td>power distance, p. 234</td></tr>
<tr><td>global product structure, p. 225</td><td>standardization, p. 222</td></tr>
<tr><td>global stage, p. 219</td><td>transnational model, p. 239</td></tr>
<tr><td>global teams, p. 232</td><td>uncertainty avoidance, p. 234</td></tr>
</table>

## ■ Discussion Questions

1. Under what conditions should a company consider adopting a global geographic structure as opposed to a global product structure?
2. Name some companies that you think could succeed today with a globalization strategy and explain why you selected those companies. How does the globalization strategy differ from a multidomestic strategy?
3. Why would a company want to join a strategic alliance rather than go it alone in international operations? What do you see as the potential advantages and disadvantages of international alliances?
4. Why is knowledge sharing so important to a global organization?
5. What are some of the primary reasons a company decides to expand internationally? Identify a company in the news that has recently built a new overseas facility. Which of the three motivations for global expansion described in the chapter do you think best explains the company's decision? Discuss.
6. When would an organization consider using a matrix structure? How does the global matrix differ from the domestic matrix structure described in Chapter 3?
7. Name some of the elements that contribute to greater complexity for international organizations. How do organizations address this complexity? Do you think these elements apply to an online company such as eBay that wants to grow internationally? Discuss.

8. Traditional values in Mexico support high power distance and a low tolerance for uncertainty. What would you predict about a company that opens a division in Mexico and tries to implement global teams characterized by shared power and authority and a lack of formal guidelines, rules, and structure?
9. Compare Hofstede's six dimensions with the GLOBE's nine dimensions. Which approach to national values do you find more useful? Why?
10. Do you believe it is possible for a global company to simultaneously achieve the goals of global efficiency and integration, national responsiveness and flexibility, and the worldwide transfer of knowledge and innovation? Discuss.
11. Compare the description of the transnational model in this chapter to the elements of the learning organization described in Chapter 1. Do you think the transnational model seems workable for a huge global firm? Discuss.
12. What does it mean to say that the transnational model is based on a philosophy of interdependence?

## ■ Chapter 6 Workbook: Appreciating Cultural Differences*

Go the Hofstede's website at www.geert-hofstede.com and look up scores for his five core dimensions for Canada and two other countries. Record them here.

| Country | Power Distance | Individualism | Masculinity | Uncertainty Avoidance | Long-Term Orientation |
|---------|----------------|---------------|-------------|-----------------------|-----------------------|
| Canada  |                |               |             |                       |                       |
|         |                |               |             |                       |                       |
|         |                |               |             |                       |                       |

### Questions

1. What similarities and differences did you observe?
2. How can managers use Hofstede's dimensions when working internationally?

*Copyright © 2008 by Ann Armstrong.

## Case for Analysis: Ivanhoe Mines*

Mining magnate Robert Friedland has made a career of dancing on the knife's edge. His Ivanhoe Mines Ltd., for example, operates in Mongolia, Myanmar and Kazakhstan—countries where, to varying degrees, governments can be oppressive and unstable, civil unrest can break out without warning, contracts can be abandoned with impunity, corruption may run rampant, or all of the above. Friedland's appetite for risk is not unique: surging metals prices have renewed interest for mining in unstable countries with promising ore bodies. Recent turmoil at Ivanhoe's property in Myanmar, however, provides a

sobering reminder of what can go wrong. Which, in this case, includes pretty much everything.

While other foreign investors fled Myanmar (commonly known by its former name, Burma) because of its unfriendly business climate and opposition from shareholders and consumers, Vancouver-based Ivanhoe charged headlong into the Southeast Asian country during the 1990s. The fruit of its efforts is the Monywa Copper Project, an open-pit mine located on the lowland plains west of Mandalay. Ivanhoe owns half of the joint venture company; its partner is No. 1 Mining Enterprise, which is controlled by the State Peace and Development Council (SPDC). The mine has become mired in international sanctions and disputes over taxation and permits. Ivanhoe is now in talks to sell a significant portion of its interest in the project to Asian buyers.

Much of Monywa's problems stem from Friedland's choice of business partners. The SPDC is a military junta that seized control of Burma in 1988 and held onto power despite democratic opposition and its loss of an election in 1990. Its international image is poor. According to the U.S. State Department, the SPDC maintains its control by censoring information, suppressing ethnic minorities and repressing the rights of its people. Amnesty International accuses it of restricting freedom of movement, employing forced labour and keeping more than 1,300 political prisoners in custody. And Human Rights Watch, a nongovernmental organization, claims that "the junta's pledges of democratic reform and respect for human rights continue to be empty rhetoric." Assuming that the SPDC earns the same amount of income from the mine as Ivanhoe, Monywa provided the junta with nearly US$23 million last year. Given the SPDC's international unpopularity, one might think that windfall would give the regime ample reason to keep Ivanhoe happy. In fact, relations between the two parties have evidently soured.

One threat commonly faced by mining companies abroad is called tax risk. "The rates of import duties, royalties, withholding taxes and corporate income taxes can have a big effect on the profitability of a project," explained Nabil Khodadad, a London-based partner with international law firm Chadbourne & Parke LLP, in a 2005 paper about mining risks. "The local regime can break a project by making it unprofitable." Ivanhoe became embroiled in a dispute when the Myanmar government imposed a commercial tax on copper exported from Monywa, applied retroactively from the beginning of 2003. This would amount to US$11 million from Ivanhoe's pockets, the company claims, plus the increased ongoing costs. As far as Ivanhoe is concerned, its joint-venture agreement precludes such a tax, and it has sought a written legal opinion from the attorney general of Myanmar to that effect. Even if Ivanhoe's interpretation is correct, however, it is dealing with an authoritarian government with little respect for the rule of law.

When operating in developing countries, mining firms also must worry about whether the government will expropriate a property, revoke licences or otherwise interfere with their ability to operate—which is known as political risk. Monywa includes the Sabetaung and Kyisintaung "S&K" deposits and the much larger Letpadaung ore body. The grade of ore extracted at S&K deteriorated significantly last year, and Ivanhoe announced plans to increase capacity. It then ordered the necessary mining equipment. But the SPDC has so far not issued the required import permits, so the equipment sits offshore, idle and depreciating. This year, Ivanhoe predicts that copper production from S&K will drop by more than half.

As for Letpadaung, Ivanhoe has long planned to develop it. But the Canadian company has so far not been able to obtain the necessary approvals from the SPDC, for unspecified reasons. These are serious problems. "Without a substantial increase in mining capacity, these two deposits cannot be economically developed," the company's recently released 2005 annual report warned. Mines that cannot be economically developed are effectively worthless and must be shut down.

International politics create more challenges. In 1997, the U.S. government prohibited its citizens and U.S. companies from making new investments in Myanmar. In 2003, it added a ban on imports and the export of financial services to the country following an attack on the convoy of the National League for Democracy's Aung San Suu Kyi, the prominent opposition leader. (The European Union, Australia, Canada, Japan and Korea have applied their own sanctions.) As a result of the U.S. sanctions, both Monywa's insurance broker and its offshore bank terminated their relationship with Ivanhoe 2002. As Ivanhoe explained candidly in its annual report, the sanctions "have started to seriously impact the mine's ability to function in a normal way." And Ivanhoe doesn't have anything to fall back on: the company isn't insured for political or environmental risks.

These difficulties could have profound financial consequences. Ivanhoe currently estimates its stake in Monywa to be worth nearly US$140 million, or roughly 35 percent of total assets on its balance sheet. Ivanhoe has said that if it cannot resolve problems there, it may be forced to write down that value significantly. Meanwhile, Monywa also accounts for the lion's share of Ivanhoe's income; the company has recorded 26 consecutive quarters of negative free cash flow.

It would seem, though, that shareholders are taking it all in stride: Ivanhoe's stock (TSX: IVN) has risen in the months since Monywa's troubles were revealed. The reason is that Monywa is not their focus. Ivanhoe's appeal to investors has largely been rooted in its Oyu Tolgoi property in Mongolia's Gobi Desert, where the company says it is focused on exploring and developing "a major discovery of copper and gold." As such, Ivanhoe is widely seen as an exploration firm, and such companies are expected to burn cash. The cash flow generated by Monywa pales in comparison to the outside investment Ivanhoe relies on to fund its operations. In late April, the company closed a $189-million bought-deal financing without any apparent difficulty.

Ivanhoe's predicament at Monywa could become more acute should it erode confidence in the company's ability to manage government relations in Mongolia and bring Oyu Tolgoi into production. (Ivanhoe recently announced that John Macken, the president and COO, will become CEO "to assemble and guide the team that will build a world-class copper and gold mine at Oyu Tolgoi.") Ivanhoe has been negotiating with the Mongolian government to reach a formal agreement on how to develop Oyu Tolgoi since 2003, and those discussions recently sparked protests in the capital, Ulan Bator, by critics who want more mineral-generated wealth to stay in the country. The protests apparently worked: on May 12, the Mongolian parliament approved a surprise windfall-profits tax on foreign miners. The move helped send Ivanhoe stock into a tailspin; it fell nearly 22 percent in one day of trading.

But there's another problem. Such is Oyu Tolgoi's importance—Ivanhoe estimates the project could produce an annual average of more than one billion pounds of copper and 330,000 ounces of gold for at least 35 years—that the Canadian company is considering the sale of "non-core assets" to fund it. This apparently includes Monywa. Ivanhoe's annual report claimed that the company signed a memorandum of understanding with "an established large Korean corporation" to sell a significant portion of its interest in Monywa. More recently, in mid-April, *The Korea Herald* reported that a consortium of three South Korean companies had signed a preliminary agreement with Ivanhoe to jointly develop Monywa, and pay US$120 million to buy half of Ivanhoe's stake. One of the consortium's members, Korea Resources Corp., said the deal is subject to due diligence; even if prospective buyers are comfortable with having the SPDC as a business partner, Monywa's misfortunes can only reduce Friedland's bargaining position in getting the best value for shareholders. Moreover, the non-binding agreement with the Koreans is subject to regulatory approval from the SPDC. And Myanmar's generals, it seems, have not been in an accommodating mood of late.

## Assignment Questions

1. What problems did Ivanhoe Mines encounter when it invested in Myanmar?
2. Do you think that Ivanhoe Mines' approach to risk is appropriate? Why or why not?

---

*M. McClearn, "Mine Games: Ivanhoe Mines," *Canadian Business* (May 22, June 4, 2006) at http://www.canadianbusiness.com/shared/print.jsp?content=20060522_77851_77851 (accessed July 16, 2008). Used with permission.

## Case for Analysis: The "Pianistic Other" in Shenzhen*

### The Stage
The day was close to the Chinese lunar New Year's Eve in 2004, the lunar 28th of the 12th month. According to Chinese folk custom, this date is believed to be one of the most significant days preceding the lunar New Year. At this time households clean up all trash symbolizing "the oldness" or even "the misfortune," in order to forecast a new life in the subsequent lunar year. In Chen's native Tantou village, such a day is still well observed. During my visit, cold showers made the day even more miserable for young children who had piano lessons like Chen's. For one thing, one would have to warm up for a considerable time before playing the piano, because there is no heat inside ordinary apartments and houses in Shenzhen. For another, as the day is right before the New Year, Chinese people would be in a festive mood, and that would be especially true of the children. Yet, the day was just another Sunday for Chen: his teaching day.

### Scene 1—"Just Because She Is a Girl…"
A thirteen-year-old girl, Xiaoxin, accompanied by her mother, came to Chen's house for her piano lesson. When asked why she sends her daughter for piano lessons, the mother sighed, "*Nv zai ma*…" [English translation: Just because she is a girl] To her, it seemed natural or commonsense to send a girl for piano lessons. The mother continued, "How could people like us understand these things?…. Her Hong Kong cousin plays the piano, so [I] sent her over here." While Xiaoxin was warming up for the lesson, I asked to take a picture of her. The mother, interestingly, asked whether or not I could include her in the picture as well. Meanwhile, she asked Xiaoxin to pose more elegantly, though the girl seemed a bit uneasy. The mother seemed kept commenting that Chen was a strict teacher whose teaching and playing the piano is "up to standard," that Chen graduated from a brand music conservatory, and that Chen had a good local reputation in piano playing since his childhood.

### Scene 2—"Look at Her Long Fingers…"
The first family I visited had two children: an 11-year-old boy and his 9-year-old sister. Before starting the lessons, Chen suggested the girl warm up a bit. Chen sighed, "See this kid? [She] just does not want to practise. She is really talented…. See her long fingers? Very good condition [for playing the piano]." The older brother came in. Presumably, he was going to refill his cup for another drink or to get another snack after a long while in front of his beloved computer screen. Chen pointed to the boy and told me, "This is her brother. See him? Smart boy…. His fingers

are even better [for playing the piano]. He quit.... See, now, he is so much into playing the computer games." I could tell how disappointed Chen was because of the boy's decision to stop his piano lessons. Chen proceeded, "If I were at this age..." At that moment, the girl's voice came to our ears, "Teacher Chen, I am ready..." Chen got up and ordered the girl to play a series of scales—a routine essential to build the strength of one's fingers (in particular, those naturally weaker fingers, such as the fourth and fifth fingers)—and significant mapping techniques on the keyboard for major and minor keys on the piano.

### Scene 3—"Teacher Chen Said..."
The second family had only one child, a five-year-old girl. This child's parents were present, both of whom, as I would have expected, were busy with cleaning, both inside and outside their apartment. However, the mother was willing to offer her insight into her perceptions of piano education for young amateurs. She was particularly interested in learning more about the general issues and situations of piano education for amateurs in the Special Economic Zone (SEZ).

She had a strong belief that playing the piano from childhood would boost one's intelligence, because the more "exercise" the two little hands have, the more stimuli both hemispheres of the brain would have as well. She said that Teacher Chen would occasionally convey similar ideas to her to support her strong desire for her little daughter's piano efforts. I noticed that the little girl seemed hesitant to play. Chen assured me that she probably was afraid of a stranger observing her playing, because her hesitancy to play was unusual. I was amazed by the little girl's discipline. The mother believed that it was because of learning the piano that she had cultivated discipline, as she was too naughty to even sit down before taking up the piano. I wonder whether the passing years might have resulted in her becoming more self-disciplined. Chen assured me that this little girl was one of his most promising students, given her young age in taking up the instrument, her proficiency, and her relatively strong family support (particularly from her mother).

### Scene 4—"I Pledge..."
The Wen/Tan family was the last one I visited with Chen. The family lives in a two-floor townhouse, near the Shenzhen-Guangzhou Expressway. The family owned a grocery store on the first floor, and lived on the second floor in a studio with an extended balcony where the piano sat. The balcony was also the bedroom of their beloved 10-year-old daughter, Wenshi Tan.

Wenshi's mother, Yeyun, expressed her appreciation for Chen's admission of her daughter as his student. Yeyun commented on Chen's good reputation for being a committed piano teacher, and appreciated the fact that Chen is a native of Tantou. Yeyun was grateful that Chen accepted Wenshi, because Wenshi had been unwilling to

play or practise before. Chen confirmed that Wenshi was sometimes a rebellious child who would not listen to his admonitions to practise more often, and that Wenshi often repeated the same mistakes (wrong notes, wrong finger positions, etc.). This is indicated by Wenshi's handwritten pledge.

*[Author's Translation:] I promise I will [properly] curve my fingers without bending my palm. When I practise alone, I promise to be attentive: I will play half an hour every day. I will play while reading the scores [carefully]. No wrong notes. Play attentively, read [the scores] attentively, read the notes attentively, look at the teacher's finger positions carefully. [To decide] which notes are higher (i.e., mapping the corresponding key based on the staff notation), I, myself, will listen attentively to what the teacher says about what to do and how to do it.*

That handwritten pledge was attached to Wenshi's piano lesson notebook. Although neither Chen nor Yeyun asked Wenshi to write it, school-age children are normally asked to write a pledge when they violate a school code.

Through my visit, Wenshi remained silent, except when Chen ordered her to sing along the melody while playing the piano.

### Epilogue
I was fortunate to visit many families of Chen's students during this special period of the year. Indeed, portraits of Chen's students offered an occasion that I would not have experienced, had I visited their village at any other time. Interactions between Chen's students, their parents, and me could not be repeated, due to the unique sociocultural context brought by the Chinese lunar New Year. Given that particular period of the year, villagers were more likely to be themselves and live their lives by their own free will.

### Assignment Questions
1. Using Hofstede's framework, discuss what cultural value elements constitute the Chinese "Pianistic Other" phenomenon.
2. What have you learned about cultural values in the changing Chinese (rural) society?
3. Evaluate the applicability of Hofstede's cultural value dimensions to the Chinese piano phenomenon (e.g., collectivism vs. individualism, masculinity vs. femininity, etc.).
4. If you were to study the Chinese piano culture through the lens of cultural value orientations, what potential conclusions will you draw?

---

*Case written by Xiao Chen for the second Canadian edition, excerpted from Chen, Xiao (2007). The Pianistic Other in Shenzhen (1978–2007). Master of Arts thesis, Center for Chinese Studies, University of Michigan, Ann Arbor.

## ■ Chapter 6 Workshop: Working Abroad*

Working in your class teams, identify the country of origin of each team member. After each member provides some information about his or her country, select one country that you are all interested in learning more about. Collect information on that country's (1) social practices, (2) cultural mores, (3) religious and other belief systems, (4) politics, and (5) business and professional practices.

The research is to be done in class, so ensure that at least one team member has his or her laptop. Once the information has been identified and classified under the five topics, discuss how best to present the material to the whole class during the following session. The presentation should be an informational one designed to help employees who are about to go on a two-year international posting. The employees need to know how to behave—and how not to behave—in the country.

At the next session, two teams will present for seven to ten minutes and will be expected to answer questions. This process will continue during the term until all teams have presented.

The order of the presentations will be random and the instructor will ensure at the first session that each team is researching a different country.

### Questions

1. As you worked on your team's country, what was your most significant learning? Please explain.
2. Now that you have heard all the presentations, what do you think are the main considerations to ensure a good international work assignment?

*Copyright © 2008 by Ann Armstrong.

PART 4

# Internal Design Elements

# 7 Manufacturing and Service Technologies

© Fitzroy Face/Urbanologymag.com. Used with permission.

Purpose of This Chapter

**Core Organization Manufacturing Technology**
Manufacturing Firms • Strategy, Technology, and Performance

**Contemporary Applications**
Flexible Manufacturing Systems • Lean Manufacturing
• Performance and Structural Implications

**Core Organization Service Technology**
Service Firms • Designing the Service Organization

**Noncore Departmental Technology**
Variety • Analyzability • Framework

**Department Design**

**Workflow Interdependence among Departments**
Types • Structural Priority • Structural Implications

**Impact of Technology on Job Design**
Job Design • Sociotechnical Systems

**Summary and Interpretation**

## Manitobah Mukluks

In 1990, two Métis siblings, Heather and Sean McCormick, started Manitobah Mukluks as a trading post. Aboriginal artisans traded handmade mukluks and moccasins for the McCormicks' tanned leather skins and furs. In 1997, the McCormicks created a corporation and, by 2006, their moccasins and mukluks were being worn by celebrities. Manitobah Mukluks is now an international brand. The company has partnered with Aboriginal celebrities, in particular, to serve as product and cultural ambassadors. For example, former Olympian Waneek Horn-Miller works to inspire younger Aboriginals to learn the history and spirit of the craft by making the products themselves.[1]

In addition, the company has created an innovative high-abrasion Vibram sole that is suitable for urban markets.[2] Manitobah Mukluks manufactures some of its products in Canada, including the Classic Mukluks with the Vibram sole; deerskin products; and Storyboots, which are handcrafted by elders and artisans in Aboriginal communities. Some of its products are manufactured in China; as a result, Manitobah Mukluks has been criticized for not being authentic enough. Sean McCormick counters the criticism by explaining that

> Manitobah Mukluks IS proudly Canadian. As an Aboriginal Canadian, authentic to me means being engaged in and contributing to my community. It also means respecting our history while creating positive change for the future. The best way for me to make the biggest impact is to get as many people wearing Manitobah Mukluks as possible. It's simple[;] for every pair of Manitobah Mukluks we sell, we are able to make a bigger impact.[3]*

Each Manitobah product comes with a certificate of authenticity that describes the role of Aboriginal business in its design and manufacture. Besides, the company invests heavily in Capital for Aboriginal Prosperity and Entrepreneurship (CAPE) whose mission is "to further a culture of economic independence, ownership, entrepreneurship and enterprise management among Aboriginal peoples through the creation and growth of successful businesses."[4]

---

**M**anufacturers in North America are being threatened as never before. Many companies have found it more advantageous to outsource manufacturing to contractors in other countries that can do the work less expensively, as we see in Manitobah Mukluks. Overall, manufacturing has been on the decline in Canada and other developed countries for years, with services becoming an increasingly greater part of the economy. However, some manufacturing organizations, like Manitobah Mukluks, are applying new technologies to traditional crafts to gain a new competitive edge.

This chapter explores both service and manufacturing technologies, and how technology is related to organizational structure. Technology is a broad concept as it refers to the work processes, techniques, machines, and actions used to transform organizational inputs (materials, information, ideas) into outputs (products and services).[5] **Technology** is an organization's production process and includes work procedures as well as machinery. Take a couple of minutes now to complete the You and Design feature to see which type of technology you prefer.

---

*© Manitobah Mukluks. Used with permission.

An organization's **core technology** is the work process that is directly related to the its mission, such as teaching in a university, medical services in a health clinic, or design and manufacturing at Manitobah Mukluks. For example, at Manitobah Mukluks, the core technology begins with raw materials (e.g., leather, beads, fur). Employees take action on the raw material to make a change in it (they design different styles), thus transforming the raw material into the output of the organization (moccasins and mukluks). For a service organization such as Purolator Courier, the core technology includes the production equipment (e.g., sorting machines, package-handling equipment, trucks, airplanes), and procedures for delivering packages and overnight mail. In addition, as at companies like Purolator Courier, computers and new information technology have revolutionized work processes in both manufacturing and service organizations.

# YOU & DESIGN

## Manufacturing versus Service

The questions that follow ask you to describe your behaviour. For each question, check the answer that best describes you.

1. I am usually running late for class or other appointments:
   a. Yes
   b. No

2. When taking a test I prefer:
   a. Subjective questions (discussion or essay)
   b. Objective questions (multiple choice)

3. When making decisions, I typically:
   a. Go with my gut—what feels right
   b. Carefully weigh each option

4. When solving a problem, I would more likely:
   a. Take a walk, mull things over, then discuss
   b. Write down alternatives, prioritize them, then pick the best

5. I consider time spent daydreaming as:
   a. A viable tool for planning my future
   b. A waste of time.

6. To remember directions, I typically:
   a. Visualize the information
   b. Make notes

7. My work style is mostly:
   a. Juggle several things at once.
   b. Concentrate on one task at a time until complete

8. My desk, work area, or laundry area are typically:
   a. Cluttered
   b. Neat and organized

**Scoring:** Count the number of checked "a" items and "b" items. Each "a" represents right-brain processing, and each "b" represents left-brain processing. If you scored 6 or higher on either, you have a distinct processing style. If you checked fewer than 6 for either, you probably have a balanced style.

**Interpretation:** People have two thinking processes—one visual and intuitive in the right half of the brain, and the other verbal and analytical in the left half of the brain. The thinking process you prefer predisposes you to certain types of knowledge and information—technical reports, analytical information, and quantitative data (left brain) vs. talking to people, thematic impressions, and personal intuition (right brain)—as effective input to your thinking and decision making. Manufacturing organizations typically use left-brain processing to handle data based on physical, measurable technology. Service organizations typically use right-brain processing to interpret less-tangible situations and serve people in a direct way. Left-brain processing has been summarized as based on logic; right-brain processing has been summarized as based on love.

Source: Adapted from Carolyn Hopper, *Practicing Management Skills* (Houghton Mifflin, 2003), and Jacquelyn Wonder and Priscilla Donovan, "Mind Openers," *Self* (March 1984).

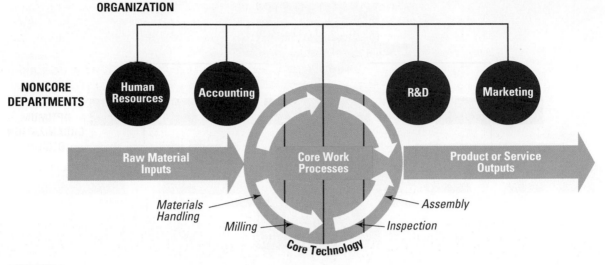

**EXHIBIT 7.1**
Core Transformation Process for a Manufacturing Company

Exhibit 7.1 features an example of core technology for a manufacturing plant. Note how the core technology consists of raw material inputs and a transformation work process (materials handling, milling, inspection, assembly) that changes and adds value to the raw material and produces the ultimate product or service output that is sold to consumers in the environment. In today's large, complex organizations, core work processes vary widely and sometimes can be hard to pinpoint. A core technology can be partly understood by examining the raw materials flowing into the organization,[6] the variability of work activities,[7] the degree to which the production process is mechanized,[8] the extent to which one task depends on another in the workflow,[9] or the number of new product or service outputs.[10]

An important theme in this chapter is how core technology influences organizational structure. Understanding core technology provides insight into how an organization can be structured for efficient performance.[11]

Organizations are made up of many departments, each of which may use a different work process (technology) to provide a good or service within the organization. A **noncore technology** is a department work process that is important to the organization but is not directly related to its primary mission. In Exhibit 7.1, noncore work processes are illustrated by the departments of human resources (HR), accounting, research and development (R&D), and marketing. Thus, R&D transforms ideas into new products, and marketing transforms inventory into sales, each using a somewhat different work process. The output of the HR department is people to work in the organization, and accounting produces accurate statements about the organization's financial condition.

## ■ Purpose of This Chapter

In this chapter, we will discuss both core and noncore work processes and their relationship to designing organizational structure. The optimal organizational design is based on a variety of elements. Exhibit 7.2 illustrates that forces affecting organizational design come from both outside and inside the organization. External strategic needs, such as environmental conditions, strategic direction, and organizational goals, create

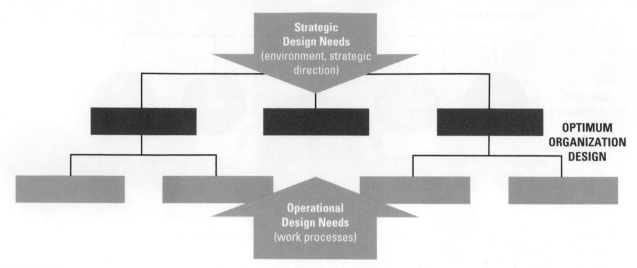

**EXHIBIT 7.2**
**Pressures Affecting Organizational Design**
Source: Based on David A. Nadler and Michael L. Tushman, with Mark B. Nadler, *Competing by Design: The Power of Organizational Architecture* (New York: Oxford University Press, 1997), 54. By permission of Oxford University Press, Inc.

top-down pressure for designing the organization in such a way as to fit the environment and accomplish goals. These pressures on design have been discussed in previous chapters. However, decisions about design should also take into consideration pressures from the bottom up—from the work processes that are performed to produce the organization's products or services. The operational work processes will influence the structural design associated with both the core technology and noncore departments. Thus, the subject with which this chapter is concerned is, "How should the organization be designed to accommodate and facilitate its operational work processes?"

The remainder of the chapter will unfold as follows. First, we examine how the technology for the organization as a whole influences organizational structure and design. This discussion includes both manufacturing and service technologies. Next, we examine differences in departmental technologies and how the technologies influence the design and management of organizational subunits. Third, we explore how interdependence—flow of materials and information—among departments affects structure.

## Core Organization Manufacturing Technology

Manufacturing technologies include traditional manufacturing processes and contemporary applications, such as flexible manufacturing and lean manufacturing.

### Manufacturing Firms

The first and most influential study of manufacturing technology was conducted by Joan Woodward, a British industrial sociologist. Her research began as a field study of management principles in South Essex, England. The prevailing management wisdom at the time (1950s) was contained in what were known as universal principles of management. These principles were "one best way" prescriptions that effective organizations were expected to adopt. Woodward surveyed 100 manufacturing firms firsthand to learn how they were organized.[12] She and her research team visited each firm, interviewed managers, examined company records, and observed the manufacturing operations. Her data included a wide range of structural characteristics (span of control, levels of management), dimensions of management style (written versus oral communications, use of rewards), and types of manufacturing process. Data were also obtained that reflected commercial success of the firms.

Woodward developed a scale and organized the firms according to technical complexity of the manufacturing process. **Technical complexity** represents the extent of mechanization of the manufacturing process. High technical complexity means most of the work is performed by machines. Low technical complexity means workers play a larger role in the production process. Woodward's scale of technical complexity originally had ten categories, as summarized in Exhibit 7.3. These categories were further consolidated into three basic technology groups:

**Apply**

Apply Woodward's typology to three different organizations with which you are familiar. What differences do you observe and what accounts for them?

- *Group I: Small-batch and unit production.* **Small-batch production** firms tend to be job shop operations that manufacture and assemble small orders to meet specific needs of customers. Custom work is the norm. Small-batch production relies heavily on the human operator; it is thus not highly mechanized. Schleese Saddlery Service, in Holland Landing, Ontario, makes customized saddles that are designed to fit a particular rider and horse.[13] Similarly, Kiln Art in Chester Basin, Nova Scotia, makes small batches of fused glass plates and bowls.[14] Both organizations and their founders have been recognized for the quality of their customized products.

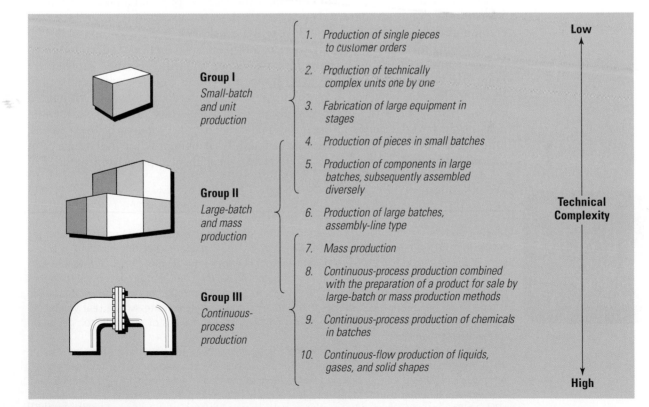

**EXHIBIT 7.3**
**Woodward's Classification of 100 British Firms According to Their Systems of Production**
Source: Adapted from Joan Woodward, *Management and Technology* (London: Her Majesty's Stationery Office, 1958). Licensed under the Open Government Licence v1.0. http://www.nationalarchives.gov.uk/doc/open-government-licence/open-government-licence.htm

- *Group II: Large-batch and mass production.* **Large-batch production** is a manufacturing process characterized by long production runs of standardized parts. Output often goes into inventory from which orders are filled because customers do not have special needs. Examples include most assembly lines, such as for cars, trucks, or trailer homes.
- *Group III: Continuous-process production.* In **continuous-process production**, the entire process is mechanized. There is no starting and stopping. This represents mechanization and standardization one step beyond those in an assembly line. Automated machines control the continuous process, and outcomes are highly predictable. Examples include chemical plants, oil refineries, beer makers, pharmaceuticals, and nuclear power plants.

Using this classification of technology, Woodward's data made sense. The number of management levels and the manager-to-total-personnel ratio, for example, show definite increases as technical complexity increases from unit production to continuous process. This indicates that greater management intensity is needed to manage complex technology. The direct-to-indirect labour ratio decreases with technical complexity because more indirect workers are required to support and maintain complex machinery. Other characteristics, such as span of control, formalized procedures, and centralization, are high for mass-production technology because the work is standardized, but low for other technologies. Unit-production and continuous-process technologies require highly skilled workers to run the machines and verbal communication to adapt to changing conditions. Mass production is standardized and routinized, so few exceptions occur, little oral communication is needed, and employees are less skilled.

Overall, the management systems in both unit-production and continuous-process technology are characterized as organic, as defined in Chapter 4. They are more free-flowing and adaptive, with fewer procedures and less standardization. Mass production, however, is mechanistic, with standardized jobs and formalized procedures. Woodward's discovery about technology thus provided substantial new insight into the causes of organizational structure. In Woodward's own words, "[different] technologies impose different kinds of demands on individuals and organizations, and those demands had to be met through an appropriate structure."[15]

## In Practice
### Maple Leaf Foods Inc. (Maple Leaf)

Maple Leaf was founded over 100 years ago and now employs about 21,000 people around the world. In 1991, a merger of Maple Leaf Mills Limited and Canada Packers Inc. resulted in Maple Leaf. Maple Leaf gained both notoriety and approbation for its handling of the 2008 listeriosis outbreak. The day after the outbreak of the food-borne illness, the plant that produced the meat was shut down. The CEO, Michael McCain, was immediately visible through press conferences and the company used print and video media. It posted an apology on its website. Maple Leaf weathered the crisis even though it claimed 22 lives and cost Maple Leaf millions of dollars in compensation to the affected families.[16]

More recently, Maple Leaf has decided to streamline its hotdog manufacturing process. In 2010, the company made hotdogs using 78 different recipes and made them in 50 different sizes! A hotdog can take about four hours to make and goes thorough many machines and processes and even goes to different plants. Maple Leaf is moving to reduce its production costs. It has developed a $1.3 billion dollar turnaround plan that includes getting rid of its old plants and building a large state-of-the-art facility that uses the latest technology.[17]

## ■ Strategy, Technology, and Performance

Another portion of Woodward's study examined the success of the firms along dimensions such as profitability, market share, stock price, and reputation. As indicated in Chapter 2, the measurement of effectiveness is neither simple nor precise, but Woodward was able to rank firms on a scale of commercial success according to whether they displayed above-average, average, or below-average performance on strategic objectives.

Woodward compared the structure–technology relationship against commercial success and discovered that successful firms tended to be those that had complementary structures and technologies. Many of the organizational characteristics of the successful firms were near the average of their technology category. Below-average firms tended to depart from the structural characteristics for their technology type. Another conclusion was that structural characteristics could be interpreted as clustering into organic and mechanistic management systems. Successful small-batch and continuous-process organizations had organic structures, and successful mass-production organizations had mechanistic structures. Subsequent research has replicated Woodward's findings.[18]

This illustrates for today's organizations that strategy, structure, and technology need to be aligned, especially when competitive conditions change.[19] For example, computer makers had to realign strategy, structure, and technology to compete with Dell in the personal computer market. Manufacturers such as IBM that once tried to differentiate their products and charge a premium price, switched to a low-cost strategy, adopted new technology to enable them to customize PCs, revamped supply chains, and began outsourcing manufacturing to other companies that could do the job more efficiently.

Today, many North American manufacturers farm out production to other companies. Doepker Industries of Annaheim, Saskatchewan, however, has gone in the opposite direction and achieved success by carefully aligning technology, structure, and management processes to achieve strategic objectives.

---

**In Practice**
**Doepker Industries (Doepker)**

Six Doepker brothers started the family business as a repair shop in 1948. They then ventured into farm equipment manufacturing, and, in 1972, produced their first grain trailer. Doepker now manufactures trailers for a number of industries, including agriculture, commercial, industrial/construction, and forestry. Doepker has expanded but kept its head office in Annaheim, Saskatchewan, a town of 220. Doepker has 6,996 square metres of production and office space in Annaheim, 2,267 square metres in Moose Jaw, 2,676 square metres of production space and 799 square metres of office space in Humboldt, and 23,000 square metres in Salmon Arm, B.C. The plants employ 500 people, use modern equipment such as a state-of-the-industry paint department, 3-D solids modelling engineering and design software, robotics, and CNC equipment technology.[20]

The location of each of the plants was chosen strategically to be close to Doepker's largest markets in Western Canada. Doepker is looking at realigning its dealer network in Eastern Canada to create a strong distribution network there. Doepker is expanding into the U.S. market where it has already a few outlets selling its specialized trailers.[21]

In 2005, Dave Doepker, executive chairman of the board of Doepker Industries, announced the appointment of Gurcan Kocdag to the position of president. Kocdag is the first nonfamily member named to the position of president in the company's 57-year history. Part of his mandate is to continue to operate the company as a family business.[22]

Today's increased global competition means more volatile markets, shorter product life cycles, and more sophisticated and knowledgeable consumers; flexibility to meet these new demands has become a strategic imperative for many companies.[23] Manufacturing companies can adopt new technologies to support the strategy of flexibility. However, organizational structures and management processes must also be realigned, as a highly mechanistic structure hampers flexibility and prevents the company from reaping the benefits of the new technology.[24] Managers should always remember that the technological and human systems of an organization are intertwined. This chapter's Book Mark provides a different perspective on technology by looking at the dangers of failing to understand the human role in managing technological advances.

## Contemporary Applications

In the years since Woodward's research, new developments have occurred in manufacturing technology. While the manufacturing sector in Canada has faced many shocks, recent research suggests that Canada is not de-industrializing. Rather, "... in the face of intense international competition and rising resource prices, Canadian manufacturers raised their productivity by an annual average of 1.1 percent, shifting manufacturing shares in durable goods industries to resemble that of the United States.[25] However, the factory of today is far different from the industrial firms Woodward studied in the 1950s. In particular, computers have revolutionized all types of manufacturing—small batch, large batch, and continuous process. Oil and gas companies, as well as chemical and mining and power companies have used electronic technology "to drive significant improvements in their operating results...while reducing their costs and meeting regulatory compliance and safety standards."[26] An example in continuous-process manufacturing comes from Shell's unionized petrochemical plant in Sarnia, Ontario. Technicians who would have once manually monitored hundreds of complex processes now focus their energy on surveying long-term production trends. Controlling the continuous production of petrochemicals today is handled faster, smarter, more precisely, and more economically by computer. The Sarnia plant was one of Shell's most productive plants. The next In Practice highlights the integration of old and new technologies to manufacture handcrafted signs.

## In Practice
### Eyecandy Signs Inc. (Eyecandy)

Eyecandy was founded in 1998 in Halifax and has worked closely with the local arts community. It works with students from the Nova Scotia College of Art and Design as well as local entrepreneurs. It has been active in building the economic community of the north end of the city.[27] Eyecandy consists of two partners and eight employees. Creativity is encouraged as each employee has a few free hours a week to play on the machines and to create new designs that are not intended for any particular client.

Eyecandy's employees no longer make signs from scratch; rather they build on machine-carved designs. "What sets Eyecandy apart is a dedication to craft—what sign making was when hand-carving was usually the only option."[28] It competes by creating custom designs while maintaining its digital-print technology for everyday work. Much of the design is done collaboratively. While Eyecandy is well known in Eastern Canada, it has not yet grown across the country.

# Book Mark 7.0    HAVE YOU READ THIS BOOK?

## Inviting Disaster: Lessons from the Edge of Technology
By James R. Chiles

Dateline: Paris, France, July 25, 2000. Less than two minutes after Air France Concorde Flight 4590 departs Charles DeGaulle Airport, something goes horribly wrong. Trailing fire and billowing black smoke, the huge plane rolls left and crashes into a hotel, killing all 109 people aboard and four more on the ground. It's just one of the technological disasters James R. Chiles describes in his book, *Inviting Disaster: Lessons from the Edge of Technology*. One of Chiles's main points is that advancing technology makes possible the creation of machines that strain the human ability to understand and safely operate them. Moreover, he asserts, the margins of safety are thinner as the energies we harness become more powerful and the time between invention and use grows shorter. Chiles believes that today, "For every twenty books on the pursuit of success, we need a book on how things fly into tiny pieces despite enormous effort and the very highest ideals." All complex systems, he reminds us, are destined to fail at some point.

### HOW THINGS FLY INTO PIECES: EXAMPLES OF SYSTEM FRACTURES

Chiles uses historical calamities such as the sinking of the *Titanic* and modern disasters such as the explosion of the space shuttle *Challenger* (the book was published before the 2003 crash of the *Columbia* shuttle) to illustrate the dangers of system fracture, a chain of events that involves human error in response to malfunctions in complex machinery. Disaster begins when one weak point links up with others.

- *Sultana* (American steamboat on the Mississippi River near Memphis, Tennessee), April 25, 1865. The boat, designed to carry a maximum of 460 people, was carrying more than 2,000 Union ex-prisoners north—as well as 200 additional crew and passengers—when three of the four boilers exploded, killing 1,800 people. One of the boilers

had been temporarily patched to cover a crack, but the patch was too thin. Operators failed to compensate by resetting the safety valve.
- Piper Alpha (offshore drilling rig in the North Sea), July 6, 1988. The offshore platform processed large volumes of natural gas from other rigs via pipe. A daytime work crew that didn't complete a repair of a gas-condensate pump relayed a verbal message to the next shift, but workers turned the pump on anyway. When the temporary seal on the pump failed, a fire trapped crewmen with no escape route, killing 167 crew and rescue workers.
- Union Carbide (India) (release of highly toxic chemicals into a community), Bhopal, Mahdya Pradesh, India, December 3, 1984. There are three competing theories for how water got into a storage tank, creating a violent reaction that sent highly toxic methyl isocyanate for herbicides into the environment, causing an estimated 7,000 deaths: (1) poor safety maintenance, (2) sabotage, or (3) worker error.

### WHAT CAUSES SYSTEM FRACTURES?

There is a veritable catalogue of causes that lead to such disasters, from design errors, insufficient operator training, and poor planning, to greed and mismanagement. Chiles wrote this book as a reminder that technology takes us into risky locales, whether into outer space, up a 600 metre tower, or into a chemical processing plant. Chiles also cites examples of potential disasters that were averted by quick thinking and appropriate response. To help prevent system fractures, managers can create organizations in which people throughout the company are expert at picking out the subtle signals of real problems—and where they are empowered to report them and take prompt action.

*Inviting Disaster: Lessons from the Edge of Technology*, by James R. Chiles, is published by Harper Business, 2002.

---

Mass production manufacturing has seen similar transformations. Two significant contemporary applications of manufacturing technology are flexible manufacturing systems and lean manufacturing.

## ▪ Flexible Manufacturing Systems

Most of today's factories use a variety of new manufacturing technologies, including robots, numerically controlled machine tools, radio-frequency identification (RFID), wireless technology, and computerized software for product design, engineering analysis, and remote control of machinery. The ultimate automated factories are referred to as **flexible manufacturing systems** (FMS).[29] Also called computer-integrated manufacturing, smart factories, advanced manufacturing technology, agile manufacturing, or the factory of the future, FMS link manufacturing components that previously stood alone. Thus, robots, machines, product design, and engineering analysis are coordinated by a single computer.

The result has already revolutionized the shop floor, enabling large factories to deliver a wide range of custom-made products at low mass-production costs.[30] Flexible manufacturing also enables small companies to go toe-to-toe with larger factories and lower-cost competitors. The manufacturing process at Weyerhaeuser Company's Chemainus Sawmill on Vancouver Island, while similar to traditional sawmilling in that it uses hydraulic and pneumatic technology, also uses computerized precision scanning technology to get value out of the logs for different orders. The sawmill was the company's first manufacturing facility to achieve ISO 14001 registration.[31]

Flexible manufacturing is typically the result of three subcomponents:

- *Computer-aided design (CAD)*. Computers are used to assist in the drafting, design, and engineering of new parts. Designers guide their computers to draw specified configurations on the screen, including dimensions and component details. Hundreds of design alternatives can be explored, as can scaled-up or scaled-down versions of the original.[32]
- *Computer-aided manufacturing (CAM)*. Computer-controlled machines in materials handling, fabrication, production, and assembly greatly increase the speed at which items can be manufactured. CAM also permits a production line to shift rapidly from producing one product to any variety of other products by changing the instruction tapes or software codes in the computer. CAM enables the production line to quickly honour customer requests for changes in product design and product mix.[33]
- *Integrated information network*. A computerized system links all aspects of the firm—including accounting, purchasing, marketing, inventory control, design, production, and so forth. This system, based on a common data and information base, enables managers to make decisions and direct the manufacturing process in a truly integrated fashion.

The combination of CAD, CAM, and integrated information systems means that a new product can be designed on the computer and a prototype can be produced untouched by human hands. The ideal factory can switch quickly from one product to another, working quickly and with precision, without paperwork or recordkeeping to bog down the system.[34] CAD/CAM can be used for a variety of products. For example, Montréal's Foot Crafters makes personalized insoles and foot orthoses. Using a computer and a graphic interface, it visualizes in real time a foot's pressure distribution and enables two- or three-dimensional shape analysis. The data are then sent internally or online to its manufacturing site. The manufacturing process of the orthesis is completely computer assisted. A numerically controlled milling machine then creates the orthesis. The time from order to manufacture has decreased considerably.[35]

Designersilversmiths.com, located in Devon, England, uses CAD/CAM software to design jewellery. According to Hillary Corney, owner of Designersilversmiths, "[Projects] that would have taken months can now be completed in weeks. [Another] advantage is that any duplicated elements can be reproduced almost instantly."[36]

Some advanced factories have moved to a system called product life-cycle management (PLM). PLM software can manage a product from idea through development, manufacturing, testing, and even maintenance in the field. The PLM software provides three primary advantages for product innovation. PLM (1) stores data on ideas and products from all parts of the company; (2) links product design to all departments (and even outside suppliers) involved in new product development; and (3) provides three-dimensional images of new products for testing and maintenance. PLM has been used to coordinate people, tools, and facilities around the world for the design, development, and manufacture of products as diverse as product packaging for Procter & Gamble consumer products and Tesla's cars.[37]

## ■ Lean Manufacturing

Flexible manufacturing reaches its ultimate level to improve quality, customer service, and cost cutting when all parts are used interdependently and combined with flexible management processes in a system referred to as lean manufacturing. **Lean manufacturing** uses highly trained employees at every stage of the production process, and they take a painstaking approach to details and problem solving to cut waste and improve quality. Lean manufacturing incorporates technological elements, such as CAD/CAM and PLM, but the heart of lean manufacturing is not machines or software, but people. Lean manufacturing requires changes in organizational systems, such as decision-making processes and management processes, as well as an organizational culture that supports active employee participation. Employees are trained to "think lean," which means attacking waste and striving for continuous improvement in all areas.[38] Canada Post, for example, adopted a lean manufacturing approach when it eliminated a large automated sorting machine and replaced it with a much smaller manual cell. "I used to think that we weren't a manufacturing company; we didn't produce anything," said Don McLellan, director, Mail Operations, at the Calgary facility, "but you can lean out mail operations. What we're looking for is flow; in one door and out another."[39]

The application of lean thinking is not limited to manufacturing organizations but is used in service organizations as well. Mt. Sinai Hospital and Women's College Hospital have adopted lean principles to improve their services by reducing wait times for access to MRIs.[40] Other hospitals in Ontario have also adopted lean principles to improve their services. The Rouge Valley Health System has engaged in extensive training and process mapping to determine how best to become more efficient to streamline the referral process for individuals waiting for placement in a long-term care facility.[41]

Lean manufacturing is not without its critics. It is criticized for creating workplace stress, as there is an obsessive focus on achieving perfection, that is no errors and no waste. There is no margin for error. Its no-waste focus—cutting flab—may result in ignoring other crucial parameters such as employee wellness and corporate social responsibility. Its here-and-now focus can result in reducing experimentation and long-term thinking and action.[42] A 2011 survey of 100 executives whose companies had implemented lean manufacturing techniques revealed disappointing results. Nearly 70 percent indicated that the techniques had not reduced costs by 5 percent, the researchers' minimum benchmark for productivity improvements to be deemed successful. Most of the executives said the savings were temporary;

**EXHIBIT 7.4**
Have a Quality Focus!

13 percent managed to sustain three-quarters or more of the previous year's savings. Even so, and surprisingly, 91 percent considered their re-engineering efforts to be effective.[43]

Japan's Toyota Motor Corporation, which pioneered lean manufacturing, is often considered the premier manufacturing organization in the world although its reputation was tarnished considerably in 2010 when some of its cars were believed to have faulty acceleration pedals. The famed Toyota Production System combines techniques such as just-in-time inventory, product life-cycle management, continuous-flow production, quick changeover of assembly lines, continuous improvement, and preventive maintenance with a management system that encourages employee involvement and problem solving. Any employee can stop the production line at any time to solve a problem. In addition, designing equipment to stop automatically so that a defect can be fixed is a key element of the system.[44] The next In Practice highlights the use of lean manufacturing techniques to address the demands of global competition. And, the cartoon in Exhibit 7.4 shows us why it is important to have a quality focus!

*act!*

**Compare**

Compare the application of lean manufacturing principles in a service organization and a manufacturing organization. What are some key differences?

## In Practice
### Sealy

Faced with cost pressures brought about by global competition combined with a recession, manufacturers can't afford to tie up hundreds of millions of dollars in raw materials that sit in factories for months or have partially finished products taking up floor space. Sealy managers have positioned their company for success in tough times by using lean manufacturing techniques.

Sealy operates 25 factories in North America and sells mattresses through thousands of retail outlets. The company conducts a *kaizen* (continuous improvement) event each month at every factory. In the beginning, Sealy focused on cutting unnecessary parts movement, eliminating waste, and eliminating unnecessary handling of materials. Employees are trained to "think lean" and look for any area of potential improvement. Previously, workers produced dozens of unfinished mattresses at a time that sat on the factory floor waiting for the next step. After implementing lean processes, teams of workers produce a complete mattress at a time matched closely to customer orders, which cuts the amount of time handling and moving materials. Today, Sealy has taken lean thinking even further, applying it to product design, for instance, to take waste out of engineering processes and design products that can be manufactured with less time and waste.

Using lean manufacturing helped Sealy reduce its scrap by 69 percent. Raw materials inventory is down 50 percent, to 16 days' worth, and the reduction in piles of partially finished mattresses freed up enough space that managers could combine two shifts, further slashing manufacturing costs. During the recent recession, Sealy maintained its commitment to continuous improvement and employee involvement. "Because of our lean culture we continued to get better…despite a downturn in volume," said Mike Hofmann, executive vice president of operations. "We're trying to keep our plants in condition by pushing *kaizen* and lean initiatives. When the market does return, if we can produce product in 20 percent to 30 percent less time than our competitors, we could seize market share."[45]

Many North American organizations have studied the Toyota Production System and seen dramatic improvements in productivity, inventory reduction, and quality. Garrison Guitars of St. John's, Newfoundland and Labrador, used Toyota's ideas to create some of the world's best acoustic guitars.

**In Practice**

**Garrison Guitars (Garrison)**

Chris Griffiths started Garrison when he was 19. Garrison guitars are now used by performers such as Alanis Morrisette, Stompin' Tom Connors, Tom Cochrane, The Tragically Hip, and Eric Clapton. Garrison guitars are sold in 35 countries through a dealer network of more than 450 music retailers worldwide. The guitars retail from $400 to more than $3,000. In 2007, the company had annual sales of $5 million. In the same year, Garrison was sold to Nashville-based Gibson Guitar so that it could reach a larger market while managing its costs.[46]

Garrison started off as a one-person guitar repair shop but has grown into a manufacturer of specially designed guitars. Griffiths had an epiphany in 1995 after visiting some guitar manufacturers. He wondered, "[Wouldn't] it be more efficient if we could make all the braces out of one piece?" Griffiths was the first person to make the guitar's bracing system out of artificial materials while the rest of the guitar was made of wood. In 2000, Griffiths got the patents for the design and then raised $3.5 million to build a 1,858-square-metre production facility that uses robotics and laser technology.

At Garrison, it takes 45 seconds to complete a guitar frame rather than the two hours it takes to machine and to assemble 30 wooden pieces using the traditional approach to manufacturing guitars. The Garrison system uses injection moulding to build a single-piece guitar frame that is 40 percent glass. The remainder of the moulding is Griffiths's "secret sauce."[47] Garrison is able to sell its guitars for 25 percent less than its competitors. "The [manufacturing] system also makes the guitar sound better—an unexpected side effect caused by reducing the number of parts and their vibrations—and last longer as there's less wood to be affected by humidity and temperature changes."[48] Garrison also applied the Toyota Production System to the plant to maximize its efficiency.

Griffiths is not concerned, however, about any hollowing out of the Canadian guitar industry. As Griffiths says, "I just don't see how we could have grown as exponentially as we're about to grow by just continuing on in our current path" as he plans to quintuple production in 12 months so that the Garrison Guitar produces 60 guitars a day.[49]

Lean manufacturing and flexible manufacturing systems paved the way for **mass customization**, which refers to using mass-production technology to quickly and cost-effectively assemble goods that are uniquely designed to fit the demands of individual customers.[50] Mass customization first took hold when Dell Computer Corporation began building computers to order, and has since expanded to products as diverse as farm machinery, water heaters, clothing, and industrial detergents. Today, you can buy jeans customized for your body, glasses moulded to precisely fit and flatter your face, windows in the exact shape and size you want for your new home, and pills with the specific combination of vitamins and minerals you need.[51] Dell, described in the Leading by Design, provides a useful example of the flexible manufacturing needed to make mass customization work.

Auto manufacturers, too, are moving toward mass customization. Sixty percent of the cars BMW sells in Europe are built to order while only 15 percent were custom-built in 2010 in North America.[52] North American manufacturers are building and remodelling plants to catch up with Japanese manufacturers such as Nissan and Honda in the ability to offer customers personalized products. For example, Ford's Kansas City, Missouri, plant, one of the largest manufacturing facilities in the world, produces around 490,000 F-150s, Ford Escapes, and Mazda Tributes a year. With just a little tweaking, the assembly lines in Kansas City can be programmed to manufacture any kind of car or truck Ford makes. The new F-150 has so many options that there are more than 1 million possible configurations of that model alone. Robots in wire cages do most of the work, while people act as assistants, taking measurements, refilling parts, and altering the system if something goes wrong. Assembly is synchronized by computers, right down to the last rearview mirror. Ford's flexible manufacturing system is projected to save the company $2 billion.[53] Plant efficiency experts believe the trend toward mass customization will grow as flexible manufacturing systems become even more sophisticated and adaptive.

**Think**

Can you think of other organizations that use mass customization? Why are they using mass customization?

# Leading *by Design*

## Dell Computer

It's a tough time in the computer industry, and Dell Computer is rumoured to be laying off a significant number of employees.[54] Even so, competitors agree that there is just no better way to make, sell, and deliver personal computers (PCs) than the way Dell does it. Dell PCs are made to order and are delivered directly to the consumer. Each customer gets exactly the machine he or she wants—and gets it faster and cheaper than Dell's competitors could provide it.

Dell's speedy, flexible, cost-efficient system is illustrated by the company's newest factory, the Topfer Manufacturing facility near Dell headquarters in Round Rock, Texas, where Dell created a new way of making PCs that helped spur the company from number three to number one in PC sales. The process combines just-in-time delivery of parts from suppliers with a complicated, integrated computer manufacturing system that practically hands a worker the right part—whether it be any of a dozen different microprocessors or a specific combination of software—at just the right moment. The goal is to not only slash costs but also save time by reducing the number of worker-touches per machine. Dell used to build computers in progressive assembly-line fashion, with up to 25 different people building one machine. Now, teams of three to seven workers build a complete computer from start to finish by following precise guidelines and using the components that arrive in carefully indicated racks in front of them. The combination of baskets, racks, and traffic signals that keeps the whole operation moving is called the Pick-to-Light system. Pick-to-Light is based on an up-to-the-minute database and software tying it to a stockroom system. That means the system can make sure teams have everything they need to complete an order, whether it be for one PC or 200. The system keeps track of which materials need replenishing and makes sure the racks and baskets are supplied with the proper components. Precise coordination, aided by sophisticated supply-chain software, means that Dell can keep just two hours' worth of parts inventory and replenish only what it needs throughout the day. The flexible system works so well that 85 percent of orders are built, customized, and shipped within eight hours.

Dell's new system has dramatically improved productivity, increasing manufacturing speed and throughput of custom-made computers by 150 percent. Employees are happier too because they now use more skills and build a complete machine within the team rather than performing the same boring, repetitive task on an assembly line. The system that began at one cutting-edge factory has been adopted at all of the company's manufacturing plants. With this kind of flexibility, no wonder Dell *was* number one.[55]

Like Toyota, Dell has faced quality problems and has been sued. Some of the documents from that suit indicate that the employees were aware of the quality problems and had played them down. "Dell, as a company, was the model everyone focused on.... But when you combine missing a variety of shifts in the industry with management turmoil, it's hard not to have the shine come off your reputation."[56]

## Performance and Structural Implications

The advantage of flexible manufacturing is that products of different sizes, types, and customer requirements freely intermingle on the assembly line. Bar codes imprinted on a part enable machines to make instantaneous changes—such as putting a larger screw in a different location—without slowing the production line. A manufacturer can turn out an infinite variety of products in unlimited batch sizes. As illustrated in Exhibit 7.5, in the traditional manufacturing systems studied by Woodward, the choices were limited to those illustrated on the diagonal. Small batch allowed for high product flexibility and custom orders, but because of the

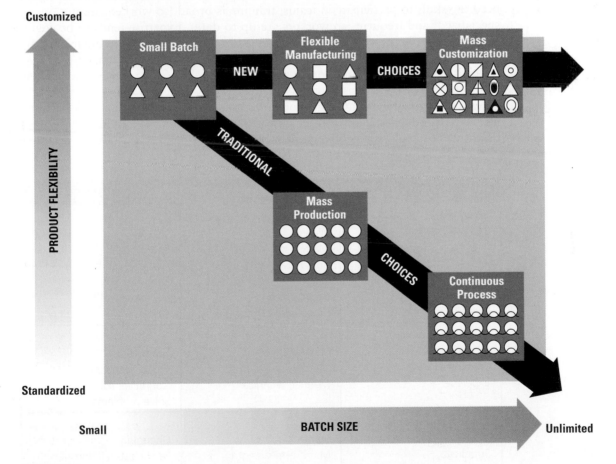

**EXHIBIT 7.5**
**Relationship of Flexible Manufacturing Technology to Traditional Technologies**
Source: Based on Jack Meredith, "The Strategic Advantages of New Manufacturing Technologies for Small Firms," *Strategic Management Journal* 8 (1987), 249–258; Paul Adler, "Managing Flexible Automation," *California Management Review* (Spring 1988), 34–56; and Otis Port, "Custom-made Direct from the Plant," *BusinessWeek/21st Century Capitalism* (November 18, 1994), 158–159.

"craftsmanship" involved in custom-making products, batch size was necessarily small. Mass production could have large batch size, but offered limited product flexibility. Continuous process could produce a single standard product in unlimited quantities. Flexible manufacturing systems (FMS) allow plants to break free of this diagonal relationship and to increase both batch size and product flexibility at the same time. When taken to its ultimate level, FMS allows for mass customization, with each specific product tailored to customer specification. This high-level use of FMS has been referred to as computer-aided craftsmanship.[57]

Studies suggest that with FMS, machine utilization is more efficient, labour productivity increases, scrap rates decrease, and product variety and customer satisfaction increase.[58] Some North American manufacturing companies are reinventing the factory using FMS and lean manufacturing systems to increase productivity.

Research into the relationship between FMS and organizational characteristics is beginning to emerge, and the patterns are summarized in Exhibit 7.6. Compared with traditional mass-production technologies, FMS has a narrow span of control, few hierarchical levels, adaptive tasks, low specialization, and decentralization, and the overall environment is characterized as organic and self-regulating. Employees need the skills to participate in teams; training is broad (so workers are not overly specialized) and frequent (so workers are up to date). Expertise tends to be cognitive so workers can process abstract ideas and solve problems. Interorganizational relationships in FMS firms are characterized by changing demand from customers—which is easily handled with the new technology—and close relationships with a few suppliers that provide top-quality raw materials.[59]

Technology alone cannot give organizations the benefits of flexibility, quality, increased production, and greater customer satisfaction. Research suggests that FMS can become a competitive burden rather than a competitive advantage unless

**EXHIBIT 7.6**
Comparison of Organizational Characteristics Associated with Mass Production and Flexible Manufacturing Systems

| CHARACTERISTIC | MASS PRODUCTION | FMS |
|---|---|---|
| **Structure** | | |
| Span of control | Wide | Narrow |
| Hierarchical levels | Many | Few |
| Tasks | Routine, repetitive | Adaptive, craft-like |
| Specialization | High | Low |
| Decision making | Centralized | Decentralized |
| Overall | Bureaucratic, mechanistic | Organic, self-regulating |
| **Human Resources** | | |
| Interactions | Standalone | Teamwork |
| Training | Narrow, one time | Broad, frequent |
| Expertise | Manual, technical | Cognitive, social Solve problems |
| **Interorganizational** | | |
| Customer demand | Stable | Changing |
| Suppliers | Many, arm's length | Few, close relationships |

Source: Based on Patricia L. Nemetz and Louis W. Fry, "Flexible Manufacturing Organizations: Implications for Strategy Formulation and Organization Design," *Academy of Management Review* 13 (1988), 627–638; Paul S. Adler, "Managing Flexible Automation," *California Management Review* (Spring 1988), 34–56; and Jeremy Main, "Manufacturing the Right Way," *Fortune* (May 21, 1990) 54–64.

organizational structures and management processes are redesigned to exploit the new technology.[60] However, when top managers make a commitment to implement new structures and processes that empower workers and support a learning and knowledge-creating environment, FMS can help companies be more competitive.[61]

# Core Organization Service Technology

Another big change occurring in the technology of organizations is the growing service sector. The percentage of the workforce employed in manufacturing continues to decline, not only in Canada, but also in the United States, France, Germany, the United Kingdom, and Sweden.[62] The service sector has increased three times as quickly as the manufacturing sector in the North American economy. Service technologies are different from manufacturing technologies and, in turn, require a specific organizational structure.

## Service Firms

**Definition.** Although manufacturing organizations achieve their primary purpose through the production of products, service organizations accomplish their primary purpose through the production and provision of services, such as education, health care, transportation, banking, and hospitality. Studies of service organizations have focused on the unique dimensions of service technologies. While both manufacturing and service technologies involve many components, "service components are usually not physical entities, but rather are a combination of processes, people skills, and materials that must be appropriately integrated to yield the 'planned' or 'designed' service."[63] Exhibit 7.7 compares the characteristics of service and manufacturing technologies.

The most obvious difference is that **service technology** produces an intangible output, rather than a tangible product, such as a refrigerator produced by a manufacturing firm. A service is abstract and often consists of knowledge and ideas rather than a physical product. Thus, whereas manufacturers' products can be inventoried for later sale, services are characterized by simultaneous production and consumption. A client meets with a doctor or lawyer, for example, and students and teachers come together in the classroom or over the Internet. A service is an intangible product that does not exist until it is requested by the customer. It cannot be stored, inventoried, or viewed as a finished good. If a service is not consumed immediately upon production, it disappears.[64] This typically means that service firms are labour- and knowledge-intensive, with many employees needed to meet the needs of customers, whereas manufacturing firms tend to be capital-intensive, relying on mass production, continuous process, and flexible manufacturing technologies.[65]

Direct interaction between customer and employee is generally very high with services, while there is little direct interaction between customers and employees in the technical core of a manufacturing firm. This direct interaction means that the human element (employees) becomes extremely important in service firms. While most people never meet the workers who manufactured their cars, they interact directly with the salesperson who sold them their Honda Element or Toyota Prius. The treatment received from the salesperson—or from a doctor, lawyer, or hairstylist—affects the perception of the service received and the customer's level of satisfaction. The quality of a service is perceived, and cannot be directly measured and compared in the same

**Service Technology**
1. Intangible output
2. Production and consumption take place simultaneously
3. Labour- and knowledge-intensive
4. Customer interaction generally high
5. Human element very important
6. Quality is perceived and difficult to measure
7. Rapid response time is usually necessary
8. Site of facility is extremely important

**Manufacturing Technology**
1. Tangible product
2. Products can be inventoried for later consumption
3. Capital asset-intensive
4. Little direct customer interaction
5. Human element may be less important
6. Quality is directly measured
7. Longer response time is acceptable
8. Site of facility is moderately important

| Service | Product and Service | Product |
|---|---|---|
| Airlines | Fast-food outlets | Soft drink companies |
| Hotels | Cosmetics | Steel companies |
| Consultants | Real estate | Automobile manufacturers |
| Health care | Stockbrokers | Mining corporations |
| Law firms | Retail stores | Food-processing plants |

**EXHIBIT 7.7**
**Differences between Manufacturing and Service Technologies**
Source: Based on F. F. Reichheld and W. E. Sasser, Jr., "Zero Defections: Quality Comes to Services," *Harvard Business Review* 68 (September/October 1990), 105–111; and David E. Bowen, Caren Siehl, and Benjamin Schneider, "A Framework for Analyzing Customer Service Orientations in Manufacturing," *Academy of Management Review 14* (1989), 75–95.

way that the quality of a tangible product can. Another characteristic that affects customer satisfaction and perception of quality service is rapid response time. A service must be provided when the customer wants and needs it. When you take a friend to dinner, you want to be seated and served in a timely manner; you would not be very satisfied if the host or manager told you to come back tomorrow when there would be more tables or servers available to accommodate you.

The final defining characteristic of service technology is that site selection is often much more important than with manufacturing. Because services are intangible, they have to be located where the customer wants to be served. The next In Practice addresses the importance of not losing customer focus so that the organization is able to offer service in a timely way.

**In Practice**
**Home Depot**

Home Depot became the world's largest home improvement retailer largely through the service skills of its employees. It often hired former plumbers, carpenters, and other skilled tradespeople who understood the products and took pride in helping "do-it-yourselfers."

However, to cut costs in recent years, Home Depot began hiring more part-time employees and established a salary cap that made the work less appealing to experienced and skilled workers. In addition, managers began measuring every aspect of the stores' productivity, such as how long it took to unload shipments or how many extended warranties each employee sold weekly. What got overlooked, though, was how well employees were providing service. Customers began to complain that they couldn't find anyone and if they could find someone, he or she was not knowledgeable enough to help them. Home Depot began to lose customers.

As a result, managers are hiring more full-time employees and instituting new training programs. The CEO even approached the founders of Home Depot for advice on how to restore its previous lustre.[66]

---

In reality, it is difficult to find organizations that reflect 100 percent service or 100 percent manufacturing characteristics. Some service firms take on characteristics of manufacturers, and vice versa. Many manufacturing firms are placing a greater emphasis on customer service to differentiate themselves and be more competitive. In addition, manufacturing organizations have departments such as purchasing, HR, and marketing that are based on service technology. For example, Lo-Pel Manufacturing, a family-owned company founded in 2001, located in Rosenort, Manitoba, not only manufactures earthmoving scrapers but also provides service support for its customers. According to Ken Rempel, designer of the scraper, "[If] anyone has a problem, we address it quickly and efficiently to reach a solution; that has built a lot of faith in our company."[67] On the other hand, organizations such as gas stations, stockbrokers, retail stores, and restaurants belong to the service sector, but the provision of a product is a significant part of the transaction. The vast majority of organizations involve some combination of products and services. The important point is that all organizations can be classified along a continuum that includes both manufacturing and service characteristics, as illustrated in Exhibit 7.7.

**New Directions in Services.** Service firms have always tended toward providing customized output—that is, providing exactly the service each customer wants and needs. When you visit a hairstylist, you don't automatically get the same cut the stylist gave the three previous clients. The stylist cuts your hair the way you request it. However, the trend toward mass customization that is revolutionizing manufacturing has had a significant impact on the service sector as well. Customer expectations of what constitutes good service are rising.[68] Service companies such as the Ritz-Carlton Hotels and Bell Canada use new technology to keep customers coming back. All Ritz-Carlton hotels are linked to a database filled with the preferences of half a million guests, allowing any desk clerk or bellhop to find out what your favourite wine is, whether you're allergic to feather pillows, and how many extra towels you want in your room.[69] At Bell Canada, much of its customer service is performed online but there are customer service representatives available as well.

The expectation for better service is also pushing service firms in industries from package delivery to banking to take a lesson from manufacturing. Japan Post, under pressure to cut a $191 million loss on operations, hired Toyota's Toshihiro Takahashi to help apply the Toyota Production System to the collection, sorting, and delivery of mail. In all, Takahashi's team came up with 370 improvements and reduced the post office's person-hours by 20 percent. The waste reduction is expected to cut costs by around $350 million a year.[70]

## ■ Designing the Service Organization

The feature of service technologies with a distinct influence on organizational structure and control systems is the need for technical core employees to be close to the customer.[71] The differences between service and product organizations necessitated by customer contact are summarized in Exhibit 7.8.

**EXHIBIT 7.8**
Configuration and Structural Characteristics of Service Organizations versus Product Organizations

|  | SERVICE | PRODUCT |
|---|---|---|
| **Structural Characteristic** | | |
| 1. Separate boundary roles | Few | Many |
| 2. Geographical dispersion | Much | Little |
| 3. Decision making | Decentralized | Centralized |
| 4. Formalization | Lower | Higher |
| **Human Resources** | | |
| 1. Employee skill level | Higher | Lower |
| 2. Skill emphasis | Interpersonal | Technical |

The impact of customer contact on organizational structure is reflected in the use of boundary roles and structural disaggregation.[72] Boundary roles are used extensively in manufacturing firms to handle customers and to reduce disruptions for the technical core. They are used less in service firms because a service is intangible and cannot be passed along by boundary spanners, so service customers must interact directly with technical employees, such as doctors or brokers.

A service firm deals in information and intangible outputs and does not need to be large. Its greatest economies are achieved through disaggregation into small units that may be located close to customers. Stockbrokers, doctors' clinics, consulting firms, and banks disperse their facilities into regional and local offices. Some quick service chains, such as Tim Hortons, are taking this a step further, selling coffee, muffins, and sandwiches anywhere people gather—war zones, airports, gas stations, university or college campuses, or street corners.

Manufacturing firms, on the other hand, tend to aggregate operations in a single area that has raw materials and an available workforce. A large manufacturing firm can take advantage of economies derived from expensive machinery and long production runs.

Service technology also influences internal organization characteristics used to direct and control the organization. For one thing, the skills of technical core employees typically need to be higher. These employees need enough knowledge and awareness to handle customer problems rather than just enough to perform mechanical tasks. Employees need social and interpersonal skills as well as technical skills.[73] Because of higher skills and structural dispersion, decision making often tends to be decentralized in service firms, and formalization tends to be low. In general, employees in service organizations have more freedom and discretion on the job. However, some service organizations, such as many fast-food chains, have set rules and procedures for customer service. The U.K. chain Pret a Manger hopes to differentiate itself in the fast-food market by taking a different approach.

**act!**

**Apply**

Describe a service organization that you know well. Does it apply the design attributes highlighted in Exhibit 7.8?

# In Practice

**Pret a Manger (Pret)**

"Would you like fries with that?" The standard line is rattled off by fast-food workers who have been taught to follow a script in serving customers. But at Pret, a fast-growing chain based in London, you won't hear any standard lines. Employees aren't given scripts for serving customers or pigeonholed into performing the same repetitive tasks all day long. Managers want people to let their own personalities come through in offering each customer the best service possible. "Our customers say, 'I like to be served by human beings,'" explains Ewan Stickley, head of employee training. London's *Sunday Times* has ranked Pret as one of the top 50 companies to work for in Britain—the only restaurant to make the cut. Pret turns over roughly £150 million a year and is working to make a 9 percent profit.

"Pret opened in London in 1986. College friends Sinclair and Julian made proper sandwiches using natural, preservative-free ingredients. The two of them had woefully little experience in the world of business. They created the sort of food they craved but couldn't find anywhere else."[74]

Pret a Manger (faux French for "ready to eat") operates 150 outlets in the United Kingdom and is expanding into the United States. "Nobody has ever gone to America, the home of fast food, with a concept that turned out to be a successful national chain. We think we can do that," says chairman and CEO Andrew Rolfe. Translating that confidence into success in the United States has been a struggle. To help make the transition, Pret has allied itself with a powerful partner— McDonald's. Some worry that McDonald's might corrupt the company's values and emphasis on fresh, healthy food and individualized service, but Rolfe believes he and his employees are up to the challenge.

Pret's concept is based on organizing a mass-market service business around innovation rather than standardization. The menu is based on salads, fresh-made sandwiches, hot soups, sushi, and a variety of yogurt parfaits and blended juices. Menu items are constantly changing, based on what sells and what customers want. Pret has built in a number of mechanisms for getting fast feedback. The CEO reviews customer and employee comments every Friday. Employees who send in the best ideas for changes to products or procedures can win up to $1,500. Managers spend one day each quarter working in a store to keep in touch with customers and see how their policies affect employees. In addition, "[Whenever] a customer calls or writes to congratulate a member of our staff for being helpful, professional or simply great, off goes a [solid silver custom-designed] Tiffany Star to the staff member. We are thrilled to have awarded hundreds and hundreds over the years."[75]

In its native England, Pret has been a huge hit. Pret supports dozens of charities helping the homeless by offering unsold sandwiches to them at the end of each day. The Pret Charity Run collects and distributes over 12,000 meals to the homeless every week of the year. Many charities collect directly from the Pret shops at the end of each day too.[76]

---

Understanding the nature of its service technology helps managers at Pret a Manger align strategy, structure, and management processes that are quite different from those for a product-based or traditional manufacturing technology. For example, the concept of separating complex tasks into a series of small jobs and exploiting economies of scale is a cornerstone of traditional manufacturing, but researchers have found that applying it to service organizations often does not work so well.[77] Some service firms have redesigned jobs to separate low- and high-customer contact activities, with more rules and standardization in the low-contact jobs. High-touch service jobs, like those at Pret a Manger, need more freedom and less control to satisfy customers.

E-commerce organizations also need to understand how to provide service that satisfies their customers. E-service is defined as "the initial landing on the home page until the requested service has been completed or the final product has been delivered and is *fit for use*."[78] If customers see value in the e-service, they are likely to make repeat purchases. One credit union, for example, offered a 0.25 percent discount to its customers if they applied online and provided a computer kiosk to make it easy to do so. The use of the credit union's e-service rose dramatically as a result.[79] Recent research suggests that consistency is an important element to e-service and customer retention as "[consistency] reinforces e-loyalty."[80]

In addition to e-commerce, f-commerce organizations are starting to develop; those that do commerce within Facebook. Companies such as Best Buy and Proctor & Gamble have a commerce site within Facebook so that consumers can buy their products without leaving Facebook.[81] There are three types of f-commerce; (1) on Facebook (f-stores, credits), (2) on the Web (using Facebook open-graph/social plug-ins/FB storefronts with web stores), and (3) in-store (using Facebook open-graph/social plug-ins/deals for bricks-and-mortar retail). While f-commerce organizations are still quite new, some estimate that that they will soon account for 10 to 15 percent of consumer spending.[82]

Understanding service technology is important for manufacturing firms, too, especially as they put greater emphasis on customer service. Managers can use these concepts and ideas to strengthen their company's service orientation. Similarly, service organizations continue to automate their processes through machines such as self-service lanes in grocery stores. AVT Inc., a vending machine company, is now designing a fully automated gas station that will provide all services without any attendant.[83]

Now let's turn to another perspective on technology, that of production activities within specific organizational departments. Departments often have characteristics similar to those of service technology, providing services to other departments within the organization.

**Compare**

Compare the service challenges between e-commerce and in-person service organizations.

# Noncore Departmental Technology

This section shifts to the department level of analysis for departments not necessarily within the technical core. Each department in an organization has a production process that consists of a distinct technology. General Motors has departments for engineering, R&D, HR, advertising, quality control, finance, and dozens of other functions. This section analyzes the nature of noncore departmental technology and its relationship with departmental structure.

The framework that has had the greatest impact on the understanding of departmental technologies was developed by Charles Perrow.[84] Perrow's model has been useful for a broad range of technologies, which made it ideal for research into departmental activities.

## ■ Variety

Perrow specified two dimensions of departmental activities that were relevant to organizational structure and process. The first is the number of exceptions in the work. This refers to **task variety**, which is the frequency of unexpected and novel events that occur in the conversion process. Task variety concerns whether work processes are performed the same way every time or differ from time to time as employees transform the organization's inputs into outputs.[85] When individuals encounter a large number of unexpected situations, with frequent problems, variety is considered high. When there are few problems, and when day-to-day job requirements are repetitious, technology contains little variety. Variety in departments can range from repeating a single act, such as on a traditional assembly line, to working on a series of unrelated problems or projects.

## ■ Analyzability

The second dimension of technology concerns the **analyzability** of work activities. When the conversion process is analyzable, the work can be reduced to mechanical steps and participants can follow an objective, computational procedure to solve problems. Problem solution may involve the use of standard procedures, such as instructions and manuals, or technical knowledge, such as that in a textbook. On the other hand, some work is not analyzable; when problems arise, it is difficult to identify the correct solution. There is no store of techniques or procedures to tell a person exactly what to do. The cause of or solution to a problem is not clear, so employees rely on accumulated experience, intuition, and judgment. Philippos Poulos, a tone regulator at Steinway & Sons, has an unanalyzable technology. Tone regulators carefully check each piano's hammers to ensure they produce the proper Steinway sound.[86] These quality-control tasks require years of experience and practice; standard procedures will not tell a person how to do such tasks.

## Framework

The two dimensions of technology and examples of departmental activities on Perrow's framework are shown in Exhibit 7.9. The dimensions of variety and analyzability form the basis for four major categories of technology: routine, craft, engineering, and nonroutine.

**Routine technologies** are characterized by little task variety and the use of objective, computational procedures. The tasks are formalized and standardized. Examples include an automobile assembly line and a bank teller department.

**Craft technologies** are characterized by a fairly stable stream of activities, but the conversion process is not analyzable or well understood. Tasks require extensive

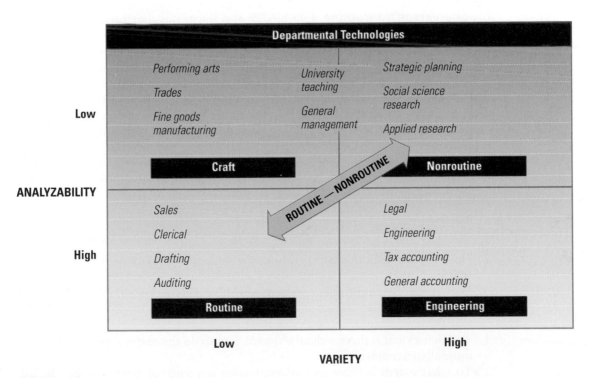

**EXHIBIT 7.9**
Framework for Department Technologies
Source: Copyright © 1978, by The Regents of the University of California. Adapted from Richard Daft and Norman Macintosh, "A New Approach to Design and Use of Management Information," *California Management Review*, Vol. 21, No. 1. 82–92. By permission of The Regents.

training and experience because employees respond to intangible factors on the basis of wisdom, intuition, and experience. Although advances in machine technologies seem to have reduced the number of craft technologies in organizations, craft technologies are still important. For example, steel furnace engineers continue to mix steel based on intuition and experience, pattern makers at apparel firms convert rough designers' sketches into saleable garments, and teams of writers for television series such as *CSI* or *DeGrassi* convert ideas into story lines.

**Engineering technologies** tend to be complex because there is substantial variety in the tasks performed. However, the various activities are usually handled on the basis of established formulas, procedures, and techniques. Employees normally refer to a well-developed body of knowledge to handle problems. Engineering and accounting tasks usually fall in this category.

**Nonroutine technologies** have high task variety, and the conversion process is not analyzable or well understood. In nonroutine technology, a great deal of effort is devoted to analyzing problems and activities. Several equally acceptable options typically can be found. Experience and technical knowledge are used to solve problems and perform the work. Basic research, strategic planning, and other work that involves new projects and unexpected problems are nonroutine. The complex biotechnology industry also represents a nonroutine technology. Breakthroughs in understanding metabolism and physiology at a cellular level depend on highly trained employees who use their experience and intuition as well as scientific knowledge. A scientist manipulating the chemical rungs on a DNA molecule has been compared to a musician playing variations on a theme.[87]

**Routine versus Nonroutine.** Exhibit 7.9 also illustrates that variety and analyzability can be combined into a single dimension of technology. This dimension is called routine versus nonroutine technology, and it is the diagonal line in Exhibit 7.9. The analyzability and variety dimensions are often correlated in departments, meaning that technologies high in variety tend to be low in analyzability, and technologies low in variety tend to be analyzable. Departments can be evaluated along a single dimension of routine versus nonroutine that combines both analyzability and variety, which is a useful shorthand measure for analyzing departmental technology.

The following questions show how departmental technology can be analyzed for determining its placement on Perrow's technology framework in Exhibit 7.9.[88] Employees normally circle a number on a seven-point scale response to each question.

*Variety:*

1. To what extent would you say your work is routine?
2. Do most people in this unit do about the same job in the same way most of the time?
3. Do you think unit members perform repetitive activities when doing their jobs?

*Analyzability:*

1. To what extent is there a clearly known way to do the major types of work you normally encounter?
2. To what extent is there an understandable sequence of steps that can be followed in doing your work?
3. To do your work, to what extent can you actually rely on established procedures and practices?

**Think**

Think about Perrow's dimensions. What sort of department would make the best use of your talents?

If answers to the above questions indicate high scores for analyzability and low scores for variety, the department would have a routine technology. If the opposite occurs, the technology would be nonroutine. Low variety and low analyzability indicate a craft technology, and high variety and high analyzability indicate an engineering technology. As a practical matter, most departments fit somewhere along the diagonal and can be most easily characterized as routine or nonroutine.

## Department Design

Once the nature of a department's technology has been identified, the appropriate structure can be determined. Department technology tends to be associated with a cluster of departmental characteristics, such as the skill level of employees, formalization, and pattern of communication. Definite patterns exist in the relationship between work-unit technology and structural characteristics, which are associated with departmental performance.[89] Key relationships between technology and other dimensions of departments are described in this section and are summarized in Exhibit 7.10.

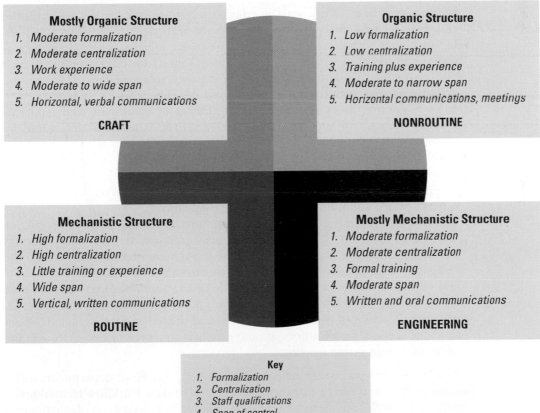

**Mostly Organic Structure**
1. Moderate formalization
2. Moderate centralization
3. Work experience
4. Moderate to wide span
5. Horizontal, verbal communications

**CRAFT**

**Organic Structure**
1. Low formalization
2. Low centralization
3. Training plus experience
4. Moderate to narrow span
5. Horizontal communications, meetings

**NONROUTINE**

**Mechanistic Structure**
1. High formalization
2. High centralization
3. Little training or experience
4. Wide span
5. Vertical, written communications

**ROUTINE**

**Mostly Mechanistic Structure**
1. Moderate formalization
2. Moderate centralization
3. Formal training
4. Moderate span
5. Written and oral communications

**ENGINEERING**

**Key**
1. Formalization
2. Centralization
3. Staff qualifications
4. Span of control
5. Communication and coordination

**EXHIBIT 7.10**
Relationship of Department Technology to Structural and Management Characteristics

The overall structure of departments may be characterized as either organic or mechanistic. Routine technologies are associated with a mechanistic structure and processes, with formal rules and rigid management processes. Nonroutine technologies are associated with an organic structure, and department management is more flexible and free flowing. The specific design characteristics of formalization, decentralization, worker skill level, span of control, and communication and coordination vary, depending on work-unit technology.

1. *Formalization*. Routine technology is characterized by standardization and division of labour into small tasks that are governed by formal rules and procedures. For nonroutine tasks, the structure is less formal and less standardized. When variety is high, as in a research department, fewer activities are covered by formal procedures.[90]

2. *Decentralization*. In routine technologies, most decision making about task activities is centralized to management.[91] In engineering technologies, employees with technical training tend to acquire moderate decision authority because technical knowledge is important to task accomplishment. Production employees who have long experience obtain decision authority in craft technologies because they know how to respond to problems. Decentralization to employees is greatest in nonroutine settings, where many decisions are made by employees.

3. *Worker skill level*. Work staff in routine technologies typically require little education or experience, which is congruent with repetitious work activities. In work units with greater variety, staff are more skilled and often have formal training in technical schools or universities. Training for craft activities, which are less analyzable, is more likely to be through job experience. Nonroutine activities require both formal education and job experience.[92]

4. *Span of control*. Span of control is the number of employees who report to a single manager or supervisor. This characteristic is normally influenced by departmental technology. The more complex and nonroutine the task, the more problems arise in which the supervisor becomes involved. Although the span of control may be influenced by other factors, such as skill level of employees, it typically should be smaller for complex tasks because on such tasks the supervisor and subordinate must interact frequently.[93]

5. *Communication and coordination*. Communication activity and frequency increase as task variety increases.[94] Frequent problems require more information sharing to solve problems and ensure proper completion of activities. The direction of communication is typically horizontal in nonroutine work units and vertical in routine work units.[95] The form of communication varies by task analyzability.[96] When tasks are highly analyzable, statistical and written forms of communication (memos, reports, rules, and procedures) are frequent. When tasks are less analyzable, information typically is conveyed face-to-face, over the telephone, or in group meetings.

Two important points are reflected in Exhibit 7.10. First, departments differ from one another and can be categorized according to their workflow technology.[97] Second, structural and management processes differ based on departmental technology. Managers should design their departments so that requirements based on technology can be met. Design problems are most visible when the design is clearly inconsistent with technology. Studies have found that when structure and communication characteristics did not reflect technology, departments tended to be less effective.[98] Employees could not communicate with the frequency needed to solve problems. Consider how the design characteristics of Aravind Eye Hospital contribute to a smoothly functioning department.

**In Practice**
**Aravind Eye Hospital (Aravind)**

In 1976, Dr. Govindappa Venkataswamy founded a 12-bed eye hospital in Madurai, India. Now, his family and siblings run five hospitals that perform more than 180,000 operations annually. Seventy percent of the patients cannot pay while the remainder seek Dr. Venkataswamy's services as he was a cataract surgeon of international renown.

When Dr. Venkataswamy started the hospital, there were about eight ophthalmologists in India and 20 million people with cataracts. Now, Aravind Eye Hospital is the world's largest single provider of eye surgery in the world. In 1998, the Aravind hospitals saw 1.2 million outpatients and performed 183,000 cataract operations. In 2005, the five hospitals performed 200,000 surgeries and treated 2 million people. Although Dr. Venkataswamy died in 2006, his work continues.[99]

In addition to the hospitals, Aravind has its own laboratory, Aurolab, which pioneered the development of high-quality, low-cost intraocular lenses. Aurolab produces 750,000 lenses annually for Aravind and other organizations.

Seeing 400 patients is a slow day at Aravind. The hospital grounds are full with the families and friends of the patients. "[A] slow day at Aravind would drive most [North] American hospital officials mad."[100] It costs Aravind $10 for one cataract surgery. Two or more patients are put in the same operating theatre so that the surgeon can go easily from patient to patient. Each patient in the theatre is prepped and ready for the surgery. Avarind's surgeons have created equipment that allows them to swivel around to work on the next patient as soon as they have performed the ten-minute surgery on their first patient. Post-op patients are wheeled out and new patients are wheeled in. There have been no problems with infections.

No one at Aravind uses the term *the poor*. According to Dr. Venkataswamy, "[To] think of certain people as 'the poor' puts you in a superior position, blinds you to the ways in which you are poor—and in the West there are many such ways: emotionally and spiritually, for example. You have comforts in [North] America, but are afraid of each other."[101]

# Workflow Interdependence among Departments

So far, this chapter has explored how organization and department technologies influence structural design. The final characteristic of technology that influences structure is called interdependence. **Interdependence** means the extent to which departments depend on each other for resources or materials to accomplish their tasks. Low interdependence means that departments can do their work independently of each other and have little need for interaction, consultation, or exchange of materials. High interdependence means departments must constantly exchange resources.

## Types

James Thompson defined three types of interdependence that influence organizational structure.[102] These interdependencies are illustrated in Exhibit 7.11 and are discussed in the following sections.

**EXHIBIT 7.11**
Thompson's
Classification of
Interdependence
and Management
Implications

| Form of Interdependence | Demands on Horizontal Communication, Decision Making | Types of Coordination Required | Priority for Locating Units Close Together |
|---|---|---|---|
| **Pooled (bank)**  Clients | Low communication | Standardization, rules, procedures<br><br>Divisional structure | Low |
| **Sequential (assembly line)**  Client | Medium communication | Plans, schedules, feedback<br><br>Task forces | Medium |
| **Reciprocal (hospital)** 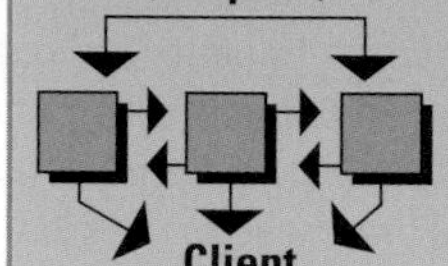 Client | High communication | Mutual adjustment, cross-departmental meetings, teamwork<br><br>Horizontal structure | High |

**Pooled.** **Pooled interdependence** is the lowest form of interdependence among departments. In this form, work does not flow between units. Each department is part of the organization and contributes to the common good of the organization, but works independently. Subway restaurants or branch banks are examples of pooled interdependence. An outlet in Kelowna need not interact with an outlet in Peterborough. Pooled interdependence may be associated with the relationships within a divisional structure, defined in Chapter 3. Divisions or branches share financial resources from a common pool, and the success of each division contributes to the success of the overall organization.

Thompson proposed that pooled interdependence would exist in firms with what he called a mediating technology. A **mediating technology** provides products or services that mediate or link clients from the external environment and, in so doing, allows each department to work independently. Banks, brokerage firms, and real estate offices all mediate between buyers and sellers, but the offices work independently within the organization.

The management implications associated with pooled interdependence are quite simple. Thompson argued that managers should use rules and procedures to standardize activities across departments. Each department should use the same procedures and financial statements so the outcomes of all departments can be measured and pooled. Very little day-to-day coordination is required among units.

**Sequential.** When interdependence is of serial form, with parts produced in one department becoming inputs to another department, it is called **sequential interdependence**.

The first department must perform correctly for the second department to perform correctly. This is a higher level of interdependence than pooled interdependence, because departments exchange resources and depend on others to perform well. Sequential interdependence creates a greater need for horizontal mechanisms such as integrators or task forces.

Sequential interdependence occurs in what Thompson called **long-linked technology**, which "refers to the combination in one organization of successive stages of production; each stage of production uses as its inputs the production of the preceding stage and produces inputs for the following stage."[103] An example of sequential interdependence comes from the shipbuilding industry. Until recently, ship designers made patterns and moulds out of paper and plywood, which were passed on to assembly. Mistakes in measurements or pattern mix-ups, though, often caused errors in the cutting and assembly process, leading to delays and increased costs. Naval architect Filippo Cali created a complex software program that serves as a bridge between design and assembly. The software eliminates the need for paper and plywood moulds by putting that crucial part of the design process in a computer program.[104] Another example of sequential interdependence would be an automobile assembly line, which must have all the parts it needs, such as engines, steering mechanisms, and tires, to keep production rolling.

The management requirements for sequential interdependence are more demanding than those for pooled interdependence. Coordination among the linked plants or departments is required. Since the interdependence implies a one-way flow of materials, extensive planning and scheduling are generally needed. Department B needs to know what to expect from Department A so both can perform effectively. Some day-to-day communication among plants or departments is also needed to handle unexpected problems and exceptions that arise.

**Reciprocal.** The highest level of interdependence is **reciprocal interdependence**. This exists when the output of operation A is the input to operation B, and the output of operation B is the input back again to operation A. The outputs of departments influence those departments in reciprocal fashion.

Reciprocal interdependence tends to occur in organizations with what Thompson called **intensive technologies**, which provide a variety of products or services in combination to a client. Hospitals, such as Aravind (described in the In Practice), are an excellent example because they provide coordinated services to patients. A patient may move back and forth between X-ray, surgery, and physical therapy as needed to be cured. A firm developing new products, such as IDEO, is another example. Intense coordination is needed between design, engineering, manufacturing, and marketing to combine all their resources to suit the customer's product need.

Management requirements are greatest in the case of reciprocal interdependence. Because reciprocal interdependence requires that departments work together intimately and be closely coordinated, a horizontal structure may be appropriate. The structure must allow for frequent horizontal communication and adjustment. Extensive planning is required, but plans will not anticipate or solve all problems. Daily interaction and mutual adjustment among departments are required. Managers from several departments are jointly involved in face-to-face coordination, teamwork, and decision making. Reciprocal interdependence is the most complex interdependence for organizations to handle.

## Structural Priority

As indicated in Exhibit 7.11, because decision making, communication, and coordination problems are greatest for reciprocal interdependence, reciprocal interdependence should receive first priority in organizational structure. New product development is one area of reciprocal interdependence that is of growing concern to managers as companies face increasing pressure to get new products to market quickly. Many firms are revamping the design–manufacturing relationship by closely integrating CAD and CAM technologies discussed earlier in this chapter.[105] Activities that are reciprocally interdependent should be grouped close together in the organization so managers have easy access to one another for mutual adjustment. These units should report to the same person on the organizational chart and should be physically close so the time and effort for coordination can be minimized. A horizontal structure, with linked sets of teams working on core processes, can provide the close coordination needed to support reciprocal interdependence. Poor coordination will result in poor performance for the organization. If reciprocally interdependent units are not located close together, the organization should design mechanisms for coordination, such as daily meetings between departments or an intranet to facilitate communication. The next priority is given to sequential interdependencies, and finally to pooled interdependencies.

This strategy of organizing keeps the communication channels short where coordination is most critical to organizational success. For example, the Toronto facility of Celestica underwent a significant organizational redesign with the objective of reducing costs, accelerating the rate of new product introduction, and increasing response timeliness and capability. As a result of the redesign, there have been considerable performance improvements; productivity has doubled, manufacturing cycle times were reduced, and quality has improved.[106]

## Structural Implications

Most organizations experience various levels of interdependence, and structure can be designed to fit these needs.[107] In a manufacturing firm, new product development entails reciprocal interdependence among the design, engineering, purchasing, manufacturing, and sales departments. Perhaps a horizontal structure or crossfunctional teams could be used to handle the back-and-forth flow of information and resources. Once a product is designed, its actual manufacture would be sequential interdependence, with a flow of goods from one department to another, such as among purchasing, inventory, production control, manufacturing, and assembly. The actual ordering and delivery of products is pooled interdependence, with warehouses working independently. Customers could place an order with the nearest facility, which would not require coordination among warehouses, except in unusual cases such as a stock outage.

| | BASEBALL | FOOTBALL | BASKETBALL |
|---|---|---|---|
| Interdependence | Pooled | Sequential | Reciprocal |
| Physical dispersion of players | High | Medium | Low |
| Coordination | Rules that govern the sport | Game plan and position roles | Mutual adjustment and shared responsibility |
| Key management roles | Select players and develop their skills | Prepare and execute game | Influence flow of game |

**EXHIBIT 7.12**
Relationships among Interdependence and Other Characteristics of Team Play

Source: Based on William Pasmore, Carol E. Francis, and Jeffrey Haldeman, "Sociotechnical Systems: A North American Reflection on the Empirical Studies of the 70s," *Human Relations 35* (1982), 1179–1204.

**In Practice**
**Sports Teams**

A major difference between baseball, football, and basketball is the interdependence among players. Baseball is low in interdependence, football is medium, and basketball represents the highest player interdependence. The relationships among interdependence and other characteristics of team play are illustrated in Exhibit 7.12.

In baseball, interdependence among team players is low and can be defined as pooled. Each member acts independently, taking a turn at bat and playing his or her own position. When interaction does occur, it is between only two or three players, as in a double play. Players are physically dispersed, and the rules of the game are the primary means of coordinating players. Players practise and develop their skills individually, such as by taking batting practice and undergoing physical conditioning. Management's job is to select good players. If each player is successful as an individual, the team should win.

In football, interdependence among players is higher and tends to be sequential. The line first blocks the opponents to enable the backs to run or pass. Plays are performed sequentially from first down to third down. Physical dispersion is medium, which allows players to operate as a coordinated unit. The primary mechanism for coordinating players is developing a game plan along with rules that govern the behaviour of team members. Each player has an assignment that fits with other assignments, and management designs the game plan to achieve victory.

In basketball, interdependence tends to be reciprocal. The game is free flowing, and the division of labour is less precise than in other sports. Each player is involved in both offence and defence, handles the ball, and attempts to score. The ball flows back and forth among players. Team members interact in a dynamic flow to achieve victory. Management skills involve the ability to influence this dynamic process, either by substituting players or by working the ball into certain areas. Players must learn to adapt to the flow of the game and to one another as events unfold.

Interdependence among players is a primary factor explaining the difference among the three sports. Baseball is organized around an autonomous individual, football around groups that are sequentially interdependent, and basketball around the free flow of reciprocal players.[108]

## Impact of Technology on Job Design

So far, this chapter has described models for analyzing how manufacturing, service, and department technologies influence structure and management processes. The relationship between a new technology and organization seems to follow a pattern, beginning with immediate effects on the content of jobs followed (after a longer period) by impact on design of the organization. The ultimate impact of technology on employees can be partially understood through the concepts of job design and sociotechnical systems.

## ■ Job Design

**Job design** includes the assignment of goals and tasks to be accomplished by employees. Managers may consciously change job design to improve productivity or worker motivation. For example, when workers are involved in performing boring, repetitive tasks, managers may introduce **job rotation**, which means moving employees from job to job to give them a greater variety of tasks. However, managers may also unconsciously influence job design through the introduction of new technologies, which can change how jobs are done and the very nature of jobs.[109] Managers should understand how the introduction of a new technology may affect employees' jobs. The common theme of new technologies in the workplace is that they in some way substitute machinery for human labour in transforming inputs into outputs. Automated teller machines (ATMs) have replaced thousands of human bank tellers, for example.

In addition to actually replacing human workers, technology may have several different effects on the human jobs that remain. Research has indicated that mass-production technologies tend to produce **job simplification**, which means that the variety and difficulty of tasks performed by a single person are reduced. The consequence is boring, repetitive jobs that generally provide little satisfaction. More advanced technology, on the other hand, tends to cause **job enrichment**, meaning that the job provides greater responsibility, recognition, and opportunities for growth and development. These technologies create a greater need for employee training and education because workers need higher-level skills and greater competence to master their tasks. For example, ATMs took most of the routine tasks (deposits and withdrawals) away from bank tellers and left them with the more complex tasks that require higher-level skills. Studies of flexible manufacturing found that it produces three noticeable results for employees: more opportunities for intellectual mastery and enhanced cognitive skills for workers; more worker responsibility for results; and greater interdependence among workers, enabling more social interaction and the development of teamwork and coordination skills.[110] Flexible manufacturing technology may also contribute to **job enlargement**, which is an expansion of the number of different tasks performed by an employee. Fewer workers are needed with the new technology, and each employee has to be able to perform a greater number and variety of tasks.

With advanced technology, workers have to keep learning new skills because technology is changing so rapidly. Advances in information technology are having a significant effect on jobs in the service industry, including doctors' offices and medical clinics, law firms, financial planners, and libraries. Workers may find that their jobs change almost daily because of new software programs, increased use of the Internet, and other advances in information technology.

Advanced technology does not always have a positive effect on employees, but research findings in general are encouraging, suggesting that jobs for workers are enriched rather than simplified, engaging their higher mental capacities, offering opportunities for learning and growth, and providing greater job satisfaction.

# ■ Sociotechnical Systems

The **sociotechnical systems approach** recognizes the interaction of technical and human needs in effective job design, combining the needs of people with the organization's need for technical efficiency. The *socio* portion of the approach refers to the people and groups that work in organizations and how work is organized and coordinated. The *technical* portion refers to the materials, tools, machines, and processes used to transform organizational inputs into outputs.

Exhibit 7.13 illustrates the three primary components of the sociotechnical systems model.[111] The social system includes all human elements—such as individual and team behaviours, organizational culture, management practices, and degree of communication openness—that can influence the performance of work. The technical system refers to the type of production technology, the level of interdependence, the complexity of tasks, and so forth. The goal of the sociotechnical systems approach is to design the organization for **joint optimization**, which means that an organization functions best only when the social and technical systems are designed to fit the needs of one another. Designing the organization to meet human needs while ignoring the technical systems, or changing technology to improve efficiency while ignoring human needs, may inadvertently cause performance problems. The sociotechnical systems approach attempts to find a balance between what workers want and need and the technical requirements of the organization's production system.[112]

One example comes from a museum that installed a closed-circuit TV system. Rather than having several guards patrolling the museum and grounds, the television could easily be monitored by a single guard. Although the technology saved money because only one guard was needed per shift, it led to unexpected performance problems. Guards had previously enjoyed the social interaction provided by patrolling; monitoring a closed-circuit television led to alienation and boredom. When a federal agency did an 18-month test of the system, only 5 percent of several thousand experimental covert intrusions were detected by the guard.[113] The system was inadequate because human needs were not taken into account.

**EXHIBIT 7.13**
Sociotechnical Systems Model

Source: Based on T. Cummings, "Self-Regulating Work Groups: A Socio-Technical Synthesis," *Academy of Management Review* 3 (1978), 625–634; Don Hellriegel, John W. Slocum, and Richard W. Woodman, *Organizational Behavior*, 8th ed. (Cincinnati, Ohio: South-Western, 1998), 492; and Gregory B. Northcraft and Margaret A. Neale, *Organizational Behavior: A Management Challenge*, 2nd ed. (Fort Worth, Tex.: The Dryden Press, 1994), 551.

Sociotechnical principles evolved from the work of the Tavistock Institute, a research organization in England, during the 1950s and 60s.[114] There are 11 core principles that underlie sociotechnical systems thinking and design. They are

1. *Compatibility*—the process used to redesign must be compatible with its objectives.
2. *Minimum critical specification*—design should specify no more than is necessary.
3. *Variance control*—control any variances not removed through technology at the point closest to their origin.
4. *Boundary location*—locate boundaries so that a team can regulate itself.
5. *Information flow*—have information go first to the point of action.
6. *Power and authority*—empower employees.
7. *Multifunctional/multiskills*—each team and each person should have more than one function or skill.
8. *Support congruence*—design systems of social support to reinforce the behaviours that the organizational structure is designed to elicit.
9. *Design and human values*—design the organization to achieve a high quality of working life.
10. *Bridging the transition*—minimize stressors during redesign.
11. *Incompletion*—design is an iterative process.[115]

## In Practice
### General Electric at Bromont, Québec (Bromont)

The Bromont plant began operations in 1983; it manufactures compressor airfoils for aircraft engines, led by the CFM56, the most widely used commercial jet engine. The plant's mandates are to (1) use innovative technologies and manufacturing processes; (2) achieve cost superiority, (3) maintain optimum quality, and (4) optimize both its technical and social systems. Its mission statement states, "Manufacture Six Sigma quality blades at lowest cost."[116]*

Bromont's manufacturing process of more than 100 steps involves precision forging, grinding, and turning, up to tolerances of one 1/500th of a centimetre. The process is a very technical one. Once the product is manufactured, it is shipped to a plant in the United States where the jet engines are assembled. Bromont uses a variety of automated systems in the manufacture of the compressor airfoils. They include robots, robotic vision systems, programmable controllers, five axis CNC (computer numerical control) milling machines, and updated quality and maintenance information online.

The plant's design was based on core values that focus on participation, personal development, social climate and structure, justice, family and community involvement, and organizational renewal. The plant was structured around five production businesses, each of which represents one of the technologies used in the manufacturing process. They are forging, pinch and roll, vanes, small rotors, and large rotors. The first two involve forming the product and the latter three involve machining the product.

Bromont has three levels of hierarchy: production teams of operators in each business; supervisory teams for each business and support teams for the plant as a whole; and the senior management team. The plant has various standing committees to manage plant-wide issues. They include committees to manage the gain-sharing system, social activities, safety procedures, and communications. Bromont is guided by a steering committee, which comprises senior representatives from operations.

The plant has been seen as a model plant as it has had stellar productivity rates and has produced high net income for GE. In 2005, GE invested further in Bromont, creating 100 more jobs to bring the total number of employees to more than 700. According to Philippe Simonato, Bromont's plant manager, "[this] new production mandate for more than 200,000 airfoils a year is an acknowledgement of the exceptional quality of the work done in Bromont."[117]

*Armstrong, A. (1993) Pay for Knowledge and Skill Systems: A Multilevel Exploratory Investigation, Doctoral Dissertation, University of Toronto; Normand Charron, HR Manager at General Electronic, Bromont, Quebec (2008), Personal communication with text researcher, April 17, 2008. Used with permission.

The GE plant at Bromont is one of the world's best examples of the sociotechnical systems principles in practice. Examples of organizational change using sociotechnical systems principles have occurred in numerous organizations, including General Motors, Volvo, Celestica, and Procter & Gamble.[118] Although there have been failures, in many of these applications the joint optimization of changes in technology and structure to meet the needs of people also improved efficiency, performance, safety, quality, absenteeism, and turnover. In some cases, work design was not the most efficient based on technical and scientific principles, but worker involvement and commitment more than made up for the difference. Thus, once again research shows that new technologies need not have a negative impact on workers, because the technology often requires higher-level mental and social skills and can be organized to encourage the involvement and commitment of employees, thereby benefiting both the employee and the organization.

The sociotechnical systems principle that people should be viewed as resources with much potential and provided with appropriate skills, meaningful work, and suitable rewards becomes even more important in today's world of growing technological complexity.[119] One study of paper manufacturers found that organizations that put too much faith in machines and technology and pay little attention to the appropriate management of people do not achieve advances in productivity and flexibility. Today's most successful companies strive to find the right mix of machines, computer systems, and people, and the most effective way to coordinate them.[120]

Although many principles of sociotechnical systems theory are still valid, current scholars and researchers are also arguing for an expansion of the approach to capture the dynamic nature of today's organizations, the chaotic environment, and the shift from routine to nonroutine jobs brought about by advances in technology.[121]

## Summary and Interpretation

This chapter reviewed several frameworks and key research findings on the topic of organizational technology. The potential importance of technology as a factor in organizational structure was discovered during the 1960s. Since then, a flurry of research activity has been undertaken to understand more precisely the relationship of technology to other characteristics of organizations.

Five ideas in the technology literature stand out. The first is Woodward's research into manufacturing technology. Woodward went into organizations and collected practical data on technology characteristics, organizational structure, and management systems. She found clear relationships between technology and structure in high-performing organizations. Her findings are so clear that managers can analyze their own organizations on the same dimensions of technology and structure. In addition, technology and structure can be co-aligned with organizational strategy to meet changing needs and provide new competitive advantages.

The second important idea is that service technologies differ in a systematic way from manufacturing technologies. Service technologies are characterized by intangible outcomes and direct client involvement in the production process. Service firms do not have the fixed, machine-based technologies that appear in manufacturing organizations; hence, organizational design often differs as well. E-commerce and f-commerce organizations present new service challenges.

The third significant idea is Perrow's framework applied to department technologies. Understanding the variety and analyzability of a technology tells you about the management style, structure, and process that should characterize that department. Routine technologies are characterized by mechanistic structure and nonroutine technologies by organic structure. Applying the wrong management system to a department will result in dissatisfaction and reduced efficiency.

The fourth important idea is interdependence among departments. The extent to which departments depend on each other for materials, information, or other resources determines the amount of coordination required between them. As interdependence increases, demands on the organization for coordination increase. Organizational design must allow for the correct amount of communication and coordination to handle interdependence across departments.

The fifth important idea is that new flexible manufacturing systems are being adopted by organizations and affecting organizational design. For the most part, the impact is positive, with shifts toward more organic structures both on the shop floor and in the management hierarchy. These technologies replace routine jobs, give employees more autonomy, produce more challenging jobs, encourage teamwork, and let the organization be more flexible and responsive. The new technologies are enriching jobs to the point where organizations are happier places to work.

Several principles of sociotechnical systems theory, which attempts to design the technical and human aspects of an organization to fit one another, are increasingly important as advances in technology alter the nature of jobs and social interaction in today's organizations.

## ■ Key Concepts

analyzability, p. 272
continuous process production, p. 256
core technology, p. 252
craft technologies, p. 273
engineering technologies, p. 274
flexible manufacturing systems, p. 260
intensive technologies, p. 279
interdependence, p. 277
job design, p. 282
job enlargement, p. 282
job enrichment, p. 282
job rotation, p. 282
job simplification, p. 282
joint optimization, p. 283
large-batch production, p. 256
lean manufacturing, p. 261

long-linked technology, p. 279
mass customization, p. 263
mediating technology, p. 278
noncore technology, p. 253
nonroutine technologies, p. 274
pooled interdependence, p. 278
reciprocal interdependence, p. 279
routine technologies, p. 273
sequential interdependence, p. 278
service technology, p. 267
small-batch production, p. 255
sociotechnical systems approach, p. 283
task variety, p. 272
technical complexity, p. 255
technology, p. 251

## ■ Discussion Questions

1. Where would your university or college department be located on Perrow's technology framework? Look for the underlying variety and analyzability characteristics when making your assessment. Would a department devoted exclusively to teaching be put in a different quadrant from a department devoted exclusively to research?

2. Explain Thompson's levels of interdependence. Identify an example of each level of interdependence in the university or college setting. What kinds of coordination mechanisms should an administration develop to handle each level of interdependence?

3. Describe Woodward's classification of organizational technologies. Explain why each of the three technology groups is related differently to organizational structure and management processes.

4. What relationships did Woodward discover between supervisor span of control and technological complexity?

5. How do flexible manufacturing and lean manufacturing differ from other manufacturing technologies? Why are these new approaches needed in today's environment?

6. What is a service technology? Are different types of service technologies likely to be associated with different structures? Explain.

7. Mass customization of products has become a common approach in manufacturing organizations. Discuss ways in which mass customization can be applied to service firms as well.

8. In what primary ways does the design of service firms typically differ from that of product firms? Why?

9. A top executive claimed that top-level management is a craft technology because the work contains intangibles, such as handling people, interpreting the environment, and coping with unusual situations that have to be learned through experience. If this is true, is it appropriate to teach management in a business school? Does teaching management from a textbook assume that the manager's job is analyzable, and hence that formal training rather than experience is most important?

10. In which quadrant of Perrow's framework would a mass-production technology be placed? Where would small-batch and continuous process technologies be placed? Why? Would Perrow's framework lead to the same recommendation about organic versus mechanistic structures that Woodward made? Why?

11. To what extent does the development of new technologies simplify and routinize the jobs of employees? How can new technology lead to job enlargement? Discuss.

12. Describe the sociotechnical systems model. Why might some managers oppose a sociotechnical systems approach?

## ■ Chapter 7 Workbook: Bistro Technology*

You will be analyzing the technology used in three different restaurants—McDonald's, Subway, and a typical family-owned restaurant. Your instructor will tell you whether to do this assignment as individuals or in a group.

You must visit all three restaurants and infer how the work is done, according to the following criteria. You are not allowed to interview any employees, but instead you will be an observer. Take lots of notes when you are there.

| Criteria | McDonald's | Subway | Family-owned Restaurant |
|---|---|---|---|
| Organization goals: Speed, service, atmosphere, etc. | | | |
| Authority structure | | | |
| Type of technology using Woodward's model | | | |
| Organizational structure: Mechanistic or organic? | | | |
| Team versus individual: Do people work together or alone? | | | |

*(Continued)*

| Criteria | McDonald's | Subway | Family-owned Restaurant |
|---|---|---|---|
| Interdependence: How do employees depend on each other? | | | |
| Tasks: Routine versus nonroutine | | | |
| Specialization of tasks by employees | | | |
| Standardization: How varied are tasks and products? | | | |
| Expertise required: Technical versus social | | | |
| Decision making: Centralized versus decentralized | | | |

## Questions

1. Is the technology used the best one for each restaurant, considering its goals and environment?
2. From the preceding data, determine if the structure and other characteristics fit the technology.

3. If you were part of a consulting team assigned to improve the operations of each organization, what recommendations would you make and why?

## Case for Analysis: Metropolitan College

Mary Clark, manager of Student Services at Metropolitan College, was preparing for the start of the new school year. It was August 10th, and in another four weeks, Mary's department of eight people would be responsible for registering approximately 1,000 students as they arrived for the fall term. Clark was not satisfied with the registration process of the previous year, which had resulted in long lines, frustrated staff and unhappy students. She wanted to identify opportunities for improvements for this year.

### The Registration Process

Each year, students arrived on Metropolitan's campus in the first week of September, termed Orientation Week, with classes beginning the following week. During Orientation Week, all students registered (or, the case of returning students, are reregistered), confirmed their initial course selection, paid their tuition fees and participated in a variety of orientation activities.

Mary identified several steps and the associated times required to perform the registration process, as shown in Exhibit 1. She found that each step was assigned to a different person. To process the large volume of registrations in a short period of time, a temporary office was set up

**EXHIBIT 1**
Metropolitan College Registration Process

| STEP | AVERAGE TIME TO PERFORM (MINUTES) |
|---|---|
| 1. Review registration information | 2 |
| 2. Out-of-province medical coverage (25 percent of students) | 3 |
| 3. Sign up for college services | 2 |
| 4. Fee payment | 1 |
| 5. Photograph student | 1.5 |
| 6. Produce and code card | 5 |
| 7. Issue card | 1 |

on the third floor of the college administration building during the first week of September. The first four steps were performed at this location. The office was open from 8 a.m. to 4:30 p.m. and was closed between 12 p.m. to 12:30 p.m. for lunch.

All students were required to have their registration data reviewed and confirmed, including their address, program-based tuition and course selection. Students living in one of the college's residences took the longest time to process. Approximately 10 percent of students did not complete their registration forms correctly and had to have them reviewed again.

Students from outside the province, roughly one-quarter of the total, were required to enrol in the college's out-of-province health coverage plan (Step 2). In the third step, students could sign up for a variety of services such as meal plans, bus passes and parking; these fees were then added to the student's invoice. Payment of fees and tuition was performed in the fourth step. Students had the option to use a cheque or debit card when making their payments.

After students had finished paying, they would proceed to the Student Services Office on the first floor of the administration building to have their photograph taken (Step 5) and their student card coded and issued (Steps 6 and 7, respectively). Students would enter the office, where they would take a number and wait to be called for their photograph. Each student would then hand his or her receipt to a staff member who would prepare the student card, including coding it for various services (e.g. meal plans). Students would sit in a waiting area while their cards were prepared.

Mary found that Steps 1, 2, 3 and 7 were handled by temporary staff members who were each paid $15 per hour. Payment of fees (Step 4), as dictated by college policy, had to be handled by an approved member of the Registrar's Office at a cost of $25 per hour. Steps 5 and 6 were performed by members of the college staff association, who received $20 per hour. Each step had one staff person assigned, with the exception of Step 6, where two staff members produced the student cards.

Mary wanted to avoid the problems that occurred the previous year. The college had recently announced plans for expansion, and Mary knew that enrolments would be rising in the coming years. As a starting point, she wanted to explore opportunities to make changes that would improve the student registration process.

## Assignment Questions

1. What is Mary trying to achieve by implementing a process change?
2. At what point in the process is variability likely to occur? How will that affect the performance of the process and the customer experience?

# 8

# Organization Size, Life Cycle, and Decline

JOSEPH BARRAK/AFP/Getty Images

## Interpol

The International Criminal Police Organization (Interpol) was created in 1923 and is the world's largest police organization. Interpol has a membership from 190 countries and 11 territories; its permanent headquarters is in Lyon, France. Interpol works with countries around the globe, fostering cooperation among people with different cultural values, languages, and legal and political systems. Interpol operates through National Central Bureaus in its member countries. Canada joined Interpol in 1949, and the Royal Canadian Mounted Police (RCMP) was delegated responsibility for Interpol in Canada.[1] In 2005, the Secretary General of Interpol, Ronald Noble (see photo), visited Canada. "In a world where the law enforcement community faces increasing and changing threats from criminals and terrorists, the need for international police co-operation and communication has never been greater," he said. "Canada, through the RCMP, has recognized the need for increased integration and coordination, and continues to play an important role in supporting Interpol and the world's police."[2]

When Interpol works, it works very well, leading to the quick capture of international terrorists, murderers, and other fugitives. But when Noble took over the international police organization in 2000, it wasn't working very well. Rather than a fast moving, crime-fighting organization, Noble found at Interpol a clumsy, slow-moving, bureaucratic agency that was ill equipped to respond to the massive challenges of a world increasingly reliant on worldwide coordinated law enforcement to prevent tragedies such as the World Trade Center attacks of September 2001. If a request for assistance and information on Mohammed Atta, one of the terrorist leaders, for example, came into Interpol on a weekend, too bad—the agency was closed until Monday morning. Interpol "Red Notices" (urgent, global wanted-persons alerts) took up to six months to process and were sent out by third-class mail to save postage costs.

Noble knew that kind of slow response had to change. Since taking over as head of Interpol, he has moved the organization forward by leaps and bounds, reducing bureaucracy and transforming Interpol into a modern, fast-moving organization. Keeping Interpol open 24 hours a day, seven days a week, was one of his first changes. A policy of issuing red alerts for terrorists within 24 hours and notices for less-threatening criminals within 72 hours went into effect immediately after the U.S. attacks on September 11, 2001. Noble has reorganized Interpol to increase speed and flexibility and to focus on the "customer" (law enforcement groups in its member countries). Today, the most critical notices are translated immediately, posted online, and sent by express-delivery service.

The reorganization also includes mechanisms for better coordination and information gathering. Noble's goal is for Interpol to become the number-one global police agency, one that coordinates and leads a multidimensional crime-fighting approach. Combating terrorism and organized crime, Noble knows, requires that everyone have the information they need when they need it and that local police, judicial, intelligence, diplomatic, and military services all work together. A major step toward a more coordinated worldwide effort came when Interpol recently appointed its first-ever representative to the United Nations.[3]

---

As organizations grow large and complex, they need more complex systems and procedures for guiding and controlling the organization. Unfortunately, these characteristics can also cause problems of inefficiency, rigidity, and slow response time. Every organization—from international agencies to locally owned restaurants and auto body shops—wrestles with questions about organizational size, bureaucracy, and control. Most entrepreneurs who start a business want their organization to grow. Yet, as organizations become larger, they often find it difficult to respond quickly to changes in the environment. Today's organizations are looking for ways to be more flexible and responsive to a rapidly changing environment while continuing to grow.

During the 20th century, large organizations became widespread, and bureaucracy has become a major topic of study in organizational theory.[4] Most large organizations have bureaucratic characteristics, which can be very effective. These organizations provide us with abundant goods and services and accomplish astonishing feats—explorations of Mars, overnight delivery of packages to any location in the world, scheduling and coordination of thousands of airline flights a day—that are testimony to their effectiveness. On the other hand, bureaucracy is also accused of creating inefficiency, rigidity, and demeaning routinized work that alienates both employees and the customers an organization is trying to serve.

Now, take a few minutes to complete the You and Design feature to see whether you prefer to work for a small or large organization.

# YOU & DESIGN

## What Size Organization for You?

How do your work preferences fit organization size? Answer the following questions as they reflect your likes and dislikes. Please answer whether each item is Mostly True or Mostly False for you.

| | Mostly True | Mostly False |
|---|---|---|
| 1. I value stability and predictability in the organization I work for. | ____ | ____ |
| 2. Rules are meant to be broken. | ____ | ____ |
| 3. Years of service should be an important determinant of pay and promotion. | ____ | ____ |
| 4. I generally prefer to work on lots of different things rather than specialize in a few things. | ____ | ____ |
| 5. Before accepting a job, I would want to make sure the company had good benefits. | ____ | ____ |
| 6. I would rather work on a team where managerial responsibility is shared than work in a department with a single manager. | ____ | ____ |
| 7. I would like to work for a large, well-known company. | ____ | ____ |
| 8. I would rather earn $90,000 a year in a small company than earn $100,000 a year as a middle manager in a big company. | ____ | ____ |

**Scoring:** Give yourself one point for each odd-numbered item you marked as Mostly True and one point for each even-numbered item you marked Mostly False.
**Interpretation:** Working in a large organization is a very different experience from working in a small organization. The large organization is well-established, has good benefits, is stable, and has rules, well-defined jobs, and a clear management hierarchy of authority. A small organization may be struggling to survive, has excitement, multitasking, risk, and sharing of responsibility. If you scored 6 or more, a large organization may be for you. If you scored 3 or less, you may be happier in a smaller organization.

Source: From HELLRIEGEL/JACKSON/SLOCUM. Managing, 11E. © 2008 South-Western, a part of Cengage Learning, Inc. Reproduced by permission. www.cengage.com/permissions.

## ■ Purpose of This Chapter

In this chapter, we explore the question of large versus small organizations and how size relates to structure and control. Organization size is a contextual variable that influences organizational design and functioning in the same way as the contextual variables—technology, environment, goals—discussed in previous chapters. In the first section, we look at the advantages of large versus small size. Then, we explore an organization's life cycle and the structural characteristics at each stage. Next, we examine the historical need for bureaucracy as a means to control large organizations and compare bureaucratic control to various other control strategies. Finally, the chapter looks at the causes of organizational decline and discusses some methods for dealing with downsizing. By the end of this chapter, you should be able to recognize when bureaucratic control can make an organization effective and when other types of control are more appropriate.

**Apply**

Apply your result from the You and Design feature to your career planning. Map out possible organizations for your career.

# Organization Size: Is Bigger Better?

The question of big versus small begins with the notion of growth and the reasons so many organizations feel the need to grow large.

## ■ Pressures for Growth

The vision of practically every businessperson is to have his or her company become a member of the Fortune 500 list—to grow fast and to grow large.[5] Sometimes this goal is more urgent than to make the best products or show the greatest profits. A decade ago, analysts and management scholars were heralding a shift away from "bigness" toward small, nimble companies that could quickly respond in a fast-changing environment. Yet, despite the proliferation of new, small organizations, the giants such as Procter & Gamble, Toyota, General Electric (GE), and Canadian Pacific Railway Ltd. (CPR) continue to grow. GE, for example, founded in 1878, now has 300,000 employees in 100 countries and competes in a variety of industries such as energy, transportation, finance, and television.[6] Similarly, CPR is growing through acquisition; it bought Dakota Minnesota & Eastern Railroad for $1.48 billion as its first step in its multibillion-dollar plan to haul U.S. coal.[7]

Today, the business world has entered an era of the mega-corporation. Merger mania has given rise to behemoths such as DaimlerChrysler AG and Citigroup.[8] The advertising industry is controlled by four giant agencies: the Omnicom Group and the Interpublic Group of Companies, both with headquarters in New York; London's WPP Group; and Publicis Groupe, based in Paris.[9] These huge conglomerates own scores of companies that soak up more than half the ad industry's revenues and reach into the advertising, direct-mail marketing, and public relations of every region on the planet. Moreover, these agencies grew primarily to better serve their clients, which were themselves growing larger and more global. Companies in all industries, from aerospace to consumer products to media, strive for growth to acquire the size and resources needed to compete on a global scale, to invest in new technology, and to control distribution channels and guarantee access to markets.[10]

There are other pressures for organizations to grow. Many executives have observed that firms must grow to stay economically healthy and believe that to stop growing is to stagnate. To be stable means that customers may not have their demands fully met or that competitors will increase market share at the expense of your organization. For example, Digital Extremes, a London, Ontario–based computer games creator, has the goal of creating at least one new product each year. Digital Extremes was founded in 1994 and has 63 employees and generates about $8 million a year in revenues. According to the company's chief financial officer (and brother of the founder), Michael Schmalz, "[What] you need to survive, much less prosper today, are blockbuster releases, . . . [better] yet what you want to do is to create a new game that will become a franchise, with each release breaking ground for the next."[11] Similarly, Neal Brothers Foods Inc., which sells organic snacks and food items, is looking to expand beyond its regional bases of Ontario and Québec across the country. It is facing pressure from the large food brands as they have "deep pockets" and "coast-to-coast name recognition."[12] Growth alone, however, is insufficient for success as companies such as The Loewen Group, Cinar Films, and 724 Solutions illustrate—their global promise fizzled out.[13]

Scale is crucial to economic success in marketing-intensive companies such as Coca-Cola, Procter & Gamble, and Molson-Coors. Greater size gives these companies power in the marketplace and thus increases revenues.[14] In addition, growing organizations can be vibrant, exciting places to work, which enables these companies to attract and keep quality employees. When the number of employees is expanding, an organization can offer many challenges and opportunities for advancement.

**Compare**

Compare two organizations that are different in size. What are three significant differences you observe?

## ■ Dilemmas of Large Size

Organizations feel compelled to grow, but how much and how large? What size organization is better poised to compete in a global environment? The arguments are summarized in Exhibit 8.1.

**Large.** Huge resources and economies of scale are needed for many organizations to compete globally. Only large organizations can build a massive pipeline in the North. Only a large corporation like Airbus Industrie can afford to build the A380, the world's first double-deck passenger airline, and only a large Virgin Atlantic Airways can buy it. Only a large Johnson & Johnson can invest hundreds of millions in new products such as bifocal contact lenses and a patch that delivers contraceptives through the skin. In addition, large organizations have the resources to be a supportive economic and social force in difficult times. In 2006, the Canadian Government undertook the largest evacuation in our country's history. Over 14,000 citizens were evacuated from Lebanon to Cyprus and Turkey in ships and airplanes chartered by the government. While there was considerable criticism of the evacuation, only a large organization like the federal government would have been able to mobilize the necessary resources to conduct the rescue. Large organizations also are able to get back to business more quickly following a disaster, giving employees a sense of security and belonging during an uncertain time.

Large companies are standardized, often mechanistically run, and complex. The complexity offers hundreds of functional specialties within the organization to perform multifaceted tasks and to produce varied and complicated products.

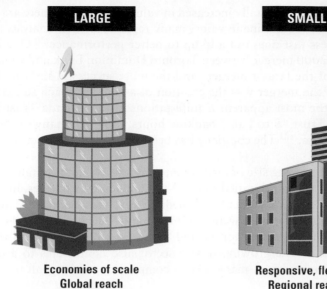

**LARGE**

Economies of scale
Global reach
Vertical hierarchy, mechanistic
Complex
Stable market
Employee longevity, raises, and promotions

**SMALL**

Responsive, flexible
Regional reach
Flat structure, organic
Simple
Niche finding
Entrepreneurs

**EXHIBIT 8.1**
**Differences between Large and Small Organizations**
Source: Based on John A. Byrne, "Is Your Company Too Big?" *BusinessWeek* (March 27, 1989), 84–94; and Lawler, III, E.E. (1997) "Rethinking Organization Size," *Organizational Dynamics* 26, 2, 24–35.

Moreover, large organizations, once established, can be a presence that stabilizes a market for years and at which managers can work for many years. The organization can provide longevity, raises, and promotions.

**Small.** The competing argument says small is beautiful because the crucial requirements for success in a global economy are responsiveness and flexibility in fast-changing markets. Small scale can provide significant advantages in terms of quick reaction to changing customer needs or shifting environmental and market conditions.[15]

Small organizations have a flat structure and an organic, free-flowing management style that encourages entrepreneurship and innovation. Today's leading biotechnological drugs, for example, were all discovered by small, young firms, such as Montréal's Theratechnologies, which is developing a compound to treat HIV lipodystrophy, rather than by huge pharmaceutical companies.[16] Moreover, the personal involvement of employees in small firms encourages entrepreneurial motivation and commitment, because employees personally identify with the company's mission.

Although the North American economy contains many large and successful organizations, research shows that as global trade has accelerated, smaller organizations have become the norm. Since the mid-1960s, most of the then-existing large businesses have lost market share worldwide.[17] Many large companies have grown even larger through merger or acquisition in recent years, yet research indicates that few of these mergers live up to their expected performance levels.[18] A study of ten of the largest mergers of all time, including AOL/Time Warner, Glaxo/SmithKline, and Daimler/Chrysler, showed a significant decline in shareholder value for eight of the ten combined companies. Only two, Exxon/Mobil and Travelers/Citicorp, actually increased in value.[19] Although there are numerous factors involved in the decline in value, many researchers and analysts agree that, frequently, bigness just does not add up to better performance.[20] One interesting exception is the 2000 merger between Toronto Dominion Bank and Canada Trust. It remains one of the largest mergers and the most successful in Canada. One of the outcomes of the merger was the creation of a new approach to customer service: "[One] of the most apparent manifestations of the Canada Trust DNA is in the TD Canada Trust "8 to Late" banking hours, in which many of the branches stay open until 8 pm."[21] The company has been recognized for its customer service initiatives.

Despite the increasing size of many companies, the economic vitality of Canada, as well as most of the world, is tied to small and mid-sized businesses. In 2001, there were more than 1.5 million small and medium-sized businesses in Canada. Fifty-eight percent of the businesses were in Ontario and Québec.[22] By 2004, small and medium-sized firms accounted for 87 and 11 percent, respectively, of the firms in the private sector.[23] The growing service sector also contributes to a decrease in average organization size, as many service companies remain small to better serve customers.

**Think**

Think about why so many mergers have failed. What factors might explain the failures?

**Big-Organization/Small-Organization Hybrid.** The paradox is that the advantages of small organizations sometimes enable them to succeed and, hence, grow large. Most of the 100 firms on Fortune's list of the fastest-growing companies are small firms characterized by an emphasis on being fast and flexible in responding to the environment.[24] Small companies, however, can become victims of their own success as they grow large, shifting to a mechanistic structure emphasizing vertical hierarchies and spawning "corporate drones" rather than entrepreneurs. Giant companies are "built for optimization, not innovation."[25] Big companies may become committed to their existing products and technologies, and have a hard time supporting innovation for the future.

The solution is what Jack Welch, retired chairman of GE, called the "big-company/small-company hybrid" that combines a large corporation's resources and reach with a small company's simplicity and flexibility. Full-service global firms need a strong resource base and sufficient complexity and hierarchy to serve clients around the world. Size is not necessarily at odds with speed and flexibility, as evidenced by large companies such as GE, eBay, and Apple, which continue to try new things and move quickly to change the rules of business. The divisional structure, described in Chapter 3, is one way some large organizations attain a big/small design. By reorganizing into groups of small companies, huge corporations such as Johnson & Johnson capture the mind-set and advantages of smallness. Johnson & Johnson is actually a group of 204 separate companies. When a new product is created in one of Johnson & Johnson's 56 labs, a new company is created along with it.[26] According to the late Steve Jobs, Apple is still a start-up even though it is the world's largest technology company. He kept the start-up culture at Apple by (1) focusing the company's strategy on one cohesive vision, (2) encouraging debate and eliminating passive-aggressiveness about ideas, and (3) setting up cross-disciplinary reviews of how the company would succeed.[27]

The development of new organizational forms, with an emphasis on decentralizing authority and cutting out layers of the hierarchy, combined with the increasing use of information technology, is making it easier than ever for organizations to be simultaneously large and small, thus capturing the advantages of each. Big companies also find a variety of ways to act both large and small. Retail giants Home Depot and Walmart, for example, use the advantage of size in areas such as advertising, purchasing, and raising capital; however, they also give each individual store the autonomy needed to serve customers as if it were a small, hometown shop.[28] To encourage innovation, the giant corporation Royal Dutch/Shell created a strategy in its exploration-and-production division to set aside 10 percent of the division's research budget for so-called outlandish ideas. Anyone can apply for the funds, and decisions are made not by managers but by a small group of nonconformist employees. [29] Small organizations that are growing can also use these ideas to help them retain the flexibility and customer focus that fuelled their growth.

**Apply**

How might you apply the idea of the small giant to how you manage your career?

---

# Book Mark 8.0    HAVE YOU READ THIS BOOK?

## Small Giants: Companies That Choose to Be Great Instead of Big
### By Bo Burlingham

The conventional business mind-set is to equate growth with success. But Bo Burlingham, an editor-at-large at *Inc.* magazine, reminds us that there is a different class of great companies that focus not on getting bigger, but on getting better. He calls them *Small Giants*. In his book of the same name, Burlingham looks at 14 small companies that are admired in their industries and recognized for their accomplishments—and in which managers have made a conscious decision *not* to significantly expand, go public, or become part of a larger firm.

### WHAT GIVES SMALL GIANTS THEIR MOJO?
The companies Burlingham profiles come from a wide range of industries and vary a great deal in terms of number of employees, corporate structure, management approach, and stage of the life cycle. What makes them similar? Burlingham describes seven shared characteristics that give these companies an almost magical quality.

Here are three of them:

- The founders and leaders made a mindful choice to build the kind of business they wanted to "live in," rather than accommodating to a business shaped by outside forces. Danny Meyer, owner of the Union Square Café, says he "earned more money by choosing the right things to say no to than by choosing things to say yes to." Fritz Maytag of Anchor Brewery, content to limit his distribution to northern California, even helped rival brewers develop their skills to accommodate growing demand for his kind of beer.

- Each of the small giants is intimately connected with the community in which it does business. CitiStorage, the premier independent records-storage company in the United States, built its warehouse in a depressed inner-city neighbourhood to save money. But it quickly bonded with the community by hiring local residents, opening the facility for community events, and making generous donations to the local school.

- Their leaders have a passion for the business. Whether it's making music, creating special effects, designing and manufacturing constant torque hinges, brewing beer, or planning commercial construction projects, the leaders of these companies show a true passion for the subject matter as well as a deep emotional commitment to the business and its employees, customers, and suppliers.

### DO YOU WANT TO BUILD A SMALL GIANT?
One beneficial outcome of Burlingham's book has been to prove to new or aspiring entrepreneurs that better doesn't have to mean bigger. For some, this eases the urge to seize every opportunity to expand. But Burlingham warns that resisting the pressures for growth takes strength of character. This fun-to-read book provides great insight into some entrepreneurs and managers who summoned the fortitude to make the choices that were right for them.

*Small Giants: Companies That Choose to Be Great Instead of Big*, by Bo Burlingham, is published by Portfolio, a division of the Penguin Group, 2007.

## Organizational Life Cycle

A useful way to think about organizational growth and change is the concept of an organizational **life cycle**,[30] which suggests that organizations are born, grow older, and eventually die. Organizational structure, leadership style, and administrative systems follow a fairly predictable pattern through stages in the life cycle. Stages are sequential and follow a natural progression. See the next In Practice for an example of an aspiring small giant.

<table>
<tr><td>

**In Practice**

**The Grackle Coffee Company (Grackle)**

</td><td>

The Grackle Coffee Company was founded in 2006 and in its first year of operation made $500! Since then, it has steadily increased its sales and profits. The Grackle Coffee Company is located in Schomberg, a small Ontario town, and is situated on its main street. Its mission is to "provide good, healthy food and drink that make sense both environmentally and economically, . . . [using] high quality materials, with as much local sourcing and fair trading as possible, and ensuring it is skillfully prepared."[31] It now offers not only coffee but also ice cream, sandwiches, and various sweet treats from organizations that share its values. It sells fair trade coffee and chocolate and supports local artists and artisans by showcasing and selling their work. One of Grackle's baristas successfully competed against baristas from large coffee chains, and made it to the finals of the 2008 Canadian Barista Championship held in Montréal.

One of its distinguishing features is its green commitment. It uses biodegradable cups and spoons, which are more expensive than nonbiodegradable ones, to demonstrate its commitment to the environment. Grackle produces an occasional quarterly newsletter to share its financial successes and its plans for improvement of its facilities and its offerings. It appears not to have any interest in getting larger but is focused on improving the local customer experience. Grackle has continued to increase its sales and profit, year over year. As the owners note, "[so] this is good! We seem to have a grasp on the new products and pricing of same, we sold most of what we bought, and in generally [sic] things are pretty ok."[32]

</td></tr>
</table>

## ■ Stages of Life-Cycle Development

Research on organizational life cycle suggests that four major stages characterize organizational development.[33] These stages are illustrated in Exhibit 8.2, along with the problems associated with transition to each stage. Growth is not easy. Each time an organization enters a new stage in the life cycle, it enters a whole new arena with a new set of rules for how the organization functions internally and how it relates to the external environment.[34] For technology companies today, life cycles are getting shorter; to stay competitive, companies such as eBay and Google have to successfully progress through stages of the cycle faster.

1. *Entrepreneurial stage.* The **entrepreneurial stage** is the start-up of an organization. When an organization is born, the emphasis is on creating a product or service and surviving in the marketplace. The founders are entrepreneurs, and they devote their full energies to the technical activities of production and marketing. The organization is informal and nimble. The hours of work are long. Control is based on the owners' personal supervision. Growth is from a creative

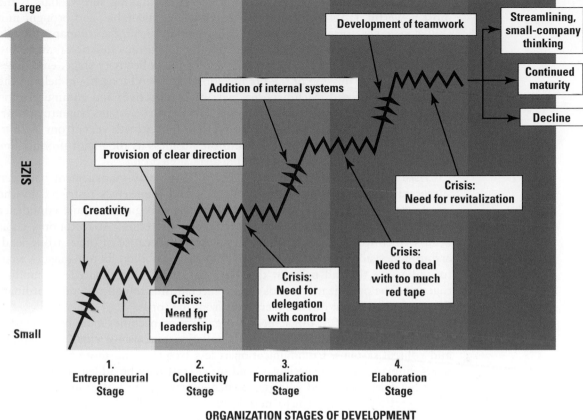

**EXHIBIT 8.2**
Organizational Life Cycle
Source: Adapted from Robert E. Quinn and Kim Cameron, Organizational Life Cycles and Shifting Criteria of Effectiveness: Some Preliminary Evidence, *Management Science* 29 (1983), 33–51; and Larry E. Greiner, Evolution and Revolution as Organizations Grow, *Harvard Business Review* 50 (July–August 1972), 37–46.

new product or service. Apple was in the entrepreneurial stage when it was created by Steve Jobs and Stephen Wozniak in Wozniak's parents' garage.

*Crisis: Need for leadership.* As the organization starts to grow, the larger number of employees causes problems. The creative and technically oriented owners are confronted with management issues, but they may prefer to focus their energies on making and selling the product or inventing new products and services. At this time of crisis, entrepreneurs must either adjust the structure of the organization to accommodate continued growth or else bring in strong managers who can do so. When Apple began a period of rapid growth, A.C. Markkula was brought in as a leader because neither Jobs nor Wozniak was qualified or cared to manage the expanding company.

2. *Collectivity stage.* In the **collectivity stage**, the organization grows and develops a more elaborate design. If the leadership crisis is resolved, strong leadership is obtained and the organization begins to develop clear goals and direction. Departments are established along with a hierarchy of authority, job assignments, and a beginning division of labour. Web search engine Google has quickly moved from the entrepreneurial to the collectivity stage. Founders Larry

Page and Sergey Brin devoted their full energy to making sure Google is the most powerful, fastest, and simplest search engine available, and brought in a skilled manager, former Novell CEO Eric Schmidt, to run the company. Google has hired other experienced executives to manage various functional areas and business units as the organization grows.[35] In the collectivity stage, employees identify with the mission of the organization and spend long hours helping the organization succeed. Members feel part of a collective, and communication and control are mostly informal although a few formal systems begin to appear. Apple was in the collectivity stage during the rapid-growth years from 1978 to 1981. Employees threw themselves into the business as the major product line was established and more than 2,000 dealers signed on.

*Crisis: Need for delegation with control.* If the new management has been successful, lower-level employees gradually find themselves restricted by the strong top-down leadership. Lower-level managers begin to acquire confidence in their own functional areas and want more discretion. An autonomy crisis occurs when top managers, who were successful because of their strong leadership and vision, do not want to give up responsibility. Top managers want to make sure that all parts of the organization are coordinated and pulling together. The organization needs to find mechanisms to control and coordinate departments without direct supervision from the top.

3. *Formalization stage.* At this stage, the organization becomes more bureaucratic. The **formalization stage** involves the installation and use of rules, procedures, and control systems. Communication is less frequent and more formal. Engineers, human resource specialists, and other staff may be added. Top management becomes concerned with issues such as strategy and planning, and leaves the operations of the firm to middle management. Product groups or other decentralized units may be formed to improve coordination. Incentive systems based on profits may be implemented to motivate managers to work toward what is best for the overall company. When effective, the new coordination and control systems enable the organization to continue growing by establishing linkage mechanisms between top management and field units. Apple was in the formalization stage in the mid-to-late 1980s.

*Crisis: Need to deal with too much red tape.* At this point in the organization's development, the proliferation of systems and programs may begin to strangle middle-level executives. The organization seems bureaucratized. Middle management may resent the intrusion of staff. Innovation may be restricted. The organization seems too large and complex to be managed through formal programs. It was at this stage of Apple's growth that Jobs resigned from the company and a new CEO took control and faced his own management challenges.

4. *Elaboration stage.* In the **elaboration stage,** the organization becomes more flexible in its design. The solution to the red-tape crisis is a new sense of collaboration and teamwork. Throughout the organization, managers develop skills for confronting problems and working together. Bureaucracy may have reached its limit. Social control and self-discipline reduce the need for additional formal controls. Managers learn to work within the bureaucracy without adding to it. Formal systems may be simplified and replaced by manager teams and task forces. To achieve collaboration, teams are often formed across functions or divisions of the company. The organization may also be split into multiple divisions to maintain a small-company philosophy. Apple is currently in the

elaboration stage of the life cycle. Apple is looking at ways to increase its three percent market share in the computer industry. The Macintosh had limited retail presence, so Apple ran a pilot project in 2006 with Best Buy to get shelf space for Macs. It was projected that, by the end of 2007, there would be Macs in 300 Best Buy stores; however, Best Buy did not agree to place Macs in all its stores.[36] Nevertheless, by 2010, Best Buy was selling iPads in all its stores.[37]

*Crisis: Need for revitalization.* After the organization reaches maturity, it may enter periods of temporary decline.[38] A need for renewal may occur every 10 to 20 years. The organization shifts out of alignment with the environment or perhaps becomes slow moving and over-bureaucratized and must go through a stage of streamlining and innovation. Top managers are often replaced during this period. At Apple, the top spot has changed hands a number of times as the company struggled to revitalize. CEOs John Sculley, Michael Spindler, and Gilbert Amelio were each ousted by the board as Apple's problems worsened. Steve Jobs returned in mid-1997 to run the company he had founded nearly 25 years earlier. During those 25 years, Jobs had gained management skills and experience he needed to help Apple through its problems. An older and smarter Jobs quickly reorganized the company, weeded out inefficiencies, and refocused Apple on innovative products for the consumer market, introducing a sleek new iMac in one of the hottest new product launches ever. Even more importantly, Jobs brought the entrepreneurial spirit back to Apple by moving the company into a whole new direction with the iPod music system. The iPod jump-started growth at Apple as the personal computer market continued to decline. Sales and profits are booming at Apple thanks to the iPod and an expanding line of innovative consumer electronics products.[39] In 2010, Apple surpassed Microsoft to become the world's largest technology company and maintained its position in 2013.[40] All mature organizations have to go through periods of revitalization or they will decline, as shown in the last stage of Exhibit 8.2.

*act!*

**Compare**

Compare the types of crises at each stage. What managerial skills are the most useful at each stage?

**Summary.** Eighty-four percent of organizations that make it past the first year still fail within five years because they can't make the transition from the entrepreneurial stage.[41] The transitions become even more difficult as organizations progress through future stages of the life cycle as you will see from the Nike example. Organizations that do not successfully resolve the problems associated with these transitions are restricted in their growth and may even fail. From within an organization, the life-cycle crises are very real. For example, Sam the Record Man was not able to survive the significant decline in CD sales as consumers shifted to digital downloading as their preferred method for buying music. In the first quarter of 2007, CD sales dropped 35 percent in Canada! According to Bobby Sniderman, son of the founder, "[we] are making a responsible decision [to close on June 30, 2007] in recognizing the status of the record industry and the increasing impact of technology."[42]

Nike has always been sort of the "bad boy" of sports marketing. Phil Knight and his college track coach, Bill Bowerman, started the company with $500 each and got the inspiration for their first training shoe from a waffle iron (the shoe was named the Waffle Trainer because of its unique treads). Nike reveres creativity above all; leaders have supported a free-wheeling culture and seemed to almost scoff at the business side of things. Until recently, the company had been run largely on instinct and bravado.

In Practice
**Nike**

But Nike began to suffer from its anti-establishment attitude, and Phil Knight recently made some major changes to move the company out of its lingering adolescence into a new stage of the life cycle. After hitting the $9.6 billion mark in 1998, sales stagnated. The company's previous approach of guessing how many shoes to manufacture and then flooding the market with them backfired when Nikes were left gathering dust on store shelves. A series of poorly conceived acquisitions and accusations that workers were being exploited in Nike's Asian factories didn't help matters. Nike didn't have the discipline and the formal systems it needed to cope with these kinds of problems. Consider that for a couple of years in the 1990s, the huge company didn't even have a chief financial officer. When Nike's French division went millions over budget in a promotional effort, Wall Street started asking if anyone was in charge at the company.

Although the Nike culture was powerful in terms of design and marketing, Knight realized the company could no longer operate like it was a young, small, entrepreneurial firm. Getting the basic pieces of the business side right—operating principles, financial management, supply chain and inventory management, and so forth—became a priority. He started by putting together a new team of experienced managers, including some Nike veterans but also some outsiders, such as CFO Donald Blair, who was lured from Pepsi. These managers, in turn, have brought the discipline Nike needs, such as establishing clear lines of authority, setting up top-flight systems for inventory and supply-chain management, and creating a department to deal with labour issues.

Nike seems to have successfully moved into the formalization stage, and the new-found discipline is paying off. After four years under the new management team, Nike's sales climbed 15 percent and the company earned almost $1 billion.[43]

Phil Knight's management overhaul didn't stop until it reached the top. In early 2005, Knight retired as CEO of the company and picked Bill Perez, former CEO of S.C. Johnson Company, as his successor. Some observers worried that without Knight, Nike would again founder. However, Knight believed Perez was the right leader for the organization's current stage of the life cycle. Knight continues to provide vision and guidance in his role as chairman, but the day-to-day running of the company is now in the hands of others.[44] Mark Parker became president and chief executive officer in 2006.

Nike has had to deal with significant criticism about the working conditions of its factories. The global anti-sweatshop movement has been targeting Nike since 1996 as it is the world's largest shoe supplier.[45] Nike responded by setting up an inspection system whereby its staff inspects several hundred factories a year, grades them on labour standards, and works with managers to improve problems. Nike also allows random factory inspections by the Fair Labour Association.[46]

## ■ Organizational Characteristics During the Life Cycle

As organizations evolve through the four stages of the life cycle, changes take place in structure, control systems, innovation, and goals. The organizational characteristics associated with each stage are summarized in Exhibit 8.3.

**Entrepreneurial.** Initially, the organization is small, nonbureaucratic, and a one-person show. The top manager provides the structure and control system. Organizational energy is devoted to survival and the production of a single product or service. For example, Michael Cowpland, founder of Corel Corporation and co-founder of Mittel, took over the tiny ZIM Technologies International in 2001 so he could "get his hands dirty and work with start-up companies [again]."[47]

**Collectivity.** This is the organization's youth. Growth is rapid, and employees are excited and committed to the organization's mission. The structure is still mostly informal, although some procedures are emerging. Strong charismatic leaders like

**EXHIBIT 8.3**
Organization Characteristics During Four Stages of the Life Cycle

| CHARACTERISTIC | 1. ENTREPRENEURIAL NONBUREAUCRATIC | 2. COLLECTIVITY PRE-BUREAUCRATIC | 3. FORMALIZATION BUREAUCRATIC | 4. ELABORATION VERY BUREAUCRATIC |
|---|---|---|---|---|
| Structure | Informal, one-person show | Mostly informal, some procedures | Formal procedures, division of labour, new specialties added | Teamwork within bureaucracy, small-company thinking |
| Products or services | Single product or service | Major product or service, with variations | Line of products or services | Multiple product or service lines |
| Reward and control systems | Personal, paternalistic | Personal, contribution to success | Impersonal, formalized systems | Extensive, tailored to product and department |
| Innovation | By owner-manager | By employees and managers | By separate innovation group | By institutionalized R&D department |
| Goal | Survival | Growth | Internal stability, market expansion | Reputation, complete organization |
| Top management style | Individualistic, entrepreneurial | Charismatic, direction-giving | Delegation with control | Team approach, attack bureaucracy |

Source: Adapted from Larry E. Greiner, "Evolution and Revolution as Organizations Grow," *Harvard Business Review* 50 (July–August 1972), 37–46; G. L. Lippitt and W. H. Schmidt, "Crises in a Developing Organization," *Harvard Business Review* 45 (November–December 1967), 102–112; B. R. Scott, "The Industrial State: Old Myths and New Realities," *Harvard Business Review* 51 (March–April 1973), 133–148; Robert E. Quinn and Kim Cameron, "Organizational Life Cycles and Shifting Criteria of Effectiveness," *Management Science* 29 (1983), 33–51.

Steve Jobs of Apple or Phil Knight at Nike provide direction and goals for the organization. Continued growth is a major goal.

**Formalization.** At this point, the organization is entering mid-life. Bureaucratic characteristics emerge. The organization adds staff support groups, formalizes procedures, and establishes a clear hierarchy and division of labour. At the formalization stage, organizations may also develop complementary products to offer a complete product line. Innovation may be achieved by establishing a separate innovation department. Major goals are internal stability and market expansion. Top management delegates, but it also implements formal control systems.

At this stage, for example, Microsoft founder Bill Gates turned the daily management of the company over to Steven Ballmer, who developed and implemented formal planning, management, and financial systems throughout the company. Gates wanted someone who could manage daily business operations so that he could focus his energies on technological innovation.[48]

**Elaboration.** The mature organization is large and bureaucratic, with extensive reward and control systems, rules, and procedures. Top managers attempt to develop a team orientation within the bureaucracy to prevent further bureaucratization.

**EXHIBIT 8.4**
Perils of Smallness!
Source: DILBERT © 2004 Scott Adams. Used By permission of UNIVERSAL UCLICK. All rights reserved.

Their goal is to establish a complete organization that provides multiple product or service lines well. Innovation is institutionalized through an R&D department. Management may attack the bureaucracy and streamline it.

**Summary.** Growing organizations move through stages of a life cycle, and each stage is associated with specific characteristics of structure, control systems, goals, and innovation. The life-cycle phenomenon is a powerful concept used for understanding problems facing organizations and how managers can respond in a positive way to move an organization to the next stage. Exhibit 8.4 highlights the perils of being small!

# Organizational Bureaucracy and Control

As organizations progress through the life cycle, they usually take on bureaucratic characteristics as they grow larger and more complex. The systematic study of bureaucracy was launched by Max Weber, a sociologist who studied government organizations in Europe and developed a framework of administrative characteristics that would make large organizations rational and efficient.[49] Weber wanted to understand how organizations could be designed to play a positive role in the larger society.

## What Is Bureaucracy?

Although Weber perceived bureaucracy as a threat to basic personal liberties, he also recognized it as the most efficient possible system of organizing. He predicted the triumph of bureaucracy because of its ability to ensure more efficient functioning of organizations in both business and government settings. Weber identified a set of organizational characteristics, listed in Exhibit 8.5, that could be found in successful bureaucratic organizations.

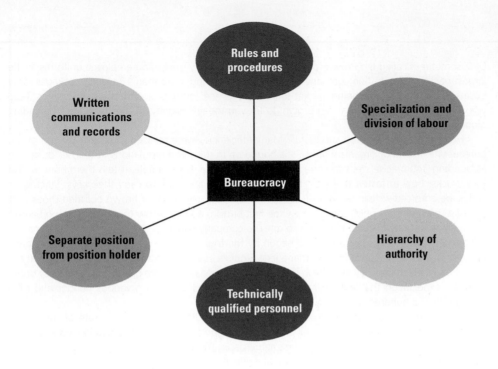

**EXHIBIT 8.5**
Weber's Dimensions
of Bureaucracy

In a **bureaucracy,** rules and standard procedures enable organizational activities to be performed in a predictable, routine manner. Specialized duties mean that each employee had a clear task to perform. Hierarchy of authority provides a sensible mechanism for supervision and control. Technical competence was the basis by which people were hired rather than friendship, family ties, and favouritism, which dramatically increased work performance. The separation of the position from the position holder means that individuals did not own or have an inherent right to the job, which promoted efficiency. Written records provided an organizational memory and continuity over time.

Although bureaucratic characteristics carried to an extreme are widely criticized today, the rational control introduced by Weber was a significant idea and a new form of organization. Bureaucracy provided many advantages over organization forms based on favouritism, social status, family connections, or graft. For example, when he was appointed as commissioner of internal revenue in the Philippines some 30 years ago, Efren Plana found massive corruption, including officials hiring their relatives for high-ranking jobs and tax assessors winning promotions by bribing their superiors.[50] In Mexico, an American lawyer had to pay a $500 bribe to get a telephone. The tradition of giving government posts to relatives is widespread in places such as China; however, China's emerging class of educated people does not like seeing the best jobs going to children and other relatives of officials.[51] By comparison, the logical and rational form of organization described by Weber allows work to be conducted efficiently and according to established rules.

The bureaucratic characteristics listed in Exhibit 8.5 can have a positive impact on many large firms. Consider United Parcel Service (UPS), one of the most efficient large organizations in North America.

## In Practice
### United Parcel Service (UPS)

UPS, sometimes called Big Brown for the colour of its delivery trucks and employee uniforms, is the largest package-distribution company in the world, delivering more than 13 million packages every business day. UPS is also gaining market share in air service, logistics, and information services. Television commercials ask, "What can Brown do for you today?" signifying the company's expanding global information services.

How did UPS become so successful? Many efficiencies were realized through adoption of the bureaucratic model of organization. UPS is bound up in rules and regulations. It teaches drivers an astounding 340 precise steps to correctly deliver a package. For example, it tells them how to load their trucks, how to fasten their seat belts, how to walk, and how to carry their keys. Strict dress codes are enforced—clean uniforms (called *browns*) every day, black or brown polished shoes with non-slip soles, no shirt unbuttoned below the first button, no hair below the shirt collar, no beards, no smoking in front of customers, and so on. The company conducts three-minute physical inspections of its drivers each day, a practice begun by the founder in the early 1900s. There are safety rules for drivers, loaders, clerks, and managers. Employees are asked to clean off their desks at the end of each day so they can start fresh the next morning. Managers are given copies of policy books with the expectation that they will use them regularly, and memos on various policies and rules circulate by the hundreds every day.

Despite the strict rules, employees are satisfied and UPS has a retention rate of more than 90 percent. Employees are treated well and paid well, and the company has maintained a sense of equality and fairness. Everyone is on a first-name basis. The policy book states, "A leader does not have to remind others of his authority by use of a title. Knowledge, performance, and capacity should be adequate evidence of position and leadership." Technical qualification, not favouritism, is the criterion for hiring and promotion. Top executives started at the bottom—the current chief executive, James Kelly, for example, began as a temporary holiday-rush driver. The emphasis on equality, fairness, and a promote-from-within mentality inspires loyalty and commitment throughout the ranks.

UPS has also been a leader in using new technology to enhance reliability and efficiency. Drivers use a computerized clipboard, called DIAD (Delivery Information Acquisition Device), to record everything from drivers' miles per gallon to data on parcel delivery. Technology is enabling UPS to expand its services and become a global mover of knowledge and information as well as packages. Top managers know the new technology means some of UPS's rigid procedures may have to bend. However, it's likely they won't bend too far. When you're moving more than 13 million items a day, predictability and stability are the watchwords, whether you're using the company's first Model T Ford or its latest technological wizardry.[52]

---

UPS illustrates how bureaucratic characteristics increase with large size. UPS is so productive and dependable that it dominates the small package–delivery market. As it expands and transitions into a global, knowledge-based logistics business, UPS managers may need to find effective ways to reduce bureaucracy. The new technology and new services place more demands on workers, who may need more flexibility and autonomy to perform well. Now, let's look at some specific ways size affects organizational structure and control.

## ■ Size and Structural Control

In the field of organizational theory, organization size has been described as an important variable that influences structural design and methods of control. Should an organization become more bureaucratic as it grows larger? In what size organizations are bureaucratic characteristics most appropriate? More than 100 studies have attempted to answer these questions.[53] Most of these studies indicate that large organizations are different from small organizations along several dimensions of structure, including formalization, centralization, and personnel ratios.

**Formalization and Centralization. Formalization,** as described in Chapter 1, refers to rules, procedures, and written documentation, such as policy manuals and job descriptions, that prescribe the rights and duties of employees.[54] The evidence supports the conclusion that large organizations are more formalized, as at UPS. The reason is that large organizations rely on rules, procedures, and paperwork to achieve standardization and control across their large numbers of employees and departments, whereas top managers can use personal observation to control a small organization.[55]

**Centralization** refers to the level of hierarchy with authority to make decisions. In centralized organizations, decisions tend to be made at the top. In decentralized organizations, similar decisions would be made at a lower level.

Decentralization represents a paradox because, in the perfect bureaucracy, all decisions would be made by the top administrator, who would have perfect control. However, as an organization grows larger and has more people and departments, decisions cannot be passed to the top because senior managers would be overloaded. Thus, the research on organization size indicates that larger organizations permit greater decentralization.[56] Consider Microsoft, where former CEO Steven Ballmer and Chairman Bill Gates used to make every important decision. In a company with 50,000 employees and multiple product lines, however, the traditional structure was too top-heavy; decision making had slowed to a snail's pace. Ballmer reorganized the 50,000-employee firm into seven divisions and gave division heads greater decision-making authority.[57] In small start-up organizations, on the other hand, the founder or top executive can effectively be involved in every decision, large and small.

**Personnel Ratios.** Another characteristic of bureaucracy relates to **personnel ratios** for administrative, clerical, and professional support staff. The most frequently studied ratio is the administrative ratio.[58] Two patterns have emerged. The first is that the ratio of top administration to total employees is actually smaller in large organizations,[59] indicating that organizations experience administrative economies as they grow larger. The second pattern concerns clerical and professional support staff ratios.[60] These groups tend to *increase* in proportion to organization size. The clerical ratio increases because of the greater communication and reporting requirements needed as organizations grow larger. The professional staff ratio increases because of the greater need for specialized skills in larger, complex organizations.[61]

The net effect for direct workers is that they decline as a percentage of total employees. In summary, whereas top administrators do not make up a disproportionate number of employees in large organizations, the idea that proportionately greater overhead is required in large organizations is supported. Although large organizations reduced overhead during the difficult economic years of the 1980s, overhead costs for many North American corporations began creeping back up again as revenues soared during the late 1990s.[62] With the declining North American economy following the crash of the technology sector, threats of war and terrorism, and general feelings of uncertainty, many companies have again been struggling to cut overhead costs. Keeping costs for administrative, clerical, and professional support staff low represents an ongoing challenge for large organizations.[63] Similarly, organizations, particularly those in the United States, that are trying to recover from the 2008–2009 recession are neither hiring individuals nor creating jobs.[64]

# Bureaucracy in a Changing World

Weber's prediction of the triumph of bureaucracy proved accurate. Bureaucratic characteristics have many advantages and have worked extremely well for many of the needs of the industrial age.[65] By establishing a hierarchy of authority and specific rules and procedures, bureaucracy provided an effective way to bring order to large groups of people and prevent abuses of power. Impersonal relationships based on roles rather than people reduced the favouritism and nepotism characteristic of many pre-industrial organizations. Bureaucracy also provided for systematic and rational ways to organize and manage tasks too complex to be understood and handled by a few individuals, thus greatly improving the efficiency and effectiveness of large organizations.

The world is rapidly changing, however, and the machine-like bureaucratic system of the industrial age no longer works so well as organizations face new challenges. With global competition and uncertain environments, many organizations are fighting against increasing formalization and professional staff ratios. The problems caused by over-bureaucratization are evident in the inefficiencies of some government organizations. Some agencies have so many clerical staff members and confusing job titles so that no one is really sure who does what. Some confusing titles include initiative officer, undersecretary to the subcommittee, and associate vice president![66]

Some critics have blamed government bureaucracy for intelligence, communication, and accountability failures related to the September 11, 2001, terrorist attacks in the United States; the space shuttle disasters; the December 2004 tsunami; and the 2010 earthquake in Haiti. "Every time you add a layer of bureaucracy, you delay the movement of information up the chain of command.... And you dilute the information because at each step some details are taken out."[67] Many business organizations, too, need to reduce formalization and bureaucracy. Narrowly defined job descriptions, for example, tend to limit the creativity, flexibility, and rapid response needed in today's knowledge-based organizations.

## Organizing Temporary Systems for Flexibility and Innovation

How can organizations overcome the problems of bureaucracy in rapidly changing environments? Some are implementing innovative structural solutions. One structural concept, called the **incident command system** (ICS), is commonly used by organizations, such as police and fire departments or other emergency management agencies, that have to respond rapidly to emergency or crisis situations. The incident command system was developed to maintain the efficiency and control benefits of bureaucracy yet prevent the problem of slow response to crises.[68] The approach is being adapted by other types of organizations to help them respond quickly to new opportunities, unforeseen competitive threats, or organizational crises.

The basic idea behind the ICS is that the organization can glide smoothly between a highly formalized, hierarchical structure that is effective during times of stability and a more flexible, loosely structured one needed to respond well to unexpected and demanding environmental conditions. The hierarchical side with its rules, procedures, and chain of command helps maintain control and ensure adherence to rules that have been developed and tested over many years to cope with well-understood problems and situations. However, during times of high uncertainty, the most effective structure is one that loosens the lines of command and enables people to work across departmental and hierarchical lines to anticipate, avoid, and solve unanticipated problems within the context of a clearly understood mission and guidelines.

The approach can be seen on the deck of a nuclear aircraft carrier, where there is a rigid chain of command and people are expected to follow orders promptly and without question.[69] Formalization is high, with manuals detailing proper procedures for every known situation. However, at times of high uncertainty, such as the launching and recovery of planes during real or simulated warfare, an important shift occurs. The rigid hierarchy seems to dissolve, and a loosely organized, collaborative structure in which sailors and officers work together as colleagues takes its place. People discuss the best procedures to use, and everyone typically follows the lead of whoever has the most experience and knowledge in a particular area. During this time, no one is thinking about job titles, authority, or chain of command; they are just thinking about the best way to accomplish the mission safely.

A variety of mechanisms ensure smooth functioning of the ICS.[70] For example, despite the free-flowing and flexible nature of crisis response, someone is always in charge. The *incident commander* is ultimately responsible for all activities that occur, and everyone knows clearly who is in charge of what aspect of the situation. This helps maintain order in a chaotic environment. The key is that, whereas formal authority relationships are fixed, decision-making authority is dispersed to individuals who best understand the particular situation. The system is based on trust that lower-level workers have a clear understanding of the mission and make decisions and take actions within guidelines that support the organization's goals. Developing an ICS requires a significant commitment of time and resources, but it offers great potential for organizations that require extremely high reliability, flexibility, and innovation. One organization that effectively uses the incident command model is the Salvation Army, as described in this chapter's Leading by Design box.

## ■ Other Approaches to Reducing Bureaucracy

Organizations are taking a number of other, less-dramatic steps to reduce bureaucracy. Many are cutting layers of the hierarchy, keeping headquarters staff small, and giving lower-level workers greater freedom to make decisions rather than burdening them with excessive rules and regulations. The point is to ensure that organizations are not top-heavy with lawyers, accountants, and financial analysts who inhibit the flexibility and autonomy of divisions. The rise in the Canadian dollar has challenged the manufacturing sector to become lean and flexible so that it can better compete globally. Manufacturers such as Edson and Elettra Technologies in Hamilton, Ontario, have responded by streamlining their internal processes and organizational designs.[71]

Of course, many companies must be large to have sufficient resources and complexity to produce products for a global environment, but companies such as 3M, Coca-Cola, Weyerhaeuser, and Heinz are striving toward greater decentralization and leanness. They are giving frontline workers more authority and responsibility to define and direct their own jobs, often by creating self-directed teams that find ways to coordinate work, improve productivity, and better serve customers.

# Leading *by Design*

## The Salvation Army

The Salvation Army has been called "the most effective organization in the world" by leading management scholar the late Peter Drucker. One reason the organization is so effective and powerful is its approach to organizing, which makes use of the incident command system to provide the right amount of structure, control, and flexibility to meet the requirements of each situation. The Salvation Army refers to its approach as "organizing to improvise."

The Salvation Army provides day-to-day assistance to homeless and economically disadvantaged people. In addition, the organization rushes in whenever there is a major disaster—whether a tornado, flood, hurricane, airplane crash, or terrorist attack—to network with other agencies to provide disaster relief. Long after the most desperate moments of the initial crisis have passed, the Salvation Army continues helping people rebuild their lives and communities—offering financial assistance; meeting physical needs for food, clothing, and housing; and providing emotional and spiritual support to inspire hope and help people build a foundation for the future. The Army's management realizes that emergencies demand high flexibility. At the same time, the organization must have a high level of control and accountability to ensure its continued existence and meet its day-to-day responsibilities. As a former national commander puts it, "We have to have it both ways. We can't choose to be flexible and reckless or to be accountable and responsive.... We have to be several different kinds of organizations at the same time."

In the early emergency moments of a crisis, the Salvation Army deploys a temporary organization that has its own command structure. People need to have a clear sense of who's in charge to prevent the rapid response demands from degenerating into chaos. For example, when the Army responds a crisis, manuals clearly specify in advance who is responsible for talking to the media, who is in charge of supply inventories, who liaises duties with other agencies, and so forth. This model for the temporary organization keeps the Salvation Army responsive and consistent. In the later recovery and rebuilding phases of a crisis, supervisors frequently give people general guidelines and allow them to improvise the best solutions. There isn't time for supervisors to review and sign off on every decision that needs to be made to get families and communities re-established. On September 11, 2001, the Salvation Army in Corner Brook, Newfoundland and Labrador, had to support 150 people whose flight had been diverted to Stephenville. According to Major Ross Bungay, "[It] was an operation of mercy in a crisis environment, and even in situations we had not been specifically trained for...the cumulative talent and expertise served us all well."[72]

The Salvation Army has people simultaneously working in all different types of organizational structures, from traditional vertical command structures, to horizontal teams, to a sort of network form that relies on collaboration with other agencies. Operating in such a fluid way enables the organization to accomplish amazing results. It has been recognized as a leader in putting money to maximal use, meaning donors are willing to give because they trust the organization to be responsible and accountable at the same time it is flexible and innovative in meeting human needs.[73]

Another attack on bureaucracy is from the increasing professionalism of employees. Professionalism is defined as the length of formal training and experience of employees. More employees need college or university degrees, MBAs, and other professional degrees to work as lawyers, researchers, or doctors at large organizations. Internet-based companies may be staffed entirely by well-educated knowledge workers. Studies of professionals show that formalization is not needed because professional training regularizes a high standard of behaviour for employees that acts as a substitute for bureaucracy.[74] Organizations also enhance this trend when they provide ongoing training for *all* employees, from the front office to the shop floor, in a push for continuous individual and organizational learning. Increased training substitutes for bureaucratic rules and procedures that can constrain the creativity of employees in solving problems and increases organizational capability.

A form of organization called professional partnership has emerged that is made up completely of professionals.[75] These organizations include medical practices, law firms, and consulting firms, such as McKinsey & Company and the now defunct Monitor Company.[76] The general finding concerning professional partnerships is that branches have substantial autonomy and decentralized authority to make necessary decisions. They work with a consensus orientation rather than the top-down direction typical of traditional business and government organizations. Thus, the trend of increasing professionalism, combined with rapidly changing environments, is leading to less bureaucracy in North America.

# Organizational Control Strategies

Even though many organizations are trying to decrease bureaucracy and reduce rules and procedures that constrain employees, every organization needs systems for guiding and controlling the organization. Employees may have more freedom in today's organizations, but control is still a major responsibility of management.

Managers at the top and middle levels of an organization can choose among three overall control strategies. These strategies come from a framework for organizational control proposed by William Ouchi. Ouchi suggested three control strategies that organizations could adopt—bureaucratic, market, and clan.[77] Each form of control uses different types of information. However, all three types may appear simultaneously in an organization. The requirements for each control strategy are given in Exhibit 8.6.

## ▪ Bureaucratic Control

**Bureaucratic control** is the use of rules, policies, hierarchy of authority, written documentation, standardization, and other bureaucratic mechanisms to standardize behaviour and assess performance. Bureaucratic control uses the bureaucratic characteristics defined by Weber and illustrated in the UPS In Practice feature. The primary purpose of bureaucratic rules and procedures is to standardize and control employee behaviour.

Recall that as organizations progress through the life cycle and grow larger, they become more formalized and standardized. Within a large organization, thousands of work behaviours and information exchanges take place both vertically and horizontally. Rules and policies evolve through a process of trial and error to regulate these behaviours. Some degree of bureaucratic control is used in virtually every organization. Rules, regulations, and directives contain information about a range of behaviours.

| TYPE | REQUIREMENTS |
|------|--------------|
| Bureaucracy | Rules, standards, hierarchy, legitimate authority |
| Market | Prices, competition, exchange relationship |
| Clan | Tradition, shared values and beliefs, trust |

**EXHIBIT 8.6**
Three Organizational Control Strategies

Source: Based on William G. Ouchi, "A Conceptual Framework for the Design of Organizational Control Mechanisms," *Management Science* 25 (1979), 833–848.

To make bureaucratic control work, managers must have the authority to maintain control over the organization. Weber argued that legitimate, rational authority granted to managers was preferred over other types of control (e.g., favouritism or payoffs) as the basis for organizational decisions and activities. Within the larger society, however, Weber identified three types of authority that could explain the creation and control of a large organization.[78]

**Rational-legal authority** is based on employees' belief in the legality of rules and the right of those elevated to positions of authority to issue commands. Rational-legal authority is the basis for both creation and control of most government organizations and is the most common base of control in organizations worldwide. **Traditional authority** is the belief in traditions and in the legitimacy of the status of people exercising authority through those traditions. Traditional authority is the basis for control for monarchies, religious institutions, and some organizations in Latin America and the Middle East. **Charismatic authority** is based on devotion to the exemplary character or to the heroism of an individual person and the order defined by him or her. Revolutionary military organizations are often based on the leader's charisma, as are North American organizations led by charismatic individuals such as Steve Jobs. The organization reflects the personality and values of the leader.

More than one type of authority—such as long tradition and the leader's special charisma—may exist in organizations, but rational-legal authority is the most widely used form to govern internal work activities and decision making, particularly in large organizations. Bureaucratic control can be highly effective, but when carried to an extreme it can also create problems. Consider the following examples.

## In Practice

**Shizugawa Elementary School Evacuation Centre and Toyota Motors**

One newspaper reporter recently characterized Japan as "a rule-obsessed nation with a penchant for creating bureaucracy, designating titles and committees for even the most mundane of tasks." When the fishing village of Minamisanriku was ravaged by a tsunami in the spring of 2011, that propensity served a valuable purpose. The creation of rules, procedures, and authority structures helped create a sense of normalcy and comfort at the Shizugawa Elementary School Evacuation Centre. The group of evacuees created six divisions to oversee various aspects of daily life, such as cooking, cleaning, inventory control, and medical care, and each function had detailed rules and procedures to follow. The cleaning crews, for instance, followed an instruction sheet describing in minute detail how to separate types of garbage and recyclables, how to replace the garbage bags, and so forth. The exhaustive and meticulous procedures kept the centre running smoothly and helped people cope with a devastating situation. "The Japanese people are the type to feel more reassured the more rules are in place," said Shintaro Goto, a 32-year-old actor and electrician who moved back to the village from Tokyo just months before the tsunami.

However, while rules, procedures, and detailed lists were highly beneficial at the tsunami evacuation centres, they have been partially blamed for quality and safety problems that have plagued Japan's Toyota Motors in recent years. "The bottom line is that we succumbed to 'Big Company Disease,'" said Shinichi Sasaki, a Toyota board member and executive vice president in charge of quality. "That has led us to question some of our basic assumptions." Toyota's strong top-down bureaucratic system helped obscure problems. For example, the company wanted suppliers, dealers, and other partners, as well as employees, to follow strict guidelines to the letter. The rules and checklists got in the way of executives seeing when things started going wrong, however, and customer complaints started piling up. Toyota has since implemented a number of reforms to its operations, many of them designed to overcome the problems brought about by large size and bureaucracy.[79]

Toyota isn't the only large company to find that too many rules can get in the way of serving customers. Employees at Starbucks, which grew rapidly from six stores in 1987 into a huge corporation with thousands of stores around the world, are being strangled by meticulous rules and policies that no longer work. Consistency is important for any company, and rules and procedures that facilitated predictable outcomes enabled Starbucks to grow and succeed. However, applying rules inflexibly and blindly soon started to cause problems. One software entrepreneur and *Inc.* magazine contributor tells a story about an order taker in a Starbucks store who got into a prolonged shouting match with a customer who wanted to pick up her sandwich at the front counter. "They're not allowed to give it to you up here!" the employee kept shouting at the shocked and frustrated customer.[80]

## ■ Market Control

**Market control** occurs when price competition is used to evaluate the output and productivity of an organization. The idea of market control originated in economics.[81] A dollar price is an efficient form of control, because managers can compare prices and profits to evaluate the efficiency of their corporation. Top managers nearly always use the price mechanism to evaluate performance in organizations. Corporate sales and costs are summarized in a profit-and-loss statement that can be compared against performance in previous years or with that of other corporations.

The use of market control requires that outputs be sufficiently explicit for a price to be assigned and for competition to exist. Without competition, the price does not accurately reflect internal efficiency. Increasingly, governments and nonprofit organizations are turning to market control. For example, nonprofits are entering the market through social purpose businesses that integrate both financial and social bottom lines.[82] Market control was once used primarily at the level of the entire organization, but it is increasingly used in product divisions. Profit centres are self-contained product divisions, such as those described in Chapter 3. Each division contains resource inputs needed to produce a product. Each division can be evaluated on the basis of profit or loss compared with other divisions. Asea Brown

## In Practice
### Imperial Oil Limited

In the early 1990s, Imperial Oil's R&D was a monopoly service provider allocated an annual budget of about $45 million. However, Imperial Oil felt that this method of operating gave the 200 scientists and staff little incentive to control costs or advance quality.

Today, R&D receives a much smaller budget and essentially supports itself through applied research and lab-services contracts negotiated with internal and external customers. Contracts spell out the costs of each program, analysis, or other service, and cost-conscious Imperial Oil managers can shop for lower prices among external labs.

R&D has even introduced competition within its own small unit. For example, research teams are free to buy some lab services outside the company if they feel their own laboratories are overpriced or inefficient. However, quality and efficiency have dramatically improved at Imperial Oil's R&D, and the unit's high-quality, low-cost services are attracting a great deal of business from outside the company. Canadian companies routinely send samples of used motor oil to the R&D labs for analysis, manufacturers use R&D to autopsy equipment failures, and vehicle makers such as General Motors and Ford test new engines at Imperial Oil's R&D's chassis dynamometer lab. According to John Charlton, Imperial Oil's corporate strategic planning manager, applying market control to R&D has led to an increase in the amount of work the unit does, as well as a 12 percent reduction in internal costs.[83]

Boveri (ABB), a multinational electrical contractor and manufacturer of electrical equipment, includes three different types of profit centres, all operating according to their own bottom line and all interacting through buying and selling with one another and with outside customers.[84] The network organization, also described in Chapter 3, illustrates market control as well. Different companies compete on price to provide the functions and services required by the hub organization. The organization typically contracts with the company that offers the best price and value.

Some firms require that individual departments interact with one another at market prices—buying and selling products or services among themselves at prices equivalent to those quoted outside the firm. To make the market control system work, internal units also have the option to buy and sell with outside companies, as Imperial Oil did.

Market control can be used only when the output of an organization, division, or department can be assigned a dollar price and when there is competition. Organizations are finding that they can apply the market control concept to internal departments such as accounting, data processing, legal, and information services.

## ■ Clan Control

**Clan control** is the use of social characteristics, such as organizational culture, shared values, commitment, traditions, and beliefs, to control behaviour. Organizations that use clan control require shared values and trust among employees.[85] Clan control is important when ambiguity and uncertainty are high. High uncertainty means the organization cannot put a price on its services, and things change so quickly that rules and regulations are not able to specify every correct behaviour. Under clan control, people may be hired because they are committed to the organization's purpose, such as in a religious organization. New employees may be subjected to a long period of socialization to gain acceptance by colleagues. Clan control is most often used in small, informal organizations or in organizations with a strong culture, because of personal involvement in and commitment to the organization's purpose. For example, St. Luke's Communications Ltd., a London, England, advertising firm committed to equal employee ownership, is especially careful to bring in only new employees who believe in the agency's philosophy and mission. The company even turned down a $90 million contract because it meant rapidly recruiting new employees who might not fit with St. Luke's distinctive culture. Clan control works for St. Luke's; the agency is highly respected and its revenues continue to grow.[86] It is London's longest-running creative agency in which every employee has a share. In addition, in 2000 it became the first carbon-neutral ad agency and made the first carbon–offset TV campaign in 2004. It is also ISO:14001 accredited.[87]

Traditional control mechanisms based on strict rules and close supervision are ineffective for controlling behaviour in conditions of high uncertainty and rapid change.[88] In addition, the growing use of computer networks and the Internet, which often leads to a democratic spread of information throughout the organization, may force many companies to depend less on bureaucratic control and more on shared values that guide individual actions for the corporate good.[89] Labatt Brewing Company Limited, described in the next In Practice, represents a good example of clan control.

Labatts is successfully using clan control, but the story illustrates that large size increases the demands on managers to maintain strong cultural values that support this type of control. Today's companies that are trying to become learning organizations often use clan control or self-control rather than relying on rules and regulations. Self-control is similar to clan control, but whereas clan control is a function of being socialized into a group, **self-control** stems from the values, goals, and standards of individuals. The organization attempts to induce a change such that individual employees' own internal values and work preferences are brought in line with the organization's values and goals.[90] With self-control, employees generally set their own goals and monitor their own performance, yet companies relying on self-control need strong leaders who can clarify boundaries within which employees exercise their own knowledge and discretion.

## In Practice
### Labatt Brewing Company Limited (Labatts)

"Don't expect working life [at Labatts] to be like one continuous beer commercial."[91] New employees learn immediately that they need to fit into the organization's culture or leave. They are told, on their first day at work, that those who cannot or will not embrace the InBev Way are in the wrong organization. (InBev SA is the Belgium-based company that owns Labatts.) According to John Stacey, vice president, People Matters, it is not enough to deliver results; people must fit into Labatts or leave. He says, "You may think that it's a harsh comment but we want both [fit and performance]."[92] He goes on to say that there's zero tolerance for complacency at Labatts and describes Labatts as a hard-driving environment.

John Stacey's principal role at Labatts is to ensure that the InBev Way—the values—permeate the organization. InBev has a global training program so that it can develop its own leadership from within the organization. Management trainees spend ten months learning all aspects of the business and then they are assigned junior management positions. The trainees are selected through a rigorous process—only 14 of more than 3,000 applicants are hired.

Labatts has been through several organizational changes and now brews more than 60 brands of beer worldwide. The InBev Way is designed to inspire and to control behaviour among the 3,200 Canadian employees.

Clan control or self-control may also be used in some departments, such as strategic planning, where uncertainty is high and performance is difficult to measure. Managers of departments that rely on these informal control mechanisms must not assume that the absence of written, bureaucratic control means no control is present. Clan control is invisible yet very powerful. One study found that the actions of employees were controlled even more powerfully and completely with clan control than with a bureaucratic hierarchy.[93] When clan control works, bureaucratic control is not needed.

*act!*

**Think**
Think about the various types of control. Which one would you prefer? Why?

## Organizational Decline and Downsizing

Earlier in the chapter, we discussed the organizational life cycle, which suggests that organizations are born, grow older, and eventually die. Every organization goes through periods of temporary decline. In addition, a reality in today's environment is that for some organizations, continual growth and expansion may not be possible.

All around, we see evidence that some organizations have stopped growing, and many are declining. Huge organizations such as Enron, WorldCom, and Arthur Andersen have collapsed partly as a result of rapid growth and ineffective control.

The Catholic Church continues to lose membership following reports of child molestation by priests and the failure in higher levels of the organization to remove molesters and prevent further abuse. Municipalities have been forced to close schools and lay off teachers as tax revenues have declined. Many big companies, including DaimlerChrysler, Bell Canada, General Motors, and General Electric, have had significant job cuts in recent years, and hundreds of Internet companies that once looked poised for rapid growth have gone out of business.

In this section, we examine the causes and stages of organizational decline and then discuss how leaders can effectively manage the downsizing that is often a reality in today's organizations.

## ■ Definition and Causes

The term **organizational decline** is used to define a condition in which a substantial, absolute decrease in an organization's resource base occurs over a period.[94] Organizational decline is often associated with environmental decline in the sense that an organizational domain experiences either a reduction in size (such as shrinkage in customer demand or erosion of a city's tax base) or a reduction in shape (such as a shift in customer demand). In general, three factors are considered to cause organizational decline.

1. *Organizational atrophy.* Atrophy occurs when organizations grow older and become inefficient and overly bureaucratized. The organization's ability to adapt to its environment deteriorates. Often, atrophy follows a long period of success, because an organization takes success for granted, becomes attached to practices and structures that worked in the past, and fails to adapt to changes in the environment.[95] For example, Blockbuster, which was king of the video-store industry in the 1980s and 1990s, had trouble adapting to the new world of video-on-demand (VOD) and digital downloading. Blockbuster was way behind upstarts like Netflix in pay-VOD delivery because managers had trouble giving up the traditional successful approach of renting out videos in stores and online. Blockbuster declared bankruptcy in Canada in 2011 and had sought Chapter 11 protection in 2010 in the United States.[96] Experts warn that companies risk becoming obsolete by sticking to patterns that were successful in the past but might no longer be effective.[97] Some warning signals for organizational atrophy include excess administrative and support staff, cumbersome administrative procedures, lack of effective communication and coordination, and outdated organizational structure.[98]

2. *Vulnerability.* Vulnerability reflects an organization's strategic inability to prosper in its environment. This often happens to small organizations that are not yet fully established. They are vulnerable to shifts in consumer tastes or in the economic health of the larger community. Small e-commerce companies that had not yet become established were the first to go out of business when the technology sector began to decline. Some organizations are vulnerable because they are unable to define the correct strategy to fit the environment. Vulnerable organizations typically need to redefine their environmental domain to enter new industries or markets.

3. *Environmental decline or competition.* Environmental decline refers to reduced energy and resources available to support an organization. When the environment has less capacity to support organizations, the organization has to either scale down operations or shift to another domain.[99] New competition increases

the problem, especially for small organizations. Consider what's happening to North American toolmakers, the companies that make the dies, moulds, jigs, fixtures, and gauges used on factory floors to manufacture everything from car doors to laser-guided bombs. Many have gone out of business in recent years, unable to compete with the super-low prices their counterparts in China are offering. As a result, there was a decrease of eight percent, between 1997 and 2004, in the number of workers employed in the toolmaker sector.[100]

## ■ A Model of Decline Stages

Based on an extensive review of organizational decline research, a model of decline stages has been proposed and is summarized in Exhibit 8.7. This model suggests that decline, if not managed properly, can move through five stages, resulting in organizational dissolution. [101]

1. *Blinded stage.* The first stage of decline is the internal and external change that threatens long-term survival and may require the organization to tighten up. The organization may have excess personnel, cumbersome procedures, or lack of harmony with customers. Leaders often miss the signals of decline at this point, and the solution is to develop effective scanning and control systems that indicate when something is wrong. With timely information, alert executives can bring the organization back to top performance.
2. *Inaction stage.* The second stage of decline is called inaction, in which denial occurs despite signs of deteriorating performance. Leaders may try to persuade

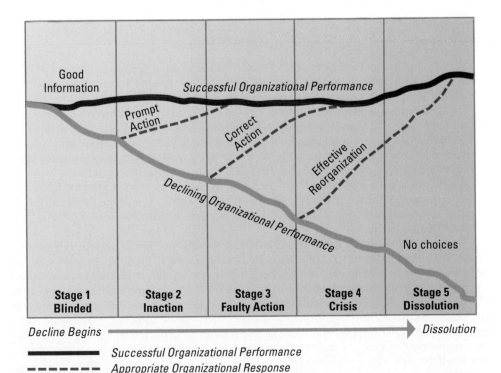

**EXHIBIT 8.7**
**Stages of Decline and the Widening Performance Gap**
Source: Reprinted from "Decline in Organizations: A Literature Integration and Extension," by William Weitzel and Ellen Jonsson, published in *Administrative Science Quarterly, 34,* no. 1 (March 1989), by permission of Administrative *Science Quarterly.* © Johnson Graduate School of Management, Cornell University.

employees that all is well. "Creative accounting" may make things look fine during this period. The solution is for leaders to acknowledge decline and take prompt action to realign the organization with the environment. Leadership actions may include new problem-solving approaches, increasing decision-making participation, and encouraging expression of dissatisfaction to learn what is wrong.

3. *Faulty action stage.* In the third stage, the organization is facing serious problems, and indicators of poor performance cannot be ignored. Failure to adjust to the declining spiral at this point can lead to organizational failure. Leaders are forced by severe circumstances to consider major changes. Actions may involve retrenchment, including downsizing personnel. Leaders should reduce employee uncertainty by clarifying values and providing information. A major mistake at this stage decreases the organization's chance for a turnaround.

4. *Crisis stage.* In the fourth stage, the organization still has not been able to deal with decline effectively and is facing a panic. The organization may experience chaos, efforts to go back to basics, sharp changes, and anger. If managers cannot prevent a stage-4 crisis, then the only solution is major reorganization. The social fabric of the organization is eroding, and dramatic actions, such as replacing top administrators and revolutionary changes in structure, strategy, and culture, are necessary. Workforce downsizing may be severe.

5. *Dissolution stage.* This stage of decline is irreversible. The organization is suffering loss of markets and reputation, the loss of its best personnel, and capital depletion. The only available strategy is to close down the organization in an orderly fashion and reduce the separation trauma of employees.

The following example of a once-respected Canadian retailer shows how failure to respond appropriately to signs of decline can lead to disaster.

## In Practice

### T. Eaton Company Limited (Eaton's)

Eaton's was founded by Timothy Eaton in 1869 on Yonge Street in downtown Toronto. His first venture, a bakery in St. Marys, Ontario, failed but he successfully changed the shop from a bakery to a dry goods store. He worked very hard and took the view that " ... we never close the store in the evening while there is anybody on the street."[102] Timothy Eaton was an innovator—he pioneered "sales in cash only" and "satisfaction guaranteed or money refunded" approaches to retail. By the mid-1880s, Eaton's had electric lights and a sprinkler system and, in 1884, Eaton's distributed its first mail-order catalogue. The Eaton family ran the company without interruption for many years. During World War II, Eaton's had a staff of 30,000. Eaton's had a strong culture—employees referred to themselves proudly as Eatonians. Eatonians received lavish presents from the family considered by many to be royalty. Even so, workers tried, unsuccessfully, to unionize Eaton's in 1952 in response to the long hours and low wages that they endured. In 1984, they tried again and failed again to unionize the chain.[103]

From the 1960s onward, Eaton's faced increasing competition from Simpsons-Sears and boutiques across the country. In 1997, the Eaton family, who owned all the shares in Eaton's, sought bankruptcy protection. At the time, Eaton's had 90 stores and 24,500 employees. In 1998, Eaton's went public and reduced the number of its stores to 64. Even so, Eaton's suffered a net loss of $72 million and in 1999 it closed more stores and restructured. In August 1999, after its share price had plummeted from a June 1998 high of $16 to 71¢, Eaton's went bankrupt.[104] The restructuring effort had failed and what was once the largest privately held department chain in the world became not much more than a real estate play. The Royal Canadian Air Farce gave Eaton's a funeral and noted that Eaton's was Walmarted![105]

While there are many possible explanations for the chain's demise, one important factor was Timothy Eaton's children's and grandchildren's lack of interest in the business. "Fundamentally, it appears that the problem-sensing ability of management was missing at the troubled Eaton's."[106] Sears Canada bought the rights to the Eaton name but, on February 26, 2002, conceded defeat in its efforts to relaunch Eaton's as an upscale retailer. Sears Canada is now facing significant threats to its future. It has sold five of its properties, including its flagship store in the Eaton Centre. Nordstrom Inc., an American high-end retail chain, will open its flagship Canadian store in Sears' space in the Eaton Centre.[107]

---

As this example shows, properly managing organizational decline is necessary if an organization is to avoid dissolution. Leaders have a responsibility to detect the signs of decline, acknowledge them, implement necessary action, and reverse course. Some of the most difficult decisions pertain to downsizing, which refers to intentionally reducing the size of a company's workforce.

## ■ Downsizing Implementation

The economic downturn that began in 2000 has made **downsizing** a common practice in North American corporations. When an organization is downsized, individuals are laid off permanently or are not replaced when they retire. In addition, downsizing is a part of many change initiatives in today's organizations.[108] Re-engineering projects, mergers and acquisitions, global competition, and the trend toward outsourcing have all led to job reductions.[109]

Some researchers have found that massive downsizing has often not achieved the intended benefits and in some cases has significantly harmed the organization.[110] Nevertheless, there are times when downsizing is a necessary part of managing organizational decline. During the most recent recession, U.S.-based banks cut 65,000 employees and many companies around the world also cut back their workforce.[111] A number of techniques can help smooth the downsizing process and ease tensions for employees who leave and for those who remain.[112]

1. *Communicate more, not less.* Some organizations seem to think the less that's said about a pending layoff, the better. Not so. Organizational managers should provide advance notice with as much information as possible. At 3Com Corporation, managers drew up a three-stage plan as they prepared for layoffs. First, they warned employees several months ahead that layoffs were inevitable. Soon thereafter, they held on-site presentations at all locations to explain to employees why the layoffs were needed and to provide as much information as they could about what employees should expect. Employees being cut were given the required full 60 days' notice.[113] Managers should remember that it is impossible to over-communicate during turbulent times. Remaining employees need to know what is expected of them, whether future layoffs are a possibility, and what the organization is doing to help co-workers who have lost their jobs.

2. *Provide assistance to displaced workers.* The organization has a responsibility to help displaced workers cope with the loss of their jobs and get re-established in the job market. The organization can provide training, severance packages, extended benefits, and outplacement assistance. In addition, counselling services for both employees and their families can ease the trauma associated with a job loss. Another key step is to allow employees to leave with dignity, giving them an opportunity to say goodbye to colleagues and meet with leaders to express their hurt and anger.

3. *Help the survivors cope.* Leaders should remember the emotional needs of survivors as well. Many people experience survivor guilt, anger, confusion, and sadness after the loss of colleagues, and these feelings should be acknowledged. Survivors might also be concerned about their own jobs and have difficulty adapting to the changes in job duties, responsibilities, and so forth.

Even the best-managed organizations may sometimes need to lay off employees in a turbulent environment or to revitalize the organization and reverse decline. Leaders can attain positive results if they handle downsizing in a way that lets departing employees leave with dignity and enables remaining organization members to be motivated, productive, and committed to a better future.

## In Practice
### Dofasco (now ArcelorMittal Dofasco)

C. W. Sherman created the Dominion Steel Casting Company in 1912 to make steel castings for Canadian railways. It was not until 1918 that its name was changed to Dofasco. In 1938, Dofasco became the first Canadian manufacturer to introduce profit sharing. "[World War II] put added pressure on Canada's heavy industries. In 1941, production started at Dofasco's armour plate shop. Every inch of armour plate used to protect Canadian soldiers was manufactured by Dofasco."[114]

In the 1970s, the North American steel industry shrank considerably—32 percent of its steelmaking capacity disappeared. Dofasco, however, survived by improving customer service and automating many of its processes. A 1985 article in *The Globe and Mail* reported that "steel industry watchers are beginning to run out of superlatives to describe the continued robust performance of Dofasco."[115] However, in the late 1980s and early 1990s, Dofasco downsized considerably. The number of employees dropped from 12,800 to 7,000 through attrition and voluntary early retirements.

In April 1994, when 650 employees were laid off, their layoffs were handled through the Canadian Steel Trade and Employment Congress, a joint venture between Canadian steel companies and the United Steelworkers of America. The Congress provides various services to steel industry workers such as worker adjustment services, helping workers affected by layoff and/or shutdowns, and providing training services for the workforce.[116] Dofasco created an action committee from all its stakeholders and 14 people were assigned to develop a program to assist employees to adjust to the layoffs. The resulting program was called the Dofasco Transition Assistance Program. The laid-off workers received new skills training, career counselling, and job placement. At the same time, Dofasco introduced a program called Play-to-Win designed to reduce the negative impact of the layoffs on those who were not laid off. The program consisted of a three-day experiential session that focused on topics such as coping with change, rebuilding trust, and working together in a team environment.[117]

## Summary and Interpretation

The material covered in this chapter contains several important ideas about organizations. Organizations evolve through distinct life cycle stages as they grow and mature. Organizational structure, internal systems, and management issues are different for each stage of development. Growth creates crises and revolutions along the way toward large size. A major task of managers is to guide the organization through the entrepreneurial, collectivity, formalization, and elaboration stages of development. As organizations progress through the life cycle and grow larger and more complex, they generally take on bureaucratic characteristics, such as rules, division of labour, written records, hierarchy of authority, and impersonal procedures.

Bureaucracy is a logical form of organizing that lets firms use resources efficiently. However, in many large corporate and government organizations, bureaucracy has come under attack with attempts to decentralize authority, flatten organizational structure, reduce rules and written records, and create a small-company mind-set. These companies are willing to trade economies of scale for responsive, adaptive organizations. Many companies are subdividing to gain small-company advantages. Another approach to overcoming the problems of bureaucracy is to use a structural concept called the incident command system, which enables the organization to glide smoothly between a highly formalized, hierarchical style that is effective during times of stability and a more flexible, loosely structured one needed to respond to unexpected or volatile environmental conditions.

In large organizations, greater support is required from clerical and professional staff specialists. This is a logical outcome of employee specialization and the division of labour. By dividing an organization's tasks and having specialists perform each part, the organization can become more efficient.

All organizations, large and small, need systems for control. Managers can choose among three overall control strategies: bureaucratic, market, and clan. Bureaucratic control relies on standard rules and the rational-legal authority of managers. Market control is used where product or service outputs can be priced and competition exists. Clan control and self-control are associated with uncertain and rapidly changing organization processes. They rely on commitment, tradition, and shared values for control. Managers may use a combination of control approaches to meet the organization's needs.

Many organizations have stopped growing, and some are declining. Organizations go through stages of decline, and it is the responsibility of managers to detect the signs of decline, implement necessary action, and reverse course. One of the most difficult decisions is downsizing the workforce. To smooth the downsizing process, managers should communicate with employees and provide as much information as possible, provide assistance to displaced workers, and remember to address the emotional needs of those who remain with the organization.

## ■ Key Concepts

bureaucracy, p. 305
bureaucratic control, p. 311
centralization, p. 307
charismatic authority, p. 312
clan control, p. 314
collectivity stage, p. 299
downsizing, p. 319
elaboration stage, p. 300
entrepreneurial stage, p. 298
formalization stage, p. 300

formalization, p. 307
incident command system, p. 308
life cycle, p. 298
market control, p. 313
organizational decline, p. 316
personnel ratios, p. 307
rational-legal authority, p. 312
self-control, p. 315
traditional authority, p. 312

## ■ Discussion Questions

1. Discuss the key differences between large and small organizations. Which kinds of organizations would be better off acting as large organizations, and which are best trying to act as big-company/small-company hybrids?

2. Why do large organizations tend to be more formalized?

3. If you were managing a department of university or college professors, how might you structure the department differently than if you were managing a department of book-keepers? Why?

4. Apply the concept of life cycle to an organization with which you are familiar, such as a university or college, or a local business. What stage is the organization in now? How did the organization handle or pass through its life-cycle crises?

5. Describe the three bases of authority identified by Weber. Is it possible for each of these types of authority to function at the same time within an organization?

6. In writing about types of control, William Ouchi said, "The Market is like the trout and the Clan like the salmon, each a beautiful highly specialized species which requires uncommon conditions for its survival. In comparison, the bureaucratic method of control is the Catfish—clumsy, ugly, but able to live in the widest range of environments and ulti- mately, the dominant species." Discuss what Ouchi meant by that analogy.

7. Government organizations often seem more bureaucratic than for-profit organizations. Could this partly be the result of the type of control used in government organizations? Explain.

8. The incident command system has been used primarily by organizations that regularly deal with crisis situations. Discuss whether this approach seems workable for a large media company that wants to reduce bureaucracy. How about for a manufacturer of cell phones?

9. Refer to the Air Canada case at the beginning of Chapter 1 and discuss how Air Canada illustrates the various stages of the organizational life cycle. In what stage of the life cycle does Air Canada seem to be today?

10. Do you think a "no growth" philosophy of management should be taught in business schools? Why?

## ■ Chapter 8 Workbook: Control Mechanisms*

Think of two situations in your life: your school and your work experiences. How is control exerted? Fill out the tables.

### On the Job

| Your Job Responsibilities | How Your Boss Controls | Positives of This Control | Negatives of This Control | How You Would Improve Control |
|---|---|---|---|---|
|  |  |  |  |  |
|  |  |  |  |  |
|  |  |  |  |  |
|  |  |  |  |  |

### At the University

| Items | How Professor A (Small Class) Controls | How Professor B (Large Class) Controls | How These Controls Influence You | What You Think Is a Better Control |
|---|---|---|---|---|
| Exams |  |  |  |  |
| Assignments/papers |  |  |  |  |
| Class participation |  |  |  |  |
| Attendance |  |  |  |  |
| Other |  |  |  |  |

*From DAFT. *Organization Theory and Design*, 10E. © 2010 South-Western, a part of Cengage Learning, Inc. Reproduced by permission. www.cengage.com/permissions

## Questions

1. What are the advantages and disadvantages of the various controls?
2. What happens when there is too much control? Too little?
3. Does the type of control depend on the situation and the number of people involved?
4. How do the control mechanisms of your team mates compare to those of other students?

## Case for Analysis: Daily Grind Coffee Inc.*

### The Challenge

Massimo Iafolla, principal owner and manager of *Daily Grind Coffee Inc.*, and Tom Paquette, a supporting investor and assistant manager, looked out their front door and started counting the eating establishments within an easy walk of their front door. With a Subway literally next door, a Starbucks in the Safeway in the same retail complex, a McDonald's on the far corner of the lot, a Tim Hortons, a Pizza Hut and a Joey's Seafood just a short jaunt across the two streets the mall fronted on, the number of alternatives competing for the same eat-out dollar was formidable.

And these were big companies with lots of advertising support and high brand-name recognition. The two Winnipeg restaurateurs wondered: How could they differentiate their eating establishment, Daily Grind Coffee Inc., from the plethora of chains and franchises?

### The Background

In 2005, Mr. Iafolla launched a specialty coffeehouse on west Portage Avenue in Winnipeg. Mr. Iafolla, who graduated in 1999 from the Asper School of Business at the University of Manitoba, had two passions: food and entrepreneurship. These two interests came together in his decision to launch a specialty coffeehouse, which he called Daily Grind Coffee.

Known informally by customers as The Daily Grind, the restaurant operated in a 1,500-square-foot space in a strip mall in the Winnipeg neighbourhood of Westwood and it had seating for about 40 patrons. The business began with the intent of offering specialty coffees, breakfasts and lunches, as well as an assortment of desserts and gelatos.

### The Problem

Being a small independent like Daily Grind Coffee was not without its challenges. As the opening vignette suggested, there were lots of other eating options with a significant number in very close proximity. These restaurants had all kinds of advertising support and brand recognition that little guys could only dream about.

Mr. Iafolla and Mr. Paquette could offer customers no smiling clown, no national spokesperson who lost dozens of pounds by eating the company's sandwiches, no annual promotion involving rolling up the edges of cups in a search for prizes. Given all the things they couldn't do, what could they do instead in order to compete against the prominent chain operations?

### The Solution

Mr. Iafolla and Mr. Paquette have sought to define and defend their turf by doing what the big guys can't, or at least can't do as easily — began to differentiate themselves two years ago by offering an array of dishes that score heavy on the 'home made' element. Sales have increased every month since they were introduced.

Whether it's offering home made soups, such as their special Hungarian mushroom or West African peanut, or specialty baked products, Daily Grind Coffee has sought and found a way to differentiate itself by offering something different and desirable. The efforts have met with approval from customers and local organizations.

For example, a local school recently contacted The Daily Grind to cater a staff appreciation day with soups and sandwiches. And a number of local church groups have made it a point to 'congregate' at The Grind after church for Sunday lunch.

Mr. Iafolla and Mr. Paquette have also made it a point to get to know many of these customers—by name and by palate. The common theme running through these experiences points to a larger lesson potentially relevant for all smaller players: Offer customers what they want, and what the big guys can't, and you will create a basis for sustainable co-existence. And as the experience of Daily Grind Coffee suggests, you can get out of the 'daily grind' of competing against clowns, spokesmen and contests.

Or as Mr. Iafolla puts it: "Part of me is starting to believe that the three most important things to success are not 'location, location, location,' but 'hard work, good quality and treating your customers right.'"

## Assignment Questions

1. How well do you think that The Daily Grind defines its distinctive niche?
2. What are future challenges the organization should anticipate?

*Source: Reg Litz "How a Small Coffee Shop Took on the Big Guys," Special to *Globe and Mail Update, The Globe and Mail*, accessed from http://www.umanitoba.ca/faculties/management/media/201101210-How-a-small-coffee-shop-took-on-the-big-guys.pdf on February 6, 2011. Reproduced by permission of the author.

## Case for Analysis: I Love Rewards Inc.*

Razor Suleman started out creating T-shirts and other inexpensive items while he was a university student. He has turned that fledgling business into a growing player in the consumer reward/incentive industry with a strong footing in Canada and a toehold in the massive U.S. market.

Razor Suleman has a plan. Over the next five years, he wants to build I Love Rewards Inc., the company he started in his dorm room at Waterloo, Ont.'s Wilfrid Laurier University, into a $1-billion, online powerhouse. He can see the company, which today generates less than $10-million in sales, becoming to loyalty rewards what Google is to search engines.

"I think it is supremely doable," he says. "Loyalty rewards programs are enormously popular across North America and we have found a business model that will extend them to the Internet, which is wide open territory right now."

Loyalty rewards are simple programs where merchants give customers points with each purchase. Those points can be redeemed for a range of goods and services. Think Aeroplan, Air Miles, Amex Membership Rewards and even Petro-points.

I Love Rewards recently moved into the consumer rewards field. It won its spurs creating employee incentive programs for clients such as ING, KPMG and Rogers Communications. The expansion into the consumer field seemed a natural move, Mr. Suleman says.

"Our first client was a large packaged food company that made those corndogs on a stick," he explains. "We created a program where consumers would buy the product and look for a code on the package. They could then go to a dedicated Web site, enter the code and receive rewards points.

"When they amassed enough points they could trade them for electronics from Sony, things like MP3 players. It worked well and that led to other, similar promotions."

But as he was turning out online incentive programs for others, an idea struck him. Why not do it for himself? Why not create RazorPoints and enlist online merchants without incentive programs to sign up as clients? For them, it would be an administrative no brainer. All they had to do was decide what level of RazorPoints to offer per $1 spent; I LoveRewards would handle the rest.

Razorpoints.com becomes a reality this fall. In March, Mr. Suleman began testing a version among employees, friends and the employees of clients. Membership is by invitation only. How it works is simple.

Visitors go to the site, become members of the program and create a home page, which effectively becomes their personal launching point for all the sites they visit on the Internet. Each time they take an online shopping spree that starts from the Razorpoints.com site, participating merchants award a fixed number of RazorPoints based on a percentage of the sale before taxes. Some might offer 5 percent while others may offer up to 10 percent, he says.

Each RazorPoint will be worth 1¢. Collectors can cash them in for a variety of merchandise, travel-related and service rewards such as Apple iPods and BestBuy Gift Cards, up to golf holidays with Tiger Woods. RazorPoints makes its money by cashing in the dollar value of those points with merchants and on the spread between what it pays for its rewards and what it redeems them for.

"The idea is to get teenagers in the habit of using the site as their home base," he says. "Loyalty programs rely on habit. If you get teens engaged, then the chances are you will have them as collectors for life."

He can also see an enormous appeal for his program among small merchants who cannot afford to create their own loyalty program and larger ones who have been shut out of programs such as Air Miles because those programs offer exclusivity within certain categories to participating merchants.

"We have added to our management team to tackle this project. We hired a new marketing vice-president formerly with the Disney organization. This is a whole new business and its future is terribly exciting," he says.

Mr. Suleman's enthusiasm has carried him a long way since he started the predecessor to I Love Rewards in his second year of university. The idea was to create T-shirts, sweatshirts, mugs and other items that the student union could sell to undergraduates.

"It made me enough that I graduated without any debt," he says.

After graduation, the idea of working for anyone else had little appeal. He thought there might be a market for employee incentive programs based on his T-shirts in the corporate world. As it turned out, he was right, but not in the way he was moving.

His first client was ING, the Dutch virtual bank. ING wanted T-shirts to motivate its call centre staff and to create a sort of team spirit as they sold GICs, mortgages and such. "They came to us and said: 'This is not as effective as we would like. Can you create a more results-oriented incentive program?'"

Mr. Suleman devised an incentive program based on point rewards. Sell a mortgage or a GIC and earn a corresponding number of rewards. For rewards, he used the catalogue of items I Love Rewards was selling to clients and expanded it to include hot, low-cost electronics such as iPods, and the program took off.

"ING found it was indeed a profound motivational tool," he says. "Sales took off."

Rogers Communications became his next major client, starting with a trial program covering one division and now expanded to include the entire company. KPMG is using one of the company's incentive programs to reward employees who show they adhere to and practise the company's core values.

Two years ago, I Love Rewards entered the consumer space with its Pogo Points program. Today, corporate programs generate 70 percent of the revenues while consumer programs account for the balance.

To crack the vast U.S. market, Mr. Suleman opened an office in New York City. "U.S. companies want to do business with U.S. companies," he says. "If we wanted to crack the U.S. market, we had to put a U.S. face on the company."

So far, that strategy is successful, he says. I Love Rewards is picking up U.S. clients.

The company has also won a reputation for its employment policies. It has been named one of the 100 best employers in Canada and one of the top 50 in Toronto. It gives staff time off for charitable and community involvement and, this fall, it will introduce an employment share ownership plan.

"We have grown 5,000 percent in the past five years," Mr. Suleman says. "And I think that is just the beginning. As I say, we have the potential to be a billion-dollar company in five to 10 years."

## I Love Rewards Inc.

Head office: Toronto, Ont.
Business sector: Incentive rewards and loyalty programs
Market: North America
Number of Employees: 44
2007 Revenues: $10 million
Website: www.iloverewards.com

## Assignment Questions

1. What risks does I Love Rewards Inc. face as it expands?
2. Razor Suleman comments that his company could be a billion-dollar company in five to ten years. What are some challenges he may face then?

---

*Source: "Feature Entrepreneur Profile: I Love Rewards Inc.," *Financial Post*, June 18, 2007. Material reprinted with the express permission of National Post Inc.

PART 5
# Managing Dynamic Processes

# 9

# Organizational Culture and Ethical Values

© Gary Knight/VII/VII/Corbis

## Birks & Mayors Inc. (Birks)

In 1879, Henry Birks founded Henry Birks & Sons, an exclusive jewellery store that emphasized quality and service. It dominated Canada's market for many years and has been recognized internationally for its innovative designs in diamond jewellery. In 1993, Regaluxe Investment bought Birks and, in 2002, Birks acquired a controlling interest in Mayors Jewelers Inc.[1] In 2007, Birks was selected as the official jeweller for the Vancouver 2010 Winter Olympic Games.

The 2006 film *Blood Diamond,* starring Leonardo DiCaprio, raised global awareness about the horrors of blood (or conflict) diamonds. Blood diamonds are those diamonds that are mined, often by children (see photo), in war zones and sold to finance armed conflicts and civil wars.

Partnership Africa Canada in Sierra Leone reports that more than 50,000 people have been killed, many more displaced, and much of the country's infrastructure ruined. Meanwhile, the underground trade of illicit diamonds is booming. Conflict diamonds are valued between four percent and 15 percent of the world's total and generate annual trade revenues of $7.5 billion.[2]

In response to the advocacy of the United Nations and many nonprofit organizations around the world, the Kimberley Process Certification Scheme was created in 2003. The Kimberley Process requires that signatory countries certify that all rough-diamond exports are conflict-free and that the country will allow importation of diamonds only from participating countries.

Birks has implemented measures to comply with the Kimberley Process and notifies its vendors of the requirement to comply with the Kimberley Process Certification Scheme. It sources diamonds only from cutters who declare on their invoices that the diamonds have been obtained in compliance with the Kimberley Process.[3]

However, in a new initiative, Birks has gone beyond compliance to the Kimberley Process. Birks is launching a new line of jewellery using diamonds from Botswana. The line will be sourced exclusively through Diamond Trade Company Botswana, which is part of DeBeers. According to John Orrico, Birks' senior vice president, as the diamonds will be cut and polished in Botswana, "[You] can feel good that it's giving back to the people from whose country it was originally mined."[4]

## ■ Purpose of This Chapter

This chapter explores ideas about organizational culture and ethical values, and how these are influenced by organizations. The first section describes the nature of organizational culture, its origins and purpose, and how to identify and interpret culture through ceremonies, stories, and symbols. We then examine how culture reinforces the strategy and structural design the organization needs to be effective in its environment and discuss the important role of culture in organizational learning and high performance. Next, the chapter turns to ethical values and social responsibility. We consider how managers implement the structures and systems that influence ethical and socially responsible behaviour. The chapter also discusses how leaders shape culture and ethical values in a direction suitable for strategy and performance outcomes. The chapter closes with a brief overview of the complex cultural and ethical issues managers face in an international environment. Complete the You and Design feature to see what sort of organizational culture you prefer.

## YOU & DESIGN

### Organization Culture Preference

The fit between a manager or employee and culture can determine both personal success and satisfaction. To understand your culture preference, rank the following items from 1 to 8 based on the strength of your preference (1 = highest preference; 8 = lowest preference).

1. The organization is very personal, much like an extended family. _____

2. The organization is dynamic and changing, where people take risks. _____

3. The organization is achievement oriented, with the focus on competition and getting jobs done. _____

4. The organization is stable and structured, with clarity and established procedures. _____

5. Management style is characterized by teamwork and participation. _____

6. Management style is characterized by innovation and risk-taking. _____

7. Management style is characterized by high performance demands and achievement. _____

8. Management style is characterized by security and predictability. _____

**Scoring:** To compute your preference for each type of culture, add together the scores for each set of two questions as follows:

Clan culture—total for questions 1, 5:_____
Adaptability culture—total for questions 2, 6:_____
Mission culture—total for questions 3, 7:_____
Bureaucratic culture—total for questions 4, 8:_____

**Interpretation:** Each of the preceding questions pertains to one of the four types of culture in Exhibit 9.4. A lower score means a stronger preference for that specific culture.

You will likely be more comfortable and more effective as a manager in a corporate culture that is compatible with your personal preferences. A higher score means the culture would not fit your expectations, and you would have to change your style to be effective. Review the text discussion of the four culture types. Do your cultural preference scores seem correct to you?

Source: Adapted from Kim S. Cameron and Robert D. Quinn, *Diagnosing and Changing Organizational Culture* (Reading, Massachusetts: Addison-Wesley, 1999).

## Organizational Culture

Every organization, like Birks, has a set of values that characterize how people behave and how the organization carries out everyday business. Sometimes, these values get out of alignment with the environment and cause problems for the organization. One of the most important jobs organizational leaders do is instill and support the kind of values needed for the company to thrive.

Strong cultures can have a profound impact, which can be either positive or negative for the organization. For example, Teva Neuroscience in Montréal, which was selected in 2007 as the best small company to work for, based on a survey of 120 organizations, conducted by Queen's University and Hewitt Associates, "borders on the obsessive to living its values."[5] It works to hire the right people to keep staff well informed and to collect feedback from its employees. According to Jon Congleton, "[We] focus on three clarities: clarity of structure: Where do I fit in with this company? Clarity of direction: Where am I going? And clarity of measurement: How do I know I did a good job?"[6] In 2011, for example, Teva Neuroscince was honoured for the second consecutive year with a Stevie Award for the best sales team of the year. According to Vice President of Sales Paul Ritman, "This recognition is the direct result of the strong teamwork, superior performance and patient focus of our sales force, and the ongoing support from our field and home office partners. Congratulations to everyone...this was truly a team effort."[7]

Negative cultural norms, however, can damage an organization just as powerfully as positive ones can strengthen it. Consider the case of Enron, where the organizational culture supported pushing everything to the limits: business practices, rules, personal behaviour, and laws. Executives drove expensive cars, challenged employees to participate in risky competitive behaviour, and often celebrated big deals by heading off to a bar or dance club.[8] A related concept concerning the influence of norms and values on how people work together and how they treat one another and customers is called *social capital*. **Social capital** refers to the quality of interactions among people and whether they share a common perspective. In organizations with a high degree of social capital, for example, relationships are based on trust, mutual understandings, and shared norms and values that enable people to cooperate and coordinate their activities to achieve organizational goals.[9] An organization can have either a high or a low level of social capital. One way to think of social capital is as *goodwill*. When relationships both within the organization and with customers, suppliers, and partners are based on honesty, trust, and respect, a spirit of goodwill exists and people willingly cooperate to achieve mutual benefits. A high level of social capital enables frictionless social interactions and exchanges that help to facilitate smooth organizational functioning.

Think of eBay, which relies largely on social capital to bring millions of buyers and sellers together on its website. eBay's 2013 enabled commerce volume increased 21 percent, its revenue grew 14 percent, and its net income climbed.[10] The company builds goodwill through mechanisms such as a feedback system that enables buyers and sellers to rate one another, discussion boards that build a sense of community among site users, and regular all-day focus groups with representative buyers and sellers. Another example of a company with high social capital is Deloitte & Touche, LLP, Calgary. According to Esther Colwill, now a partner, the firm recognizes everyone as individuals. She recounts what happened when she shared her goal of scaling the Seven Summits—the highest mountain in each continent. "[The organization] gave her a satellite phone and asked her to leave messages now and then. The firm also gave her tens of thousands of dollars in sponsorship money and accommodated the six months off she needed over five years to complete her goal, including her three-month Everest expedition in 2005 that gave her 15 cold, dizzying minutes at the top of the world. 'I joined Deloitte...wondering if at some point I would have to leave,' says Colwill. 'I really had no idea how open they would be, but they were amazing.'"[11]

Other organizations also build social capital by being open and honest and cultivating positive social relationships among employees and with outsiders. Relationships based on cutthroat competition, self-interest, and subterfuge, such as those at Enron, can be devastating to a company. Social capital relates to both organizational culture and ethics, which is the focus of this chapter.

The popularity of the organizational culture topic raises a number of questions. Can we identify cultures? Can culture be aligned with strategy? How can cultures be managed or changed? The best place to start is by defining culture and explaining how it can be identified in organizations.

**Apply**

How can you apply the practice of building *your* social capital in your career?

# What Is Culture?

**Culture** is the set of values, norms, guiding beliefs, and understandings that is shared by members of an organization and is taught to new members.[12] It represents the unwritten, feeling part of the organization. Everyone participates in culture, but culture generally goes unnoticed. It is only when organizations try to implement new strategies or programs that go against basic cultural norms and values that they come face-to-face with the power of culture.

Organizational culture exists at two levels, as illustrated in Exhibit 9.1. On the surface are visible artifacts and observable behaviours—the ways people dress and act, and the symbols, stories, and ceremonies organization members share. The visible elements of culture, however, reflect deeper values in the minds of organization members. These underlying values, assumptions, beliefs, and thought processes are the true culture.[13] For example, The Body Shop incorporated an on-site biological sewage treatment system in a greenhouse near its Toronto headquarters. "Beauty and function combine in the botanical and biological workings of the system, [enabling] the company to show off its corporate philosophy, [a commitment to sustainability]. Every drop reused is a drop of municipal water saved and a drop less discharged."[14] The attributes of culture display themselves in many ways but

**EXHIBIT 9.1**
Levels of Organizational Culture

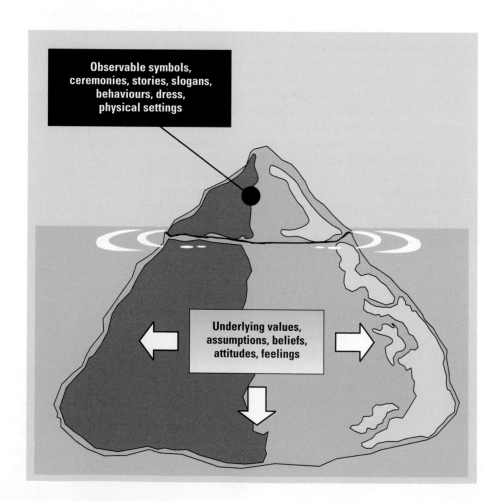

Observable symbols, ceremonies, stories, slogans, behaviours, dress, physical settings

Underlying values, assumptions, beliefs, attitudes, feelings typically evolve into a patterned set of activities carried out through social interactions.[15] The patterns can be used to interpret culture.

## ■ Emergence and Purpose of Culture

Culture provides members with a sense of organizational identity and generates in them a commitment to beliefs and values that are larger than themselves. Though ideas that become part of culture can come from anywhere within the organization, an organization's culture generally begins with a founder or early leader who articulates and implements particular ideas and values as a vision, philosophy, or business strategy.

When these ideas and values lead to success, they become institutionalized, and an organizational culture emerges that reflects the vision and strategy of the founder or leader.[16] For example, the culture at ExtendMedia (now part of Cisco Systems), a dot-com-bust survivor that provides software and services to distribute content through the Web, reflects the founder's vision of being a cool company. As Keith Kocho puts it "There was never that big IPO or home run acquisition, but we've always been in advance of being cool...We had an open concept workplace with stock options and a beer fridge and people's kids and dogs running around before Silicon Valley was even waking up to these kinds of ideas."[17]

Cultures serve two critical functions in organizations: (1) to integrate members so that they know how to relate to one another, and (2) to help the organization adapt to the external environment. **Internal integration** means that members develop a collective identity and know how to work together effectively. It is culture that guides day-to-day working relationships and determines how people communicate within the organization, what behaviour is acceptable or not acceptable, and how power and status are allocated. Culture is a potent force in shaping organizational identity. It provides cues to help organizational actors make sense of their organizations. "Organizational identities, then, provide the context within which members interpret and assign profound meaning to surface-level behaviour."[18] **External adaptation** refers to how the organization meets goals and deals with outsiders. Culture helps guide the daily activities of workers to meet certain goals. It can help the organization respond rapidly to customer needs or the moves of a competitor.

The organization's culture also guides employee decision making in the absence of written rules or policies.[19] Thus, both functions of culture are related to building the organization's social capital, by forging either positive or negative relationships both within the organization and with outsiders.

**Compare**

Compare the cultures of two organizations you know well. What did you observe and then what inferences did you make?

---

Tony Hsieh joined Zappos.com in 2000 and by 2009, the company had a market value of $1.2 billion when it was bought by Amazon. Zappos is an extraordinary e-commerce success; it is one of the largest online shoe and apparel stores in the world. Zappos has 50,000 types of shoes and 1000 brands and provides free shipping. Seventy-five percent of its business is from repeat customers.[20]

Hsieh has described his business philosophy in *Delivering Happiness: A Path to Profits, Passion, and Purpose*. In his view, organizational culture needs to be a top priority for leaders. At Zappos, all employees attend a four-week training session and commit the core values to memory. At the end of training, they're offered $2,000 to resign if they believe they aren't a good fit with the culture. Every year, Zappos puts out a *Culture Book*, in which employees share their own stories about what the Zappos culture means to them. Core values are supported by structures, processes, and systems that give them concrete reality and keep them in the forefront of employees' attention, and performance reviews are based in part on how well people participate in the culture.

**In Practice**
**Zappos.com (Zappos)**

Zappos has a set of ten core values that include *Create fun and a little weirdness; Deliver WOW through service; Embrace and drive change; Be adventurous, creative, and open-minded; Pursue growth and learning;* and *Be humble.* Significantly Hsieh didn't dictate the values from on high. He sent an e-mail to all employees asking them what values should guide the company. The responses were discussed, condensed, and combined to come up with the final list.

Zappos continues to evolve its management processes and structures to complement its values. It has decided to remove manager roles; employees will work in circles, engaging in various roles and responsibilities. It has adopted the 'holacracy' structure which is essentially a series of circles of authority that allow everyone to put their ideas on the table. It does not, however, completely flatten the organization. Holocracy is still quite untested as an organizational design choice.[21]

## ■ Interpreting Culture

To identify and interpret culture requires that people make inferences based on observable artifacts. Artifacts can be studied but are hard to decipher accurately. An award ceremony in one company may have a different meaning than in another company. To decipher what is really going on in an organization requires detective work and probably some experience as an insider. Some of the typical and important observable aspects of culture are rites and ceremonies, stories, symbols, and language.[22]

**Rites and Ceremonies.** Important artifacts for culture are **rites and ceremonies**, the elaborate, planned activities that make up a special event and are often conducted for the benefit of an audience. Managers can hold rites and ceremonies to provide dramatic examples of what a company values. These are special occasions that reinforce specific values, create a bond among people for sharing an important understanding, and anoint and celebrate heroes who symbolize important beliefs and activities.[23]

Four types of rites that appear in organizations are summarized in Exhibit 9.2. Rites of passage facilitate the transition of employees into new social roles. Rites of enhancement create stronger social identities and increase the status of employees. Rites of renewal reflect training and development activities that improve organization functioning. Rites of integration create common bonds and good feelings among

**EXHIBIT 9.2**
A Typology of Organization Rites and Their Social Consequences

| TYPES OF RITE | EXAMPLE | SOCIAL CONSEQUENCES |
|---|---|---|
| Passage | Induction and basic training, Canadian military | Facilitate transition of persons into social roles and statuses that are new for them |
| Enhancement | Annual awards night | Enhance social identities and increase status of employees |
| Renewal | Organization development activities | Refurbish social structures and improve organization functioning |
| Integration | Office holiday party | Encourage and revive common feelings that bind members together and commit them to the organization |

Source: Adapted from Harrison M. Trice and Janice M. Beyer, "Studying Organizational Cultures through Rites and Ceremonials," *Academy of Management Review* 9 (1984), 653–669; permission conveyed through Copyright Clearance Center, Inc.

employees and increase commitment to the organization. The following examples illustrate how these rites and ceremonies are used by top managers to reinforce important cultural values:

- At the first offering of the Internationally Trained Lawyers Program at the University of Toronto, students from 20 countries started their training with orientation week. "Orientation week—a rite of passage for so many Canadians—proved a novelty to most of these students.... Many simply wanted to get down to the business of studying and preparing for their exams. But they all embraced Orientation quickly!"[24] This is a rite of passage.
- Mary Kay Cosmetics Company holds elaborate awards ceremonies, presenting gold and diamond pins, furs, and luxury cars to high-achieving sales consultants. The most successful consultants are introduced by film clips, such as the kind used to introduce award nominees in the entertainment industry. This is a rite of enhancement.
- An important event at Walt Disney Company is the "Gong Show." Three times a year, executives hold events around the United States at which any employee, down to the level of secretaries, janitors, and mailroom personnel, can pitch movie ideas to top executives. The fun event is a way to symbolize and support the company's commitment to employee involvement and innovation.[25] This is a rite of renewal.
- Whenever a Walmart executive visits one of the stores, he or she leads employees in the Walmart cheer: "Give me a W! Give me an A! Give me an L! Give me a squiggly! (All do a version of the twist.) Give me an M! Give me an A! Give me an R! Give me a T! What's that spell? Walmart! What's that spell? Walmart! Who's No. 1? THE CUSTOMER!" The cheer strengthens bonds among employees and reinforces their commitment to common goals.[26] This is a rite of integration.

**Stories.** **Stories** are narratives based on true events that are frequently shared among organizational employees and told to new employees to inform them about an organization. Many stories are about company **heroes** who serve as models or ideals for serving cultural norms and values. Some stories are considered **legends** because the events are historic and may have been embellished with fictional details. Other stories are **myths,** which are consistent with the values and beliefs of the organization but are not supported by facts.[27] Stories keep alive the primary values of the organization and provide a shared understanding among all employees. Examples of how stories shape culture are as follows:

- At 3M, the story is told of a vice president who was fired early in his career for persisting with a new product even after his boss had told him to stop because the boss thought it was a stupid idea. After the worker was fired, he stayed in an unused office, working without a salary on the new product idea. Eventually he was rehired, the product was a success, and he was promoted to vice president. The story symbolizes the 3M value of persisting in what you believe in.[28]
- In the Canadian Pacific Railway (CPR) hotels, now operating under the Fairmont banner, William Cornelius Van Horne's statement that "if we can't export the scenery, we'll import the tourists!"[29] is still repeated as part of the lore about the creation of the chain of grand hotels across Canada.

**Symbols.** Another tool for interpreting culture is the symbol. A **symbol** is something that represents another thing. In one sense, ceremonies, stories, slogans, and rites are all

**EXHIBIT 9.3**
Strong Cultures!

**Think**

Think about the rituals at your university or college. How do they shape culture?

symbols; they symbolize deeper values of an organization. Another symbol is a physical artifact of the organization. Physical symbols are powerful because they focus attention on a specific item. Symbols can also represent negative elements of organizational culture. At Enron, premium parking spots were symbols of power, wealth, and winning at any cost. At the company's London (U.K.) office, executives submitted blind e-mail bids for the limited spaces. One top manager paid more than $6,000 to use a well-placed company spot for a year.[30] On a sardonic note, see Exhibit 9.3, which shows the power of culture to get people to do what they might not otherwise do.

**Language.** The final technique for influencing culture is **language**. Many organizations use a specific saying, slogan, metaphor, or other form of language to convey special meaning to employees. Slogans can be readily picked up and repeated by employees as well as customers of the company. Hudson's Bay Company's motto "We are Canada's merchants" applies to employees and customers but has become an ironic motto as the company is now American-owned. Averitt Express, a trucking company, uses the slogan "Our driving force is people" to emphasize the importance of treating employees as well as they are expected to treat customers. Drivers and customers, not top executives, are seen as the power that fuels the company's success. Other significant uses of language to shape culture are as follows:

- At Environics Communications, the ESRA (*arse* spelled backwards!) awards are designed to get staff laughing at their embarrassing moments and the Five for Five program allows employees to go to other countries; in their fifth year of employment, they are given $5,000, an extra week of holiday, and encouraged to go anywhere.[31]
- Tourism British Columbia holds monthly CEO mouth-abouts to update staff on decisions made by a rotating employee committee whose mandate is to make organizational values go beyond words on a page.[32]

Recall that culture exists at two levels—the underlying values and assumptions and the visible artifacts and observable behaviours. The slogans, symbols, and ceremonies just described are artifacts that reflect underlying company values. These visible artifacts and behaviours can be used by managers to shape company values and to strengthen organizational culture.

# Organizational Design and Culture

Organizational culture should reinforce the strategy and structural design that the organization needs to be effective within its environment. For example, if the external environment requires flexibility and responsiveness, such as the environment for Internet-based companies like eBay, the culture should encourage adaptability. The correct relationship among cultural values, organizational strategy and structure, and the environment can enhance organizational performance.[33]

Culture can be assessed along many dimensions, such as the extent of collaboration versus isolation among people and departments, the importance of control and where control is concentrated, or whether the organization's time orientation is short range or long range.[34] Here, we will focus on two specific dimensions: (1) the extent to which the competitive environment requires flexibility or stability; and (2) the extent to which the organization's strategic focus and strength are internal or external. Four categories of culture associated with these differences, as illustrated in Exhibit 9.4, are adaptability, mission, clan, and bureaucratic.[35] These four categories relate to the fit among cultural values, strategy, structure, and the environment. Each can be successful, depending on the needs of the external environment and the organization's strategic focus. In addition, we look at the culture of discipline.

## The Adaptability Culture

The **adaptability culture** is characterized by strategic focus on the external environment through flexibility and change to meet customer needs. The culture encourages entrepreneurial values, norms, and beliefs that support the capacity of the organization to detect, interpret, and translate signals from the environment into new behaviour responses. This type of organization, however, doesn't just react quickly to environmental changes—it actively creates change. Innovation, creativity, and risk taking are valued and rewarded.

**NEEDS OF THE ENVIRONMENT**

**EXHIBIT 9.4**
Relationship of Environment and Strategy to Organizational Culture

Source: Based on Daniel R. Denison and Aneil K. Mishra, "Toward a Theory of Organizational Culture and Effectiveness," *Organization Science* 6, no. 2 (March–April 1995), 204–223; R. Hooijberg and F. Petrock, "On Cultural Change: Using the Competing Values Framework to Help Leaders Execute a Transformational Strategy," *Human Resource Management* 32 (1993), 29–50; and R. E. Quinn, *Beyond Rational Management: Mastering the Paradoxes and Competing Demands of High Performance* (San Francisco: Jossey-Bass, 1988).

An example of the adaptability culture is 3M, a company whose values promote individual initiative and entrepreneurship. All new employees attend a class on risk taking, where they are told to pursue their ideas even if it means defying their supervisors. IBM has been shifting to an adaptability culture to support a new strategy that requires flexibility, speed, and innovation. IBM has implemented practices and procedures that support teamwork, egalitarianism, and creativity, such as dismantling the 92-year-old executive committee that previously ruled the company and replacing it with three cross-functional and cross-hierarchical teams for strategy, operations, and technology, and a clear external focus.[36] Most e-commerce companies, such as eBay, Amazon, and Google, as well as companies in the marketing, electronics, and cosmetics industries, use this type of culture because they must move quickly to satisfy customers.

An example of an adaptability culture is Sandvine, a tech start-up founded in 2001 in the Kitchener-Waterloo region, which provides networking equipment. In 2007, it was named one of Canada's best places to work.[37] In 2013, Sandvine continued to be recognized as one of the "Best Workplaces in Canada."[38] It is listed on the Toronto and London Stock Exchanges and in 2014 had a market cap of about $426.55 million.[39]

## ■ The Mission Culture

An organization concerned with serving specific customers in the external environment, but without the need for rapid change, is suited to the mission culture. The **mission culture** is characterized by emphasis on a clear vision of the organization's purpose and on the achievement of goals, such as sales growth, profitability, or market share, to help achieve the purpose. Individual employees may be responsible for a specified level of performance, and the organization promises specified rewards in return. Managers shape behaviour by envisioning and communicating a desired future state for the organization. Because the environment is stable, they can translate the vision into measurable goals and evaluate employee performance for meeting them. In some cases, mission cultures reflect a high level of competitiveness and a profit-making orientation.

In Practice
**Sandvine**

Sandvine was founded from the ashes of the telecom industry's meltdown. David Caputo, the current president of Sandvine, learned that Cisco Systems was closing down the organization that it had bought from him. In response, Caputo told his 30 engineers to think about the future of the Internet while he raised some capital to create a new company. As Caputo puts it, "It was like we had gone from the best of times to the worst of times almost overnight.... But we also saw that the tech crash had created a huge pool of talented people that all of a sudden had some time on their hands."[40]

On August 31, 2001, Sandvine was born. At the all-employee meeting, Caputo revealed the Sandvine Way, an eight-point statement* that is on every employee's ID.[41] The eight points are (1) customer first, (2) showcase flexibility, (3) underpromise and overdeliver, (4) amazing tool utilization, (5) teamwork, (6) knowledge sharing, (7) zero politics, and (8) risk taking. The Sandvine culture, according to Caputo, was engineered "[as] we're a bunch of engineers."[42] In Caputo's view, an organization's culture is of such importance that he designed the Sandvine Way even before he knew what Sandvine was going to produce.

Sandvine's leaders are required to follow the *Leaders 10 Commandments** to ensure that the culture of Sandvine is reinforced. The Commandments state (1) Treat your team with respect. Have fun. (2) Disagree and then commit to new company strategies. (3) Make decisions, communicate

*The Leaders 10 Commandments (and the Eight Points) provided by Sandvine Public Affairs, June 2007. Used with permission.

decisions. (4) Always explain "why" something needs to be done. (5) Never complain downward in the organization. (6) Openly praise, privately criticize. (7) Coach—don't fix. (8) Meet with your team as a team regularly. (9) Meet your team members individually regularly. (10) Encourage each team member to have/own a minimum of three objectives.[43]

**Apply**

If you were starting a nonprofit organization, would you want to apply the mission or the clan culture? Why or why not?

## ■ The Clan Culture

The **clan culture** has a primary focus on the involvement and participation of the organization's members and on rapidly changing expectations from the external environment. This culture is similar to the clan form of control described in Chapter 8. More than any other, this culture focuses on the needs of employees as the route to high performance. Involvement and participation create a sense of responsibility and ownership and, hence, greater commitment to the organization.

In a clan culture, an important value is taking care of employees and making sure they have whatever they need to help them be satisfied as well as productive. Companies in the fashion and retail industries often adopt this culture because it releases the creativity of employees to respond to rapidly changing tastes. Mountain Equipment Co-op is an example of an organization that combines attributes of the clan and mission cultures; for example, it looks for "people who share our passion for wild spaces, outdoor activities, and great gear. If you think a job should be more than a paycheque, check out our current postings."[44]

As described in Chapter 3, MEC was started in 1971 by a group of students at the University of British Columbia. It sold sporting equipment not otherwise available in Canada such as avalanche beacons, climbing rope, and ice crampons. The students charged a one-time membership fee of five dollars. The founders insisted that MEC should never make a profit and did no advertising.

Since then, MEC has become a large "anti-retailer"[45] with stores across Canada and a website that both educates and sells. MEC's Vancouver head office is housed in a converted building formerly used as an auto parts warehouse, and many of the fixtures were salvaged from other buildings. MEC's buildings are award winning—the Ottawa and Winnipeg stores were the first and second retail buildings in Canada to comply with Canada's C2000 Green Building Standard—a Natural Resources Canada program that acknowledges buildings that achieve a 50 percent reduction in energy consumption over conventional structures. In addition, in 1998, MEC was one of the first Canadian retailers to have rooftop gardens on its stores.

The green building program rests on four principles: (1) Reduce—Avoid using unnecessary materials, (2) Reuse—Incorporate existing materials, (3) Recycle—Incorporate existing materials in new ways, and (4) Rethink—Look for new and better building solutions.

MEC reinforces its commitment to sustainability in various ways. It has recycle bins in its stores for used polyester clothing, which it turns into new clothing and resells. It uses environmentally responsible paper made with a minimum of 30 percent postconsumer waste. In 2007, MEC announced that it had joined the One Percent for the Planet, an alliance of 500 companies in more than 20 countries that pledge to give 1 percent of their revenue to environmental causes. In 2009, MEC donated just under $2.5 million (1 percent of the previous year's sales) to various green initiatives.[46]

MEC's core values of ethical conduct and respect for others and the environment are enshrined in its first logo, two mountain peaks and the name of the co-op, as it is seen as a declaration of social responsibility. In 2006, MEC released its first annual accountability report and was the only Canadian retailer to make the top ten companies to report their labour practices transparently.[47] The Conference Board of Canada recognized MEC for incorporating sustainability in all aspects of its strategy. MEC received the prestigious Conference Board of Canada/Spencer Stuart 2008 national awards in governance in two categories—nonprofit organizations and all organizations.[48] In addition, in 2014, MEC was ranked first on the *Corporate Knight's* Best 50 Corporate Citizens in Canada.[49] MEC is Canada's leader in carbon productivity; in 2012, it cuts its carbon footprint by 31 percent. According to MEC's CEO, David Labistour, "We're at a point where we've picked the low-hanging 'sustainability fruit,'…additional gains are becoming tougher to achieve, but we're up for the challenge."[50]

**Compare**

Do some research to compare two well-known green organizations such as MEC and Evergreen. What are their most notable design features?

## ■ The Bureaucratic Culture

The **bureaucratic culture** has an internal focus and a consistency orientation for a stable environment. This organization has a culture that supports a methodical approach to doing business. Symbols, heroes, and ceremonies support cooperation, tradition, and following established policies and practices as ways to achieve goals. Personal involvement is somewhat lower here, but that is outweighed by a high level of consistency, conformity, and collaboration among members. This organization succeeds by being highly integrated and efficient.

Today, most managers are shifting away from bureaucratic cultures because of a need for greater flexibility. However, one thriving company, Pacific Edge Software, has successfully implemented some elements of a bureaucratic culture, ensuring that all its projects are on time and on budget. The co-founders implanted a culture of order, discipline, and control from the moment they founded the company. The emphasis on order and focus means employees can generally go home by 6:00 p.m. rather than working all night to finish an important project. The co-founders insist that the company's culture isn't rigid or uptight, just *careful*. Although sometimes being careful means being slow, so far Pacific Edge has managed to keep pace with the demands of the external environment.[51]

## ■ A Culture of Discipline

Collins identifies a number of characteristics that define truly great companies. One aspect is a culture of discipline, in which everyone in the organization is focused on doing whatever is needed to keep the company successful.[52] How is a culture of discipline built? Here are some of the key factors:

- *Level 5 leadership.* All good-to-great companies begin with a top leader who exemplifies what Collins calls level 5 leadership. Level 5 leaders are characterized by an almost complete lack of personal ego, coupled with a strong will and ambition for the success of the organization. They develop a strong corps of leaders throughout the organization so that when they leave, the company can grow even more successful. Values of selfishness, greed, and arrogance have no place in a great company.
- *The right values.* Leaders build a culture based on values of individual freedom and responsibility, but within a framework of organizational purpose, goals, and systems. People have the autonomy to do whatever it takes—within well-defined boundaries and clear, consistent guidelines—to move the organization toward achieving its goals and vision.
- *The right people in the right jobs.* Leaders of good-to-great organizations look for self-disciplined people who embody values that fit the culture. These people are described using terms such as *determined, diligent, precise, systematic, consistent,*

*focused*, *accountable*, and *responsible*. They are willing to go the extra mile to become the best they can be and help the organization continuously improve.

- *Knowing where to go*. Good-to-great companies base their success on a deep understanding throughout the organization of three essential ideas, conceptualized as three intersecting circles: what they can be the best in the world at, what they are deeply passionate about, and what makes economic sense for the organization. This understanding is translated into a vision and strategy that guides all actions.

No company makes the leap from good to great in one fell swoop. The process is one of buildup followed by breakthrough, similar to pushing a giant flywheel in one direction, turn after turn, building momentum until a breakthrough is reached. Once leaders get the right people in the right jobs, support the right values, and focus on activities that fit within the three intersecting circles, people begin to see positive results, which pushes the flywheel to full momentum. As success builds on success, the organization makes the move from good to great.

## Culture Strength and Organizational Subcultures

A strong organizational culture can have a powerful impact on company performance. **Culture strength** refers to the degree of agreement among members of an organization about the importance of specific values. If widespread consensus exists about the importance of those values, the culture is cohesive and strong; if little agreement exists, the culture is weak.[53]

A strong culture is typically associated with the frequent use of ceremonies, symbols, stories, heroes, and slogans. These elements increase employee commitment to the values and strategy of a company. In addition, managers who want to create and maintain strong organizational cultures often emphasize the selection and socialization of employees.[54] At the Lannick Group of Companies, potential employees can participate in a one-day job shadow and meet employees from across the organization. Once they are hired, they receive orientation and training.[55]

However, culture is not uniform throughout the organization, particularly in large companies. Even in organizations that have strong cultures, there are several sets of subcultures. **Subcultures** develop to reflect the common problems, goals, and experiences that members of a team, department, or other unit share. An office, branch, or unit of a company that is physically separated from the company's main operations may also take on a distinctive subculture. Sometimes, subcultures are so different in an organization that employees feel cultural anxieties when they have to move to other units or when their organizations are taken over by mergers or acquisitions.[56]

For example, although the dominant culture of an organization may be a mission culture, various departments may also reflect characteristics of adaptability, clan, or bureaucratic cultures. The manufacturing department of a large organization may thrive in an environment that emphasizes order, efficiency, and obedience to rules, whereas the research and development (R&D) department may be characterized by employee empowerment, flexibility, and customer focus. This is similar to the concept of differentiation described in Chapter 4, where employees in manufacturing, sales, and research departments studied by Paul Lawrence and Jay Lorsch[57] developed different values with respect to time horizon, interpersonal relationships, and formality in order to perform the job of each particular department most effectively. The credit division of Pitney Bowes, a huge corporation that manufactures postage meters, copiers, and other office equipment, developed a distinctive subculture to encourage innovation and risk taking. Pitney Bowes has long thrived in an environment of order and predictability. Its headquarters reflects a typical corporate environment and an orderly culture with its blank walls and bland carpeting. But step onto the third floor of the Pitney Bowes building in Shelton, Connecticut, and you might think you're at a different company. The domain of Pitney Bowes Credit Corporation looks more like an indoor theme park, featuring cobblestone-patterned carpets, faux gas lamps, and an ornate town square-style clock. It also has a French-style café, a 1950s-style diner, and the "Cranial Kitchen," where employees sit in cozy booths to surf the Internet or watch training videos. The friendly hallways encourage impromptu conversations, where people can exchange information and share ideas they would not otherwise share.[58]

Subcultures typically include the basic values of the dominant organizational culture and additional values unique to members of the subculture. However, subcultural differences can sometimes lead to conflicts between departments, especially in organizations that do not have strong overall organizational cultures. When subcultural values become too strong and outweigh the corporate cultural values, conflicts may emerge and hurt organizational performance. Conflict will be discussed in detail in Chapter 12.

## Organizational Culture, Learning, and Performance

Culture can play an important role in creating an organizational climate that enables learning and innovative response to challenges, competitive threats, or new opportunities. A strong culture that encourages adaptation and change enhances organizational performance by energizing and motivating employees, unifying people around shared goals and a higher mission, and shaping and guiding employee behaviour so that everyone's actions are aligned with strategic priorities. Thus, creating and influencing an adaptive culture is one of the most important jobs for organizational leaders. The right culture can drive high performance, as we can see in the WestJet case below.[59]

A number of studies have found a positive relationship between culture and performance.[60] In *Corporate Culture and Performance*, John P. Kotter and James L. Heskett provided evidence that companies that intentionally managed cultural values outperformed similar companies that did not. Some companies have developed systematic ways to measure and manage the impact of culture on organizational performance. At Home Depot, leaders identified key aspects of the culture that needed to be changed to meet more demanding performance goals. They use various tools to strengthen the business and to modify its culture. They use tools such as strategic operating and resource planning, disciplined talent reviews, store manager learning forums, Monday morning conference calls of the organization's top 15 executives, employee task forces, as well an array of leadership and employee development programs.[61]

Strong cultures that don't encourage adaptation, however, can hurt the organization. A danger for many successful organizations is that the culture becomes set and the company fails to adapt as the environment changes. When organizations are successful, the values, ideas, and practices that helped attain success become institutionalized. As the environment changes, these values may become detrimental to future performance. Many organizations become victims of their own success, clinging to outmoded and even destructive values and behaviours. Thus, the impact of a strong culture is not necessarily positive. Typically, healthy cultures not only provide for smooth internal integration but also encourage adaptation to the external environment. Nonadaptive cultures encourage rigidity and stability. Strong adaptive cultures often incorporate the following values:

1. *The whole is more important than the parts, and boundaries between parts are minimized.* People are aware of the whole system, how everything fits together, and the relationships among various organizational parts. All members consider how their actions affect other parts and the total organization. This emphasis on the whole reduces boundaries both within the organization and with other companies. Although subcultures may form, everyone's primary attitudes and behaviours reflect the organization's dominant culture. The free flow of people, ideas, and information allows coordinated action and continuous learning.

2. *Equality and trust are primary values.* The culture creates a sense of community and caring for one another. The organization is a place for creating a web of relationships that allows people to take risks and develop to their full potential. The emphasis on treating everyone with care and respect creates a climate of safety and trust that allows experimentation, frequent mistakes, and learning. Managers emphasize honest and open communications as a way to build trust.

# Leading *by Design*

## WestJet Airlines Ltd. (WestJet)

I am convinced now that THE COMPETITIVE ISSUE OF OUR TIME IS CULTURE AS EXPRESSED IN VOICE. Firms that use voice and an adult culture of genuine care will destroy those that use scripts and efficiency.

What on Earth do I mean by that? Let me illustrate by offering up a few things that happened to me while flying WestJet last week.

1. We land at Pearson. The FA comes on and says, "Please be careful and stay buckled up as there is always a chance that we may have to stop suddenly if we get caught in traffic." Wow—someone did not give us orders but gave us context for remaining buckled up. On Air Canada, everyone is fiddling with their stuff well before the ramp. Why—because of the tone of voice—On most airlines we are lectured to.

2. We have 2 unaccompanied minors on the return flight. Members of the crew played cards, chatted and generally fooled around with them the entire trip. They were really well looked after—not just the mundane look after—but genuinely cared for as people. Caring is not the same as service. There was no script. Children have great bullshit detectors and these men passed. By the way it was the male FA's who were front and centre with the kids.

3. On our approach into Moncton, we suddenly hit very bad turbulence—amongst the worst in 50 years of flying. We were suddenly being tossed all over the sky. The First Officer came on immediately—Flight Attendants grab a seat! Now folks we are entering the jet-stream at 29,000 and we will come out the other side at 23,000. Just hang on a few minutes and it will be smooth again." Well we all looked at each other and gasped. Someone had told us what was really happening. With context and [an adult peer-to-peer tone] we were all calm. At AC the seat belt sign would have come on. If we were lucky this Test Pilot Voice would tell us to buckle up as we were having some turbulence. At WestJet, the FA safety was dealt with immediately and we were all taken in to the confidence as adults by the flight deck.

What we all experienced was that the real service issue is not doing things—there are no meals on WestJet. It is how you are and how you related to each other and then with the customer. At WestJet we are all called "Guests." Words mean something. A Guest is someone you legitimately care for. A passenger or a customer is someone you are paid to do things for.

So what is wrong with most organizations today? They use the voice of the grumpy teacher. [They] confuse doing things with love and with care. When confronted with a culture of care, they look and feel terrible.[62]

Source: "WestJet - The Difference that Culture makes" - Posted by Robert Paterson on June 29, 2004, at 04:45 PM in Organizations and Culture. smartpei.typepad.com/robert_patersons_weblog/2004/06/westjet_the_dif.html. Used with permission.

|  | ADAPTIVE CULTURES | MALADAPTIVE CULTURES |
|---|---|---|
| Core Values | Managers care deeply about customers, stockholders, and employees. They value processes that can create useful change. | Managers care about themselves and their immediate work group, and value orderly and risk-reducing processes. They value short-term gains. |
| Common Behaviours | Managers pay attention to their stakeholders and initiate change to serve their interests. They create an organizational climate that is supportive of employee participation, development, and creativity. | Managers tend to be somewhat isolated, political, and bureaucratic. They tend to resist change and when they must change, they tend to push ideas down the hierarchy and restrict employee creativity. |

**EXHIBIT 9.5**
Adaptive versus Maladaptive Organizational Cultures

Source: Kotter, J.P. and J. Heskett (1992) *Corporate Culture and Performance* (New York: The Free Press; and Cangemi, J. and R. Miller (2007) "Breaking-out-of-the-box in Organizations," *Journal of Management Development* 26, 5, 401–410).

3. *The culture encourages risk taking, change, and improvement.* A basic value is to question the status quo. Constant questioning of assumptions opens the gates to creativity and improvement. The culture rewards and celebrates the creators of new ideas, products, and work processes. To symbolize the importance of taking risks, an adaptive culture may also reward those who fail in order to learn and grow.

As illustrated in Exhibit 9.5, adaptive organizational cultures have different values and behaviour patterns than maladaptive cultures.[63] In adaptive cultures, managers are concerned with customers and employees as well as with the internal processes and procedures that bring about useful change. Behaviour is flexible and managers initiate change when needed, even if it involves risk. In maladaptive cultures, managers are more concerned about themselves or their own special projects, and their values discourage risk taking and change. Thus, strong, healthy cultures, such as those in learning organizations, help them adapt to the external environment, whereas strong, unhealthy cultures can encourage an organization to march resolutely in the wrong direction. Lululemon, described in the next In Practice, has a strong culture that some consider healthy and others believe is cult-like. It has also faced some significant ethical issues recently.

## In Practice

### Lululemon athletica inc. (Lululemon)

Lululemon was founded in 1998 by Chip Wilson, now chairman of the board and chief designer of product. According to Wilson, his original goal was to have one store in Kitsilano and not to expand. "But then I surrounded myself with great twenty-five-to-thirty-five-year-old people…[who wanted] a future and a family and a mortgage. In order to keep these people, I had to expand."[64] In 2008, Christine Day was appointed COO, President, and CEO Designate. Day enjoyed an illustrious career at Starbucks where she started as an office manager and became the head of the $1.5 billion Asia Pacific Group. Lululemon, headquartered in Vancouver's North Shore, is traded on both the Nasdaq and Toronto exchanges. For the fiscal year ended January 31, 2011, Lululemon's net revenue increased 57 percent to $711.7 million from $452.9 million in fiscal 2009. Its diluted earnings per share (EPS) in fiscal 2010 increased 106 percent to $1.69 on net income of $121.8 million compared to an EPS of $0.82 on a net income of $58.3 million in fiscal 2009. Day remarked that "[while] we will see some cost pressures in 2011, we are confident in our ability to maintain our business model through disciplined management, operating efficiencies and leverage on higher sales."[65] Even so, it faced some inventory issues in 2011, in part as its demand forecasts were not very accurate. While some analysts have expressed concern about the inventory shortages and increasing costs of flying in inventory, others believe that the inventory shortage is helping to create pent-up demand.[66] Lululemon, however, continues to enjoy market success; income from operations increased by 4 percent to $391.4 million, from $376.4 million in fiscal 2012. As a percentage of net revenue, income from operations decreased to 24.6 percent compared to 27.5 percent of net revenue in fiscal 2012.[67]

Lululemon's mission is "creating components for people to live a longer, healthier, more fun life."[68] Lululemon's approach to creating and managing its culture has been deliberate. Its sales staff are called educators, and its employees are instructed to *be* yoga, not merely to *do* yoga. Its employees practise what Lululemon preaches about a healthy lifestyle; for example, the accounting department goes running together three days at week at 4:45 PM.[69] Besides, Lululemon's Manifesto, which has 31 sayings, is printed on its bags and includes ideas such as "Do one thing a day that scares you" and "Friends are more important than money." However, in 2008, Lululemon faced a controversy when some of its bags were found to have hidden risqué messages about how regular aerobic activity results in a high similar to that from drugs or sex as well as one that mentioned that we would be dead in 30,000 days. According to Lululemon, the message was not an error but was not meant to be read by the public. The company then covered up the messages rather than destroying the bags so as not to be wasteful. When it turned out that the messages were still visible in some of its bags, Lululemon removed the remaining bags. Even so, "[We'll] continue to strive to inspire people to open their minds to new ideas and experiences as it's what drives us as a company."[70]

In another controversy, Lululemon had to back away, in 2007, from claims that its seaweed fibre had health benefits. It claimed that its VitaSea shirts reduced stress and provided many other benefits, which were not supported by any scientific evidence.[71] According to Ethical Shopping, independent laboratory tests showed that the VitaSea shirts did not even contain seaweed.[72] Lululemon continues to face controversy. Some its yoga pants were discovered in 2013 to be see-through and 17 percent of them were recalled. To add to the controversy, Chip Wilson responded, "There has always been pilling. The thing is that women will wear seatbelts that don't work or they'll wear a purse that doesn't work or, quite frankly, some women's bodies just don't work for [the pants]."[73]...It's really about the rubbing through the thighs, how much pressure is there."[74] Wilson's comments were not well received. He resigned as Chair; Day had earlier resigned as CEO.

Chip Wilson had shaped the culture of Lululemon around his own views of self-actualization. He integrated training by the Landmark Forum seminars, designed by a former scientologist; Brian Tracy's books; and Rhonda Byrne's book *The Secret*.[75] It is Lululemon's affiliation with the Landmark Forum that has been another and long-term controversial aspect of the company. Employees receive Landmark Forum seminars as recognition for one year of service at Lululemon. According to Lululemon, the seminars have been very successful in helping its employees achieve lives they would not have otherwise.[76] However, not all employees have appreciated the seminars and see the seminars as tools to create a cult. When challenged about Lululemon's affiliation with Landmark Forum, Wilson comments that

> Every business has to start a certain way and evolve in some ways. It shows up like a cult because it has become a very simple concept that releases people from a lot of blocks in life. When people are released from these blocks, it has that aura. People who don't understand greatness are scared by greatness. Canadians especially, I find, are like a wall of mediocrity. The whole socialist backlog that we've heard for so many years that it's wrong to be rich, that it's wrong to be powerful, that it's wrong to be great, that's it's wrong to be an individual—that's just wrong.[77]

# Ethical Values and Social Responsibility

Of the values that make up an organization's culture, ethical values are now considered among the most important. Widespread corporate accounting scandals, allegations that top managers of some organizations made personal use of company funds, and charges of insider trading have blanketed the Internet and airwaves in recent years.

Top corporate managers are under scrutiny from the public as never before, and even small companies are finding a need to put more emphasis on ethics to restore trust among their customers and the community. As the University of Calgary's Gregory Daneke notes "[in] the aftermath of major corporate scandals, such as Enron and Hollinger, it is high time that ethics and economics become reacquainted."[78]

## ■ Sources of Individual Ethical Principles

**Ethics** is the code of moral principles and values that governs the behaviours of a person or group with respect to what is right or wrong. An individual manager's values can be shaped by his or her background and experiences. Ethical values set standards as to what is good or bad in conduct and decision making.[79] Ethics are personal and unique to each individual, although in any given group, organization, or society there are many areas of consensus about what constitutes ethical behaviour.[80] Exhibit 9.6 illustrates the varied sources of individual ethical principles. Each person is a creation of his or her time and place in history. National culture, religious heritage, historical background, and so forth lead to the development of societal morality, or society's view of what is right and wrong. Societal morality is often reflected in norms of behaviour and values about what makes sense for an orderly society. Some principles are codified into laws and regulations, such as laws against drunk driving, robbery, or murder.

These laws, as well as unwritten societal norms and values, shape the local environment within which each individual acts, such as a person's community, family, and place of work. Individuals absorb the beliefs and values of their family, community, culture, society, religious community, and geographic environment, typically discarding some and incorporating others into their own personal ethical standards.

**EXHIBIT 9.6**
Sources of Individual
Ethical Principles and
Actions
Source: Thanks to Susan H. Taft
and Judith White for providing
this exhibit.

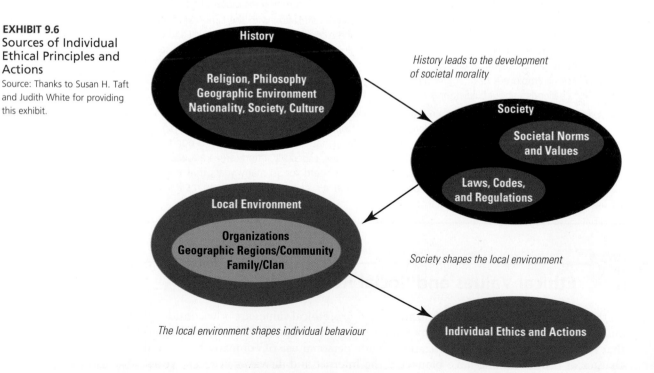

Each person's ethical stance is thus a blending of his or her historical, cultural, societal, and family backgrounds and influences.

It is important to look at individual ethics because ethics always involve an individual action, whether it be a decision to act or the failure to take action against wrongdoing by others. In organizations, an individual's ethical stance may be affected by peers, subordinates, and supervisors, as well as by the organizational culture. Organizational culture often has a profound influence on individual choices and can support and encourage ethical actions or promote unethical and socially irresponsible behaviour.

## ■ Managerial Ethics and Social Responsibility

Recent events have demonstrated the powerful influence of organizational standards on ethical behaviour. Strict ethical standards are becoming part of the formal policies and informal cultures of many organizations, and courses in ethics are taught in many business schools. Many of the scandals in the news have dealt with people and corporations that broke the law. But it is important to remember that ethics goes far beyond behaviours governed by law.[81] The **rule of law** arises from a set of codified principles and regulations that describe how people are required to act, that are generally accepted in society, and that are enforceable in the courts.[82]

## Book Mark 9.0    HAVE YOU READ THIS BOOK?

### The Corporation: The Pathological Pursuit of Profit and Power
By Joel Bakan

*The Corporation*, written by Joel Bakan, a professor at the University of British Columbia's Law School, is both controversial and uplifting. Bakan argues that corporations are rapacious entities interested only in power and profits. Bakan goes on to show some parallels in the behaviours of corporations and psychopaths. He writes that "as a psychopathic creature, the corporation can neither recognize nor act upon moral reasons to refrain from harming others. Nothing in its legal makeup limits what it can do to others in pursuit of its selfish ends, and it is compelled to cause harm when the benefits of doing so outweigh the costs."[83]

Bakan suggests that corporations pursue socially and environmentally responsible actions, not for altruistic reasons, but for strategic reasons designed to enhance their own performance. He acknowledges that corporate social responsibility initiatives can do good, although he believes that often they are token responses. While his is a depressing account of the ruthless power of the corporation, Bakan remains an optimist. He believes that it is vital that the regulatory systems affecting corporations are reconceived and legitimated "as the principal means for bringing corporations under democratic control and ensuring that they respect the interests of citizens, communities, and the environment."[84] He also believes that there should be tighter restrictions on lobbying and that we need to create a stronger social sphere where fundamental social services are offered by organizations other than corporations.

The film of the same name has received critical acclaim and received eight audience choice awards, including one from the Sundance Film Festival. Noam Chomsky of the Massachusetts Institute of Technology comments that "[This] vivid and often mesmerizing film lifts the veil from one of the most important and least understood features of modern age: the extraordinary powers that have been bestowed on virtually unaccountable private tyrannies, required by law to act in ways that severely undermine democracy and the most elementary human rights, and that pose a serious threat even to survival."[85]

*The Corporation: The Pathological Pursuit of Profit and Power*, by Joel Bakan, is published by Penguin, 2004.

Ethical standards for the most part apply to behaviour not covered by the law, and the rule of law applies to behaviours not necessarily covered by ethical standards. Our laws often reflect combined moral judgments, but not all moral judgments are codified into law. The morality of aiding a drowning person, for example, is not specified by law, and driving on the right-hand side of the road has no moral basis; but in acts such as robbery or murder, rules and moral standards overlap.

Unethical conduct in organizations is surprisingly widespread. More than 54 percent of human resource (HR) professionals polled by the Society for Human Resource Management and the Ethics Resource Center reported observing employees lying to supervisors or coworkers, falsifying reports or records, or abusing drugs or alcohol while on the job.[86] Many people believe that if you are not breaking the law, then you are behaving in an ethical manner, but this is not necessarily true. Many behaviours have not been codified, and managers must be very sensitive to emerging norms and values. Increasingly, a stellar track record does not protect a CEO from scrutiny; for example, (former) Boeing CEO Harry Stonecipher was fired in 2005 over a romance with an employee. "It used to be that as long as an executive performed well on the job, no one much cared about what they were doing in their free time—or even behind closed doors in the office....But a sea change has occurred, with every aspect of managers' conduct being scrutinized—and ever more closely the higher up one goes."[87]

**Managerial ethics** are principles that guide the decisions and behaviours of managers with regard to whether they are right or wrong. The notion of **social responsibility** is an extension of this idea and refers to management's obligation to make choices and take action so that the organization contributes to the welfare and interest of all organizational stakeholders, such as employees, customers, shareholders, the community, and the broader society.[88]

Examples of the need for managerial ethics are as follows:[89]

- Top executives are considering promoting a rising sales manager who consistently brings in $70 million a year and has cracked open new markets in places such as Brazil and Turkey that are important to the organization's international growth. However, female employees have been complaining for years that the manager is verbally abusive to them, tells offensive jokes, and throws temper tantrums if female employees don't do exactly as he says.
- The manager of a beauty supply store is told that she and her salespeople can receive large bonuses for selling a specified number of boxes of a new product, a permanent-wave solution that costs nearly twice as much as what most of her salon customers typically use. She orders the salespeople to store the old product in the back and tell customers there's been a delay in delivery.
- The project manager for a construction planning project wondered whether some facts should be left out of a report because the community where the facility would be built might object if they discovered certain environmental aspects of the project.
- A North American manufacturer operating abroad was asked to make cash payments (a bribe) to government officials and was told the practice was consistent with local customs, despite being illegal in North America.

As these examples illustrate, ethics and social responsibility are about making decisions. Managers make choices every day about whether to be honest or deceitful with suppliers, treat employees with respect or disdain, and be a good or a harmful corporate citizen. Some issues are exceedingly difficult to resolve and often represent ethical dilemmas. An **ethical dilemma** arises in a situation concerning right and wrong in which values are in conflict.[90] Right or wrong cannot be clearly identified in such situations. For example, for a salesperson at the beauty supply store, the value conflict is between being honest with customers and adhering to the boss's expectations. The manufacturing manager may feel torn between respecting and following local customs in a foreign country or adhering to domestic laws concerning bribes. Sometimes, both alternatives seem undesirable.

Ethical dilemmas are not easy to resolve, but top executives can aid the process by establishing organizational values that provide people with guidelines for making the best decision from a moral standpoint.

## ■ Does It Pay to Be Good?

The relationship of an organization's ethics and social responsibility to its performance concerns both organizational managers and organization scholars. Studies have provided varying results but generally have found that there is a small positive relationship between ethical and socially responsible behaviour and financial results.[91] For example, a recent study of the financial performance of large U.S. corporations considered "best corporate citizens" found that they have both superior reputations and superior financial performance.[92] Similarly, Governance Metrics International, an independent corporate governance ratings agency, found that the stocks of companies run on more selfless principles perform better than those run in a self-serving manner. According to another study, corporate philanthropy adds to shareholder wealth: "businesses that have earned a reputation for being generous through acts of philanthropy are given the benefit of the doubt when negative events occur."[93] Of course, philanthropy is not confined to corporations; for example, members of the Union of Food and Commercial Workers of Canada raised about $1.5 million in 2007 for the Leukemia & Lymphoma Society and have raised $28,700,00 since 1985.[94]

As discussed earlier in the chapter, long-term organizational success relies largely on social capital, which means companies need to build a reputation for honesty, fairness, and doing the right thing. Researchers have found that people prefer to work for companies that demonstrate a high level of ethics and social responsibility, so these companies can attract and retain high-quality employees.[95] Timberland, for example, which gives employees 40 hours of unpaid leave annually to do community volunteer work and supports a number of charitable causes, is consistently ranked on *Fortune's* list of the 100 best companies to work for. One vice president says she has turned down lucrative offers from other companies because she prefers to work at a company that puts ethics and social responsibility ahead of just making a profit.[96]

Customers pay attention, too. A study by Walker Research indicates that, price and quality being equal, two-thirds of people say they would switch brands to do business with a company that makes a high commitment to ethics.[97]

Companies that put ethics on the back burner in favour of fast growth and short-term profits ultimately suffer. To gain and keep the trust of employees, customers, investors, and the general public, organizations must put ethics first. "Just saying you're ethical isn't very useful," says Charles O. Holliday, Jr., chairman and CEO of DuPont Co. "You have to earn trust by what you do every day."[98]

Bruce Poon Tip, founder and CEO of GAP Adventures, says "[It] is my duty as the founder and CEO...to help preserve our planet, her people and to make sure her treasures are around for the next generation of eager travellers and wide-eyed explorers."[99] Through his Planeterra Foundation, he has supported community projects around the world by matching individual donations and paying administration costs so that all the monies go to support the projects.

## Sources of Ethical Values in Organizations

Ethics in organizations is both an individual and an organizational matter. The standards for ethical or socially responsible conduct are embodied within each employee as well as within the organization itself. In addition, external stakeholders can influence standards of what is ethical and socially responsible. The immediate forces that impact on ethical decisions in organizations are summarized in Exhibit 9.7. Individual beliefs and values, a person's ethical decision framework, and moral development influence personal ethics. Organizational culture, as we have already discussed, shapes the overall framework of values within the organization. Moreover, formal organizational systems influence values and behaviours according to the organization's policy framework and reward systems. Companies also respond to numerous stakeholders in determining what is right. They consider how their actions may be viewed by customers, government agencies, shareholders, and the general community, as well as the impact each alternative course of action may have on other stakeholders. All of these factors can be explored to understand ethical and socially responsible decisions in organizations.[100]

**EXHIBIT 9.7**
Forces That Shape
Managerial Ethics

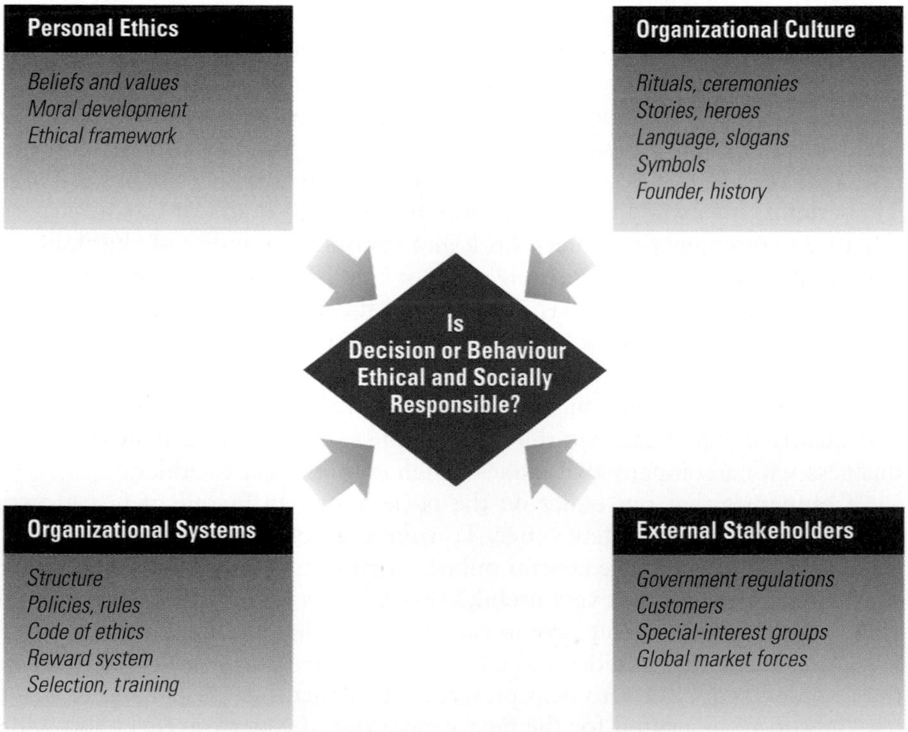

**Personal Ethics**

Beliefs and values
Moral development
Ethical framework

**Organizational Culture**

Rituals, ceremonies
Stories, heroes
Language, slogans
Symbols
Founder, history

**Is Decision or Behaviour Ethical and Socially Responsible?**

**Organizational Systems**

Structure
Policies, rules
Code of ethics
Reward system
Selection, training

**External Stakeholders**

Government regulations
Customers
Special-interest groups
Global market forces

# Personal Ethics

Every individual brings a set of personal beliefs and values into the workplace. Personal values and the moral reasoning that translates these values into behaviour are an important aspect of ethical decision making in organizations.[101]

As we discussed earlier, the historical, cultural, family, religious, and community backgrounds of managers shape their personal values and provide principles by which they carry out business. In addition, people go through stages of moral development that affect their ability to translate values into behaviour. For example, children have a low level of moral development, making decisions and behaving to obtain rewards and avoid punishment. At an intermediate level of development, people learn to conform to expectations of good behaviour as defined by colleagues and society. Most managers are at this level, willingly upholding the law and responding to societal expectations. At the highest level of moral development are people who develop an internal set of standards. These are self-chosen ethical principles that are more important to decisions than external expectations. Only a few people reach this high level, which can mean breaking laws if necessary to sustain higher moral principles.[102]

The other personal factor is whether managers have developed an *ethical framework* that guides their decisions. *Utilitarian theory*, for example, argues that ethical decisions should be made to generate the greatest benefits for the largest number of people. This framework is often consistent with business decisions because costs and benefits can be calculated in dollars. The *personal liberty* framework argues that decisions should be made to ensure the greatest possible freedom of choice and liberty for individuals. Liberties include the freedom to act on your own conscience, freedom of speech, due process of law, and the right to privacy. The *distributive justice* framework holds that moral decisions are those that promote equity, fairness, and impartiality with respect to the distribution of rewards and the administration of rules, which are essential for social cooperation.[103]

One promising tool to give guidance to CEOs of corporations has been developed by Roger Martin, of the Rotman School of Management, in Toronto. Martin developed a conceptual framework for addressing critical questions about responsibility such as (1) What drives the market for responsible corporate behaviour? (2) What creates the public demand for greater responsibility? (3) Why does globalization raise concerns about corporate responsibility? (4) What are the barriers to increasing responsible behaviours? and (5) What forces can add to the supply of corporate responsibility?[104] A virtue matrix shows the forces that generate corporate social responsibility. The bottom two quadrants are the civil foundation, which consists of norms, customs, and laws that govern corporate behaviours. Corporations either choose to comply with the requirements of the civil foundation or are mandated to do so. The upper two quadrants of the matrix are the frontier where innovations in socially responsible behaviour occur either for the benefit of the shareholders and society or for society alone. Each quadrant raises questions that need to be answered before developing a corporate social responsibility strategy. (The Workshop at the end of this chapter has the questions to use in identifying socially responsible activities for an organization.)

# Organizational Culture

Rarely can ethical or unethical business practices be attributed entirely to the personal ethics of a single individual. Business practices also reflect the values, attitudes, and behaviour patterns of an organization's culture. To promote ethical behaviour in the workplace, companies should make ethics an integral part of the organization's culture. Raymond Royer, president and CEO of Domtar Corporation, came to the realization that Domtar and environmental groups shared the same goals, i.e., to have sustainability in the forest. He comments that "[you] have to put yourself in the position of whoever does business with you... [at] the end of the day, we are taking fibre, so like it or not, we have to be involved with the environment."[105]

Organizational culture has a powerful impact on individual ethics because it helps to guide employees in making daily decisions. When the culture supports wrongdoing, it is easier for individual employees to go along. One young Enron employee explained how he slid into unethical decisions and practices in his job: "It was easy to get into, 'Well, everybody else is doing it, so maybe it isn't so bad.'"[106]

The third category of influences that shape managerial ethics is formal organizational systems. This includes the basic architecture of the organization, such as whether ethical values are incorporated in policies and rules; whether an explicit code of ethics is available and issued to members; whether organizational rewards, including praise, attention, and promotions, are linked to ethical behaviour; and whether ethics is a consideration in the selection and training of employees. These formal efforts can reinforce ethical values that exist in the informal culture.

Many companies have established formal ethics programs. For example, Alcan Inc. has a 32-page Worldwide Code of Employee and Business Conduct that codifies its values of integrity, accountability, teamwork, trust, and transparency.[107] Alcan ranks eighth on the 2007 Global 100 Most Sustainable Corporations in the World and is the highest-ranked Canadian organization.[108]

## ■ External Stakeholders

Managerial ethics and social responsibility are also influenced by a variety of external stakeholders, groups outside the organization that have a stake in the organization's performance. Ethical and socially responsible decision making recognizes that the organization is part of a larger community and considers the impact of a decision or action on all stakeholders.[109] Important external stakeholders are government agencies, customers, and special-interest groups such as those concerned with the natural environment.

Companies must operate within the limits of certain government regulations, such as safety laws, environmental protection requirements, and many other laws and regulations. Numerous companies, including Hollinger, WorldCom, Merrill Lynch, and Xerox, have come under investigation by the U.S. Securities and Exchange Commission for alleged violations of laws related to financial controls and accounting practices. Health care organizations have to respond to numerous laws and regulations, as do organizations such as schools and day care centres. Customers are another important stakeholder group. Customers are primarily concerned about the quality, safety, and availability of goods and services. For example, McDonald's reduced trans-fatty acids in its fried foods in response to growing customer concerns about health risks associated with a fast-food diet.[110]

Special-interest groups continue to be one of the largest stakeholder concerns that companies face. Today, those concerned with corporate responsibility to the natural environment are particularly vocal. Thus, environmentalism is becoming an integral part of organizational planning and decision making for leading companies. The concept of *sustainable development*, a dual concern for economic growth and

Chapter 9: Organizational Culture and Ethical Values

environmental sustainability, has been gaining ground among many business leaders. The public is no longer comfortable with organizations focusing solely on profit at the expense of the natural environment. For example, Ron Dembo, founder of Algorithmics, has started Zerofootprint, an Internet hub providing information, products, and services to help organizations and individuals reduce their environmental impact.[111] Environmental sustainability—meaning that what is taken out of the environmental system for food, shelter, clothing, energy, and other human uses is restored to the system in waste that can be reused—is a part of strategy for companies such as IKEA, Electrolux, Scandic Hotels, MacMillan-Bloedel, and Interface. Interface, a $1 billion leader in the floor-covering industry, is instituting changes that will allow the company to manufacture without pollution, waste, or fossil fuels. From the factory floor to the R&D lab, sustainability is as important a consideration at Interface as profitability. The emphasis on environmentalism hasn't hurt Interface. Over a one-year period, sales increased from $800 million to $1 billion. During that time, the amount of raw materials used by the company dropped almost 20 percent per dollar of sales.[112]

## How Leaders Shape Culture and Ethics

In a study of ethics policy and practice in successful, ethical companies such as Johnson & Johnson and General Mills, no point emerged more clearly than the role of top management in providing commitment, leadership, and examples for ethical behaviour.[113] The CEO and other top managers must be committed to specific values and demonstrate constant leadership in tending and renewing the values. Values can be communicated in a number of ways—speeches, company publications, policy statements, and, especially, personal actions. Top leaders are responsible for creating and sustaining a culture that emphasizes the importance of ethical behaviour for all employees every day. When the CEO engages in unethical practices or fails to take firm and decisive action in response to the unethical practices of others, this attitude filters down through the organization. Formal ethics codes and training programs are worthless if leaders do not set and live up to high standards of ethical conduct.[114] The next In Practice describes what may be a watershed leadership moment at the Harvard Business School.

---

In an unprecedented move, the Dean of the Harvard Business School (HBS), Nitin Nohria, made a public apology for HBS's past behaviour toward women. He noted that in the past, HBS had treated its female students and professors badly. Nohria acknowledged that there were times when women felt "disrespected, left out, and unloved by the school. I'm very sorry on behalf of the business school... The school owed you better, and I promise it will be better."[115] Nohria made his apology in January 2014 at the first alumni chapter event that celebrated women.

HBS had been under scrutiny after the publication of a *New York Times* article on HBS's attempts to deal with gender inequality. The article triggered much discussion on the Twitterverse and elsewhere. Nohria announced several initiatives to address gender inequality at HBS. They included (1) doubling the percentage of women who are protagonists in its teaching cases from nine to 20 percent, (2) launching a program to help more women to serve on boards, and (3) encouraging better mentorship programs for women at HBS. While there is much work to do, Betsy Massar, an attendee at the event, comments:

**In Practice**
Harvard
Business
School (HBS)

> I too am from HBS in the 80's, and I was even one of the honorees at the dinner. I think that it's a shame that the problems he's pointing out are still problems. And I am grateful that he is standing up and saying something about it. I would have liked it to be otherwise, but guess what, he's talking about it. And he's putting the resources of a great institution behind the change. Thank goodness.[116]

The following sections examine how managers signal and implement values through leadership as well as through the formal systems of the organization.

## ■ Values-based Leadership

The underlying value system of an organization cannot be managed in the traditional way. Issuing an authoritative directive, for example, has little or no impact on an organization's value system. Organizational values are developed and strengthened primarily through **values-based leadership,** a relationship between a leader and followers that is based on shared, strongly internalized values that are advocated and acted upon by the leader.[117]

Leaders influence cultural and ethical values by clearly articulating a vision for organizational values that employees can believe in, communicating the vision throughout the organization, and institutionalizing the vision through everyday behaviour, rituals, ceremonies, and symbols, as well as through organizational systems and policies. The Vancouver 2010 Winter Olympic Games used environmentally friendly construction and operation of all events in Whistler. The Games showcased its use of alternative energy sources; it worked with wind-generation companies and planned to have a wind-monitoring station in the mountain in time for the Games.[118] However, any sustainability kudos were overshadowed by the death of Georgian luger, Nodar Kumaritashvili, in a training run. After his death, there was an outcry about the safety of the track and the judgment of the Games' officials in designing the particular track. The Olympic officials shortened the course by 174 metres.[119]

Managers should remember that every statement and action has an impact on culture and values. For example, a survey of readers of the magazine *The Secretary* found that employees are acutely aware of their bosses' ethical lapses. Something as simple as having a secretary notarize a document without witnessing the signature may seem insignificant, but it communicates that the manager doesn't value honesty.[120] Employees learn about values, beliefs, and goals from watching managers, just as students learn which topics are important for an exam, what professors like, and how to get a good grade from watching professors. To be effective values-based leaders, executives often use symbols, ceremonies, speeches, and slogans that match the values. Citigroup's former CEO, Charles Prince, devoted a tremendous amount of time to talking about values with both employees and customers. Prince knew that for a company the size of Citigroup, just strengthening rules and systems wasn't enough. To get the company to "internalize" a strong code of ethics around the globe, Prince made a visible commitment to values through speeches, video addresses, and regular communication.[121] Prince also said he would be "ruthless" with managers and employees who don't follow the rules. Actions speak louder than words, so values-based leaders "walk their talk."[122] In late 2007, Prince himself faced a crisis, and he resigned from Citigroup. As he put it, "[It] is my judgment that given the size of the recent losses in our mortgage-backed securities business, the only honourable course for me to take as chief executive officer is to step down."[123]

Values-based leaders engender a high level of trust and respect from employees, based not only on their stated values but also on the courage, determination, and self-sacrifice they demonstrate in upholding them. Leaders can use this respect and trust to motivate employees toward high-level performance and a sense of purpose in achieving the organizational vision. When leaders are willing to make personal sacrifices for the sake of values, employees also become more willing to do so. This element of self-sacrifice puts a somewhat spiritual connotation on the process of leadership. Indeed, one writer in organizational theory, Karl Weick, has said that "managerial work can be viewed as managing myth, symbols, and labels…; because managers traffic so often in images, the appropriate role for the manager may be evangelist rather than accountant."[124]

**Think**

Think about a values-based leader you know. What are his or her most notable behaviours?

John Tu and David Sun, cofounders of Kingston Technology Co., which manufactures memory products for personal computers, laser printers, digital cameras, and other products, provide an example of values-based leadership. "Business is not about money," says Sun, vice president and CEO of the U.S.–based company, "It's about relationships." Sun and president Tu strive to develop deep, caring, trusting relationships with employees. "They are part of the team," says one employee of the partnership that workers feel with leaders at Kingston. "They are not owners; they are employees. And that…value system is passed on." Sun and Tu believe everyone in the company is a leader, so they share the wealth with employees. When the two sold 80 percent of Kingston to Softbank of Japan for $1.5 billion, they set aside $100 million of the proceeds for employee bonuses. The initial distribution of $38 million went to about 550 employees who were with the company at the time of its sale. Another $40 million has since been divvied up among the company's current 1,500 workers. Sun and Tu seem genuinely puzzled by people's astonishment that they would give $100 million to employees. It seems only right to them.[125]

## ■ Formal Structure and Systems

Another set of tools leaders can use to shape cultural and ethical values is the formal structure and systems of the organization. These systems have been especially effective in recent years for influencing managerial ethics.

**Structure.** Managers can assign responsibility for ethical values to a specific position. This not only allocates organization time and energy to the problem but also symbolizes to everyone the importance of ethics. One example is an **ethics committee**, which is a cross-functional group of executives who oversee company ethics. The committee provides rulings on questionable ethical issues and assumes responsibility for disciplining wrongdoers. By appointing top-level executives to serve on the committee, the organization signals the importance of ethics.

Today, many organizations are setting up ethics departments that manage and coordinate all corporate ethics activities. These departments are headed by a **chief ethics officer**, a high-level company executive who oversees all aspects of ethics, including establishing and broadly communicating ethical standards, setting up ethics training programs, supervising the investigation of ethical problems, and advising managers on the ethical aspects of corporate decisions.[126] The title of chief ethics officer was almost unheard of a decade ago, but recent ethical and legal problems have created a growing demand for these specialists. Membership in the Ethics & Compliance Officer Association, a trade group, soared from only 12 companies in 1992 to more than 1,200 in 30 countries in 2011.[127]

Ethics offices sometimes also work as counselling centres to help employees resolve difficult ethical dilemmas. The focus is as much on helping employees make the right decisions as on disciplining wrongdoers. Most ethics offices have confidential **ethics hotlines** that employees can use to seek guidance as well as report questionable behaviour. One organization calls its hotline a "Guide Line" to emphasize its use as a tool for making ethical decisions as well as reporting lapses.[128] Holding organizations accountable depends to some degree on individuals who are willing to speak up if they suspect illegal, dangerous, or unethical activities. According to Gary Edwards, president of the Ethics Resource Center, between 65 and 85 percent of calls to hotlines in the organizations he advises are calls for counsel on ethical issues. Randstad Canada, a placement agency, encourages honesty and integrity through its phone line where employees can report misconduct anonymously.[129]

**Disclosure Mechanisms.** Organizations can establish policies and procedures to support and protect whistle-blowers. **Whistle-blowing** is employee disclosure of illegal, immoral, or illegitimate practices on the part of the organization.[130] One value of corporate policy is to protect whistle-blowers so they will not be transferred to lower-level positions or fired because of their ethical concerns. A policy can also encourage whistle-blowers to stay within the organization—for instance, to quietly blow the whistle to responsible managers.[131] Whistle-blowers still have the option to stop organizational activities by going to newspaper or television reporters, but, instead, as a last resort. As ethical problems in the corporate world increase, many companies are looking for ways to protect whistle-blowers. In addition, calls are increasing for stronger legal protection for those who report illegal or unethical business activities.[132] When there are no protective measures, whistle-blowers suffer, and the company may continue its unethical or illegal practices.

Many whistle-blowers suffer financial and personal loss to maintain their personal ethical standards. In 1992, Joanna Gualtieri, then a young lawyer working for the Canadian government, wrote some reports critical of the residences and offices of Canadian diplomats overseas. According to Gualtieri, her efforts were thwarted by her bosses for two years. Then, as a way to go public with her claims, she sued her former bosses at the Department of Foreign Affairs and International Trade. She argues that "[it] is just so simple. If there is respect for the truth...?, let your people speak."[133] Similarly, when five RCMP officers and staff exposed a scandal about the force's pension plan, their claims were met with three years of inertia, denials, and career reprisals. According to the special investigator looking into their claims, "[It] was their perseverance in tracking misdeeds in the force's pension fund that revealed a horribly broken management culture out of step with the RCMP's own values of honesty and accountability."[134] The five whistle-blowers received the force's highest honour, the Commissioner's Commendation in June 2007. Even so, when the whistle-blowers were asked if it was worth it, "...each, in separate interviews, [paused] long and hard."[135]

A recent study of Canadian organizations found that fewer than half of the firms had any guidelines to support whistle-blowers. In addition, the same study found that only half of the responding firms had created an ombudsperson role or department, a mechanism vital for fostering ethical behaviours.[136] Enlightened organizations, however, strive to create a climate and a culture in which employees feel free to point out problems, and managers take swift action to address concerns about unethical or illegal activities. Organizations can view whistle-blowing as a benefit to the company, helping to prevent the kind of disasters that have hit companies such as Enron, Arthur Andersen, and WorldCom, and make dedicated efforts to encourage and protect whistle-blowers.

**Code of Ethics.** A survey of Fortune 1000 companies found that 98 percent address issues of ethics and business conduct in formal corporate policies, and 78 percent have separate codes of ethics that are widely distributed to employees.[137] A **code of ethics** is a formal statement of the company's values concerning ethics and social responsibility; it clarifies to employees what the company stands for and its expectations for employee conduct. Codes of ethics may cover a broad range of issues, including statements of the company's guiding values; guidelines related to issues such as workplace safety, the security of proprietary information, or employee privacy; and commitments to environmental responsibility, product safety, and other matters of concern to stakeholders.

Some companies use broader values statements within which ethics is a part. These statements define ethical values as well as organizational culture and contain language about company responsibility, quality of product, and treatment of employees. A formal statement of values can serve as a fundamental organizational document that defines what the organization stands for, and legitimizes value choices for employees.[138] For example, Citigroup implemented a statement of cultural and ethical values after being stung by a series of scandals in the United States, Japan, and Europe. Charles Prince, then CEO, explained: "Our goal is to make explicit what is implicit. Every employee, starting with me, has the ability to refocus our reputation and our integrity."[139]

Written codes of ethics are important because they clarify and formally state the company's values and expected ethical behaviours. However, it is essential that top managers support and reinforce the codes through their actions, including rewards for compliance and discipline for violations. Otherwise, a code of ethics is nothing more than a piece of paper. Indeed, one study found that companies with a written code of ethics are just as likely as those without a code to be found guilty of illegal activities.[140]

**Training Programs.** To ensure that ethical issues are considered in daily decision making, companies can supplement a written code of ethics with employee training programs.[141] All Texas Instruments (TI) employees go through an eight-hour ethics training course that includes case examples, giving people a chance to wrestle with ethical dilemmas. In addition, TI incorporates an ethics component into every training course it offers.[142] TI's commitment was established at its outset and continues today. TI focuses on teaching its employees to "Know what's right. Value what's right. Do what's right."[143] Similarly, all TELUS employees are required to take an e-learning ethics course.[144]

Ethics programs also often include frameworks for ethical decision making, such as the utilitarian approach described earlier in this chapter. Learning these frameworks helps managers act autonomously and still think their way through a difficult decision. In a few companies, managers are also taught about the stages of moral development, which helps to bring them to a high level of ethical decision making. This training has been an important catalyst for establishing ethical behaviour and integrity as critical components of strategic competitiveness.[145]

These formal systems and structures can be highly effective. However, they alone are not sufficient to build and sustain an ethical company. Leaders should integrate ethics into the organizational culture and support and renew ethical values through their words and actions. For example, since 1995, TELUS has been an Imagine Caring Company, a designation by Imagine Canada (formerly the Canadian Centre for Philanthropy). Caring companies donate more than one percent of their pretax profits to charitable purposes each year. In addition, in 2010 alone, TELUS and its employees and retirees contributed $37.5 million to charitable and not-for-profit organizations and volunteered more than 550,000 hours to local communities.[146] As part of its corporate social responsibility initiatives, TELUS has created community boards across Canada that have so far distributed $25,100,000 in five years.[147]

Darren Entwistle, CEO of TELUS for 14 years, is striving to integrate ethical and socially responsible values into the very core of TELUS. In doing so, he is making organizational integrity and community engagement a part of day-to-day business. Only when employees are convinced that ethical values play a key role in all management decisions and actions can they become committed to making them a part of their everyday behaviour. Organizations that operate on a global scale also face challenges related to culture and ethics.

## In Practice
### TELUS

Community boards have been established in Vancouver, Edmonton, Calgary, Toronto, Ottawa, Montréal, and Rimouski. Prominent community representatives and senior TELUS team members make up the community boards, which are designed to support and expand TELUS's investment in smaller grassroots efforts. Selection of community board members is based on the needs of each community, usually focusing on one of TELUS's key areas of investment: arts and culture, education and sports, and health and well-being.

The TELUS community boards have five principal goals: (1) to determine where and how to invest resources to optimize the benefits that accrue to the community; (2) to determine whether or not the benefits envisioned mutually were successfully created; (3) to identify opportunities that may have been overlooked; (4) to secure additional partners in order to optimize the good to be achieved; and (5) to identify where best to deploy human capital—TELUS executives who are willing to lend their time to serve communities.

In May 2006, TELUS launched the TELUS Toronto Community Board as part of its national philanthropic program. As a result, Toronto community initiatives will receive an increase of $500,000 annually from TELUS. According to (former) President and CEO Darren Entwistle, "[Members of] the TELUS Toronto Community Board will help provide the local insight, knowledge and inspiration to determine where and how we can donate funds to maximize the benefits that accrue to the community. They will also play key roles in helping TELUS identify where best to deploy our executives who are excited to lend their time to serve the Toronto community and business organizations. At TELUS, we are deeply committed to supporting the communities where we live, work and serve."[148]

## Organizational Culture and Ethics in a Global Environment

A Hudson Institute report, *Workforce 2020*, states, "The rest of the world matters to a degree that it never did in the past."[149] Managers are finding this to be true not only in terms of economics or HR issues, but also in terms of cultural and ethical values. Organizations operating in many different areas of the world have a tough time because of the various cultural and market factors they must address. The greater complexities of the environment and organizational domain creates a greater potential for ethical problems or misunderstandings.[150] Consider that in Europe, privacy has been defined as a basic human right and there are laws limiting the amount and kind of information companies can collect and governing how they use it. How do managers translate the ideas for developing strong organizational cultures to a complex global environment? How do they develop ethics codes or other ethical structures and systems that address the complex issues associated with doing business on a global scale?

Organizational culture and national culture are often intertwined, and the global diversity of many of today's companies presents a challenge to managers trying to build a strong organizational culture. Employees who come from different countries often have varied attitudes and beliefs that make it difficult to establish a sense of community and cohesiveness based on the organizational culture. In fact, research has indicated that national culture has a greater impact on employees than does organizational culture.[151] For example, a study of effectiveness and cultural values in Russia found that flexibility and collectivism (working together in groups), which are key values in the national culture, are considerably more important to organizational effectiveness than they are for most U.S.–based companies.[152] However, a more recent study of international joint ventures found, in contrast, that the impact of organizational culture was stronger than that of national culture.[153] When these values are not incorporated into the organizational culture, employees do not perform as well. Another study found that differences in national cultural values and preferences also create significant variance in ethical attitudes among people from different countries.[154]

Some companies have been successful in developing a broad global perspective that permeates the entire organizational culture. For example, Omron, a global company with headquarters in Kyoto, Japan, has offices on six continents. However, until a few years ago, Omron had always assigned Japanese managers to head them. Today, it relies on local expertise in each geographical area and blends the insights and perspectives of local managers into a global whole. Global planning meetings are held in offices around the world. In addition, Omron established a global database and standardized its software to ensure a smooth exchange of information among its offices worldwide. It takes time to develop a broad cultural mind-set and spread it throughout the company, but firms such as Omron try to bring a multicultural approach to every business issue.[155]

Vijay Govindarajan, a Dartmouth College professor of international business, offers some guidance for managers trying to build a global culture. His research indicates that, even though organizational cultures may vary widely, specific components characterize a global culture. These include an emphasis on multicultural rather than national values, basing status on merit rather than nationality, being open to new ideas from other cultures, showing excitement rather than trepidation when entering new cultural environments, and being sensitive to cultural differences without being limited by them.[156]

Global ethics is also challenging today's organizations to think more broadly. Many are using a wide variety of mechanisms to support and reinforce their ethics initiatives on a global scale. One of the most useful mechanisms for building global ethics is the **social audit**, which measures and reports the ethical, social, and environmental impact of a company's operations.[157] Concerns about the labour practices and working conditions of many major U.S. corporations' overseas suppliers originally spurred the Council on Economic Priorities Accreditation Agency to propose a set of global social standards to deal with issues such as child labour, low wages, and unsafe working conditions. Today, the Social Accountability 8000, or SA 8000, is the only auditable social standard in the world. The system is designed to work like the ISO 9000 quality-auditing system of the International Standards Organization.

Many companies, such as Avon Products, Nike, and Toys "R" Us, are taking steps to ensure that their factories and suppliers meet SA 8000 standards. Organizations can also ask an outside firm to perform an independent social audit to measure how well the company is living up to its ethical and social values, and how it is perceived by different stakeholder groups. An interesting Canadian example is Me to We [Responsible Design]. It is a social enterprise that also provides ethically manufactured apparel for the socially conscious consumer. The product line is domestically produced, sweatshop-free, and made using certified organic cotton and bamboo. Fifty percent of the profit goes to Free the Children, to support development projects in rural and impoverished areas across the world.[158]

In the coming years, organizations will continue to evolve in their ability to work with varied cultures, combine them into a cohesive whole, live up to high social and ethical standards worldwide, and cope with the conflicts that may arise when working in a multicultural environment.

## Summary and Interpretation

This chapter covered a range of material on organizational culture, the importance of cultural and ethical values, and techniques managers can use to influence these values. Cultural and ethical values help determine the organization's social capital, and the right values can contribute to organizational success.

Culture is the set of key values, beliefs, and norms shared by members of an organization. Organizational cultures serve two critically important functions—to integrate members so that they know how to relate to one another and to help the organization adapt to the external environment. Culture can be observed and interpreted through rites and ceremonies, stories and heroes, symbols, and language.

Organizational culture should reinforce the strategy and structure that the organization needs to be successful in its environment. Five types of culture that may exist in organizations are adaptability culture, mission culture, clan culture, bureaucratic culture, and discipline culture. When widespread consensus exists about the importance of specific values, the organizational culture is strong and cohesive. However, even in organizations with strong cultures, several sets of subcultures may emerge, particularly in large organizations. Strong cultures can be either adaptive or maladaptive. Adaptive cultures have different values and different behaviour patterns than maladaptive cultures. Strong but unhealthy cultures can be detrimental to an organization's chances for success. On the other hand, strong adaptive cultures can play an important role in creating high performance and innovative response to challenges, competitive threats, or new opportunities.

An important aspect of organizational values is managerial ethics, which is the set of values governing behaviour about what is right or wrong. Ethical decision making in organizations is shaped by many factors: personal characteristics, which include personal beliefs, moral development, and the adoption of ethical frameworks for decision making; organizational culture, which is the extent to which values, heroes, traditions, and symbols reinforce ethical decision making; organizational systems, which pertain to the formal structure, policies, codes of ethics, and reward systems that reinforce ethical or unethical choices; and the interests and concerns of external stakeholders, which include government agencies, customers, and special-interest groups.

The chapter also discussed how leaders can shape culture and ethics. One important idea is values-based leadership, which means leaders define a vision of proper values, communicate it throughout the organization, and institutionalize it through everyday behaviour, rituals, ceremonies, and symbols. We also discussed formal systems that are important for shaping ethical values. Formal systems include an ethics committee, an ethics department, disclosure mechanisms for whistle-blowing, ethics training programs, and a code of ethics or values statement that specifies ethical values. As business increasingly crosses geographical and cultural boundaries, leaders face difficult challenges in establishing strong cultural and ethical values with which all employees can identify and agree. Organizations that develop global cultures emphasize multicultural values, base status on merit rather than nationality, are excited about new cultural environments, remain open to ideas from other cultures, and are sensitive to different cultural values without being limited by them. Social audits are important tools for organizations trying to maintain high ethical standards on a global basis.

## Key Concepts

adaptability culture, p. 337
bureaucratic culture, p. 340
chief ethics officer, p. 355
clan culture, p. 339
code of ethics, p. 357
culture strength, p. 341
culture, p. 332
ethical dilemma, p. 348
ethics committee, p. 355
ethics hotlines, p. 356
ethics, p. 346
external adaptation, p. 333
heroes, p. 335
internal integration, p. 333
language, p. 336

legends, p. 335
managerial ethics, p. 348
mission culture, p. 338
myths, p. 335
rites and ceremonies, p. 334
rule of law, p. 347
social audit, p. 359
social capital, p. 331
social responsibility, p. 348
stories, p. 335
subcultures, p. 341
symbol, p. 335
values-based leadership, p. 354
whistle-blowing, p. 356

## Discussion Questions

1. Describe observable symbols, ceremonies, dress, or other aspects of culture and the underlyinsg values they represent for an organization where you have worked.
2. What might be some of the advantages of having several subcultures within an organization? the disadvantages?
3. Explain the concept of social capital. Name an organization currently in the business news that seems to have a high degree of social capital and one that seems to have a low degree.
4. Do you think a bureaucratic culture would be less employee oriented than a clan culture? Discuss.
5. Why is values-based leadership so important to the influence of culture? Does a symbolic act communicate more about company values than an explicit statement? Discuss.

6. Are you aware of a situation in which either you or someone you know was confronted by an ethical dilemma, such as being encouraged to inflate an expense account? Do you think the person's decision was affected by individual moral development or by the accepted values within the company? Explain.

7. Why is equality an important value to support learning and innovation? Discuss.

8. What importance would you attribute to leadership statements and actions for influencing ethical values and decision making in an organization?

9. How do external stakeholders influence ethical decision making in an organization? Discuss how globalization has contributed to more complex ethical issues related to external stakeholders.

10. Codes of ethics have been criticized for transferring responsibility for ethical behaviour from the organization to the individual employee. Do you agree? Do you think a code of ethics is valuable for an organization?

11. In the recent global economic meltdown, many senior executives made money while many lost their jobs and their houses. What ethical issues does this situation raise? How do you think this affects the social capital of these organizations?

## ■ Chapter 9 Workbook: Shop 'Til You Drop: Organizational Culture in the Retail World*

To understand more about organizational culture, visit two retail stores and compare them according to various factors. Go to one discount or low-end store, such as Giant Tiger or Walmart and to one high-end store, such as Holt Renfrew or Simons. Do not interview any employees, but instead be an observer or a shopper. After your visits, fill out the following table for each store. Spend at least two hours in each store on a busy day and be very observant.

| Culture Item | Discount Store | High-End Store |
|---|---|---|
| Mission of store: What is it, and is it clear to employees? | | |
| Individual initiative: Is it encouraged? | | |
| Reward system: What are employees rewarded for? | | |
| Teamwork: Do people within one department or across departments work together or talk with each other? | | |
| Company loyalty: Is there evidence of loyalty or of enthusiasm to be working there? | | |
| Dress: Are there uniforms? Is there a dress code? How strong is it? How do you rate employees' personal appearance in general? | | |
| Diversity or commonality of employees: Is there diversity or commonality in age, education, race, personality, and so on? | | |
| Service orientation: Is the customer valued or tolerated? | | |
| Human resource development: Is there opportunity for growth and advancement? | | |

*From DAFT. *Organization Theory and Design*, 10E. © 2010 South-Western, a part of Cengage Learning, Inc. Reproduced by permission. www.cengage.com/permissions

## Questions

1. How does the culture seem to influence employee behaviour in each store?
2. What effect does employees' behaviour have on customers?
3. Which store was more pleasant to be in? How does that relate to the mission of the store?

## Case for Analysis: Closing the Gap Healthcare Group*

Connie Clerici valued the work she did in a nursing home as a teenager, but her employer certainly didn't. She wasn't told that outright, but the message was clear. During lunch or coffee breaks, registered nurses sat together at the best tables, where the sun streamed in through the windows, while nursing assistants and cleaning staff huddled in the dark back corners. The groups didn't mingle; the RNs were deemed superior and the doctors were that much higher. "It was one of the most demoralizing experiences of my life," says Clerici. "I swore I would never in my career as a nurse—never mind as an entrepreneur—treat anybody like that."

Clerici has stayed true to her word. Since launching her home health-care company Closing the Gap Health-care Group in 1980, Clerici has worked hard to nurture a corporate culture based on the values she holds dear: respect, integrity, trust, teamwork and quality care. To Clerici, that means treating everyone equally, regardless of title or education; empowering employees; doing what's morally right, even if it's not the best business decision; and always leading by example. "At a very basic level, it's all about valuing people," says Clerici. "All of us have a role in the organization, and when you put the whole thing together, we all become successful."

Such principles, believes Clerici, have played a key role in growing Mississauga, Ont.–based Closing the Gap, which provides health services such as nursing, physio-therapy, speech-language pathology, [and] dietary counseling in clients' homes, to six offices, 500 employees and annual revenue of $25 million.

Whether it is actively managed or not, every company has a corporate culture—the collective consciousness that's infused in your organization and employees, including values, beliefs, processes and encouraged behaviours. If that sounds like a touchy-feely issue you can put on the back burner while you deal with more concrete concerns, think again. Your company's culture plays an important role in attracting and keeping top talent, [and] boosting morale, active learning and higher productivity and performance. According to a 2006 study of Fortune 500 firms by Palo Alto, Calif.–based consultancy Crawford Leadership Corp. and HR.com, companies with strong leadership and adaptive corporate cultures—those that engage staff and help them respond quickly to changing markets and environments—financially outperform those that do not. The good news is, there are management practices that can help you shape and maintain the culture you want in your business.

Money wasn't Clerici's motivation. From the get-go, she was inspired by a simple premise: to treat people the way she wanted to be treated. Over the years, that mantra has evolved and merged with concepts to form the four core values that Cleric says her company embodies: quality care, ethical behaviour, teamwork and innovation. "This is at the heart of who we really are," says Clerici.

But there's a big difference between saying and being. So, Closing the Gap gives employees the policies and tools they need to live those values. For starters, its professional health-care workers—including nurses, physical and occupational therapists, speech pathologists and dieticians—have autonomy to set their own schedules, from when to visit patients to how long to stay. "We don't micro-manage," says Clerici. "We trust our workforce to decide what's best for clients." Over the years, a few employees have broken that trust, admits Clerici, but by and large, staff do not abuse their power. For that reason, Clerici refuses to set policies "aimed at the lowest denominator." Instead, she handles incidents as they come up.

With the majority of Closing the Gap's employees working remotely, many in rural areas, the firm built a comprehensive employee-only section on its website to provide staff with the clinical tools, education materials and best-practice guidelines to enable staff to make the most appropriate decisions in line with best clinical practices. Such tools provide the benchmarks and current standards of quality care that make Closing the Gap unique in its industry, says Clerici, and means employees are never left to guess when it comes to making the best decisions regarding patient care during home visits.

While many competitors take a haphazard approach to training, Clerici deliberately promotes a learning culture that compels staff to be the best they can be. To help employees stay current in their fields, the firm facilitates ongoing development, from attending conferences and workshops, to regularly bringing professionals in-house to review practices and teach new theories. And there are performance-measurement processes in place to ensure that staff stay appropriately qualified and service-oriented. Investing in resources and staff development beefs up employees' skill sets. It also signals a commitment to giving them the tools they need to deliver top-notch care, as well as promoting an environment in which employees want to excel.

That translates into a workforce that routinely delivers outstanding patient care, says Clerici, citing a case where a physical therapist faced a high-risk situation in a post-operative client, and not only accompanied the patient to the local emergency department but stayed with him until he was seen by a doctor.

Other points of differentiation: Closing the Gap has developed its own comprehensive ethics framework, including ethics training for all staff. And its privacy officer ensures the firm adheres to privacy legislation, and always reports breaches. "While it may be uncomfortable to report a weakness, it's the right thing to do," says Clerici. "When we say we're a company of integrity, we mean that."

One of Closing the Gap's biggest challenges is keeping its mobile employees connected to both their co-workers and the company. To help them stay plugged in to the firm's goals and strategies, the company produces a quarterly newsletter and an annual report—a rarity for a private company. Its website includes both a "What's New" page strictly for employees, plus a "Talk to the CEO" component, which encourages staff to e-mail Clerici with questions or concerns. (She receives about 50 per month.) She also makes a point of occasionally accompanying staff on home visits to ensure she stays in touch with the needs and challenges of front-line workers.

At the local level, Clerci developed a system for employees to stay in touch with the office via daily phone calls and weekly meetings with their immediate supervisor; there are also monthly meetings, teleconferences, training sessions and social gatherings. Such get-togethers promote a team environment in which staff feel comfortable calling on each other for advice or support, be it to collaborate with joint patient visits or meeting in the field for lunch to compare notes. That's important because with so many of her employees on the road, says Clerici, "It's not like they can walk down the hall and ask for help."

Despite operating in an industry famous for chewing up and spitting out burned-out workers, Closing the Gap is in the enviable position whereby employees instinctively perform above job expectations. Take, for example, the occupational therapist who voluntarily moved a roomful of heavy furniture, including dismantling a bed that was too high, to accommodate an elderly patient who had just returned home from hip-replacement surgery.

The proof of its employee engagement is in the numbers: Closing the Gap boasts an employee turnover rate of just 2 percent, significantly lower than the industry average of about 10 percent, says Clerici.

Surprisingly, Clerici says another big challenge is staying true to her values. "There are so many outside forces coming in," she says, "whether it's regulatory bodies, customers, external legal counsel or accountants—they're all giving you advice that could pull you away from your value system." Clerici says she relies on her management team to help her consistently stay true to her values. But Kathy Underwood, Closing the Gap's COO, says in fact it's Clerici herself who is the company's role model—and that's a good thing, because it's crucial for the CEO to walk the talk. "She sets the bar high," says Underwood. "And while I've worked at a number of health organizations before, this is the first one where I can say everyone is really committed to trying to live out values." Underwood says Clerici encourages her staff to ask questions, voice their opinions and continuously ask if the decisions the company makes are in line with "what we say we do."

For Clerici, the litmus test is always. "Can I go home and sleep at night? It's not like we pull our mission, vision and values off the shelf once a year," she says. "We're not that kind of company. We embrace it every day."

## Assignment Questions

1. How would you characterize the culture at Closing the Gap Healthcare Group?
2. What is the CEO's role in creating and sustaining the culture?
3. Would you like to work there? Why?

---

*Myers, J. "Company Culture: Invisible Weapon," *Profit Magazine*, March 2010, accessed from http://www.canadianbusiness .com/entrepreneur/human_resources/article.jsp?content= 20100219_111306_6768 on March 26, 2011. Reproduced by permission of the author.

## Case for Analysis: Queen's Returns Radler Gift*

Queen's Board of Trustees has decided to return all monies received in relation to a gift pledge from David Radler and remove the Radler name from a wing of its School of Business and from Queen's Benefactor Wall.

"This was not an easy decision. However, we were guided by the simple principle of what is the right thing to do in this particular situation," says Vice-Principal (Advancement) George Hood.

Mr. Radler entered a plea of guilty to fraud in a U.S. federal court last Tuesday. The following day, the board made its decision, which was communicated in a public statement by the university on Thursday.

The gift pledge of $1 million (of which $915,180 has been received by the university) was to Goodes Hall building fund. It involved donations from Mr. Radler and from a number of corporate newspaper organizations with which he has been associated. The university plans to take immediate steps to return all monies to these donors. "This gift was given and received in good faith by the university and in accordance with approved parameters of its Gift Acceptance Policy and used according to the intended philanthropic purpose," the statement says.

"The quality of Queen's learning and research environment depends heavily on the generosity and support of our alumni and other supporters. We feel in this case, however, that the integrity of this gift to the university has been compromised."

"These actions by the university are in keeping with our policies and with our primary commitment to act in the best interest of our students, our alumni, other members of the Queen's community, our donors, and the general public."

"Ethics and corporate social responsibility are a cornerstone of good business practice, and we take them very seriously at Queen's," says School of Business Dean David Saunders. "Our decision to return Mr. Radler's gift is consistent with what we teach our students, and I have received nothing but supportive comments from alumni, students, faculty and others. It is unfortunate we were faced with this decision but we made the right one."

A number of post-secondary institutions have faced similar issues with respect to gift acceptance and donor recognition. While there doesn't appear to be a comparable Canadian precedent, the Washington-based Council for the Advancement and Support of Education (CASE) cites a number of U.S. schools which have encountered similar issues, including the universities of Harvard, Princeton, Brown, Cornell, Michigan, and North Carolina at Chapel Hill.

There don't appear, however, to be any consistent guidelines or policies within the higher education philanthropic sector for dealing with such donor matters. Responses in these U.S. cases have ranged broadly from no action or maintaining status quo to the removal of named recognition only or removal of naming coupled with return of funds. "It appears that each situation has been handled through case-by-case review and relied ultimately upon the judgement of the university's administrators, staff, trustees, and faculty in examining their particular circumstance," says Mr. Hood. The two main university policies that informed the board's decision are the Queen's University Naming Policy and the Gift Acceptance Policy.

The naming policy notes that "ultimate authority to discontinue the designated name of a building, room, or area, or to transfer the name to another building room or area" at Queen's rests with the Board of Trustees. It goes on to say that "no naming will be approved or (once approved) continued that will call into serious question the public respect of the university."

A recent *Globe and Mail* editorial suggested that charities should not return donations. "Clearly, there will be many different opinions on this," says George Hood. "Queen's thoroughly discussed all the ramifications of this matter and decided what it felt was the best course of action."

## Assignment Questions

1. What are the most important ethical issues in the case?
2. Should Queen's have returned the gift? Why?
3. Does returning the gift establish some sort of precedent?

---

*Kershaw, A. (2006) "Queen's returns Radler Gift," *Queen's Gazette* 36 (14). Used with permission of Queen's University.

---

## ■ Chapter 9 Workshop: Where to Begin—A Framework for Developing Your CSR Strategy*

Using an organization you know well, answer the questions for each of the quadrants in the virtue matrix. What ideas do you have for improving the social responsibility of the organization?

### Civil Foundation—Compliance Quadrant Questions

1. To what extent do we seek to be in full compliance with the key laws and regulations to which we are subject?

2. And if so, how do we ensure, demonstrate and communicate that we meet all laws and regulations?
3. What are the two or three priorities, if any, for overcoming compliance issues?

### Civil Foundation—Choice Quadrant Questions

1. What are the key norms and customs in the industry?
2. To what extent are we currently a leader or a laggard in adopting the norms?

3. What are our aspirations for leading in adherence to customs and norms?
4. What two or three initiatives would be most important to improve adherence to customs and norms?

## Strategic Frontier Quadrant Questions

1. What are activities that your corporation's customers, employees, shareholders, or suppliers want that you could provide if you chose?
2. How could we develop a business case to overcome the impediment to undertaking such new practices?
3. What two or three initiatives would be of the highest priority?

## Structural Frontier Quadrant Questions

1. What practices that are desired by customers/employees/shareholders/stakeholders would require collective action among firms in the industry to make them happen?
2. How would a coalition of interested firms be pulled together for each potential practice?
3. What governmental/non-governmental organizations might your corporation include in a coalition?
4. What two or three new initiatives would be of the highest priority?

---

*Martin, Roger, "Where to Begin: A Framework for Developing Your CSR Strategy," Microsoft Social Responsibility Series Part 2, *Canadian Business*, Summer 2005. Used with permission.

# 10 Innovation and Change

Norm Betts/Bloomberg/Getty Images

## Toyota Motor Corporation

In auto manufacturing, Japanese companies have ruled, and one manufacturer outshines them all. Toyota dominates the global auto market, achieving its goal of overtaking General Motors (GM) as the world's number-one automaker. The basis of Toyota's supremacy lies primarily in its steady stream of technological and product innovation. Toyota executives created the doctrine of *kaizen*, or continuous improvement, and the company applies it relentlessly. Toyota hands the responsibility for continuous improvement to every employee. People on the shop floor can get cash rewards for searching out production glitches and finding ways to solve them.

Although thinking big can be important, Toyota knows that sweating the details is just as critical for driving innovation. Consider this: Toyota made a small change to its production lines (see photo) by using a single master brace to hold automobile frames in place as they were welded, instead of the dozens of braces used in a standard auto factory. It seemed almost insignificant in the context of the company's complex manufacturing system, yet it was a radical manufacturing innovation. That one change, referred to now as the Global Body Line system, slashed 75 percent from the cost of retrofitting a production line and made it possible for Toyota to produce different car and truck models on a single line. The result has been billions of dollars in annual cost savings.

For developing new models, Toyota applies the concept of *obeya*, which literally means "big room." To ensure all the critical factors are considered from the beginning, product development teams made up of manufacturing and product engineers, designers, marketers, and suppliers hold regular face-to-face brainstorming sessions. New software programs, including product life cycle management software, also make it possible for these cross-functional teams to collaborate digitally, viewing product design changes and associated costs. That way, if a designer makes a change that conflicts with manufacturing's needs or a supplier's capability, it can be noted and adjusted immediately. This collaborative process created Toyota's sturdy small truck, the Hilux, which is sold mostly in developing countries and is favoured by oil companies and other organizations working in areas where a pickup breakdown can mean life or death. An updated version of the Hilux has been key to Toyota's strategy of overtaking GM.[1] In the first quarter of 2007, Toyota passed GM as the world's number-one automaker and maintained the ranking through 2013.[2]

---

Canada has had a long and interesting history of innovation and invention. Pablum cereal, kerosene, and the electron microscope were invented in Canada. In 1927, the Creed telegraph system was designed; it was the first teleprinter that combined transmitting and receiving. This innovation resulted in the expansion of news wire services and increased the amount of news available to newspapers. In 1937, the self-propelled combine harvester, built by Thomas Carroll, transformed agriculture by rolling all the stages of wheat harvesting into one operation. The innovation has benefited farmers across the world. In addition, the first North American commercial jet was built in Toronto.[3] The ubiquitous BlackBerry was invented in 1999, even as the company faces a fight for its survival now.

Today, every organization, whether Canadian or global, must change and innovate to survive. New discoveries and inventions quickly replace standard ways of doing things. Organizations such as Toyota, Microsoft, Apple, and Bombardier are searching for any innovation edge they can find. Some companies, such as 3M, the maker of Post-it Notes, Thinsulate insulation, Scotch-Brite scouring pads, and thousands of other products, are known for innovation. 3M's culture supports a risk-taking and entrepreneurial spirit that keeps it bubbling over with new ideas and new products. However, many large, established companies have a hard time being entrepreneurial and continually look for ways to encourage change and innovation to keep pace with changes in the external environment.

The pace of change is revealed in the fact that the parents of today's postsecondary-age students grew up without debit cards, video on demand, iPhones, laser checkout systems, cellular phones, instant messaging, and the Internet. The idea of communicating instantly with people around the world was unimaginable to many people as recently as two decades ago. Take a few minutes now to assess how innovative you are by completing the You and Design feature.

# YOU & DESIGN

## Are You Innovative?

Think about your current life. Indicate whether each of the following items is Mostly True or Mostly False for you.

| | Mostly True | Mostly False |
|---|---|---|
| 1. I am always seeking new ways to do things. | _____ | _____ |
| 2. I consider myself creative and original in my thinking and behaviour. | _____ | _____ |
| 3. I rarely trust new gadgets until I see whether they work for people around me. | _____ | _____ |
| 4. In a group or at work I am often sceptical of new ideas. | _____ | _____ |
| 5. I typically buy new foods, gear, and other innovations before other people do. | _____ | _____ |
| 6. I like to spend time trying out new things. | _____ | _____ |
| 7. My behaviour influences others to try new things. | _____ | _____ |
| 8. Among my co-workers, I will be among the first to try out a new idea or method. | _____ | _____ |

**Scoring:** To compute your score on the Personal Innovativeness scale, add the number of Mostly True answers to items 1, 2, 5, 6, 7, 8 and the Mostly False answers to items 3 and 4 for your score.

**Interpretation:** *Personal Innovativeness* reflects the awareness of a need to innovate and a readiness to try new things. Innovativeness is also thought of as the degree to which a person adopts innovations earlier than other people in the peer group. Innovativeness is considered a positive for people in creative companies, creative departments, venture teams, and for corporate entrepreneurship. A score of 6–8 indicates that you are very innovative and likely are one of the first people to adopt changes. A score of 4–5 would suggest that you are average or slightly above average in innovativeness compared to others. A score of 0–3 means that you may prefer the tried and true and hence are not excited about new ideas or innovations. As a manager, a high score suggests you will emphasize innovation and change.

Source: Based on H. Thomas Hurt, Katherine Joseph, and Chester D. Cook, "Scales for the Measurement of Innovativeness," *Human Communication Research* 4, no. 1 (1977), 58–65; and John E. Ettlie and Robert D. O'Keefe, "Innovative Attitudes, Values, and Intentions in Organizations," *Journal of Management Studies* 19, no. 2 (1982), 163–182.

## ■ Purpose of This Chapter

This chapter will explore how organizations change and how managers can direct the innovation and change process. We discuss the difference between incremental and radical change, the four types of change—technology, product, structure, people—occurring in organizations, and how to manage change successfully. Note that innovation and change are not synonymous. Innovation can create change and can result from change; however, change may not necessarily create or result in innovation. The organizational structure and management approach for facilitating each type of change is then discussed. Management techniques for influencing both the creation and implementation of change are also covered.

## Innovate or Perish: The Strategic Role of Change

If there is one theme or lesson that emerges from previous chapters, it is that organizations must run quickly to keep up with changes taking place all around them. Large organizations must find ways to act like small, nimble organizations. Manufacturing firms need to reach out for new, flexible manufacturing technology and service firms for new information technology (IT). The impact of IT as a source of organizational change cannot be over-emphasized. It has resulted in smaller organizations, decentralized structures, improved horizontal coordination, improved interorganizational relationships, and the creation of network structures such as Impact Hub, described in Chapter 6.

Today's organizations must poise themselves to innovate and change, not only to prosper but also to survive in a world of increased competition.[4] As illustrated in Exhibit 10.1, a number of environmental forces drive this need for major organizational change. Powerful forces associated with advancing technology, international economic integration, the maturing of domestic markets, and the shift to capitalism in formerly communist regions have brought about a globalized economy that affects every business, from the largest to the smallest, creating more threats as well as more opportunities. To recognize and manage the threats and take advantage of the opportunities, today's organizations are undergoing dramatic changes in all areas of their operations.

As we have seen in previous chapters, many organizations are responding to global forces by adopting self-directed teams and horizontal structures that enhance communication and collaboration, streamlining supply and distribution channels, and overcoming barriers of time and place through IT and e-business. Others become involved in joint ventures or consortia to exploit opportunities and extend operations or markets internationally. Some adopt structural innovations such as the virtual network approach to focus on their core competencies while outside specialists handle other activities. In addition, today's organizations face a need for dramatic strategic and cultural change and for rapid and continuous innovations in technology, services, products, and processes. A key element of the success of companies such as 3M Corporation, Celestica, and Google, highlighted in the Leading by Design feature, has been their passion for creating and sustaining change.

**EXHIBIT 10.1**
Forces Driving
the Need for Major
Organizational
Change
Source: Based on John P.
Kotter, *The New Rules: How
to Succeed in Today's Post-
Corporate World* (New York:
The Free Press, 1995).

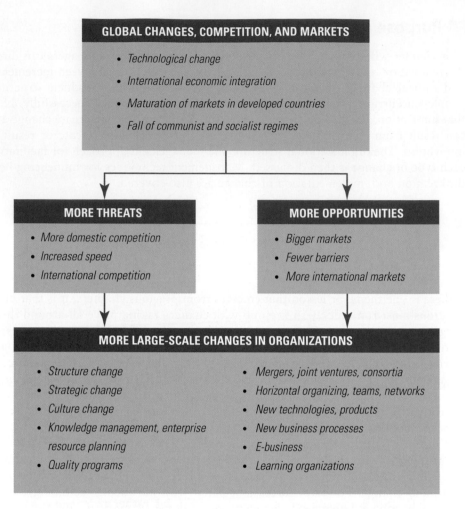

Recently, we have been seeing significant innovation in Canada by entrepreneurs who are developing ways to address environmental sustainability and making money doing so. They are known as eco-capitalists who are addressing such complex green issues as destruction of our forests, water conservation, and alternative energy sources. This chapter's Book Mark describes the work of several eco-capitalists. We are also seeing more companies—even large resource and manufacturing companies— becoming more green to enhance their public image and their bottom line. Between 1990 and 2008, there were significant declines in energy consumption in industries such as copper mining and dairy production.[5]

Change, rather than stability, is the norm today. Whereas change once occurred incrementally and infrequently, today it is often dramatic and constant.

**Apply**

Apply your results from the You and Design feature to see how you might become more innovative still.

## Incremental Versus Radical Change

The changes used to adapt to the environment can be evaluated according to scope—that is, the extent to which changes are incremental or radical for the organization.[6] As summarized in Exhibit 10.2, **incremental change** represents a series of continual progressions that maintain the organization's general equilibrium and

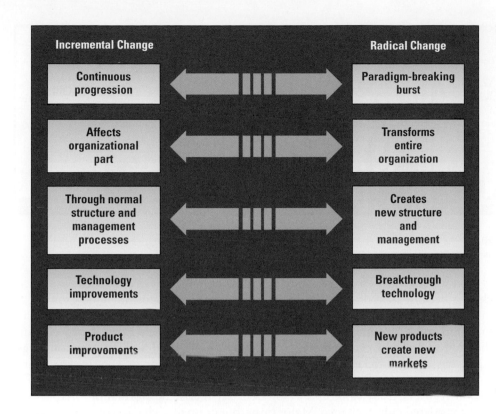

**EXHIBIT 10.2**
Incremental versus
Radical Change
Source: Based on Alan D.
Meyer, James B. Goes, and
Geoffrey R. Brooks, "Organiza-
tions in Disequilibrium: Envi-
ronmental Jolts and Industry
Revolutions," in George Huber
and William H. Glick, eds.,
Organizational Change and
Redesign (New York: Oxford
University Press, 1992), 66–111,
and Harry S. Dent, Jr., "Growth
through New Product Develop-
ment," Small Business Reports
(November 1990), 30–40.

often affect only one organizational part. **Radical change**, by contrast, breaks the frame of reference for the organization, often transforming the entire organiza- tion. For example, an incremental change is the implementation of sales teams in the marketing department, whereas a radical change is shifting the entire orga- nization from a vertical to a horizontal structure, with all employees who work on specific core processes brought together in teams rather than being separated into functional departments such as marketing, finance, production, and so forth. Although bold, transforming change gets a lot of attention and can be powerful for an organization, recent research indicates that incremental change—the con- stant implementation of small ideas, such as at Toyota—more often results in a sustainable competitive advantage. At the two Honda plants in Alliston, Ontario, for example, New Honda (NH) quality circles try to find cost-cutting or efficiency improvements through teamwork. One NH circle modified the way the stamping press line could be changed so that the hood and frame could be stamped from one metal sheet, which resulted in an annual saving of $500,000.[7] Google, based in Mountain View, California, also thrives on a culture that encourages continuous incremental change. Exhibit 10.3 highlights what can happen when there is too much change in an organization!

Incremental change occurs mainly through the established structure and man- agement processes, and it may include technology improvements—such as the introduction of flexible manufacturing systems—or product improvements—such as Procter & Gamble's addition to Tide detergent of cleaning agents that protect colours and fabrics. Radical change involves the creation of a new structure and new management processes. The technology is likely to be breakthrough, and new products thereby created will establish new markets.

**EXHIBIT 10.3**
How to Manage Innovation!

**Compare**

Research the approaches to innovation that are used by Celestica or Google and by the 3M Corporation to compare their similarities and differences.

As we have just discussed, there is a growing emphasis on the need for radical change because of today's turbulent, unpredictable environment.[8] One example of radical change is Apple, which has transformed itself from a personal computer (PC) manufacturer to a dominant force in the digital entertainment business. By creating the iPod and iTunes online store, giving people easy, legal access to lots of songs, Apple has changed the rules of the game in consumer electronics, entertainment, and software.[9] Organizational turnarounds and transformations such as Tembec's successful recovery from bankruptcy[10] or Lou Gerstner's transformation of IBM, are also considered radical change. Major turnarounds involve changes in all areas of the organization, including structure, management systems, culture, technology, and products or services. The cartoon highlights how not to manage innovation!

## ■ Strategic Types of Change

Managers can focus on four types of change within organizations to achieve strategic advantage. These four types of change are changes of products and services, strategy and structure, culture, and technology. We touched on overall leadership and organizational strategy in Chapter 2 and on organizational culture in Chapter 9. These factors provide an overall context within which the four types of change serve as a competitive wedge to achieve an advantage in the international environment. Each organization has a unique configuration of products and services, strategy and structure, culture, and technology that can be focused for maximum impact upon its chosen markets.[11]

**Product and service changes** pertain to the product or service outputs of an organization. New products include small adaptations of existing products or entirely new product lines. New products and services are normally designed to increase the market share or to develop new markets, customers, or clients. Toyota's Hilux truck is a product designed to increase market share, whereas Apple's iPod was a new product that created a new market for the company. An example of a new service designed to reach new markets and customers is IKEA's entry into low-income housing, which is being piloted in Gateshead, the United Kingdom.[12]

**Strategy and structure changes** pertain to the administrative domain in an organization. The administrative domain involves the supervision and management of the organization. These changes include changes in organizational structure, strategic management, policies, reward systems, labour relations, coordination devices, management information and control systems, and accounting and budgeting systems. Structure and system changes are usually top-down, that is, mandated by top management, whereas product and technology changes may often come from the bottom up. A system change instituted by management in a university might be a new merit-pay plan. Corporate downsizing and the shift to horizontal teams are other examples of top-down structure change.

**Culture changes** refer to changes in the values, attitudes, expectations, beliefs, abilities, and behaviour of employees. Culture changes pertain to changes in how employees think; these are changes in mind-set rather than technology, structure, or products.

**Technology changes** are changes in an organization's production process, including its knowledge and skill base, that enable distinctive competence. These changes are designed to make production more efficient or to produce greater volume. Changes in technology involve the techniques for making products or services. They include work

# Leading *by Design*

## Google

Google quickly became the most popular search engine on the Internet with its smarter, faster approach to providing users with what they are looking for. But to maintain that success, managers knew the company needed to continuously innovate.

Marissa Mayer, then vice president of Product Management, suggested that the company come up with new ideas the same way its search engine scours the Web. To provide users with the best Web search experience possible, Google searches far and wide, combing through billions of documents. Then it ranks the search results by relevance and sends them to the user quickly. The idea search process works much the same way by casting a wide net across the organization. The process begins with an easy-to-use intranet. Even employees with limited technology expertise can quickly set up a page of ideas. "We never say, 'This group should innovate and the rest should just do their jobs,'" says Jonathan Rosenberg, former vice president of product management. "Everyone spends a fraction of [the] day on R&D." The intranet has also tapped into more ideas from technologically savvy Google employees who may not be very vocal or assertive in meetings. Mayer said some engineers had lots of good ideas but were shy about putting them forth in open meetings. Now, employees can post their ideas on the intranet and see what kind of response they get.

Mayer searched the site each day to see which ideas were generating the most excitement and comments. Once a week, she sat down with a team to hash out the ideas and fleshed out at least six or seven that could be fast-tracked into development. In addition to the internal search process, users continued to play a key role in innovation.

Ten full-time employees read and respond to user e-mails and pass along ideas to project teams, who are constantly tweaking Google's service. Engineers work in teams of three and have the authority to make any changes that improve the quality of the user experience and get rid of anything that gets in the way. Moreover, Google allows all software developers to integrate its search engine into their own applications. The download is easy and the licence is free. It sounds crazy to some businesses, but Google says it "turns the world into Google's development team."[13]

Google's organic approach to innovation has been highly successful. Indeed, the company is no longer just a hugely successful search engine. Google has evolved into a software company that is a major threat to Microsoft's dominance. While Microsoft has been struggling to catch up in the game of search, Google has quietly been launching products such as desktop search; Gmail; software to manage, edit, and send digital photos; and programs for creating, editing, and posting documents. The idea that Google could one day marginalize Microsoft's operating system and bypass Windows applications is being taken seriously by Microsoft managers. Microsoft is ten times the size of Google and has plenty of cash with which to compete. But Microsoft leaders know that, for now, Google's innovation process gives it an edge. "Here Microsoft was spending $600 million a year in R&D for MSN [Microsoft Networks], $1 billion a year for Office, and $1 billion a year for Windows, and Google [got] desktop search out before us," said a Microsoft executive. "It was a real wake-up call."[14] Not surprisingly, Google's track record of innovation, as well as its culture, has made it the employer of first choice for recent business school graduates.[15]

methods, equipment, and workflow. For example, a technology change at UPS was the implementation of the DIAD (Delivery Information Acquisition Device). When a customer signs for a package on a computerized clipboard, the device automatically transmits the information to the website, where the sender can verify that the package has been delivered before the driver even gets back to the truck.[16]

The four types of change are interdependent—a change in one often means a change in another. A new product may require changes in the production technology, or a change in structure may require new employee skills. For example, during the 1999 merger of TD and Canada Trust, the largest merger in the history of Canadian financial services, much attention was directed at getting the most efficient technological solutions by drawing on the expertise in both organizations. The merger required significant structural and technological changes. Organizations are interdependent systems, and changing one part often has implications for other organization elements.

# Elements for Successful Change

**Think**

Think about how organizations can achieve Drucker's definition of innovation.

Regardless of the type or scope of change, there are identifiable stages of innovation, which generally occur as a sequence of events, though innovation stages may overlap.[17] In the research literature on innovation, **organizational change** is considered the adoption of a new idea or behaviour by an organization.[18] **Organizational innovation**, in contrast, is the adoption of an idea or behaviour that is new to the organization's industry, market, or general environment.[19] Similarly, the late Peter Drucker, a global thought leader in for-profit and not-for-profit management, defined innovation as "change that creates a new dimension of performance."[20]

The first organization to introduce a new product is considered the innovator, and organizations that copy are considered to adopt changes. Innovations typically are assimilated into an organization through a series of steps or elements. Organization members first become aware of a possible innovation, evaluate its appropriateness, and then evaluate and choose the idea.[21] Tom Kelley, general manager of IDEO, the internationally renowned design firm, has identified the ten "faces" of innovation.[22] The ten faces provide insight into the many stages and components of innovation. Exhibit 10.4 highlights the ten and their principal characteristics.

**EXHIBIT 10.4**
**The Ten Faces of Innovation**
Source: Based on Tom Kelley, *The Ten Faces of Innovation* (New York: Currency Doubleday, 2005) 8–12.

| Learning Faces | Anthropologist—looks at human interactions |
|---|---|
| | Experimenter—prototypes new ideas |
| | Cross-Pollinator—explores other industries and cultures |
| Organizing Faces | Hurdler—develops ways to deal with roadblocks |
| | Collaborator—brings together an eclectic group |
| | Director—sparks creative talents |
| Building Faces | Experience Architect—creates experiences that go beyond product/service's functionality |
| | Set Designer—creates the right space |
| | Caregiver—delivers special service |
| | Storyteller—builds internal morale and external awareness |

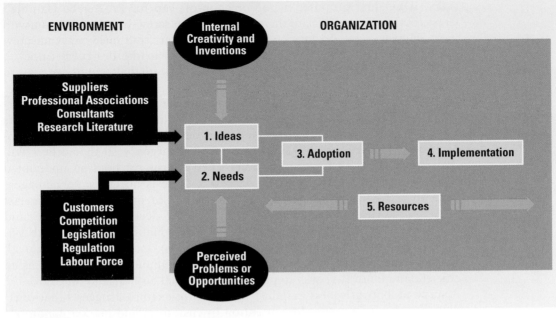

**EXHIBIT 10.5**
Sequence of Elements for Successful Change

The required elements of successful change are summarized in Exhibit 10.5. For a change to be successfully implemented, managers must ensure each element occurs in the organization. If one of the elements is missing, the **change process** will fail. For purposes of managing change, however, the terms *innovation* and *change* will be used interchangeably because the change process within organizations tends to be similar whether a change is early or late with respect to other organizations in the environment.

1. *Ideas*. No company can remain competitive without new ideas; change is the outward expression of those ideas.[23] An idea is a new way of doing things. It may be a new product or service, a new management concept, or a new procedure for working together in the organization. Ideas can come from within or from outside the organization. Internal creativity is a dramatic element of organizational change. **Creativity** is the generation of novel ideas that may meet perceived needs or respond to opportunities. Umbra, for example, has brought high design to everyday objects while making them affordable. One of its signature objects, the Garbino wastepaper basket with its tulip shape, its opalescent glow, and its handles, is on permanent display in New York's Museum of Modern Art. "Applying innovative designs to standard products and seeing the potential in new technology are hallmarks of Umbra's work."[24] In 2007, Umbra opened its architecturally innovative retail store in Toronto to make its designs more accessible still.

   Some techniques for spurring internal creativity are to increase the diversity within the organization, ensure employees have plenty of opportunities to interact with people different from themselves, give employees time and freedom for experimentation, and support risk taking and making mistakes.[25] At IDEO, prototypes are developed rapidly and then shared with the end users. IDEO first proposed a pop-on, pop-off cap for Procter & Gamble's Crest toothpaste to alleviate the problem of the screw-on cap filling up with paste. However, the designers noticed that the users continued to try unscrew the cap even when told about the new design. So the designers came up with a hybrid—a twist-off cap with a short thread that would be easy to clean.[26]

2. *Needs*. Ideas are generally not seriously considered unless there is a perceived need for change. A perceived need for change occurs when managers see a gap between actual performance and desired performance in the organization. Managers try to establish a sense of urgency so that others will understand the need for change. Sometimes a crisis provides an undoubted sense of urgency. In many cases, however, there is no crisis, so managers have to recognize a need and communicate it to others.[27] Over the last 20 years, Nortext of Nunavut has pioneered the development of fonts and programs to publish in approximately 40 Aboriginal languages in both syllabic and Roman orthographies. It organizes "co-operative printing runs," sharing materials and costs among Aboriginal communities and regions as an efficient and innovative way to promote Aboriginal authors and illustrators.[28] A study of innovativeness in industrial firms, for example, suggests that organizations that encourage close attention to customers and market conditions and support for entrepreneurial activity produce more ideas and are more innovative.[29]

3. *Adoption*. Adoption occurs when decision makers choose to proceed with a proposed idea. Key managers and employees need to be in agreement to support the change. For a major organizational change, the decision might require the signing of a legal document by the board of directors. For a small change, adoption might occur with informal approval by a middle manager.

4. *Implementation*. Implementation occurs when organization members, in fact, use a new idea, technique, or behaviour. Materials and equipment may have to be acquired, and workers may have to be trained to use the new idea. Implementation is a very important step because, without it, previous steps are to no avail. Implementation of change is often the most difficult part of the change process. Until people use the new idea, no change has actually taken place.

5. *Resources*. Human energy and activity are required to bring about change. Change does not happen on its own; it requires time and resources, for both creating and implementing a new idea. Employees have to provide energy to see both the need and the idea to meet that need. Someone must develop a proposal and provide the time and effort to implement it. 3M has an unwritten but widely understood rule that its 8,300 researchers can spend up to 15 percent of their time working on any idea of their choosing, without management approval. Most innovations go beyond ordinary budget allocations and require special funding. At 3M, exceptionally promising ideas become "pacing programs" and receive high levels of funding for further development.[30] In addition, 3M's CEO boosted research and development (R&D) funding to $1.5 billion in 2007 and directed much of the funding to 3M's core product lines of abrasives, flexible electronics, and nanotechnology.[31] Some companies use task forces, as described in Chapter 3, to focus resources on a change. Others set up seed funds or venture funds that employees with promising ideas can access.

In Practice
**Cirque du Soleil**

Cirque du Soleil was cofounded by Guy Laliberté and Daniel Gauthier in Montréal, and has grown from a band of street performers to a large innovative organization that has transformed the essence of a circus. Cirque's primary audience is adults, not children, and it does not use any animals in its shows. It offers a combination of feats of aerobatics with theatre, opera, and original music; it has created a new art form. It has its own record label, a retail operation, and a deal with Carnival Cruise Lines. Its 2012 revenues, from its 22 shows and its merchandise, are expected to surpass $1 billion.[32] According to Mario D'Amico, chief marketing officer for Cirque du Soleil, the organization invented a new market by inventing a new brand of circus by using a "blue ocean" strategy. (A blue ocean strategy suggests that organizations should be less concerned with their competitors; instead they should look for ways to compete against themselves.)[33] Cirque du Soleil has created a new market, creating a true innovation and, as a result, transformed our understanding of a circus. It made decisions about four key competitive issues: (1) Which of the factors that the industry takes for granted should be eliminated? (2) Which factors should be reduced well below the industry's standard? (3) Which factors should be raised well above the industry's standard? and (4) Which factors should be created that the industry has never offered?[34] Cirque du Soleil aims to maintain a constant delicate tension between art and commerce. D'Amico also emphasizes the importance of building failure into the creative process, noting that the organization routinely spends time and money developing acts that never make it into a performance. "Any time spent pursuing an idea is time well spent."[35]

**Apply**

How can you apply the idea of building failure into the creative process for your personal and/or career development?

One point about Exhibit 10.5 is especially important. Needs and ideas are listed simultaneously at the beginning of the change sequence. Either may occur first. Most organizations adopted the computer, for example, because it seemed a promising way to improve efficiency. The search for a vaccine against the AIDS virus, on the other hand, was stimulated by a critical need. Whether the need or the idea occurs first, for the change to be accomplished, each of the steps in Exhibit 10.5 must be completed.

## Technology Change

In today's business world, any company that isn't continually developing, acquiring, or adapting new technology will likely be out of business in a few years. However, organizations face a contradiction when it comes to technology change, because the conditions that promote new ideas are not generally the best for implementing those ideas for routine production. An innovative organization is characterized by flexibility and empowered employees and the absence of rigid work rules.[36] As discussed earlier in this book, an organic, free-flowing organization is typically associated with change and is considered the best organization form for adapting to a chaotic environment.

The flexibility of an organic organization contributes to people's freedom to be creative and introduce new ideas. Organic organizations encourage a bottom-up innovation process. Ideas bubble up from middle- and lower-level employees because they have the freedom to propose ideas and to experiment. A mechanistic structure, in contrast, stifles innovation with its emphasis on rules and regulations, but it is often the best structure for efficiently producing routine products. The challenge for managers is to create both organic and mechanistic conditions within the organization to achieve both innovation and efficiency. To attain both aspects of technological change, many organizations use the ambidextrous approach.

## ■ The Ambidextrous Approach

Recent thinking has refined the idea of organic versus mechanistic structures with respect to innovation creation versus innovation utilization. For example, sometimes an organic structure generates innovative ideas but is not the best structure for using those ideas.[37] In other words, the initiation and the utilization of change are two distinct processes. Organic characteristics such as decentralization and employee freedom are excellent for initiating ideas; but these same conditions often make it hard to implement a change because employees are less likely to comply. Employees can ignore the innovation because of decentralization and a generally loose structure.

How does an organization solve this dilemma? One remedy is for the organization to use an **ambidextrous approach**—to incorporate structures and management processes that are appropriate to both the creation and the implementation of innovation.[38] Another way to think of the ambidextrous approach is to look at the organizational design elements that are important for *exploring* new ideas versus the design elements that are most suitable for *exploiting* current capabilities. Exploration means encouraging creativity and developing new ideas, whereas exploitation means implementing those ideas to produce routine products. The organization can be designed to behave in an organic way for exploring new ideas and in a mechanistic way to exploit and use the ideas. Exhibit 10.6 illustrates how one department is structured organically to explore and develop new ideas, and another department is structured mechanistically for routine implementation of innovations. Research has shown that organizations that use an ambidextrous approach by designing for both exploration and exploitation are significantly more successful in launching innovative new products or services.[39]

For example, a study of long-established Japanese companies such as Honda and Canon that have succeeded in breakthrough innovations found that these companies use an ambidextrous approach.[40] To develop ideas related to a new technology, the companies assign teams of young staff members who are not entrenched in the "old way of doing things" to work on the project. The teams are headed by an esteemed elder and are charged with doing whatever is needed to develop new ideas and products, even if it means breaking rules that are important in the larger organization.

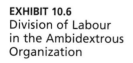

**EXHIBIT 10.6**
Division of Labour in the Ambidextrous Organization

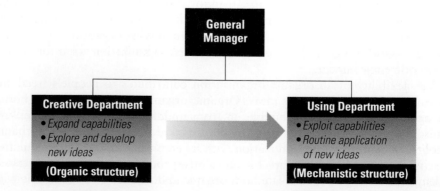

# ■ Techniques for Encouraging Technology Change

Some of the techniques used by companies to maintain an ambidextrous approach are switching structures, separate creative departments, venture teams, and corporate entrepreneurship.

**Switching Structures. Switching structures** means an organization creates an organic structure when such a structure is needed for the initiation of new ideas.[41] Some of the ways organizations have switched structures to achieve the ambidextrous approach are as follows:

- For example, Tesco of the United Kingdom experiments with new store formats and nonfood offerings while achieving record profits in its core business.[42]
- Corus Entertainment is creating an ambidextrous organization that is adept at managing core business activities while encouraging innovation and exploring new business models. Corus Entertainment maintains a fund to support employee innovations, which had resulted in 15 new projects as of 2007.[43]
- The NUMMI plant, a Toyota subsidiary located in Fremont, California, creates a separate, organically organized, cross-functional subunit, called the Pilot Team, to design production processes for new car and truck models. When the model they are preparing moves into production, workers return to their regular jobs on the shop floor.[44]

Each of these organizations found creative ways to be ambidextrous, establishing organic conditions for developing new ideas in the midst of more mechanistic conditions for implementing and using those ideas.

**Separate Creative Departments.** In many large organizations the initiation of innovation is assigned to separate **creative departments.**[45] Staff departments, such as research and development, engineering, design, and systems analysis, create changes for adoption in other departments. Departments that initiate change are organically structured to facilitate the generation of new ideas and techniques. Departments that use those innovations tend to have a mechanistic structure more suitable for efficient production.

One example of a creative department is the research lab at Oksuka Pharmaceutical Company. Although most large North American drug firms have switched to using robots and other high-tech tools to perform large-scale drug experiments, Japanese companies such as Oksuka are achieving success by continuing to emphasize human creativity. To get the kind of creative spirit that is willing to try new things and look for the unexpected, Oksuka's president Tatsuo Higuchi says its research labs "put a high value on weird people."[46] However, in the department that manufactures drugs, where routine and precision is important, a pharmaceutical company would prefer to have less unusual people who are comfortable following rules and standard procedures.

Another type of creative department is the **idea incubator,** an increasingly popular way to facilitate the development of new ideas within the organization. An idea incubator provides a safe harbour where ideas from employees throughout the organization can be developed without interference from company bureaucracy or politics.[47] The incubator gives people throughout the organization a place to go rather than having to shop a new idea all over the company and hope someone will pay attention. In 2003, the Sudbury Centre of Innovation and Technology was created as a business incubator for the community. According to its founder, Mark Charbonneau, "[the] idea is more inventions are hatched over a cup of coffee than anything else."[48] Similarly, in 2007, the Government of Alberta created Canada's first idea incubator for agri-food entrepreneurs, to bring together up to eight organizations at a time to support the development of creative ideas.[49]

**Venture Teams.** **Venture teams** are a technique used to give free rein to creativity within organizations. Venture teams are often given a separate location and facilities so they are not constrained by organizational procedures. A venture team is like a small company within a large company. Numerous organizations have used the venture team concept to free creative people from the bureaucracy of a large corporation. At 3M, a program called *3M Acceleration* allows an employee with a promising idea for a new technology or product to recruit people from around the company to serve on a new venture team. 3M provides the space, funding, and freedom the team needs to fast-track the idea into a marketable product.[50] Many established companies that have successful Internet-based operations have set them up as venture teams so they have the freedom and authority to explore and develop the new technology. To create the Macintosh, for example, Steve Jobs created a separate physical space to let the engineers and designers do their innovative work.

One type of venture team is called a *skunkworks*.[51] A **skunkworks** is a separate, small, informal, highly autonomous, and often secretive group that focuses on breakthrough ideas for the business. The original skunkworks was created by Lockheed Martin in the United States more than 50 years ago and is still in operation. The essence of a skunkworks is that highly talented people are given the time and freedom to let creativity reign. Much of the design work on the Razr cell phone was done at Moto City, a Chicago innovation lab decorated in stylish colours rather than at Motorola's traditional research and development facility outside Chicago, Illinois. Care is taken to design open team-based facilities to encourage communication. Skunkworks are also known as mosh pits of creativity![52] A variation of the venture team concept is the **new-venture fund**, which provides financial resources for employees to develop new ideas, products, or businesses.

**Corporate Entrepreneurship.** Corporate entrepreneurship attempts to develop an internal entrepreneurial spirit, philosophy, and structure that will produce a higher-than-average number of innovations. Corporate entrepreneurship may involve the use of creative departments and new venture teams, but it also attempts to release the creative energy of all employees in the organization. Managers can create systems and structures that encourage entrepreneurship. The MaRS Venture Group, for example, focuses on supporting Canadian organizations by securing investment from the seed stage onward from Canadian and international venture capitalists. The MaRS Discovery Centre opened in 2005 to improve Canada's ability to innovate and to commercialize its innovations.[53] One of MaRS's tenants, Skymeter, has developed a black box to be attached to the windshield of a car. The box contains a GPS receiver, a memory chip, a processor, and a telecommunications chip. The GPS receiver computes where it is and uploads its history to a data centre to generate the bill. The vehicle measures its own use and a bill is itemized like a cell phone bill.[54] The box can be used for services such as pay-as-you-drive insurance.

An important outcome of corporate entrepreneurship is to facilitate **idea champions**. These go by a variety of names, including *advocate, intrapreneur,* or *change agent.* Idea champions provide the time and energy to make things happen.

They fight to overcome resistance to change and to convince others of the merit of a new idea.[55] Idea champions need not be within the organization. Some companies have found that fostering idea champions among regular customers can be a highly successful approach.[56] The importance of the idea champion is illustrated by a fascinating fact discovered by Texas Instruments (TI): when TI reviewed 50 successful and unsuccessful technical projects, it discovered that every failure was characterized by the absence of a volunteer champion. There was no one who passionately believed in the idea, who pushed the idea through every obstacle to make it work. TI took this finding so seriously that now its number-one criterion for approving new technical projects is the presence of a zealous champion.[57]

Idea champions usually come in two types. The **technical champion,** or *product champion*, is the person who generates or adopts and develops an idea for a technological innovation and is devoted to it, even to the extent of risking position or prestige. The **management champion** acts as a supporter and sponsor to shield and promote an idea within the organization.[58] The management champion sees the potential application, and has the prestige and authority to get the idea a fair hearing and to allocate resources to it. Technical and management champions often work together because a technical idea will have a greater chance of success if a manager can be found to sponsor it. Numerous studies have identified the importance of idea champions as a factor in the success of new products.[59]

Companies encourage idea champions by providing freedom and slack time to creative people. Companies such as IBM, General Electric, and 3M allow employees to develop new technologies without company approval. Known as bootlegging, the unauthorized research often pays big dividends. As one IBM executive said, "We wink at it. It pays off. It's just amazing what a handful of dedicated people can do when they are really turned on."[60]

---

## In Practice
### Pratt & Whitney Canada (P&WC)

Pratt & Whitney Canada (P&WC), whose head office is in Longueuil, Québec, designs, develops, manufactures, and markets turboprop, turbofan, and turboshaft engines. It also provides support and maintenance services, which account for half of its revenues. P&WC has customers in over 170 countries, more than a dozen domestic plants, and a network of service centres around the world.

Its competitors include General Electric, Honeywell, and Rolls Royce-Allison. In 1999, P&WC controlled about 24 percent of the increasingly fragmented and global market, which was moving toward a mass customization approach. As a response to the difficult competitive environment, P&WC increased its engine models and cut production times so that it could deliver customized orders in a timely way. Between June 1996 and January 1999, P&WC implemented an ERP system as one way to deal with the changing demands of its environment. (ERP, or enterprise resource planning, is a software system designed to assist in managing all aspects of manufacturing from product planning and inventory management to order tracking. It is uses relational database systems to integrate the information necessary for effective manufacturing processes.)

The implementation is considered a particularly successful one. There are three key reasons for its success. First, at the strategic level, senior managers created a clear vision of the role of the ERP project, created a sense of urgency around the project, and supported the change with sufficient resources. Second, at the tactical level, PW&C redesigned its organization, took on technological partners, and used an established methodology and process. The company also used clear metrics to gauge progress. At the operational level, change leadership and knowledge-transfer teams were used to be sensitive to employee needs throughout the change. Employees were involved in the training, which helped both the transfer of knowledge and the acceptance of the implementation.[61]

# New Products and Services

Although the ideas just discussed are important to product and service as well as technology changes, other factors also need to be considered. In many ways, new products and services are a special case of innovation because they are used by customers outside the organization. Since new products are designed for sale in the environment, uncertainty about the suitability and success of an innovation is very high.

## New Product Success Rate

Research has explored the enormous uncertainty associated with the development and sale of new products.[62] To understand what this uncertainty can mean to organizations, just consider flops such as the Bricklin car with its distinctive gull-wing design. American promoter Malcolm Bricklin wanted to build his own U.S.-designed sports car, and, enticed by loan guarantees and other investments, he set up shop in Saint John and Minto, New Brunswick, where the fibreglass bodies were made. Production was delayed as both the gull wings and the fibreglass body were difficult to build. The company owed $23 million to the provincial government, at which point the government refused to grant more aid unless the private sector provided 50 percent of the financing. The private sector would not, and Bricklin fell into receivership. During 1974 and 1975, only 2,857 cars were made and sent to the United States.[63]

The Avro *Arrow* (CF-105) is another spectacular failure. The *Arrow* was a supersonic interceptor jet developed in the 1950s to counter the perceived threat to the Canadian North from Soviet bombers. The costs for building the plane skyrocketed to $12.5 million per aircraft. In 1959, the government cancelled the project, which had already cost $400 million. As a result, 14,000 employees were fired, and all plans and prototypes were ordered destroyed. Many of the research scientists and engineers left Canada to work in the aircraft industry in the United States.[64] The Avro *Arrow* story is one of failure and also of mystery as speculation continues about the reasons for destroying the plans and the prototypes.

Experts estimate that about 80 percent of new products fail upon introduction and another 10 percent disappear within five years. Considering that it can cost $50 million or more to successfully launch a new product, new product development is a risky, high-stakes game for organizations. Nevertheless, more than 25,000 new products appeared in one year alone, including more than 5,000 new toys.[65] A survey some years ago examined 200 projects in 19 chemical, drug, electronics, and petroleum laboratories to learn about success rates.[66] To be successful, the new product had to pass three stages of development: technical completion, commercialization, and market success. On the average, only 57 percent of all projects undertaken in the R&D laboratories achieved technical objectives, which means all technical problems were solved and the projects moved on to production. Of all projects that were started, less than one-third (31 percent) were fully marketed and commercialized. Several projects failed at this stage because production estimates or test market results were unfavourable. Finally, only 12 percent of all projects originally undertaken achieved economic success. Most of the commercialized products did not earn sufficient returns to cover the cost of development and production. This means that only about one project in eight returned a profit to the company.

## Reasons for New Product Success

The next question to be answered by research was why some products are more successful than others. Other studies indicated that innovation success is related to collaboration between technical and marketing departments. Successful new products and services seem to be technologically sound and also carefully tailored to customer needs.[67] A study called Project SAPPHO[68] examined 17 pairs of new product innovations, with one success and one failure in each pair, and concluded the following:

1. Successful innovating companies had a much better understanding of customer needs and paid much more attention to marketing.
2. Successful innovating companies made more effective use of outside technology and outside advice, even though they did more work in-house.
3. Top management support in the successful innovating companies was from people who were more senior and had greater authority.

Thus, there is a distinct pattern of tailoring innovations to customer needs, making effective use of technology, and having influential top managers support the project. These ideas taken together indicate that the effective design for new product innovation is associated with horizontal coordination across departments.

## Horizontal Coordination Model

The organizational design for achieving new product innovation involves three components—departmental specialization, boundary spanning, and horizontal coordination. These components are similar to the horizontal coordination mechanisms discussed in Chapter 3, such as teams, task forces, and project managers, and the differentiation and integration ideas discussed in Chapter 4. Exhibit 10.7 illustrates these components in the **horizontal coordination model**.

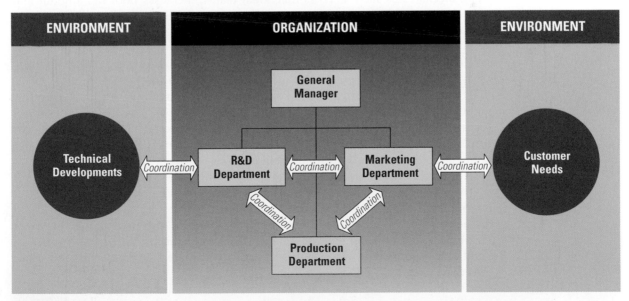

**EXHIBIT 10.7**
Horizontal Coordination Model for New Product Innovations

**Specialization.** The key departments in new product development are R&D, marketing, and production. The specialization component means that the personnel in all three of these departments are highly competent at their own tasks. The three departments are differentiated from each other and have skills, goals, and attitudes appropriate for their specialized functions.

**Boundary Spanning.** This component means each department involved with new products has excellent linkage with relevant sectors in the external environment. R&D personnel are linked to professional associations and to colleagues in other R&D departments. They are aware of recent scientific developments. Marketers need to be closely linked to customer needs. They listen to what customers have to say, and they analyze competitor products and suggestions from distributors. For example, Puretracks listened to its customers and started selling some songs online without copy protection in early 2007. The unprotected catalogue includes music from The Barenaked Ladies and Sarah McLachlan. Besides, the songs will be playable on devices that they did not work on previously such as iPods.[69] Puretracks continues to innovate, for example, by providing customized music opportunities for retailers. It worked with The Children's Place, to increase the sale of The Children's Place gift cards by creating an instant win game card that accompanied the gift cards that featured Puretrack music downloads and other prizes.[70]

**Horizontal Coordination.** This component means that technical, marketing, and production people share ideas and information. Research people inform marketing of new technical developments to learn whether the developments are applicable to customers. Marketing people provide customer complaints and information to R&D to use in the design of new products. People from both R&D and marketing coordinate with production because new products have to fit within production capabilities so costs are not exorbitant. The decision to launch a new product is ultimately a joint decision among all three departments. Horizontal coordination, using mechanisms such as cross-functional teams, increases both the amount and the variety of information for new product development, enabling the design of products that meet customer needs and circumventing manufacturing and marketing problems.[71]

Recall the chapter-opening example of Toyota, which uses a product development technique called *obeya*. The idea behind *obeya* is to change the way people think about product innovation and development by changing how they share information. "There are no taboos in *obeya*," explains Takeshi Yoshida, chief engineer for the 2003 Corolla. "Everyone in that room is an expert. They all have a part to play in building the car."[72] Consumer products firm Procter & Gamble is also taking a bold new approach to innovation.

Research findings show that collaboration with other firms and with customers can be a significant source of product innovation, and can even stimulate stronger internal coordination. Cooperating with external parties requires the involvement of people from different areas of the company, which in turn necessitates that organizations set up stronger internal coordination mechanisms.[73] Companies such as Procter & Gamble and Corel routinely turn to customers and other organizations for advice.

Such companies use the concept of horizontal coordination to achieve competitive advantage. Famous innovation failures—such as McDonald's Arch Deluxe or the baby-food company Gerber's Singles for Adults—usually violate the horizontal linkage model. Employees fail to connect with customer needs and market forces or internal departments fail to adequately share needs and coordinate with one another. Recent research has confirmed a connection between effective boundary spanning that keeps the organization in touch with market forces, smooth coordination among departments, and successful product development.[74]

**In Practice**
**Procter & Gamble (P&G)**

A few years ago, Procter & Gamble (P&G) was a stodgy (over 160-year-old) consumer products company selling successful but tired brands such as Tide, Crest, and Pampers. Today, the 174-year-old company has reemerged as a master brand builder and a hot growth company, thanks largely to a new approach to innovation initiated by CEO A. G. Lafley. Between 2002 and 2004, P&G raised its new product hit rate from 70 percent to 90 percent.[75] Products such as Olay Regenerist, Swiffer dusters, and Mr. Clean AutoDry have made Procter & Gamble look like a nimble start-up company.

There are several key elements to Lafley's innovation machine. One is a stronger connection with consumers. Rather than relying on focus groups, P&G marketers now spend time with people in their homes, watching how they wash their dishes or clean their floors, and asking questions about their habits and frustrations with household chores or child rearing. Another key is getting people from different functions and divisions to exchange ideas and collaborate. Lafley conducts half-day "innovation reviews" in each unit once a year and evaluates how well marketers and researchers are sharing ideas. Besides opportunities for face-to-face meetings and internal trade shows, an internal website called InnovationNet connects employees from all divisions and departments worldwide. R&D people located in 20 technical facilities in nine countries can post a question such as, "How can you clean without rinsing?" and get suggestions from employees across the company and around the world. The technologies that enabled Mr. Clean AutoDry (discontinued in 2010) a power gun that sprays your car clean and dry, came from P&G's Cascade division, which knew how to reduce water spots on dishes, and the PuR water filter unit, which had a technology for reducing minerals in water.

The most revolutionary part of Lafley's approach is encouraging collaboration with outside people and other firms, even competitors. "The idea, since dubbed 'connect and develop,' was a radical departure from P&G's invent-it-ourselves culture, which relied mostly on 7,500 company scientists to churn out new products."[76] For example, Glad Press 'n Seal was developed collaboratively with Clorox, which competes fiercely with P&G in floor mops and water purification products. Lafley is pushing for half of P&G's innovations to be derived from outside sources. "Inventors are evenly distributed in the population," he says, "and we're as likely to find invention in a garage as in our labs."[77]

Lafley was CEO until 2009 but was brought back in 2013 after the sudden retirement of his successor. P&G's shares rose 4 percent on the news.[78]

## ■ Achieving Competitive Advantage: The Need for Speed

The rapid development of new products is becoming a major strategic weapon in the shifting international marketplace.[79] To remain competitive, companies are learning to develop ideas into new products and services incredibly quickly. Whether the approach is called the *horizontal linkage model, concurrent engineering, companies without walls, the parallel approach,* or *simultaneous coupling of departments*, the point is the same—get people working together simultaneously on a project rather than in sequence. Many companies are learning to sprint to market with new products.

**Time-based competition** means delivering products and services faster than competitors, giving companies a competitive edge. Some companies use what are called fast-cycle teams as a way to support highly important projects and deliver products and services faster than competitors. A fast-cycle team is a multifunctional, and sometimes multinational, team that works under stringent timelines and is provided with high levels of company resources and empowerment to accomplish an accelerated product development project.[80] Using virtual reality, collaborative software, and a horizontal, integrated design process, GM has cut its time from concept to production on a new vehicle model to a mere 18 months. Not so long ago, it took GM an astounding four years to complete that process. The new approach to product development gave GM a speed advantage over competitors in the design and production of hot new car models that capitalize on fashion trends and capture the market for younger car buyers.[81]

Another critical issue is designing products that can compete on a global scale and successfully marketing those products internationally. Companies such as Quaker Oats, Häagen Dazs, and Levi's are trying to improve horizontal communication and collaboration across geographical regions, recognizing that they can pick up winning product ideas from customers in other countries. Many new product development teams today are global teams because organizations have to develop products that will meet diverse needs of consumers all over the world.[82] GM's collaborative, computer-based product development system enables engineers and suppliers from all over the world to work together on a project. Ford Motor Company also uses an intranet and global teleconferencing to link car design teams around the world into a single unified group.[83] When companies enter the arena of intense international competition, horizontal coordination across countries is essential to new product development.

## Strategy and Structure Change

The preceding discussion focused on new production processes and products, which are based in the technology of an organization. The expertise for such innovation lies within the technical core and professional staff groups, such as research and engineering. This section turns to an examination of strategy and structure changes.

All organizations need to make changes in their strategies, structures, and administrative procedures from time to time. In the past, when the environment was relatively stable, most organizations focused on small, incremental changes to solve immediate problems or take advantage of new opportunities. Organizations across the world have faced the need to make radical changes in strategy, structure, and management processes to adapt to new competitive demands.[84] Many organizations are cutting out layers of management and decentralizing decision making. There is a strong shift toward more horizontal structures, with teams of frontline workers empowered to make decisions and solve problems on their own. Some companies are breaking completely from traditional organization forms and shifting toward virtual network strategies and structures. Numerous companies are reorganizing and shifting their strategies as the expansion of e-business changes the rules. Global competition and rapid technological change will likely lead to even greater strategy-structure realignments over the next decade.

These types of changes are the responsibility of the organization's top managers, and the overall process of change is typically different from the process for innovation in technology or new products.

## ■ The Dual-Core Approach

The **dual-core approach** to organizational change compares administrative and technical changes. Administrative changes pertain to the design and structure of the organization itself, including restructuring, downsizing, teams, control systems, information systems, and departmental grouping. Research into administrative change suggests two things. First, administrative changes occur less frequently than do technical changes. Second, administrative changes occur in response to different environmental sectors and follow a different internal process than do technology-based changes.[85] The dual-core approach to organizational change identifies the unique processes associated with administrative change.[86]

Organizations—schools, hospitals, municipal governments, welfare agencies, government bureaucracies, and many business firms—can be conceptualized as having two cores: *a technical core* and an *administrative core*. Each core has its own employees, tasks, and environmental domain. Innovation can originate in either core.

The administrative core is above the technical core in the hierarchy. The responsibility of the administrative core includes the structure, control, and coordination of the organization itself and concerns the environmental sectors of government, financial resources, economic conditions, human resources, and competitors. The technical core is concerned with the transformation of raw materials into organizational products and services, and involves the environmental sectors of customers and technology.[87]

The point of the dual-core approach is that many organizations—especially not-for-profit and government organizations—must adopt frequent administrative changes and need to be structured differently from organizations that rely on frequent technical and product changes for competitive advantage.

## ■ Organizational Design for Implementing Administrative Change

The findings from research comparing administrative and technical change suggest that a mechanistic organizational structure is appropriate for frequent administrative changes, including changes in goals, strategy, structure, control systems, and human resources.[88] Administrative changes in policy, regulations, or control systems are more critical than technical changes in many government organizations that are bureaucratically structured. Organizations that successfully adopt many administrative changes often have a larger administrative ratio, are larger in size, and are centralized and formalized compared with organizations that adopt many technical changes.[89] The reason is the top-down implementation of changes in response to changes in the government, financial, or legal sectors of the environment. If an organization has an organic structure, lower-level employees have more freedom and autonomy and, hence, may resist top-down initiatives.

The innovation approaches associated with administrative versus technical change are summarized in Exhibit 10.8. Technical change, such as changes in production techniques and innovation technology for new products, is facilitated by

**EXHIBIT 10.8**
Dual-Core Approach
to Organizational
Change

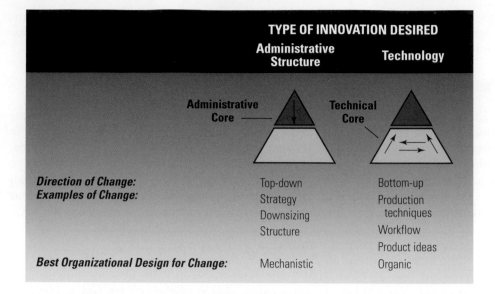

an organic structure, which allows ideas to bubble upward from lower-and middle-level employees. Organizations that must adopt frequent administrative changes, in contrast, tend to use a top-down process and a mechanistic structure. For example, policy changes, such as the adoption of no-smoking policies, sexual harassment policies, or new safety procedures, are facilitated by a top-down approach. Downsizing and significant restructuring are nearly always managed top-down. When Bobby Genovese took over the moribund Clearly Canadian Beverage Corp in 2006, he installed a new management team, which developed a new strategy of new products, celebrity-filled marketing, and the company's own reality-TV series.[90] In 2010, its restructuring application was approved by the Supreme Court of B.C.[91]

Research into civil service reform found that the implementation of administrative innovation was extremely difficult in organizations that had an organic technical core. The professional employees in a decentralized agency could resist civil service changes. By contrast, organizations that were considered more bureaucratic in the sense of high formalization and centralization adopted administrative changes readily.[92]

What about business organizations that are normally technologically innovative in bottom-up fashion but suddenly face a crisis and need to reorganize? Or a technically innovative, high-tech firm that must reorganize frequently to accommodate changes in production technology or the environment? Technically innovative firms may suddenly have to restructure, reduce the number of employees, alter pay systems, disband teams, or form a new division.[93] The answer is to use a top-down change process. The authority for strategy and structure change lies with top management, who should initiate and implement the new strategy and structure to meet environmental circumstances. Employee input may be sought, but top managers have the responsibility to direct the change.

Some top-down changes, particularly those related to restructuring and downsizing, can be very painful for employees, so top managers should move quickly and authoritatively to make them as humane as possible.[94] A study of successful corporate transformations, which frequently involve painful changes, found that managers followed a fast, focused approach. When top managers spread difficult changes such as downsizing over a long time period, employee morale suffers and the change is much less likely to lead to positive outcomes.[95] Top managers should also remember that top-down change means initiation of the idea occurs at upper levels and is implemented downward. It does not mean that lower-level employees are not educated about the change or allowed to participate in it.

# Culture Change

Organizations are made up of people and their relationships with one another. Changes in strategy, structure, technologies, and products do not happen on their own, and changes in any of these areas involve changes in people as well. Employees must learn how to use new technologies, or market new products, or work effectively in a team-based structure. Sometimes achieving a new way of thinking requires a focused change in the underlying cultural values and norms. Changing organizational culture fundamentally shifts how work is done in an organization and can lead to renewed commitment and empowerment of employees and a stronger bond between the company and its customers.[96] In one intriguing example of cultural change, potential employees at the Cherwell School in Oxford, the United Kingdom are interviewed by the children. Teachers seeking senior management positions are interviewed by a panel consisting of students aged 13 and above, who receive training in reading individual cues, as well as several panels of adults. According to the assistant head, who was herself hired through this innovative process, "… far from being out of their depth in the recruitment process, students often provide a great deal of insight …" and "[the] more input we get from students the more likely we are to make a good decision."[97]

## Forces for Culture Change

A number of recent trends have contributed to a need for cultural makeovers at companies such as the merged Canada Trust and Toronto Dominion Bank, IBM, and Canada Revenue Agency.[98] Some of the primary changes requiring a shift in culture and employee mind-set are re-engineering and the move toward horizontal forms of organizing, greater employee and customer diversity, and the shift to the learning organization.

**Re-engineering and Horizontal Organizing.** As described in Chapter 3, re-engineering involves redesigning a vertical organization along its horizontal workflows. This changes the way managers and employees need to think about how work is done and requires greater focus on employee empowerment, collaboration, information sharing, and meeting customer needs. In his book, *The Reengineering Revolution*, Michael Hammer refers to people change as "the most perplexing, annoying, distressing, and confusing part" of re-engineering.[99] Managers may confront powerful emotions as employees react to rapid, massive change with fear or anger.

In the horizontal organization, managers and front-line workers need to understand and embrace the concepts of teamwork, empowerment, and cooperation. Managers shift their thinking to view workers as colleagues rather than cogs in a wheel, and workers learn to accept not only greater freedom and power, but also the

**Compare**

Compare traditional approaches to teacher recruitment to the innovative example above. What are their strengths and weaknesses?

higher level of responsibility that comes with them. Mutual trust, risk taking, and tolerance for mistakes become key cultural values in the horizontal organization.

**Diversity.** Diversity is a fact of life for today's organizations, and many are implementing new recruiting, mentoring, and promotion methods; diversity training programs; tough policies regarding sexual harassment and racial discrimination; and new benefits programs that respond to a more diverse workforce. However, if the underlying culture of an organization does not change, all other efforts to support diversity will fail. Managers at Mitsubishi are still struggling with this reality. Even though the company settled a sexual harassment lawsuit filed by women at its Normal, Illinois, plant; established a zero-tolerance policy; and fired workers who were guilty of blatant sexual or racial harassment, employees said the work environment at the plant remained deeply hostile to women and minorities. Incidents of blatant harassment declined, but women and various minority workers still felt threatened and powerless because the culture that allowed the harassment to occur had not changed.[100]

**The Learning Organization.** The learning organization involves breaking down boundaries both within and between organizations to create companies that are focused on knowledge sharing and continuous learning. Recall from Chapter 1 that shifting to a learning organization involves changes in a number of areas. For example, structures become horizontal and involve empowered teams working directly with customers. There are few rules and procedures for performing tasks, and knowledge and control of tasks are located with employees rather than supervisors. Information is broadly shared rather than being concentrated with top managers. In addition, employees, customers, suppliers, and partners all play a role in determining the organization's strategic direction. Clearly, all of these changes require new values, new attitudes, and new ways of thinking and working together. A learning organization cannot exist without a culture that supports openness, equality, adaptability, and employee participation. WestJet Airlines Ltd. has tried, from its founding, to create a culture of openness and employee participation.

## In Practice
### WestJet Airlines Ltd. (WestJet)

WestJet sees itself as part of the hospitality industry rather than the airline industry. From the outset, it wanted a culture that encouraged innovation and a passion to succeed. WestJet's co-founder, Don Bell, is considered its culture guru, its spiritual leader who championed teamwork and rewarded innovation. According to Bell, the culture of WestJet is its greatest strategic advantage. He notes that "[everyone] is unique, and if you embrace people's personalities rather than turn them into robots, and give them the guidelines and the working environment to blossom, it creates something that's very hard to reckon with."[101]

It is a youthful and fun culture. There is a committee of flight attendants called WestJesters whose job is to write comedy for the end of flights. There is a demonstrated commitment to minimize status differences. Everyone, including former President Clive Beddoes, helps pick up garbage at the end of a flight. As Bell comments, "I always say [a great culture] starts by the actions of the leaders." As Sherril Hatch, a call centre attendant put it, "Everyone here is first-class."[102]

At least once a year, employees attend small chat sessions with management to raise concerns, ask questions, and make suggestions. An employee-based Pro-Active Communication System provides one way to deal with issues before they become a problem. Employees participate in a profit-sharing system and can have some of their pay in the form of WestJet stock.

In 2010, WestJet was named to the Corporate Culture Hall of Fame. In order to be inducted to the Hall of Fame, organizations must have been named to the Waterstone Human Capital's Canada's 10 Most Admired Corporate Cultures program four times. WestJet is admired for its entrepreneurial spirit, its winning attitude, and for living up to its commitments. "We are thrilled to see the Canadian business community recognize our corporate culture for the fifth straight year," said Ferio Pugliese, WestJet's executive vice president, People and Culture. "Keeping our culture vibrant and relevant as we grow, exploring exciting opportunities and striving to become one of the top five international airlines can be challenging. But the passion and hard work of our WestJetters ensures that our culture evolves as WestJet evolves."[103]

## ■ Organization Development Interventions for Culture Change

Managers use a variety of approaches and techniques for changing organizational culture, some of which we discussed in Chapter 9. One method of bringing about culture change is known as **organization development** (OD), which focuses on the human and social aspects of the organization as a way to improve the organization's ability to adapt and solve problems. OD emphasizes the values of human development, fairness, openness, freedom from coercion, and individual autonomy, which allow workers to perform the job as they see fit, within reasonable organizational constraints.[104] In the 1970s, OD evolved as a separate field that applied the behavioural sciences in a process of planned organization-wide change, with the goal of increasing organizational effectiveness. Today, the concept has been enlarged to examine how people and groups can change to a learning organization culture in a complex and turbulent environment. Organization development is not a step-by-step procedure to solve a specific problem but a process of fundamental change in the human and social systems of the organization, including organizational culture.[105]

OD uses knowledge and techniques from the behavioural sciences to create a learning environment through increased trust, open confrontation of problems, employee empowerment and participation, knowledge and information sharing, the design of meaningful work, cooperation and collaboration between groups, and the full use of human potential.

OD interventions involve training specific groups or everyone in the organization. For OD interventions to be successful, senior management in the organization must see the need for OD and provide visible support for the change. Techniques used by many organizations for improving people skills through OD include the following.

**Large Group Intervention.** Most early OD activities involved small groups and focused on incremental change. However, in recent years, there has been growing interest in the application of OD techniques to large group settings, which are more attuned to bringing about radical or transformational change in organizations operating in complex environments.[106] The large group intervention approach[107] brings together participants from all parts of the organization—often including key stakeholders from outside the organization as well—in an off-site setting to discuss problems or opportunities and plan for change. A **large group intervention** might involve 50 to 500 people and last for several days. The off-site setting limits interference and distractions, enabling participants to focus on new ways of doing things. General Electric's "Work Out" program, an ongoing process of solving problems, learning, and improving, begins with large-scale off-site meetings that get people talking across functional, hierarchical, and organizational boundaries. Hourly and salaried workers come together from many different parts of the organization and join with customers and suppliers to discuss and solve specific problems.[108] The process forces a rapid analysis of ideas, the creation of solutions, and the development of a plan for implementation. Over time, Work Out creates a culture where ideas are rapidly translated into action and positive business results.[109]

**Team Building.** **Team building** promotes the idea that people who work together can work as a team. A work team can be brought together to discuss conflicts, goals, the decision-making process, communication, creativity, and leadership. The team can then plan to overcome problems and improve results. Team-building activities are also used in many companies to train task forces, committees, and new product development groups. These activities enhance communication and collaboration and strengthen the cohesiveness of organizational groups and teams.

**Interdepartmental Activities.** Representatives from different departments are brought together in a mutual location to expose problems or conflicts, diagnose the causes, and plan improvements in communication and coordination. This type of intervention has been applied to union–management conflict, headquarters–field office conflict, interdepartmental conflict, and mergers.[110] A box-storage business, which stores archived records for other companies, found interdepartmental meetings to be a key means of building a culture based on team spirit and customer focus. People from different departments met for hour-long sessions every two weeks and shared their problems, told stories about their successes, and talked about things they'd observed in the company. The meetings helped people understand the problems faced in other departments and see how everyone depended on each other to do their jobs successfully.[111]

One current area in which OD can provide significant value is in spurring culture change toward valuing diversity.[112] In addition, today's organizations are continuously adapting to environmental uncertainty and increasing global competition, and OD interventions can respond to these new realities as organizations strive to create greater capability for learning and growth.[113]

# Strategies for Implementing Change

Managers and employees can think of inventive ways to improve the organization's technology, creative ideas for new products and services, fresh approaches to strategies and structures, or ideas for fostering adaptive cultural values, but until the ideas are put into action, they are worthless to the organization. Implementation is the most crucial part of the change process, but it is also the most difficult. Change is frequently disruptive and uncomfortable for managers as well as employees. Change is complex, dynamic, and messy, and implementation requires strong and persistent leadership. In this final section, we briefly discuss the role of leadership for change, some reasons for resistance to change, and techniques that managers can use to overcome resistance and successfully implement change.

## Leadership for Change

The pressures on organizations to change will probably increase over the next few decades. Leaders must develop the personal qualities, skills, and methods needed to help their companies remain competitive. Indeed, some management experts argue that to survive the upheaval of the early 21st century, managers must turn their organizations into *change leaders* by using the present to actually create the future—breaking industry rules, creating new market space, and routinely abandoning outmoded products, services, and processes to free up resources to build the future.[114]

## Book Mark 10.0    HAVE YOU READ THIS BOOK?

### The New Entrepreneurs: Building a Green Economy for the Future
By Andrew Heintzman

Heintzman begins his engaging account of those who are in the forefront of Canadian environmental capitalism by quoting from a key thought leader in the field of green commerce, Paul Hawken. In an address Hawken gave in 2009, he said

> [if] you look at the science about what is happening on earth and aren't pessimistic, you don't understand the data. But if you meet the people who are working to restore the earth and the lives of the poor, and you aren't optimistic, you haven't got a pulse.[115]

Heintzman's thesis is that we need to go back to our Canadian roots while we create new organizational responses to address the needs of the future. He argues that we must build business practices that are sustainable as we now know that our natural resources, so central in our history as "hewers of wood and drawers of water,"[116] are not limitless. We cannot continue to take from our environment without environmental and social consequences.

Heintzman describes various entrepreneurs and their work. He does so by focusing on several innovative entrepreneurs across Canada. He describes Triton Logging's work to recover trees from the bottom of Ootsa Lake in B.C. Triton Logging, in which Heintzman has a financial interest. It is one of the few companies in the world dedicated to logging $50 billion of forests that were submerged by the building of hydro-electricity plants. Triton Logging is what Heintzman describes as "the reinvention of an old industry for a new time."

We learn that innovation in water is now about water conservation, rather than water purification. Heintzman describes the development of innovative processes to detect water pipe thicknesses to estimate where leaks might occur. As much of our water pipes were installed before the Second World War, such an estimation capability could save municipalities a significant amount of money. Echologics and Pure Technologies are two companies that have helped create Canadian expertise in water conservation. Similarly, Saltworks has developed a pioneering desalination technology that was profiled by *The Economist.*

The book has many examples of innovative people developing innovative and commercial technologies and processes. Another to highlight is the work of First Power. It is working with the Hesquiaht First Nation to provide an alternative energy source to propane-generated power, which is both polluting and expensive. Together they are working to provide renewable energy and energy independence for the remote community. Heintzman concludes that Canada will look different in 30 years if we embrace the path set by the innovative green entrepreneurs he describes. He says that "[if] we do it well, we will be not only a less wasteful society, but a more prosperous society too."

His is an optimistic book but well grounded in the distressing environmental legacy that we have created. In his review of the book, Toby Heaps, the president, editor, and co-founder of Corporate Knights, comments that "[quibbles] aside, Heintzman's authentic vision for Canada's green industrial revolution and compelling portraits of the initial revolutionaries already making it happen in the trenches is an inspiring read."[117]

*The New Entrepreneurs: Building a Green Economy for the Future,* by Andrew Heintzman, is published by Anansi Press Inc., 2010.

The need for change within organizations and the need for leaders who can successfully manage change continue to grow. The leadership style of the top executive sets the tone for how effective the organization is at continuous adaptation and innovation. One style of leadership, referred to as *transformational leadership*, is particularly suited for bringing about change. Top leaders who use a transformational leadership style enhance organizational innovation both directly, by creating a compelling vision, and indirectly, by creating an environment that supports exploration, experimentation, risk taking, and sharing of ideas.[118]

Successful change can happen only when employees are willing to devote the time and energy needed to reach new goals, as well as endure possible stress and hardship. Having a clearly communicated vision that embodies flexibility and openness to new ideas, methods, and styles sets the stage for a change-oriented organization and helps employees cope with the chaos and tension associated with change.[119] Leaders also build organization-wide commitment by taking employees through three stages of the change commitment process.[120] In the first stage, *preparation*, employees hear about the change through memos, meetings, speeches, or personal contact, and become aware that the change will directly affect their work. In the second stage, *acceptance*, leaders should help employees develop an understanding of the full impact of the change and the positive outcomes of making the change. When employees perceive the change as positive, the decision to implement is made. In the third stage, the true *commitment* process begins. The commitment stage involves the steps of installation and institutionalization. Installation is a trial process for the change, which gives leaders an opportunity to discuss problems and employee concerns, and build commitment to action. In the final step, *institutionalization*, employees view the change not as something new but as a normal and integral part of organizational operations.

## ■ Barriers to Change

Visionary leadership is crucial for change; however, leaders should expect to encounter resistance as they attempt to take the organization through the three stages of the change commitment process. It is understandable that people to resist change, and many barriers to change exist at the individual and organizational levels.[121]

1. *Excessive focus on costs.* Management may possess the mind-set that costs are all-important and may fail to appreciate the importance of a change that is not focused on costs—for example, a change to increase employee motivation or customer satisfaction.
2. *Failure to perceive benefits.* Any significant change will produce both positive and negative reactions. Education may be needed to help managers and employees perceive more positive than negative aspects of the change. In addition, if the organization's reward system discourages risk taking, a change process might falter because employees think that the risk of making the change is too high.
3. *Lack of coordination and cooperation.* Organizational fragmentation and conflict often result from the lack of coordination for change implementation.

**Think**

Think about any barriers to change that you have observed in organizations. How did the organizations try to overcome the barriers?

Moreover, in the case of new technology, the old and new systems must be compatible.

4. *Uncertainty avoidance.* At the individual level, many employees fear the uncertainty associated with change. Constant communication is needed so that employees know what is going on and understand how it affects their jobs.

5. *Fear of loss.* Managers and employees may fear the loss of power and status—or even their jobs. In these cases, implementation should be careful and incremental, and all employees should be involved as closely as possible in the change process.

Implementation can typically be designed to overcome many of the organizational and individual barriers to change. The next In Practice describes an innovative company that has created a tool to help with change implementation.

## In Practice
### Experience-Point

James Chisholm and Greg Warman, graduates of the B.Comm. program at Queen's University, co-founded ExperiencePoint in 1996. They are ardent fans of video games and used their passion to create learning games. The two built their business in what Chisholm describes as "the old-fashioned way, one customer at a time."[122] Like any startup, ExperiencePoint had some lean years in the beginning but persisted and has grown into a world leader in game-based learning experiences for business professionals. ExperiencePoint's clients are varied and range from universities to nonprofit organizations to public- and private-sector organizations such as the Judge Business School at Cambridge University, Habitat for Humanity, the United Nations, and GE, to name a few.

ExperiencePoint has designed simulations on change management in manufacturing, change management in health care, social responsibility and, most recently, design thinking, for which it received the Edison Award for innovation. (The Edison Awards are named after Thomas Alva Edison [1847–1931], whose extraordinary new product development methods garnered him 1,093 U.S. patents and made him a household name around the world.)[123]

According to Warman, "Sim U" has become increasingly important in education. He notes that the military, which often uses simulations, "has recognized that simulation is better than the School of Hard Knocks for reasons that extend well beyond risk mitigation. Simulations save leaders and their organizations time, money and are ultimately more effective at delivering powerful learning."[124]

One of ExperiencePoint's most popular change simulations, GlobalTech, challenges learners to lead change at an organization that is facing a significant strategic challenge. While the game has evolved considerably since its initial launch, the core processes of (1) understanding change, (2) planning for change, (3) implementing the change, and (4) reflecting on the change remain the core activities in the simulation. The simulation is now web-based and highly interactive. Participants receive a budget of money and time and ongoing feedback as to how they are doing to achieve their vision and plan. The simulation can be played in teams or alone. However, playing the simulation in a team format is the most rewarding as each team member can learn not only about planned change, but also about team dynamics and their influence on decision making.

ExperiencePoint's GlobalTech simulation is grounded in a variation of the Kotter model (see Exhibit 10. 9 for the ExperienceChange Model). It has seven steps that guide the participants through an entire change process from understanding the need for change and ending with consolidating the change in the organization so that it sticks. As the model illustrates, change management is a deliberate process that follows a sequence of steps that must be followed in order. In each of the

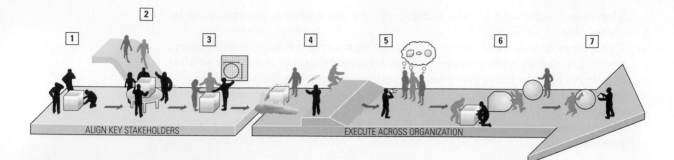

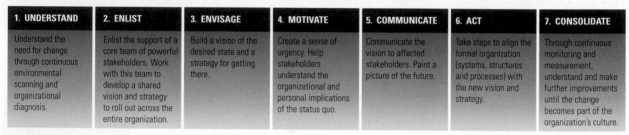

**EXHIBIT 10.9**
**ExperienceChange Model**
Source: Reproduced by permission of ExperiencePoint Inc.

steps, the timing of the tactics to execute the step properly is critical. Even so, the simulation has many different ways to achieve success. It is a sophisticated and innovative simulation that cannot be "gamed." ExperiencePoint remains one of the pioneers of the serious-gaming industry, developing simulations that allow organizations and individuals to practise their skills in a realistic but safe virtual space.

## ■ Techniques for Implementation

Top leaders articulate the vision and set the tone, but managers and employees throughout the organization are involved in the process of change. A number of techniques can be used to successfully implement change. This list of techniques draws heavily on the work of change guru John Kotter, who has influenced many organizations through his thinking presented in books such as *A Sense of Urgency, The Iceberg is Melting,* and *The Heart of Change* with Dan Cohen.

1. *Establish a sense of urgency for change.* Once managers identify a true need for change, they need to thaw resistance by creating a sense of urgency that change is really needed. Organizational crises can help unfreeze employees and make them willing to invest the time and energy needed to adopt new techniques or procedures. However, in many cases, there is no public or apparent crisis and managers have to make others aware of the need for change.

2. *Establish a coalition to guide the change.* Change managers have to build a coalition of people throughout the organization who have enough power and influence to steer the change process. For implementation to be successful, there must be a shared commitment to the need and possibilities for change.

Top management support is crucial for any major change project, and lack of top management support is one of the most frequent causes of implementation failure.[125] In addition, the coalition should involve lower-level supervisors and middle managers from across the organization. For smaller changes, the support of influential managers in the affected departments is important.

3. *Create a vision and strategy* for *change*. Leaders who have taken their organizations through major successful transformations often have one thing in common: they focus on formulating and articulating a compelling vision and strategy that will guide the change process. Even for a small change, a vision of how the future can be better and strategies to get there are important motivations for change.

4. *Find an idea that fits the need*. Finding the right idea often involves search procedures—talking with other managers, assigning a task force to investigate the problem, sending out a request to suppliers, or asking creative people within the organization to develop a solution. The creation of a new idea requires organic conditions. This is a good opportunity to encourage employee participation, because employees need the freedom to think about and explore new options.[126] Toyota's suggestion system has generated an estimated 20 million suggestions over 40 years and the average number of suggestions per employees is estimated at 50.[127]

5. *Develop plans to overcome resistance to change*. Many good ideas are never used because managers failed to anticipate or prepare for resistance to change by consumers, employees, or other managers. No matter how impressive the performance characteristics of an innovation, its implementation will conflict with some interests and jeopardize some alliances in the organization. To increase the chance of successful implementation, management must acknowledge the conflict, threats, and potential losses perceived by employees. Several strategies can be used by managers to overcome the resistance problem:

   - *Alignment with needs and goals of users*. The best strategy for overcoming resistance is to make sure change meets a real need. Employees in R&D often come up with great ideas that solve nonexistent problems. This happens because initiators fail to consult with the intended users. Resistance can be frustrating for managers, but moderate resistance to change is good for an organization. Resistance provides a barrier to frivolous changes and to change for the sake of change. The process of overcoming resistance to change normally requires that the change be good for its users.

   - *Communication and training*. Communication means informing users about the need for change and the consequences of a proposed change, preventing rumours, misunderstanding, and resentment. In one study of change efforts, the most commonly cited reason for failure was that employees learned of the change from outsiders. Top managers concentrated on communicating with the public and shareholders but failed to communicate with the people who would be most intimately involved with and most affected by the change—their own employees.[128] Open communication often gives management an opportunity to explain what steps will be taken to ensure that the change will have no adverse consequences for employees. Training is also needed to help employees understand and cope with their role in the change process.

- *An environment that affords psychological safety.* Psychological safety means that people feel a sense of confidence that they will not be embarrassed or rejected by others in the organization. People need to feel secure and capable of making the changes that are asked of them.[129] Change requires that people be willing to take risks and do things differently, but many people are fearful of trying something new if they think they might be embarrassed by mistakes or failure. Managers support psychological safety by creating a climate of trust and mutual respect in the organization. "Not being afraid someone is laughing at you helps you take genuine risks," says Andy Law, one of the founders of St. Luke's, an advertising agency based in London, England.[130]
- *Participation and involvement.* Early and extensive participation in a change should be part of implementation. Participation gives those involved a sense of control over the change activity. They understand it better, and they become committed to successful implementation. One study of the implementation and adoption of technology systems at two companies showed a much smoother implementation process at the company that introduced the new technology using a participatory approach.[131] The team-building and large group intervention activities described earlier can be effective ways to involve employees in a change process.
- *Forcing and coercion.* As a last resort, managers may overcome resistance by threatening employees with the loss of jobs or promotions or by firing or transferring them. In other words, management power is used to overwhelm resistance. In most cases, this approach is not advisable because it leaves people angry at change managers, it gets compliance at best, and the change may be sabotaged. However, this technique may be needed when speed is essential, such as when the organization faces a crisis. It may also be required for needed administrative changes that flow from the top down, such as downsizing the workforce.[132]

6. *Create change teams.* Throughout this chapter the need for resources and energy to make change happen has been highlighted. Separate creative departments, new-venture groups, and ad hoc teams or task forces are ways to focus energy on both creation and implementation. A separate department has the freedom to create a new technology that fits a genuine need. A task force can be created to see that implementation is completed. The task force can be responsible for communication, involvement of users, training, and other activities needed for change.

7. *Foster idea champions.* One of the most effective weapons in the battle for change is the idea champion. The most effective champion is a volunteer champion who is deeply committed to a new idea. The idea champion sees that all technical activities are correct and complete. An additional champion, such as a manager sponsor, may also be needed to persuade people about implementation, even using coercion if necessary.

Current thinking on change management is grounded in the pioneering work of Kurt Lewin. In the 1950s, he proposed a model that explains change as a process with three distinct phases—unfreezing, changing and refreezing. The first phase—unfreezing—involves both understanding the current situation and breaking it down. Then the changes are implemented in the changing phase. Once the changes have been implemented in the second phase, it is important to solidify the changes in the refreezing phase. That way, the changes stick and are locked into an organization's culture until such time that the process needs to start again.[133] One of Lewin's useful change tools is the forcefield analysis technique. The tool helps change agents identify and weight forces that are helping change and those that are hindering it. The tool can be used to understand the current situation and potential levers for change.

## Summary and Interpretation

Organizations face a dilemma. Managers prefer to organize day-to-day activities in a predictable, routine manner. However, change—not stability—is the natural order of things in today's global environment. Thus, organizations need to build in change as well as stability, to facilitate innovation as well as efficiency.

Most change in organizations is incremental, but there is a growing emphasis on the need for radical change. Four types of change—technology, products and services, strategy and structure, and culture—may give an organization a competitive edge, and managers need to make certain each of the necessary ingredients for change is present.

For technical innovation, which is of concern to most organizations, an organic structure that encourages employee autonomy works best because it encourages a bottom-up flow of ideas. Other approaches are to establish a separate department charged with creating new technical ideas, establish venture teams or idea incubators, and encourage idea champions. New products and services generally require cooperation among several departments, so horizontal linkage is an essential part of the innovation process.

For changes in strategy and structure, a top-down approach is typically best. These innovations are in the domain of top administrators who take responsibility for restructuring, for downsizing, and for changes in policies, goals, and control systems.

Culture changes are also generally the responsibility of top management. Some recent trends that may create a need for broad-scale culture change in the organization are re-engineering, the shift to horizontal forms of organizing, greater organizational diversity, and the learning organization. All of these changes require significant shifts in employee and manager attitudes and ways of working together. One method for bringing about this level of culture change is organization development (OD). OD focuses on the human and social aspects of the organization and uses behavioural science knowledge to bring about changes in attitudes and relationships.

Finally, the implementation of change is difficult. Strong leadership is needed to guide employees through the turbulence and uncertainty and build organization-wide commitment to change. A number of barriers to change exist, including excessive focus on cost, failure to perceive benefits, lack of coordination and cooperation, individual uncertainty avoidance, and fear of loss. Managers can thoughtfully plan how to deal with resistance to increase the likelihood of success. Techniques that will facilitate implementation are to establish a sense or urgency for change; establish a coalition to guide the change; create a vision and strategy for change; develop plans to overcome resistance by aligning with the needs and goals of users, creating communication and training, providing psychological safety, encouraging participation and involvement, and, in rare cases, forcing the innovation if necessary; creating change teams; and fostering idea champions.

## ■ Key Concepts

| | |
|---|---|
| ambidextrous approach, p. 380 | organization development, p. 393 |
| change process, p. 377 | organizational change, p. 376 |
| creative departments, p. 381 | organizational innovation, p. 376 |
| creativity, p. 377 | product and service changes, p. 374 |
| culture changes, p. 375 | radical change, p. 373 |
| dual-core approach, p. 389 | skunkworks, p. 382 |
| horizontal coordination model, p. 385 | strategy and structure changes, p. 374 |
| idea champion, p. 382 | switching structures, p. 381 |
| idea incubator, p. 381 | team building, p. 394 |
| incremental change, p. 372 | technical champion, p. 383 |
| large group intervention, p. 393 | technology changes, p. 375 |
| management champion, p. 383 | time-based competition, p. 388 |
| new-venture fund, p. 382 | venture teams, p. 382 |

## ■ Discussion Questions

1. How is the management of radical change likely to differ from the management of incremental change?
2. How are organic characteristics related to changes in technology? to administrative changes?
3. Describe the dual-core approach. How does administrative change normally differ from technology change? Discuss.
4. How might organizations manage the dilemma of needing both stability and change?
5. Why do organizations experience resistance to change? What steps can managers take to overcome this resistance?
6. "Bureaucracies are not innovative." Discuss.
7. A noted organization theorist said, "Pressure for change originates in the environment; pressure for stability originates within the organization." Do you agree? Discuss.
8. Of the seven elements required for successful change, which element do you think managers are most likely to overlook? Discuss.
9. How do the underlying values of organization development compare to the values underlying other types of change? Why do the values underlying OD make it particularly useful in shifting to a learning organization?
10. The manager of R&D for a drug company said that only five percent of the company's new products ever achieve market success. He also said the industry average is 10 percent and wondered how his organization might increase its success rate. If you were acting as a consultant, what advice would you give him concerning organizational structure?
11. Review the seven stages for implementing change illustrated in Exhibit 10.9. What sort of resistance might you expect at stages 2,4 and 6? Explain.

## ■ Chapter 10 Workbook: Innovation Climate*

In order to examine differences in the level of innovation encouragement in organizations, you will be asked to rate two organizations. The first should be an organization in which you have worked, or your college or university. The second should be someone else's workplace, that of a family member, a friend, or an acquaintance. You will have to interview that person to answer the questions below. You should put your own answers in column A, your interviewee's answers in column B, and what you think would be the ideal in column C.

## Innovation Measures

| Item of Measure | A<br>Your<br>Organization | B<br>Other<br>Organization | C<br>Your<br>Ideal |
|---|---|---|---|
| **Score items 1–5 on this scale:**<br>1 = disagree completely to 5 = agree completely | | | |
| 1. Creativity is encouraged here.* | | | |
| 2. People are allowed to solve the same problems in different ways.* | | | |
| 3. I get to pursue creative ideas.** | | | |
| 4. The organization publicly recognizes and also rewards those who are innovative.** | | | |
| 5. Our organization is flexible and always open to change.* | | | |
| **Score items 6–10 on the opposite scale:**<br>1 = agree completely to 5 = don't agree at all | | | |
| 6. The primary job of people here is to follow orders that come from the top.* | | | |
| 7. The best way to get along here is to think and act like the others.* | | | |
| 8. This place seems to be more concerned with the status quo than with change.* | | | |
| 9. People are rewarded more if they don't rock the boat.** | | | |
| 10. New ideas are great, but we don't have enough people or money to carry them out.** | | | |

*These items indicate the organization's innovation climate.
**These items show resource support.

## Questions

1. What comparisons in terms of innovation climate can you make between these two organizations?
2. How might productivity differ between a climate that supports innovation and a climate that does not?
3. Where would you rather work? Why?

---

## **Case for Analysis:** Change at Defence Research and Development—DRDC Toronto*

DRDC Toronto is a research centre whose mission is "to ensure that the Canadian Defence and National Security capabilities exploit the full potential of Human Effectiveness S&T [science and technology]." It is one of nine centres across Canada that are governed by several core values: trust and respect, commitment, client focus, creativity and innovation, teamwork, leadership, and professionalism and integrity. DRDC Toronto was founded in 1939 when the Department of National Defence (DND) recognized the importance of human factors by establishing the interdepartmental Associate Committee on Aviation Medical Research. Sir Frederick Banting, the co-discoverer of insulin, chaired the committee. DRDC Toronto has built on its early history of scientific excellence in human factors design and now serves both the Canadian forces and industrial clients with an internationally recognized combination of research facilities and expertise.

DRDC Toronto has developed a range of S&T products and processes for military and industrial clients. For example, its diving tables are used around the world to reduce the risk of decompression sickness; the STING (Sustained Tolerance to INcreased G) system, provides superior G protection to jet fighter pilots; and the "Clothe the Soldier" project provided human engineering support to the Canadian Army in acquiring over 24 new items of state-of-the-art soldier protective clothing and personal equipment. These are just a few of the projects DRDC Toronto has been involved in but they are illustrative of the range and the variety of its work.[1]

DRDC Toronto began "a change journey" to design an organization that both integrated and acknowledged its scientific expertise while becoming more efficient and relevant to its military client. It was a particularly challenging change as there were various stakeholders within the organization who had different mental maps that shaped their behaviour. As Exhibit 10.10 shows, a mix of military, scientific, technical, and administrative staff reported ultimately to the director general, a well-published researcher in psychology. However, the military members (Canadian Forces personnel) also reported

through a separate chain of command to the military commanding officer and associate director general. Dr. Pigeau was the change agent for DRDC Toronto's "Partnership through Professionalism"—an initiative designed to promote an organizational culture of mutual respect so that all staff worked together collaboratively. He brought in external consultants as well as engaging his own personnel. He wanted to create a community of professionals dedicated to using and sharing its expertise to work on projects that would have direct and lasting benefits for its clients. The organization was to become client-driven rather than remaining a largely "silo-ed" organization where scientists did pure research of interest to them. Besides, the organization was to become better integrated and more cohesive while still recognizing the professional expertise of the various units.

As part of its change, the Professional Partnership Initiative (PPI) recognized four professional streams—corporate, technical, science, and management—which cut across the hierarchy and affected both military and civilian staff. Each stream has members at different levels of experience who also have roles and responsibilities that are distinct to the stream. What is key in the design is that each stream is considered to be of equal value in serving the goals of DRDC Toronto's clients. The streams do not replace the organization's design (illustrated in Exhibit 10.10) nor do

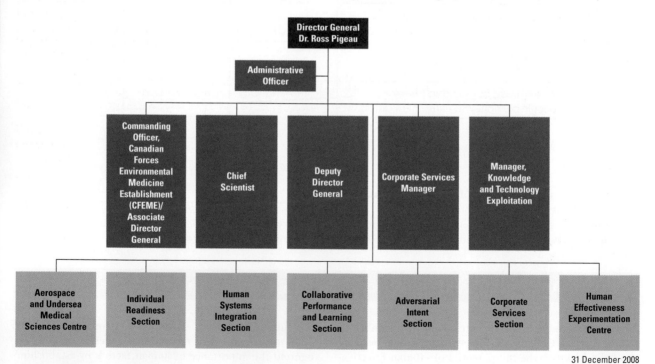

31 December 2008

**EXHIBIT 10.10**
Organization Chart for DRDC Toronto (n.d.)

| STREAM | OBSERVATIONS |
|---|---|
| Corporate | Coming from a military family, I can tell you that change is always constant. In fact, I get jumpy when there is no change—change is healthy and it means that we are trying to do things better. |
| Technical | The professional partnership philosophy is a critical concept and success enabler for any interdependent multidiscipline organization. Explicitly recognizing the essential contribution of each distinct professional stream is refreshing. |
| Science | A supportive and enabling partnership is built up with people, as a house with stones, but a collection of people without a common purpose is no more a partnership than a heap of stones is a house. |
| Management | The professional partnership philosophy gives me hope that each person at DRDC Toronto will be able to recognize his or her contributions to the successes of the lab and feel satisfaction that success brings. |

**EXHIBIT 10.11**
**Some Observations about the PPI**
Source: *Partnership through Professionalism: An Organizational Journey*, Defence Research and Development Canada, Toronto: April (2010), vi, vii, 2, 7.

they challenge the military chain of command. "Rather, [the system of streams] complements it by allowing members of professional streams, civilian and military, to see how their efforts yield tangible, mission-specific effects."[2] The organizational design has two dimensions, vertical and horizontal, that establish task accountability and unity of effort, respectively.

According to Dr. Pigeau, the PPI will be a successful change when it has achieved three significant outcomes: each professional stream will be able (1) to self-organize, (2) to partner well with other streams, and (3) to contribute directly to achieving the mission and vision of DRDC Toronto.

See Exhibit 10.11 for observations from one member of each stream.

## Assignment Questions

1. What are the change challenges for DRDC Toronto?
2. What is your assessment of the PPI?

This case is dedicated to the memory of Colonel Carl Walker, Commanding Officer of the Canadian Forces Environmental Medicine Establishment and Associate Director General, DRDC Toronto, 2004–2008, who embodied the spirit of collaboration and integration.

[1]About Defence Research and Development Canada (DRDC) (September 30, 2010) at www. toronto.drdc-rddc.gc.ca/about-apropos/index-eng.asp (accessed April 13, 2011).
[2]*Partnership through Professionalism: An Organizational Journey*, Defence Research and Development Canada, Toronto: April (2010), vi, vii, 2, 7.

*Copyright © 2011 by Ann Armstrong.

# Case for Analysis: Osoyoos Band*

Over the last decade*, British Columbia's Osoyoos Band has been on an economic tear. With nine businesses—including the year-old Desert Cultural Centre—going strong, and an entrepreneurial chief unafraid to shun tradition, it's no wonder there are more jobs than band members. A case study in self-sustainability.

Evening light pours across the land like a thick golden liquid and the shadows grow long. Waves of bunch grass morph between yellow, saffron and deep magenta as the sun dips toward Kobau Mountain across the valley.

In the softening light, tiny yellow flowers become visible on the twisted branches of antelope brush, a stoic desert plant that sends deep tap roots into the seared earth of the south Okanagan in search of moisture. Lofty Ponderosa pines, with their fire-protective skins of thick bark, gather in shallow draws like old men stopping to chat about the weather.

Moments ago on this pleasant May evening, I was relaxing with my feet up in a plush spa resort condo. Now I walk gingerly amongst the antelope brush, alert for clumps of prickly pear cactus or perhaps the venomous Western rattlesnake coiled and concealed somewhere underfoot.

If you could project the cartoon setting of the Road Runner and Wile E. Coyote into some kind of three-dimensional, metaphysical reality, it might resemble this extraordinary landscape, right here in Canada's desert country in the south Okanagan. Home to myriad fascinating rare plant and animal species, this is also the traditional territory of the Osoyoos people, an upstart Native band that is striking an enterprising balance between their traditional roots and a progressive approach to economic development that is the talk of Canada's aboriginal community and the tourism industry at large.

Admittedly, vineyards, golf courses, spa hotels and RV parks aren't exactly hallmarks of traditional Native culture, but the Osoyoos Indian Band has no problem keeping one foot in the past while striding confidently forward with the other.

One year ago, the band celebrated the opening of the deluxe Nk'Mip (pronounced "ink-a-meep") Desert Cultural Centre, showcasing both the flora and fauna of the region and the ingenuity of an ancient culture that flourished here for millennia. With a $9-million price tag mostly paid for with government grants, this 12,000-square-foot facility houses interpretive displays, a theatre and a rattlesnake research program, forming the cultural cornerstone of an extensive tourist development that includes a golf course, the award-winning Nk'Mip Wine Cellars and the Spirit Ridge Resort and Spa, my home for the past several days.

"We're not perfect. This centre has been talked about since the early '90s and a lot of debate went into this, but we're proud of the result," explains Clarence Louie, the tough-talking entrepreneurial chief of the Osoyoos Indian Band. "It was worth the time and effort to advance and preserve our heritage and culture."

Though the Osoyoos are proud of their past, they're not content to be simply a museum culture. They're growing a business empire. By striving for economic self-sufficiency, the 450-strong band is slowly overcoming some of the social ills of drug and alcohol abuse, unemployment and the crippling dependence fostered over years on spoon-fed, ill-conceived government handouts and programs. Capitalizing on its south Okanagan location, the Osoyoos Indian Band is setting a high benchmark for Native entrepreneurship in the local economy. The band owns nine businesses with annual revenues of $14.5 million, marking significant growth from 1997 when revenues were a mere $1.45 million.

[In 2006], Chief Louie and his economic team penned a unique agreement with the Province of British Columbia that will accommodate the development of nearby Mount Baldy—located on traditional band land—into a destination resort by its owners, Idaho-based Winter Recreation ULC. The band also has a small 2.5 percent equity in the Mt. Baldy Ski Corporation and is close to inking a deal with Bellstar Resorts and Hotels Inc. to buy a 25 percent share in its Spirit Ridge development. With all its business holdings, the band creates more jobs than it has working-age band members, a fact Chief Louie is fond of trumpeting during speeches to other Native bands, government bureaucrats and business leaders.

Four years ago, Alberta-based Bellstar decided to seriously consider a desert country investment after witnessing the Osoyoos Indian Band's efforts to balance economic development with cultural and ecological conservation. Last fall, Bellstar completed the $23-million first phase of its Spirit Ridge Spa and Resort complex, all on leased band land. The next phase, worth roughly $50 million, will bring the total number of resort suites and villas to 226, complete with conference facilities and a business centre.

"We liked how the chief spoke about business. The band council was willing to listen but they never strayed from their vision of economic development," says Ed Romanewski, president and CEO of Bellstar, over the phone from his Calgary office.

"Frankly, in our previous experience with Indian bands, we didn't see that kind of focus. We saw this as a great investment in a truly unique part of Canada."

To understand where the Osoyoos people are today, you need to dust off the history books and gaze into their past—and at the landscape that has defined them.

Their tenacity and pride has roots that date back to well before the tourist town of Osoyoos sprang up on the shores of its namesake lake, now buzzing with powerboats and Jet Skis. In 1915, when aboriginal culture was being torn asunder by the residential school and reservation system, then-Osoyoos chief Baptiste George stood firm. With uncanny foresight, he persuaded the federal government of the day to allow the band to build and manage its own school. Seven months later, the Nk'Mip Day School welcomed its first students. In the early years, the school struggled to retain teachers, opening and closing its doors as overwhelmed instructors came and went. Then in 1932, a visionary young man named Anthony Walsh arrived at the school. It was a fortuitous meeting.

Given the troubled times of white–Native politics, Walsh had unusual empathy toward indigenous culture. Rather than suppress the Native language and traditional values of his young pupils, he encouraged them. Subsequently, Osoyoos culture flowered during Walsh's tenure. This unique synergy between student and teacher reached far beyond the sleepy backwater of the south Okanagan. Thanks to Walsh's knack for promotion, in 1936 a Nativity scene painted on buckskin by young Francis Baptiste was singled out for distinction at the Royal Drawing Society's

Annual Exhibition at London's Guildhall Gallery. The following year, a portfolio of drawings and sketches by Osoyoos youth depicting ancient and modern Osoyoos life was shown at the Cizek Juvenile Art Centre in Vienna. Then, in 1938, Walsh toured Europe, exhibiting the children's work in Dublin, London, Glasgow and Paris.

Today the legacy of these precocious Osoyoos youngsters lives on in a new exhibit at the Nk'Mip Centre, where visitors get a taste of the south Okanagan beyond beach blankets and wine tours.

"The centre is here to serve the community, but also to share in the rich living culture of the Okanagan people," says manager Charlotte Sanders, adding that it exceeded first-year expectations by welcoming more than 12,750 visitors [in 2006].

There's no question, scientists across Canada recognize traditional Osoyoos land as a threatened biological treasure, home to more at-risk species than any other ecosystem in British Columbia. Not surprisingly, people are naturally drawn to the pleasant Okanagan climate and its proximity to lakes and beaches. Golf courses, vineyards, resorts and urban development sprawl across a landscape once blanketed in sage and antelope brush. The Osoyoos Natives have also seen fit to bulldoze sections of the desert to make way for vineyards, fairways and condos. Chief Louie doesn't apologize.

"Conservation of the desert is important but we also need to develop land, create jobs and generate revenue for our people. If this land wasn't in Osoyoos band hands, I bet every square inch of this desert would be developed," Chief Louie says with characteristic candor.

In what's left of the desert, like the land adjacent to the Nk'Mip Centre, extreme temperatures and severe aridity combine to create one of the country's most unusual and rich ecosystems. There is nothing frivolous or extravagant about life here. It lacks the exuberance and fecundity of a West Coast rainforest, yet its riches and subtleties are revealed upon closer inspection. Like, for example, the curious tapestry of lichens and mosses underfoot, known in scientific circles as the sci-fi-sounding "cryptogamic crust." Essential for maintaining sensitive soil structures and preserving moisture, this crust is so sensitive that it can be destroyed by an afternoon of grazing Herefords, rendering this biological marvel irreparable. At-risk species like the Western rattlesnake, the spadefoot toad, the burrowing owl and even the antelope brush also cling to a precarious existence.

"There are so many species here that are at the margins of their habitat," says Bob Lincoln, retired wildlife branch manager for the B.C. Environment Ministry's Okanagan Region and a full-time conservation activist. "It's also one of the richest areas because you can go from aquatic to riparian to desert to cliffs in a span of a few kilometres."

As I hike through this surreal landscape of cactus, snakes and sagebrush next to the Nk'Mip Centre, I ponder life in an environment like this. It's spring and a recent rainfall has infused the land with a freshness that could be misleading. During summer, temperatures frequently soar into the punishing mid-40°C range; enough to wilt even the hardiest desert traveller. Just as the stubborn flora and fauna of the south Okanagan persevere in the extremes, the Osoyoos people have survived and are now making their distinct mark on the future of Canada's aboriginal peoples.

## Assignment Questions

1. How does the Osoyoos band integrate its traditions with its businesses?
2. How has the Osoyoos band changed the paradigm of development?

---

*Findlay, A. (2007) "High and Dry - How the Okanagan's Osoyoos Band Turned Aboriginal Tourism on its Head," *Up!*, May, pp. 51–59. Used with permission of the author.

The Canadian Press/Thunder Bay Chronicle/BRENT LINTON

## Anishinabek Nation

In March 2007, Grand Council Chief John Beaucage pledged to do more to preserve the water of the Great Lakes and to take better care of the environment. He created the Anishinabek Women's Water Commission to advise the Union of Ontario Indians; the Commission provides advice on all aspects of the management of the Great Lakes. According to the Chief, "[We] need to ensure that First Nations, especially our women, maintain their role as stewards of the water and give a voice to our most precious resource."[1] The founding Chief Commissioner is Josephine Mandamin (see photo), an elder from Wikwemikong Unceded Nation. She notes that "[water] is a great uniter...Hearing Mother Earth cry about how ill she is and how she is having a hard time feeding her children is a reminder to us all that our women feel the same way. We must unite in this momentous task."[2] Mandamin created the Mother Earth Water Walk and leads walks around each of the Great Lakes.

Chief Beaucage notes that First Nations are dedicated to the principles of co-management: "[We] acknowledge Ontario's jurisdiction in managing the Great Lakes on behalf of their citizens, while we [are] asserting traditional management principles on behalf of our citizens.[3] The Anishinabek Nation signed a memorandum of understanding with the Ministry of Natural Resources that strengthens the relationship between them. The memorandum commits the Government of Ontario and the Anishinabek Nation (1) to hold an annual meeting between the Anishinabek Grand Council Chief and the Minister of Natural Resources, (2) to establish a joint Great Lakes Charter Annex Agreement Implementation Committee, and (3) to help build Anishinabek Nation advisory and technical capacity through the Union of Ontario Indians by retaining a technical advisor, as well as other measures.

---

Every organization grows, prospers, or fails as a result of decisions by its managers, and decisions can be risky and uncertain, without any guarantee of success. Sometimes, decision making is a trial-and-error process, in which top managers continue to search for appropriate ways to solve complex problems. Decision making is done amid constantly changing factors, unclear information, and conflicting points of view. The 2002 decision to merge Hewlett-Packard (HP) and Compaq, for example, was highly controversial. Former HP CEO Carly Fiorina and her supporters believed it was essential for HP's future success, but other managers and board members argued that it was ill advised to risk HP's printer business and move the company more deeply into the highly competitive computer world. Fiorina's side ultimately won out, but results of the merger were disappointing. HP's board ousted Fiorina in early 2005, partly due to issues related to the Compaq merger.[4] Similarly, Canadian Tire Corporation's 1982 purchase of White Stores, a money-losing Texas-based chain of automotive parts, furniture, and appliance stores cost the CEO, Dean Muncaster, his job. The decision to buy White Stores cost Canadian Tire $300 million in three years.[5]

Many organizational decisions are complete failures. A classic example is the 1985 introduction of New Coke, which Coca-Cola executives were sure was the company's answer to winning back market share from Pepsi. Within three months, the company had gotten more than 400,000 angry letters and phone calls, and New Coke quietly faded from store shelves.[6] Even the most successful companies sometimes make big blunders. DreamWorks, the studio that made *Shrek 2*, the biggest box-office hit of 2004, poured tens of millions into marketing for the DVD release of the monster hit. Sales during the initial release period boomed, so DreamWorks flooded the market. Managers got a shock when retailers began returning millions of unsold copies. Based on patterns in the past, DreamWorks wrongly assumed the strong early sales would continue and perhaps even grow.[7]

Yet managers also make many successful decisions every day. Meg Whitman made eBay today's model of what an Internet company should be by steering clear of get-rich-quick schemes and keeping the company focused on nurturing its community of buyers and sellers. Cadillac managers' decision to ditch stuffy golf and yachting sponsorships in favour of tying in with popular Hollywood movies has boosted sales and revived Cadillac's image. And Carlos Ghosn implemented

## YOU & DESIGN

### Making Important Decisions

How do you make important decisions? To find out, think about a time when you made an important career decision or made a major purchase or investment. To what extent does each of the following words describe how you reached the final decision? Please check five words that best describe how you made your final choice.

1. Logic _____
2. Inner knowing _____
3. Data _____
4. Felt sense _____
5. Facts _____
6. Instincts _____
7. Concepts _____
8. Hunch _____
9. Reason _____
10. Feelings _____

**Scoring:** Give yourself one point for each odd-numbered item you checked, and subtract one point for each even-numbered item you checked. The highest possible score is 15 and the lowest possible score is –5.

**Interpretation:** The odd-numbered items pertain to a linear decision style and the even-numbered items pertain to a nonlinear decision approach. Linear means using logical *rationality* to make decisions.

Nonlinear means to use primarily *intuition* to make decisions. If you scored from –3 to –5, then intuition and a satisficing model is your dominant approach to major decisions. If you scored +3 to +5, then the rational model of decision making as described in the text is your dominant approach. The rational approach is taught in business schools, but many managers use intuition based on experience, especially at senior management levels when there is little tangible data to evaluate.

Source: Adapted from Charles M. Vance, Kevin S. Groves, Yongsun Paik, and Herb Kindler, "Understanding and Measuring Linear-Nonlinear Thinking Style for Enhanced Management Education and Professional Practice," *Academy of Management Learning & Education* 6, no. 2 (2007), 167–185.

structural, management, and product changes that transformed Nissan from a directionless, debt-ridden company into one of the more dynamic and profitable automakers in the world.[8]

## ■ Purpose of This Chapter

At any time, an organization may be identifying problems and implementing alternatives for hundreds of decisions. Managers and organizations somehow muddle through these processes.[9] The purpose here is to analyze these processes to learn what decision making is, in fact, like in organizational settings. Decision-making processes can be thought of as the brain and nervous system of an organization. Decision making is the end use of the information and control systems. Decisions are made about organization strategy, structure, innovation, and acquisitions. This chapter explores how organizations make decisions about these issues. Before reading any further, complete the You and Design to assess your decision-making style.

The first section defines decision making. The next section examines how individual managers make decisions. Then several models of organizational decision making are explored. Each model is used in a different organizational situation. The final sections in this chapter combine the models into a single framework that describes when and how they should be used, and discuss special issues, such as decision mistakes.

## Definitions

**Organizational decision making** is formally defined as the process of identifying and solving problems. The process has two major stages. In the **problem identification** stage, information about environmental and organizational conditions is monitored to determine if performance is satisfactory and to diagnose the cause of shortcomings. The **problem solution** stage occurs when alternative courses of action are considered and one alternative is selected and implemented.

Organizational decisions vary in complexity and can be categorized as programmed or nonprogrammed.[10] **Programmed decisions** are repetitive and well defined, and procedures exist for resolving the problem. They are well structured because criteria of performance are normally clear, good information is available about current performance, alternatives are easily specified, and there is relative certainty that the chosen alternative will be successful. Examples of programmed decisions include decision rules, such as when to replace an office copy machine, when to reimburse managers for travel expenses, or whether an applicant has sufficient qualifications for an assembly-line job. Many companies adopt rules based on experience with programmed decisions. For example, a rule for large hotels staffing banquets is to allow one server per 30 guests for a sit-down function and one server per 40 guests for a buffet.[11]

**Nonprogrammed decisions** are novel, ill structured, and poorly defined, and no procedure exists for solving the problem. They are used when an organization has not seen a problem before and may not know how to respond. Clear-cut decision criteria do not exist. Alternatives are fuzzy. There is uncertainty about whether a proposed solution will solve the problem. Typically, few alternatives can be developed for a nonprogrammed decision, so a single solution is custom-tailored to the problem.

Many nonprogrammed decisions involve strategic planning because uncertainty is significant and decisions are complex. One example of a nonprogrammed decision comes from Tupperware, the maker of food storage products and kitchen gadgets traditionally sold at home Tupperware parties. Managers hit a home run with the decision to set up booths in shopping malls and push sales over the Internet. Thus, a further push into retail sales by placing Tupperware in a retail chain in the United States, with volunteer salespeople to demonstrate the products, seemed destined for success. But moving into Target turned out to be one of the biggest disasters in Tupperware's history. Some Target stores and shoppers didn't know how to deal with the influx of Tupperware salespeople, who ended up feeling slighted and stopped volunteering for store duty. Sales were slow. At the same time, the availability of Tupperware in the retail stores decreased the interest in home parties, further hurting sales and alienating independent sales representatives. Although overseas sales remained strong, sales of Tupperware in North America fell to a three-year low and profits plummeted nearly 50 percent. To address the decline in U.S. earnings Tupperware cut costs and stepped up its sales force recruiting efforts. In addition, the company moved into direct mail, for the first time sending out unsolicited catalogues in 1992.[12] However, by 2010, Forbes named Tupperware the second most admired company for a second year in a row and Tupperware now gets 44 percent of its sales from domestic markets.[13]

Particularly complex nonprogrammed decisions have been referred to as "wicked" decisions, because simply defining the problem can turn into a major task. Wicked problems are associated with manager conflicts over objectives and alternatives, rapidly changing circumstances, and unclear linkages among decision elements. Managers dealing with a wicked decision may hit on a solution that merely proves they failed to correctly define the problem to begin with.[14]

Today's managers and organizations are dealing with a higher percentage of nonprogrammed decisions because of the rapidly changing business environment. As outlined in Exhibit 11.1, today's environment has increased both the number and complexity of decisions that have to be made and has created a need for new decision-making processes. Managers in rapidly changing e-business departments, for example, often have to make quick decisions based on very limited information. Another example is globalization. The trend toward moving production to low-wage countries has managers all over North America struggling with ethical decisions concerning working conditions in the developing world and the loss of manufacturing jobs in North America.

**Apply**

How can you apply the distinction between programmed and nonprogrammed decisions to your career planning?

## Individual Decision Making

Individual decision making by managers can be described in two ways. The first is the **rational approach**, which suggests how managers should try to make decisions. The second is the **bounded rationality perspective**, which describes how decisions actually have to be made under severe time and resource constraints. The rational approach is an ideal that managers may work toward but never reach.

### Rational Approach

The rational approach to individual decision making stresses the need for systematic analysis of a problem followed by choice and implementation in a logical,

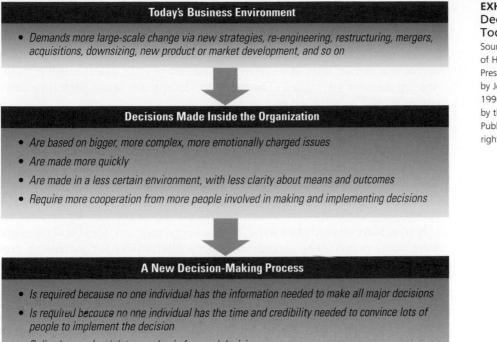

**EXHIBIT 11.1**
**Decision Making in Today's Environment**
Source: Reprinted by permission of Harvard Business School Press. From *Leading Change* by John P. Kotter. Boston, MA, 1996, p. 56. Copyright © 1996 by the Harvard Business School Publishing Corporation, all rights reserved.

step-by-step sequence. The rational approach was developed to guide individual decision making because many managers were observed to be unsystematic and arbitrary in their approach to organizational decisions.

Although the rational model is not fully achievable in the real world of uncertainty, complexity, and rapid change highlighted in Exhibit 11.1, the model does help managers think about decisions more clearly and rationally. Managers should use systematic procedures to make decisions whenever possible. When managers have a deep understanding of the rational decision-making process, it can help them make better decisions even when there is a lack of clear information. According to the rational approach, decision making can be broken down into *eight sequential* steps. The eight steps are demonstrated by a retail sector example. (The retail sector had sales of $457.4 billion in 2011, up from $439.5 billion in 2010, and employed 12 percent of the country's workforce).[15]

1. *Monitor the decision environment.* In the first step, a manager monitors internal and external information that will indicate deviations from planned or acceptable behaviour. She talks to colleagues and reviews financial statements, performance evaluations, industry indices, competitors' activities, and so forth. For example, during the pressure-packed five-week winter holiday season, the general manager of a retail store checks out competitors around the mall, eyeing whether they are marking down merchandise. She also scans printouts of her store's previous day's sales to learn what is or is not moving.[16]

2. *Define the decision problem.* The manager responds to deviations by identifying essential details of the problem: where, when, who was involved; who was affected; and how current activities are influenced. The general manager needs to determine if store profits are low because overall sales are less than expected or because certain lines of merchandise are not moving as expected.

3. *Specify decision objectives.* The manager determines what performance outcomes should be achieved by a decision.

4. *Diagnose the problem.* In this step, the manager digs below the surface to analyze the cause of the problem. Additional data might be gathered to facilitate this diagnosis. Understanding the cause enables appropriate treatment—the cause of slow sales, for example, might be competitors' marking down of merchandise or the store's failure to display hot-selling items in a visible location.

5. *Develop alternative solutions.* Before a manager can move ahead with a decisive action plan, she must have a clear understanding of the various options available to achieve desired objectives. The manager may seek ideas and suggestions from other people. The general manager's alternatives for increasing profits could include buying fresh merchandise, running a sale, or reducing the number of employees.

6. *Evaluate alternatives.* This step may involve the use of statistical techniques or personal experience to gauge the probability of success. The merits of each alternative are assessed, as well as the probability that it will reach the desired objectives.

7. *Choose the best alternative.* This step is the core of the decision process. The manager uses her analysis of the problem, objectives, and alternatives to select a single alternative that has the best chance for success. The general manager may choose to reduce the number of staff as a way to meet the profit goals rather than increase advertising or markdowns.

8. *Implement the chosen alternative.* Finally, the manager uses managerial, administrative, and persuasive abilities and gives directions to ensure that the decision is carried out. The monitoring activity (step 1) begins again as soon as the solution is implemented. The decision cycle should be a continuous process, with new decisions made daily based on monitoring her environment for problems and opportunities.

The first four steps in this sequence are the problem identification stage, and the next four steps are the problem solution stage of decision making. A manager normally goes through all eight steps in making a decision, although each step may not be a distinct element. Managers may know from experience exactly what to do in a situation, so one or more steps will be minimized.

The following In Practice illustrates how the rational approach can be used to make a decision about a challenging human resource problem.

**Compare**

Compare the eight-sequential-step model with the case analysis approach you use in your case courses. What do you observe?

1. *Monitor the decision environment.* It is Monday morning, and Joe DeFoe, Alberta's accounts receivable supervisor, is absent again.

2. *Define the decision problem.* This is the fourth consecutive Monday DeFoe has been absent. Company policy forbids unexcused absenteeism, and DeFoe has been warned about his excessive absenteeism on the last two occasions. A final warning is in order but can be delayed, if warranted.

3. *Specify decision objectives.* DeFoe should attend work regularly and establish the invoice collection levels of which he is capable. The time period for solving the problem is two weeks.

4. *Diagnose the problem.* Discreet discussions with DeFoe's co-workers and information gleaned from DeFoe indicate that DeFoe has a drinking problem. He apparently uses Mondays to dry out from weekend binges. Discussion with other company sources confirms that DeFoe is a problem drinker.

5. *Develop alternative solutions.* (1) Fire DeFoe. (2) Issue a final warning without comment. (3) Issue a warning and accuse DeFoe of being an alcoholic to let him know you are aware of his problem. (4) Talk with DeFoe to see if he will discuss his drinking. If he admits he has a drinking problem, delay the final warning and suggest that he enrol in the company's new employee assistance program for help with personal problems, including alcoholism. (5) Talk with DeFoe to see if he will discuss his drinking. If he does not admit he has a drinking problem, let him know that the next absence will cost him his job.

6. *Evaluate alternatives.* The cost of training a replacement is the same for each alternative. Alternative 1 ignores cost and other criteria. Alternatives 2 and 3 do not adhere to company policy, which advocates counselling where appropriate. Alternative 4 is designed for the benefit of both DeFoe and the company. It might save a good employee if DeFoe is willing to seek assistance. Alternative 5 is primarily for the benefit of the company. A final warning might provide some incentive for DeFoe to admit he has a drinking problem. If so, dismissal might be avoided, but further absences will no longer be tolerated.

7. *Choose the best alternative.* DeFoe does not admit that he has a drinking problem. Choose alternative 5.

8. *Implement the chosen alternative.* Write up the situation and issue the final warning.

---

In the preceding example, issuing the final warning to Joe DeFoe was a programmed decision. The standard of expected behaviour was clearly defined, information on the frequency and cause of DeFoe's absence was readily available, and acceptable alternatives and procedures were described. The rational procedure works best in such cases, when the decision maker has sufficient time for an orderly, thoughtful process. Moreover, Alberta Consulting had mechanisms in place to implement the decision, once made.

When decisions are nonprogrammed, ill defined, and piling on top of one another, the individual manager should still try to use the steps in the rational approach, but he or she often will have to take shortcuts by relying on intuition and experience. Deviations from the rational approach are explained by the bounded rationality perspective.

## ■ Bounded Rationality Perspective

The point of the rational approach is that managers should try to use systematic procedures to arrive at good decisions. When organizations are facing little competition and are dealing with well-understood issues, managers generally use rational procedures to make decisions.[17] Yet research into managerial decision making shows that often managers are *unable* to follow an ideal procedure. Many decisions must be made very quickly. Time pressure, a large number of internal and external factors affecting a decision, and the ill-defined nature of many problems make systematic analysis virtually impossible. Managers have only so much time and mental capacity and, hence, cannot evaluate every goal, problem, and alternative. Mintzberg's research in the 1970s found that

**Think**

Think about a complex decision you faced. What were the
trade-offs and constraints that
you had to address?

managerial work is demanding, open-ended, fragmented, and full of brevity, variety and interruption.[18] The attempt to be rational is bounded (limited) by the enormous complexity of many problems. There is a limit to how rational managers can be. For example, an executive in a hurry may have a choice of 20 shirts but will take the first or second one that matches his or her suit. The executive doesn't carefully weigh all 20 alternatives because the short amount of time and the large number of plausible alternatives would be overwhelming. The manager simply selects the first solution that addresses the problem and moves on quickly to the next task.

**Constraints and Trade-offs.** Not only are large organizational decisions too complex to fully comprehend, but several other constraints impinge on the decision maker, as illustrated in Exhibit 11.2. For many decisions, the circumstances are ambiguous, requiring social support, a shared perspective on what happens, and acceptance and agreement. In the SARS outbreak in Toronto in 2003, for example, many complex decisions needed to be made in trying circumstances by many different health care practitioners. Setting the correct priorities was vital in responding to the many demands of the crisis. According to a 2004 study, "[In] the midst of a crisis such as SARS where guidance is incomplete, consequences uncertain, and information constantly changing, where hour-by-hour decisions involve life and death, fairness is more important rather than less."[19]

Organizational culture and ethical values also influence decision making, as discussed in Chapter 9. This chapter's Leading by Design box describes how

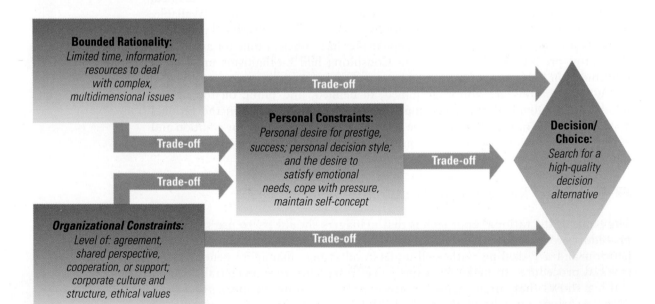

**EXHIBIT 11.2**
**Constraints and Trade-offs during Nonprogrammed Decision Making**
Source: Adapted from Irving L. Janis, *Crucial Decisions* (New York: Free Press, 1989); and A. L. George, *Presidential Decision Making in Foreign Policy: The Effective Use of Information and Advice* (Boulder, Colo.: Westview Press, 1980).

Nicole Rycroft and her organization, Canopy Planet, are influencing decision makers to make green decisions.

Managers also often make decisions within a context of trying to please upper managers, people who are perceived to have power within the organization, or others they respect and want to emulate.[20] Personal constraints—such as decision style, work pressure, desire for prestige, or simple feelings of insecurity—may constrain either the search for alternatives or the acceptability of an alternative. All of these factors constrain a perfectly rational approach that should lead to an obviously ideal choice.[21] Even seemingly straightforward decisions, such as selecting a job on graduation from university, can quickly become so complex that a bounded rationality approach is used. Graduating students have been known to search for a job until they have two or three acceptable job offers, at which point their search activity rapidly diminishes. Many firms may be available for interviews, and two or three job offers fall short of the maximum number that would be possible if students made the decision based on perfect rationality.

**The Role of Intuition.** The bounded rationality perspective is often associated with intuitive decision processes. In **intuitive decision making**, experience and judgment rather than sequential logic or explicit reasoning are used to make decisions.[22] Intuition is not arbitrary or irrational because it is based on years of practice and hands-on experience, often stored in the subconscious. When managers use their intuition based on long experience with organizational issues, they more rapidly perceive and understand problems, and they develop a gut feeling or hunch about which alternative will solve a problem, speeding the decision-making process.[23] The value of intuition for effective decision making is supported by a growing body of research from psychology, organizational science, and other disciplines.[24] Indeed, many universities are offering courses in creativity and intuition so business students can learn to understand and use these processes.

In a situation of great complexity or ambiguity, previous experience and judgment are needed to incorporate intangible elements at both the problem identification and problem solution stages.[25] Bits and pieces of unrelated information from informal sources result in a pattern in the manager's mind. One study of managerial problem finding, for example, showed that 30 of 33 problems were ambiguous and ill defined.[26] A simplistic view of a complex problem is often associated with decision failure.[27] Intuition plays an increasingly important role in problem identification in today's fast-paced and uncertain environment.

Intuitive processes are also used in the problem solution stage. Executives frequently make decisions without explicit reference to the impact on profits or to other measurable outcomes.[28] As we saw in Exhibit 11.2, many intangible factors—such as a person's decision style, desire for prestige, and ability to deal with pressure—influence selection of the best alternative. These factors cannot be quantified in a systematic way, so intuition guides the choice of a solution. Managers may make a decision based on what they sense to be right rather than on what they can document with hard data. A survey of managers conducted in 2002 by executive search firm Christian & Timbers found that 45 percent of corporate executives say they rely more on instinct than on facts and figures to make business decisions.[29]

# Leading *by Design*

## Canopy Planet (Canopy)

Nicole Rycroft, Executive Director of Canopy Planet, founded the organization more than a decade ago. Rycroft has been recognized for her work by Ashoka and is an Ashoka Fellow. Ashoka is a global organization to support social entrepreneurship and social innovation. Canopy's mission is to "[make] the conservation of wild places a reality. We work to protect the world's forests, species and climate by harnessing the power of the marketplace to create the economic and political leverage for conservation and sustainable solutions." Canopy is structured as an independent nonprofit governed by five core values. They are "(1) Restless Leadership—We aim to challenge ourselves and inspire the people we work with to build a sustainable world, (2) Collaboration—We create and magnify our successes through partnerships that culminate in action, (3) Solutions Focused—We rise to the challenge of today's ecological realities and direct our work toward tangible results and systemic change, (4) Creative Playfulness—We bring an element of play that energizes and inspires our work, and (5) Integrity—We cultivate these values in ourselves, our organization, and the world at large."[30]

Canopy works to influence publishers, paper producers, and printers to make green purchasing decisions. As 50 percent of the forests logged in Canada end up in pulp and paper products, Canopy's work in influencing paper purchasing decisions is of vital importance. Through its work to shift publishers and printers away from papers originating from carbon- and species-rich forests to eco-friendly alternatives, Canopy has saved millions of trees and been a key driver behind landmark conservation initiatives such as the Canadian Boreal Forest Agreement.

Its best-known success is the greening of the *Harry Potter* series. As the following time line shows, there were many significant decision-making points and processes.

- *2000*—Canopy, formerly Markets Initiative, a one-person Vancouver-based environmental organization, begins conversations with Raincoast Books (the Canadian Harry Potter publisher) and other publishers to start using more environmental papers in its print runs. At this time, no publishers are consistently printing on Ancient Forest Friendly (AFF) papers, as they are unavailable in book grade.
- *2001*—Canopy works with Raincoast Books to develop an Ancient Forest Friendly paper policy for all of its titles. The environmental group also works with 20 other Canadian book publishers, including McClelland & Stewart, Random House Canada, and Douglas & McIntyre to develop new, environmental paper purchasing policies.

- *2001*—The first Ancient Forest Friendly book grade paper is developed in response to publishers' requests. Alice Munro is the first big-name author to print her book on Ancient Forest Friendly paper in 2001.
- *2002*—Raincoast Books asks Canopy for help shifting its reprints of the first four books in the *Harry Potter* series onto Ancient Forest Friendly papers; this amounts to 1.15 million books.
- *2002*—Canopy works with Greenpeace to expand its work with Canadian book publishers into Europe and supports campaigns in seven countries.
- *2003*—Raincoast Books prints *Harry Potter and the Order of the Phoenix* on Ancient Forest Friendly paper, the only publisher to do so internationally. In doing this, Raincoast saves more than 39,320 trees and greenhouse gases equivalent to driving a car 5.3 million kilometres. Raincoast worked closely with Canopy to ensure this title is printed on an Ancient Forest Friendly paper as well as building the green paper into the core marketing strategy for the book.
- *2003*—J.K. Rowling issues a personal statement about the Ancient Forest Friendly initiative that appears on the front page of the Canadian edition of the book.
- *2003*—Canopy meets with Rowling's agent about other international publishers printing on Ancient Forest Friendly papers for future books.
- *2005*—*Harry Potter and the Half Blood Prince* is printed on Ancient Forest Friendly paper in both official Canadian languages, as well as on eco-friendly papers in seven other countries including Israel, the United Kingdom, Germany, and France.
- *2005*—Scholastic fails to print the U.S. edition of *Harry Potter* on eco-friendly paper. Canopy exposes Scholastic's reluctance to shift to a more environmental friendly paper through a widely read *The New York Times* article and other mainstream and industry media stories.
- *2007*—*Harry Potter and the Deathly Hallows* proves to be the greenest book in publishing history to date. The last installment of the Potter series is to be printed on eco-friendly papers in 23 countries and in at least 8 languages. From the United States (Scholastic developed a new policy for the last Potter book and for all of its book titles) to Australia, Canada to Israel, [and] the UK to Argentina....[31]

Canopy is now working to make straw-based papers a commercial reality in North America. It has launched the Wheat Sheet, a paper that uses a combination of recycled fibre, and FSC-second-growth forest fibre. Straw is a by-product

*(Continued)*

of the food harvest, and is often burnt or discarded. It has half the ecological footprint of the tree fibre used in paper production. In 2008, *Canadian Geographic* trialed the Wheat Sheet, which was well received by the paper industry, advertisers, and readers alike. Canopy now faces the strategic challenge of determining how best to create or encourage the right kind of mills to produce enough of the Wheat Sheet to meet market demand.[32] Margaret Atwood partnered with Canopy in 2011, to print 300 copies of *In Other Words: SF and the Human Imagination* on second-harvest paper. It is the first book in North America printed on straw.[33]

Canopy has created the Canopy Club, comprising leading CEOs across Canada, some of whom are Canopy's most impassioned environmental advocates. Rycroft also notes that "[the] Canadian book industry is the greenest on the planet and has sparked an international movement, with green publishing initiatives in 13 other countries."[34]

Sources: About Us, Canopy, accessed from http://www.canopyplanet .org/index.php?page=about-mi on April 2, 2011; and How We Worked with Harry Potter to Change Publishing as We Know it, accessed from http://canopyplanet.org/index.php?page=the-markets-initiative-harry-potter-timeline on April 2, 2011. Reproduced by permission of Canopy.

## Book Mark 11.0    HAVE YOU READ THIS BOOK?

### Blink: The Power of Thinking without Thinking
By Malcolm Gladwell

Snap decisions can be just as good as—and sometimes better than—decisions that are made cautiously and deliberately. Yet they can also be seriously flawed or even dangerously wrong. That's the premise of Malcolm Gladwell's *Blink: The Power of Thinking without Thinking*. Gladwell, a Canadian working in New York City, explores how our "adaptive unconscious" arrives at complex, important decisions in an instant—and how we can train it to make those decisions good ones.

#### SHARPENING YOUR INTUITION
Even when we think our decision making is the result of careful analysis and rational consideration, Gladwell says, most of it actually happens subconsciously in a split second. This process, which he refers to as "rapid cognition," provides room for both amazing insight and grave error. Here are some tips for improving rapid cognition:

• *Remember that more is not better.* Gladwell argues that giving people too much data and information hampers their ability to make good decisions. He cites a study showing that emergency room doctors who are best at diagnosing heart attacks gather less information from their patients than other doctors do. Rather than overloading on information, search out the most meaningful parts.
• *Practise thin-slicing.* The process Gladwell refers to as "thin-slicing" is what harnesses the power of the adaptive unconscious and enables us to make smart decisions with minimal time and information. Thin-slicing means focusing on a thin slice of pertinent data or information

and allowing your intuition to do the work for you. Gladwell cites the example of a Pentagon war game, in which an enemy team of commodities traders defeated a U.S. Army that had "an unprecedented amount of information and intelligence" and "did a thoroughly rational and rigorous analysis that covered every conceivable contingency." The commodities traders were used to making thousands of instant decisions an hour based on limited information. Managers can practise spontaneous decision making until it becomes second nature.

• *Know your limits.* Not every decision should be based on intuition. When you have a depth of knowledge and experience in an area, you can put more trust in your gut feelings. Gladwell also cautions to be aware of biases that interfere with good decision making. *Blink* suggests that we can teach ourselves to sort through first impressions and figure out which are important and which are based on subconscious biases such as stereotypes or emotional baggage.

#### CONCLUSION
*Blink* is filled with lively and interesting anecdotes, such as how firefighters can "slow down a moment" and create an environment where spontaneous decision making can take place. Gladwell asserts that a better understanding of the process of split-second decision making can help people make better decisions in all areas of their lives, as well as help them anticipate and avoid miscalculations.

*Blink: The Power of Thinking without Thinking*, by Malcolm Gladwell, is published by Little, Brown, 2005.

Howard Schultz turned Starbucks into a household name by pursuing his intuition that the leisurely caffeine-and-conversation *caffe* model he observed in Italy would work in the United States, despite market research that indicated Americans would never pay $3 or more for a cup of coffee. Jerry Jones based his decision to buy the losing Dallas Cowboys on intuition, then made a series of further intuitive decisions that turned the team back into a winner. Similarly, the vice president for talent development and casting at MTV relied on intuition to create the show *The Osbournes*. "We never tested the show," he says. "We just knew it would make great TV."[35]

However, there are also many examples of intuitive decisions that turned out to be complete failures.[36] This chapter's Book Mark discusses how managers can give their intuition a better chance of leading to successful decisions.

Managers may walk a fine line between two extremes: on the one hand, making arbitrary decisions without careful study, and on the other, relying obsessively on numbers and rational analysis.[37] Remember that the bounded rationality perspective and the use of intuition apply mostly to nonprogrammed decisions. The novel, unclear, complex aspects of nonprogrammed decisions mean hard data and logical procedures are not available. One study of executive decision making found that managers simply could not use the rational approach for nonprogrammed decisions, such as when to buy a CT (computed tomography) scanner for an osteopathic hospital or whether a city had a need for and could reasonably adopt an enterprise resource planning system.[38] In those cases, managers had limited time and resources, and some factors simply couldn't be measured and analyzed. Trying to quantify such information may cause mistakes because it may oversimplify decision criteria. Intuition can also balance and supplement rational analysis to help organization leaders make better decisions. At Paramount Pictures, a top management team combined intuition and analysis to keep the studio consistently profitable.

*act!*
_____

**Apply**

In what circumstances would you apply intuition to reach a decision? Why?

## In Practice

**Paramount Pictures (Paramount)**

When she was head of Paramount Pictures, Sherry Lansing and her boss, Jonathan Dolgen, head of Viacom Entertainment Group, made a powerful team. Unlike many studios, which lose money despite successful box-office films, Paramount consistently turned a profit every year Lansing and Dolgen were in charge.[39]

As a former independent producer, Lansing relied on her experience and intuition to pick good scripts and the right actors to make them work. Consider 1994's *Forrest Gump*. "It was a film about a guy on a bench," said Lansing. "It was one of the riskiest films ever made." But Lansing's intuition told her that Tom Hanks sitting on a bench talking about life being "like a box of chocolates" would work, and the film reaped $329 million at the box office. Other successes under the leadership of Lansing and Dolgen included *Along Came a Spider, Vanilla Sky*, and *Lara Croft: Tomb Raider*. Dolgen, a former lawyer, provided the analytical side of the partnership. Dolgen's intelligence and careful attention to detail helped Paramount generate consistently good returns. Sometimes, his analysis would suggest that a risk was just not worth taking, even though it meant the studio turned down a potential blockbuster.

Lansing and Dolgen were considered one of the most effective management teams in Hollywood. They combined their natural strengths—one intuitive, the other analytical—to make good decisions that kept Paramount consistently profitable in a difficult, high-risk, unpredictable business. Although Paramount has turned out a string of well-planned, reliable movies, top executives at Viacom pushed the studio to take bigger risks and come up with some box-office blockbusters. Lansing left Paramount and a new leader will try his hand at the business of picking successful movies. Like Lansing, though, he will likely rely largely on intuition. There's no formula for accurately predicting which stories will resonate with today's fickle movie-going audience.[40]

# Organizational Decision Making

Organizations are composed of managers who make decisions using both rational and intuitive processes; but organization-level decisions are not usually made by a single manager. Many organizational decisions involve several managers. Problem identification and problem solution involve many departments, multiple viewpoints, and even other organizations, which are beyond the scope of an individual manager.

The processes by which decisions are made in organizations are influenced by a number of factors, particularly the organization's own internal structures and the degree of stability or instability of the external environment.[41] Research into organization-level decision making has identified four primary types of organizational decision-making processes: the management science approach, the Carnegie model, the incremental decision process model, and the garbage can model.

## ■ Management Science Approach

The **management science approach** to organizational decision making is the analogue to the rational approach by individual managers. Management science came into being during the Second World War.[42] At that time, mathematical and statistical techniques were applied to urgent, large-scale military problems that were beyond the ability of individual decision makers.

Mathematicians, physicists, and operations researchers used systems analysis to develop artillery trajectories, antisubmarine strategies, and bombing strategies such as salvoing (discharging multiple shells simultaneously). Consider the problem of a battleship trying to sink an enemy ship several miles away. The calculation for aiming the battleship's guns should consider distance, wind speed, shell size, speed and direction of both ships, pitch and roll of the firing ship, and curvature of the earth. Methods for performing such calculations using trial and error and intuition are not accurate, take far too long, and may never achieve success.

This is where management science came in. Analysts were able to identify the relevant variables involved in aiming a ship's guns and could model them with the use of mathematical equations. Distance, speed, pitch, roll, shell size, and so on could be calculated and entered into the equations. The answer was immediate, and the guns could begin firing. Factors such as pitch and roll were soon measured mechanically and fed directly into the targeting mechanism. Today, the human element is completely removed from the targeting process. Radar picks up the target, and the entire sequence is computed automatically.

Management science yielded astonishing success for many military problems. This approach to decision making diffused into corporations and business schools, where techniques were studied and elaborated. Today, many corporations have assigned departments to use these techniques. The computer department develops quantitative data for analysis. Operations research departments use mathematical models to quantify relevant variables and develop a quantitative representation of alternative solutions and the probability of each one solving the problem. These departments also use devices such as linear programming, Bayesian statistics, PERT (Program Evaluation and Review Technique) charts, and computer simulations. Management science is an excellent device for organizational decision making when problems are analyzable and when the variables can be identified and measured. Mathematical models can contain a thousand or more variables, each one relevant in some way to the ultimate outcome. Management science techniques have been used to correctly solve problems as diverse as finding the right spot for a church camp, test-marketing the first of a new family of products, drilling for oil, and radically altering the distribution of telecommunications services.[43] Other problems amenable to management science techniques are the scheduling of ambulance technicians, telephone operators, and toll collectors.[44]

**In Practice**

**Algorithms Rule!**

Three professors at the Rotman School of Management, Opher Baron, Oded Berman, and Dimitry Krass, developed a complex algorithm that reduces waiting times for many services from lining up to get a cup of coffee to waiting times for hospital services. The three researchers used a three-pronged approach to the waiting problem by accounting for the regulation of demand, capacity versus waiting time, and the cost versus the number and locations of facilities. The algorithm is dynamic so it can account for variables such as politics, which are hard to quantify.[45]

"Algorithms, they say, are taking over the world. They hold the answers to everything from designing better cars to finding the perfect mate...."[46] While the trio has not commercialized their algorithm, according to Dr. Berman, "That is part of the research game....We may work at a business school but in truth we are researchers and scientists, not business people."[47] Even so, the type of research they do in advanced mathematics is being used in a partnership between McMaster University in Hamilton, Ontario, and the world-renowned Princess Margaret Hospital in Toronto to determine the optimal level of radiation for cancer patients.[48]

"Mathematical models are bound to play a greater role in business and even personal decision making," Dr. Baron predicts.[49] For example, MapQuest uses algorithms to work out optimal routes for drivers.

Management science can accurately and quickly solve problems that have too many explicit variables for human processing. This system is at its best when applied to problems that are analyzable, are measurable, and can be structured in a logical way. Increasingly sophisticated computer technology and software programs are allowing the expansion of management science to cover a broader range of problems than ever before. For example, some retailers, including Home Depot, Hudson's Bay Company, and Club Monaco, now use software to analyze current and historical sales data and determine when, where, and how much to mark down prices. Managers at Harrah's Entertainment have turned the company into one of the hottest operators of casinos by amassing plenty of data about customers and using sophisticated computer systems to make decisions about everything from casino layout to hotel room pricing. Prices quoted for rooms, for instance, are based on a complex mathematical formula that takes into account how long the customers typically stay, what games they play and how often, and other details.[50]

Management science has also produced many failures.[51] Now, many banks use computerized scoring systems to rate those applying for credit, but some argue that human judgment is needed to account for extenuating circumstances.

One problem with the management science approach is that quantitative data are not rich and do not convey tacit knowledge. Informal cues that indicate the existence of problems have to be sensed on a more personal basis by managers.[52] The most sophisticated mathematical analyses are of no value if the important factors cannot be quantified and included in the model. Things such as competitor reactions, consumer tastes, and product warmth are qualitative dimensions. In these situations, the role of management science is to supplement manager decision making. Quantitative results can be given to managers for discussion and interpretation along with their informal opinions, judgment, and intuition. The final decision can include both qualitative factors and quantitative calculations.

## ■ Carnegie Model

The **Carnegie model** of organizational decision making is based on the work of Richard Cyert, James March, and Herbert Simon, who were all associated with Carnegie-Mellon University.[53] Their research helped formulate the bounded rationality approach to individual decision making, as well as provide new insights about organizational decisions.

Until their work, research in economics assumed that business firms made decisions as a single entity, as if all relevant information were funnelled to the top decision maker for a choice. Research by the Carnegie group indicated that organization-level decisions involved many managers and that a final choice was based on a coalition among those managers. A **coalition** is an alliance among several managers who agree about organizational goals and problem priorities.[54] It could include managers from line departments, staff specialists, and even external groups, such as powerful customers, bankers, or union representatives.

Management coalitions are needed during decision making for two reasons. First, organizational goals are often ambiguous, and operative goals of departments are often inconsistent. When goals are ambiguous and inconsistent, managers disagree about problem priorities. They must bargain about problems and build a coalition around the question of which problems to solve.

The second reason for coalitions is that individual managers intend to be rational but function with human cognitive limitations and other constraints, as described earlier. Managers do not have the time, resources, or mental capacity to identify all dimensions and to process all information relevant to a decision. These limitations lead to coalition-building behaviour. Managers talk to each other and exchange points of view to gather information and reduce ambiguity. People who have relevant information or a stake in a decision outcome are consulted. Building a coalition will lead to a decision that is supported by interested parties. As Exhibit 11.3 shows, decision-making processes are often politicized!

**EXHIBIT 11.3**
Politicized Decision Making
Source: DILBERT © 2007 Scott Adams. Used By permission of UNIVERSAL UCLICK. All rights reserved.

The process of coalition formation has several implications for organizational decision behaviour. First, decisions are made to *satisfice* rather than to optimize problem solutions. **Satisficing** means organizations accept a satisfactory rather than a maximum level of performance, enabling them to achieve several goals simultaneously. In decision making, the coalition will accept a solution that is perceived as satisfactory to all coalition members. Second, managers are concerned with immediate problems and short-run solutions. They engage in what Cyert and March called *problemistic search*.[55]

**Problemistic search** means managers look around in the immediate environment for a solution to quickly resolve a problem. Managers don't expect a perfect solution when the situation is ill defined and conflict laden. This contrasts with the management science approach, which assumes that analysis can uncover every reasonable alternative. The Carnegie model says that search behaviour is sufficient to produce a satisfactory solution and that managers typically adopt the first satisfactory solution that emerges.

Discussion and bargaining are especially important in the problem identification stage of decision making. Unless coalition members perceive a problem, action will not be taken.

The decision process described in the Carnegie model is summarized in Exhibit 11.4. The Carnegie model points out that building agreement through a managerial coalition is a major part of organizational decision making. This is especially true at upper management levels. Discussion and bargaining are time consuming, so search procedures are usually simple and the selected alternative satisfices rather than optimizes problem solution. When problems are programmed—are clear and have been seen before—the organization will rely on previous procedures and routines. Rules and procedures prevent the need for renewed coalition formation and political bargaining. Nonprogrammed decisions, however, require bargaining and conflict resolution.

Organizations suffer when managers are unable to build a coalition around goals and problem priorities, as illustrated by the case of Encyclopaedia Britannica.

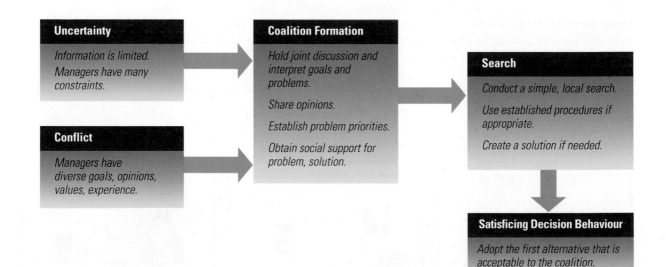

**EXHIBIT 11.4**
Choice Processes in the Carnegie Model

For most of its 231-year history, the *Encyclopaedia Britannica* had been viewed as an illustrious repository of cultural and historical knowledge—almost a national treasure. Generations of students and librarians relied on the *Britannica*—but that was before the Internet became the study tool of choice. Suddenly, the 32-volume collection of encyclopedias, stretching four feet on a bookshelf and costing as much as a personal computer, seemed destined to fade into history.

When Swiss-based financier Joseph Safra bought Britannica, he discovered one of the reasons. For nearly a decade, managers had bickered over goals and priorities. Some top executives believed the company needed to invest more in electronic media, but others supported Britannica's traditional direct-to-home sales force. Eventually, the company's Compton unit, a CD-ROM pioneer was sold, leaving Britannica without any presence in the new market. In the 1980s, Microsoft had approached Britannica to develop a CD-ROM encyclopedia; when it didn't work out, Microsoft went with Funk & Wagnalls and developed Encarta. Microsoft arranged to have Encarta preinstalled on PCs, so the CD-ROM was essentially free to new PC buyers. When Britannica finally came out with its CD-ROM version, however, it was priced at a staggering $1,200. The squabbling among managers, owners, and editors about product development, pricing, distribution, and other important decisions contributed to the company's decline.

The first step in Safra's turnaround strategy was to install a new top management team, led by one of his long-time advisers. The team immediately coalesced around the important problem of establishing a presence in the world of electronic media. With this goal, the company rushed out a revamped, lower-cost CD-ROM package and launched the Britannica.com website, which allows users to view encyclopedia entries online as well as get a list of links to related websites. The team also created a separate digital media division to focus on new product development, such as for wireless Web technology. Managers are looking toward the wireless Web as the best route to a successful future and have teamed up with numerous wireless carriers and licensed Britannica's content to other websites.

Building a coalition focused on common goals rather than having managers pushing and pulling in different directions got Britannica off the critical list by helping it cross the bridge to the digital era. Managers are in the process of evaluation to see what new decisions need to be made to help the company thrive in the digital world.[56]

The Carnegie model is particularly useful at the problem identification stage. However, a coalition of key department managers is also important for smooth implementation of a decision, particularly a major reorganization. Top executives at Britannica realized the importance of building coalitions for decision making to keep the company moving forward. When top managers perceive a problem or want to make a major decision, they need to reach agreement with other managers to support the decision.[57]

## ■ Incremental Decision Process Model

Henry Mintzberg and his colleagues at McGill University approached organizational decision making from a different perspective. They identified 25 decisions made in organizations and traced the events associated with these decisions from beginning to end.[58] Their research identified each step in the decision sequence. This approach to decision making, called the **incremental decision process model**, places less emphasis on the political and social factors described in the Carnegie model, but tells more about the structured sequence of activities undertaken from the discovery of a problem to its solution.[59]

Sample decisions in Mintzberg's research included choosing which aircraft to acquire for a regional airline, developing a new supper club, developing a new container terminal in a harbour, identifying a new market for a deodorant, installing a controversial new medical treatment in a hospital, and firing a star radio announcer.[60] The scope and importance of these decisions are revealed in the length of time taken to complete them. Most of these decisions took more than a year, and one-third of them took more than two years. Most of these decisions were nonprogrammed and required custom-designed solutions.

One discovery from this research is that major organizational choices are usually a series of small choices that combine to produce the major decision. Thus, many organizational decisions are a series of nibbles rather than a big bite. Organizations move through several decision points and may hit barriers along the way. Mintzberg called these barriers *decision interrupts*. An interrupt may mean an organization has to cycle back through a previous decision and try something new. Decision loops or cycles are one way the organization learns which alternatives will work. The ultimate solution may be very different from what was initially anticipated.

The pattern of decision stages discovered by Mintzberg and his associates is shown in Exhibit 11.5. Each box indicates a possible step in the decision sequence. The steps take place in three major decision phases: identification, development, and selection.

**Identification Phase.** The identification phase begins with *recognition*. Recognition means one or more managers become aware of a problem and the need to make a decision. Recognition is usually stimulated by a problem or an opportunity. A problem exists when elements in the external environment change or when internal performance is perceived to be below standard. In the case of firing a radio announcer, comments about the announcer came from listeners, other announcers, and advertisers. Managers interpreted these cues until a pattern emerged that indicated a problem had to be addressed.

The second step is *diagnosis*, in which more information is gathered if needed to define the problem situation. Diagnosis may be systematic or informal, depending upon the severity of the problem. Severe problems do not allow time for extensive diagnosis; the response must be immediate. Mild problems are usually diagnosed in a more systematic manner.

**Development Phase.** In the development phase, a solution is shaped to solve the problem defined in the identification phase. The development of a solution takes one of two directions. First, *search* procedures may be used to seek out alternatives within the organization's repertoire of solutions. For example, in the case of firing a star announcer, managers asked what the radio station had done the last time an announcer had to be let go. To conduct the search, organization participants may look into their own memories, talk to other managers, or examine the formal procedures of the organization. The screen routine is used when search is expected to generate more ready-made alternatives than can be practically evaluated. Screening "is a superficial routine, more concerned with eliminating what is infeasible than with defining what is appropriate."[61]

The second direction of development is to *design* a custom solution. This happens when the problem is novel so that previous experience has no value. Mintzberg found that in these cases, key decision makers have only a vague idea of the ideal solution. Gradually, through a trial-and-error screening process, a custom-designed alternative will emerge. Development of the solution is a groping, incremental procedure, like building a house brick by brick.

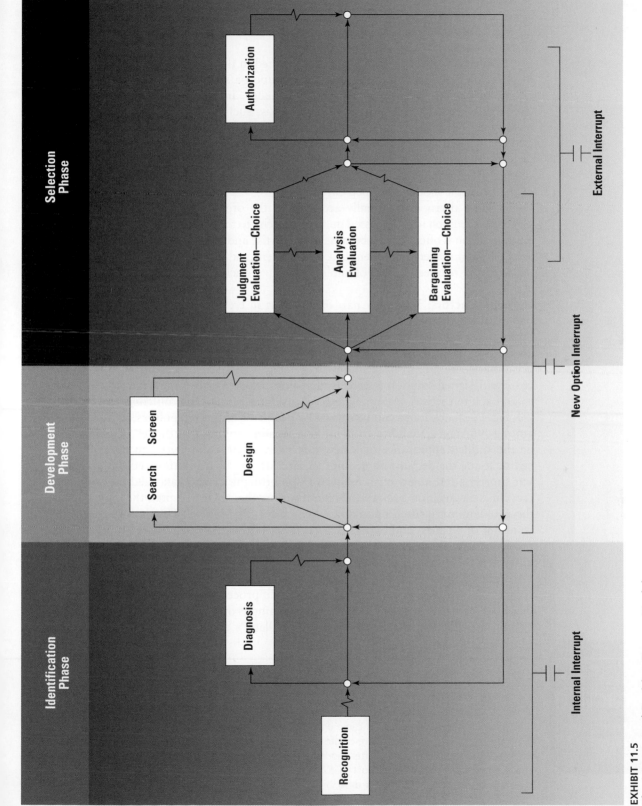

**EXHIBIT 11.5**

## The Incremental Decision Process Model

Adapted and reprinted from "The Structure of Unstructured Decision Processes," by Henry Mintzberg, Duru Raisinghani, and Andre Theorêt, published in *Administrative Science Quarterly* 21, no. 2 (1976), 266, by permission of *The Administrative Science Quarterly*. Copyright © 1976 Cornell University.

**Selection Phase.** The selection phase is when the solution is chosen. This phase is not always a matter of making a clear choice among alternatives. In the case of custom-made solutions, selection is more an evaluation of the single alternative that seems feasible.

Evaluation and choice may be accomplished in three ways. The *judgment* form of selection is used when a final choice falls upon a single decision maker, and the choice involves judgment based upon experience. In *analysis evaluation*, alternatives are evaluated on a more systematic basis, such as with management science techniques. Mintzberg found that most decisions did not involve systematic analysis and evaluation of alternatives. *Bargaining* occurs when selection involves a group of decision makers. Each decision maker may have a different stake in the outcome, so conflict emerges. Discussion and bargaining occur until a coalition is formed, as in the Carnegie model described earlier.

When a decision is formally accepted by the organization, *authorization* takes place. The decision may be passed up the hierarchy to the responsible hierarchical level. Authorization is often routine because the expertise and knowledge rest with the lower-level decision makers who identified the problem and developed the solution. A few decisions are rejected because of implications not anticipated by lower-level managers.

**Dynamic Factors.** The lower part of the chart in Exhibit 11.5 shows lines running back toward the beginning of the decision process. These lines represent loops or cycles that take place in the decision process. Organizational decisions do not follow an orderly progression from recognition through authorization. Minor problems arise that force a loop back to an earlier stage. These are decision interrupts. If a custom-designed solution is perceived as unsatisfactory, the organization may have to go back to the very beginning and reconsider whether the problem is truly worth solving. Feedback loops can be caused by problems of timing, politics, disagreement among managers, inability to identify a feasible solution, turnover of managers, or the sudden appearance of a new alternative. For example, when a small local airline made the decision to acquire jet aircraft, the board authorized the decision, but shortly after, a new chief executive was brought in who cancelled the contract, recycling the decision back to the identification phase. He accepted the diagnosis of the problem but insisted upon a new search for alternatives. Then a foreign airline went out of business and two used aircraft became available at a bargain price. This presented an unexpected option, and the chief executive used his own judgment to authorize the purchase of the aircraft.[62]

Because most decisions take place over an extended period of time, circumstances change. Decision making is a dynamic process that may require a number of cycles before a problem is solved. An example of the incremental process and cycling that can take place is illustrated in Gillette's decision to create a new razor.

## In Practice
### Gillette Company

The Gillette Company uses incremental decision making to perfect the design of razors such as the Sensor, the Mach3, and the vibrating M3Power. Consider the development of the Mach3. While searching for a new idea to increase sales in Gillette's mature shaving market, researchers at the company's British research lab came up with a bright idea to create a razor with three blades to produce a closer, smoother, more comfortable shave (recognition and diagnosis). Ten years later, the Mach3 reached the market, after thousands of shaving tests, numerous design modifications, and a development and tooling cost of $750 million, roughly the amount a pharmaceutical firm invests in developing a blockbuster drug.

The technical demands of building a razor with three blades that would follow a man's face and also be easy to clean had several blind alleys. Engineers first tried to find established techniques (search, screen), but none fit the bill. Eventually a prototype called Manx was built (design), and in shaving tests it "beat the pants off" Gillette's Sensor Excel, the company's best-selling razor at the time. However, Gillette's CEO insisted that the razor had to have a radically new blade edge so the razor could use thinner blades (internal interrupt), so engineers began looking for new technology that could produce a stronger blade (search, screen). Eventually, the new edge, known as DLC for diamond-like carbon coating, would be applied atom by atom with chip-making technology (design).

The next problem was manufacturing (diagnosis), which required an entirely new process to handle the complexity of the triple-bladed razor (design). Although the board gave the go-ahead to develop manufacturing equipment (judgment, authorization), some members became concerned because the new blades, which are three times stronger than stainless steel, would last longer and cause Gillette to sell fewer cartridges (internal interrupt). The board eventually made the decision to continue with the new blades, which have a blue indicator strip that fades to white and signals when it's time for a new cartridge.

The board gave final approval for production of the Mach3 to begin in the fall of 1997. The new razor was introduced in the summer of 1998 and began smoothly sliding off shelves. Gillette recovered its huge investment in record time. Gillette then started the process of searching for the next shaving breakthrough all over again, using new technology that can examine a razor blade at the atomic level and high-speed video that can capture the act of cutting a single whisker. The company has moved ahead in increments; in 2006, Gillette launched its Fusion Power line of razors, which took eight years of innovation to develop. The line has 20 patented features.[63]

At Gillette, the identification phase occurred because executives were aware of the need for a new razor and became alert to the idea of using three blades to produce a closer shave. The development phase was characterized by the trial-and-error custom design leading to the Mach3. During the selection phase, certain approaches were found to be unacceptable, causing Gillette to cycle back and redesign the razor, including using thinner, stronger blades. Advancing once again to the selection phase, the Mach3 passed the judgment of top executives and board members, and manufacturing and marketing budgets were quickly authorized. This decision took more than a decade, finally reaching completion in the summer of 1998.

# The Learning Organization

At the beginning of this chapter, we discussed how the rapidly changing external business environment is creating greater uncertainty for decision makers. Some organizations that are particularly affected by this trend are shifting to the learning organization concept. These organizations are marked by a tremendous amount of uncertainty at both the problem identification and problem solution stages. Two approaches to decision making have evolved to help managers cope with this uncertainty and complexity. One approach is to combine the Carnegie and incremental process models just described. The second is a unique approach called the garbage can model.

## Combining the Incremental Process and Carnegie Models

The Carnegie description of coalition building is especially relevant for the problem identification stage. When issues are ambiguous, or if managers disagree about

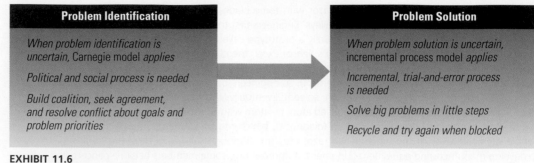

**EXHIBIT 11.6**
Decision Process When Problem Identification and Problem Solution Are Uncertain

problem severity, discussion, negotiation, and coalition building are needed. Once agreement is reached about the problem to be tackled, the organization can move toward a solution.

The incremental process model tends to emphasize the steps used to reach a solution. After managers agree on a problem, the step-by-step process is a way of trying various solutions to see what will work. When problem solution is unclear, a trial-and-error solution may be designed. For example, in 1999, executives from three of the world's largest music companies formed a coalition to provide online consumers with a legal alternative to the digital piracy of Internet song-swapping services. However, making the joint venture MusicNet an appealing choice was a challenge. As originally conceived, the service didn't provide music lovers with the features they wanted, so managers took an incremental approach to try to make MusicNet more user-friendly by enabling customized downloads and subscription services distributed through providers such as Yahoo!, AOL, and Virgin Digital. As one executive put it, "This is a business of trial and error."[64] Managers continued to use an incremental approach as the industry evolved with the development of Apple's iTunes and other new distribution channels. In 2007, MusicNet expanded its content and changed its name to MediaNet Digital. The MN Open platform allows customers to add music and media content to their websites or applications easily and quickly.[65]

The incremental process and Carnegie models do not disagree with one another. They describe how organizations make decisions when either problem identification or solution is uncertain. The application of these two models to the stages in the decision process is illustrated in Exhibit 11.6. When both parts of the decision process are simultaneously highly uncertain, which is often the case in learning organizations, the organization is in an extremely difficult position. Decision processes in that situation may be a combination of Carnegie and incremental process models, and this combination may evolve into a situation described in the garbage can model. The following In Practice highlights how Bombardier used a combination decision-making approach as it recovered from the shocking events of September 11, 2001.

## In Practice
### Bombardier Inc.

The events of September 11, 2001, had a significant impact on Bombardier and other plane manufacturers, That same year, Bombardier expanded considerably through acquisitions in its rail and recreational groups. According to Pierre Beaudoin, CEO since 2008, "...[as a result,] a lot of the rocks came to the surface in terms of Bombardier's capabilities and structure." He notes that "...in 2001, we had an organization that was very proud of being number one...But when we talked to our customers, they were saying we weren't very good."[66]

Beaudoin and his leadership team soon realized that the company's managers, while acknowledging that there were problems, insisted that the problems were not in their departments. They surveyed their employees and the employees observed that the company focused too much on hardware. Based on the survey results and on observing the managers, Beaudoin realized that Bombardier would need to move beyond particular fixes and needed to get to the core of the company. As Beaudoin put it, "[We] needed employees to understand we were flying people, not planes."[67] Beaudoin then made the decision to focus on culture to transform Bombardier.

Beaudoin indentified identified three priorities—creating a rewarding and safe workplace, providing excellent customer service, and reducing waste—and then asked Bombardier's top leaders how they would realize the priorities. One of the many challenges that Beaudoin faced was employees wondering why he had decided to focus on "soft" issues such as creating a rewarding workplace. However, Beaudoin also emphasized that "hard" goals needed to be met, for example a $500 million performance improvement gain. Bombardier has enjoyed a financial performance above analysts' expectations. In the three months ending January 2011, Bombardier's income was $325 million; analysts commented that "the results…signalled strong opportunities for a turnaround"[68]

## ◼ Garbage Can Model

The **garbage can model** is one of the interesting descriptions of organizational decision processes. It is not directly comparable to the earlier models, because the garbage can model deals with the pattern or flow of multiple decisions within organizations, whereas the incremental and Carnegie models focus on how a single decision is made. The garbage can model helps managers think of the whole organization and the frequent decisions being made by managers throughout.

**Organized Anarchy.** The garbage can model was developed to explain the pattern of decision making in organizations that experience extremely high uncertainty, such as the growth and change required in a learning organization. Michael Cohen, James March, and Johan Olsen, the originators of the model, called the highly uncertain conditions an **organized anarchy**, which describes an extremely organic organization.[69] Organized anarchies do not rely on the normal vertical hierarchy of authority and bureaucratic decision rules. They result from three characteristics:

1. *Problematic preferences.* Goals, problems, alternatives, and solutions are ill defined. Ambiguity characterizes each step of a decision process.
2. *Unclear, poorly understood technology.* Cause-and-effect relationships within the organization are difficult to identify. An explicit database that applies to decisions is not available.
3. *Turnover.* Organizational positions experience turnover of participants. In addition, employees are busy and have only limited time to allocate to any one problem or decision. Participation in any given decision will be fluid and limited.

An organized anarchy is characterized by rapid change and a collegial, nonbureaucratic environment. No organization fits this extremely organic circumstance all the time, although learning organizations and today's Internet-based companies may experience it much of the time. Many organizations will occasionally find themselves in positions of making decisions under unclear, problematic circumstances. The garbage can model is very useful for understanding the pattern of these decisions.

**Compare**

Compare the decision-making models presented so far. What other similarities do you observe?

**Streams of Events.** The unique characteristic of the garbage can model is that the decision process is not seen as a sequence of steps that begins with a problem and ends with a solution. Indeed, problem identification and problem solution may not be connected to each other. An idea may be proposed as a solution when no problem is specified. A problem may exist and never generate a solution. Decisions are the outcome of independent streams of events within the organization. The four streams relevant to organizational decision making are as follows:

1. *Problems*. Problems are points of dissatisfaction with current activities and performance. They represent a gap between desired performance and current activities. Problems are perceived to require attention. However, they are distinct from solutions and choices. A problem may lead to a proposed solution or it may not. Problems may not be solved when solutions are adopted.

2. *Potential solutions*. A solution is an idea somebody proposes for adoption. Such ideas form a flow of alternative solutions through the organization. Ideas may be brought into the organization by new personnel or may be invented by existing personnel. Participants may simply be attracted to certain ideas and push them as logical choices regardless of problems. Attraction to an idea may cause an employee to look for a problem to which the idea can be attached and, hence, justified. The point is that solutions exist independent of problems.

3. *Participants*. Organization participants are employees who come and go throughout the organization. People are hired, reassigned, and fired. Participants vary widely in their ideas, perception of problems, experience, values, and training. The problems and solutions recognized by one manager will differ from those recognized by another manager.

4. *Choice opportunities*. Choice opportunities are occasions when an organization usually makes a decision. They occur when contracts are signed, people are hired, or a new product is authorized. They also occur when the right mix of participants, solutions, and problems exists. Thus, a manager who happened to learn of a good idea may suddenly become aware of a problem to which it applies and, hence, can provide the organization with a choice opportunity. Match-ups of problems and solutions often result in decisions.

With the concept of four streams, the overall pattern of organizational decision making takes on a random quality. Problems, solutions, participants, and choices all flow through the organization. In one sense, the organization is a large garbage can in which these streams are being stirred, as illustrated in Exhibit 11.7. When a problem, solution, and participant happen to connect at one point, a decision may be made and the problem may be solved; however, if the solution does not fit the problem, the problem may not be solved.

Thus, when viewing the organization as a whole and considering its high level of uncertainty, you can see problems arise that are not solved and solutions tried that do not work. Organization decisions are disorderly and not the result of a logical, step-by-step sequence. Events may be so ill defined and complex that decisions, problems, and solutions act as independent events. When they connect, some problems are solved, but many are not.[70] One study of 2,476 white-collar workers in 21 Japanese companies, using a computer simulation, found some support for the garbage can model and underscored the usefulness of the model in saving time in decision making.[71]

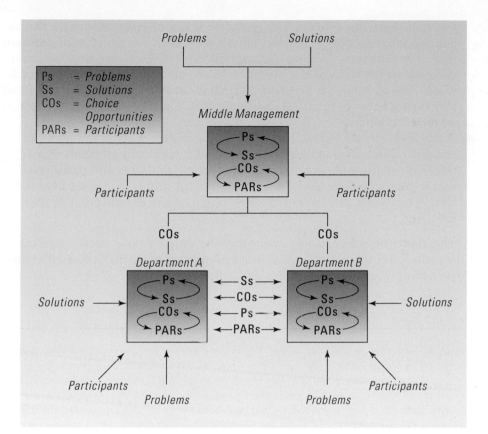

**EXHIBIT 11.7**
Illustration of
Independent Streams
of Events in the
Garbage Can Model
of Decision Making

**Consequences.** There are four specific consequences of the garbage can decision process for organizational decision making:

1. *Solutions may be proposed even when problems do not exist.* An employee might be sold on an idea and might try to sell it to the rest of the organization. An example was the adoption of computers by many organizations during the 1970s. The computer was an exciting solution and was pushed by both computer manufacturers and systems analysts within organizations. The computer did not solve any problems in those initial applications. Indeed, some computers caused more problems than they solved.

2. *Choices are made without solving problems.* A choice such as creating a new department may be made with the intention of solving a problem; but, under conditions of high uncertainty, the choice may be incorrect. Moreover, many choices just seem to happen. People decide to quit, the organization's budget is cut, or a new policy bulletin is issued. These choices may be oriented toward problems but do not necessarily solve them.

3. *Problems may persist without being solved.* Organization participants get used to certain problems and give up trying to solve them, or participants may not know how to solve certain problems because the technology is unclear. For example, a Canadian university was placed on probation by the American Association of University Professors because a professor had been denied

tenure without due process. The probation was a nagging annoyance that the administrators wanted to remove. Fifteen years later, the nontenured professor died. The probation continues because the university did not acquiesce to the demands of the heirs of the professor to reevaluate the case. The university would like to solve the problem, but administrators are not sure how, and they do not have the resources to allocate to it. The probation problem persists without a solution.

4. *A few problems are solved*. The decision process does work in the aggregate. In computer simulations of the garbage can model, important problems were often resolved. Solutions do connect with appropriate problems and participants so that a good choice is made. Of course, not all problems are resolved when choices are made, but the organization does move in the direction of problem reduction.

The effects of independent streams and the rather chaotic decision processes of the garbage can model can be seen in the production of David O. Russell's movie *I ♥Huckabees*, which has been called an "existential comedy."

## In Practice
### I ♥ Huckabees

Screenwriter and director David O. Russell has become known for creating intelligent, original movies such as *Flirting with Disaster* and *Three Kings*. His 2004 film *I ♥ Huckabees* might be the most original—or some would say just plain weirdest—so far. *The New York Times* noted that the film "will probably drive some audiences bonkers. Loud, messy, aggressively in your face and generally played for the back row in the theater, the film doesn't offer up solutions, tender any comfort or rejoice in the triumph of the human spirit." Yet the movie got decent critical reviews and was picked by the *Village Voice* as one of the best films of 2004.[72]

Russell had a vision of what he wanted the movie to be from the beginning, but few others could grasp what that was. Most of the actors who signed on to star in *I ♥ Huckabees* admit that they didn't really understand the script, but trusted Russell's vision and imagination. Two of the biggest actors in Hollywood, Jude Law and Gwyneth Paltrow, signed on to play employees at a department store chain called Huckabees. But Paltrow backed out before filming ever started. Nicole Kidman was interested but had a conflict. Jennifer Aniston became—and as quickly unbecame—a possibility. Finally, Naomi Watts, who had been Russell's original choice for the role, was able to free herself from scheduling conflicts to take the part. The casting wasn't quite set though. Jude Law dropped out for unknown reasons—but just as quickly dropped back in.

Filming was chaotic. As the actors were on camera saying the lines they'd memorized, Russell was a few feet away continually calling out new lines to them. In one scene, Law became so exhausted and frustrated that he started pounding his fists in the grass and shouting expletives. Russell loved the improvisation and kept the cameras rolling. Actors were unsure of how to develop their characterizations, so they just did whatever seemed right at the time, often based on Russell's efforts to keep them off balance. Scenes were often filmed blindly with no idea of how they were supposed to fit in the overall story.

After Russell's hours in the editing room, the final film turned out to be quite different from what the actors thought they'd shot. Some major scenes, including one that was supposed to articulate the film's theme that everything is connected, were cut entirely.

Amazingly, considering the chaos on the set, the film was completed on schedule and on budget. Although *I ♥ Huckabees* is emotionally and intellectually dense, and not the kind of movie that reaps big bucks, the haphazard process worked to create the movie David O. Russell wanted to make.[73]

The production of *I ♥ Huckabees* was not a rational process that started with a clear problem and ended with a logical solution. Many events occurred by chance and were intertwined, which characterizes the garbage can model. Everyone from the director to the actors continuously added to the stream of new ideas for the story. Some solutions were connected to emerging problems: Naomi Watts cleared her schedule just in time to take the role after Gwyneth Paltrow dropped out, for example. The actors (participants) daily made personal choices regarding characterization that proved to be right for the story line. The garbage can model, however, doesn't always work—in the movies or in organizations. A similar haphazard process during the filming of *Waterworld* led to the most expensive film in Hollywood history and a decided box-office flop for Universal Pictures.[74]

**Think**

Think about a decision-making situation in which you played a significant role. How did you reach a solution and how would you classify your solution?

# Contingency Decision-Making Framework

This chapter has covered several approaches to organizational decision making, including management science, the Carnegie model, the incremental decision process model, and the garbage can model. It has also discussed rational and intuitive decision processes used by individual managers. Each decision approach is a relatively accurate description of the actual decision process, yet all differ from each other. Management science, for example, reflects a different set of decision assumptions and procedures than does the garbage can model.

One reason for having different approaches is that they appear in different organizational situations. The use of an approach is contingent on the organization setting. Two characteristics of organizations that determine the use of decision approaches are (1) problem consensus and (2) technical knowledge about the means to solve those problems.[75] Analyzing organizations along these two dimensions suggests which approach will be used to make decisions.

## ■ Problem Consensus

**Problem consensus** refers to the agreement among managers about the nature of a problem or opportunity and about which goals and outcomes to pursue. This variable ranges from complete agreement to complete disagreement. When managers agree, there is little uncertainty—the problems and goals of the organization are clear, and so are standards of performance. When managers disagree, organization direction and performance expectations are in dispute, creating a situation of high uncertainty. One example of problem uncertainty occurred at Walmart stores regarding the use of parking lot patrols. Some managers presented evidence that golf-cart patrols significantly reduced auto theft, assault, and other crimes in the stores' lots and increased business because they encouraged more shopping at night. These managers argued that the patrols should be used, but others believed the patrols were not needed and were too expensive, emphasizing that parking lot crime was a society problem rather than a store problem.[76]

Problem consensus tends to be low when organizations are differentiated, as described in Chapter 4. Recall that uncertain environments cause organizational departments to differentiate from one another in goals and attitudes to specialize in specific environmental sectors. This differentiation leads to disagreement and conflict, so managers must make a special effort to build coalitions during decision making. For example, NASA has been criticized for failing to identify problems with the *Columbia* space shuttle that might have prevented the February 2003 disaster. Part of the reason was high differentiation and conflicting opinions between safety managers and scheduling managers, in which pressure to launch on time overrode safety concerns. In addition, after the launch, engineers three times requested—and were denied—better photos to assess the damage from a piece of foam debris that struck the shuttle's left wing just seconds after launch. Investigations now indicate that the damage caused by the debris may have been the primary physical cause of the explosion. Mechanisms for hearing dissenting opinions and building coalitions can improve decision making at NASA and other organizations dealing with complex problems.[77]

Problem consensus is especially important for the problem identification stage of decision making. When problems are clear and agreed on, they provide clear standards and expectations for performance. When problems are not agreed on, problem identification is uncertain and management attention must be focused on gaining agreement about goals and priorities.

## ■ Technical Knowledge About Solutions

**Technical knowledge** refers to understanding and agreement about how to solve problems and reach organizational goals. This variable can range from complete agreement and certainty to complete disagreement and uncertainty about cause–effect relationships leading to problem solution. One example of low technical knowledge occurred at PepsiCo's 7Up division. Managers agreed on the problem to be solved—they wanted to increase market share from six to seven percent. However, the means for achieving this increase in market share were not known or agreed on. A few managers wanted to use discount pricing in supermarkets. Other managers believed they should increase the number of soda fountain outlets in restaurants and fast-food chains. A few other managers insisted that the best approach was to increase advertising through radio and television. Managers did not know what would cause an increase in market share. Eventually, the advertising judgment prevailed at 7Up, but it did not work very well. The failure of its decision reflected the managers' low technical knowledge about how to solve the problem.

When means (methods) are well understood, the appropriate alternatives can be identified and calculated with some degree of certainty. When means are poorly understood, potential solutions are ill defined and uncertain. Intuition, judgment, and trial and error become the basis for decisions.

## ■ Contingency Framework

Exhibit 11.8 describes the **contingency decision-making framework**, which brings together the two dimensions of problem consensus and technical knowledge about solutions. Each cell represents an organizational situation that is appropriate for the decision-making approaches described in this chapter.

**Cell 1.** In cell 1 of Exhibit 11.8, rational decision procedures are used because problems are agreed on and cause–effect relationships are well understood, so there is little uncertainty. Decisions can be made in a computational manner. Alternatives can be identified and the best solution adopted through analysis and calculations. The rational models described earlier in this chapter, both for individuals and for organizations, are appropriate when problems and the means for solving them are well defined.

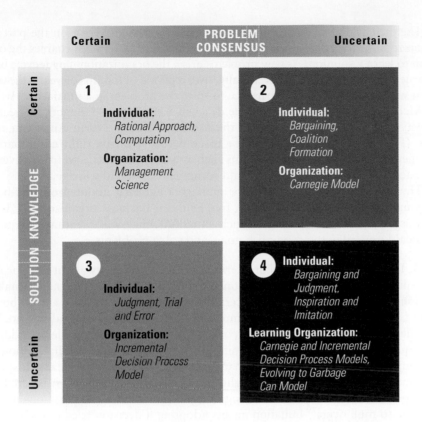

**EXHIBIT 11.8**
Contingency Framework for Using Decision Models

**Cell 2.** In cell 2, there is high uncertainty about problems and priorities, so bargaining and compromise are used to reach consensus. Tackling one problem might mean the organization must postpone action on other issues. The priorities given to problems are decided through discussion, debate, and coalition building.

Managers in this situation should use broad participation to achieve consensus in the decision process. Opinions should be surfaced and discussed until compromise is reached. The organization will not otherwise move forward as an integrated unit. In the case of Walmart, managers discussed conflicting opinions about the benefits and costs of parking lot patrols.

The Carnegie model applies when there is dissension about organizational problems. When groups within the organization disagree, or when the organization is in conflict with constituencies (such as government regulators, suppliers, unions), bargaining and negotiation are required. The bargaining strategy is especially relevant to the problem identification stage of the decision process. Once bargaining and negotiation are completed, the organization will have support for one direction.

**Cell 3.** In a cell 3 situation, problems and standards of performance are certain, but alternative technical solutions are vague and uncertain. Techniques to solve a problem are ill defined and poorly understood. When an individual manager faces this situation, intuition will be the decision guideline. The manager will rely on past experience and judgment to make a decision. Rational, analytical approaches are not effective because the alternatives cannot be identified and calculated. Hard facts and accurate information are not available.

The incremental decision process model reflects trial and error on the part of the organization. Once a problem is identified, a sequence of small steps enables the organization to learn a solution. As new problems arise, the organization may recycle back to an earlier point and start over. Eventually, over a period of months or years, the organization will acquire sufficient experience to solve the problem in a satisfactory way.

McDonald's provides an example of a cell 3 situation. Managers are searching for ways to revive flagging sales at the fast-food chain's North American restaurants. They are using trial and error to come up with the right combination of management changes, new menu items such as assorted salads, and fresh advertising approaches that will rekindle sales and recharge McDonald's image.[78]

The situation in cell 3, of senior managers agreeing about problems but not knowing how to solve them, occurs frequently in business organizations. If managers use incremental decisions in such situations, they will eventually acquire the technical knowledge to accomplish goals and solve problems.

**Cell 4.** The situation in cell 4, characterized by high uncertainty about both problems and solutions, is difficult for decision making. An individual manager making a decision under this high level of uncertainty can employ techniques from both cell 2 and cell 3. The manager can attempt to build a coalition to establish goals and priorities and use judgment, intuition, or trial and error to solve problems. Additional techniques, such as inspiration and imitation, also may be required. **Inspiration** refers to an innovative, creative solution that is not reached by logical means. Inspiration sometimes comes like a flash of insight, but—similar to intuition—it is often based on deep knowledge and understanding of a problem that the unconscious mind has had time to mull over.[79] **Imitation** means adopting a decision tried elsewhere in the hope that it will work in this situation.

For example, in one university, accounting department faculty were unhappy with their current circumstances but could not decide on the direction the department should take. Some faculty members wanted a greater research orientation, whereas others wanted greater orientation toward business firms and accounting applications. The disagreement about goals was compounded because neither group was sure about the best technique for achieving its goals. The ultimate solution was inspirational on the part of the dean. An accounting research centre was established with funding from major accounting firms. The funding was used to finance research activities for faculty interested in basic research and to provide contact with business firms for other faculty. The solution provided a common goal and unified people within the department to work toward that goal.

When an entire organization is characterized by high uncertainty regarding both problems and solutions, as in learning organizations, elements of the garbage can model will appear. Managers may first try techniques from both cells 2 and 3, but logical decision sequences starting with problem identification and ending with problem solution will not occur. Potential solutions will precede problems as often as problems precede solutions. In this situation, managers should encourage widespread discussion of problems and idea proposals to facilitate the opportunity to make choices. Eventually, through trial and error, the organization will solve some problems.

Research has found that decisions made following the guidelines of the contingency decision-making framework tend to be more successful; the study noted that nearly six of ten strategic management decisions failed to follow the framework, leading to a situation in which misleading or missing information decreased the chance of an effective decision choice.[80]

# Special Decision Circumstances

In a highly competitive world beset by global competition and rapid change, decision making seldom fits the traditional rational, analytical model. Today's managers have to make high-stakes decisions more often and more quickly than ever before in an environment that is increasingly less predictable. For example, interviews with CEOs in high-tech industries found that they strive to use some type of rational process, but the uncertainty and change in the industry often make that approach unsuccessful. These managers actually reach decisions through a complex process of interacting with other managers, subordinates, environmental factors, and organizational events.[81]

Three issues of particular concern for today's decision makers are coping with high-velocity environments, learning from decision mistakes, and avoiding escalating commitment.

## High-Velocity Environments

In some industries today, the rate of competitive and technological change is so extreme that market data are either unavailable or obsolete; strategic windows open and shut quickly, perhaps within a few months; and the cost of poor decisions is company failure. Research has examined how successful companies make decisions in these **high-velocity environments**, especially to understand whether organizations abandon rational approaches or have time for incremental implementation.[82]

A comparison of successful with unsuccessful decisions in high-velocity environments found the following patterns:

- Successful decision makers tracked information in real time to develop a deep and intuitive grasp of the business. Two to three intense meetings per week with all key players were usual. Decision makers tracked operating statistics about cash, scrap, backlog, work in process, and shipments to constantly feel the pulse of what was happening. Unsuccessful firms were more concerned with future planning and forward-looking information, with only a loose grip on immediate happenings.
- During a major decision, successful companies began immediately to build multiple alternatives. Implementation of alternatives sometimes ran in parallel before management finally settled on a final choice. Companies that made decisions slowly developed just one alternative, moving to another only after the first one failed.
- Fast, successful decision makers sought advice from everyone and depended heavily on one or two savvy, trusted colleagues as counsellors. Slow companies were unable to build trust and agreement among the best people.
- Fast companies involved everyone in the decision and tried for consensus; but if consensus did not emerge, the top manager made the choice and moved ahead. Waiting for everyone to be on board created more delays than was warranted. Slow companies delayed decisions to achieve a uniform consensus.
- Fast, successful choices were well integrated with other decisions and the overall strategic direction of the company. Less successful choices considered the decision in isolation from other decisions; the decision was made in the abstract.[83]

When speed matters, a slow decision is as ineffective as the wrong decision. As we discussed in Chapter 10, speed is a crucial competitive weapon in a growing number of industries, and companies can learn to make decisions quickly. To improve the chances of a good decision under high-velocity conditions, some organizations stimulate constructive conflict through a technique called **point-counterpoint**, which divides decision makers into two groups and assigns them different, often competing, responsibilities.[84] The groups develop and exchange proposals and debate options until they arrive at a common set of understandings and recommendations. Groups can often make better decisions because multiple and diverse opinions are considered. In the face of complexity and uncertainty, the more people who have a say in the decision making, the better. At Intel, the decision-making process typically involves people from several different areas and levels of hierarchy, "jousting with one another about the pros and cons of this or that," says (former) CEO Craig Barrett.[85]

In group decision making, a consensus may not always be reached, but the exercise gives everyone a chance to consider options and state their opinions, and it gives top managers a broader understanding. Typically, those involved support the final choice. However, if a very speedy decision is required, top managers are willing to make the decision and move forward. Once a decision has been made at Intel, for example, it is everyone's responsibility to be involved and commit, even if they disagree. As Barrett says, "No backbiting, no second-guessing. We make a decision, we charge ahead."[86]

## ■ Decision Mistakes and Learning

Organizational decisions result in many errors, especially when made in conditions of great uncertainty. Managers simply cannot determine or predict which alternative will solve a problem. In these cases, the organization must make the decision—and take the risk—often in the spirit of trial and error. If an alternative fails, the organization can learn from it and try another alternative that better fits the situation. Each failure provides new information and insight. The point for managers is to move ahead with the decision process despite the potential for mistakes. "Chaotic action is preferable to orderly inaction."[87]

In some organizations, managers are encouraged to instill a climate of experimentation to facilitate creative decision making. If one idea fails, another idea should be tried. Failure often lays the groundwork for success, such as when technicians at 3M developed Post-it Notes based on a failed product—a not-very-sticky glue. Companies such as PepsiCo believe that if all their new products succeed, they're doing something wrong, not taking the necessary risks to develop new markets.[88]

Only by making mistakes can managers and organizations go through the process of **decision learning** and acquire sufficient experience and knowledge to perform more effectively in the future. Robert Townsend, who was president at Avis Corporation, gives the following advice:

> Admit your mistakes openly, maybe even joyfully. Encourage your associates to do likewise by commiserating with them. Never castigate. Babies learn to walk by falling down. If you beat a baby every time he falls down, he'll never care much for walking.
>
> My batting average on decisions at Avis was no better than a .333. Two out of every three decisions I made were wrong. But my mistakes were discussed openly and most of them corrected with a little help from my friends.[89]

## ■ Escalating Commitment

A much more dangerous mistake is to persist in a course of action when it is failing, a tendency referred to as **escalating commitment**. Research suggests that organizations often continue to invest time and money in a solution despite strong evidence that it is not working. Two explanations are given for why managers escalate commitment to a failing decision. The first is that managers block or distort negative information when they are personally responsible for a negative decision. They simply don't know when to pull the plug. In some cases, they continue to throw good money after bad even when a strategy seems incorrect and goals are not being met.[90]

A second explanation is that consistency and persistence are valued in contemporary society. Consistent managers are considered better leaders than those who switch from one course of action to another. Even though organizations learn through trial and error, organizational norms value consistency. These norms may result in a course of action being maintained, resources being squandered, and learning being inhibited. Senior managers, however, seem less likely to engage in escalating commitment.[91] For example, Ballard Power Systems had maintained its automotive division by pouring millions of dollars into developing a hydrogen-powered car. It claimed that the division was a key component of its business. Developing a hydrogen car was "the holy grail Ballard has chased for two and half decades."[92] In 2007, Ballard Power Systems announced that it was "reviewing strategic alternatives" with Daimler AG and the Ford Motor Company in what analysts described as an admission that the holy grail was unattainable. The automotive division was sold in November 2007. Twenty percent of Ballard's R&D employees were transferred to a newly created private company, managed and funded by Daimler AG and the Ford Motor Company, which "will be positioned for success in automotive fuel cell technology over the longer term...."[93]

Failure to admit a mistake and adopt a new course of action should be replaced by an attitude that tolerates mistakes to encourage learning. Based on what has been said about decision making in this chapter, we can expect companies to be ultimately successful in their decision making by adopting a learning approach toward solutions. They will make mistakes along the way, but they will resolve uncertainty through the trial-and-error process. The next In Practice highlights what can happen when mistakes are made but are *not* addressed as learning opportunities.

**In Practice**
**BlackBerry**

The once mighty Research in Motion—renamed BlackBerry—is fighting for its life again. It was once Canada's biggest company by market capitalization; RIM shed about $30 billion in value in 2011. At the time, investors called for action by the board of directors. Investors were concerned that the board was not truly independent and therefore not serving the interests of the investors. At the time, "Amid the carnage, a growing chorus of investors and analysts [called] for RIM's independent directors to take firmer control of the company, either by forcing a big strategic shift, selling the company or ousting co-Chief Executives Jim Balsillie and Mike Lazaridis who also serve as co-chairmen."[94] Some investors were particularly angry as the Board included two governance experts who were not acting as the investors expected from independent directors.

BlackBerry's attempts to recover have been marred by a series of poor decisions. BlackBerry's attempt at a professional tablet, the Playbook, was not successful. By the time the PlayBook went on sale, RIM had fired two different advertising agencies and the company's marketing director and two of his deputies had resigned. The company's head of global sales and marketing said the

PlayBook was aimed at both ordinary consumers and business users who want to enhance the abilities of a BlackBerry.[95]

BlackBerry's next attempt to compete against Apple and Samsung showed much more promise. However, the decision to launch the Z10 line of smartphones before all were available was met with concern. At the March 2013 launch, Thorsten Heins, CEO of BlackBerry, attributed the delay to not getting technical certification from US carriers. However, an analyst noted the delay was easy to avoid.[96] The demand for the Z10 and Q10 smartphones was lower than expected and the anticipated BlackBerry enterprise upgrade did not occur. The appointment of Alicia Keys as the company's global creative director was an ineffective decision. She was apparently even spotted using a competitor's smartphone! Her involvement ended January 30, 2014. Executives were fired and others left.

John Chen, a turnaround specialist, is now the CEO and "faces a massive challenge—how to enhance BlackBerry's encrypted servers, messaging platforms...to offset a halving of revenues thanks to tanking handset sales..."[97] Many questions remain about the decisions made at and for BlackBerry. Its future remains uncertain.

## Summary and Interpretation

The most important idea in this chapter is that most organizational decisions are not made in a logical, rational manner. Most decisions do not begin with a careful analysis of a problem, followed by systematic analysis of alternatives, and finally implementation of a solution. On the contrary, decision processes are characterized by conflict, coalition building, trial and error, speed, and mistakes. Managers operate under many constraints that limit rationality; hence, intuition and hunch often are the criteria for choice.

Another important idea is that individuals make decisions, but organizational decisions are not made by a single individual. Organizational decision making is a social process. Only in rare circumstances do managers analyze problems and find solutions by themselves. Many problems are not clear, so widespread discussion and coalition building take place. Once goals and priorities are set, alternatives to achieve those goals can be tried. When a manager does make an individual decision, it is often a small part of a larger decision process. Organizations solve big problems through a series of small steps. A single manager may initiate one step but should be aware of the larger decision process to which it belongs.

The greatest amount of conflict and coalition building occurs when problems are not agreed on. Priorities must be established to indicate which goals are important and what problems should be solved first. If a manager attacks a problem other people do not agree with, the manager will lose support for the solution to be implemented. Thus, as the Carnegie model suggests, time and activity should be spent building a coalition in the problem identification stage of decision making. Then the organization can move toward solutions. Under conditions of low technical knowledge, the solution unfolds through an incremental decision process that will gradually lead to an overall solution. In contrast, the management science approach works well when problems are analyzable.

The most novel description of decision making is the garbage can model. This model describes how decision processes can seem almost random in highly organic organizations such as learning organizations. Decisions, problems, ideas, and people flow through these organizations and mix together in various combinations.

Through this process, the organization gradually learns. Some problems may never be solved, but many are, and the organization will move toward maintaining and improving its level of performance.

Finally, many organizations must make decisions with speed, which means staying in immediate touch with operations and the environment. Moreover, in an uncertain world, organizations will make mistakes, and mistakes made through trial and error should be encouraged to facilitate organizational learning. On the other hand, an unwillingness to change from a failing course of action can have serious negative consequences for an organization. Norms for consistency and the desire to prove a decision correct can lead to continued investment in a useless course of action.

## ■ Key Concepts

bounded rationality perspective, p. 412
Carnegie model, p. 423
coalition, p. 423
contingency decision-making
    framework, p. 436
decision learning, p. 440
escalating commitment, p. 441
garbage can model, p. 431
high-velocity environments, p. 439
imitation, p. 438
incremental decision process model, p. 425
inspiration, p. 438
intuitive decision making, p. 417

management science approach, p. 421
nonprogrammed decisions, p. 411
organizational decision making, p. 411
organized anarchy, p. 431
point–counterpoint, p. 440
problem consensus, p. 435
problem identification, p. 411
problem solution, p. 411
problemistic search, p. 424
programmed decisions, p. 411
rational approach, p. 412
satisficing, p. 424
technical knowledge, p. 436

## ■ Discussion Questions

1. When you are faced with choosing between several valid options, how do you typically make your decision? How do you think managers typically choose between several options? What are the similarities between your decision process and what you think managers do?
2. A professional economist once told her class, "An individual decision maker should process all relevant information and select the economically rational alternative." Do you agree? Why or why not?
3. Do you think intuition is a valid way to make important business decisions? Why or why not?
4. The Carnegie model emphasizes the need for a political coalition in the decision-making process. When and why are coalitions necessary?
5. What are the three major phases in Mintzberg's incremental decision process model? Why might an organization recycle through one or more phases of the model?
6. An organization theorist once told his class, "Organizations never make big decisions. They make small decisions that eventually add up to a big decision." Explain the logic behind this statement.
7. How would you make a decision to select a building site for a new waste-treatment plant in South Africa? Where would you start with this complex decision, and what steps would you take? Explain which decision model in the chapter best describes your approach.

8. Why would managers in high-velocity environments worry more about the present than the future? Discuss.
9. Describe the four streams of events in the garbage can model of decision making. Do you think those streams are independent of each other? Why?
10. Why are decision mistakes, usually accepted in organizations, penalized in university courses and exams that are designed to train managers?

## ■ Chapter 11 Workbook: Decision Styles*

Think of some recent decisions that have influenced your life. Choose two significant decisions that you made and two decisions that other people made. Fill out the following table, using Exhibit 11.8 to determine decision styles.

| Your Decisions | Approach Used | Advantages and Disadvantages | Your Recommended Decision Style |
|---|---|---|---|
| 1. | | | |
| 2. | | | |
| Decisions by Others | | | |
| 1. | | | |
| 2. | | | |

*From DAFT. *Organization Theory and Design*, 10E. © 2010 South-Western, a part of Cengage Learning, Inc. Reproduced by permission. www.cengage.com/permissions.

### Questions

1. How can a decision approach influence the outcome of the decision? What happens when the approach fits the decision? when it doesn't fit?

2. How can you know which approach is best?

## Case for Analysis: The Big Carrot*

The Big Carrot is a democratically structured and worker-owned organic foods retailer. Since its founding in 1983 as a small store in Toronto's east end that employed nine, it has expanded to a supermarket with a staff of 187 of which 65 are members, and with annual sales in the fiscal year 2007–2008 of $27 million. The Big Carrot is also one-third owner of Carrot Common, a small mall in which it is housed. As the business has grown, The Big Carrot has expanded and taken over other stores in the mall creating an organic fresh meat store, a body care shop, a supplement department called The Wholistic Dispensary, and an Organic Juice Bar, and now is expanding the supermarket itself. Of the profits that The Big Carrot receives from Carrot Common, one third goes to an organization called Carrot Cache, which provides loans and grants to organizations related to organic agriculture and other co-operative businesses, both in Canada and internationally.

### Background

Six of the founders of The Big Carrot were employees of another organic-foods retailer in Toronto, a sole proprietorship which the employees believed would be sold to them. The owner did sell 46 percent of the shares and also permitted the employees to manage the operation. It was during this period that the core group of The Big Carrot's founders received their first taste of workplace democracy. The store prospered, sales doubled, and business experience was acquired. However, the majority owner decided to return to the business as "boss," and the six employees who were managing the store in his absence determined that their energies could be better used to establish their own enterprise. Well prepared to operate their own store, they nevertheless lacked previous experience in starting a business, particularly one with worker ownership, a matter that required much research on their part.

Financing was a challenge, and is acknowledged as one for worker-owned businesses in general. There should be no mystery as to why this is so: Business financing requires assets and credibility and, in the eyes of the financial community, ordinary working people and the unemployed do not achieve high ratings on either of these. To the members of The Big Carrot without jobs or substantial savings, the $125,000 required for the original market seemed overwhelming. Personal loans totaling $25,000 ($5,000 for five members) were secured from a small credit union. To secure an additional $20,000, four more people were accepted as members. With $45,000 in hand, $25,000 was borrowed from friends and relatives. The most difficult step was a $50,000 bank loan to purchase equipment. The bank manager hesitated, requesting a market survey, collateral, and the name of the persons or entity "in charge." Five members of the co-operative were made individually liable, and three members had to use their homes as security.

In all, it took nine discouraging months to arrange the financial package. At times, it seemed doubtful that the business would ever become operational. The financial package placed a lot of pressure on The Big Carrot to achieve sales that would permit it to break even. Interest charges were very high and the arrangements were cumbersome. In order to establish a substantial member investment in the enterprise, The Big Carrot had to take on more members than seemed prudent, given the projected sales at start-up. And instead of the co-operative being collectively responsible for the bank loan, as is usual for a business loan, members were treated individually. However, the business took off and by the first year-end, sales passed $1 million, and by the second year-end, annual sales were $2 million.

The financing required for expansion in 1987 to the supermarket and mall was far greater than for the initial store, but the co-operative had acquired credibility. Its customers purchased $265,000 of nonvoting preferred shares at 10 percent interest. Good fortune was also needed—in this case, a benevolent real estate developer, David Walsh, and the availability of a parking lot across the street with the necessary space for an 8,000-square-foot supermarket and a 14-store mall (Carrot Common). In total, the deal came to $6.5 million, with Walsh arranging the financing. The Big Carrot financed $700,000, which covered the costs of constructing and equipping the supermarket, in addition to making a token investment in the mall. Despite support from its customers and the deal with Walsh, the financial community was resistant. Before a loan was arranged, The Big Carrot was turned down by three banks, two trust companies, and the Credit Union Central of Ontario. Finally, the Federal Business Development Bank (often a small-business lender of last resort) agreed to a five-year $250,000 loan. Unlike the bank loan for the first store, board members who signed limited their liability. The remaining financing was from store revenues ($70,000) and supplier credits ($115,000).

Short-term repayment costs on the loan caused the co-operative to sustain business losses of $250,000 in the two years after the expansion. However, sales continued to increase, expenses were brought under control as the loans were paid down, and the store started turning a profit.

## Workers With a Difference

The full-time workers at The Big Carrot are also members, each with one vote in meetings. To become a member, workers must commit to a one-year probation, which permits both the applicant and the co-operative to determine whether the arrangement is mutually beneficial. After acceptance, $5,000 is invested in class-B par value shares, which are deposited into a capital account and accumulate interest at 10 percent per year. This investment entitles the member to a common (Class C) share with a nominal value of one dollar and bearing one vote (one member/ one vote). Although the investment in the co-operative is a prerequisite, members must work at least 24 hours per week, that is, be full-time workers. If members want to take a leave, they cease to have voting rights until they resume working the minimum hours. In this way, The Big Carrot has associated the right to vote with labour, a standard practice in a worker co-operative. In addition to the full-time staff who become members, The Big Carrot has a cadre of part-time employees, on average about 122, who work during peak hours, typically the weekend. This is common practice in grocery retailing.

Like the Mondragon Cooperative Corporation in the Basque region of Spain, which influenced its structure, The Big Carrot has endeavoured to assure that membership remains affordable by holding the initial investment at a constant amount. In that respect, The Big Carrot differs from a worker co-operative that permits its shares to be tied to the market value of the firm like conventional businesses in general. If those companies are successful, then the price of membership can become prohibitive, and the end result is often a sale to private owners.

At The Big Carrot, both the membership fee and the rights of membership are set up to assure continuance of the co-operative. Not only has the membership fee been maintained at a constant amount, and therefore at a discount in constant dollars, but the co-operative also loans new members the $5,000 and permits them to pay off the loan by a small check-off against salary.

One issue that arises in organizations of this sort is what percentage of the current members should have to approve a new member. Originally, The Big Carrot required unanimous approval of existing members, but to facilitate new membership, the requirement has been reduced so that at least 80 percent of members must vote and of the voters 80 percent must vote yes. This is still a high proportion, reflecting the importance of having new members who fit well with the existing group. In addition to the technical skills needed for their job, members require a commitment to organic foods and the ability to participate in a democratically governed business. Finding this combination can be challenging.

## Pay and Benefits

As a self-governing business, the members of The Big Carrot have had to decide how much to pay for various jobs, that is, to pay themselves. When the co-operative was first formed, pay was egalitarian and very low. As sales increased, members with greater experience wanted this recognized in their compensation, and after lengthy discussions, the members agreed to recognize responsibilities and experience in compensation, but enshrined within its bylaws a maximum ratio of 3:1 between the highest and lowest paid—though in practice the differences have been less. The current hourly pay ranges from $10 to $24.25.

One of the challenges in determining pay is that The Big Carrot must be competitive in a low-wage industry. The Big Carrot has deviated from the norms of the industry in trying to avoid traditional gender patterns of employment. Thus, it has limited its use of part-time workers and strived for lower turnover. The end result is a larger number of staff, usually members, in the middle of the pay structure and salaries lower than industry norms for senior management. Nevertheless, industry standards inevitably influence the salary scale at The Big Carrot, as prices must be competitive.

Because each member is a worker as well as an owner, any discussion about earnings is often challenging. Nevertheless, The Big Carrot has attempted to define its earnings' policy around principles based upon fairness and the productivity of each worker. Any year-end surplus is generally divided as follows: 10 percent for the community; 20 percent for the collective reserve, retained in perpetuity in the business; and 70 percent as labour dividends to be divided among the members according to hours of work. Labour dividends are allocated to each member's account, not immediately paid out, and in effect become a reinvestment in the business. (The account also contains each member's initial investment of $5,000 and 10 percent annual interest.) Under current policy, the labour dividends are paid out as cash flow allows. Due to increased profits over the past few years, members have also been paid bonuses prior to the determination of dividends.

The Big Carrot's procedure for allocating surplus earnings is adapted from the Mondragon Cooperative Corporation, the difference being that for Mondragon the total money in the capital account is retained until a member leaves the co-operative. This has the practical advantage of providing the co-operative with a pool of investment capital, but has the disadvantage of creating a large drain of capital if many longtime members retire simultaneously. It also means that members have to forego access to part of their earnings until retirement. To avoid the problem of a run on its capital, and to give its members better earnings in the short term, The Big Carrot modified the Mondragon by-law to suit its own needs.

Another Mondragon by-law that was adopted had to do with the allocation of losses. The founders of The Big Carrot, assuming quite optimistically that losses were unlikely, agreed that they should be divided according to the same formula as surpluses—that is, 70 percent would be applied to individual capital accounts. In the period following the expansion, however, there were sizable losses, resulting in an unfair burden upon the original members. These same people, who had already experienced very low earnings when the expansion occurred, now were faced with a total loss of the accumulated labour dividends in their capital accounts because they took the risk to expand. Finally, it was agreed that the losses be dealt with through a special "start-up loss" account that would be amortized over five years and would be shared by all members during that period.

Although The Big Carrot is owned by its members, ownership rights are partial and do not include the right to sell the store for personal gain. In the event of dissolution, members are entitled only to the amount in their capital account. Monies in addition would go to the co-operative movement or to some appropriate organization designated by the members.

## Governance

As is evident in the preceding discussion, the members of The Big Carrot are responsible for its policies, that is, for the policies that affect them. Each member has one vote in electing the board of directors (the legal governance) from among its group and in meetings. The seven-person board of directors meets every week with the general manager attending. During its 25 years, the co-operative has relied upon different management styles, sometimes selecting the general manager from among its group and other times hiring outside. Members attempt to reach consensus on major issues at the long and lively meetings scheduled every other Wednesday.

From the beginning, The Big Carrot experimented with its decision-making processes in an effort to strike a balance between effective decision making and meaningful participation. When there were only nine members, the firm was a participatory democracy in which all issues were decided collectively. As the operations became more complex, decisions were delegated and there was greater selectivity about group matters. Knowing which issues were appropriate for the board and which were the domain of the total membership required experimentation. Similarly, there were ongoing discussions about the decisions that management could make without consulting the board.

The Big Carrot has had an ongoing tradition for ad hoc committees that take on specific issues and that make recommendations to the governance. To address concerns of individual workers, there are procedures including formal grievances as well as a solid harassment policy.

As owners-in-common, the members of The Big Carrot are highly motivated in their work. There is a strong emphasis on worker self-management, relative to other similar businesses. However, because of the democratic structures, decision making can be time consuming and change can be challenging. Although the democratic structures of The Big Carrot have created a high degree of worker involvement, democracy can come with a price. The role of management is constantly discussed, and management's powers can be challenged by both the board and the members in general. Traditional business training does not prepare managers properly for this challenge. Heather Barclay, a 20-year member and the current president of the board of directors and office manager, highlights the challenge for members and management:

*There always seems to be a constant "pull" between the necessity for a hierarchical system to run the business and the need for the "equality" of the membership. In members meetings, we are all equal but as soon as we go downstairs our roles shift. This can and often has led to some conflict, especially for those members that do not hold managerial positions.*

## Assignment Questions

1. What do you think of the decision-making processes at The Big Carrot?
2. What do you believe are the main advantages and disadvantages of organizational and ownership arrangements of The Big Carrot?
3. If you were creating a business, would you consider this structure? Why?

*An earlier article by Mary Lou Morgan and Jack Quarter, *A Start-up Experience: The Case of The Big Carrot,* served as resource material for this case study. I would like to thank Mary Lou Morgan, the first manager of The Big Carrot, and Heather Barclay, the current president of the board of directors, office manager, and a 20-year member, for their insights on the organization and for their assistance with this case study.

Source: Quarter, J., Mook, L. and Armstrong, A. (2009), "Case for Analysis: The Big Carrot," from *Understanding the Social Economy: A Canadian Perspective,* © University of Toronto Press, Inc. pp. 33-39. Reprinted with permission of the publisher.

## Case for Analysis: Nackawic Community Story*

Nackawic, New Brunswick, is the home of the world's largest axe and is also New Brunswick's newest town. It is situated in the Saint John River Valley where the Nackawic stream meets the Saint John River. Nackawic gets its name from the Maliseet word meaning "straight" or "not in the direction it seems to be." The town was designated Canada's forestry capital in 1991. Forestry has been the primary industry in the area for many generations.

The town's mission's statement reads "[By] committing ourselves to necessary change and improved quality, we are dedicated to providing cost effective and reliable municipal services for the long term benefit of the residents of the Town...and, where mutually agreed upon, to the communities surrounding the Town."[1] The town's population is 1,100 and the population in the surrounding area is 7,000.

In September 2004, 400 mill workers were locked out of the St. Anne Pulp and Paper Mill. In addition, the woods workers, construction workers, contractors, truck drivers and suppliers lost work. "One by one, small business owners in the town and surrounding villages closed up shop and a pall of loss and grief settled over the area."[2] In response, the town council hired a consultant to hold strategic planning sessions and created a committee called the Nackawic Regional Economic Development Team. The work of the committee resulted in the sale of the mill to an Indian company; the mill was reopened in 2006 as AV Nackawic. The reopening, however, was not without its problems. While some of the locked-out workers were rehired, the company also hired new workers from the surrounding communities. Further, as the pension fund had been underfunded, pensioners lost about 35 percent of their retirement funds as the limited funds had to be shared among all the pensioners. The reopening pitted family members against one another and local communities against one another. There was a fear that the mill would not last as there was a downturn in the forestry market. Area residents were anxious.

A local nonprofit organization, the Neighbourhood Alliance of North York (NANY), decided that action was necessary to deal with the negative attitudes in the town of Nackawic and the surrounding communities. "[NANY] felt it was time to take stock of what [existed] and to scrutinize the potential for growth and development in the area."[3] NANY decided to use a decision-making tool called Asset Mapping. Asset Mapping is a method used both to collect information on the positive attributes of a community and to discover why people value them. It produces a common view of what is considered important in a community. It provides a useful starting point, potentially leading to a strategic planning process and/or community/organizational development. There are three approaches to Asset Mapping: Storytelling, Heritage, and Whole Assets. NANY used the Whole Assets approach, which involves the following eight steps.

1. First, each participant is encouraged to identify the top six assets in his or her community, and record these assets on three separate cards.
2. The participants post their cards under asset categories on a wall. Examples of asset categories include Built, Social, Service, Natural, and Economic.
3. The group is encouraged to discuss why these assets are important. Possible questions to ask include "Were there any surprises?" and "What do those surprises mean?"
4. Afterwards, each participant identifies the most important asset in each category by posting a dot beside that item. The item containing the most dots becomes the most important asset for the group.
5. The participants are divided into smaller groups of five to seven people. Each group selects the asset category with which they would like to work.
6. Each small group discusses asset supports and threats, and identifies ways in which the asset can be preserved or strengthened.

7. The small groups present a summary of their thoughts to all participants.
8. Finally, the larger group is encouraged to determine next steps.[4]

Over ten weeks, NANY held five formal meetings and conducted numerous telephone interviews/conversations. In total, 300 people participated. The Whole Assets approach yielded many insights. The people of Nackawic identified the natural beauty of the Saint John River Valley as its most valuable asset. Participants felt that the protection of the river was critical as there are many threats to the river. Second, the participants noted that Nackawic, although a rural area, has infrastructure more typical of urban areas. Its education system has been recognized all over the world for its inclusive curriculum. Educators from Sweden, China, Iceland, Spain, Mexico, and other countries have visited Nackawic. The participants also identified various economic assets including a well-trained (if ageing) work force and a variety of potential employers such as an expanding call centre, a trucking company, a log home manufacturer, and a poker chip plant.

Many asked if there was going to be any follow-up to the process. Focus groups have since been formed to address opportunities for riverfront development, small business, youth, promotion, community linkages, and seniors. The town and the community are now galvanized—"[We] must get out there and sell ourselves. It is not wrong to promote what we hold as valuable."[5]

## Assignment Questions

1. What is asset mapping?
2. How might asset mapping work within an organization?

---

[1]Town of Nackawic, "Mission Statement" (2011) at www.nackawic.com/content/4057 (accessed June 5, 2011).
[2]Canada's Rural Partnership, "Community Decision-Making Toolkit—Nackawic CaseStudy" (2011) at www.rural.gc.ca/RURAL/display-afficher.do?id=1238609114220&lang=eng (accessed June 5, 2011).
[3]Ibid.
[4]Ibid.
[5]Ibid.

---

*Ann Armstrong. This case references the report prepared by J.A. Stone, "Nackawic Community Story: Asset Mapping Project," posted at www.rural.gc.ca/decision/nackawic/nackawic_e.phtml#1 (accessed September 29, 2008).

# ■ **Chapter 11 Workshop:** Mist Ridge*

It is approximately 9 a.m. on August 23, and you and four friends are about to set off on an all day hike in the mountains of Southwestern Alberta. Having driven southwest from Calgary, Alberta, you have arrived at Kananaskis Provincial Park, located on the boundary between British Columbia and Alberta. Just off Highway 40, you turn into the Mist Creek day use area and have just parked the car. You can see a sign indicating the beginning of the Mist Ridge trail, which you have selected for your hike, but you know that from there on, the trail proceeds along unmarked paths and logging roads. You can also see another sign that allows campfires only in designated rest areas.

Since it is mid-week, few others should be on the Mist Ridge trail. You and your friends are looking forward to an enjoyable day walking the long grass and rock ridge as it is usually dry and sunny at this time of the year, when a mere few kilometres away across the valley Mist Mountain can be covered in rain clouds. Hiking from the parking lot to the ridge, then along the whole top of the ridge to Rickert's Pass, then returning at ground level alongside the Mist Creek is, at minimum, an eight hour trip. In guidebooks it is classified as a long day hike covering a distance of 23 kilometres with a height gain of 808 metres and a maximum elevation of 2515 metres.

The weather at the moment is cool but not cold, and the sun is beaming down, beginning to heat the air. In general, the climate of Southwestern Alberta is cold continental, having long cold winters and cool summers, though summers do have brief hot spells. Annual precipitation peaks in the summer and thunderstorms occur regularly. Hikers at this time of year must be prepared for rain or cold weather. Snow has been known to fall by the middle of August in this area, with accumulations on the ground of up to 20 centimetres. Also, the weather can be somewhat changeable and unpredictable. What starts out as a warm, sunny morning could easily change into a cold, snowy afternoon. Therefore, experienced hikers will make sure that they have adequate reserve clothing for the rain or snow that could develop. It is also known that temperatures are expected to be cooler at the top of the ridge, as temperatures decrease, in general, 2 degrees Celsius for every 300 metres of altitude.

There are a few dangers to watch out for during your hike. If you get soaked crossing a river, loss of body heat may result in hypothermia, even when temperatures are above freezing. Death from hypothermia is quite possible within a few hours of the first symptoms if proper care is not taken. On the other hand, the exertions of walking and climbing will probably cause you to sweat. Dehydration can increase your chance of sunstroke and hypothermia. In terms of animals, you may encounter a bear looking for berries. While bear attacks on humans are not common, they are not unusual either. It is also possible that elk or moose may be encountered. These large plant eaters are not usually dangerous to humans, but should be avoided during the mating season. There are also some insects to be considered. Ticks can carry Rocky Mountain Spotted Fever, which can be fatal if left untreated. Bees can also be dangerous if the person stung has a strong allergic reaction.

You are all currently dressed in warm clothes including wool socks and sturdy hiking boots, and each person has a day pack in which to carry those items that you deem necessary.

## Part I: Individual Decision

There are 15 items listed below. Before you set out on your hike your task is to rank these items according to their general importance for a hiker, not for you specifically. Rank the items from 1, the most important, to 15, the least important. No ties are allowed. You might want to consider "If a hiker was allowed to take only one item, what would it be?" That item would be ranked number 1. Then, "If a hiker was allowed only one more item, what would it be?" That item would rank number 2. Write your rankings in the column below titled "Your Ranking." It is important to remember that the decisions that you are making are for your group as a whole and should not be influenced by factors affecting you as an individual.

## Part II: Group Decision

Now form into groups. Take a few minutes to examine and discuss your individual assumptions before you begin to discuss how to rank specific items. Use constructive controversy decision rules to guide your decision method and rank the 15 items again. To refresh [your] memory, they are: (1) be critical of ideas, not people; (2) focus on making the best possible decision, not on winning; (3) encourage everyone to participate in the discussion; (4) listen to everyone's ideas, even if you do not agree; (5) restate what someone has said if their point is not clear to you; (6) bring out the ideas and facts supporting both sides of the argument and then try to integrate them; (7) try to understand both sides of the issue under discussion; and (8) change your mind if the

| Items | Your Ranking | Group Ranking | Expert Ranking | Your Score | Group Score |
|---|---|---|---|---|---|
| Canteen with water | | | | | |
| Matches | | | | | |
| Compass | | | | | |
| Hat | | | | | |
| Repair kit (includes short length of cord, string, duct tape, and shoelaces) | | | | | |
| First aid kit (includes blister protection and aspirin) | | | | | |
| Five sleeping bags | | | | | |
| Sunglasses | | | | | |
| Flashlight | | | | | |
| Topographic map and Kananaskis Country Trail guide book | | | | | |
| Food | | | | | |
| 5-person tent with waterproof fly | | | | | |
| Sunscreen | | | | | |
| Rain gear | | | | | |
| Insect repellent | | | | | |

evidence clearly indicates that you should do so (from Johnson, D.W. & R.T. Johnson [1992] *Cooperation and Competition: Intellectual Challenge in the Classroom*, Edina, MN: Interaction Book.)

Write your group's answers in the "Group Ranking" column.

## Part III: Scoring

Your instructor will inform you of how experts have ranked these 15 items. Write these rankings into the column titled "Expert Ranking." To calculate your personal score, calculate for each of the 15 items the absolute difference between your ranking and the expert's ranking, then sum these 15 absolute value differences. Determine your group's score in the same manner. Write these scores and summary statistics into the spaces below.

Your total score _____
Average of the individual scores in your group _____

Your group's total score _____
Number of individuals in our group having a lower score than your group's total score _____

# 12

# Conflict, Power, and Politics

The Canadian Press/FRANK GUNN

## Harold Ballard and the Toronto Maple Leafs

Harold Ballard was—and remains—arguably the most reviled team owner in the history of the National Hockey League. In 1961, Ballard, along with John Bassett and Conn Smythe's son, Stafford Smythe, bought Smythe's controlling interest in the Toronto Maple Leafs (see photo). In 1971, Ballard took control of Maple Leaf Gardens as well. "He quickly developed a reputation for only thinking of the bottom line, and letting players and fans suffer for it."[1] For example, Ballard refused to have the players' names sewn onto the back of their jerseys as he thought that having the players easily identifiable would hurt program sales. After being fined $2000 a day by the league, he had the names sewn on in the same colour as the jerseys so that they would be difficult to read.

In 1972, Ballard was found guilty on 48 of 50 charges of theft and fraud. According to the judge, Ballard had demonstrated "a clear pattern of fraud" including using monies that belonged to Maple Leaf Gardens to renovate his house.[2] Ballard was sentenced to three consecutive one-year terms. He spent one year in Millhaven penitentiary, which he compared to a motel, complete with luxuries such as golf, beer, and steak.

The Toronto Maple Leafs last won the Stanley Cup in 1967. The 1970s were marred by Ballard's tyrannical rule: "[his] antics included firing Red Kelley, hiring Roger Nielson, firing him and hiring him back, and once again firing him along with Bob Davidson—all in the span of weeks."[3] Ballard is reputed to have told Nielson that he had to wear a bag over his head when he was rehired; Nielson refused.

In 1981, Ballard was in conflict with his oldest son, Bill Ballard, and bought shares owned by his son Harold Ballard, Jr. for $25 million to prevent the possibility of a takeover of the team and the Gardens. According to Harold Ballard, "Bill and Molson [Breweries] were trying to get control of the place.... It would have given them control. But I've pretty much got all of it now, and I'm going to make a private company to buy up the public's stock too. I told Molson that if they ever set foot into the building, I'll have them thrown out."[4] When Ballard died in 1990, the Toronto Maple Leafs were struggling both on and off the ice.

---

According to *Toronto Star* columnist Damien Cox, the Toronto Maple Leafs' bumbling history continues today. "In all, it's as big of a tangled web of intrigue now as it was during the days of Smythe-Bassett-Ballard, or when Fletcher was fighting Stavro, or when Dryden and Smith were trying to get each other fired. It's the Leaf way."[5] Although the conflicts at the Toronto Maple Leafs organization are an extreme example, all organizations are a complex mix of individuals and groups pursuing various goals and interests. Conflict is a natural and inevitable outcome of the close interaction of people who may have diverse opinions and values, pursue different objectives, and have differential access to information and resources within the organization. Individuals and groups will use power and political activity to handle their differences and manage conflict.[6] Too much conflict can be harmful to an organization, as was the case during Harold Ballard's reign. However, conflict can also be a positive force because it challenges the status quo, encourages new ideas and approaches, and leads to change.[7] Some degree of conflict occurs in all human relationships—between friends, life partners, and teammates, as well as between

# YOU & DESIGN

## Political Skills

How good are you at influencing people across an organization? To learn something about your political skills, answer the questions that follow. Please answer whether each item is Mostly True or Mostly False for you.

| | Mostly True | Mostly False |
|---|---|---|
| 1. I am able to communicate easily and effectively with others. | _____ | _____ |
| 2. I spend a lot of time at work developing connections with people outside my area. | _____ | _____ |
| 3. I instinctively know the right thing to say or do to influence others. | _____ | _____ |
| 4. I am good at using my connections outside my area to get things done at work. | _____ | _____ |
| 5. When communicating with others I am absolutely genuine in what I say and do. | _____ | _____ |
| 6. It is easy for me to reach out to new people. | _____ | _____ |
| 7. I make strangers feel comfortable and at ease around me. | _____ | _____ |
| 8. I am good at sensing the motivations and hidden agendas of others. | _____ | _____ |

**Scoring:** Give yourself one point for each item marked as Mostly True.

**Interpretation:** Having some basic political skill helps a manager gain broad support and influence. Political skills help a manager build personal and organizational relationships that enhance your team's outcomes. A score of 6 or higher suggests active political skills and a good start for your career, especially in an organization in which things get done politically. If you scored three or less, you may want to focus more on building collegial and supportive relationships as you progress in your career. If not, perhaps join an organization in which decisions and actions are undertaken by rational procedures rather than by support of key coalitions.

Source: Adapted from Gerald R. Ferris, Darren C. Treadway, Robert W. Kolodinsky, Wayne A. Hochwarter, Charles J. Kacmer, Ceasar Douglas, and Dwight D. Frink, "Development and Validation of the Political Skill Inventory," *Journal of Management* 31 (February 2005), 126–152.

**Apply**

How can you apply what you learned about your political skills to managing your boss?

parents and children, teachers and students, and bosses and employees. Conflict results from the normal interaction of varying human interests. Within organizations, individuals and groups frequently have different interests and goals they wish to achieve through the organization. In learning organizations, which encourage a democratic push and pull of ideas, the forces of conflict, power, and politics may be particularly evident. Managers in all organizations regularly deal with conflict and struggle with decisions about how to get the most out of employees, enhance job satisfaction and team identification, and realize high organizational performance. Take a few minutes to complete the You and Design feature to assess your political skills.

## ■ Purpose of This Chapter

In this chapter, we discuss the nature of conflict and the use of power and political tactics to manage and reduce conflict among individuals and groups. The notion of conflict has appeared in previous chapters. In Chapter 3, we talked about horizontal linkages such as task forces and teams that encourage collaboration among functional departments. Chapter 4 introduced the concept of differentiation, which means that different departments pursue different goals and may have different attitudes and values. Chapter 9 discussed the emergence of subcultures, and in Chapter 11, coalition building was proposed as one way to resolve disagreements among departments.

The first sections of this chapter explore the nature of intergroup conflict, characteristics of organizations that contribute to conflict, and the use of a political versus a rational model of organization to manage conflicting interests. Subsequent sections examine individual and organizational power, power versus authority, the vertical and horizontal sources of power for managers and other employees, and how power is used to attain organizational goals. The latter part of the chapter looks at politics, which is the application of power and authority to achieve desired outcomes. We also discuss some tactics managers can use to enhance collaboration among people and departments.

## Intergroup Conflict in Organizations

Intergroup conflict requires three ingredients: group identification, observable group differences, and frustration. First, employees have to perceive themselves as part of an identifiable group or department.[8] Second, there has to be an observable group difference of some sort. Groups may be located on different floors of the building, members may have different social or educational backgrounds, or members may work in different departments. The ability to self-identify as a part of one group and to observe differences in comparison with other groups is necessary for conflict.[9] The third ingredient is frustration. Frustration means that if one group achieves its goal, the other will not; it will be blocked. Frustration need not be severe and needs only to be anticipated to set off intergroup conflict. Intergroup conflict will appear when one group tries to advance its position in relation to other groups. **Intergroup conflict** can be defined as the behaviour that occurs among organizational groups when participants identify with one group and perceive that other groups may block their group's goal achievement or expectations.[10] Conflict means that groups clash directly, that they are in fundamental opposition. Conflict is similar to competition but more severe. **Competition** is rivalry among groups in the pursuit of a common prize, whereas conflict presumes direct interference with goal achievement.

Intergroup conflict within organizations can occur horizontally across departments or vertically between different levels of the organization.[11] The production department of a manufacturing company may have a dispute with quality control because new quality procedures reduce production efficiency. Teammates may argue about the best way to accomplish tasks and achieve goals. Workers may clash with bosses about new work methods, reward systems, or job assignments. Another typical area of conflict is between groups such as unions and management or franchise owners and headquarters. For example, there have been many conflicts between the Canadian Auto Workers (CAW), the country's largest private-sector union, and General Motors, the Ford Motor Company, and Daimler-Chrysler. The founding of the CAW in 1985 was itself fraught with conflict. "The decision of the Canadian section of the United Auto Workers (UAW) to form its own Canadian union was rooted in the different responses of unionists in … Canada and the United States to an increasing belligerence on the part of the corporations. While this break from an 'international' union was not the first such action within the Canadian labour movement, it was perhaps the most dramatic and certainly the most significant."[12] Similarly, franchise owners for McDonald's, Taco Bell, Burger King, and KFC have clashed with headquarters because of the increase of company-owned stores in neighbourhoods that compete directly with franchisees.[13] Conflict can also occur between different divisions or business units within an organization, such as between the auditing and consulting units of big firms such as PricewaterhouseCoopers and Deloitte Touche Tohmatsu International.[14] In global organizations, conflicts between regional managers and business division managers, among different divisions, or between divisions and headquarters are common because of the complexities of international business, as described in Chapter 6. Conflicts often occur after a merger or acquisition; for example, Porsche's takeover of the Volkswagen (VW) Group brought together two different organizational cultures and, as a result, a power struggle emerged. The conflict began when "Porsche CEO Wendelin Wiedeking, alarmed about the considerable influence of the VW's labour representatives...said that nothing could be considered sacred. According to Wiedeking, all things should be questioned to determine whether they are still timely and in keeping with corporate strategy."[15] Similarly, conflict has occurred between the different artisans who make up Etsy, an online artisanal organization. In November 2013, Etsy changed the rules for sellers and allowed them to have their products manufactured by others. However, some "Etsians" have quit the site to protest what they consider to be a selling out of their values to the interests of business.[16]

## ■ Sources of Conflict

Some specific organizational characteristics can generate conflict. These **sources of intergroup conflict** are goal incompatibility, differentiation, task interdependence, and limited resources. These characteristics of organizational relationships are determined by the contextual factors of environment, size, technology, strategy and goals, and organizational structure, which have been discussed in previous chapters. These characteristics, in turn, help shape the extent to which a rational model of behaviour versus a political model of behaviour is used to accomplish objectives.

**Goal Incompatibility.** Goal incompatibility is probably the greatest cause of intergroup conflict in organizations.[17] The goals of each department reflect the specific objectives members are trying to achieve. The achievement of one department's goals often interferes with another department's goals. University police, for example, have a goal of providing a safe and secure campus. They can achieve their goal by locking all buildings on evenings and weekends and not distributing keys. Without easy access to buildings, however, progress toward the science department's research goals will proceed slowly. On the other hand, if scientists come and go at all hours and security is ignored, police goals for security will not be met. Goal incompatibility throws the departments into conflict with each other.

The potential for conflict is perhaps greater between marketing and manufacturing than between other departments because the goals of these two departments are frequently at odds. Exhibit 12.1 shows examples of goal conflict between typical marketing and manufacturing departments. Marketing strives to increase the breadth of the product line to meet customer tastes for variety. A broad product line means short production runs, so manufacturing has to bear higher costs.[18] Other areas of goal conflict are quality, cost control, and new products or services. For example, when a human resources (HR) department wants to implement a new self-service benefits system that would let employees manage their benefits from their home computers, the high price of the software licences conflicts with the finance department's goal of controlling costs.[19] Goal incompatibility exists among departments in most organizations.

| GOAL CONFLICT | MARKETING VERSUS MANUFACTURING | |
| | OPERATIVE GOAL IS CUSTOMER SATISFACTION | OPERATIVE GOAL IS PRODUCTION EFFICIENCY |
| --- | --- | --- |
| **Conflict Area** | **Typical Comment** | **Typical Comment** |
| Breadth of product line | "Our customers demand variety." | "The product line is too broad—all we get are short, uneconomical runs." |
| New product introduction | "New products are our lifeblood." | "Unnecessary design changes are prohibitively expensive." |
| Product scheduling | "We need faster response. Our customer lead times are too long." | "We need realistic commitments that don't change like wind direction." |
| Physical distribution | "Why don't we ever have the right merchandise in inventory?" | "We can't afford to keep huge inventories." |
| Quality | "Why can't we have reasonable quality at lower cost?" | "Why must we always offer options that are too expensive and offer little customer utility?" |

**EXHIBIT 12.1**
**Marketing–Manufacturing Areas of Potential Goal Conflict**
Source: Based on Benson S. Shapiro, "Can Marketing and Manufacturing Coexist?" *Harvard Business Review* 55 (September–October 1977), 104–114, and Victoria L. Crittenden, Lorraine R. Gardiner, and Antonie Stam, "Reducing Conflict between Marketing and Manufacturing," *Industrial Marketing Management* 22 (1993), 299–309.

**Differentiation.** *Differentiation* was defined in Chapter 4 as "the differences in cognitive and emotional orientations among managers in different functional departments." Functional specialization requires people with specific education, skills, attitudes, and time horizons. For example, people may join a sales department because they have ability and aptitude consistent with sales work. After becoming members of the sales department, they are influenced by departmental norms and values. Departments or divisions within an organization often differ in values, attitudes, and standards of behaviour, and these subcultural differences lead to conflicts.[20] See how Bennett Jones LLP addresses these sorts of issues in the following Leading by Design.

**Task Interdependence.** Task interdependence refers to the dependence of one unit on another for materials, resources, or information. As described in Chapter 7, *pooled interdependence* means there is little interaction; *sequential interdependence* means the output of one department goes to the next department; and *reciprocal interdependence* means that departments mutually exchange materials and information.[21] Generally, as interdependence increases, the potential for conflict increases.[22] In the case of pooled interdependence, units have little need to interact. Conflict is at a minimum. Sequential and reciprocal interdependence require employees to spend time coordinating and sharing information. Employees must communicate frequently, and differences in goals or attitudes will surface. Conflict is especially likely to occur when agreement is not reached about the coordination of services to each other. Greater interdependence means departments often exert pressure for a fast response because departmental work has to wait on other departments.[23]

# Leading *by Design*

## Bennett Jones LLP

Bennett Jones LLP was founded in 1922 in Calgary, Alberta, and began as Bennett, Hannah & Sanford. It has had many name changes as partners came and went. In the 1980s, the firm felt that it was time to have a name that would be institutionalized. It took the last name of the founding partner, R. B. Bennett, our Prime Minister from 1930–1935, and the last name of the most senior living partner, Mac Jones.

Bennett Jones has expanded rapidly from its Alberta base. It followed a go-east strategy. "Bennett Jones' East/West strategy lets the firm "breathe with two lungs," servicing two very different markets and bringing together the best practices from each market to benefit the firm. It also means that the firm is less exposed to the cyclical nature of business in any market centre."[24] The growth in the Toronto office has been extraordinary. "What makes this situation unique, says [Hugh] MacKinnon [Chair and CEO], is that... senior lawyers chose to decamp from long-time partnerships at prestigious, well-regarded Toronto firms, opting to join the Bennett Jones fold."[25]

According to MacKinnon, Bennett Jones has an egalitarian culture, and functions as a meritocracy. Bennett Jones has appeared on the Top 50 Employers in Canada list every year since 2003 and ranked fourth in 2006. The firm placed eighth in the 2011 best employers in Canada survey conducted by Aon Hewitt for *Maclean's* and Queen's

University School of Business.[26] Bennett Jones continues to be recognized as an employer of choice. "Bennett Jones was... recognized as One of Canada's Top Employers for young people, and was selected in 2013 as one of the top three Best employers in the GTA, a Top 60 Employer in Alberta and 3rd Best Employer in Canada."[27]

Bennett Jones states that it has three core values: "To be the law firm of choice having earned a reputation as being one of the very best providers of legal services in all areas in which we practice, to provide individuals in the firm with an opportunity to perform stimulating, interesting, and rewarding work in a collegial team environment, and to promote an atmosphere of excellence through strong personal commitment and the encouragement of a balanced life.[28]

Professional firms, like law firms, are often fraught with conflict. Sources of conflict in law firms include divergent goals, differences in individual style, status conflicts, value differences, role pressures, dysfunctional organizational structures, limited resources, and unsatisfactory communications.[29] Bennett Jones seems to be the exception. As MacKinnon puts it, "[The] difference between Bennett Jones and other firms is in the execution[;] internally and externally the way our law firm interacts with our lawyers and with our clients."[30]

---

**Limited Resources.** Another major source of conflict involves competition between groups for what members perceive as limited resources.[31] Organizations have limited money, physical facilities, and human resources to share among departments. In their desire to achieve goals, groups want to increase their own resources. This throws them into conflict. Managers may develop strategies, such as inflating budget requirements or working behind the scenes, to obtain a desired level of resources.

Resources also symbolize power and influence within an organization. The ability to obtain resources enhances prestige. Departments typically believe they have a legitimate claim on additional resources. However, exercising that claim results in conflict. For example, in almost every organization, conflict occurs during the annual budget exercise, often creating political activity.

## ■ Rational Versus Political Model

The sources of intergroup conflict are listed in Exhibit 12.2. The degree of goal incompatibility, differentiation, task interdependence, and conflict over limited resources determines whether a rational or political model of behaviour is used within the organization to accomplish goals.

**Compare**

Compare the sources of conflict. Which one(s) do you think would contribute to creating a toxic culture?

| Sources of Potential Intergroup Conflict | When Conflict Is Low, Rational Model Describes Organization | | When Conflict Is High, Political Model Describes Organization |
|---|---|---|---|
| • Goal incompatibility<br>• Differentiation<br>• Task interdependence<br>• Limited resources | Consistent across participants | **Goals** | Inconsistent, pluralistic within the organization |
| | Centralized | **Power and control** | Decentralized, shifting coalitions and interest groups |
| | Orderly, logical, rational | **Decision process** | Disorderly, result of bargaining and interplay among interests |
| | Norm of efficiency | **Rules and norms** | Free play of market forces; conflict is legitimate and expected |
| | Extensive, systematic, accurate | **Information** | Ambiguous; information is used and withheld strategically |

**EXHIBIT 12.2**
Sources of Conflict and Use of Rational versus Political Model

When goals are in alignment, there is little differentiation, departments are characterized by pooled interdependence, and resources seem abundant, managers can use a **rational model** of organization, as outlined in Exhibit 12.2. As with the rational approach to decision making described in Chapter 11, the rational model of organization is an ideal that is not fully achievable in the real world, though managers strive to use rational processes whenever possible. In the rational organization, behaviour is not random or accidental. Goals are clear and choices are made in a logical way. When a decision is needed, the goal is defined, alternatives are identified, and the choice with the highest probability of success is selected. The rational model is also characterized by centralized power and control, extensive information systems, and an efficiency orientation.[32] The opposite view of organizational processes is the **political model**, also described in Exhibit 12.2. When differences are great, organization groups have separate interests, goals, and values. Disagreement and conflict are normal, so power and influence are needed to reach decisions. Groups will engage in the push and pull of debate to decide goals and reach decisions. Information is ambiguous and incomplete. The political model particularly describes organizations that strive for democracy and participation in decision making by empowering workers. Purely rational procedures do not work in democratic organizations, such as learning organizations.

Both rational and political processes are normally used in organizations. In most organizations, neither the rational model nor the political model characterizes things fully, but each will be used some of the time. At Amazon.com, founder and CEO Jeff Bezos emphasizes a rational approach to planning and decision making whenever possible. "The great thing about fact-based decisions," he says, "is that they overrule the hierarchy. The most junior person in the company can win an argument with the most senior person with a fact-based decision." For decisions and situations that are complex, ill defined, and controversial, however, Bezos uses a political model, discussing the issues with people, building agreement among senior executives, and then relying on his own judgment.[33]

**Think**

Think about how you can use Bezos's approach to planning and decision making in your career.

Managers may strive to adopt rational procedures but will find that politics is needed to accomplish objectives. The political model means managers learn to acquire, develop, and use power to accomplish objectives.

## Power and Organizations

Power is an intangible force in organizations. It cannot be seen, but its effect can be felt. *Power* is often defined as the potential ability of one person (or department) to influence other people (or departments) to carry out orders[34] or to do something he or she would not otherwise have done.[35] Other definitions stress that power is the ability to achieve goals or outcomes that power holders desire.[36] The achievement of desired outcomes is the basis of the definition used here: **power** is the ability of one person or department in an organization to influence other people to bring about desired outcomes. It is the potential to influence others within the organization with the goal of attaining desired outcomes for power holders. Exhibit 12.3 shows us how to wield power through delegation!

Power exists only in a relationship between two or more people, and it can be exercised in either vertical or horizontal directions. The source of power often derives from an exchange relationship in which one position or department provides scarce or valued resources to other departments. When one person is dependent on another person, a power relationship emerges in which the person with the resources has greater power.[37] Sometimes power is described as a relationship of asymmetric or unequal dependence between two or more individuals in a department.[38] When power exists in a relationship, the power holders can achieve compliance with their requests. Powerful individuals are often able to get bigger budgets for their departments, more favourable production schedules, and more control over the organization's agenda.[39]

As an illustration, consider how power is shifting in the game of baseball. Seasoned team managers, who typically base their decisions on instinct and experience, are losing power to general managers using business theories and new analytical tools to come up with statistical benchmarks and operational

**EXHIBIT 12.3**
Power to Delegate!

standards that are believed to improve performance. As a result of their increased power, some general managers are now suggesting player lineups, handpicking members of the coaching staff, and generally telling team managers how to run the team.[40]

## ■ Individual Versus Organizational Power

In popular literature, power is often described as a personal characteristic, and a frequent topic is how one person can influence or dominate another person.[41] You probably recall from an earlier management or organizational behaviour course that managers have five sources of personal power.[42] *Legitimate power* is the authority granted by the organization to the formal management position a manager holds. *Reward power* stems from the ability to bestow rewards—a promotion, raise, or pat on the back—to other people. The authority to punish or recommend punishment is called *coercive power*. *Expert power* derives from a person's greater skill or knowledge about the tasks being performed. The last, *referent power,* is derived from personal characteristics: people admire the manager and want to be like or identify with the manager out of respect and admiration. Each of these sources may be used by individuals within organizations.

Power in organizations, however, is often the result of *structural* characteristics.[43] Organizations are large, complex systems that contain hundreds, even thousands, of people. These systems have a formal hierarchy in which some tasks are more important regardless of who performs them. In addition, some positions have access to greater resources, or their contribution to the organization is more critical. Thus, the important power processes in organizations reflect larger organizational relationships, both horizontal and vertical.

**Apply**

How can you apply the idea of asymmetric dependence to increase your power?

## ■ Power Versus Authority

Anyone in an organization can exercise power to achieve desired outcomes. When the Discovery Channel wanted to extend its brand beyond cable television, Tom Hicks began pushing for a focus on the Internet. Even though Discovery's CEO favoured exploring interactive television, Hicks organized a grassroots campaign that eventually persuaded the CEO to focus instead on Web publishing, indicating that Hicks had power within the organization. Today, Hicks runs Discovery Channel Online.[44] The concept of formal authority is related to power but is narrower in scope. **Authority** is also a force for achieving desired outcomes, but only as prescribed by the formal hierarchy and reporting relationships. Three properties identify authority:

1. *Authority is vested in organizational positions*. People have authority because of the positions they hold, not because of personal characteristics or resources.
2. *Authority is accepted by subordinates*. Subordinates comply because they believe position holders have a legitimate right to exercise authority.[45] In most North American organizations, employees accept that supervisors can legitimately tell them what time to arrive at work, the tasks to perform while they're there, and what time they can go home.
3. *Authority flows down the vertical hierarchy.*[46] Authority exists along the formal chain of command, and positions at the top of the hierarchy are vested with more formal authority than are positions at the bottom.

Organizational power can be exercised upward, downward, and horizontally in organizations. Formal authority is exercised downward along the hierarchy and is the same as legitimate power. In the following sections, we will examine vertical and horizontal sources of power for employees throughout the organization.

## ■ Vertical Sources of Power

All employees along the vertical hierarchy have access to some sources of power. Although a large amount of power is typically allocated to top managers by the organizational structure, employees throughout the organization often obtain power disproportionate to their formal positions and can exert influence in an upward direction, as Tom Hicks did at the Discovery Channel. There are four major sources of vertical power: formal position, resources, control of decision premises and information, and network centrality.[47]

**Formal Position.** Certain rights, responsibilities, and prerogatives accrue to top positions. People throughout the organization accept the legitimate right of top managers to set goals, make decisions, and direct activities. Thus, the power from formal position is sometimes called *legitimate power*.[48] Senior managers often use symbols and language to perpetuate their legitimate power, both in the workplace and their homes. For example, an intriguing economic study shows a negative correlation between CEOs buying lavish houses and the price of their organizations' shares. "It gives you some insight into the CEO's mindset... entrenched [CEOs perceive themselves] as immune from discipline by [their] board and [are] uninterested in maintaining or improving [their] performance to attract outside offers."[49] The amount of power provided to middle managers and lower-level participants can be built into the organization's structural design. The allocation of power to middle managers and staff is important because power enables employees to be productive. When job tasks are nonroutine, and when employees participate in self-directed teams and problem-solving task forces, employees are encouraged to be flexible and creative and to use their own discretion. Allowing people to make their own decisions increases their power.

Power is also increased when a position encourages contact with high-level people. Access to powerful people and the development of a relationship with them provide a strong base of influence.[50] For example, in some organizations an administrative assistant to the president will have more power than a department head because the assistant has access to the senior executive on a daily basis.

The logic of designing positions with more power assumes that an organization does not have a limited amount of power to be allocated among high-level and low-level employees. The total amount of power in an organization can be increased by designing tasks and interactions along the hierarchy so everyone can exert more influence. Former eBay CEO Meg Whitman, for example, topped *Fortune*'s list of the most powerful women in American business. Yet Whitman believes that to have power, you have to give it away. She made sure executives and employees at eBay had the power and authority they needed to contribute to the company's success.[51] Similarly, Sylvia Vogel, founder and CEO of Québec's Canderm Pharma Inc. and one of the most powerful women entrepreneurs in Canada,[52] believes that "[the] company... is like my home." For example, Vogel enforces her approach to organizational values by decreeing that no personal assistant or secretary is allowed to serve coffee in the office. "People are people and they have to be respected," she insists.[53] Both CEOs recognize that if the distribution of power is skewed too heavily toward the top, the organization will be less effective.[54]

**Resources.** Organizations allocate huge amounts of resources. Buildings are constructed, salaries are paid, and equipment and supplies are purchased. Each year, new resources are allocated in the form of budgets. These resources are allocated downward from top managers. Top managers often own stock, which gives them property rights over resource allocation. However, in some of today's organizations, employees throughout the organization also share in ownership, as they do at WestJet, which increases their power.

In most cases, top managers control the resources and, hence, can determine their distribution. Resources can be used as rewards and punishments, which are additional sources of power. Resource allocation also creates a dependency relationship. Lower-level participants depend on top managers for the financial and physical resources needed to perform their tasks. Top management can exchange resources in the form of salaries and bonuses, stock options, personnel, promotions, and physical facilities for compliance with the outcomes they desire.

**Control of Decision Premises and Information.** Control of **decision premises** means that top managers place constraints on decisions made at lower levels by specifying a decision frame of reference and guidelines. In one sense, top managers make big decisions, whereas lower-level participants make small decisions. Top management decides which goal an organization will try to achieve, such as increased market share. Lower-level participants then decide how the goal is to be reached. In one company, top management appointed a committee to select a new marketing vice president. The CEO provided the committee with detailed qualifications that the new vice president should have. He also selected people to serve on the committee. In this way, the CEO shaped the decision premises within which the marketing vice president would be chosen. Top manager actions and decisions such as these place limits on the decisions of lower-level managers and thereby influence the outcome of their decisions.[55] The control of information can also be a source of power. Managers in today's organizations recognize that information is a primary business resource and that by controlling what information is collected, how it is interpreted, and how it is shared, they can influence how decisions are made.[56] In some of today's companies, especially in learning organizations, information is openly and broadly shared, which increases the power of people throughout the organization. However, top managers generally have access to more information than do other employees. This information can be released as needed to shape the decision outcomes of other people.

Control of information can also be used to shape decisions for self-serving, unethical, and even illegal purposes. For example, at Hollinger International, which owned newspapers including the *Chicago Sun-Times* and *Jerusalem Post*, the board approved a series of transactions that allowed then CEO Lord Conrad Black and his colleagues to improperly draw off millions of dollars from the company for personal gain. Although the board has been criticized for its lax governance, several directors insist that their decisions were based on false, skewed, or misleading information provided by Lord Black.[57] On July 13, 2007, Conrad Black was found guilty of three counts of mail fraud and one count of obstruction of justice. His three co-defendants were convicted of three counts each of mail fraud.[58] In October 2010, after several legal victories that let Black leave jail after serving just over two years of his six and a half year sentence, Black had only two of his four convictions overturned. His convictions for one count of fraud and one count of obstruction of justice stood. The presiding judge "made it clear that the panel had grudgingly reversed the fraud charges, and he noted that the arguments raised had 'barely' met the test for a retrial."[59] Despite further legal representations, Black returned to prison in late 2011. In 2014, Canada stripped him of his Order of Canada and from the Queen's Privy Council for Canada.[60]

Middle managers and lower-level employees may also have access to information that can increase their power. A secretary to a senior executive can often control information that other people want and will thus be able to influence those people. Top executives depend on people throughout the organization for information about problems or opportunities. Middle managers or lower-level employees may manipulate the information they provide to top managers in order to influence decision outcomes.

**Network Centrality.** **Network centrality** means being centrally located in the organization and having access to information and people who are critical to the company's success. Top executives are more successful when they put themselves at the centre of a communication network, building connections with people throughout the company. Sir Howard Stringer, former CEO of Sony, is known as a skilled corporate politician who builds trust and alliances across different divisions and hierarchical levels. Stringer has been praised for his ability to network with almost everyone. He needed those political skills to gain an understanding of the sprawling Sony empire and to get the various divisions working together. "He's the only one I know who can manage the Japanese [electronics side] and the show-bizzers [entertainment side]," said a former head of Sony Pictures Entertainment.[61] Stringer continued with his ambitious vision for Sony—in 2008, he announced that "[we] want to restore the TV to the center of the home."[62] His ambitions were thwarted by recent developments such as the March 2011 earthquake and tsunami as well as by cyber attacks, which have cost Sony billions of dollars.[63] In 2013, Stringer announced his retirement from Sony; he was replaced by Kazuo Hirai who was the head of the video-game unit. Stringer was pleased to retire and leave Sony in Hirai's hands as "I saw in him the right mix of skills to lead Sony, and I knew it was the right time to bring about generational change...."[64]

Middle managers and lower-level employees can also use the ideas of network centrality. For example, at PricewaterhouseCoopers (PwC), two trainees, Amy Middelburg and James Shaw, were asked to write a proposal about what values should shape the merging firm. They proposed that PwC measure its business success not only by financial goals but also by global social impact. The recommendation was a radical one in a culture that was very focused on a single financial bottom line. The two passed their proposal to a partner who passed it on to another. Even so, the proposal went nowhere. Middelburg and Shaw then started to network, talking with PwC's global managing partner at a conference; recruiting a friend, Fabio Sgaragli, to help; and tailoring their message carefully to different members of their networks. The three became lead members of a team looking at ways that might revolutionize the way PwC does business. "We've had an impact on the firm because we're starting conversations," Sgaragli said. "I'm absolutely convinced that we've already planted some seeds."[65] He was also quoted as saying, "Few industries in the world are as innately conservative as the accountancy profession, yet the multi-million dollar initiatives spawned by this group were part of a major industry rethink about how to measure value."[66] Employees also have more power when their jobs are related to current areas of concern or opportunity. When a job pertains to pressing organizational problems, power is more easily accumulated. For example, managers at all levels who possess crisis leadership skills have gained power in today's world of terror alerts, major natural disasters, and general uncertainty. A communications manager at the U.S. company Empire Blue Cross and Blue Shield, for instance, gained power following the September 11, 2001, terrorist attacks in New York because he acted on his own and worked around the clock to get phone lines and voice mail restored.[67] Employees increase their network centrality by becoming knowledgeable and expert about certain activities or by taking on difficult tasks and acquiring specialized knowledge that makes them indispensable to managers above them. People who show initiative, work beyond what is expected, take on undesirable but important projects, and show interest in learning about the company and industry often find themselves with influence. Physical location also helps because some locations are in the centre of things. Central location lets a person be visible to key people and become part of important interaction networks.

**People.** Top leaders often increase their power by surrounding themselves with a group of loyal executives.[68] Loyal managers keep the top leader informed and in touch with events, and report possible disobedience or troublemaking in the organization. Top executives can use their central positions to build alliances and exercise substantial power when they have a management team that is fully in support of their decisions and actions.

This works in the opposite direction too. Lower-level people have greater power when they have positive relationships and connections with higher-ups. By being loyal and supportive of their bosses, employees sometimes gain favourable status and exert greater influence.

It is not uncommon for CEOs to surround themselves with their loyal allies as one way to reinforce their power base. According to Richard Breeden's report on Conrad Black, Hollinger Inc. was "a corporate kleptocracy" and "unfortunately, most members of the Board also saw Hollinger as Black's Company. They weren't selected by institutional shareholders for board seats, they were selected by Black."[69] Similarly, according to a senior banker from a rival firm, in describing the situation after the merger between Morgan Stanley and Dean Witter Discover & Co., "What do you really have here? A CEO who isn't terribly popular, who gets rid of any executive who isn't loyal to him. He packs the board with his pals, and the company's stock performance is mediocre. So what? That's like most companies on the S&P 500." Indeed, many top executives strive to build a cadre of loyal and supportive executives to help them achieve their goals for the organization. The U.S. government, for example, handpicked the advisers and committee members who would influence decisions made by the interim Iraqi government.[70]

## ■ The Power of Empowerment

In forward-thinking organizations, top managers want lower-level employees to have greater power so they can do their jobs more effectively. These managers intentionally push power down the hierarchy and share it with employees to enable them to achieve goals. Empowerment is power sharing, the delegation of power or authority to subordinates in an organization.[71] Increasing employee power heightens motivation for task accomplishment because people improve their own effectiveness, choosing how to do a task and using their creativity.[72]

*act!*

**Compare**

Compare the changes over time in a sport that you know well. What changes do you observe in the relative power of the players, coaches, owners, and fans?

Empowering employees involves giving them three elements that enable them to act more freely to accomplish their jobs: information, knowledge, and power.[73]

1. *Employees receive information about company performance.* In companies where employees are fully empowered, all employees have access to all financial and operational information.
2. *Employees have knowledge and skills to contribute to company goals.* Companies use training programs and other development tools to help people acquire the knowledge and skills they need to contribute to organizational performance.
3. *Employees have the power to make substantive decisions.* Empowered employees have the authority to directly influence work procedures and organizational performance, such as through quality circles or self-directed work teams.

Many of today's organizations are implementing empowerment programs, but they are empowering employees to varying degrees. At some companies, empowerment means encouraging employees' ideas while managers retain final authority for decisions; at others it means giving people almost complete freedom and power to make decisions and exercise initiative and imagination.[74] The continuum of empowerment can run from a situation in which front-line employees have almost no discretion, such as on a traditional assembly line, to full empowerment, where employees even participate in formulating organizational strategy. One organization that pushes empowerment to the maximum is Semco.

**In Practice**
**Semco**

The Brazil-based company Semco's fundamental operating principle is to harness the wisdom of all its employees. It does so by letting people control their work hours, location, and even pay plans. Employees also participate in all organizational decisions, including what businesses Semco should pursue.

Semco leaders believe economic success requires creating an atmosphere that puts power and control directly in the hands of employees. People can veto any new product idea or business venture. They choose their own leaders and manage themselves to accomplish goals. Information is openly and broadly shared so that everyone knows where they and the company stand. Instead of dictating Semco's identity and strategy, leaders allow it to be shaped by individual interests and efforts. People are encouraged to seek challenge, explore new ideas and business opportunities, and question the ideas of anyone in the company.

This high level of employee empowerment has helped Semco achieve decades of high profitability and growth despite fluctuations in the economy and shifting markets. "At Semco, we don't play by the rules," says Ricardo Semler. Semler, whose father started the company in the 1950s, says it doesn't unnerve him to "step back and see nothing on the company's horizon." He is happy to watch the company and its employees "ramble through their days, running on instinct and opportunity..."[75]

## ■ Horizontal Sources of Power

Horizontal power pertains to relationships across departments or divisions. All vice presidents are usually at the same level on the organizational chart. Does this mean each department has the same amount of power? No. Horizontal power is not defined by the formal hierarchy or the organizational chart. Each department makes a unique contribution to organizational success. Some departments will have

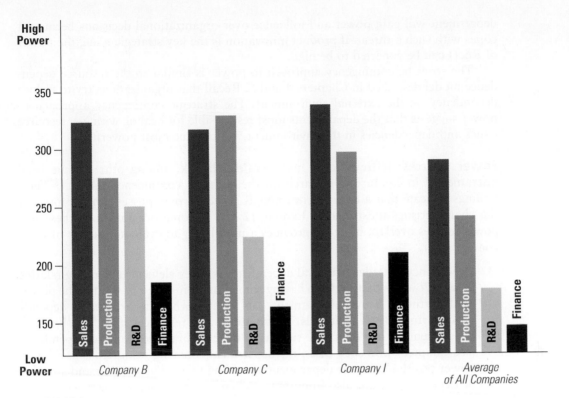

**EXHIBIT 12.4**
Ratings of Power among Departments in Industrial Firms
Source: Charles Perrow, "Departmental Power and Perspective in Industrial Firms," in Mayer N. Zald, ed., *Power in Organizations* (Nashville, Tenn.:, 1970), 64. Used with permission.

greater say and will achieve their desired outcomes, whereas others will not. For example, Charles Perrow surveyed managers in several industrial firms.[76] He bluntly asked, "Which department has the most power?" among four major departments: production, sales and marketing, R&D, and finance and accounting. Partial survey results are given in Exhibit 12.4.

In most firms, sales had the greatest power. In a few firms, production was also quite powerful. On average, the sales and production departments were more powerful than R&D and finance, although substantial variation existed. Differences in the amount of horizontal power clearly occurred in those firms. Today, IT departments have growing power in many organizations.

Horizontal power is difficult to measure because power differences are not defined on the organizational chart. However, some initial explanations for departmental power differences, such as those shown in Exhibit 12.4, have been found. The theoretical concept that explains relative power is called strategic contingencies.[77]

**Strategic Contingencies. Strategic contingencies** are events and activities both inside and outside an organization that are essential for attaining organizational goals. Departments involved with strategic contingencies for the organization tend to have greater power. Departmental activities are important when they provide strategic value by solving problems or crises for the organization. For example, if an organization faces an intense threat from lawsuits and regulations, the legal department will gain power and influence over organizational decisions because it copes with such a threat. If product innovation is the key strategic issue, the power of R&D can be expected to be high.

The strategic contingency approach to power is similar to the resource dependence model described in Chapters 4 and 5. Recall that organizations try to reduce dependency on the external environment. The strategic contingency approach to power suggests that the departments most responsible for dealing with key resource issues and dependencies in the environment will become most powerful.

**Power Sources.** Jeffrey Pfeffer and Gerald Salancik, among others, have been instrumental in conducting research on the strategic contingency theory.[78] Their findings indicate that a department rated as powerful may possess one or more of the characteristics illustrated in Exhibit 12.5.[79] In some organizations these five **power sources** overlap, but each provides a useful way to evaluate sources of horizontal power.

1. **Dependency.** Interdepartmental dependency is a key element underlying relative power. Power is derived from having something someone else wants. The power of department A over department B is greater when department B depends on department A.[80] Materials, information, and resources may flow between departments in one direction, such as in the case of sequential interdependence (see Chapter 7). In such cases, the department receiving resources is in a lower power position than the department providing them. The number and strength of dependencies are also important. When seven or eight departments must

**EXHIBIT 12.5**
**Strategic Contingencies That Influence Horizontal Power among Departments**
Source: Based on D.J. Hickson, C.R. Hinings, C.A. Lee, R.E. Schneck, and J.M. Pennings, "A Strategic Contingencies' Theory of Intraorganizational Power" *Administrative Science Quarterly* 16 (1971), 216–229.

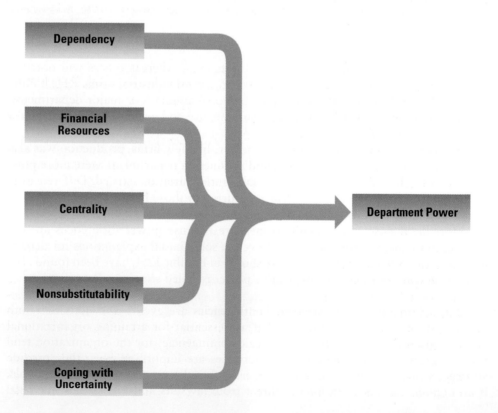

come for help to the engineering department, for example, engineering is in a strong power position. In contrast, a department that depends on many other departments is in a low power position. Likewise, a department in an otherwise low power position might gain power through dependencies. If a factory cannot produce without the expertise of maintenance workers to keep the machines working, the maintenance department is in a strong power position because it has control over a strategic contingency.

## In Practice
### Dr. Nancy Olivieri and Apotex

In 1996, Dr. Olivieri discovered an unexpected risk during her clinical trials of one of Apotex's drugs for the treatment of thalassemia, a potentially fatal blood disorder. When she tried to inform her patients of the risk, Apotex ended the trials early and warned her of legal action should she disclose the risk to anyone. Some time later, Olivieri found another, more significant risk and was warned again of possible legal action. Even so, Olivieri informed her patients and published her research in 1998 in a leading scientific journal. At the same time, the University of Toronto had reached an agreement in principle with Apotex to receive what would have been the largest donation ever received by the university.

The Canadian Association of University Teachers, in its review of the case, found that "[from] 1996 onward, Dr. Olivieri was subjected to a series of strongly adverse actions, by senior staff [at the Hospital for Sick Children], the Hospital Board of Trustees, officers at Apotex and others, some of them highly public."[81] When the Report of the Committee of Inquiry on the Case Involving Dr. Nancy Olivieri, the Hospital for Sick Children, the University of Toronto, and Apotex was released, Dr. Olivieri noted that the report vindicated her position and had found that some of the administrators at the Hospital for Sick Children had tried to discredit her and her work. This much-layered conflict was a catalyst for positive change in the university's policies on industry-sponsored research. The current policy states that scientists can no longer be prevented from disclosing risks to patients.[82]

2. **Financial resources.** There's a so-called golden rule in the business world: "The person with the gold makes the rules."[83] Control over resources is an important source of power in organizations. Money can be converted into other kinds of resources that are needed by other departments. Money generates dependency; departments that provide financial resources have something other departments want. Departments that generate income for an organization have greater power. Exhibit 12.4 showed sales as the most powerful unit in most industrial firms. This is because salespeople find customers and bring in money, thereby removing an important problem for the organization. An ability to provide financial resources also explains why certain departments are powerful. For example, fundraising departments in universities are often powerful as they bring in the funds necessary for research.

Power enables those departments that bring in or provide resources that are highly valued by an organization to obtain more of the scarce resources allocated within the organization.[84] "Power derived from acquiring resources is used to obtain more resources, which in turn can be employed to produce more power—the rich get richer."[85]

3. **Centrality.** Centrality reflects a department's role in the primary activity of an organization.[86] One measure of centrality is the extent to which the work of the department affects the final output of the organization. For example,

the production department is more central and usually has more power than staff groups (assuming no other critical contingencies). Centrality is associated with power because it reflects the contribution made to the organization. The corporate finance department of an investment bank generally has more power than the stock research department. By contrast, in the industrial firms described in Exhibit 12.4, finance tends to be low in power. When the finance department has the limited task of recording money and expenditures, it is not responsible for obtaining critical resources or for producing the products of the organization. Today, however, finance departments have greater power in many organizations because of the greater need for controlling costs.

4. **Nonsubstitutability.** Power is also determined by *nonsubstitutability*, which means that a department's function cannot be performed by other readily available resources. Similarly, if an employee cannot be easily replaced, his or her power is greater. If an organization has no alternative sources of skill and information, a department's power will be greater. This can be the case when management uses outside consultants. Consultants might be used as substitutes for staff people to reduce the power of staff groups.

   The impact of substitutability on power was studied for programmers in computer departments.[87] When computers were first introduced, programming was a rare and specialized occupation. Programmers controlled the use of organizational computers because they alone possessed the knowledge to program them. Over a period of about ten years, computer programming became a more common activity. People could be substituted easily, and the power of programming departments dropped.

5. **Coping with uncertainty.** Elements in the environment can change swiftly and can be unpredictable and complex. In the face of uncertainty, little information is available to managers on appropriate courses of action. Departments that reduce this uncertainty for the organization will increase their power.[88] When market research personnel accurately predict changes in demand for new products, they gain power and prestige because they have reduced a critical uncertainty. But forecasting is only one technique. Sometimes uncertainty can be reduced by taking quick and appropriate action after an unpredictable event occurs. Departments can cope with critical uncertainties by (1) obtaining prior information, (2) prevention, and (3) absorption.[89] Obtaining prior information means a department can reduce an organization's uncertainty by forecasting an event. Departments increase their power through prevention by predicting and forestalling negative events. Absorption occurs when a department takes action after an event to reduce its negative consequences.

Horizontal power relationships in organizations change as strategic contingencies change. In a hospital dealing with a major health crisis, the public relations department might gain power, for example, by soothing public fears and keeping people informed about the hospital's efforts to control the spread of disease. As another example, large retailers such as Walmart and Home Depot attempting to build new stores often face challenges from community activists fighting urban sprawl. The public relations department can gain power by helping the organization present a positive side to the story and counteract the arguments of protestors. Departments that help organizations cope with new strategic issues will have greater power.

# Political Processes in Organizations

Politics, like power, is intangible and difficult to measure. It is hidden from view and is hard to observe in a systematic way. Two surveys uncovered the following reactions of managers toward political behaviour.[90]

1. Most managers have a negative view toward politics and believe that politics will more often hurt than help an organization in achieving its goals.
2. Most managers believe that political behaviour is common in all organizations.
3. Most managers think that political behaviour occurs more often at upper rather than lower levels in organizations.
4. Most managers believe that political behaviour arises in certain decision domains, such as structural change, but is absent from other decisions, such as handling employee grievances.

Based on these surveys, politics seems more likely to occur at the top levels of an organization and around certain issues and decisions. Moreover, managers do not approve of political behaviour. The remainder of this chapter explores more fully what political behaviour is, when it should be used, the type of issues and decisions most likely to be associated with politics, and some political tactics that may be effective.

## Definition

Power is the ability of one person or department in an organization to influence other people to bring about desired outcomes. *Politics* is the use of power to influence decisions in order to achieve those outcomes. The exercise of power and influence has led to two ways to define politics—as self-serving behaviour or as a natural organizational decision process. The first definition emphasizes that politics is self-serving and involves activities that are not sanctioned by the organization.[91] In this view, politics involves deception and dishonesty for purposes of individual self-interest and leads to conflict and disharmony within the work environment. This dark view of politics is widely held by laypeople, and political activity certainly can be used in this way. Recent studies have shown that workers who perceive this kind of political activity within their companies often have related feelings of anxiety and job dissatisfaction. Studies also support the belief that inappropriate use of politics is related to low employee morale, inferior organizational performance, and poor decision making.[92] This view of politics explains why managers in the surveys described above did not approve of political behaviour.

Although politics can be used in a negative, self-serving way, the appropriate use of political behaviour can serve organizational goals.[93] The second view sees politics as a natural organizational process for resolving differences among organizational interest groups.[94] Politics is the process of bargaining and negotiation that is used to overcome conflicts and differences of opinion. In this view, politics is similar to the coalition-building decision processes defined in Chapter 11.

The organizational theory perspective views politics as described in the second definition—as a normal decision-making process. Politics is simply the activity through which power is exercised in the resolution of conflicts and uncertainty. Politics is neutral and is not necessarily harmful to the organization. The formal definition of organizational politics is as follows: **Organizational politics** involves activities to acquire, develop, and use power and other resources to obtain the outcome when there is uncertainty or disagreement about choices.[95] Political behaviour can be either a positive or a negative force. Uncertainty and conflict are natural and inevitable, and politics is the mechanism for reaching agreement. Politics includes informal discussions that enable participants to arrive at consensus and make decisions that otherwise might be stalemated or unsolvable.

## ■ When Is Political Activity Used?

Politics is a mechanism for arriving at consensus when uncertainty is high and there is disagreement over goals or problem priorities. Recall the rational versus political models described in Exhibit 12.2. The political model is associated with conflict over goals, shifting coalitions and interest groups, ambiguous information, and uncertainty. Thus, political activity tends to be most visible when managers confront nonprogrammed decisions, as discussed in Chapter 11, and is related to the Carnegie model of decision making. Because managers at the top of an organization generally deal with more nonprogrammed decisions than do managers at lower levels, more political activity will appear at higher levels. Moreover, some issues are associated with inherent disagreement. Resources, for example, are critical for the survival and effectiveness of departments, so resource allocation often becomes a political issue. Rational methods of allocation do not satisfy participants. Three **domains of political activity** (areas in which politics plays a role) in most organizations are structural change, management succession, and resource allocation.

Structural reorganizations strike at the heart of power and authority relationships. Reorganizations such as those discussed in Chapter 3 change responsibilities and tasks, which also affects the underlying power base from strategic contingencies. For these reasons, a major reorganization can lead to an explosion of political activity.[96] Managers may actively bargain and negotiate to maintain the responsibilities and power bases they have. Mergers and acquisitions also frequently create tremendous political activity, as we saw with the Porsche–VW example.

Organizational changes such as hiring new executives, promotions, and transfers have great political significance, particularly at top organizational levels where uncertainty is high and networks of trust, cooperation, and communication among executives are important.[97] Hiring decisions can generate uncertainty, discussion, and disagreement. Managers can use hiring and promotion to strengthen network alliances and coalitions by putting their own people in prominent positions.

The third area of political activity is resource allocation. Resource allocation decisions encompass all resources required for organizational performance, including salaries, operating budgets, employees, office facilities, equipment, use of the company airplane, and so forth. Resources are so vital that disagreement about priorities exists, and political processes help resolve the dilemmas.

**Think**

Think about situations when you would engage in political behaviour. When is such behaviour appropriate, in your view?

<table>
<tr><td>

**In Practice**

**Liberal Party of Canada**

</td><td>

On June 2, 2002, Jean Chrétien fired Paul Martin, Jr. as his finance minister. Martin had served for nearly a decade in the position. According to Chrétien, he had replaced Martin for nongovernment reasons: "[We] agreed that for the good of the governance of the country...it was better that he [Paul Martin] was not to be the minister of finance."[98] Martin claimed, however, that the differences were related to differences in government policy. Chrétien and Martin had had a professional working relationship until March 2000 when Chrétien heard that a "pro-Martin cabal

</td></tr>
</table>

was plotting his overthrow...."[99] In addition, the prime minister's supporters were well aware of the power brokers behind the so-called PM-in-waiting. "A relatively small but well-connected lobbying and consulting firm, Earnscliffe, had been dubbed the shadow PMO."[100] As a result, there was a public division between Chrétien's supporters and Martin's supporters. Martin charged that Chrétien had punished Liberals who were working against Chrétien. Chrétien responded by saying that he had never acted against those who had financially supported his political opponents. Some of Chrétien's cabinet ministers called Martin's allegations unfair and insisted that Chrétien would be supported by a majority of Liberals at the February 2003 leadership review.[101] After Chrétien resigned, Paul Martin became leader of the Liberal Party. "The Liberal gathering at Toronto's Air Canada Centre [was] more of a coronation than a convention. Martin [had] rock stars singing his praises and, more importantly, the vote of almost every single delegate in the building."[102] In Martin's first election as prime minister, the Liberal government was reduced to a minority government and, in the 2006 election, the Liberal Party was defeated by the Conservative Party. When Martin then announced that he would not continue as Liberal leader, "[not] even Liberals shed many tears for the departure of Paul Martin."[103] In 2008, Stéphane Dion, Martin's successor, faced questions about his leadership and his future. And he was replaced the following year by Michael Ignatieff. Ignatieff suffered a humiliating defeat by losing his own seat and leaving a decimated Liberal Party in 2011.

# Using Power, Politics, and Collaboration

One theme in this chapter has been that power in organizations is not primarily a phenomenon of the individual. It is related to the resources departments command, the role departments play in an organization, and the environmental contingencies with which departments cope. Position and responsibility, more than personality and style, determine a manager's influence on outcomes in the organization.

Power is used through individual political behaviour, however. Individual managers seek agreement about a strategy to achieve their departments' desired outcomes. Individual managers negotiate decisions and adopt tactics that enable them to acquire and use power. In addition, managers develop ways to increase cooperation and collaboration within the organization to reduce damaging conflicts.

To fully understand the use of power within organizations, it is important to look at both structural components and individual behaviour.[104] Although the power comes from larger organizational forms and processes, the political use of power involves individual-level activities. For instance, all managers use tactics to exert influence, but research indicates that managers in HR departments may use softer, more subtle approaches than do managers in more powerful finance departments. In one study, HR executives, who were not seen as having centrality to the firm's mission, took a low-key approach to try to influence others, whereas finance executives, who had a more central and powerful position, used harder, more direct influence tactics.[105] The following sections briefly summarize various tactics that managers can use to increase the power base of their departments, political tactics they can use to achieve desired outcomes, and tactics for increasing collaboration. These tactics are summarized in Exhibit 12.6.

**EXHIBIT 12.6**
Power and Political
Tactics in
Organizations

| TACTICS FOR INCREASING THE POWER BASE | POLITICAL TACTICS FOR USING POWER | TACTICS FOR ENHANCING COLLABORATION |
|---|---|---|
| Enter areas of high uncertainty<br>Create dependencies<br>Provide scarce resources<br>Satisfy strategic contingencies | Build coalitions and expand networks<br>Assign loyal people to key positions<br>Control decision premises<br>Enhance legitimacy and expertise<br>Make a direct appeal | Create integration devices<br>Use confrontation and negotiation<br>Schedule intergroup consultation<br>Practise member rotation<br>Create shared mission and superordinate goals |

## ■ Tactics for Increasing Power

Four **tactics for increasing power** for the organization are as follows:

1. *Enter areas of high uncertainty.* One source of departmental power involves coping with critical uncertainties.[106] If department managers can identify key uncertainties and take steps to remove those uncertainties, the department's power base will be enhanced. Uncertainties could arise from stoppages on an assembly line, from the quality demanded of a new product, or from the inability to predict a demand for new services. Once an uncertainty is identified, the department can take action to cope with it. By their very nature, uncertain tasks will not be solved immediately. Trial and error will be needed, which is to the advantage of the department. The trial-and-error process provides experience and expertise that cannot easily be duplicated by other departments.

2. *Create dependencies.* Dependencies are another source of power.[107] When the organization depends on a department for information, materials, knowledge, or skills, that department will hold power over others. This power can be increased by incurring obligations. Doing additional work that helps out other departments will obligate the other departments to respond at a future date. The power accumulated by creating a dependency can be used to resolve future disagreements in the department's favour. An equally effective and related strategy is to reduce dependency on other departments by acquiring necessary information or skills. IT departments have created dependencies in many organizations because of the continuous rapid changes in this area. Employees in other departments depend on the IT unit to master complex software programs, changing use of the Internet, and other advances so that they will have the information they need to perform effectively.

3. *Provide scarce resources.* Resources are always important to organizational survival. Departments that accumulate resources and provide them to an organization in the form of money, information, or facilities will be powerful. For example, sales departments are powerful in industrial firms because they bring in financial resources.

4. *Satisfy strategic contingencies.* The theory of strategic contingencies says that some elements in the external environment and within the organization are especially important for organizational success. A contingency could be a critical

event, a task for which there are no substitutes, or a central task that is interdependent with many others in the organization. An analysis of the organization and its changing environment will reveal strategic contingencies. To the extent that contingencies are new or are not being satisfied, there is room for a department to move into those critical areas and increase its importance and power.

In summary, the allocation of power in an organization is not random. Power is the result of organizational processes that can be understood and predicted. The abilities to reduce uncertainty, increase dependency on one's own department, obtain resources, and cope with strategic contingencies all enhance a department's power. Once power is available, the next challenge is to use it to attain helpful outcomes.

## ■ Political Tactics for Using Power

The use of power in organizations requires both skill and willingness. Many decisions are made through political processes because rational decision processes do not fit; uncertainty or disagreement is too high. **Political tactics for using power** to influence decision outcomes include the following:

1. *Build coalitions and expand networks.* Coalition building means taking the time to talk with other managers to persuade them to a point of view.[108] Most important decisions are made outside formal meetings; managers discuss issues with each other and reach agreement. Effective managers are those who huddle, meeting in groups of twos and threes to resolve key issues.[109] Effective managers also build networks of relationships across hierarchical and functional boundaries. Networks can be expanded by (1) reaching out to establish contact with additional managers and (2) coopting dissenters. One research study found that the ability to build networks had a positive impact on both employees' perception of a manager's effectiveness and the ability of the manager to influence performance.[110] Establishing contact with additional managers means building good interpersonal relationships based on liking, trust, and respect. Reliability and the motivation to work with rather than exploit others are part of both networking and coalition building.[111] The second approach to expanding networks, cooptation, is the act of bringing a dissenter into one's network. One example of cooptation involved a university committee whose membership was based on promotion and tenure. Several professors who were critical of the tenure and promotion process were appointed to the committee. Once a part of the administrative process, they could see the administrative point of view. Cooptation effectively brought them into the administrative network.[112]

2. *Assign loyal people to key positions.* Another political tactic is to assign trusted and loyal people to key positions in the organization or department. Top managers as well as department heads often use the hiring, transfer, and promotion processes to place in key positions people who are sympathetic to the outcomes of the department, thus helping achieve departmental goals.[113] Top leaders frequently use this tactic, as we discussed earlier. For example, when he became CEO at Merrill Lynch & Co., Stan O'Neal removed a whole generation of top talent and moved in other managers who supported his vision and goals for the organization. He then brought back a popular retired executive, countering charges that he was stacking the management ranks only with people who wouldn't challenge his power and authority.[114]

3. *Control decision premises.* To control decision premises means to constrain the boundaries of a decision. One technique is to choose or limit information provided to other managers. A common method is simply to put the department's best foot forward, such as selectively presenting favourable criteria. A variety of statistics can be assembled to support the departmental point of view. A university department that is growing rapidly and has a large number of students can make claims for additional resources by emphasizing its growth and large size. Such objective criteria do not always work, but they are a valuable step.

    Decision premises can be further influenced by limiting the decision process. Decisions can be influenced by the items put on an agenda for an important meeting or even by the sequence in which items are discussed.[115] Items discussed last, when time is short and people want to leave, receive less attention than those discussed earlier. Calling attention to specific problems and suggesting alternatives also will affect outcomes. Stressing a specific problem to get it—rather than problems not relevant to one's department—on the agenda is an example of agenda setting.

4. *Enhance legitimacy and expertise.* Managers can exert the greatest influence in areas in which they have recognized legitimacy and expertise. If a request is within the task domain of a department and is consistent with the department's vested interest, other departments will tend to comply. Members can also identify external consultants or other experts within the organization to support their cause.[116] For example, a financial vice president in a large retail firm wanted to fire the director of HR management. She hired a consultant to evaluate the HR projects undertaken to date. A negative report from the consultant provided sufficient legitimacy to fire the director, who was replaced with a director loyal to the financial vice president.

5. *Make a direct appeal.* If managers do not ask, they seldom receive. Political activity is effective only when goals and needs are made explicit so the organization can respond. Managers should bargain aggressively and be persuasive. An assertive proposal may be accepted because other managers have no better alternatives. Moreover, an explicit proposal will often receive favourable treatment because other alternatives are ambiguous and less well defined. Effective political behaviour requires sufficient forcefulness and risk taking to at least ask for what is needed to achieve desired outcomes.

The use of power, however, should not be obvious.[117] If managers formally draw on their power base in a meeting by saying, "My department has more power, so the rest of you have to do it my way," their power will be diminished. Power works best when it is used quietly. To call attention to power is to lose it. People know who has power. Explicit claims to power are not necessary and can even harm the department's cause.

When using any of the preceding tactics, recall that most people think self-serving behaviour hurts rather than helps an organization. If managers are perceived to be throwing their weight around or pursuing goals that are self-serving rather than beneficial to the organization, they will lose respect. On the other hand, managers must recognize the relational and political aspect of their work. It is not sufficient to be rational and technically competent. Politics is a way to reach agreement. This chapter's Book Mark describes some basic psychological principles that underlie successful political influence tactics. Managers can use this understanding to assert influence and get things done within the organization. When managers ignore political tactics, they may find themselves failing without understanding why. This is partly the reason Tim Koogle failed to accomplish a key acquisition at Yahoo!, described in the next In Practice.

# Book Mark 12.0  HAVE YOU READ THIS BOOK?

## Influence: Science and Practice
By Robert B. Cialdini

Managers use a variety of political tactics to influence others and bring about desired outcomes. In his book *Influence: Science and Practice*, Robert Cialdini examines the social and psychological pressures that cause people to respond favourably to these various tactics. Over years of study, Cialdini, Regents' Professor of Psychology at Arizona State University, has identified some basic *influence principles*, "those that work in a variety of situations, for a variety of practitioners, on a variety of topics, for a variety of prospects."

### INFLUENCE PRINCIPLES
Having a working knowledge of the basic set of persuasion tools can help managers predict and influence human behaviour, which is valuable for interacting with colleagues, employees, customers, partners, and even friends. Some basic psychological principles that govern successful influence tactics are as follows:

- *Reciprocity*. The principle of reciprocity refers to the sense of obligation people feel to give back in kind what they have received. For example, a manager who does favours for others creates in them a sense of obligation to return the favours in the future. Smart managers find ways to be helpful to others, whether it be helping a colleague finish an unpleasant job or offering compassion and concern for a subordinate's personal problems.
- *Liking*. People say yes more often to those they like. Companies such as Tupperware have long understood that familiar faces and congenial characteristics sell products. In-home Tupperware parties allow customers to buy from a friend instead of an unknown salesperson. Salespeople in all kinds of companies often try to capitalize on this principle

by finding interests they share with customers as a way to establish rapport. In general, managers who are pleasant, generous with praise, cooperative, and considerate of others' feelings find that they have greater influence.
- *Credible authority*. Legitimate authorities are particularly influential sources. However, research has discovered that the key to successful use of authority is to be knowledgeable, credible, and trustworthy. Managers who become known for their expertise, who are honest and straightforward with others, and who inspire trust can exert greater influence than those who rely on formal position alone.
- *Social validation*. One of the primary ways people decide what to do in any given situation is to consider what others are doing. That is, people examine the actions of others to validate correct choices. For instance, when homeowners were shown a list of neighbours who had donated to a local charity during a fundraiser, the frequency of contributions increased dramatically. By demonstrating, or even implying, that others have already complied with a request, managers gain greater cooperation.

### THE PROCESS OF SOCIAL INFLUENCE
Because life as a manager is all about influencing others, learning to be genuinely persuasive is a valuable management skill. Cialdini's book helps managers understand the basic psychological rules of persuasion—how and why people are motivated to change their attitudes and behaviours. When managers use this understanding in an honest and ethical manner, they improve their effectiveness and the success of their organizations.

*Influence: Science and Practice* (4th edition), by Robert B. Cialdini, is published by Allyn & Bacon, 2001.

## In Practice
### Yahoo!

In late March 2000, Yahoo! began negotiating to buy online auction leader eBay. Tim Koogle, Yahoo!'s CEO at the time, was fully in support of the deal, believing it would enable the company to beef up its e-commerce revenues and bring needed new blood to the increasingly insular Yahoo! culture. But the deal never happened, and while Yahoo!'s fortunes flagged, eBay's revenues and net income continued to climb.

What happened? Jeffrey Mallett, Yahoo!'s president, opposed the acquisition of eBay, and he used political tactics to quash it. Koogle had always been a consensus-style manager. He believed the top leaders would debate the pros and cons of the acquisition and arrive at the best decision. In addition, he felt sure the merits of the eBay deal would ultimately win the day. But Mallett, who insiders say was already angling to take over the CEO job, began courting co-founders Jerry Yang and David

Filo. Eventually, he convinced them that the eBay culture was a poor fit with Yahoo!. With Koogle outnumbered, the deal fell apart. A former Yahoo! manager called it management by persuasion.

By failing to build a coalition, Koogle allowed Mallett to control this important decision. It's only one example of several that ultimately led to Koogle being pushed out as CEO. Despite Mallett's political moves, he was passed over for the top job in favour of an outsider who board members felt could turn the struggling company around. Koogle took the decision to seek a new CEO calmly and blamed himself for not keeping a closer eye on Mallett.[118]

## ■ Tactics for Enhancing Collaboration

Power and political tactics are important means for getting things done within organizations. Most organizations today have at least moderate interunit conflict. An additional approach in many organizations is to overcome conflict by stimulating cooperation and collaboration among departments to support the attainment of organizational goals. **Tactics for enhancing collaboration** include the following:

1. *Create integration devices.* As described in Chapter 3, teams, task forces, and project managers who span the boundaries between departments can be used as integration devices. Bringing together representatives from conflicting departments in joint problem-solving teams is an effective way to enhance collaboration because representatives learn to understand each other's point of view.[119] Sometimes a full-time integrator is assigned to achieve cooperation and collaboration by meeting with members of the various departments and exchanging information. The integrator has to understand each group's problems and must be able to move both groups toward a solution that is mutually acceptable.[120]

   Teams and task forces reduce conflict and enhance cooperation because they integrate people from different departments. Integration devices can also be used to enhance cooperation between labour and management, as the example of the Brotherhood of Locomotive Engineers, the United Transportation Union, and Canadian Pacific Railway shows.

**In Practice**

**Brotherhood of Locomotive Engineers, United Transportation Union, and Canadian Pacific Railway (CPR)**

"Canadian Pacific Railway was founded in 1881 to link Canada's populated centres with the vast potential of its relatively unpopulated West. This incredible engineering feat was completed on [November] 7, 1885—six years ahead of schedule—when the last spike was driven at Craigellachie, B.C.... Canadian Pacific Railway was formed to physically unite Canada and Canadians from coast to coast."[121] It now provides freight transportation services over a 22,400 kilometre network in Canada and the United States.

In the 1980s–1990s, railroad companies in North America were selling or abandoning branch lines that they considered peripheral to their core routes. Union leaders from the Brotherhood of Locomotive Engineers and the United Transportation Union approached both CPR and Canadian National to join them to study what could be done instead of selling or abandoning the lines. The organizations began their study in 1994. In order to reduce labour costs by 30 percent and to maintain the levels of employee wages and benefits, the study committee recommended "revolutionary changes to turn two branch lines into...internal short-line operations."[122] Employees would jointly manage the lines through a process of co-determination. Co-determination entailed (1) senior labour–management participation on an oversight advisory board, (2) self-managed work groups, (3) minimally specified work rules, (4) multitasking, and (5) a new pay plan made up of salary and profit-sharing components.

As a result of the joint study committee's work, union workers were able to keep their jobs and CPR was able to keep two lines that would have been lost. "Based on the generally positive results of the two short-line railways, CPR has developed five criteria to judge potential, additional short-line railways [for] CPR: (1) the potential for the property to be self-managed, (2) the ratio of capital investment to potential revenue, (3) the degree of self-containment of the property, (4) the profits from the property must be low enough to make it desirable to convert to a short line and potential profits must be high enough to make it viable on its own, and (5) the interests of the unions and the company must be in alignment."[123]

**Labour–management teams,** which are designed to increase worker participation and provide a cooperative model for solving union–management problems, are increasingly being used at companies such as Goodyear, Ford Motor Company, and Xerox. In the steel industry, American companies such as USX and Wheeling-Pittsburgh Steel have signed pacts that give union representatives seats on the board.[124] Although unions continue to battle over traditional issues such as wages, these integration devices are creating a level of cooperation that many managers would not have believed possible just a few years ago.

2. *Use confrontation and negotiation.* **Confrontation** occurs when parties in conflict directly engage one another and try to work out their differences. **Negotiation** is the bargaining process that often occurs during confrontation and that enables the parties to systematically reach a solution. These techniques bring appointed representatives from the departments together to work out a serious dispute. Confrontation and negotiation involve some risk. There is no guarantee that discussions will focus on a conflict or that emotions will not get out of hand. However, if members are able to resolve the conflict on the basis of face-to-face discussions, they will find new respect for each other, and future collaboration becomes easier. The beginnings of relatively permanent attitude change are possible through direct negotiation.

Confrontation and negotiation are successful when managers engage in a *win–win strategy*. Win–win means both sides adopt a positive attitude and strive to resolve the conflict in a way that will benefit each other.[125] If the negotiations deteriorate into a strictly win–lose strategy (each group wants to defeat the other), the confrontation will be ineffective. The differences between win–win and win–lose strategies of negotiation are shown in Exhibit 12.7. With a win–win strategy—which includes defining the problem as mutual, communicating openly, and avoiding threats—understanding can be changed while the dispute is resolved.

One type of negotiation, used to resolve a disagreement between workers and management, is referred to as **collective bargaining.** The bargaining process is usually accomplished through a union and results in an agreement that specifies each party's responsibilities for the next two to three years. For example, Teamsters Canada and Molson Coors negotiated a team design for some warehouse, shipping, and garage operations as well as multiskill premiums for client service activities and for brewing operations.[126]

3. *Schedule intergroup consultation.* When conflict is intense and enduring, and department members are suspicious and uncooperative, top managers may intervene as third parties to help resolve the conflict or bring in third-party consultants from outside the organization.[127] This process, sometimes called *workplace mediation*, is a strong intervention to reduce conflict because it

**EXHIBIT 12.7**
Negotiating Strategies

| WIN–WIN STRATEGY | WIN–LOSE STRATEGY |
|---|---|
| Define the conflict as a mutual problem. | Define the problem as a win–lose situation. |
| Pursue joint outcomes. | Pursue own group's outcomes. |
| Find creative agreements that satisfy both groups. | Force the other group into submission. |
| Be open, honest, and accurate in communicating the group's needs, goals, and proposals. | Be deceitful, inaccurate, and misleading in communicating the group's needs, goals, and proposals. |
| Avoid threats (to reduce the other's defensiveness). | Use threats (to force submission). |
| Communicate flexibility of position. | Communicate strong commitment (rigidity) regarding position. |

Source: Adapted from JOHNSON & JOHNSON, *JOINING TOGETHER: GROUP THEORY & GROUP SKILLS*, 3rd, ©1987. Printed and Electronically reproduced by permission of Pearson Education, Inc., Upper Saddle River, New Jersey.

involves bringing the disputing parties together and allowing each side to present its version of the situation. The technique has been developed by psychologists such as Robert Blake, Jane Mouton, and Richard Walton.[128]

Department members attend a workshop, which may last for several days, away from day-to-day work problems. This approach is similar to the organization development (OD) approach described in Chapter 10. The conflicting groups are separated, and each group is invited to discuss and make a list of its perceptions of itself and the other group. Group representatives publicly share these perceptions, and together the groups discuss the results.

Intergroup consultation can be quite demanding for everyone involved. Although it is fairly easy to have conflicting groups list perceptions and identify discrepancies, exploring their differences face-to-face and agreeing to change is more difficult. If handled correctly, these sessions can help department employees understand each other much better and lead to improved attitudes and better working relationships for years to come.

4. *Practise member rotation.* Rotation means that individuals from one department can be asked to work in another department on a temporary or permanent basis. The advantage is that individuals become submerged in the values, attitudes, problems, and goals of the other department. In addition, individuals can explain the problems and goals of their original departments to their new colleagues. This enables a frank, accurate exchange of views and information. Rotation works slowly to reduce conflict but is very effective for changing the underlying attitudes and perceptions that promote conflict.[129]

5. *Create shared mission and superordinate goals.* Another strategy is for top management to create a shared mission and establish superordinate goals that require cooperation among departments.[130] As discussed in Chapter 9, organizations with strong, adaptive cultures, where employees share a larger vision for their company, are more likely to have a united, cooperative workforce. Studies have shown that when employees from different departments see that their goals are linked, they will openly share resources and information.[131] To be effective, superordinate goals must be substantial, and employees must be granted the time and incentives to work cooperatively in pursuit of the superordinate goals rather than departmental subgoals.

## Summary and Interpretation

The central message of this chapter is that conflict, power, and politics are natural outcomes of organizing. Differences in goals, backgrounds, and tasks are necessary for organizational excellence, but these differences can throw groups into conflict. Managers use power and politics to manage and resolve conflict. Two views of organization were presented. The rational model of organization assumes that organizations have specific goals and that problems can be logically solved. The other view, the political model of organization, is the basis for this chapter. This view argues that the goals of an organization are not specific or agreed upon. Departments have different values and interests, so managers come into conflict. Decisions are made on the basis of power and political influence. Bargaining, negotiation, persuasion, and coalition building decide outcomes.

The chapter also discussed the vertical and horizontal sources of power. Vertical sources of power include formal position, resources, control of decision premises and information, and network centrality. In general, managers at the top of the organizational hierarchy have more power than people at lower levels. However, positions all along the hierarchy can be designed to increase the power of employees. As organizations face increased competition and environmental uncertainty, top executives are finding that increasing the power of middle managers and lower-level employees can help the organization be more competitive. Research into horizontal power processes has revealed that certain characteristics make some departments more powerful than others. Factors such as dependency, resources, centrality, nonsubstitutability, and coping with uncertainty determine the influence of departments.

Managers can use political tactics such as building coalitions and expanding networks, assigning loyal people to key positions, controlling decision premises, enhancing legitimacy and expertise, and making a direct appeal to help departments achieve desired outcomes. Many people distrust political behaviour, fearing that it will be used for selfish ends that benefit the individual but not the organization. However, politics is often needed to achieve the legitimate goals of a department or organization. Three areas in which politics often plays a role are structural change, management succession, and resource allocation because these are areas of high uncertainty. Although conflict and political behaviour are natural and can be used for beneficial purposes, managers also strive to enhance collaboration so that conflict between groups does not become too strong. Tactics for enhancing collaboration include integration devices, confrontation and negotiation, intergroup consultation, member rotation, and shared mission and superordinate goals.

## ■ Key Concepts

authority, p. 461
centrality, p. 469
collective bargaining, p. 479
competition, p. 455
confrontation, p. 479
coping with uncertainty, p. 470
decision premises, p. 463
dependency, p. 468

domains of political activity, p. 472
financial resources, p. 469
intergroup conflict, p. 455
labour–management teams, p. 479
negotiation, p. 479
network centrality, p. 464
nonsubstitutability, p. 470
organizational politics, p. 471

political model, p. 459
political tactics for using power, p. 475
power, p. 460
power sources, p. 468
rational model, p. 459

sources of intergroup conflict, p. 465
strategic contingencies, p. 467
tactics for enhancing collaboration, p. 478
tactics for increasing power, p. 474

## ■ Discussion Questions

1. Give an example from your personal experience of how differences in tasks, personal background, and training lead to conflict among groups. How might task interdependence have influenced that conflict?
2. A noted expert on organizations said that some conflict is beneficial to organizations. Discuss.
3. In a rapidly changing organization, are decisions more likely to be made using the rational or political model of organization? Discuss.
4. What is the difference between power and authority? Is it possible for a person to have formal authority but no real power? Discuss.
5. Discuss ways in which a department in a hospital could help the CEO respond to changes in provincial health-care policies.
6. In Exhibit 12.4, R&D has greater power in company B than in the other firms. Discuss possible strategic contingencies that give R&D greater power in this firm.
7. What are some sources of power for university or college students? What are some sources of power for university professors and administrators? How might students increase their power?
8. A bookkeeper tried for several years to expose fraud in an organization's accounting department, but couldn't get anyone to pay attention to his claims. How would you evaluate this employee's power? What might he have done to increase his power and call notice to the ethical and legal problems at the organization?
9. The engineering school at a major university brings in three times as many government research dollars as does the rest of the university combined. Engineering appears wealthy and has many professors on full-time research status. Yet, when internal research funds are allocated, engineering gets a larger share of the money, even though it already has substantial external research funds. Why would this happen?
10. Which do you believe would have a greater long-term impact on changing employee attitudes toward increased collaboration—intergroup consultation or confrontation and negotiation? Discuss.

## ■ Chapter 12 Workbook: How Do You Handle Conflict?*

Think of some disagreements you have had with a friend, relative, manager, or co-worker. Then indicate how frequently you engage in each of the following behaviours.

There are no right or wrong answers, so answer the items honestly. Respond to all items using the following scale from 1 to 7.

Scale

| Always | Very often | Often | Sometimes | Seldom | Very seldom | Never |
|--------|-----------|-------|-----------|--------|-------------|-------|
| 1 | 2 | 3 | 4 | 5 | 6 | 7 |

_____ 1. I blend my ideas to create new alternatives for resolving a disagreement.

_____ 2. I shy away from topics that are sources of disputes.

_____ 3. I make my opinion known in a disagreement.

_____ 4. I suggest solutions that combine a variety of viewpoints.

_____ 5. I steer clear of disagreeable situations.

_____ 6. I give in a little on my ideas when the other person also gives in.

_____ 7. I avoid the other person when I suspect that he or she wants to discuss a disagreement.

_____ 8. I integrate arguments into a new solution from the issues raised in a dispute.

_____ 9. I will go 50–50 to reach a settlement.

_____ 10. I raise my voice when I'm trying to get the other person to accept my position.

_____ 11. I offer creative solutions in discussions of disagreements.

_____ 12. I keep quiet about my views in order to avoid disagreements.

_____ 13. I give in if the other person will meet me halfway.

_____ 14. I downplay the importance of a disagreement.

_____ 15. I reduce disagreements by making them seem insignificant.

_____ 16. I meet the other person at a midpoint in our differences.

_____ 17. I assert my opinion forcefully.

_____ 18. I dominate arguments until the other person understands my position.

_____ 19. I suggest we work together to create solutions to disagreements.

_____ 20. I try to use the other person's ideas to generate solutions to problems.

_____ 21. I offer tradeoffs to reach solutions in disagreements.

_____ 22. I argue insistently for my stance.

_____ 23. I withdraw when the other person confronts me about a controversial issue.

_____ 24. I sidestep disagreements when they arise.

_____ 25. I try to smooth over disagreements by making them appear unimportant.

_____ 26. I insist my position be accepted during a disagreement with the other person.

_____ 27. I make our differences seem less serious.

_____ 28. I hold my tongue rather than argue with the other person.

_____ 29. I ease conflict by claiming our differences are trivial.

_____ 30. I stand firm in expressing my viewpoints during a disagreement.

*Scoring and interpretation:* Three categories of conflict-handling strategies are measured in this instrument: solution oriented, nonconfrontational, and control. By comparing your scores on the following three scales, you can see which of the three is your preferred conflict-handling strategy.

To calculate your three scores, add the individual scores for the items and divide by the number of items measuring the strategy. Then subtract each of the three mean scores from seven.

*Solution oriented:* Items 1, 4, 6, 8, 9, 11, 13, 16, 19, 20, 21 (total = 11)

*Nonconfrontational:* Items 2, 5, 7, 12, 14, 15, 23, 24, 25, 27, 28, 29 (total = 12)

*Control:* Items 3, 10, 17, 18, 22, 26, 30 (total = 7)

*Solution-oriented strategies* tend to focus on the problem rather than on the individuals involved. Solutions reached are often mutually beneficial, with neither party defining himself or herself as the winner and the other party as the loser.

*Nonconfrontational strategies* tend to focus on avoiding the conflict by either avoiding the other party or by simply allowing the other party to have his or her way.

These strategies are used when there is more concern with avoiding a confrontation than with the actual outcome of the problem situation.

*Control strategies* tend to focus on winning or achieving an individual's goals without regard for the other party's needs or desires. Individuals using these strategies often rely on rules and regulations in order to win the battle.

## Questions

1. Which strategy do you find easiest to use? Most difficult? Which strategy do you use more often?
2. How would your answers have differed if the other person was a friend, family member, or co-worker?
3. What is it about the conflict situation or strategy that tells you which strategy to use in dealing with a conflict situation?

## Case for Analysis: The Irving Dynasty to End?*

In November 2007, there were media reports that the three Irving brothers, J.K., Arthur, and Jack, were going to break up their 125-year-old family business. "The reason, as in most family splits, is a succession impasse...."[1] While the three brothers had been able to make decisions collegially, their five children have not been able to do so. J.K.'s two sons run J. D. Irving Limited, the forestry side of the business. Arthur's two sons run the refinery side of the business and Jack's son, who has a Harvard MBA, "is a bit of an enigma."[2]

As the tensions between the cousins escalated, the three brothers were afraid of having the sort of internecine clashes that the McCain family had endured. As part of a planned restructuring, the family members will be offered the choice of cash or business interests. No assets will be sold to outsiders.

J. D. Irving established a sawmill in the late 1800s and K. C. Irving founded Irving Oil, both in Boutouche, New Brunswick. In 2008, the town was selected as the only finalist from Canada for the global Tourism for Tomorrow awards. Boutouche, located near Moncton, has a long Acadian history as well as being the original home of the Irving empire.[3]

K. C. Irving's first business was a small service station; he lived in the apartment above the station. In just over 80 years, it has grown into a $6 billion regional energy processing, transportation, retail, media, and marketing company headquartered in Saint John. It is privately owned and has 7,000 employees, 800 retail sites, operations from 13 marine terminals, and a fleet of tractor-trailers. It operates Canada's largest refinery and produces over 300,000 barrels of finished energy products daily.[4] It has also operations in Eastern Canada, Québec, and New England. According to the *Canadian Business* 2007 list of the richest Canadians, the Irvings are the fifth richest family in Canada, after the Thomsons, Edward (Ted) Rogers, the Westons, and Paul Desmarais, Sr.[5]

In 2006, Irving Oil announced that it was planning to build a second refinery in Saint John so that it could double its capacity. While the provincial government has responded positively to the proposed refinery, environmentalists are suing the federal government; they allege that federal government ignored its own laws by restricting the environmental assessment of the proposed refinery.[6] The lawsuit was launched by Ecojustice for the Conservation Council of New Brunswick, the Fundy Baykeeper, and the Friends of the Earth-Canada.

Both Irving Oil and the Irvings themselves are part of the lore of New Brunswick. Much of the Irving mythology revolves around the life and times of K. C. Irving:

*[He is seen] as [a] powerful tycoon, a work-obsessed, hard-nosed dealmaker who took no prisoners, who crushed unions and competitors without pity, who would sue anyone who dared touch an errant Irving-branded log, and who used vertical integration as if it were an evil conspiracy. He is seen by some as a man with too much power, a man who couldn't give a square damn about the environment, who owned rather than employed people, and who took his fortune and hoarded it in a Caribbean tax haven.[7]*

There is even a website—www.irvingsucks.com—which provides a mixture of news and criticism of Irving Oil. To counter its reputation for secrecy about its human resource policies, the company sends its leaders on executive development programs. Kenneth Irving, Arthur Irving's eldest son, was one of the first people to take the course and has emphasized the value of such courses for helping managers address issues as varied as refinery operations to email overload.[8]

The future of the Irving family and its empire remains uncertain. There are 24 grandchildren who may want to work in the various businesses. What is certain is that "[the] ownership structure [created by K. C. Irving] can't survive."[9]

### Assignment Questions

1. Why would a family business like Irving Oil generate such antipathy?
2. What changes are necessary if the organization is to continue?

*Source: Ann Armstrong.

[1]G. Pitts and J. McNish, "Irving Brothers Look to Break Up Empire," *The Globe and Mail* (November 21, 2007).
[2]G. Pitts and J. McNish, "The Irvings: Shaking the Family Tree," *The Globe and Mail* (November 22, 2007), B1.
[3]C. Alphonso, "Historic Boutouche Wins a Tourism Boost," *The Globe and Mail* (February 7, 2007), A10.
[4]Irving Oil, "About Us" (2008) at www.irvingoil.com/company (accessed June 27, 2008).
[5]J. Gray, M. Harman, L. McKeon, Z. Olijnyk, and R. Ray, "The Rich 100: Canada's Wealthiest People" (November 30, 2007) at www.canadianbusiness.com/after_hours/article.jsp?content=20071131_198701_198701
[6]"Lawsuit Challenges Ottawa over Irving Oil Refinery" (January 14, 2008) at www.cbc.ca/canada/new-brunswick/story/2008/01/14/nb-environmentalists.html?ref=rss (accessed May 19, 2011).
[7]H. Sawler, *Twenty-First Century Irvings* (Halifax: Nimbus Publishing, 2007), xiii.
[8]K. Cox, "Irving Oil Fuels Its Leaders," *The Globe and Mail* (April 21, 2004).
[9]G. Pitts and J. McNish (2007) "Irving Brothers Look to Break Up Empire," *supra*, note 1.

## Case for Analysis: The National Hockey League Collective Bargaining Agreement*

*Jeremy Yip, Phil Ward and Steve Dempsey prepared this case under the supervision of Professor Michael Sider solely to provide material for class discussion. The authors do not intend to illustrate either effective or ineffective handling of a managerial situation. The authors may have disguised certain names and other identifying information to protect confidentiality. Ivey Management Services prohibits any form of reproduction, storage or transmittal without its written permission. Reproduction of this material is not covered under authorization by any reproduction rights organization. To order copies or request permission to reproduce materials, contact Ivey Publishing, Ivey Management Services, c/o Richard Ivey School of Business, The University of Western Ontario, London, Ontario, Canada, N6A 3K7; phone (519) 661-3208; fax (519) 661-3882; e-mail cases@ivey.uwo.ca. Copyright © 2004, Ivey Management Services. Version: (A) 2007-12-07. One time permission to reproduce granted by Richard Ivey School of Business Foundation on January 24, 2014.*

### Introduction

On March 3, 2004, Bob Goodenow, executive director of the National Hockey League Players' Association (NHLPA), sat in his office staring at a calendar on his wall. On September 15, 2004, the collective bargaining agreement (CBA) between the National Hockey League (NHL) and the NHLPA would expire. With approximately six months left to contract expiration, Goodenow had to develop a communications strategy that would effectively communicate the position of the NHLPA on the players' salary cap issue to the owners and, at the same time, avoid alienating loyal hockey fans. The stakes were high: sports commentators were predicting a possible lockout if the NHLPA and NHL did not reach an agreement. Goodenow knew that few hockey fans sympathized with the players, and that the general public was fed up with the issue: on Thursday, February 19, 2004, the *Globe and Mail* had published the results of an on-line survey, which asked readers which group in the NHL labor dispute they sided with. Of the 2,126 responses, 900 of them, or 42 percent, said, "the owners," while only 175, or eight percent, responded "the players." The remaining 1,051 respondents, or 49 percent, said, "neither."

### The National Hockey League Players' Association

The National Hockey League Players' Association (NHLPA) dated back to June 1967, when player representatives

from the original six NHL clubs met to adopt a constitution and elect a director. There was widespread belief among the players that without proper representation the owners would exploit the players by maintaining low salaries, while thriving off the ticket and merchandise sales that the players were largely responsible for. The NHLPA was a labor union whose members were the players of the NHL and whose mandate was to represent their interests. Headquartered in Toronto, the NHLPA had a staff of approximately 50 employees who worked in such varied disciplines as labor law, product licensing and community relations. While the management of daily operations was the responsibility of an executive director (currently Robert W. Goodenow), ultimate power over all NHLPA activities resided with the players who each year elected representatives from their respective NHL teams in order to form an executive board. Overseeing the board was an executive committee, which consisted in 2004 of President Trevor Linden and Vice-Presidents, Bob Boughner, Vincent Damphousse, Daniel Alfredsson and Bill Guerin. The NHLPA had an overall mandate to provide its members with the opportunity to sell their services in a free-and-open-market context. Bob Goodenow, executive director of the NHLPA, represented the players at all meetings with the NHL and communicated their collective opinions.

### Past Collective Bargaining Agreement Negotiations

Despite the development of the NHLPA, the NHL existed with minimal labor disputes over the years. However, in September 1994, the NHL owners, led by Gary Bettman, the league's commissioner since 1993, forced a lockout preventing the players from reporting to training camp.[1] The work stoppage eventually ended in mid-January of 1995, but only after 34 regular season games had been

---

*This case has been written on the basis of published sources only. Consequently, the interpretation and perspectives presented in this case are not necessarily those of The National Hockey League Players' Association or any of its employees.

[1]Gary Bettman became the NHL's first Commissioner on February 1, 1993. Bettman was responsible for the operations of the league and represented the 30 privately held clubs and their owners. Bettman was hired away from the marketing-savvy National Basketball Association (NBA). In his new role, Bettman was responsible for guiding the transformation of the NHL through ambitious franchise expansion and relocation. Originally pitched as a viable route to broaden the sport's exposure, Bettman's attempt to introduce hockey in nontraditional markets resulted in half-full arenas, hemorrhaging cash flows and "franchise for-sale" signs.

lost. The major premise for the 1994 lockout was the owners' attempt to impose a salary cap on players' rising salaries. There was a surging belief among the owners that players' salaries were escalating to levels that were not sustainable. Worsening the situation, many of the new expansion teams had not generated the expected returns and the sheer number of players in the league had "depreciated" the talent pool. However, despite their reputation as "over-paid athletes," the players were able to deflect attention from themselves as the source of failure and focus media attention on the owners who were claiming to lose money, but not producing any type of documentation to support these losses. Many times throughout the labor dispute, the owners avoided media attention and failed to deliver a unified message to the general public, including the fans. In the end, only a limited salary cap, an entry-level cap restricting how much a player could earn in his first few years, was imposed. This CBA was set to expire on September 15, 2004.

## The National Hockey League/Owners' Perspective

As the time neared for the expiration of this CBA, the NHL sought changes to the new agreement. The league claimed that there were several major deficiencies in the current contract that had led to significant financial losses and a competitive imbalance. This competitive imbalance referred to the fact that smaller teams were not able to compete fairly with larger teams, and, as a result, the league as a whole could not be competitive with other professional sports and pastimes. The NHL had hoped that the current CBA would control rapid growth in player salaries and form a direct link between salary growth and the league's revenues. Although the CBA satisfactorily did so for a number of years, the league claimed that recently it had broken down, resulting in significant losses for NHL teams.

The league claimed that the root of the current CBA's ineffectiveness was the league's transition from locally based markets to league-based markets. In the past, teams could establish budgets for player payrolls based on the realities of their local markets, and retain the star players needed to make them competitive. In the new millennium, however, a league-wide marketplace had emerged, and small-market teams, which generated comparatively low revenue, were at a disadvantage. These teams were increasingly forced to lose their talented players to wealthier teams once the league-wide marketplace rendered them no longer affordable, which often occurred before the agreed-upon date for those players with unrestricted free-agent status. The only other option to the clubs was to spend greater and greater proportions of revenue to retain players; hence, clubs' spending became directly impacted by what other clubs spent.

The existing CBA was unsuccessful at dealing with these pressures. Although an entry-level salary cap had been imposed, this cap was rendered ineffective due to

signing bonuses. Moreover, restricted free agents were withholding their services until they could obtain a better contract and prices for unrestricted free agents were rapidly inflating, though unsupported by increases in productivity.

The NHL argued that the existing CBA had led to the drastic overpricing of players. League revenue grew at an unprecedented rate of 173 percent over the term of the existing CBA. On the other hand, players' salaries outpaced this growth by 261 percent over the same period.[2] Players' salaries currently accounted for 75 percent of revenues—a far higher percentage than other professional sports leagues.[3] The NHL claimed that these costs were unsustainable and made the sport uncompetitive, leading to large losses for its franchises.

In the annual Unified Report of Operations (URO), the NHL disclosed that the league had lost a substantial sum of money in recent years. It stated that the majority of teams had lost money, including both high-revenue and low-revenue teams.

Based on the URO, the NHL claimed that it was in a dire financial situation, with astronomical losses, stagnant or decreasing franchise values, and a diminishing pool of available investment capital. The league claimed that these problems were evidence that the current economic system was not working and that mechanisms were needed to control player salaries and tie them to revenue. It proposed a salary cap for players that would be tied to, or forced to grow proportionately to, revenue, and argued that this change was necessary for the NHL's survival.

## The Players' Perspective

A principal responsibility of the NHLPA was to negotiate, on behalf of the players, the terms of the CBA with the NHL. Ultimately, the CBA governed all aspects of a player's rights and responsibilities relative to his employment with an NHL club, so this upcoming negotiation was of great importance. From the NHLPA's perspective, the conditions of the current CBA were favorable to the players and, therefore, they did not want to modify those conditions. There were three main arguments against the owners' proposed solutions:

1. Free market forces should determine players' salaries.
2. The validity of owners' financial statements and situations was questionable.
3. The recent financial losses of underperforming teams and the bankruptcy of the Buffalo Sabres and Ottawa Senators were due to poor business decisions rather than players' high salaries.

In the end, the NHLPA knew that the proposed salary cap would translate into a salary cut for the players. However, despite the union's adversarial relationship with the owners

---

[2]Player costs accounted for 64 percent of revenues in the NFL, and 58 percent in the NBA—nhlcbanews.com
[3]nhlcbanews.com

on this issue, Goodenow was well aware that the future of the NHLPA depended on the overall success of the NHL.

## The Levitt Report

On February 12, 2004, the NHL held a media conference and released a report conducted by Arthur Levitt, a successful businessman and former chairman of the Securities and Exchange Commission (SEC). Levitt had conducted a thorough audit of the NHL's teams and its URO to verify the accuracy of the financial numbers released by the league. Many of the figures in the URO were open to interpretation. For example, definitions of both "hockey-related revenue" and "player costs" could differ widely according to each club. After thousands of hours of research, Levitt concluded that the URO was accurate in all material respects, and that, conservatively speaking, the NHL had a combined operating loss of $273 million in the 2002–2003 season.

## The National Hockey League's Communications Strategy

Throughout the controversy surrounding the CBA renewal, the NHL followed an open strategy of communication. Its message was simple: it believed the league was financially sick, and the only way to restore its health was to impose a salary cap. The NHL stressed that a prolonged lockout or strike would have serious adverse effects for the sport, and that several teams would likely be forced to cease operations, causing the loss of many player jobs. The NHL took the stance that it was concerned with the very survival of professional hockey. In addition, it stressed that it had nothing to hide and earnestly wanted to reach a fair and viable solution.

To convey its message, the NHL disclosed its financial situation to the public through various channels. The NHL established the website www.nhlcbanews.com to present its arguments to fans and to explain the situation, including a detailed analysis of the URO. The website also provided a vehicle to gain public feedback and address concerns.

The NHL also used the media effectively. Numerous articles on the upcoming CBA agreement were published in sports magazines, such as the *Sports Business Journal* and *Sports Illustrated*, and general news publications, such as the *Globe and Mail* and *MacLean's* (see Exhibit 1). The authors of these articles almost unanimously sided with the league, accepting the NHL's precarious financial position and the need for change and urging the NHLPA to make the concessions necessary for the league's survival.

The NHL made extensive use of facts and statistics to show the overpayment of players, and to contrast hockey-players' salaries to salaries in other more successful sports leagues. It released its URO along with a guide to aid understanding and emphasize the current financial crisis it faced. It also made a strong effort to achieve credibility by funding the Levitt report to support its claims. Levitt's integrity was widely accepted, and he took several steps to ensure his neutrality in conducting the report, such as being paid beforehand and declaring that the report would be released to the public, no matter what the results. The league also gained the support of several well-respected spokespeople such as "the Great One," Wayne Gretzky, who made statements supporting the case.

Finally, the league's message appealed to the emotions of the fans who desperately wished to avoid losing a season of their favorite sport. The multimillion-dollar contracts of hockey stars were common knowledge. When these salaries were emphasized by the NHL, fans on the whole did not feel much sympathy for the players, as indicated by surveys where the majority stated that they believed players were overpaid. Moreover, ticket prices had increased drastically over the last few years, and many fans related this increase to the players' growing salaries.

The NHL's strategy was highly successful in gaining the support of the media and the public. The Levitt report and the league's openness appealed to the media who definitively sided against the players. This "pro-owner" media support, in turn, increased the public exposure of the NHL's

**EXHIBIT 1**
Excerpts from the Media

"Hockey fans are backing NHL owners in their showdown with the players' union over a new collective bargaining agreement, according to the results of a poll released on Thursday.... The league claims its member teams lost more than $300 million last season and is demanding "costs linked to revenues guarantees" in any new deal.... The NHL Players' Association translates this as nothing more than a salary cap, something it says it will never accept even if it means shutting down the league for two seasons."

Reuters *news agency, March 5, 2004*

"That the NHL game is in a financial crisis is inarguable. Players are welcome to dispute all they wish the owners' claim of losing $300 million (U.S.) a year; fans who actually pay for their tickets know every time they come up to the gate that this game is an economic disaster."

Globe and Mail *columnist Roy MacGregor, March 4, 2004*

*(Continued)*

## Excerpts from the Media *(Continued)*

"Any reminder we needed that the NHL system is broken and needs to be fixed arrived with word Friday that Washington had traded Robert Lang, the league's leading scorer, to Detroit for draft picks and a prospect. Can anyone imagine, say, Baltimore trading Ray Lewis to Green Bay in December, or San Antonio shipping Tim Duncan to New Jersey at the NBA trade deadline? The league wouldn't allow it. But with the financial state of teams like the Capitals now, the NHL has no choice. All the more reason for the league to stick to its guns when collective bargaining agreement talks get serious this summer."

Palm Beach Post *writer Brian Biggane, February 29, 2004*

"The players appear oblivious to the NHL's declining attendance and microscopic TV ratings. If they are so blind to the league's problems and so thick-headed that the NHL will be forced to shut down next season, it probably would be a blessing for hockey fans in Buffalo and many other league cities."

Rochester Democrat & Chronicle *columnist Bob Matthews, February 28, 2004*

"Say what you want about Bettman but you can't suggest for one second he's hiding from anything. Unlike his rather quiet NHLPA counterpart, Bob Goodenow, who will not acknowledge the NHL's problems and has thus provided little in the way of constructive solutions, Bettman is working hard at quelling the masses who stand to be the biggest losers in the inevitable lockout. As The War of 2004 heats up, the commish has laid all his cards on the table. All he's waiting for now is someone to deal with.

"Doing well to ensure owners continue to win the battle for public support in the looming CBA impasse, Bettman has done well to outline the issue. Decide how the pool of $2 billion in revenues can be grown and split by 700 players, while still providing ownership across the league with a meaningful portion."

Calgary Sun *columnnist Eric Francis, February 27, 2004*

case and aided greatly in swaying public opinion. The success of the NHL's campaign was evident in a number of fan surveys conducted by independent sources, which indicated strong public support for the league.[4]

## The Problem

While the NHL had made a significant effort to communicate both financial and qualitative information to the players and the public, the NHLPA had remained relatively silent on the issue. When the Levitt report was first released, Goodenow launched a press conference to question the validity of the report (Exhibit 2). Since then, he

[4]The fans' opinions were made clear in several surveys. The Hockey News (March 16, 2004) published results showing 39 percent support for 'Owners' and only 12 percent for 'Players.' The Globe and Mail released a survey on February 19, in which 42 percent indicated that they sided with the owners, as opposed to 8 percent for the players.

**EXHIBIT 2**
**Press Release by Bob Goodenow Addressing the Levitt Report**
Source: Reproduced by permission of the National Hockey League Players' Association.

TORONTO—Bob Goodenow, NHLPA Executive Director, had the following comments in response to the League commissioned report by Arthur Levitt:

"We understand the Levitt report took 12 months and thousands of hours to complete. Because we received the report from the League late this morning, it will take more than a couple of hours of review to fully comment. Selected media outlets received this report days before us, which speaks volumes about its intended audience. Without a detailed review of all the underlying documents one can only make preliminary comments on the report:

1.  The owners and their commissioner Gary Bettman have obviously found it necessary to retain a new spokesman/ consultant to provide general conclusions about League finances while still not disclosing any individual team information or providing an opportunity to examine the actual records upon which the conclusions are allegedly based.

2. We understand that 12 months ago, Levitt was retained by the League's commissioner through two New York City based law firms. The League did not advise the NHLPA of this initiative and there has been no discussion of it by the parties, even though we had many discussions of issues flowing from the URO process during the substantive economic discussions and collective bargaining sessions we have had over the last 12 months. Against this background, it is clear the Levitt report is simply another League public relations initiative. To suggest the report is in any way independent is misleading.

3. We have consistently stated that one critical issue of disagreement between the NHLPA and the League on finances is how to define the complete business of owning an NHL franchise, and how to address the significant inconsistencies contained in the NHL's voluntary and unaudited URO reporting process. At the outset it is clear the Levitt report, commissioned by the League, is fundamentally flawed when the author "elects" to define hockey revenues on the same basis as used in the NBA and NFL for defining revenues in their salary cap systems.

4. We were given access to the UROs for 30 clubs, but were only able to conduct a thorough review of four NHL clubs. On those four clubs alone we found just over $52 million in hockey related revenues and benefits not reported in the League's voluntary and unaudited URO process. If we are given similar access to all of the other individual teams' financial information, presumably used in the Levitt report, we will be in a position to provide further comment.

*We continue to believe that a market system, not a team of hired-gun accountants, provides the best measure of the value of the hockey business. In a market system, the owner decides how much to pay the players. The owner knows the value of his business better than any paid consultant or league employee and the owner uses this knowledge when he sets player salaries. In our view, there is no better indicator of the true value of the players and the business."*

*Source: Reproduced by permission of the National Hockey League Players' Association.

had done very little to sway public opinion. With approximately six months until contract expiration, Goodenow realized that he must devise a communications strategy that would place the NHLPA in a strong bargaining position for the upcoming negotiation in September 2004 with the NHL owners and, at the same time, retain fan loyalty.

## Assignment Questions

1. What are Goodenow's goals and objectives?
2. What factors could help him reach his objectives? How?

## ■ Chapter 12 Workshop: Understanding Conflict in Your Teams*

You need to do this workshop activity with your teammates.

1. Describe a recent conflict that your team has experienced.
2. Discuss what caused the conflict.
3. How did you resolve the conflict? If you did not resolve the conflict, what should you have done differently and why?

4. What have you learned about conflict and power dynamics in your team?

*Source: Ann Armstrong.

# Integrative Cases

## Integrative Case 1.0

## IKEA: Scandinavian Style*

*"Behind the mountain there are people too."*

Old Swedish Proverb

As one of the world's most successful businessmen, Ingvar Kamprad never forgot the dreams, aspirations, and hard work of rural people, or their ability to find solutions to difficult problems. Growing up on the farmland of southern Sweden, Kamprad embodied many of the traits of the hearty men and women who surrounded him and, as an ambitious working boy, revealed the business traits that would contribute to his later success and reputation. As a child, Kamprad learned the concept of serving the needs of ordinary people by purchasing matches in bulk, which he then sold to rural customers at a profit. While still in his teens, he expanded his retail operation to sell everything from pencils to Christmas cards and upgraded the efficiency of his distribution by using the regional milk-delivery system.

### Beginnings

In 1943, at age 17, Kamprad formed IKEA with initials representing his first and last names, along with that of the family farm (Elmtaryd) and the nearby village (Agunnaryd). Anticipating the rising consumerism amid the rebuilding boom that would follow the war, IKEA moved quickly to provide families with low-cost furniture designs through the convenience of catalogue sales. With the opening of the company's first showroom in 1953, Kamprad created a model of vertical integration, uniting a variety of suppliers under the IKEA umbrella, coordinating long run production schedules, and controlling distribution. That model expanded in 1964 with the introduction of the first warehouse store, eliminating an entire step in product distribution by allowing warehouse container pick-up by customers.

*The business lessons Kamprad mastered as a boy entrepreneur were evidenced at the corporate level in many ways. For example, the bulk purchasing of matches in his youth was a forerunner to the bulk purchase of fabric that expanded upholstery choices for consumers and made the luxury of fabric options, formerly limited to the wealthy, available to all customers. Likewise, IKEA used imaginative distribution and delivery options, such as when an IKEA employee cleverly discovered the company's "flat box" approach in 1955. While attempting to load a table into a customer's automobile, an employee simply removed the table legs, enabling a new vision of selling furniture—unassembled. Practical solutions wedded to a low-cost promise created a new IKEA formula of "knock-down" furniture, flat-box*

*storage and shipping, and assembly by consumers armed with IKEA-developed assembly tools and visual instructions. This formula revolutionized the home furnishings industry.*

A major strength of IKEA lies in its pioneering distribution created through unique corporate-supplier relationships. In the earliest days of the company, Swedish fine furniture manufacturers attempted to boycott IKEA and drive it out of business for selling furniture at such low cost. Kamprad outmaneuvered them by forging new partnerships with other Scandinavian manufacturers, providing assurances of long production runs. Moreover, top managers learned that affordable furniture can be provided without the necessity of owning the factories. IKEA is something of a "hollow" or virtual corporation because nearly all of its manufacturing is outsourced. IKEA uses normal short-term purchasing contracts with suppliers, which means it can quickly adjust orders to changes in demand and not be saddled with huge unsold inventory. Suppliers are also in competition with one another to keep costs low. IKEA has indirect control over suppliers because it often purchases 90 to 100 percent of a supplier's production. Aware of the importance of supplier relationships, IKEA maintains a constant vigilance in working with suppliers to find ways to cut costs while keeping quality standards high, occasionally even agreeing to underwrite supplier technical assistance. That can-do attitude with suppliers has served IKEA well over time.

### Supplier Relationships

Today, with 1,300 suppliers in 53 countries, IKEA's integrated design, production, and distribution faces new problems. The sheer numbers can weaken long production runs and disperse supply lines. Global reach also means that domestic requirements vary from one region to another or that certain areas, such as Eastern Europe, have few suppliers capable of high-quality, low-cost production. In addition, furniture competitors have not been idly sitting by, but have garnered lessons from the furniture giant. In the face of these challenges, IKEA continues to believe in the power of its ingenuity. Design teams work with suppliers in imaginative ways. For example, the need for expertise in bent-wood design for a popular armchair resulted in a partnership with ski-makers. Likewise, the need throughout Scandinavia for affordable housing resulted in IKEA's expansion into manufactured homes, built on supplier factory floors and delivered to construction sites, ready to be filled with IKEA furnishings, conveniently assisted through $500 in IKEA gift certificates to the homeowner.

**1.0**

From the outset, IKEA represented more than catch phrases such as low price and convenience. Looking out for the families of modest incomes leads to IKEA's constant adherence to frugality, which is reflected in a cultural abhorrence for corporate office perks such as special parking or dining facilities. IKEA executives are expected to fly "coach." In his effort to bring "a little bit of Sweden to the world," Kamprad created a lifestyle model that would mold consumer habits and attitudes. True to the rural values of his homeland, Kamprad nurtured the ideal of the *IKEA family*, referring to employees as *co-workers*, and bestowing the name *Tillsammans* (Swedish for "Together") on the corporate center.

## Mission and Culture

The higher cultural purpose of IKEA was reaffirmed in 1976 with the publication of Kamprad's *Testament of a Furniture Dealer*, which states explicitly that IKEA is about "creating a better everyday life for the majority of people." He went on, "In our line of business, for instance, too many new and beautifully designed products can be afforded by only a small group of better-off people. IKEA's aim is to change this situation." The purpose of providing fine-looking furniture to the masses was to be met via an internal culture that Kamprad described with words such as the following: "informal, cost conscious, humbleness, down to earth, simplicity, will-power, making do, honesty, common sense, facing reality, and enthusiasm." Achieving this purpose meant employees had to have direct personal experience with the needs of the customer majority.

Visualizing the constantly changing needs of a customer base comprised of farmers and college students, young professionals, and on-the-go families, Kamprad defined IKEA's business mission as *"to offer a wide variety of home furnishing items of good design and function at prices so low that the majority of people can afford to buy them."* This is "place-holder" furniture, filling the constantly changing needs in the lives of individuals and families. But the company would go further than merely providing the solution to a consumer's immediate needs. From furniture design to catalogue layout or the arrangement of warehouse showrooms, Kamprad and his co-workers gently imprinted Swedish style and cultural values of home, frugality, and practicality. As CEO Anders Dahlvig explained in a 2005 interview for *Business Week*, "IKEA isn't just about furniture. It's a lifestyle."

That lifestyle is reflected in the consumer shopping experience. The convenience of helpful touches—providing tape measures and pencils, a playroom that frees parents for leisurely shopping, a restaurant midway through the building to provide a shopping break—is a key part of the IKEA experience. Also familiar is the gray pathway, guiding the shopper along wide aisles through the 300,000-square-foot store. A veritable labyrinth, the route provides the charm of surprise as shoppers venture past the showrooms or leads to total confusion for those who venture off the intended path. Everything is carefully orchestrated; price tags are draped always to the left of the object, large bins lure with the promise of practical and inexpensive "must-haves," and room arrangements include special touches that spark vision and stimulate add-on purchases.

IKEA's attention to detail is honed through a variety of strategies that link management and co-workers at all levels to their customers. *Anti-bureaucracy week* places executives on stock-room and selling floors, tending registers, answering customer queries, or unloading merchandise from trucks. IKEA's *Loyalty Program* and *Home Visits* program allow company researchers entrance to consumer homes in order to better determine individual and community needs for furniture designs. The results of such efforts can be practical, such as specially designed storage units for urban apartment dwellers, or deeper drawers to meet the wardrobe needs of Americans. They can also help in detecting or anticipating cultural shifts. IKEA was the first retailer to acknowledge through its advertising the broadening definition of family to include multi-racial, multi-generational, and single-sex family arrangements and to promote its openness to "all families."

## Challenges

Over the decades, efforts at strengthening IKEA and consumer family ties and encouraging repeat business as customers moved from one phase of life into another produced a unique global brand famous for innovation. The company's devotion to lifestyle solutions led to rapid movement on two fronts, the expansion of product lines (now over 9,500 products) and the expansion of global markets. By 2010 there were 332 IKEA stores in 41 countries. Global economic woes of recent years—including slumps in world stock markets, rising unemployment, and personal financial insecurity—increased sales and profits for IKEA. As consumers searched for ways to trim overall expenses and cut home furnishing costs, the company continued experiencing steady growth with a sales increase of 7.7 percent to 23.1 billion Euros.

However, the company's rapid global expansion and the rise of imitators in providing low-cost, quality home furnishings led some critics to believe IKEA had abandoned its maverick methods and relinquished its innovative edge. They detected a loosening of the company's strict core values, established more than half a century ago and reinforced in the training of co-workers in the *IKEA Way*.

Other critics take the opposite view and claim that IKEA is provincial. The problems from this viewpoint are the result of those strict core values, monitored on a regular basis through *Commercial Reviews*, measuring how closely the various stores adhere to the IKEA Way. IKEA repeatedly surveys customers, visitors, suppliers, and co-workers about their satisfaction with the IKEA relationship. Repeating the surveys provides clear feedback and even measures important trends, especially if the results venture from the expected 5's toward the dreaded 1's. The critics would argue that the constant pressure for Kamprad's "little bit of Sweden" creates a culture that scorns strategic planning, is slow to react to cultural nuance in new locations, and offers limited opportunity for professional growth or advancement for non-Swedes. They could point out that the notion of *people behind the mountain* should work both ways.

## Globalization

Global expansion into non-European markets, including the United States, Japan, and China, magnified the problems and the need for flexibility. Examples abound. The focus on standardization rather than adaptation poses problems for an industry giant such as IKEA, particularly as it enters Asian markets that are culturally different. IKEA's dependence on standardization for everything from store layout to the Swedish names of all products presented translation problems when informing Asian consumers about shopping and shipping procedures. Addressing cultural differences (women are the prime decision-makers and purchasers for the home), store and product specifications (for example, lowering store shelves and adjusting the length of beds), or consumer purchasing power (a worker may need up to a year and a half to purchase a product) was critical to company success in China. Furthermore, IKEA managers realized the need to shift focus from selling furniture to providing home decorating advice when they discovered that many skilled consumers could use the convenient tape measures and pencils to sketch pieces which they could then build for themselves at home.

In the U.S. market, IKEA was slow to make allowances, such as a shift from measuring in meters to feet and inches. While consumers embraced low pricing and the convenience of break-down furniture, the company's delay in bed size designation to the familiar king, queen, and twin drove U. S. customers bonkers because "160 centimeters" meant nothing to them. Co-worker issues also arose. Angry American workers in locations such as Danville, Virginia moved to unionize amid complaints of discrepancies in pay ($8.00 per hour compared to the $19.00 per hour for workers in Sweden), vacation (12 days annually for U.S. workers compared to five weeks for their counterparts in Sweden), and the constant demands by strict managers in requiring, for example, mandatory overtime.

Officials with IKEA admit they "almost blew it" in America and that they are committed to being both global and local. They insist they are responsive to issues and people. The company points to a history of standing against corruption and to its own quick response when a subcontractor's bribery efforts brought the hint of scandal to IKEA's door. CEO Mikael Ohlsson proudly points to the company's recent record in looking out for the needs of ordinary people through charitable projects such as IKEA Social Initiatives, benefiting over 100 million children. Service to people "behind the mountain" also requires acknowledgement of the mountain. IKEA places a priority on sustainability, working to improve company energy efficiency as reflective of its commitment to thrift, the wise use of natural resources, and a family level regard for stewardship of the earth. From the elimination of wood pallets and the ban on use of plastic bags to the installation of solar panels and the phasing out of sales on incandescent light bulbs, IKEA leads consumers and competitors by example and demonstration of its core values.

**1.0**

## Behind the Curtain

Despite the concerns of critics, those values established by Kamprad remain intact through the combination of co-worker training in the IKEA Way and a carefully crafted organization structure that leaves little room for cultural or corporate change. Although retired (since 1986), Kamprad remains senior advisor on a board dominated by fellow Swedes. Organization structure resembles the IKEA flat box, with only four layers separating the CEO and the cashier on the sales floor. And the culture is in good hands with current CEO Mikael Ohlsson, who says bluntly, "we hate waste," as he points with pride at a sofa that his engineers found a way to ship in one-half the container space, thus shaving €100 from the price—and sharply reducing carbon-dioxide emissions while transporting it.

Historically, financial details about IKEA have been kept tight and neat and, until recently, secretive. The full public disclosure of information such as sales, profits, assets, and liabilities appeared for the first time in 2010 on the heels of a Swedish documentary. The ability to maintain such an opaque organization dates back 30 years. Nineteen eighty-two marked the transfer of IKEA ownership to Ingka Holding, held by Stichting INGKA Foundation (a Dutch non-profit). Kamprad chairs the foundation's five-member executive committee.

The IKEA trademark is owned by IKEA Systems, another private Dutch company whose parent, IKEA Holding, is registered in Luxembourg and owned by Interogo, a Liechtenstein foundation controlled by the Kamprad family. This complex organizational setup enables IKEA to minimize taxes, avoid disclosure, and through strict guidelines protect Kamprad's vision while minimizing the potential for takeover.

### The Future

The vision remains, but with global expansion IKEA's corporate culture ventured into ways to use technology to bond loyal IKEA customers while tapping into their ideas and valuable feedback. The company expanded its e-commerce sales and initiated the *IKEA Family Club* in order to strengthen ties with existing customers and build long-term relationships. Family club members assist in sharing values and ideas and providing co-creating value for everything from product development to improvements in stores and service. Members are encouraged to increase their visits to stores, on-site "experience rooms," and the website to familiarize themselves with products and to build ties of shared-development in finding real-life solutions to the home furnishings challenges they encounter at various stages of their lives. This latest development in the long history of IKEA reinforces the decades-old goal of the founder to continue to look behind the mountain to meet the needs of the ordinary people.

### ■ Sources

Laura Collins, "House Perfect: Is the IKEA Ethos Comfy or Creepy?" *The New Yorker* (October 3, 2011), 54–66.

Colleen Lief, "IKEA: Past, Present & Future," *IMD International* (June 18, 2008), http://www.denisonconsulting.com/Libraries/Resources/-IMD-IKEA.sflb.ashx (accessed January 4, 2012).

Kerry Capell, "IKEA: How the Swedish Retailer Became a Global Cult Brand," *BusinessWeek* (November 14, 2005), 96–106.

Bo Edvardsson and Bo Enquist, "'The IKEA Saga': How Service Culture Drives Service Strategy," *The Services Industry Journal* 22, no. 4 (October 2002), 153–186.

Katarina Kling and Ingela Goteman, "IKEA CEO Anders Dahlvig on International Growth and IKEA's Unique Corporate Culture and Brand Identity," *Academy of Management Executive* 17, no. 1 (2003), 31–37.

Anonymous, "The Secret of IKEA's Success: Lean Operations, Shrewd Tax Planning, and Tight Control," *The Economist* (February 26, 2011), 57–58.

"IKEA: Creativity Key to Growth," *Marketing Week* (July 19, 2007), 30.

Gareth Jones, "IKEA Takes Online Gamble," *Marketing* (May 25, 2007), 14.

Bob Trebilcock, "IKEA Thinks Global, Acts Local," *Modern Material Handling* 63 no. 2 (February 2008), 22.

Anonymous, "IKEA Focuses on Sustainability," *Professional Services Close-Up* (September 26, 2011).

D. Howell, "IKEA 'LEEDS' the Way," *Chain Store Age* special issue (2006), 97–98.

Ulf Johansson and Asa Thelander, "A Standardized Approach to the World," *International Journal of Quality & Service Sciences* 1, no. 2 (2009), 199–219.

Anonymous, "IKEA Aims to Have 15 Stores in China by 2015," *Asia Pulse* (June 24, 2011).

Mei Fong, "IKEA Hits Home in China: The Swedish Design Giant, Unlike Other Retailers, Slashes Prices for the Chinese," *The Wall Street Journal* (March 3, 2006), B.1.

Ali Yakhlef, "The Trinity of International Strategy: Adaptation, Standardization, and Transformation," *Asian Business & Management* 19, no. 1 (November 2009), 47–65.

M. Roger, P. Grol and C. Schoch, "IKEA: Culture as Competitive Advantage," *ECCH Collection* (1998), available for purchase at http://www.ecch.com/educators/products/view?id=22574 (Case reference # 398-173-1).

## Integrative Case 2.0

### The Hospital for Sick Children (SickKids®)*

The Hospital for Sick Children, commonly and affectionately known as SickKids, is located in hospital row in Toronto. SickKids is a world-renowned teaching and research hospital and is one of Toronto's best-known and much-loved landmarks.

### Background

In 1875, Elizabeth McMaster led a group of determined socially prominent women to found the hospital. The Ladies Committee ran the hospital for 17 years. McMaster was actively involved in the management of the hospital; in 1891, motivated by a spiritual commitment to social action, she became a trained nurse and served as lady superintendent.[1] When the hospital started to expand, its governance was transferred to a board of trustees, an organizational design that continues today.

Throughout its history SickKids has had many accomplishments: (1) in 1908, the hospital installed the first milk pasteurization plant in Canada, 30 years before it was legally mandated; (2) it pioneered renowned surgical developments such as the Salter operation to repair the dislocation of a hip and the Mustard operation to correct an often-fatal heart detect; (3) in the 1960s, it opened one of the first intensive care units in North America devoted exclusively to the care of critically ill newborn and premature babies; and (4) its researchers determined that humidity is an ineffective therapy for the common childhood ailment croup.[2]

SickKids has also piloted the use of PEBBLES (Providing Education By Bringing Learning Environments to Students). PEBBLES allows students to maintain a connection to their regular educational environment from an isolated and unusual setting, such as a hospital. PEBBLES is a joint undertaking by the Centre for Learning Technologies at Ryerson University, the Adaptive Technology Resource Centre at the University of Toronto, and Telebotics.[3]

In 2006, SickKids launched the SickKids Learning Institute whose purpose is to enhance training and education by coordinating activities across professions and specialties. According to Dr. Susan Tallett, director of the institute, "[by] making SickKids' expertise more accessible, we will build local, national, and international networks of educators and learners that can work together on key

child care issues."[4] (To see many more milestones at SickKids, visit http://www.sickkids.ca/AboutHSC/section.asp?s=History+and+Milestones&sID=11889&ss=Milestones&ssID=488).

### Current Strategy

SickKids has a clear and compelling vision—*Healthier children. A better world.*™ SickKids is guided by five strategic directions: (1) to lead nationally and internationally; (2) to enhance system capabilities by partnering with other organizations so that children have equitable access to health care; (3) to integrate further its activities of care, education, and research; (4) to establish its own focus areas in care, education, and research; and (5) to achieve operational excellence so that evidence-based decision making, accountability, information management, and accountability are institutionalized in the SickKids' culture.[5]

### Emergency Department

For many Ontario residents, the Emergency Department is the first and only contact they have with SickKids. It is a time of acute anxiety for both children and parents. The triage nurse is the first person that the children and parents meet. She/He must determine the severity of the child's condition to ensure that those with acute conditions receive treatment first. The child is then seen by a nurse, followed by one or more physicians. The Emergency Department pediatrician has final responsibility for the child's care. Specialists may be called for consultation.[6]

### One Emergency Room Story—Caitlin

Caitlin had just turned two and she appeared to be the picture of health. But her mother, Natalie, was concerned about her stomach, which seemed to be distended. She took Caitlin to their family doctor, who sent them to a local hospital for blood tests. Doctors there knew something wasn't right and immediately transferred her to SickKids for further examination.

In the Emergency Department, doctors re-ran all the blood tests to confirm the diagnosis of leukemia. Caitlin was admitted to the Hematology/Oncology inpatient unit, where she had to endure even more tests. Doctors discovered that many of her organs were enlarged from the disease, and started her on chemotherapy immediately.

*Written by Ann Armstrong, 2008, for the first Canadian edition. The author is most grateful to Lutfi Haj-Assaad, Director of Emergency Medicine, Poison Information Centre, Motherisk Program, Division of Infectious Diseases, Pediatric Medicine and Respiratory Medicine, for his insights and support.

Caitlin was initially at SickKids for over seven weeks. Although she responded well to treatment, she had her ups and downs. When she first started chemotherapy, there were numerous complications, including several bouts of bowel inflammation. Since many of the chemotherapy drugs she was taking can result in pneumatosis, her treatment had to be delayed until she recovered. She was so ill at one point that the Critical Care team at SickKids was on standby in case she had to be transferred to the Critical Care Unit.

She received chemotherapy as an outpatient at her local hospital, which was set up as one of the satellite oncology centres. There, pediatricians and nurses trained at SickKids administered chemotherapy and took care of central lines. Though she was treated at a satellite local hospital, she still came to SickKids every 12 weeks for checkups, blood tests, and lumbar punctures.

Caitlin recently celebrated a big milestone—she finished her chemotherapy treatment for the leukemia she's fought for two-and-a-half years.[7]

## Emergency Department Reorganization

In 2002, approximately 50 members of the Emergency Department team participated in a facilitated strategic retreat. Lutfi Haj-Assaad, the director of the department, asked participants to work on the following three assignments: (1) what we want the Emergency Department to be—for patients, the department, and ourselves: Creating a vision for the Emergency Department; (2) how we need to function to make the vision happen: The vision starts with us; and (3) how we will improve Emergency Department decision making: The proposed departmental structure. At the retreat, Haj-Assaad described a possible structure, a shared governance model. Participants were divided into six working groups for the day. Following each assignment, each working group presented the results of their work to the larger group. The detailed results are presented in Exhibit 1 on page 498.

Forty-seven participants evaluated the retreat and forty-three gave a positive assessment of the experience. See Table 1 for their responses.

The retreat resulted in five immediate action steps: (1) circulating the facilitator's notes to all staff and physicians of the department; (2) inviting staff feedback and questions regarding the draft vision created during the strategic retreat and proposed organizational structure within two weeks; (3) asking Emergency Department staff to sign up to participate in one of the decision-making councils; (4) assigning Haj-Assaad to chair the first meeting of each decision-making council to help facilitate the development of council ground rules and terms of references, and to help select a chairperson; and (5) scheduling the Governance Council's first meeting in April 2002.

The shared governance model splits decision making into six councils: policy and practice, education, research, human resource and scheduling, social, and quality and ethics. The Governance Council is charged with strategic planning, goal setting, and performance monitoring. It is the formal link between the six councils and deals with any issues that are not within the councils' purview. (See Figure 1.)

The Policy and Practice Council has three mandates: (1) to review, promote and evaluate professional and clinical practice; (2) to develop, review and approve policies and procedures within the department; and (3) to foster continuous patient care improvement. The Education Council has four mandates: (1) to provide a forum for education that enhances professional practice,

**TABLE 1**
Retreat Evaluation Data

| WHAT WAS GOOD ABOUT THE DAY? (PERCENTAGE OF PARTICIPANTS) | WHAT COULD HAVE BEEN BETTER? (PERCENTAGE OF PARTICIPANTS) |
|---|---|
| Constructive discussion and brainstorming, 34% | More concrete solutions/direction, 23% |
| Team and multidisciplinary participation, 28% | More information about shared governance, 17% |
| Worked like a team/worked in teams, 19% | More planning of committees and shared governance, 13% |
| Solution/positive focused, 17% | |
| Got to know/meet members of team, 13% | More of the Emergency Department doctors present, 4% |
| Feeling there's hope, 9% | Agenda in advance, 4% |
| Feeling there's leadership, 9% | Talk about conflict resolution re: staff who won't "play ball," 4% |
| Lunch, 6% | |
| Shared governance model, 4% | More staff participation, 2% |
| We have a common vision, 2% | Discussion geared to medical stakeholders, 2% |
| Structure of the day/we were on time, 2% | More staff present, 2% |

**FIGURE 1**
Emergency
Department Structure,
October 2007

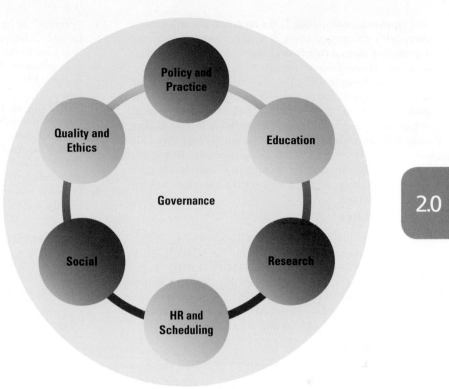

(2) to identify staff learning needs, (3) to develop plans to meet staff educational needs, and (4) to develop an equitable system to reimburse staff educational expenses. The HR and Scheduling Council's mandate spans the range of human resource activities from work assignment to employee selection to skills assessment to developing rules for schedule changes. The Ethics and Quality Management Council has four mandates: (1) to provide a forum for discussion of ethical situations, (2) to monitor risk and quality management issues, (3) to develop audit tools and to conduct audits, and (4) to recommend change, as necessary. The Social Council's mandate to develop tactics to boost morale and to plan activities based on staff interest. Lastly, the Research Council is responsible for approving any studies conducted in the department and ensuring that all research follows appropriate ethics protocols.

Each council has a chair—he/she works on the front line in the department. In late 2007, three were chaired by physicians, two by nurses, and one by a volunteer and an employee of the Child Life Specialist. Haj-Assaad chairs the governance Council. All the councils are open to all the Emergency Department staff. However, only the permanent members of a particular council can vote on the council's decisions. Membership on a council is attained by being an active participant in the council's work. Councils make many difficult and sometimes con-

tentious decisions. In the five years of the shared governance model experience, Haj-Assaad has not had to veto any council decisions.

The shared governance model was a radical departure from the previous departmental structure. In addition, it is a structure that is not used in other hospitals' emergency rooms in the way it is implemented at SickKids. The structure is guided by three core principles—the structure must be first in the best interests of the patients, then the department as a whole, and, lastly, the different disciplines. The structure allows for decisions to be made as close as possible to point of service and, as a result, is empowering. It also requires accountability and "there's no place for non-participation or non-ownership of the process."[8]

## Haj-Assaad's Reflections on the Design

Staff engagement in the operation of the department is extremely powerful and important to the success of our work. The integrity and sincerity of the department's leadership in supporting the shared governance structure is paramount. The understanding of the staff members of what the structure is and/or is not makes implementing and living it much easier. The design was meant to increase the department effectiveness and provide a context for partnership, equity, accountability, and ownership. On many occasions, the staff needed to be reminded that this design is not democratic-based as much as it's accountability-based.

Any time new staff is hired, the structure is explained to them with the expectation that every employee of the department plays a role in decision making either through councils' representation or decision implementation.

Often the staff will go to the managers with an issue and it's always tempting to make a decision and solve the problem. However, the manager has to be conscious of not doing so and must direct the employee to take his/her issue with potential solutions to the appropriate council.

Having used this design for over five years, I can't imagine the Emergency Department staff accepting any ... alternative decision-making structure.

### ■ Notes

1. J. Young, "A Divine Mission: Elizabeth Mc-Master and the Hospital for Sick Children, 1875–92," *CBMH/BCHM* 11 (1994), 71–90.
2. "SickKids History" (December 15, 2005) at http://www.sickkids.ca/AboutHSC/section.asp?s=History+and+Milestones&sID=11889&ss=SickKids+History&ssID=211 (accessed July 11, 2008).
3. "Pebbles" at http://www.ryerson.ca/pebbles (accessed July 12, 2008); and A. Blackburn-Evans, "Connecting Sick Kids to the Classroom," *Edge* 4 (2003), 1.
4. *The Hospital for Sick Children 2006–07 Annual Report*, 13.
5. Ibid.
6. "Welcome to Emergency" (September 7, 2007) at http://www.sickkids.ca/FamilyInformation/section.asp?s=Emergency&sID=7388&ss=Welcome+to+Emergency&ssID=7389 (accessed July 12, 2008).
7. "Meet Caitlin" (2007) at http://www.sickkidsfoundation.com/believe/caitlin.asp# (accessed July 12, 2008).
8. Personal communication with Lutfi Haj-Assaad, February 10, 2008.

### ■ Assignment Questions

1. What was effective in Haj-Assaad's approach? What was not?
2. What do you think of the new governance model?

---

**EXHIBIT 1**
Detailed Findings from Retreat

**A. What we want Emergency Department to be—for patients, the department, and ourselves: Creating a vision for the Emergency Department.**

**Background**

- The Emergency Department has been operating in a crisis management mode.
- There is a lot of energy within the Department—lots of people doing lots of things—but this activity could be more focused.
- Decisions are not being made, accepted, and/or implemented.
- Resources are strained and the scarcity is fragmenting the team.
- The Emergency Department has no guiding vision or directing principles to help focus activity, energy, and decision making.

**The Assignment**

- Form six groups and write a great vision statement that clearly communicates your aspirations for the Emergency Department—what *you* want it to be—in the future.
- Include in your vision statement your aspirations of how the Emergency Department will be for patients, the staff who work there, and the hospital.

**Results**

- The six groups presented their vision statements to the entire group.
- During the break, participants voted for the **two** vision statements that best captured their aspirations for the department.
- Each participant has two votes, but could not vote for the vision statement created by [his/her] own group.

- There was a clear favourite among the six vision statements, with a total of 27 votes.
- The Emergency Department will deliver family-centred patient care through dedicated, skilled professionals.
- We will create a supportive environment of mutual respect and responsiveness to the individual needs of all families and staff.
- We will foster partnerships to develop innovative therapies to set the gold standard for children's care.
- There was a high degree of overlap or commonality between the six vision statements. Some of the common themes included aspirations about:
  - Being the best—"exceptional," "gold standard," "leader in delivery," and "world-class."
  - How team members would treat each other (and patients/families)—words such as "mutually supportive, morale-enhancing academic environment," "supportive environment of mutual respect," "tolerance and respect for all," "respecting cultural and religious diversity," and "great place to work and learn."
  - Being responsive to patients' needs (and staff needs)—"timely accessible family-centred car," "timely evidence-based holistic," and "responsive to the needs of families and ourselves."
  - Continuous learning and improvement—"outcome-based, quality-based," "innovative ideas," "continuously re-evaluated," and "innovative therapies."
  - Collaboration—"community involvement and collaboration with agencies and intra-hospital services" and "foster partnerships."
  - The team—"committed staff" and "dedicated, skilled professionals."

**B. How we need to function to make the vision happen: The vision starts with us.**

**Background**

- The visions created in the previous exercise are not apparent in the Emergency Department today.
- There are plenty of issues outside the Emergency Department that need to be resolved before the Department's vision can be realized.
- There are also plenty of things we can do that will make a substantial difference inside the Emergency Department to move toward the vision.
- We need to change within the Emergency Department before we can change the Emergency Department.

**The Assignment**

- Form six groups and identify how we need to operate or function within the Emergency Department to start making the vision real—what can we do as individuals and as a group to change the Emergency Department?
  - **State** clearly what needs to change inside the Emergency Department that is related to how we behave (e.g., what we do and how we do it).
  - Briefly explain why this is a potential roadblock to realizing the vision.
  - Propose at least one solution.
- "Thought-starters" for the assignment: orientation, professionalism, standards, training, education, morale, disagreement, quality work-life, teamwork, communication, decision making, attitude, feedback, conflict, measurement, management leadership decisions.
- Each team will present its findings to the large group.

(Continued)

2.0

**Detailed Findings from Retreat** *(Continued)*

**Results**

- The six groups presented the issues they identified to the larger group, along with some of their solutions.
- There was a high degree of overlap between the issues identified by groups, and a high degree of consensus among participants that these issues are important.
- The key issues are listed below:
  - Patient flow
  - Physical resource allocation and use (including skill mix versus need)
  - Communication between team members and teams
  - Quality assurance and measurement
  - Protocols, guidelines, and standards being met/followed
  - Mutual respect/morale/how we treat each other
  - Education, orientation, and mentoring
- In the discussion following the presentation of the Emergency Department internal issues, three issues surfaced:
  - It was noted that the tension and pressure inherent in an Emergency Department often result in people treating each other in ways they otherwise wouldn't. Under stress, respect, courtesy, and dignity are often compromised.
  - There is a high degree of frustration inside the Emergency Department that was fuelling this stress; frustration at the lack of progress and change, and a feeling of powerlessness to effect change.
  - While the morning exercises were valuable, the group *had* created a vision and identified a similar list of issues confronting the Division four years ago. Nothing has changed in the interim.
- The ensuing discussion focused on accountability, summarized by the following questions:
  1. Is each of us accountable for how we treat others—for what we say and how we behave? What are we saying about ourselves when we say the stress and tension of the Emergency Department make us behave in ways we're not accountable for? Are we or are we not accountable for our own actions?
  2. Nothing has changed in four years since these issues were first identified—who is accountable for allowing this to continue? What are we now holding accountable for making the necessary changes we've discussed today? Who will we point the finger at if the changes don't happen over the next four years: ourselves or someone else?
  3. Does each of us feel *personally* accountable for moving the Emergency Department toward the vision?

**C. How we'll improve Emergency Department decision making: The proposed departmental structure.**

**Background**

- There is frustration within the Emergency Department at the lack of positive meaningful change and decision making.
- People feel powerless to effect change.
- We each need to be more accountable for moving the Emergency Department in the direction of the vision.

- Shared governance was introduced as a means of putting decision making and accountability in the hands of the Emergency Department team.
- Six decision-making groups were described: education, research, human resources and scheduling, social, quality and ethics, and policy and practice. The seventh group, the Governance Council, was introduced as the link between the six groups as well as providing direction and counsel.
- Group decision-making processes need to be decided and worked out by the team.
- Group composition, membership, and rules of conduct need to be established.
- When asked for comments or questions, there was mostly silence from participants. A couple of people in the team remarked that the concept sounded positive.
- Mostly people seemed either shocked by the idea or puzzled as to what it really meant and how it would affect them and the Emergency Department.

**The Assignment**

- The Challenge: Again, form six groups. Each will be assigned to one of the six councils. Pick one of the high-priority issues from the list that you think is most closely related to your council's mandate. Decide (1) what to do about the issue and (2) the best process for deciding what to do about it.

**Results**

- The six groups wrestled with their issues. Some had heated discussions.
    - The groups presented their findings to the entire group.
    - [They] presented lists of ideas and potential solutions, but little in the way of decisions.
    - Others presented decisions, and processes for making future decisions.
    - In this exercise, participants experienced a little of what shared governance is about.
    - Participants were asked, in the context of shared governance, what they wanted from their leadership. Here's what they said:

        1. Trust our decisions.
        2. Support our decisions and, when you can't, give us direction.
        3. Be visible in the department.
        4. Take an interest in what we're doing, and what we're confronting.
        5. Be responsive with feedback: if it can't be done, tell us why not, and if it can, tell us when.
        6. Keep us on track and focused on the vision in shared governance groups.
        7. Help us deal with conflict and group impasse in our shared governance decision making.
        8. Give us more information about shared governance (e.g., how it works, history, philosophy, principles, and examples).

2.0

## Integrative Case 3.0

## Costco: Join the Club*

Following high school, James Sinegal worked for discount warehouse Fed Mart unloading mattresses. Then, in the 1970s as an employee of California-based Price Club, he absorbed every detail of the high-volume, low-cost warehouse club formula pioneered by Sol Price.

Armed with knowledge and ideas, Sinegal partnered with Jeffrey Brotman to establish Costco Wholesale Corporation. The duo opened their first store in Seattle in 1983. Today, nearing 30 years in business, Sinegal's vision and success not only eclipsed those of his mentor but led to the merger of Costco and Price Club.

**3.0**

### No Frills

In 2010, Costco's reputation for rock-bottom pricing and razor-thin profit margins helped the company maintain its position as the nation's fourth-largest retailer and the number-one membership warehouse retailer with 572 stores (425 in the United States), 142,000 employees, and 55 million members. Sales reached $76 billion, up 9.1 percent and reflecting, in part, a consumer tendency in a poor economy to focus on value, but more significantly a unique corporate culture that gives not only lip-service to the value of its employees, but maintains a reputation for honouring that value.

The no-frills warehouse-club concept exemplifies the much-maligned "big box" store—merchandise stacked floor to ceiling on wooden pallets, housed in 150,000 square footage of bare concrete, and illuminated by fluorescent lighting. Customers flash member cards and push oversized carts or flatbeds down wide aisles, unadorned by advertising or display. Costco reflects industry standards and consumer expectations for providing limited selection, volume buying, and low pricing.

### Valuing People

But the owners believe the secret to Costco's success lies in the many ways the company ventures from the norm by overturning conventional wisdom. Because the owners view people as the organization's "competitive edge," labour and benefits comprise 70 percent of Costco's operating costs. Despite Wall Street criticism, the company maintains its devotion to a well-compensated workforce and scoffs at the notion of sacrificing the well-being of employees for the sake of profits. The 2010 Annual Report declares, "With respect to expenses relating to the compensation of our employees, our philosophy is not to seek to minimize the wages and benefits they earn. Rather, we believe

that achieving our longer-term objectives of reducing turnover and enhancing employee satisfaction requires maintaining compensation levels that are better than the industry average." The report admits Costco's willingness to "absorb costs" of higher wages that other retailers routinely squeeze from their workforce. As a result, what the company lacks in margin per item, management believes it makes up in volume, in maintaining "pricing authority" by "consistently providing the most competitive values," and in purchased loyalty memberships which, Sinegal points out, "locks them into shopping with you."

Sinegal is a no-nonsense CEO whose annual salary ($550,000) is a fraction of the traditional pay for large corporate executives and reflects an organizational culture that attempts to minimize disparity between management and workers. Luxury corporate offices are out of the question. Sinegal dresses in casual attire, wears a nametag, answers his own phone, and like all members of management, spends a significant amount of time (upwards of 200 days annually) on the warehouse sales floor.

This unorthodox employer-employee relationship is in sharp contrast to the industry norm, with employees in most companies feeling the added stress of infrequent site visits by suited corporate executives. During an interview for ABC's news magazine "20/20" in 2006, Sinegal provided a simple explanation for the frequency of warehouse visits. "The employees know that I want to say hello to them, because I like them." Indeed, Costco employees marvel at the CEO's ability to remember names and to connect with them as individuals. It is that "in the trenches together" mind-set that defines Costco's corporate culture, contributing to a level of mutual support, teamwork, empowerment, and rapid response that can be activated for confronting any situation. A dramatic example occurred when employees instantly created a Costco emergency brigade, armed with forklifts and fire extinguishers, whose members organized themselves and rushed to offer first aid and rescue trapped passengers following the wreck of a commuter train behind a California warehouse store.

Costco's benevolent and motivational management approach manifests itself most dramatically in wages and benefits. Employees sign a one-page employment contract and then join co-workers as part of the best-compensated workforce in retail. Hourly wages of $17.00 smash those of competitors ($10 to $11.50 per hour). Rewards

*From Daft. Organization Theory and Design, 11E. © 2013 South-Western, a part of Cengage Learning, Inc. Reproduced by permission. www.cengage.com/permissions

and bonuses for implementation of time-saving ideas submitted by an individual employee can provide up to 150 shares of company stock. In addition, employees receive a generous benefits package including health care (82 percent of premiums are paid by the company) as well as retirement plans.

Costco's generosity to employees flies in the face of industry and Wall Street conventional wisdom whereby companies attempt to improve profits and shareholder earnings by keeping wages and benefits low. Sinegal insists the investment in human capital is good business. "You get what you pay for," he asserts. As a result, Costco enjoys the reputation of a loyal, highly productive workforce, and store openings attract thousands of quality applicants.

By turning over inventory rather than people, Costco can boast an annual employee turnover of only six percent, compared to retail's dismal 50 percent average. Taking into account the cost of worker replacement (1.5 to 2.5 times the individual's annual salary), the higher wages and benefits package pays off in the bigger picture with higher retention levels, a top-quality workforce, low shrinkage from theft (0.2 percent), and greater sales per employee. The combination results in increased operating profit per hour. Whether used for attracting customers or employees, the need for PR or advertising is nonexistent. Sinegal told ABC that the company doesn't spend a dime on advertising, as it already has over 140,000 enthusiastic ambassadors scattered through Costco's warehouses.

## Design to Fit

Equal care has been given to organization design. Sinegal's belief in a "flat, fast, and flexible" organization encourages de-facto CEO designation for local warehouse managers who have the freedom and authority to make quick, independent decisions that suit the local needs of customers and employees. The only requirement is that any decision must fit into the organization's five-point code of ethics. Decisions must be lawful, serve the best interests of customers and employees, respect suppliers, and reward shareholders. Likewise, employee training places a high priority on coaching and empowerment over command and control.

All of this fits together in a culture and structure in which the focus on meeting customer needs goes beyond rock-bottom pricing. Costco's new store location efforts seek "fit" between the organization and the community it serves. Typical suburban locations emphasize the bulk shopping needs of families and small businesses, and Costco has extended its own private label, Kirkland Signature. While other companies downsize or sell their private labels, Costco works to develop Kirkland, which now accounts for approximately 400 of Costco's 4,000 in-stock items. The private label provides additional savings of up to 20 percent off of products produced by top-manufacturers, such as tires made by Michelin specifically for the Kirkland label. Additional efforts to better meet the needs of customers contributed to Costco's decision to run selected stores as test labs. Over the past decade, selected Costco stores paved the way for launching a variety of ancillary businesses, including pharmacies, optical services, and small business services to better serve the one-stop-shopping needs of the company's suburban customers.

Meanwhile, urban Costco locations acknowledge the customer's desire to purchase in bulk while also serving the upscale shopping desires of condo-dwellers. In these locations, the urgency to "purchase before it's gone" tempts consumers into treasure hunts with special deals on luxury items such as Dom Pérignon Champagne, Waterford crystal, or Prada watches.

The rapid growth of Costco from one store in Seattle to America's warehouse club leader and global retailer has come with a share of growing pains as the organization attempts to adapt to its various environments. The merger with Price Club brought an infusion of unionized workers, forcing Sinegal and management officials to push Costco's "superior" wages and benefits as a way to negate the need for unionization.

## New Issues

Costco's own reputation for high ethical standards and self-regulation has, in the face of rapid expansion, come up against myriad new problems ranging from complaints about a lack of notification for management job openings to persistent complaints of a glass-ceiling that provides few opportunities for the advancement of women within the organization. In response, the company instituted online job postings, automated recruiting, the use of an outside vendor for hiring, and a recommitment to equity in promotion.

International issues are often more complex and often run up against local needs and perceptions. For example, efforts to expand into Cuernavaca, Mexico, were viewed from the company perspective as a win-win situation, opening a new market and providing jobs and high-quality, low-priced items for area shoppers. When the site of a dilapidated casino became available, Costco moved quickly, but suddenly found itself facing charges of cultural insensitivity in Mexico. Accusations in Cuernavaca that Costco was locating a parking lot over an area with significance in artistic and national heritage led to negotiations under which Costco set aside millions of dollars to preserve landscape, restore murals, and work alongside city planners and representatives of the Mexican Institute of Fine Arts & Literature in the building of a state-of-the-art cultural center and museum.

3.0

The story illustrates the emphasis on moral leadership that has come to characterize Costco and its senior management. Business decisions based strictly on financial terms take a back seat to success based on broader criteria: Are we creating greater value for the customer? Are we doing the right thing for employees and other stakeholders? Management believes that the answers to these broader questions help keep the company relevant to the issues and trends shaping the future of business.

Indications are bright for Costco's future, but questions loom on the horizon. Company visionary Sinegal signals no plans to retire, but everyone from Wall Street pundits to customers, shareholders, and employees wonders how the organization might change after he has stepped down. Will future leaders be willing to maintain the modest levels of compensation for top management and maintain the company's above-average wages and benefits for employees? And how will increased globalization alter the strong corporate culture?

**3.0**

## ■ Sources

Richard L. Daft, "Costco Wholesale Corporation, Parts One–Six," in *Management*, 8th ed. (Mason, OH: Southwestern, 2008).

"Table of Contents, Item 7—Management's Discussion and Analysis of Financial Conditions," *Costco 2010 Annual Report.*

Wayne F. Cascio, "The High Cost of Low Wages," *Harvard Business Review* 84, no. 2 (December 2006).

Alan B. Goldberg and Bill Ritter, "Costco CEO Finds Pro-Worker Means Profitability," ABC News 20/20, August 2, 2006, http://abcnews.go.com/2020/Business/story?id=1362779 (accessed January 4, 2012).

Doug Desjardins, "Culture of Inclusion: Where Top Executives Lead by Example and Honesty and Frugality Are Valued Virtues," *DSN Retailing Today* (December 2005).

Michelle V. Rafter, "Welcome to the Club," *Workforce Management* 84, no. 4 (April 2005), 40–46.

# Integrative Case 4.0

## "Ramrod" Stockwell*

The Benson Metal Company employs about 1,500 people, is listed on the stock exchange, and has been in existence for many decades. It makes a variety of metals that are purchased by manufacturers or specialized metal firms. It is one of the five or six leading firms in the specialty steel industry. This industry produces steels in fairly small quantities with a variety of characteristics. Orders tend to be in terms of pounds rather than tons, although a 1,000-pound order is not unusual. For some of the steels, 100 pounds is an average order.

The technology for producing specialty steels in the firm is fairly well established, but there is still a good deal of guesswork, skill, and even some "black magic" involved. Small changes are made in the ingredients going into the melting process, often amounting to the addition of a tiny bit of expensive alloying material in order to produce varieties of specialty steels. Competitors can analyze one another's products and generally produce the same product without too much difficulty, although there are some secrets. There are also important variations stemming from the type of equipment used to melt, cog, roll, and finish the steel.

In the period that we are considering, the Benson Company and some of its competitors were steadily moving into more sophisticated and technically more difficult steels, largely for the aerospace industry. The aerospace products were far more difficult to make, required more research skills and metallurgical analysis, and required more "delicate" handling in all stages of production, even though the same basic equipment was involved. Furthermore, they were marketed in a different fashion. They were produced to the specifications of government subcontractors, and government inspectors were often in the plant to watch all stages of production. One firm might be able to produce a particular kind of steel that another firm could not produce even though it had tried. These steels were considerably more expensive than the specialty steels, and failures to meet specifications resulted in more substantial losses for the company. At the time of the study about 20 percent of the cash value output was in aerospace metals.

The chairman, Fred Benson, had been president (managing director) of the company for two decades before moving up to this position. He is an elderly man but has a strong will and is much revered in the company for having built it up to its present size and influence. The president,

Tom Hollis, has been in office for about four years; he was formerly the sales director and has worked closely with Fred Benson over many years. Hollis has three or four years to go before expected retirement. His assistant, Joe Craig, had been a sales manager in one of the smaller offices. It is the custom of this firm to pick promising people from middle-management and put them in the "assistant-to" position for perhaps a year to groom them for higher offices in their division. For some time these people had come from sales, and they generally went back as managers of large districts, from whence they might be promoted to a sales manager position in the main office.

Dick Benson, the executive vice president (roughly, general manager), is the son of Fred Benson. He is generally regarded as being willing, fairly competent, and decent, but weak and still much under his father's thumb. Traditionally, the executive vice president became president. Dick is not thought to be up to that job, but it is believed that he will get it anyway.

Ramsey Stockwell, vice president of production, had come into the organization as an experienced engineer about six years before. He rose rather rapidly to his present position. Rob Bronson, vice president of sales, succeeded Dick Benson after Benson had a rather short term as vice president of sales. Alan Carswell, the vice president of research, has a doctorate in metallurgy and some patents in his name, but he is not considered an aggressive researcher or an aggressive in-fighter in the company.

## The Problem

When the research team studied Benson Metal, there were the usual problems of competition and price-cutting, the difficulties with the new aerospace metals, and inadequate plant facilities for a growing industry and company. However, the problem that particularly interests us here concerned the vice president of production, Ramsey Stockwell. He was regarded as a very competent production man. His loyalty to the company was unquestioned. He managed to keep outdated facilities operating and still had been able to push through the construction of quite modern facilities in the finishing phases of the production process. But he was in trouble with his own staff and with other divisions of the company, principally sales.

It was widely noted that Stockwell failed to delegate authority to his subordinates. A steady stream of people came into his office asking for permission for this and that or bringing questions to him. People who took some

*Charles Perrow, Yale University. Reprinted by permission.

4.0

action on their own could be bawled out unmercifully at times. At other times they were left on their own because of the heavy demands on Stockwell's time, given his frequent attention to details in some matters, particularly those concerning schedules and priorities. He "contracted" the lines of authority by giving orders directly to a manager or even to a head foreman rather than by working through the intermediate levels. This violated the chain of command, left managers uninformed, and reduced their authority. It was sometimes noted that he had good people under him but did not always let them do their jobs.

The key group of production people rarely met in a group unless it was to be bawled out by Stockwell. Coordinating committees and the like existed mainly on paper.

More serious perhaps than this was the relationship to sales. Rob Bronson was widely regarded as an extremely bright, capable, likable, and up-and-coming manager. The sales division performed like a well-oiled machine and also had the enthusiasm and flashes of brilliance that indicated considerable adaptability. Morale was high, and identification with the company was complete. However, sales personnel found it quite difficult to get reliable information from production as to delivery dates or even what stage in the process a product was in.

Through long tradition, they were able to get special orders thrust into the work flow when they wanted to, but they often could not find out what this was going to do to normal orders, or even how disruptive this might be. The reason was that Stockwell would not allow production people to give any but the most routine information to sales personnel. In fact, because of the high centralization of authority and information in production, production personnel often did not know themselves. "Ramrod" Stockwell knew, and the only way to get information out of him was to go up the sales line to Rob Bronson. The vice president of sales could get the information from the vice president of production.

But Bronson had more troubles than just not wanting to waste his time by calling Stockwell about status reports. At the weekly top-management meeting, which involved all personnel from the vice presidential level and above, and frequently a few from below that level, Bronson would continually ask Stockwell whether something or other could be done. Stockwell always said that he thought it could be. He could not be pressed for any better estimations, and he rarely admitted that a job was, in fact, not possible. Even queries from President Tom Hollis could not evoke accurate forecasts from Stockwell. Consequently, planning on the part of sales and other divisions was difficult, and failures on the part of production were many because it always vaguely promised so much. Stockwell was willing to try anything, and worked

his head off at it, but the rest of the group knew that many of these attempts would fail.

While the people under Stockwell resented the way he took over their jobs at times and the lack of information available to them about other aspects of production, they were loyal to him. They admired his ability and they knew that he fought off the continual pressure of sales to slip in special orders, change schedules, or blame production for rejects. "Sales gets all the glory here" said one. "At the semiannual company meeting last week, the chairman of the board and the managing director of the company couldn't compliment sales enough for their good work, but there was only the stock 'well done' for production; 'well done given the trying circumstances.' Hell, Sales is what is trying us." The annual reports over the years credited sales for the good years and referred to equipment failures, crowded or poor production facilities, and the like in bad years. But it was also true that problems still remained even after Stockwell finally managed to pry some new production facilities out of the board of directors.

Stockwell was also isolated socially from the right group of top personnel: He tended to work later than most, had rougher manners, was less concerned with cultural activities, and rarely played golf. He occasionally relaxed with the manager of aerospace sales, who, incidentally, was the only high-level sales person who tended to defend Stockwell. "Ramrod's a rough diamond; I don't know that we ought to try to polish him," he sometimes said.

But polishing was in the minds of many. "Great production man—amazing what he gets out of that mill. But he doesn't know how to handle people. He won't delegate; he won't tell us when he is in trouble with something; he builds a fence around his people, preventing easy exchange," said the president. "Bullheaded as hell—he was good a few years ago, but I would never give him the job again," said the chairman of the board. He disagreed with the president that Stockwell could change. "You can't change people's personalities, least of all production men." "He's in a tough position," said the vice president of sales, "and he has to be able to get his people to work with him, not against him, and we all have to work together in today's market. I just wish he would not be so uptight."

A year or so before, the president had approached Stockwell about taking a couple of weeks off and joining a leadership training session. Stockwell would have nothing to do with it and was offended. The president waited a few months, then announced that he had arranged for the personnel manager and each of the directors to attend successive four-day T-group sessions run by a well-known organization. This had been agreed on at one of the directors' meetings, though no one had taken it very seriously.

One by one, the directors came back with marked enthusiasm for the program. "It's almost as if they had our company in mind when they designed it," said one. Some started having evening and weekend sessions with their staff, occasionally using the personnel manager, who had had more experience with this than the others. Stockwell was scheduled to be the last one to attend the four-day session, but he canceled at the last minute—there were too many crises in the plant, he said, to go off that time. In fact, several had developed over the previous few weeks.

That did it, as far as the other vice presidents were concerned. They got together themselves, then with the president and executive vice president, and said that they had to get to the bottom of the problem. A top-level group session should be held to discuss the tensions that were accumulating. The friction between production and sales was spilling over into other areas as well, and the morale of management in general was suffering. They acknowledged that they put a lot of pressure on production, and were probably at fault in this or that matter, and thus a session would do all the directors good, not just Stockwell. The president hesitated. Stockwell, he felt, would just ride it out. Besides, he added, the "Old Man" (chairman of the board) was skeptical of such techniques. The executive vice president was quite unenthusiastic. It was remarked later that Stockwell had never recognized his official authority, and thus young Dick feared any open confrontation.

But events overtook the plan of the vice presidents. A first-class crisis had developed involving a major order for their oldest and best customer, and an emergency top management meeting was called, which included several of their subordinates. Three in particular were involved: Joe Craig, assistant to the president, who knows well the problems at the plant in his role as troubleshooter for the managing director; Sandy Falk, vice president of personnel, who is sophisticated about leadership training programs and in a position to watch a good bit of the bickering at the middle and lower levels between sales and production; Bill Bletchford, manager of finishing, who is loyal to Stockwell and who has the most modern-equipped phase of the production process and the most to do with sales. It was in his department that the jam had occurred, due to some massive scheduling changes at the rolling phase and to the failure of key equipment.

In the meeting, the ground is gone over thoroughly. With their backs to the wall, the two production men, behaving somewhat uncharacteristically in an open meeting, charge sales with devious tactics for introducing special orders and for acting on partial and misinterpreted information from a foreman. Joe Craig knows, and admits, that the specialty A sales manager made promises to the customer without checking with the vice president of sales, who could have checked with Stockwell. "He was

right," says Vice President Bronson. "I can't spend all my time calling Ramsey about status reports; if Harrison can't find out from production on an official basis, he has to do the best he can." Ramsey Stockwell, after his forceful outburst about misleading information through devious tactics, falls into a hardened silence, answering only direct questions, and then briefly. The manager of finishing and the specialty A sales manager start working on each other. Sandy Falk, of personnel, knows they have been enemies for years, so he intervenes as best he can. The vice president of research, Carswell, a reflective man, often worried about elusive dimensions of company problems, then calls a halt with the following speech:

*You're all wrong and you're all right. I have heard bits and pieces of this fracas a hundred times over the last two or three years, and it gets worse each year. The facts of this damn case don't matter unless all you want is to score points with your opponents. What is wrong is something with the whole team here. I don't know what it is, but I know that we have to radically rethink our relations with one another. Three years ago this kind of thing rarely happened; now it is starting to happen all the time. And it is a time when we can't afford it. There is no more growth in our bread-and-butter line, specialty steels. The money, and the growth, is in aerospace; we all know that. Without aerospace we will just stand still. Maybe that's part of it. But maybe Ramsey's part of it too; this crisis is over specialty steel, and more of them seem to concern that than aerospace, so it can't be the product shift or that only. Some part of it has to be people, and you're on the hot seat, Ramsey.*

Carswell let that sink in, then went on.

*Or maybe it's something more than even these.... It is not being pulled together at the top, or maybe, the old way of pulling it together won't work anymore. I'm talking about you, Tom [Hollis], as well as Fred [Benson, the chairman of the board, who did not attend these meetings] and Dick [the executive vice president, and heir apparent]. I don't know what it is, here are Ramsey and Rob at loggerheads; neither of them are fools, and both of them are working their heads off. Maybe the problem is above their level.*

There is a long silence. Assume you break the silence with your own analysis. What would that be?

### ■ Assignment Questions

1. What are Stockwell's vertical sources of power?
2. What are the horizontal sources of power?
3. How could empowerment improve this situation?
4. What do you recommend for this company?

## Integrative Case 5.0

## Make Green Delicious: Sustainability at Jamie Kennedy Kitchens*

*Melissa Leithwood wrote this case under the supervision of Professor Oana Branzei solely to provide material for class discussion. The authors do not intend to illustrate either effective or ineffective handling of a managerial situation. The authors may have disguised certain names and other identifying information to protect confidentiality. Ivey Management Services prohibits any form of reproduction, storage or transmittal without its written permission. Reproduction of this material is not covered under authorization by any reproduction rights organization. To order copies or request permission to reproduce materials, contact Ivey Publishing, Ivey Management Services, c/o Richard Ivey School of Business, The University of Western Ontario, London, Ontario, Canada, N6A 3K7; phone (519) 661-3208; fax (519) 661-3882; e-mail cases@ivey.uwo.ca. Copyright © 2007, Ivey Management Services. Version: (A) 2007-12-07. One time permission to reproduce granted by Richard Ivey School of Business Foundation on January 24, 2014.*

**5.0**

"Growing past the artisan stage doesn't make sense to me," thought Jamie Kennedy, one of Canada's most celebrated chefs on May 18, 2007, as he was pondering several expansion options for his Toronto-based corporation, Jamie Kennedy Kitchens (JKK), comprised of the Jamie Kennedy Wine Bar (the Wine Bar), the Jamie Kennedy Restaurant (the Restaurant) and the Jamie Kennedy Gardiner (the Gardiner). With gross margins before taxes of 6.7 percent in an industry typically averaging 2.8 to 5.5 percent,[1] global accolades, and rave reviews from acclaimed local food critics, such as Marion Kane, Joanne Kates, and Steven Davey,[2] the JKK was poised to grow.

### The Sustainability Challenge: Growth Plus Values

Kennedy, JKK's founder, co-owner and executive chef, was concerned that meeting the rapidly increasing consumer demand for his exquisite dish and wine pairings could clash with the deeply held values that had inspired his cuisine for over three decades. In his 33 years in the restaurant business, Kennedy had become known as much for culinary harmony (see Exhibit 1 on page 515) as for his legendary commitment to environmental issues and his support for organic agriculture, local producers and traditional methods (see Exhibit 2 on page 516).

*Fundamental to everything Jamie Kennedy does is an underlying respect for the products he buys and sells, and the world we live in. This translates into choices about the fish we buy, the meat and vegetables we serve and increasingly the wines we choose to offer.*

*Jamie makes every effort to minimize the impact of our operations on the environment and we continuously search out like-minded suppliers and better methods of work.[3]*

But could Kennedy grow JKK in ways that respected the natural environment and offered a socially responsible consumption experience that promoted health, quality and pleasure in everyday life? Kennedy's two partners, Dan Donovan and Ken Steele, who each owned 15 percent of the corporation's shares, and his chefs de cuisine (see Exhibit 3 on page 517) shared Kennedy's passion for marrying cuisine with sustainability. But his competitors didn't (see Exhibit 4 on page 518).

Mark McEwan a fellow graduate of George Brown Chef School, one of Toronto's best chefs and a highly successful proprietor in Canada's foodservice industry, was growing his operations rapidly and successfully by promoting an uncontrived experience of luxury in taste and the consumption experience. With a massive catering business, two established restaurants (By Mark and North 44) and a recent new launch (One, in Toronto's most fashionable area), McEwan's recipe for success measured well financially (see Exhibit 4). For Mark McEwan, Kennedy's focus on local sourcing was unduly constraining:

*If you limit yourself to the Canadian market, you'll be serving beets and roots all winter. There's California, Florida, and South America, it's a very small world we live in now in terms of transportation and distribution so you can basically bring in food from anywhere.[4]*

For like-minded Canadian chefs, such as Stratford-based Paul Finkelstein, Jamie Kennedy's beliefs did not go far enough. According to Finkelstein, growth needed to reverse unsustainable consumption patterns. Finkelstein's Screaming Avocado Cafe was reacquainting underprivileged school kids with healthy food and land stewardship from soil to pan. His Food for Thought nutrition program with Health Canada was introducing healthy snacks and organic foods to schools' underprivileged communities.

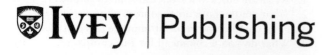

Food critics, such as Marion Kane of the *Toronto Star*, felt that Kennedy's philosophy added value to the fine dining experience. But although Kennedy's sustainability values strengthened the JKK brand, they also constrained his growth. He did not simply desire a larger footprint or greater profits. He was searching for expansion options that could help him support locally rooted supply chains of organic producers and advocate sustainable consumption beyond the taste of the tongue.

Kennedy's focus on local and seasonal foods had helped Kennedy define and refine his unique cooking style:

*I find the older I get the more focused I am on the local and less so on the world. It's like when you experiment as an artist and you are experimenting with color for the first time let's say … you just want to pick up every single color on your canvas because you are so enamored of … or infatuated with these new feelings … over time you develop restraint and focus and then over more time you develop an individual identify that people can relate to and people can say that looks like Jamie Kennedy's work. And that to me it is the highest compliment when someone recognizes your work as opposed to somebody else's work.*

His ideology now blended his roles as chef, environmental steward and social advocate:

*The trade of a cook is the building block to where I am today with respect to my feelings about sustainable agriculture and how I feel about the world ….It's about putting into practice what I believe in my soul….Being in business means I am part of the community and by being part of the community I want to support other people in my community.*

## The Ingredients: Organic Plus Local

Kennedy had very clear criteria about the ingredients he used in his kitchen: he always preferred earth over hydroponics and organic over conventional. If he couldn't source an organic ingredient then he opted for the conventional alternative as long as it was from the earth. Kennedy had never understood why people were importing broccoli and strawberries from California out of season.[5] Beets, carrots, potatoes, beef, cabbage and onions did not have to be imported—they were all local. For Kennedy, working with a set of familiar ingredients from Canada never proved mundane, rather, he found himself noticing ever more subtle differences and finer nuances in the taste of the local, seasonal ingredients:

*You don't need to have, as your source of inspiration, rare ingredients that amaze people. You can, if you're a cook, look around in your own backyard and figure out something that is raised from the mundane, just from your ability to work with those ingredients that you have right there in front of you.*

Other chefs resented such sourcing criteria as too restrictive. But Kennedy felt that each additional constraint stimulated his creativity:

*It's about becoming more restrained…it's about imposing more limitations so that you're creating a world that can be identified with you.…Just spending time focusing on one thing and not being distracted by other things, takes you to different levels of understanding about that one thing, and you can be inspired or have those moments where you go "oh yes" this is interesting.…You are pushing yourself, coming to a certain level, and then moving onto another level of understanding. You've created this work that you can follow over time.*

Kennedy's commitment to seasonal ingredients became a source of differentiation (Exhibit 5, on page 519, has a sample of his menu offerings at the Wine Bar and the Restaurant). First a fan and quickly a champion of the slow food movement[6]—a counter current to the standardization of taste and supermarket homogenization, which strived to promote awareness of local food choices in order to restore the cultural dignity of food, preserve biodiversity and strengthen partnerships between chefs and growers in the community—Kennedy relied on seasonal ingredients to set the tone for the dining experience. Fine dining at JKK was all about enjoying food, culture and community, while being respectful to the environment.

*We live in a seasonal environment in Canada, a seasonal place, so the idea of taking advantage of summer's bounty and trying to capture that for service in the winter, is not only an endeavor that has an aesthetic beauty, but it's also one that is born of another time when having access to fresh vegetables and fruits in the winter was just impossible. So the only way you could have fruits or vegetables in the winter was if you preserved them somehow… through a whole culture of canning and bottling.*

Launched in 2003, Kennedy's canning facility on his farm in Ontario's Prince Edward County helped him preserve foods harvested during the growing season for winter cooking. His signature wall of preserves had been greeting customers when they entered the Wine Bar (see Exhibit 6 on page 520). Kennedy was now thinking about diversifying the output of the canning facility on his rural property. This product line of canned harvested fruits and vegetables could supply all the JKK restaurants in Toronto and perhaps sell more broadly through gourmet outlets. The canning operation was environmentally sustainable and well aligned with his philosophy, yet upstream expansion of his value chain might compete against the local networks of artisan producers he wanted to support.

Wine sourcing decisions were even more challenging. Since 2004, Kennedy had been experimenting with the production of local wines in his Prince Edward County

**5.0**

vineyard. The Gardiner carried only local Ontario wines. But at the Wine Bar, where the 400-plus vintages, which paired so well with Hokkaido sea scallops or grilled short ribs that they rivaled New York and Chicago's finest dining,[7] only 17 percent of the bottled wines were Canadian. The Wine Bar served 23 wines by the glass—always one white and one red from Canada, and 60 percent of their dessert wines were Canadian. Ultra-premium Canadian wines sold well, but 88 percent of JKK's overall wine revenues still came from internationally sourced wines. These procurement choices were driven by consumers—who still preferred access to global varieties. However, Jamie Drummond,[8] JKK's renowned sommelier, used education to instill a greater appreciation for local wines:[9]

*If you do look at the lists I put together, you can tell what my current passions are. Right now I'm going really crazy for Ontario Riesling. I recently had verticals from Cave Spring and from Henry of Pelham that were fascinating. Riesling is one of the things Ontario does quite well, and it was great to taste 96, 97, 98 and 99.... Once people are educated about a wine they become quite receptive. So I tell them about how this Pinot Grigio comes from a very low yield, one ton per acre (or something crazy like that) and that we actually have 10 percent of the total production, or whatever. And with the back-story they're willing to try it again and often say. "Oh, that's quite nice."*

Kennedy had made sourcing decisions, some controversial at the time, to give voice to his sustainability values. In 2002, Kennedy partnered with other chefs, restaurateurs and conservationists to form the Endangered Fish Alliance, whose mission was to keep endangered fish off the dinner plates of Canadians by providing information on which fish were good to serve and which were on the brink of extinction. In 2004, he powered his farm and vineyard (and his home) with renewable energy, becoming a founding member of Bullfrog Power.[10] In 2005, he passionately joined the Canadian seafood boycott to protect the seals—he would keep snow crab off his menus until the slaughter of seals stopped. In 2006, Kennedy rallied at Queen's Park for Michael Schmidt—a local farmer arrested by the Canadian federal government for selling raw, unpasteurized, milk. Unpasteurized milk was illegal under the FDA, because it could contain viruses and bacteria harmful to the human body.[11] Jamie Kennedy held a media conference and raised funds at the Wine Bar for Schmidt's legal defense in support of the right to safe and alternative food choices:

*I am a spokesperson for this school of thought in jkkitchens, I grew it within the organization, within and reaching out. In reaching out, environmental causes, taking an interest in the Raw Milk question and saying from a gastronomic point of view, from a restaurateur's point of view, how important the issue of choice is with respect to access of ingredients*

*that we as restaurateurs believe are of a higher level and quality than the status quo. We would like to have access to that, we would also like to foster relationships with people like Mr. Schmidt because he is an artisan producer of raw milk and raw milk products. So you step outside and voice an opinion and you get enough support around that opinion then maybe at some point we are going to revisit the question of WHY we insist that raw milk be pasteurized. And what may have been current and valid in 1935 maybe isn't quite as valid today. And let's maybe take a look at changing that, so then I become a spokesperson for this place.*

Kennedy felt that such tough choices helped him create more than a unique cuisine:

*I think what I have created here is a school of thought ... because we are in a creative process each and every day and we bring our feelings and the things we learn about food sources, for example, endangered fish. These are issues we learn about and apply to our creativity. These things just get discussed in a casual way that is all a part of our daily role.*

### The Cuisine: Sustenance Plus Art

For Kennedy, food had always been a form of expression—"not just to provide food and sustenance, but sustenance plus art!"

The food at all three JKK ventures—the Wine Bar, the Restaurant and the Gardiner—had been produced on-site, and whenever possible, from organic ingredients supplied by local artisans. The menus featured seasonally driven offerings of Kennedy's unique Canadian interpretation of international classics (see Exhibit 5). All offerings changed with the season, except at the Wine Bar, where the menu featured different daily combinations of foods in season and local preserves.

The widely acclaimed Wine Bar had also been a bold move to democratize the art of fine dining—to encourage people to experience different tastes and to better understand the provenance of ingredients. The experience was designed to be casual and fun. Kennedy wanted to move away from the fine-dining realm he once inhabited at the Royal Ontario Museum (ROM) and create a wine bar with popular pricing, featuring tapas-style dishes (priced from $3 to $14)[12] with wine that could be bought by the glass (at $8 to $60) or by the bottle. The Wine Bar had an open kitchen bar where customers could sit and watch their food being prepared and ask the cooks about the food and where it had been sourced. Service was attentive, but friendly and unpretentious. This deliberate design, Kennedy felt, broadened the appeal to people on many different levels, be it 19-year-olds trying out a restaurant with food and wine for the first time or business professionals entertaining clients:

*What they get is professional advice delivered in a casual way that is not threatening or intimidating. We think food and wine culture should be a natural extension of society and so it's very successful. So that's been observed and that's been emulated, by other operators, three years ago a wine bar style of restaurant did not exist in gastronomy, now I could name five or six, three years later, it's something that works.*

By 2007, local imitators had reached double digits, and Jamie Kennedy Wine Bar had been named A Wine Lover's Top 10 in Toronto, one of Readers' Favourite Restaurants, a Top Five MMM (Most Memorable Meals) Nominees, one of the 10 Top Toques and was mentioned in Toronto Neighbourhoods and Night Moves.[13] Food critics such as Steven Davey[14] gave top marks to the exquisite food–wine pairings:

*We begin with a buttery slice of the house paté sided with Jardinière Vegetables, crunchy pickled green beans and cauliflower over a slaw-like julienne of celery root ($6). Note how the 3-ounce flute of sweet Hungarian dessert wine (1995 Tokaji, $2.90) accentuates the subtlety of the smooth terrine, especially once spread on paper-thin toasts made from the house's walnut baguette.*

*Kennedy's swoonsome Mediterranean fish Soup ($10) tastes like it's caught to order. A tremendously flaky white filet of flounder-like fluke swims in a rich near-bouillabaisse cream garnished with eggy saffron aioli, a tangle of fennel threads and slim Melba toasts. Similarly balanced, melt-in-the-mouth braised oxtail ($7) arrives deboned and shredded in a puddle of deeply flavoured jus scattered with diced carrots. A wisp of wilted leek offers visual and textural contrast, while a pair of crisps slathered with marrow add salty bite.*

For Kennedy, the Wine Bar was part of a broader mission of customer conversion:[15]

*We took ourselves out of the fine dining realm by having more popular pricing to enable the public to consider us, even though what we are offering them is of a much higher level in terms of quality, of cost, in terms of how the food is prepared and the added value. Also the educational part of things, when you walk into the wine bar all of a sudden you are assailed with all this information about relationships and the community and about what kinds of fish are endangered and why we don't serve them. You are getting all kinds of messages that you don't get at other restaurants, social consciousness messages.*

This message had become the core of his brand identity—the Wine Bar was well known as a place where people gathered to enjoy food, culture and local tastes. The gastronomic themes of harmony and seasonality played out in the interior design: the wall of jarred preserves, the mural of a vineyard stretched across the dining room wall and a mural of Kennedy's handwritten recipes (see Exhibit 6):

*Stuff is interconnected, at the wine bar the idea of the shelves of preserves is a very strong statement, a couth statement, and it's also a season's statement. And on the other side of the restaurant is the wall of wine and everything on the other side of the wine bar is about things to do with wine and wine culture. So when people walk into the space they get this feeling that food and wine is being explained to them on many different levels, so the idea of gastronomy comes through in the décor of the room.*

But many saw Jamie Kennedy's initial move as a risky one—in order to democratize the dining experience, he was putting a lid on the revenue side but building up the cost side. Open for 19 hours out of 24 (7 a.m. to 2 a.m.) in a 6,000-square-foot heritage location leased for $180,000 a year, the Wine Bar averaged between 0.5 and 1.5 turns at lunch and three turns at dinner. The average dining check was $50 per cover, split evenly between food and wine. Despite the low prices, the Wine Bar contributed about half of JKK's revenues and three quarters of EBITDA, even after adding its share of corporate overhead.[16]

Wine markups were in part driving the margins. For bottles costing less than $20, the markup was 100 percent—selling for $40. The markup declined with the purchase cost: 80 percent for bottles costing between $20 and $40, 70 percent for bottles costing between $40 and $60, 60 percent for bottles costing between $60 and $80 and 50 percent for bottles costing more than $80. On average, most non-holiday sales were accrued from the wines in the less than $20 category and in the $20 to $40 range. During the holiday season sales most purchases came from bottles in the $40+ range. Ninety-five percent of wines were direct imports—bottles not accessible to the public for retail sale through a Liquor Control Board of Ontario (LCBO) outlet. The markups were significantly below the industry average of 200 percent to 400 percent, but in line with Kennedy's core belief and philosophy that wine should be accessible. Rather than having people judge a wine based on price, they encouraged an overall experience based on taste and enjoyment, an experience that encouraged customers to return because the food was great and the wine they had never tried before offered a taste experience that they would (and could) enjoy again.

With excellent pairings, an attractive wine selection and affordable prices, the Wine Bar was in high demand—customers often waited two hours for a seat at the Wine Bar. Kennedy was wondering how he could reduce this wait to 30 or 35 minutes per seat. One option was to extend the seating for the Wine Bar, which currently occupied 25 percent of the Church Street locale (the Restaurant seating took another 25 percent; the rest was shared between the common cook-to-order kitchen and the production kitchen shared by all JKK ventures, including catering).

As another option, Kennedy considered moving the production kitchen off-site, to a lower-cost location that met his environmental priorities. Relocating to a larger,

5.0

greener building with more energy-efficient heating and lighting systems could simultaneously support profitable growth through catering while furthering Kennedy's environmental goals. A larger production kitchen would also allow Jamie Kennedy to market some of his value-add products (especially the baked goods) to an even broader base of customers, furthering the democratization of the eating experience and reaching new customer targets with a sustainable consumption message.

## The Restaurant

Sharing a heritage building in the historic St. Lawrence Market district with the Wine Bar, the Restaurant seated 30 and was open for, dinner only (5 p.m. to 11 p.m. daily). The total revenues of the restaurant (about 1.15 million a year) were split roughly 61/39 between food and wine. Across all JKK's operations, the average cost of the food sold was 30 percent; the average cost of the wine sold was 56 percent. At the restaurant, the menu items were larger and pricier than the tapas-style entries at the Wine Bar (see Exhibit 5). The menu changed seasonally and each dish was listed with suggested wine pairings, With an average of 1.5 daily turns per cover, the restaurant was often fully booked by reservations.

### The Gardiner

The Gardiner venue was described by Steven Davey as a "local wunderkind's return to Yorkville.... The serene space is minimally appointed, all concrete walls surprisingly free of ornament, hard wooden floors and modish stacking tables and chairs." Located in a heritage building turned "from dowdy to downtown" by Toronto-based Kuwabara Payne McKenna Blumberg,[17] the Gardiner featured complete meals for $60 per person, including all taxes, tip and a glass of Ontario wine. The average mains were $18, and food costs accounted for 22 percent of the price. The Gardiner was open daily for lunch, 11:30 a.m. to 3:30 p.m., and was staffed 8 a.m. to 5 p.m.—except on Fridays, when the locale was open for dinner, and during two to three catering events and one to two cocktail events each week, when the Gardiner stayed open until 2 a.m.

One of the popular organic and locally sourced dishes on the Gardiner menu had been conceived by Kennedy with Stadtlander more than 20 years ago at Palmerston: "thick slices of rustic-crusted house-baked multigrain that arrived plated on a chainsaw-fashioned wooden plank, coupled with a ramekin each of whipped butter and heavenly roasted eggplant-sweet bell pepper spread."[18] According to *NOW Magazine*'s, food critic, the mouth-watering dishes were also very reasonably priced. For example:

*A plump, exquisitely grilled scallop swims in an intensely fresh and buttery cream of Ontario corn soup ($10), strewn with a tiny chiffonade of chives. Thirteen bucks for a green salad is a bit much even for a swanky joint like*

*dis, but it only takes one bite of the home-grown heirloom tomatoes coupled with rich Quebecois chèvre and leafy arugula in a simply herbed vinaigrette to remind us what tomatoes used to taste like worth every Proustian cent....*

*Another main finds gorgeously fatty but easily trimmed slices of seared 'n' roasted duck breast exploding over wilted red stalks of Swiss chard and oven-tender wedges of incredibly coloured summer squash ($18). An artfully puddled pool of cassis-kicked jus and another of plum reduction provide counterpoint....*

*Sure to become JKG's newest signature dish, Kennedy's spectacular charcuterie platter ($14) showcases substantial slices of house-cured duck alongside gauzy Serrano ham and a dazzlingly rich scoop of chicken liver paté. His farm-pickled veggies, some sheep's milk cheese and an oversized tuille made from a length of walnut loaf complete the plate, er, log.*

At the Gardiner, food sales contributed about 74 percent of the revenues, Canadian wines, 26 percent. Catering generated revenues of about l.7 million a year, roughly 76 percent from the sales of food.

The Wine Bar was JKK's flagship location—the most popular among consumers and the most profitable (see Exhibit 7 on page 521). The Gardiner came second in revenues, largely due to its catering events. However, profit margins on catering were thin, and scaling up the catering business could strain JKK's cash-flows (the average repayment period for catering events was 40 days). Despite having the highest menu prices, the JKK Restaurant came third in terms of revenues. Kennedy felt that the three establishments effectively reached different customer segments and could help JKK achieve greater operational efficiencies, while economizing on marketing and advertising through generating positive word of mouth across target segments. Given that overall the profit margin was twice as high as the industry average, Kennedy pondered whether profitability, efficiency or popularity should be the main considerations for his next expansion.

## Advocacy: The Ark of Taste

Several prestigious chefs had taken up taste for a cause, both locally (see Exhibit 4) and globally (see Exhibit 8 on page 522). But social enterprises, such as Finkelstein's Screaming Avocado Café and Jamie Oliver's Fifteen, were not Kennedy's bread and butter. Kennedy wanted to do something to further the environmental and social causes he had invested in (see Exhibit 2). Since 1989, when Kennedy had helped found the Knives and Forks Alliance, a group of chefs and farmers with a shared commitment to promoting mixed farming and locally grown produce,[19] Kennedy had been a champion of local produce. He had co-founded Feast of Fields,[20] a non-profit organization that promoted awareness building about fresh organic delicacies for the food connoisseur and offered an annual sumptuous experience celebrating the sustainable growth, preparation and consumption of organic food. Kennedy was organizing the 2007 event, with the theme "Sustainability Starts with Your Local Organic Farm."

Kennedy, was also closely involved in the Toronto chapter of Slow Food,[21] which he had helped found in 2003.[22] Kennedy was a member of the steering committee, a dedicated group of activists striving for a collective reconsideration of the cultural, environmental, historical and economic meanings of food. The steering committee was already working at asserting the rights of local food communities to make a just living and at furthering development of sustainable systems that support food security for the people of Toronto and beyond.

Kennedy had long been an active proponent and user of local, seasonal organic food—starting in April 2007, he also became an active member of Green Living, by participating in the first Green Living Show.[23] He was also engaged in the Slow Food Green Link,[24] a gathering that brought together professional kitchens with artisan producers and farmers.

Some of his advocacy infused his own operations—at times blurring the fine line between helping local producers and jkkitchens and often sharpening the very edge of his environmental and social values. In 2005, the Wine Bar hosted a food education discussion, Feeding your Mind. He had cooked for the Riverdale Farm community and supported the farmers market at the Dufferin Grove Park.

## Feeding a Cause

Kennedy found that social advocacy was harder to reconcile with his high cuisine. However, eating together, Kennedy thought, could be a good means to a great end. He wanted to play a part, however small, in promoting collective well-being. For the past 15 years, Kennedy had become selectively but actively involved with several social causes. In 1993, he raised money for Anishnawbe Health Toronto, an Aboriginal community-based health center. Since then, he had helped raise money for the Princess Margaret Hospital and other organizations. In 2006, he began supporting St. Francis Table's program to feed the homeless. Kennedy contemplated whether and how he could better bridge his social and environmental interests while he grew his business.

## Food for Thought

Education in particular was becoming increasingly important for Jamie Kennedy. He wanted to expose as many people as possible to this school of thought and this practice. Kennedy was taking his educational role seriously, at all the levels. He felt that an important part of education was to represent the wine and the food in a gastronomic sense, and he knew he needed people to actually talk about it, sell it and explain it. His staff members were educated in the locality of ingredients and served staff meals reflective of the menu's offerings, so they could in turn create opportunities for the customers to learn about wines and dish pairings.

Kennedy was on the board of directors of the Stratford Chefs School. He also made several guest chef appearances at Stratford Northwestern Secondary School (home of chef Paul Finkelstein's Screaming Advocado Café), where he lectured and demonstrated seasonal and local cooking.

## Sustainable Growth Options

Looking forward, Kennedy was struggling to balance opportunity and constraint. He wanted to draw closer bridges between his operations and his sustainable values. Growth could enable him to have a positive impact on the consumer (through democratizing fine taste; advocating slow, seasonal, organic foods and supporting local artisan producers). But growth could also upset the growing harmony between his values and cooking style.

## Closed-Loop Cuisine

One of the options ahead was closing the loop on his supply chain. Kennedy's dream had long been to become self-sufficient—to turn his rural Canadian farm into an outpost of Jamie Kennedy Kitchens. He envisioned the farm as a place where members of the community, customers and staff could visit, experience, work and further their understanding of the relationships that existed between themselves, the community and their food sources:

*So part of our community is the farm, and growing things and processing them, and bringing them back to the restaurant, using them in the restaurant; closing the circle so we become our own source of supply.... This farm project, I want to start working on it in earnest this year, and hope by the end of this growing season we will have a lot of supply coming our way. I have also set up a canning facility out of the farm. And the winery is happening at the same time, the vines are in the ground just a matter of getting it all under control, getting it to the point where it's feeding back into the flow of things.*

## Messaging the Customer

Kennedy also wanted to create a consumption experience with a social and environmental message. Many other chefs thought he was pushing the envelope too far, that he was spending a lot of time and extra money connecting with people, and that the public was not yet ready. But Kennedy felt that the timing was just right. He imagined a new foundation that could integrate many of his efforts: educate the public about the slow food philosophy, offer dedicated programs for future chefs, hold guest speaker sessions featuring leaders in sustainability and host city versions of annual fundraisers that would involve and promote local farmers and winemakers. A foundation would cater to the soul, but would it get in the way of the cuisine? Would he have the skills needed to run a foundation or would he need to partner with a local non governmental organization (NGO)? On the other hand, if the foundation

5.0

took off, would that help or hinder brand differentiation? Jamie Kennedy was torn between his need for action and impact on one hand and his desire to remain an example of local, sustainable artisan cuisine on the other.

## Notes

1. Source: 2006 Foodservice Operations Report, p. 8, available at http://www.crfa.ca/products/pdf/foodserviceoperationsreport_sample.pdf, last accessed on December 2, 2007.
2. Marcy Cornblum, Celeb Kitchens, http://metronews.ca/column.aspx?id=16900; Joanne Kates, "Colborne Lane," *Globe and Mail*, April 20, 2007, available at http://www.theglobeandmail.com/servlet/story/RTGAM.20070310.wxkates10/BNStory/lifeFoodWine, accessed on July 15, 2007.
3. Everything Olive, "Chef Jamie Kennedy," available at http://www.everythingolive.com/jamiekennedy.html, accessed on July15, 2007.
4. Mark McEwan, personal interview, February 6, 2007.
5. Over three-fourths of U.S. strawberry production comes from California and the primary market of U.S. fresh strawberries is Canada. See http://findarticles.com/p/articles/mi_m3723/is_nll_v4/ai_13290970.
6. Slow Food is "a non-profit, eco-gastronomic member-supported organization that was founded in 1986 to counteract fast food and fast life, the disappearance of local food traditions and people's dwindling interest in the food they eat, where it comes from, how it tastes and how our food choices affect the rest of the world." Today, the organization brings together more than 80,000 members across 104 countries. Source: http//www.slowfood.com/, accessed on July 15, 2007. The core tenets of the slow food movement are summarized in a humorous news review of the Mouth Revolution, available on the You Tube at http://multimedia.slowfood.it/index.php?method=multimedia&action=zoom&id=2035, produced on February 21, 2007 and last accessed on July 15, 2007.
7. "Toronto's Time," *Travel + Leisure*. April 2007, available at http://www.travelandleisure.com/articles/torontos-time/?page=2, accessed on November 5, 2007.
8. Drummond was promoted to head of sommeliers at Jamie Kennedy Wine Bar, with an assistant working under him. He also produced podcasts for Jamie Kennedy Wine Bar featuring guest speakers from biodynamic wineries. Source: Personal interview with Jamie Kennedy, January 25, 2007.
9. Malcolm Jolley, "Jamie Drummond Interview," available at http://gremolata.com/drummond.htm, accessed on July 15, 2007.
10. "From the kitchen, to the dining room, to the great outdoors, a healthy environment is something worth striving for. We have a responsibility as tenants of this earth to exercise responsible stewardship in preserving and protecting our environment. Supporting

renewables by becoming a bullfrogpowered home is one essential ingredient in accomplishing this goal." Source: "Jamie Kennedy, Bullfrog Founders Club," available at http://www.bullfrogpower.com/powered/kennedy.cfm, accessed on July 15, 2007.
11. According to Health Canada, unpasteurized milk is illegal because it contravenes Food and Drug Regulations, http://www.hc-sc.gc.ca/ahc-asc/media/advisories-avis/2006/2006_65_e.html, accessed November 25, 2007.
12. All funds in Canadian dollars unless specified otherwise.
13. "Jamie Kennedy Wine Bar," *Where Toronto,* available at http://www.where.ca/toronto/guide_listing~listing_id~2217.htm, accessed on November 5, 2007.
14. "Kennedy Can: Jamie Kennedy Comes Back Strong with a New Wine Bar," http://www.nowtoronto.com/issues/2003-12-18/goods_foodfeature.php, accessed on November 5, 2007.
15. And there was safety in numbers. As the popular appeal of the Wine Bar grew, it became the most profitable venture in the stable of JK Kitchens. Source: Jamie Kennedy, personal interview, January 25, 2007.
16. Overhead costs were split among locales based on their percentage contribution to the corporation's revenues, and included maintenance fees of $6,000 per month, accessories costs of $4,500 per month, $20,000 a year for laundry, $22,000 a year for garbage/waste removal and recycling, $140,000 for call center staff, $120,000 a year for the sommelier, and $100,000 for accounting staff.
17. Steven Davey, "Gusto at the Gardiner: It May Be Too Loud, but Jamie Kennedy at the Gardiner is Oh So Tasty," *NOW Magazine*, August 31–September 6, 2006, available at http://www.nowtoronto.com/issues/2006-08-31/goods_foodfeature.php, accessed on September 4, 2007.
18. Ibid.
19. The Knives and Forks Alliance created one of the first local organic marketplaces. Local organic growers set up stations, and chefs purchased ingredients from the growers on a weekly basis and took the opportunity to interact with other chefs.
20. The Feast of Fields website, http://www.feastoffields.org/, accessed on July 15, 2007. At this annual fundraising event, chefs created and prepared dishes at a rural location alongside a vending farmer, paired their dishes with local wines, and presented and spoke about their cooking creations to the public.
21. Slow Food celebrated worldwide diversity in food cultures through Terra Madra, a biannual conference held in Turin, Italy, where approximately 5,000 small-enterprise food producers from around the globe exchanged and promoted ways to grow, create and distribute food that respects the environment and health of consumers. Each local chapter organized specialized events. Slow Food convivas (i.e., individually run chapters) connected with home

food enthusiasts locally and helped build a stronger sense of community through programs that strengthened awareness of local food availability and choices. Slow Food's Ark of Taste catalogued and sought to protect foods on the brink of extinction, recovered recipes and recorded local food varieties and tastes.

22. The Slow Food organization "promotes gastronomic culture, develops taste education, preserves agricultural biodiversity and protects traditional foods at risk of extinction." Source: Slow Food Toronto, available at http://toronto.slowfood.ca/index.php/C15/, accessed on July 15, 2007.

23. The Green Living show website, http://www.greenlivingshow.ca/, accessed on July 15, 2007.

24. Malcolm Jolley, "Wanted: A Truck Driver," Gremolata. March 2007, available at http://gremolata.com/greenlink.htm, accessed on July 15, 2007.

---

### ■ Assignment Questions

1. What are the key challenges of designing a restaurant in a sustainable way?
2. What are the key drivers of sustainability at Jamie Kennedy Kitchens?
3. What are the current trade-offs between sustainability and growth at Jamie Kennedy Kitchens?
4. Which growth option would allow Jamie Kennedy Kitchens to grow most sustainably?

**EXHIBIT 1**
## Jamie Kennedy's Accolades

Jamie Kennedy started his cooking apprenticeship at the Windsor Arms Hotel in Toronto, Canada, and at the Grand National Hotel in Switzerland, where he experimented with the many different tastes and harmonies in French cooking, much like an artist wanting to experiment with all the colors on the palette for the first time.

In 1980, Kennedy became Executive Chef at Scaramouche. There he realized the gaping disconnect between cuisine and food supply. Kennedy became interested in the farmer behind the fruit. In 1983, Kennedy started his own catering company; and two years later he opened Palmerston restaurant with friend and fellow slow food supporter Michael Stadtlander.

His thematic gastronomic dining experiences came together in the mid-1990s when Kennedy founded his restaurant at the Royal Ontario Museum. From 1994 to 2003, the J.K. at the ROM restaurant was a popular lunch spot with à la carte dining complemented by private events held in the evening.

In April 2000, Kennedy's contribution to Canadian cuisine through his showcasing of local, seasonal and organic ingredients was recognized by the Ontario Hostelry Institute's Chef of the Year award.[1]

In October 2000, he published a successful cook book, *Jamie Kennedy's Seasons*.[2]

In 2003, Kennedy won the Award of Excellence for the "Best savoury use of regional ingredients" for his signature poutine with aged cheddar served with lamb and Concord grape sauce.[3]

Isaiah Trickey/FilmMagic/Getty Images

The Jamie Kennedy Wine Bar, opened in 2003, earned him local and international acclaim. In April 2006, the JKK Wine Bar was named as one of "Toronto's Top 20 Restaurants" in the respected *Toronto Life* magazine; in May, *Condé Nast Traveler* placed it on its 2006 Hot List.

To satisfy demand for a more conventionally styled menu and to allow patrons to make reservations, the Jamie Kennedy Restaurant was opened in August 2005, an equally hot dining spot according to *Condé Nast Traveler*.

In June 2006, he launched a new restaurant, Jamie Kennedy at the Gardiner in the newly renovated Gardiner Museum. The Gardiner is open daily for lunch and is available for evening group events, for up to 120 people for formal plated dinners and for up to 300 people for cocktails.

[1]http://www.everythingolive.com/jamiekennedy.html
[2]Ibid.
[3]http://www.thecounty.ca/taste/awards_2003.html, accessed on July 15, 2007.

**EXHIBIT 2**
**A History of Jamie Kennedy's Initiatives**

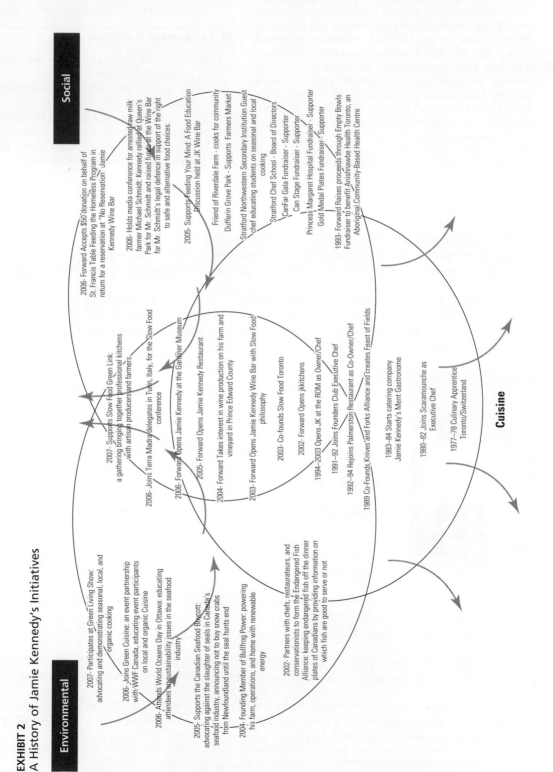

**Environmental**

**Social**

**Cuisine**

2007- Participates at Green Living Show: advocating and demonstrating seasonal, local, and organic cooking

2006- Joins Green Cuisine: an event partnership with WWF Canada, educating event participants on local and organic Cuisine

2006- Attends World Oceans Day in Ottawa: educating attendees in sustainability issues in the seafood industry

2005- Supports the Canadian Seafood Boycott: advocating against the slaughter of seals in Canada's seafood industry, announcing not to buy snow crabs from Newfoundland until the seal hunts end

2004- Founding Member of Bullfrog Power: powering his farm, operations, and home with renewable energy

2002- Partners with chefs, restaurateurs, and conservationists to form the Endangered Fish Alliance: keeping endangered fish off the dinner plates of Canadians by providing information on which fish are good to serve or not

2007- Supports Slow Food Green Link: a gathering bringing together professional kitchens with artisan producers and farmers

2006- Joins Terra Madra delegates in Turin, Italy, for the Slow Food conference

2006- Forward Opens Jamie Kennedy at the Gardiner Museum

2005- Forward Opens Jamie Kennedy Restaurant

2004- Forward Takes interest in wine production on his farm and vineyard in Prince Edward County

2003- Forward Opens Jamie Kennedy Wine Bar with Slow Food philosophy

2003- Co-founds Slow Food Toronto

2002- Forward Opens jkkitchens

1994–2003 Opens JK at the ROM as Owner/Chef

1991–92 Joins Founders Club Executive Chef

1992–94 Rejoins Palmerston Restaurant as Co-Owner/Chef

1989 Co-Founds Knives and Forks Alliance and creates Feast of Fields

1983–84 Starts catering company Jamie Kennedy's Ment Gastronome

1980–82 Joins Scaramounche as Executive Chef

1977–78 Culinary Apprentice Toronto/Switzerland

2006- Forward Accepts $50 donation on behalf of St. Francis Table Feeding the Homeless Program in return for a reservation at "No Reservation" Jamie Kennedy Wine Bar

2006- Holds media conference for arrested raw milk farmer Michael Schmidt: Kennedy rallied at Queen's Park for Mr. Schmidt and raised funds at the Wine Bar for Mr. Schmidt's legal defence in support of the right to safe and alternative food choices.

2005- Supports Feeding Your Mind: A Food Education Discussion held at JK Wine Bar

Friend of Riverdale Farm - cooks for community

Dufferin Grove Park - Supports Farmers Market

Stratford Northwestern Secondary Institution Guest chef educating students on seasonal and local cooking

Stratford Chef School - Board of Directors

CanFar Gala Fundraiser - Supporter

Can Stage Fundraiser - Supporter

Princess Margaret Hospital Fundraiser - Supporter

Gold Medal Plates Fundraiser- Supporter

1993- Forward Raises proceeds through Empty Bowls Fundraiser to benefit Anishnawbe Health Toronto, an Aboriginal Community-Based Health Centre

5.0

**EXHIBIT 3**
Jamie Kennedy Kitchens' Organizational Chart

## JAMIE KENNEDY KITCHENS' ORGANIZATIONAL CHART

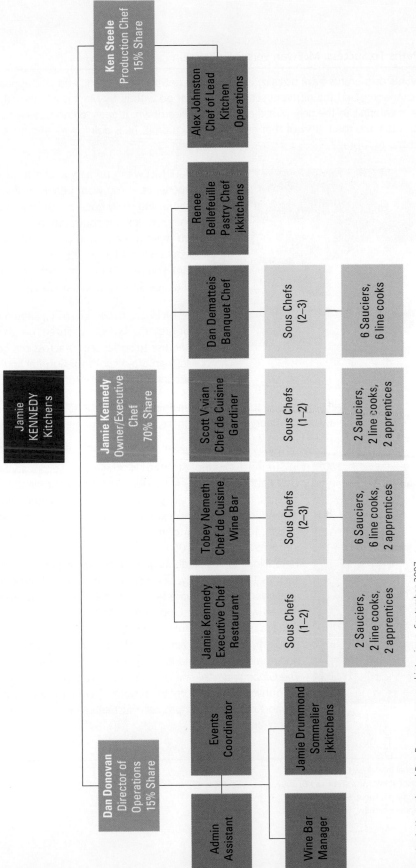

Source: Jamie Kennedy and Dan Donovan, personal interviews, September 2007.

5.0

**EXHIBIT 4**
Alternative Paths To Success: McEwan versus Finkelstein

Mark McEwan's restaurants have pizzazz, wow, they've got that jazzy, slick, and chic appeal—if you want a nice bottle of champagne, and the different set of beliefs that go with it. By Mark is a high-end restaurant, it's $250 for two, and he is catering to the rich. [But the money] trickles down, it goes to chefs, waiters, dishwashers, and the guys who produce the food. It's not that he is getting rich on it, he is doing well, and if his restaurant does well it's good for the economy.[1]

Mark McEwan's primary goal is to provide a memorable experience: "You want people walking away from your property feeling really good about having been there, and that's what it is. It's not about fashion or about how cool or stylish you think you are. That can happen in our industry, some people get a little caught up, you get a little press, and you think you're an artist. You get a little carried away, when what you should be is a good proprietor."[2]

For McEwan, good citizenship should not constrain cuisine, nor growth. As a good citizen, he often lends his catering expertise to social causes across the greater Toronto area. McEwan often cooks for hospital and medical research fundraisers for Sick Kids Hospital, AIDS and breast cancer.

(Photographer: Nikki Leigh McKean, www.generalpurposepictures.com)

But what is the point of teaching people to make crème caramel if they are not feeding their children a proper breakfast? We need to be aware of hungry people out there, or the environment, or how we are growing our foods.[3]

In Stratford, Ontario, Stratford Northwestern Secondary School teacher and chef Paul Finkelstein is reinventing the way his students "know" food. Finkelstein's innovative culinary program, which he created and heads, is the first of its kind in Canada: kids learn about healthy food and land stewardship from soil to pan, from morning to mid-afternoon. They take this knowledge and cook lunch for more than 100 students at the school's Screaming Avocado Café. Here, Finkelstein's students gain on-the-job experience. High-profile guest chefs, such as Jamie Kennedy, often stop in to cook and speak with students. In the schoolyard, 3,000 square feet of school property have been turned into a market garden where organic crops are tended and farmed by the students. Health Canada is now test-piloting Finkelstein's *Food for Thought: Schools and Nutrition* program, an initiative aimed at introducing healthy snacks and organic foods to underprivileged communities.[4] Finkelstein has been featured in *Time* magazine, *The Globe and Mail* and on Food TV's program *Chefs at Large*. He has used his publicity in his efforts to convince City of Toronto councilors to design and support initiatives that promote sustainable eating in Canada's schools and school-aged children.

Terry Manzo www.terrymanzo.com

[1]Marion Kane, personal interview, February 9, 2007.
[2]Mark McEwan, personal interview, February 6, 2007.
[3]Marion Kane, personal interview, February 9, 2007.
[4]Marion Kane, personal interview, February 9, 2007.

## EXHIBIT 5
## Jamie Kennedy's Menus

Yukon Gold Fries                                      5
with Lemon and Mayonnaise
   *2005 Domaine Lafond Roc-Epine Tavel Rosé*
   *Southern Rhône Blend  4.50 ~ 9*

Grilled Flatbread with Three Dips           7
   *2003 Morella "Terre Rosse"*
   *Primitivo/Malbec  6.40 ~ 12.80*

Yukon Gold Fries                                      9
as Braised Lamb Poutine
   *1999 Abadia de San Quirce "Reserva"*
   *Tempranillo  15.10 ~ 28.30*

Mushroom Soup                                         7
   *2004 Domaine Jo Pithon*
   *"Les 4 Villages" Côteaux du Layon*
   *Chenin Blanc  5 (1oz) ~ 10 (2oz)*

Chicken Liver Pâté with Walnut Tuiles      9
   *2004 Rolly Gassman "Weingarten de Rorschwihr"*
   *Gewürztraminer  9.30 ~ 18.55*

Winter Salad with Marinated Beets,       11
Organic Greens and Pumpkinseeds
   *2004 Schloss Gobelsburg "Tradition"*
   *Gruner Veltliner  7.50 ~ 15*

Sheep's Milk Cheese Sandwich               10
   *2005 Taltle*
   *Sauvignon Blanc  7.90 ~ 15.80*

Northern Woods Mushrooms on Toast       11
   *2000 Gabriel Meffre Gigondas "Lauren"*
   *Southern Rhône Blend  7.65 ~ 15.30*

Seared Sea Scallops                                12
with Organic Carrots and Chili Sauce
   *2005 Taltle*
   *Sauvignon Blanc  7.90 ~ 15*

Grilled Octopus with Fennel Salad          11
   *2005 Val de Sarego*
   *Albariño  5.10 ~ 10.30*

Black Cod Marmitako                            12
   *2005 Thirty Bench "Small Lot ~ Triangle Vineyard"*
   *Riesling  6.10 ~ 12.30*

Roast Cornish Hen Breast                       12
with Braised Endive
   *2004 Jean Luc Colombo Condrieu*
   *Viognier  15.50 ~ 31*

Peanut Mole with Grilled Cornish Hen     10
   *2004 Albert Mann "Grand H"*
   *Pinot Noir  11.10 ~ 22.30*

Swedish Meatballs                                 10
with Mashed Potatoes
   *2000 Gabriel Meffre Gigondas "Lauren"*
   *Southern Rhône Blend  7.65 ~ 15.30*

Grilled Shortribs                                    10
with Wild Arugula Salad
   *2004 Tackurbe "Only Sun"*
   *Tempranillo  6.90 ~ 13.80*
   or
   *2003 Morella "Terre Rosse"*
   *Primitivo/Malbec  6.40 ~ 12.80*

Entrecote of Beef                                  14
with Root Vegetable Purée
   *1988 Château Taillefer*
   *Bordeaux Blend  11.40 ~ 22.85*
   or
   *2003 Penfolds R.W.T.*
   *Shiraz  19.30 ~ 39*

Artisanal Cheeses                                 14
   *2004 Cantina di Bertiola*
   *Picolit  16 (1oz) ~ 32 (2oz)*
   or
   *1991 Niepoort Colheita*
   *Port  9 (1oz) ~ 18 (2oz)*

Selection of House-Made Bread                 3

Sparkling Sorbets                                    5
Plum and Apricot
   *NV Champalou Fauvray "Petillant"*
   *Chenin Blanc  4.90 ~ 9.80*

Chocolate Cherry Torte                            6
with Cashew Ice Cream
   *2004 Bunny Dixon "Reserva"*
   *Barbera  9 (1oz) ~ 18 (2oz)*

Ricotta-Rosemary Cake                            6
with Candied Oranges and Caramel
   *2005 Turbrock "The Bothie"*
   *Muscat  9 (1oz) ~ 18 (2oz)*

Crème Brûlée                                          6
with Biscotti
   *2001 Château Roumieu-Lacoste*
   *Sauternes  12 (1oz) ~ 24 (2oz)*

Thursday, January 11, 2007

Thanks,
Wine Bar Chef, Tobey Nemeth
Executive Chef, Jamie Kennedy

---

**Winter 2006-2007**
**First Courses and Soups**

Frisée Salad with Grilled Fresh Goat's Cheese
   and Olive Toasts . . . . . .15⁻

Torn Radicchio with Poached Organic Egg
   and Lardons . . . . . . . .16⁻

Marinated Wild Salmon with Kohlrabi
   and Beet Salad . . . . . . .17⁻

Chestnut Soup with Crème Fraîche and
   Parsley Oil . . . . . . .14⁻

Chicken Broth with Liver Dumpling . . .14⁻

Potato Gnocchi with Roasted Shiitake Mushrooms
   and Velouté Sauce . . . . . .17⁻

Black and White Gratin . . . . . .22⁻

Streets of Toronto . . . . . . . .19⁻

Executive Chef   Jamie Kennedy

---

**Winter 2006-2007**
**Vegetarian, Fish, Meats**

Three Vegetarian Dishes . . . .25⁻

Grilled Squid and Octopus
with Spanish Paprika and Braised
          Beans . . . .35⁻

Fluke in Wild Rice Meunière with
Pickled Wild Leeks and Winter Greens . . .37⁻

Confit and Roast of Duck
       with Tangerine . . . . .39⁻

Roast Pork with Red Cabbage
and Iced Apple Sauce . . . .36⁻

Pepper Steak Gratin with Steamer
  of Winter Vegetables . . . .40⁻

Venison Ossobucco with
  Printanière of Vegetables . . . .40⁻

Restaurant Chef Daniel Muia

---

Note: The printed menu for the JKK Restaurant (on the left) changes seasonally. The handwritten menu for the Wine Bar (on the right) changes 2–3 times daily. Although a few signature dishes, such as Jamie Kennedy's famous poutine, are always available, their flavour is different every day.

**EXHIBIT 6**
Jamie Kennedy Wine Bar and Restaurant

Tasting Wine Bar, with Jamie Drummond

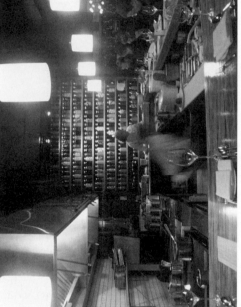

Open Kitchen Featuring Wall of Preserves

Wine Wall

Ontario Vineyard Mural

Front Signage & Seating

Recipe Thought Process Mural

**EXHIBIT 7**
JKK Annual Income Statement[1]

| | JK RESTAURANT | | WINE BAR | | GARDINER | | CATERING | | TOTAL | |
|---|---|---|---|---|---|---|---|---|---|---|
| | Annual | % | Annual | % | Annual | % | Annual | % | Annual | % |
| Revenue | 1,150,200 | 100 | 3,210,480 | 100 | 976,320 | 100 | 1,776,000 | 100 | 7,113,000 | 100 |
| Food | 696,600 | 61 | 1,698,480 | 53 | 729,360 | 75 | 1,320,000 | 74 | 4,444,440 | 62 |
| Wine | 453,600 | 39 | 1,512,000 | 47 | 246,960 | 25 | 456,000 | 26 | 2,668,560 | 38 |
| Total COGS | 462,996 | 40 | 1,356,264 | 42 | 357,106 | 37 | 651,360 | 37 | 2,827,726 | 40 |
| Gross Margin | 687,204 | 60 | 1,854,216 | 58 | 619,214 | 63 | 1,124,640 | 63 | 4,285,274 | 60 |
| Payroll | 355,150 | 31 | 784,790 | 24 | 337,270 | 35 | 757,970 | 43 | 2,235,180 | 31 |
| Benefits | 46,170 | 4 | 102,023 | 3 | 43,845 | 4 | 68,217 | 4 | 260,255 | 4 |
| Lease | 80,000 | 7 | 180,000 | 6 | 55,000 | 7 | 130,000 | 7 | 455,000 | 6 |
| Utilities | 20,000 | 2 | 60,000 | 2 | 18,000 | 2 | 38,000 | 2 | 136,000 | 2 |
| Other General & Admin | 80,000 | 7 | 220,000 | 7 | 68,000 | 7 | 160,000 | 9 | 528,000 | 7 |
| Operating Income (EBITDA) | 105,885 | 9 | 507,403 | 16 | 87,099 | 9 | −29,547 | −2 | 670,840 | 9 |
| Dep | 40,000 | 3 | 40,000 | 1 | 40,000 | 4 | 40,000 | 2 | 160,000 | 2 |
| Interest | 8,000 | 1 | 8,000 | 2 | 8,000 | 1 | 8,000 | .5 | 32,000 | .4 |
| EBT | 57,885 | 5 | 459,403 | 14 | 39,099 | 4 | −77,547 | −4 | 478,840 | 7 |
| Tax | 17,365 | 2 | 137,821 | 4 | 11,730 | 1 | −23,264 | −1 | 143,652 | 2 |
| Net Income | 40,519 | 4 | 321,582 | 10 | 27,370 | 3 | −54,283 | −3 | 335,188 | 5 |

[1]The financial data has been disguised to protect confidentiality.

5.0

**EXHIBIT 8**
Do Something!

World renowned for his cuisine, Jamie Oliver turned his breakout TV shows, *The Naked Chef*, into a campaign to ban junk food in schools. In 2005, the U.K. government pledged £280 million for school dinners. As acknowledged by Prime Minister Tony Blair, the program revolutionized kids' appreciation for healthy nutritious foods and education of organic choices. But *Jamie's School Dinners* were not Oliver's first engagement with activity meant to improve quality of life. In 2002, Oliver had founded Fifteen, a charity restaurant in London that would eventually open three sister locations around the globe where disadvantaged youth would learn to cook and work in the hospitality industry. This social enterprise had since become a profitable and self-sustaining venture. All profits go back into the model and are supplemented by fundraising events, applications to companies, charitable trusts, franchise fees and royalties alongside individual donations.[1]

[1]http:/www.fifteen.net/Pages/default.aspx, accessed on July 25, 2007.

5.0

## Integrative Case 6.0

## The Donor Services Department*

Joanna Reed was walking home through fallen tree blossoms in Guatemala City. Today, however, her mind was more on her work than the natural beauty surrounding her. She unlocked the gate to her colonial home and sat down on the porch, surrounded by riotous toddlers, pets, and plants, to ponder the recommendations she would make to Sam Wilson. The key decisions she needed to make about his Donor Services Department concerned who should run the department and how the work should be structured.

Joanna had worked for a sponsorship agency engaged in international development work with poor people for six years. She and her husband moved from country to country setting up new agencies. In each country, they had to design how the work should be done, given the local labor market and work conditions.

After a year in Guatemala, Joanna, happily pregnant with her third child, had finished setting up the Donor Services Department for the agency and was working only part-time on a research project. A friend who ran a "competing" development agency approached her to do a consulting project for him. Sam Wilson, an American, was the national representative of a U.S.-based agency that had offices all over the world. Sam wanted Joanna to analyze his Donor Services Department, because he'd received complaints from headquarters about its efficiency. Since he'd been told that his office needed to double in size in the coming year, he wanted to get all the bugs worked out beforehand. Joanna agreed to spend a month gathering information and compiling a report on this department.

Sponsorship agencies, with multimillion-dollar budgets, are funded by individuals and groups in developed countries who contribute to development programs in less-developed countries (LDCs). Donors contribute approximately $20.00 per month plus optional special gifts. The agencies use this money to fund education, health, community development, and income-producing projects for poor people affiliated with their agency in various communities. In the eyes of most donors, the specific benefit provided by sponsorship agencies is the personal relationship between a donor and a child and his or her family in the LDC. The donors and children write back and forth, and the agency sends photos of the child and family to the donors. Some donors never write the family they sponsor; others write weekly and visit the family on their vacations. The efficiency of a Donor Services Department and the quality of their translations are key ingredients to keeping

*Joyce S. Osland, San Jose State University.

donors and attracting new ones. Good departments also never lose sight of the fact that sponsorship agencies serve a dual constituency—the local people they are trying to help develop and the sponsors who make that help possible through their donations.

### What Is a Donor Services Department in a Sponsorship Agency Anyway?

The work of a Donor Services Department consists of more than translating letters, preparing annual progress reports on the families, and answering donor questions directed to the agency. It also handles the extensive, seemingly endless paperwork associated with enrolling new families and assigning them to donors, reassignments when either the donor or the family stops participating, and the special gifts of money sent (and thank you notes for them). Having accurate enrollment figures is crucial because the money the agency receives from headquarters is based upon these figures and affects planning.

### The Department Head

Joanna tackled the challenge of analyzing the department by speaking first with the department head (see the organizational chart in Exhibit 1). José Barriga, a charismatic, dynamic man in his forties, was head of both Donor Services and Community Services. In reality, he spent virtually no time in the Donor Services Department and was not bilingual. "My biggest pleasure is working with the community leaders and coming up with programs that will be successful. I much prefer being in the field, driving from village to village talking with people, to supervising paperwork. I'm not sure exactly what goes on in Donor Services, but Elena, the supervisor, is very responsible. I make it a point to walk through the department once a week and say hello to everyone, and I check their daily production figures."

### The Cast of Characters in the Department

Like José, Sam was also more interested in working with the communities on projects than in immersing himself in the details of the more administrative departments. In part, Sam had contracted Joanna because he rightfully worried that Donor Services did not receive the attention it deserved from José, who was very articulate and personable but seldom had time to look at anything beyond case histories. José never involved himself in the internal affairs of the department. Even though he was not

6.0

considered much of a resource to them, he was well liked and respected by the staff of Donor Services, and they never complained about him.

## The Supervisor

This was not the case with the supervisor José had promoted from within. Elena had the title of departmental supervisor, but she exercised very little authority. A slight, single woman in her thirties, Elena had worked for the organization since its establishment ten years earlier. She was organized, meticulous, dependable, and hard working. But she was a quiet, non-assertive, nervous woman who was anything but proactive. When asked what changes she would make if she were the head of the department, she sidestepped the question by responding, "It is difficult to have an opinion on this subject. I think that the boss can see the necessary changes with greater clarity."

Elena did not enjoy her role as supervisor, which was partly due to the opposition she encountered from a small clique of long-time translators. In the opinion of this subgroup, Elena had three strikes against her. One, unlike her subordinates, she was not bilingual. "How can she be the supervisor when she doesn't even know English well? One of us would make a better supervisor." Bilingual secretaries in status-conscious Guatemala see themselves as a cut above ordinary secretaries. This group looked down on Elena as being less skilled and educated than they were, even though she was an excellent employee. Second, Elena belonged to a different religion than the organization itself and almost all the other employees. This made no difference to Sam and José but seemed important to the clique who could be heard making occasional derogatory comments about Elena's religion.

The third strike against Elena was her lack of authority. No one had ever clarified how much authority she really possessed, and she herself made no effort to assume control of the department. "My instructions are to inform Don José Barriga of infractions in my daily production memo. I'm not supposed to confront people directly when infractions occur, although it might be easier to correct things if I did." ("Don" is a Latin American honorific used before the first name to denote respect.)

This subgroup showed their disdain and lack of respect for Elena by treating her with varying degrees of rudeness and ignoring her requests. They saw her as a watchdog, an attitude furthered by José who sometimes announced, "We (senior management) are not going to be here tomorrow, so be good because Elena will be watching you." When Sam and José left the office, the clique often stopped working to socialize. They'd watch Elena smolder out of the corner of their eyes, knowing she would not reprimand them. "I liked my job better before I became

**6.0**

supervisor," said Elena. "Ever since, some of the girls have resented me, and I'm not comfortable trying to keep them in line. Why don't they just do their work without needing me to be the policeman? The only thing that keeps me from quitting is the loyalty I feel for the agency and Don José."

## The Workers

In addition to the clique already mentioned, there were three other female translators in the department. All the translators but one had the same profile: in their twenties, of working-class backgrounds, and graduates of bilingual secretary schools, possessing average English skills. (As stated earlier, in Latin America, being a bilingual secretary is a fairly prestigious occupation for a woman.) The exception in this group was the best translator, Magdalena, a college-educated recent hire in her late thirties who came from an upper-class family. She worked, not because she needed the money, but because she believed in the mission of the agency. "This job lets me live out my religious beliefs and help people who have less advantages than I do." Magdalena was more professional and mature than the other translators. Although all the employees were proud of the agency and its religious mission, the clique members spent too much time socializing and skirmishing with other employees within and without the department.

The three translators who were not working at full capacity were very close friends. The leader of this group, Juana, was a spunky, bright woman with good oral English skills and a hearty sense of humor. A long-time friend of Barriga's, Juana translated for English-speaking visitors who came to visit the program sites throughout the country. The other translators, tied to their desks, saw this as a huge perk. Juana was the ringleader in the occasional mutinies against Elena and in feuds with people from other departments. Elena was reluctant to complain about Juana to Barriga, given their friendship. Perhaps she feared Juana would make her life even more miserable.

Juana's two buddies (*compañeras*) in the department also had many years with the agency. They'd gotten into the habit of helping each other on the infrequent occasions when they had excessive amounts of work. When they were idle or simply wanted to relieve the boredom of their jobs, they socialized and gossiped. Juana in particular was noted for lethal sarcasm and pointed jokes about people she didn't like. This clique was not very welcoming to the newer members of the department. Magdalena simply smiled at them but kept her distance, and the two younger translators kept a low profile to avoid incurring their disfavor. As one of them remarked, "It doesn't pay to get on Juana's bad side."

Like many small offices in Latin America, the agency was located in a spacious former private home. The Donor Services Department was housed in the 40 × 30-foot living room area. The women's desks were set up in two rows, with Elena's desk in the back corner. Since the offices of both Wilson and Barriga were in former back bedrooms, everyone who visited them walked through the department, greeting and stopping to chat with the long-time employees (Elena, Juana, and her two friends). Elena's numerous visitors also spent a good deal of time working their way through the department to reach her desk, further contributing to the amount of socializing going on in the department.

Elena was the only department member who had "official" visitors since she was the liaison person who dealt with program representatives and kept track of enrollments. The translators each were assigned one work process. For example, Marisol prepared case histories on new children and their families for prospective donors while Juana processed gifts. One of the newer translators prepared files for newly enrolled children and did all the filing for the entire department (a daunting task). Most of the jobs were primarily clerical and required little or no English. The letter translations were outsourced to external translators on a piece-work basis and supervised by Magdalena. Hers was the only job that involved extensive translation; for the most part, however, she translated simple messages (such as greeting cards) that were far below her level of language proficiency. The trickier translations, such as queries from donors in other countries, were still handled by Wilson's executive secretary.

Several translators complained that, "We don't have enough opportunity to use our English skills on the job. Not only are we not getting any better in English, we are probably losing fluency because most of our jobs are just clerical work. We do the same simple, boring tasks over and over, day in and day out. Why did they hire bilingual secretaries for these jobs anyway?"

Another obvious problem was the uneven distribution of work in the office. The desks of Magdalena and the new translators were literally overflowing with several months' backlog of work while Juana and her two friends had time to kill. Nobody, including Elena, made any efforts to even out the work assignments or help out those who were buried. The subject had never been broached.

The agency was growing at a rapid pace, and there were piles of paperwork sitting around waiting to be processed. Joanna spent three weeks having each department member explain her job (in mind-numbing detail), drawing up flow charts of how each type of paperwork was handled, and poking around in their files. She found many unnecessary steps that resulted in slow turnaround times for various processes. There were daily output reports submitted to Barriga, but no statistics kept on the length of time it took to respond to requests for information or process paperwork. No data were shared with the translators, so they had no idea how the department was faring and little sense of urgency about their work. The only goal was to meet the monthly quota of case histories, which only affected Marisol. Trying to keep up with what came across their desks summed up the entire focus of the employees.

Joanna found many instances of errors and poor quality, not so much from carelessness as lack of training and supervision. Both Barriga and Wilson revised the case histories, but Joanna was amazed to discover that no one ever looked at any other work done by the department. Joanna found that the employees were very accommodating when asked to explain their jobs and very conscientious about their work (if not the hours devoted to it). She also found, however, the employees were seldom able to explain why things were done in a certain way, because they had received little training for their jobs and only understood their small part of the department. Morale was obviously low, and all the employees seemed frustrated with the situation in the department. With the exception of Magdalena who had experience in other offices, they had few ideas for Joanna about how the department could be improved.

6.0

**EXHIBIT 1**
Organizational Chart—Donor
Services Department

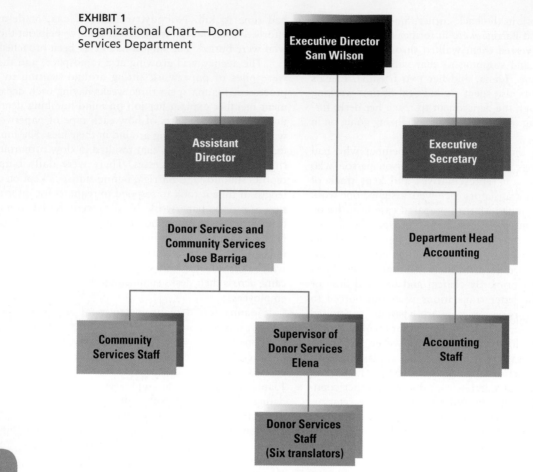

6.0

## Integrative Case 7.0

## The War of the Woods: A Forestry Giant Seeks Peace*

The case examines the difficult strategic decision before MacMillan Bloedel, the largest forest company in British Columbia at the time. The company had been battered by economic downturns in key markets, long-standing protests and criticism from environmentalists for its logging methods of old-growth forests, accidents and safety problems in its operations, and loss of confidence by its investors. With the prospect of losing key European customers to its increasingly tarnished image, the company goes about examining its options to get out of this quagmire and regain respect and profitability in the marketplace. The CEO strikes a high-level, internal task force and grants this 'Forest Project' 90 days to comprehensively review all options. Now the often conflicting recommendations are in. Should MacMillan Bloedel opt for major, but risky, innovations? Or should it stay with the perhaps equally risky status quo?

- Sustainable strategy
- Triple bottom line
- Strategic decision-making
- Stakeholder conflict
- Profitability
- Organisational change
- Forest Industry

*Minika I. Winn; Charlene Zietma,"War of the Woods: A Forestry Giant Seeks Peace", *Greener Management International* (Winter 2004/2005, Issue 48.) © Greenleaf Publishing. Reprinted with Permission.

Monika Winn is Associate Professor of Business Strategy and Sustainability. Her research focuses on organisational and institutional change related to the challenges of sustainability (including climate change impacts on strategy, marketing for the poorest of the poor, stakeholder conflicts, and social to strategic issue transformation (salmon farming). Monika has published in *Organization Studies, Academy of Management Review, Business and Society* and *The Journal of Business Venturing*. She co-founded and chaired the Academy of Management's 'Organisations and the Natural Environment' group.

Charlene Zietsma is an assistant professor of Strategy at the Ivey Business School, University of Western Ontario. She completed her PhD at the University of British Columbia. Charlene's research interests focus on processes of emergence and change, especially in the context of corporate conflicts with social and environmental stakeholders. She has studied processes of institutional change, organisational learning, dynamic capability emergence, and opportunity recognition. She has served on a number of boards and committees for non-profit, professional and government organisations.

'Bill, can I talk to you?' Tom Stephens, CEO of Macmillan Bloedel Ltd, the giant of British Columbia's forest industry, ushered Bill Cafferata, his Chief Forester, into his office.

'What's up, Tom?' Cafferata asked, trying to sound casual. Stephens had been CEO of MacMillan Bloedel (MB) (and Cafferata's boss) for exactly six months. During that time, he had replaced nearly the entire senior team with their former subordinates. Cafferata had survived the cleansing, and, after 26 years with the company, he was not especially anxious to end his career that day.

'I hear you've been having troubles with the Forest Project team. There is talk about some pretty loud arguments. My consultants tell me you guys were going to self-destruct, and that I'd better have a back-up plan in place. What do you think? Are you going to make it?'

Cafferata paused, knowing the next few words could give him enough rope to hang himself with. 'Yep, I think we're going to make it,' he said.

'Okay, go to it,' Stephens said.

A little relieved, a little uneasy, Cafferata went back to his office, determined to come up with a way to make the Forest Project work. The Forest Project was a cross-functional team of senior managers and experts that were charged with finding a new way of managing forestry. Cafferata's first meeting with Stephens about the forest project one-and-a-half months earlier had been just as short. Stephens had conducted a 90-day strategic review of the company to determine what needed to be done to turn it around. Every aspect of the company had come under the scrutiny of Stephens and his 'Council', 'a team of high-priced, best-of-breed consultants', according to Cafferata. The management team from each division made a presentation to the council. They were told to make the business case for their units, mindful of Stephens's admonition: 'Sell it, milk it or grow it: get off your lazy assets.' Change came with a heavy dose of fear. The results of these presentations had become corporate legend: middle managers would come into work the day after their team presented to find that the team ranks had been decimated, and they were now in charge of making the 'revised' presentation. Any indication of MB's typical bureaucratic, divisionalised thinking was punishable by pink slip (i.e., termination of employment).

When Stephens took the helm in September 1997, MB had had six consecutive quarters of sizeable losses, and the losses were growing. Stephens was fond of saying 'MB

7.0

is worth more dead than alive.' The company's market capitalisation was lower than the amount that could be generated by breaking it up and selling the parts. MB's five-year financial data are shown in Table 1. But Stephens felt that MB had other problems . . .

The 90-day review turned up several priority areas in need of major overhaul. One issue particularly critical for regaining financial success was how MB secured its supply of raw material, wood. As soon as the review was complete, Stephens had invited Cafferata, MB Chief Forester and VP, into his office.

'Bill, we need to find a new way to do forestry. I'd like you to form a team to find some solutions. I'll give you a budget of $1 million, and a time frame of 90 days. Are you willing to take on this challenge?'

And so the Forest Project began.

## The Forest Project team

Cafferata put together a cross-functional team comprising senior managers and experts in the areas of logging, silviculture,[1] conservation biology, forest ecology, forest growth and yield projections, and the social aspects of environmental affairs. The team included Cafferata himself, a professional forester. The team consulted outside experts from academia, government and industry research groups, along with internal experts.

Each team member brought a particular perspective to the table. Group members had gone to considerable lengths just to *understand* each other's issues, and disagreements had been fierce. In some ways, the diverse and often contradictory views in this group mirrored the myriad of conflicting views and pressures the company was exposed to externally. In line with corporate objectives for 'safety, respectability and outrageous success', the group agreed that they needed to find a way to:

- Increase conservation of old-growth forests
- Find a harvesting compromise to suit environmentalists and the public
- Achieve both of the above in ways that would enable the company to:
  - Protect employee safety first and foremost

**TABLE 1**

Macmillan Bloedel Five-Year Financial Data (all Dollar items, Except Market Price Range, are in Canadian $ Millions)

| | 1997 | 1996 | 1995 | 1994 | 1993 |
|---|---|---|---|---|---|
| **Financial position** | | | | | |
| Total assets | $4,559 | $4,830 | $5,271 | $4,679 | $4,397 |
| Current liabilities | 724 | 833 | 1,102 | 973 | 544 |
| Long-term debt and liabilities | 2,239 | 2,000 | 2,068 | 1,828 | 2,124 |
| Shareholders' equity | 1,596 | 1,997 | 2,101 | 1,878 | 1,729 |
| Total liabilities and shareholders' equity | 4,559 | 4,830 | 5,271 | 4,679 | 4,397 |
| **Results of operations** | | | | | |
| Sales | $4,521 | $4,267 | $4,327 | $3,781 | $3,121 |
| Costs and expenses | 4,624 | 4,179 | 3,897 | 3,373 | 2,818 |
| Operating earnings (loss) | (103) | 88 | 430 | 408 | 303 |
| Other income and expenses | (265) | (37) | (150) | (227) | (249) |
| Net earnings (loss) | (368) | 51 | 280 | 181 | 54 |
| **Financial and statistical data** | | | | | |
| Capital expenditures in continuous operations ($ millions) | 90 | 220 | 503 | 232 | 167 |
| Market price range     High | 21.70 | 20.10 | 21.62 | 23.50 | 23.62 |
|     Low | 14.15 | 16.50 | 16.00 | 15.50 | 16.12 |
| Earnings (loss) as percentage of sales—continuous operations | (3%) | 2% | 7% | 6% | 6% |
| Return on average common shareholders' equity | (22%) | 2% | 15% | 11% | 3% |
| Common shares outstanding (000s) | 124,414 | 124,377 | 124,336 | 123,754 | 123,732 |
| Number of employees (excludes discontinued operations) | 10,592 | 10,966 | 10,523 | 10,189 | 9,810 |

*Source*: MB 1998 Annual Report.

– Achieve forest certification (ISO 14001, FSC [Forest Stewardship Council], etc.) to ensure market access
– Maintain employment at current levels
– Meet or exceed regulatory obligations
– Improve profitability

It was a wish list: no one really dreamed they would be able to meet all of the objectives, especially since many of them seemed directly in conflict and would involve trade-offs. However, this list of objectives gave each member of the group a set of targets to aim for. The team then decided that the best approach would be to split up into subcommittees, each of which was charged with becoming an expert in one of the key aspects of forestry that were currently at odds: biodiversity and conservation, harvest levels, yield and employment, safety, silviculture, social issues and profitability. The subcommittees had six weeks to do their research and generate recommendations for discussion by the whole team.

## Company history, products and markets

MacMillan Bloedel had grown from a small British Columbia-based company at the start of the (20th) century, to one of the world's foremost forest products companies. The company managed 5 million acres (2 million ha) of productive timberlands (2.7 million acres [1.1 million ha] in British Columbia), which supplied most of its fibre requirements. Timber from these lands was cut in MB sawmills and further processed into lumber, panel boards, engineered lumber, containerboard and corrugated containers. Over decades of expansion, MB had entered and exited such businesses as pulp and paper, shipping, lumber distribution, and others, and had made investments and acquisitions in Europe, the United States, Hong Kong, Australia and across Canada. By the late 1960s, MB had become Canada's 14th largest industrial corporation based on sales, and by the late 1970s employed 24,500 people in logging camps, sawmills and panel board plants, newsprint, pulp, fine-paper and paper bag plants in Canada, the United States and the United Kingdom.

In 1996, MacMillan Bloedel had sales of Can $5.043 billion, 13,497 employees, and harvested 5,716,000 cubic metres of logs, the equivalent of approximately 5.7 million telephone poles (1 m$^3$ = 35.315 cubic feet). The company consisted of three major business segments: building materials as its core business segment (67 percent of sales), paper (14 percent) and packaging (17 percent). Both paper and packaging were industries in overcapacity; MB's largest growth came from its building materials segment, particularly its value-added wood products. Figure I illustrates the products that come from the forest industry. MB had operations in each of these areas, and a research centre that developed new value-added wood products. MB also had a network of distribution centres across Canada and the United States.

The biggest forest products company in British Columbia (BC), a Canadian province that depended heavily on forestry for both employment and revenue, MacMillan Bloedel had come under heavy fire from many sides. Environmentalists filled the media with negative publicity about MB's practice of clear-cut logging old-growth forests and organised boycotts on company products. The early symptoms of the Asian financial crisis gave management serious headaches: 40 percent of their lumber sales went to Asia. MB's biggest market was the United States, but it could not easily sell its product there because the Softwood Lumber Agreement imposed restrictive quotas on Canadian lumber exports. Growing environmental concerns by customers in Europe, plus demands for environmental certification, limited access to that market. By the late 1980s and early 1990s, environmental controversies in coastal British Columbia had focused international media attention on the company's logging operations. Now, environmental groups had pressured several of MB's customers into cancelling purchasing contracts because of its logging practices. It seemed like the whole world was changing, but MB was out of step. Stephens claimed that MB was in danger of losing its 'social licence to operate' in BC.

Inside the company the situation was equally difficult. Devastating confrontations with unions had led to labour disruptions. A poor safety record did little to improve labour relations or cost efficiency. Low productivity, combined with the highest wages in the industry, placed MacMillan Bloedel at a big competitive disadvantage in global markets. And British Columbia, with its strong unions, high wages, complex forestry legislation, and significant environmental pressures already had a reputation for its 'unfriendly' business climate. Industry experts spoke of the 'BC discount', the lower stock prices (relative to earnings) accorded to BC logging companies.

Facing such tough times, MB executives talked about cutting costs and waiting for things to turn around. Investors, however, decided they would wait no longer and initiated a shareholders' revolt. CEO Robert B. Findlay was replaced by Tom Stephens, a seasoned corporate veteran from Denver, in September 1997.

## The environment

### ■ Government regulation

For many years, forestry had been the largest employer in British Columbia and, through fees and tax revenues, was the largest contributor to the provincial government coffers. The forest industry accounted for 50 percent of all BC exports and employed 275,000 people in BC. The government owned and managed 95 percent

**7.0**

**FIGURE 1**
From Trees to Products: British Columbia Forest Industry Value Chain

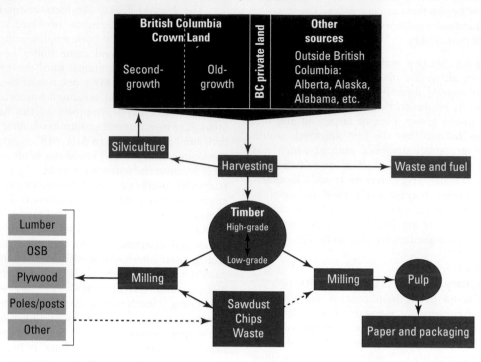

of the forestland in BC (about 60 million hectares or 150 million acres; 1 hectare = 2.471 acres). In other countries, forests were usually privately held. In BC, however, the government granted forest companies long-term timber licences to cut and manage particular plots of land in return for stumpage fees.[2] Forest companies were required to adhere to harvesting, replanting and environmental regulations, which included the Forest Practices Code, a complex set of regulations claimed to mandate sustainable forest management practices (though environmentalists claimed otherwise), and the government mandated Land Resource Management Planning process, requiring public consultation with stakeholders prior to the approval of logging plans for a particular area.

### ■ Environmentalists

Starting in the late 1980s, local, regional and international environmental groups waged highly visible protests against forest management in British Columbia. Their major emphasis was on the practice of clear-cutting, which sometimes caused erosion of mountainsides and destroyed fish-bearing streams, habitat for wildlife (including bears and mountain lions), and high-biodiversity, old-growth rainforests. Two other major concerns were the cutting

of old-growth forests (with trees ranging from 140 to over 1,000 years old) and the failure to preserve sufficient quantities of wilderness in parks. As the largest licence holder of public lands on the BC coast, MB was especially heavily targeted. Initially, MB ignored the environmentalists. But, when their voices became too loud, MB vigorously defended its practices of clear-cutting old growth. After all, it was largely in compliance with regulations governing logging in BC, and its practices were deemed by the forestry profession to be the best for the long-term growth and health of the forest, as well as the safest way to log.

Much of the steam behind the environmental movement in BC came from outside Canada. Money was raised in international campaigns (particularly in Europe), and large U.S. foundations funded and participated in campaigns. A number of American actors, Robert Kennedy Jr and California state senator Tom Hayden travelled to Clayoquot Sound on Vancouver Island's rainforest coast to support protests in the early 1990s. US Vice President Gore publicly pressured the Canadian government into converting public lands to parks and wilderness areas. A local logger's response to Robert Kennedy Jr's visit to BC typified the view of many BC citizens: 'I've worked hard for

7.0

44 years,' says Doug Pichette, 'and now I've got to listen to an outsider who had life given to him on a silver platter tell me what's wrong with my economy and government. Who does he think he is?'[3] Environmental groups targeted U.S. and European customers, threatening them with smear campaigns if they did not put public pressure on MB and other BC forest companies. BC observers considered it quite ironic that the United States and Europe, where most of the forests had been cut years ago, were calling on Canadians to bear the full costs for conserving a 'world resource'.

### ■ The tourism industry and native land claims

An industry of growing importance, tourism, was also against clear-cutting: ugly bald clear-cut patches on mountainsides destroyed 'viewscapes' along the 'inside passage' to Alaska, the route travelled by a large number of cruise ships. Native land claims also created an element of uncertainty for BC forest companies. BC's aboriginal peoples claimed areas in excess of the total land area of the province (due to overlapping claims among different native groups). In the landmark 'Delgamuukw' decision, the Supreme Court of Canada ruled in December 1997 that aboriginal groups have rights in lands used or occupied by their ancestors, ranging from limited use up to aboriginal title. This decision called the security of long-term tenures on the lands licensed from the government into question. Until treaties were negotiated and court challenges settled, however, it was difficult to predict exactly what effect native land claims would have.

### ■ Changing global markets

BC forest companies exported 83.3 percent of their products (for revenues of approximately Can $13.24 billion) in 1998. The largest customer was the US, followed by Japan and Europe. The Softwood Lumber Agreement, negotiated between Canada and the United States to run until 2001, restricted the volume of softwood lumber that could be exported into the US. Because MB had historically sold to the Asian market, a very small amount of U.S. quota was allocated to it. When the 'Asian Flu' (Asia's financial crisis) hit in 1997, MB turned its attention to 'greener' European markets, which had become increasingly competitive. MB had a very poor environmental image in Europe because of environmental groups' campaigns there. Already, two of MB's customers had cancelled their contracts. And, now, a number of other customers were starting to ask MB staff what they were going to do to get the environmentalists off their back.

Environmentalists were calling for forest products to be independently certified as coming from sustainably managed forests. Three major certification schemes were emerging in BC forestry, each with different criteria. Environmentalists favoured the Forest Stewardship Council scheme, of which European furniture giant IKEA was a founding member. The Forest Stewardship Council had not yet developed criteria for certification of forestry in BC, but indications of what would be required could be identified based on criteria already established in other forest ecosystems.

### Stephens sets new strategic objectives

When Stephens took the helm of MB in September 1997, the board of directors had given him a broad mandate for change. He refocused MB'S strategy on its core building materials business and aggressively addressed the areas that hampered cost-competitiveness in its BC base. Under the new CEO, MB exited the paper business and medium-density fibreboard, closed its MB Research Center and shut down large numbers of distribution centres, sawmills, wood remanufacturing and packaging plants all over Canada and the United States. By late 1998, he had downsized MB's workforce to 9,000 from 13,500 employees worldwide, and he had completely restructured the senior management team.

During the restructuring, MB's formerly bureaucratic culture was to be shaken to its core: everyone in the company, managers and unionised employees, clerks, loggers and executives, would co-manage projects to turn the company around. Three key objectives were to guide every corporate action: to become the safest forest company, to become the most respected forest company, and to be outrageously successful. Given the company's recent dismal performance in each of these three areas, many observers thought they might as well be shooting for the moon.

### The Forest Project subcommittees report their findings

In the spring of 1998, the Forest Project team met as a whole, for what was going to be a long day of heated debate. Six in-depth reports and memos summarising their recommendations had been distributed to all a few days earlier. It was clear that differences in perspectives had become more pronounced. Over the six weeks, each subcommittee had gained both a deeper understanding and a greater appreciation of their respective positions. The mood was tense. No one knew how to resolve what appeared to be unsolvable differences. The meeting started promptly at 8 a.m. With executive summaries of the six research reports in front of Team Leader Bill Cafferata and each team member, each of the six subcommittees presented its recommendations.

### The Forest Project team disagrees

After the reports were presented, lively discussion ensued and generated some additional considerations:

- Harvest levels in the past few years had declined by 20 percent because of environmental controversies,

**7.0**

and were currently holding at 5.7 million m³. This number could be expected to go down further if no environmental solution was found. If the environmental controversy died down, it would be conceivable that the company could access all 6.2 million m³ of its potential annual allowable cut, though of course that amount would have to be reduced by whatever amount was committed to old-growth preservation or variable retention

- Some of the wood that was usually removed from the clear-cut site was waste wood (e.g. deadfalls); it currently did not count in cut calculations, but needed to be removed from the site because of government guidelines. This wood was actually important habitat for species, and thus should be retained on-site. It was estimated that considering this waste wood could make up approximately four percent of that retained. Furthermore, about five percent of the total area (1.1 million hectares) logged by MB was already preserved owing to forest practice code regulations protecting areas along-side stream beds (important salmon spawning grounds) and on hillsides (because of erosion issues)
- Current regulations required that not only the best trees, but also the poor trees were taken out of the forest. The poorer trees might be those that had decay

or timber 'defects' such as large knots or branch structures that reduced their timber value. Trees that were too small to yield timber of a size demanded by the market also had to be cut. All of these trees were uneconomic to cut. For preserving biodiversity and habitat, however, they were often as well suited as any other tree. Leaving such trees was a win–win for habitat and economics. Special habitats such as ravines, wetlands and rock outcrops typically had higher plant diversity, yet lower timber values. Leaving these sites as part of permanent reserves would help maintain biodiversity. Uneconomic trees accounted for an average of five percent of the total harvest. Not cutting those trees would save the company a significant amount in handling costs

## Cafferata ponders the decision

Cafferata thought again about his options and what he and the Forest Project team were going to do next. A complete halt to cutting old-growth forest would virtually be the end of MB in BC, since there would not be enough volume left to sustain operations. However, if the company failed to make any move on old growth, environmental groups would be unlikely to stop the customer campaigns and to give MB some peace. On the other

**BOX 1**
**Technical Report of The Harvest Level Subcommittee to The Forest Project Team**

## EXECUTIVE SUMMARY

**Task.** Assess alternative logging methods' impact on current and future yield of fibre.

**Clear-cutting.** Any replacement of clear-cutting with a partial cutting method (variable retention) will increase cost significantly and lead to an immediate drop in harvest levels due to cutting fewer logs. Current methods allow us to cut an average of 8 cubic metres (m³) of timber per year per hectare. To estimate the annual cut using variable retention (and ignoring the future declining yield effect), we subtract the percentage of retention from 8 m³ per hectare, and multiply by the hectares planned to cut per year.

We also expect a future volume reduction. Using studies and simulation, we also expect the forest to regenerate more slowly as the trees left standing reduce the light to and growth of the 'understorey' tree crop. There are no studies or data for periods longer than 5 years on the effect of alternative silvicultural systems in coastal BC. The following are our best projections of yield reductions: at an average 25% retention rate, over 5 years: negligible; over 10 years: 2–3%; over 20 years: 5–6%.

Other considerations: Any variable retention system requires more and better roads, which have a very negative environmental effect. Also, clear-cutting mimics natural disturbances, providing a diversity of habitats for various species. Further, switching away from clear-cutting methods would cause a backlash from loggers, their unions, the industry and others in BC for giving in and selling out to environmentalist demands.

**Old growth.** About half of the 5.7 million acres in BC managed by MB currently contains old growth; the other half is second growth. However, second-growth forests are not ready to cut, requiring about 80-year cycles. Old growth will continue to account for the majority of MB's harvest for another 25 years. Many environmentalists are calling for a complete halt to the cutting of old-growth forests and to clear-cutting. If MB stopped both, harvest levels would be reduced to 20–25% of current harvest levels in the short term, to average about 2 million m³ per year over 20 years. MB could not afford to maintain its operations at that harvest level, with implications not just for the solid wood business, but also for nearly every other business we are involved in.

**Recommendation.** In sum, our projections of yield reductions would hurt MB financially and would lead to lay-offs, plant shutdowns and devastation of the many forest dependent communities, all of which is clearly contrary to our landlord's, the government's, objectives for forest land use and social welfare. The harvest level subcommittee therefore recommends that it is critical to protect our access to fibre and that we must continue the use of clear-cutting old growth (except in designated preservation areas). If we continue to fight the environmentalist threat, eventually our customers will ignore environmentalists because they need secure access to wood.

**BOX 2**
Technical Report to The Forest Project Team: Biodiversity and Conservation

## EXECUTIVE SUMMARY

**Task.** Assess MB's role in retaining habitat conservation and biodiversity.

**Biodiversity.** Based on data from ecological and biological studies, large, contiguous blocks of old-growth forests are important for the maintenance of habitat and for plant and animal species biodiversity. Current parkland, though substantial, may not be of sufficient size or contiguity. Our estimates suggest that approximately 10% of MB's current old-growth holdings is in fragmented blocks of insufficient size to maintain biodiversity. Our old-growth strategy then should focus on cutting those fragmented blocks and retaining more of the wood in the large, contiguous blocks.

**Wildlife habitat.** Other areas provide valuable habitat for animal or plant species, but would not require the same level of preservation and high retention as the contiguous old-growth sections. These 'habitat zones' make up approximately 25% of our land base. The remaining 65% of the land base is prime timberland that could be subject to intensive forestry. These numbers are our best estimate.

**Other values.** Aesthetic and other values must also be considered, although results will depend on a social decision process and will likely be subject to significant controversy (e.g. road building carves up habitat; tourism requires access so that people can view wildlife). To determine exactly which blocks are to be preserved and to what extent, whether to conserve habitat, biodiversity or other values, we need to commission further scientific studies, and we need to develop a process that considers multiple stakeholders.

**Recommendation.** The biodiversity and conservation subcommittee concludes that, to meet market demands, it is essential for MB to show commitment to retaining old-growth forests; this should be done by distinguishing forest areas based on their primary value for biodiversity, for wildlife habitat, for primary logging and for aesthetic values.

**BOX 3**
Technical Report on Silvicultural Options to The Forest Project Team

## EXECUTIVE SUMMARY

**Task.** Review and assess MB's options to harvest, regenerate and grow forest crops.

**Review.** The two principal silvicultural systems available are clear-cut (removing all trees in an area) and selection (maintaining continuous, uneven-aged forest cover). To maximise the growth and yield of trees. MB has relied mostly on clear-cut (e.g. 93% from 1994 to 1996).

**Variable retention.** This selection system, developed to address a wide array of forest management goals, offers an alternative to clear-cut systems that focus exclusively on tree growth and yield. Variable retention follows nature's model by retaining part of the forest after harvesting. We know that dead standing trees, decaying wood on the forest floor, and diverse tree sizes and canopy levels are important as wildlife habitat. Variable retention retains these structural features, as habitat for a host of forest organisms, ensuring managed stands will be more similar to natural forests.

Different levels of retention can be used in different areas. Retention can be dispersed throughout a cutblock (individual trees or small groups) or aggregated (clumps or patches). For both safety and ecological reasons, aggregates are preferable. Clumps of trees are also more attractive to look at than a clear-cut site. Studies from other regions suggest that at 70% retention of ecologically sensitive areas, the effect on wildlife, biodiversity and aesthetics is negligible. At

*(Continued)*

40% retention, biodiversity may be affected, and aesthetics are obviously affected, but wildlife habitat is likely to be sufficient for most species. At 25% retention, habitat is affected, as are viewscapes. This level of retention may be best suited to areas that provide relatively poor habitat to begin with. At 10% retention, this method is not very distinguishable from clear-cutting.

**Recommendation.** A switch to variable retention will allow for other forest values such as habitat, aesthetic appearance and biodiversity. Variable retention is flexible enough to be adapted to specific terrain and it allows us to use high-value trees more effectively. While the annual harvest level would be somewhat lower, and trees do not grow as quickly or as plentifully under variable retention, we are convinced we could maintain forest productivity over the long term. Furthermore, we could obtain environmental kudos by being the first in BC to broadly implement this harvesting method.

**BOX 4**
Technical Report of The Safety Subcommittee to The Forest Project Team

## EXECUTIVE SUMMARY

**Task.** Assess implications and feasibility of selection logging methods on worker safety.

**Technical assessment.** Using a partial harvest system (i.e. selection or variable retention logging) is more hazardous than clear-cut logging. Interlaced canopies of old-growth forests are littered with broken limbs and debris, and workers may be exposed to falling debris if they must work under or near a partial canopy. The risk can be reduced significantly through planning and training with deliberate attention to safety. An example is to develop harvest plans that allow loggers to fell trees into open areas; this is more easily achieved when trees retained on the site are clustered, instead of dispersed. Extensive retraining of loggers would be needed as well. With both, we might be able to log almost as safely using a partial harvesting system as we do now with clear-cutting.

**Costs and risks.** Safety is critical to MB, and we are already spending considerable resources to improve our safety record. Additional costs would be required to retrain loggers in a new method. There is also the risk that workers' compensation premiums would go up. We have worked with the BC Workers' Compensation Board to examine safety records of partial cutting systems elsewhere. The Board concedes that partial harvesting may be done safely and is willing to take a close look at a new system before deciding whether to increase our insurance rates upwards, if we adopt such a system.

For years, MB has been adamant that partial harvesting is hazardous and MB (and the industry) has argued that clear-cutting is the only safe way to log. It would be difficult to now try to convince our employees otherwise; it would be an especially hard sell to our unions. Logging safely can only be achieved with a new system if union members are willing to participate in training and to be flexible during the initial experimental stage.

**Recommendation.** The subcommittee concludes that selection logging can be done safely, only if we invest in the necessary planning and training, can convince the loggers of the new system, and can gain the trust of and work closely with the unions throughout the transition and learning phase.

**BOX 5**
Research Report to The Forest Project Team: Stakeholder Management

## EXECUTIVE SUMMARY

**Task.** Assess MB's key stakeholder groups and gauge their reaction to MB changing its logging practices to methods other than clear-cutting.

**Overview.** The report is based on focus groups, discussions and formal modelling methods of stakeholder groups to identify their needs, values and 'zones of tolerance' (the range of actions within which they are unlikely to complain about MB). We summarise perspectives of these key stakeholders: customers, environmentalists, competitors, government, unions, workers and communities, and the general public.

**Customers.** Many MB customers face significant pressure from environmental groups to publicly announce that they will no longer purchase products from old-growth forests and, particularly, forest products from MB. Examples are threats by Greenpeace to initiate consumer boycotts, media stunts targeting specific companies, and company email systems jammed with thousands of protest emails. Some customers have succumbed to the bullying tactics, cancelling contracts; others want MB to defuse the problem. Meanwhile, worldwide supplies of industrial wood fibre are abundant. BC is one of the world's largest producers of high-valued appearance-grade wood from old-growth forests, but, once customers find other sources, winning them back may be impossible. A good option for MB is to get certified using either ISO 14001 or Canadian Standards Association criteria for forest practices. MB may find itself with serious market access problems in the very near future, unless environmentalists' customer campaigns can be stopped.

**Environmentalists.** Local and international groups would likely welcome a proactive move by MB but, over the long term, might want no cutting in BC. Besides, environmentalists are generally distrustful of corporate interests and may interpret any proactive move cynically.

**Government.** Two ministries have jurisdiction over forestry. Owing to Ministry of Forests regulatory constraints, it is currently difficult to change silviculture systems: one, the full utilisation policy does not allow us to leave behind deadfalls and clumps of trees; and, two, requirements for average annual cuts over 5 years mean we could lose some of our timber land allocation if we depart from clear-cutting. If our alternatives can successfully deal with environmentalists' concerns, and they do not result in job losses, government officials may be flexible with respect to these regulations. They understand that logging of all old growth on the coast may be at risk if we don't make changes. The government, as owner of the majority of the forestlands managed by MB in BC, has the final say. MB must also continue to participate in the land resource management planning process, which covers five-year periods. The Ministry of the Environment supports a move to alternative silviculture methods that protect the biodiversity of plant and animal species better than does clear-cutting, so they are less likely to impede a change in practices.

**Unions, Workers, Communities.** The **unions** are concerned with maintaining logging and sawmilling jobs, the long-term future of the industry in BC, and worker safety. **Workers** themselves are also currently concerned with safety issues, feeling that their safety is compromised by environmentalists (they have experienced nasty confrontations during blockades, and terrorist acts such as vandalism of equipment, tree spiking and the burning of a bridge). Moving to a variable retention system raises other issues. For years, the industry has asserted (in part to defend itself from environmentalists) that clear-cutting is the only safe way to log. Using another system may be difficult for employees to accept. Workers also fear that their jobs and communities will disappear if environmentalists succeed in converting logging lands to parks. Workers have also experienced being painted as 'the bad guys' by environmentalists, losing respect in their communities, and some saw their children harassed at school. In sum, we predict that workers and unions would accept a compromise that preserved current employment levels or reduced them by only up to 10%, while maintaining worker safety. The many remote forestry-dependent **communities** in BC lobby heavily for logging companies to continue to work in their areas and to provide high-paying jobs. Without regular forestry work, these towns would die, as little other work exists. Some communities attempt to diversify (e.g. into tourism) and to preserve the beauty of their towns, and would prefer to have trees left for aesthetic purposes in certain areas.

**Competitors in BC.** Fellow BC coastal forestry firms and our industry lobby group, the Forest Alliance, were mostly against changing to a selection harvest system. Such a decision would be 'caving in' to environmentalists' demands and giving away BC's economic prosperity, with new demands sure to follow. They favour continuing to resist environmental pressures. To date, MB has been the primary target, bearing the brunt of this fight, and others have few incentives to change. Some companies expressed support for new practices, recognising they could be the next targets, and that market access could become blocked for all BC logging firms.

**The 'general public'.** BC citizens have grown weary of the war of the woods, with cynical views about both companies and environmentalists: companies want only profit and are against conservation; environmentalists are extreme, and international groups are not sensitive to the economic dependence of BC on the forest industry. One result from focus groups was that people would trust only what environmentalists and forest industry people could agree on.

**Recommendation.** MB's objective is to become the most respected forest company. We recommend moving to variable retention in the most proactive way we can. We identified as potential benefits: rebuilding trust with the public and regaining a good reputation; reduced pressure from environmentalists on us and our customers; providing us with breathing room to develop a long-term strategy. We see no other option.

**BOX 6**
Report of The Profit Subcommittee to The Forest Project Team

## EXECUTIVE SUMMARY

**Task.** Assess cost and profitability factors of switching to selective harvest methods.

**Current conditions.** The lumber market is currently in a down cycle and, after fees paid to the government, MB loses money on wood cut on public lands. Profits from private land are used to offset those losses. The reason behind this is that government regulations (designed to maintain stable employment levels for forestry and sawmill workers) require that annual cuts be maintained within certain limits. We expect government to be somewhat flexible with respect to changes in silvicultural and harvesting systems, but it is politically unlikely that large variations in employment levels would be tolerated. MB itself would have trouble retaining good workers if our cut varied significantly from year to year. Not all lumber prices are in down cycles at the same time, however (e.g. hemlock prices may be high when cedar prices are low). Currently, we have no choice but to cut all types of trees together, taking whatever price the market provides.

**New scenarios.** If we moved to a variable retention harvesting system, we could cut for value, not volume: we could focus on taking the trees out of the forest that have the highest value at a given time, providing we maintain forest biodiversity over time. We can maximise economic benefits by harvesting stands when their dominant species command the best price. To work, this approach requires a sufficient inventory of government approved cutblocks—something we are currently unable to get. Focusing on positive margin stands could increase the average margin and net earnings of the company, but reduce the harvest, and leave trees for habitat, aesthetics and other non-timber values on sites not currently profitable to log.

Significant capital is required to transition to new harvesting systems. Large equipment currently used for clear-cutting requires large logging roads, and road building is very expensive and has a large ecological impact. If cut sites are to be significantly reduced in size to accommodate clumps of trees in retention, we must consider other options and we may not have enough new equipment, if we convert to a variable retention system. A surprising finding from our models is that harvesting options such as helicopter and skyline logging have become more economical; regulations have reduced sizes of clear-cut sites to the point where the cost of road building is only slightly below the cost of other logging practices on many types of terrain; sometimes, it is more expensive. In variable retention, with cut sites much smaller, the cost differential is diminished further. Logging for value instead of volume, as noted above, may offset some of the costs.

In sum, we estimate that variable retention logging will add about 5% to the cost of cutting trees. While lumber prices fluctuate with the market, we based our estimates on an average of Can$400/$m^3$ in sales, and profits at 5–7% of sales at Can$24/$m^3$. Cost and other risk factors include: availability and cost of equipment; start-up costs; time to retrain loggers; and unions reluctant to agree to variable retention. Benefits and potential cost recovery would come from technological improvements, higher prices, productivity improvements and better access to trees due to fewer conflicts with environmental groups.

**Recommendation.** Cost increases run counter to current efforts to cut costs and improve efficiency. We cannot expect a green premium for changing to variable retention, which means any cost increases must be recovered through other means. There is the possibility to make variable retention work economically, but it is a very high-risk strategy.

hand, moving to a variable retention system would answer the environmentalists' demands to end clear-cutting, but it would involve significant investment in new harvesting equipment and employee training. It might also be unpopular with loggers who had spent their lives clear-cutting, and it was sure to be unpopular with the other forest companies. Some accommodation by the government would also be necessary to ensure that the changes did not result in charges of violating the Forest Practices Code.

One thing was sure: MB had to do something to get the environmental monkey off its back, and a strong move might give the company a competitive advantage with

customers, at least in the short term. It might be costly, however. A weak move could intensify the pressure on MB, if environmentalists cried 'too little, too late'. In the long term, the pressure was sure to return no matter what decision was made, as there were many environmentalists who wanted no logging of old-growth timber in BC at all.

Thinking back to the 90-day review process, Cafferata remembered Tom Stephens's admonition to business unit managers to 'sell it, milk it or grow it'. Milking the forest assets would involve cutting and selling as much as possible, until social or government forces moved to stop them, then exiting the business. The company's reputation would be likely to suffer from a milking strategy but, if the company exited the business, it might not matter. On the other hand, selling the assets immediately could be a viable option. Although the assets would not be likely to fetch a high price given the 'BC discount', the company's market capitalisation currently valued them at zero: the stock price reflected only the value of the non-BC assets. Selling would bring in some cash that could be used to grow the business in other areas, and would be likely to increase the company's stock price and get the investment community of MB's back.

If the Forest Project team did recommend keeping the assets, they needed to present a unified front to the board of directors when they made recommendations—and they needed to present a decision that was acceptable to the board and the institutional investors. At this point, that seemed only a distant possibility. Cafferata could take the team's input under advisement and then make the decision himself as to what to recommend to the board. Or

he could use his power as the team leader to push people in one direction. However, the people on the team were just the starting point. If he couldn't get agreement among these people, what hope did he have of getting buy-in from all the other parties involved: the employees and unions, the government, the environmentalists, customers and aboriginal groups?

### ■ Notes

1. Silviculture refers to the cultivation of trees; it aims to maximise long-term growth and yield of the forests through activities such as planting, thinning, fertilising and pruning.
2. Stumpage refers to a volume-based tax paid by BC forest companies for timber they harvest on public lands; it is a substantial source of revenue for the government.
3. *Globe and Mail*, 6 November 1993, A1.

7.0

## Integrative Case 8.0

## Chiquita In Colombia*

| | |
|---|---|
| *Cuando sonó la trompeta, estuvo todo preparado en la tierra, y Jehová repartió el mundo a Coca-Cola Inc., Anaconda, Ford Motors, y otras entidades: la Compañía Frutera Inc. se reservó lo más jugoso, la costa central de mi tierra, la dulce cintura de América.* | *When the trumpet blared everything on earth was prepared and Jehovah distributed the world to Coca-Cola Inc., Anaconda, Ford Motors and other entities: United Fruit Inc. reserved for itself the juiciest, the central seaboard of my land, America's sweet waist.* |

—Pablo Neruda, "La United Fruit Co."
(translation by Jack Schmitt)[1]

In 1997, executives at the Chiquita Brands Banadex subsidiary in Urabá, Colombia, left a meeting with Carlos Castaño, the leader of Autodefensas Unidas de Colombia (AUC), a paramilitary group, and several other AUC representatives. Castaño and his group had just put a deal on the table—for every dollar's worth of bananas Banadex exported, AUC would receive a penny. In return, AUC would offer protection for the employees of this Chiquita subsidiary, keeping them safe from the murder and violence that characterized this region. It was common knowledge that Chiquita had paid similar "taxes" to the Marxist guerilla group the Fuerzas Armadas Revolucionarias de Colombia (FARC) in the 1980s and early 1990s. The AUC representatives had chased FARC out of Colombia's Urabá region, home to some of Chiquita's banana plantations, and now wanted Chiquita to pay them. The executive team struggled with how to respond, especially in light of its past practices, the presence of few alternatives to making the payments, and existing U.S. federal law—specifically, the Foreign Corrupt Practices Act (FCPA), passed in 1977— that mandated

*This case was prepared by Jenny Mead, Senior Researcher, Andrew C. Wicks, Associate Professor of Business Administration, and Heidi White, Editor, Business Roundtable Institute for Corporate Ethics. It was written as a basis for class discussion rather than to illustrate effective or ineffective handling of an administrative situation.

reporting such payments and levied financial penalties for making them. As a result of the FCPA of 1977, businesses were under more scrutiny as to how they conducted themselves abroad. No longer was it acceptable to be "paying or offering to pay, directly or indirectly, money or anything of value to a 'foreign official' to obtain or retain business."[2] Extenuating circumstances were no longer considered; self-defense was not warranted. "Funding a terrorist organization can never be treated as a cost of doing business," U.S. Attorney Jeffrey Taylor said.[3] The FCPA considered payments to terrorist organizations as crimes; therefore, it was the responsibility of corporations to find alternative ways to operate within the requirements of the law while remaining competitive.

### Chiquita at a Glance

Chiquita Brands had its origins in 1899 as the United Fruit Company (UFC). The company refined the process of fresh produce distribution (painting its ships white to reflect the sun and keep the bananas cooler and later building refrigerated ships) so that it could sell its produce to regions far away. Costa Rica and Panama were the first countries to transport bananas; however, UFC soon expanded trade, providing bananas from Nicaragua, Honduras, and Colombia. In 1900, the United Fruit Company produced its first annual report; it was listed on the New York Stock Exchange in 1903 After battling several seasons of diseased bananas, the company began researching and developing disease-resistant varieties. By 1930, UFC had a fleet of 95 ships, but during the Second World War, the boats were used by the United States and Great Britain for military purposes, and the banana industry suffered for several years.

UFC became Chiquita in 1944, and in the mid-1950s was handling more than 2.7 billion pounds of fruit. In 1963, the company "[b]egan the largest branding program

8.0

ever undertaken by a produce marketer, accompanied by a record-breaking ad campaign which included affixing the trademark blue sticker to bananas: 'This seal outside means the best inside.'" In the mid-1960s, Chiquita began selling in Europe, with more than four billion pounds shipped worldwide each year. To keep the bananas from ripening during shipment, Chiquita invented a low-oxygen packing/shipping box. In 1989, UFC became Chiquita Brands International, Inc., taking advantage of and emphasizing the company's highest profile brand. By 1995, Chiquita had approximately a 25 percent share of the world banana market. Its two closest competitors were Dole Foods (22 percent to 23 percent) and Fresh Del Monte Produce (15 percent to 16 percent).

### ■ Chiquita's rough-and-tumble past

Over the years, Chiquita—as the United Fruit Company—had gained a reputation of paying bribes and being linked to coups in Central America. (In fact, "banana republic," a pejorative term coined by the American writer O. Henry, came from the influence large fruit and banana companies such as UFC had on Central and South American governments). The United Fruit Company's reputation for interfering in governments and controlling politics whenever possible led to its nickname: *El Pulpo* (the Octopus). One of the most horrific events—1928's "Banana Massacre," in which the Colombian army gunned down UFC workers demonstrating for better pay and conditions (and formal contracts with the company)—was memorialized (with some exaggeration) by Gabriel García Márquez in his 1967 book, *One Hundred Years of Solitude*. UFC's less than savory reputation, however, was not confined to Colombia. Throughout Latin America, the company was "often regarded as the quintessential representative of American imperialism in Central and South America."[4] In 1954, UFC was involved in a CIA-led coup against a Guatemalan president in favor of land reform. The suicide of Chiquita's chairman, Eli Black, in 1975, was the apparent result of an impending public announcement in the news that the company had bribed Honduran government officials. Chiquita also routinely pressed the government to send in troops to break up labor strikes on the banana plantations.

### Bananas

Bananas were large, herbaceous plants, quick-growing and, because of their sensitivity to cold (the smallest frost would kill a plant for that year), required a tropical environment. They were propagated by suckers that appeared at the base of the plant and took 10 to 15 months to become fruit. This fruit ripened not on the tree but after it was cut and placed in a warm environment. Bananas grew year-round, and, because they had to be harvested daily with the stems cut by hand (or machete), they were extremely labor-intensive. Since bananas ripened almost immediately after being cut, they needed to be transported quickly and stored in a cool atmosphere until the point of sale.

In the 1880s, bananas were a foreign fruit to Americans. The United Fruit Company and its competitor, Standard Fruit, changed that when they introduced the banana to North America. By the end of the 1890s, bananas "were being sold in major American cities in individually wrapped tinfoil packages as luxury goods."[5] A decade later, the banana was commonplace, a familiar and inexpensive fruit. By the early 20th century, bananas had become ubiquitous in America, marketed as an excellent source of nutrition, a perfect baby food (because of the texture), and an important ingredient for housewives to add to their families' diets. Another advantage of the banana was that it did not depend on seasonal changes; the fruit was grown all year long in warmer climates.

One of the banana's proponents, trying to head off a banana tariff in 1913, waxed eloquent about the fruit:

*The only fruit that comes every day in the year, year in and year out, almost unvarying in price, within the reach of all, nutritious, healthy in its germ-proof coat, is the gold ranks of the incoming tide of bananas, 40,000,000 bunches a year, two to four billion golden satisfiers of American desires.*[6]

Americans' dietary changes throughout the 20th century affected the popularity of bananas. With the advent of processed foods in the 1950s (which included canned fruits and vegetables), per capita consumption of bananas decreased. Then, growing consciousness in the 1970s of the health benefits of fresh fruit led Americans to abandon much of those processed foods and consume more bananas.

### ■ Bananas in Colombia

Most Colombian banana exports originated from medium to large plantations located along two Atlantic coast regions of the country: Urabá, comprising parts of Antioquía and Chocó departments near the border with Panama, and Magdalena department, which included the port city of Santa Marta. In the mid-1990s, about 85 percent of all Colombia's banana production was exported, and almost half that number was destined for the United States. In 1995, total banana production was estimated at 1.7 million tons, of which 1.5 million tons were exported. In 1996, Chiquita sourced approximately 30 percent of its bananas from Panama. Other source countries were Colombia, Costa Rica, Ecuador, Guatemala, and Honduras (ranging from 5 percent to 21 percent). The company owned 90,000 acres and leased 40,000 acres of improved land, primarily in Costa Rica, Panama, and Honduras. Approximately two-thirds of Chiquita's bananas were produced by subsidiaries, with the rest purchased from growers.

8.0

According to the Colombian banana growers association (AUGURA), productivity on Latin and Central American plantations was three times greater than in the Caribbean, and costs to import were 50 percent lower.[7]

## Colombia

Colombia, the fourth-largest and second-most densely populated country in South America, was colonized by the Spanish in 1499. The country achieved independence from Spain in 1819, but suffered a long history of violent battles between Conservatives and Liberals from its inception. The Conservative party was composed of the upper strata and social elite such as the landholders, plantation owners, and owners of mining operations. The Conservatives believed in a strong central government, limited voting rights for the lower class, close collaboration with the Catholic Church, and the importance of maintaining a social and clerical hierarchy. The Liberals, on the other hand, believed in a federalist government and complete separation of church and state; this group comprised the country's merchants, farmers, working people, and reformers. The labor unions that developed in the mid-20th century were the work of the Liberals.

Shortly after United Fruit arrived in Colombia, the Conservatives took power, with poet, journalist, and statesman Rafael Nuñez as president through 1894; under him, Colombia experienced remarkable economic growth. Nuñez centralized the government, strengthened the church, and sought to protect local industry and promote national exports. Over the next century, Colombia seesawed between ruling parties, with the Liberals in power from 1930 until the 1948 assassination of Jorge Gaitán, the labor leader and Liberal candidate for president, which resulted in rioting and bloodshed on a massive scale. Five years later, in a coup supported by both parties, General Gustavo Rojas Pinilla took power as dictator, which he held for five years; in 1957, a referendum supported the ratification of the National Front, a coalition government of Liberals and Conservatives agreeing to alternate power between the two parties. The coalition continued until the ratification of a new constitution in 1991.

Post-Second World War, Colombian and Central American companies experienced a growth in nationalism and a rise in power of the labor unions. There was a great deal of tension between paramilitary groups and unions and, as violence escalated, UFC and other foreign companies had to adapt their corporate strategies in these countries. As the 20th century went on, UFC shifted its operations in Colombia more to marketing than producing. Starting in the 1950s, the company sold off production assets such as plantations and relied more heavily on local planters.

### ■ Relentless violence

Latin American countries traditionally had the highest homicide rates in the world, with Colombia standing at the top. In the 1990s, the country had 30,000 murders annually. In 1996, there were 69.4 murders for each 100,000 Colombians. By contrast, Ecuador had 14 murders per 100,000; Venezuela had 22.3 per 100,000; the United States, 7.7; and Canada, 2. The murder rates in Colombia had risen dramatically in the 1980s and 1990s. Colombia's justice system had also broken down, making it less of a deterrent for criminal activity.

Violence in Colombia emanated from a variety of groups: the military and paramilitary forces, the drug traders, and the various guerrilla groups that acted "in semicollusive fashion to keep the spoils of war going."[8] There were a number of guerrilla groups, active for decades but formalized in the 1960s. These included the Fuerzas Armadas Revolucionarias de Colombia (FARC), the Ejército de Liberación Nacional (ELN), and the Movimiento 19 de Abril (M-19). Such groups were continually at war with the government. In 1985, three presidential candidates were assassinated, and the M-19 seized control of the Colombian Justice Palace and murdered many judges. The violence grew as the decade ended, and the government warred constantly with the Unión Patriótica political party, founded by a former M-19 member.

AUC was just one of the paramilitary groups that formed throughout Colombia. Some members came from private armies created by landowners to protect their property, and some came from the Colombian military itself. Until the early 1990s, the Colombian government had actually used the paramilitary groups to fight the guerrillas, but by 1997, realized that "it had created a monster by legalizing paramilitary groups."[9] It tried shutting down the groups but with little success. Similar to the other groups, AUC was notorious for torture, murder, brutal violence, and the killing of any civilians suspected of being sympathetic to the guerrilla groups. Estimates were that AUC was responsible for almost 70 percent of the human rights violations in Colombia. Its operational expenses came from supporters and from cocaine sales.

As cocaine overtook marijuana in popularity, the drug market grew larger, and drug traffickers joined the melee. A new constitution and a new, inclusive president in the early 1990s led to a small decline in violence, but the drug cartels, most notably those in Medellín and Cali, grew even more powerful. According to an *America's Watch Report* from the early 1990s, "political violence continues to take more lives in Colombia than in any other country in the Western Hemisphere."[10] Colombian citizens often did not know where the greatest threat lay because the Colombian Army, the guerrillas, and right-wing death squads all terrorized the country, often shooting inhabitants on a whim.

**8.0**

To the rest of the world, emblematic of Colombia's violence was the murder in 1994 of Colombian soccer player Andrés Escobar Saldarriaga, also known as *El Caballero del Fútbol* ("the gentleman of football"). Although the reason he was gunned down outside a Medellín bar was never determined, most people suspected that Escobar's unwitting goal against his own team (i.e., the Colombian National Soccer Team) during the 1994 World Cup, which eliminated the team in an early round, had earned him the ire of fellow Colombians.

Despite the ongoing violence in Colombia, Chiquita was not the only multinational with a presence there. Others—such as Coca-Cola, Occidental Petroleum, ExxonMobil, and Drummond Coal—set up shop in Colombia to access "cheap labor, an abundance of resources, low taxes, few labor restrictions, ample corporate freedom and accessibility to the world market."[11] The Colombian government encouraged the presence of these corporations for the economic and development benefits they provided the communities. As had Chiquita, Colombia Coca-Cola also experienced intimidation, kidnapping threats, murders, and blackmail during the 1990s. Paramilitaries warned employees they would be killed if they dared to participate in labor unions or their activities. Union leaders, on the other hand, pointed the finger at government hostility and the ongoing four-decade-old civil war in Colombia.

## Unpleasant Option

Chiquita's executives knew they had limited options. Carlos Castaño had made it clear that not paying AUC would result in harm to Chiquita and its employees. The executives could refuse to make the payments to AUC and risk the safety of their employees. Already, AUC had purportedly killed 50 Chiquita employees. More killings—along with kidnappings—were probable. Chiquita could quit its operations in the country, leaving behind an extremely profitable enterprise. Or Chiquita could pay the money. Although this second option seemed the simplest, it was rife with all sorts of hazards, since payments might only encourage the extortion and perhaps would be used to fund other AUC atrocities throughout the region and the country. Chiquita executives were aware that other multinationals throughout the world had been accused of protection payments (Coca-Cola in Colombia;

Daimler-Chrysler in Argentina; ExxonMobil in Indonesia, and Chevron in Nigeria), but none had been tried in court, and Chiquita executives did not know any details of the alleged payments. In addition, the potential damage to Chiquita's reputation, if those companies' payments were revealed, could be enormous.

■ **Notes**

1. Pablo Neruda, "La United Fruit Co.," *Canto General*, 1950, trans. Jack Schmitt, translator, Berkeley and Los Angeles, CA: University of California Press, 2000.
2. "FCPA Enforcement," http://www.fcpaenforcement.com/index.aspx (accessed December 14, 2009).
3. Jill St. Claire, "Chiquita Brands International Pleads Guilty to Making Payments to a Designated Terrorist Organization and Agrees to Pay $25 Million Fine," http://www.homelandsecurityus.net/chiquita_brands_international_pl.htm (accessed January 27, 2010).
4. Marcelo Bucheli, *Bananas and Business: The United Fruit Company in Colombia, 1899–2000* (New York: New York University Press, 2005), 3.
5. Bucheli, 24.
6. Bucheli, 29.
7. Julien Roche, *The International Banana Trade* (Cambridge, UK: Woodhead Publishing Limited, 1998), chap. 6.
8. Nazih Richani, "The Political Economy of Violence: the War-System in Colombia," *Journal of Interamerican Studies and World Affairs* 39 (1997): 37–81.
9. Luz Estella Nagle, "Survey: Solving Problems Facing International Law Today: Global Terrorism in Our Own Backyard: Colombia's Legal War Against Illegal Armed Groups," *Transnational Law & Contemporary Problems* 5, no. 18 (2005): 19.
10. Adrian Karatnycky, ed., Freedom in the World: The Annual Survey of Political Rights and Civil Liberties, (Edison, NJ: Transaction Publishers, 2002), 169.
11. Tara Patel, "Colombian Trade Unions: A Target for Intimidation and Assassination," Council on Hemispheric Affairs, August 3, 2009, http://www.coha.org/colombian-trade-unions-a-target-for-intimidation-and-assassination/ (accessed December 11, 2009).

8.0

## Integrative Case 9.0

## Genocide in Rwanda: Leadership, Ethics and Organizational 'Failure' in a Post-Colonial Context*

In 1993, the United Nations appointed a small peace-keeping force—the United Nations Assistance Mission for Rwanda (UNAMIR)—to oversee a peace agreement between the Rwanda Government Forces (RGF) and a rebel force known as the Rwandese Patriotic Army (RPA). Two Canadian military officers—Lieutenant-General Roméo Dallaire and his deputy, Major Brent Beardsley—led the peace mission. The RGF and the RPA had signed a peace agreement to end a brutal civil war that had raged for two and a half years. The agreement was to come into effect later that year. Dallaire and his UN peacekeepers were to monitor the situation and attempt to prevent further bloodshed, which might jeopardize the peace agreement. However, it soon became apparent to Dallaire that forces sponsored by the Rwandan government were fostering ethnic disagreements to encourage mass murder. Dallaire notified UN headquarters, requesting extra resources to mount a pre-emptive action against those planning the mass murders.

Far from receiving assistance, Dallaire encountered bureaucratic, diplomatic, and leadership resistance. UN officials eventually ordered the withdrawal of all but 270 peacekeepers in the face of a genocide that "would prove to be the fastest, most efficient killing spree of the 20th century." Over the course of 100 days in 1994, approximately 800,000 Rwandans were killed in a genocidal campaign launched by Hutu extremists against Tutsi and politically moderate Hutu.

With the situation in Rwanda changing rapidly and hundreds of thousands of people being murdered, the United Nations seemed incapable of responding to Dallaire's numerous requests for assistance. Mired in excessive bureaucratic regulations and structures shaped by conflicting political interests, the United Nations had to undergo an elaborate series of international meetings, bargaining, and negotiation to provide any material support. The UN's political will was strongly influenced by Western nations who not only failed to halt the killing, but were involved in the period leading up to its commencement, with evidence showing not only negligence, but also complicity.

The case focuses on the organizational factors (i.e., United Nations, UN Security Council, UN Department of Peacekeeping Operations, UNAMIR) that played a role in "failing" to prevent genocide in Rwanda. In particular, it focuses on the interplay between the UNAMIR military leader, General Roméo Dallaire, the United Nations, and its member states—particularly the United States, Belgium, and France, as well as the Rwandan government.

The case works at several levels:

- It allows the instructor to draw on rich materials to engage the students in discussing the impact of organizational arrangements on such things as stress, decision-making, organizational politics, etc.
- It encourages students to consider the relationship between organizational arrangements (i.e., structures and processes) and the potentially devastating outcomes of decision-making
- By discussing the operation of an international organization such as the United Nations, the case contextualizes the notion of globalization and its relationship to organizations and their activities

Perhaps above all else, the case provides a stark discussion point for consideration of the relationship between ethics and organizational behaviour.

### Introduction

The Rwandan genocide in 1994 resulted in the deaths of over 800,000 people. The killings occurred against a backdrop of politicking between key western members of the United Nations, whose peacekeeping role was described as at best ineffectual and at worst culpable. The role of the United Nations in the Rwandan genocide is the focus of this case.

The Republic of Rwanda is a small, landlocked, mountainous, heavily populated African nation without significant natural or geographical resources. A country of some 8.5 million people, it borders Uganda to its north, the Democratic Republic of the Congo to its north-north-west, Tanzania to its east-south-east, and Burundi to its south (see Figure 1). Kigali is the nation's capital.

The people fall into two main groups—the Hutus, who form the majority of the population, and the Tutsis. Although both groups share a common Bantu culture, they have been engaged in a series of wars for much of the second half of the 20th century, including a fierce civil war that tore the country apart in the early part of the 1990s.

**9.0**

*Brad S. Long, Jim Grant, Albert J. Mills, Ellen Rudderham-Gaudet, and Amy Warren, "4.4. Genocide in Rwanda: leadership, ethics and organizational 'failure' in a post-colonial context" (Greenleaf Publishing) © 2009. Reprinted with permission.

On August 4, 1993, the government of the Republic of Rwanda and the Rwanda Patriotic Army (RPA) signed a peace agreement in Arusha, Tanzania.[1] The Arusha Peace Agreement, as it became known, was designed to end the bitter civil war and open up the democratic political process in the country. It was also agreed that the United Nations would monitor the implementation of the peace agreement.

Two Canadian military officers, Lieutenant-General Roméo Dallaire and his deputy, Major Brent Beardsley, led the UN peacekeeping operation. Their mission was to monitor the situation and prevent further bloodshed which might jeopardize the peace agreement. It soon became apparent, however, that Rwandan government-sponsored forces were fostering ethnic disagreements to encourage mass murder. Nonetheless, from the very beginning Dallaire encountered bureaucratic, diplomatic, and leadership resistance to his various requests for resources and authority to take decisive action.

Far from providing assistance, UN officials—under political pressure from national governments—ordered the withdrawal of all but 270 peacekeepers at a critical time. In the process, UN peacekeepers were unable to prevent the murder of ten Belgian peacekeepers and a genocidal campaign launched by Hutu extremists against the Tutsi and politically moderate Hutu that saw over 800,000 Rwandans killed over the course of 100 days in 1994.

Clearly the mission was a terrible failure, and Dallaire went on to blame his lack of leadership skills, arguing:

*When you're in command, you are in command. There's 800,000 gone, the mission turned into catastrophe, and you're in command. I feel I did not convince my superiors and the international community. I didn't have enough of the skills to be able to influence that portion of the problem.[2]*

The Belgian government, who blamed him in part for the death of their ten paratroopers, also openly criticized him. Dallaire returned to Canada a broken man, feeling victimized, angry, and suicidal. Yet it is clear that, despite horrendous obstacles, his actions actually saved the lives of some 20,000 people who would otherwise have perished in the genocide.

So why was Dallaire unable to act effectively to prevent "the fastest, most efficient killing spree of the 20th century"?[3] To answer that question we need to examine the role of the United Nations and its member states.

### Dallaire's problem simply stated: how to develop an effective peacekeeping force

On August 19, 1993, a small 18-member UN team arrived in the Rwandan capital, Kigali, led by General Roméo Dallaire and Major Brent Beardsley. The role of Dallaire and his team was to assess the situation and make recommendations to the United Nations on the requirements needed for an effective peacekeeping force. With time being of the essence, Dallaire had 12 days to report his findings.

An initial part of Dallaire's assessment was to decide *if* the UN should commit to sending a full-fledged peacekeeping force to Rwanda, and he stressed to all who would listen that he was on a fact-finding mission. His assessment of the situation had to take into account a number of different considerations, including humanitarian, political, military and administrative factors. He was also on a tight schedule because the Arusha Peace Agreement had designated September 10, 1993 as the day when a new transitional government would be established. The new transitional government was to consist of a coalition of all the various groups who were party to the Peace Agreement. Dallaire knew that the UN would be unable to send even a token force to Rwanda by September 10, but promised that, should a peacekeeping force be agreed to, he would do what he could to get it to Rwanda in record time. Although optimistic that a peacekeeping force would be dispatched in due course, Dallaire began to sense that his "fact-finding" objective was dampening expectations, and his own optimism was tempered by concern as he began his assessment.

### Background to the Peace Agreement

In order to make any assessment, Dallaire needed to know something about the background to the Peace Agreement and he needed to know quickly. What he found out was disquieting and encouraged him to press for a large peacekeeping force with the power to intervene with force of arms if necessary.

#### ■ Humanitarian concerns[4]

Chief among Dallaire's humanitarian concerns was the decades-old ethnic violence between the Hutus and the Tutsis. Not only was that violence in danger of erupting at any point, it had also created hundreds of thousands of refugees, mainly from the minority Tutsis who had over the years fled to neighbouring countries.

As Dallaire was to discover, much of the ethnic disagreements were rooted in an extended period of colonial dominance. The Belgians took over the territory following the defeat of Germany in the first World War. The new colonial administration and a powerful group of Roman Catholic missionaries (called the White Fathers) were obsessed with notions of race and, based on little evidence, began the process of classifying the Hutus and Tutsis as distinct "races" of people. In effect, they reduced a number of highly complex issues of heredity, class, and social obligation to racial differences. The Tutsis were deemed to be "sub-Aryan" and of Christian ancestry, while the Hutus were treated as lowly Bantus. These classifications were exacerbated by administrative changes, complete with the

9.0

Issuance of racial identification cards that ensured Tutsis were privileged over Hutus. Tutsis played important roles in the developing "native administration" and even in the priesthood.[5]

Following the Second World War, as people throughout the colonial world struggled for independence, Rwandan liberation forces were deeply divided along ethnic lines. The Union nationale rwandaise (UNAR) was formed and led by Tutsi monarchists determined to retain their political privileges in a post-colonial state. The Mouvement démocratique républicain (MDR), on the other hand, was formed by a self-proclaimed Hutu leader, Gregorie Kayibanda, with the aim of fostering social revolution, first against Tutsi rule and then the colonial administration. The ensuring struggles resulted in pogroms against the Tutsis, with over 300,000 fleeing to Uganda and Burundi. Arguably, the MDR's focus on the Tutsis coincided with Belgian interests in prolonging colonial rule: certainly they did not intervene to prevent the widespread violence against the Tutsis. In 1962, however, Belgium finally granted independence to Rwanda and Kayibanda became the country's president.

Several times over the next few years, Tutsi refugees attempted to invade Rwanda. This led to further repression of those Tutsis still living in the country. In 1973, Juvénal Habyarimana staged a coup. Kayibanda was removed, the national assembly was closed down, and the MDR was banned. Habyarimana ruled as a dictator for the next two decades. In 1981, he formed his only political party, the Mouvement républicain nationale pour la démocratie et le dévelopement (MRND), whose hand-picked delegates presided over a restored, but sham, national assembly.

Meanwhile, in the late 1980s, Tutsi refugees organized themselves into a guerilla army called the Rwandese Patriotic Front (RPF). In 1990 they invaded Rwanda and, by 1991, were in control of two northern provinces until their advance was blocked by French troops who were deployed to defend Habyarimana. The French also put pressure on Habyarimana to establish multi-party elections. In 1992 he formed a new multi-party government and began peace talks with the RPF, which led to the Arusha Peace Agreement.

The problem of how to deal with the massive repatriation of potentially hundreds of thousands of people while avoiding a renewal of violence crossed Dallaire's mind as he paid attention to his other concerns.

## 9.0

### ■ Political concerns

Political problems confronted Dallaire as soon as he set foot on Rwandan soil. As he delved into the background to the Peace Agreement, it was hard to know how committed each side was. He was quickly reassured by his meeting with the Rwandan foreign minister, Anastase Gasana, a member of the MDR,

who was very much in support of the Arusha accords. Yet the reaction from the Rwandan Ambassador to the United Nations, Jean-Damascène Bizimana, was disquieting. Bizimana seemed less than thrilled by the Peace Agreement. Dallaire was also concerned that the Rwandan government had made no attempt to arrange a meeting between him and the president. As Dallaire pondered this, he felt it was an ominous sign. However, he had cause for optimism once more as he met with the leadership of the RPF, who strongly supported the Peace Agreement. Optimism turned to disquiet as the RPF leaders raised concerns about the fact that some of the country's 600,000 displaced people had begun to return to their homes in the designated demilitarized zone. When Dallaire suggested that this was to be expected and that the United Nations should attempt to make the area safe for their return, he was met with resistance. The RPF leaders expressed the concern that the situation could compromise the RPF's security, but Dallaire began to wonder that day whether it may have also had something to do with the resettlement ambitions of displaced Tutsis currently living in Uganda. Finally, when Dallaire met with Juvénal Habyarimana he was worried that the president had yet to publicly embrace the UN mission; nonetheless, it appeared at face value that he was committed to begin the peace process.

Dallaire could see that the various humanitarian problems were going to be difficult to deal with in the face of both entrenched and emerging political ambitions. These political factors were surely containable, but they would make the problem that much harder—especially given the administrative problems the country faced as it prepared for a new, multi-party, multi-ethnic state.

### ■ Administrative concerns

Given the background to the war almost two decades of dictatorial rule and the immense problems facing the country, Dallaire was concerned about the lack of a supportive administrative system. He needed to create a sense of structure to deal with a number of factors, including the repatriation of refugees, the reintegration of people into the life of the country, the establishment of a new interim government, a planned demobilization of troops, and an associated distribution of pensions and retraining for the demobilized soldiers. He also needed an administrative structure to help with the establishment of a democratic parliamentary system, complete with a new police force and armed services. Much of the latter depended on the will of Juvénal Habyarimana, a former dictator, who still retained control of the national army and much of the police forces (the Gendarmerie).

On this front Dallaire hoped to gain some administrative assistance from the United Nations, but he would have to rely on a military presence to contain any potential social breakdown that could result from the restructuring of the government and armed forces. To that end, he decided that if the UN determined to send a mission he would situate it south of the demilitarized zone, in the sector controlled by the existing Rwandan Government Forces (RGF).

### ■ Military concerns

For Dallaire, the military situation was highly problematic. In addition to the RGF and the military wing of the RPF—the Rwandese Patriotic Army (RPA)—any UN peacekeeping force would have to contend with the 6,000-strong Gendarmerie, the 1,500-strong Presidential Guard, and various militia groups estimated to consist of between 15,000 and 30,000 members.

When Dallaire first visited the leaders of the RPF and the RPA, he did what he could to assess their military strength. From what he could see, the army was well led, well trained, and highly motivated. Although he had some concerns about the military threat posed by the RPF's combat-proven and battle-ready army, he had a different order of concern about the undisciplined character of the RGF. Unlike the RPF, the RGF leadership was far from committed to the peace process and some openly spoke of their hatred of the RPF. Dallaire was troubled not only by the lack of discipline among the RGF, but also by a double standard in the treatment of their soldiers. He found that the main army consisted of poorly trained and ill-equipped soldiers who lacked discipline and whose morale was low. Dallaire worried that these troops could pose a threat to law and order as the country moved to implement the terms of the Peace Agreement.

The elite units of the RGF posed a threat of a different kind, particularly the Presidential Guard that Major Brent Beardsley observed, which consisted of highly trained but aggressive and arrogant officers and men. Dallaire knew that it would be difficult to handle this unit (and others like it) in a handover of power that would lead to many of them losing their elite status through either reintegration back into civilian life of being rolled into the new integrated army. Then there were the various militia, including:

- The Interahamwe—a militant youth wing of the MRND who dressed in fatigues and carried machetes
- The Impuzamugambi—the militant youth wing of the Coalition pour la Défense de la République (CDR)
- A violently anti-Tutsi splinter group of the MRND that refused to sign the Arusha Peace Agreement

As he weighed his various concerns, Dallaire was torn between recommending a classic "chapter-six" *peacekeeping* operation, whereby the United Nations would send a small peacekeeping force to monitor and oversee the peace process, or a "chapter-seven" peace *enforcement* mission, whereby the United Nations would send a coalition of armed military forces to invade the country and impose peace on the warring groups. He had ruled out recommending diplomatic pressure alone to contain the problem.

### Dallaire makes his decision

Dallaire knew that a chapter-seven recommendation would not be acceptable to UN headquarters. It was rarely used. It was first used in Korea in the early 1950s, and then in the Gulf War in 1991. More recently it had been used in Somalia in 1992, but the death of several US and Pakistani soldiers had made UN member states more cautious to take future action of this kind.

Although Dallaire believed that a classic peacekeeping (chapter-six) mission could be successful, he had two major concerns:

1. It had to be implemented almost immediately
2. UN troops should be authorized to use whatever force was necessary, including deadly force, to prevent crimes against humanity

It was this modified chapter-six recommendation that Dallaire sent on to the United Nations. In it he set out four options for troop deployment.

- Option 1 was based on estimates from previous UN assessments and called for 8,000 UN troops
- Option 2 called for 5,500 troops and was based on Dallaire's best estimate of what he would "Ideally" need to manage the situation
- Option 3, which Dallaire dubbed a "reasonable viable option," called for 2,500 troops but it would involve considerable risks
- Option 4 called for 500–1,000 troops and was based on estimates by the United States, France, and Russia.

Feeling this last option could not work, Dallaire only included it to deal with the concerns of interested foreign governments and to lay out the dangers involved in such a course of action.

### The UN responds

The United Nations, established in 1945, is one of the world's best-known and largest organizations, with 191 member states and an annual budget in excess of $2.5 billion. Peacekeeping operations at the United Nations come under the jurisdiction of the Department of Peacekeeping Operations (DPKO), which in 1993 (until 1996) was run by the Under-Secretary-General for Peacekeeping Operations, Kofi Annan. Annan was assisted by Iqbal Riza (Assistant Secretary-General), and Maurice Baril (head of the military division).

When Roméo Dallaire first visited the UN building in New York he was surprised to find that, in contrast to the grandeur of the general assembly chambers, the offices of the DPKO were by far the drabbest and most

**9.0**

cramped offices. This was in keeping with its relatively low political status at the United Nations. It was clearly, or so it seemed to Dallaire, well below the Department of Political Affairs (DPA), which on many occasions interfered in the work of peacekeeping missions without consulting the DPKO's political staff.

He was made aware of the political manoeuvring at the United Nations when it was strongly suggested that, to gain Security Council approval, he needed to recommend a mission to Rwanda that was small and inexpensive. This weighed strongly on his mind as he balanced his options at the end of his technical mission on September 5, and it was why, despite his own preference for a larger force, he spent some time developing an option that only called for 2,500 troops.

Despite the urgency of the situation and Dallaire's concern to move quickly, he was forcefully reminded that it could take at least three months or more for an agreement to deploy any troops. Dallaire was asked to prepare a report with a recommendation for the immediate deployment of a small force. Thus, before the process was put in motion, Dallaire's choices were already limited to options 3 or 4.

Dallaire's report was then passed on to the DPKO leadership before being sent forward as a formal report to the UN Secretary-General, Boutros Boutros-Ghali. Once it reached this stage the report would then be passed on to the Security Council. If successful, the recommendation would then go to a vote to be ratified. As expected, the process began very slowly and gave every impression of being set to take considerable time to reach resolution. Only the dramatic intervention of the leadership of the RPF, who flew to New York to lobby the United Nations, broke the impasse and sped up the process. On October 5, the Security Council approved the United Nations Assistance Mission for Rwanda (UNAMIR) mandate and agreed to deploy, in phases, a total of 2,600 troops. Roméo Dallaire was duly appointed force commander.

## Dallaire returns to Rwanda

Anxious to get under way, Dallaire returned to Rwanda on October 22 and began the process of monitoring the fragile peace. Over the next 12 weeks, he would encounter a number of challenges—both on the ground and with UN bureaucracy. It would take every ounce of Dallaire's leadership skills to deal with the overwhelming problems that were facing him. His efforts to patrol the demilitarized zone (an area 120 km long and 20 km wide) were severely hampered by a number of problems, including a severe lack of resources, political in-fighting between departments, and a lack of cooperation on the part of the political head of the mission, Jacques-Roger Booh-Booh, the Special Representative of the UN Secretary-General. The presence of the UN's Belgian

peacekeeping troops was also problematic because these soldiers were negatively associated with the previous colonial rule. As Dallaire struggled with these bureaucratic issues, he was faced with growing tension and a series of unsolved killings. In addition, the country's main radio station, RTLM, stirred up racial hatred against the Tutsis and orchestrated a campaign against the presence of Belgian peacekeeping troops.

## Problem areas and bureaucratic responses

Dallaire's problems multiplied as soon as he returned to Rwanda. The day he left New York there was a *coup d'état* in neighbouring Burundi that threatened the fragile peace in Rwanda and eventually saw some 300,000 refugees flooding into the country. When Dallaire appealed to the United Nations for extra troops to deal with the situation, he was turned down because he had not included the request in his original report in September.

The resource issues included:

- An initial lack of blue berets and other UN regalia that took weeks to arrive
- An acute shortage of food and lodgings for his troops
- A mishmash of unserviced vehicles
- Poorly armed, officer-heavy troops
- A general lack of equipment, including pens and paper

A request for the latter was turned down for budgetary reasons. Part of the problem with the food shortage was that, when a country donated troops to a peacekeeping mission, they are, under UN rules, supposed to bring enough rations to be self-sufficient for two months. Bangladesh, which supplied a large contingent of troops to Rwanda, didn't follow this rule and it was left to Dallaire to cope with the problem. He dealt with the issue by sharing supplies, including those for himself and his fellow officers. In the face of shortages among his men, Dallaire was shocked to find that the head of the mission (Booh-Booh) expected him to commandeer a large house, fancy car, and a range of perks. Dallaire decided to live as modestly as possible. He returned his Mercedes staff car and rented a small house that he shared with two other officers and a driver. He was determined to send a firm signal to his troops and the people of Rwanda that he was there on humanitarian grounds and would not jeopardize the mission by being seen to live high above everyone else.

With most countries reluctant to supply troops, it was left to Bangladesh, Tunisia, and Belgium to supply them. The Bangladeshi troops were grossly under-armed and led by an over-abundance of officers. The Belgians, on the other hand, were well armed, but as former colonizers they were a problem for the mission and Dallaire would have to do what he could do dampen tensions against their presence. This was not helped by the fact that RTLM was stirring up local feeling against the Belgian troops or that the Belgian

9.0

troops themselves acted aggressively to the local population and used racist language to describe how they had previously dealt with Africans in Somalia. Dallaire attempted to deal with the radio station by appealing to the United States to Jam the transmissions; the US refused.

Washington, still reeling from a humiliating retreat in Somalia, could see nothing to be gained from another intervention in Africa. With estimates of $8,500 per flight-hour, the exercise was also seen as too costly. President Clinton would later apologize for U.S. inaction, saying that they just didn't know the extent of the killings. Thwarted by the U.S. government, Dallaire could nonetheless deal directly with the Belgian troops, telling them that he would not tolerate "racist statements, colonialist attitudes, unnecessary aggression, or other abuses of power."[6] However, Dallaire was unable to overcome ingrained racist attitudes that were embedded in the official operating rules of the Belgian army. Told that they had to sleep in tents to be close to the airport they were sent to protect, the Belgians refused, citing a regulation that stated that Belgian soldiers should live in buildings and not under canvas because it was important that they "maintain a correct presence in front of the Africans."[7] As a result Dallaire agreed to allow the Belgian troops to be spread out across the city in various buildings. Little did he know that it was a decision that would come back to haunt him.

## Making UNAMIR's presence known

With few resources, Dallaire faced a monumental problem of ensuring that UNAMIR's presence was known throughout Rwanda. He decided to deal with the problem by arranging for a flag-raising ceremony. Dallaire had always been interested in what he called "the showcase occasions put on to influence and impress people and bring home the symbolism of events."[8] Dallaire felt that holding a flag-raising ceremony in the demilitarization zone would not only signal the UN's presence, but also serve to stress the urgency of the peace process. To that end, he chose a mountaintop that had been the site of fierce struggle but was subsequently rendered neutral territory. At the symbolic ceremony, the troops of the Organization of African Unity (OAU) handed over control of the zone to Dallaire and his UNAMIR troops.

## Big problems and petty politics

When Dallaire first returned to Rwanda, he was effectively in charge of both the political and military operation until someone could be found to serve as head of the mission. On November 22, exactly one month after Dallaire's return, Jacques-Roger Booh-Booh arrived in Rwanda to take over the political aspects of the mission and to act as its overall head. Dallaire's hopes that this would signal the beginning of greater political pressures to deal with the many problems at hand were soon dashed by Booh-Booh's work ethic and political approach. In the face of a massive human tragedy, Booh-Booh and his staff adopted diplomatic office hours, working from nine in the morning to five at night, with a long lunch break. There were also tensions over differential treatment of civilian office staff and the military, with the local chief administration officer, Per Q. Hallqvist, assigning more resources to the civilians on the basis that soldiers are only there for the short term and thus should make do, while the office staff were there for the long haul and should be taken care of. Dallaire's attempts to have Hallqvist overruled were rejected by the DPKO, who argued that Hallqvist was acting within his UN authority.

A week before Booh-Booh arrived in Rwanda, there had been a series of killings within the demilitarized zone. Dallaire's investigations had not been able to find the perpetrators, but in the process he uncovered weapons caches. The knowledge of these caches gave Dallaire several sleepless nights as he deliberated what he should do about them. Finally he recommended to Booh-Booh that he be allowed to search and seize the weapons caches. A horrified Booh-Booh refused the request, saying that the action was likely to damage the peace process as the UN forces would be seen as taking action only against the government side (who were the likely owners of the caches). Dallaire accepted the decision but very reluctantly. It was another decision that was to haunt him later.

At the end of December, Dallaire and Beardsley drafted a required three-month report to the DPKO. Although optimistic in what had and could be achieved, the report stressed an urgent need for logistical support and the deployment of phase two troops ahead of schedule. It was then given to Booh-Booh to include in his overall report, but, as Dallaire was only to find out much later, his report was watered down to reassure the Security Council that slow but steady progress was being made. As a result, Dallaire did not get the extra assistance required.

## A warning letter

Perhaps the first signs of an impending genocide came on December 3 when Dallaire received a letter from a group of senior RGF and Gendarmerie officers who warned that elements close to the president were out to undermine the peace process by massacring Tutsis. Not sure how to react to the letter, Dallaire established his own unofficial two-person intelligence unit to investigate the claims. It was through these investigations that the weapons caches came to light.

In the New Year, on January 10, a top-level military trainer with the MRND approached the UNAMIR and asked for a secret meeting, stating that he had important information on the intentions of Hutu extremists in the MRND party. He informed

9.0

Lue Marchal, one of Dallaire's deputies, that the MRND had established a number of highly efficient death squads—organized through the Interahawe—to murder massive numbers of Tutsis. Part of the plan was also to murder ten Belgian soldiers because the extremist Hutu leaders believed that Belgium would have no stomach for taking further casualties and would withdraw their troops from Rwanda. This was to prove prophetic.

Dallaire did not take time to think about his next step this time. He made the decision to mount a search-and-seize operation within 36 hours, and he took the unprecedented step of going over Booh-Booh's head by making his request directly to DPKO (see Appendix). Dallaire slept that night excited that UNAMIR would finally take the Initiative by showing the warring parties that the United Nations was prepared to enforce the peace process where necessary.

The next day Dallaire was unprepared for the reply from UN headquarters. He was told that not only was he not to use deterrent operations such as he proposed, but that he was to strictly remain within the limits of a chapter-six mandate. Furthermore, he was required to hand over the information from the informant to President Habyarimana. Worst still, Dallaire gained the distinct impression that DPKO now saw him as a loose cannon rather than a determined force commander.

## Pressure mounts to end the mission

Tensions mounted over the first three months of 1994, and the establishment of an interim government—one of the key aspects of the peace process—had not progressed. Yet when Dallaire flew to New York on March 29 to press for increased assistance, he was surprised to find that the UN was thinking of withdrawing from Rwanda. In particular, the United States was strongly pressing the Security Council to end the UNAMIR mission and the Rwandan representative who, as of January 1, 1994 had a seat on the 15-member Security Council, was supporting them. Only the urging of the French and the Belgians, fearful that they would have to deal with the situation alone, ensured that the mission would continue for at least 60 more days.

On April 6 the Security Council passed Resolution 909, which extended the UNAMIR mandate for six weeks, after which it would likely be withdrawn. Remarkably, to Dallaire's total surprise, the mission's budget was also cut. But that day of April 6 was to be overshadowed by a more immediate and critical incident.

### April 6: the Peace Agreement explodes and the genocide is unleashed

At the beginning of April there had been some hope that the peace process would move forward, with President Habyarimana flying off to Dares Salaam to discuss the process. On the evening of April 6, the plane carrying Habyarimana and members of his armed forces was shot down over Kigali and all were killed, Hutu extremists used this as the signal to launch genocide against Tutsis and politically moderate Hutus.

The entire administrative mechanism governing Rwanda was used to deliver a meticulously planned extermination of Tutsis, and all Hutus were implored and equipped to do their share. The presence of UN peacekeepers was used as a rallying point for the genocide as evidence of continued Western interference, and the peacekeepers became a convenient target upon which blame for the death of the president could be laid. In the first 24 hours, ten Belgian peacekeepers had been killed.

### The UN retreat

The death of peacekeepers so early into this conflict was an ominous sign for members of the UN Security Council, who were still scarred by the recent loss of life in Somalia in what was supposed to be a simple humanitarian mission. In particular, Somalia marked a dramatic turning point in the US administration's perspective toward peacekeeping operations as they watched television images of dead American soldiers being dragged through the streets of Mogadishu.

From this disaster emerged Presidential Decision Directive No. 25 (PDD-25), in which President Clinton outlined limitations on future U.S. involvement with the UN unless strict conditions were met. Primary among these was that future participation in peace operations would be limited to those cases that directly advanced US interests. Belgium, as had been predicted by Hutu extremist earlier on, was insistent on an immediate withdrawal of its forces from Rwanda, but did not want to be seen as acting independently. It found an ally in the United States, who moved for a withdrawal of all peacekeepers.[9]

On April 21, a meeting of the Security Council was convened and Resolution 912 was passed, which reduced the number of UN troops to a token force of 270 peacekeepers. In an unintended ironic turn of phrase. US Secretary of State Madeleine Albright described the reduced force as enough "to show the will of the international community."[10]

Dallaire, who had been surprised many times by the inefficiencies, caution, and politics of the UN, was not prepared for the withdrawal of most of his troops in the face of rampant killings. He had "expected the ex-colonial white countries to stick it out even if they took casualties."[11] Later he would summarize the situation thus:

*Ultimately, led by the United States, France, and the United Kingdom, [the UN Security Council] aided and abetted genocide in Rwanda. No amount of its cash and aid will ever wash its hands of Rwandan blood.[12]*

**9.0**

# A question of genocide

One of the things that allowed the Security Council to withdraw most of its troops was the characterization of the bloodshed as civil war or, worse, "tribal war." The US Ambassador to Rwanda, for example, waited almost a month into the genocide before declaring a "state of disaster," but then minimized the problem by characterizing it as "tribal killings."[13] Eventually, under some pressure to respond to the scale of the killings, the U.S. State Department spoke of "acts of genocide." When asked how many "acts of genocide" it took to make "genocide," a spokesperson for the U.S. State Department responded: "That's just not a question that I'm in a position to answer."[14]

Dallaire made constant attempts to get the United Nations to characterize the killings as genocide, knowing that this would require it to act more decisively. Defined as "a criminal act, with the intention of destroying an ethnic, national, or religious group,"[15] the UN—under its 1948 Convention on the Prevention and Punishment of the Crime of Genocide—has an obligation to respond where genocide is acknowledged to be occurring. Article VIII of this treaty states:

*Any Contracting Party may call upon the competent organs of the United Nations to take such action under the Charter of the United Nations as they consider appropriate for the prevention and suppression of acts of genocide...*[16]

Not only does the word "genocide," first coined to describe Hitler's designs for the extermination of Jews, carry a legal obligation, it further has been imbued with moral judgement.

By defining events as "tribal killings," "civil war," or even "acts of genocide," the United Nations was able to defer taking more decisive action. As Dallaire and his remaining troops did what they could to protect people, the distinction between a civil war and genocide became critical in the events in Rwanda in 1994. Had the attacks on Tutsis been labelled as genocide, it would have triggered the machinery of the United Nations to take firm and decisive action to prevent it. However, the United Nations was slow to act and has since been criticized for the time it took it to actually label the events in Rwanda as genocide, waiting until June 28, 1994 to make the initial declaration and until July for a panel of experts within the United Nations to confirm it was indeed genocide. The United Nations was finally satisfied that the events that were going on in Rwanda met the criteria established under the 1948 Convention, by which time 800,000 people had already been murdered. As some commentators have noted:

*For an event that was so widely covered by the media, the genocide in Rwanda largely remains misunderstood by the international community.*[17]

As international awareness of the genocide grew, the member states of the United Nations could no longer simply ignore the situation in Rwanda. UN Resolution 919, authorized well into the genocide, sought to establish an expanded UNAMIR II humanitarian mission to help protect the population. The chair of the Security Council, however, admitted that the expansion was a fiction, as the resolution had been gutted by the United States which was intent on successfully brokering a ceasefire before peacekeeping troops were committed. Even then, the continued characterization of the conflict in Rwanda as a civil was between two feuding parties, and not genocide, contributed to the weakness of the Security Council. Moreover, the fact that the United States worked actively and effectively against an effective UNAMIR was one of the most significant failures, far exceeding the failings of the United Nations itself.

## The aftermath: globalization, leadership, organizational failure, and post-colonial values

The tragic events in Rwanda in 1994 could easily be seen as something well beyond the reach of organizational analysis, well beyond the apparently mundane analysis of organizational processes and structures. Yet the genocide itself was well organized, relying on structured militia, government, and police forces. The fact that genocide was able to progress and at such a rapid pace was also due to a failure of organization, in particular the United Nations, which is one of the largest institutions in the world. Thus, the ingredients of this case are very much about organizational analysis and deal with key issues such as leadership, ethics, organizational structure and culture, and globalization.

General Roméo Dallaire has since blamed himself and his lack of leadership skills for failing to convince the United Nations and its DPKO of the severity of the situation, but he has harsh words for the United Nations itself. He contends that the UN's process of peacekeeping is deeply flawed, arguing that:

*Even if he had received the political and humanitarian training the job demanded, the UN's rules would have robbed him of the ability to use his military skills.*[18]

The troops under his operational command:

*...were ultimately under the command of their nations, so...if a national capital feels that a [rescue] mission is unwarranted, or too risk, or something, the soldiers can turn around and say, "No, I can't do it."*[19]

He recommends that the UN should undergo a renaissance that is:

*...not limited to the Secretariate. Its administration, and bureaucrats, but must encompass the member nations,*

9.0

*who need to rethink their roles and recommit to a renewal of purpose. Otherwise the hope that we will ever truly enter an age of humanity will die as the UN continues to decline into irrelevance.*[20]

Dallaire saves his harshest words for key member states of the United Nations. He claims that, while countries argued over the characterization of the killings, "they knew how many people were dying,"[21] adding that no matter what word was used the action was racist. Commenting on the difference between the enormous efforts that the United Nations put into Yugoslavia compare with Rwanda, Dallaire felt that:

*Africans don't count; Yugoslavians do. More people were killed, injured, internally displaced, and refugeed in 100 days in Rwanda than in the whole eight to nine years of the Yugoslavia campaign.*[22]

Yet, while peacekeeping troops remain in the former Yugoslavia, they are "off the radar" in Rwanda.[23] And, finally, Dallaire asks:

*Why didn't the world react to scenes where women were held as shields so nobody could shoot back while the militia shot into the crowd? Where ... boys were drugged up and turned into child soldiers, slaughtering families? ... Where girls and women were systematically raped before they were killed? Babies ripped out of their stomachs? ... Why didn't the world come?*[24]

His answer:

*Because there was no self-interest ... No oil. They didn't come because some humans are [considered] less human than others.*[25]

## Glossary[26]

**Kofi Annan:** As the Under-Secretary-General for Peacekeeping Operations, oversaw the UN's Department of Peacekeeping Operations from 1993 to 1996.

**Arusha Peace Agreement:** Signed in Arusha, Tanzania, it agreed to end the civil war between the Rwandan Government Forces (RGF) and the Rwandese Patriotic Army (RPA).

**Maurice Baril:** Head of the military division of the DPKO during the Rwanda genocide.

**Major Brent Beardsley:** Roméo Dallaire's military assistant.

**Jean-Damascène Bizimana:** The Rwandan Ambassador to the UN at the time of the peace accord. Later, the Rwandan representative on the UN Security Council.

**Jacques-Roger Booh-Booh:** In charge of the UNAMIR mission from November 1993 to May 1994.

**Boutros Boutros-Ghali:** Secretary-General of the UN from 1992 to 1997.

**Chapter-seven:** Refers to Chapter 7 of the United Nations Charter, which lays out a course of peacekeeping activities.

**Chapter-six:** Refers to Chapter 6 of the United Nations Charter, which lays out a course of peacekeeping activities.

**CDR (Coalition pour la défense de la république):** A violently anti-Tutsi splinter group of the MRND that refused to sign the Arusha Peace Agreement.

**Lieutenant-General Roméo Dallaire:** Commander of the United Nations peace mission UNAMIR.

**DPA:** United Nations Department of Political Affairs.

**DPKO:** United Nations Department of Peacekeeping Operations.

**Anastase Gasana:** A leading member of the MRND who served as the Rwandan foreign minister at the time of the peace accord.

**Gendarmerie:** A para-military police force of the Rwandan government.

**Major General Juvénal Habyarimana:** The President of Rwanda and head of the ruling MRND party; the main signatory to the agreement for the RGF.

**Per O. Hallqvist:** The Chief Administration Officer in Rwanda until February 1994.

**Impuzamugambl:** The militant youth wing of the CDR.

**Inteahamwe:** The militant youth wing of the MRND.

**MDR (Mouvement démocratique républicain):** The main opposition party to the MRND and which was a part of the Rwandan coalition government that signed the peace agreement.

**MRND (Mouvement républicain pour la démocratie et le développement):** Led the peace talks on behalf of the Rwandan government.

**OAU:** The Organization of African Unity.

**Presidential Guard:** Habyarimana's personal guard.

**Iqbal Riza:** Assistant Secretary-General of peacekeeping at the DPKO during the Rwanda genocide.

**RTLM (Radio Télévision Libre des Mille Collines):** The main radio station that stirred up hatred against the Tutsis.

**RGF (Rwandan Government Forces):** The armed forces of Rwanda.

**RPA (Rwandese Patriotic Army):** The military wing of the RPF.

**RPF (Rwandese Patriotic Front):** Led the talks on behalf of the Tutsi-dominated rebel forces.

**UN (United Nations):** One of the main international witnesses to the peace agreement and agreed to monitor the peace process.

**UNAMIR (United Nations Assistance Mission for Rwanda):** Established by UN Security Council Resolution 872, October 5, 1993, as a response for assistance in the implementation of the Arusha Peace Agreement.

## Appendix: Timeline

### ■ 1992

**3 December.** UN Resolution 794 authorizes a chapter-seven mission in Somalia, which allowed an invasion force to use "all means necessary" to create a secure environment for the delivery of humanitarian aid: 37,000 troops from 20 countries are committed to the mission.

**9.0**

**9 December.** UN troops led by US forces come ashore, without opposition, on the shores of Mogadishu.

### 1993
**4 August.** Arusha Peace Agreement signed.
**19 August.** Dallaire and his UN team arrive in Rwanda to undertake an assessment.
**5 September.** Dallaire takes his recommendation to the UN offices in New York.
**10 September.** Deadline for the establishment of a transitional government.
**3 October.** Eighteen US soldiers killed and 84 wounded in an ambush in Mogadishu as part of the UN chapter-seven mission in Somalia.
**5 October.** The UN Security Council approves the UNAMIR mandate and appoints Dallaire as force commander.
**22 October.** Dallaire returns to Rwanda.
**26 October.** Belgian army reconnaissance group arrives in Rwanda.
**18 November.** A series of killings occur in the demilitarized zone.
**19 November.** Seventy-five members of the Belgian contingent arrive in Rwanda.
**22 November.** Jacques-Roger Booh-Booh arrives to take over as head of the UN mission.
**3 December.** A group of senior RGF and Gendarmerie officers warn of impending massacre of Tutsis.
**4 December.** Last of the Belgians arrive, including Colonel Lue Marchal.
**15 December.** Bangladeshi contingent arrives in Rwanda. French paratroop battalion leaves Rwanda.

### 1994
**10 January.** Informant warns of death squads and plans to assassinate ten Belgian soldiers.
**11 January.** Dallaire sends coded message to DPKO requesting support for search-and-seizure action.
**12 January.** DPKO refuses Dallaire's request.
**9 February.** Contingent of Ghanaian troops arrive in Rwanda.
**6 April.** Security Council passes Resolution 909 to extend the UNAMIR mandate by six weeks. Juvénal Habyarimana is killed when his plane is shot down.

## References
Allen, T.J. "The General and the Genocide" (www.arnnestyusa.org/amnestynow/general_and_genocide.html, January 31, 2006).
Berry, J.A., and C.P. Berry (1999) *Genocide in Rwanda: A Collective Memory* (Washington, DC: Howard University Press).
Dallaire, R. (2003) *Shake Hands with the Devil* (Toronto: Vintage Canada).
Destexhe, A. (1995) *Rwanda and Genocide in the Twentieth Century* (New York: New York University Press).
Melvern, L. (2000). *A People Betrayed: The Role of the West in Rwanda's Genocide* (New York: Zeb Books).
Mthembu-Salter, G. (2002) "Rwanda," selfdetermine.irc-online.org/conflicts/rwanda_body.html, accessed January 31, 2005.
Power, S. (2002) *A Problem from Hell: America and the Age of Genocide* (New York: Basic Books).

## Discussion Questions
1. Who was responsible for the genocide in Rwanda?
2. Discuss the moral obligation of external governments and international organizations to become involved in the prevention of genocide, and the arguments for and against an earlier intervention in Rwanda.
3. Identify the major stakeholders of UNAMIR's goals and activities. Discuss the stakeholders' varying and conflicting interests and how the lack of interest influenced the course of events leading to the genocide.
4. Describe the main features of the organizational design of UNAMIR in Rwanda. Be sure to consider the issues of the division of labour, standardization, hierarchy, degree of centralization and formalization, the form of departmentalization, and whether the mission has a mechanistic or organic structure, as well as UNAMIR's relationship to the United Nations.
5. Roméo Dallaire was very committed and motivated as the force commander of UNAMIR and adamantly fought to keep the peacekeeping mission going in Rwanda, despite its failure to prevent genocide. Assess Dallaire's leadership capabilities using concepts such as power, contingency theory, motivation, leadership traits, and ability to manage change.
6. Compare and contrast a mainstream organizational approach (e.g., contingency theory) with post-colonial theory in explaining the inaction by the United Nations to stop the genocide.
7. What can be learned from the Rwandan genocide that can help stop such a tragedy from happening again?

### Notes
1. The text of the agreement can be downloaded from www.incore.ulst.ac.uk/services/cds/agreements/pdf/rwan1.pdf.
2. Quoted in Allen 2006.
3. Power 2002: 334,
4. Much of this section is based on Mthembu-Salter 2002.
5. Until the post–Second World War era, only Tutsis were allowed to become priests.
6. Dallaire 2003: 113.
7. Dallaire 2003: 121.
8. Dallaire 2003: 103.
9. Melvern 2000: 163.
10. Quoted in Allen 2005.
11. Quoted in Power 2002: 364.
12. Dallaire 2003: 323.
13. Allen 2006.
14. Quoted in Power 2002:364.
15. Destexhe 1995: 5.

9.0

16. Convention on the Prevention and Punishment of the Crime of Genocide, www.unhchr.ch/html/menu3/b/p_genoci.htm.
17. Berry and Berry 1999: 4.
18. Allen 2006.
19. Ibid.
20. Dallaire 2003: 520.
21. Allen 2006.
22. Quated in Allen 2006.
23. Allen 2006.
24. Ibid.
25. Ibid.
26. Many of these definitions and descriptions are based on the glossary in Dallaire 2003: 523, 44.

9.0

## Integrative Case 10.0

### The International Career Opportunity: From Dream to Nightmare in Eight Weeks*[1]

### Introduction

It was a dream come true for Matt Sosnowski. In October 2003 Matt had been chosen as a candidate for the management training program at Elietl[2]—a giant German food discounter with plans to expand into the Canadian market. As a management trainee, Matt was offered a salary and benefits package worth almost $100,000 Cdn. During the training period all of Matt's living expenses would be covered including accommodation, meals, an Audi A6 (including weekly car washes, gas, and repairs), and a return flight to Canada every six months. Matt was told that after a two-year intensive training period he would return to Canada to assume an executive position in Elietl's planned Canadian operations. It was the opportunity of a lifetime.

By the end of January 2004, the dream management training program was becoming a nightmarish test of endurance and wills. Matt found Elietl extremely autocratic. From his perspective, the company used a demoralizing approach to people management. He had seen even the most minor of mistakes severely and publicly punished. Grueling 90- to 100-hour work weeks were the norm. The most difficult issue for Matt to cope with, however, was the company's promise to secure a visa for his wife so that she could join him for the duration of the training period. The visa never materialized. Demoralized, exhausted, and frustrated, Matt was faced with the decision—to stay or to resign?

### Matt Sosnowski

Pursuing a career in international business was Matt's passion. Matt grew up in Poland and spent almost two years in Germany before coming to Canada at age 11. Matt completed three years of the BBA program at Wilfrid Laurier University (Waterloo, Ontario). He then worked for two months in Germany before completing his bachelor's degree at the University of Alicante in Spain. In December 2000, only a few months after graduation, Matt landed a market research/sales job with a German company that allowed him to travel around the world. Already fluent in Polish, German, Spanish, and English, Matt learned

French, Portuguese, and Italian. At 24 years of age Matt was on top of the world. Every month he was on a different continent gaining priceless international experience. Not to mention the fact he was back in Europe with 40 days of paid vacations and two flights home to Canada a year. While studying at Laurier, Matt met and fell in love with Larisa, a dentist who had come to Canada from Colombia to study English for a month. He was looking for somebody to help him practice his Spanish and she was looking for someone to help her with her English. Not long after they met, Larisa returned to Colombia and Matt was getting ready for his final year in Spain. They did not see each other for 16 months, but kept in touch. Over the next three years Matt and Larisa would see each other twice a year, summer vacation and Christmas holidays, and each time they traveled—through Europe, Colombia, or North America.

Matt spent 2 1/2 years working in Germany. His plans to have Larisa work in Germany did not work out. Matt resigned his job in Germany in order to get married in Colombia and bring his bride to Canada to start a new life together. Quitting that job was a difficult decision, but Matt was convinced that he made the right choice. Leaving Germany was even more difficult. He was leaving a job he loved, and leaving Europe meant that he was giving up the opportunity to work in a multilingual environment.

In May 2003 Matt and Larisa came to Canada. Starting over in Canada was not an easy task. Matt believed that his experience in international business and language skills would land him at least a middle-management-level job. After three months of searching, Matt was still unemployed. He was stuck in a trap between being overqualified and underqualified, and the only jobs he was getting were in the fields of door-to-door sales, insurance sales, and telemarketing. Despite having over three years of international business experience, Matt was forced to dramatically lower his salary expectations. In August 2003, Matt finally secured a position with a company he liked. It paid $36,000, less than a half of what he was making three years ago when he first graduated. Doing phone interviews was not his favourite activity, but it gave him the opportunity to use his foreign language skills. Meanwhile, Matt kept his eyes open for other opportunities.

### The Elietl Opportunity

It was late October when Matt found a posting on the Internet:

10.0

*A large German food discounter is looking to expand to Canada. We are looking for young and energetic individuals to be area managers. There will be a two-year training period in Germany, and upon completion the candidates will receive a substantial increase in salary.*

*We offer a very high salary and a car for the duration of your training. Upon the return to Canada, the candidates will also have a company vehicle.*

*Requirements:*

- *A completed university degree.*
- *Knowledge of German a must. French an asset.*
- *No previous experience necessary. We will train.*

Matt did a quick check on the Internet and learned that the grocery discounter Elietl Stiftung was Germany's second-largest retailer. Its stores are comparable in size to Shoppers Drug Mart. By 2003 there were approximately 5,600 stores employing 80,000 people throughout Europe with half of them in Germany. Elietl offers a limited range of good-quality products at a low price. Elietl was planning an aggressive expansion to Canada—400 stores in Quebec and Ontario in the first few years. The company was planning to offer a hybrid between large grocery stores (Zehrs, No Frills, Dominion) and convenience stores. Elietl sought Canadians who spoke German to fill key management positions.

Matt e-mailed his résumé to the company. Elietl scheduled an interview for early November.

## The Interview: November 10 Mississauga

Matt recalled his feelings as he drove to the interview.

Was I nervous? No way, I was too excited to be nervous. There were two things I was sure of: I had the qualifications they were looking for, and there was no one who wanted this job more than I did. My international experience and my knowledge of foreign languages, things that seemed of little value to Canadian employers, were finally going to be recognized. The opportunity to live and work in Europe was very attractive.

Shortly after he arrived at Elietl's offices in Mississauga, just west of Toronto, Matt was greeted by two tall men in their 40s.

"Herr Sosnowski, Guten Tag. Ich bin Herr Backer." (*Mr. Sosnowski. Good Day. My name is Mr. Backer.*)

The entire interview was conducted in German. Precise, professional, and straight to the point—just the way I recall the German approach to business. They only asked me three questions: "Why did I want to work for Elietl? What was my previous work experience? How soon could I start?"

The entire interview lasted 25 minutes. I asked them specifics about the company and the training program. I didn't ask about the weekly hourly commitment, I didn't think it was an appropriate question for an initial interview. Besides, Germany has very strict laws that prohibit employment of over 50 hours per week.

It was a two-year management training program. In year one, I would be a store employee (six weeks); a store manager (2 months); involved in general training in the areas of purchasing, sales, and marketing (two months); substituting store manager (2 months); and finally, area manager (five months). In year two, I would be involved in training at the Headquarters in Heilbronn. This portion of the program was unique to the Canadian trainees since I would be one of Elietl's Canadian pioneers.

Four days after the interview there was a contract in my email inbox. After carefully studying the contract, I had no doubt this was the job of a lifetime. A week and a half later I was back in the same office in Mississauga to discuss employment details.

Herr Gopp, the vice-president of Elietl Canada welcomed me with a firm handshake. He had a stack of papers ready for me to sign.

"In Germany you will be given an Audi A6. All expenses for the car including gas, repairs, car washes are paid by the company. In Germany we will provide you with a hotel where you can stay for the duration of your work. If you want to move to an apartment you may, and the company will pay for it. We will give you an additional $60/day (tax free) to spend on food or whatever else you need to buy. Any other expenses, including phone (for business purposes), medical expenses etc. you will pay, and send us a receipt and we will reimburse you. Two times a year a company will pay for a return trip to Canada. Any questions?"

"Herr Gopp," I started. "I am married and would like my wife to come with me for the duration of my contract. Do you foresee any difficulties?"

"Herr Sosnowski, that's your life, you can do whatever you wish. She can come, but Elietl will not cover any of her costs."

"That's understandable. The problem though, is that she is a landed immigrant from Colombia. I've already found out how to apply for her visa, but I know it can take some time. I know from experience that if Elietl applies for visas for my wife and I at the same time it will be a much easier and faster process. I will of course cover all of her costs."

"Don't worry about it. We have advisors in Germany and they will take care of it."

"Ok, thank you, so when am I flying out, so that I can make a reservation for her?"

"You will be flying out on November 28 at 16:00. Here is your flight schedule. There will be a car waiting for you at the airport."

"But that's in 12 days! I haven't resigned my job yet."

10.0

Of course I wasn't going to quit my job until I was 100 percent sure I was going. And besides, from experience I know that it can take a company a few months to get a work visa for a potential employee. That's why I was surprised with such a quick turnaround. I didn't understand the rush, but I did not question it.

"Herr Sosnowski, you said you could start in two weeks. We have a training program already for you in place and we need you there starting December 1. Here is the airline ticket. If you can't make it, we'll find somebody else who can."

"I understand Herr Gopp." "I will be on that plane. Please do your best with your advisors so that my wife can join me soon."

"Don't worry. There are people from many countries that come for the training in Germany. Our people have dealt with much more complicated issues. This is their full-time job."

I left the meeting with mixed feelings, I liked my current employer but I was very happy about going to Germany. I still didn't know where exactly in Germany I was going, but with a fast car and autobahns without speed limits, I couldn't be any further than six hours from my beloved Dusseldorf. I was going to be back in Europe, again be able to use all my language skills and this time I will be with Larisa. And above all, this was a beginning of an amazing career. This is the break I was looking for. The fact that the total package was worth close to $100,000/year was a bonus.

## Departure for Germany: Friday, November 28, 2003

"Was mochten Sie zum Trinken? (*What would you like to drink?*)

"Coke with red wine" (This was also known as Calimocho—a popular drink in southern Spain). To my left sat Anas. We met earlier this morning in Mississauga, and he too was going to Germany for the training. Anas was going to work in Stuttgart, and I to Warden, a small town between Saarbrucken and Trier. I was happy with my location. Being close to the French border meant going to France whenever I wanted and practicing French. We both thought it was odd that they were in such a rush to send us to Germany. And at the same time they waited until the day of the flight to tell us where we were going. We knew that this program involved more Canadians, but any further details were secret. We agreed this was not a typical behaviour for German companies, but we were too excited to worry.

## The Elietl Experience: Week 1

### ■ Monday, December 1—Heilbronn

In the morning I drove to Elietl's head office. The building was impressive. The parking lot was full of beautiful new cars, almost all of them Audis. When I entered the building I noticed that everyone was impeccably dressed in expensive suits and polished shoes. "This is where I will make a career," I said to myself. I was ready to give 100 percent, no matter the cost. Larisa and I agreed that the following two years were an investment in our future. Ms. Langnbruner, my boss's assistant took my passport and my contract and told me to come back the next day. It was 8:03 in the morning and I had a whole day to myself.

### ■ Tuesday, December 2—Heilbronn

It was 8:00 a.m. and I was ready to meet my boss. Instead, his assistant Ms. Langnbruner greeted me. She told me that my work visa has not been issued yet, and that I needed to come back the following day. They were in such a rush to get me over to Germany and they don't even have a work visa for me? Why were they in such a rush? Ms. Langnbruner told me I would need to move to a different hotel; my hotel was fully booked for that evening. Upon returning to the hotel (10 minutes later) there was a message on my phone from Ms. Langnbruner to call her back and tell her if I already found another hotel. "What's the rush? It's not like I won't find another hotel by myself." I stepped out for a few minutes and when I returned there were three more messages from Ms. Langnbruner and the phone was ringing—it was Ms. Langnbruner. This anecdote illustrates the military-style environment where "sofort" (right away) was the only answer an employee was allowed to give.

### ■ Wednesday, December 3—Heilbronn

8:00 a.m. When I arrived at work, Ms. Langnbruner showed me into my boss's office. I smiled and was just started to introduce myself when I was interrupted in mid-sentence.

"Herr Sosnowski, you have to show more initiative. It is expected of you, just like the rest of the employees here at Elietl. When you are told to do something like for example find a hotel, you should do that immediately."

Well, that was a little different from a standard introduction I was used to.

"We have some difficulties getting you the visa, but don't worry, we have a representative at the government level, and he will get it done. Now, we can't waste any more time. Did you check out already?"

"Of course."

"Good, so get in your car and start driving. You are already one day late with your program!"

As I drove westwards I wondered what was going to happen next. I failed to make a good first impression, but I knew that through hard work I would make it up.

At 11:30 a.m. I arrived at Saarbrucken (Elietl's western headquarters). Just like the main headquarters, this office was the size of three Canadian Costco stores. I was introduced to Miss Schmidt who right away took me downstairs and gave me the blue and yellow work uniform along with safety boots.

10.0

"I'm so excited," I told her. "I always wanted to work in a store but never had the chance."

She looked at me in disbelief. "It's hard work. Monday until Saturday, early morning till evening." I thought she was joking. We drove to the store in the little town of Warden, my home for the next few months. After checking into the hotel, Miss Schmidt took me for a ride in her Audi. We went to a few stores and I was told that I was to test the cashier. I was to try and steal a chocolate bar by hiding it in the cart underneath a carton of juices. This was the standard test they conducted on the cashiers. I felt sorry for the women working at the cash register. I am sure most Canadian cashiers would have failed this test. How can you tell the customers to lift up the carton in their shopping cart? This seemed so rude. At Elietl, every cashier was supposed to do this. If not, they received a warning. A few warnings and they were gone. I was thankful the cashier passed the test.

Miss Schmidt explained how the store should look.

"It will be your responsibility Mr. Sosnowski that the store always looks great. There can be no dirt, all products must *always* be displayed in a nice and presentable fashion and the shelves always have to be full. This will be controlled, and if something doesn't look perfectly tidy, there will be trouble. The worst thing you can do is to take a lunch break when the store is not perfect. So what are you going to do?"

"Well, first get to know my co-workers and find out about the culture in the store. I need to find out how things are done first."

"No, you don't have time for that. You are in charge, and the things will be done the way you like them to be, regardless of the past."

"But isn't this authoritative approach demoralizing?"

She grinned. "If you want to be successful at Elietl, you had better forget that word. 'Morale' is not an Elietl word."

## End of Week 2

### ■ Thursday, December 11, Warden

Miss Schmidt wasn't joking when she said I would be working Monday to Saturday morning till evening. I had worked 85 hours in my first week and I was exhausted. None of the employees worked more than eight hours a day, or more than five days a week. There was clearly some mistake. I talked to the store manager Mrs. Schlieman and she did not have any information on my schedule. So I called Elietl Canada.

"Herr Gopp, this must be a mistake. I need a work schedule. I have worked 85 hours. I think they are trying to kill me."

"Herr Sosnowski, you were warned in the interview that it was going to be hard work."

"But if I work so much, I can't even go shopping, nor get any personal things done. The only day I have free is Sunday, and Sunday everything is closed."

"That's your problem, Mr. Sosnowski. You are being paid to work and not to go shopping nor do your personal things. If you can't get your shopping done, find someone else who can do it for you. You have food and a place to sleep. What else do you want?"

I was left speechless. I thought about quitting but quitting was not an option. Soon it became clear to me—it was all a test of my endurance, physical strength, initiative, commitment, and perseverance. They can't have me working like this forever. Nobody works like this—they would burn out. My only concern was that I still didn't have my work visa—a basic requirement for my wife to apply for a visa. I was confident though that the company would take care of it.

### Friday, December 12, Zweibrucken

I was invited to the Elietl Christmas party. Before the party, all area managers had a training session that was led by Mr. Mikorai and Ms. Milock—the regional sales coordinators. I was still working in a store but was invited to the meeting as I was considered a district sales coordinator in training. Most of the district sales coordinators were around my age, some of them even younger. The meeting was anything but friendly. It was not intended to promote a group discussion, but rather delegate what needed to be done and point out what wasn't done correctly. Only last names were used, and two-way communication and suggestions were not welcomed....

"But Mr. Mikorai, the way you wanted the coffee displayed in the aisle isn't appealing," suggested Mr. Muller, of the district sales coordinators

"Mr. Muller, when I tell you to nail a yogurt to the wall, you do it! Understand? It will be done as I say. Any other suggestions?"

"Yes, are we going to get computers in the stores? A computerized system would save us a lot of money."

"*No!* No computers."

This is Germany, a fast-paced technically sophisticated country. And here is Elietl—no computers, nothing. Just recently they installed a scanner at the checkout, and it works only for some articles. All of the bookkeeping is done with old paper (recycled so many times that it looks gray), and a black pen. Other colours are not acceptable. Each store has an old fax machine and phone, both of which break down frequently.

Over the last week I had worked like never before, and met some of the most unpleasant people. I missed my wife and the visa process was stalled. I was told my working visa was ready a week before coming to Germany. Three weeks had passed and the visa was not there yet. I was frustrated and close to burning out.

10.0

And then the strangest thing happened. I felt that I really liked what I was doing. There was something about the company and the people whom I admired. Whether it is the sense of power, strength, or dominance, I don't know, but one thing was clear—Elietl was an amazing organization.

Christmas and New Years came and went; I was in Germany and Larisa was in Canada. It was not a good holiday. The relationship with my wife was on a slide. I was confident that by the middle of December Larisa would have received her visa.[3] Under that assumption we gave up our apartment in Toronto and Larisa moved in with my parents in Barrie, Ontario (a small city approximately one hour north of Toronto). The relationship between my wife and my parents was strained and soon Larisa was desperate to return to Colombia. Our evening phone conversations were increasingly marked by conflict. After 16-hour workdays, I was simply too tired to listen to and be supportive of my wife.

## Week 6

### ■ January 5—Warden

I had been an Elietl employee for over one month. As time went on, my responsibilities increased, and now I was averaging 93 hours a week. In order to save money the stores were terribly understaffed. In a 16-hour workday, I rarely had more than a one-hour break. I was in fear that Miss Schmidt would come when I was on break. She said that in order to go for lunch the store needed to be perfect. With 50 customers in the store and three employees (including me), it was nearly impossible to keep the store in perfect condition. But for Elietl, I soon learned, customer service was not as important as saving money. Physically I was doing fine except for the fact that my lower back was killing me from lifting heavy items. I addressed my concerns of heavy lifting to one of my co-workers.

"You just need to get needles and you'll be fine. I get them all the time."

That's not the answer I wanted to hear. I was under constant pressure to work faster and faster, and each time Miss Schmidt or Ms. Milock came, they had something negative to say.

"You're too slow. Mr. Muller, when he was working here, he was on his knees unpacking boxes. He would sweat so much he needed to change his clothes twice a day. That's expected of you. If you are not sweating and falling on your face, you are not working hard enough. If at the end of the day you still have strength left to watch TV, you are not working hard enough. If you don't spend the whole Sunday sleeping, you are not working hard enough," commented one of my co-workers. And that was perfectly true and perfectly normal at Elietl. That night I called Anas. His situation wasn't any different. We both came to the conclusion that this is the Elietl world.

Until you worked there, you can't imagine that something like this exists.

At Elietl you always felt like a thief. I addressed this issue with Miss Schmidt, and she replied it was the only way to control so many stores. At Elietl there was on an average $300 worth of food thrown out a day. A farmer would come each morning and take the food. An employee taking anything would be considered as committing misconduct. One former employee took an old bun to feed the sea gulls and was fired on the spot. Any employee purchase had to be accompanied by a receipt. The receipt had to be signed by two different co-workers with a black pen (any other colour ink was not acceptable and could lead to reprimand) and the receipt had to be taped to the item with transparent tape. This wasn't a bad idea but the process became ridiculous. I purchased a cooking pan that I used at work every day for a month; I had to keep on regluing the receipt. If you bought more than one apple, to which apple do you attach the receipt? Failure to meet the rules on product receipts led to trouble.

As area manager I had the right to search the employees' pockets, any personal belongings, and their personal vehicles at any time without any justification. Checking lockers and employee vehicles was a routine exercise the area managers were expected to do. After a month of work, the company would leave me alone every evening to count the money. The store made on an average between 10,000–20,000 euros/day. Any money missing would come out of my pocket. I had the right, though, to fire any employees suspected of stealing money.

What morale and motivation are to other companies, fear and mistrust are to Elietl. The customers were treated similarly. The customers were expected to put everything from the basket on the belt. One time there was a man who bought eight bags of dog food (10 kg each), and placed only one bag on the belt. I had to ask him to place all of the bags on the belt to see if maybe he was hiding a 20-cent chocolate on the bottom basket. When I first started I felt really uncomfortable asking customers to remove every single item from their grocery cart, but after a month at Elietl shame wasn't an issue. If the customer is upset and never came back, too bad, I did my job according to the rules. So, what's the upside? Well, I did prevent the possibility of theft. I had no choice but to act in this way, because any of these customers could be an Elietl employee doing a test on me. If I failed the test, I would be in serious trouble.

## Week 7

### ■ January 12, 2004—Warden

With six weeks of work experience at Elietl, I was adapting. Now Ms. Schlieman would leave me alone with the employees and the store was my sole responsibility. My weekly work hours

**10.0**

reached 102 hours. But I was healthy and physically fit. I estimated that I walked or ran about 140 km each week thorough the store and lifted a few tons of product. I was overworked, but knew that soon Larisa and I were going to be together. The conversations in the evenings were on an upward turn again.

Although I considered myself physically fit, my brain was not responding. I was so overworked that even basic arithmetic was difficult. I had to count cans in a box: 6 across, 5 wide and 3 high + 4 extra. How many cans were there? It took me a minute and I still had it wrong. In the evenings I had to count the money, and that was the worst. To not make a mistake, I would do everything extra slowly and triple-check it. As a result, I was at the store until midnight; the next day at 5:45 a.m. I was back, unpacking vegetables.

The curious thing was that none of the district sales coordinators was married. I wasn't sure if it was because working at Elietl consumed all of their time and energy, or because their personality changed while working at the company. To be successful at Elietl, you had to be, pardon my language but there is no other way to describe it, a total selfish bastard, and treat others like crap. If you didn't have this personality, Elietl wasn't a place for you. I've worked and lived in Germany before, and let me tell you this has nothing to do with Germany. It is not the German culture, it is the Elietl culture.

### January 14—Warden

As soon as I got to the hotel (11:30 at night) the phone rang. It was my father. My wife and my mom were in a car accident. Larisa was driving. The car was demolished and my mom was in hospital. I was deeply conflicted about where I should be and what I should be doing.

## Week 8

### January 20—Heilbronn

Today I was in Heilbronn again. It was a meeting for all Canadians involved in this program. I was looking forward to sharing my experience with others. I didn't know how many Canadians were in Germany or their locations. When I got there, I didn't see anyone. We all had our interviews at different times so that we wouldn't meet each other. I entered the office and a warm smile greeted me. Mr. Leonard sat me down and talked to me like I was a human being. He asked me how I was, so I brought up the issue with my wife. He promised to look into it. He asked me if I have been overworked, and then said not to worry.

"They just want to see if you can work, that's all. In your second year of training you will be here at head office, then it becomes more normal—60 to 70 hours max."

I left Heilbronn convinced that this training marathon was just a test. Only a test! I knew it

was all going to be good. Larisa would soon be here. I trusted Mr. Leonard to get the things done. The next 10 months were going to be difficult, but after that I will collect dividends. I will work at the head office, I will be an executive, I will perfect my German and we will live in Europe. Ten more months to go! Despite sleeping only two hours (again), I was pumped, I was ready and loving it.

### January 21—Warden

I called Mrs. Morchett at the Trier City Hall to find out if the papers for my wife's visa were ready. Not yet. This night I called Larisa and we got into another fight. She wanted to go back home to Colombia, and I told her to stop acting selfish. She said she doesn't want to stay in my parents' house any longer. My response was: "That's your problem. You've got food, you've got a place to sleep. Smarten up, it is expected of you." She called me a bastard and slammed down the phone. This had never happened before. Then I realized that I had changed. I was becoming part of Elietl culture. I was becoming an "Elietl person." But I was too tired to think about it, and in three hours I had to be up.

### January 22—Warden

I called Mrs. Morchett seven times to finally get hold of her.

"Yes, your papers have arrived."

"Is everything okay? Can you send them to Canada?"

"No, I can't, Mr. Sosnowski. Your work permit doesn't permit you to invite your wife."

She started explaining the details, but I was too furious to understand. In addition, the area manager Mr. Zimmer came in and gave me a dirty look.

"Mr. Sosnowski, look at all these unpacked boxes. They needed to be unpacked at 12:00. It's now 11:45 and you haven't started."

I wanted to jump into the car and see Mrs. Morchett. There was nothing more important in this life than going there right now. I told the store manager I had to go, but she refused. She said they needed me to help with the boxes, but that I could go tomorrow. I was devastated. I didn't know what to do. In the morning I was motivated, but after this phone call, I felt flat. Shortly after the call, I cut my finger to the bone with a knife while cutting one of the boxes. I needed stitches. My coworkers looked at it and laughed:

"That's nothing. Get back to work."

I taped my finger and put a coke bottle cap on top of it to shield it from any type of pressure. For the rest of the day I was slow. Later in the afternoon the store manager told me that there were serious complaints from the head office that my personal problems are getting in the way of my work, and if this continued I would be fired.

This was followed by a phone call from Mr. Backer from Canada with the same message. I didn't want to

**10.0**

beat around the bush. I explained to him, it is not personal problems that were affecting my work, but rather Elietl's inability to get their things done. He was blunt in his comments: "Mr. Sosnowski, we don't feel it is a good idea that your wife comes over. She doesn't speak German and being in a foreign country will not be easy. With you working all the time, you won't have any time for her and she will get very lonely. And this will not have a good effect on your work."

"Whether my wife comes or not is my decision, and not Elietl's."

"Well, that's your opinion. It's not Elietl's responsibility to help your wife come over."

## ■ January 23—Warden

In the morning I drove to meet Mrs. Morchett. She explained to me that the work permit I have authorizes me to work, but not to sponsor my wife. I asked to see my file. She didn't want to show me, and hinted that she was given instructions not to show my file to me. I was furious.

"This is my file, my information and I want to see it. I don't care about the instructions you were given, I have a right to look at my personal records!"

She showed me the file. It weighed about 2 kg and had all of my information, much of it confidential in nature. They had all the information about me, including addresses of all of my previous employers and my home addresses. I had no idea they had all the information about me. She wanted to get me out of the office fast, but I wasn't going to leave until she answered all of my questions. At this point she was the only person I trusted. She saw my determination and my hopelessness and became cooperative. She explained that with the work visa that I had, my wife would never be able to come, and that all the work I have done until this point was useless.

"How hard would it have been for Elietl to make my contract in such way that she could come?"

"Not hard at all. All they needed to do was request it at the time your visa was issued in December."

I left the office devastated. There was no doubt in my mind Elietl did it purposely. The company didn't want my wife to come, and they had done everything that they could so she wouldn't. They pretended to be helpful and understanding, and tricked me to give up all I had in Canada. Elietl has a department that deals with getting visas for foreign workers, and they have their own people in the local governments. One phone call from Mr. Gopp from Canada to the local government and Larisa would be on the plane to Germany. But that's not what they wanted to do. Mr. Gopp said he would talk to the people in Germany to help with my wife's visa, and said that my visa was already done. In reality, my visa took over a month, and there was nothing done for my wife. Mr. Leonard's role was to be the "good cop" and delay the process. Mr. Muller in the city hall at Heilbronn knew that all the paperwork I was doing was totally useless, but he kept his mouth shut. And the regional sales coordinator at Saarbrucken was supposed to keep me so busy that I wouldn't have the time or the means to get anything done like find an apartment or visit the city hall. What were they thinking? That I would give up my marriage for Elietl? Some Elietl managers have gone down that path.

As I came out of the city hall I was welcomed by a warm and sunny day. I sat on a rock to think about what had happened. It was 11:00 a.m. They were expecting me back by 10:00 a.m., and I was going to be in trouble. I was devastated; not angry, but sad. I saw a young couple with two children walking through the park. I felt tears in my eyes. That's what I wanted. That was why I was here, so that I would have a future where I could walk through the park with my wife and children. Why don't I have the right to do this? Why can't I have a normal life?

Everyone told me to quit, that I wasn't going to make it, that I was going to be in the 80 percent that don't make it. I was so determined to prove them wrong. Two months ago I left Canada as a winner. Larisa and I had plans to work extremely hard over the next two years, do whatever it took, and in two years buy a house and have children. Two years from now I was going to be an executive, and would make our dreams come true. If I quit now, I will shatter our dreams. If I go back to Canada, I will be a loser. I will have to move into my parents' house with my wife and sit in my parents' basement for the next few months and look for a job. What job am I going to land? Another telemarketing job for $13/hour? Or admit defeat and return to my old job? They would probably take me back, but I don't think I would be able to go back. What am I going to say to my family and friends? That I quit, that I didn't make it because the work was too tough? Mr. Leonard said that the second year will be normal working hours. It is all just a test, only a test. I can still win this. I can physically stand working the 90–100 hour weeks. As far as mentally, as soon as the problems with my wife are solved, my mind will be clear. We'll make it through the first year, and the second will be easier. Upon return to Canada, we will have enough money to buy a house in two years. We can still make this dream reality.

As I was driving back to Elietl, I shifted between anger and hope. I knew that upon my return to the store there would be a group of people to "greet me." What should I say? I've been lied to and feel used. Mr. Zimmer's black Audi was at the Elietl's parking lot in Warden. Surely he had a speech ready for me. A showdown would occur. What should I do? What would you do?

**10.0**

## Notes

1. The authors gratefully acknowledge that financial support for this research was received from a grant partly funded by WLU Operating funds and partly by the SSHRC Institutional Grant awarded to WLU.

2. The company and employee names have been disguised.

3. According to the German rules, I was not allowed to invite my wife until I had an apartment, not a hotel. The company prohibited me from getting an apartment, because they needed me to be mobile. Thanks to my good relationship with the store manager, Mrs. Schlieman, I was able to get her to sign a document stating that I was living in an apartment at her home. I could finally start the application for Larisa's visa. Since I was working Monday to Saturday morning to evening I had no chance to find an apartment. I talked to the regional sales coordinator, Ms. Milock, and asked for a free day to look for an apartment.

"Mr. Sosnowski, we don't think it is a good idea. You shouldn't look for an apartment, because at any time the company can change their mind and send you to another part of the country. You need to remain flexible and remain in the hotel."

"Ms. Milock, for me it doesn't matter, I can stay in the hotel. But if I don't get an apartment, my wife can't come."

"That's your problem, Mr. Sosnowski. But understand, we all have personal problems, and we don't let it influence our work. You are not any different."

## Assignment Questions

1. Describe the interview approach used by Elietl. How did Matt manage himself in the interview? How would you characterize Matt's effectiveness in the interview? What questions could he (should he) have asked?

2. How can people such as Matt "do their homework" far more effectively before they take on "expat" assignments around the world?

3. With respect to organizational culture, identify the underlying values and beliefs at Elietl. What are the effects of this culture on employee morale?

4. What form of organizational control does Elietl use? What are the strengths and limitations to this form of control?

5. Describe Matt's attempts to make sense of his situation. What motivates Matt to stay with Elietl? What courses of action are open to Matt? What do you recommend that he do?

10.0

# References

## Chapter 1

1. Much of the description of Air Canada comes from CBC News Indepth: Air Canada at http://www.cbc.ca/news/background/aircanada/index.html and much of the information on WestJet comes from http://www.flightnetwork.com/airlines/westjet (both accessed May 30, 2008) as well as from each airline's website.

2. "WestJet's CEO Named One of Canada's Most Respected (January 2005) at http://findarticles.com/p/articles/mi_hb5559/is_20050/ai_n23470045 (accessed July 5, 2008).

3. C. Sorenson, "WestJet Apologizes to Air Canada for Snooping," *Financial Post* (May 30, 2006) at http://www.canada.com/nationalpost/financialpost/story.html?id=6ca8461a-fb61-4bcc-be49-002f092c337f&k=61096 (accessed March 5, 2014).

4. Transcript: Robert Milton, Chairman & CEO, ACE Aviation (October 9, 2006) at edition.cnn.com/2006/BUSINESS/10/06/boardroom.milton (accessed March 5, 2014).

5. J. McNish, "Calin Rovinescu's Second Shot at 'Unfinished Business,'" *The Globe and Mail* (October 5, 2010) at http://www.ctv.ca/generic/generated/static/business/article759636.html (accessed February 3, 2011).

6. D. Olive, Air Canada Looks to Stay on Course, *Toronto Star* (January 18, 2014), B2.

7. Ibid, B1.

8. J. Castaldo and M. Luxe, "Canada's Three New Discount Airlines Get Ready to Rumble," *Canadian Business* (July 19, 2013) at http://www.canadianbusiness.com/companies-and-industries/air-wars/ (accessed March 5, 2014).

9. G. Pitts, "Ganong Finds Its Profits Are Not as Sweet," *The Globe and Mail* (March 23, 2007), B3.

10. G. Pitts, "Shaken by Chocolate Woes, Ganong Goes Outside for Help," *The Globe and Mail* (July 8, B3) at http://gold.globeinvestor.com/servlet/story/LAC.2008079.RGANONG9/APStory/?query=ganong+2008+pitts+shaken&pageRequested=all (accessed May 28, 2011).

11. Ann Harrington, "The Big Ideas," *Fortune* (November 22, 1999), 152–154; Robert Kanigel, *The One Best Way: Frederick Winslow Taylor and the Enigma of Efficiency* (New York: Viking, 1997); and Alan Farnham, "The Man Who Changed Work Forever," *Fortune* (July 21, 1997), 114. For a discussion of the impact of scientific management on American industry, government, and nonprofit organizations, also see Mauro F. Guillen, "Scientific Management's Lost Aesthetic: Architecture, Organization, and the Taylorized Beauty of the Mechanical," *Administrative Science Quarterly* 42 (1997), 682–715.

12. Amanda Bennett, *The Death of the Organization Man* (New York: William Morrow, 1990).

13. Harry G. Barkema, Joel A. C. Baum, and Elizabeth A. Mannix, "Management Challenges in a New Time," *Academy of Management Journal* 45, 5 (2002), 916–930; Eileen Davis, "What's on American Managers' Minds?" *Management Review* (April 1995), 14–20.

14. Barkema et al., "Management Challenges."

15. Samsung Electronics, "About Samsung Electronics" (2009) at http://www.samsung.com/us/aboutsamsung/sustainability/sustainabilityreports/download/2009/2009%20About%20Samsung%20Electronics.pdf (accessed February 26, 2014).

16. Keith H. Hammonds, "Smart, Determined, Ambitious, Cheap: The New Face of Global Competition," *Fast Company* (February 2003), 9–97; William J. Holstein, "Samsung's Golden Touch," *Fortune* (April 2002), 89–94; Pete Engardio, Aaron Bernstein, and Manjeet Kripalani, "Is Your Job Next?" *BusinessWeek* (February 3, 2003), 50–60.

17. Joann S. Lublin, "Travel Expenses Prompt Yale to Force Out Institute Chief," *The Wall Street Journal* (January 10, 2005), B1.

18. S. Puzic, "CEO of Scandal-plagued Ontario Hospital Fired, *The Ottawa Citizen* (March 4, 2011) at http://www.ottawacitizen.com/scandal+plagued+Ontario+hospital+fired/443896/story.html (accessed May 28, 2011).

19. Andy Serwer, "Inside the Rolling Stones Inc.," *Fortune* (September 30, 2002), 58–72; and William J. Holstein, "Innovation, Leadership, and Still No

Satisfaction," *The New York Times* (December 9, 2004), Section 3, 11.

20. Lucy Kellaway, "The Rolling Stones Flout Every Business Rule, and Win," *The Globe and Mail* (July 8, 2013) at http://www.theglobeandmail.com/report-on -business/careers/careers-leade.../the-rolling-stones -flout-every-business-rule-and-win/article13078812/ (accessed September 6, 2013).

21. David Wessel, "Venal Sins: Why the Bad Guys of the Boardroom Emerged en Masse," *The Wall Street Journal* (June 20, 2002), A1, A6.

22. G. Morgan, *Freedom, Ethical Values and Leadership (presentation to the Canadian Centre for Ethics and Corporate Policy* (Toronto: October 3, 2007).

23. Bernard Wysocki Jr., "Corporate Caveat: Dell or Be Delled," *The Wall Street Journal* (May 10, 1999), A1.

24. Andy Reinhardt, "From Gearhead to Grand High Pooh-Bah," *BusinessWeek* (August 28, 2000), 129–130.

25. G. Pascal Zachary, "Mighty Is the Mongrel" (June 2000) at http://www.fastcompany.com/magazine/36/mongrel .html (accessed March 5, 2014).

26. McKinsey & Company, "Diversity of Backgrounds" at http://www.mckinsey.com/careers/is_mckinsey_right_ for_me/diversity_of_backgrounds.aspx (accessed May 28, 2011).

27. Canadian Heritage, "Annual Report on the Operation of the Canadian Multiculturalism Act, 2005–2006" (2007) at http://www.multiculturalism.pch.gc.ca (accessed May 30, 2008).

28. "Capitalizing on Canada's Diversity Is Key to Nation's Future Prosperity," RBC Financial Group Special Reports at http://www.rbc.com/ newstoom/2005020diversity.html (accessed April 1, 2007).

29. Debra E. Meyerson and Joyce K. Fletcher, "A Modest Manifesto for Shattering the Glass Ceiling," *Harvard Business Review* (January–February 2000), 27–36; Annie Finnigan, "Different Strokes," *Working Woman* (April 200), 42–48; Joline Godfrey, "Been There, Doing That," *Inc.* (March 1996), 2–22; Paula Dwyer, Marsha Johnston, and Karen Lowry Miller, "Out of the Typing Pool, into Career Limbo," *BusinessWeek* (April 5, 1996), 92–94.

30. Howard Aldrich, *Organizations and Environments* (Englewood Cliffs, NJ: Prentice Hall, 1979), 3.

31. This section is based largely on Peter F. Drucker, *Managing the Non-Profit Organization: Principles and Practices* (New York: HarperBusiness, 1992); and Thomas Wolf, *Managing a Nonprofit Organization* (New York: Fireside/Simon & Schuster, 1990).

32. Christine W. Letts, William Ryan, and Allen Grossman, *High Performance Nonprofit Organizations* (New York: John Wiley & Sons, 1999), 30–35.

33. J. Foley, "Joining of Big Brothers & Big Sisters Orga- nizations Signals Trend Towards Alliances" (2001) at http://www.charityvillage.com/cv/archive/acov/acov0/ acov045.hmtl (accessed April 8, 2007).

34. Jack Quarter, Laurie Mook and Ann Armstrong, *Understanding the Social Economy: A Canadian Perspective* (Toronto: University of Toronto Press, 2009), 107.

35. Robert N. Stern and Stephen R. Barley, "Organizations and Social Systems: Organization Theory's Neglected Mandate," *Administrative Science Quarterly* 4 (996), 146–162.

36. Brent Schlender, "The New Soul of a Wealth Machine," *Fortune* (April 5, 2004), 102–110.

37. Schlender, "The New Soul of a Wealth Machine"; and Keith H. Hammonds, "Growth Search," *Fast Company* (April 2003), 75–80.

38. Steven Levy, "The Inside Story of the Moto X, The Phone that Reveals Why Google Bought Motorola," *Wired* (August 1, 2013) at http://www.wired.com/ gadgetlab/2013/08/inside-story-of-moto-x/ (accessed March 5, 2014).

39. James D. Thompson, *Organizations in Action* (New York: McGraw-Hill, 1967), 4–13.

40. Henry Mintzberg, *The Structuring of Organizations* (Englewood Cliffs, NJ: Prentice Hall, 1979), 215–297; and Henry Mintzberg, "Organization Design: Fashion or Fit?" *Harvard Business Review* 59 (January– February 1981), 103–116.

41. The following discussion was heavily influenced by Richard H. Hall, *Organizations: Structures, Processes, and Outcomes* (Englewood Cliffs, NJ: Prentice Hall, 99); D. S. Pugh, "The Measurement of Organization Structures: Does Context Determine Form?" *Organiz- ational Dynamics* (Spring 973), 9–34; and D. S. Pugh, D. J. Hickson, C. R. Hinings, and C. Turner, "Dimensions of Organization Structure," *Administrative Science Quarterly* 3 (968), 65–9.

42. Quote from http://www.ellisdon.com/ed/about (accessed April 8, 2007).

43. EllisDon, "EllisDon Ranked #2 Best Employer in Canada" at http://www.ellisdon.com/bg/news/-/asset _publisher/FB9x/content/id/29129 (accessed March 5, 2014).

44. Quote from http://www.ellisdon.com/ed/about (accessed April 8, 2007).

45. Quotes are from http://www.mocca.toronto.on.ca (accessed July 19, 2011) and personal communication.

46. *Information Systems Today*, 2nd Canadian Edition, Supplementary Online Cases, Pearson Education Canada, 2008, at http://wps.pearsoned.ca/wps/media/ objects/4065/4162990/ch07_supp_cases.pdf (accessed May 17, 2011).

47. M. Aspan and J. Saba, "Google Takes Wraps off Pay-by-Phone System," *Reuters* (May 26, 2011) at www.reuters.com/article/2011/05/26/us-google -idUSTRE74P5FJ20110526 (accessed March 5, 2014).

48. T. Donaldson and L. E. Preston, "The Stakeholder Theory of the Corporation: Concepts, Evidence, and Implications," *Academy of Management Review* 20 (1995), 65–91; Anne S. Tusi, "A Multiple-Constituency

Model of Effectiveness: An Empirical Examination at the Human Resource Subunit Level," *Administrative Science Quarterly* 35 (1990), 458–483; Charles Fombrun and Mark Shanley, "What's in a Name? Reputation Building and Corporate Strategy," *Academy of Management Journal* 33 (1990), 233–258; Terry Connolly, Edward J. Conlon, and Stuart Jay Deutsch, "Organizational Effectiveness: A Multiple-Constituency Approach," *Academy of Management Review* 5 (1980), 211–217.

49. Charles Fishman, "The Wal-Mart You Don't Know—Why Low Prices Have a High Cost," *Fast Company* (December 2003), 68–80.

50. Connolly, Conlon, and Deusch, "Organizational Effectiveness: A Multiple-Constituency Approach."

51. Fombrun and Shanley, "What's in a Name?"

52. Information from http://www.mackenziegasproject.com/theProject (accessed May 18, 2011); Article 13—CSR best practice cases studies—Mackenzie Valley Pipeline, www.article13.com/A13_ContentList.asp?strAction+ GetPublication&PNID=1162 and K. Hoggan Mackenzie Valley Gas Controversy May Put $5 Billion Project on Hold, *Aboriginal Times* (2003) at http://www.aboriginaltimes.com/economic-development/oil%20pipeline/view (accessed April 9, 2007).

53. Ibid.

54. Joint Review Panel Hearing Phase Concludes, *The MGP Exchange*, 14, 1, February 2008.

55. M. McDiamid, "Mackenzie Valley Pipeline Facing Possible Revival," CBC (October 25, 2013) at http://www.cbc.ca/news/politics/mackenzie-valley-pipeline-facing-possible-revival-1.2224291 (accessed January 15, 2014).

56. Johannes M. Pennings, "Structural Contingency Theory: A Reappraisal," *Research in Organizational Behavior* 14 (1992), 267–309.

57. This discussion is based in part on Toby J. Tetenbaum, "Shifting Paradigms: From Newton to Chaos," *Organizational Dynamics* (Spring 1998), 21–32.

58. William Bergquist, *The Postmodern Organization* (San Francisco: Jossey-Bass, 1993).

59. Based on Tetenbaum, "Shifting Paradigms: From Newton to Chaos," and Richard T. Pascale, "Surfing the Edge of Chaos," *Sloan Management Review* (Spring 1999), 83–94.

60. C. White, *Seismic Shifts—Leading in Times of Change* (Toronto: United Church Publishing House, 2006), 3.

61. Information from http://www.kairos.org and www.united-church.ca.

62. Organizational Chart of the United Church of Canada (January 2007) at http://www.united-church.ca.

63. Polly LaBarre, "This Organization Is Disorganization," *Fast Company* (June–July 996), 77–81.

64. "Conversations on Work and Well-Being—Response-Ability and Power to Please—Delta Hotels" at http://www.vifamily.ca.

65. David K. Hurst, *Crisis and Renewal: Meeting the Challenge of Organizational Change* (Boston, Mass.: Harvard Business School Press, 1995), 32–52.

66. Information from http://www.magna.com (accessed May 29, 2008).

67. Information from http://archives.cbc.ca/300c.asp??id=-69-377 and J. P. Sheppard and S. D. Chowdhury, "Riding the Wrong Wave: Organizational Failure as a Failed Turnaround," *Long Range Planning*, 38 (2005), 250.

68. Information from http://www.bostonpizza.com/?q=bostonpizza_aboutus_history (accessed May 30, 2008).

69. The In Practice draws heavily on Ann Armstrong, "Environmental Leadership in Education: Evergreen Canada" in Gallagher, D. R., ed., *Environmental Leadership: A Reference Handbook*, Vol 2 (Los Angeles, CA: Sage Publications).

70. Ushnish Sengupta, G. Cape, S. Irvine, P. Bertrand, and A. Armstrong. (2008). Evergreen Brick Works: Planning for Success in a Triple Bottom-Line Enterprise. In J. A. F. S. and C. Wankel (ed.), *Global Sustainability Initiatives: New Models and New Approaches* (2008), 15–32. Charlotte, NC: Information Age Publishing.

71. E. Mumford, The Story of Socio-technical Design: Reflections on its Successes, Failures and Potential. *Information Systems Journal*, 16 (2006) 317–342.

72. Robert House, Denise M. Rousseau, and Melissa Thomas-Hunt, "The Meso Paradigm: A Framework for the Integration of Micro and Macro Organizational Behavior," *Research in Organizational Behavior* 17 (1995), 71–114.

73. Culture is seen here as a contingency and/or a process variable. It is typically seen as a contingency.

74. Ali Mir, "The Hegemonic Discourse of Management Texts," *Journal of Management Education*, 27, 6 (December 2003), 734–738.

# Chapter 2

1. "Double, Double? Now You Can Look It Up" (July 5, 2004) at http://www.cbc.ca/arts/story/2004/06/30/doubledouble040630.html (accessed June 1, 2008).

2. "Tim Hortons Touches Down in Kandahar (June 2, 2006) at http://www.cbc.ca/world/story/2006/06/2/tim-hortons-kandahar.html (accessed May 18, 2011).

3. Francine Kupin, "Tim Hortons Looks to Grow with 700 more Canadian Stores and New Food Items" (March 6, 2012) at http://www.thestar.com/business/2012/03/06/tim_hortons_looks_to_grow_with_700_more_canadian_stores_and_new_food_items.html (accessed March 5, 2014).

4. "Canadian Donut War: Krispy Kreme vs. Tim Hortons" (July 13, 2002) News and Media Center, NACS Online.

5. Tim Hortons, "Tim Hortons Named One of World's Hottest Brands" (2011) at http://www.timhortons.com/us/en/about/3315.html (accessed June 1, 2011).

6. "Tim Hortons Raises C$783 Million in Initial Offering" (March 23, 2006) at http://quote.bloomberg.com/apps/

news?pid=10000103&sid=aVbau_WUTixk&refer=news_index (accessed May 18, 2011).

7. John Grey, "Staying Power: Strong Brands" *Canadian Business* (November 6–19, 2006) at http://www.canadianbusiness.com/managing/strategy/article.jsp?content=20061106_82398_82398 (accessed June 3, 2008).

8. J. Nelson," Companies We Love," *Canadian Business* (May 19, 2011) at http://www.canadianbusiness.com/article/26490-companies-we-love (accessed June 1, 2011).

9. Ipsos Reid, "Two New Brands Join Top 10 Most Influential Brands in Canada: Ipsos Reid" (January 28, 2014) at ahttps://www.ipsos-na.com/news-polls/pressrelease.aspx?id=6406 (accessed April 7, 2014).

10. Interbrand, "Interbrand Announces Canada's 2010 Best Brands by Value" (May 17, 2011) at http://www.interbrand.com/en/news-room/press-releases/2010-05-17.aspx (accessed June 1, 2011).

11. CNW Group, "Canada's Top Performing Brands Valued by Interbrand" at http://www.newswire.ca/en/releases/archive/July2006/24/c8737.html (accessed June 3, 2008).

12. "Timmies: An Iconic Canadian Brand" (2005) http://www.wendys-invest.com/fin/annual/2005/wen05ar_th.pdf (accessed June 3, 2008).

13. Amitai Etzioni, *Modern Organizations* (Englewood Cliffs, NJ: Prentice Hall, 1964), 6.

14. Francine Kupin, "Tim Hortons Looks to Grow with 700 more Canadian Stores and New Food Items" (March 6, 2012) at http://www.thestar.com/business/2012/03/06/tim_hortons_looks_to_grow_with_700_more_canadian_stores_and_new_food_items.html (accessed March 5, 2014).

15. Marina Strauss, "Can Tim Hortons Fight off McDonald's Attack?," *The Globe and Mail* (February 23, 2013) at http://www.theglobeandmail.com/globe-investor/can-tim-hortons-fight-off-mcdonalds-attack/article8993325/?page=all (accessed March 5, 2014).

16. Tim Hortons (2011) Tim Hortons Named One of World's Hottest Brands, accessed from www.timhortons.com/us/en/about/3315.html (accessed July 28, 2013).

17. John P. Kotter, "What Effective General Managers Really Do," *Harvard Business Review* (November–December 1982), 156–167; Henry Mintzberg, *The Nature of Managerial Work* (New York: Harper & Row, 1973).

18. Building on Strength: Improving Governance and Accountability in Canada's Voluntary Sector. Panel on Accountability and Governance in the Voluntary Sector. Final Report (February 1999) at http://www.voluntary-sector.ca/eng/publications/1999/building_strength.pdf (accessed June 3, 2008).

19. Charles C. Snow and Lawrence G. Hrebiniak, "Strategy, Distinctive Competence, and Organizational Performance," *Administrative Science Quarterly* 25 (1980), 317–335.

20. Amy Barrett, "Staying on Top," *BusinessWeek* (May 5, 2003), 60–68.

21. T. Ready, "Can CEOs Cure Cancer?" *Fast Company*, Issue 117 (July 2007), 35.

22. Johnson & Johnson, Diversity Awards and Recognition, at http://www.jnj.com/about-jnj/diversity/awards (accessed March 7, 2014).

23. Forest R. David and Fred R. David, "It's Time to Redraft Your Mission Statement," *Journal of Business Strategy* (January–February 2003), 11–14; John Pearce and Fred David, "Corporate Mission Statements: The Bottom Line," *Academy of Management Executive* 1, 2 (May 1987), 109–116; and Christopher Bart "The Relationship Between Mission Statements and Firm Performance: An Exploratory Study," *Journal of Management Studies* 35, 6 (1998), 823–853.

24. James C. Collins and Jerry I. Porras, "Building Your Company's Vision," in *On Strategy*, Harvard Business School Publishing Corporation, 2011, pp. 77–102.

25. Barbara Bartkus, Myron Glassman, and R. Bruce McAfee, "Mission Statements: Are They Smoke and Mirrors?" *Business Horizons* (November–December 2000), 23–28.

26. Mark C. Suchman, "Managing Legitimacy: Strategic and Institutional Approaches," *Academy of Management Review* 20, 3 (1995), 571–610.

27. Kurt Eichenwald, "Miscues, Missteps, and the Fall of Andersen," *The New York Times* (May 8, 2002), C1, C4; Ian Wilson, "The Agenda for Redefining Corporate Purpose: Five Key Executive Actions," *Strategy & Leadership* 32, no. 1 (2004), 21–26.

28. Bill George, "The Company's Mission is the Message," *Strategy & Business*, Issue 33 (Winter 2003), 13–14; Jim Collins and Jerry Porras, *Built to Last: Successful Habits of Visionary Companies* (New York: Harper-Business, 1994).

29. Charles Perrow, "The Analysis of Goals in Complex Organizations," *American Sociological Review* 26 (1961), 854–866.

30. Johannes U. Stoelwinder and Martin P. Charns, "The Task Field Model of Organization Analysis and Design," *Human Relations* 34 (1981), 743–762; Anthony Raia, *Managing by Objectives* (Glenview, IL: Scott, Foresman, 1974).

31. Swapalease, "Audi Pushes Fast Growth with New Models in 2011" at http://www.swapalease.com/news/Audi-pushes-fast-growth-with-new-models-in-2011-800507628.aspx (accessed March 7, 2014).

32. N. Averill, "Diversity Matters: Changing the Face of Public Boards, The Maytree Foundation" at www.maytree.com/PDF_Files/DiversityMatters.pdf (accessed March 7, 2014).

33. Service Measurement Framework Report, submitted to Treasury Board of Canada, Secretariat (March 1, 2005) at http://www.tbs-sct.gc.ca/si-as/initiative/2004/smfr-rcms/smfr-rcms00-eng.asp (accessed March 7, 2014).

34. Leslie Ferenc "United Way Toronto: 2012 Campaign Raises $116.1 million and Exceeds Goal" *Toronto Star* (January 31, 2013) at http://www.thestar.com/news/gta/2013/01/31/united_way_toronto_2012_campaign_raises_1161_million_and_exceeds_goal.html (accessed March 7, 2014).

35. Jeffrey N. Ross, "New Honda Fit Ousts Toyota Prius as Japan's Top Selling Car Last Month," *Autoblog* (November 11, 2013) at http://www.autoblog.com/2013/11/11/honda-fit-best-selling-car-in-japan (accessed April 7, 2014).

36. Joseph Pereira and Christopher J. Chipello, "Battle of the Block Makers," *The Wall Street Journal* (February 4, 2004), B1.

37. K. Kapoor, "Wellington West Named One of Canada's Best Managed Companies" (February 22, 2011) at http://www.newswire.ca/en/releases/archive/February2011/22/c3830.html?view=print (accessed March 5, 2014).

38. "50 Best Employers in Canada," *The Globe and Mail*, December 20, 2005, at http://www.theglobeandmail.com/servlet/story/RTGAM.20051220.rm50best1223/BNStory/specialROBmagazine (accessed May 18, 2011).

39. Michael Arndt, "3M: A Lab for Growth?" *BusinessWeek* (January 21, 2002), 50–51.

40. "The World's 50 Most Innovative Companies," *Fast Company*, at http://www.fastcompany.com/most-innovative-companies/2014 (accessed April 7, 2014).

41. Kim Cross, "Does Your Team Measure Up?" Business2.com (June 12, 2001), 22–28; J. Lynn Lunsford, "Lean Times: With Airbus on Its Tail, Boeing is Rethinking How It Builds Planes," *The Wall Street Journal* (September 5, 2001), A11.

42. P.T. Lee and N. Krause, "The Impact of a Worker Health Study on Working Conditions," *Journal of Public Health Policy*, 23, 3 (2002), 268–285.

43. Unite Here, "Our History" (2006) at http://www.unitehere.org/about/history.php (accessed May 18, 2011).

44. Andrea C. Poe, "Keeping Hotel Workers: It Takes More Than Money to Retain Lower-Paid Employees—Employment & Staffing Agenda" *HR Magazine* 48, 2 (February 2003), 91–93.

45. Ibid.

46. Alex Markels, "Dishing It Out in Style," *U.S. News and World Report*, 52–53 (April 15, 2007).

47. T. Wiedmann and M. Lenzen, Triple-Bottom Line Accounting of Social and Environmental Indicators–A New Life—Cycle Software Tool for UK Businesses, Third Annual International Sustainable Development Conference, November 15–16, 2006, Perth, Scotland.

48. The Honourable Dennis R. O'Connor, Report of the Walkerton Inquiry: The Events of May 2000 and Related Issues Ontario. Part One: A Summary. Ministry of the Attorney General, Queen's Printer for Ontario 2002.

49. James D. Thompson, *Organizations in Action* (New York: McGraw-Hill, 1967), 83–98.

50. Michael E. Porter, "What Is Strategy?" *Harvard Business Review* (November–December 1996), 61–78.

51. G. Keenan, "Magna to Make Move on Bigger Targets, *The Globe and Mail* (January 13, 2011), B3.

52. David Barry and Michael Elmes, Strategy Retold: Toward a Narrative View of Strategic Discourse, *Academy of Management Review*, 22, 2, 429–452 (1987).

53. Toby Harfield, Strategic Management and Michael Porter: a Postmodern Reading, *Electronic Journal of Radical Organisation Theory* 4, no. 1 (1998).

54. Michael E. Porter, *Competitive Strategy: Techniques for Analyzing Industries and Competitors* (New York: Free Press, 1980).

55. Zena Olijnyk, "Beat China on Quality: Cervélo Bets on Premium Design to Win," *Canadian Business* (November 7–20, 2005).

56. N. Williams, "Why It's (Still) Good to be WestJet," *Strategy Magazine* (November 2005) at http://www.strategymag.com/articles/magazine/20051101/westjet.html (accessed May 18, 2011).

57. Lauren Krugel, "WestJet CEO Apologizes for Tier-Service Confusion," *The Globe and Mail* (July 31, 2013), B14.

58. Bertrand Maroote, Héroux-Devtek Profit Hit by Cuts in Military Spending, *The Globe and Mail* (May 24, 2013) at http://www.theglobeandmail.com/report-on-business/restructured-heroux-devtek-posts-lower-profit/article12125062/ (accessed March 5, 2014).

59. Reuters, "Puma Q4 Sales Jump 16 [percent], Maintains 2010 Dividend" (February 15, 2011) at http://www.reuters.com/article/2011/02/15/puma-idUSFAB01592620110215 (accessed March 5, 2014).

60. Michael E. Porter, "Strategy and the Internet," *Harvard Business Review* (March 2001), 63–78; and John Magretta, "Why Business Models Matter," *Harvard Business Review* (May 2002), 86.

61. Millar, D. (1992) The Generic Strategy Trap, *Journal of Business Strategy*, 13, 1, 37–42; and C. Baden-Fullen and J. Stopford, *Rejuvenating the Mature Business* (Cambridge: HBS Press, 1992).

62. Raymond E. Miles and Charles C. Snow, *Organizational Strategy, Structure, and Process* (New York: McGraw-Hill, 1978).

63. Nicholas Casey, "New Nike Sneaker Targets Jocks, Greens, Wall Street," *The Wall Street Journal* (February 15, 2008), B1.

64. Norihiko Shirouzu, "Chinese Begin Volvo Overhaul," *The Wall Street Journal* (June 7, 2011), B1.

65. Frances Innis, "Bonnie Brooks Ends Her Five-year Reign as HBC President," *Toronto Life* (June 18, 2013) at http://www.torontolife.com/style/toronto-stores/2013/06/18/bonnie-brooks-hudsons-bay-promotion/ (accessed April 7, 2014).

66. Broverman, "Target Coming to Canada: What Can We Expect?" (January 27, 2011) at http://www.walletpop.ca/blog/2011/01/27/target-coming-to-canada-what-can-we-expect (accessed February 17, 2011).

67. "Miles and Snow: Enduring Insights for Managers: Academic Commentary by Sumantra Ghoshal," *Academy of Management Executive* 17, 4 (2003), 109–114.

68. Pallavi Gogoi and Michael Arndt, "Hamburger Hell," *BusinessWeek* (March 3, 2003), 104–108; and Michael Arndt, "McDonald's: Fries with That Salad?" *BusinessWeek* (July 5, 2004), 82–84.

69. B. Horovitz, "McDonald's Revamps Stores to Look More Upscale," *USA Today* (May 9, 2011) at http://www.usatoday.com/money/industries/food/2011-05-06-mcdonalds-revamp_n.htm (accessed June 1, 2011).

70. "On the Staying Power of Defenders, Analyzers, and Prospectors: Academic Commentary by Donald C. Hambrick," *Academy of Management Executive* 17, 4 (2003), 115–118.

71. Etzioni, *Modern Organizations*, 8.

72. Etzioni, *Modern Organizations*, 8; and Gary D. Sandefur, "Efficiency in Social Service Organizations," *Administration and Society* 14 (1983), 449–468.

73. Richard M. Steers, *Organizational Effectiveness: A Behavioral View* (Santa Monica, CA: Goodyear, 1977), 51.

74. Karl E. Weick and Richard L. Daft, "The Effectiveness of Interpretation Systems," in Kim S. Cameron and David A. Whetten, eds., *Organizational Effectiveness: A Comparison of Multiple Models* (New York: Academic Press, 1982).

75. David L. Blenkhorn and Brian Gaber, "The Use of 'Warm Fuzzies' to Assess Organizational Effectiveness," *Journal of General Management*, 21, 2 (Winter 1995), 40–51.

76. Steven Strasser, J. D. Eveland, Gaylord Cummins, O. Lynn Deniston, and John H. Romani, "Conceptualizing the Goal and Systems Models of Organizational Effectiveness—Implications for Comparative Evaluation Research," *Journal of Management Studies* 18 (1981), 321–340.

77. The discussion of the resource-based approach is based in part on Michael V. Russo and Paul A. Fouts, "A Resource-Based Perspective on Corporate Environmental Performance and Profitability," *Academy of Management Journal* 40, 3 (June 1997), 534–559; and Jay B. Barney, J. L. "Larry" Stempert, Loren T. Gustafson, and Yolanda Sarason, "Organizational Identity within the Strategic Management Conversation: Contributions and Assumptions," in *Identity in Organizations: Building Theory through Conversations*, David A. Whetten and Paul C. Godfrey, eds. (Thousand Oaks, CA: Sage Publications, 1998), 83–98.

78. Lucy Mccauley, "Unit of One: Measure What Matters," *Fast Company* (May 1999), 97.

79. Richard I. Priem, "Is the Resource-Based 'View' a Useful Perspective for Strategic Management Research?" *Academy of Management Review* 26, 1 (2001), 22–40.

80. Chris Argyris, *Integrating the Individual and the Organization* (New York: Wiley, 1964); Warren G. Bennis, *Changing Organizations* (New York: McGraw-Hill, 1966); Rensis Likert, *The Human Organization* (New York: McGraw-Hill, 1967); and Richard Beckhard, *Organization Development Strategies and Models* (Reading, Mass.: Addison-Wesley, 1969).

81. Cheri Ostroff and Neal Schmitt, "Configurations of Organizational Effectiveness and Efficiency," *Academy of Management Journal* 36 (1993), 1345–1361; Peter J. Frost, Larry F. Moore, Meryl Reise Louis, Craig C. Lundburg, and Joanne Martin, *Organizational Culture* (Beverly Hills, CA: Sage Publications, 1985).

82. J. Barton Cunningham, "Approaches to the Evaluation of Organizational Effectiveness," *Academy of Management Review* 2 (1977), 463–474; Beckhard, *Organization Development*.

83. "Living on the Edge at American Apparel" at http://www.businessweek.com/magazine/content/05_26/b3939108_mz017.htm?chan=search (accessed May 18, 2011).

84. M. Sanati "Last Stand at American Apparel," *The Globe and Mail* (October 28, 2010) (accessed October 31, 2010).

85. L. Chernikoff, "Good News for Dov Charney: American Apparel Stays Afloat With $15M Cash Injection" (April 22, 2011) at http://fashionista.com/2011/04/good-news-for-dov-charney-american-apparel-stays-afloat-with-15m-cash-injection (accessed March 11, 2014).

86. Robert Levering and Milton Moskowitz, "The 100 Best Companies to Work For," *Fortune* (January 24, 2005), 72–90.

87. James L. Price, "The Study of Organizational Effectiveness," *Sociological Quarterly* 13 (1972), 3–15.

88. "Ridership Growth Strategy" (March 2003) at www.toronto.ca/ttc/textonly/textonly%20-%20ridership%20growth%20strategy.htm (accessed June 3, 2008).

89. "City Council Builds a Cleaner, Greener and More Transit-friendly Toronto with an Approved Five-Year Capital Plan" (March 7, 2007) at http://wx.toronto.ca/inter/it/newsrel.nsf/9da959222128b9e885256618006646d3/340c0d4612969fe485257297007f7b4c?OpenDocument (accessed March 11, 2014).

90. CBC News.ca "TTC Faces Driver Dilemma as Ridership Rockets" (January 8, 2007) at http://www.cbc.ca/canada/toronto/story/2007/01/08/ttc-ridership.html (accessed May 18, 2011).

91. Richard H. Hall and John P. Clark, "An Ineffective Effectiveness Study and Some Suggestions for Future Research," *Sociological Quarterly* 21 (1980), 119–134; Price, "The Study of Organizational Effectiveness" and Perrow, "Analysis of Goals."

92. Diavik Diamond Mines, "Vision" at http://www.diavik.ca/vs.htm (accessed June 3, 2008).

93. GlobeAdvisor.com, "A Simple Loblaw Equation" (July 10, 2007) at https://secure.globeadvisor.com/servlet/ArticleNews/story/RTGAM/20070710/wrdecloet10 (accessed May 18, 2011).

94. Loblaw, "Loblaw Companies Limited Reports Second Quarter 2010 Results" (July 22, 2011) at www.loblaw.ca/English/Media-Centre/news-releases/news-releasedetails/default.aspx?PressReleaseId=9dab8b2d-43a8-4765-aaf9-4d406b9497f2 (accessed June 1, 2011).

95. Hollie Shaw, Loblaw's Business Strategy Needs Freshening Up," *Financial Post* (May 18, 2012) at http://business.financialpost.com/2012/05/18/loblaws-business-strategy-needs-some-freshening-up (accessed March 11, 2014).

96. Alexandra Posadz, "George Weston Will Look to Health and Wellness Space for Future Acquisitions," *Macleans* (July 30, 2013) at http://www2.macleans.ca/2013/07/30/george-weston-will-look-to-health-and-wellness-space-for-future-acquisitions/ (accessed March 11, 2014).

97. Eric J. Walton and Sarah Dawson, "Managers' Perceptions of Criteria of Organizational Effectiveness," *Journal of Management Studies* 38, 2 (2001), 173–199.

98. Beth Dickey, "NASA's Next Step," *Government Executive* (April 15, 2004), 341.

99. Robert E. Quinn and John Rohrbaugh, "A Spatial Model of Effectiveness Criteria: Toward a Competing Values Approach to Organizational Analysis," *Management Science* 29 (1983), 363–377.

100. Regina M. O'Neill and Robert E. Quinn, "Editor's Note: Applications of the Competing Values Framework," *Human Resource Management* 32 (Spring 1993), 1–7.

101. Robert E. Quinn and Kim Cameron, "Organizational Life Cycles and Shifting Criteria of Effectiveness: Some Preliminary Evidence," *Management Science* 29 (1983), 33–51.

102. Robert Kaplan and David Norton, "The Balanced Scorecard: Measures That Drive Performance," *Harvard Business Review* (January–February 1992), 71–79; "On Balance," a CFO Interview with Robert Kaplan and David Norton, *CFO* (February 2001), 73–78; Chee W. Chow, Kamal M. Haddad, and James E. Williamson, "Applying the Balanced Scorecard to Small Companies," *Management Accounting* 79, no. 2 (August 1997), 21–27; and Meena Chavan, "The Balanced Scorecard: A New Challenge," *Journal of Management Development* 28, no. 5 (2009), 393–406.

# Chapter 3

1. Desjardins Group, "2007 Social Responsibility and Cooperative Report" at http://www.desjardins.com/en/a_propos/publications/bilans_sociaux/responsabilite-sociale07.pdf (accessed April 9, 2014). Used with permission from the Desjardins Group.

2. Monique F. Leroux, "About Desjardins" at www.desjardins.com/en/a_propos/qui-nous-sommes/conseil-administration/monique_fleroux-direction.jsp (accessed May 18, 2011).

3. J. Nelson, "Desjardins Group to Buy State Farm Canada," *The Globe and Mail* (January 15, 2014) at http://www.theglobeandmail.com/report-on-business/desjardins-to-buy-state-farm-canada/article16342689 (accessed March 11, 2014).

4. Daniel J. Wakin, "Following a Shifting Flock: As Some Churches Falter and Others Grow, Catholic Church Plans Overhaul" (October 26, 2003) at http://query.nytimes.com/gst/fullpage.html?res=9c00e2dd1031f935a15753c1a9659c8b63&sec=&spon=&pagewanted=print (accessed March 11, 2014).

5. Editorial Board, "Pope Francis' Reforms," *The New York Times* (January 15, 2014) at http://www.nytimes.com/2014/01/16/opinion/pope-francis-reforms.html?_r=0 (accessed March 11, 2014).

6. John Child, *Organization* (New York: Harper & Row, 1984).

7. Stuart Ranson, Bob Hinings, and Royston Greenwood, "The Structuring of Organizational Structures," *Administrative Science Quarterly* 25 (1980), 1–17; and Hugh Willmott, "The Structuring of Organizational Structure: A Note,"

8. This section is based on Frank Ostroff, *The Horizontal Organization: What the Organization of the Future Looks Like and How It Delivers Value to Customers* (New York: Oxford University Press, 1999).

9. David Nadler and Michael Tushman, *Strategic Organization Design* (Glenview, IL: Scott Foresman, 1988).

10. William C. Ouchi, "The Implementation of a Decentralized Organization Design in Three Large Public School Districts: Edmonton, Seattle, and Houston" (unpublished manuscript, Anderson School of Management, University of California–Los Angeles, 2004).

11. "Country Managers: From Baron to Hotelier," *The Economist* (May 11, 2002), 55–56.

12. Based on Jay R. Galbraith, *Designing Complex Organizations* (Reading, Mass.: Addison-Wesley, 1973), and *Organization Design* (Reading, Mass.: Addison-Wesley, 1977), 81–127.

13. Rochelle Garner and Barbara Darrow, "Oracle Plots Course," *CRN* (January 24, 2005), 3; and Anthony Hilton, "Dangers behind Oracle's Dream," *Evening Standard* (February 11, 2005), 45.

14. Lee Iacocca with William Novak, *Iacocca: An Autobiography* (New York: Phantom Books, 1984), 152–153.

15. Based on Galbraith, *Designing Complex Organizations*.

16. "Mandate 2003: Be Agile and Efficient," *Microsoft Executive Circle* (Spring 2003), 46–48.

17. Jay Galbraith, Diane Downey, and Amy Kates, "How Networks Undergird the Lateral Capability of an Organization—Where the Work Gets Done," *Journal of Organizational Excellence* (Spring 2002), 67–78.

18. Amy Barrett, "Staying on Top," *BusinessWeek* (May 5, 2003), 60–68.

19. Task Management Guide "Task Force—Definition, Guidelines and Software" (2011) at www.taskmanagementguide.com/setting-tasks/task-force-

definition-guidelines-software.php (accessed March 11, 2014); Walter Kiechel III, "The Art of the Corporate TaskCAForce," *Fortune* (January 28, 1991), 104–105; and William J. Altier, "Task Forces: An Effective Management Tool," *Management Review* (February 1987), 52–57.

20. Neal E. Boudette, "Marriage Counseling: At DaimlerChrysler, a New Push to Make Its Units Work Together," *The Wall Street Journal* (March 12, 2003), A1, A15.

21. Daimler A.G. at http://topics.nytimes.com/top/news/business/companies/daimler_ag/index.html (accessed June 30, 2008).

22. Keith Naughton and Kathleen Kerwin, "At GM, Two Heads May Be Worse Than One," *BusinessWeek* (August 14, 1995), 46.

23. Paul R. Lawrence and Jay W. Lorsch, "New Managerial Job: The Integrator," *Harvard Business Review* (November–December 1967), 142–151.

24. Imagination, "Our Company" (2007) at http://www.imagination.com/our_company (accessed June 4, 2008).

25. C. Fishman, Total Teamwork—Imagination Ltd., *Fast Company* 33 (2000), 156.

26. Charles Fishman, "Total Teamwork: Imagination Ltd.," *Fast Company* (April 2000), 156–168.

27. Thomas L. Legare, "How Hewlett-Packard Used Virtual Cross-Functional Teams to Deliver Healthcare Industry Solutions," *Journal of Organizational Excellence* (Autumn 2001), 29–37.

28. "The Stalling of Motor City," *BusinessWeek* (November 1, 2004), 128.

29. "Ford Unveils a New Plug-in Hybrid" (December 3, 2007) at http://www.greenlivingonline.com/gettingaround/ford-unveils-a-new-plug-in-hybrid (accessed June 30, 2008).

30. S. Deveau, "Ford Takes Canada Sales Crown," *The Vancouver Sun* (January 5, 2011) at www.vancouversun.com/cars/Ford+takes+Canada+sales+crown/4057344/story.html (accessed May 18, 2011).

31. S. Duffy, "Hybrid Car Global Sales Set to Explode to 7.8 Million Units By 2020" at http://www.hybridcar.com (accessed April 15, 2007).

32. Chuck Salter, "Ford's Escape Route," *Fast Company* (October 2004), 106–110; "Ford Escape Hybrid Named Best Truck in Detroit," *The Jakarta Post* (January 27, 2005), 18; and Bernard Simon, "Ford Aims to Build on Escape Hybrid's Success," *National Post* (January 26, 2005), FP10.

33. Henry Mintzberg, *The Structuring of Organizations* (Englewood Cliffs, NJ: Prentice Hall, 1979).

34. Based on Robert Duncan, "What Is the Right Organization Structure?" *Organizational Dynamics* (Winter 1979), 59–80; and W. Alan Randolph and Gregory G. Dess, "The Congruence Perspective of Organization Design: A Conceptual Model and Multivariate Research Approach," *Academy of Management Review* 9 (1984), 114–127.

35. Rahul Jacob, "The Struggle to Create an Organization for the 21st Century," *Fortune* (April 3, 1995), 90–99.

36. Jack Quarter, Laurie Mook and Ann Armstrong (2009) *The Social Economy: A Canadian Perspective*, Toronto: UTP, 241–245.

37. "FAQS about MEC and Co-ops" at www.mec.ca/AST/ContentPrimary/AboutMEC/AboutOurCoOp/CoOpFaqs.jsp (accessed January 20, 2014).

38. "Internal Environment, Organizational Structure" at http://michelandmp.wordpress.com/internal-environment (accessed January 20, 2014).

39. Joseph Weber, "A Big Company That Works," *BusinessWeek* (May 4, 1992), 124–132; and Elyse Tanouye, "Johnson & Johnson Stays Fit by Shuffling Its Mix of Businesses," *The Wall Street Journal* (December 22, 1992), A1, A4.

40. Robert A. Guth, "Midlife Correction; Inside Microsoft, Financial Managers Winning New Clout," *The Wall Street Journal* (July 23, 2003), A1, A6; and Michael Moeller, with Steve Hamm and Timothy J. Mullaney, "Remaking Microsoft," *BusinessWeek* (May 17, 1999), 106–114.

41. Omar El Akkad, "At Microsoft, Many Become One," *The Globe and Mail* (July 12, 2013), B1.

42. Ibid., B5.

43. Based on Duncan, "What Is the Right Organization Structure?"

44. Weber, "A Big Company That Works."

45. Phred Dvorak and Merissa Marr, "Stung by iPod, Sony Addresses a Digital Lag," *The Wall Street Journal* (December 30, 2004), B1.

46. Maisie O'Flanagan and Lynn K. Taliento, "Nonprofits: Ensuring That Bigger Is Better," *McKinsey Quarterly* 2 (2004), 112ff.

47. "MSF Charter" at http://www.msf.ca/about/msf-charter (accessed June 30, 2008).

48. "What We Do" at http://www.msf.ca/about/what-we-do (accessed June 30, 2008).

49. "40 Degrees in the Sudanese Shade" (October 30) at http://www.msf.ca/blogs/mikew.php (accessed June 4, 2008).

50. Stanley M. Davis and Paul R. Lawrence, *Matrix* (Reading, Mass.: Addison-Wesley, 1977), 11–24.

51. Erik W. Larson and David H. Gobeli, "Matrix Management: Contradictions and Insight," *California Management Review* 29 (Summer 1987), 126–138

52. Davis and Lawrence, *Matrix*, 155–180.

53. Defence Research and Development Canada, "Delivering Science and Technology for Impact" at www.drdc-rddc.gc.ca/ststrategy/delivering1_e.asp (accessed June 4, 2008).

54. Robert C. Ford and W. Alan Randolph, "Cross-Functional Structures: A Review and Integration of Matrix Organizations and Project Management," *Journal of Management* 18 (June 1992), 267–294;

and Duncan, "What Is the Right Organization Structure?"

55. Lawton R. Burns, "Matrix Management in Hospitals: Testing Theories of Matrix Structure and Development," *Administrative Science Quarterly* 34 (1989), 349–368.

56. Carol Hymowitz, "Managers Suddenly Have to Answer to a Crowd of Bosses," *The Wall Street Journal* (August 12, 2003), B1; and Michael Goold and Andrew Campbell, "Making Matrix Structures Work: Creating Clarity on Unit Roles and Responsibilities," *European Management Journal* 21, 3 (June 2003), 351–363.

57. Christopher A. Bartlett and Sumantra Ghoshal, "Matrix Management: Not a Structure, a Frame of Mind," *Harvard Business Review* (July–August 1990), 138–145.

58. This case was inspired by John E. Fogerty, "Integrative Management at Standard Steel" (unpublished manuscript, Latrobe, Penn., 1980); Stanley Reed with Adam Aston, "Steel: The Mergers Aren't Over Yet," *BusinessWeek* (February 21, 2005), 6; Michael Amdt, "Melting Away Steel's Costs," *BusinessWeek* (November 8, 2004), 48; and "Steeling for a Fight," *The Economist* (June 4, 1994), 63.

59. Michael Hammer, "Process Management and the Future of Six Sigma," *Sloan Management Review* (Winter 2002), 26–32; and Michael Hammer and Steve Stanton, "How Process Enterprises Really Work," *Harvard Business Review* 77 (November–December 1999), 108–118.

60. Hammer, "Process Management and the Future of Six Sigma."

61. Based on Ostroff, *The Horizontal Organization*, and Richard L. Daft, *Organization Theory and Design*, 6th ed. (Cincinnati, Ohio: South-Western, 1998), 250–253.

62. Ann Armstrong, "Pay for Knowledge and Skill Systems: A Multilevel Exploratory Investigation" (1993) unpublished University of Toronto Ph.D. Dissertation, 201.

63. Ibid.

64. Melissa A. Schilling and H. Kevin Steensma, "The Use of Modular Organizational Forms: An Industry-Level Analysis," *Academy of Management Journal* 44, 6 (2001), 1149–1168; Jane C. Linder, "Transformational Outsourcing," *MIT Sloan Management Review* (Winter 2004), 52–58; and Denis Chamberland, "Is It Core or Strategic? Outsourcing as a Strategic Management Tool," *Ivey Business Journal* (July–August 2003), 1–5.

65. A. Kakabadse and N. Kakabadse, "Outsourcing: Current and Future Trends" (2005) *Thunderbird International Business Review*, 47(2) 183–204.

66. Denis Chamberland, "Is It Core or Strategic?"; Philip Siekman, "The Snap-Together Business Jet," *Fortune* (January 21, 2002), 104[A]–104[H]; Keith H. Hammonds, "Smart, Determined, Ambitious, Cheap: The New Face of Global Competition," *Fast Company* (February 2003), 91–97; Kathleen Kerwin, "GM: Modular Plants Won't Be a Snap," *BusinessWeek* (November 9, 1998), 168–172; and Giuseppe Bonazzi and Cristiano Antonelli, "To Make or To Sell? The Case of In-House Outsourcing at Fiat Auto," *Organization Studies* 24, 4 (2003), 575–594.

67. Schilling and Steensma, "The Use of Modular Organizational Forms"; Raymond E. Miles and Charles C. Snow, "The New Network Firm: A Spherical Structure Built on a Human Investment Philosophy," *Organizational Dynamics* (Spring 1995), 5–18; and R. E. Miles, C. C. Snow, J. A. Matthews, G. Miles, and H. J. Coleman Jr., "Organizing in the Knowledge Age: Anticipating the Cellular Form," *Academy of Management Executive* 11, 4 (1997), 7–24.

68. Paul Engle, "You Can Outsource Strategic Processes," *Industrial Management* (January–February 2002), 13–18.

69. Don Tapscott, "Rethinking Strategy in a Networked World," *Strategy & Business* 24 (Third Quarter, 2001), 34–41.

70. Miles and Snow, "The New Network Firm"; Gregory G. Dess, Abdul M. A. Rasheed, Kevin J. McLaughlin, and Richard L. Priem, "The New Corporate Architecture," *Academy of Management Executive* 9, 2 (1995), 7–20; and Engle, "You Can Outsource Strategic Processes."

71. The discussion of weaknesses is based on Engle, "You *Can* Outsource Strategic Processes"; Henry W. Chesbrough, and David J. Teece, "Organizing for Innovation: When Is Virtual Virtuous?" *Harvard Business Review* (August 2002), 127–134; Dess et al., "The New Corporate Architecture"; and N. Anand, "Modular, Virtual, and Hollow Forms of Organization Design," working paper, London Business School, 2000.

72. Based on Ostroff, *The Horizontal Organization*, 29–44.

73. S. Helgesen, *The Web of Inclusion: Architecture for Building Great Organizations* (New York: Beard Books, 2005).

74. The Web of Inclusion: A New Architecture for Building Great Organizations at http://www.sallyhelgesen.com/books.cfm?isbn=0385423640 (accessed July 24, 2011).

75. "The Canadian Inquisition" at http://torquiz.freeshell.org/about/about.html (accessed March 13, 2014).

76. L. Mann, Personal Communication, September 13, 2007.

77. Based on Child, *Organization*, Ch. 1; and Jonathan D. Day, Emily Lawson, and Keith Leslie, "When Reorganization Works," *The McKinsey Quarterly*, 2003 Special Edition: The Value in Organization, 21–29.

78. G. Morgan, *Images of Organization* (Updated Edition) (Thousand Oaks, CA: Sage Publications, 2006), 4.

79. Ibid., 366.

80. "The Boundaryless Organization: The Phrase" at www.trainingmag.com/article/boundaryless-organization-phrase (accessed May 18, 2011).

81. R. Ashkenas, D. Ulrich, T. Jick, and S. Kerr, *The Boundaryless Organization: Breaking the Chains of*

*Organizational Structure* (San Francisco: Jossey-Bass, 1995).

82. S. Falk, "Organizational Evolution in a 'Boundaryless' Organization" at web.mit.edu/org-ev/www/documents/samthesis.pdf (accessed May 18, 2011).

# Chapter 4

1. David Pringle, "Wrong Number; How Nokia Chased Top End of Market, Got Hit in Middle," *The Wall Street Journal* (June 1, 2004), A1; and Andy Reinhardt with Moon Ihlwan, "Will Rewiring Nokia Spark Growth?" *BusinessWeek* (February 14, 2005), 46ff.

2. "Nokia, Microsoft Form Smartphone Alliance," ABC News (February 11, 2011) at www.abc.net.au/news/stories/2011/02/11/3136888.htm (accessed March 13, 2014).

3. Andrew Yeh, "China Set to Be Nokia's Top Market," *Financial Times* (February 24, 2005), 24; and Reinhardt and Ihlwan, "Will Rewiring Nokia Spark Growth?"

4. Juliette Garside, "Nokia Bounces Back to Profit on Smartphone Demand," *The Guardian* (January 24, 2013) at http://www.theguardian.com/technology/2013/jan/24/nokia-returns-to-profit-smartphones (accessed April 15, 2014).

5. Mark Scott, "Nokia Struggles to Project a Bright Future Without Phones," *The New York Times* (January 23, 2014) at http://www.nytimes.com/2014/01/24/business/international/Nokia-Reports-Fourth-Quarter-Earnings.html?_r=0 (accessed March 13, 2014).

6. Tim Arango, "A Hot Social Networking Site Cools as Facebook Flourishes," *The New York Times* (January 12, 2011), A1; and Geoffrey A. Fowler, "Facebook's Web of Frenemies," *The Wall Street Journal* (February 15, 2011), B1.

7. Jason Abbruzzese, "Facebook Teen Decline Is Real but Leveling Off," Mashable at http://mashable.com/2014/01/21/report-teens-declines-on-facebook-similar-to-broader-trend/ (accessed March 13, 2014).

8. Salvador Rodrigues, "Could Facebook Really Lose 80% of Users by 2017? Not Likely," *Los Angeles Times* (January 22, 2014) at http://www.latimes.com/business/technology/la-fi-tn-facebook-lose-80-users-2017-not-likely-20140122,0,5369746.story#axzz2rFOFhVSC (accessed March 13, 2014).

9. Paul Keegan, "Is the Music Store Over?" *Business 2.0* (March 2004), 115–118; Tom Hansson, Jurgen Ringbeck, and Markus Franke, "Fight for Survival: A New Business Model for the Airline Industry," Strategy + Business, Issue 31 (Summer 2003), 78–85.

10. Paul Shrivastava, "CASTRATED Environment: GREENING Organizational Studies," *Organization Studies* 15, 5 (1994) 705–726.

11. "The NHLPA and the David Suzuki Foundation Announce 'Green' Partnership" (December 7, 2007) at www.davidsuzuki.org/latestnews/dsfnews12070702.asp (accessed June 5, 2008); NHLPA, "523 NHLPA Members go Green with David Suzuki" (2008) at www.nhlpa.com/News/H-7EE42671-E30A-429A-A2EF-24AC39BF4C52/523-NHLPA-Members-Go-Green-With-David-Suzuki (accessed May 31, 2011).

12. Tim Arango and David Carr, "Netflix's Move Onto the Web Stirs Rivalries," *The New York Times* (November 25, 2010, A1); and Cecilia Kang, "Netflix Could Upend Telecom Industry," *Pittsburg Post-Gazette* (March 6, 2011), A4.

13. David Carr, "Giving Viewers What They Want," *The New York Times* (February 24, 2013) at www.nytimes.com/2013/02/25/business/media/for-house-of-cards-using-big-data-to-guarantee-its-popularity.html?pagewanted=all&_r=0 (accessed April 7, 2014).

14. Dana Milbank, "Aluminum Producers, Aggressive and Agile, Outfight Steelmakers," *The Wall Street Journal* (July 1, 1992), A1.

15. Roman Friedrich, Michael Peterson, and Alex Koster, "The Rise of Generation C," *Strategy + Business*, Issue 62 (Spring 2011), http://www.strategy-business.com/article/11110 (accessed March 13, 2014).

16. "The Skills Gap in Canada: The Knowledge Intensity of Canadians' Jobs is Growing Rapidly" (December 21, 2006) at www.ccl-cca.ca/CCL/Reports/LessonsInLearning/LinL20061220SkillsGap.htm (accessed June 6, 2008).

17. M. J. Douglas, "The Challenges of a Canadian Workforce," http://content.monster.ca/7249_en-CA_p1.asp (accessed June 6, 2008).

18. Andrew Pollack, "Yet Another Sector Embraces Outsourcing to Asia: Life Sciences," *International Herald Tribune* (February 25, 2005), 17.

19. S. Forbes, "Kraft's Miracle Woman Whips up Strategy," *Forbes* (November 5, 2010) at www.forbes.com/2010/11/05/shareholder-kraft-foods-intelligent-investing-rosenfeld.html (accessed May 31, 2011).

20. Kim Bashin, "The Kraft Foods Split is the Grand Finale of an Epic Transformation," *Business Insider* (August 4, 2011) at http://www.businessinsider.com/kraft-foods-split-strategy-2011-8 (accessed March 13, 2014).

21. Samuel Loewenberg, "Europe Gets Tougher on U.S. Companies," *The New York Times* (April 20, 2003), Section 3, 6.

22. Canadian Press, "Canada's Foreign-born Population Soars to 6.8 Million," CBC News (May 8, 2013) at http://www.cbc.ca/news/canada/canada-s-foreign-born-population-soars-to-6-8-million-1.1308179 (accessed March 13, 2014).

23. V. Galt, "Diversity at Work: 77 People, 27 Languages," *The Globe and Mail* (December 5, 2007), C1–2.

24. David Kirkpatrick and Daniel Roth, "Why There's No Escaping the Blog," *Fortune* (January 10, 2005), 44–50.

25. International Telecommunication Union, "Estimated 100 Million Blogs Worldwide in Early 2006" at www.itu.int/osg/spu/newslog/Estimated+100+Million+Blogs+Worldwide+In+Early+2006.aspx (accessed May 18, 2011).

26. Pingdom, "Internet 2010 in Numbers" at http://royal.pingdom.com/2011/01/12/internet-2010-in-numbers (accessed March 13, 2014).

27. Robert Frank, "Silver Lining; How Terror Fears Brought Tiny Firm to Brink of Success," *The Wall Street Journal* (May 8, 2003), A1, A14.

28. Mark Landler, "Woes at Two Pillars of German Journalism," *The New York Times* (January 19, 2004), C8.

29. "When Fortune Frowned," *The Economist* (October 9, 2008) at www.economist.com/node/12373696/print (accessed March 13, 2014).

30. "Canada's Auto Sector Could Lose 15,000 Jobs by 2009: Conference Board," CBC News (November 25, 2008) at www.cbc.ca/news/business/story/2008/11/25/autos-conference-board.html (accessed March 13, 2014).

31. Andrew Kupfer, "How American Industry Stacks Up," *Fortune* (March 9, 1992), 36–46.

32. "Sapporo Acquisition of Sleeman on Tap" (August 11, 2006) at www.cbc.ca/money/story/2006/08/11/sapporo-sleeman.html (accessed May 18, 2011).

33. "Methane to Markets" (n.d.) at http://www.methanetomarkets.org (accessed June 5, 2008).

34. R. Harris, "Ogilvy & Mather," *Marketing* (November 12, 2007).

35. Devin Leonard, "Nightmare on Madison Avenue Media Fragmentation, Recession, Fed-up Clients,TiVo—It's All Trouble, and the Ad Business Is Caught up in the Wake," CNN Money (June 28, 2004) at http://money.cnn.com/magazines/Fortune/Fortune_archive/2004/06/28/374368/index.htm (accessed June 9, 2011); and Brian Steinberg, "Agency Cost-Accounting Is under Trial," *The Wall Street Journal* (January 28, 2005), B2.

36. H. Lacroix, "Message from the President and CEO" (n.d.) at www.cbc.radio-canada.ca/submissions/plan/2009/pdf/message-e.pdf (accessed May 31, 2011).

37. Randall D. Harris, "Organizational Task Environments: An Evaluation of Convergent and Discriminant Validity," *Journal of Management Studies* 41, 5 (July 2004), 857–882; Allen C. Bluedorn, "Pilgrim's Progress: Trends and Convergence in Research on Organizational Size and Environment," *Journal of Management* 19 (1993), 163–191; Howard E. Aldrich, *Organizations and Environments* (Englewood Cliffs, NJ: Prentice Hall, 1979); and Fred Emery and Eric L. Trist, "The Casual Texture of Organizational Environments," *Human Relations* 18 (1965), 21–32.

38. Gregory G. Dess and Donald W. Beard, "Dimensions of Organizational Task Environments," *Administrative Science Quarterly* 29 (1984), 52–73; Ray Jurkovich, "A Core Typology of Organizational Environments," *Administrative Science Quarterly* 19 (1974), 380–394; Robert B. Duncan, "Characteristics of Organizational Environment and Perceived Environmental Uncertainty," *Administrative Science Quarterly* 17 (1972), 313–327.

39. Christine S. Koberg and Gerardo R. Ungson, "The Effects of Environmental Uncertainty and Dependence on Organizational Structure and Performance: A Comparative Study," *Journal of Management* 13 (1987), 725–737; and Frances J. Milliken, "Three Types of Perceived Uncertainty about the Environment: State, Effect, and Response Uncertainty," *Academy of Management Review* 12 (1987), 133–143.

40. Mike France with Joann Muller, "A Site for Soreheads," *BusinessWeek* (April 12, 1999), 86–90; Kirkpatrick and Roth, "Why There's No Escaping the Blog."

41. J. A. Litterer, *The Analysis of Organizations,* 2nd ed. (New York: Wiley, 1973), 335.

42. Constance L. Hays, "More Gloom on the Island of Lost Toy Makers," *The New York Times* (February 23, 2005) at http://www.nytimes.com (accessed June 9, 2008).

43. "Mattel CEO: 'Rigorous Standards' after Massive Toy Recall" (November 15, 2007) at www.cnn.com/2007/US/08/14/recall (accessed March 13, 2014).

44. Rosalie L. Tung, "Dimensions of Organizational Environments: An Exploratory Study of Their Impact on Organizational Structure," *Academy of Management Journal* 22 (1979), 672–693.

45. Joseph E. McCann and John Selsky, "Hyper-turbulence and the Emergence of Type 5 Environments," *Academy of Management Review* 9 (1984), 460–470.

46. S. D. Nonato, "Canadians Drinking Less Beer, Turning to Imported Wine: Report, Financial Post" (March 26, 2012) at http://business.financialpost.com/2012/03/26/canadians-drinking-less-beer-turning-to-imported-wine-report (accessed March 13, 2014).

47. Vera Ovanin, "Former WestJetters Look at New Airline" (October 22, 2007) at http://calsun.canoe.ca/News/Alberta/2007/10/22/pf-4596698.html (accessed June 9, 2008).

48. Enerjet "About Enerjet" (2011) at http://www.enerjet.ca/aboutenerjet.html (accessed June 1, 2011).

49. James D. Thompson, *Organizations in Action* (New York: McGraw-Hill, 1967), 20–21.

50. Sally Solo, "Whirlpool: How to Listen to Consumers," *Fortune* (January 11, 1993), 77–79.

51. David B. Jemison, "The Importance of Boundary Spanning Roles in Strategic Decision-Making," *Journal of Management Studies* 21 (1984), 131–152; and Mohamed Ibrahim Ahmad At-Twaijri and John R. Montanari, "The Impact of Context and Choice on the Boundary-Spanning Process: An Empirical Extension," *Human Relations* 40 (1987), 783–798.

52. Michelle Cook, "The Intelligentsia," *Business 2.0* (July 1999), 135–136.

53. Robert C. Schwab, Gerardo R. Ungson, and Warren B. Brown, "Redefining the Boundary-Spanning Environment Relationship," *Journal of Management* 11 (1985), 75–86.

54. Innovation in Canada (October 28, 2005) at www.innovationstrategy.gc.ca/gol/innovation/site.nsf/en/in03621.html (accessed June 5, 2008).

55. Steve Mossop, "Companies Not Spending Enough on Business Intelligence Activities" (November 24, 2005) at www.ipsos-na.com/news/pressrelease.cfm?id=2874# (accessed March 13, 2014).

56. Pia Nordlinger, "Know Your Enemy," *Working Woman* (May 2001), 16.

57. Ken Western, "Ethical Spying," *Business Ethics* (September/October 1995), 22–23; Stan Crock, Geoffrey Smith, Joseph Weber, Richard A. Melcher, and Linda Himelstein, "They Snoop to Conquer," *Business-Week* (October 28, 1996), 172–176; and Kenneth A. Sawka, "Demystifying Business Intelligence," *Management Review* (October 1996), 47–51.

58. Edwin M. Epstein, "How to Learn from the Environment about the Environment—A Prerequisite for Organizational Well-Being," *Journal of General Management* 29, 1 (Autumn 2003), 68–80.

59. "Snooping on a Shoestring," *Business 2.0* (May 2003), 64–66.

60. Mike France with Joann Muller, "A Site for Soreheads," *BusinessWeek* (April 12, 1999), 86–90.

61. Emily Wexler, "Not Your Average Joe" (2005) at www.citylifemagazine.ca/sucessstory_joe.php (accessed June 9, 2008).

62. Ibid.

63. "Joe Fresh Style Launched in Toronto," Fashion Monitor Toronto at http://toronto.fashion-monitor.com/news.php/fashion/2006031307fresh-fashion-launch (accessed June 18, 2008).

64. "First, Joe Fresh Takes Manhattan, Pilot Store in NYC to Open This Fall" at http://www2.macleans.ca/2011/02/23/first-joe-fresh-takes-manhattan (accessed March 13, 2014).

65. CBC News, "Joe Fresh Vows to Be 'Force for Good' in Bangladesh," CBC News (May 2, 2013) at http://www.cbc.ca/news/business/joe-fresh-vows-to-be-force-for-good-in-bangladesh-1.1329098 (accessed March 13, 2014).

66. Jay W. Lorsch, "Introduction to the Structural Design of Organizations," in Gene W. Dalton, Paul R. Lawrence, and Jay W. Lorsch, eds. (Homewood, IL: Irwin and Dorsey, 1970), 5.

67. Paul R. Lawrence and Jay W. Lorsch, *Organization and Environment* (Homewood, IL: Irwin, 1969).

68. Lorsch, "Introduction to the Structural Design of Organizations," 7.

69. Jay W. Lorsch and Paul R. Lawrence, "Environmental Factors and Organizational Integration," in J. W. Lorsch and Paul R. Lawrence, eds., *Organizational Planning:*

*Cases and Concepts* (Homewood, IL: Irwin and Dorsey, 1972), 45.

70. Tom Burns and G. M. Stalker, *The Management of Innovation* (London: Tavistock, 1961).

71. John A. Courtright, Gail T. Fairhurst, and L. Edna Rogers, "Interaction Patterns in Organic and Mechanistic Systems," *Academy of Management Journal* 32 (1989), 773–802.

72. Dennis K. Berman, "Crunch Time," *BusinessWeek Frontier* (April 24, 2000), F28–F38.

73. Robert A. Guth, "Eroding Empires: Electronics Giants of Japan Undergo Wrenching Change," *The Wall Street Journal* (June 20, 2002), A1, A9.

74. Thomas C. Powell, "Organizational Alignment as Competitive Advantage," *Strategic Management Journal* 13 (1992), 119–134; Mansour Javidan, "The Impact of Environmental Uncertainty on Long-Range Planning Practices of the U.S. Savings and Loan Industry," *Strategic Management Journal* 5 (1984), 381–392; Tung, "Dimensions of Organizational Environments," 672–693; and Thompson, *Organizations in Action.*

75. Ian Wylie, "There Is No Alternative To …," *Fast Company* (July 2002), 106–110.

76. "Manitoba Telcom Services, Inc." (n.d.) at http://www.referenceforbusiness.com/history2/76/Manitoba-Telecom-Services-Inc.html (accessed July 7, 2008) and at www.mts.ca/portal/site/mts/menuitem.e21815bb3f30fc8e7ee558c3408021a0/?vgnextoid=13ef82cd24bf1110VgnVCM1000000408120aRCRD&vgnextfmt=print General (accessed July 7, 2008).

77. Ibid.

78. J. Swayze and A. Bromilow, *"Not Just an Operator"—How the Manitoba Telephone System (MTS) & Communication, Energy & Paperworkers Union (CEP) Jointly Implemented Work Redesign* (1993).

79. Ibid.

80. David Ulrich and Jay B. Barney, "Perspectives in Organizations: Resource Dependence, Efficiency, and Population," *Academy of Management Review* 9 (1984), 471–481; and Jeffrey Pfeffer and Gerald Salancik, *The External Control of Organizations: A Resource Dependent Perspective* (New York: Harper & Row, 1978).

81. Andrew H. Van de Ven and Gordon Walker, "The Dynamics of Interorganizational Coordination," *Administrative Science Quarterly* (1984), 598–621; and Huseyin Leblebici and Gerald R. Salancik, "Stability in Interorganizational Exchanges: Rulemaking Processes of the Chicago Board of Trade," *Administrative Science Quarterly* 27 (1982), 227–242.

82. Kevin Kelly and Zachary Schiller with James B. Treece, "Cut Costs or Else: Companies Lay Down the Law to Suppliers," *BusinessWeek* (March 22, 1993), 28–29.

83. G. Pascal Zachary, "Many Journalists See a Growing Reluctance to Criticize Advertisers," *The Wall Street Journal* (February 6, 1992), A1, A9.

84. Judith A. Babcock, Organizational Responses to Resource Scarcity and Munificence: Adaptation and Modification in Colleges within a University (Ph.D. diss., Pennsylvania State University, 1981).

85. Peter Smith Ring and Andrew H. Van de Ven, "Developmental Processes of Corporative Interorganizational Relationships," *Academy of Management Review* 19 (1994), 90–118; Jeffrey Pfeffer, "Beyond Management and the Worker: The Institutional Function of Management," *Academy of Management Review* 1 (April 1976), 36–46; and John P. Kotter, "Managing External Dependence," *Academy of Management Review* 4 (1979), 87–92.

86. Bryan Borys and David B. Jemison, "Hybrid Arrangements as Strategic Alliances: Theoretical Issues in Organizational Combinations," *Academy of Management Review* 14 (1989), 234–249.

87. McMillan Binch Mendelsohn, "M&A Developments in Canada," *Securities Bulletin* (February 2007), 2.

88. B. Marotte, B. Erman, and J. Parttridge, "TMX Group Formed as Toronto, Montréal Exchanges Merge," *The Globe and Mail* (December 10, 2007), A1.

89. Ibid.

90. R. Trichur, "Toronto, Montreal Exchanges Tie the Knot," *Toronto Star* (December 10, 2007) at www.thestar.com/Business/article/284166 (accessed March 13, 2014).

91. Dana Flavelle, Toronto-London Stock Exchange Merger Terminated, *Toronto Star* (June 29, 2011) at http://www.thestar.com/business/2011/06/29/torontolondon_stock_exchange_merger_terminated.html (accessed June 11, 2014).

92. Julie Cohen Mason, "Strategic Alliances: Partnering for Success," *Management Review* (May 1993), 10–15.

93. Teri Agins and Alessandra Galloni, "After Gianni; Facing a Squeeze, Versace Struggles to Trim the Fat," *The Wall Street Journal* (September 30, 2003), A1, A10; John F. Love, *McDonald's: Behind the Arches* (New York: Bantam Books, 1986).

94. Zachary Schiller and Wendy Zellner with Ron Stodghill, II, and Mark Maremont, "Clout! More and More, Retail Giants Rule the Marketplace," *BusinessWeek* (December 21, 1992), 66–73.

95. Borys and Jemison, "Hybrid Arrangements as Strategic Alliances."

96. "Joint Venture with Canada to Expand Nickel Production to 49,000 Tons" (April 19, 2006) at http://granmai.cubasi.cu/ingles/2006/abril/mier19/17niquel.html (accessed May 18, 2011).

97. Donald Palmer, "Broken Ties: Interlocking Directorates and Intercorporate Coordination," *Administrative Science Quarterly* 28 (1983), 40–55; F. David Shoorman, Max H. Bazerman, and Robert S. Atkin, "Interlocking Directorates: A Strategy for Reducing Environmental Uncertainty," *Academy of Management Review* 6 (1981), 243–251; and Ronald S. Burt, *Toward a Structural Theory of Action* (New York: Academic Press, 1982).

98. James R. Lang and Daniel E. Lockhart, "Increased Environmental Uncertainty and Changes in Board Linkage Patterns," *Academy of Management Journal* 33 (1990), 106–128; and Mark S. Mizruchi and Linda Brewster Stearns, "A Longitudinal Study of the Formation of Interlocking Directorates," *Administrative Science Quarterly* 33 (1988), 194–210.

99. Kotter, "Managing External Dependence."

100. William C. Symonds, with Farah Nayeri, Geri Smith, and Ted Plafker, "Bombardier's Blitz," *BusinessWeek* (February 6, 1995), 62–66; and Joseph Weber, with Wendy Zellner and Geri Smith, "Loud Noises at Bombardier," *BusinessWeek* (January 26, 1998), 94–95.

101. "Canadian Companies Lobby for Missile Shield Contracts" (March 17, 2004) at www.cbc.ca/canada/story/2004/03/16/missileshield040316.html (accessed June 9, 2008).

102. L. McQuaig, "Harper Bids to Be Bush's "Poodle" (June 12, 2007) at www.lindamcquaig.com/Columns/ViewColumn.cfm?REF=33 (accessed March 13, 2014).

103. Jeanne Cummings, "Joining the PAC; Wal-Mart Opens for Business in a Tough Market: Washington," *The Wall Street Journal* (March 24, 2004), A1.

104. "Quebec Court of Appeal Declines to Hear Wal-Mart Case" (May 16, 2006) at www.nupge.ca/news_2006/n16my06a.htm (accessed March 13, 2014); "Wal-Mart Store Closing Chills Union Drive in 25 Canada Outlets" (April 29, 2005) at www.bloomberg.com/apps/news?pid=71000001&refer=canada&sid=alpljhOyZjW4 (accessed March 13, 2014).

105. David B. Yoffie, "How an Industry Builds Political Advantage," *Harvard Business Review* (May–June 1988), 82–89; and Jeffrey H. Birnbaum, "Chief Executives Head to Washington to Ply the Lobbyist's Trade," *The Wall Street Journal* (March 19, 1990), A1, A16.

106. Anthony J. Daboub, Abdul M. A. Rasheed, Richard L. Priem, and David A. Gray, "Top Management Team Characteristics and Corporate Illegal Activity," *Academy of Management Review* 20, 1 (1995), 138–170.

107. I. Austen, "WestJet Settles Spy Case with Rival Air Canada" (May 31, 2006) at www.iht.com/articles/2006/05/30/business/canair.php (accessed July 2, 2008).

108. Barry M. Staw and Eugene Szwajkowski, "The Scarcity-Munificence Component of Organizational Environments and the Commission of Illegal Acts," *Administrative Science Quarterly* 20 (1975), 345–354; and Kimberly D. Elsbach and Robert I. Sutton, "Acquiring Organizational Legitimacy through Illegitimate Actions: A Marriage of Institutional and Impression Management Theories," *Academy of Management Journal* 35 (1992), 699–738.

109. K. Donovan, "Toronto Charity ICAN Suspended by Federal Regulator," *Toronto Star* (November 30, 2007), A10.

## Chapter 5

1. "14 Management Principles from the World's Greatest Manufacturer" (February 1, 2006) at www.industryweek.com/PrintArticle.aspx?ArticleID=11303 (accessed May 18, 2011).
2. N. Kehler, "Interorganizational Relationships and Learning; Deep Supplier Relationships Drive Automakers' Success" (July 6, 2005) at http://Knowledge.wpcarey.asu.edu/index.cfm?fa=viewfeature&id=1061 (accessed May 11, 2011); and J. Teresko "Learning from ToyotaAgain" (February 1, 2006) at www.industryweek.com/PrintArticle.aspx?ArticleID=11301 (accessed May l8, 2011).
3. Christine Oliver, "Determinants of Interorganizational Relationships: Integration and Future Directions," *Academy of Management Review* 15 (1990), 241–265.
4. S. Dubois, "Apple, Why It's Admired" (2001) at http://money.cnn.com/magazines/Fortune/mostadmired/2011/snapshots/670.html (accessed May 18, 2011) and *Fortune* (2013) World's Most Admired Companies, at http://money.cnn.com/magazines/Fortune/most-admired (accessed March 13, 2014).
5. James Moore, *The Death of Competition: Leadership and Strategy in the Age of Business Ecosystems* (New York: HarperCollins, 1996); Brent Schlender, "How Big Can Apple Get?" *Fortune* (February 21, 2005), 66–76.
6. D. George-Cosh, "Hello, Magna: Apples's iPhone Contains Surprise Component" (July 4, 2007) *The Globe and Mail*, B3.
7. Howard Muson, "Friend? Foe? Both? The Confusing World of Corporate Alliances," *Across the Board* (March–April 2002), 19–25; and Devi R. Gnyawali and Ravindranath Madhavan, "Cooperative Networks and Competitive Dynamics: A Structural Embeddedness Perspective," *Academy of Management Review* 26, 3 (2001), 431–445.
8. Thomas Petzinger, Jr., *The New Pioneers: The Men and Women Who Are Transforming the Workplace and Marketplace* (New York: Simon & Schuster, 1999), 53–54.
9. James Moore, "The Death of Competition," *Fortune* (April 15, 1996), 142–144.
10. J. Markoff. "Intel, in Shift, Joins Project on Education," *The New York Times* (July 14, 2007 at http://www.nytimes.com/2007/07/14/business/14chip.html (accessed April 9, 2014).
11. Greg Ferenstein, "In a Cutthroat World, Some Web Giants Thrive by Cooperating," *The Washington Post* (February 19, 2011), http://www.washingtonpost.com/business/in-a-cutthroat-world-some-web-giants-thrive-by-cooperating/2011/02/19/ABmYSYQ_story.html (accessed March 13, 2014); Sam Grobart, "Gadgetwise: Body Browser Is a Google Earth for the Anatomy," *The New York Times* (December 23, 2010), B7; Andrew Dowell, "The Rise of Apps, iPad, and Android," *The Wall Street Journal Online* (December 28, 2010), http://online.wsj.com/article/SB10001424052748704774604576035611315663944.html (accessed March 13, 2014); and Beth Kowitt, "100 Million Android Fans Can't Be Wrong," *Fortune* (June 16, 2011), http://tech.Fortune.cnn.com/2011/06/16/100-million-android-fans-cant-be-wrong (accessed March 13, 2014).
12. Ferenstein, "In a Cutthroat World, Some Web Giants Thrive by Cooperating;" and Jessica E. Vascellaro and Yukari Iwatani Kane, "Apple, Google Rivalry Heats Up," *The Wall Street Journal* (December 11, 2009), B1.
13. T. Wong, "Rivals Unite to Build Film Studio," *Toronto Star* (July 5. 2007), B1, B4.
14. Ibid.
15. E. Vlessing, "Lights on at Toronto's Filmport, But Nobody's Home," *Reuters*, August 21, 2008) at www.reuters.com/article/2008/08/21/industry-filmport-dc-idUSN2149447220080821 (accessed March 13, 2014).
16. Pinewood Toronto Studios, "Pinewood Toronto Studios Named 'One of the Reasons to Love Toronto'" (March 16, 2011) at www.pinewoodtorontostudios.com/content/pinewood-toronto-studios-named-one-reasons-love-toronto (accessed March 13, 2014).
17. Ashante Infantry, " Pinewood Looks to Further Expansion," *Toronto Star* (October 4, 2013) at http://www.thestar.com/news/gta/2013/10/04/pinewood_looks_to_further_expansion.html (accessed March 27, 2014).
18. Sumantra Ghoshal and Christopher A. Bartlett, "Changing the Role of Top Management: Beyond Structure and Process" *Harvard Business Review* (January–February 1995), 86–96.
19. "GBC History" at www.gbcimpact.org/live/about/history.php (accessed July 7, 2009).
20. J. Pfeffer and G. R. Salancik, *The External Control of Organizations: A Resource Dependence Perspective* (New York: Harper & Row, 1978).
21. Derek S. Pugh and David J. Hickson, *Writers on Organizations*, 5th ed. (Thousand Oaks, CA: Sage Publications, 1996).
22. A. J. Armstrong-Doherty, "Resource Dependence-based Perceived Control: An Examination of Canadian Interuniversity Athletics," *Journal of Sports Management* (1996) 10, 1, 49–64.
23. L. Thibault and J. Harvey, "Fostering Interorganizational Linkages in the Canadian Sport Delivery System," *Journal of Sports Management* (1997) 11, 1, 45–68 and K. Babiak, "Determinants of Interorganizational Relationships: The Case of a Canadian Nonprofit Sport Organizations," *Journal of Sports Management* (2007) 21, 3, 3.

24. "Canadian National Swim Team Helps Red Cross Kick off Water Safety Week with a Splash," *Canada Newswire* (June 1, 2006).

25. This discussion is based on Matthew Schifrin, "The Big Squeeze," *Forbes* (March 11, 1996), 45–46; Wendy Zellner with Marti Benedetti, "CLOUT!" *Business Week* (December 21, 1992), 62–73; Kevin Kelly and Zachary Schiller with James B. Treece, "Cut Costs or Else," *Business Week* (March 22, 1993), 28–29; and Lee Berton, "Push from Above," *The Wall Street Journal* (May 23, 1996), R24.

26. "Fitting In; In Bow to Retailers' New Clout, Levi Strauss Makes Alterations," *The Wall Street Journal* (June 17, 2004), A1.

27. "AMR Research Announces Rankings of Its 2010 Supply Chain Top 25" at www.gartner.com/it/page .jsp?id=1379730 (accessed March 13, 2014).

28. Robert A. Guth and Don Clark, "Peace Program; Behind Secret Settlement Talks: New Power of Tech Customers," *The Wall Street Journal* (April 5, 2004), A1.

29. M. K. Foster and A. Meinhard, "Women's Voluntary Organizations in Canada: Bridgers, Bonders or Both?" *Voluntas: International Journal of Voluntary and Nonprofit Organizations*, 16, 2 (2005), 143–159.

30. Mitchell P. Koza and Arie Y. Lewin, "The Co-Evolution of Network Alliances: A Longitudinal Analysis of an International Professional Service Network," *Center for Research on New Organizational Forms*, Working Paper 98–09–02; and Kathy Rebello with Richard Brandt, Peter Coy, and Mark Lewyn, "Your Digital Future," *Business Week* (September 7, 1992), 56–64.

31. Christine Oliver, "Determinants of Inter-organizational Relationships: Integration and Future Directions," *Academy of Management Review*, 15 (1990), 241–265; Ken G. Smith, Stephen J. Carroll, and Susan Ashford, "Intra- and Interorganizational Cooperation: Toward a Research Agenda," *Academy of Management Journal* 38 (1995), 7–23.

32. Timothy M. Stearns, Alan N. Hoffman, and Jan B. Heide, "Performance of Commercial Television Stations as an Outcome of Interorganizational Linkages and Environmental Conditions," *Academy of Management Journal* 30 (1987), 71–90; and David A. Whetten and Thomas K. Kueng, "The Instrumental Value of Interorganizational Relations: Antecedents and Consequences of Linkage Formation," *Academy of Management Journal* 22 (1979), 325–344.

33. "Angiotech's Corporate Partner, Boston Scientific, Announces Japanese Launch of TAXUS Express2 Coronary Stent System" (May 2007) at www.medicalnewstoday .com/articles/70342.php (accessed March 13, 2014).

34. Muson, "Friend? Foe? Both?"

35. "Leave No Trace" (n.d.) at www.leavenotrace.ca/ about/founding.html (accessed June 10, 2008).

36. Ontario Craft Brewers, "News on Tap" (June 2005) at www.ontariocraftbrewers.com/content2.php?

nextpage=ocb_press_release_june3 (accessed March 13, 2014).

37. "Ontario Microbreweries Thriving," *Ontario News* (July 28, 2012) at http://news.ontario.ca/medt/ en/2012/07/ontario-microbreweries-thriving.html (accessed March 27, 2014).

38. Keith G. Provan and H. Brinton Milward, "A Preliminary Theory of Interorganizational Network Effectiveness: A Comparative of Four Community Mental Health Systems," *Administrative Science Quarterly* 40 (1995), 1–33.

39. Myron Magnet, "The New Golden Rule of Business," *Fortune* (February 21, 1994), 60–64; Grittner, "Four Elements of Successful Sourcing Strategies"; and Jeffrey H. Dyer and Nile W. Hatch, "Using Supplier Networks to Learn Faster," MIT *Sloan Management Review* (Spring 2004), 57–63.

40. Peter Smith Ring and Andrew H. Van de Ven, "Developmental Processes of Corporate Interorganizational Relationships," *Academy of Management Review* 19 (1994), 90–118; Jeffrey H. Dyer, "How Chrysler Created an American Keiretsu," *Harvard Business Review* (July–August 1996), 42–56; Grittner, "Four Elements of Successful Sourcing Strategies"; Magnet, "The New Golden Rule of Business"; and Mick Marchington and Steven Vincent, "Analysing the Influence of Institutional, Organizational and Interpersonal Forces in Shaping Inter-Organizational Relationships," *Journal of Management Studies* 41, 6 (September 2004), 1029–1056.

41. Pete Engardio, "The Barons of Outsourcing," *Business Week* (August 28, 2000), 177–178.

42. Philip Siekman, "The Snap-Together Business Jet," *Fortune* (January 21, 2002), 104[A]–104[H].

43. Ibid.

44. Andrew Raskin, "Who's Minding the Store?" *Business 2.0* (February 2003), 70–74.

45. Marchington and Vincent, "Analysing the Influence of Institutional, Organizational and Interpersonal Forces in Shaping Inter-Organizational Relationships."

46. Fred R. Blekley, "Some Companies Let Suppliers Work on Site and Even Place Orders," *The Wall Street Journal* (January 13, 1995), A1, A6.

47. This section draws from Joel A. C. Baum, "Organizational Ecology," in Stewart R. Clegg, Cynthia Hardy, and Walter R. Nord, eds., *Handbook of Organization Studies* (Thousand Oaks, CA: Sage Publications, 1996); Jitendra V. Singh, *Organizational Evolution: New Directions* (Newbury Park, CA: Sage Publications, 1990); Howard Aldrich, Bill McKelvey, and Dave Ulrich, "Design Strategy from the Population Perspective," *Journal of Management* 10 (1984), 67–86; Howard E. Aldrich, *Organizations and Environments* (Englewood Cliffs, NJ: Prentice Hall, 1979); Michael Hannan and John Freeman, "The Population Ecology of Organizations," *American Journal of Sociology* 82 (1977), 929–964; Dave Ulrich, "The Population

Perspective: Review, Critique, and Relevance," *Human Relations* 40 (1987), 137–152; Jitendra V. Singh and Charles J. Lumsden, "Theory and Research in Organizational Ecology," *Annual Review of Sociology* 16 (1990), 161–195; Howard E. Aldrich, "Understanding, Not Integration: Vital Signs from Three Perspectives on Organizations," in Michael Reed and Michael D. Hughes, eds., *Rethinking Organizations: New Directions in Organizational Theory and Analysis* (London: Sage Publications, 1992); Jitendra V. Singh, David J. Tucker, and Robert J. House, "Organizational Legitimacy and the Liability of Newness," *Administrative Science Quarterly* 31 (1986), 171–193; and Douglas R. Wholey and Jack W. Brittain, "Organizational Ecology: Findings and Implications," *Academy of Management Review* 11 (1986), 513–533.

48. Pugh and Hickson, *Writers on Organizations*; and Lex Donaldson, *American Anti-Management Theories of Organization* (New York: Cambridge University Press, 1995).

49. Bullfrog Power (n.d). at http://www.bullfrogpower.com/about/about.cfm (accessed June 10, 2008).

50. Thomas Moore, "The Corporate University: Transforming Management Education" (presentation in August 1996; Thomas Moore is the Dean of the Arthur D. Little University).

51. Peter Newcomb, "No One Is Safe," *Forbes* (July 13, 1987), 121; "It's Tough Up There," *Forbes* (July 13, 1987), 145–160.

52. D. Crane, "Striking a Balance on Foreign Ownership," *Toronto Star* (July 23, 2007), B5.

53. "Canadian National RF to Buy Most of EJ&E from US Steel Subsidiary" (September 27, 2007) at http://chestertontribune.com/business/9273%20canadian_national_rr_to_buy_most.htm (accessed July 8, 2008).

54. K. Kotarski, "McJobs Becoming the Norm?" *The Vancouver Sun* (May 7, 2011) at www.vancouversun.com/health/McJobs+becoming+norm/4744957/story.html (accessed June 1, 2011).

55. "McDonald's Canada Announces Next Phase of Balanced Lifestyles Initiative" (2005) at www.crfa.ca/research/resources/foodandfitnessfacts/news/mcdonalds_announces_next_phase_of_initiative.asp (accessed July 7, 2008).

56. M. Brandau, "Papa John's, "KFC and BK Post Gains," *Nation's Restaurant News*, June 15, 2010) at www.nrn.com/article/mcdonalds-sees-drop-customer-satisfaction (accessed March 13, 2014).

57. "SDC Partners with Shazam to Create Simple, Secure Music Download," *M2Presswire* (February 14, 2005), 1; Steve McClure, "Shazam Works Its Magic," *Billboard* (August 21, 2004), 60; Adam Jolly, "Going for a Song and Growth," *Sunday Times* (June 13, 2004), 17; Michael Parsons, "I Got Music, I Got Algorithm," *Red Herring* (May 2002), 54–57; and "MTV and Shazam Lead Japanese Market Extending Music Recognition Offering to KDDI Subscribers and Expanding Local Music Database," *M2Presswire* (February 16, 2005), 1.

58. James Parducci (n.d.) "Alternatives to Shazam, Ehow Tech" at http://www.ehow.com/info_8462642_alternatives-shazam.html (accessed March 13, 2014).

59. *Business Wire,* "SoundHound Now Enabling Its 170 Million Global Users to Sync, Save and Transfer Music Search & Discovery History across Multiple Devices and in the Cloud" (September 20, 2013) at http://www.businesswire.com/news/home/20130920005824/en/SoundHound-Enabling-170-Million-Global-Users-Sync#.UuP9Pv30Cek (accessed March 13, 2014).

60. T. Watson "A State of Bliss in Steeltown," *Canadian Business* (June 18, 2007).

61. David J. Tucker, Jitendra V. Singh, and Agnes G. Meinhard, "Organizational Form, Population Dynamics, and Institutional Change: The Founding Patterns of Voluntary Organizations," *Academy of Management Journal* 33 (1990), 151–178; Glenn R. Carroll and Michael T. Hannan, "Density Delay in the Evolution of Organizational Populations: A Model and Five Empirical Tests," *Administrative Science Quarterly* 34 (1989), 411–430; Jacques Delacroix and Glenn R. Carroll, "Organizational Foundings: An Ecological Study of the Newspaper Industries of Argentina and Ireland," *Administrative Science Quarterly* 28 (1983), 274–291; Johannes M. Pennings, "Organizational Birth Frequencies: An Empirical Investigation," *Administrative Science Quarterly* 27 (1982), 120–144; David Marple, "Technological Innovation and Organizational Survival: A Population Ecology Study of Nineteenth-Century American Railroads," *Sociological Quarterly* 23 (1982), 107–116; and Thomas G. Rundall and John O. McClain, "Environmental Selection and Physician Supply," *American Journal of Sociology* 87 (1982), 1090–1112.

62. Robert D. Hof and Linda Himelstein, "eBay vs. Amazon.com," *BusinessWeek* (May 31, 1999), 128–132; and Maria Mallory with Stephanie Anderson Forest, "Waking Up to a Major Market," *BusinessWeek* (March 23, 1992), 70–73.

63. Arthur G. Bedeian and Raymond F. Zammuto, *Organizations: Theory and Design* (Orlando, Fla.: Dryden Press, 1991); and Richard L. Hall, *Organizations: Structure, Process and Outcomes* (Englewood Cliffs, NJ: Prentice Hall, 1991).

64. The Rich 100: 11, www.canadianbusiness.com/article.jsp?content=23143 (accessed July 30, 1999).

65. P. Waldie, "Apotex Founder Hits Hard in Legal Family Feud" (October 26, 2007) at www.theglobeandmail.com/servlet/story/LAC.20071026.RSHERMAN26/PPVStory?URL_Article_ID=LAC.20071026.RSHERMAN26&DENIED=1 (accessed July 8, 2008).

66. "Corporate Overview" at www.apotex.com/ca/en/aboutapotex/corporate.asp (accessed July 8, 2008).

67. T. Talaga, "AIDS Drugs Fiasco a Tale of Red Tape," *Toronto Star* (August 9, 2007) at www.thestar.com/article/244582 (accessed March 13, 2014).

68. "Rwanda to Override Patents and Import Cheaper Generic AIDS Drugs," *International Herald Tribune* (July 20, 2007) at http://www.canadianbusiness.com/business-strategy/pandemic-polemics (accessed April 3, 2014); E. Pooley, "Pandemic Polemics," *Canadian Business* (September 11–24, 2006).

69. M. Tina Dacin, Jerry Goodstein, and W. Richard Scott, "Institutional Theory and Institutional Change: Introduction to the Special Research Forum," *Academy of Management Journal* 45, 1 (2002), 45–47. Thanks to Tina Dacin for her material and suggestions for this section of the chapter.

70. J. Meyer and B. Rowan, "Institutionalized Organizations: Formal Structure as Myth and Ceremony," *American Journal of Sociology* 83 (1990), 340–363.

71. Mark C. Suchman, "Managing Legitimacy: Strategic and Institutional Approaches," *Academy of Management Review* 20 (1995), 571–610.

72. Corporate Knights, "Best 50 Corporate Citizens 2010" (June 1, 2011). At www.corporateknights.ca/report/9th-annual-best-50-corporate-citizens-canada/best-50-corporate-citizens (accessed March 13, 2014).

73. CBERN, "Corporate Knights Release 11th Annual Report on "50 Best Corporate Citizens" (June 18, 2012) at http://cbernblog.ca/2012/06/cbern-11th-annual-50-best-corporate-citizens-gala (accessed April 9, 2014).

74. M. Connor, "Johnson & Johnson, Under Investigation, Tops CSR Index" (2010) at http://business-ethics.com/2010/10/13/1602-johnson-johnson-under-investigation-tops-csr-reputation-index (accessed March 14, 2014).

75. Richard J. Martinez and Patricia M. Norman, "Whither Reputation? The Effects of Different Stakeholders," *Business Horizons* 47, 5 (September–October 2004), 25–32.

76. "Ryanair News" at www.ryanair.com/en/news/ryanair-s-full-year-profit-rises-204-percent-to-319m-euro-fares-fall-13-percent-as-traffic-grows-14-percent-to-67m-passengers-ryanair-to-pay-dividend-of-500m-euro-in-october (accessed March 14, 2014).

77. "World's Biggest Retailer Wal-Mart Closes Up Shop in Germany" (July 28, 2006) at www.dw-world.de/dw/article/0,2144,2112746,00.html (accessed March 14, 2014).

78. M. Lander, "Wal-Mart Gives Up Germany" (July 29, 2006) at www.iht.com/articles/2006/07/28/business/walmart.php (accessed May 18, 2011).

79. "Wal-Mart Is Canada's Largest Purchaser of Green Power" (June 8, 2007) at Execdigital June News at www.canada-digital.com/wal-mart-is-canada-s-largest-purchaser-of-green-power-_514.aspx (accessed July 7, 2008).

80. Jerry Useem, "Should We Admire Wal-Mart?" *Fortune* (March 8, 2004), 118–120; Charles Fishman, "The Wal-Mart You Don't Know: Why Low Prices Have a High Cost," *Fast Company* (December 2003), 68–80; Ronald Alsop, "In Business Ranking, Some Icons Lose Luster," *The Wall Street Journal* (November 15, 2004), B1; and

Ronald Alsop, "Corporate Scandals Hit Home," *The Wall Street Journal* (February 19, 2004), B1.

81. "Ten Steps to Turn Around Wal-Mart" at http://blog.fastcompany.com/archives/2005/12/02/ten_steps_to_turn_around_walmart.html#more (accessed May 18, 2011).

82. Air Scoop, "Ryanair's Skyrocketing Success: Flying on Thin Air? An In-depth Analysis of Ryanair's Business Model," http://www.air-scoop.com/.../In-Depth-Analysis-Ryanair-Business-Model-Air- Scoop-Nov2010.pdf (accessed March 5, 2011) p. 119.

83. Pamela S. Tolbert and Lynne G. Zucker, "The Institutionalization of Institutional Theory," in Stewart R. Clegg, Cynthia Hardy, and Walter R. Nord, eds., *Handbook of Organization Studies* (Thousand Oaks, CA: Sage Publications, 1996).

84. Pugh and Hickson, *Writers on Organizations*; and Paul J. DiMaggio and Walter W. Powell, "The Iron Cage Revisited: Institutional Isomorphism and Collective Rationality in Organizational Fields," *American Sociological Review* 48 (1983), 147–160.

85. This section is based largely on DiMaggio and Powell, "The Iron Cage Revisited"; Pugh and Hickson, *Writers on Organizations*; and W. Richard Scott, *Institutions and Organizations* (Thousand Oaks, CA: Sage Publications, 1995).

86. Ellen R. Auster and Mark L. Sirower, "The Dynamics of Merger and Acquisition Waves," *The Journal of Applied Behavioral Science* 38, 2 (June 2002), 216–244.

87. William McKinley, Jun Zhao, and Kathleen Garrett Rust, "A Sociocognitive Interpretation of Organizational Downsizing," *Academy of Management Review* 25, 1 (2000), 227–243.

88. Barry M. Staw and Lisa D. Epstein, "What Bandwagons Bring: Effects of Popular Management Techniques on Corporate Performance, Reputation, and CEO Pay," *Administrative Science Quarterly* 45, 3 (September 2000), 523–560.

89. Jeremy Kahn, "Deloitte Restates Its Case," *Fortune* (April 29, 2002), 64–72.

# Chapter 6

1. A. Hoffman, "Not in My Backfjord, Icelanders Tell Alcan," *The Globe and Mail* (April 3, 2007) B11.

2. Ibid., B1, B11.

3. "Bjork Leads Protest against Iceland Energy Sale" (July 19, 2010) at www.reuters.com/article/2010/07/19/us-iceland-idUSTRE66I4L720100719 (accessed March 13, 2014); "Magma's Iceland Subsidiary HS Orka Signs New Energy Agreement with Silica Company" (February 17, 2011) at http://finance.yahoo.com/news/Magma-Iceland-Subsidiary-HS-cnw-3750025632.html?x=0&.v=1 (accessed March 9, 2011).

4. PR Newswire, "Alterra Power Sells 25% of Iceland Subsidiary HS Orka to Icelandic Pension Funds and Buys 1.5% from Icelandic Municipalities" (May 31, 2011)

at http://www.prnewswire.com/news-releases/alterra-power-sells-25-of-iceland-subsidiary-hs-orka-to-icelandic-pension-funds-and-buys-15-from-icelandic-municipalities-122861734.html (accessed January 25, 2014).

5. T. Watson, "Beat China in Asia: Magna Faces a New World Order" (November 7–20, 2005) at www.canadianbusiness.com/managing/strategy/article.jsp?content=20060109_155853_4528 (accessed July 8, 2008).

6. The *Wired* 40 (March 2007) at www.wired.com/wired/archive/15.04/wired40_list.html (accessed March 13, 2014).

7. J. Yarrow and K. Angelova, "Chart of the Day: Hopefully You Invested In Baidu When Google Left China (February 1, 2011) www.businessinsider.com/chart-of-the-day-google-baidu-stock-2011-2 (accessed May 18, 2011).

8. Dara Kerr, "Bing Falls to 5th Global Search Engine, Surpassed by Yandex," CNET News (February 7, 2013) at http://news.cnet.com/8301-1023_3-57568315-93/bing-falls-to-5th-global-search-engine-surpassed-by-yandex (accessed March 13, 2014).

9. Sam Byford, "Sony Has Sold over 5.3 Million PlayStation 4 Consoles Worldwide," *The Verge* (February 18, 2014) moblile.theverge.com (accessed April 10, 2014).

10. Cole + Parker, "1 for Many" (2014) at http://coleandparker.co/1-for-many (accessed March 13, 2014).

11. "Boréalis Puts Corporate Social Responsibility on the World Map" at www.bdc.ca/EN/about/mediaroom/news_releases/Pages/Borealis_puts_corporate_social_responsibility_on_world_map.aspx (accessed March 13, 2014).

12. CNN, "Global 500 by Country" at http://money.cnn.com/magazines/Fortune/global500/2010 (accessed June 1, 2011).

13. Paola Hject, "The Fortune Global 500," *Fortune* (July 26, 2004), 159–180; "*Fortune* Global 500" (July 23, 2007) at http://money.cnn.com/magazines/Fortune/global500/2007 (accessed July 8, 2008). This discussion is based heavily on Christopher A. Bartlett and Sumantra Ghoshal, *Transnational Management: Text, Cases, and Readings in Cross-Border Management*, 3rd ed. (Boston, MA: Irwin McGraw-Hill, 2000), 94–96; and Anil K. Gupta and Vijay Govindarajan, "Converting Global Presence into Global Competitive Advantage," *Academy of Management Executive* 15, 2 (2001), 45–56.

14. J. McIntosh, "The Marathon Man," *Maclean's* (August 6, 2007), 44; John Vomhof Jr., "Running Room, Other New Tenants Opening at Mall of America," *Minneapolis/St. Paul Business Journal*, at http://www.bizjournals.com/twincities/news/2014/02/19/running-room-new-tenants-mall-of-america.html (accessed March 30, 2014).

15. Ibid.

16. B. Marotte, "First la Belle Province, then the World," *The Globe and Mail* (July 7, 2007), B3.

17. Jim Carlton, "Branching Out; New Zealanders Now Shear Trees Instead of Sheep," *The Wall Street Journal* (May 29, 2003), A1, A10.

18. "Little Trouble in Big China," *FSB* (March 2004), 56–61; "Trade Gap," sidebar in *Fast Company* (June 2004), 42.

19. R. Luciw, "Gildan Activewear Profits with Offshore Moves" (February 8, 2007) at http://www.reportonbusiness.com/servlet/story/RTGAM.20070802.wgildan0802/BNStory/robNEWS/home (accessed July 2, 2008).

20. R. R. Luciw, "Gildan Takes $21.5-million (U.S.) Charge to Shutter Plants" at www.theglobeandmail.com.com/servlet/story/RTGAM.20070327.wgildanstaff0327/BNStory/Business/home (accessed March 27, 2007).

21. Sandro Contenta, Made in Canada: How Globalization has Hit the Canadian Apparel Industry, *Toronto Star* (May 27 2013) at http://www.thestar.com/news/insight/2013/05/27/made_in_canada_how_globalization_has_hit_the_canadian_apparel_industry.html (accessed March 14, 2014).

22. Todd Zaun, Gregory L. White, Norihiko Shirouzu, and Scott Miller, "More Mileage: Auto Makers Look for Another Edge Farther from Home," *The Wall Street Journal* (July 31, 2002), A1, A8.

23. Ken Belson, "Outsourcing, Turned Inside Out," *The New York Times* (April 11, 2004), Section 3, 1.

24. David Lewis and Karl Moore, "The Origins of Globalization: A Canadian Perspective," *Ivey Business Journal* (June 2009) at http://iveybusinessjournal.com/topics/the-organization/the-origins-of-globalization-a-canadian-perspective#.UuVHVv30DjA (accessed January 25, 2014).

25. Noah Smith, "The Dark Side of Globalization: Why the Seattle's 1999 Protesters Were Right," *The Atlantic* (January 6, 2014) at http://www.theatlantic.com/business/archive/2014/01/the-dark-side-of-globalization-why-seattles-1999-protesters-were-right/282831 (accessed March 14, 2014).

26. Globalization 101, "IMF/World Bank" at http://www.globalization101.org/category/issues-in-depth/imfworld-bank / (accessed March 14, 2014).

27. Based on Nancy J. Adler, *International Dimensions of Organizational Behavior*, 4th ed. (Cincinnati, OH: South-Western, 2002); Theodore T. Herbert, "Strategy and Multinational Organizational Structure: An Interorganizational Relationships Perspective," *Academy of Management Review* 9 (1984), 259–271; and Laura K. Rickey, "International Expansion—U.S. Corporations: Strategy, Stages of Development, and Structure" (unpublished manuscript, Vanderbilt University, 1991).

28. S. Prashad, "Couple Bake Their Way to Business Perfection," *Toronto Star* (January 27, 2007), D1, D20.

29. Walmart, "Wal-Mart Reports Record Sales and Earnings" (2003) at http://investors.walmartstores.com/

phoenix.zhtml?c=112761&p=irol-newsArticle&ID=411445&highlight= (accessed June 1, 2011).

30. B. Jopson, "Walmart's US Sales Struggle," FT.com (May 17, 2011) at www.ft.com/cms/s/0/78dd23bc-808a-11e0-adca-00144feabdc0,s01=1.html#axzz1O4QsREpi (accessed March 14, 2014).

31. Michael E. Porter, "Changing Patterns of International Competition," *California Management Review* 28 (Winter 1986), 9–40.

32. William J. Holstein, "The Stateless Corporation," *Business Week* (May 14, 1990), 98–115.

33. Debra Sparks, "Partners," *Business Week*, Special Report: Corporate Finance (October 25, 1999), 106–112.

34. "QLT Inc." at www.qltinc.com/Qlinc/main/mainpages.cfm?InternetPageID=194 (accessed March 14, 2014).

35. David Lei and John W. Slocum, Jr., "Global Strategic Alliances: Payoffs and Pitfalls," *Organizational Dynamics* (Winter 1991), 17–29.

36. Joseph Weber with Amy Barrett, "Volatile Combos," *Business Week*, Special Report: Corporate Finance (October 25, 1999), 122; and Lei and Slocum, "Global Strategic Alliances."

37. Stratford Sherman, "Are Strategic Alliances Working?" *Fortune* (September 21, 1992), 77–78; and David Lei, "Strategies for Global Competition," *Long-Range Planning* 22 (1989), 102–109.

38. J. McDonald, "Chinese Car Companies in Tie-Up," *Toronto Star* (July 31, 2007), B3.

39. Carol Matlack, "Nestlé Is Starting to Slim Down at Last; But Can the World's No. 1 Food Colossus Fatten Up Its Profits As It Slashes Costs?" *Business Week* (October 27, 2003), 56ff.

40. Ron Grover and Richard Siklos, "When Old Foes Need Each Other," *Business Week*, Special Report: Corporate Finance (October 25, 1999), 114, 118.

41. K. Fitchard, "Nortel Used Joint Ventures to Advance in Asian Market," *Telephony* (January 31, 2005), 16–17.

42. "Joint Venture Agreement and Resource Acquisition by Robex," *PR Newswire* (March 8, 2005), 1.

43. "Iron Mine in Quebec and Labrador Closer with Tata Deal," CBC (March 7, 2011) at www.cbc.ca/news/business/story/2011/03/07/iron-ore-quebec-labrador-tata.html (access March 14, 2014).

44. "ICICI Announces General Insurance Foray with Lombard of Canada" (October 1, 2000) at http://www.icicibank.com/pfsuser/aboutus/investorelations/pressrelease/oct04-2000.htm (accessed June 14, 2008).

45. Sparks, "Partners."

46. Sparks, "Partners."

47. Kevin Kelly and Otis Port, with James Treece, Gail DeGeorge, and Zachary Schiller, "Learning from Japan," *Business Week* (January 27, 1992), 52–60; and Gregory G. Dess, Abdul M. A. Rasheed, Kevin J. McLaughlin, and Richard L. Priem, "The New Corporate Architecture," *Academy of Management Executive* 9, no. 3 (1995), 7–20.

48. Brandaid Project, "Vision" (August 10, 2010) at http://brandaidproject.com/about (accessed May 18, 2011).

49. J. Leeder, "Jacmel Artists Win Clinton Bush Grant" (August 10, 2010) at http://www.theglobeandmail.com/news/world/project-jacmel/the-artisans/jacmel-artists-win-clinton-bush-grant/article1668670 (accessed March 14, 2014); and J. Leeder, "A Brandaid Solution for Damaged Artisans" (March 2, 2010), *The Globe and Mail* at www.theglobeandmail.com/news/world/project-jacmel/a-brandaid-solution-for-damaged-artisans/article1486312 (accessed March 14, 2014).

50. CBC News (2013) Haitian Artisan to Sell Products though Hudson Bay's Stores, November 21 at http://www.cbc.ca/news/business/haitian-artisans-to-sell-products-through-hudson-s-bay-stores-1.2435704 (accessed January 25, 2014).

51. Kenichi Ohmae, "Managing in a Borderless World," *Harvard Business Review* (May–June 1989), 152–161.

52. N. Buck, "Tapping into 'A Very Lucrative Market,'" *The Globe and Mail* (June 13, 2007), B6.

53. Constance L. Hays, "From Bentonville to Beijing and Beyond" (December 6, 2004) at www.nytimes.com/2004/12/06/business/businessspecial2/06walmart.html?_r=1&scp=1&sq=bentonville+beijing+hays&st=nyt&oref=slogin (accessed March 14, 2014).

54. Conrad de Aenlle, "Famous Brands Can Bring Benefit, or a Backlash," *The New York Times* (October 19, 2003), Section 3, 7.

55. Cesare R. Mainardi, Martin Salva, and Muir Sanderson, "Label of Origin: Made on Earth," *Strategy & Business* 15 (Second Quarter 1999), 42–53; and Joann S. Lublin, "Place vs. Product: It's Tough to Choose a Management Model," *The Wall Street Journal* (June 27, 2001), A1, A4.

56. Ian Rowley, "Toyota's Watanabe will talk to Ford," *Business Week* (January 15, 2007) at http://www.businessweek.com/stories/2007-01-15/toyotas-watanabe-will-talk-to-ford (accessed April 15, 2014).

57. Gupta and Govindarajan, "Converting Global Presence into Global Competitive Advantage."

58. José Pla-Barber, "From Stopford and Wells's Model to Bartlett and Ghoshal's Typology: New Empirical Evidence," *Management International Review* 42, 2 (2002), 141–156.

59. Sumantra Ghoshal and Nitin Nohria, "Horses for Courses: Organizational Forms for Multinational Corporations," *Sloan Management Review* (Winter 1993), 23–35; and Roderick E. White and Thomas A. Poynter, "Organizing for Worldwide Advantage," *Business Quarterly* (Summer 1989), 84–89.

60. Robert J. Kramer, *Organizing for Global Competitiveness: The Country Subsidiary Design* (New York: The Conference Board, 1997), 12.

61. Laura B. Pincus and James A. Belohlav, "Legal Issues in Multinational Business: To Play the Game, You Have to Know the Rules," *Academy of Management Executive* 10, 3 (1996), 52–61.

62. John D. Daniels, Robert A. Pitts, and Marietta J. Tretter, "Strategy and Structure of U.S. Multinationals: An Exploratory Study," *Academy of Management Journal* 27 (1984), 292–307.

63. Robert J. Kramer, *Organizing for Global Competitiveness: The Product Design* (New York: The Conference Board, 1994).

64. Robert J. Kramer, *Organizing for Global Competitiveness: The Business Unit Design* (New York: The Conference Board, 1995), 18–19.

65. Carol Matlack, "Nestlé Is Starting to Slim Down."

66. Based on Robert J. Kramer, *Organizing for Global Competitiveness: The Geographic Design* (New York: The Conference Board, 1993).

67. Carol Matlack, "Nestlé Is Starting to Slim Down."

68. McCain Foods Limited, "Good Employees" (2014) at http://mccain.com/GOODPEOPLE/EMPLOYEES/Pages/default.aspx (accessed April 10, 2014).

69. "McCain Foods" at http://www.mccain.com/mc_home.htm (accessed August 3, 2007); and D. McMurdy (2001) "Frying the Competition" at www.canadianbusiness.com/shared/print.jsp?content=41265 (accessed July 30, 2007).

70. Ibid.

71. Ibid.

72. "McCain Business Empire has Deep Roots" (March 19, 2004) at www.cbc.ca/money/story/2004/03/19/mccainbiz_040319.html (accessed May 18, 2011).

73. Matthew Karnitschnig, "Identity Question; For Siemens, Move into U.S. Causes Waves Back Home," *The Wall Street Journal* (September 8, 2003) at http://buiznt.cob.calpoly.edu/cob/MGT/Pendergast/Wall%20Street%20Journal/Identity%20Questions%20for%20Siemens.htm (accessed June 9, 2011).

74. B. De Wit and R. Meyer, *Strategy: Process Content, Context, An International Perspective*, 4th ed. (Hampshire, UK: Cengage Learning EMEA, 2010), 210.

75. William Taylor, "The Logic of Global Business: An Interview with ABB's Percy Barnevik," *Harvard Business Review* (March–April 1991), 91–105; Carla Rappaport, "A Tough Swede Invades the U.S.," *Fortune* (January 29, 1992), 76–79; Raymond E. Miles and Charles C. Snow, "The New Network Firm: A Spherical Structure Built on a Human Investment Philosophy," *Organizational Dynamics* (Spring 1995), 5–18; and Manfred F. R. Kets de Vries, "Making a Giant Dance," *Across the Board* (October 1994), 27–32.

76. Gupta and Govindarajan, "Converting Global Presence into Global Competitive Advantage."

77. Robert Frank, "Withdrawal Pains: In Paddies of Vietnam, Americans Once Again Land in a Quagmire," *The Wall Street Journal* (April 21, 2000), A1, A6.

78. "InoWeb" at http://www.inowebinc.com/#home (accessed July 8, 2008).

79. The discussion of these challenges is based on Bartlett and Ghoshal, *Transnational Management*.

80. Paul De Grauwe and F. Camerman, *How Big Are the Big Multinational Companies?* (2002), Working paper.

81. Ian Katz and Elisabeth Malkin, "Battle for the Latin American Net," *BusinessWeek* (November 1, 1999), 194–200; and Pamela Drukerman and Nick Wingfield, "Lost in Translation: AOL's Big Assault in Latin America Hits Snags in Brazil," *The Wall Street Journal* (July 11, 2000), A1; Neil King Jr., "Competition from China and India Is Changing the Way Businesses Operate" and "Little Trouble in Big China."

82. Shirley Leung, "McHaute Cuisine: Armchairs, TVs, and Espresso—Is It McDonald's?" *The Wall Street Journal* (August 30, 2002), A1, A6.

83. Michel Bachman, "How the Hub Found its Center," *Stanford Social Innovation Review* (Winter, 2014), 22.

84. Impact Hub, "What Is Impact Hub" at http://www.impacthub.net/what-is-impact-hub (accessed March 14, 2014).

85. Bachman, "How the Hub Found Its Center," 27.

86. P. Ingrassia, "Industry Is Shopping Abroad for Good Ideas to Apply to Products," *The Wall Street Journal* (April 29, 1985), A1.

87. Based on Gupta and Govindarajan, "Converting Global Presence into Global Competitive Advantage."

88. Vijay Govindarajan and Anil K. Gupta, "Building an Effective Global Business Team," *MIT Sloan Management Review* 42, 4 (Summer 2001), 63–71.

89. Charlene Marmer Solomon, "Building Teams across Borders," *Global Workforce* (November 1998), 12–17.

90. Charles C. Snow, Scott A. Snell, Sue Canney Davison, and Donald C. Hambrick, "Use Transnational Teams to Globalize Your Company," *Organizational Dynamics* 24, 4 (Spring 1996), 50–67.

91. Jane Pickard, "Control Freaks Need Not Apply," *People Management* (February 5, 1998), 49.

92. Snow et al., "Use Transnational Teams to Globalize Your Company."

93. Robert J. Kramer, *Organizing for Global Competitiveness: The Corporate Headquarters Design* (New York: The Conference Board, 1999).

94. Manly and Sorkin, "At Sony, Diplomacy Trumps Technology."

95. These roles are based on Christopher A. Bartlett and Sumantra Ghoshal, *Managing across Borders: The Transnational Solution*, 2nd ed. (Boston, MA: Harvard Business School Press, 1998), 231–249.

96. See Jay Galbraith, "Building Organizations around the Global Customer," *Ivey Business Journal* (September–October 2001), 17–24, for a discussion of both formal and informal lateral networks used in multinational companies.

97. This section is based on Morten T. Hansen and Nitin Nohria, "How to Build Collaborative Advantage," *MIT Sloan Management Review* (Fall 2004), 22ff.

98. Geert Hofstede, "The Interaction between National and Organizational Value Systems," *Journal of Management Studies* 22 (1985), 347–357; and Geert Hofstede, *Cultures and Organizations: Software of the Mind* (London: McGraw-Hill, 1991).

99. Geert Hofstede "Cultural Dimensions" at http://www .geert-hofstede.com (accessed July 8, 2008).

100. Dimensions of National Cultures, at www .geerthofstede.nl/culture/dimensions-of-national -cultures.aspx (accessed May 18, 2011).

101. This discussion is based on "Culture and Organization," Reading 2–2 in Christopher A. Bartlett and Sumantra Ghoshal, *Transnational Management*, 3rd ed. (Boston, MA: Irwin McGraw-Hill, 2000), 191–216, excerpted from Susan Schneider and Jean-Louis Barsoux, *Managing across Cultures* (London: Prentice Hall, 1997).

102. See Mansour Javidan and Robert J. House, "Cultural Acumen for the Global Manager: Lessons from Project GLOBE," *Organizational Dynamics* 29, no. 4 (2001), 289–305; and R. J. House, M. Javidan, Paul Hanges, and Peter Dorfman, "Understanding Cultures and Implicit Leadership Theories across the Globe: An Introduction to Project GLOBE," *Journal of World Business* 37 (2002), 3–10.

103. R. R. Gesteland, *Cross-Cultural Business Behaviour* (Copenhagen: Handelshojskolens Forlag, 1997).

104. Based on Bartlett and Ghoshal, *Managing across Borders*, 181–201.

105. Martin Hemmert, "International Organization of R&D and Technology Acquisition Performance of High-Tech Business Units," *Management International Review* 43, 4 (2003), 361–382.

106. Jean Lee, "Culture and Management—A Study of a Small Chinese Family Business in Singapore," *Journal of Small Business Management* 34, 3 (July 1996), 63ff; "Olivier Blanchard and Andrei Shleifer, "Federalism with and without Political Centralization: China versus Russia," *IMF Staff Papers* 48 (2001), 171ff.

107. Nailin Bu, Timothy J. Craig, and T. K. Peng, "Reactions to Authority," *Thunderbird International Business. Review* 43, 6 (November–December 2001), 773–795.

108. Sumantra Ghoshal and Christopher Bartlett, "The Multinational Corporation as an Inter-organizational Network," *Academy of Management Review* 15 (1990), 603–625.

109. The description of the transnational organization is based on Bartlett and Ghoshal, *Transnational Management* and *Managing across Borders*.

# Chapter 7

1. Adam Azimov, VIDEO: Manitobah Mukluks—Behind the Boots Worn by Kate Moss and Megan Fox, CBC Live (February 12, 2012), from http://www.cbc.ca/ live/manitobah-mukluks-the-story-behind-the-boots- worn-by-kate-moss-and-megan-fox-1.html (accessed March 14, 2014).

2. Manitobah Mukluks History, from http://www .manitobah.ca/manitobahhistory.php (accessed September 16, 2013).

3. Sean McCormick (Manitobah Mukluks), Facebook Q&A (August 14, 2012) at https://www.facebook.com/ manitobahmukluks/posts/515611181798614 (accessed March 14, 2014).

4. Authenticity (Manitobah Mukluks), from http://www .manitobah.ca/authenticity.php (accessed September 16, 2013).

5. Charles Perrow, "A Framework for the Comparative Analysis of Organizations," *American Sociological Review* 32 (1967), 194–208; and R. J. Schonberger, *World Class Manufacturing: The Next Decade* (New York: The Free Press, 1996).

6. Linda Argote, "Input Uncertainty and Organizational Coordination in Hospital Emergency Units," *Administrative Science Quarterly* 27 (1982), 420–434; Charles Perrow, *Organizational Analysis: A Sociological Approach* (Belmont, CA: Wadsworth, 1970); and William Rushing, "Hardness of Material as Related to the Division of Labor in Manufacturing Industries," *Administrative Science Quarterly* 13 (1968), 229–245.

7. Lawrence B. Mohr, "Organizational Technology and Organization Structure," *Administrative Science Quarterly* 16 (1971), 444–459; and David Hickson, Derek Pugh, and Diana Pheysey, "Operations Technology and Organization Structure: An Empirical Reappraisal," *Administrative Science Quarterly* 14 (1969), 378–397.

8. Joan Woodward, *Industrial Organization: Theory and Practice* (London: Oxford University Press, 1965); and Joan Woodward, *Management and Technology* (London: Her Majesty's Stationery Office, 1958).

9. Hickson, Pugh, and Pheysey, "Operations Technology and Organization Structure"; and James D. Thompson, *Organizations in Action* (New York: McGraw-Hill, 1967).

10. Edward Harvey, "Technology and the Structure of Organizations," *American Sociological Review* 33 (1968), 241–259.

11. Wanda J. Orlikowski, "The Duality of Technology: Rethinking the Concept of Technology in Organizations," *Organization Science* 3 (1992), 398–427.

12. Based on Woodward, *Industrial Organization and Management and Technology*.

13. Diane McCurdy "You, Inc." (September 2007) at www .chatelaine.com/english/moneymavens/article.jsp?content= 20070607_155708_4940 (accessed June 16, 2008).

14. Kiln Art, "About Us" at http://www.kilnart.ca/aboutus .php (accessed July 10, 2008).

15. Woodward, *Industrial Organization*, vi.

16. "Maple Leaf Foods Recovers from Listeria Crisis," *Toronto Star*, July 29, 2009, at www.thestar.com/ article/673527 (accessed March 14, 2014).

17. T. Perkins, "Old Dogs New Tricks," *The Globe and Mail* (February 25, 2011), B1, B4.

18. William L. Zwerman, New Perspectives on *Organizational Theory* (Westport, Conn.: Greenwood, 1970); and Harvey, "Technology and the Structure of Organizations."

19. Dean M. Schroeder, Steven W. Congden, and C. Gopinath, "Linking Competitive Strategy and Manufacturing Process Technology," *Journal of Management Studies* 32, 2 (March 1995), 163–189.

20. "What's New" at http://www.doepker.com/what'snew.html (accessed June 16, 2008).

21. Ibid.

22. Ibid.

23. Fernando F. Suarez, Michael A. Cusumano, and Charles H. Fine, "An Empirical Study of Flexibility in Manufacturing," *Sloan Management Review* (Fall 1995), 25–32.

24. Raymond F. Zammuto and Edward J. O'Connor, "Gaining Advanced Manufacturing Technologies' Benefits: The Roles of Organization Design and Culture," *Academy of Management Review* 17, no. 4 (1992), 701–728; and Schroeder, Congden, and Gopinath, "Linking Competitive Strategy and Manufacturing Process Technology."

25. John Baldwin and Ryan Macdonald, "The Canadian Manufacturing Sector: Adapting to Challenges," Statistics Canada (July 2009) at http://www.statcan.gc.ca/pub/11f0027m/11f0027m2009057-eng.pdf (accessed March 14, 2014).

26. C. Rogers, "Pacesetting Strategies for the Paper Industry," *Pulp & Paper Canada* 107, 1 (2006), 30.

27. Colleen Cosgrove, "Signs of Success for Eyecandy," *Chronicle Herald Business* (February 28, 2012) at http://thechronicleherald.ca/business/68161-signs-success-eyecandy (accessed March 14, 2014).

28. Josh O'Kane, "Marketing Ye Olde Handcrafted Signs in a Digital Age," *The Globe and Mail* (January 23, 2014) at http://www.theglobeandmail.com/report-on-business/small-business/sb-growth/the-challenge/marketing-ye-olde-handcrafted-charm-in-a-digital-age/article16431977/ (accessed March 14, 2014).

29. Jack R. Meredith, "The Strategic Advantages of the Factory of the Future," *California Management Review* 29 (Spring 1987), 27–41; Jack Meredith, "The Strategic Advantages of the New Manufacturing Technologies for Small Firms," *Strategic Management Journal* 8 (1987), 249–258; and Althea Jones and Terry Webb, "Introducing Computer Integrated Manufacturing," *Journal of General Management* 12 (Summer 1987), 60–74.

30. Raymond F. Zammuto and Edward J. O'Connor, "Gaining Advanced Manufacturing Technologies' Benefits: The Roles of Organization Design and Culture," *Academy of Management Review* 17 (1992), 701–728.

31. "Weyerhaeuser's BC Coastal Group Units Achieve New Certifications" (December 5, 2000) at http://forests.org/archive/Canada/weybccgr.htm (March 14,

2014); Ann Armstrong, "Chemainus Sawmill Division of MacMillan Bloedel: Its Pay for Knowledge and Skill System," *ASTD Casebook Volume II* (1999).

32. Paul S. Adler, "Managing Flexible Automation," *California Management Review* (Spring 1988), 34–56.

33. Bela Gold, "Computerization in Domestic and International Manufacturing," *California Management Review* (Winter 1989), 129–143.

34. Graham Dudley and John Hassard, "Design Issues in the Development of Computer Integrated Manufacturing (CIM)," *Journal of General Management* 16 (1990), 43–53; David M. Upton, "What Really Makes Factories Flexible?" *Harvard Business Review* (July–August 1995), 74–84.

35. ShoeInfoNet at www.shoeinfonet.com/technology/cad%20cam/NA/cadcam_ca.htm (accessed June 16, 2008).

36. news.delcam, Issue 1 (2007), 12.

37. Tom Massung, "Manufacturing Efficiency," *Microsoft Executive Circle* (Winter 2004), 28–29; and 3DS (2010) Tesla Motors Selects Dassault Systèmes' V6 PLM Solution, September 29 athttp://www.3ds.com/press-releases/single/tesla-motors-selects-dassault-systemes-v6-plm-solution/ (accessed March 14, 2014).

38. Brian Heymans, "Leading the Lean Enterprise," *Industrial Management* (September–October 2002), 28–33; and Fara Warner, "Think Lean," *Fast Company* (February 2002), 40, 42.

39. "New LEI Case Study—Canada Post" (August 26, 2005) at www.leanblog.org/2005/08/new-lei-case-study-canada-post.html (accessed June 16, 2008).

40. Canadian College of Health Service Executives, 3M Health Care Quality Team Awards (2010), 8.

41. A. Dresseckie, "'Lean' Helps to Improve Long-term Care Placement Process" (2010) at www.centraleastlhin.on.ca/newsroom_display.aspx?id=16474 (accessed March 14, 2014).

42. N. Nayab, "Criticism of Lean Manufacturing" (August 2, 2011) at http://www.brighthubpm.com/methods-strategies/105933-criticism-of-lean-manufacturing/ (accessed March 14, 2014).

43. Michael McCollough, Lean Manufacturing's Oversized Claims, *Canadian Business* (October 20, 2011) at http://www.canadianbusiness.com/business-strategy/lean-manufacturings-oversized-claims/ (accessed March 14, 2014).

44. Peter Strozniak, "Toyota Alters Face of Production," *IndustryWeek* (August 13, 2001), 46–48.

45. Jake Stiles, "Lean Initiatives Help Sealy Prepare for Market Rebound," *IndustryWeek.com* (May 6, 2009) http://www.industryweek.com/articles/lean_initiatives_help_sealy_-prepare_for_market_rebound_19073.aspx?ShowAll=1 (accessed March 14, 2014); "Stiles Associates, LLC: Lean Companies Gain Even Greater Edge in Recessionary Times," *Science Letter* (March 17, 2009), 4089; Paul Davidson, "Lean Manufacturing

Helps Companies Survive Recession," *USA Today*, November 1, 2009; and "About Sealy: Environmental Footprint," Sealy.com, http://www.sealy.com/About-Sealy/Environmental-Footprint.aspx (accessed August 17, 2011).

46. Mora Baird, "Garrison Guitars Sold to Gibson," *The Telegram* (July 4, 2007) at http://www.thetelegram.com/Employment/2007-07-04/article-1446367/Garrison-Guitars-sold-to-Gibson/1 (accessed March 30, 2014).

47. T. Shufelt, "Gibson Grooves on Garrison's Guitars," *The Globe and Mail* (July 5, 2007), B5.

48. A. Holloway, "Between the Rock and a Hard Place," *Canadian Business* (December 2004).

49. T. Shufelt, "Gibson Grooves on Garrison's Guitars."

50. B. Joseph Pine II, *Mass Customization: The New Frontier in Business Competition* (Boston: Harvard Business School Press, 1999).

51. Barry Berman, "Should Your Firm Adopt a Mass Customization Strategy?" *Business Horizons* (July–August 2002), 51–60.

52. Erick Schonfeld, "The Customized, Digitized, Have-It-Your-Way Economy," *Fortune* (September 28, 1998), 115–124; and Joann Muller, "BMW's Push for Made-to-Order Cars," *Forbes*, September 9, 2010) at http://www.forbes.com/forbes/2010/0927/companies-bmw-general-motors-cars-bespoke-auto.html (accessed April 15, 2014).

53. Grainger David, "One Truck a Minute," and Scott McMurray, "Ford F-150: Have It Your Way," *Business 2.0* (March 2004), 53–55.

54. Julie Bort, "REPORT: Dell Layoffs Are About to Hit And Could Be Huge, *Business Insider* (January 9, 2014) at http://www.businessinsider.com/report-of-layoffs-at-dell-2014-1 (accessed March 14, 2014).

55. Kathryn Jones, "The Dell Way," *Business 2.0* (February 2003), 61–66; Stewart Deck, "Fine Line," CIO (February 1, 2000), 88–92; Andy Serwer, "Dell Does Domination," *Fortune* (January 21, 2002), 71–75; and Betsy Morris, "Can Michael Dell Escape the Box?" *Fortune* (October 16, 2000), 93–110.

56. A. Vance, "Suit over Faulty Computers Highlights Dell's Decline," *The New York Times* (June 28, 2010) at www.nytimes.com/2010/06/29/technology/29dell.html (accessed March 14, 2014).

57. Joel D. Goldhar and David Lei, "Variety Is Free: Manufacturing in the Twenty-First Century," *Academy of Management Executive* no. 4 (1995), 73–86.

58. Meredith, "The Strategic Advantages of the Factory of the Future."

59. Patricia L. Nemetz and Louis W. Fry, "Flexible Manufacturing Organizations: Implementations for Strategy Formulation and Organization Design," *Academy of Management Review* 13 (1988), 627–638; Paul S. Adler, "Managing Flexible Automation," *California Management Review* (Spring 1988), 34–56; Jeremy

Main, "Manufacturing the Right Way," *Fortune* (May 21, 1990), 54–64; and Frank M. Hull and Paul D. Collins, "High-Technology Batch Production Systems: Woodward's Missing Type," *Academy of Management Journal* 30 (1987), 786–797.

60. Goldhar and Lei, "Variety Is Free: Manufacturing in the Twenty-First Century"; P. Robert Duimering, Frank Safayeni, and Lyn Purdy, "Integrated Manufacturing: Redesign the Organization before Implementing Flexible Technology," *Sloan Management Review* (Summer 1993), 47–56; Zammuto and O'Connor, "Gaining Advanced Manufacturing Technologies' Benefits."

61. Goldhar and Lei, "Variety Is Free: Manufacturing in the Twenty-First Century."

62. "Manufacturing's Decline," *Johnson City Press* (July 17, 1999), 9; Ronald Henkoff, "Service Is Everybody's Business," *Fortune* (June 27, 1994), 48–60; Ronald Henkoff, "Finding, Training, and Keeping the Best Service Workers," *Fortune* (October 3, 1994), 110–122.

63. S. M. Goldstein, R. Johnston, J. Duffy, and J. Rao, "Service Concept: The Missing Link in Service Design Research?" *Journal of Operations Management* 20, 2 (2002), 121.

64. Byron J. Finch and Richard L. Luebbe, *Operations Management: Competing in a Changing Environment* (Fort Worth, Tex.: The Dryden Press, 1995), 51.

65. David E. Bowen, Caren Siehl, and Benjamin Schneider, "A Framework for Analyzing Customer Service Orientations in Manufacturing," *Academy of Management Review* 14 (1989), 79–95; Peter K. Mills and Newton Margulies, "Toward a Core Typology of Service Organizations," *Academy of Management Review* 5 (1980), 255–265; Peter K. Mills and Dennis J. Moberg, "Perspectives on the Technology of Service Operations," *Academy of Management Review* 7 (1982), 467–478; and G. Lynn Shostack, "Breaking Free from Product Marketing," *Journal of Marketing* (April 1977), 73–80.

66. A. Zimmerman, "Home Depot Tries to Make Nice to Customers," *The Wall Street Journal* (February 20, 2007), D1.

67. "Ken, Greta and Phyllis Rempel Win BDC's Young Entrepreneur Award for Manitoba" (October 18, 2005) at www.bdc.ca/en/about/mediaroom/news_releases/2005/2005101810.htm (accessed June 16, 2008).

68. Ron Zemke, "The Service Revolution: Who Won?" *Management Review* (March 1997), 10–15; and Wayne Wilhelm and Bill Rossello, "The Care and Feeding of Customers," *Management Review* (March 1997), 19–23.

69. Schonfeld, "The Customized, Digitized, Have-It-Your-Way Economy."

70. Paul Migliorato, "Toyota Retools Japan," *Business 2.0* (August 2004), 39–41.

71. Richard B. Chase and David A. Tansik, "The Customer Contact Model for Organization Design," *Management Science* 29 (1983), 1037–1050.

72. Ibid.

73. David E. Bowen and Edward E. Lawler III, "The Empowerment of Service Workers: What, Why, How, and When," *Sloan Management Review* (Spring 1992), 31–39; Gregory B. Northcraft and Richard B. Chase, "Managing Service Demand at the Point of Delivery," *Academy of Management Review* 10 (1985), 66–75; and Roger W. Schmenner, "How Can Service Businesses Survive and Prosper?" *Sloan Management Review* 27 (Spring 1986), 21–32.

74. "About Our Company" at http://www.pret.com/about (accessed June 16, 2008).

75. "Our Customers" at http://www.pret.com/about/customers.htm (accessed June 16, 2008).

76. Scott Kirsner, "Recipe for Reinvention," *Fast Company* (April 2002), 38–42.

77. Richard Metters and Vincente Vargas, "Organizing Work in Service Firms," *Business Horizons* (July–August 2000), 23–32.

78. K. K. Boyer, R. Hallowell, and A. V. Roth, "E-services: Operating Strategy—A Case Study and a Method for Analyzing Operational Benefits," *Journal of Operations Management* 20, 2 (2002), 178.

79. Ibid.

80. Ibid.

81. Joel, "F-commerce: Rise of the Facebook Consumer, *The Vancouver Sun* (March 18, 2010) at www.vancouversun.com/news/commerce+Rise+Facebook+consumer/4462774/story.html (accessed June 2, 2011).

82. P. Marsden, "F-commerce" (April 4, 2011) at http://socialcommercetoday.com/f-commerce-statistics-roundup-facebook-commerce-by-the-numbers/ (accessed June 2, 2011).

83. A. Semuels, "U.S. Retail Workers Latest Casualty of Automation," *Toronto Star* (March 12, 2011), A11.

84. Perrow, "A Framework for Comparative Analysis" and *Organizational Analysis*.

85. Brian T. Pentland, "Sequential Variety in Work Processes," *Organization Science* 14, 5 (September–October 2003), 528–540.

86. Jim Morrison, "Grand Tour. Making Music: The Craft of the Steinway Piano," *Spirit* (February 1997), 42–49, 100.

87. Stuart F. Brown, "Biotech Gets Productive," *Fortune*, special section, "*Industrial Management and Technology*" (January 20, 2003), 170[A]–170[H].

88. Michael Withey, Richard L. Daft, and William C. Cooper, "Measures of Perrow's Work Unit Technology: An Empirical Assessment and a New Scale," *Academy of Management Journal* 25 (1983), 45–63.

89. Christopher Gresov, "Exploring Fit and Misfit with Multiple Contingencies," *Administrative Science Quarterly* 34 (1989), 431–453; and Dale L. Goodhue and Ronald L. Thompson, "Task-Technology Fit and Individual Performance," *MIS Quarterly* (June 1995), 213–236.

90. Gresov, "Exploring Fit and Misfit with Multiple Contingencies"; Charles A. Glisson, "Dependence of Technological Routinization on Structural Variables in Human Service Organizations," *Administrative Science Quarterly* 23 (1978), 383–395; and Jerald Hage and Michael Aiken, "Routine Technology, Social Structure and Organizational Goals," *Administrative Science Quarterly* 14 (1969), 368–379.

91. Gresov, "Exploring Fit and Misfit with Multiple Contingencies"; A. J. Grimes and S. M. Kline, "The Technological Imperative: The Relative Impact of Task Unit, Modal Technology, and Hierarchy on Structure," *Academy of Management Journal* 16 (1973), 583–597; Lawrence G. Hrebiniak, "Job Technologies, Supervision and Work Group Structure," *Administrative Science Quarterly* 19 (1974), 395–410; and Jeffrey Pfeffer, *Organizational Design* (Arlington Heights, IL: AHM, 1978), Chapter 1.

92. Patrick E. Connor, *Organizations: Theory and Design* (Chicago: Science Research Associates, 1980); Richard L. Daft and Norman B. Macintosh, "A Tentative Exploration into Amount and Equivocality of Information Processing in Organizational Work Units," *Administrative Science Quarterly* 26 (1981), 207–224.

93. Paul D. Collins and Frank Hull, "Technology and Span of Control: Woodward Revisited," *Journal of Management Studies* 23 (1986), 143–164; Gerald D. Bell, "The Influence of Technological Components of Work upon Management Control," *Academy of Management Journal* 8 (1965), 127–132; and Peter M. Blau and Richard A. Schoenherr, *The Structure of Organizations* (New York: Basic Books, 1971).

94. W. Alan Randolph, "Matching Technology and the Design of Organization Units," *California Management Review* 22–23 (1980–81), 39–48; Daft and Macintosh, "Tentative Exploration into Amount and Equivocality of Information Processing"; and Michael L. Tushman, "Work Characteristics and Subunit Communication Structure: A Contingency Analysis," *Administrative Science Quarterly* 24 (1979), 82–98.

95. Andrew H. Van de Ven and Diane L. Ferry, *Measuring and Assessing Organizations* (New York: Wiley, 1980); and Randolph, "Matching Technology and the Design of Organization Units."

96. Richard L. Daft and Robert H. Lengel, "Information Richness: A New Approach to Managerial Behavior and Organization Design," in Barry Staw and Larry L. Cummings, eds., *Research in Organizational Behavior,* vol. 6 (Greenwich, CT: JAI Press, 1984), 191–233; Richard L. Daft and Norman B. Macintosh, "A New Approach into Design and Use of Management Information," *California Management Review* 21 (1978), 82–92; Daft and Macintosh, "A Tentative Exploration into Amount and Equivocality of Information Processing"; W. Alan Randolph, "Organizational Technology and the Media and Purpose Dimensions of

Organizational Communication," *Journal of Business Research* 6 (1978), 237–259; Linda Argote, "Input Uncertainty and Organizational Coordination in Hospital Emergency Units," *Administrative Science Quarterly* 27 (1982), 420–434; and Andrew H. Van de Ven and Andre Delbecq, "A Task Contingent Model of Work Unit Structure," *Administrative Science Quarterly* 19 (1974), 183–197.

97. Peggy Leatt and Rodney Schneck, "Criteria for Grouping Nursing Subunits in Hospitals," *Academy of Management Journal* 27 (1984), 150–165; and Robert T. Keller, "Technology-Information Processing," *Academy of Management Journal* 37, 1 (1994), 167–179.

98. Gresov, "Exploring Fit and Misfit with Multiple Contingencies"; Michael L. Tushman, "Technological Communication in R&D Laboratories: The Impact of Project Work Characteristics," *Academy of Management Journal* 21 (1978), 624–645; and Robert T. Keller, "Technology-Information Processing Fit and the Performance of R&D Project Groups: A Test of Contingency Theory," *Academy of Management Journal* 37, 1 (1994), 167–179.

99. Richard I. Litwin, "Govindappa Venkataswamy, MD: 1918 to 2006," Cataract & Refractive Surgery Today (September 2006), 1.

100. R. Rubin, "The Perfect Vision of Dr. V.," *Fast Company*, January, 43 (2001), 146.

101. Ibid.

102. James Thompson, *Organizations in Action* (New York: McGraw-Hill, 1967).

103. Ibid., 40.

104. Gene Bylinsky, "Shipmaking Gets Modern," *Fortune*, special section, "*Industrial Management* and Technology" (January 20, 2003), 170[K]–170[L].

105. Paul S. Adler, "Interdepartmental Interdependence and Coordination: The Case of the Design/Manufacturing Interface," *Organization Science* 6, 2 (March–April 1995), 147–167.

106. R. Dyck, "Team-based Organization at Celestica," *Journal for Quality and Participation* (September–October 1999).

107. Christopher Gresov, "Effects of Dependence and Tasks on Unit Design and Efficiency," *Organization Studies* 11 (1990), 503–529; Andrew H. Van de Ven, Andre Delbecq, and Richard Koenig, "Determinants of Coordination Modes within Organizations," *American Sociological Review* 41 (1976), 322–338; Linda Argote, "Input Uncertainty and Organizational Coordination in Hospital Emergency Units"; Jack K. Ito and Richard B. Peterson, "Effects of Task Difficulty and Interdependence on Information Processing Systems," *Academy of Management Journal* 29 (1986), 139–149; and Joseph L. C. Cheng, "Interdependence and Coordination in Organizations: A Role-System Analysis," *Academy of Management Journal* 26 (1983), 156–162.

108. Robert W. Keidel, "Team Sports Models as a Generic Organizational Framework," *Human Relations* 40 (1987), 591–612; Robert W. Keidel, "Baseball, Football, and Basketball: Models for Business," *Organizational Dynamics* (Winter 1984), 5–18; and Nancy Katz, "Sports Teams as a Model for Workplace Teams: Lessons and Liabilities," *Academy of Management Executive* 15, 3 (2001), 56–67.

109. Michel Liu, Hélène Denis, Harvey Kolodny, and Bengt Stymne, "Organization Design for Technological Change," *Human Relations* 43 (January 1990), 7–22.

110. Stephen P. Robbins, *Organizational Behavior* (Upper Saddle River, NJ: Prentice Hall, 1998), 521.

111. Gerald I. Susman and Richard B. Chase, "A Sociotechnical Analysis of the Integrated Factory," *Journal of Applied Behavioral Science* 22 (1986), 257–270; and Paul Adler, "New Technologies, New Skills," *California Management Review* 29 (Fall 1986), 9–28.

112. Based on Don Hellriegel, John W. Slocum, Jr., and Richard W. Woodman, *Organizational Behavior*, 8th ed. (Cincinnati, OH: South-Western, 1998), 491–495; and Gregory B. Northcraft and Margaret A. Neale, *Organizational Behavior: A Management Challenge*, 2nd ed. (Fort Worth, TX: The Dryden Press, 1994), 550–553.

113. W.F. Cascio, *Managing Human Resources* (New York: McGraw-Hill, 1986), 19.

114. F. Emery, "Characteristics of Sociotechnical Systems," Tavistock Institute of *Human Relations*, document 527 (1959); William Pasmore, Carol Francis, and Jeffrey Haldeman, "Sociotechnical Systems: A North American Reflection on Empirical Studies of the 70s," *Human Relations* 35 (1982), 1179–1204; and William M. Fox, "Sociotechnical System Principles and Guidelines: Past and Present," *Journal of Applied Behavioral Science* 31, 1 (March 1995), 91–105.

115. Albert Cherns, The Principles of Sociotechnical Design, *Human Relations*, 29, 8 (1976), 783–792; Eric Trist and Hugh Murray, eds., *The Social Engagement of Social Science: A Tavistock Anthology*, vol. II (Philadelphia: University of Pennsylvania Press, 1993); and William A. Pasmore, "Social Science Transformed: The Socio-Technical Perspective," *Human Relations* 48, 1 (1995), 1–21.

116. Ann Armstrong, "Pay for Knowledge and Skill Systems: A Multilevel Exploratory Investigation," Doctoral Dissertation (1993), University of Toronto; Normand Charron, HR Manager, GE Aviation, Bromont, Personal Communication (April 17, 2008).

117. A. Bruns, "Something in the Air," *Site Selection* (September, 2005).

118. R. E. Walton, "From Control to Commitment in the Workplace," *Harvard Business Review* 63, no. 2 (1985), 76–84; E. W. Lawler, III, High Involvement Management (London: Jossey-Bass, 1986), 84; and

Hellriegel, Slocum, and Woodman, *Organizational Behavior*, 491.

119. J. C. Taylor and D. F. Felten, *Performance by Design: Sociotechnical Systems in North America* (Upper Saddle River, NJ: Prentice Hall, 1993).

120. William A. Pasmore, "Social Science Transformed: The Socio-Technical Perspective," *Human Relations* 48, 1 (1995), 1–21.

121. Pasmore, "Social Science Transformed: The Socio-Technical Perspective"; H. Scarborough, "Review Article: The Social Engagement of Social Science: A Tavistock Anthology, Vol. II," *Human Relations* 48, 1 (1995), 23–33.

## Chapter 8

1. RCMP Interpol Ottawa (February 2, 2007) at www.rcmp-grc.gc.ca/intpolicing/interpol_e.htm (accessed June 18, 2008).

2. "Secretary General of Interpol to Visit Canada from March 29–31" (March 23, 2005) at www.rcmp-grc.gc.ca/news/2005/adv_0504_e.htm (accessed September 21, 2007).

3. Chuck Salter, "Terrorists Strike Fast ... Interpol Has to Move Faster…Ron Noble Is on the Case," *Fast Company* (October 2002), 96–104; and "Interpol Pushing to Be UN Globocop," *The New American* (November 1, 2004), 8.

4. James Q. Wilson, *Bureaucracy* (New York: Basic Books, 1989); and Charles Perrow, *Complex Organizations: A Critical Essay* (Glenview, IL: Scott, Foresman, 1979), 4.

5. Tom Peters, "Rethinking Scale," *California Management Review* (Fall 1992), 7–29.

6. Government of Canada, "GE Canada, Complete Profile" (2011) at www.ic.gc.ca/app/ccc/srch/nvgt.do?sbPrtl=&prtl=1&estblmntNo=900401970000&profile=cmpltPrfl&profileId=1421&app=sold&lang=eng (accessed June 3, 2011).

7. B. Jang, "CPR Eyes Big League of U.S. Carriers," *The Globe and Mail* (September 6, 2007), B1.

8. Matt Murray, "Critical Mass: As Huge Companies Keep Growing, CEOs Struggle to Keep Pace," *The Wall Street Journal* (February 8, 2001), A1, A6.

9. Stuart Elliott, "Advertising's Big Four: It's Their World Now," *The New York Times* (March 31, 2002), Section 3, 1, 10.

10. Donald V. Potter, "Scale Matters," *Across the Board* (July–August 2000), 36–39.

11. Entrepreneur, *National Post*, January 29, 2007, FP14.

12. Barb Gormely, "Toronto's Neal Brothers Aims to Sell Speciality Organic Foods from Coast to Coast," *Star Business Club* (January 21, 2014) at http://www.starbusinessclub.ca/sales/torontos-neal-brothers-aims-to-sell-speciality-organic-foods-from-coast-to-coast/ (accessed March 17, 2014).

13. D. Calleja, "Get Big—or Die Tryin'," *The Globe and Mail* (June 22, 2007).

14. James B. Treece, "Sometimes, You've Still Gotta Have Size," *BusinessWeek/Enterprise* (1993), 200–201.

15. Frits K. Pil and Matthias Holweg, "Exploring Scale: The Advantages of Thinking Small," MIT *Sloan Management Review* (Winter 2003), 33–39.

16. F. Taylor, "Theratech Drug Gets Encouraging Word," *The Globe and Mail* (September 21, 2007), B15.

17. David Friedman, "Is Big Back? Or Is Small Still Beautiful?" *Inc.* (April 1998), 23–28.

18. David Henry, "Mergers: Why Most Big Deals Don't Pay Off," *BusinessWeek* (October 14, 2002), 60–70.

19. Keith H. Hammonds, "Size Is Not a Strategy," *Fast Company* (September 2002), 78–86.

20. See Hammonds, "Size Is Not a Strategy"; Henry, "Mergers: Why Most Big Deals Don't Pay Off"; and Tom Brown, "How Big Is Too Big?" *Across the Board* (July–August 1999), 15–20, for a discussion.

21. Industry Awards Recognize CATD Canada Trust's Customer Service, at www.makeitbusiness.com/featurearticles/THE-RBCs-OF-LENDING (accessed May 18, 2011).

22. "Key Small Business Financing Statistics" at http://sme-fdi.gc.ca/epic/site/sme_fdi-prf_pme.nsf/en/01259e.html (accessed September 17, 2007).

23. L. Earl, "Are Small Businesses Positioning Themselves for Growth? A Comparative Look at the Use of Selected Management Practices by Firm Size," Statistics Canada, 2006.

24. "The Hot 100," *Fortune* (September 5, 2005), 75–80.

25. Gary Hamel, quoted in Hammonds, "Size Is Not a Strategy."

26. Richard A. Melcher, "How Goliaths Can Act Like Davids," *BusinessWeek/Enterprise* (1993), 192–201.

27. N. Merchant, "Apple's Startup Culture," Bloomberg *BusinessWeek* (June 14, 2010) at www.businessweek.com/print/innovate/content/jun2010/id20100610_525759.htm (accessed May 18, 2011).

28. Melcher, "How Goliaths Can Act like Davids."

29. Hammonds, "Size Is Not a Strategy."

30. John R. Kimberly, Robert H. Miles, and associates, *The Organizational Life Cycle* (San Francisco: Jossey-Bass, 1980); Ichak Adices, "Organizational Passages—Diagnosing and Treating Lifecycle Problems of Organizations," *Organizational Dynamics* (Summer 1979), 3–25; Danny Miller and Peter H. Friesen, "A Longitudinal Study of the Corporate Life Cycle," *Management Science* 30 (October 1984), 1161–1183; and Neil C. Churchill and Virginia L. Lewis, "The Five Stages of Small Business Growth," *Harvard Business Review* 61 (May–June 1983), 30–50.

31. Sales Increase! *The Grackle View* (March 31, 2007) at http://gracklecoffee.com/Grackle%20View%20newsletter%20Q1-2007.pdf (accessed May 18, 2011).

32. Graph-tastic! *The Grackle View* (January 2014) at http://www.gracklecoffee.com/Grackle%20View%20newsletter%20Q1-2014.pdf (accessed January 29, 2014).

33. Larry E. Greiner, "Evolution and Revolution as Organizations Grow," *Harvard Business Review* 50 (July–August 1972), 37–46; and Robert E. Quinn and Kim Cameron, "Organizational Life Cycles and Shifting Criteria of Effectiveness: Some Preliminary Evidence," *Management Science* 29 (1983), 33–51.

34. George Land and Beth Jarman, "Moving beyond Breakpoint," in Michael Ray and Alan Rinzler, eds., *The New Paradigm* (New York: Jeremy P. Tarcher/Perigee Books, 1993), 250–266; and Michael L. Tushman, William H. Newman, and Elaine Romanelli, "Convergence and Upheaval: Managing the Unsteady Pace of Organizational Evolution," *California Management Review* 29 (1987), 1–16.

35. Adam Lashinsky, "Google Hires a Grown-Up," *Business 2.0* (February 2002), 22.

36. R. Stross, "A Window of Opportunity for Macs, Soon to Close" (September 16, 2007) at www.nytimes.com/2007/09/16/technology/16digi.html?_r=1&sq=window%20opportunity%20macs%20soon%20to%20close&st=nyt&oref=slogin&scp=1&pagewanted=print (accessed March 17, 2014).

37. M. Tilman, "iPad Sales Expanding to All Best Buy Stores" (September 14, 2010), *MacLife* at www.maclife.com/article/ipad/ipad_sales_expanding_all_best_buy_stores_sept_26th (accessed March 17, 2014).

38. David A. Whetten, "Sources, Responses, and Effects of Organizational Decline," in John R. Kimberly, Robert H. Miles, and associates, *The Organizational Life Cycle*, 342–374.

39. Brent Schlender, "How Big Can Apple Get?" *Fortune* (February 21, 2005), 67–76; and Josh Quittner with Rebecca Winters, "Apple's New Core—Exclusive: How Steve Jobs Made a Sleek Machine That Could Be the Home-Digital Hub of the Future," *Time* (January 14, 2002), 46.

40. D. Tweney, "Apple Passes Microsoft as World's Largest Tech Company," *Wired*, May 26,2010) at www.wired.com/epicenter/2010/05/apple-passes-microsoft (accessed March 18, 2014); Rick Whiting, "The 25 Biggest Tech Companies on the Fortune 500,"(May 14, 2010) at http://www.crn.com/slide-shows/channel-programs/240154736/the-25-biggest-tech-companies-on-the-fortune-500.htm/pgno/0/25?itc=nextpage (accessed March 30, 2014).

41. Land and Jarman, "Moving beyond Breakpoint."

42. D. Black, "Sam the Record Man Finally Signs Off" (May 30, 2007) at www.thestar.com/printArticle/219252 (accessed May 18, 2011).

43. Stanley Holmes, "The New Nike," *BusinessWeek* (September 20, 2004), 78–86.

44. Daniel Roth, "Can Nike Still Do It without Phil Knight?" *Fortune* (April 4, 2005), 58–68.

45. Global Exchange, "Sweatfree Communities" (October 28, 2007) at www.globalexchange.org/campaigns/sweatshops/nike/faq.html (accessed July 11, 2008).

46. A. Bernstein "Online Extra: Nike's New Game Plan for Sweatshops" (September 20, 2004) at www.businessweek.com/magazine/content/04_38/b3900011_mz001.htm (accessed March 18, 2014).

47. "Corel Founder Cowpland Resurfaces at Tiny Zim Technologies," *CRN* (February 6, 2001) at www.crn.com/it-channel/18835301 (accessed May 18, 2011).

48. Jay Greene, "Microsoft's Midlife Crisis," *BusinessWeek* (April 19, 2004), 88–98.

49. Max Weber, *The Theory of Social and Economic Organizations*, translated by A. M. Henderson and T. Parsons (New York: Free Press, 1947).

50. Tina Rosenberg, "The Taint of the Greased Palm," *The New York Times Magazine* (August 10, 2003), 28.

51. John Crewdson, "Corruption Viewed as a Way of Life," Bryan-College Station Eagle (November 28, 1982), 13A; Barry Kramer, "Chinese Officials Still Give Preference to Kin, Despite Peking Policies," *The Wall Street Journal* (October 29, 1985), 1, 21.

52. Kelly Barron, "Logistics in Brown," *Forbes* (January 10, 2000), 78–83; Scott Kirsner, "Venture Vérité: United Parcel Service," *Wired* (September 1999), 83–96; and Kathy Goode, Betty Hahn, and Cindy Seibert, United Parcel Service: The Brown Giant (unpublished manuscript, Texas A&M University, 1981).

53. Allen C. Bluedorn, "Pilgrim's Progress: Trends and Convergence in Research on Organizational Size and Environment," *Journal of Management Studies* 19 (Summer 1993), 163–191; John R. Kimberly, "Organizational Size and the Structuralist Perspective: A Review, Critique, and Proposal," *Administrative Science Quarterly* (1976), 571–597; Richard L. Daft and Selwyn W. Becker, "Managerial, Institutional, and Technical Influences on Administration: A Longitudinal Analysis," *Social Forces* 59 (1980), 392–413.

54. James P. Walsh and Robert D. Dewar, "Formalization and the Organizational Life Cycle," *Journal of Management Studies* 24 (May 1987), 215–231.

55. Nancy M. Carter and Thomas L. Keon, "Specialization as a Multidimensional Construct," *Journal of Management Studies* 26 (1989), 11–28; Cheng-Kuang Hsu, Robert M. March, and Hiroshi Mannari, "An Examination of the Determinants of Organizational Structure," *American Journal of Sociology* 88 (1983), 975–996; Guy Geeraerts, "The Effect of Ownership on the Organization Structure in Small Firms," *Administrative Science Quarterly* 29 (1984), 232–237; Bernard Reimann, "On the Dimensions of Bureaucratic Structure: An Empirical Reappraisal," *Administrative Science Quarterly* 18 (1973), 462–476; Richard H. Hall, "The Concept of Bureaucracy: An Empirical Assessment," *American Journal of Sociology* 69 (1963), 32–40; and William A. Rushing, "Organizational Rules and Surveillance: A Proposition in Comparative

Organizational Analysis," *Administrative Science Quarterly* 10 (1966), 423–443.

56. Jerald Hage and Michael Aiken, "Relationship of Centralization to Other Structural Properties," *Administrative Science Quarterly* 12 (1967), 72–91.

57. Steve Lohr and John Markoff, "You Call This a Midlife Crisis?" *The New York Times* (August 31, 2003), Section 3, 1.

58. Peter Brimelow, "How Do You Cure Injelitance?" *Forbes* (August 7, 1989), 42–44; Jeffrey D. Ford and John W. Slocum, Jr., "Size, Technology, Environment and the Structure of Organizations," *Academy of Management Review* 2 (1977), 561–575; and John D. Kasarda, "The Structural Implications of Social System Size: A Three-Level Analysis," *American Sociological Review* 39 (1974), 19–28.

59. Graham Astley, "Organizational Size and Bureaucratic Structure," *Organization Studies* 6 (1985), 201–228; Spyros K. Lioukas and Demitris A. Xerokostas, "Size and Administrative Intensity in Organizational Divisions," *Management Science* 28 (1982), 854–868; Peter M. Blau, "Interdependence and Hierarchy in Organizations," *Social Science Research* 1 (1972), 1–24; Peter M. Blau and R. A. Schoenherr, *The Structure of Organizations* (New York: Basic Books, 1971); A. Hawley, W. Boland, and M. Boland, "Population Size and Administration in Institutions of Higher Education," *American Sociological Review* 30 (1965), 252–255; Richard L. Daft, "System Influence on Organization Decision-Making: The Case of Resource Allocation," *Academy of Management Journal* 21 (1978), 6–22; and B. P. Indik, "The Relationship between Organization Size and the Supervisory Ratio," *Administrative Science Quarterly* 9 (1964), 301–312.

60. T. F. James, "The Administrative Component in Complex Organizations," *Sociological Quarterly* 13 (1972), 533–539; Daft, "System Influence on Organization Decision-Making"; E. A. Holdaway and E. A. Blowers, "Administrative Ratios and Organization Size: A Longitudinal Examination," *American Sociological Review* 36 (1971), 278–286; and John Child, "Parkinson's Progress: Accounting for the Number of Specialists in Organizations," *Administrative Science Quarterly* 18 (1973), 328–348.

61. Richard L. Daft and Selwyn Becker, "School District Size and the Development of Personnel Resources," *Alberta Journal of Educational Research* 24 (1978), 173–187.

62. Thomas A. Stewart, "Yikes! Deadwood Is Creeping Back," *Fortune* (August 18, 1997), 221–222.

63. Cathy Lazere, "Resisting Temptation: The Fourth Annual SG&A Survey," *CFO* (December 1997), 64–70.

64. T. Grant, "Job Seekers Faced with Wary Employers," *The Globe and Mail* (April 29, 2010) at www.theglobeandmail.com/report-on-business/economy/job-seekers-faced-with-wary-employers/article1494454 (accessed March 18, 2014).

65. Based on Gifford and Elizabeth Pinchot, *The End of Bureaucracy and the Rise of the Intelligent Organization* (San Francisco: Berrett-Koehler Publishers, 1993), 21–29.

66. Listoff, "Confusing Job Titles" (June 26, 2007) at http://listoff.blogspot.com/2007/06/confusing-job-titles.html (accessed March 18, 2014).

67. Scott Shane, "The Beast That Feeds on Boxes: Bureaucracy" (April 10, 2005) at www.nytimes.com/2005/04/10/weekinreview/10shane.html?sq=The%20Beast%20That%20Feeds%20on%20Boxes:%20Bureaucracy&st=cse&scp=1&pagewanted=print&position (accessed March 18, 2014).

68. Gregory A. Bigley and Karlene H. Roberts, "The Incident Command System: High-Reliability Organizing for Complex and Volatile Task Environments," *Academy of Management Journal* 44, no. 6 (2001), 1281–1299.

69. Robert Pool, "In the Zero Luck Zone," *Forbes ASAP* (November 27, 2000), 85.

70. Based on Bigley and Roberts, "The Incident Command System."

71. L. G. Marr, "Lean and Mean," *The Hamilton Spectator* (January 2005).

72. "Local Salvation Army Response to 9-11 Happenings Recalled by Mayor" (September 14, 2006) at www.salvationarmy.ca/2006/09/14/local-salvation-army-response-to-9-11-happenings-recalled-by-major (accessed March 18, 2014).

73. This Leading by Design box is based, in large part, on information from Robert A. Watson and Ben Brown, *The Most Effective Organization in the U.S.: Leadership Secrets of the Salvation Army* (New York: Crown Business, 2001), 159–181.

74. Philip M. Padsakoff, Larry J. Williams, and William D. Todor, "Effects of Organizational Formalization on Alienation among Professionals and Nonprofessionals," *Academy of Management Journal* 29 (1986), 820–831.

75. Royston Greenwood, C. R. Hinings, and John Brown, "'P2-Form' Strategic Management: Corporate Practices in Professional Partnerships," *Academy of Management Journal* 33 (1990), 725–755; Royston Greenwood and C. R. Hinings, "Understanding Strategic Change: The Contribution of Archetypes," *Academy of Management Journal* 36 (1993), 1052–1081.

76. *The Economist,* "Monitor's End" (November 14, 2013) at http://www.economist.com/blogs/schumpeter/2012/11/consulting (accessed March 18, 2014).

77. William G. Ouchi, "Markets, Bureaucracies, and Clans," *Administrative Science Quarterly* 25 (1980), 129–141; idem, "A Conceptual Framework for the Design of Organizational Control Mechanisms," *Management Science* 25 (1979), 833–848.

78. Weber, *The Theory of Social and Economic Organizations*, 328–340.

79. Daisuke Wakabayashi and Toko Sekiguchi, "Disaster in Japan: Evacuees Set Rules to Create Sense of Normalcy," *The Wall Street Journal* (March 26, 2011),

A8; and Chester Dawson and Yoshio Takahashi, "A Year Later, Toyota Quietly Tackles Quality," *The Wall Street Journal* (February 23, 2011), B2.

80. Joel Spolsky, "Good System, Bad System; Starbucks' Meticulous Policy Manual Shows Employees How to Optimize Profits. Too Bad It Undercuts Basic Customer Service," *Inc.* (August 2008), 67.

81. Oliver A. Williamson, *Markets and Hierarchies: Analyses and Antitrust Implications* (New York: Free Press, 1975).

82. Jack Quarter, Laurie Mook, and Ann Armstrong, *The Social Economy: A Canadian Perspective* (Toronto: UTP, 2009).

83. Anita Micossi, "Creating Internal Markets," *Enterprise* (April 1994), 43–44.

84. Raymond E. Miles, Henry J. Coleman, Jr., and W. E. Douglas Creed, "Keys to Success in Corporate Redesign," *California Management Review* 37, no. 3 (Spring 1995), 128–145.

85. William G. Ouchi, "Markets, Bureaucracies, and Clans," *Administrative Science Quarterly* 25 (1980), 129–141; idem, "A Conceptual Framework for the Design of Organizational Control Mechanisms," *Management Science* 25 (1979), 833–848

86. Anna Muoio, ed., "Growing Smart," *Fast Company* (August 1998), 73–83.

87. St. Luke's, "Who We Are" (2011) at http://www.stlukes.co.uk/who-we-are (accessed June 3, 2011).

88. Richard Leifer and Peter K. Mills, "An Information Processing Approach for Deciding upon Control Strategies and Reducing Control Loss in Emerging Organizations," *Journal of Management* 22, no. 1 (1996), 113–137.

89. Stratford Sherman, "The New Computer Revolution," *Fortune* (June 14, 1993), 56–80.

90. Leifer and Mills, "An Information Processing Approach for Deciding upon Control Strategies"; and Laurie J. Kirsch, "The Management of Complex Tasks in Organizations: Controlling the Systems Development Process," *Organization Science* 7, 1 (January–February 1996), 1–21.

91. V. Galt, "Don't Like it Here? Don't Bother Crying in Your Beer," *The Globe and Mail* (September 8, 2007), B18.

92. Ibid.

93. James R. Barker, "Tightening the Iron Cage: Concertive Control in Self-Managing Teams," *Administrative Science Quarterly* 38 (1993), 408–437.

94. Kim S. Cameron, Myung Kim, and David A. Whetten, "Organizational Effects of Decline and Turbulence," *Administrative Science Quarterly* 32 (1987), 222–240.

95. Danny Miller, "What Happens after Success: The Perils of Excellence," *Journal of Management Studies* 31, 3 (May 1994), 325–358.

96. CBC, "Blockbuster's Bankruptcy: What Does the Loss of Video Stores Mean to You?" (May 6, 2011) at www.cbc.ca/news/yourcommunity/2011/05/blockbusters-bankruptcy-what-does-the-loss-of-video-stores-mean-to-you.html (accessed June 3, 2011).

97. Kris Frieswick, "The Turning Point: What Options Do Companies Have When Their Industries Are Dying?" (April 1, 2005) at www.cfo.com/printable/article.cfm/3786531/c_3805512?f=options (accessed March 18, 2014).

98. Leonard Greenhalgh, "Organizational Decline," in Samuel B. Bacharach, ed., *Research in the Sociology of Organizations* 2 (Greenwich, CT: JAI Press, 1983), 231–276; and Peter Lorange and Robert T. Nelson, "How to Recognize—and Avoid—Organizational Decline," *Sloan Management Review* (Spring 1987), 41–48.

99. Kim S. Cameron and Raymond Zammuto, "Matching Managerial Strategies to Conditions of Decline," *Human Resources Management* 22 (1983), 359–375; and Leonard Greenhalgh, Anne T. Lawrence, and Robert I. Sutton, "Determinants of Workforce Reduction Strategies in Organizations," *Academy of Management Review* 13 (1988), 241–254.

100. Service Canada, "Tool and Die Makers" (March 31, 2007) at www.jobfutures.ca/noc/7232p4.shtml (accessed June 19, 2008).

101. William Weitzel and Ellen Jonsson, "Reversing the Downward Spiral: Lessons from W. T. Grant and Sears Roebuck," *Academy of Management Executive* 5 (1991), 7–21; William Weitzel and Ellen Jonsson, "Decline in Organizations: A Literature Integration and Extension," *Administrative Science Quarterly* 34 (1989), 91–109.

102. R. Corelli, "Eaton's: A Dynasty in Decline" (March 10, 1997) at www.thecanadianencyclopedia.com/index.cfm?PgNm=TCE&Params=M1ARTM0011178 (accessed March 18, 2014).

103. "Eaton's: A Canadian Institution, December 8, 1869–February 18, 2002" at http://archives.cbc.ca/300i.asp?id=1-69-377 (accessed September 23, 2007).

104. K. Noble, "Eaton's Goes Bankrupt" (August 30, 1999) at www.thecanadianencyclopedia.com/index.cfm?PgNm=TCE&Params=M1ARTM0012007 (accessed March 18, 2014).

105. "Eaton's: A Canadian Institution, December 8, 1869–February 18, 2002."

106. J.P. Sheppard and S.D. Chowdhury, "Riding the Wrong Wave: Organizational Failure as a Failed Turnaround," *Long Range Planning*, 38 (2005), 256.

107. Hollie Shaw, "Nordstrom to Open Store in Toronto Eaton Centre as Sears Departs," *Financial Post* (January 15, 2014) at http://business.financialpost.com/2014/01/15/nordstrom-to-open-store-in-eaton-centre-after-sears-departs/ (accessed March 18, 2014).

108. William McKinley, Carol M. Sanchez, and Allen G. Schick, "Organizational Downsizing: Constraining, Cloning, Learning," *Academy of Management Executive* 9, 3 (1995), 32–42.

109. Gregory B. Northcraft and Margaret A. Neale, *Organizational Behavior: A Management Challenge,*

2nd ed. (Fort Worth, TX: The Dryden Press, 1994), 626; and A. Catherine Higgs, "Executive Commentary" in McKinley, Sanchez, and Schick, "Organizational Downsizing: Constraining, Cloning, Learning," 43–44.

110. Wayne Cascio, "Strategies for Responsible Restructuring," *Academy of Management Executive* 16, no. 3 (2002), 80–91; James R. Morris, Wayne F. Cascio, and Clifford E. Young, "Downsizing after All These Years: Questions and Answers about Who Did It, How Many Did It, and Who Benefited from It," *Organizational Dynamics* (Winter 1999), 78–86; Stephen Doerflein and James Atsaides, "Corporate Psychology: Making Downsizing Work," *Electrical World* (September–October 1999), 41–43; and Brett C. Luthans and Steven M. Sommer, "The Impact of Downsizing on Workplace Attitudes," *Group and Organization Management* 2, 1 (1999), 46–70.

111. F. Gandolfi, "Unravelling Downsizing—What Do We Know about the Phenomenon?" *Review of International Comparative Management* 10, 3 (2009), 414–426.

112. These techniques are based on Bob Nelson, "The Care of the Un-Downsized," *Training and Development* (April 1997), 40–43; Shari Caudron, "Teach Downsizing Survivors How to Thrive," *Personnel Journal* (January 1996), 38; Joel Brockner, "Managing the Effects of Layoffs on Survivors," *California Management Review* (Winter 1992), 9–28; Ronald Henkoff, "Getting beyond Downsizing," *Fortune* (January 10, 1994), 58–64; Kim S. Cameron, "Strategies for Successful Organizational Downsizing," *Human Resource Management* 33, no. 2 (Summer 1994), 189–211; and Doerflein and Atsaides, "Corporate Psychology: Making Downsizing Work."

113. Matt Murray, "Stress Mounts as More Firms Announce Large Layoffs, But Don't Say Who or When" (Your Career Matters column), *The Wall Street Journal* (March 13, 2001), B1, B12.

114. Dofasco, "1940–1960" at http://www.dofasco.ca/bins/content_page.asp?cid=339-9516-9556-9650 (accessed May 18, 2011).

115. Ibid.

116. Canadian Case Study: Steel Industry Worker Adjustment Program, Asia-Pacific Economic Co-operation, 2001.

117. Ibid.

# Chapter 9

1. "A Journey Milestone" at www.birksandmayors .com/index.asp?cs=386&css=390 (accessed July 9, 2008); and "Stronger Together" at http://www .birksandmayors.com/index.asp?cs=386&css=391 (accessed July 9, 2008).

2. P. P. Brown, "Blood Diamonds" (December 13, 2005) at www.worldpress.org/africa/2193.cfm (accessed March 18, 2014).

3. "Birks FAQ" at http://www.birks.com/index.asp? cFlag=content&incFile=faq&langid=1 (accessed May 18, 2011).

4. R. Mendleson, "Your Bling Can Save the World" (June 11, 2008) at www.macleans.ca/business/ companies/article.jsp?content=20080611_45238_45237 (accessed July 9, 2008).

5. C. Silverman, "How One Firm Saw the Light on Hiring," *The Globe and Mail* (January 31, 2007), C1, C3.

6. Ibid.

7. Teva, "Teva Neuroscience Honored at Stevie Awards NA (Miami Florida) (2014) at http://www.tevapharm .com/Career/Awards/Pages/Neuroscience.aspx (accessed March 30, 2014).

8. Anita Raghavan, Kathryn Kranhold, and Alexei Barrionuevo, "Full Speed Ahead: How Enron Bosses Created a Culture of Pushing Limits," *The Wall Street Journal* (August 26, 2002), A1, A7.

9. Mark C. Bolino, William H. Turnley, and James M. Bloodgood, "Citizenship Behavior and the Creation of Social Capital in Organizations," *Academy of Management Review* 27, no. 4 (2002), 505–522; and Don Cohen and Laurence Prusak, *In Good Company: How Social Capital Makes Organizations Work* (Boston, Mass.: Harvard Business School Press, 2001), 3–4.

10 Yahoo, "eBay Inc. Reports Fourth Quarter and Full Year 2013 Results," Yahoo Finance (January 22, 2014) at http://finance.yahoo.com/news/ebay-inc-reports -fourth-quarter-211500331.html (accessed March 30, 2014).

11. Esther Colwill, Best Workplaces at a Glance (April 23, 2007) at www.canadianbusiness.com/managing/ career/article.jsp?content=20070425_85422_85422 (accessed June 24, 2008); Deloitte & Touche (2009) "55 New Leaders with the Passion to Perform" (2009) at www.deloitte.com/assets/Dcom-Canada/Local% 20Assets/Documents/Alumni/ca_en_con_new_partners _ad_122209.pdf (accessed March 18, 2014).

12. W. Jack Duncan, "Organizational Culture: 'Getting a Fix' on an Elusive Concept," *Academy of Management Executive* 3 (1989), 229–236; Linda Smircich, "Concepts of Culture and Organizational Analysis," *Administrative Science Quarterly* 28 (1983), 339–358; and Andrew D. Brown and Ken Starkey, "The Effect of Organizational Culture on Communication and Information," *Journal of Management Studies* 31, 6 (November 1994), 807–828.

13. Edgar H. Schein, "Organizational Culture," *American Psychologist* 45 (February 1990), 109–119.

14. "The Body Shop Canada Living Machine Effluent Reuse" (2001) at www.ecowerks.ca/clients.htm (accessed March 18, 2014).

15. Harrison M. Trice and Janice M. Beyer, "Studying Organizational Cultures through Rites and Ceremonials," *Academy of Management Review* 9 (1984), 653–669; Janice M. Beyer and Harrison M. Trice, "How an

Organization's Rites Reveal Its Culture," *Organizational Dynamics* 15 (Spring 1987), 5–24; Steven P. Feldman, "Management in Context: An Essay on the Relevance of Culture to the Understanding of Organizational Change," *Journal of Management Studies* 23 (1986), 589–607; and Mary Jo Hatch, "The Dynamics of Organizational Culture," *Academy of Management Review* 18 (1993), 657–693.

16. This discussion is based on Edgar H. Schein, *Organizational Culture and Leadership*, 2nd ed. (Homewood, IL: Richard D. Irwin, 1992); and John P. Kotter and James L. Heskett, *Corporate Culture and Performance* (New York: Free Press, 1992).

17. S. Valentine, "ExtendMedia—Courting Jane Q. Public" (May 27, 2007) at www.redcanary.ca/view/extendmedia-courting (accessed July 12, 2008).

18. Advide Ravasi and Majken Schultz, "Responding to Organizational Identity Threats: Exploring the Role of Organizational Culture," *Academy of Management Journal* (2006) 49. 3, 437.

19. Larry Mallak, "Understanding and Changing Your Organization's Culture," *Industrial Management* (March–April 2001), 18–24.

20. August Iskandar, "When Culture Is Everything, a Brief Lesson from Zappos.com" (2013) at http://www.slideshare.net/justalittleslide/20130110-when-culture-is-everything-v11?from_search=2 (accessed March 18, 2014).

21. Eleanor Bloxham, "Zappos and the Search for a Better Way to Run a Business," CNN Money (January 29, 2014) at http://management.Fortune.cnn.com/2014/01/29/zappos-holacracy/ (accessed January 30, 2014); and Vanessa Lu, "Online Retailer Zappos to Toss Manager Roles," *Toronto Star* (January 20, 2014) at http://www.thestar.com/business/2014/01/20/online_retailer_zappos_to_toss_manager_roles.html (accessed March 18, 2014).

22. For a list of various elements that can be used to assess or interpret corporate culture, see "10 Key Cultural Elements," sidebar in Micah R. Kee, "Corporate Culture Makes a Fiscal Difference," *Industrial Management* (November–December 2003), 16–20.

23. Charlotte B. Sutton, "Richness Hierarchy of the Cultural Network: The Communication of Corporate Values" (unpublished manuscript, Texas A&M University, 1985); and Terrence E. Deal and Allan A. Kennedy, "Culture: A New Look through Old Lenses," *Journal of Applied Behavioral Science* 19 (1983), 498–505.

24. Faculty of Law, "Global Student Group Starts Internationally Trained Lawyers Program" at www.law.utoronto.ca/visitors_content.asp?itempath=5/5/0/0/0&specNews=808&cType=NewsEvents (accessed June 3, 2011).

25. Jennifer A. Chatman and Sandra Eunyoung Cha, "Leading by Leveraging Culture," *California Management Review* 45, no. 4 (Summer 2003), 20–34.

26. Don Hellriegel and John W. Slocum, Jr., *Management*, 7th ed. (Cincinnati, OH: South-Western, 1996), 537.

27. Trice and Beyer, "Studying Organizational Cultures through Rites and Ceremonials."

28. Sutton, "Richness Hierarchy of the Cultural Network"; and Terrence E. Deal and Allan A. Kennedy, *Corporate Cultures: The Rites and Rituals of Corporate Life* (Reading, Mass.: Addison-Wesley, 1982).

29. S. Foster, "Our Love Affair with Trains" at www.crossculturedtraveler.com/Archives/Nov2003/Canada.htm (accessed May 18, 2011).

30. Raghavan, Kranhold, and Barrionuevo, "Full Speed Ahead."

31. A. Wahl, J. Castaldo, Z. Olijnyk, E. Pooley, and A. Jezovit, "Best Workplaces '07" (April 25, 2007) at http://www.canadianbusiness.com/managing/career/article.jsp?content=20070425_133041_5516 (accessed July 12, 2008).

32. Ibid.

33. Jennifer A. Chatman and Sandra Eunyoung Cha, "Leading by Leveraging Culture," *California Management Review* 45, no. 4 (Summer 2003), 20–34; and Abby Ghobadian and Nicholas O'Regan, "The Link between Culture, Strategy, and Performance in Manufacturing SMEs," *Journal of General Management* 28, 1 (Autumn 2002), 16–34.

34. James R. Detert, Roger G. Schroeder, and John J. Mauriel, "A Framework for Linking Culture and Improvement Initiatives in Organizations," *Academy of Management Review* 25, 4 (2000), 850–863.

35. Based on Daniel R. Denison, *Corporate Culture and Organizational Effectiveness* (New York: Wiley, 1990), 11–15; Daniel R. Denison and Aneil K. Mishra, "Toward a Theory of Organizational Culture and Effectiveness," *Organization Science* 6, 2 (March–April 1995), 204–223; R. Hooijberg and F. Petrock, "On Cultural Change: Using the Competing Values Framework to Help Leaders Execute a Transformational Strategy," *Human Resource Management* 32 (1993), 29–50; and R. E. Quinn, *Beyond Rational Management: Mastering the Paradoxes and Competing Demands of High Performance* (San Francisco: Jossey-Bass, 1988).

36. Steve Lohr, "Big Blue's Big Bet: Less Tech, More Touch," *The New York Times* (January 25, 2004), Sec. 3, 1.

37. A. Wahl, "Canada's Best Workplaces: Overview," *Canadian Business* (April 26, 2007).

38. Best Workplaces in Canada 2013, at http://www.greatplacetowork.ca/best-workplaces/best-workplaces-in-canada (accessed March 18, 2014).

39. S. Valentine, "The Sandvine Way" (2006) at www.theredcanary.com/print?articleID=130 (accessed June 24, 2008).

40. "Sandvine Corp." *Globe Investor* (March 28, 2014) at http://www.theglobeandmail.com/globe-investor/markets/stocks/summary/?q=svc-T (accessed March 30, 2014).

41. "Best Workplaces in Canada 2007" at www
.greatplacetowork.ca/best/list-ca-2007.htm (accessed
July 12, 2008).

42. Ibid.

43. The Leaders 10 Commandments (and the Eight Points)
provided by Sandvine Public Affairs, June 2007. Used
with permission.

44. "Jobs at MEC" at www.mec.ca/Main/content_text.
jsp;jsessionid=L5TrWB4sVyyNvntKVhVMpdfJHhp0
QJffsLvLX6FGWG3BMGK22qZD!-1599383407?FO
LDER%3C%3Efolder_id=1408474396038661&FO
LDER%3C%3EbrowsePath=1408474396038661&b
mUID=1215909419636 (accessed July 14, 2008).

45. G. Harris cited in Mountain Equipment Co-op (profile)
at http://thecanadianencyclopedia.com/PrinterFriendly
.cfm?Params=M1ARTM0012398 (accessed May 18,
2011).

46. MEC, Accountability Performance 2009 Interim
Report at http://images.mec.ca/media/Images/pdf/
accountability/MEC_2009_Accountability_Report_
v1_m56577569830970401.pdf (accessed March 18,
2014).

47. "Mountain Equipment Co-op" at http://
dotherightthing.com/companies/mountain-equipment
-co-op (accessed July 12, 2008); A. Holloway, "It's
All in the Details," *Canadian Business* (December
25–January 14,2006); "Mountain Equipment Co-op
(profile)" at http://thecanadianencyclopedia.com/
PrinterFriendly.cfm?Params=M1ARTM0012398
(accessed May 18, 2011); R. de Lazzer, "Clothing
Retailer Pledges 1 Percent of Revenue to Planet,"
*The Globe and Mail* (April 5, 2007), Q12;
S. Prashad, "Good Green Goals," *Toronto Star*
(April 22, 2007), A12; and "Ethical Sourcing:
What it Means to Us" at http://www.mec.ca/Main/
content_text.jsp?FOLDER%3C%3Efolder_id=14084
74396038947&FOLDER%3C%3EbrowsePath=1408
474396038947&bmUID=1203874207701 (accessed
May 18, 2011).

48. "MEC Wins Canada's Governance Award"
(February 2, 2008) at www.8264.net/article.php?id=881
(accessed July 12, 2008).

49. Tara Perkins, "The Tallest Mountain: Why Outdoor
Gear and Clothing Retailer Mountain Equipment
Co-op Topped this Year's Best 50," *Corporate Knights*,
(Summer 2014), 44.

50. Brenda Bouw, Who's Pushing that Shopping Cart?
Global Retail Ranking (2013) at http://www
.corporateknights.com/report/2013-global-retail
-ranking/whos-pushing-shopping-cart (accessed
March 18, 2014).

51. Rekha Balu, "Pacific Edge Projects Itself," *Fast
Company* (October 2000), 371–381.

52. Jim Collins, *Good to Great: Why Some Companies
Make the Leap ... and Others Don't* (New York:
HarperCollins, 2001), 120–133.

53. Bernard Arogyaswamy and Charles M. Byles, "Organizational Culture: Internal and External Fits," *Journal of
Management* 13 (1987), 647–659.

54. Chatman and Cha, "Leading by Leveraging Culture";
and J. Collins, *From Good to Great* (New York:
HarperCollins, 2001).

55. "Best Workplaces in Canada 2006" at www
.greatplacetowork.ca/best/list-ca-2006.htm (accessed
May 18, 2011).

56. A. Styhre, S. Börjesson, and J. Wickenberg, "Managed
by the Other: Cultural Anxieties in Two Anglo-
Americanized Swedish Firms," *International Journal of
Human Resource Management* 17, 7 (2006), 1293–1306.

57. Paul R. Lawrence and Jay W. Lorsch, *Organization
and Environment* (Homewood, IL: Irwin, 1969).

58. Scott Kirsner, "Designed for Innovation," *Fast
Company* (November 1998), 54, 56.

59. Chatman and Cha, "Leading by Leveraging Culture";
Jeff Rosenthal and Mary Ann Masarech, "High-
Performance Cultures: How Values Can Drive Business
Results," *Journal of Organizational Excellence*
(Spring 2003), 3–18.

60. Ghobadian and O'Regan, "The Link between Culture,
Strategy and Performance"; G. G. Gordon and N.
DiTomaso, "Predicting Corporate Performance from
Organisational Culture," *Journal of Management
Studies* 29, 6 (1992), 783–798; and G. A. Marcoulides
and R. H. Heck, "Organizational Culture and Perfor-
mance: Proposing and Testing a Model," *Organization
Science* 4 (1993), 209–225.

61. R. Charan, "Home Depot's Blueprint for Culture
Change," *Harvard Business Review* (April 2006), 4.

62. Robert Paterson, "WestJet—The Difference that Culture Makes" (June 29, 2004) at smartpei.typepad.com/
robert_patersons_weblog/2004/06/westjet_the_dif.html
(accessed May 18, 2011). (Used with permission.)

63. John P. Kotter and James L. Heskett, *Corporate Culture
and Performance* (New York: The Free Press, 1992).

64. L. Bogomolny, "Toned and Ready: Lululemon
Transitions," *Canadian Business Online* (April 24,
2006) at www.canadianbusiness.com/managing/
strategy/article.jsp?content=20060424_76424_76424
(accessed May 18, 2011).

65. "lululemon athletica inc. Announces Fourth Quarter
and Full Year Fiscal 2010 Results"(March 17,
2011) at http://investor.lululemon.com/releasedetail.
cfm?ReleaseID=558393 (accessed March 18, 2014).

66. M. Strauss, "Lululemon's Problem? Customers Can't
Get Enough," *The Globe and Mail* (March 17,
2011) at www.theglobeandmail.com/globe-investor/
lululemons-problem-customers-cant-get-enough/
article1945253 (accessed March 18, 2014).

67. lululemon, "Mission Statement" (2011) at http://www
.lululemon.com/about/culture (accessed June 3, 2011).

68. Lululemon, "lululemon athletica inc. Announces Fourth
Quarter and Full Year Fiscal 2013 Results" (2014) at

http://investor.lululemon.com/releases.cfm (accessed March 30, 2014).

69. L. Bogomolny, "Toned and Ready: Lululemon Transitions," *Canadian Business Online* (April 24, 2006) at www.canadianbusiness.com/managing/strategy/article.jsp?content=20060424_76424_76424 (accessed May 18, 2011).

70. "Controversial Message Uncovered in Lululemon Bags," ctvtoronto.ca (April 16, 2008) at www.ctv.ca/CTVNews/TopStories/20080416/Lululemon_controversy_080416 / (accessed March 18, 2014).

71. M. Strauss and P. Waldie, "Lululemon Ditches Tags Touting Health Benefits," *The Globe and Mail* (November 17, 2007) at www.theglobeandmail.com/report-on-business/article797885.ece (accessed May 18, 2011).

72. "Lululemon Athletica's 'Seaweed' Clothing Contains No Seaweed (November 15, 2007) at www.ethicalshopper.com/clothing-accessories/clothes/lululemon-athleticas-seaweed-clothing-contains-no-seaweed.html (accessed May 18, 2011).

73. CTV BC, "Lululemon Founder Blames Women's Bodies for Pants Problems," CTV (November 2013) at http://bc.ctvnews.ca/lululemon-founder-blames-women-s-bodies-for-pants-problems-1.1531351 (accessed March 18, 2014).

74. CBC News, "Chip Wilson, Lululemon Founder, Steps Down," CBC (December 13, 2013) at http://www.cbc.ca/news/business/chip-wilson-lululemon-founder-steps-down-1.2457958 (accessed January 29, 2014).

75. D. Sacks, "Lululemon's Cult of Selling," *Fast Company* (March 18, 2009) at www.fastcompany.com/magazine/134/om-my.html (accessed May 18, 2011).

76. Ibid.

77. M. Stewart, "Lululemon Boss Rides Creative Wave," *Business Edge* 8, 10 (May 16, 2008) at www.businessedge.ca/archives/article.cfm/lululemon-boss-rides-creative-wave-17862 (accessed March 18, 2014).

78. G. Danake, cited in D. Haskayne, *Northern Tigers—Building Ethical Canadian Corporate Champions, A Memoir and a Manifesto* (Toronto: Key Porter Books, 2007), 284.

79. Gordon F. Shea, *Practical Ethics* (New York: American Management Association, 1988); Linda K. Trevino, "Ethical Decision Making in Organizations: A Person–Situation Interactionist Model," *Academy of Management Review* 11 (1986), 601–617; and Linda Klebe Trevino and Katherine A. Nelson, *Managing Business Ethics: Straight Talk about How to Do It Right*, 2nd ed. (New York: John Wiley & Sons, Inc., 1999).

80. Thanks to Susan H. Taft, Kent State University, and Judith White, University of Redlands, for this overview of the sources of individual ethics.

81. Dawn-Marie Driscoll, "Don't Confuse Legal and Ethical Standards," *Business Ethics* (July–August 1996), 44.

82. LaRue Tone Hosmer, *The Ethics of Management*, 2nd ed. (Homewood, IL: Irwin, 1991).

83. Joel Bakan, *The Corporation: The Pathological Pursuit of Power* (Toronto: Penguin, 2004), 60.

84. Ibid., 161.

85. Noam Chomsky (n.d.) at www.thecorporation.com/index.cfm?page_id=7 (accessed March 18, 2014).

86. Geanne Rosenberg, "Truth and Consequences," *Working Woman* (July–August 1998), 79–80.

87. D. Schwarz in C. Hymowitz, "Ain't Misbehavin'—Increasingly, That's What Firms Are Demandin'," *The Globe and Mail* (June 20, 2007), C8.

88. N. Craig Smith, "Corporate Social Responsibility: Whether or How?" *California Management Review* 45, no. 4 (Summer 2003), 52–76; and Eugene W. Szwajkowski, "The Myths and Realities of Research on Organizational Misconduct," in James E. Post, ed., *Research in Corporate Social Performance and Policy*, vol. 9 (Greenwich, CT: JAI Press, 1986), 103–122.

89. Some of these incidents are from Hosmer, *The Ethics of Management*.

90. Linda K. Trevino and Katherine A. Nelson, *Managing Business Ethics: Straight Talk about How to Do It Right* (New York: John Wiley & Sons, 1995), 4.

91. Curtis C. Verschoor and Elizabeth A. Murphy, "The Financial Performance of Large U.S. Firms and Those with Global Prominence: How Do the Best Corporate Citizens Rate?" *Business and Society Review* 107, no. 2 (Fall 2002), 371–381; Homer H. Johnson, "Does It Pay to Be Good? Social Responsibility and Financial Performance," *Business Horizons* (November–December 2003), 34–40; Quentin R. Skrabec, "Playing by the Rules: Why Ethics Are Profitable," *Business Horizons* (September–October 2003), 15–18; Marc Gunther, "Tree Huggers, Soy Lovers, and Profits," *Fortune* (June 23, 2003), 98–104; Dale Kurschner, "5 Ways Ethical Business Creates Fatter Profits," *Business Ethics* (March–April 1996), 20–23. Also see various studies reported in Lori Ioannou, "Corporate America's Social Conscience," *Fortune*, special advertising section (May 26, 2003), S1–S10.

92. Verschoor and Murphy, "The Financial Performance of Large U.S. Firms."

93. P. Godfrey, "Corporate Philanthropy Adds to Shareholder Wealth, Says BYU Study" (October 28, 2005) at www.csrwire.com/print.cgi?sfArticleId=4620 (accessed June 25, 2008).

94. UFCW, "Special Partner" (2014) at http://www.llscanada.org/waystohelp/sponsorpartner/specialpartner_ufcw/ (accessed March 30, 2014).

95. Daniel W. Greening and Daniel B. Turban, "Corporate Social Performance as a Competitive Advantage in Attracting a Quality Workforce," *Business and Society* 39, 3 (September 2000), 254.

96. Christopher Marquis, "Doing Well and Doing Good," *The New York Times* (July 13, 2003), Section 3, 2; and Joseph Pereira, "Career Journal: Doing Good and Doing Well at Timberland," *The Wall Street Journal* (September 9, 2003), B1.

97. "The Socially Correct Corporate Business," in Leslie Holstrom and Simon Brady, "The Changing Face of Global Business," *Fortune*, special advertising section (July 24, 2000), S1–S38.

98. Carol Hymowitz (2002) CEOs Work Hard to Maintain The Faith in the Corner Office, The Wall Street Journal, July 9, accessed from http://online.wsj.com/news/articles/SB1026159582730334760#printMode (March 30, 2014).

99. Planeterra Annual Report, 2006–2007.

100. Linda Klebe Trevino, "A Cultural Perspective on Changing and Developing Organizational Ethics," in Richard Woodman and William Pasmore, eds., *Research and Organizational Change and Development*, vol. 4 (Greenwich, CT: JAI Press, 1990); and Lynn Sharp Paine, "Managing for Organizational Integrity," *Harvard Business Review* (March/April 1994), 106–117.

101. James Weber, "Exploring the Relationship between Personal Values and Moral Reasoning," *Human Relations* 46 (1993), 435–463.

102. L. Kohlberg, "Moral Stages and Moralization: The Cognitive-Developmental Approach," in T. Likona, ed., *Moral Development and Behavior: Theory, Research, and Social Issues* (New York: Holt, Rinehart & Winston, 1976).

103. Hosmer, *The Ethics of Management*. Toronto: McGraw-Hill, 2010.

104. R. Martin, "The Virtue Matrix: Calculating the Return on Corporate Responsibility," *Harvard Business Review* (March 2002), 68.

105. G. Pitts, "Feisty Forest Guy Royer Unafraid to Go Green," *The Globe and Mail* (May 7, 2007), B10.

106. John A. Byrne with Mike France and Wendy Zellner, "The Environment Was Ripe for Abuse," *BusinessWeek* (February 25, 2002), 118–120.

107. Alcan, "Our Values" (2008) at www.alcan.com/web/publishing.nsf/content/About+Alcan+-+Our+Values (accessed May 18, 2011).

108. Global 100, "The 2007 List" at www.global100.org/2007/index.asp (accessed June 25, 2008).

109. David M. Messick and Max H. Bazerman, "Ethical Leadership and the Psychology of Decision Making," *Sloan Management Review* (Winter 1996), 9–22; Dawn-Marie Driscoll, "Don't Confuse Legal and Ethical Standards," *Business Ethics* (July–August 1996), 44; and Max B. E. Clarkson, "A Stakeholder Framework for Analyzing and Evaluating Corporate Social Performance," *Academy of Management Review* 20, 1 (1995), 92–117.

110. Roger Parloff, "Is Fat the Next Tobacco?" *Fortune* (February 3, 2003), 51–54.

111. Cristina Howorun, "PEOPLE: Ron Dembo and Zero-footprint" (August 31, 2007) at www.redcanary.ca/view/people-ron-dembo-and-zerofootprint (accessed May 18, 2011).

112. Gwen Kinkead, "In the Future, People Like Me Will Go to Jail," *Fortune* (May 24, 1999), 190–200; "Sustainability Overview" at www.interfaceinc.com/goals/sustainability_overview.html (accessed July 12, 2008); and "Recycled and Bio-based Content in Products" at http://www.interfacesustainability.com/metrics.html (accessed July 13, 2008).

113. *Corporate Ethics: A Prime Business Asset* (New York: The Business Round Table, February 1988).

114. Andrew W. Singer, "The Ultimate Ethics Test," *Across the Board* (March 1992), 19–22; Ronald B. Morgan, "Self and Co-Worker Perceptions of Ethics and Their Relationships to Leadership and Salary," *Academy of Management Journal* 36, no. 1 (February 1993), 200–214; and Joseph L. Badaracco, Jr., and Allen P. Webb, "Business Ethics: A View from the Trenches," *California Management Review* 37, no. 2 (Winter 1995), 8–28.

115. John A. Byrne, "Harvard B-school Dean Offers Unusual Apology," CNN Money (January 29, 2014) at http://management.Fortune.cnn.com/2014/01/29/harvard-business-dean-apologizes (accessed March 18, 2014).

116. Betsy Massar, Conversation on Disqus about John A Byrne, "Harvard B-school Dean Offers Unusual Apology," CNN Money (January 29, 2014) at http://management.fortune.cnn.com/2014/01/29/harvard-business-dean-apologizes/ (accessed April 14, 2014).

117. This discussion is based on Robert J. House, Andre Delbecq, and Toon W. Taris, "Value Based Leadership: An Integrated Theory and an Empirical Test" (working paper, 1998).

118. Tamara Schweitzer, "Skiing Green" (February 2007) at www.fastcompany.com/articles/2007/02/green-ski-resorts.html?page=0%2C1 (accessed May 18, 2011).

119. S. Shields, "Luger Who Died was Terrified of Track," *The Wall Street Journal* (February 15, 2007) at http://online.wsj.com/article/SB10001424052748703447704575065492351741522.html (accessed March 18, 2014).

120. Michael Barrier, "Doing the Right Thing," *Nation's Business* (March 1998), 33–38.

121. Mitchell Pacelle, "Citigroup CEO Makes 'Value' a Key Focus," *The Wall Street Journal* (October 1, 2004), C1.

122. Thomas J. Peters and Robert H. Waterman, Jr., *In Search of Excellence* (New York: Harper & Row, 1982).

123. "Citigroup's Day of Reckoning" (November 4, 2007) at http://money.cnn.com/2007/11/04/news/companies/citigroup_prince/index.htm (accessed March 18, 2014).

124. Karl E. Weick, "Cognitive Processes in Organizations," in B. M. Staw, ed., *Research in Organizations*, vol. 1 (Greenwich, CT: JAI Press, 1979), 42.

125. Richard Osborne, "Kingston's Family Values," *IndustryWeek* (August 13, 2001), 51–54.

126. Alan Yuspeh, "Do the Right Thing," *CIO* (August 1, 2000), 56–58.

127. ECOA, "ECOA Global Network" (2011) at www .theecoa.org/imis15/ECOAPublic/ABOUT_THE _ECOA/ECOA_Global_Network/ECOAPublic/ AboutContent/Global_Network.aspx?hkey=c7be86fd -b2ec-4495-b658-98d4d69ad456 (accessed June 3, 2011).

128. Trevino and Nelson, *Managing Business Ethics*, 212.

129. A. Wahl, J. Castaldo, Z. Olijnyk, E. Pooley and A. Jezovit,"Best Workplaces '07" (April 25, 2007) at www.canadianbusiness.com/managing/career/article .jsp?content=20070425_133041_5516 (accessed July 12, 2008).

130. Janet P. Near and Marcia P. Miceli, "Effective Whistle-Blowing," *Academy of Management Review* 20, 3 (1995), 679–708.

131. Richard P. Nielsen, "Changing Unethical Organizational Behavior," *Academy of Management Executive* 3 (1989), 123–130.

132. Jene G. James, "Whistle-Blowing: Its Moral Justification," in Peter Madsen and Jay M. Shafritz, eds., *Essentials of Business Ethics* (New York: Meridian Books, 1990), 160–190; and Janet P. Near, Terry Morehead Dworkin, and Marcia P. Miceli, "Explaining the Whistle-Blowing Process: Suggestions from Power Theory and Justice Theory," *Organization Science* 4 (1993), 393–411.

133. D. Jacobs, "Whistleblower Awaits Justice after 14 Years, *Ottawa Citizen* (May 15, 2006), 2.

134. T. MacCharles, "High Cost of Whistleblowing," *Toronto Star* (June 30, 2007), A15.

135. Ibid.

136. J. B. Singh, "Ethics Programs in Canada's Largest Corporations," *Business and Society Review*, 111, 2 (2006), 119–136.

137. Linda Klebe Trevino, Gary R. Weaver, David G. Gibson, and Barbara Ley Toffler, "Managing Ethics and Legal Compliance: What Works and What Hurts?" *California Management Review* 41, 2 (Winter 1999), 131–151.

138. Carl Anderson, "Values-Based Management," *Academy of Management Executive* 11, 4 (1997), 25–46.

139. "Citigroup Begins Implementing 5-Point Ethics Program," Dow Jones Newswires (March 1, 2005) at http://online.wsj.com.

140. Ronald E. Berenbeim, *Corporate Ethics Practices* (New York: The Conference Board, 1992).

141. James Weber, "Institutionalizing Ethics into Business Organizations: A Model and Research Agenda," *Business Ethics Quarterly* 3 (1993),419–436.

142. Mark Henricks, "Ethics in Action," *Management Review* (January 1995), 53–55; Dorothy Marcic, *Management and the Wisdom of Love* (San Francisco: Jossey-Bass, 1997); and Beverly Geber, "The Right

and Wrong of Ethics Offices," *Training* (October 1995), 102–118.

143. TI, "Values and Ethics of TI (n.d.) at www.ti.com/ corp/docs/csr/corpgov/ethics/statement.shtml (accessed March 18, 2014).

144. Elearning, "Case Study" (Winter 2005) at http:// elearning.b2bmediaco.com/issues/winter05/ casestudy01_0205.html (accessed May 18, 2011).

145. Susan J. Harrington, "What Corporate America Is Teaching about Ethics," *Academy of Management Executive* 5 (1991), 21–30.

146. TELUS, "Community Investment" (2011) at http://ar.telus.com/investor_overview/about_telus/ community_investment (accessed June 4, 2011).

147. Ibid.

148. TELUS, "We're Committed to Developing Athletes" (n.d.) at http://about.telus.com/community/community _boards/index.html (accessed June 25, 2008).

149. Richard W. Judy and Carol D'Amico, *Workforce 2020: Work and Workers in the 21st Century* (Indianapolis, Ind.: Hudson Institute, 1997).

150. Jerry G. Kreuze, Zahida Luqmani, and Mushtaq Luqmani, "Shades of Gray," *Internal Auditor* (April 2001), 48.

151. S. C. Schneider, "National vs. Corporate Culture: Implications for Human Resource Management," *Human Resource Management* (Summer 1988), 239.

152. Carl F. Fey and Daniel R. Denison, "Organizational Culture and Effectiveness: Can American Theory Be Applied in Russia?" *Organization Science* 14, 6 (November–December 2003), 686–706.

153. X. V. Pothukuchi, F. Damanpour, J. Choi, C. Chen, and S. Park, "National and Organizational Differences and International Joint Venture Performance," *Journal of International Business Studies* 33, 2 (2002), 243–265.

154. Terence Jackson, "Cultural Values and Management Ethics: A 10-Nation Study," *Human Relations* 54, 10 (2001), 1267–1302.

155. Gail Dutton, "Building a Global Brain," *Management Review* (May 1999), 34–38.

156. Ibid.

157. Homer H. Johnson, "Corporate Social Audits—This Time Around," *Business Horizons* (May–June 2001), 29–36.

158. "Me to We, Our Story" at http://www.metowestyle .com/ourstory_aboutus_s/134.htm (accessed July 12, 2008).

## Chapter 10

1. Robert D. Hof, "Building an Idea Factory," *BusinessWeek* (October 11, 2004), 194–200; Brian Bremner and Chester Dawson, "Can Anything Stop Toyota?" *BusinessWeek* (November 17, 2003), 114–122; and Norihiko Shirouzu and Jathon Sapsford, "Heavy Load; For Toyota, a New Small Truck Carries Hopes

for Topping GM," *The Wall Street Journal* (May 12, 2005), A1, A6.

2. "Hans Greimel, "Toyota Keeps No. 1 Crown after Outselling GM, VW in 2013," *Automotive News* (January 23, 2014) at http://www.autonews.com/article/20140123/COPY01/301239962/toyota-keeps-no.-1-crown-after-outselling-gm-vw-in-2013 (accessed April 1, 2014).

3. "Innovation in Canada" (n.d.) at www.mta.ca/faculty/arts/canadian_studies/english/about/innovation/index.htm (accessed June 24, 2008).

4. Based on John P. Kotter, *Leading Change* (Boston, Mass.: Harvard Business School Press, 1996), 18–20.

5. M. Lewis, "Business Rises to Eco Challenge," *Toronto Star* (March 26, 2011), B1–2.

6. David A. Nadler and Michael L. Tushman, "Organizational Frame Bending: Principles for Managing Reorientation," *Academy of Management Executive* 3 (1989), 194–204; and Michael L. Tushman and Charles A. O'Reilly III, "Ambidextrous Organizations: Managing Evolutionary and Revolutionary Change," *California Management Review* 38, no. 4 (Summer 1996), 8–30.

7. R. Colman, "Shifting into High Gear—Honda Canada Drives Process Innovation with Its Employees" (October 1, 2002) at www.allbusiness.com/automotive/motor-vehicle-models-motorcycles/10602037-1.html (accessed July 13, 2008).

8. William A. Davidow and Michael S. Malone, *The Virtual Corporation* (New York: HarperBusiness, 1992); and Gregory G. Dess, Abdul M. A. Rasheed, Kevin J. McLaughlin, and Richard L. Priem, "The New Corporate Architecture," *Academy of Management Executive* 9, no. 3 (1995), 7–20.

9. Brent Schlender, "How Big Can Apple Get?" *Fortune* (February 21, 2005), 66–76.

10. F. Taylor, "Don't Knock on Wood," *The Globe and Mail* (February 22, 2011) at www.theglobeandmail.com/report-on-business/rob-magazine/dont-knock-wood/article1915986 (accessed March 19, 2014)

11. Joseph E. McCann, "Design Principles for an Innovating Company," *Academy of Management Executive* 5 (May 1991), 76–93.

12 Loz Blain, "IKEA's Ingenious Affordable Housing System," gizmag (April 15, 2007) at http://www.gizmag.com/go/7108 (accessed April 3, 2014).

13. K. Hammonds, "How Google Grows…and Grows…and Grows," *Fast Company* (March 31, 2003) at www.fastcompany.com/magazine/69/google.html?page=0%2C2 (accessed March 19, 2014).

14. Fara Warner, "How Google Searches Itself," *Fast Company* (July 2002), 50–52; Fred Vogelstein, "Search and Destroy," *Fortune* (May 2, 2005), 72–82; and Keith H. Hammonds, "How Google Grows…and Grows…and Grows," *Fast Company* (April 2003), 74.

15. K. Vijayraghavan, "Google Most Preferred Employer in B-schools," *The Economic Times* (2010) at http://articles.economictimes.indiatimes.com/2010-12-21/news/27590400_1_fmcg-sector-google-india-shailesh-rao (accessed March 19, 2014).

16. Kelly Barron, "Logistics in Brown," *Forbes* (January 10, 2000), 78–83; and Scott Kirsner, "Venture Vérité: United Parcel Service," *Wired* (September 1999), 83–96.

17. Richard A. Wolfe, "Organizational Innovation: Review, Critique and Suggested Research Directions," *Journal of Management Studies* 31, 3 (May 1994), 405–431.

18. John L. Pierce and Andre L. Delbecq, "Organization Structure, Individual Attitudes and Innovation," *Academy of Management Review* 2 (1977), 27–37; and Michael Aiken and Jerald Hage, "The Organic Organization and Innovation," *Sociology* 5 (1971), 63–82.

19. Richard L. Daft, "Bureaucratic versus Non-bureaucratic Structure in the Process of Innovation and Change," in Samuel B. Bacharach, ed., *Perspectives in Organizational Sociology: Theory and Research* (Greenwich, CT: JAI Press, 1982), 129–166.

20. The Peter F. Drucker Award for Nonprofit Innovation, at www.cgu.edu/pages/4126.asp (accessed May 18, 2011).

21. Alan D. Meyer and James B. Goes, "Organizational Assimilation of Innovations: A Multilevel Contextual Analysis," *Academy of Management Journal* 31 (1988), 897–923.

22. T. Kelley, *The Ten Faces of Innovation* (New York: Currency Doubleday, 2005).

23. Richard W. Woodman, John E. Sawyer, and Ricky W. Griffin, "Toward a Theory of Organizational Creativity," *Academy of Management Review* 18 (1993), 293–321; and Alan Farnham, "How to Nurture Creative Sparks," *Fortune* (January 10, 1994), 94–100.

24. D. Flavelle, "Where Design Meets Function," *Toronto Star* (April 1, 2007), A12.

25. Robert I. Sutton, "Weird Ideas That Spark Innovation," *MIT Sloan Management Review* (Winter 2002), 83–87; Robert Barker, "The Art of Brainstorming," *Business-Week* (August 26, 2002), 168–169; Gary A. Steiner, ed., *The Creative Organization* (Chicago, IL: University of Chicago Press, 1965), 16–18; and James Brian Quinn, "Managing Innovation: Controlled Chaos," *Harvard Business Review* (May–June 1985), 73–84.

26. J. M. Pethokousis, "The Design of Design—From the Computer Mouse to the Newest Swiffer, IDEO Is the Firm Behind the Scenes," *U.S. News and World Report* (September 24, 2006) at www.usnews.com/usnews/biztech/articles/060924/2best_print.htm (accessed May 18, 2011).

27. J. Kotter, *Leading Change*, 20–25; and John P. Kotter, "Leading Change," *Harvard Business Review* (March–April 1995), 59–67.

28. J. Nortext, "First Language Schoolbooks" (n.d.) at http://www.nortext.com/schoolbooks.htm (accessed May 18, 2011).

29. J. G. Tomas M. Hult, Robert F. Hurley, and Gary A. Knight, "Innovativeness: Its Antecedents and Impact on Business Performance," *Industrial Marketing Management* 33 (2004), 429–438.

30. J. L. D. DiSimone, comments about 3M in "How Can Big Companies Keep the Entrepreneurial Spirit Alive?" *Harvard Business Review* (November–December 1995), 184–185; and Thomas A. Stewart, "3M Fights Back," *Fortune* (February 1996), 94–99.

31. J. B. Hindo, "At 3M, A Struggle between Efficiency and Creativity" (June 11, 2007) at www.businessweek.com/magazine/content/07_24/b4038406.htm (accessed March 19, 2014).

32. J. Zinoman, "Defiant Showman Demands His 'Wow,'" *The New York Times* (June 3, 2011) at www.nytimes.com/interactive/2011/06/05/theater/20110605-cirque.html (accessed June 7, 2011).

33. Chad Brooks, "What Is Blue Ocean Strategy?" *Business News Daily* (December 17, 2013) at http://www.businessnewsdaily.com/5647-blue-ocean-strategy.html (accessed April 1, 2014).

34. "What Is Blue Ocean Strategy?" *The Wall Street Journal Online* (2009), http://guides.wsj.com/management/strategy/what-is-blue-ocean-strategy/ (accessed March 19, 2014).

35. J. L. Tischler, "Join the Circus," *Fast Company*, 96 (2005), 53; and John Gustavson, "Meeting the Green Challenge (February 2007) at www.the-cma.org/?WCE=C=47%7CK=226716 (accessed May 28, 2011).

36. J. D. Bruce Merrifield, "Intrapreneurial Corporate Renewal," *Journal of Business Venturing* 8 (September 1993), 383–389; Linsu Kim, "Organizational Innovation and Structure," *Journal of Business Research* 8 (1980), 225–245; and Tom Burns and G. M. Stalker, *The Management of Innovation* (London: Tavistock Publications, 1961).

37. J. James Q. Wilson, "Innovation in Organization: Notes toward a Theory," in James D. Thompson, ed., *Approaches to Organizational Design* (Pittsburgh, PA: University of Pittsburgh Press, 1966), 193–218.

38. Charles A. O'Reilly III and Michael L. Tushman, "The Ambidextrous Organization," *Harvard Business Review* (April 2004), 74–81; M. L. Tushman and C. A. O'Reilly III, "Building an Ambidextrous Organization: Forming Your Own 'Skunk Works,'" *Health Forum Journal* 42, no. 2 (March–April 1999), 20–23; J. C. Spender and Eric H. Kessler, "Managing the Uncertainties of Innovation: Extending Thompson (1967)," *Human Relations* 48, no. 1 (1995), 35–56; and Robert B. Duncan, "The Ambidextrous Organization: Designing Dual Structures for Innovation," in Ralph H. Killman, Louis R. Pondy, and Dennis Slevin, eds., *The Management of Organization*, vol. 1 (New York: North-Holland, 1976), 167–188.

39. C. A. O'Reilly III and M. L. Tushman, "The Ambidextrous Organization."

40. Tushman and O'Reilly, "Building an Ambidextrous Organization."

41. Edward F. McDonough III and Richard Leifer, "Using Simultaneous Structures to Cope with Uncertainty," *Academy of Management Journal* 26 (1983), 727–735.

42. J. Birkinshaw, "The Ambidextrous Organization—Driving Leadership" (2006) at www.mannaz.com/Mail.asp?MailID=102&TopicID=1160 (accessed March 19, 2014).

43. John Gustavson, "Meeting the Green Challenge."

44. Paul S. Adler, Barbara Goldoftas, and David I. Levine, "Ergonomics, Employee Involvement, and the Toyota Production System: A Case Study of NUMMI's 1993 Model Introduction," *Industrial and Labor Relations Review* 50, no. 3 (April 1997), 416–437.

45. Judith R. Blau and William McKinley, "Ideas, Complexity, and Innovation," *Administrative Science Quarterly* 24 (1979), 200–219.

46. Peter Landers, "Back to Basics; With Dry Pipelines, Big Drug Makers Stock Up in Japan," *The Wall Street Journal* (November 24, 2003), A1, A7.

47. Sherri Eng, "Hatching Schemes," *The Industry Standard* (November 27–December 4, 2000), 174–175.

48. I. Ross, "Making His Mark," *Northern Ontario Business* (March 2004), 1.

49. "Alberta Opens First Canadian Incubator for CA Food Processors" (May 16, 2007) at www.gov.ab.ca/home/NewsFrame.cfm?ReleaseID=/acn/200705/2146695822D72-0272-3519-73F8E08198276853.html (accessed May 18, 2011).

50. Christine Canabou, "Fast Ideas for Slow Times," *Fast Company* (May 2003), 52.

51. Christopher Hoenig, "Skunk Works Secrets," *CIO* (July 1, 2000), 74–76.

52. J. Weber, "'Mosh Pits' of Creativity" (November 7, 2005) at www.businessweek.com/magazine/content/05_45/b3958078.htm (accessed March 19, 2014).

53. "MaRS Services" (2007) at www.marsdd.com/mars/MaRS-Services.html (accessed July 13, 2008).

54. J. Steed, "Kicking out the Jams" (February 19, 2007) at www.thestar.com/article/183136 (accessed March 19, 2014).

55. Jane M. Howell and Christopher A. Higgins, "Champions of Technology Innovation," *Administrative Science Quarterly* 35 (1990), 317–341; and Jane M. Howell and Christopher A. Higgins, "Champions of Change: Identifying, Understanding, and Supporting Champions of Technology Innovations," *Organizational Dynamics* (Summer 1990), 40–55.

56. Peter F. Drucker, "Change Leaders," *Inc.* (June 1999), 65–72; and Peter F. Drucker, *Management Challenges for the 21st Century* (New York: HarperBusiness, 1999).

57. Thomas J. Peters and Robert H. Waterman, Jr., *In Search of Excellence* (New York: Harper & Row, 1982).

58. Peter J. Frost and Carolyn P. Egri, "The Political Process of Innovation," in L. L. Cummings and Barry M. Staw, eds., *Research in Organizational Behavior*, vol. 13 (New York: JAI Press, 1991), 229–295; Jay R. Galbraith, "Designing the Innovating Organization," *Organizational Dynamics* (Winter 1982), 5–25; and Marsha Sinatar, "Entrepreneurs, Chaos, and Creativity—Can Creative People Really Survive Large Company Structure?" *Sloan Management Review* (Winter 1985), 57–62.

59. See Lionel Roure, "Product Champion Characteristics in France and Germany," *Human Relations* 54, no. 5 (2001), 663–682 for a recent review of the literature related to product champions.

60. Ibid., 205.

61. A. Tchokogué, C. Bareil, and C.R. Duguay, "Key Lessons from the Implementation of an ERP at Pratt & Whitney Canada," *International Journal of Production Economics*, 95 (2005), 151–163.

62. Christopher Power with Kathleen Kerwin, Ronald Grover, Keith Alexander, and Robert D. Hof, "Flops," *BusinessWeek* (August 16, 1993), 76–82; Modesto A. Maidique and Billie Jo Zirger, "A Study of Success and Failure in Product Innovation: The Case of the U.S. Electronics Industry," *IEEE Transactions in Engineering Management* 31 (November 1984), 192–203.

63. "Bricklin" at www.thecanadianencyclopedia.com/index.cfm?PgNm=TCE&Params=A1ARTA0000983 (accessed May 18, 2011).

64. Avro Arrow at www.thecanadianencyclopedia.com/index.cfm?PgNm=TCE&Params=A1ARTA0000425 (accessed May 18, 2011).

65. Cliff Edwards, "Many Products Have Gone Way of the Edsel," *Johnson City Press* (May 23, 1999), 28, 30; Paul Lukas, "The Ghastliest Product Launches," *Fortune* (March 16, 1998), 44; Robert McMath, *What Were They Thinking? Marketing Lessons I've Learned from Over 80,000 New-Product Innovations and Idiocies* (New York: Times Business, 1998).

66. Edwin Mansfield, J. Rapaport, J. Schnee, S. Wagner, and M. Hamburger, *Research and Innovation in Modern Corporations* (New York: Norton, 1971); and Antonio J. Bailetti and Paul F. Litva, "Integrating Customer Requirements into Product Designs," *Journal of Product Innovation Management* 12 (1995), 3–15.

67. Shona L. Brown and Kathleen M. Eisenhardt, "Product Development: Past Research, Present Findings, and Future Directions," *Academy of Management Review* 20, 2 (1995), 343–378; F. Axel Johne and Patricia A. Snelson, "Success Factors in Product Innovation: A Selective Review of the Literature," Journal of Product Innovation Management 5 (1988), 114–128; and Science Policy Research Unit, University of Sussex, *Success and Failure in Industrial Innovation* (London: Centre for the Study of Industrial Innovation, 1972).

68. R. V. Curnow and G. G. Moring, "Project Sappho: A Study in Industrial Innovation," *Futures* 1, 2 (1969) 82–90; and R. Rothwell, C. Freeman, A. Horsley, V. T. P. Jervis, A. B. Robertson, and J. Townsend, "SAPPHO Updated—Project SAPPHO Phase II," *Research Policy* 22, 2 (1993), 110.

69. P. Nowak, "Puretracks Takes Lead in Rights Fight" (February 22, 2007) at www.financialpost.com/story.html?id=c4fe4fe1-bd7c-489b-bfdf-54991a0587be (accessed March 19, 2014).

70. The Children's Place, at http://corporate.puretracks.com/success.htm (accessed May 18, 2011).

71. Brown and Eisenhardt, "Product Development"; Dan Dimancescu and Kemp Dwenger, "Smoothing the Product Development Path," *Management Review* (January 1996), 36–41.

72. Fara Warner, "In a Word, Toyota Drives for Innovation," *Fast Company* (August 2002), 36–38.

73. Bettina von Stamm, "Collaboration with Other Firms and Customers"; Bas Hillebrand and Wim G. Biemans, "Links between Internal and External Cooperation in Product Development: An Exploratory Study," *The Journal of Product Innovation Management* 21 (2004), 110–122.

74. Kenneth B. Kahn, "Market Orientation, Interdepartmental Integration, and Product Development Performance," *The Journal of Product Innovation Management* 18 (2001), 314–323; and Ali E. Akguèn, Gary S. Lynn, and John C. Byrne, "Taking the Guesswork Out of New Product Development: How Successful High-Tech Companies Get That Way," *Journal of Business Strategy* 25, no. 4 (2004), 41–46.

75. "A. G. Lafley," *Reference for Business*, at www.referenceforbusiness.com/biography/F-L/Lafley-A-G-1947.html (accessed April 13, 2014).

76. Alex Markels, "Turning the Tide at P&G" (October 22, 2006) at www.usnews.com/usnews/news/articles/061022/30lafley_2.htm (accessed May 18, 2011).

77. Patricia Sellers, "P&G: Teaching an Old Dog New Tricks," *Fortune* (May 31, 2004), 167–180; Robert D. Hof, "Building an Idea Factory"; and Bettina von Stamm, "Collaboration with Other Firms and Customers: Innovation's Secret Weapon," *Strategy & Leadership* 32, 3 (2004), 16–20.

78. Max Nisen, "Here's Why Wall Street Loves the Return of P&G's OLD CEO," *Business Insider* (May 24, 2013) at http://www.businessinsider.com/ag-lafley-rehired-as-pg-ceo-2013-5 (accessed April 1, 2014).

79. John A. Pearce II, "Speed Merchants," *Organizational Dynamics* 30, no. 3 (2002), 191–205; Kathleen M. Eisenhardt and Behnam N. Tabrizi, "Accelerating Adaptive Processes: Product Innovation in the Global Computer Industry," *Administrative Science Quarterly* 40 (1995), 84–110; D. Dougherty and C. Hardy, "Sustained Product Innovation in Large, Mature Organizations," *Academy of Management Journal* 39 (1996), 1120–1153; and Karne Bronikowski, "Speeding

New Products to Market," *Journal of Business Strategy* (September–October 1990), 34–37.

80. V. K. Narayanan, Frank L. Douglas, Brock Guernsey, and John Charnes, "How Top Management Steers Fast Cycle Teams to Success," *Strategy & Leadership* 30, 3 (2002), 19–27.

81. Steve Konicki, "Time Trials," *InformationWeek* (June 3, 2002), 36–44.

82. Edward F. McDonough III, Kenneth B. Kahn, and Gloria Barczak, "An Investigation of the Use of Global, Virtual, and Colocated New Product Development Teams," *The Journal of Product Innovation Management* 18 (2001), 110–120.

83. Dimancescu and Dwenger, "Smoothing the Product Development Path."

84. Raymond E. Miles, Henry J. Coleman, Jr., and W. E. Douglas Creed, "Keys to Success in Corporate Redesign," *California Management Review* 37, 3 (Spring 1995), 128–145.

85. Fariborz Damanpour and William M. Evan, "Organizational Innovation and Performance: The Problem of 'Organizational Lag,'" *Administrative Science Quarterly* 29 (1984), 392–409; David J. Teece, "The Diffusion of an Administrative Innovation," *Management Science* 26 (1980), 464–470; John R. Kimberly and Michael J. Evaniski, "Organizational Innovation: The Influence of Individual, Organizational and Contextual Factors on Hospital Adoption of Technological and Administrative Innovation," *Academy of Management Journal* 24 (1981), 689–713; Michael K. Moch and Edward V. Morse, "Size, Centralization, and Organizational Adoption of Innovations," *American Sociological Review* 42 (1977), 716–725; and Mary L. Fennell, "Synergy, Influence, and Information in the Adoption of Administrative Innovation," *Academy of Management Journal* 27 (1984), 113–129.

86. Richard L. Daft, "A Dual-Core Model of Organizational Innovation," *Academy of Management Journal* 21 (1978), 193–210.

87. Daft, "Bureaucratic versus Nonbureaucratic Structure"; Robert W. Zmud, "Diffusion of Modern Software Practices: Influence of Centralization and Formalization," *Management Science* 28 (1982), 1421–1431.

88. Daft, "A Dual-Core Model of Organizational Innovation"; Zmud, "Diffusion of Modern Software Practices."

89. Fariborz Damanpour, "The Adoption of Technological, Administrative, and Ancillary Innovations: Impact of Organizational Factors," *Journal of Management* 13 (1987), 675–688.

90. J. Castaldo, "Refreshing! A Clearly Canadian Comeback" (September 11, 2006) at www.canadian business.com/managing/strategy/article.jsp?content=20060911_80201_80201 (accessed July 13, 2008).

91. "Supreme Court of British Columbia Approves Clearly Canadian Restructuring Proposal" (May 3, 2010) at http://www.clearly.ca/pdfs/May032010_Release.pdf (accessed June 4, 2011).

92. Gregory H. Gaertner, Karen N. Gaertner, and David M. Akinnusi, "Environment, Strategy, and the Implementation of Administrative Change: The Case of Civil Service Reform," *Academy of Management Journal* 27 (1984), 525–543.

93. Claudia Bird Schoonhoven and Mariann Jelinek, "Dynamic Tension in Innovative, High Technology Firms: Managing Rapid Technology Change through Organization Structure," in Mary Ann Von Glinow and Susan Albers Mohrman, eds., *Managing Complexity in High Technology Organizations* (New York: Oxford University Press, 1990), 90–118.

94. David Ulm and James K. Hickel, "What Happens after Restructuring?" *Journal of Business Strategy* (July–August 1990), 37–41; and John L. Sprague, "Restructuring and Corporate Renewal: A Manager's Guide," *Management Review* (March 1989), 34–36.

95. Stan Pace, "Rip the Band-Aid Off Quickly," *Strategy & Leadership* 30, 1 (2002), 4–9.

96. Benson L. Porter and Warrington S. Parker, Jr., "Culture Change," *Human Resource Management* 31 (Spring–Summer 1992), 45–67.

97. H. Richardson, "When Pupils Sit on Teachers' Job Interview Panels," BBC News-Education & Family (March 28, 2011) at www.bbc.co.uk/news/education-12883110 (accessed March 19, 2014).

98. I. Cinite and H. Kolodny, *Culture Change at Canada Revenue Agency: Implementing Alternate Dispute Resolution* (n.d.),unpublished case study, Rotman School of Business, University of Toronto.

99. Quoted in Anne B. Fisher, "Making Change Stick," *Fortune* (April 17, 1995), 122.

100. PBS, "Isolated Incidents?" (April 26, 1996) at www.pbs.org/newshour/bb/business/april96/mitsubishi_4-26.html (accessed June 4, 2011).

101. A. Wahl, "Culture Shock: A Survey of Canadian Executives Reveals That Corporate Culture Is in Need of Improvement" (October 10–23, 2005) at www.canadianbusiness.com/managing/employees/article.jsp?content=20060106_160426_5512 (accessed May 18, 2011); and G. Seijts, *WestJet Airlines (A): the Culture that Breeds a Passion to Succeed* (Ivey Management Services, 2001).

102. M. Magnan, "People Power" (October 10, 2005) at www.canadianbusiness.com/managing/strategy/article.jsp?content=20051010_71478_71478 (accessed July 13, 2008).

103. "WestJet Named to Corporate Culture Hall of Fame" (February 1, 2010) at www.cnw.ca/en/releases/archive/February2010/01/c5612.html (accessed March 19, 2014).

104. W. Warner Burke, "The New Agenda for Organization Development," in Wendell L. French, Cecil H. Bell, Jr., and Robert A. Zawacki, *Organization Development and Transformation: Managing Effective Change* (Burr Ridge, IL: Irwin McGraw-Hill, 2000), 523–535.

105. W. Warner Burke, *Organization Development: A Process of Learning and Changing*, 2nd ed. (Reading, MA: Addison-Wesley, 1994); and Wendell L. French and Cecil H. Bell, Jr., "A History of Organization Development," in French, Bell, and Zawacki, *Organization Development and Transformation*, 20–42.

106. French and Bell, "A History of Organization Development."

107. The information on large group intervention is based on Kathleen D. Dannemiller and Robert W. Jacobs, "Changing the Way Organizations Change: A Revolution of Common Sense," *The Journal of Applied Behavioral Science* 28, no. 4 (December 1992), 480–498; Barbara B. Bunker and Billie T. Alban, "Conclusion: What Makes Large Group Interventions Effective?" *The Journal of Applied Behavioral Science* 28, no. 4 (December 1992), 570–591; and Marvin R. Weisbord, "Inventing the Future: Search Strategies for Whole System Improvements," in French, Bell, and Zawacki, *Organization Development and Transformation*, 242–250.

108. J. Quinn, "What a Workout!" *Performance* (November 1994), 58–63; and Bunker and Alban, "Conclusion: What Makes Large Group Interventions Effective?"

109. Dave Ulrich, Steve Kerr, and Ron Ashkenas, with Debbie Burke and Patrice Murphy, *The GE Work Out: How to Implement GE's Revolutionary Method for Busting Bureaucracy and Attacking Organizational Problems—Fast!* (New York: McGraw-Hill, 2002).

110. Paul F. Buller, "For Successful Strategic Change: Blend OD Practices with Strategic Management," *Organizational Dynamics* (Winter 1988), 42–55.

111. Norm Brodsky, "Everybody Sells" (Street Smarts column) *Inc. Magazine* (June 2004), 53–54.

112. Richard S. Allen and Kendyl A. Montgomery, "Applying an Organizational Development Approach to Creating Diversity," *Organizational Dynamics* 30, no. 2 (2001), 149–161.

113. Jyotsna Sanzgiri and Jonathan Z. Gottlieb, "Philosophic and Pragmatic Influences on the Practice of Organization Development, 1950–2000," *Organizational Dynamics* (Autumn 1992), 57–69.

114. Bernard M. Bass, "Theory of Transformational Leadership Redux," *Leadership Quarterly* 6, no. 4 (1995), 463–478; and Dong I. Jung, Chee Chow, and Anne Wu, "The Role of Transformational Leadership in Enhancing Organizational Innovation: Hypotheses and Some Preliminary Findings," *The Leadership Quarterly* 14 (2003), 525–544.

115. P. Hawken, "Commencement Address, University of Portland (2009), at www.up.edu/commencement/default.aspx?cid=9456 (accessed March 21, 2014).

116. E. Knowles, "Hewers of Wood and Drawers of Water," *The Oxford Dictionary of Phrase and Fable* (2006) at www.encyclopedia.com/doc/1O214 -hewersofwoodanddrawrsfwtr.html (accessed March 21, 2014).

117. T. Heaps, "Green Tycoons," *Literary Review of Canada* (November 2010) at http://reviewcanada.ca/reviews/2010/11/01/green-tycoons (accessed March 21, 2014).

118. Ronald Recardo, Kathleen Molloy, and James Pellegrino, "How the Learning Organization Manages Change," *National Productivity Review* (Winter 1995/96), 7–13.

119. Drucker, *Management Challenges for the 21st Century*; Tushman and O'Reilly, "Ambidextrous Organizations"; Gary Hamel and C. K. Prahalad, "Seeing the Future First," *Fortune* (September 4, 1994), 64–70; and Linda Yates and Peter Skarzynski, "How Do Companies Get to the Future First?" *Management Review* (January 1999), 16–22.

120. Based on Daryl R. Conner, *Managing at the Speed of Change* (New York: Villard Books, 1992), 146–160.

121. Based on Carol A. Beatty and John R. M. Gordon, "Barriers to the Implementation of CAD/CAM Systems," *Sloan Management Review* (Summer 1988), 25–33.

122. M. A-T Yew, "Software Firm's Got Game," *Toronto Star* (September 10, 2007) at www.thestar.com/Business/article/254706 (accessed March 21, 2014).

123. The Edison Awards at http://www.edisonawards.com/Awards.php (accessed May 18, 2011).

124. G. Warman "Sim U, Front Lines, *The Globe and Mail* (March 7, 2006) at http://gold.globeinvestor.com/servlet/story/RTGAM.20060206.gtflWarmanfeb6/APStory/?query=experiencepoint&pageRequested=all (accessed May 18, 2011).

125. Everett M. Rogers and Floyd Shoemaker, *Communication of Innovations: A Cross Cultural Approach*, 2nd ed. (New York: Free Press, 1971); Stratford P. Sherman, "Eight Big Masters of Innovation," *Fortune* (October 15, 1984), 66–84.

126. Richard L. Daft and Selwyn W. Becker, *Innovation in Organizations* (New York: Elsevier, 1978); and John P. Kotter and Leonard A. Schlesinger, "Choosing Strategies for Change," *Harvard Business Review* 57 (1979), 106–114.

127. "Employee Suggestion Systems" (September 19, 2001) at http://www.hi.is/~joner/eaps/ds_esug.htm (accessed May 18, 2011).

128. Peter Richardson and D. Keith Denton, "Communicating Change," *Human Resource Management* 35, 2 (Summer 1996), 203–216.

129. Edgar H. Schein and Warren Bennis, *Personal and Organizational Change via Group Methods* (New York: Wiley, 1965); and Amy Edmondson, "Psychological Safety and Learning Behavior in Work Teams," *Administrative Science Quarterly* 44 (1999), 350–383.

130. Diane L. Coutu, "Creating the Most Frightening Company on Earth; An Interview with Andy Law

of St. Luke's," *Harvard Business Review* (September–October 2000), 143–150.

131. Philip H. Mirvis, Amy L. Sales, and Edward J. Hackett, "The Implementation and Adoption of New Technology in Organizations: The Impact on Work, People, and Culture," *Human Resource Management* 30 (Spring 1991), 113–139; Arthur E. Wallach, "System Changes Begin in the Training Department," *Personnel Journal* 58 (1979), 846–848, 872; and Paul R. Lawrence, "How to Deal with Resistance to Change," *Harvard Business Review* 47 (January–February 1969), 4–12, 166–176.

132. Dexter C. Dunphy and Doug A. Stace, "Transformational and Coercive Strategies for Planned Organizational Change: Beyond the O.D. Model," *Organizational Studies* 9 (1988), 317–334; and Kotter and Schlesinger, "Choosing Strategies for Change."

133. Mindtools, "Lewin's Change Management Model" (n.d.) at http://www.mindtools.com/pages/article/newPPM_94.htm (accessed March 21, 2014).

# Chapter 11

1. "Anishinabek Nation Appoints Women's Water Commission" (March 27, 2007) at www.anishinabek.ca/index.php?option=com_content&task=view&id=167&Itemid=47 (accessed June 27, 2008).

2. Ibid.

3. Anishinabek/Ontario Agreements Pledge Cooperation, www.anishinabek.ca/index.php?option=com_content&task=view&id=162&Itemid=2.

4. Carol J. Loomis, "Why Carly's Big Bet Is Failing," *Fortune* (February 7, 2005), 50–64; David Bank and Joann S. Lublin, "For H-P, No Shortage of Ideas; Turnaround Experts Offer Wide Range of Conflicting Strategies," *Asian Wall Street Journal* (February 14, 2005), M5; and James B. Stewart, "Common Sense: Finding a New CEO Won't Help Unless H-P Finds New Products," *The Wall Street Journal* (February 23, 2005), D3.

5. C. Boyd, Canadian Tire (A), College of Commerce, University of Saskatchewan, 1989).

6. Alex Markels, "10 Biggest Business Blunders," *U.S. News & World Report* (November 8, 2004), EE2–EE8.

7. Merissa Marr, "Return of the Ogre; How Dream-Works Misjudged DVD Sales of Its Monster Hit," *The Wall Street Journal* (May 31, 2005), A1, A9.

8. Saul Hansell, "Meg Whitman and eBay, Net Survivors," *The New York Times* (May 5, 2002), 17; Michael V. Copeland and Owen Thomas, "Hits (& Misses)," *Business 2.0* (January–February 2004), 126; Carlos Ghosn, "Saving the Business without Losing the Company," *Harvard Business Review* (January 2002), 37–45.

9. Charles Lindblom, "The Science of 'Muddling Through,'" *Public Administration Review* 29 (1954), 79–88.

10. Herbert A. Simon, *The New Science of Management Decision* (Englewood Cliffs, NJ: Prentice Hall, 1960), 1–8.

11. Paul J. H. Schoemaker and J. Edward Russo, "A Pyramid of Decision Approaches," *California Management Review* (Fall 1993), 9–31.

12. Funding Universe, "Tupperware Corporation" (2011) at www.fundinguniverse.com/company-histories/Tupperware-Corporation-Company-History.html (accessed June 4, 2011).

13. J. Lazor, "The Tupperware Success Story" (2010) at www.helium.com/items/1935941-tupperware-history-tupperware-careers-food-storage-tips-how-to-use-tupperware-buy-tupperware (accessed June 5, 2011); Rick Brooks, "Sealing Their Fate; A Deal with Target Put Lid on Revival at Tupperware," *The Wall Street Journal* (February 18, 2004), A1, A9.

14. Michael Pacanowsky, "Team Tools for Wicked Problems," *Organizational Dynamics* 23, 3 (Winter 1995), 36–51.

15. Industry Canada OCA, "Key Facts from Industry Canada's Consumer Trends Update" (August 22, 2013) at http://www.ic.gc.ca/eic/site/oca-bc.nsf/eng/ca02865.html (accessed February 1, 2014).

16. Based on Francine Schwadel, "Christmas Sales' Lack of Momentum Test Store Managers' Mettle," *The Wall Street Journal* (December 16, 1987), 1.

17. James W. Dean, Jr., and Mark P. Sharfman, "Procedural Rationality in the Strategic Decision-Making Process," *Journal of Management Studies* 30 (1993), 587–610.

18. H. Mintzberg, *The Nature of Managerial Work* (New York: Harper & Row, 1993).

19. J. A. H. Bell, S. Hyland, T. DePellegrin, R. E. G. Upshur, M. Bernstein, and D. K. Martin, "SARS and Hospital Priority Setting: A Qualitative Case Study and Evaluation," *BMC Health Services Research*, 4 (2004), 36.

20. Art Kleiner, "Core Group Therapy," *Strategy & Business* 27 (Second Quarter, 2002), 26–31.

21. Irving L. Janis, *Crucial Decisions: Leadership in Policymaking and Crisis Management* and (New York: The Free Press, 1989); and Paul C. Nutt, "Flexible Decision Styles and the Choices of Top Executives," *Journal of Management Studies* 30 (1993), 695–721.

22. Herbert A. Simon, "Making Management Decisions: The Role of Intuition and Emotion," *Academy of Management Executive* 1 (February 1987), 57–64; and Daniel J. Eisenberg, "How Senior Managers Think," *Harvard Business Review* 62 (November–December 1984), 80–90.

23. Stefan Wally and J. Robert Baum, "Personal and Structural Determinants of the Pace of Strategic Decision Making," *Academy of Management Journal* 37, 4 (1994), 932–956; and Orlando Behling and Norman L. Eckel, "Making Sense Out of Intuition," *Academy of Management Executive* 5, 1 (1991), 46–54.

24. Gary Klein, *Intuition at Work: Why Developing Your Gut Instincts Will Make You Better at What You Do* (New York: Doubleday, 2002); Milorad M. Novicevic, Thomas J. Hench, and Daniel A. Wren, "'Playing by Ear…in an Incessant Din of Reasons': Chester Barnard and the History of Intuition in Management Thought," *Management Decision* 40, 10 (2002), 992–1002; Alden M. Hayashi, "When to Trust Your Gut," *Harvard Business Review* (February 2001), 59–65; Brian R. Reinwald, "Tactical Intuition," *Military Review* 80, 5 (September–October 2000), 78–88; Thomas A. Stewart, "How to Think with Your Gut," *Business 2.0* (November 2002) at http://www.manyworlds.com/exploreco .aspx?coid=CO111120210263240 (accessed May 18, 2011); Bill Breen, "What's Your Intuition?" *Fast Company* (September 2000), 290–300; and Henry Mintzberg and Frances Westley, "Decision Making: It's Not What You Think," *MIT Sloan Management Review* (Spring 2001), 89–93.

25. Thomas F. Issack, "Intuition: An Ignored Dimension of Management," *Academy of Management Review* 3 (1978), 917–922.

26. Marjorie A. Lyles, "Defining Strategic Problems: Subjective Criteria of Executives," *Organizational Studies* 8 (1987), 263–280; and Marjorie A. Lyles and Ian I. Mitroff, "Organizational Problem Formulation: An Empirical Study," *Administrative Science Quarterly* 25 (1980), 102–119.

27. Marjorie A. Lyles and Howard Thomas, "Strategic Problem Formulation: Biases and Assumptions Embedded in Alternative Decision-Making Models," *Journal of Management Studies* 25 (1988), 131–145.

28. Ross Stagner, "Corporate Decision-Making: An Empirical Study," *Journal of Applied Psychology* 53 (1969), 1–13.

29. Reported in Eric Bonabeau, "Don't Trust Your Gut," *Harvard Business Review* (May 2003), 116ff.

30. "About Us" Canopy, at http://www.canopyplanet.org/ index.php?page=about-mi (accessed May 18, 2011). (Reproduced by permission of Canopy.)

31. "How We Worked with Harry Potter to Change Publishing as We Know It" at http://canopyplanet.org/ index.php?page=the-markets-initiative-harry-potter-timeline (accessed March 21, 2014). (Reproduced by permission of Canopy.)

32. Q. N. Y. Lee, "Protecting Ancient Forests with Harry Potter, Orato" (2010) at www.orate.com/business -career/canopy-greening-businesses-for-earth (accessed April 2, 2011).

33. Ashante Infantry, "Atwood Special-Edition Book Printed on Straw," *Toronto Star* (October 11, 2011)_ at http://canopyplanet.org/news/77/310/Atwood-special-edition-book-printed-on-straw-Toronto-Star (accessed April 3, 2014).

34. E. Birnbaum, "In Conversation with Nicole Rycroft," SEE Change Magazine (2010) at www.seechangemagazine .ca/articles/interviews/198-in-conversation-with-nicole -rycroft (accessed March 21, 2014).

35. Thomas George, "Head Cowboy Gets Off His High Horse," *The New York Times* (December 21, 2003), Section 8, 1; Stewart, "How to Think with Your Gut."

36. Bonabeau, "Don't Trust Your Gut."

37. Ann Langley, "Between 'Paralysis by Analysis' and 'Extinction by Instinct,'" *Sloan Management Review* (Spring 1995), 63–76.

38. Paul C. Nutt, "Types of Organizational Decision Processes," *Administrative Science Quarterly* 29 (1984), 414–450.

39. G. Fabrikant, "The Paramount Team Puts Profit over Splash" (June 30, 2002) from www.nytimes .com/2002/06/30/business/the-paramount-team-puts -profit-over-splash.html (accessed March 21, 2014).

40. Geraldine Fabrikant, "The Paramount Team Puts Profit Over Splash," *The New York Times* (June 30, 2002), 1, 15.

41. Nandini Rajagopalan, Abdul M. A. Rasheed, and Deepak K. Datta, "Strategic Decision Processes: Critical Review and Future Decisions," *Journal of Management* 19 (1993), 349–384; Paul J. H. Schoemaker, "Strategic Decisions in Organizations: Rational and Behavioral Views," *Journal of Management Studies* 30 (1993), 107–129; Charles J. McMillan, "Qualitative Models of Organizational Decision Making," *Journal of Management Studies* 5 (1980), 22–39; and Paul C. Nutt, "Models for Decision Making in Organizations and Some Contextual Variables Which Stimulate Optimal Use," *Academy of Management Review* 1 (1976), 84–98.

42. Hugh J. Miser, "Operations Analysis in the Army Air Forces in World War II: Some Reminiscences," *Interfaces* 23 (September–October 1993), 47–49; Harold J. Leavitt, William R. Dill, and Henry B. Eyring, *The Organizational World* (New York: Harcourt Brace Jovanovich, 1973), chap. 6.

43. Stephen J. Huxley, "Finding the Right Spot for a Church Camp in Spain," *Interfaces* 12 (October 1982), 108–114; James E. Hodder and Henry E. Riggs, "Pitfalls in Evaluating Risky Projects," *Harvard Business Review* (January–February 1985), 128–135.

44. Edward Baker and Michael Fisher, "Computational Results for Very Large Air Crew Scheduling Problems," *Omega* 9 (1981), 613–618; Jean Aubin, "Scheduling Ambulances," *Interfaces* 22 (March–April, 1992), 1–10.

45. F. Di Meglio, "B-Schools Profs Want to Know, *BusinessWeek* (October 7, 2007) at www.businessweek .com/bschools/content/oct2007/bs2007107_843692 .htm (accessed March 21, 2014).

46. Terrence Belford, "Where Best to Set up Shop? Do the Math" (November 13, 2007) at www.theglobeandmail .com/servlet/story/RTGAM.20071113.winnomath13/ BNStory/Technology (accessed May 18, 2011).

47. Ibid.

48. Ibid.

49. Ibid.

50. Julie Schlosser, Markdown Lowdown," *Fortune* (January 12, 2004), 40; Christina Binkley, "Numbers Game; Taking Retailers' Cues, Harrah's Taps Into Science of Gambling," *The Wall Street Journal* (November 22, 2004), A1, A8.

51. Harold J. Leavitt, "Beyond the Analytic Manager," *California Management Review* 17 (1975), 5–12; and C. Jackson Grayson, Jr., "Management Science and Business Practice," *Harvard Business Review* 51 (July–August 1973), 41–48.

52. Richard L. Daft and John C. Wiginton, "Language and Organization," *Academy of Management Review* (1979), 179–191.

53. Based on Richard M. Cyert and James G. March, *A Behavioral Theory of the Firm* (Englewood Cliffs, NJ: Prentice Hall, 1963); and James G. March and Herbert A. Simon, *Organizations* (New York: Wiley, 1958).

54. William B. Stevenson, Joan L. Pearce, and Lyman W. Porter, "The Concept of 'Coalition' in Organization Theory and Research," *Academy of Management Review* 10 (1985), 256–268.

55. Cyert and March, *A Behavioral Theory of the Firm*, 120–222.

56. Pui-Wing Tam, "One for the History Books: The Tale of How Britannica Is Trying to Leap from the Old Economy Into the New One," *The Wall Street Journal* (December 11, 2000), R32; and Richard A. Melcher, "Dusting Off the Britannica," *BusinessWeek* (October 20, 1997), 143–146.

57. Lawrence G. Hrebiniak, "Top-Management Agreement and Organizational Performance," *Human Relations* 35 (1982), 1139–1158; and Richard P. Nielsen, "Toward a Method for Building Consensus during Strategic Planning," *Sloan Management Review* (Summer 1981), 29–40.

58. Based on Henry Mintzberg, Duru Raisinghani, and André Théorêt "The Structure of 'Unstructured' Decision Processes," *Administrative Science Quarterly* 21 (1976), 246–275.

59. Lawrence T. Pinfield, "A Field Evaluation of Perspectives on Organizational Decision Making," *Administrative Science Quarterly* 31 (1986), 365–388.

60. Mintzberg et al., "The Structure of 'Unstructured' Decision Processes."

61. Henry Mintzberg, Duru Raisinghani, and André Théorêt, "The Structure of 'Unstructured' Decision Processes," *Administrative Science Quarterly* 21, no. 2 (June 1976), 257.

62. Mintzberg et al., "The Structure of 'Unstructured' Decision Processes," 270.

63. William C. Symonds with Carol Matlack, "Gillette's Edge," *BusinessWeek* (January 19, 1998), 70–77; William C. Symonds, "Would You Spend $1.50 for a Razor Blade?" *BusinessWeek* (April 27, 1998), 46; Peter J. Howe, "Innovative; For the Past Half Century, 'Cutting Edge' Has Meant More at Gillette Co. Than a Sharp Blade," Boston Globe (January 30, 2005), D1; and FAQ at http://www.gillettefusion.com/us/custom/en_US/ (accessed July 13, 2008).

64. Anna Wilde Mathews, Martin Peers, and Nick Wingfield, "Off-Key: The Music Industry Is Finally Online, but Few Listen," *The Wall Street Journal* (May 7, 2002), A1, A20; and "Medianet Overview" at http://www.musicnet.com/about/overview.html (accessed July 13, 2008).

65. Medianet, "About MediaNet" (2011) at http://www.mndigital.com/about-us (accessed June 5, 2011).

66. B. Simpson, "'Flying People, not Planes': The CEO of Bombardier on Building a World-class Culture," *McKinsey Quarterly*, at https://www.mckinseyquarterly.com/Flying_people_not_planes_The_CEO_of_Bombardier_on_building_a_world-class_culture_2755 (accessed May 18, 2011).

67. Ibid.

68. C. Noronha, "Bombardier 4Q Income Soars to $325M," *AP* (March 31, 2011) http://finance.yahoo.com/news/Bombardier-4Q-income-soars-to-apf-1706674796.html?x=0&.v=5 (accessed June 13, 2011).

69. Michael D. Cohen, James G. March, and Johan P. Olsen, "A Garbage Can Model of Organizational Choice," *Administrative Science Quarterly* 17 (March 1972), 1–25; and Michael D. Cohen and James G. March, *Leadership and Ambiguity: The American College President* (New York: McGraw-Hill, 1974).

70. Michael Masuch and Perry LaPotin, "Beyond Garbage Cans: An AI Model of Organizational Choice," *Administrative Science Quarterly* 34 (1989), 38–67.

71. N. Takahashi, "A Single Garbage Can Model and the Degree of Anarchy in Japanese Firms," *Human Relations* 50, 1 (1997), 91–109.

72. Manohla Dargis "On a Stroll in Angstville with Dots Disconnected." (October 1, 2004) at http://movies.nytimes.com/2004/10/01/movies/01HUCK.html (accessed May 18, 2011).

73. Sharon Waxman, "The Nudist Buddhist Borderline-Abusive Love-In," *The New York Times* (September 19, 2004), Section 2, 1; and V. A. Musetto, "Crix Pick Best Pix," *The New York Post* (May 29, 2005), 93.

74. Thomas R. King, "Why 'Waterworld,' with Costner in Fins, Is Costliest Film Ever," *The Wall Street Journal* (January 31, 1995), A1.

75. Adapted from James D. Thompson, *Organizations in Action* (New York: McGraw-Hill, 1967), chap. 10; and McMillan, "Qualitative Models of Organizational Decision Making," 25.

76. Louise Lee, "Courts Begin to Award Damages to Victims of Parking-Area Crime," *The Wall Street Journal* (April 23, 1997), A1, A8.

77. Beth Dickey, "NASA's Next Step," *Government Executive* (April 15, 2004), 34ff; and Jena McGregor, "Gospels of Failure," *Fast Company* (February 2005), 61–67.

78. Dowden, "Fast Food that's Good for You," *Evening Standard* (n.d.) at www.dailymail.co.uk/health/article-176850/Fast-food-thats-good-you.html (accessed March 21, 2014).

79. Mintzberg and Wheatley, "Decision Making: It's Not What You Think."

80. Paul C. Nutt, "Selecting Decision Rules for Crucial Choices: An Investigation of the Thompson Framework," *The Journal of Applied Behavioral Science* 38, 1 (March 2002), 99–131; and Paul C. Nutt, "Making Strategic Choices," *Journal of Management Studies* 39, no. 1 (January 2002), 67–95.

81. George T. Doran and Jack Gunn, "Decision Making in High-Tech Firms: Perspectives of Three Executives," *Business Horizons* (November–December 2002), 7–16.

82. L. J. Bourgeois III and Kathleen M. Eisenhardt, "Strategic Decision Processes in High Velocity Environments: Four Cases in the Microcomputer Industry," *Management Science* 34 (1988), 816–835.

83. Kathleen M. Eisenhardt, "Speed and Strategic Course: How Managers Accelerate Decision Making," *California Management Review* (Spring 1990), 39–54.

84. David A. Garvin and Michael A. Roberto, "What You Don't Know about Making Decisions," *Harvard Business Review* (September 2001), 108–116.

85. James Surowiecki, *The Wisdom of Crowds: Why the Many Are Smarter Than the Few and How Collective Wisdom Shapes Business, Economies, Societies, and Nations* (New York: Doubleday, 2004); Doran and Gunn, "Decision Making in High-Tech Firms."

86. Doran and Gunn, "Decision Making in High-Tech Firms."

87. Karl Weick, *The Social Psychology of Organizing*, 2nd ed. (Reading, MA: Addison-Wesley, 1979), 243.

88. Christopher Power with Kathleen Kerwin, Ronald Grover, Keith Alexander, and Robert D. Hof, "Flops," *BusinessWeek* (August 16, 1993), 76–82.

89. Robert Townsend, *Up the Organization* (New York: Knopf, 1974), 115.

90. Helga Drummond, "Too Little Too Late: A Case Study of Escalation in Decision Making," *Organization Studies* 15, 4 (1994), 591–607; Joel Brockner, "The Escalation of Commitment to a Failing Course of Action: Toward Theoretical Progress," *Academy of Management Review* 17 (1992), 39–61; Barry M. Staw and Jerry Ross, "Knowing When to Pull the Plug," *Harvard Business Review* 65 (March–April 1987), 68–74; and Barry M. Staw, "The Escalation of Commitment to a Course of Action," *Academy of Management Review* 6 (1981), 577–587.

91. S. B. Salter, and D. D. Sharp, "Agency Effects and Escalation of Commitment: Do Small National Culture Differences Matter?" *The International Journal of Accounting* 36, 1 (2001), 33–45.

92. N. VanderKlippe, "Hydrogen Highway Hits Dead End (November 5, 2007) at www.financialpost .com/story.html?id=356bed57-656b-4ffd-b3b0-f7f5a96ace29&k=80493 (accessed March 21, 2014).

93. "Ballard Power to Sell Auto Fuel Cell Assets to Ford, Daimler" (November 8, 2007) at www.theglobeandmail .com/servlet/story/RTGAM.20071108.wballard1108/BNStory/Business (accessed July 13, 2008).

94. Will Connors, "Directors at RIM Urged to Exert Control," *Wall Street Journal* (December 27, 2011) at http://online.wsj.com/news/articles/SB100014240529702036862045771167517856711184 (accessed March 21, 2014).

95. Phred Dvorak, Suzanne Vranica, and Spencer E. Ante, "BlackBerry Maker's Issue: Gadgets for Work or Play?" *The Wall Street Journal Online* (September 30, 2011), http://online.wsj.com/article/SB100014240529702044224045765976061591715344.html (accessed September 30, 2011).

96. Michael Lewis, "BlackBerry, One Year Later," *Toronto Star* (January 25, 2014), B1.

97. Ibid., B4.

# Chapter 12

1. "Harold Ballard Convicted of Fraud" at http://archives.cbc.ca/sports/hockey/clips/1290 (accessed March 21, 2014).

2. Ibid.

3. Hockey Fans, "Toronto Maple Leafs" at http://www .hockey-fans.com/northeast/mapleleafs (accessed May 18, 2011).

4. "Leafs' President Averts Possibility of Takeover" (June 22, 1989) at http://query.nytimes.com/gst/fullpage.html?res=950DEFD91538F931A15755C0A96F948260&scp=1&sq=Leafs%92+President+Averts+Possibility+of+Takeover&st=nyt (accessed March 21, 2014).

5. "The Leaf Way" (March 2006) at http://mirtle.blogspot.com/2006_03_01_archive.html (accessed March 21, 2014).

6. Lee G. Bolman and Terrence E. Deal, *Reframing Organizations: Artistry, Choice, and Leadership* (San Francisco: Jossey-Bass, 1991).

7. Paul M. Terry, "Conflict Management," *The Journal of Leadership Studies* 3, no. 2 (1996), 3–21; and Kathleen M. Eisenhardt, Jean L. Kahwajy, and L. J. Bourgeois III, "How Management Teams Can Have a Good Fight," *Harvard Business Review* (July–August 1997), 77–85.

8. Clayton T. Alderfer and Ken K. Smith, "Studying Intergroup Relations Imbedded in Organizations," *Administrative Science Quarterly* 27 (1982), 35–65.

9. Muzafer Sherif, "Experiments in Group Conflict," *Scientific American* 195 (1956), 54–58; and Edgar H. Schein, *Organizational Psychology*, 3rd ed. (Englewood Cliffs, NJ: Prentice Hall, 1980).

10. M. Afzalur Rahim, "A Strategy for Managing Conflict in Complex Organizations," *Human Relations* 38 (1985), 81–89; Kenneth Thomas, "Conflict and

Conflict Management," in M.D. Dunnette, ed., *Handbook of Industrial and Organizational Psychology* (Chicago, IL: Rand McNally, 1976); and Stuart M. Schmidt and Thomas A. Kochan, "Conflict: Toward Conceptual Clarity," *Administrative Science Quarterly* 13 (1972), 359–370.

11. L. David Brown, "Managing Conflict among Groups," in David A. Kolb, Irwin M. Rubin, and James M. McIntyre, eds., *Organizational Psychology: A Book of Readings* (Englewood Cliffs, NJ: Prentice Hall, 1979), 377–389; and Robert W. Ruekert and Orville C. Walker, Jr., "Interactions between Marketing and R&D Departments in Implementing Different Business Strategies," *Strategic Management Journal* 8 (1987), 233–248.

12. S. Ginden," Breaking Away: The Formation of the Canadian Auto Workers" at http://www.caw.ca/whoweare/ourhistory/gindin_index.asp (accessed June 27, 2008). Joseph B. White, Lee Hawkins, Jr., and Karen Lundegaard, "UAW Is Facing Biggest Battles in Two Decades," *The Wall Street Journal* (June 10, 2005), B1.

13. Amy Barrett, "Indigestion at Taco Bell," *Business Week* (December 14, 1994), 66–67; Greg Burns, "Fast Food Fight," *Business Week* (June 2, 1997), 34–36.

14. Nanette Byrnes, with Mike McNamee, Ronald Grover, Joann Muller, and Andrew Park, "Auditing Here, Consulting Over There," *Business Week* (April 8, 2002), 34–36.

15. D. Hawranek, "Porsche and VW Battle It Out" (September 19, 2007) at www.businessweek.com/globalbiz/content/sep2007/gb20070919_640245_page_3.htm (accessed May 18, 2011).

16. *The Economist,* "The Art and Craft of Business" (January 4, 2014) at http://www.economist.com/node/21592656/print (accessed March 21, 2014).

17. Thomas A. Kochan, George P. Huber, and L. L. Cummings, "Determinants of Intraorganizational Conflict in Collective Bargaining in the Public Sector," *Administrative Science Quarterly* 20 (1975), 10–23.

18. Victoria L. Crittenden, Lorraine R. Gardiner, and Antonie Stam, "Reducing Conflict between Marketing and Manufacturing," *Industrial Marketing Management* 22 (1993), 299–309; and Benson S. Shapiro, "Can Marketing and Manufacturing Coexist?" *Harvard Business Review* 55 (September–October 1977), 104–114.

19. Ben Worthen, "Cost-Cutting versus Innovation: Reconcilable Differences," *CIO* (October 1, 2004), 89–94.

20. Eric H. Neilsen, "Understanding and Managing Intergroup Conflict," in Jay W. Lorsch and Paul R. Lawrence, eds., *Managing Group and Intergroup Relations* (Homewood, IL: Irwin and Dorsey, 1972), 329–343; and Richard E. Walton and John M. Dutton, "The Management of Interdepartmental Conflict: A Model and Review," *Administrative Science Quarterly* 14 (1969), 73–84.

21. James D. Thompson, *Organizations in Action* (New York: McGraw-Hill, 1967), 54–56.

22. Walton and Dutton, "The Management of Interdepartmental Conflict."

23. Joseph McCann and Jay R. Galbraith, "Interdepartmental Relations," in Paul C. Nystrom and William H. Starbuck, eds., *Handbook of Organizational Design*, vol. 2 (New York: Oxford University Press, 1981), 60–84.

24. B. Cline, Hugh MacKinnon: The Managing Partner behind Bennett Jones' Rapid Expansion," *The Lawyers Weekly* (August 24, 2007) at www.lawyersweekly.ca/index.php?section=article&articleid=526 (accessed March 21, 2014).

25. Ibid.

26. "Bennett Jones Tops Employer List" at www.lawtimesnews.com/201011087839/Inside-Story/Monday-Nov-8-2010 (accessed May 18, 2011).

27. J. Melnitzer, "Bennett Jones, McCarthy Tetrault Make Top 100 Employers List," *Legal Post* (October 21, 2013) at http://business.financialpost.com/2013/10/21/bennett-jones-mccarthy-tetrault-make-top-100-employers-list (accessed March 21, 2014).

28. Values at http://www.bennettjones.ca/about_values.aspx (accessed May 18, 2011)

29. J. W. Zinober, "Resolving Conflict in the Firm," *Law Practice Management*, 16, 6 (1990), 20.

30. B. Cline, "Hugh MacKinnon: The Managing Partner behind Bennett Jones' Rapid Expansion."

31. Roderick M. Cramer, "Intergroup Relations and Organizational Dilemmas: The Role of Categorization Processes," in L. L. Cummings and Barry M. Staw, eds., *Research in Organizational Behavior*, vol. 13 (New York: JAI Press, 1991), 191–228; Neilsen, "Understanding and Managing Intergroup Conflict"; and Louis R. Pondy, "Organizational Conflict: Concepts and Models," *Administrative Science Quarterly* 12 (1968), 296–320.

32. Jeffrey Pfeffer, *Power in Organizations* (Marshfield, Mass.: Pitman, 1981).

33. Alan Deutschman, "The Mind of Jeff Bezos," *Fast Company* (August 2004), 53–58.

34. Robert A. Dahl, "The Concept of Power," *Behavioral Science* 2 (1957), 201–215.

35. W. Graham Astley and Paramijit S. Sachdeva, "Structural Sources of Intraorganizational Power: A Theoretical Synthesis," *Academy of Management Review* 9 (1984), 104–113; Abraham Kaplan, "Power in Perspective," in Robert L. Kahn and Elise Boulding, eds., *Power and Conflict in Organizations* (London: Tavistock, 1964), 11–32.

36. Gerald R. Salancik and Jeffrey Pfeffer, "The Bases and Use of Power in Organizational Decision-Making: The Case of the University," *Administrative Science Quarterly* 19 (1974), 453–473.

37. Richard M. Emerson, "Power-Dependence Relations," *American Sociological Review* 27 (1962), 31–41.

38. D. Mechanic, "Sources of Power of Lower Participants in Complex Organizations," *Administrative Science Quarterly* 7, 3 (1962), 349–364.

39. Rosabeth Moss Kanter, "Power Failure in Management Circuits," *Harvard Business Review* (July–August 1979), 65–75.

40. Sam Walker, "On Sports: Meet the Micro Manager," *The Wall Street Journal* (July 11, 2003), W12.

41. Examples are Robert Greene and Joost Elffers, *The 48 Laws of Power* (New York: Viking, 1999); Jeffrey J. Fox, *How to Become CEO* (New York: Hyperion, 1999).

42. John R. P. French, Jr., and Bertram Raven, "The Bases of Social Power," in D. Cartwright and A. F. Zander, eds., *Group Dynamics* (Evanston, IL: Row Peterson, 1960), 607–623.

43. Ran Lachman, "Power from What? A Reexamination of Its Relationships with Structural Conditions," *Administrative Science Quarterly* 34 (1989), 231–251; and Daniel J. Brass, "Being in the Right Place: A Structural Analysis of Individual Influence in an Organization," *Administrative Science Quarterly* 29 (1984), 518–539.

44. Michael Warshaw, "The Good Guy's Guide to Office Politics," *Fast Company* (April–May 1998), 157–178.

45. A. J. Grimes, "Authority, Power, Influence, and Social Control: A Theoretical Synthesis," *Academy of Management Review* 3 (1978), 724–735.

46. Astley and Sachdeva, "Structural Sources of Intraorganizational Power."

47. Jeffrey Pfeffer, *Managing with Power: Politics and Influence in Organizations* (Boston, Mass.: Harvard Business School Press, 1992).

48. Robert L. Peabody, "Perceptions of Organizational Authority," *Administrative Science Quarterly* 6 (1962), 479.

49. M. Brush, "CEO Mansions: A Stock Indicator?" (April 11, 2007) at articles.moneycentral.msn.com/Investing/CompanyFocus/CEOMansionsAStockIndicator.aspx (accessed May 18, 2011).

50. Richard S. Blackburn, "Lower Participant Power: Toward a Conceptual Integration," *Academy of Management Review* 6 (1981), 127–131.

51. Patricia Sellers, "eBay's Secret," *Fortune* (October 18, 2004), 161–178.

52. Women's Executive Network at http://www.wxnetwork.com/top100.html (accessed June 27, 2008).

53. "Sylvia Vogel" at http://www.chronicle.ca/vogel_eng.html (accessed June 27, 2008).

54. Kanter, "Power Failure in Management Circuits," 70.

55. Jeffrey Pfeffer, *Power in Organizations* (Marshfield, Mass.: Pitman, 1981).

56. Erik W. Larson and Jonathan B. King, "The Systemic Distortion of Information: An Ongoing Challenge to Management," *Organizational Dynamics* 24, no. 3 (Winter 1996), 49–61; and Thomas H. Davenport, Robert G. Eccles, and Laurence Prusak, "Information Politics," *Sloan Management Review* (Fall 1992), 53–65.

57. Robert Frank and Elena Cherney, "Paper Tigers; Lord Black's Board: A-List Cast Played Acquiescent Role," *The Wall Street Journal* (September 27, 2004), A1.

58. P. Waldie and J. McNish, "U.S. Court Upholds Two Charges against Black," *The Globe and Mail* (October 29, 2010) at http://www.theglobeandmail.com/report-on-business/us-court-upholds-two-charges-against-black/article1777946 (accessed March 21, 2014).

59. "Black Found Guilty of Obstruction, Mail Fraud" (July 13, 2007) at http://www.cbc.ca/money/story/2007/07/13/black-verdict.html (accessed May 18, 2011).

60. CBC News, "Conrad Black Removed from Order of Canada" (January 31, 2014) at http://www.cbc.ca/news/canada/conrad-black-removed-from-order-of-canada-1.2519299 (accessed March 21, 2014).

61. Lorne Manly and Andrew Ross Sorkin, "At Sony, Diplomacy Trumps Technology" (March 8, 2005) at http://www.nytimes.com/2005/03/08/business/worldbusiness/08reconstruct.html?scp=1&sq=At+Sony%2C+Diplomacy+Trumps+Technology&st=nyt (accessed March 21, 2014).

62. Kenji Hall, "Stringer, Sony Step on the Gas" (June 26, 2008) at http://www.businessweek.com/globalbiz/content/jun2008/gb20080626_493388.htm?campaign_id=rss_tech (accessed July 13, 2008).

63. *The Economist*, "Stringer Theory: Critics Call Howard Stringer a Failure. They Are Wrong" (May 26, 2011) at http://www.economist.com/node/18745381 (accessed March 21, 2014).

64. Associated Press, "Chairman of Sony Announces Retirement," *The New York Times* (March 10, 2013) at http://www.nytimes.com/2013/03/11/business/sonys-chairman-howard-stringer-announces-his-retirement.html?_r=0 (accessed April 3, 2014).

65. B. Breen, and C. Dahle, "Fire Starters," *Fast Company*, 30 (1999), 386.

66. Paul Gibbons, "From Managing to Leading: Making the Leap," *Academy of Management MSR Newsletter*, Winter 2003, 4–7.

67. Carol Hymowitz, "Companies Experience Major Power Shifts as Crises Continue" (In the Lead column), *The Wall Street Journal* (October 9, 2001), B1.

68. Astley and Sachdeva, "Structural Sources of Intraorganizational Power"; and Noel M. Tichy and Charles Fombrun, "Network Analysis in Organizational Settings," *Human Relations* 32 (1979), 923–965.

69. Report of Investigation by the Special Committee of the Board of Directors of Hollinger International Inc. at http://www.sec.gov/Archives/edgar/data/868512/000095012304010413/y01437exv99w2.htm (accessed March 21, 2014), 4.

70. Greg Ip, Kate Kelly, Susanne Craig, and Ianthe Jeanne Dugan, "A Bull's Market; Dick Grasso's NYSE Legacy: Buffed Image, Shaky Foundation," *The Wall Street Journal* (December 30, 2003), A1, A6; Yochi J. Dreazen and Christopher Cooper, "Lingering Presence;

Behind the Scenes, U.S. Tightens Grip on Iraq's Future," *The Wall Street Journal* (May 13, 2004), A1.

71. Edwin P. Hollander and Lynn R. Offermann, "Power and Leadership in Organizations," *American Psychologist* 45 (February 1990), 179–189.

72. Jay A. Conger and Rabindra N. Kanungo, "The Empowerment Process: Integrating Theory and Practice," *Academy of Management Review* 13 (1988), 471–482.

73. David E. Bowen and Edward E. Lawler III, "The Empowerment of Service Workers: What, Why, How, and When," *Sloan Management Review* (Spring 1992), 31–39; and Ray W. Coye and James A. Belohav, "An Exploratory Analysis of Employee Participation," *Group and Organization Management* 20, 1 (March 1995), 4–17.

74. Robert C. Ford and Myron D. Fottler, "Empowerment: A Matter of Degree," *Academy of Management Executive* 9, no. 3 (1995), 21–31.

75. Ricardo Semler, "Out of This World: Doing Things the Semco Way," *Global Business and Organizational Excellence* (July–August 2007), 13–21.

76. Charles Perrow, "Departmental Power and Perspective in Industrial Firms," in Mayer N. Zald, ed., *Power in Organizations* (Nashville, TN: Vanderbilt University Press, 1970), 59–89.

77. D. J. Hickson, C. R. Hinings, C. A. Lee, R. E. Schneck, and J. M. Pennings, "A Strategic Contingencies Theory of Intraorganizational Power," *Administrative Science Quarterly* 16 (1971), 216–229; and Gerald R. Salancik and Jeffrey Pfeffer, "Who Gets Power—and How They Hold onto It: A Strategic-Contingency Model of Power," *Organizational Dynamics* (Winter 1977), 3–21.

78. Pfeffer, *Managing with Power*; Salancik and Pfeffer, "Who Gets Power"; C. R. Hinings, D. J. Hickson, J. M. Pennings, and R. E. Schneck, "Structural Conditions of Intraorganizational Power," *Administrative Science Quarterly* 19 (1974), 22–44.

79. Carol Stoak Saunders, "The Strategic Contingencies Theory of Power: Multiple Perspectives," *Journal of Management Studies* 27 (1990), 1–18; Warren Boeker, "The Development and Institutionalization of Sub-Unit Power in Organizations," *Administrative Science Quarterly* 34 (1989), 388–510; and Irit Cohen and Ran Lachman, "The Generality of the Strategic Contingencies Approach to Sub-Unit Power," Organizational Studies 9 (1988), 371–391.

80. Richard M. Emerson, "Power-Dependence Relations," *American Sociological Review* 27 (1962), 31–41.

81. J. Thompson, P. A. Baird, and J. Downie, "The Olivieri Case: Context and Significance" (December 2005) at http://www.ecclectica.ca/issues/2005/3/index.asp?Article=2 (accessed May 18, 2011).

82. J. Thompson, P.A. Baird, and J. Downie, "The Olivieri Case: Context and Significance."

83. Jeffrey Pfeffer, *Managing with Power: Politics and Influence in Organizations* (Boston, Mass.: Harvard Business School Press, 1992).

84. Jeffrey Pfeffer and Gerald Salancik, "Organizational Decision-Making as a Political Process: The Case of a University Budget," *Administrative Science Quarterly* (1974), 135–151.

85. Gerald R. Salancik and Jeffrey Pfeffer, "Who Gets Power—and How They Hold onto It: A Strategic-Contingency Model of Power," *Organizational Dynamics* (Winter 1977), 3–21.

86. D. J. Hickson, C. R. Hinings, C. A. Lee, R. E. Schneck, and J. M. Pennings, "A Strategic Contingencies Theory of Intraorganizational Power," *Administrative Science Quarterly* 16 (1971), 216–229.

87. A.M. Pettigrew, *The Politics of Organizational Decision-Making* (Tavistock, 1973).

88. D. J. Hickson, C. R. Hinings, C. A. Lee, R. E. Schneck, and J. M. Pennings, "A Strategic Contingencies Theory of Intraorganizational Power," *Administrative Science Quarterly* 16 (1971), 216 -229.

89. Ibid.

90. Jeffrey Gantz and Victor V. Murray, "Experience of Workplace Politics," *Academy of Management Journal* 23 (1980), 237–251; and Dan L. Madison, Robert W. Allen, Lyman W. Porter, Patricia A. Renwick, and Bronston T. Mayes, "Organizational Politics: An Exploration of Managers' Perception," *Human Relations* 33 (1980), 79–100.

91. Gerald R. Ferris and K. Michele Kacmar, "Perceptions of Organizational Politics," *Journal of Management* 18 (1992), 93–116; Parmod Kumar and Rehana Ghadially, "Organizational Politics and Its Effects on Members of Organizations," *Human Relations* 42 (1989), 305–314; Donald J. Vredenburgh and John G. Maurer, "A Process Framework of Organizational Politics," *Human Relations* 37 (1984), 47–66; and Gerald R. Ferris, Dwight D. Frink, Maria Carmen Galang, Jing Zhou, Michele Kacmar, and Jack L. Howard, "Perceptions of Organizational Politics: Prediction, Stress-Related Implications, and Outcomes," *Human Relations* 49, 2 (1996), 233–266.

92. Ferris et al., "Perceptions of Organizational Politics: Prediction, Stress-Related Implications, and Outcomes"; John J. Voyer, "Coercive Organizational Politics and Organizational Outcomes: An Interpretive Study," *Organization Science* 5, 1 (February 1994), 72–85; and James W. Dean, Jr., and Mark P. Sharfman, "Does Decision Process Matter? A Study of Strategic Decision-Making Effectiveness," *Academy of Management Journal* 39, 2 (1996), 368–396.

93. Jeffrey Pfeffer, *Managing with Power: Politics and Influence in Organizations* (Boston, Mass.: Harvard Business School Press, 1992).

94. Amos Drory and Tsilia Romm, "The Definition of Organizational Politics: A Review," *Human Relations* 43 (1990), 1133–1154; and Vredenburgh and Maurer, "A Process Framework of Organizational Politics"; and Lafe Low, "It's Politics, As Usual," *CIO* (April 1, 2004), 87–90.

95. Jeffrey Pfeffer, *Power in Organizations* (Marshfield, Mass.: Pitman, 1981).

96. Madison et al., "Organizational Politics"; Jay R. Galbraith, *Organizational Design* (Reading, Mass.: Addison-Wesley, 1977).

97. Gantz and Murray, "Experience of Workplace Politics"; Pfeffer, *Power in Organizations*.

98. "Prime Minister Chrétien Fires Paul Martin" at http://www.mapleleafweb.com/old/education/spotlight/issue_16/?q=education/spotlight/issue_16 (accessed October 7, 2007).

99. CBC.ca, "The Feud Boils Over" (June 2, 2004) at http://archives.cbc.ca/IDC-1-73-2148-13114/politics_economy/paul_martin/clip1 (accessed May 18, 2011).

100. S. Anderson, "Martin's Shadow PMO," NOW Magazine Online Edition 21 (2002), 52.

101. "PM Says He Never Punished Liberals who Supported Paul Martin" (July 17, 2002) at http://www.cbc.ca/canada/story/2002/07/16liberals0...(accessed October 7, 2007).

102. CBC.ca, "The Paul Martin Era Begins" (November 14, 2003) at http://archives.cbc.ca/IDC-1-73-2148-13115/politics_economy/paul_martin/clip1 (accessed May 19, 2011).

103. John Gray, "Whatever Became of Paul Martin?" (January 24, 2006) at http://www.cbc.ca/canadavotes/realitycheck/martin.html (accessed July 13, 2008).

104. Daniel J. Brass and Marlene E. Burkhardt, "Potential Power and Power Use: An Investigation of Structure and Behavior," *Academy of Management Journal* 38 (1993), 441–470.

105. Harvey G. Enns and Dean B. McFarlin, "When Executives Influence Peers, Does Function Matter?" *Human Resource Management* 4, 2 (Summer 2003), 125–142.

106. Hickson et al., "A Strategic Contingencies Theory."

107. Jeffrey Pfeffer, *Power in Organizations* (Marshfield, Mass.: Pitman, 1981).

108. Ibid.

109. V. Dallas Merrell, *Huddling: The Informal Way to Management Success* (New York: AMACON, 1979).

110. Ceasar Douglas and Anthony P. Ammeter, "An Examination of Leader Political Skill and Its Effect on Ratings of Leader Effectiveness," *The Leadership Quarterly* 15 (2004), 537–550.

111. Vredenburgh and Maurer, "A Process Framework of Organizational Politics."

112. Jeffrey Pfeffer, *Power in Organizations* (Marshfield, Mass.: Pitman, 1981).

113. Ibid.

114. Ann Davis and Randall Smith, "Merrill Switch: Popular Veteran Is In, Not Out," *The Wall Street Journal* (August 13, 2003), C1.

115. Jeffrey Pfeffer, *Power in Organizations* (Marshfield, Mass.: Pitman, 1981).

116. Ibid.

117. Kanter, "Power Failure in Management Circuits"; Pfeffer, *Power in Organizations*.

118. Ben Elgin, "Inside Yahoo!" *BusinessWeek* (May 21, 2001), 114–122.

119. Robert R. Blake and Jane S. Mouton, "Overcoming Group Warfare," *Harvard Business Review* (November–December 1984), 98–108.

120. Blake and Mouton, "Overcoming Group Warfare"; Paul R. Lawrence and Jay W. Lorsch, "New Management Job: The Integrator," *Harvard Business Review* 45 (November–December 1967), 142–151.

121. Canadian Pacific, "A Brief History" (n.d.) at http://www8.cpr.ca/cms/English/General+Public/Heritage/A+Brief+History.htm (accessed June 27, 2008).

122. D. Shenfield, A. Ponak, and B. Painter, "Beyond Collision: High Integrity Labour Relations—CPR Shortline Railway Case Study" (June 1, 2007) at http://www.hrsdc.gc.ca/en/lp/wid/articles/article6.shtml (accessed May 18, 2011).

123. Ibid.

124. Aaron Bernstein, "Look Who's Pushing Productivity," *BusinessWeek* (April 7, 1997), 72–75.

125. Robert R. Blake, Herbert A. Shepard, and Jane S. Mouton, *Managing Intergroup Conflict in Industry* (Houston: Gulf Publishing, 1964); Doug Stewart, "Expand the Pie before You Divvy It Up," *Smithsonian* (November 1997), 78–90.

126. Suzanne Payette, "Innovative Practices in Collective Agreements" (Summer 2005) at http://www.hrsdc.gc.ca/en/lp/wid/win/presentation_2005.shtml (accessed May 19, 2011).

127. Patrick S. Nugent, "Managing Conflict: Third-Party Interventions for Managers," *Academy of Management Executive* 16, 1 (2002), 139–155.

128. Blake and Mouton, "Overcoming Group Warfare"; Schein, *Organizational Psychology*; Blake, Shepard, and Mouton, *Managing Intergroup Conflict in Industry*; and Richard E. Walton, *Interpersonal Peacemaking: Confrontation and Third-Party Consultations* (Reading, Mass.: Addison-Wesley, 1969).

129. Neilsen, "Understanding and Managing Intergroup Conflict"; McCann and Galbraith, "Interdepartmental Relations."

130. Neilsen, "Understanding and Managing Intergroup Conflict"; McCann and Galbraith, "Interdepartmental Relations"; Sherif et al., *Intergroup Conflict and Cooperation.*

131. Dean Tjosvold, Valerie Dann, and Choy Wong, "Managing Conflict between Departments to Serve Customers," *Human Relations* 45 (1992), 1035–1054.

# Glossary

## A

**adaptability culture** a culture characterized by strategic focus on the external environment through flexibility and change to meet customer needs (p. 337).

**administrative principles** a closed system's management perspective that focuses on the total organization and grows from the insights of practitioners (p. 8).

**ambidextrous approach** a characteristic of an organization that can behave in both an organic and a mechanistic way (p. 380).

**analyzability** a dimension of technology in which work activities can be reduced to mechanical steps and participants can follow an objective, computational procedure to solve problems (p. 272).

**analyzer** a business strategy that seeks to maintain a stable business while innovating on the periphery (p. 65).

**authority** a force for achieving desired outcomes that is prescribed by the formal hierarchy and reporting relationships (p. 461).

## B

**boundary-spanning roles** activities that link and coordinate an organization with key elements in the external environment (p. 153).

**bounded rationality perspective** how decisions are made when time is limited, a large number of internal and external factors affect a decision, and the problem is ill-defined (p. 412).

**buffering roles** activities that absorb uncertainty from the environment (p. 152).

**bureaucracy** an organizational framework marked by rules and procedures, specialization and division of labour, hierarchy of authority, technically qualified personnel, separation of position and person, and written communications and records (p. 305).

**bureaucratic control** the use of rules, policies, hierarchy of authority, written documentation, standardization, and other bureaucratic mechanisms to standardize behaviour and assess performance (p. 311).

**bureaucratic culture** a culture that has an internal focus and a consistency orientation for a stable environment (p. 340).

**bureaucratic organization** an organization design that emphasizes management on an impersonal, rational basis through elements such as clearly defined authority and responsibility, formal record keeping, and uniform application of standard rules (p. 8).

## C

**Carnegie model** organizational decision making involving many managers and a final choice based on a coalition among those managers (p. 423).

**centrality** a trait of a department whose role is in the primary activity of an organization (p. 469).

**centralization** the level of hierarchy with authority to make decisions (p. 307).

**chain of command** formal line of authority in a hierarchy (p. 96).

**change process** the way in which planned changes occur in an organization (p. 377).

**change strategy** a plan to guide an organizational change (p. 6).

**chaos theory** a scientific theory that suggests that relationships in complex, adaptive systems are made up of numerous interconnections that create unintended effects and render the environment unpredictable (p. 30).

**charismatic authority** based on devotion to the exemplary character or heroism of an individual and the order defined by him or her (p. 312).

**chief ethics officer** high-level executive who oversees all aspects of ethics, including establishing and broadly communicating ethical standards, setting up ethics training programs, supervising the investigation of ethical problems, and advising managers in the ethical aspects of decisions (p. 355).

**clan control** the use of social characteristics, such as culture, shared values, commitments, traditions, and beliefs, to control behaviour (p. 314).

**clan culture** a culture that focuses primarily on the involvement and participation of the organization's members and on rapidly changing expectations from the external environment (p. 339).

**closed system** a system that is autonomous, enclosed, and not dependent on its environment (p. 19).

**coalition** an alliance among several managers who agree through bargaining about organizational goals and problem priorities (p. 423).

**code of ethics** a formal statement of the company's values concerning ethics and social responsibility (p. 357).

**coercive forces** external pressures such as legal requirements exerted on an organization to adopt structures, techniques, or behaviours similar to other organizations (p. 200).

**collaborative network** an emerging perspective whereby organizations allow themselves to become dependent on other organizations to increase value and productivity for all (p. 187).

**collective bargaining** the negotiation of an agreement between management and workers (p. 479).

**collectivity stage** the life-cycle phase in which an organization has strong leadership and begins to develop clear goals and direction (p. 299).

**competing-values model** a perspective on organizational effectiveness that combines diverse indicators of performance that represent competing management values (p. 75).

**competition** rivalry between groups in the pursuit of a common prize (p. 455).

**confrontation** a situation in which parties in conflict directly engage one another and try to work out their differences (p. 479).

**consortia** groups of firms that venture into new products and technologies (p. 220).

**contextual dimensions** traits that characterize the whole organization, including its size, technology, environment, and goals (p. 22).

**contingency** a theory meaning one thing depends on other things; the organization's situation dictates the correct management approach (p. 29).

**contingency decision-making framework** a perspective that brings together the two organizational dimensions of problem consensus and technical knowledge about solutions (p. 436).

**continuous process production** a completely mechanized manufacturing process in which there is no starting or stopping (p. 256).

**cooptation** when leaders from important sectors in the environment are made part of an organization (p. 162).

**coping with uncertainty** a source of power for a department that reduces uncertainty for other departments by obtaining prior information, prevention, and absorption (p. 470).

**core technology** the work process that is directly related to the organization's mission (p. 252).

**craft technology** technology characterized by a fairly stable stream of activities but in which the conversion process is not analyzable or well-understood (p. 273).

**creative departments** organizational departments that initiate change, such as research and development, engineering, design, and systems analysis (p. 381).

**creativity** the generation of novel ideas that may meet perceived needs or respond to opportunities (p. 377).

**culture** the set of values, guiding beliefs, understandings, and ways of thinking that are shared by members of an organization and are taught to new members as correct (p. 332).

**culture changes** changes in the values, attitudes, expectations, beliefs, abilities, and behaviour of employees (p. 375).

## D

**decentralized** decision making and communication are spread out across the company (p. 95).

**decision learning** a process of recognizing and admitting mistakes that allows managers and organizations to acquire the experience and knowledge to perform more effectively in the future (p. 440).

**decision premises** constraining frames of reference and guidelines placed by top managers on decisions made at lower levels (p. 463).

**defender** a business strategy that seeks stability or even retrenchment rather than innovation or growth (p. 64).

**departmental grouping** a structure in which employees share a common supervisor and resources, are jointly responsible for performance, and tend to identify and collaborate with each other (p. 103).

**dependency** one aspect of horizontal power: when one department is dependent on another, the latter is in a position of greater power (p. 468).

**differentiation** the cognitive and emotional differences among managers in various functional departments of an organization and formal structure differences among these departments (p. 154).

**differentiation strategy** strategy organizations use to distinguish their products or services from others in the industry/sector (p. 62).

**direct interlock** a situation that occurs when a member of the board of directors of one company sits on the board of another (p. 162).

**divisional grouping** a grouping in which people are organized according to what the organization produces (p. 103).

**divisional structure** the structuring of the organization according to individual products, services, product groups, major projects, or profit centres; also called product structure or strategic business units (p. 105).

**domain** an organization's chosen environmental field of activity (p. 142).

**domains of political activity** areas in which politics plays a role. Three domains in organizations are structural change, management succession, and resource allocation (p. 472).

**domestic stage** the first stage of international development in which a company is domestically oriented while managers are aware of the global environment (p. 218).

**downsizing** intentionally reducing the size of a company's workforce by laying off employees (p. 319).

**dual-core approach** an organizational change perspective that identifies the unique processes associated with administrative change compared to those associated with technical change (p. 389).

# E

**economies of scale** achieving lower costs through large volume production; often made possible by global expansion (p. 216).

**economies of scope** achieving economies by having a presence in many product lines, technologies, or geographic areas (p. 216).

**effectiveness** the degree to which an organization achieves its goals (p. 26).

**efficiency** the amount of resources used to produce a unit of output (p. 26).

**elaboration stage** the organizational life-cycle phase in which the red-tape crisis is resolved through the development of a new sense of teamwork and collaboration (p. 300).

**engineering technology** technology in which there is substantial variety in the tasks performed, but activities are usually handled on the basis of

established formulas, procedures, and techniques (p. 274).

**entrepreneurial stage** the life-cycle phase in which an organization is born and its emphasis is on creating a product and surviving in the marketplace (p. 298).

**escalating commitment** persisting in a course of action when it is failing; occurs because managers block or distort negative information and because consistency and persistence are valued in contemporary society (p. 441).

**ethical dilemma** when each alternative choice or behaviour seems undesirable because of a potentially negative ethical consequence (p. 348).

**ethics** the code of moral principles and values that governs the behaviour of a person or group with respect to what is right or wrong (p. 346).

**ethics committee** a group of executives appointed to oversee company ethics (p. 355).

**ethics hotline** a telephone number that employees can call to seek guidance and to report questionable behaviour (p. 356).

**external adaptation** the manner in which an organization meets goals and deals with outsiders (p. 333).

# F

**factors of production** supplies necessary for production, such as land, raw materials, and labour (p. 217).

**financial resources** control over money is an important source of power within an organization (p. 469).

**flexible manufacturing systems (FMS)** using computers to link manufacturing components such as robots, machines, product design, and engineering analysis to enable fast switching from one product to another (p. 260).

**focus strategy** a strategy in which an organization concentrates on a specific regional market or buyer group (p. 62).

**formalization** the degree to which an organization has rules, procedures, and written documentation (p. 307).

**formalization stage** the phase in an organization's life cycle involving the installation and use of rules, procedures, and control systems (p. 300).

**functional grouping** the placing together of employees who perform similar functions or work processes or who bring similar knowledge and skills to bear on a task (p. 103).

**functional matrix** a structure in which functional bosses have primary authority, and product or project managers simply coordinate product activities (p. 114).

**functional structure** the grouping of activities by common function (p. 104).

## G

**garbage can model** model that describes the pattern or flow of multiple decisions within an organization (p. 431).

**general environment** includes those sectors that may not directly affect the daily operations of a firm but will indirectly influence it (p. 144).

**generalist** an organization that offers a broad range of products or services and serves a broad market (p. 195).

**global company** a company that no longer thinks of itself as having a home country (p. 219).

**global geographical structure** a form in which an organization divides its operations into world regions, each of which reports to the CEO (p. 225).

**global matrix structure** a form of horizontal linkage in an international organization in which both product and geographical structures are implemented simultaneously to achieve a balance between standardization and globalization (p. 227).

**global product structure** a form in which product divisions take responsibility for global operations in their specific product areas (p. 225).

**global stage** the stage of international development in which the company transcends any one country (p. 219).

**global teams** work groups comprising multinational members whose activities span multiple countries; also called *transnational teams* (p. 232).

**globalization strategy** the standardization of product design and advertising strategy throughout the world (p. 222).

**goal approach** an approach to organizational effectiveness that is concerned with output and whether the organization achieves its output goals (p. 70).

**green environment** our natural environment (p. 142).

## H

**Hawthorne Studies** a series of experiments on worker productivity begun in 1924 at the Hawthorne plant of Western Electric Company in Illinois; attributed employees' increased output to managers' better treatment of them during the study (p. 8).

**heroes** organizational members who serve as models or ideals for serving cultural norms and values (p. 335).

**high-velocity environments** industries in which competitive and technological change is so extreme that market data are either unavailable or obsolete, strategic windows open and shut quickly, and the cost of a decision error is company failure (p. 439).

**horizontal coordination model** a model of the three components of organizational design needed to achieve new product innovation: departmental specialization, boundary spanning, and horizontal linkages (p. 385).

**horizontal grouping** the organizing of employees around core work processes rather than by function, product, or geography (p. 103).

**horizontal linkage** the amount of communication and coordination that occurs horizontally across organizational departments (p. 97).

**horizontal structure** a structure that virtually eliminates both the vertical hierarchy and departmental boundaries by organizing teams of employees around core work processes; the end-to-end work, information, and material flows that provide value directly to customers (p. 117).

**human relations emphasis** emphasis on an aspect of the competing-values model that incorporates the values of an internal focus and a flexible structure (p. 77).

**hybrid structure** a structure that combines characteristics of various structural approaches (functional, divisional, geographical, horizontal) tailored to specific strategic needs (p. 123).

## I

**idea champions** organizational members who provide the time and energy to make things happen; sometimes called *advocates*, *intrapreneurs*, and *change agents* (p. 382).

**idea incubator** safe harbour where ideas from employees throughout the organization can be developed without interference from bureaucracy or politics (p. 381).

**imitation** the adoption of a decision tried elsewhere in the hope that it will work in the present situation (p. 438).

**incident command system** developed to maintain the efficiency and control benefits of bureaucracy yet prevent the problems of slow response to crises (p. 308).

**incremental change** a series of continual progressions that maintains an organization's general equilibrium and often affects only one organizational part (p. 372).

**incremental decision process model** a model that describes the structured sequence of activities undertaken from the discovery of a problem to its solution (p. 425).

indirect interlock a situation that occurs when a director of one company and a director of another are both directors of a third company (p. 162).

inspiration an innovative, creative solution that is not reached by logical means (p. 438).

institutional environment norms and values from stakeholders (customers, investors, boards, government, etc.) that organizations try to follow in order to please stakeholders (p. 197).

institutional perspective a view that holds that, under high uncertainty, organizations imitate others in the same institutional environment (p. 196).

institutional similarity the emergence of common structures, management approaches, and behaviours among organizations in the same field (p. 199).

integration the quality of collaboration between departments of an organization (p. 155).

integrator a position or department created solely to coordinate several departments (p. 99).

intensive technologies a variety of products or services provided in combination to a client (p. 279).

interdependence the extent to which departments depend on each other for resources or materials to accomplish their tasks (p. 277).

intergroup conflict behaviour that occurs between organizational groups when participants identify with one group and perceive that other groups may block their group's goal achievements or expectations (p. 455).

interlocking directorate a formal linkage that occurs when a member of the board of directors of one company sits on the board of another company (p. 162).

internal integration a state in which organization members develop a collective identity and know how to work together effectively (p. 333).

internal-process approach an approach that looks at internal activities and assesses effectiveness by indicators of internal health and efficiency (p. 71).

internal-process emphasis an aspect of the competing-values model that reflects the values of internal focus and structural control (p. 76).

international division a division that is equal in status to other major departments within a company and has its own hierarchy to handle business in various countries (p. 224).

international stage the second stage of international development, in which the company takes exports seriously and begins to think multidomestically (p. 219).

interorganizational relationships the relatively enduring resource transactions, flows, and linkages that occur among two or more organizations (p. 181).

intuitive decision making the use of experience and judgment, rather than sequential logic or explicit reasoning, to solve a problem (p. 417).

## J

job design the assignment of goals and tasks to be accomplished by employees (p. 282).

job enlargement the designing of jobs to expand the number of different tasks performed by an employee (p. 282).

job enrichment the designing of jobs to increase responsibility, recognition, and opportunities for growth and achievement (p. 282).

job rotation moving employees from job to job to give them a greater variety of tasks and alleviate boredom (p. 282).

job simplification the reduction of the number and difficulty of tasks performed by a single person (p. 282).

joint optimization the goal of the sociotechnical systems approach, which states that an organization will function best only if its social and technical systems are designed to fit the needs of one another (p. 283).

joint venture a separate entity for sharing development and production costs and penetrating new markets that is created with two or more active firms as sponsors (p. 220).

## L

labour–management teams teams designed to increase worker participation and to provide a cooperative model for addressing union–management issues (p. 479).

language slogans, sayings, metaphors, or other expressions that convey a special meaning to employees (p. 336).

large-batch production a manufacturing process characterized by long production runs of standardized parts (p. 256).

large group intervention an approach that brings together participants from all parts of the organization (and may include outside stakeholders as well) to discuss problems or opportunities and plan for change (p. 393).

lean manufacturing uses highly trained employees at every stage of the production process who take a painstaking approach to details and continuous problem solving to cut waste and improve quality (p. 261).

learning organization an organization in which everyone is engaged in identifying and solving problems, enabling the organization to continuously experiment, improve, and increase its capability (p. 30).

**legends** stories of events based in history that may have been embellished with fictional details (p. 335).

**legitimacy** the general perspective that an organization's actions are desirable, proper, and appropriate within the environment's system of norms, values, and beliefs (p. 197).

**level of analysis** in systems theory, the subsystem on which the primary focus is placed; four levels of analysis normally characterize organizations (p. 34).

**liaison role** the function of a person located in one department who is responsible for communicating and achieving coordination with another department (p. 98).

**life cycle** a perspective on organizational growth and change that suggests that organizations are born, grow older, and eventually die (p. 298).

**long-linked technology** the combination, within one organization, of successive stages of production, with each stage using as its inputs the production of the preceding stage (p. 279).

**low-cost leadership strategy** a strategy that tries to increase market share by emphasizing low cost when compared with competitors' products (p. 63).

# M

**management champion** a manager who acts as a supporter and sponsor of a technical champion to shield and promote an idea within the organization (p. 383).

**management science approach** organizational decision making that is the analogue to the rational approach by individual managers (p. 421).

**managerial ethics** principles that guide the decisions and behaviours of managers with regard to whether they are morally right or wrong (p. 348).

**market control** a situation that occurs when price competition is used to evaluate the output and productivity of an organization (p. 313).

**mass customization** the use of computer-integrated systems and flexible work processes to enable companies to mass produce a variety of products or services designed to exact customer specification (p. 263).

**matrix structure** a strong form of horizontal linkage in which both product and functional structures (horizontal and vertical) are implemented simultaneously (p. 111).

**mechanistic** an organization system marked by rules, procedures, a clear hierarchy of authority, and centralized decision making (p. 156).

**mediating technology** the provision of products or services that mediate or link clients from the external environment and allow each department to work independently (p. 278).

**meso theory** a new approach to organization studies that integrates both micro and macro levels of analysis (p. 35).

**mimetic forces** under conditions of uncertainty, the pressure to copy or model other organizations that appear to be successful in the environment (p. 199).

**mission** the organization's reason for its existence (p. 56).

**mission culture** a culture that places emphasis on a clear vision of the organization's purpose and on the achievement of specific goals (p. 338).

**multidomestic** company that deals with competitive issues in each country independent of other countries (p. 219).

**multidomestic strategy** competition in each country is handled independently of competition in other countries (p. 222).

**multifocused grouping** a structure in which an organization embraces structural grouping alternatives simultaneously (p. 103).

**multinational stage** the stage of international development in which a company has marketing and production facilities in many countries and more than one-third of its sales outside its home country (p. 219).

**myths** stories that are consistent with the values and beliefs of the organization but are not supported by facts (p. 335).

# N

**negotiation** the bargaining process that often occurs during confrontation and enables the parties to systematically reach a solution (p. 479).

**network centrality** top managers increase their power by locating themselves centrally in an organization and surrounding themselves with loyal subordinates (p. 464).

**new-venture fund** a fund that provides financial resources to employees to develop new ideas, products, or businesses (p. 382).

**niche** a domain of unique environmental resources and needs (p. 192).

**noncore technology** a department work process that is important to the organization but is not directly related to its central mission (p. 253).

**nonprogrammed decisions** novel and poorly defined, these are made when no procedure exists for solving the problem (p. 411).

**nonroutine technology** technology in which there is high task variety and the conversion process is not analyzable or well understood (p. 274).

**nonsubstitutability** a trait of a department whose function cannot be performed by other readily available resources (p. 470).

**normative forces** pressures to adopt structures, techniques, or management processes because they are considered by the community to be up-to-date and effective (p. 201).

# O

**official goals** the formally stated definition of business scope and outcomes the organization is trying to achieve; another term for *mission* (p. 56).

**open system** a system that must interact with the environment to survive (p. 19).

**open-systems emphasis** an aspect of the competing-values model that reflects a combination of external focus and flexible structure (p. 76).

**operative goals** descriptions of the ends sought through the actual operating procedures of the organization; these explain what the organization is trying to accomplish (p. 57).

**organic** an organization system marked by free-flowing, adaptive processes, an unclear hierarchy of authority, and decentralized decision making (p. 156).

**organization development** a behavioural science field devoted to improving performance through trust, open confrontation of problems, employee empowerment and participation, the design of meaningful work, cooperation between groups, and the full use of human potential (p. 393).

**organization theory** a macro approach to organizations that analyzes the whole organization as a unit (p. 35).

**organizational behaviour** a micro approach to organizations that focuses on the individuals within organizations as the relevant units for analysis (p. 35).

**organizational change** the adoption of a new idea or behaviour by an organization (p. 376).

**organizational decision making** the organizational process of identifying and solving problems (p. 411).

**organizational decline** a condition in which a substantial, absolute decrease in an organization's resource base occurs over a period of time (p. 316).

**organizational ecosystem** a system formed by the interaction of a community of organizations and their environment, usually cutting across traditional industry lines (p. 182).

**organizational environment** all elements that exist outside the boundary of the organization and have the potential to affect all or part of the organization (p. 141).

**organizational form** an organization's specific technology, structure, products, goals, and personnel (p. 192).

**organizational goal** a desired state of affairs that the organization attempts to reach (p. 70).

**organizational innovation** the adoption of an idea or behaviour that is new to an organization's industry, market, or general environment (p. 376).

**organizational politics** activities to acquire, develop, and use power and other resources to obtain a preferred outcome when there is uncertainty or disagreement about choices (p. 471).

**organizational structure** designates formal reporting relationships, including the number of levels in the hierarchy and the span of control of managers and supervisors; identifies the grouping together of individuals into departments and of departments into the total organization; and includes the design of systems to ensure effective communication, coordination, and integration of efforts across departments (p. 93).

**organized anarchy** extremely organic organizations characterized by highly uncertain conditions (p. 431).

**outsourcing** contracting out certain functions, such as manufacturing, information technology, or credit processing, to other organizations (p. 121).

# P

**personnel ratios** the proportions of administrative, clerical, and professional support staff (p. 307).

**point–counterpoint** a decision-making technique that divides decision makers into two groups and assigns them different, often competing, responsibilities (p. 440).

**political model** a definition of an organization as being made up of groups that have separate interests, goals, and values in which power and influence are needed to reach decisions (p. 459).

**political tactics for using power** these include building coalitions, expanding networks, controlling decision premises, enhancing legitimacy and expertise, and making a direct appeal (p. 475).

**pooled interdependence** the lowest form of interdependence among departments, in which work does not flow between units (p. 278).

**population** a set of organizations engaged in similar activities with similar patterns of resource utilization and outcomes (p. 191).

**population-ecology perspective** a perspective in which the focus is on organizational diversity and adaptation within a community or population or organizations (p. 191).

**power** the ability of one person or department in an organization to influence others to bring about desired outcomes (p. 460).

**power distance** the level of inequality people are willing to accept within an organization (p. 234).

**power sources** there are five sources of horizontal power in organizations: dependency, financial resources, centrality, nonsubstitutability, and the ability to cope with uncertainty (p. 468).

**problem consensus** the agreement among managers about the nature of problems or opportunities and about which goals and outcomes to pursue (p. 435).

**problem identification** the decision-making stage in which information about environmental and organizational conditions is monitored to determine if performance is satisfactory and to diagnose the cause of shortcomings (p. 411).

**problem solution** the decision-making stage in which alternative courses of action are considered and one alternative is selected and implemented (p. 411).

**problemistic search** when managers look around in the immediate environment for a solution to resolve a problem quickly (p. 424).

**process** organized group of related tasks and activities that work together to transform inputs into outputs that create value for customers (p. 117).

**product and service changes** changes in an organization's product or service outputs (p. 374).

**product matrix** a variation of the matrix structure in which project or product managers have primary authority, and functional managers simply assign technical personnel to projects and provide advisory expertise (p. 114).

**programmed decisions** repetitive and well-defined procedures that exist for resolving problems (p. 411).

**prospector** a business strategy characterized by innovation, risk taking, seeking out new opportunities, and growth (p. 64).

# R

**radical change** a breaking of the frame of reference for an organization, often creating a new equilibrium because the entire organization is transformed (p. 373).

**rational approach** a process of decision making that stresses the need for systematic analysis of a problem followed by choice and implementation in a logical sequence (p. 412).

**rational-goal emphasis** an aspect of the competing-values model that reflects values of structural control and external focus (p. 76).

**rational-legal authority** based on employees' belief in the legality of rules and the right of those in authority to issue commands (p. 312).

**rational model** a description of an organization characterized by a rational approach to decision making, extensive and reliable information systems, central power, a norm of optimization, uniform values across groups, little conflict, and an efficiency orientation (p. 459).

**reactor strategy** a business strategy in which environmental threats and opportunities are responded to in an ad hoc fashion (p. 66).

**reciprocal interdependence** the highest level of interdependence, in which the output of one operation is the input of a second, and then the output of the second operation becomes the input of the first (for example, a hospital) (p. 279).

**re-engineering** redesigning a vertical organization along its horizontal workflows and processes (p. 117).

**resource dependence** a situation in which organizations depend on the environment, but strive to acquire control over resources to minimize their dependence (p. 160).

**resource-based approach** an organizational perspective that assesses effectiveness by observing how successfully the organization obtains, integrates, and manages valued resources (p. 71).

**retention** the preservation and institutionalization of selected organizational forms (p. 194).

**rites and ceremonies** the elaborate, planned activities that make up a special event and often are conducted for the benefit of an audience (p. 334).

**role** a part in a dynamic social system that allows an employee to use his or her discretion and ability to achieve outcomes and meet goals (p. 31).

**routine technologies** technologies characterized by little task variety and the use of objective, computational procedures (p. 273).

**rule of law** that which arises from a set of codified principles and regulations that describe how people are required to act, are generally accepted in society, and are enforceable in the courts (p. 347).

# S

**satisficing** the acceptance by organizations of a satisfactory rather than a maximum level of performance (p. 424).

**scientific management** a classical approach that claims decisions about organization and job design should be based on precise, scientific procedures (p. 8).

**sectors** subdivisions of the external environment that contain similar elements (p. 142).

**selection** the process by which organizational variations are determined to fit the external environment; variations that fail to fit the needs of the environment are "selected out" and fail (p. 193).

**self-control** a person's values are brought into line with the organization's values to control behaviour (p. 315).

**sequential interdependence** a serial form of interdependence in which the output of one operation becomes the input to another operation (p. 278).

**service technology** technology characterized by simultaneous production and consumption, customized output, customer participation, intangible output, and being labour intensive (p. 267).

**simple-complex dimension** the number and dissimilarity of external elements relevant to an organization's operation (p. 148).

**skunkworks** separate, small, informal, highly autonomous, and often secretive group that focuses on breakthrough ideas for the business (p. 382).

**small-batch production** a manufacturing process, often custom work, that is not highly mechanized and relies heavily on the human operator (p. 255).

**social audit** measures and reports the ethical, social, and environmental impact of an organization's operations (p. 359).

**social capital** the quality of interactions among people, affected by whether they share a common perspective (p. 331).

**social responsibility** management's obligation to make choices and take action so that the organization contributes to the welfare and interest of society as well as itself (p. 348).

**sociotechnical systems approach** an approach that combines the needs of people with the needs of technical efficiency (p. 283).

**sources of intergroup conflict** factors that generate conflict, including goal incompatibility, differentiation, task interdependence, and limited resources (p. 456).

**specialist** an organization that has a narrow range of goods or services or serves a narrow market (p. 195).

**stable–unstable dimension** the state of an organization's environmental elements (p. 148).

**stakeholder** any group within or outside an organization that has a stake in the organization's performance (p. 27).

**stakeholder approach** also called the *constituency approach*, this perspective assesses the satisfaction of stakeholders as an indicator of the organization's performance (p. 27).

**standardization** a policy that ensures all branches of the company at all locations operate in the same way (p. 222).

**stories** narratives based on true events that are frequently shared among organizational employees and told to new employees to inform them about an organization (p. 335).

**strategic contingencies** events and activities inside and outside an organization that are essential for attaining organizational goals (p. 467).

**strategy** the current set of plans, decisions, and objectives that have been adopted to achieve the organization's goals (p. 61).

**strategy and structure changes** changes in the administrative domain of an organization, including structure, policies, reward systems, labour relations, coordination devices, management information control systems, and accounting and budgeting (p. 374).

**structural dimensions** descriptions of the internal characteristics of an organization (p. 22).

**structure** the formal reporting relationships, groupings, and systems of an organization (p. 67).

**struggle for existence** a principle of the population ecology model that holds that organizations are engaged in a competitive struggle for resources and fighting to survive (p. 195).

**subcultures** cultures that develop within an organization to reflect the common problems, goals, and experiences that members of a team, department, or other unit share (p. 341).

**subsystems** divisions of an organization that perform specific functions for the organization's survival; organizational subsystems perform the essential functions of boundary spanning, production, maintenance, adaptation, and management (p. 19).

**switching structures** an organization creates an organic structure when such a structure is needed for the initiation of new ideas (p. 381).

**symbol** something that represents another thing (p. 335).

**symptoms of structural deficiency** signs of the organization structure being out of alignment, including delayed or poor-quality decision making, failure to respond innovatively to environmental changes, and too much conflict (p. 127).

**system** a set of interacting elements that acquires inputs from the environment, transforms them, and discharges outputs to the external environment (p. 19).

# T

**tactics for enhancing collaboration** techniques such as integration devices, confrontation and negotiation, intergroup consultation, member rotation, and shared mission and superordinate goals that enable groups to overcome differences and work together (p. 478).

**tactics for increasing power** these include entering areas of high uncertainty, creating dependencies, providing resources, and satisfying strategic contingencies (p. 474).

**task** a narrowly defined piece of work assigned to a person (p. 31).

**task environment** sectors with which the organization interacts directly and that have a direct effect on the organization's ability to achieve its goals (p. 142).

**task force** a temporary committee composed of representatives from each department affected by a problem (p. 98).

**task variety** the frequency of unexpected and novel events that occur in the conversion process (p. 272).

**team building** activities that promote the idea that people who work together can work together as a team (p. 394).

**teams** permanent task forces often used in conjunction with a full-time integrator (p. 100).

**technical champion** a person who generates or adopts and develops an idea for a technological innovation and is devoted to it, even to the extent of risking position or prestige; also called *product champion* (p. 383).

**technical complexity** the extent of mechanization in the manufacturing process (p. 255).

**technical knowledge** understanding and agreement about how to solve problems and reach organizational goals (p. 436).

**technology** the tools, techniques, and actions used to transform organizational inputs into outputs (p. 251).

**technology changes** changes in an organization's production process, including its knowledge and skills base, that enable distinctive competence (p. 375).

**time-based competition** delivering products and services faster than competitors, giving companies a competitive edge (p. 388).

**traditional authority** based in the belief in traditions and the legitimacy of the status of people exercising authority through those traditions (p. 312).

**transnational model** a form of horizontal organization that has multiple centres, subsidiary managers who initiate strategy and innovations for the company as a whole, and unity and coordination achieved through organizational culture and shared vision and values (p. 239).

# U

**uncertainty** occurs when decision makers do not have sufficient information about environmental factors and have a difficult time predicting external changes (p. 147).

**uncertainty avoidance** the level of tolerance for, and comfort with, uncertainty and individualism within a culture (p. 234).

# V

**values-based leadership** a relationship between a leader and followers that is based on strongly shared values that are advocated and acted upon by the leader (p. 354).

**variation** appearance of new organizational forms in response to the needs of the external environment; analogous to mutations in biology (p. 193).

**venture teams** a technique to foster creativity within organizations in which a small team is set up as its own company to pursue innovations (p. 382).

**vertical information system** the periodic reports, written information, and computer-based communications distributed to managers (p. 97).

**vertical linkages** communication and coordination activities connecting the top and bottom of an organization (p. 95).

**virtual cross-functional teams** teams comprising individuals from different functions who are separated in space and time as well (p. 100).

**virtual network grouping** organization that is a loosely connected cluster of separate components (p. 103).

**virtual network structure** the organization subcontracts many or most of its major processes to separate companies and coordinates their activities from a small headquarters organization (p. 121).

**virtual team** made up of organizationally or geographically dispersed members who are linked through advanced information and communications technologies. Members frequently use the Internet and collaborative software to work together, rather than meeting face to face (p. 100).

# W

**whistle-blowing** employee disclosure of illegal, immoral, or illegitimate practices on the part of the organization's employees (p. 356).

# Name Index

# Organization Index

# Subject Index